JAN 1 7 2023

Federal Tax Handbook Quick Reference
2022 Tax Rates and Key Figures

D1229397

Single Taxpayers

Taxable Income	Amount of tax
Not over $ 10,275	10% of taxable income
Over $ 10,275 but not over $ 41,775	$ 1,027.50 plus 12% of the excess over $10,275
Over $ 41,775 but not over $ 89,075	$ 4,807.50 plus 22% of the excess over $41,775
Over $ 89,075 but not over $170,050	$ 15,213.50 plus 24% of the excess over $89,075
Over $170,050 but not over $215,950	$ 34,647.50 plus 32% of the excess over $170,050
Over $ 215,950 but not over $539,900	$ 49,335.50 plus 35% of the excess over $215,950
Over $539,900	$162,718 plus 37% of the excess over $539,900

Married Taxpayers Filing Separate Returns

Taxable Income	Amount of tax
Not over $10,275	10% of taxable income
Over $10,275 but not over $41,775	$1,027.50 plus 12% of the excess over $10,275
Over $41,775 but not over $89,075	$ 4,807.50 plus 22% of the excess over $41,775
Over $89,075 but not over $170,050	$ 15,213.50 plus 24% of the excess over $89,075
Over $170,050 but not over $215,950	$ 34,647.50 plus 32% of the excess over $170,050
Over $215,950 but not over $323,925	$ 49,335.50 plus 35% of the excess over $215,950
Over $323,925	$87,126.75 plus 37% of the excess over $323,925

Married Taxpayers Filing Joint Returns and Qualifying Widows and Widowers

Taxable Income	Amount of tax
Not over $ 20,550	10% of taxable income
Over $ 20,550 but not over $ 83,550	$ 2,055 plus 12% of the excess over $ 20,550
Over $ 83,550 but not over $ 178,150	$ 9,615 plus 22% of the excess over $ 83,550
Over $ 178,150 but not over $340,100	$ 30,427 plus 24% of the excess over $ 178,150
Over $ 340,100 but not over $ 431,900	$ 69,295 plus 32% of the excess over $ 340,100
Over $ 431,900 but not over $ 647,850	$ 98,671 plus 35% of the excess over $ 431,900
Over $ 647,850	$ 174,253.50 plus 37% of the excess over $ 647,850

Estates and Trusts

Taxable Income	Amount of tax
Not over $ 2,750	10% of taxable income
Over $ 2,750 but not over $ 9,850	$ 275 plus 24% of the excess over $2,750
Over $ 9,850 but not over $13,450	$1,979 plus 35% of the excess over $9,850
Over $ 13,450	$ 3,239 plus 37% of the excess over $13,450

Heads of Household

Taxable Income	Amount of tax
Not over $ 14,650	10% of taxable income
Over $ 14,650 but not over $ 55,900	$ 1,465 plus 12% of the excess over $ 14,650
Over $ 55,900 but not over $ 89,050	$ 6,415 plus 22% of the excess over $ 55,900
Over $ 89,050 but not over $ 170,050	$ 13,708 plus 24% of the excess over $ 89,050
Over $ 170,050 but not over $ 215,950	$ 33,148 plus 32% of the excess over $ 170,050
Over $ 215,950 but not over $ 539,900	$ 47,836 plus 35% of the excess over $ 215,950
Over $ 539,900	$ 161,218.50 plus 37% of the excess over $ 539,900

2022 Unified Gift and Estate Tax Rates

If the amount with respect to which the tentative tax to be computed is:	The tentative tax is:
Not over $10,000.	18% of such amount.
Over $10,000 but not over $20,000.	$1,800, plus 20% of the excess over $10,000.
Over $20,000 but not over $40,000.	$3,800, plus 22% of the excess over $20,000.
Over $40,000 but not over $60,000.	$8,200, plus 24% of the excess over $40,000.
Over $60,000 but not over $80,000.	$13,000, plus 26% of the excess over $60,000.
Over $80,000 but not over $100,000.	$18,200, plus 28% of the excess over $80,000.
Over $100,000 but not over $150,000.	$23,800, plus 30% of the excess over $100,000.
Over $150,000 but not over $250,000.	$38,800, plus 32% of the excess over $150,000.
Over $250,000 but not over $500,000.	$70,800, plus 34% of the excess over $250,000.
Over $500,000 but not over $750,000.	$155,800, plus 37% of the excess over $500,000.
Over $750,000 but not over $1,000,000.	$248,300, plus 39% of the excess over $750,000.
Over $1,000,000.	$345,800, plus 40% of the excess over $1,000,000.

Subject to the applicable exclusion amount for US citizens and residents.

Standard Deductions

Basic*

Single or married filing separate	$ 12,950
Married filing joint and surviving spouses	$ 25,900
Head of household	$ 19,400

Additional (for 65 or over and/or blind)

Unmarried (including head of household)	$ 1,750
Married or surviving spouse (whether or not joint return)	$ 1,400

* For individuals who can be claimed as a dependent by another taxpayer, limited to the greater of (a) $1,150, or (b) the sum of $400 plus the earned income of the individual claimed as a dependent.

3.8% Tax on Individuals' Net Investment Income

Individuals with modified AGI (MAGI) over $200,000 ($250,000 for joint filers or surviving spouses; $125,000 for married separate filers) must pay the Net Investment Income Tax, which is 3.8% of the lesser of: (1) "net investment income" (interest, dividends, etc.), or (2) MAGI over these thresholds.

Federal Tax Handbook Quick Reference Card
2022 Tax Rates and Key Figures

Standard Mileage Rates
(Jan. 1, 2022—June 30, 2022)

Business use of auto	58.5¢ a mile
Charitable	14¢ a mile
Medical	18¢ a mile
Moving expenses	18¢ a mile*

* For tax years 2018-2025, the moving expense deduction is limited to members of the U.S. Armed Forces on active duty who meet certain criteria

Standard Mileage Rates
(July 1, 2022—Dec. 31, 2022)

Business use of auto	62.5¢ a mile
Charitable	14¢ a mile
Medical	22¢ a mile
Moving expenses	22¢ a mile

Itemized Deductions Percentage Limitations

Medical expenses	7.5% of adjusted gross income (AGI)—floor
Personal interest	0%
Net nonbusiness casualty losses	10%* of AGI (after $100 per casualty limitation) — floor
Charitable contributions	60%** of AGI—ceiling on deductible amount
Miscellaneous itemized deductions	Suspended through 2025

* Only if attributable to a federally declared disaster
** Other limits apply depending on type of gift and/or recipient

Personal Exemption

Personal exemption is suspended for 2018-2025.

Alternative Minimum Tax

AMT rates on taxable excess (i.e., on alternative minimum taxable income (AMTI), less AMT exemption amount):

	AMTI threshhold	AMT rate
Individual,	$0 – $206,100	26%
estate, trust*	over $206,100	28%
Married filing	$0 – $103,050	26%
separately*	over $103,050	28%

* Tax rate on net capital gain and qualified dividend income is the same as for regular tax.

	AMT Exemption Amounts	Phaseout range
Single or head of household	$75,900	$539,900–843,500
Married filing separately**	$59,050	$539,900–776,100
Joint filers or surviving spouse	$118,100	$1,079,800–1,552,200
Estate, trust	$26,500	$88,300-$194,300

** Must also add the lesser of the following to AMTI: (1) 25% of the excess of AMTI over $776,100, or (2) $59,050

Corporations

Flat rate of 21%

Social Security Tax

FICA	Tax base	Rate	Maximum tax
Social Security	$147,000	6.2%	$9,114
Medicare			
Married	$250,000	1.45%	$3,625
filing jointly	over $250,000	2.35%	no limit
Married	$125,000	1.45%	$1,812.50
filing separate	over $125,000	2.35%	no limit
All other	$200,000	1.45%	$2,900
individuals	over $200,000	2.35%	no limit

Capital gains and qualified dividend income*— Individuals, Estates & Trusts

Net short-term (held one year or less) **capital gain** is taxed at: ordinary income rates

Long-term (more than one year) capital gain and qualified dividend income* are taxed at:
15% (0% for adjusted net taxable gain that's below the maximum zero rate amount; 20% for adjusted net taxable gain that's above the maximum 15% rate amount)

***Except** the maximum tax on:

Unrecaptured section 1250 gain (attributable to real estate depreciation) is:	25%
Collectibles gain (on works of art, rugs, antiques, etc.) is:	28%
Section 1202 gain (from the sale of small business stock eligible for partial exclusion from gross income) is:	28%

* Equals dividends from domestic corporations and qualified foreign corporations that meet specified holding period requirements. Exclusions may apply.

3.8% net investment income tax may also apply.

Self-Employment Tax

FICA	Tax base	Rate	Maximum tax
Social Security	$147,000	12.4%	$18,228
Medicare			
Married	$250,000	2.9%	$7,250
filing jointly	over $250,000	3.8%	no limit
Married	$125,000	2.9%	$3,625
filing separate	over $125,000	3.8%	no limit
All other	$200,000	2.9%	$5,800
individuals	over $200,000	3.8%	no limit

Federal Tax Handbook

Nancy Hawkins
(J.D.)
*Vice President,
Product & Editorial*

Catherine E. Murray
(LL.M., NY Bar)
Director, Editorial

Kay Alexander
(J.D., WA Bar)
*Senior Director,
Editorial*

Kersten Behrens
(J.D., NY, NJ Bar)
*Senior Manager,
Editorial*

Adam Gretz
*Product
Manager*

Steve Brylski
(LL.M., NY Bar)
Executive Editor

Simon Schneebalg
(LL.M., NY Bar)
Senior Specialist Editor

Shannon M. Christensen
(J.D., M.B.T., MN Bar)

Tola Ozim
(J.D., NY Bar)

Harris Abrams
(LL.M., PA Bar)
Senior Specialist Editor

Richard H. Sternberg
(LL.M., NY Bar)
Senior Specialist Editor

Gregory J. Evanella
(J.D., NJ Bar)

Julie S. Rose
(J.D., CT Bar)

James Seidel
(LL.M., NY Bar)

Gary S. Bronstein
(LL.M., CA, MA Bar)
Senior Specialist Editor

Natalie Tal
(LL.M., NY Bar)
Senior Specialist Editor

Jonathan D. Grossberg
(LL.M., NY, PA Bar)

Dara R. Siegel
(J.D., NY Bar)

James A. Chapman
(LL.M., MI Bar)
Senior Specialist Editor

Anne Wagenbrenner
(LL.M., NY, CT Bar)
Senior Specialist Editor

Robert O. Heroux
(LL.M., C.P.A.,
NY, CT Bar)

Kristina G. Smith
(J.D., NY, DC, WY Bar)

Karen A. Rennie
(LL.M., NY Bar)
Senior Specialist Editor

Scott E. Weiner
(J.D., NY Bar)
Senior Specialist Editor

Elizabeth McLeod
(J.D., NY Bar)

Catherine Daleo
*Senior Tax Editorial
Associate*

E.H. Rubinsky
(LL.M., NY Bar)
Senior Specialist Editor

Patricia Brandstetter
(LL.M., Ph.D, NY Bar)

John Melazzo
(J.D., NJ Bar)

Cara O'Brien
(LL.M., NY, CO Bar)

Thomson Reuters/Tax & Accounting
3 Times Sq.
New York, NY 10036-6564

ISBN 978-0-7811-0580-4

To order additional copies of this publication, please call Toll Free 1-800-950-1216, ext. 1, or visit our Product Store at tax.tr.com/store.

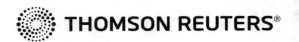

2023 Federal Tax Handbook

The 2023 edition of the Thomson Reuters Federal Tax Handbook is designed to answer the tax questions and resolve the tax problems that arise in everyday business and personal transactions. It helps in preparing 2022 federal income tax returns and provides specific guidance about the tax consequences of transactions occurring in 2023. It is prepared by the professional staff that prepares Thomson Reuters' comprehensive federal tax service on Checkpoint, the Federal Tax Coordinator 2d, and is derived from that tax service.

The 2023 Federal Tax Handbook reflects all federal tax legislation passed by Congress to date of publication, including the Inflation Reduction Act of 2022 (Inflation Reduction Act; P.L. 117-169, 8/16/2022) and the 2022 CHIPS and Science Act (CHIPS Act; P.L. 117-167, 8/9/2022). The Handbook also reflects regulations and other guidance issued by IRS to implement past years' legislation, including rules clarifying cryptocurrency reporting requirements and changes to the Code Sec. 30D electric vehicle credit. It also reflects other key developments (such as new regulations, rulings, and revenue procedures) affecting 2022 returns and the 2023 tax year. The Handbook also includes inflation-adjusted 2023 tax figures (issued by IRS) throughout.

caution: For highlights of significant later-enacted tax laws that affect the 2023 edition, consult the homepage dedicated to handbook users (tax.thomsonreuters.com/federaltaxhandbookupdates).

The Handbook discusses and explains common tax problems in clear, concise, nontechnical language, and, where appropriate, includes:

illustration: To clarify the tax rules and problems discussed, with simple, easy-to-follow examples.

caution: To warn of dangers that arise in particular tax situations and, where appropriate, to indicate what should be done.

recommendation: To provide specific, carefully studied guides to action to keep taxes at a legal minimum.

observation: For professional analysis or commentary that is not part of cited authorities.

Forms to use: The Handbook explains which IRS forms to use to report transactions, pay taxes, make elections, etc. For a complete list of all official forms discussed, with references to the paragraph where they are discussed, see the "Forms" entry in the Topic Index.

References: The Handbook uses the following references:

. . . "Code Sec." references are to sections of the Internal Revenue Code.

. . . "Reg §" references are to sections of the federal tax regulations. "Prop Reg §" references are to proposed regulations, which are only cited in the text where IRS has indicated that "Taxpayers may rely" on them.

. . . Footnote references beginning with a single letter are to paragraphs in the Federal Tax Coordinator 2d and RIA's Analysis of Federal Taxes: Income. However, RIA's Analysis of Federal Taxes: Income doesn't include coverage of estate, gift and excise taxes. Accordingly, references to ¶Q-1000 *et seq.* (gift tax), ¶R-1000 *et seq.* (estate tax), and ¶W-1000 *et seq.* (excise taxes) are only to paragraphs in the Federal Tax Coordinator 2d.

¶ 105. What's New on the 2022 Form 1040?

Here are the current draft changes affecting the 2022 Form 1040 and related forms and schedules, cross-referenced to where they are discussed in the Handbook. Note that the draft versions of these forms and schedules are subject to change.

FORM 1040—UNNUMBERED LINES ON PAGE 1

Filing status. The Qualifying widow(er) (QW) language and acronym are changed to Qualifying surviving spouse (QSS).

Question about virtual currency (e.g., cryptocurrency). The virtual currency question has been modified once again. For 2022, it's set out with a bold **Digital Assets** heading and is expanded and clarified. To that end, the question clarifies that receiving digital assets includes doing so via rewards, awards, or compensation; specifically includes gifts as disposition; and replaces "virtual currency" with the broader "digital asset" terminology. Thus, the question on the 2022 Form 1040 now asks: "At any time during 2022, did you: (a) receive (as a reward, award, or payment for property or services); or (b) sell, exchange, **gift**, or otherwise dispose of a **digital asset** (or a financial interest in a digital asset)?"

FORM 1040—NUMBERED LINES ON PAGES 1 AND 2

Line 1. Wages, salaries, tips, etc. For 2022, Form 1040 also expands Line 1 from what used to be a single line item to include a number of new subsections for reporting out particular types of relevant income.

Line 6. Social Security benefits. For 2022, Form 1040 adds a new subsection "c" to line 6, adding a checkbox for using the lump-sum election method.

Line 8. Other income. As gross income is broadly defined, taxpayers should be aware that it includes both more conventional income items, such as employee wages, as well as income earned from working in the gig economy and sundry other items. Also, for 2022, third-party settlement organizations, including banks and on-line payment networks, are required to report payments exceeding $600, regardless of the number of transactions involved, which is a significant change from the $20,000/200 transactions reporting threshold that applied to years before 2022 (payments are reported on Forms 1099-K, issued to IRS and payees such as taxpayers who rent out vacation homes, gig workers, and others crossing the threshold). (¶1200)

Line 9. Total income. There is a minor change on line 9, changing the cross-reference to line 1 to line 1z, to account for the new subsections added for line 1. (see above)

Line 12. Standard deduction or itemized deductions. The temporary charitable deduction for non-itemizers that was included on line 12b on the 2021 Form 1040 has been removed for 2022 (along with line 12c) as that deduction is no longer available. (¶2100)

Line 12. Standard deduction in general (regular standard deduction). The regular standard deduction has been increased for 2022 to $12,950 for those filing single or married filing separately; $25,900 for those filing married filing jointly or as qualifying surviving spouse; and $19,400 for those filing as head of household. (¶3110)

Additional standard deduction for older or blind taxpayers. For 2022, the additional standard deduction for married taxpayers who are 65 or over or blind is $1,400 (married or a surviving spouse). That amount is increased to $1,750 for those who are single or head of household (not surviving spouse). (¶3110)

Limited standard deduction for dependents. For an individual who can be claimed as a dependent on another's return, the standard deduction for 2022 is $1,150 or $400 plus the individual's earned income, whichever is greater. But this amount may not exceed the regular standard deduction. (¶3110)

Line 15. Taxable income. There is a minor wording modification, but the entry is otherwise unchanged.

Lines 19 and 28. Child tax credit and credit for other dependents. For 2022, lines 19 and 28 remove the refundable/nonrefundable language that was included in the 2021 Form 1040, reflecting the fact that the *fully* refundable (and advance) credit relief was for the 2021 tax year only (see American Rescue Plan Act (ARPA, §9611 and §9612, PL 117-2, 3/11/2021)), and is no longer available. However, the general child tax credit rules and provisions, including the partially refundable ("additional" credit), still apply. (¶2350)

Line 27. Earned income credit. The 2021 line 27 subsections, reflecting expanded EIC relief for 2021 (see American Rescue Plan Act (ARPA, §9626(a), PL 117-2, 3/11/2021)), including among other things the provisional lookback period and expanded age limits, have been removed as those expansions don't apply to 2022. That aside, the EIC, which serves to assist moderate and lower income households, is still in place for 2022 subject to regular rules and phaseouts. (¶2338)

Line 30. The entry that was on the 2021 Form 1040, line 30, for the Recovery Rebate Credit has also been removed from the 2022 Form 1040 as that program has expired, although the line itself is at present still on the form as "Reserved for future use."

Line 32. There is a small conforming change to account for the changes to line 27 (see above).

Line 37. Amount you owe. There is a minor modification in the placement of the "amount you owe" wording on line 37. Also, for details on how to pay, line 37 now points filers to both the instructions as well as the IRS website.

FORM 1040—SCHEDULE 1, ADDITIONAL INCOME AND ADJUSTMENTS TO INCOME

LINE ITEM HIGHLIGHTS

Line 8. Other income. Following the expansion of line 8 that was made on the 2021 Schedule 1, the 2022 Schedule 1 further expands the subsections to specify additional items coming under other income, including scholarship and fellowship grants that are not included on Form W-2, nontaxable amount of Medicaid waiver payments included on Form 1040 (new lines 1a or 1d), wages earned while incarcerated, and more. Also, the 2021 Schedule 1 entry entitled Taxable Health Savings Account distribution (2021 line 8e) is modified for 2022, such that lines 8e and 8f now specify income from Form 8853 (Archer MSAs and Long-Term Care Insurance Contracts) and Form 8889 (Health Savings Accounts (HSAs)), respectively.

Line 11. Educator expenses. For 2022, eligible elementary and secondary school teachers can claim an above-the-line deduction for up to $300 of expenses paid for books and certain other supplies used in the classroom ($600 if married filing jointly and both spouses are eligible educators, although not more than $300 each). (¶2224)

Line 14. Moving expenses for members of the Armed Forces. A taxpayer can deduct moving expenses if he or she is a member of the Armed Forces on active duty and, due to a military order, moves because of a permanent change of station. The 2022 standard mileage rate for moving expenses for qualified active-duty members of the Armed Forces is 18¢ per mile (up 2¢ from the 2021 rate) for expenses paid or incurred on or after Jan. 1, 2022 and before July 1, 2022, and 22¢ per mile for expenses paid or incurred after June 30, 2022. (¶1627)

Line 20. IRA deduction. In general, a taxpayer who isn't an active participant in certain employer-sponsored retirement plans, and whose spouse isn't an active participant, may deduct an IRA contribution up to the lesser of: (1) a statutory dollar limit, or (2) 100% of the compensation that's includible in his or her gross income. Also, if the taxpayer or the taxpayer's spouse is covered by a retirement plan at work, the deduction phases out over a specified dollar range of modified AGI (MAGI). For 2022, the statutory dollar limit on contributions remains at $6,000, plus an additional $1,000 for those age 50 or older. And the deduction phase-out limits are as follows: for taxpayers who are covered by a retirement plan at work, the deduction phases out ratably for MAGI between $68,000 and $78,000 for those filing as single or head of household, or between $109,000 and $129,000 for those filing as married filing joint or as qualifying widow(er). If only the taxpayer's spouse is covered by a retirement plan at work, the deduction phases out ratably for those filing jointly between $204,000 and $214,000. Note that for taxpayers who are married filing separately, there is a $10,000 MAGI limit when either the taxpayer or the spouse is covered by a retirement plan at work. (¶4342)

Line 21. Student loan interest deduction. For 2022, the student loan interest deduction phases out ratably for taxpayers other than joint filers with MAGI between $70,000 and $85,000, unchanged from 2021. For joint filers however, the phase-out has been moderately increased for 2022 to MAGI between $145,000 and $175,000 (vs. $140,000/$170,000 for 2021). (¶2220)

Line 24. Other adjustments. There are minor conforming changes on line 24b and 24c to match the changes made to line 8, above.

FORM 1040—SCHEDULE 2, ADDITIONAL TAXES

IN GENERAL

Other taxes and Other additional taxes. The expansion that was made to the 2021 Schedule 2, expanding both the page 1 line items as well as the page 2 line 17 subsections for "other additional taxes," stays in place largely unchanged for 2022.

LINE ITEM HIGHLIGHTS

Line 1. Alternative minimum tax. For 2022, the AMT exemption amounts are $118,100 for joint filers or surviving spouses; $75,900 for unmarried individuals other than surviving spouses; and $59,050 for married individuals filing separately. The income levels at which the AMT exemption begins to phase out for 2022 are $539,900 for married individuals filing separately and unmarried individuals other than surviving spouses, or $1,079,800 if married filing jointly or qualifying surviving spouse. (¶3203)

Line 4. Self-employment tax. For 2022, the maximum amount of self-employment income subject to FICA tax is $147,000. (¶1109)

Line 19. The 2021 entry on then-new line 19 for "Additional tax from Schedule 8812," which was used to figure child tax credits (CTC), to report advance CTC payments received, and figure additional tax owed if one received excess advance CTC payments during 2021, has been removed. Taxpayers are reminded that the *advance* credit program has expired (see also the extant/*additional* credit scheme noted under Form 1040, lines 19 and 28, above). (¶2350)

Line 21. Total other taxes. There is a minor conforming change on line 21 to match the change made to line 19.

FORM 1040—SCHEDULE 3, ADDITIONAL CREDITS AND PAYMENTS

LINE ITEM HIGHLIGHTS

Line 13b, 13h. Qualified sick and family leave credits. The 2021 entries for "Qualified sick and family leave credits from Schedule(s) H and Form(s) 7202 for leave taken..." are changed for 2022 to "Credit for qualified sick and family leave wages paid in 2022 from Schedule(s) H for leave taken...," reflecting expiration of Credits for Sick Leave and Family Leave for Certain Self-Employed Individuals (Form 7202).

Line 13g. The 2021 child and dependent care expense credit entry on line 13g has been removed for 2022. Taxpayers should note that the expansions which were made for the 2021 tax year for this credit were for 2021 only and do not apply to 2022. (¶2347)

FORM 1040-SR—U.S. TAX RETURN FOR SENIORS

Form 1040-SR, U.S. Tax Return for Seniors, may be used by persons who are age 65 or older. The schedules discussed above and below are schedules for both the 2022 Form 1040 and Form 1040-SR and the changes noted above and below are the same for both.

FORM 1040—SCHEDULE A, ITEMIZED DEDUCTIONS

Line 1. Medical and dental expenses. The 2021 16¢ per mile standard mileage rate for medically-related use of an auto increased in increments for 2022, increasing to 18¢ per mile for expenses paid or incurred from 1/1/2022 through 6/30/2022, and then to 22¢ per mile for expenses after 6/30/2022. (¶2148)

Line 3. Medical expense floor. The adjusted gross income (AGI) threshold for deducting medical and dental expenses remains at 7.5%. (¶2141)

Line 8d. Mortgage insurance premiums. The former entry for mortgage insurance premiums on line 8d has been removed as the deduction for same doesn't apply in respect to amounts paid or accrued after 2021. (¶1730)

Line 8e. There is a minor conforming change on 8e to match the change to 8d.

Line 12. Gifts to charity, other than by cash or check. Per statute, the standard mileage rate for use of an auto in rendering gratuitous services to a charitable organization remains at 14¢ per mile, and isn't indexed for inflation. (¶2120)

FORM 1040—SCHEDULE B, INTEREST AND ORDINARY DIVIDENDS

Part I, Line 3. Excludable interest on series EE and I U.S. savings bonds issued after '89. There is an exclusion for education-related savings bond interest, but the exclusion phases out at higher income levels. For 2022, the exclusion phases out for a taxpayer whose modified AGI (MAGI) exceeds $85,800 ($128,650 for joint filers). (¶2218)

Part III, Caution. Foreign Accounts and Trusts. For 2022, the "caution" section under Part III, which previously included a reminder about potential penalties exposure for failing to file FinCEN Form 114 (FBAR), now includes both that reminder as well as a new affirmative reminder that taxpayers may also be required to file Form 8938, Statement of Specified Foreign Financial Assets. (¶4746)

Part III, Line 7b. For 2022, line 7b has minor wording changes to account for the possibility of multiple foreign accounts in different foreign countries (the wording of this line on the 2021 form was in the singular).

FORM 1040—SCHEDULE C, PROFIT OR LOSS FROM BUSINESS

Line 9. Car and truck expenses. The standard mileage rate for business travel received two bumps for 2022, moving up to 58.5¢ per mile (up from 2021's 56¢) for travel from 1/1/2022 through 6/30/2022, and then up to 62.5¢ per mile for travel after 6/30/2022. (¶1553)

Line 13. Depreciation and section 179 expense. See entries for Form 4562, below.

FORM 4562, DEPRECIATION AND AMORTIZATION

Part I. Election to expense certain tangible property under Sec. 179. For tax years beginning in 2022, the maximum section 179 expense deduction is $1,080,000. This limit is reduced by the amount by which the cost of section 179 property placed in service during the tax year exceeds $2,700,000. (¶1935)

Part V. Listed property. The first-year luxury auto limit for vehicles placed in service in 2022 that are eligible for bonus first-year depreciation is $19,200 for autos, light trucks and vans. (¶1945)

FORM 1040—SCHEDULE D, CAPITAL GAINS AND LOSSES

Disposal of Qualified Opportunity Fund investment. A QOF is any investment vehicle that is organized as a corporation or partnership for the purpose of investing in eligible property located in a qualified opportunity zone. For taxpayers who disposed of any investment in a QOF during the tax year, the box on the top line on Schedule D above Part I should be checked, Form 8949 should be attached, and per the instructions, Part III of Form 8997 must be completed as well. (¶2427)

FORM 1040—SCHEDULE E, SUPPLEMENTAL INCOME AND LOSS

Standard mileage rate. The 2022 standard mileage rate for miles driven in connection with business is 58.5¢ per mile for travel from 1/1/2022 through 6/30/2022, and 62.5¢ per mile for travel after 6/30/2022. (¶1553)

FORM 1040—SCHEDULE F, PROFIT OR LOSS FROM FARMING

Line 10. Car and truck expenses. The 2022 standard mileage rate for business travel is 58.5¢ per mile for travel from 1/1/2022 through 6/30/2022, and 62.5¢ per mile for travel after 6/30/2022. (¶1553)

¶1000. Tax Calendar—2023 Due Dates.

Here are the principal 2023 tax due dates. The effect of Saturdays, Sundays, and federal (but not State) holidays has been taken into account.

January 17, 2023

Individuals.

Make a payment of estimated tax for 2022 if not enough 2022 income tax has been withheld. Use Form 1040-ES, or pay by various electronic means. This is the final installment date for 2022 estimated tax. However, individuals needn't make this payment if they file their 2022 returns (Form 1040) and pay any tax due by Jan. 31, 2023.

Farmers and fishermen.

Pay estimated tax for 2022 by using Form 1040-ES or via various electronic means. Farmers and fishermen can then file their 2022 income tax returns (Form 1040) by Apr. 18 (as Apr. 15 falls on a Saturday, and Apr. 17 is D.C. Emancipation Day). If they don't make this estimated payment at this time, they must file their 2022 returns and pay any tax due by Mar. 1, 2023, to avoid an estimated tax penalty.

January 31, 2023

Individuals.

File income tax return (Form 1040) for 2022, if the last installment of estimated tax wasn't paid by Jan. 17. Filing the return now prevents any penalty for late payment of the last installment.

Employers.

Give employees their copies of Form W-2 for 2022.

File Form W-3 along with Copy A of all the Form W-2s issued for 2022.

"Applicable large employers" must furnish copies of Forms 1095-C to full-time employees, and all other providers of minimum essential coverage must furnish copies of Forms 1095-B to responsible individuals.

Businesses.

Give an annual information statement to recipients of certain payments made by the business during 2022. (Use a copy of the appropriate Form 1099.)

File Form 1099-MISC if reporting (whether electronically or by paper) nonemployee compensation payments in box 7. (For all other payments, file Form 1099-MISC by Feb. 28, 2023 on paper, or Mar. 31, 2023, electronically.)

February 15, 2023

Individuals.

Individuals who claimed exemption from income tax withholding for 2022 on the Form W-4 given to the employer must file a new Form W-4 by this date to continue the exemption for another year.

Businesses.

Give an annual information statement to recipients of certain payments (e.g., proceeds from broker and barter transactions) made by the business during 2022. (Use a copy of the appropriate Form 1099.)

February 28, 2023

Businesses.

File an information return (Form 1099) with IRS for certain payments made by the business during 2022. There are different versions of Form 1099 for different types of payments. For a 30-day extension of time to file, use Form 8809. The due date for electronic filers is Mar. 31, 2023.

Large food and beverage establishment employers.

File Form 8027 to report tip income and allocated tips. Use Form 8027-T to summarize and transmit Form 8027 if employer has more than one establishment. The due date for electronic filers is Mar. 31, 2023.

March 1, 2023

Farmers and fishermen.

File the 2022 income tax return (Form 1040) and pay any tax due. However, farmers and fishermen have until Apr. 18 if they paid their 2022 estimated tax by Jan. 17, 2022.

March 15, 2023

Partnerships.

File a 2022 calendar-year return (Form 1065), and provide each partner with a copy of Schedule K-1. For an automatic 6-month extension to file the return and provide Schedule K-1 or a substitute Schedule K-1, file Form 7004. Then file Form 1065 by Sept. 15.

S corporations.

File a 2022 calendar-year income tax return (Form 1120S), pay any tax still due, and provide each shareholder with a copy of Schedule K-1. For an automatic 6-month extension, file Form 7004 and deposit an estimate of the tax owed.

S elections.

File Form 2553 to choose to be treated as an S corporation for calendar year 2023 and thereafter. If Form 2553 is filed late, S treatment will begin with calendar year 2024 (unless the taxpayer qualifies for late election relief).

March 31, 2023

Electronic filers of information returns.

Electronically file those information returns listed under Feb. 28, above (e.g., Form 1099s, Form W-2s, etc.). (Feb. 28 is the due date for non-electronic filers.)

Large food and beverage establishment employers.

Electronically file Form 8027 to report tip income and allocated tips. Employers with more than one establishment should use Form 8027-T to summarize and transmit Form 8027. (Mar. 1, 2023 is the due date for non-electronic filers.)

April 18, 2023

Individuals.

File an income tax return (Form 1040) for 2022 and pay any tax due.

U.S. citizens and resident aliens living and working (or on military duty) outside the U.S. and Puerto Rico get an automatic 2-month extension (to June 15) to file their returns and pay any tax due.

Make the first installment payment of 2023 estimated tax.

Last day to make contributions to an IRA, Roth IRA, HSA, Archer MSA or Coverdell ESA for 2022.

C corporations.

File 2022 calendar-year income tax returns (Form 1120) and make any required income tax payments. Corporations needing additional time (beyond April 18) to *file* should file

Form 7004, and deposit the tax they owe, by April 18, 2023, to obtain an extension to file the return. The filing extension date won't go beyond Oct. 18, 2023. And, that extension doesn't extend the time to pay the tax beyond April 18, 2023.

Corporations.

Calendar-year corporations deposit the first installment of estimated income tax for 2023.

June 15, 2023

Individuals.

Make the second installment payment of 2023 estimated tax.

U.S. citizens or resident aliens living and working (or on military duty) outside the U.S. and Puerto Rico file their 2022 Forms 1040 and pay any tax, interest and penalties due (under the 60-day extension to which they're entitled). For further extension to Oct. 16, file Form 4868 and check the box on line 8. For taxpayers serving in a combat zone, the filing deadline is extended further.

Corporations.

Calendar-year corporations deposit the second installment of estimated income tax for 2023.

July 17, 2023

Employers.

Employers that maintain an employee benefit plan, such as a pension, profit-sharing, or stock bonus plan, file Form 5500 or Form 5500-EZ for plan years that ended in Sept., Oct., or Nov. of 2022. Employers with Forms 5500 due between Mar. 31, 2023, and July 17, 2023 because of a previously filed extension request, file the Form 5500.

July 31, 2023

Employers.

Employers that maintain an employee benefit plan, such as a pension, profit-sharing, or stock bonus plan, file Form 5500 or Form 5500-EZ for calendar year 2022. Employer that use a fiscal year as the plan year file the form by the last day of the seventh month after the plan year ends.

September 15, 2023

Individuals.

Make the third installment payment of 2023 estimated tax, if not enough 2023 income tax is being withheld. Use Form 1040-ES, or pay by various electronic means.

S corporations.

If under a 6-month extension, file a 2022 calendar-year income tax return (Form 1120S), and pay any tax due.

Corporations.

Calendar-year corporations must deposit the third installment of estimated income tax for 2023.

Partnerships.

If under a 6-month extension, file a 2022 calendar-year return (Form 1065).

October 16, 2023

Individuals.

Individuals with an automatic 6-month extension to file income tax returns for 2022, file Form 1040 and pay any tax, interest, and penalties due.

C corporations.

File a 2022 calendar-year income tax return (Form 1120), and pay any tax due if under an automatic 6-month extension.

During November, 2023

Employers.

Request that employees whose withholding exemptions will be different in 2024 fill out a new Form W-4.

December 15, 2023

Corporations.

Calendar-year corporations must deposit the fourth installment of estimated income tax for 2023.

2023 FEDERAL TAX HANDBOOK

Contents

Table of Contents—Main Topics

Chapter 1   Tax Rates and Tables

¶ 1100   Tax Rates and Tables.

Different rates apply for federal income (¶1101 *et seq.*), gift (¶1114), excise (¶1116), and other taxes. The draft income tax tables are reflected at ¶1111.

¶ 1101   Income tax rates for individuals—single taxpayers, married filing jointly, married filing separately, heads of households.

Code Sec. 1 applies different tax rates to:

. . . single taxpayers (¶1102);

. . . married persons filing joint returns (see rates at ¶1103 and discussion at ¶4705) and qualified widows and widowers (¶1103);

. . . married persons filing separate returns (¶1104); and

. . . heads of households (¶1105).

Bankruptcy estates of individuals compute their tax using the same rate schedule as married individuals filing separate tax returns.[1]

Individuals with taxable income under a ceiling amount ($100,000) may compute their tax using tax tables (Code Sec. 3); see ¶1111.

For the 3.8% surtax on "unearned income," see ¶1107.

For capital gains rates, see ¶2600 *et seq.*

¶ 1102   Income tax rates for single individuals.

Under Code Sec. 1, taxpayers who aren't married *at year's end* and who don't qualify as surviving spouses or heads of household, and certain married taxpayers living apart compute their tax under the following tax rates for single persons if they can't use the tax tables.

The rates for 2022 are:

If taxable income is:	The tax is:
Not over $10,275	10% of taxable income
Over $10,275 but not over $41,775	$1,027.50 plus 12% of the excess over $10,275
Over $41,775 but not over $89,075	$4,807.50 plus 22% of the excess over $41,775
Over $89,075 but not over $170,050	$15,213.50 plus 24% of the excess over $89,075
Over $170,050 but not over $215,950	$34,647.50 plus 32% of the excess over $170,050
Over $215,950 but not over $539,900	$49,335.50 plus 35% of the excess over $215,950
Over $539,900	$162,718 plus 37% of the excess over $539,900

---

1. ¶C-9707

References beginning with a single letter are to paragraphs in Federal Tax Coordinator 2d and RIA's Analysis of Federal Taxes: Income.

The rates for 2023 are:

If taxable income is:	The tax is:
Not over $11,000	10% of taxable income
Over $11,000 but not over $44,725	$1,100 plus 12% of the excess over $11,000
Over $44,725 but not over $95,375	$5,147 plus 22% of the excess over $44,725
Over $95,375 but not over $182,100	$16,290 plus 24% of the excess over $95,375
Over $182,100 but not over $231,250	$37,104 plus 32% of the excess over $182,100
Over $231,250 but not over $578,125	$52,832 plus 35% of the excess over $231,250
Over $578,125	$174,238.25 plus 37% of the excess over $578,125

¶ 1103   Income tax rates for married filing joint returns and surviving spouses.

Under Code Sec. 1, married taxpayers filing joint returns and surviving spouses who can't use the tax tables compute their tax on the basis of the rates indicated below.

The rates for 2022 are:

If taxable income is:	The tax is:
Not over $20,550	10% of taxable income
Over $20,550 but not over $83,550	$2,055 plus 12% of the excess over $20,550
Over $83,550 but not over $178,150	$9,615 plus 22% of the excess over $83,550
Over $178,150 but not over $340,100	$30,427 plus 24% of the excess over $178,150
Over $340,100 but not over $431,900	$69,295 plus 32% of the excess over $340,100
Over $431,900 but not over $647,850	$98,671 plus 35% of the excess over $431,900
Over $647,850	$174,253.50 plus 37% of the excess over $647,850

The rates for 2023 are:

If taxable income is:	The tax is:
Not over $22,000	10% of taxable income
Over $22,000 but not over $89,450	$2,200 plus 12% of the excess over $22,000
Over $89,450 but not over $190,750	$10,294 plus 22% of the excess over $89,450
Over $190,750 but not over $364,200	$32,580 plus 24% of the excess over $190,750
Over $364,200 but not over $462,500	$74,208 plus 32% of the excess over $364,200
Over $462,500 but not over $693,750	$105,664 plus 35% of the excess over $462,500
Over $693,750	$186,601.50 plus 37% of the excess over $693,750

¶ 1104   Income tax rates for married filing separate returns.

Under Code Sec. 1, married taxpayers filing separate returns who can't use the tax tables compute their tax on the basis of the rates indicated below.

The rates for 2022 are:

If taxable income is:	The tax is:
Not over $10,275	10% of taxable income
Over $10,275 but not over $41,775	$1,027.50 plus 12% of the excess over $10,275
Over $41,775 but not over $89,075	$4,807.50 plus 22% of the excess over $41,775

If taxable income is:	The tax is:
Over $89,075 but not over $170,050	$15,213.50 plus 24% of the excess over $89,075
Over $170,050 but not over $215,950	$34,647.50 plus 32% of the excess over $170,050
Over $215,950 but not over $323,925	$49,335.50 plus 35% of the excess over $215,950
Over $323,925	$87,126.75 plus 37% of the excess over $323,925

The rates for 2023 are:

If taxable income is:	The tax is:
Not over $11,000	10% of taxable income
Over $11,000 but not over $44,725	$1,100 plus 12% of the excess over $11,000
Over $44,725 but not over $95,375	$5,147 plus 22% of the excess over $44,725
Over $95,375 but not over $182,100	$16,290 plus 24% of the excess over $95,375
Over $182,100 but not over $231,250	$37,104 plus 32% of the excess over $182,100
Over $231,250 but not over $346,875	$52,832 plus 35% of the excess over $231,250
Over $346,875	$93,300.75 plus 37% of the excess over $346,875

¶ 1105   Head-of-household status—tax rates.

Those who qualify for head-of-household status (see ¶3127), and who can't use the tax tables, compute their tax on the basis of the rates indicated below.

The rates for 2022 are:

If taxable income is:	The tax is:
Not over $14,650	10% of taxable income
Over $14,650 but not over $55,900	$1,465 plus 12% of the excess over $14,650
Over $55,900 but not over $89,050	$6,415 plus 22% of the excess over $55,900
Over $89,050 but not over $170,050	$13,708 plus 24% of the excess over $89,050
Over $170,050 but not over $215,950	$33,148 plus 32% of the excess over $170,050
Over $215,950 but not over $539,900	$47,836 plus 35% of the excess over $215,950
Over $539,900	$161,218.50 plus 37% of the excess over $539,900

The rates for 2023 are:

If taxable income is:	The tax is:
Not over $15,700	10% of taxable income
Over $15,700 but not over $59,850	$1,570 plus 12% of the excess over $15,700
Over $59,850 but not over $95,350	$6,868 plus 22% of the excess over $59,850
Over $95,350 but not over $182,100	$14,678 plus 24% of the excess over $95,350
Over $182,100 but not over $231,250	$35,498 plus 32% of the excess over $182,100
Over $231,250 but not over $578,100	$51,226 plus 35% of the excess over $231,250
Over $578,100	$172,623.5 plus 37% of the excess over $578,100

¶ 1106   Income tax rates for trusts and estates.

The income tax on trusts and decedent's estates is imposed at graduated rates on their taxable income. (Code Sec. 1(e)) For capital gains rates, see ¶2600.

The rates for 2022 are:

If taxable income is:	The tax is:
Less than $2,750	10% of taxable income
Over $2,750 but not over $9,850	$275 plus 24% of the excess over $2,750
Over $9,850 but not over $13,450	$1,979 plus 35% of the excess over $9,850
Over $13,450	$3,239 plus 37% of the excess over $13,450

The rates for 2023 are:

If taxable income is:	The tax is:
Not over $2,900	10% of taxable income
Over $2,900 but not over $10,550	$290 plus 24% of the excess over $2,900
Over $10,550 but not over $14,450	$2,126 plus 35% of the excess over $10,550
Over $14,450	$3,491 plus 37% of the excess over $14,450

¶ 1107   3.8% surtax on "unearned income."

Certain unearned income of individuals, trusts, and estates is subject to a surtax (i.e., it's payable on top of any other tax payable on that income). For individuals, the surtax is 3.8% of the lesser of (1) "net investment income" or (2) the excess of modified adjusted gross income (MAGI) over the threshold amount ($250,000 for joint filers or surviving spouses, $125,000 for a married individual filing a separate return, and $200,000 in any other case). Special computations apply to estates and trusts. (Code Sec. 1411(a)(1), Code Sec. 1411(b))[2] For details, see ¶3142 *et seq.*

¶ 1108   FICA (Social Security and Medicare) tax rates for employers and employees.

Both employee and employer are liable for taxes under the Federal Insurance Contributions Act (FICA).[3]

For 2023, under Code Sec. 3111, an employer is required to pay a 7.65% FICA tax, consisting of:

(a) 6.20% Social Security tax on the first $160,200 of an employee's wages (maximum tax is $9,932.40 [6.20% of $160,200]), plus

(b) 1.45% Medicare tax on the employee's total wages (no ceiling).

And, under Code Sec. 3101 employees are required to pay:

(a) a 6.20% Social Security tax on the first $160,200 of wages (maximum tax is $9,932.40 [6.20% of $160,200]), plus

(b) a 1.45% Medicare tax on the first $200,000 of wages ($250,000 for joint returns; $125,000 for married taxpayers filing a separate return), plus

(c) a 2.35% Medicare tax (regular 1.45% Medicare tax + 0.9% additional Medicare tax) on all wages in excess of $200,000 ($250,000 for joint returns; $125,000 for married taxpayers filing a separate return). (Code Sec. 3101(b)(2))

---

2. ¶A-6361   3. ¶H-4687

For 2022, under Code Sec. 3111, an employer is required to pay a 7.65% FICA tax, consisting of:

(a) 6.20% Social Security tax on the first $147,000 of an employee's wages (maximum tax is $9,114 [6.20% of $147,000]), plus

(b) 1.45% Medicare tax on the employee's total wages (no ceiling).

And, under Code Sec. 3101 employees are required to pay:

(a) a 6.20% Social Security tax on the first $147,000 of wages (maximum tax is $9,114 [6.20% of $147,000]), plus

(b) a 1.45% Medicare tax on the first $200,000 of wages ($250,000 for joint returns; $125,000 for married taxpayers filing a separate return), plus

(c) a 2.35% Medicare tax (regular 1.45% Medicare tax + 0.9% additional Medicare tax) on all wages in excess of $200,000 ($250,000 for joint returns; $125,000 for married taxpayers filing a separate return). (Code Sec. 3101(b)(2))

The 0.9% additional Medicare tax applies only to employees, not employers. Employers must begin withholding the additional Medicare tax once an employee's wages exceed $200,000, even if the employee may not ultimately be liable for the additional tax (e.g., employee earns $210,000, his or her spouse earns $25,000, and they file a joint return). Any excess additional Medicare tax withheld will be credited against the total tax liability shown on the employee's income tax return. Conversely, the 0.9% additional Medicare tax may be owed on the employee's income tax return where there was no withholding for it (e.g., employee earns $175,000 and her spouse earns $150,000).[4]

¶ **1109**   **Self-employment tax—OASDI, Medicare and additional Medicare taxes.**

For 2023, the self-employment tax on self-employed people is:

* 12.40% OASDI on the first $160,200 of self-employment income, for a maximum tax of $19,864.80 (12.40% of $160,200); plus

* 2.90% Medicare tax on the first $200,000 of self-employment income ($250,000 of combined self-employment income on a joint return, $125,000 on a separate return), (Code Sec. 1401(a), Code Sec. 1401(b)); plus

* 3.8% (2.90% regular Medicare tax + 0.9% additional Medicare tax) on all self-employment income in excess of $200,000 ($250,000 of combined self-employment income on a joint return, $125,000 for married taxpayers filing a separate return). (Code Sec. 1401(b)(2))

For 2022, the self-employment tax on self-employed people is:

* 12.40% OASDI on the first $147,000 of self-employment income, for a maximum tax of $18,228 (12.40% of $147,000); plus

* 2.90% Medicare tax on the first $200,000 of self-employment income ($250,000 of combined self-employment income on a joint return, $125,000 on a separate return), (Code Sec. 1401(a), Code Sec. 1401(b)); plus

* 3.8% (2.90% regular Medicare tax + 0.9% additional Medicare tax) on all self-employment income in excess of $200,000 ($250,000 of combined self-employment income on a joint return, $125,000 for married taxpayers filing a separate return). (Code Sec. 1401(b)(2))

The above $250,000, $125,000, and $200,000 thresholds are reduced (but not below zero)

4. ¶H-4687

by the amount of wages taken into account in determining the additional 0.9% HI tax on wages (i.e., the taxpayer's FICA tax, see ¶1108). (Code Sec. 1401(b)(2)(B))[5]

illustration: A single taxpayer has $150,000 in self-employment income and $120,000 in wages. The taxpayer's wages didn't exceed $200,000, so the taxpayer's employer didn't withhold the 0.9% tax. However, the $120,000 in wages reduces the $200,000 threshold for the 0.9% additional Medicare tax to $80,000, so the taxpayer owes the 0.9% tax on $70,000 of self-employment income (i.e., the extent to which the taxpayer's $150,000 in self-employment income exceeds the $80,000 threshold). (Reg § 1.1401-1(d)(2), Ex 3)

observation: Sole proprietors and partners are subject to Medicare tax on their entire self-employment income even if the income isn't distributed (unlike shareholders in an S corporation, who aren't subject to the self-employment tax on their share of the corporation's net income whether distributed or not, see ¶3135).

observation: Amounts subject to self-employment tax are excluded from "investment income" for purposes of the 3.8% net investment income tax (¶1107).

¶ 1110 Federal unemployment tax (FUTA) imposed on employers.

Employers pay a 6.0% (Code Sec. 3301) tax on the first $7,000 paid each employee as wages during the calendar year. (Code Sec. 3306(b)) This tax may be offset by a credit of up to 5.4% for contributions paid into state unemployment funds, effectively reducing the net FUTA tax rate for the majority of employers to 0.6% (i.e., 6.0% − 5.4%). However, the amount of the 5.4% credit can be reduced for employers in states that borrowed funds from the federal government to pay unemployment benefits and defaulted on repayment of the loan.[6]

---

5. ¶A-6001.2

6. ¶H-4801; ¶H-4802; ¶H-4808

¶ 1111   Tax Table for Individuals.

2022 Tax Table

See the instructions for line 16 to see if you must use the Tax Table below to figure your tax.

Example. A married couple are filing a joint return. Their taxable income on Form 1040, line 15, is $25,300. First, they find the $25,300-25,350 taxable income line. Next, they find the column for married filing jointly and read down the column. The amount shown where the taxable income line and filing status column meet is $2,628. This is the tax amount they should enter in the entry space on Form 1040, line 16.

Sample Table

At Least	But Less Than	Single	Married filing jointly*	Married filing separately*	Head of a household
			Your tax is—		
25,200	25,250	2,822	2,616	2,822	2,734
25,250	25,300	2,828	2,622	2,828	2,740
25,300	25,350	2,834	(2,628)	2,834	2,746
25,350	25,400	2,840	2,634	2,840	2,752

If line 15 (taxable income) is—		And you are—			
At least	But less than	Single	Married filing jointly*	Married filing separately	Head of a household
			Your tax is—		
0	5	0	0	0	0
5	15	1	1	1	1
15	25	2	2	2	2
25	50	4	4	4	4
50	75	6	6	6	6
75	100	9	9	9	9
100	125	11	11	11	11
125	150	14	14	14	14
150	175	16	16	16	16
175	200	19	19	19	19
200	225	21	21	21	21
225	250	24	24	24	24
250	275	26	26	26	26
275	300	29	29	29	29
300	325	31	31	31	31
325	350	34	34	34	34
350	375	36	36	36	36
375	400	39	39	39	39
400	425	41	41	41	41
425	450	44	44	44	44
450	475	46	46	46	46
475	500	49	49	49	49
500	525	51	51	51	51
525	550	54	54	54	54
550	575	56	56	56	56
575	600	59	59	59	59
600	625	61	61	61	61
625	650	64	64	64	64
650	675	66	66	66	66
675	700	69	69	69	69
700	725	71	71	71	71
725	750	74	74	74	74
750	775	76	76	76	76
775	800	79	79	79	79
800	825	81	81	81	81
825	850	84	84	84	84
850	875	86	86	86	86
875	900	89	89	89	89
900	925	91	91	91	91
925	950	94	94	94	94
950	975	96	96	96	96
975	1,000	99	99	99	99

1,000

If line 15 (taxable income) is—		And you are—			
At least	But less than	Single	Married filing jointly*	Married filing separately	Head of a household
			Your tax is—		
1,000	1,025	101	101	101	101
1,025	1,050	104	104	104	104
1,050	1,075	106	106	106	106
1,075	1,100	109	109	109	109
1,100	1,125	111	111	111	111
1,125	1,150	114	114	114	114
1,150	1,175	116	116	116	116
1,175	1,200	119	119	119	119
1,200	1,225	121	121	121	121
1,225	1,250	124	124	124	124
1,250	1,275	126	126	126	126
1,275	1,300	129	129	129	129
1,300	1,325	131	131	131	131
1,325	1,350	134	134	134	134
1,350	1,375	136	136	136	136
1,375	1,400	139	139	139	139
1,400	1,425	141	141	141	141
1,425	1,450	144	144	144	144
1,450	1,475	146	146	146	146
1,475	1,500	149	149	149	149
1,500	1,525	151	151	151	151
1,525	1,550	154	154	154	154
1,550	1,575	156	156	156	156
1,575	1,600	159	159	159	159
1,600	1,625	161	161	161	161
1,625	1,650	164	164	164	164
1,650	1,675	166	166	166	166
1,675	1,700	169	169	169	169
1,700	1,725	171	171	171	171
1,725	1,750	174	174	174	174
1,750	1,775	176	176	176	176
1,775	1,800	179	179	179	179
1,800	1,825	181	181	181	181
1,825	1,850	184	184	184	184
1,850	1,875	186	186	186	186
1,875	1,900	189	189	189	189
1,900	1,925	191	191	191	191
1,925	1,950	194	194	194	194
1,950	1,975	196	196	196	196
1,975	2,000	199	199	199	199

2,000

If line 15 (taxable income) is—		And you are—			
At least	But less than	Single	Married filing jointly*	Married filing separately	Head of a household
			Your tax is—		
2,000	2,025	201	201	201	201
2,025	2,050	204	204	204	204
2,050	2,075	206	206	206	206
2,075	2,100	209	209	209	209
2,100	2,125	211	211	211	211
2,125	2,150	214	214	214	214
2,150	2,175	216	216	216	216
2,175	2,200	219	219	219	219
2,200	2,225	221	221	221	221
2,225	2,250	224	224	224	224
2,250	2,275	226	226	226	226
2,275	2,300	229	229	229	229
2,300	2,325	231	231	231	231
2,325	2,350	234	234	234	234
2,350	2,375	236	236	236	236
2,375	2,400	239	239	239	239
2,400	2,425	241	241	241	241
2,425	2,450	244	244	244	244
2,450	2,475	246	246	246	246
2,475	2,500	249	249	249	249
2,500	2,525	251	251	251	251
2,525	2,550	254	254	254	254
2,550	2,575	256	256	256	256
2,575	2,600	259	259	259	259
2,600	2,625	261	261	261	261
2,625	2,650	264	264	264	264
2,650	2,675	266	266	266	266
2,675	2,700	269	269	269	269
2,700	2,725	271	271	271	271
2,725	2,750	274	274	274	274
2,750	2,775	276	276	276	276
2,775	2,800	279	279	279	279
2,800	2,825	281	281	281	281
2,825	2,850	284	284	284	284
2,850	2,875	286	286	286	286
2,875	2,900	289	289	289	289
2,900	2,925	291	291	291	291
2,925	2,950	294	294	294	294
2,950	2,975	296	296	296	296
2,975	3,000	299	299	299	299

(Continued)

* This column must also be used by a qualifying surviving spouse.

Draft as of October 12, 2022.

2022 Tax Table — *Continued*

If line 15 (taxable income) is—		And you are—				If line 15 (taxable income) is—		And you are—				If line 15 (taxable income) is—		And you are—			
At least	But less than	Single	Married filing jointly *	Married filing separately	Head of a household	At least	But less than	Single	Married filing jointly *	Married filing separately	Head of a household	At least	But less than	Single	Married filing jointly *	Married filing separately	Head of a household
		Your tax is—						Your tax is—						Your tax is—			
3,000						**6,000**						**9,000**					
3,000	3,050	303	303	303	303	6,000	6,050	603	603	603	603	9,000	9,050	903	903	903	903
3,050	3,100	308	308	308	308	6,050	6,100	608	608	608	608	9,050	9,100	908	908	908	908
3,100	3,150	313	313	313	313	6,100	6,150	613	613	613	613	9,100	9,150	913	913	913	913
3,150	3,200	318	318	318	318	6,150	6,200	618	618	618	618	9,150	9,200	918	918	918	918
3,200	3,250	323	323	323	323	6,200	6,250	623	623	623	623	9,200	9,250	923	923	923	923
3,250	3,300	328	328	328	328	6,250	6,300	628	628	628	628	9,250	9,300	928	928	928	928
3,300	3,350	333	333	333	333	6,300	6,350	633	633	633	633	9,300	9,350	933	933	933	933
3,350	3,400	338	338	338	338	6,350	6,400	638	638	638	638	9,350	9,400	938	938	938	938
3,400	3,450	343	343	343	343	6,400	6,450	643	643	643	643	9,400	9,450	943	943	943	943
3,450	3,500	348	348	348	348	6,450	6,500	648	648	648	648	9,450	9,500	948	948	948	948
3,500	3,550	353	353	353	353	6,500	6,550	653	653	653	653	9,500	9,550	953	953	953	953
3,550	3,600	358	358	358	358	6,550	6,600	658	658	658	658	9,550	9,600	958	958	958	958
3,600	3,650	363	363	363	363	6,600	6,650	663	663	663	663	9,600	9,650	963	963	963	963
3,650	3,700	368	368	368	368	6,650	6,700	668	668	668	668	9,650	9,700	968	968	968	968
3,700	3,750	373	373	373	373	6,700	6,750	673	673	673	673	9,700	9,750	973	973	973	973
3,750	3,800	378	378	378	378	6,750	6,800	678	678	678	678	9,750	9,800	978	978	978	978
3,800	3,850	383	383	383	383	6,800	6,850	683	683	683	683	9,800	9,850	983	983	983	983
3,850	3,900	388	388	388	388	6,850	6,900	688	688	688	688	9,850	9,900	988	988	988	988
3,900	3,950	393	393	393	393	6,900	6,950	693	693	693	693	9,900	9,950	993	993	993	993
3,950	4,000	398	398	398	398	6,950	7,000	698	698	698	698	9,950	10,000	998	998	998	998
4,000						**7,000**						**10,000**					
4,000	4,050	403	403	403	403	7,000	7,050	703	703	703	703	10,000	10,050	1,003	1,003	1,003	1,003
4,050	4,100	408	408	408	408	7,050	7,100	708	708	708	708	10,050	10,100	1,008	1,008	1,008	1,008
4,100	4,150	413	413	413	413	7,100	7,150	713	713	713	713	10,100	10,150	1,013	1,013	1,013	1,013
4,150	4,200	418	418	418	418	7,150	7,200	718	718	718	718	10,150	10,200	1,018	1,018	1,018	1,018
4,200	4,250	423	423	423	423	7,200	7,250	723	723	723	723	10,200	10,250	1,023	1,023	1,023	1,023
4,250	4,300	428	428	428	428	7,250	7,300	728	728	728	728	10,250	10,300	1,028	1,028	1,028	1,028
4,300	4,350	433	433	433	433	7,300	7,350	733	733	733	733	10,300	10,350	1,034	1,033	1,034	1,033
4,350	4,400	438	438	438	438	7,350	7,400	738	738	738	738	10,350	10,400	1,040	1,038	1,040	1,038
4,400	4,450	443	443	443	443	7,400	7,450	743	743	743	743	10,400	10,450	1,046	1,043	1,046	1,043
4,450	4,500	448	448	448	448	7,450	7,500	748	748	748	748	10,450	10,500	1,052	1,048	1,052	1,048
4,500	4,550	453	453	453	453	7,500	7,550	753	753	753	753	10,500	10,550	1,058	1,053	1,058	1,053
4,550	4,600	458	458	458	458	7,550	7,600	758	758	758	758	10,550	10,600	1,064	1,058	1,064	1,058
4,600	4,650	463	463	463	463	7,600	7,650	763	763	763	763	10,600	10,650	1,070	1,063	1,070	1,063
4,650	4,700	468	468	468	468	7,650	7,700	768	768	768	768	10,650	10,700	1,076	1,068	1,076	1,068
4,700	4,750	473	473	473	473	7,700	7,750	773	773	773	773	10,700	10,750	1,082	1,073	1,082	1,073
4,750	4,800	478	478	478	478	7,750	7,800	778	778	778	778	10,750	10,800	1,088	1,078	1,088	1,078
4,800	4,850	483	483	483	483	7,800	7,850	783	783	783	783	10,800	10,850	1,094	1,083	1,094	1,083
4,850	4,900	488	488	488	488	7,850	7,900	788	788	788	788	10,850	10,900	1,100	1,088	1,100	1,088
4,900	4,950	493	493	493	493	7,900	7,950	793	793	793	793	10,900	10,950	1,106	1,093	1,106	1,093
4,950	5,000	498	498	498	498	7,950	8,000	798	798	798	798	10,950	11,000	1,112	1,098	1,112	1,098
5,000						**8,000**						**11,000**					
5,000	5,050	503	503	503	503	8,000	8,050	803	803	803	803	11,000	11,050	1,118	1,103	1,118	1,103
5,050	5,100	508	508	508	508	8,050	8,100	808	808	808	808	11,050	11,100	1,124	1,108	1,124	1,108
5,100	5,150	513	513	513	513	8,100	8,150	813	813	813	813	11,100	11,150	1,130	1,113	1,130	1,113
5,150	5,200	518	518	518	518	8,150	8,200	818	818	818	818	11,150	11,200	1,136	1,118	1,136	1,118
5,200	5,250	523	523	523	523	8,200	8,250	823	823	823	823	11,200	11,250	1,142	1,123	1,142	1,123
5,250	5,300	528	528	528	528	8,250	8,300	828	828	828	828	11,250	11,300	1,148	1,128	1,148	1,128
5,300	5,350	533	533	533	533	8,300	8,350	833	833	833	833	11,300	11,350	1,154	1,133	1,154	1,133
5,350	5,400	538	538	538	538	8,350	8,400	838	838	838	838	11,350	11,400	1,160	1,138	1,160	1,138
5,400	5,450	543	543	543	543	8,400	8,450	843	843	843	843	11,400	11,450	1,166	1,143	1,166	1,143
5,450	5,500	548	548	548	548	8,450	8,500	848	848	848	848	11,450	11,500	1,172	1,148	1,172	1,148
5,500	5,550	553	553	553	553	8,500	8,550	853	853	853	853	11,500	11,550	1,178	1,153	1,178	1,153
5,550	5,600	558	558	558	558	8,550	8,600	858	858	858	858	11,550	11,600	1,184	1,158	1,184	1,158
5,600	5,650	563	563	563	563	8,600	8,650	863	863	863	863	11,600	11,650	1,190	1,163	1,190	1,163
5,650	5,700	568	568	568	568	8,650	8,700	868	868	868	868	11,650	11,700	1,196	1,168	1,196	1,168
5,700	5,750	573	573	573	573	8,700	8,750	873	873	873	873	11,700	11,750	1,202	1,173	1,202	1,173
5,750	5,800	578	578	578	578	8,750	8,800	878	878	878	878	11,750	11,800	1,208	1,178	1,208	1,178
5,800	5,850	583	583	583	583	8,800	8,850	883	883	883	883	11,800	11,850	1,214	1,183	1,214	1,183
5,850	5,900	588	588	588	588	8,850	8,900	888	888	888	888	11,850	11,900	1,220	1,188	1,220	1,188
5,900	5,950	593	593	593	593	8,900	8,950	893	893	893	893	11,900	11,950	1,226	1,193	1,226	1,193
5,950	6,000	598	598	598	598	8,950	9,000	898	898	898	898	11,950	12,000	1,232	1,198	1,232	1,198

* This column must also be used by a qualifying surviving spouse.

Draft as of October 12, 2022.

(Continued)

2022 Tax Table — *Continued*

12,000

At least	But less than	Single	Married filing jointly *	Married filing separately	Head of a household
12,000	12,050	1,238	1,203	1,238	1,203
12,050	12,100	1,244	1,208	1,244	1,208
12,100	12,150	1,250	1,213	1,250	1,213
12,150	12,200	1,256	1,218	1,256	1,218
12,200	12,250	1,262	1,223	1,262	1,223
12,250	12,300	1,268	1,228	1,268	1,228
12,300	12,350	1,274	1,233	1,274	1,233
12,350	12,400	1,280	1,238	1,280	1,238
12,400	12,450	1,286	1,243	1,286	1,243
12,450	12,500	1,292	1,248	1,292	1,248
12,500	12,550	1,298	1,253	1,298	1,253
12,550	12,600	1,304	1,258	1,304	1,258
12,600	12,650	1,310	1,263	1,310	1,263
12,650	12,700	1,316	1,268	1,316	1,268
12,700	12,750	1,322	1,273	1,322	1,273
12,750	12,800	1,328	1,278	1,328	1,278
12,800	12,850	1,334	1,283	1,334	1,283
12,850	12,900	1,340	1,288	1,340	1,288
12,900	12,950	1,346	1,293	1,346	1,293
12,950	13,000	1,352	1,298	1,352	1,298

13,000

At least	But less than	Single	Married filing jointly *	Married filing separately	Head of a household
13,000	13,050	1,358	1,303	1,358	1,303
13,050	13,100	1,364	1,308	1,364	1,308
13,100	13,150	1,370	1,313	1,370	1,313
13,150	13,200	1,376	1,318	1,376	1,318
13,200	13,250	1,382	1,323	1,382	1,323
13,250	13,300	1,388	1,328	1,388	1,328
13,300	13,350	1,394	1,333	1,394	1,333
13,350	13,400	1,400	1,338	1,400	1,338
13,400	13,450	1,406	1,343	1,406	1,343
13,450	13,500	1,412	1,348	1,412	1,348
13,500	13,550	1,418	1,353	1,418	1,353
13,550	13,600	1,424	1,358	1,424	1,358
13,600	13,650	1,430	1,363	1,430	1,363
13,650	13,700	1,436	1,368	1,436	1,368
13,700	13,750	1,442	1,373	1,442	1,373
13,750	13,800	1,448	1,378	1,448	1,378
13,800	13,850	1,454	1,383	1,454	1,383
13,850	13,900	1,460	1,388	1,460	1,388
13,900	13,950	1,466	1,393	1,466	1,393
13,950	14,000	1,472	1,398	1,472	1,398

14,000

At least	But less than	Single	Married filing jointly *	Married filing separately	Head of a household
14,000	14,050	1,478	1,403	1,478	1,403
14,050	14,100	1,484	1,408	1,484	1,408
14,100	14,150	1,490	1,413	1,490	1,413
14,150	14,200	1,496	1,418	1,496	1,418
14,200	14,250	1,502	1,423	1,502	1,423
14,250	14,300	1,508	1,428	1,508	1,428
14,300	14,350	1,514	1,433	1,514	1,433
14,350	14,400	1,520	1,438	1,520	1,438
14,400	14,450	1,526	1,443	1,526	1,443
14,450	14,500	1,532	1,448	1,532	1,448
14,500	14,550	1,538	1,453	1,538	1,453
14,550	14,600	1,544	1,458	1,544	1,458
14,600	14,650	1,550	1,463	1,550	1,463
14,650	14,700	1,556	1,468	1,556	1,468
14,700	14,750	1,562	1,473	1,562	1,474
14,750	14,800	1,568	1,478	1,568	1,480
14,800	14,850	1,574	1,483	1,574	1,486
14,850	14,900	1,580	1,488	1,580	1,492
14,900	14,950	1,586	1,493	1,586	1,498
14,950	15,000	1,592	1,498	1,592	1,504

15,000

At least	But less than	Single	Married filing jointly *	Married filing separately	Head of a household
15,000	15,050	1,598	1,503	1,598	1,510
15,050	15,100	1,604	1,508	1,604	1,516
15,100	15,150	1,610	1,513	1,610	1,522
15,150	15,200	1,616	1,518	1,616	1,528
15,200	15,250	1,622	1,523	1,622	1,534
15,250	15,300	1,628	1,528	1,628	1,540
15,300	15,350	1,634	1,533	1,634	1,546
15,350	15,400	1,640	1,538	1,640	1,552
15,400	15,450	1,646	1,543	1,646	1,558
15,450	15,500	1,652	1,548	1,652	1,564
15,500	15,550	1,658	1,553	1,658	1,570
15,550	15,600	1,664	1,558	1,664	1,576
15,600	15,650	1,670	1,563	1,670	1,582
15,650	15,700	1,676	1,568	1,676	1,588
15,700	15,750	1,682	1,573	1,682	1,594
15,750	15,800	1,688	1,578	1,688	1,600
15,800	15,850	1,694	1,583	1,694	1,606
15,850	15,900	1,700	1,588	1,700	1,612
15,900	15,950	1,706	1,593	1,706	1,618
15,950	16,000	1,712	1,598	1,712	1,624

16,000

At least	But less than	Single	Married filing jointly *	Married filing separately	Head of a household
16,000	16,050	1,718	1,603	1,718	1,630
16,050	16,100	1,724	1,608	1,724	1,636
16,100	16,150	1,730	1,613	1,730	1,642
16,150	16,200	1,736	1,618	1,736	1,648
16,200	16,250	1,742	1,623	1,742	1,654
16,250	16,300	1,748	1,628	1,748	1,660
16,300	16,350	1,754	1,633	1,754	1,666
16,350	16,400	1,760	1,638	1,760	1,672
16,400	16,450	1,766	1,643	1,766	1,678
16,450	16,500	1,772	1,648	1,772	1,684
16,500	16,550	1,778	1,653	1,778	1,690
16,550	16,600	1,784	1,658	1,784	1,696
16,600	16,650	1,790	1,663	1,790	1,702
16,650	16,700	1,796	1,668	1,796	1,708
16,700	16,750	1,802	1,673	1,802	1,714
16,750	16,800	1,808	1,678	1,808	1,720
16,800	16,850	1,814	1,683	1,814	1,726
16,850	16,900	1,820	1,688	1,820	1,732
16,900	16,950	1,826	1,693	1,826	1,738
16,950	17,000	1,832	1,698	1,832	1,744

17,000

At least	But less than	Single	Married filing jointly *	Married filing separately	Head of a household
17,000	17,050	1,838	1,703	1,838	1,750
17,050	17,100	1,844	1,708	1,844	1,756
17,100	17,150	1,850	1,713	1,850	1,762
17,150	17,200	1,856	1,718	1,856	1,768
17,200	17,250	1,862	1,723	1,862	1,774
17,250	17,300	1,868	1,728	1,868	1,780
17,300	17,350	1,874	1,733	1,874	1,786
17,350	17,400	1,880	1,738	1,880	1,792
17,400	17,450	1,886	1,743	1,886	1,798
17,450	17,500	1,892	1,748	1,892	1,804
17,500	17,550	1,898	1,753	1,898	1,810
17,550	17,600	1,904	1,758	1,904	1,816
17,600	17,650	1,910	1,763	1,910	1,822
17,650	17,700	1,916	1,768	1,916	1,828
17,700	17,750	1,922	1,773	1,922	1,834
17,750	17,800	1,928	1,778	1,928	1,840
17,800	17,850	1,934	1,783	1,934	1,846
17,850	17,900	1,940	1,788	1,940	1,852
17,900	17,950	1,946	1,793	1,946	1,858
17,950	18,000	1,952	1,798	1,952	1,864

18,000

At least	But less than	Single	Married filing jointly *	Married filing separately	Head of a household
18,000	18,050	1,958	1,803	1,958	1,870
18,050	18,100	1,964	1,808	1,964	1,876
18,100	18,150	1,970	1,813	1,970	1,882
18,150	18,200	1,976	1,818	1,976	1,888
18,200	18,250	1,982	1,823	1,982	1,894
18,250	18,300	1,988	1,828	1,988	1,900
18,300	18,350	1,994	1,833	1,994	1,906
18,350	18,400	2,000	1,838	2,000	1,912
18,400	18,450	2,006	1,843	2,006	1,918
18,450	18,500	2,012	1,848	2,012	1,924
18,500	18,550	2,018	1,853	2,018	1,930
18,550	18,600	2,024	1,858	2,024	1,936
18,600	18,650	2,030	1,863	2,030	1,942
18,650	18,700	2,036	1,868	2,036	1,948
18,700	18,750	2,042	1,873	2,042	1,954
18,750	18,800	2,048	1,878	2,048	1,960
18,800	18,850	2,054	1,883	2,054	1,966
18,850	18,900	2,060	1,888	2,060	1,972
18,900	18,950	2,066	1,893	2,066	1,978
18,950	19,000	2,072	1,898	2,072	1,984

19,000

At least	But less than	Single	Married filing jointly *	Married filing separately	Head of a household
19,000	19,050	2,078	1,903	2,078	1,990
19,050	19,100	2,084	1,908	2,084	1,996
19,100	19,150	2,090	1,913	2,090	2,002
19,150	19,200	2,096	1,918	2,096	2,008
19,200	19,250	2,102	1,923	2,102	2,014
19,250	19,300	2,108	1,928	2,108	2,020
19,300	19,350	2,114	1,933	2,114	2,026
19,350	19,400	2,120	1,938	2,120	2,032
19,400	19,450	2,126	1,943	2,126	2,038
19,450	19,500	2,132	1,948	2,132	2,044
19,500	19,550	2,138	1,953	2,138	2,050
19,550	19,600	2,144	1,958	2,144	2,056
19,600	19,650	2,150	1,963	2,150	2,062
19,650	19,700	2,156	1,968	2,156	2,068
19,700	19,750	2,162	1,973	2,162	2,074
19,750	19,800	2,168	1,978	2,168	2,080
19,800	19,850	2,174	1,983	2,174	2,086
19,850	19,900	2,180	1,988	2,180	2,092
19,900	19,950	2,186	1,993	2,186	2,098
19,950	20,000	2,192	1,998	2,192	2,104

20,000

At least	But less than	Single	Married filing jointly *	Married filing separately	Head of a household
20,000	20,050	2,198	2,003	2,198	2,110
20,050	20,100	2,204	2,008	2,204	2,116
20,100	20,150	2,210	2,013	2,210	2,122
20,150	20,200	2,216	2,018	2,216	2,128
20,200	20,250	2,222	2,023	2,222	2,134
20,250	20,300	2,228	2,028	2,228	2,140
20,300	20,350	2,234	2,033	2,234	2,146
20,350	20,400	2,240	2,038	2,240	2,152
20,400	20,450	2,246	2,043	2,246	2,158
20,450	20,500	2,252	2,048	2,252	2,164
20,500	20,550	2,258	2,053	2,258	2,170
20,550	20,600	2,264	2,058	2,264	2,176
20,600	20,650	2,270	2,064	2,270	2,182
20,650	20,700	2,276	2,070	2,276	2,188
20,700	20,750	2,282	2,076	2,282	2,194
20,750	20,800	2,288	2,082	2,288	2,200
20,800	20,850	2,294	2,088	2,294	2,206
20,850	20,900	2,300	2,094	2,300	2,212
20,900	20,950	2,306	2,100	2,306	2,218
20,950	21,000	2,312	2,106	2,312	2,224

(Continued)

* This column must also be used by a qualifying surviving spouse.

Draft as of October 12, 2022.

2022 Tax Table — *Continued*

If line 15 (taxable income) is—		And you are—			
At least	But less than	Single	Married filing jointly *	Married filing separately	Head of a household
		Your tax is—			

21,000

At least	But less than	Single	Married filing jointly *	Married filing separately	Head of a household
21,000	21,050	2,318	2,112	2,318	2,230
21,050	21,100	2,324	2,118	2,324	2,236
21,100	21,150	2,330	2,124	2,330	2,242
21,150	21,200	2,336	2,130	2,336	2,248
21,200	21,250	2,342	2,136	2,342	2,254
21,250	21,300	2,348	2,142	2,348	2,260
21,300	21,350	2,354	2,148	2,354	2,266
21,350	21,400	2,360	2,154	2,360	2,272
21,400	21,450	2,366	2,160	2,366	2,278
21,450	21,500	2,372	2,166	2,372	2,284
21,500	21,550	2,378	2,172	2,378	2,290
21,550	21,600	2,384	2,178	2,384	2,296
21,600	21,650	2,390	2,184	2,390	2,302
21,650	21,700	2,396	2,190	2,396	2,308
21,700	21,750	2,402	2,196	2,402	2,314
21,750	21,800	2,408	2,202	2,408	2,320
21,800	21,850	2,414	2,208	2,414	2,326
21,850	21,900	2,420	2,214	2,420	2,332
21,900	21,950	2,426	2,220	2,426	2,338
21,950	22,000	2,432	2,226	2,432	2,344

22,000

At least	But less than	Single	Married filing jointly *	Married filing separately	Head of a household
22,000	22,050	2,438	2,232	2,438	2,350
22,050	22,100	2,444	2,238	2,444	2,356
22,100	22,150	2,450	2,244	2,450	2,362
22,150	22,200	2,456	2,250	2,456	2,368
22,200	22,250	2,462	2,256	2,462	2,374
22,250	22,300	2,468	2,262	2,468	2,380
22,300	22,350	2,474	2,268	2,474	2,386
22,350	22,400	2,480	2,274	2,480	2,392
22,400	22,450	2,486	2,280	2,486	2,398
22,450	22,500	2,492	2,286	2,492	2,404
22,500	22,550	2,498	2,292	2,498	2,410
22,550	22,600	2,504	2,298	2,504	2,416
22,600	22,650	2,510	2,304	2,510	2,422
22,650	22,700	2,516	2,310	2,516	2,428
22,700	22,750	2,522	2,316	2,522	2,434
22,750	22,800	2,528	2,322	2,528	2,440
22,800	22,850	2,534	2,328	2,534	2,446
22,850	22,900	2,540	2,334	2,540	2,452
22,900	22,950	2,546	2,340	2,546	2,458
22,950	23,000	2,552	2,346	2,552	2,464

23,000

At least	But less than	Single	Married filing jointly *	Married filing separately	Head of a household
23,000	23,050	2,558	2,352	2,558	2,470
23,050	23,100	2,564	2,358	2,564	2,476
23,100	23,150	2,570	2,364	2,570	2,482
23,150	23,200	2,576	2,370	2,576	2,488
23,200	23,250	2,582	2,376	2,582	2,494
23,250	23,300	2,588	2,382	2,588	2,500
23,300	23,350	2,594	2,388	2,594	2,506
23,350	23,400	2,600	2,394	2,600	2,512
23,400	23,450	2,606	2,400	2,606	2,518
23,450	23,500	2,612	2,406	2,612	2,524
23,500	23,550	2,618	2,412	2,618	2,530
23,550	23,600	2,624	2,418	2,624	2,536
23,600	23,650	2,630	2,424	2,630	2,542
23,650	23,700	2,636	2,430	2,636	2,548
23,700	23,750	2,642	2,436	2,642	2,554
23,750	23,800	2,648	2,442	2,648	2,560
23,800	23,850	2,654	2,448	2,654	2,566
23,850	23,900	2,660	2,454	2,660	2,572
23,900	23,950	2,666	2,460	2,666	2,578
23,950	24,000	2,672	2,466	2,672	2,584

24,000

At least	But less than	Single	Married filing jointly *	Married filing separately	Head of a household
24,000	24,050	2,678	2,472	2,678	2,590
24,050	24,100	2,684	2,478	2,684	2,596
24,100	24,150	2,690	2,484	2,690	2,602
24,150	24,200	2,696	2,490	2,696	2,608
24,200	24,250	2,702	2,496	2,702	2,614
24,250	24,300	2,708	2,502	2,708	2,620
24,300	24,350	2,714	2,508	2,714	2,626
24,350	24,400	2,720	2,514	2,720	2,632
24,400	24,450	2,726	2,520	2,726	2,638
24,450	24,500	2,732	2,526	2,732	2,644
24,500	24,550	2,738	2,532	2,738	2,650
24,550	24,600	2,744	2,538	2,744	2,656
24,600	24,650	2,750	2,544	2,750	2,662
24,650	24,700	2,756	2,550	2,756	2,668
24,700	24,750	2,762	2,556	2,762	2,674
24,750	24,800	2,768	2,562	2,768	2,680
24,800	24,850	2,774	2,568	2,774	2,686
24,850	24,900	2,780	2,574	2,780	2,692
24,900	24,950	2,786	2,580	2,786	2,698
24,950	25,000	2,792	2,586	2,792	2,704

25,000

At least	But less than	Single	Married filing jointly *	Married filing separately	Head of a household
25,000	25,050	2,798	2,592	2,798	2,710
25,050	25,100	2,804	2,598	2,804	2,716
25,100	25,150	2,810	2,604	2,810	2,722
25,150	25,200	2,816	2,610	2,816	2,728
25,200	25,250	2,822	2,616	2,822	2,734
25,250	25,300	2,828	2,622	2,828	2,740
25,300	25,350	2,834	2,628	2,834	2,746
25,350	25,400	2,840	2,634	2,840	2,752
25,400	25,450	2,846	2,640	2,846	2,758
25,450	25,500	2,852	2,646	2,852	2,764
25,500	25,550	2,858	2,652	2,858	2,770
25,550	25,600	2,864	2,658	2,864	2,776
25,600	25,650	2,870	2,664	2,870	2,782
25,650	25,700	2,876	2,670	2,876	2,788
25,700	25,750	2,882	2,676	2,882	2,794
25,750	25,800	2,888	2,682	2,888	2,800
25,800	25,850	2,894	2,688	2,894	2,806
25,850	25,900	2,900	2,694	2,900	2,812
25,900	25,950	2,906	2,700	2,906	2,818
25,950	26,000	2,912	2,706	2,912	2,824

26,000

At least	But less than	Single	Married filing jointly *	Married filing separately	Head of a household
26,000	26,050	2,918	2,712	2,918	2,830
26,050	26,100	2,924	2,718	2,924	2,836
26,100	26,150	2,930	2,724	2,930	2,842
26,150	26,200	2,936	2,730	2,936	2,848
26,200	26,250	2,942	2,736	2,942	2,854
26,250	26,300	2,948	2,742	2,948	2,860
26,300	26,350	2,954	2,748	2,954	2,866
26,350	26,400	2,960	2,754	2,960	2,872
26,400	26,450	2,966	2,760	2,966	2,878
26,450	26,500	2,972	2,766	2,972	2,884
26,500	26,550	2,978	2,772	2,978	2,890
26,550	26,600	2,984	2,778	2,984	2,896
26,600	26,650	2,990	2,784	2,990	2,902
26,650	26,700	2,996	2,790	2,996	2,908
26,700	26,750	3,002	2,796	3,002	2,914
26,750	26,800	3,008	2,802	3,008	2,920
26,800	26,850	3,014	2,808	3,014	2,926
26,850	26,900	3,020	2,814	3,020	2,932
26,900	26,950	3,026	2,820	3,026	2,938
26,950	27,000	3,032	2,826	3,032	2,944

27,000

At least	But less than	Single	Married filing jointly *	Married filing separately	Head of a household
27,000	27,050	3,038	2,832	3,038	2,950
27,050	27,100	3,044	2,838	3,044	2,956
27,100	27,150	3,050	2,844	3,050	2,962
27,150	27,200	3,056	2,850	3,056	2,968
27,200	27,250	3,062	2,856	3,062	2,974
27,250	27,300	3,068	2,862	3,068	2,980
27,300	27,350	3,074	2,868	3,074	2,986
27,350	27,400	3,080	2,874	3,080	2,992
27,400	27,450	3,086	2,880	3,086	2,998
27,450	27,500	3,092	2,886	3,092	3,004
27,500	27,550	3,098	2,892	3,098	3,010
27,550	27,600	3,104	2,898	3,104	3,016
27,600	27,650	3,110	2,904	3,110	3,022
27,650	27,700	3,116	2,910	3,116	3,028
27,700	27,750	3,122	2,916	3,122	3,034
27,750	27,800	3,128	2,922	3,128	3,040
27,800	27,850	3,134	2,928	3,134	3,046
27,850	27,900	3,140	2,934	3,140	3,052
27,900	27,950	3,146	2,940	3,146	3,058
27,950	28,000	3,152	2,946	3,152	3,064

28,000

At least	But less than	Single	Married filing jointly *	Married filing separately	Head of a household
28,000	28,050	3,158	2,952	3,158	3,070
28,050	28,100	3,164	2,958	3,164	3,076
28,100	28,150	3,170	2,964	3,170	3,082
28,150	28,200	3,176	2,970	3,176	3,088
28,200	28,250	3,182	2,976	3,182	3,094
28,250	28,300	3,188	2,982	3,188	3,100
28,300	28,350	3,194	2,988	3,194	3,106
28,350	28,400	3,200	2,994	3,200	3,112
28,400	28,450	3,206	3,000	3,206	3,118
28,450	28,500	3,212	3,006	3,212	3,124
28,500	28,550	3,218	3,012	3,218	3,130
28,550	28,600	3,224	3,018	3,224	3,136
28,600	28,650	3,230	3,024	3,230	3,142
28,650	28,700	3,236	3,030	3,236	3,148
28,700	28,750	3,242	3,036	3,242	3,154
28,750	28,800	3,248	3,042	3,248	3,160
28,800	28,850	3,254	3,048	3,254	3,166
28,850	28,900	3,260	3,054	3,260	3,172
28,900	28,950	3,266	3,060	3,266	3,178
28,950	29,000	3,272	3,066	3,272	3,184

29,000

At least	But less than	Single	Married filing jointly *	Married filing separately	Head of a household
29,000	29,050	3,278	3,072	3,278	3,190
29,050	29,100	3,284	3,078	3,284	3,196
29,100	29,150	3,290	3,084	3,290	3,202
29,150	29,200	3,296	3,090	3,296	3,208
29,200	29,250	3,302	3,096	3,302	3,214
29,250	29,300	3,308	3,102	3,308	3,220
29,300	29,350	3,314	3,108	3,314	3,226
29,350	29,400	3,320	3,114	3,320	3,232
29,400	29,450	3,326	3,120	3,326	3,238
29,450	29,500	3,332	3,126	3,332	3,244
29,500	29,550	3,338	3,132	3,338	3,250
29,550	29,600	3,344	3,138	3,344	3,256
29,600	29,650	3,350	3,144	3,350	3,262
29,650	29,700	3,356	3,150	3,356	3,268
29,700	29,750	3,362	3,156	3,362	3,274
29,750	29,800	3,368	3,162	3,368	3,280
29,800	29,850	3,374	3,168	3,374	3,286
29,850	29,900	3,380	3,174	3,380	3,292
29,900	29,950	3,386	3,180	3,386	3,298
29,950	30,000	3,392	3,186	3,392	3,304

* This column must also be used by a qualifying surviving spouse.

(Continued)

Draft as of October 12, 2022.

2022 Tax Table — *Continued*

30,000

If line 15 (taxable income) is— At least	But less than	Single	Married filing jointly *	Married filing separately	Head of a household
30,000	30,050	3,398	3,192	3,398	3,310
30,050	30,100	3,404	3,198	3,404	3,316
30,100	30,150	3,410	3,204	3,410	3,322
30,150	30,200	3,416	3,210	3,416	3,328
30,200	30,250	3,422	3,216	3,422	3,334
30,250	30,300	3,428	3,222	3,428	3,340
30,300	30,350	3,434	3,228	3,434	3,346
30,350	30,400	3,440	3,234	3,440	3,352
30,400	30,450	3,446	3,240	3,446	3,358
30,450	30,500	3,452	3,246	3,452	3,364
30,500	30,550	3,458	3,252	3,458	3,370
30,550	30,600	3,464	3,258	3,464	3,376
30,600	30,650	3,470	3,264	3,470	3,382
30,650	30,700	3,476	3,270	3,476	3,388
30,700	30,750	3,482	3,276	3,482	3,394
30,750	30,800	3,488	3,282	3,488	3,400
30,800	30,850	3,494	3,288	3,494	3,406
30,850	30,900	3,500	3,294	3,500	3,412
30,900	30,950	3,506	3,300	3,506	3,418
30,950	31,000	3,512	3,306	3,512	3,424

31,000

At least	But less than	Single	Married filing jointly *	Married filing separately	Head of a household
31,000	31,050	3,518	3,312	3,518	3,430
31,050	31,100	3,524	3,318	3,524	3,436
31,100	31,150	3,530	3,324	3,530	3,442
31,150	31,200	3,536	3,330	3,536	3,448
31,200	31,250	3,542	3,336	3,542	3,454
31,250	31,300	3,548	3,342	3,548	3,460
31,300	31,350	3,554	3,348	3,554	3,466
31,350	31,400	3,560	3,354	3,560	3,472
31,400	31,450	3,566	3,360	3,566	3,478
31,450	31,500	3,572	3,366	3,572	3,484
31,500	31,550	3,578	3,372	3,578	3,490
31,550	31,600	3,584	3,378	3,584	3,496
31,600	31,650	3,590	3,384	3,590	3,502
31,650	31,700	3,596	3,390	3,596	3,508
31,700	31,750	3,602	3,396	3,602	3,514
31,750	31,800	3,608	3,402	3,608	3,520
31,800	31,850	3,614	3,408	3,614	3,526
31,850	31,900	3,620	3,414	3,620	3,532
31,900	31,950	3,626	3,420	3,626	3,538
31,950	32,000	3,632	3,426	3,632	3,544

32,000

At least	But less than	Single	Married filing jointly *	Married filing separately	Head of a household
32,000	32,050	3,638	3,432	3,638	3,550
32,050	32,100	3,644	3,438	3,644	3,556
32,100	32,150	3,650	3,444	3,650	3,562
32,150	32,200	3,656	3,450	3,656	3,568
32,200	32,250	3,662	3,456	3,662	3,574
32,250	32,300	3,668	3,462	3,668	3,580
32,300	32,350	3,674	3,468	3,674	3,586
32,350	32,400	3,680	3,474	3,680	3,592
32,400	32,450	3,686	3,480	3,686	3,598
32,450	32,500	3,692	3,486	3,692	3,604
32,500	32,550	3,698	3,492	3,698	3,610
32,550	32,600	3,704	3,498	3,704	3,616
32,600	32,650	3,710	3,504	3,710	3,622
32,650	32,700	3,716	3,510	3,716	3,628
32,700	32,750	3,722	3,516	3,722	3,634
32,750	32,800	3,728	3,522	3,728	3,640
32,800	32,850	3,734	3,528	3,734	3,646
32,850	32,900	3,740	3,534	3,740	3,652
32,900	32,950	3,746	3,540	3,746	3,658
32,950	33,000	3,752	3,546	3,752	3,664

33,000

At least	But less than	Single	Married filing jointly *	Married filing separately	Head of a household
33,000	33,050	3,758	3,552	3,758	3,670
33,050	33,100	3,764	3,558	3,764	3,676
33,100	33,150	3,770	3,564	3,770	3,682
33,150	33,200	3,776	3,570	3,776	3,688
33,200	33,250	3,782	3,576	3,782	3,694
33,250	33,300	3,788	3,582	3,788	3,700
33,300	33,350	3,794	3,588	3,794	3,706
33,350	33,400	3,800	3,594	3,800	3,712
33,400	33,450	3,806	3,600	3,806	3,718
33,450	33,500	3,812	3,606	3,812	3,724
33,500	33,550	3,818	3,612	3,818	3,730
33,550	33,600	3,824	3,618	3,824	3,736
33,600	33,650	3,830	3,624	3,830	3,742
33,650	33,700	3,836	3,630	3,836	3,748
33,700	33,750	3,842	3,636	3,842	3,754
33,750	33,800	3,848	3,642	3,848	3,760
33,800	33,850	3,854	3,648	3,854	3,766
33,850	33,900	3,860	3,654	3,860	3,772
33,900	33,950	3,866	3,660	3,866	3,778
33,950	34,000	3,872	3,666	3,872	3,784

34,000

At least	But less than	Single	Married filing jointly *	Married filing separately	Head of a household
34,000	34,050	3,878	3,672	3,878	3,790
34,050	34,100	3,884	3,678	3,884	3,796
34,100	34,150	3,890	3,684	3,890	3,802
34,150	34,200	3,896	3,690	3,896	3,808
34,200	34,250	3,902	3,696	3,902	3,814
34,250	34,300	3,908	3,702	3,908	3,820
34,300	34,350	3,914	3,708	3,914	3,826
34,350	34,400	3,920	3,714	3,920	3,832
34,400	34,450	3,926	3,720	3,926	3,838
34,450	34,500	3,932	3,726	3,932	3,844
34,500	34,550	3,938	3,732	3,938	3,850
34,550	34,600	3,944	3,738	3,944	3,856
34,600	34,650	3,950	3,744	3,950	3,862
34,650	34,700	3,956	3,750	3,956	3,868
34,700	34,750	3,962	3,756	3,962	3,874
34,750	34,800	3,968	3,762	3,968	3,880
34,800	34,850	3,974	3,768	3,974	3,886
34,850	34,900	3,980	3,774	3,980	3,892
34,900	34,950	3,986	3,780	3,986	3,898
34,950	35,000	3,992	3,786	3,992	3,904

35,000

At least	But less than	Single	Married filing jointly *	Married filing separately	Head of a household
35,000	35,050	3,998	3,792	3,998	3,910
35,050	35,100	4,004	3,798	4,004	3,916
35,100	35,150	4,010	3,804	4,010	3,922
35,150	35,200	4,016	3,810	4,016	3,928
35,200	35,250	4,022	3,816	4,022	3,934
35,250	35,300	4,028	3,822	4,028	3,940
35,300	35,350	4,034	3,828	4,034	3,946
35,350	35,400	4,040	3,834	4,040	3,952
35,400	35,450	4,046	3,840	4,046	3,958
35,450	35,500	4,052	3,846	4,052	3,964
35,500	35,550	4,058	3,852	4,058	3,970
35,550	35,600	4,064	3,858	4,064	3,976
35,600	35,650	4,070	3,864	4,070	3,982
35,650	35,700	4,076	3,870	4,076	3,988
35,700	35,750	4,082	3,876	4,082	3,994
35,750	35,800	4,088	3,882	4,088	4,000
35,800	35,850	4,094	3,888	4,094	4,006
35,850	35,900	4,100	3,894	4,100	4,012
35,900	35,950	4,106	3,900	4,106	4,018
35,950	36,000	4,112	3,906	4,112	4,024

36,000

At least	But less than	Single	Married filing jointly *	Married filing separately	Head of a household
36,000	36,050	4,118	3,912	4,118	4,030
36,050	36,100	4,124	3,918	4,124	4,036
36,100	36,150	4,130	3,924	4,130	4,042
36,150	36,200	4,136	3,930	4,136	4,048
36,200	36,250	4,142	3,936	4,142	4,054
36,250	36,300	4,148	3,942	4,148	4,060
36,300	36,350	4,154	3,948	4,154	4,066
36,350	36,400	4,160	3,954	4,160	4,072
36,400	36,450	4,166	3,960	4,166	4,078
36,450	36,500	4,172	3,966	4,172	4,084
36,500	36,550	4,178	3,972	4,178	4,090
36,550	36,600	4,184	3,978	4,184	4,096
36,600	36,650	4,190	3,984	4,190	4,102
36,650	36,700	4,196	3,990	4,196	4,108
36,700	36,750	4,202	3,996	4,202	4,114
36,750	36,800	4,208	4,002	4,208	4,120
36,800	36,850	4,214	4,008	4,214	4,126
36,850	36,900	4,220	4,014	4,220	4,132
36,900	36,950	4,226	4,020	4,226	4,138
36,950	37,000	4,232	4,026	4,232	4,144

37,000

At least	But less than	Single	Married filing jointly *	Married filing separately	Head of a household
37,000	37,050	4,238	4,032	4,238	4,150
37,050	37,100	4,244	4,038	4,244	4,156
37,100	37,150	4,250	4,044	4,250	4,162
37,150	37,200	4,256	4,050	4,256	4,168
37,200	37,250	4,262	4,056	4,262	4,174
37,250	37,300	4,268	4,062	4,268	4,180
37,300	37,350	4,274	4,068	4,274	4,186
37,350	37,400	4,280	4,074	4,280	4,192
37,400	37,450	4,286	4,080	4,286	4,198
37,450	37,500	4,292	4,086	4,292	4,204
37,500	37,550	4,298	4,092	4,298	4,210
37,550	37,600	4,304	4,098	4,304	4,216
37,600	37,650	4,310	4,104	4,310	4,222
37,650	37,700	4,316	4,110	4,316	4,228
37,700	37,750	4,322	4,116	4,322	4,234
37,750	37,800	4,328	4,122	4,328	4,240
37,800	37,850	4,334	4,128	4,334	4,246
37,850	37,900	4,340	4,134	4,340	4,252
37,900	37,950	4,346	4,140	4,346	4,258
37,950	38,000	4,352	4,146	4,352	4,264

38,000

At least	But less than	Single	Married filing jointly *	Married filing separately	Head of a household
38,000	38,050	4,358	4,152	4,358	4,270
38,050	38,100	4,364	4,158	4,364	4,276
38,100	38,150	4,370	4,164	4,370	4,282
38,150	38,200	4,376	4,170	4,376	4,288
38,200	38,250	4,382	4,176	4,382	4,294
38,250	38,300	4,388	4,182	4,388	4,300
38,300	38,350	4,394	4,188	4,394	4,306
38,350	38,400	4,400	4,194	4,400	4,312
38,400	38,450	4,406	4,200	4,406	4,318
38,450	38,500	4,412	4,206	4,412	4,324
38,500	38,550	4,418	4,212	4,418	4,330
38,550	38,600	4,424	4,218	4,424	4,336
38,600	38,650	4,430	4,224	4,430	4,342
38,650	38,700	4,436	4,230	4,436	4,348
38,700	38,750	4,442	4,236	4,442	4,354
38,750	38,800	4,448	4,242	4,448	4,360
38,800	38,850	4,454	4,248	4,454	4,366
38,850	38,900	4,460	4,254	4,460	4,372
38,900	38,950	4,466	4,260	4,466	4,378
38,950	39,000	4,472	4,266	4,472	4,384

* This column must also be used by a qualifying surviving spouse.

(Continued)

Draft as of October 12, 2022.

2022 Tax Table — *Continued*

39,000

At least	But less than	Single	Married filing jointly *	Married filing separately	Head of a household
39,000	39,050	4,478	4,272	4,478	4,390
39,050	39,100	4,484	4,278	4,484	4,396
39,100	39,150	4,490	4,284	4,490	4,402
39,150	39,200	4,496	4,290	4,496	4,408
39,200	39,250	4,502	4,296	4,502	4,414
39,250	39,300	4,508	4,302	4,508	4,420
39,300	39,350	4,514	4,308	4,514	4,426
39,350	39,400	4,520	4,314	4,520	4,432
39,400	39,450	4,526	4,320	4,526	4,438
39,450	39,500	4,532	4,326	4,532	4,444
39,500	39,550	4,538	4,332	4,538	4,450
39,550	39,600	4,544	4,338	4,544	4,456
39,600	39,650	4,550	4,344	4,550	4,462
39,650	39,700	4,556	4,350	4,556	4,468
39,700	39,750	4,562	4,356	4,562	4,474
39,750	39,800	4,568	4,362	4,568	4,480
39,800	39,850	4,574	4,368	4,574	4,486
39,850	39,900	4,580	4,374	4,580	4,492
39,900	39,950	4,586	4,380	4,586	4,498
39,950	40,000	4,592	4,386	4,592	4,504

40,000

At least	But less than	Single	Married filing jointly *	Married filing separately	Head of a household
40,000	40,050	4,598	4,392	4,598	4,510
40,050	40,100	4,604	4,398	4,604	4,516
40,100	40,150	4,610	4,404	4,610	4,522
40,150	40,200	4,616	4,410	4,616	4,528
40,200	40,250	4,622	4,416	4,622	4,534
40,250	40,300	4,628	4,422	4,628	4,540
40,300	40,350	4,634	4,428	4,634	4,546
40,350	40,400	4,640	4,434	4,640	4,552
40,400	40,450	4,646	4,440	4,646	4,558
40,450	40,500	4,652	4,446	4,652	4,564
40,500	40,550	4,658	4,452	4,658	4,570
40,550	40,600	4,664	4,458	4,664	4,576
40,600	40,650	4,670	4,464	4,670	4,582
40,650	40,700	4,676	4,470	4,676	4,588
40,700	40,750	4,682	4,476	4,682	4,594
40,750	40,800	4,688	4,482	4,688	4,600
40,800	40,850	4,694	4,488	4,694	4,606
40,850	40,900	4,700	4,494	4,700	4,612
40,900	40,950	4,706	4,500	4,706	4,618
40,950	41,000	4,712	4,506	4,712	4,624

41,000

At least	But less than	Single	Married filing jointly *	Married filing separately	Head of a household
41,000	41,050	4,718	4,512	4,718	4,630
41,050	41,100	4,724	4,518	4,724	4,636
41,100	41,150	4,730	4,524	4,730	4,642
41,150	41,200	4,736	4,530	4,736	4,648
41,200	41,250	4,742	4,536	4,742	4,654
41,250	41,300	4,748	4,542	4,748	4,660
41,300	41,350	4,754	4,548	4,754	4,666
41,350	41,400	4,760	4,554	4,760	4,672
41,400	41,450	4,766	4,560	4,766	4,678
41,450	41,500	4,772	4,566	4,772	4,684
41,500	41,550	4,778	4,572	4,778	4,690
41,550	41,600	4,784	4,578	4,784	4,696
41,600	41,650	4,790	4,584	4,790	4,702
41,650	41,700	4,796	4,590	4,796	4,708
41,700	41,750	4,802	4,596	4,802	4,714
41,750	41,800	4,808	4,602	4,808	4,720
41,800	41,850	4,819	4,608	4,819	4,726
41,850	41,900	4,830	4,614	4,830	4,732
41,900	41,950	4,841	4,620	4,841	4,738
41,950	42,000	4,852	4,626	4,852	4,744

42,000

At least	But less than	Single	Married filing jointly *	Married filing separately	Head of a household
42,000	42,050	4,863	4,632	4,863	4,750
42,050	42,100	4,874	4,638	4,874	4,756
42,100	42,150	4,885	4,644	4,885	4,762
42,150	42,200	4,896	4,650	4,896	4,768
42,200	42,250	4,907	4,656	4,907	4,774
42,250	42,300	4,918	4,662	4,918	4,780
42,300	42,350	4,929	4,668	4,929	4,786
42,350	42,400	4,940	4,674	4,940	4,792
42,400	42,450	4,951	4,680	4,951	4,798
42,450	42,500	4,962	4,686	4,962	4,804
42,500	42,550	4,973	4,692	4,973	4,810
42,550	42,600	4,984	4,698	4,984	4,816
42,600	42,650	4,995	4,704	4,995	4,822
42,650	42,700	5,006	4,710	5,006	4,828
42,700	42,750	5,017	4,716	5,017	4,834
42,750	42,800	5,028	4,722	5,028	4,840
42,800	42,850	5,039	4,728	5,039	4,846
42,850	42,900	5,050	4,734	5,050	4,852
42,900	42,950	5,061	4,740	5,061	4,858
42,950	43,000	5,072	4,746	5,072	4,864

43,000

At least	But less than	Single	Married filing jointly *	Married filing separately	Head of a household
43,000	43,050	5,083	4,752	5,083	4,870
43,050	43,100	5,094	4,758	5,094	4,876
43,100	43,150	5,105	4,764	5,105	4,882
43,150	43,200	5,116	4,770	5,116	4,888
43,200	43,250	5,127	4,776	5,127	4,894
43,250	43,300	5,138	4,782	5,138	4,900
43,300	43,350	5,149	4,788	5,149	4,906
43,350	43,400	5,160	4,794	5,160	4,912
43,400	43,450	5,171	4,800	5,171	4,918
43,450	43,500	5,182	4,806	5,182	4,924
43,500	43,550	5,193	4,812	5,193	4,930
43,550	43,600	5,204	4,818	5,204	4,936
43,600	43,650	5,215	4,824	5,215	4,942
43,650	43,700	5,226	4,830	5,226	4,948
43,700	43,750	5,237	4,836	5,237	4,954
43,750	43,800	5,248	4,842	5,248	4,960
43,800	43,850	5,259	4,848	5,259	4,966
43,850	43,900	5,270	4,854	5,270	4,972
43,900	43,950	5,281	4,860	5,281	4,978
43,950	44,000	5,292	4,866	5,292	4,984

44,000

At least	But less than	Single	Married filing jointly *	Married filing separately	Head of a household
44,000	44,050	5,303	4,872	5,303	4,990
44,050	44,100	5,314	4,878	5,314	4,996
44,100	44,150	5,325	4,884	5,325	5,002
44,150	44,200	5,336	4,890	5,336	5,008
44,200	44,250	5,347	4,896	5,347	5,014
44,250	44,300	5,358	4,902	5,358	5,020
44,300	44,350	5,369	4,908	5,369	5,026
44,350	44,400	5,380	4,914	5,380	5,032
44,400	44,450	5,391	4,920	5,391	5,038
44,450	44,500	5,402	4,926	5,402	5,044
44,500	44,550	5,413	4,932	5,413	5,050
44,550	44,600	5,424	4,938	5,424	5,056
44,600	44,650	5,435	4,944	5,435	5,062
44,650	44,700	5,446	4,950	5,446	5,068
44,700	44,750	5,457	4,956	5,457	5,074
44,750	44,800	5,468	4,962	5,468	5,080
44,800	44,850	5,479	4,968	5,479	5,086
44,850	44,900	5,490	4,974	5,490	5,092
44,900	44,950	5,501	4,980	5,501	5,098
44,950	45,000	5,512	4,986	5,512	5,104

45,000

At least	But less than	Single	Married filing jointly *	Married filing separately	Head of a household
45,000	45,050	5,523	4,992	5,523	5,110
45,050	45,100	5,534	4,998	5,534	5,116
45,100	45,150	5,545	5,004	5,545	5,122
45,150	45,200	5,556	5,010	5,556	5,128
45,200	45,250	5,567	5,016	5,567	5,134
45,250	45,300	5,578	5,022	5,578	5,140
45,300	45,350	5,589	5,028	5,589	5,146
45,350	45,400	5,600	5,034	5,600	5,152
45,400	45,450	5,611	5,040	5,611	5,158
45,450	45,500	5,622	5,046	5,622	5,164
45,500	45,550	5,633	5,052	5,633	5,170
45,550	45,600	5,644	5,058	5,644	5,176
45,600	45,650	5,655	5,064	5,655	5,182
45,650	45,700	5,666	5,070	5,666	5,188
45,700	45,750	5,677	5,076	5,677	5,194
45,750	45,800	5,688	5,082	5,688	5,200
45,800	45,850	5,699	5,088	5,699	5,206
45,850	45,900	5,710	5,094	5,710	5,212
45,900	45,950	5,721	5,100	5,721	5,218
45,950	46,000	5,732	5,106	5,732	5,224

46,000

At least	But less than	Single	Married filing jointly *	Married filing separately	Head of a household
46,000	46,050	5,743	5,112	5,743	5,230
46,050	46,100	5,754	5,118	5,754	5,236
46,100	46,150	5,765	5,124	5,765	5,242
46,150	46,200	5,776	5,130	5,776	5,248
46,200	46,250	5,787	5,136	5,787	5,254
46,250	46,300	5,798	5,142	5,798	5,260
46,300	46,350	5,809	5,148	5,809	5,266
46,350	46,400	5,820	5,154	5,820	5,272
46,400	46,450	5,831	5,160	5,831	5,278
46,450	46,500	5,842	5,166	5,842	5,284
46,500	46,550	5,853	5,172	5,853	5,290
46,550	46,600	5,864	5,178	5,864	5,296
46,600	46,650	5,875	5,184	5,875	5,302
46,650	46,700	5,886	5,190	5,886	5,308
46,700	46,750	5,897	5,196	5,897	5,314
46,750	46,800	5,908	5,202	5,908	5,320
46,800	46,850	5,919	5,208	5,919	5,326
46,850	46,900	5,930	5,214	5,930	5,332
46,900	46,950	5,941	5,220	5,941	5,338
46,950	47,000	5,952	5,226	5,952	5,344

47,000

At least	But less than	Single	Married filing jointly *	Married filing separately	Head of a household
47,000	47,050	5,963	5,232	5,963	5,350
47,050	47,100	5,974	5,238	5,974	5,356
47,100	47,150	5,985	5,244	5,985	5,362
47,150	47,200	5,996	5,250	5,996	5,368
47,200	47,250	6,007	5,256	6,007	5,374
47,250	47,300	6,018	5,262	6,018	5,380
47,300	47,350	6,029	5,268	6,029	5,386
47,350	47,400	6,040	5,274	6,040	5,392
47,400	47,450	6,051	5,280	6,051	5,398
47,450	47,500	6,062	5,286	6,062	5,404
47,500	47,550	6,073	5,292	6,073	5,410
47,550	47,600	6,084	5,298	6,084	5,416
47,600	47,650	6,095	5,304	6,095	5,422
47,650	47,700	6,106	5,310	6,106	5,428
47,700	47,750	6,117	5,316	6,117	5,434
47,750	47,800	6,128	5,322	6,128	5,440
47,800	47,850	6,139	5,328	6,139	5,446
47,850	47,900	6,150	5,334	6,150	5,452
47,900	47,950	6,161	5,340	6,161	5,458
47,950	48,000	6,172	5,346	6,172	5,464

* This column must also be used by a qualifying surviving spouse.

(Continued)

Draft as of October 12, 2022.

2022 Tax Table — *Continued*

At least	But less than	Single	Married filing jointly *	Married filing separately	Head of a household

Your tax is—

48,000

At least	But less than	Single	MFJ *	MFS	HoH
48,000	48,050	6,183	5,352	6,183	5,470
48,050	48,100	6,194	5,358	6,194	5,476
48,100	48,150	6,205	5,364	6,205	5,482
48,150	48,200	6,216	5,370	6,216	5,488
48,200	48,250	6,227	5,376	6,227	5,494
48,250	48,300	6,238	5,382	6,238	5,500
48,300	48,350	6,249	5,388	6,249	5,506
48,350	48,400	6,260	5,394	6,260	5,512
48,400	48,450	6,271	5,400	6,271	5,518
48,450	48,500	6,282	5,406	6,282	5,524
48,500	48,550	6,293	5,412	6,293	5,530
48,550	48,600	6,304	5,418	6,304	5,536
48,600	48,650	6,315	5,424	6,315	5,542
48,650	48,700	6,326	5,430	6,326	5,548
48,700	48,750	6,337	5,436	6,337	5,554
48,750	48,800	6,348	5,442	6,348	5,560
48,800	48,850	6,359	5,448	6,359	5,566
48,850	48,900	6,370	5,454	6,370	5,572
48,900	48,950	6,381	5,460	6,381	5,578
48,950	49,000	6,392	5,466	6,392	5,584

49,000

At least	But less than	Single	MFJ *	MFS	HoH
49,000	49,050	6,403	5,472	6,403	5,590
49,050	49,100	6,414	5,478	6,414	5,596
49,100	49,150	6,425	5,484	6,425	5,602
49,150	49,200	6,436	5,490	6,436	5,608
49,200	49,250	6,447	5,496	6,447	5,614
49,250	49,300	6,458	5,502	6,458	5,620
49,300	49,350	6,469	5,508	6,469	5,626
49,350	49,400	6,480	5,514	6,480	5,632
49,400	49,450	6,491	5,520	6,491	5,638
49,450	49,500	6,502	5,526	6,502	5,644
49,500	49,550	6,513	5,532	6,513	5,650
49,550	49,600	6,524	5,538	6,524	5,656
49,600	49,650	6,535	5,544	6,535	5,662
49,650	49,700	6,546	5,550	6,546	5,668
49,700	49,750	6,557	5,556	6,557	5,674
49,750	49,800	6,568	5,562	6,568	5,680
49,800	49,850	6,579	5,568	6,579	5,686
49,850	49,900	6,590	5,574	6,590	5,692
49,900	49,950	6,601	5,580	6,601	5,698
49,950	50,000	6,612	5,586	6,612	5,704

50,000

At least	But less than	Single	MFJ *	MFS	HoH
50,000	50,050	6,623	5,592	6,623	5,710
50,050	50,100	6,634	5,598	6,634	5,716
50,100	50,150	6,645	5,604	6,645	5,722
50,150	50,200	6,656	5,610	6,656	5,728
50,200	50,250	6,667	5,616	6,667	5,734
50,250	50,300	6,678	5,622	6,678	5,740
50,300	50,350	6,689	5,628	6,689	5,746
50,350	50,400	6,700	5,634	6,700	5,752
50,400	50,450	6,711	5,640	6,711	5,758
50,450	50,500	6,722	5,646	6,722	5,764
50,500	50,550	6,733	5,652	6,733	5,770
50,550	50,600	6,744	5,658	6,744	5,776
50,600	50,650	6,755	5,664	6,755	5,782
50,650	50,700	6,766	5,670	6,766	5,788
50,700	50,750	6,777	5,676	6,777	5,794
50,750	50,800	6,788	5,682	6,788	5,800
50,800	50,850	6,799	5,688	6,799	5,806
50,850	50,900	6,810	5,694	6,810	5,812
50,900	50,950	6,821	5,700	6,821	5,818
50,950	51,000	6,832	5,706	6,832	5,824

51,000

At least	But less than	Single	MFJ *	MFS	HoH
51,000	51,050	6,843	5,712	6,843	5,830
51,050	51,100	6,854	5,718	6,854	5,836
51,100	51,150	6,865	5,724	6,865	5,842
51,150	51,200	6,876	5,730	6,876	5,848
51,200	51,250	6,887	5,736	6,887	5,854
51,250	51,300	6,898	5,742	6,898	5,860
51,300	51,350	6,909	5,748	6,909	5,866
51,350	51,400	6,920	5,754	6,920	5,872
51,400	51,450	6,931	5,760	6,931	5,878
51,450	51,500	6,942	5,766	6,942	5,884
51,500	51,550	6,953	5,772	6,953	5,890
51,550	51,600	6,964	5,778	6,964	5,896
51,600	51,650	6,975	5,784	6,975	5,902
51,650	51,700	6,986	5,790	6,986	5,908
51,700	51,750	6,997	5,796	6,997	5,914
51,750	51,800	7,008	5,802	7,008	5,920
51,800	51,850	7,019	5,808	7,019	5,926
51,850	51,900	7,030	5,814	7,030	5,932
51,900	51,950	7,041	5,820	7,041	5,938
51,950	52,000	7,052	5,826	7,052	5,944

52,000

At least	But less than	Single	MFJ *	MFS	HoH
52,000	52,050	7,063	5,832	7,063	5,950
52,050	52,100	7,074	5,838	7,074	5,956
52,100	52,150	7,085	5,844	7,085	5,962
52,150	52,200	7,096	5,850	7,096	5,968
52,200	52,250	7,107	5,856	7,107	5,974
52,250	52,300	7,118	5,862	7,118	5,980
52,300	52,350	7,129	5,868	7,129	5,986
52,350	52,400	7,140	5,874	7,140	5,992
52,400	52,450	7,151	5,880	7,151	5,998
52,450	52,500	7,162	5,886	7,162	6,004
52,500	52,550	7,173	5,892	7,173	6,010
52,550	52,600	7,184	5,898	7,184	6,016
52,600	52,650	7,195	5,904	7,195	6,022
52,650	52,700	7,206	5,910	7,206	6,028
52,700	52,750	7,217	5,916	7,217	6,034
52,750	52,800	7,228	5,922	7,228	6,040
52,800	52,850	7,239	5,928	7,239	6,046
52,850	52,900	7,250	5,934	7,250	6,052
52,900	52,950	7,261	5,940	7,261	6,058
52,950	53,000	7,272	5,946	7,272	6,064

53,000

At least	But less than	Single	MFJ *	MFS	HoH
53,000	53,050	7,283	5,952	7,283	6,070
53,050	53,100	7,294	5,958	7,294	6,076
53,100	53,150	7,305	5,964	7,305	6,082
53,150	53,200	7,316	5,970	7,316	6,088
53,200	53,250	7,327	5,976	7,327	6,094
53,250	53,300	7,338	5,982	7,338	6,100
53,300	53,350	7,349	5,988	7,349	6,106
53,350	53,400	7,360	5,994	7,360	6,112
53,400	53,450	7,371	6,000	7,371	6,118
53,450	53,500	7,382	6,006	7,382	6,124
53,500	53,550	7,393	6,012	7,393	6,130
53,550	53,600	7,404	6,018	7,404	6,136
53,600	53,650	7,415	6,024	7,415	6,142
53,650	53,700	7,426	6,030	7,426	6,148
53,700	53,750	7,437	6,036	7,437	6,154
53,750	53,800	7,448	6,042	7,448	6,160
53,800	53,850	7,459	6,048	7,459	6,166
53,850	53,900	7,470	6,054	7,470	6,172
53,900	53,950	7,481	6,060	7,481	6,178
53,950	54,000	7,492	6,066	7,492	6,184

54,000

At least	But less than	Single	MFJ *	MFS	HoH
54,000	54,050	7,503	6,072	7,503	6,190
54,050	54,100	7,514	6,078	7,514	6,196
54,100	54,150	7,525	6,084	7,525	6,202
54,150	54,200	7,536	6,090	7,536	6,208
54,200	54,250	7,547	6,096	7,547	6,214
54,250	54,300	7,558	6,102	7,558	6,220
54,300	54,350	7,569	6,108	7,569	6,226
54,350	54,400	7,580	6,114	7,580	6,232
54,400	54,450	7,591	6,120	7,591	6,238
54,450	54,500	7,602	6,126	7,602	6,244
54,500	54,550	7,613	6,132	7,613	6,250
54,550	54,600	7,624	6,138	7,624	6,256
54,600	54,650	7,635	6,144	7,635	6,262
54,650	54,700	7,646	6,150	7,646	6,268
54,700	54,750	7,657	6,156	7,657	6,274
54,750	54,800	7,668	6,162	7,668	6,280
54,800	54,850	7,679	6,168	7,679	6,286
54,850	54,900	7,690	6,174	7,690	6,292
54,900	54,950	7,701	6,180	7,701	6,298
54,950	55,000	7,712	6,186	7,712	6,304

55,000

At least	But less than	Single	MFJ *	MFS	HoH
55,000	55,050	7,723	6,192	7,723	6,310
55,050	55,100	7,734	6,198	7,734	6,316
55,100	55,150	7,745	6,204	7,745	6,322
55,150	55,200	7,756	6,210	7,756	6,328
55,200	55,250	7,767	6,216	7,767	6,334
55,250	55,300	7,778	6,222	7,778	6,340
55,300	55,350	7,789	6,228	7,789	6,346
55,350	55,400	7,800	6,234	7,800	6,352
55,400	55,450	7,811	6,240	7,811	6,358
55,450	55,500	7,822	6,246	7,822	6,364
55,500	55,550	7,833	6,252	7,833	6,370
55,550	55,600	7,844	6,258	7,844	6,376
55,600	55,650	7,855	6,264	7,855	6,382
55,650	55,700	7,866	6,270	7,866	6,388
55,700	55,750	7,877	6,276	7,877	6,394
55,750	55,800	7,888	6,282	7,888	6,400
55,800	55,850	7,899	6,288	7,899	6,406
55,850	55,900	7,910	6,294	7,910	6,412
55,900	55,950	7,921	6,300	7,921	6,421
55,950	56,000	7,932	6,306	7,932	6,432

56,000

At least	But less than	Single	MFJ *	MFS	HoH
56,000	56,050	7,943	6,312	7,943	6,443
56,050	56,100	7,954	6,318	7,954	6,454
56,100	56,150	7,965	6,324	7,965	6,465
56,150	56,200	7,976	6,330	7,976	6,476
56,200	56,250	7,987	6,336	7,987	6,487
56,250	56,300	7,998	6,342	7,998	6,498
56,300	56,350	8,009	6,348	8,009	6,509
56,350	56,400	8,020	6,354	8,020	6,520
56,400	56,450	8,031	6,360	8,031	6,531
56,450	56,500	8,042	6,366	8,042	6,542
56,500	56,550	8,053	6,372	8,053	6,553
56,550	56,600	8,064	6,378	8,064	6,564
56,600	56,650	8,075	6,384	8,075	6,575
56,650	56,700	8,086	6,390	8,086	6,586
56,700	56,750	8,097	6,396	8,097	6,597
56,750	56,800	8,108	6,402	8,108	6,608
56,800	56,850	8,119	6,408	8,119	6,619
56,850	56,900	8,130	6,414	8,130	6,630
56,900	56,950	8,141	6,420	8,141	6,641
56,950	57,000	8,152	6,426	8,152	6,652

(Continued)

* This column must also be used by a qualifying surviving spouse.

Draft as of October 12, 2022.

2022 Tax Table — *Continued*

57,000

At least	But less than	Single	Married filing jointly *	Married filing separately	Head of a household
57,000	57,050	8,163	6,432	8,163	6,663
57,050	57,100	8,174	6,438	8,174	6,674
57,100	57,150	8,185	6,444	8,185	6,685
57,150	57,200	8,196	6,450	8,196	6,696
57,200	57,250	8,207	6,456	8,207	6,707
57,250	57,300	8,218	6,462	8,218	6,718
57,300	57,350	8,229	6,468	8,229	6,729
57,350	57,400	8,240	6,474	8,240	6,740
57,400	57,450	8,251	6,480	8,251	6,751
57,450	57,500	8,262	6,486	8,262	6,762
57,500	57,550	8,273	6,492	8,273	6,773
57,550	57,600	8,284	6,498	8,284	6,784
57,600	57,650	8,295	6,504	8,295	6,795
57,650	57,700	8,306	6,510	8,306	6,806
57,700	57,750	8,317	6,516	8,317	6,817
57,750	57,800	8,328	6,522	8,328	6,828
57,800	57,850	8,339	6,528	8,339	6,839
57,850	57,900	8,350	6,534	8,350	6,850
57,900	57,950	8,361	6,540	8,361	6,861
57,950	58,000	8,372	6,546	8,372	6,872

58,000

At least	But less than	Single	Married filing jointly *	Married filing separately	Head of a household
58,000	58,050	8,383	6,552	8,383	6,883
58,050	58,100	8,394	6,558	8,394	6,894
58,100	58,150	8,405	6,564	8,405	6,905
58,150	58,200	8,416	6,570	8,416	6,916
58,200	58,250	8,427	6,576	8,427	6,927
58,250	58,300	8,438	6,582	8,438	6,938
58,300	58,350	8,449	6,588	8,449	6,949
58,350	58,400	8,460	6,594	8,460	6,960
58,400	58,450	8,471	6,600	8,471	6,971
58,450	58,500	8,482	6,606	8,482	6,982
58,500	58,550	8,493	6,612	8,493	6,993
58,550	58,600	8,504	6,618	8,504	7,004
58,600	58,650	8,515	6,624	8,515	7,015
58,650	58,700	8,526	6,630	8,526	7,026
58,700	58,750	8,537	6,636	8,537	7,037
58,750	58,800	8,548	6,642	8,548	7,048
58,800	58,850	8,559	6,648	8,559	7,059
58,850	58,900	8,570	6,654	8,570	7,070
58,900	58,950	8,581	6,660	8,581	7,081
58,950	59,000	8,592	6,666	8,592	7,092

59,000

At least	But less than	Single	Married filing jointly *	Married filing separately	Head of a household
59,000	59,050	8,603	6,672	8,603	7,103
59,050	59,100	8,614	6,678	8,614	7,114
59,100	59,150	8,625	6,684	8,625	7,125
59,150	59,200	8,636	6,690	8,636	7,136
59,200	59,250	8,647	6,696	8,647	7,147
59,250	59,300	8,658	6,702	8,658	7,158
59,300	59,350	8,669	6,708	8,669	7,169
59,350	59,400	8,680	6,714	8,680	7,180
59,400	59,450	8,691	6,720	8,691	7,191
59,450	59,500	8,702	6,726	8,702	7,202
59,500	59,550	8,713	6,732	8,713	7,213
59,550	59,600	8,724	6,738	8,724	7,224
59,600	59,650	8,735	6,744	8,735	7,235
59,650	59,700	8,746	6,750	8,746	7,246
59,700	59,750	8,757	6,756	8,757	7,257
59,750	59,800	8,768	6,762	8,768	7,268
59,800	59,850	8,779	6,768	8,779	7,279
59,850	59,900	8,790	6,774	8,790	7,290
59,900	59,950	8,801	6,780	8,801	7,301
59,950	60,000	8,812	6,786	8,812	7,312

60,000

At least	But less than	Single	Married filing jointly *	Married filing separately	Head of a household
60,000	60,050	8,823	6,792	8,823	7,323
60,050	60,100	8,834	6,798	8,834	7,334
60,100	60,150	8,845	6,804	8,845	7,345
60,150	60,200	8,856	6,810	8,856	7,356
60,200	60,250	8,867	6,816	8,867	7,367
60,250	60,300	8,878	6,822	8,878	7,378
60,300	60,350	8,889	6,828	8,889	7,389
60,350	60,400	8,900	6,834	8,900	7,400
60,400	60,450	8,911	6,840	8,911	7,411
60,450	60,500	8,922	6,846	8,922	7,422
60,500	60,550	8,933	6,852	8,933	7,433
60,550	60,600	8,944	6,858	8,944	7,444
60,600	60,650	8,955	6,864	8,955	7,455
60,650	60,700	8,966	6,870	8,966	7,466
60,700	60,750	8,977	6,876	8,977	7,477
60,750	60,800	8,988	6,882	8,988	7,488
60,800	60,850	8,999	6,888	8,999	7,499
60,850	60,900	9,010	6,894	9,010	7,510
60,900	60,950	9,021	6,900	9,021	7,521
60,950	61,000	9,032	6,906	9,032	7,532

61,000

At least	But less than	Single	Married filing jointly *	Married filing separately	Head of a household
61,000	61,050	9,043	6,912	9,043	7,543
61,050	61,100	9,054	6,918	9,054	7,554
61,100	61,150	9,065	6,924	9,065	7,565
61,150	61,200	9,076	6,930	9,076	7,576
61,200	61,250	9,087	6,936	9,087	7,587
61,250	61,300	9,098	6,942	9,098	7,598
61,300	61,350	9,109	6,948	9,109	7,609
61,350	61,400	9,120	6,954	9,120	7,620
61,400	61,450	9,131	6,960	9,131	7,631
61,450	61,500	9,142	6,966	9,142	7,642
61,500	61,550	9,153	6,972	9,153	7,653
61,550	61,600	9,164	6,978	9,164	7,664
61,600	61,650	9,175	6,984	9,175	7,675
61,650	61,700	9,186	6,990	9,186	7,686
61,700	61,750	9,197	6,996	9,197	7,697
61,750	61,800	9,208	7,002	9,208	7,708
61,800	61,850	9,219	7,008	9,219	7,719
61,850	61,900	9,230	7,014	9,230	7,730
61,900	61,950	9,241	7,020	9,241	7,741
61,950	62,000	9,252	7,026	9,252	7,752

62,000

At least	But less than	Single	Married filing jointly *	Married filing separately	Head of a household
62,000	62,050	9,263	7,032	9,263	7,763
62,050	62,100	9,274	7,038	9,274	7,774
62,100	62,150	9,285	7,044	9,285	7,785
62,150	62,200	9,296	7,050	9,296	7,796
62,200	62,250	9,307	7,056	9,307	7,807
62,250	62,300	9,318	7,062	9,318	7,818
62,300	62,350	9,329	7,068	9,329	7,829
62,350	62,400	9,340	7,074	9,340	7,840
62,400	62,450	9,351	7,080	9,351	7,851
62,450	62,500	9,362	7,086	9,362	7,862
62,500	62,550	9,373	7,092	9,373	7,873
62,550	62,600	9,384	7,098	9,384	7,884
62,600	62,650	9,395	7,104	9,395	7,895
62,650	62,700	9,406	7,110	9,406	7,906
62,700	62,750	9,417	7,116	9,417	7,917
62,750	62,800	9,428	7,122	9,428	7,928
62,800	62,850	9,439	7,128	9,439	7,939
62,850	62,900	9,450	7,134	9,450	7,950
62,900	62,950	9,461	7,140	9,461	7,961
62,950	63,000	9,472	7,146	9,472	7,972

63,000

At least	But less than	Single	Married filing jointly *	Married filing separately	Head of a household
63,000	63,050	9,483	7,152	9,483	7,983
63,050	63,100	9,494	7,158	9,494	7,994
63,100	63,150	9,505	7,164	9,505	8,005
63,150	63,200	9,516	7,170	9,516	8,016
63,200	63,250	9,527	7,176	9,527	8,027
63,250	63,300	9,538	7,182	9,538	8,038
63,300	63,350	9,549	7,188	9,549	8,049
63,350	63,400	9,560	7,194	9,560	8,060
63,400	63,450	9,571	7,200	9,571	8,071
63,450	63,500	9,582	7,206	9,582	8,082
63,500	63,550	9,593	7,212	9,593	8,093
63,550	63,600	9,604	7,218	9,604	8,104
63,600	63,650	9,615	7,224	9,615	8,115
63,650	63,700	9,626	7,230	9,626	8,126
63,700	63,750	9,637	7,236	9,637	8,137
63,750	63,800	9,648	7,242	9,648	8,148
63,800	63,850	9,659	7,248	9,659	8,159
63,850	63,900	9,670	7,254	9,670	8,170
63,900	63,950	9,681	7,260	9,681	8,181
63,950	64,000	9,692	7,266	9,692	8,192

64,000

At least	But less than	Single	Married filing jointly *	Married filing separately	Head of a household
64,000	64,050	9,703	7,272	9,703	8,203
64,050	64,100	9,714	7,278	9,714	8,214
64,100	64,150	9,725	7,284	9,725	8,225
64,150	64,200	9,736	7,290	9,736	8,236
64,200	64,250	9,747	7,296	9,747	8,247
64,250	64,300	9,758	7,302	9,758	8,258
64,300	64,350	9,769	7,308	9,769	8,269
64,350	64,400	9,780	7,314	9,780	8,280
64,400	64,450	9,791	7,320	9,791	8,291
64,450	64,500	9,802	7,326	9,802	8,302
64,500	64,550	9,813	7,332	9,813	8,313
64,550	64,600	9,824	7,338	9,824	8,324
64,600	64,650	9,835	7,344	9,835	8,335
64,650	64,700	9,846	7,350	9,846	8,346
64,700	64,750	9,857	7,356	9,857	8,357
64,750	64,800	9,868	7,362	9,868	8,368
64,800	64,850	9,879	7,368	9,879	8,379
64,850	64,900	9,890	7,374	9,890	8,390
64,900	64,950	9,901	7,380	9,901	8,401
64,950	65,000	9,912	7,386	9,912	8,412

65,000

At least	But less than	Single	Married filing jointly *	Married filing separately	Head of a household
65,000	65,050	9,923	7,392	9,923	8,423
65,050	65,100	9,934	7,398	9,934	8,434
65,100	65,150	9,945	7,404	9,945	8,445
65,150	65,200	9,956	7,410	9,956	8,456
65,200	65,250	9,967	7,416	9,967	8,467
65,250	65,300	9,978	7,422	9,978	8,478
65,300	65,350	9,989	7,428	9,989	8,489
65,350	65,400	10,000	7,434	10,000	8,500
65,400	65,450	10,011	7,440	10,011	8,511
65,450	65,500	10,022	7,446	10,022	8,522
65,500	65,550	10,033	7,452	10,033	8,533
65,550	65,600	10,044	7,458	10,044	8,544
65,600	65,650	10,055	7,464	10,055	8,555
65,650	65,700	10,066	7,470	10,066	8,566
65,700	65,750	10,077	7,476	10,077	8,577
65,750	65,800	10,088	7,482	10,088	8,588
65,800	65,850	10,099	7,488	10,099	8,599
65,850	65,900	10,110	7,494	10,110	8,610
65,900	65,950	10,121	7,500	10,121	8,621
65,950	66,000	10,132	7,506	10,132	8,632

* This column must also be used by a qualifying surviving spouse.

(Continued)

Draft as of October 12, 2022.

2022 Tax Table — *Continued*

If line 15 (taxable income) is—		And you are—			
At least	But less than	Single	Married filing jointly *	Married filing separately	Head of a household
		Your tax is—			

66,000

At least	But less than	Single	Married filing jointly *	Married filing separately	Head of a household
66,000	66,050	10,143	7,512	10,143	8,643
66,050	66,100	10,154	7,518	10,154	8,654
66,100	66,150	10,165	7,524	10,165	8,665
66,150	66,200	10,176	7,530	10,176	8,676
66,200	66,250	10,187	7,536	10,187	8,687
66,250	66,300	10,198	7,542	10,198	8,698
66,300	66,350	10,209	7,548	10,209	8,709
66,350	66,400	10,220	7,554	10,220	8,720
66,400	66,450	10,231	7,560	10,231	8,731
66,450	66,500	10,242	7,566	10,242	8,742
66,500	66,550	10,253	7,572	10,253	8,753
66,550	66,600	10,264	7,578	10,264	8,764
66,600	66,650	10,275	7,584	10,275	8,775
66,650	66,700	10,286	7,590	10,286	8,786
66,700	66,750	10,297	7,596	10,297	8,797
66,750	66,800	10,308	7,602	10,308	8,808
66,800	66,850	10,319	7,608	10,319	8,819
66,850	66,900	10,330	7,614	10,330	8,830
66,900	66,950	10,341	7,620	10,341	8,841
66,950	67,000	10,352	7,626	10,352	8,852

67,000

At least	But less than	Single	Married filing jointly *	Married filing separately	Head of a household
67,000	67,050	10,363	7,632	10,363	8,863
67,050	67,100	10,374	7,638	10,374	8,874
67,100	67,150	10,385	7,644	10,385	8,885
67,150	67,200	10,396	7,650	10,396	8,896
67,200	67,250	10,407	7,656	10,407	8,907
67,250	67,300	10,418	7,662	10,418	8,918
67,300	67,350	10,429	7,668	10,429	8,929
67,350	67,400	10,440	7,674	10,440	8,940
67,400	67,450	10,451	7,680	10,451	8,951
67,450	67,500	10,462	7,686	10,462	8,962
67,500	67,550	10,473	7,692	10,473	8,973
67,550	67,600	10,484	7,698	10,484	8,984
67,600	67,650	10,495	7,704	10,495	8,995
67,650	67,700	10,506	7,710	10,506	9,006
67,700	67,750	10,517	7,716	10,517	9,017
67,750	67,800	10,528	7,722	10,528	9,028
67,800	67,850	10,539	7,728	10,539	9,039
67,850	67,900	10,550	7,734	10,550	9,050
67,900	67,950	10,561	7,740	10,561	9,061
67,950	68,000	10,572	7,746	10,572	9,072

68,000

At least	But less than	Single	Married filing jointly *	Married filing separately	Head of a household
68,000	68,050	10,583	7,752	10,583	9,083
68,050	68,100	10,594	7,758	10,594	9,094
68,100	68,150	10,605	7,764	10,605	9,105
68,150	68,200	10,616	7,770	10,616	9,116
68,200	68,250	10,627	7,776	10,627	9,127
68,250	68,300	10,638	7,782	10,638	9,138
68,300	68,350	10,649	7,788	10,649	9,149
68,350	68,400	10,660	7,794	10,660	9,160
68,400	68,450	10,671	7,800	10,671	9,171
68,450	68,500	10,682	7,806	10,682	9,182
68,500	68,550	10,693	7,812	10,693	9,193
68,550	68,600	10,704	7,818	10,704	9,204
68,600	68,650	10,715	7,824	10,715	9,215
68,650	68,700	10,726	7,830	10,726	9,226
68,700	68,750	10,737	7,836	10,737	9,237
68,750	68,800	10,748	7,842	10,748	9,248
68,800	68,850	10,759	7,848	10,759	9,259
68,850	68,900	10,770	7,854	10,770	9,270
68,900	68,950	10,781	7,860	10,781	9,281
68,950	69,000	10,792	7,866	10,792	9,292

69,000

At least	But less than	Single	Married filing jointly *	Married filing separately	Head of a household
69,000	69,050	10,803	7,872	10,803	9,303
69,050	69,100	10,814	7,878	10,814	9,314
69,100	69,150	10,825	7,884	10,825	9,325
69,150	69,200	10,836	7,890	10,836	9,336
69,200	69,250	10,847	7,896	10,847	9,347
69,250	69,300	10,858	7,902	10,858	9,358
69,300	69,350	10,869	7,908	10,869	9,369
69,350	69,400	10,880	7,914	10,880	9,380
69,400	69,450	10,891	7,920	10,891	9,391
69,450	69,500	10,902	7,926	10,902	9,402
69,500	69,550	10,913	7,932	10,913	9,413
69,550	69,600	10,924	7,938	10,924	9,424
69,600	69,650	10,935	7,944	10,935	9,435
69,650	69,700	10,946	7,950	10,946	9,446
69,700	69,750	10,957	7,956	10,957	9,457
69,750	69,800	10,968	7,962	10,968	9,468
69,800	69,850	10,979	7,968	10,979	9,479
69,850	69,900	10,990	7,974	10,990	9,490
69,900	69,950	11,001	7,980	11,001	9,501
69,950	70,000	11,012	7,986	11,012	9,512

70,000

At least	But less than	Single	Married filing jointly *	Married filing separately	Head of a household
70,000	70,050	11,023	7,992	11,023	9,523
70,050	70,100	11,034	7,998	11,034	9,534
70,100	70,150	11,045	8,004	11,045	9,545
70,150	70,200	11,056	8,010	11,056	9,556
70,200	70,250	11,067	8,016	11,067	9,567
70,250	70,300	11,078	8,022	11,078	9,578
70,300	70,350	11,089	8,028	11,089	9,589
70,350	70,400	11,100	8,034	11,100	9,600
70,400	70,450	11,111	8,040	11,111	9,611
70,450	70,500	11,122	8,046	11,122	9,622
70,500	70,550	11,133	8,052	11,133	9,633
70,550	70,600	11,144	8,058	11,144	9,644
70,600	70,650	11,155	8,064	11,155	9,655
70,650	70,700	11,166	8,070	11,166	9,666
70,700	70,750	11,177	8,076	11,177	9,677
70,750	70,800	11,188	8,082	11,188	9,688
70,800	70,850	11,199	8,088	11,199	9,699
70,850	70,900	11,210	8,094	11,210	9,710
70,900	70,950	11,221	8,100	11,221	9,721
70,950	71,000	11,232	8,106	11,232	9,732

71,000

At least	But less than	Single	Married filing jointly *	Married filing separately	Head of a household
71,000	71,050	11,243	8,112	11,243	9,743
71,050	71,100	11,254	8,118	11,254	9,754
71,100	71,150	11,265	8,124	11,265	9,765
71,150	71,200	11,276	8,130	11,276	9,776
71,200	71,250	11,287	8,136	11,287	9,787
71,250	71,300	11,298	8,142	11,298	9,798
71,300	71,350	11,309	8,148	11,309	9,809
71,350	71,400	11,320	8,154	11,320	9,820
71,400	71,450	11,331	8,160	11,331	9,831
71,450	71,500	11,342	8,166	11,342	9,842
71,500	71,550	11,353	8,172	11,353	9,853
71,550	71,600	11,364	8,178	11,364	9,864
71,600	71,650	11,375	8,184	11,375	9,875
71,650	71,700	11,386	8,190	11,386	9,886
71,700	71,750	11,397	8,196	11,397	9,897
71,750	71,800	11,408	8,202	11,408	9,908
71,800	71,850	11,419	8,208	11,419	9,919
71,850	71,900	11,430	8,214	11,430	9,930
71,900	71,950	11,441	8,220	11,441	9,941
71,950	72,000	11,452	8,226	11,452	9,952

72,000

At least	But less than	Single	Married filing jointly *	Married filing separately	Head of a household
72,000	72,050	11,463	8,232	11,463	9,963
72,050	72,100	11,474	8,238	11,474	9,974
72,100	72,150	11,485	8,244	11,485	9,985
72,150	72,200	11,496	8,250	11,496	9,996
72,200	72,250	11,507	8,256	11,507	10,007
72,250	72,300	11,518	8,262	11,518	10,018
72,300	72,350	11,529	8,268	11,529	10,029
72,350	72,400	11,540	8,274	11,540	10,040
72,400	72,450	11,551	8,280	11,551	10,051
72,450	72,500	11,562	8,286	11,562	10,062
72,500	72,550	11,573	8,292	11,573	10,073
72,550	72,600	11,584	8,298	11,584	10,084
72,600	72,650	11,595	8,304	11,595	10,095
72,650	72,700	11,606	8,310	11,606	10,106
72,700	72,750	11,617	8,316	11,617	10,117
72,750	72,800	11,628	8,322	11,628	10,128
72,800	72,850	11,639	8,328	11,639	10,139
72,850	72,900	11,650	8,334	11,650	10,150
72,900	72,950	11,661	8,340	11,661	10,161
72,950	73,000	11,672	8,346	11,672	10,172

73,000

At least	But less than	Single	Married filing jointly *	Married filing separately	Head of a household
73,000	73,050	11,683	8,352	11,683	10,183
73,050	73,100	11,694	8,358	11,694	10,194
73,100	73,150	11,705	8,364	11,705	10,205
73,150	73,200	11,716	8,370	11,716	10,216
73,200	73,250	11,727	8,376	11,727	10,227
73,250	73,300	11,738	8,382	11,738	10,238
73,300	73,350	11,749	8,388	11,749	10,249
73,350	73,400	11,760	8,394	11,760	10,260
73,400	73,450	11,771	8,400	11,771	10,271
73,450	73,500	11,782	8,406	11,782	10,282
73,500	73,550	11,793	8,412	11,793	10,293
73,550	73,600	11,804	8,418	11,804	10,304
73,600	73,650	11,815	8,424	11,815	10,315
73,650	73,700	11,826	8,430	11,826	10,326
73,700	73,750	11,837	8,436	11,837	10,337
73,750	73,800	11,848	8,442	11,848	10,348
73,800	73,850	11,859	8,448	11,859	10,359
73,850	73,900	11,870	8,454	11,870	10,370
73,900	73,950	11,881	8,460	11,881	10,381
73,950	74,000	11,892	8,466	11,892	10,392

74,000

At least	But less than	Single	Married filing jointly *	Married filing separately	Head of a household
74,000	74,050	11,903	8,472	11,903	10,403
74,050	74,100	11,914	8,478	11,914	10,414
74,100	74,150	11,925	8,484	11,925	10,425
74,150	74,200	11,936	8,490	11,936	10,436
74,200	74,250	11,947	8,496	11,947	10,447
74,250	74,300	11,958	8,502	11,958	10,458
74,300	74,350	11,969	8,508	11,969	10,469
74,350	74,400	11,980	8,514	11,980	10,480
74,400	74,450	11,991	8,520	11,991	10,491
74,450	74,500	12,002	8,526	12,002	10,502
74,500	74,550	12,013	8,532	12,013	10,513
74,550	74,600	12,024	8,538	12,024	10,524
74,600	74,650	12,035	8,544	12,035	10,535
74,650	74,700	12,046	8,550	12,046	10,546
74,700	74,750	12,057	8,556	12,057	10,557
74,750	74,800	12,068	8,562	12,068	10,568
74,800	74,850	12,079	8,568	12,079	10,579
74,850	74,900	12,090	8,574	12,090	10,590
74,900	74,950	12,101	8,580	12,101	10,601
74,950	75,000	12,112	8,586	12,112	10,612

(Continued)

* This column must also be used by a qualifying surviving spouse.

Draft as of October 12, 2022.

2022 Tax Table — Continued

75,000 / 76,000 / 77,000

If line 15 (taxable income) is— At least	But less than	Single	Married filing jointly *	Married filing separately	Head of a household
75,000					
75,000	75,050	12,123	8,592	12,123	10,623
75,050	75,100	12,134	8,598	12,134	10,634
75,100	75,150	12,145	8,604	12,145	10,645
75,150	75,200	12,156	8,610	12,156	10,656
75,200	75,250	12,167	8,616	12,167	10,667
75,250	75,300	12,178	8,622	12,178	10,678
75,300	75,350	12,189	8,628	12,189	10,689
75,350	75,400	12,200	8,634	12,200	10,700
75,400	75,450	12,211	8,640	12,211	10,711
75,450	75,500	12,222	8,646	12,222	10,722
75,500	75,550	12,233	8,652	12,233	10,733
75,550	75,600	12,244	8,658	12,244	10,744
75,600	75,650	12,255	8,664	12,255	10,755
75,650	75,700	12,266	8,670	12,266	10,766
75,700	75,750	12,277	8,676	12,277	10,777
75,750	75,800	12,288	8,682	12,288	10,788
75,800	75,850	12,299	8,688	12,299	10,799
75,850	75,900	12,310	8,694	12,310	10,810
75,900	75,950	12,321	8,700	12,321	10,821
75,950	76,000	12,332	8,706	12,332	10,832
76,000					
76,000	76,050	12,343	8,712	12,343	10,843
76,050	76,100	12,354	8,718	12,354	10,854
76,100	76,150	12,365	8,724	12,365	10,865
76,150	76,200	12,376	8,730	12,376	10,876
76,200	76,250	12,387	8,736	12,387	10,887
76,250	76,300	12,398	8,742	12,398	10,898
76,300	76,350	12,409	8,748	12,409	10,909
76,350	76,400	12,420	8,754	12,420	10,920
76,400	76,450	12,431	8,760	12,431	10,931
76,450	76,500	12,442	8,766	12,442	10,942
76,500	76,550	12,453	8,772	12,453	10,953
76,550	76,600	12,464	8,778	12,464	10,964
76,600	76,650	12,475	8,784	12,475	10,975
76,650	76,700	12,486	8,790	12,486	10,986
76,700	76,750	12,497	8,796	12,497	10,997
76,750	76,800	12,508	8,802	12,508	11,008
76,800	76,850	12,519	8,808	12,519	11,019
76,850	76,900	12,530	8,814	12,530	11,030
76,900	76,950	12,541	8,820	12,541	11,041
76,950	77,000	12,552	8,826	12,552	11,052
77,000					
77,000	77,050	12,563	8,832	12,563	11,063
77,050	77,100	12,574	8,838	12,574	11,074
77,100	77,150	12,585	8,844	12,585	11,085
77,150	77,200	12,596	8,850	12,596	11,096
77,200	77,250	12,607	8,856	12,607	11,107
77,250	77,300	12,618	8,862	12,618	11,118
77,300	77,350	12,629	8,868	12,629	11,129
77,350	77,400	12,640	8,874	12,640	11,140
77,400	77,450	12,651	8,880	12,651	11,151
77,450	77,500	12,662	8,886	12,662	11,162
77,500	77,550	12,673	8,892	12,673	11,173
77,550	77,600	12,684	8,898	12,684	11,184
77,600	77,650	12,695	8,904	12,695	11,195
77,650	77,700	12,706	8,910	12,706	11,206
77,700	77,750	12,717	8,916	12,717	11,217
77,750	77,800	12,728	8,922	12,728	11,228
77,800	77,850	12,739	8,928	12,739	11,239
77,850	77,900	12,750	8,934	12,750	11,250
77,900	77,950	12,761	8,940	12,761	11,261
77,950	78,000	12,772	8,946	12,772	11,272

78,000 / 79,000 / 80,000

If line 15 (taxable income) is— At least	But less than	Single	Married filing jointly *	Married filing separately	Head of a household
78,000					
78,000	78,050	12,783	8,952	12,783	11,283
78,050	78,100	12,794	8,958	12,794	11,294
78,100	78,150	12,805	8,964	12,805	11,305
78,150	78,200	12,816	8,970	12,816	11,316
78,200	78,250	12,827	8,976	12,827	11,327
78,250	78,300	12,838	8,982	12,838	11,338
78,300	78,350	12,849	8,988	12,849	11,349
78,350	78,400	12,860	8,994	12,860	11,360
78,400	78,450	12,871	9,000	12,871	11,371
78,450	78,500	12,882	9,006	12,882	11,382
78,500	78,550	12,893	9,012	12,893	11,393
78,550	78,600	12,904	9,018	12,904	11,404
78,600	78,650	12,915	9,024	12,915	11,415
78,650	78,700	12,926	9,030	12,926	11,426
78,700	78,750	12,937	9,036	12,937	11,437
78,750	78,800	12,948	9,042	12,948	11,448
78,800	78,850	12,959	9,048	12,959	11,459
78,850	78,900	12,970	9,054	12,970	11,470
78,900	78,950	12,981	9,060	12,981	11,481
78,950	79,000	12,992	9,066	12,992	11,492
79,000					
79,000	79,050	13,003	9,072	13,003	11,503
79,050	79,100	13,014	9,078	13,014	11,514
79,100	79,150	13,025	9,084	13,025	11,525
79,150	79,200	13,036	9,090	13,036	11,536
79,200	79,250	13,047	9,096	13,047	11,547
79,250	79,300	13,058	9,102	13,058	11,558
79,300	79,350	13,069	9,108	13,069	11,569
79,350	79,400	13,080	9,114	13,080	11,580
79,400	79,450	13,091	9,120	13,091	11,591
79,450	79,500	13,102	9,126	13,102	11,602
79,500	79,550	13,113	9,132	13,113	11,613
79,550	79,600	13,124	9,138	13,124	11,624
79,600	79,650	13,135	9,144	13,135	11,635
79,650	79,700	13,146	9,150	13,146	11,646
79,700	79,750	13,157	9,156	13,157	11,657
79,750	79,800	13,168	9,162	13,168	11,668
79,800	79,850	13,179	9,168	13,179	11,679
79,850	79,900	13,190	9,174	13,190	11,690
79,900	79,950	13,201	9,180	13,201	11,701
79,950	80,000	13,212	9,186	13,212	11,712
80,000					
80,000	80,050	13,223	9,192	13,223	11,723
80,050	80,100	13,234	9,198	13,234	11,734
80,100	80,150	13,245	9,204	13,245	11,745
80,150	80,200	13,256	9,210	13,256	11,756
80,200	80,250	13,267	9,216	13,267	11,767
80,250	80,300	13,278	9,222	13,278	11,778
80,300	80,350	13,289	9,228	13,289	11,789
80,350	80,400	13,300	9,234	13,300	11,800
80,400	80,450	13,311	9,240	13,311	11,811
80,450	80,500	13,322	9,246	13,322	11,822
80,500	80,550	13,333	9,252	13,333	11,833
80,550	80,600	13,344	9,258	13,344	11,844
80,600	80,650	13,355	9,264	13,355	11,855
80,650	80,700	13,366	9,270	13,366	11,866
80,700	80,750	13,377	9,276	13,377	11,877
80,750	80,800	13,388	9,282	13,388	11,888
80,800	80,850	13,399	9,288	13,399	11,899
80,850	80,900	13,410	9,294	13,410	11,910
80,900	80,950	13,421	9,300	13,421	11,921
80,950	81,000	13,432	9,306	13,432	11,932

81,000 / 82,000 / 83,000

If line 15 (taxable income) is— At least	But less than	Single	Married filing jointly *	Married filing separately	Head of a household
81,000					
81,000	81,050	13,443	9,312	13,443	11,943
81,050	81,100	13,454	9,318	13,454	11,954
81,100	81,150	13,465	9,324	13,465	11,965
81,150	81,200	13,476	9,330	13,476	11,976
81,200	81,250	13,487	9,336	13,487	11,987
81,250	81,300	13,498	9,342	13,498	11,998
81,300	81,350	13,509	9,348	13,509	12,009
81,350	81,400	13,520	9,354	13,520	12,020
81,400	81,450	13,531	9,360	13,531	12,031
81,450	81,500	13,542	9,366	13,542	12,042
81,500	81,550	13,553	9,372	13,553	12,053
81,550	81,600	13,564	9,378	13,564	12,064
81,600	81,650	13,575	9,384	13,575	12,075
81,650	81,700	13,586	9,390	13,586	12,086
81,700	81,750	13,597	9,396	13,597	12,097
81,750	81,800	13,608	9,402	13,608	12,108
81,800	81,850	13,619	9,408	13,619	12,119
81,850	81,900	13,630	9,414	13,630	12,130
81,900	81,950	13,641	9,420	13,641	12,141
81,950	82,000	13,652	9,426	13,652	12,152
82,000					
82,000	82,050	13,663	9,432	13,663	12,163
82,050	82,100	13,674	9,438	13,674	12,174
82,100	82,150	13,685	9,444	13,685	12,185
82,150	82,200	13,696	9,450	13,696	12,196
82,200	82,250	13,707	9,456	13,707	12,207
82,250	82,300	13,718	9,462	13,718	12,218
82,300	82,350	13,729	9,468	13,729	12,229
82,350	82,400	13,740	9,474	13,740	12,240
82,400	82,450	13,751	9,480	13,751	12,251
82,450	82,500	13,762	9,486	13,762	12,262
82,500	82,550	13,773	9,492	13,773	12,273
82,550	82,600	13,784	9,498	13,784	12,284
82,600	82,650	13,795	9,504	13,795	12,295
82,650	82,700	13,806	9,510	13,806	12,306
82,700	82,750	13,817	9,516	13,817	12,317
82,750	82,800	13,828	9,522	13,828	12,328
82,800	82,850	13,839	9,528	13,839	12,339
82,850	82,900	13,850	9,534	13,850	12,350
82,900	82,950	13,861	9,540	13,861	12,361
82,950	83,000	13,872	9,546	13,872	12,372
83,000					
83,000	83,050	13,883	9,552	13,883	12,383
83,050	83,100	13,894	9,558	13,894	12,394
83,100	83,150	13,905	9,564	13,905	12,405
83,150	83,200	13,916	9,570	13,916	12,416
83,200	83,250	13,927	9,576	13,927	12,427
83,250	83,300	13,938	9,582	13,938	12,438
83,300	83,350	13,949	9,588	13,949	12,449
83,350	83,400	13,960	9,594	13,960	12,460
83,400	83,450	13,971	9,600	13,971	12,471
83,450	83,500	13,982	9,606	13,982	12,482
83,500	83,550	13,993	9,612	13,993	12,493
83,550	83,600	14,004	9,621	14,004	12,504
83,600	83,650	14,015	9,632	14,015	12,515
83,650	83,700	14,026	9,643	14,026	12,526
83,700	83,750	14,037	9,654	14,037	12,537
83,750	83,800	14,048	9,665	14,048	12,548
83,800	83,850	14,059	9,676	14,059	12,559
83,850	83,900	14,070	9,687	14,070	12,570
83,900	83,950	14,081	9,698	14,081	12,581
83,950	84,000	14,092	9,709	14,092	12,592

* This column must also be used by a qualifying surviving spouse.

(Continued)

Draft as of October 12, 2022.

2022 Tax Table — *Continued*

84,000

If line 15 (taxable income) is— At least	But less than	Single	Married filing jointly *	Married filing separately	Head of a household
					Your tax is—
84,000	84,050	14,103	9,720	14,103	12,603
84,050	84,100	14,114	9,731	14,114	12,614
84,100	84,150	14,125	9,742	14,125	12,625
84,150	84,200	14,136	9,753	14,136	12,636
84,200	84,250	14,147	9,764	14,147	12,647
84,250	84,300	14,158	9,775	14,158	12,658
84,300	84,350	14,169	9,786	14,169	12,669
84,350	84,400	14,180	9,797	14,180	12,680
84,400	84,450	14,191	9,808	14,191	12,691
84,450	84,500	14,202	9,819	14,202	12,702
84,500	84,550	14,213	9,830	14,213	12,713
84,550	84,600	14,224	9,841	14,224	12,724
84,600	84,650	14,235	9,852	14,235	12,735
84,650	84,700	14,246	9,863	14,246	12,746
84,700	84,750	14,257	9,874	14,257	12,757
84,750	84,800	14,268	9,885	14,268	12,768
84,800	84,850	14,279	9,896	14,279	12,779
84,850	84,900	14,290	9,907	14,290	12,790
84,900	84,950	14,301	9,918	14,301	12,801
84,950	85,000	14,312	9,929	14,312	12,812

85,000

At least	But less than	Single	Married filing jointly *	Married filing separately	Head of a household
85,000	85,050	14,323	9,940	14,323	12,823
85,050	85,100	14,334	9,951	14,334	12,834
85,100	85,150	14,345	9,962	14,345	12,845
85,150	85,200	14,356	9,973	14,356	12,856
85,200	85,250	14,367	9,984	14,367	12,867
85,250	85,300	14,378	9,995	14,378	12,878
85,300	85,350	14,389	10,006	14,389	12,889
85,350	85,400	14,400	10,017	14,400	12,900
85,400	85,450	14,411	10,028	14,411	12,911
85,450	85,500	14,422	10,039	14,422	12,922
85,500	85,550	14,433	10,050	14,433	12,933
85,550	85,600	14,444	10,061	14,444	12,944
85,600	85,650	14,455	10,072	14,455	12,955
85,650	85,700	14,466	10,083	14,466	12,966
85,700	85,750	14,477	10,094	14,477	12,977
85,750	85,800	14,488	10,105	14,488	12,988
85,800	85,850	14,499	10,116	14,499	12,999
85,850	85,900	14,510	10,127	14,510	13,010
85,900	85,950	14,521	10,138	14,521	13,021
85,950	86,000	14,532	10,149	14,532	13,032

86,000

At least	But less than	Single	Married filing jointly *	Married filing separately	Head of a household
86,000	86,050	14,543	10,160	14,543	13,043
86,050	86,100	14,554	10,171	14,554	13,054
86,100	86,150	14,565	10,182	14,565	13,065
86,150	86,200	14,576	10,193	14,576	13,076
86,200	86,250	14,587	10,204	14,587	13,087
86,250	86,300	14,598	10,215	14,598	13,098
86,300	86,350	14,609	10,226	14,609	13,109
86,350	86,400	14,620	10,237	14,620	13,120
86,400	86,450	14,631	10,248	14,631	13,131
86,450	86,500	14,642	10,259	14,642	13,142
86,500	86,550	14,653	10,270	14,653	13,153
86,550	86,600	14,664	10,281	14,664	13,164
86,600	86,650	14,675	10,292	14,675	13,175
86,650	86,700	14,686	10,303	14,686	13,186
86,700	86,750	14,697	10,314	14,697	13,197
86,750	86,800	14,708	10,325	14,708	13,208
86,800	86,850	14,719	10,336	14,719	13,219
86,850	86,900	14,730	10,347	14,730	13,230
86,900	86,950	14,741	10,358	14,741	13,241
86,950	87,000	14,752	10,369	14,752	13,252

87,000

At least	But less than	Single	Married filing jointly *	Married filing separately	Head of a household
87,000	87,050	14,763	10,380	14,763	13,263
87,050	87,100	14,774	10,391	14,774	13,274
87,100	87,150	14,785	10,402	14,785	13,285
87,150	87,200	14,796	10,413	14,796	13,296
87,200	87,250	14,807	10,424	14,807	13,307
87,250	87,300	14,818	10,435	14,818	13,318
87,300	87,350	14,829	10,446	14,829	13,329
87,350	87,400	14,840	10,457	14,840	13,340
87,400	87,450	14,851	10,468	14,851	13,351
87,450	87,500	14,862	10,479	14,862	13,362
87,500	87,550	14,873	10,490	14,873	13,373
87,550	87,600	14,884	10,501	14,884	13,384
87,600	87,650	14,895	10,512	14,895	13,395
87,650	87,700	14,906	10,523	14,906	13,406
87,700	87,750	14,917	10,534	14,917	13,417
87,750	87,800	14,928	10,545	14,928	13,428
87,800	87,850	14,939	10,556	14,939	13,439
87,850	87,900	14,950	10,567	14,950	13,450
87,900	87,950	14,961	10,578	14,961	13,461
87,950	88,000	14,972	10,589	14,972	13,472

88,000

At least	But less than	Single	Married filing jointly *	Married filing separately	Head of a household
88,000	88,050	14,983	10,600	14,983	13,483
88,050	88,100	14,994	10,611	14,994	13,494
88,100	88,150	15,005	10,622	15,005	13,505
88,150	88,200	15,016	10,633	15,016	13,516
88,200	88,250	15,027	10,644	15,027	13,527
88,250	88,300	15,038	10,655	15,038	13,538
88,300	88,350	15,049	10,666	15,049	13,549
88,350	88,400	15,060	10,677	15,060	13,560
88,400	88,450	15,071	10,688	15,071	13,571
88,450	88,500	15,082	10,699	15,082	13,582
88,500	88,550	15,093	10,710	15,093	13,593
88,550	88,600	15,104	10,721	15,104	13,604
88,600	88,650	15,115	10,732	15,115	13,615
88,650	88,700	15,126	10,743	15,126	13,626
88,700	88,750	15,137	10,754	15,137	13,637
88,750	88,800	15,148	10,765	15,148	13,648
88,800	88,850	15,159	10,776	15,159	13,659
88,850	88,900	15,170	10,787	15,170	13,670
88,900	88,950	15,181	10,798	15,181	13,681
88,950	89,000	15,192	10,809	15,192	13,692

89,000

At least	But less than	Single	Married filing jointly *	Married filing separately	Head of a household
89,000	89,050	15,203	10,820	15,203	13,703
89,050	89,100	15,214	10,831	15,214	13,714
89,100	89,150	15,226	10,842	15,226	13,726
89,150	89,200	15,238	10,853	15,238	13,738
89,200	89,250	15,250	10,864	15,250	13,750
89,250	89,300	15,262	10,875	15,262	13,762
89,300	89,350	15,274	10,886	15,274	13,774
89,350	89,400	15,286	10,897	15,286	13,786
89,400	89,450	15,298	10,908	15,298	13,798
89,450	89,500	15,310	10,919	15,310	13,810
89,500	89,550	15,322	10,930	15,322	13,822
89,550	89,600	15,334	10,941	15,334	13,834
89,600	89,650	15,346	10,952	15,346	13,846
89,650	89,700	15,358	10,963	15,358	13,858
89,700	89,750	15,370	10,974	15,370	13,870
89,750	89,800	15,382	10,985	15,382	13,882
89,800	89,850	15,394	10,996	15,394	13,894
89,850	89,900	15,406	11,007	15,406	13,906
89,900	89,950	15,418	11,018	15,418	13,918
89,950	90,000	15,430	11,029	15,430	13,930

90,000

At least	But less than	Single	Married filing jointly *	Married filing separately	Head of a household
90,000	90,050	15,442	11,040	15,442	13,942
90,050	90,100	15,454	11,051	15,454	13,954
90,100	90,150	15,466	11,062	15,466	13,966
90,150	90,200	15,478	11,073	15,478	13,978
90,200	90,250	15,490	11,084	15,490	13,990
90,250	90,300	15,502	11,095	15,502	14,002
90,300	90,350	15,514	11,106	15,514	14,014
90,350	90,400	15,526	11,117	15,526	14,026
90,400	90,450	15,538	11,128	15,538	14,038
90,450	90,500	15,550	11,139	15,550	14,050
90,500	90,550	15,562	11,150	15,562	14,062
90,550	90,600	15,574	11,161	15,574	14,074
90,600	90,650	15,586	11,172	15,586	14,086
90,650	90,700	15,598	11,183	15,598	14,098
90,700	90,750	15,610	11,194	15,610	14,110
90,750	90,800	15,622	11,205	15,622	14,122
90,800	90,850	15,634	11,216	15,634	14,134
90,850	90,900	15,646	11,227	15,646	14,146
90,900	90,950	15,658	11,238	15,658	14,158
90,950	91,000	15,670	11,249	15,670	14,170

91,000

At least	But less than	Single	Married filing jointly *	Married filing separately	Head of a household
91,000	91,050	15,682	11,260	15,682	14,182
91,050	91,100	15,694	11,271	15,694	14,194
91,100	91,150	15,706	11,282	15,706	14,206
91,150	91,200	15,718	11,293	15,718	14,218
91,200	91,250	15,730	11,304	15,730	14,230
91,250	91,300	15,742	11,315	15,742	14,242
91,300	91,350	15,754	11,326	15,754	14,254
91,350	91,400	15,766	11,337	15,766	14,266
91,400	91,450	15,778	11,348	15,778	14,278
91,450	91,500	15,790	11,359	15,790	14,290
91,500	91,550	15,802	11,370	15,802	14,302
91,550	91,600	15,814	11,381	15,814	14,314
91,600	91,650	15,826	11,392	15,826	14,326
91,650	91,700	15,838	11,403	15,838	14,338
91,700	91,750	15,850	11,414	15,850	14,350
91,750	91,800	15,862	11,425	15,862	14,362
91,800	91,850	15,874	11,436	15,874	14,374
91,850	91,900	15,886	11,447	15,886	14,386
91,900	91,950	15,898	11,458	15,898	14,398
91,950	92,000	15,910	11,469	15,910	14,410

92,000

At least	But less than	Single	Married filing jointly *	Married filing separately	Head of a household
92,000	92,050	15,922	11,480	15,922	14,422
92,050	92,100	15,934	11,491	15,934	14,434
92,100	92,150	15,946	11,502	15,946	14,446
92,150	92,200	15,958	11,513	15,958	14,458
92,200	92,250	15,970	11,524	15,970	14,470
92,250	92,300	15,982	11,535	15,982	14,482
92,300	92,350	15,994	11,546	15,994	14,494
92,350	92,400	16,006	11,557	16,006	14,506
92,400	92,450	16,018	11,568	16,018	14,518
92,450	92,500	16,030	11,579	16,030	14,530
92,500	92,550	16,042	11,590	16,042	14,542
92,550	92,600	16,054	11,601	16,054	14,554
92,600	92,650	16,066	11,612	16,066	14,566
92,650	92,700	16,078	11,623	16,078	14,578
92,700	92,750	16,090	11,634	16,090	14,590
92,750	92,800	16,102	11,645	16,102	14,602
92,800	92,850	16,114	11,656	16,114	14,614
92,850	92,900	16,126	11,667	16,126	14,626
92,900	92,950	16,138	11,678	16,138	14,638
92,950	93,000	16,150	11,689	16,150	14,650

(Continued)

* This column must also be used by a qualifying surviving spouse.

Draft as of October 12, 2022.

2022 Tax Table — *Continued*

93,000

At least	But less than	Single	Married filing jointly *	Married filing separately	Head of a household
93,000	93,050	16,162	11,700	16,162	14,662
93,050	93,100	16,174	11,711	16,174	14,674
93,100	93,150	16,186	11,722	16,186	14,686
93,150	93,200	16,198	11,733	16,198	14,698
93,200	93,250	16,210	11,744	16,210	14,710
93,250	93,300	16,222	11,755	16,222	14,722
93,300	93,350	16,234	11,766	16,234	14,734
93,350	93,400	16,246	11,777	16,246	14,746
93,400	93,450	16,258	11,788	16,258	14,758
93,450	93,500	16,270	11,799	16,270	14,770
93,500	93,550	16,282	11,810	16,282	14,782
93,550	93,600	16,294	11,821	16,294	14,794
93,600	93,650	16,306	11,832	16,306	14,806
93,650	93,700	16,318	11,843	16,318	14,818
93,700	93,750	16,330	11,854	16,330	14,830
93,750	93,800	16,342	11,865	16,342	14,842
93,800	93,850	16,354	11,876	16,354	14,854
93,850	93,900	16,366	11,887	16,366	14,866
93,900	93,950	16,378	11,898	16,378	14,878
93,950	94,000	16,390	11,909	16,390	14,890

94,000

At least	But less than	Single	Married filing jointly *	Married filing separately	Head of a household
94,000	94,050	16,402	11,920	16,402	14,902
94,050	94,100	16,414	11,931	16,414	14,914
94,100	94,150	16,426	11,942	16,426	14,926
94,150	94,200	16,438	11,953	16,438	14,938
94,200	94,250	16,450	11,964	16,450	14,950
94,250	94,300	16,462	11,975	16,462	14,962
94,300	94,350	16,474	11,986	16,474	14,974
94,350	94,400	16,486	11,997	16,486	14,986
94,400	94,450	16,498	12,008	16,498	14,998
94,450	94,500	16,510	12,019	16,510	15,010
94,500	94,550	16,522	12,030	16,522	15,022
94,550	94,600	16,534	12,041	16,534	15,034
94,600	94,650	16,546	12,052	16,546	15,046
94,650	94,700	16,558	12,063	16,558	15,058
94,700	94,750	16,570	12,074	16,570	15,070
94,750	94,800	16,582	12,085	16,582	15,082
94,800	94,850	16,594	12,096	16,594	15,094
94,850	94,900	16,606	12,107	16,606	15,106
94,900	94,950	16,618	12,118	16,618	15,118
94,950	95,000	16,630	12,129	16,630	15,130

95,000

At least	But less than	Single	Married filing jointly *	Married filing separately	Head of a household
95,000	95,050	16,642	12,140	16,642	15,142
95,050	95,100	16,654	12,151	16,654	15,154
95,100	95,150	16,666	12,162	16,666	15,166
95,150	95,200	16,678	12,173	16,678	15,178
95,200	95,250	16,690	12,184	16,690	15,190
95,250	95,300	16,702	12,195	16,702	15,202
95,300	95,350	16,714	12,206	16,714	15,214
95,350	95,400	16,726	12,217	16,726	15,226
95,400	95,450	16,738	12,228	16,738	15,238
95,450	95,500	16,750	12,239	16,750	15,250
95,500	95,550	16,762	12,250	16,762	15,262
95,550	95,600	16,774	12,261	16,774	15,274
95,600	95,650	16,786	12,272	16,786	15,286
95,650	95,700	16,798	12,283	16,798	15,298
95,700	95,750	16,810	12,294	16,810	15,310
95,750	95,800	16,822	12,305	16,822	15,322
95,800	95,850	16,834	12,316	16,834	15,334
95,850	95,900	16,846	12,327	16,846	15,346
95,900	95,950	16,858	12,338	16,858	15,358
95,950	96,000	16,870	12,349	16,870	15,370

96,000

At least	But less than	Single	Married filing jointly *	Married filing separately	Head of a household
96,000	96,050	16,882	12,360	16,882	15,382
96,050	96,100	16,894	12,371	16,894	15,394
96,100	96,150	16,906	12,382	16,906	15,406
96,150	96,200	16,918	12,393	16,918	15,418
96,200	96,250	16,930	12,404	16,930	15,430
96,250	96,300	16,942	12,415	16,942	15,442
96,300	96,350	16,954	12,426	16,954	15,454
96,350	96,400	16,966	12,437	16,966	15,466
96,400	96,450	16,978	12,448	16,978	15,478
96,450	96,500	16,990	12,459	16,990	15,490
96,500	96,550	17,002	12,470	17,002	15,502
96,550	96,600	17,014	12,481	17,014	15,514
96,600	96,650	17,026	12,492	17,026	15,526
96,650	96,700	17,038	12,503	17,038	15,538
96,700	96,750	17,050	12,514	17,050	15,550
96,750	96,800	17,062	12,525	17,062	15,562
96,800	96,850	17,074	12,536	17,074	15,574
96,850	96,900	17,086	12,547	17,086	15,586
96,900	96,950	17,098	12,558	17,098	15,598
96,950	97,000	17,110	12,569	17,110	15,610

97,000

At least	But less than	Single	Married filing jointly *	Married filing separately	Head of a household
97,000	97,050	17,122	12,580	17,122	15,622
97,050	97,100	17,134	12,591	17,134	15,634
97,100	97,150	17,146	12,602	17,146	15,646
97,150	97,200	17,158	12,613	17,158	15,658
97,200	97,250	17,170	12,624	17,170	15,670
97,250	97,300	17,182	12,635	17,182	15,682
97,300	97,350	17,194	12,646	17,194	15,694
97,350	97,400	17,206	12,657	17,206	15,706
97,400	97,450	17,218	12,668	17,218	15,718
97,450	97,500	17,230	12,679	17,230	15,730
97,500	97,550	17,242	12,690	17,242	15,742
97,550	97,600	17,254	12,701	17,254	15,754
97,600	97,650	17,266	12,712	17,266	15,766
97,650	97,700	17,278	12,723	17,278	15,778
97,700	97,750	17,290	12,734	17,290	15,790
97,750	97,800	17,302	12,745	17,302	15,802
97,800	97,850	17,314	12,756	17,314	15,814
97,850	97,900	17,326	12,767	17,326	15,826
97,900	97,950	17,338	12,778	17,338	15,838
97,950	98,000	17,350	12,789	17,350	15,850

98,000

At least	But less than	Single	Married filing jointly *	Married filing separately	Head of a household
98,000	98,050	17,362	12,800	17,362	15,862
98,050	98,100	17,374	12,811	17,374	15,874
98,100	98,150	17,386	12,822	17,386	15,886
98,150	98,200	17,398	12,833	17,398	15,898
98,200	98,250	17,410	12,844	17,410	15,910
98,250	98,300	17,422	12,855	17,422	15,922
98,300	98,350	17,434	12,866	17,434	15,934
98,350	98,400	17,446	12,877	17,446	15,946
98,400	98,450	17,458	12,888	17,458	15,958
98,450	98,500	17,470	12,899	17,470	15,970
98,500	98,550	17,482	12,910	17,482	15,982
98,550	98,600	17,494	12,921	17,494	15,994
98,600	98,650	17,506	12,932	17,506	16,006
98,650	98,700	17,518	12,943	17,518	16,018
98,700	98,750	17,530	12,954	17,530	16,030
98,750	98,800	17,542	12,965	17,542	16,042
98,800	98,850	17,554	12,976	17,554	16,054
98,850	98,900	17,566	12,987	17,566	16,066
98,900	98,950	17,578	12,998	17,578	16,078
98,950	99,000	17,590	13,009	17,590	16,090

99,000

At least	But less than	Single	Married filing jointly *	Married filing separately	Head of a household
99,000	99,050	17,602	13,020	17,602	16,102
99,050	99,100	17,614	13,031	17,614	16,114
99,100	99,150	17,626	13,042	17,626	16,126
99,150	99,200	17,638	13,053	17,638	16,138
99,200	99,250	17,650	13,064	17,650	16,150
99,250	99,300	17,662	13,075	17,662	16,162
99,300	99,350	17,674	13,086	17,674	16,174
99,350	99,400	17,686	13,097	17,686	16,186
99,400	99,450	17,698	13,108	17,698	16,198
99,450	99,500	17,710	13,119	17,710	16,210
99,500	99,550	17,722	13,130	17,722	16,222
99,550	99,600	17,734	13,141	17,734	16,234
99,600	99,650	17,746	13,152	17,746	16,246
99,650	99,700	17,758	13,163	17,758	16,258
99,700	99,750	17,770	13,174	17,770	16,270
99,750	99,800	17,782	13,185	17,782	16,282
99,800	99,850	17,794	13,196	17,794	16,294
99,850	99,900	17,806	13,207	17,806	16,306
99,900	99,950	17,818	13,218	17,818	16,318
99,950	100,000	17,830	13,229	17,830	16,330

$100,000
or over
use the Tax
Computation
Worksheet

* This column must also be used by a qualifying surviving spouse.

Draft as of October 12, 2022.

¶ 1112   Earned Income Credit Table.

2022 Earned Income Credit (EIC) Table
Caution. This is **not** a tax table.

1. To find your credit, read down the "At least - But less than" columns and find the line that includes the amount you were told to look up from your EIC Worksheet.

2. Then, go to the column that includes your filing status and the number of qualifying children you have who have valid SSNs as defined earlier. Enter the credit from that column on your EIC Worksheet.

Example. If your filing status is single, you have one qualifying child who has a valid SSN, and the amount you are looking up from your EIC Worksheet is $2,455, you would enter $842.

If the amount you are looking up from the worksheet is—		And your filing status is— Single, head of household, or qualifying surviving spouse and the number of children you have is—			
At least	But less than	0	1	2	3
		Your credit is—			
2,400	2,450	186	825	970	1,091
2,450	2,500	189	842	990	1,114

If the amount you are looking up from the worksheet is—		Single, head of household, or qualifying surviving spouse★ and you have—				Married filing jointly and you have—			
At least	But less than	0	1	2	3	0	1	2	3
		Your credit is—				Your credit is—			
1	50	2	9	10	11	2	9	10	11
50	100	6	26	30	34	6	26	30	34
100	150	10	43	50	56	10	43	50	56
150	200	13	60	70	79	13	60	70	79
200	250	17	77	90	101	17	77	90	101
250	300	21	94	110	124	21	94	110	124
300	350	25	111	130	146	25	111	130	146
350	400	29	128	150	169	29	128	150	169
400	450	33	145	170	191	33	145	170	191
450	500	36	162	190	214	36	162	190	214
500	550	40	179	210	236	40	179	210	236
550	600	44	196	230	259	44	196	230	259
600	650	48	213	250	281	48	213	250	281
650	700	52	230	270	304	52	230	270	304
700	750	55	247	290	326	55	247	290	326
750	800	59	264	310	349	59	264	310	349
800	850	63	281	330	371	63	281	330	371
850	900	67	298	350	394	67	298	350	394
900	950	71	315	370	416	71	315	370	416
950	1,000	75	332	390	439	75	332	390	439
1,000	1,050	78	349	410	461	78	349	410	461
1,050	1,100	82	366	430	484	82	366	430	484
1,100	1,150	86	383	450	506	86	383	450	506
1,150	1,200	90	400	470	529	90	400	470	529
1,200	1,250	94	417	490	551	94	417	490	551
1,250	1,300	98	434	510	574	98	434	510	574
1,300	1,350	101	451	530	596	101	451	530	596
1,350	1,400	105	468	550	619	105	468	550	619
1,400	1,450	109	485	570	641	109	485	570	641
1,450	1,500	113	502	590	664	113	502	590	664
1,500	1,550	117	519	610	686	117	519	610	686
1,550	1,600	120	536	630	709	120	536	630	709
1,600	1,650	124	553	650	731	124	553	650	731
1,650	1,700	128	570	670	754	128	570	670	754
1,700	1,750	132	587	690	776	132	587	690	776
1,750	1,800	136	604	710	799	136	604	710	799
1,800	1,850	140	621	730	821	140	621	730	821
1,850	1,900	143	638	750	844	143	638	750	844
1,900	1,950	147	655	770	866	147	655	770	866
1,950	2,000	151	672	790	889	151	672	790	889
2,000	2,050	155	689	810	911	155	689	810	911
2,050	2,100	159	706	830	934	159	706	830	934
2,100	2,150	163	723	850	956	163	723	850	956
2,150	2,200	166	740	870	979	166	740	870	979
2,200	2,250	170	757	890	1,001	170	757	890	1,001
2,250	2,300	174	774	910	1,024	174	774	910	1,024
2,300	2,350	178	791	930	1,046	178	791	930	1,046
2,350	2,400	182	808	950	1,069	182	808	950	1,069
2,400	2,450	186	825	970	1,091	186	825	970	1,091
2,450	2,500	189	842	990	1,114	189	842	990	1,114
2,500	2,550	193	859	1,010	1,136	193	859	1,010	1,136
2,550	2,600	197	876	1,030	1,159	197	876	1,030	1,159
2,600	2,650	201	893	1,050	1,181	201	893	1,050	1,181
2,650	2,700	205	910	1,070	1,204	205	910	1,070	1,204
2,700	2,750	208	927	1,090	1,226	208	927	1,090	1,226
2,750	2,800	212	944	1,110	1,249	212	944	1,110	1,249

If the amount you are looking up from the worksheet is—		Single, head of household, or qualifying surviving spouse★ and you have—				Married filing jointly and you have—			
At least	But less than	0	1	2	3	0	1	2	3
		Your credit is—				Your credit is—			
2,800	2,850	216	961	1,130	1,271	216	961	1,130	1,271
2,850	2,900	220	978	1,150	1,294	220	978	1,150	1,294
2,900	2,950	224	995	1,170	1,316	224	995	1,170	1,316
2,950	3,000	228	1,012	1,190	1,339	228	1,012	1,190	1,339
3,000	3,050	231	1,029	1,210	1,361	231	1,029	1,210	1,361
3,050	3,100	235	1,046	1,230	1,384	235	1,046	1,230	1,384
3,100	3,150	239	1,063	1,250	1,406	239	1,063	1,250	1,406
3,150	3,200	243	1,080	1,270	1,429	243	1,080	1,270	1,429
3,200	3,250	247	1,097	1,290	1,451	247	1,097	1,290	1,451
3,250	3,300	251	1,114	1,310	1,474	251	1,114	1,310	1,474
3,300	3,350	254	1,131	1,330	1,496	254	1,131	1,330	1,496
3,350	3,400	258	1,148	1,350	1,519	258	1,148	1,350	1,519
3,400	3,450	262	1,165	1,370	1,541	262	1,165	1,370	1,541
3,450	3,500	266	1,182	1,390	1,564	266	1,182	1,390	1,564
3,500	3,550	270	1,199	1,410	1,586	270	1,199	1,410	1,586
3,550	3,600	273	1,216	1,430	1,609	273	1,216	1,430	1,609
3,600	3,650	277	1,233	1,450	1,631	277	1,233	1,450	1,631
3,650	3,700	281	1,250	1,470	1,654	281	1,250	1,470	1,654
3,700	3,750	285	1,267	1,490	1,676	285	1,267	1,490	1,676
3,750	3,800	289	1,284	1,510	1,699	289	1,284	1,510	1,699
3,800	3,850	293	1,301	1,530	1,721	293	1,301	1,530	1,721
3,850	3,900	296	1,318	1,550	1,744	296	1,318	1,550	1,744
3,900	3,950	300	1,335	1,570	1,766	300	1,335	1,570	1,766
3,950	4,000	304	1,352	1,590	1,789	304	1,352	1,590	1,789
4,000	4,050	308	1,369	1,610	1,811	308	1,369	1,610	1,811
4,050	4,100	312	1,386	1,630	1,834	312	1,386	1,630	1,834
4,100	4,150	316	1,403	1,650	1,856	316	1,403	1,650	1,856
4,150	4,200	319	1,420	1,670	1,879	319	1,420	1,670	1,879
4,200	4,250	323	1,437	1,690	1,901	323	1,437	1,690	1,901
4,250	4,300	327	1,454	1,710	1,924	327	1,454	1,710	1,924
4,300	4,350	331	1,471	1,730	1,946	331	1,471	1,730	1,946
4,350	4,400	335	1,488	1,750	1,969	335	1,488	1,750	1,969
4,400	4,450	339	1,505	1,770	1,991	339	1,505	1,770	1,991
4,450	4,500	342	1,522	1,790	2,014	342	1,522	1,790	2,014
4,500	4,550	346	1,539	1,810	2,036	346	1,539	1,810	2,036
4,550	4,600	350	1,556	1,830	2,059	350	1,556	1,830	2,059
4,600	4,650	354	1,573	1,850	2,081	354	1,573	1,850	2,081
4,650	4,700	358	1,590	1,870	2,104	358	1,590	1,870	2,104
4,700	4,750	361	1,607	1,890	2,126	361	1,607	1,890	2,126
4,750	4,800	365	1,624	1,910	2,149	365	1,624	1,910	2,149
4,800	4,850	369	1,641	1,930	2,171	369	1,641	1,930	2,171
4,850	4,900	373	1,658	1,950	2,194	373	1,658	1,950	2,194
4,900	4,950	377	1,675	1,970	2,216	377	1,675	1,970	2,216
4,950	5,000	381	1,692	1,990	2,239	381	1,692	1,990	2,239
5,000	5,050	384	1,709	2,010	2,261	384	1,709	2,010	2,261
5,050	5,100	388	1,726	2,030	2,284	388	1,726	2,030	2,284
5,100	5,150	392	1,743	2,050	2,306	392	1,743	2,050	2,306
5,150	5,200	396	1,760	2,070	2,329	396	1,760	2,070	2,329
5,200	5,250	400	1,777	2,090	2,351	400	1,777	2,090	2,351
5,250	5,300	404	1,794	2,110	2,374	404	1,794	2,110	2,374
5,300	5,350	407	1,811	2,130	2,396	407	1,811	2,130	2,396
5,350	5,400	411	1,828	2,150	2,419	411	1,828	2,150	2,419
5,400	5,450	415	1,845	2,170	2,441	415	1,845	2,170	2,441
5,450	5,500	419	1,862	2,190	2,464	419	1,862	2,190	2,464
5,500	5,550	423	1,879	2,210	2,486	423	1,879	2,210	2,486
5,550	5,600	426	1,896	2,230	2,509	426	1,896	2,230	2,509

★ Use this column if your filing status is married filing separately and you qualify to claim the EIC. See the instructions for line 27.

Draft as of October 12, 2022.

(Continued)

Earned Income Credit (EIC) Table - *Continued*

(Caution. This is not a tax table.)

If the amount you are looking up from the worksheet is—		Single, head of household, or qualifying surviving spouse★ and you have—				Married filing jointly and you have—			
At least	But less than	0	1	2	3	0	1	2	3
		Your credit is—				Your credit is—			
5,600	5,650	430	1,913	2,250	2,531	430	1,913	2,250	2,531
5,650	5,700	434	1,930	2,270	2,554	434	1,930	2,270	2,554
5,700	5,750	438	1,947	2,290	2,576	438	1,947	2,290	2,576
5,750	5,800	442	1,964	2,310	2,599	442	1,964	2,310	2,599
5,800	5,850	446	1,981	2,330	2,621	446	1,981	2,330	2,621
5,850	5,900	449	1,998	2,350	2,644	449	1,998	2,350	2,644
5,900	5,950	453	2,015	2,370	2,666	453	2,015	2,370	2,666
5,950	6,000	457	2,032	2,390	2,689	457	2,032	2,390	2,689
6,000	6,050	461	2,049	2,410	2,711	461	2,049	2,410	2,711
6,050	6,100	465	2,066	2,430	2,734	465	2,066	2,430	2,734
6,100	6,150	469	2,083	2,450	2,756	469	2,083	2,450	2,756
6,150	6,200	472	2,100	2,470	2,779	472	2,100	2,470	2,779
6,200	6,250	476	2,117	2,490	2,801	476	2,117	2,490	2,801
6,250	6,300	480	2,134	2,510	2,824	480	2,134	2,510	2,824
6,300	6,350	484	2,151	2,530	2,846	484	2,151	2,530	2,846
6,350	6,400	488	2,168	2,550	2,869	488	2,168	2,550	2,869
6,400	6,450	492	2,185	2,570	2,891	492	2,185	2,570	2,891
6,450	6,500	495	2,202	2,590	2,914	495	2,202	2,590	2,914
6,500	6,550	499	2,219	2,610	2,936	499	2,219	2,610	2,936
6,550	6,600	503	2,236	2,630	2,959	503	2,236	2,630	2,959
6,600	6,650	507	2,253	2,650	2,981	507	2,253	2,650	2,981
6,650	6,700	511	2,270	2,670	3,004	511	2,270	2,670	3,004
6,700	6,750	514	2,287	2,690	3,026	514	2,287	2,690	3,026
6,750	6,800	518	2,304	2,710	3,049	518	2,304	2,710	3,049
6,800	6,850	522	2,321	2,730	3,071	522	2,321	2,730	3,071
6,850	6,900	526	2,338	2,750	3,094	526	2,338	2,750	3,094
6,900	6,950	530	2,355	2,770	3,116	530	2,355	2,770	3,116
6,950	7,000	534	2,372	2,790	3,139	534	2,372	2,790	3,139
7,000	7,050	537	2,389	2,810	3,161	537	2,389	2,810	3,161
7,050	7,100	541	2,406	2,830	3,184	541	2,406	2,830	3,184
7,100	7,150	545	2,423	2,850	3,206	545	2,423	2,850	3,206
7,150	7,200	549	2,440	2,870	3,229	549	2,440	2,870	3,229
7,200	7,250	553	2,457	2,890	3,251	553	2,457	2,890	3,251
7,250	7,300	557	2,474	2,910	3,274	557	2,474	2,910	3,274
7,300	7,350	560	2,491	2,930	3,296	560	2,491	2,930	3,296
7,350	7,400	560	2,508	2,950	3,319	560	2,508	2,950	3,319
7,400	7,450	560	2,525	2,970	3,341	560	2,525	2,970	3,341
7,450	7,500	560	2,542	2,990	3,364	560	2,542	2,990	3,364
7,500	7,550	560	2,559	3,010	3,386	560	2,559	3,010	3,386
7,550	7,600	560	2,576	3,030	3,409	560	2,576	3,030	3,409
7,600	7,650	560	2,593	3,050	3,431	560	2,593	3,050	3,431
7,650	7,700	560	2,610	3,070	3,454	560	2,610	3,070	3,454
7,700	7,750	560	2,627	3,090	3,476	560	2,627	3,090	3,476
7,750	7,800	560	2,644	3,110	3,499	560	2,644	3,110	3,499
7,800	7,850	560	2,661	3,130	3,521	560	2,661	3,130	3,521
7,850	7,900	560	2,678	3,150	3,544	560	2,678	3,150	3,544
7,900	7,950	560	2,695	3,170	3,566	560	2,695	3,170	3,566
7,950	8,000	560	2,712	3,190	3,589	560	2,712	3,190	3,589
8,000	8,050	560	2,729	3,210	3,611	560	2,729	3,210	3,611
8,050	8,100	560	2,746	3,230	3,634	560	2,746	3,230	3,634
8,100	8,150	560	2,763	3,250	3,656	560	2,763	3,250	3,656
8,150	8,200	560	2,780	3,270	3,679	560	2,780	3,270	3,679
8,200	8,250	560	2,797	3,290	3,701	560	2,797	3,290	3,701
8,250	8,300	560	2,814	3,310	3,724	560	2,814	3,310	3,724
8,300	8,350	560	2,831	3,330	3,746	560	2,831	3,330	3,746
8,350	8,400	560	2,848	3,350	3,769	560	2,848	3,350	3,769
8,400	8,450	560	2,865	3,370	3,791	560	2,865	3,370	3,791
8,450	8,500	560	2,882	3,390	3,814	560	2,882	3,390	3,814
8,500	8,550	560	2,899	3,410	3,836	560	2,899	3,410	3,836
8,550	8,600	560	2,916	3,430	3,859	560	2,916	3,430	3,859
8,600	8,650	560	2,933	3,450	3,881	560	2,933	3,450	3,881
8,650	8,700	560	2,950	3,470	3,904	560	2,950	3,470	3,904
8,700	8,750	560	2,967	3,490	3,926	560	2,967	3,490	3,926
8,750	8,800	560	2,984	3,510	3,949	560	2,984	3,510	3,949

If the amount you are looking up from the worksheet is—		Single, head of household, or qualifying surviving spouse★ and you have—				Married filing jointly and you have—			
At least	But less than	0	1	2	3	0	1	2	3
		Your credit is—				Your credit is—			
8,800	8,850	560	3,001	3,530	3,971	560	3,001	3,530	3,971
8,850	8,900	560	3,018	3,550	3,994	560	3,018	3,550	3,994
8,900	8,950	560	3,035	3,570	4,016	560	3,035	3,570	4,016
8,950	9,000	560	3,052	3,590	4,039	560	3,052	3,590	4,039
9,000	9,050	560	3,069	3,610	4,061	560	3,069	3,610	4,061
9,050	9,100	560	3,086	3,630	4,084	560	3,086	3,630	4,084
9,100	9,150	560	3,103	3,650	4,106	560	3,103	3,650	4,106
9,150	9,200	560	3,120	3,670	4,129	560	3,120	3,670	4,129
9,200	9,250	555	3,137	3,690	4,151	560	3,137	3,690	4,151
9,250	9,300	551	3,154	3,710	4,174	560	3,154	3,710	4,174
9,300	9,350	547	3,171	3,730	4,196	560	3,171	3,730	4,196
9,350	9,400	544	3,188	3,750	4,219	560	3,188	3,750	4,219
9,400	9,450	540	3,205	3,770	4,241	560	3,205	3,770	4,241
9,450	9,500	536	3,222	3,790	4,264	560	3,222	3,790	4,264
9,500	9,550	532	3,239	3,810	4,286	560	3,239	3,810	4,286
9,550	9,600	528	3,256	3,830	4,309	560	3,256	3,830	4,309
9,600	9,650	524	3,273	3,850	4,331	560	3,273	3,850	4,331
9,650	9,700	521	3,290	3,870	4,354	560	3,290	3,870	4,354
9,700	9,750	517	3,307	3,890	4,376	560	3,307	3,890	4,376
9,750	9,800	513	3,324	3,910	4,399	560	3,324	3,910	4,399
9,800	9,850	509	3,341	3,930	4,421	560	3,341	3,930	4,421
9,850	9,900	505	3,358	3,950	4,444	560	3,358	3,950	4,444
9,900	9,950	501	3,375	3,970	4,466	560	3,375	3,970	4,466
9,950	10,000	498	3,392	3,990	4,489	560	3,392	3,990	4,489
10,000	10,050	494	3,409	4,010	4,511	560	3,409	4,010	4,511
10,050	10,100	490	3,426	4,030	4,534	560	3,426	4,030	4,534
10,100	10,150	486	3,443	4,050	4,556	560	3,443	4,050	4,556
10,150	10,200	482	3,460	4,070	4,579	560	3,460	4,070	4,579
10,200	10,250	479	3,477	4,090	4,601	560	3,477	4,090	4,601
10,250	10,300	475	3,494	4,110	4,624	560	3,494	4,110	4,624
10,300	10,350	471	3,511	4,130	4,646	560	3,511	4,130	4,646
10,350	10,400	467	3,528	4,150	4,669	560	3,528	4,150	4,669
10,400	10,450	463	3,545	4,170	4,691	560	3,545	4,170	4,691
10,450	10,500	459	3,562	4,190	4,714	560	3,562	4,190	4,714
10,500	10,550	456	3,579	4,210	4,736	560	3,579	4,210	4,736
10,550	10,600	452	3,596	4,230	4,759	560	3,596	4,230	4,759
10,600	10,650	448	3,613	4,250	4,781	560	3,613	4,250	4,781
10,650	10,700	444	3,630	4,270	4,804	560	3,630	4,270	4,804
10,700	10,750	440	3,647	4,290	4,826	560	3,647	4,290	4,826
10,750	10,800	436	3,664	4,310	4,849	560	3,664	4,310	4,849
10,800	10,850	433	3,681	4,330	4,871	560	3,681	4,330	4,871
10,850	10,900	429	3,698	4,350	4,894	560	3,698	4,350	4,894
10,900	10,950	425	3,715	4,370	4,916	560	3,715	4,370	4,916
10,950	11,000	421	3,733	4,390	4,939	560	3,733	4,390	4,939
11,000	11,050	417	3,733	4,410	4,961	560	3,733	4,410	4,961
11,050	11,100	413	3,733	4,430	4,984	560	3,733	4,430	4,984
11,100	11,150	410	3,733	4,450	5,006	560	3,733	4,450	5,006
11,150	11,200	406	3,733	4,470	5,029	560	3,733	4,470	5,029
11,200	11,250	402	3,733	4,490	5,051	560	3,733	4,490	5,051
11,250	11,300	398	3,733	4,510	5,074	560	3,733	4,510	5,074
11,300	11,350	394	3,733	4,530	5,096	560	3,733	4,530	5,096
11,350	11,400	391	3,733	4,550	5,119	560	3,733	4,550	5,119
11,400	11,450	387	3,733	4,570	5,141	560	3,733	4,570	5,141
11,450	11,500	383	3,733	4,590	5,164	560	3,733	4,590	5,164
11,500	11,550	379	3,733	4,610	5,186	560	3,733	4,610	5,186
11,550	11,600	375	3,733	4,630	5,209	560	3,733	4,630	5,209
11,600	11,650	371	3,733	4,650	5,231	560	3,733	4,650	5,231
11,650	11,700	368	3,733	4,670	5,254	560	3,733	4,670	5,254
11,700	11,750	364	3,733	4,690	5,276	560	3,733	4,690	5,276
11,750	11,800	360	3,733	4,710	5,299	560	3,733	4,710	5,299
11,800	11,850	356	3,733	4,730	5,321	560	3,733	4,730	5,321
11,850	11,900	352	3,733	4,750	5,344	560	3,733	4,750	5,344
11,900	11,950	348	3,733	4,770	5,366	560	3,733	4,770	5,366
11,950	12,000	345	3,733	4,790	5,389	560	3,733	4,790	5,389

★ Use this column if your filing status is married filing separately and you qualify to claim the EIC. See the instructions for line 27.

Draft as of October 12, 2022.

(Continued)

Earned Income Credit (EIC) Table - *Continued* **(Caution.** This is **not** a tax table.)

If the amount you are looking up from the worksheet is—		Single, head of household, or qualifying surviving spouse★ and you have—				Married filing jointly and you have—			
At least	But less than	0	1	2	3	0	1	2	3
		Your credit is—				Your credit is—			
12,000	12,050	341	3,733	4,810	5,411	560	3,733	4,810	5,411
12,050	12,100	337	3,733	4,830	5,434	560	3,733	4,830	5,434
12,100	12,150	333	3,733	4,850	5,456	560	3,733	4,850	5,456
12,150	12,200	329	3,733	4,870	5,479	560	3,733	4,870	5,479
12,200	12,250	326	3,733	4,890	5,501	560	3,733	4,890	5,501
12,250	12,300	322	3,733	4,910	5,524	560	3,733	4,910	5,524
12,300	12,350	318	3,733	4,930	5,546	560	3,733	4,930	5,546
12,350	12,400	314	3,733	4,950	5,569	560	3,733	4,950	5,569
12,400	12,450	310	3,733	4,970	5,591	560	3,733	4,970	5,591
12,450	12,500	306	3,733	4,990	5,614	560	3,733	4,990	5,614
12,500	12,550	303	3,733	5,010	5,636	560	3,733	5,010	5,636
12,550	12,600	299	3,733	5,030	5,659	560	3,733	5,030	5,659
12,600	12,650	295	3,733	5,050	5,681	560	3,733	5,050	5,681
12,650	12,700	291	3,733	5,070	5,704	560	3,733	5,070	5,704
12,700	12,750	287	3,733	5,090	5,726	560	3,733	5,090	5,726
12,750	12,800	283	3,733	5,110	5,749	560	3,733	5,110	5,749
12,800	12,850	280	3,733	5,130	5,771	560	3,733	5,130	5,771
12,850	12,900	276	3,733	5,150	5,794	560	3,733	5,150	5,794
12,900	12,950	272	3,733	5,170	5,816	560	3,733	5,170	5,816
12,950	13,000	268	3,733	5,190	5,839	560	3,733	5,190	5,839
13,000	13,050	264	3,733	5,210	5,861	560	3,733	5,210	5,861
13,050	13,100	260	3,733	5,230	5,884	560	3,733	5,230	5,884
13,100	13,150	257	3,733	5,250	5,906	560	3,733	5,250	5,906
13,150	13,200	253	3,733	5,270	5,929	560	3,733	5,270	5,929
13,200	13,250	249	3,733	5,290	5,951	560	3,733	5,290	5,951
13,250	13,300	245	3,733	5,310	5,974	560	3,733	5,310	5,974
13,300	13,350	241	3,733	5,330	5,996	560	3,733	5,330	5,996
13,350	13,400	238	3,733	5,350	6,019	560	3,733	5,350	6,019
13,400	13,450	234	3,733	5,370	6,041	560	3,733	5,370	6,041
13,450	13,500	230	3,733	5,390	6,064	560	3,733	5,390	6,064
13,500	13,550	226	3,733	5,410	6,086	560	3,733	5,410	6,086
13,550	13,600	222	3,733	5,430	6,109	560	3,733	5,430	6,109
13,600	13,650	218	3,733	5,450	6,131	560	3,733	5,450	6,131
13,650	13,700	215	3,733	5,470	6,154	560	3,733	5,470	6,154
13,700	13,750	211	3,733	5,490	6,176	560	3,733	5,490	6,176
13,750	13,800	207	3,733	5,510	6,199	560	3,733	5,510	6,199
13,800	13,850	203	3,733	5,530	6,221	560	3,733	5,530	6,221
13,850	13,900	199	3,733	5,550	6,244	560	3,733	5,550	6,244
13,900	13,950	195	3,733	5,570	6,266	560	3,733	5,570	6,266
13,950	14,000	192	3,733	5,590	6,289	560	3,733	5,590	6,289
14,000	14,050	188	3,733	5,610	6,311	560	3,733	5,610	6,311
14,050	14,100	184	3,733	5,630	6,334	560	3,733	5,630	6,334
14,100	14,150	180	3,733	5,650	6,356	560	3,733	5,650	6,356
14,150	14,200	176	3,733	5,670	6,379	560	3,733	5,670	6,379
14,200	14,250	173	3,733	5,690	6,401	560	3,733	5,690	6,401
14,250	14,300	169	3,733	5,710	6,424	560	3,733	5,710	6,424
14,300	14,350	165	3,733	5,730	6,446	560	3,733	5,730	6,446
14,350	14,400	161	3,733	5,750	6,469	560	3,733	5,750	6,469
14,400	14,450	157	3,733	5,770	6,491	560	3,733	5,770	6,491
14,450	14,500	153	3,733	5,790	6,514	560	3,733	5,790	6,514
14,500	14,550	150	3,733	5,810	6,536	560	3,733	5,810	6,536
14,550	14,600	146	3,733	5,830	6,559	560	3,733	5,830	6,559
14,600	14,650	142	3,733	5,850	6,581	560	3,733	5,850	6,581
14,650	14,700	138	3,733	5,870	6,604	560	3,733	5,870	6,604
14,700	14,750	134	3,733	5,890	6,626	560	3,733	5,890	6,626
14,750	14,800	130	3,733	5,910	6,649	560	3,733	5,910	6,649
14,800	14,850	127	3,733	5,930	6,671	560	3,733	5,930	6,671
14,850	14,900	123	3,733	5,950	6,694	560	3,733	5,950	6,694
14,900	14,950	119	3,733	5,970	6,716	560	3,733	5,970	6,716
14,950	15,000	115	3,733	5,990	6,739	560	3,733	5,990	6,739
15,000	15,050	111	3,733	6,010	6,761	560	3,733	6,010	6,761
15,050	15,100	107	3,733	6,030	6,784	560	3,733	6,030	6,784
15,100	15,150	104	3,733	6,050	6,806	560	3,733	6,050	6,806
15,150	15,200	100	3,733	6,070	6,829	560	3,733	6,070	6,829

If the amount you are looking up from the worksheet is—		Single, head of household, or qualifying surviving spouse★ and you have—				Married filing jointly and you have—			
At least	But less than	0	1	2	3	0	1	2	3
		Your credit is—				Your credit is—			
15,200	15,250	96	3,733	6,090	6,851	560	3,733	6,090	6,851
15,250	15,300	92	3,733	6,110	6,874	560	3,733	6,110	6,874
15,300	15,350	88	3,733	6,130	6,896	557	3,733	6,130	6,896
15,350	15,400	85	3,733	6,150	6,919	553	3,733	6,150	6,919
15,400	15,450	81	3,733	6,164	6,935	550	3,733	6,164	6,935
15,450	15,500	77	3,733	6,164	6,935	546	3,733	6,164	6,935
15,500	15,550	73	3,733	6,164	6,935	542	3,733	6,164	6,935
15,550	15,600	69	3,733	6,164	6,935	538	3,733	6,164	6,935
15,600	15,650	65	3,733	6,164	6,935	534	3,733	6,164	6,935
15,650	15,700	62	3,733	6,164	6,935	531	3,733	6,164	6,935
15,700	15,750	58	3,733	6,164	6,935	527	3,733	6,164	6,935
15,750	15,800	54	3,733	6,164	6,935	523	3,733	6,164	6,935
15,800	15,850	50	3,733	6,164	6,935	519	3,733	6,164	6,935
15,850	15,900	46	3,733	6,164	6,935	515	3,733	6,164	6,935
15,900	15,950	42	3,733	6,164	6,935	511	3,733	6,164	6,935
15,950	16,000	39	3,733	6,164	6,935	508	3,733	6,164	6,935
16,000	16,050	35	3,733	6,164	6,935	504	3,733	6,164	6,935
16,050	16,100	31	3,733	6,164	6,935	500	3,733	6,164	6,935
16,100	16,150	27	3,733	6,164	6,935	496	3,733	6,164	6,935
16,150	16,200	23	3,733	6,164	6,935	492	3,733	6,164	6,935
16,200	16,250	20	3,733	6,164	6,935	488	3,733	6,164	6,935
16,250	16,300	16	3,733	6,164	6,935	485	3,733	6,164	6,935
16,300	16,350	12	3,733	6,164	6,935	481	3,733	6,164	6,935
16,350	16,400	8	3,733	6,164	6,935	477	3,733	6,164	6,935
16,400	16,450	4	3,733	6,164	6,935	473	3,733	6,164	6,935
16,450	16,500	*	3,733	6,164	6,935	469	3,733	6,164	6,935
16,500	16,550	0	3,733	6,164	6,935	466	3,733	6,164	6,935
16,550	16,600	0	3,733	6,164	6,935	462	3,733	6,164	6,935
16,600	16,650	0	3,733	6,164	6,935	458	3,733	6,164	6,935
16,650	16,700	0	3,733	6,164	6,935	454	3,733	6,164	6,935
16,700	16,750	0	3,733	6,164	6,935	450	3,733	6,164	6,935
16,750	16,800	0	3,733	6,164	6,935	446	3,733	6,164	6,935
16,800	16,850	0	3,733	6,164	6,935	443	3,733	6,164	6,935
16,850	16,900	0	3,733	6,164	6,935	439	3,733	6,164	6,935
16,900	16,950	0	3,733	6,164	6,935	435	3,733	6,164	6,935
16,950	17,000	0	3,733	6,164	6,935	431	3,733	6,164	6,935
17,000	17,050	0	3,733	6,164	6,935	427	3,733	6,164	6,935
17,050	17,100	0	3,733	6,164	6,935	423	3,733	6,164	6,935
17,100	17,150	0	3,733	6,164	6,935	420	3,733	6,164	6,935
17,150	17,200	0	3,733	6,164	6,935	416	3,733	6,164	6,935
17,200	17,250	0	3,733	6,164	6,935	412	3,733	6,164	6,935
17,250	17,300	0	3,733	6,164	6,935	408	3,733	6,164	6,935
17,300	17,350	0	3,733	6,164	6,935	404	3,733	6,164	6,935
17,350	17,400	0	3,733	6,164	6,935	400	3,733	6,164	6,935
17,400	17,450	0	3,733	6,164	6,935	397	3,733	6,164	6,935
17,450	17,500	0	3,733	6,164	6,935	393	3,733	6,164	6,935
17,500	17,550	0	3,733	6,164	6,935	389	3,733	6,164	6,935
17,550	17,600	0	3,733	6,164	6,935	385	3,733	6,164	6,935
17,600	17,650	0	3,733	6,164	6,935	381	3,733	6,164	6,935
17,650	17,700	0	3,733	6,164	6,935	378	3,733	6,164	6,935
17,700	17,750	0	3,733	6,164	6,935	374	3,733	6,164	6,935
17,750	17,800	0	3,733	6,164	6,935	370	3,733	6,164	6,935
17,800	17,850	0	3,733	6,164	6,935	366	3,733	6,164	6,935
17,850	17,900	0	3,733	6,164	6,935	362	3,733	6,164	6,935
17,900	17,950	0	3,733	6,164	6,935	358	3,733	6,164	6,935
17,950	18,000	0	3,733	6,164	6,935	355	3,733	6,164	6,935
18,000	18,050	0	3,733	6,164	6,935	351	3,733	6,164	6,935
18,050	18,100	0	3,733	6,164	6,935	347	3,733	6,164	6,935
18,100	18,150	0	3,733	6,164	6,935	343	3,733	6,164	6,935
18,150	18,200	0	3,733	6,164	6,935	339	3,733	6,164	6,935
18,200	18,250	0	3,733	6,164	6,935	335	3,733	6,164	6,935
18,250	18,300	0	3,733	6,164	6,935	332	3,733	6,164	6,935
18,300	18,350	0	3,733	6,164	6,935	328	3,733	6,164	6,935
18,350	18,400	0	3,733	6,164	6,935	324	3,733	6,164	6,935

★　Use this column if your filing status is married filing separately and you qualify to claim the EIC. See the instructions for line 27.

·　If the amount you are looking up from the worksheet is at least $16,450 but less than $16,480, and you have no qualifying children who have valid SSNs, your credit is $1.

　If the amount you are looking up from the worksheet is $16,480 or more, and you have no qualifying children who have valid SSNs, you can't take the credit.

Draft as of October 12, 2022.

(Continued)

Earned Income Credit (EIC) Table - *Continued*

(**Caution.** This is **not** a tax table.)

If the amount you are looking up from the worksheet is–		Single, head of household, or qualifying surviving spouse★ and you have–				Married filing jointly and you have–			
At least	But less than	0	1	2	3	0	1	2	3
		Your credit is–				Your credit is–			
18,400	18,450	0	3,733	6,164	6,935	320	3,733	6,164	6,935
18,450	18,500	0	3,733	6,164	6,935	316	3,733	6,164	6,935
18,500	18,550	0	3,733	6,164	6,935	313	3,733	6,164	6,935
18,550	18,600	0	3,733	6,164	6,935	309	3,733	6,164	6,935
18,600	18,650	0	3,733	6,164	6,935	305	3,733	6,164	6,935
18,650	18,700	0	3,733	6,164	6,935	301	3,733	6,164	6,935
18,700	18,750	0	3,733	6,164	6,935	297	3,733	6,164	6,935
18,750	18,800	0	3,733	6,164	6,935	293	3,733	6,164	6,935
18,800	18,850	0	3,733	6,164	6,935	290	3,733	6,164	6,935
18,850	18,900	0	3,733	6,164	6,935	286	3,733	6,164	6,935
18,900	18,950	0	3,733	6,164	6,935	282	3,733	6,164	6,935
18,950	19,000	0	3,733	6,164	6,935	278	3,733	6,164	6,935
19,000	19,050	0	3,733	6,164	6,935	274	3,733	6,164	6,935
19,050	19,100	0	3,733	6,164	6,935	270	3,733	6,164	6,935
19,100	19,150	0	3,733	6,164	6,935	267	3,733	6,164	6,935
19,150	19,200	0	3,733	6,164	6,935	263	3,733	6,164	6,935
19,200	19,250	0	3,733	6,164	6,935	259	3,733	6,164	6,935
19,250	19,300	0	3,733	6,164	6,935	255	3,733	6,164	6,935
19,300	19,350	0	3,733	6,164	6,935	251	3,733	6,164	6,935
19,350	19,400	0	3,733	6,164	6,935	247	3,733	6,164	6,935
19,400	19,450	0	3,733	6,164	6,935	244	3,733	6,164	6,935
19,450	19,500	0	3,733	6,164	6,935	240	3,733	6,164	6,935
19,500	19,550	0	3,733	6,164	6,935	236	3,733	6,164	6,935
19,550	19,600	0	3,733	6,164	6,935	232	3,733	6,164	6,935
19,600	19,650	0	3,733	6,164	6,935	228	3,733	6,164	6,935
19,650	19,700	0	3,733	6,164	6,935	225	3,733	6,164	6,935
19,700	19,750	0	3,733	6,164	6,935	221	3,733	6,164	6,935
19,750	19,800	0	3,733	6,164	6,935	217	3,733	6,164	6,935
19,800	19,850	0	3,733	6,164	6,935	213	3,733	6,164	6,935
19,850	19,900	0	3,733	6,164	6,935	209	3,733	6,164	6,935
19,900	19,950	0	3,733	6,164	6,935	205	3,733	6,164	6,935
19,950	20,000	0	3,733	6,164	6,935	202	3,733	6,164	6,935
20,000	20,050	0	3,733	6,164	6,935	198	3,733	6,164	6,935
20,050	20,100	0	3,733	6,164	6,935	194	3,733	6,164	6,935
20,100	20,150	0	3,733	6,164	6,935	190	3,733	6,164	6,935
20,150	20,200	0	3,726	6,155	6,925	186	3,733	6,164	6,935
20,200	20,250	0	3,718	6,144	6,914	182	3,733	6,164	6,935
20,250	20,300	0	3,710	6,133	6,904	179	3,733	6,164	6,935
20,300	20,350	0	3,702	6,123	6,893	175	3,733	6,164	6,935
20,350	20,400	0	3,694	6,112	6,883	171	3,733	6,164	6,935
20,400	20,450	0	3,686	6,102	6,872	167	3,733	6,164	6,935
20,450	20,500	0	3,678	6,091	6,862	163	3,733	6,164	6,935
20,500	20,550	0	3,670	6,081	6,851	160	3,733	6,164	6,935
20,550	20,600	0	3,662	6,070	6,841	156	3,733	6,164	6,935
20,600	20,650	0	3,654	6,060	6,830	152	3,733	6,164	6,935
20,650	20,700	0	3,646	6,049	6,820	148	3,733	6,164	6,935
20,700	20,750	0	3,638	6,039	6,809	144	3,733	6,164	6,935
20,750	20,800	0	3,630	6,028	6,799	140	3,733	6,164	6,935
20,800	20,850	0	3,622	6,018	6,788	137	3,733	6,164	6,935
20,850	20,900	0	3,614	6,007	6,778	133	3,733	6,164	6,935
20,900	20,950	0	3,606	5,997	6,767	129	3,733	6,164	6,935
20,950	21,000	0	3,598	5,986	6,757	125	3,733	6,164	6,935
21,000	21,050	0	3,590	5,976	6,746	121	3,733	6,164	6,935
21,050	21,100	0	3,582	5,965	6,735	117	3,733	6,164	6,935
21,100	21,150	0	3,574	5,954	6,725	114	3,733	6,164	6,935
21,150	21,200	0	3,566	5,944	6,714	110	3,733	6,164	6,935
21,200	21,250	0	3,558	5,933	6,704	106	3,733	6,164	6,935
21,250	21,300	0	3,550	5,923	6,693	102	3,733	6,164	6,935
21,300	21,350	0	3,542	5,912	6,683	98	3,733	6,164	6,935
21,350	21,400	0	3,534	5,902	6,672	94	3,733	6,164	6,935
21,400	21,450	0	3,526	5,891	6,662	91	3,733	6,164	6,935
21,450	21,500	0	3,518	5,881	6,651	87	3,733	6,164	6,935
21,500	21,550	0	3,510	5,870	6,641	83	3,733	6,164	6,935
21,550	21,600	0	3,502	5,860	6,630	79	3,733	6,164	6,935

If the amount you are looking up from the worksheet is–		Single, head of household, or qualifying surviving spouse★ and you have–				Married filing jointly and you have–			
At least	But less than	0	1	2	3	0	1	2	3
		Your credit is–				Your credit is–			
21,600	21,650	0	3,494	5,849	6,620	75	3,733	6,164	6,935
21,650	21,700	0	3,486	5,839	6,609	72	3,733	6,164	6,935
21,700	21,750	0	3,478	5,828	6,599	68	3,733	6,164	6,935
21,750	21,800	0	3,470	5,818	6,588	64	3,733	6,164	6,935
21,800	21,850	0	3,462	5,807	6,578	60	3,733	6,164	6,935
21,850	21,900	0	3,454	5,797	6,567	56	3,733	6,164	6,935
21,900	21,950	0	3,446	5,786	6,556	52	3,733	6,164	6,935
21,950	22,000	0	3,438	5,775	6,546	49	3,733	6,164	6,935
22,000	22,050	0	3,430	5,765	6,535	45	3,733	6,164	6,935
22,050	22,100	0	3,422	5,754	6,525	41	3,733	6,164	6,935
22,100	22,150	0	3,414	5,744	6,514	37	3,733	6,164	6,935
22,150	22,200	0	3,406	5,733	6,504	33	3,733	6,164	6,935
22,200	22,250	0	3,398	5,723	6,493	29	3,733	6,164	6,935
22,250	22,300	0	3,390	5,712	6,483	26	3,733	6,164	6,935
22,300	22,350	0	3,382	5,702	6,472	22	3,733	6,164	6,935
22,350	22,400	0	3,374	5,691	6,462	18	3,733	6,164	6,935
22,400	22,450	0	3,366	5,681	6,451	14	3,733	6,164	6,935
22,450	22,500	0	3,358	5,670	6,441	10	3,733	6,164	6,935
22,500	22,550	0	3,350	5,660	6,430	7	3,733	6,164	6,935
22,550	22,600	0	3,342	5,649	6,420	3	3,733	6,164	6,935
22,600	22,650	0	3,334	5,639	6,409	*	3,733	6,164	6,935
22,650	22,700	0	3,327	5,628	6,399	0	3,733	6,164	6,935
22,700	22,750	0	3,319	5,617	6,388	0	3,733	6,164	6,935
22,750	22,800	0	3,311	5,607	6,377	0	3,733	6,164	6,935
22,800	22,850	0	3,303	5,596	6,367	0	3,733	6,164	6,935
22,850	22,900	0	3,295	5,586	6,356	0	3,733	6,164	6,935
22,900	22,950	0	3,287	5,575	6,346	0	3,733	6,164	6,935
22,950	23,000	0	3,279	5,565	6,335	0	3,733	6,164	6,935
23,000	23,050	0	3,271	5,554	6,325	0	3,733	6,164	6,935
23,050	23,100	0	3,263	5,544	6,314	0	3,733	6,164	6,935
23,100	23,150	0	3,255	5,533	6,304	0	3,733	6,164	6,935
23,150	23,200	0	3,247	5,523	6,293	0	3,733	6,164	6,935
23,200	23,250	0	3,239	5,512	6,283	0	3,733	6,164	6,935
23,250	23,300	0	3,231	5,502	6,272	0	3,733	6,164	6,935
23,300	23,350	0	3,223	5,491	6,262	0	3,733	6,164	6,935
23,350	23,400	0	3,215	5,481	6,251	0	3,733	6,164	6,935
23,400	23,450	0	3,207	5,470	6,241	0	3,733	6,164	6,935
23,450	23,500	0	3,199	5,460	6,230	0	3,733	6,164	6,935
23,500	23,550	0	3,191	5,449	6,220	0	3,733	6,164	6,935
23,550	23,600	0	3,183	5,438	6,209	0	3,733	6,164	6,935
23,600	23,650	0	3,175	5,428	6,198	0	3,733	6,164	6,935
23,650	23,700	0	3,167	5,417	6,188	0	3,733	6,164	6,935
23,700	23,750	0	3,159	5,407	6,177	0	3,733	6,164	6,935
23,750	23,800	0	3,151	5,396	6,167	0	3,733	6,164	6,935
23,800	23,850	0	3,143	5,386	6,156	0	3,733	6,164	6,935
23,850	23,900	0	3,135	5,375	6,146	0	3,733	6,164	6,935
23,900	23,950	0	3,127	5,365	6,135	0	3,733	6,164	6,935
23,950	24,000	0	3,119	5,354	6,125	0	3,733	6,164	6,935
24,000	24,050	0	3,111	5,344	6,114	0	3,733	6,164	6,935
24,050	24,100	0	3,103	5,333	6,104	0	3,733	6,164	6,935
24,100	24,150	0	3,095	5,323	6,093	0	3,733	6,164	6,935
24,150	24,200	0	3,087	5,312	6,083	0	3,733	6,164	6,935
24,200	24,250	0	3,079	5,302	6,072	0	3,733	6,164	6,935
24,250	24,300	0	3,071	5,291	6,062	0	3,733	6,164	6,935
24,300	24,350	0	3,063	5,281	6,051	0	3,733	6,164	6,935
24,350	24,400	0	3,055	5,270	6,041	0	3,733	6,164	6,935
24,400	24,450	0	3,047	5,259	6,030	0	3,733	6,164	6,935
24,450	24,500	0	3,039	5,249	6,019	0	3,733	6,164	6,935
24,500	24,550	0	3,031	5,238	6,009	0	3,733	6,164	6,935
24,550	24,600	0	3,023	5,228	5,998	0	3,733	6,164	6,935
24,600	24,650	0	3,015	5,217	5,988	0	3,733	6,164	6,935
24,650	24,700	0	3,007	5,207	5,977	0	3,733	6,164	6,935
24,700	24,750	0	2,999	5,196	5,967	0	3,733	6,164	6,935
24,750	24,800	0	2,991	5,186	5,956	0	3,733	6,164	6,935

★ Use this column if your filing status is married filing separately and you qualify to claim the EIC. See the instructions for line 27.

· If the amount you are looking up from the worksheet is at least $22,600 but less than $22,610, and you have no qualifying children who have valid SSNs, your credit is $0.

If the amount you are looking up from the worksheet is $22,610 or more, and you have no qualifying children who have valid SSNs, you can't take the credit.

Draft as of October 12, 2022.

(Continued)

Earned Income Credit (EIC) Table - *Continued*

(**Caution.** This is **not** a tax table.)

If the amount you are looking up from the worksheet is—		Single, head of household, or qualifying surviving spouse★ and you have—				Married filing jointly and you have—			
At least	But less than	0	1	2	3	0	1	2	3
		Your credit is—				Your credit is—			
24,800	24,850	0	2,983	5,175	5,946	0	3,733	6,164	6,935
24,850	24,900	0	2,975	5,165	5,935	0	3,733	6,164	6,935
24,900	24,950	0	2,967	5,154	5,925	0	3,733	6,164	6,935
24,950	25,000	0	2,959	5,144	5,914	0	3,733	6,164	6,935
25,000	25,050	0	2,951	5,133	5,904	0	3,733	6,164	6,935
25,050	25,100	0	2,943	5,123	5,893	0	3,733	6,164	6,935
25,100	25,150	0	2,935	5,112	5,883	0	3,733	6,164	6,935
25,150	25,200	0	2,927	5,102	5,872	0	3,733	6,164	6,935
25,200	25,250	0	2,919	5,091	5,861	0	3,733	6,164	6,935
25,250	25,300	0	2,911	5,080	5,851	0	3,733	6,164	6,935
25,300	25,350	0	2,903	5,070	5,840	0	3,733	6,164	6,935
25,350	25,400	0	2,895	5,059	5,830	0	3,733	6,164	6,935
25,400	25,450	0	2,887	5,049	5,819	0	3,733	6,164	6,935
25,450	25,500	0	2,879	5,038	5,809	0	3,733	6,164	6,935
25,500	25,550	0	2,871	5,028	5,798	0	3,733	6,164	6,935
25,550	25,600	0	2,863	5,017	5,788	0	3,733	6,164	6,935
25,600	25,650	0	2,855	5,007	5,777	0	3,733	6,164	6,935
25,650	25,700	0	2,847	4,996	5,767	0	3,733	6,164	6,935
25,700	25,750	0	2,839	4,986	5,756	0	3,733	6,164	6,935
25,750	25,800	0	2,831	4,975	5,746	0	3,733	6,164	6,935
25,800	25,850	0	2,823	4,965	5,735	0	3,733	6,164	6,935
25,850	25,900	0	2,815	4,954	5,725	0	3,733	6,164	6,935
25,900	25,950	0	2,807	4,944	5,714	0	3,733	6,164	6,935
25,950	26,000	0	2,799	4,933	5,704	0	3,733	6,164	6,935
26,000	26,050	0	2,791	4,923	5,693	0	3,733	6,164	6,935
26,050	26,100	0	2,783	4,912	5,682	0	3,733	6,164	6,935
26,100	26,150	0	2,775	4,901	5,672	0	3,733	6,164	6,935
26,150	26,200	0	2,767	4,891	5,661	0	3,733	6,164	6,935
26,200	26,250	0	2,759	4,880	5,651	0	3,733	6,164	6,935
26,250	26,300	0	2,751	4,870	5,640	0	3,733	6,164	6,935
26,300	26,350	0	2,743	4,859	5,630	0	3,723	6,150	6,921
26,350	26,400	0	2,735	4,849	5,619	0	3,715	6,140	6,910
26,400	26,450	0	2,727	4,838	5,609	0	3,707	6,129	6,900
26,450	26,500	0	2,719	4,828	5,598	0	3,699	6,119	6,889
26,500	26,550	0	2,711	4,817	5,588	0	3,691	6,108	6,879
26,550	26,600	0	2,703	4,807	5,577	0	3,683	6,098	6,868
26,600	26,650	0	2,695	4,796	5,567	0	3,675	6,087	6,858
26,650	26,700	0	2,687	4,786	5,556	0	3,667	6,077	6,847
26,700	26,750	0	2,679	4,775	5,546	0	3,659	6,066	6,837
26,750	26,800	0	2,671	4,765	5,535	0	3,651	6,056	6,826
26,800	26,850	0	2,663	4,754	5,525	0	3,643	6,045	6,816
26,850	26,900	0	2,655	4,744	5,514	0	3,635	6,034	6,805
26,900	26,950	0	2,647	4,733	5,503	0	3,627	6,024	6,794
26,950	27,000	0	2,639	4,722	5,493	0	3,619	6,013	6,784
27,000	27,050	0	2,631	4,712	5,482	0	3,611	6,003	6,773
27,050	27,100	0	2,623	4,701	5,472	0	3,603	5,992	6,763
27,100	27,150	0	2,615	4,691	5,461	0	3,595	5,982	6,752
27,150	27,200	0	2,607	4,680	5,451	0	3,587	5,971	6,742
27,200	27,250	0	2,599	4,670	5,440	0	3,579	5,961	6,731
27,250	27,300	0	2,591	4,659	5,430	0	3,571	5,950	6,721
27,300	27,350	0	2,583	4,649	5,419	0	3,563	5,940	6,710
27,350	27,400	0	2,575	4,638	5,409	0	3,555	5,929	6,700
27,400	27,450	0	2,567	4,628	5,398	0	3,547	5,919	6,689
27,450	27,500	0	2,559	4,617	5,388	0	3,539	5,908	6,679
27,500	27,550	0	2,551	4,607	5,377	0	3,531	5,898	6,668
27,550	27,600	0	2,543	4,596	5,367	0	3,523	5,887	6,658
27,600	27,650	0	2,535	4,586	5,356	0	3,515	5,877	6,647
27,650	27,700	0	2,528	4,575	5,346	0	3,507	5,866	6,637
27,700	27,750	0	2,520	4,564	5,335	0	3,499	5,855	6,626
27,750	27,800	0	2,512	4,554	5,324	0	3,491	5,845	6,615
27,800	27,850	0	2,504	4,543	5,314	0	3,483	5,834	6,605
27,850	27,900	0	2,496	4,533	5,303	0	3,475	5,824	6,594
27,900	27,950	0	2,488	4,522	5,293	0	3,467	5,813	6,584
27,950	28,000	0	2,480	4,512	5,282	0	3,459	5,803	6,573
28,000	28,050	0	2,472	4,501	5,272	0	3,451	5,792	6,563
28,050	28,100	0	2,464	4,491	5,261	0	3,443	5,782	6,552
28,100	28,150	0	2,456	4,480	5,251	0	3,435	5,771	6,542
28,150	28,200	0	2,448	4,470	5,240	0	3,427	5,761	6,531
28,200	28,250	0	2,440	4,459	5,230	0	3,419	5,750	6,521
28,250	28,300	0	2,432	4,449	5,219	0	3,411	5,740	6,510
28,300	28,350	0	2,424	4,438	5,209	0	3,403	5,729	6,500
28,350	28,400	0	2,416	4,428	5,198	0	3,395	5,719	6,489
28,400	28,450	0	2,408	4,417	5,188	0	3,387	5,708	6,479
28,450	28,500	0	2,400	4,407	5,177	0	3,379	5,698	6,468
28,500	28,550	0	2,392	4,396	5,167	0	3,371	5,687	6,457
28,550	28,600	0	2,384	4,385	5,156	0	3,363	5,676	6,447
28,600	28,650	0	2,376	4,375	5,145	0	3,355	5,666	6,436
28,650	28,700	0	2,368	4,364	5,135	0	3,347	5,655	6,426
28,700	28,750	0	2,360	4,354	5,124	0	3,339	5,645	6,415
28,750	28,800	0	2,352	4,343	5,114	0	3,331	5,634	6,405
28,800	28,850	0	2,344	4,333	5,103	0	3,323	5,624	6,394
28,850	28,900	0	2,336	4,322	5,093	0	3,315	5,613	6,384
28,900	28,950	0	2,328	4,312	5,082	0	3,307	5,603	6,373
28,950	29,000	0	2,320	4,301	5,072	0	3,299	5,592	6,363
29,000	29,050	0	2,312	4,291	5,061	0	3,291	5,582	6,352
29,050	29,100	0	2,304	4,280	5,051	0	3,283	5,571	6,342
29,100	29,150	0	2,296	4,270	5,040	0	3,275	5,561	6,331
29,150	29,200	0	2,288	4,259	5,030	0	3,267	5,550	6,321
29,200	29,250	0	2,280	4,249	5,019	0	3,259	5,540	6,310
29,250	29,300	0	2,272	4,238	5,009	0	3,251	5,529	6,300
29,300	29,350	0	2,264	4,228	4,998	0	3,243	5,519	6,289
29,350	29,400	0	2,256	4,217	4,988	0	3,235	5,508	6,278
29,400	29,450	0	2,248	4,206	4,977	0	3,227	5,497	6,268
29,450	29,500	0	2,240	4,196	4,966	0	3,219	5,487	6,257
29,500	29,550	0	2,232	4,185	4,956	0	3,211	5,476	6,247
29,550	29,600	0	2,224	4,175	4,945	0	3,203	5,466	6,236
29,600	29,650	0	2,216	4,164	4,935	0	3,195	5,455	6,226
29,650	29,700	0	2,208	4,154	4,924	0	3,187	5,445	6,215
29,700	29,750	0	2,200	4,143	4,914	0	3,179	5,434	6,205
29,750	29,800	0	2,192	4,133	4,903	0	3,172	5,424	6,194
29,800	29,850	0	2,184	4,122	4,893	0	3,164	5,413	6,184
29,850	29,900	0	2,176	4,112	4,882	0	3,156	5,403	6,173
29,900	29,950	0	2,168	4,101	4,872	0	3,148	5,392	6,163
29,950	30,000	0	2,160	4,091	4,861	0	3,140	5,382	6,152
30,000	30,050	0	2,152	4,080	4,851	0	3,132	5,371	6,142
30,050	30,100	0	2,144	4,070	4,840	0	3,124	5,361	6,131
30,100	30,150	0	2,136	4,059	4,830	0	3,116	5,350	6,121
30,150	30,200	0	2,128	4,049	4,819	0	3,108	5,340	6,110
30,200	30,250	0	2,120	4,038	4,808	0	3,100	5,329	6,099
30,250	30,300	0	2,112	4,027	4,798	0	3,092	5,318	6,089
30,300	30,350	0	2,104	4,017	4,787	0	3,084	5,308	6,078
30,350	30,400	0	2,096	4,006	4,777	0	3,076	5,297	6,068
30,400	30,450	0	2,088	3,996	4,766	0	3,068	5,287	6,057
30,450	30,500	0	2,080	3,985	4,756	0	3,060	5,276	6,047
30,500	30,550	0	2,072	3,975	4,745	0	3,052	5,266	6,036
30,550	30,600	0	2,064	3,964	4,735	0	3,044	5,255	6,026
30,600	30,650	0	2,056	3,954	4,724	0	3,036	5,245	6,015
30,650	30,700	0	2,048	3,943	4,714	0	3,028	5,234	6,005
30,700	30,750	0	2,040	3,933	4,703	0	3,020	5,224	5,994
30,750	30,800	0	2,032	3,922	4,693	0	3,012	5,213	5,984
30,800	30,850	0	2,024	3,912	4,682	0	3,004	5,203	5,973
30,850	30,900	0	2,016	3,901	4,672	0	2,996	5,192	5,963
30,900	30,950	0	2,008	3,891	4,661	0	2,988	5,182	5,952
30,950	31,000	0	2,000	3,880	4,651	0	2,980	5,171	5,942
31,000	31,050	0	1,992	3,870	4,640	0	2,972	5,160	5,931
31,050	31,100	0	1,984	3,859	4,629	0	2,964	5,150	5,920
31,100	31,150	0	1,976	3,848	4,619	0	2,956	5,139	5,910
31,150	31,200	0	1,968	3,838	4,608	0	2,948	5,129	5,899

★ Use this column if your filing status is married filing separately and you qualify to claim the EIC. See the instructions for line 27.

Draft as of October 12, 2022.

(Continued)

Earned Income Credit (EIC) Table - Continued

(**Caution.** This is **not** a tax table.)

If the amount you are looking up from the worksheet is–		Single, head of household, or qualifying surviving spouse★ and you have–				Married filing jointly and you have–			
At least	But less than	0	1	2	3	0	1	2	3
		Your credit is–				Your credit is–			
31,200	31,250	0	1,960	3,827	4,598	0	2,940	5,118	5,889
31,250	31,300	0	1,952	3,817	4,587	0	2,932	5,108	5,878
31,300	31,350	0	1,944	3,806	4,577	0	2,924	5,097	5,868
31,350	31,400	0	1,936	3,796	4,566	0	2,916	5,087	5,857
31,400	31,450	0	1,928	3,785	4,556	0	2,908	5,076	5,847
31,450	31,500	0	1,920	3,775	4,545	0	2,900	5,066	5,836
31,500	31,550	0	1,912	3,764	4,535	0	2,892	5,055	5,826
31,550	31,600	0	1,904	3,754	4,524	0	2,884	5,045	5,815
31,600	31,650	0	1,896	3,743	4,514	0	2,876	5,034	5,805
31,650	31,700	0	1,888	3,733	4,503	0	2,868	5,024	5,794
31,700	31,750	0	1,880	3,722	4,493	0	2,860	5,013	5,784
31,750	31,800	0	1,872	3,712	4,482	0	2,852	5,003	5,773
31,800	31,850	0	1,864	3,701	4,472	0	2,844	4,992	5,763
31,850	31,900	0	1,856	3,691	4,461	0	2,836	4,981	5,752
31,900	31,950	0	1,848	3,680	4,450	0	2,828	4,971	5,741
31,950	32,000	0	1,840	3,669	4,440	0	2,820	4,960	5,731
32,000	32,050	0	1,832	3,659	4,429	0	2,812	4,950	5,720
32,050	32,100	0	1,824	3,648	4,419	0	2,804	4,939	5,710
32,100	32,150	0	1,816	3,638	4,408	0	2,796	4,929	5,699
32,150	32,200	0	1,808	3,627	4,398	0	2,788	4,918	5,689
32,200	32,250	0	1,800	3,617	4,387	0	2,780	4,908	5,678
32,250	32,300	0	1,792	3,606	4,377	0	2,772	4,897	5,668
32,300	32,350	0	1,784	3,596	4,366	0	2,764	4,887	5,657
32,350	32,400	0	1,776	3,585	4,356	0	2,756	4,876	5,647
32,400	32,450	0	1,768	3,575	4,345	0	2,748	4,866	5,636
32,450	32,500	0	1,760	3,564	4,335	0	2,740	4,855	5,626
32,500	32,550	0	1,752	3,554	4,324	0	2,732	4,845	5,615
32,550	32,600	0	1,744	3,543	4,314	0	2,724	4,834	5,605
32,600	32,650	0	1,736	3,533	4,303	0	2,716	4,824	5,594
32,650	32,700	0	1,729	3,522	4,293	0	2,708	4,813	5,584
32,700	32,750	0	1,721	3,511	4,282	0	2,700	4,802	5,573
32,750	32,800	0	1,713	3,501	4,271	0	2,692	4,792	5,562
32,800	32,850	0	1,705	3,490	4,261	0	2,684	4,781	5,552
32,850	32,900	0	1,697	3,480	4,250	0	2,676	4,771	5,541
32,900	32,950	0	1,689	3,469	4,240	0	2,668	4,760	5,531
32,950	33,000	0	1,681	3,459	4,229	0	2,660	4,750	5,520
33,000	33,050	0	1,673	3,448	4,219	0	2,652	4,739	5,510
33,050	33,100	0	1,665	3,438	4,208	0	2,644	4,729	5,499
33,100	33,150	0	1,657	3,427	4,198	0	2,636	4,718	5,489
33,150	33,200	0	1,649	3,417	4,187	0	2,628	4,708	5,478
33,200	33,250	0	1,641	3,406	4,177	0	2,620	4,697	5,468
33,250	33,300	0	1,633	3,396	4,166	0	2,612	4,687	5,457
33,300	33,350	0	1,625	3,385	4,156	0	2,604	4,676	5,447
33,350	33,400	0	1,617	3,375	4,145	0	2,596	4,666	5,436
33,400	33,450	0	1,609	3,364	4,135	0	2,588	4,655	5,426
33,450	33,500	0	1,601	3,354	4,124	0	2,580	4,645	5,415
33,500	33,550	0	1,593	3,343	4,114	0	2,572	4,634	5,404
33,550	33,600	0	1,585	3,332	4,103	0	2,564	4,623	5,394
33,600	33,650	0	1,577	3,322	4,092	0	2,556	4,613	5,383
33,650	33,700	0	1,569	3,311	4,082	0	2,548	4,602	5,373
33,700	33,750	0	1,561	3,301	4,071	0	2,540	4,592	5,362
33,750	33,800	0	1,553	3,290	4,061	0	2,532	4,581	5,352
33,800	33,850	0	1,545	3,280	4,050	0	2,524	4,571	5,341
33,850	33,900	0	1,537	3,269	4,040	0	2,516	4,560	5,331
33,900	33,950	0	1,529	3,259	4,029	0	2,508	4,550	5,320
33,950	34,000	0	1,521	3,248	4,019	0	2,500	4,539	5,310
34,000	34,050	0	1,513	3,238	4,008	0	2,492	4,529	5,299
34,050	34,100	0	1,505	3,227	3,998	0	2,484	4,518	5,289
34,100	34,150	0	1,497	3,217	3,987	0	2,476	4,508	5,278
34,150	34,200	0	1,489	3,206	3,977	0	2,468	4,497	5,268
34,200	34,250	0	1,481	3,196	3,966	0	2,460	4,487	5,257
34,250	34,300	0	1,473	3,185	3,956	0	2,452	4,476	5,247
34,300	34,350	0	1,465	3,175	3,945	0	2,444	4,466	5,236
34,350	34,400	0	1,457	3,164	3,935	0	2,436	4,455	5,225

If the amount you are looking up from the worksheet is–		Single, head of household, or qualifying surviving spouse★ and you have–				Married filing jointly and you have–			
At least	But less than	0	1	2	3	0	1	2	3
		Your credit is–				Your credit is–			
34,400	34,450	0	1,449	3,153	3,924	0	2,428	4,444	5,215
34,450	34,500	0	1,441	3,143	3,913	0	2,420	4,434	5,204
34,500	34,550	0	1,433	3,132	3,903	0	2,412	4,423	5,194
34,550	34,600	0	1,425	3,122	3,892	0	2,404	4,413	5,183
34,600	34,650	0	1,417	3,111	3,882	0	2,396	4,402	5,173
34,650	34,700	0	1,409	3,101	3,871	0	2,388	4,392	5,162
34,700	34,750	0	1,401	3,090	3,861	0	2,380	4,381	5,152
34,750	34,800	0	1,393	3,080	3,850	0	2,373	4,371	5,141
34,800	34,850	0	1,385	3,069	3,840	0	2,365	4,360	5,131
34,850	34,900	0	1,377	3,059	3,829	0	2,357	4,350	5,120
34,900	34,950	0	1,369	3,048	3,819	0	2,349	4,339	5,110
34,950	35,000	0	1,361	3,038	3,808	0	2,341	4,329	5,099
35,000	35,050	0	1,353	3,027	3,798	0	2,333	4,318	5,089
35,050	35,100	0	1,345	3,017	3,787	0	2,325	4,308	5,078
35,100	35,150	0	1,337	3,006	3,777	0	2,317	4,297	5,068
35,150	35,200	0	1,329	2,996	3,766	0	2,309	4,287	5,057
35,200	35,250	0	1,321	2,985	3,755	0	2,301	4,276	5,046
35,250	35,300	0	1,313	2,974	3,745	0	2,293	4,265	5,036
35,300	35,350	0	1,305	2,964	3,734	0	2,285	4,255	5,025
35,350	35,400	0	1,297	2,953	3,724	0	2,277	4,244	5,015
35,400	35,450	0	1,289	2,943	3,713	0	2,269	4,234	5,004
35,450	35,500	0	1,281	2,932	3,703	0	2,261	4,223	4,994
35,500	35,550	0	1,273	2,922	3,692	0	2,253	4,213	4,983
35,550	35,600	0	1,265	2,911	3,682	0	2,245	4,202	4,973
35,600	35,650	0	1,257	2,901	3,671	0	2,237	4,192	4,962
35,650	35,700	0	1,249	2,890	3,661	0	2,229	4,181	4,952
35,700	35,750	0	1,241	2,880	3,650	0	2,221	4,171	4,941
35,750	35,800	0	1,233	2,869	3,640	0	2,213	4,160	4,931
35,800	35,850	0	1,225	2,859	3,629	0	2,205	4,150	4,920
35,850	35,900	0	1,217	2,848	3,619	0	2,197	4,139	4,910
35,900	35,950	0	1,209	2,838	3,608	0	2,189	4,129	4,899
35,950	36,000	0	1,201	2,827	3,598	0	2,181	4,118	4,889
36,000	36,050	0	1,193	2,817	3,587	0	2,173	4,107	4,878
36,050	36,100	0	1,185	2,806	3,576	0	2,165	4,097	4,867
36,100	36,150	0	1,177	2,795	3,566	0	2,157	4,086	4,857
36,150	36,200	0	1,169	2,785	3,555	0	2,149	4,076	4,846
36,200	36,250	0	1,161	2,774	3,545	0	2,141	4,065	4,836
36,250	36,300	0	1,153	2,764	3,534	0	2,133	4,055	4,825
36,300	36,350	0	1,145	2,753	3,524	0	2,125	4,044	4,815
36,350	36,400	0	1,137	2,743	3,513	0	2,117	4,034	4,804
36,400	36,450	0	1,129	2,732	3,503	0	2,109	4,023	4,794
36,450	36,500	0	1,121	2,722	3,492	0	2,101	4,013	4,783
36,500	36,550	0	1,113	2,711	3,482	0	2,093	4,002	4,773
36,550	36,600	0	1,105	2,701	3,471	0	2,085	3,992	4,762
36,600	36,650	0	1,097	2,690	3,461	0	2,077	3,981	4,752
36,650	36,700	0	1,089	2,680	3,450	0	2,069	3,971	4,741
36,700	36,750	0	1,081	2,669	3,440	0	2,061	3,960	4,731
36,750	36,800	0	1,073	2,659	3,429	0	2,053	3,950	4,720
36,800	36,850	0	1,065	2,648	3,419	0	2,045	3,939	4,710
36,850	36,900	0	1,057	2,638	3,408	0	2,037	3,928	4,699
36,900	36,950	0	1,049	2,627	3,397	0	2,029	3,918	4,688
36,950	37,000	0	1,041	2,616	3,387	0	2,021	3,907	4,678
37,000	37,050	0	1,033	2,606	3,376	0	2,013	3,897	4,667
37,050	37,100	0	1,025	2,595	3,366	0	2,005	3,886	4,657
37,100	37,150	0	1,017	2,585	3,355	0	1,997	3,876	4,646
37,150	37,200	0	1,009	2,574	3,345	0	1,989	3,865	4,636
37,200	37,250	0	1,001	2,564	3,334	0	1,981	3,855	4,625
37,250	37,300	0	993	2,553	3,324	0	1,973	3,844	4,615
37,300	37,350	0	985	2,543	3,313	0	1,965	3,834	4,604
37,350	37,400	0	977	2,532	3,303	0	1,957	3,823	4,594
37,400	37,450	0	969	2,522	3,292	0	1,949	3,813	4,583
37,450	37,500	0	961	2,511	3,282	0	1,941	3,802	4,573
37,500	37,550	0	953	2,501	3,271	0	1,933	3,792	4,562
37,550	37,600	0	945	2,490	3,261	0	1,925	3,781	4,552

★ Use this column if your filing status is married filing separately and you qualify to claim the EIC. See the instructions for line 27.

Draft as of October 12, 2022.

(Continued)

Earned Income Credit (EIC) Table - *Continued*   (**Caution.** This is **not** a tax table.)

If the amount you are looking up from the worksheet is—		Single, head of household, or qualifying surviving spouse★ and you have—				Married filing jointly and you have—			
At least	But less than	0	1	2	3	0	1	2	3
		Your credit is—				Your credit is—			
37,600	37,650	0	937	2,480	3,250	0	1,917	3,771	4,541
37,650	37,700	0	930	2,469	3,240	0	1,909	3,760	4,531
37,700	37,750	0	922	2,458	3,229	0	1,901	3,749	4,520
37,750	37,800	0	914	2,448	3,218	0	1,893	3,739	4,509
37,800	37,850	0	906	2,437	3,208	0	1,885	3,728	4,499
37,850	37,900	0	898	2,427	3,197	0	1,877	3,718	4,488
37,900	37,950	0	890	2,416	3,187	0	1,869	3,707	4,478
37,950	38,000	0	882	2,406	3,176	0	1,861	3,697	4,467
38,000	38,050	0	874	2,395	3,166	0	1,853	3,686	4,457
38,050	38,100	0	866	2,385	3,155	0	1,845	3,676	4,446
38,100	38,150	0	858	2,374	3,145	0	1,837	3,665	4,436
38,150	38,200	0	850	2,364	3,134	0	1,829	3,655	4,425
38,200	38,250	0	842	2,353	3,124	0	1,821	3,644	4,415
38,250	38,300	0	834	2,343	3,113	0	1,813	3,634	4,404
38,300	38,350	0	826	2,332	3,103	0	1,805	3,623	4,394
38,350	38,400	0	818	2,322	3,092	0	1,797	3,613	4,383
38,400	38,450	0	810	2,311	3,082	0	1,789	3,602	4,373
38,450	38,500	0	802	2,301	3,071	0	1,781	3,592	4,362
38,500	38,550	0	794	2,290	3,061	0	1,773	3,581	4,351
38,550	38,600	0	786	2,279	3,050	0	1,765	3,570	4,341
38,600	38,650	0	778	2,269	3,039	0	1,757	3,560	4,330
38,650	38,700	0	770	2,258	3,029	0	1,749	3,549	4,320
38,700	38,750	0	762	2,248	3,018	0	1,741	3,539	4,309
38,750	38,800	0	754	2,237	3,008	0	1,733	3,528	4,299
38,800	38,850	0	746	2,227	2,997	0	1,725	3,518	4,288
38,850	38,900	0	738	2,216	2,987	0	1,717	3,507	4,278
38,900	38,950	0	730	2,206	2,976	0	1,709	3,497	4,267
38,950	39,000	0	722	2,195	2,966	0	1,701	3,486	4,257
39,000	39,050	0	714	2,185	2,955	0	1,693	3,476	4,246
39,050	39,100	0	706	2,174	2,945	0	1,685	3,465	4,236
39,100	39,150	0	698	2,164	2,934	0	1,677	3,455	4,225
39,150	39,200	0	690	2,153	2,924	0	1,669	3,444	4,215
39,200	39,250	0	682	2,143	2,913	0	1,661	3,434	4,204
39,250	39,300	0	674	2,132	2,903	0	1,653	3,423	4,194
39,300	39,350	0	666	2,122	2,892	0	1,645	3,413	4,183
39,350	39,400	0	658	2,111	2,882	0	1,637	3,402	4,172
39,400	39,450	0	650	2,100	2,871	0	1,629	3,391	4,162
39,450	39,500	0	642	2,090	2,860	0	1,621	3,381	4,151
39,500	39,550	0	634	2,079	2,850	0	1,613	3,370	4,141
39,550	39,600	0	626	2,069	2,839	0	1,605	3,360	4,130
39,600	39,650	0	618	2,058	2,829	0	1,597	3,349	4,120
39,650	39,700	0	610	2,048	2,818	0	1,589	3,339	4,109
39,700	39,750	0	602	2,037	2,808	0	1,581	3,328	4,099
39,750	39,800	0	594	2,027	2,797	0	1,574	3,318	4,088
39,800	39,850	0	586	2,016	2,787	0	1,566	3,307	4,078
39,850	39,900	0	578	2,006	2,776	0	1,558	3,297	4,067
39,900	39,950	0	570	1,995	2,766	0	1,550	3,286	4,057
39,950	40,000	0	562	1,985	2,755	0	1,542	3,276	4,046
40,000	40,050	0	554	1,974	2,745	0	1,534	3,265	4,036
40,050	40,100	0	546	1,964	2,734	0	1,526	3,255	4,025
40,100	40,150	0	538	1,953	2,724	0	1,518	3,244	4,015
40,150	40,200	0	530	1,943	2,713	0	1,510	3,234	4,004
40,200	40,250	0	522	1,932	2,702	0	1,502	3,223	3,993
40,250	40,300	0	514	1,921	2,692	0	1,494	3,212	3,983
40,300	40,350	0	506	1,911	2,681	0	1,486	3,202	3,972
40,350	40,400	0	498	1,900	2,671	0	1,478	3,191	3,962
40,400	40,450	0	490	1,890	2,660	0	1,470	3,181	3,951
40,450	40,500	0	482	1,879	2,650	0	1,462	3,170	3,941
40,500	40,550	0	474	1,869	2,639	0	1,454	3,160	3,930
40,550	40,600	0	466	1,858	2,629	0	1,446	3,149	3,920
40,600	40,650	0	458	1,848	2,618	0	1,438	3,139	3,909
40,650	40,700	0	450	1,837	2,608	0	1,430	3,128	3,899
40,700	40,750	0	442	1,827	2,597	0	1,422	3,118	3,888
40,750	40,800	0	434	1,816	2,587	0	1,414	3,107	3,878

If the amount you are looking up from the worksheet is—		Single, head of household, or qualifying surviving spouse★ and you have—				Married filing jointly and you have—			
At least	But less than	0	1	2	3	0	1	2	3
		Your credit is—				Your credit is—			
40,800	40,850	0	426	1,806	2,576	0	1,406	3,097	3,867
40,850	40,900	0	418	1,795	2,566	0	1,398	3,086	3,857
40,900	40,950	0	410	1,785	2,555	0	1,390	3,076	3,846
40,950	41,000	0	402	1,774	2,545	0	1,382	3,065	3,836
41,000	41,050	0	394	1,764	2,534	0	1,374	3,054	3,825
41,050	41,100	0	386	1,753	2,523	0	1,366	3,044	3,814
41,100	41,150	0	378	1,742	2,513	0	1,358	3,033	3,804
41,150	41,200	0	370	1,732	2,502	0	1,350	3,023	3,793
41,200	41,250	0	362	1,721	2,492	0	1,342	3,012	3,783
41,250	41,300	0	354	1,711	2,481	0	1,334	3,002	3,772
41,300	41,350	0	346	1,700	2,471	0	1,326	2,991	3,762
41,350	41,400	0	338	1,690	2,460	0	1,318	2,981	3,751
41,400	41,450	0	330	1,679	2,450	0	1,310	2,970	3,741
41,450	41,500	0	322	1,669	2,439	0	1,302	2,960	3,730
41,500	41,550	0	314	1,658	2,429	0	1,294	2,949	3,720
41,550	41,600	0	306	1,648	2,418	0	1,286	2,939	3,709
41,600	41,650	0	298	1,637	2,408	0	1,278	2,928	3,699
41,650	41,700	0	290	1,627	2,397	0	1,270	2,918	3,688
41,700	41,750	0	282	1,616	2,387	0	1,262	2,907	3,678
41,750	41,800	0	274	1,606	2,376	0	1,254	2,897	3,667
41,800	41,850	0	266	1,595	2,366	0	1,246	2,886	3,657
41,850	41,900	0	258	1,585	2,355	0	1,238	2,875	3,646
41,900	41,950	0	250	1,574	2,344	0	1,230	2,865	3,635
41,950	42,000	0	242	1,563	2,334	0	1,222	2,854	3,625
42,000	42,050	0	234	1,553	2,323	0	1,214	2,844	3,614
42,050	42,100	0	226	1,542	2,313	0	1,206	2,833	3,604
42,100	42,150	0	218	1,532	2,302	0	1,198	2,823	3,593
42,150	42,200	0	210	1,521	2,292	0	1,190	2,812	3,583
42,200	42,250	0	202	1,511	2,281	0	1,182	2,802	3,572
42,250	42,300	0	194	1,500	2,271	0	1,174	2,791	3,561
42,300	42,350	0	186	1,490	2,260	0	1,166	2,781	3,551
42,350	42,400	0	178	1,479	2,250	0	1,158	2,770	3,541
42,400	42,450	0	170	1,469	2,239	0	1,150	2,760	3,530
42,450	42,500	0	162	1,458	2,229	0	1,142	2,749	3,520
42,500	42,550	0	154	1,448	2,218	0	1,134	2,739	3,509
42,550	42,600	0	146	1,437	2,208	0	1,126	2,728	3,499
42,600	42,650	0	138	1,427	2,197	0	1,118	2,718	3,488
42,650	42,700	0	131	1,416	2,187	0	1,110	2,707	3,478
42,700	42,750	0	123	1,405	2,176	0	1,102	2,696	3,467
42,750	42,800	0	115	1,395	2,165	0	1,094	2,686	3,456
42,800	42,850	0	107	1,384	2,155	0	1,086	2,675	3,446
42,850	42,900	0	99	1,374	2,144	0	1,078	2,665	3,435
42,900	42,950	0	91	1,363	2,134	0	1,070	2,654	3,425
42,950	43,000	0	83	1,353	2,123	0	1,062	2,644	3,414
43,000	43,050	0	75	1,342	2,113	0	1,054	2,633	3,404
43,050	43,100	0	67	1,332	2,102	0	1,046	2,623	3,393
43,100	43,150	0	59	1,321	2,092	0	1,038	2,612	3,383
43,150	43,200	0	51	1,311	2,081	0	1,030	2,602	3,372
43,200	43,250	0	43	1,300	2,071	0	1,022	2,591	3,362
43,250	43,300	0	35	1,290	2,060	0	1,014	2,581	3,351
43,300	43,350	0	27	1,279	2,050	0	1,006	2,570	3,341
43,350	43,400	0	19	1,269	2,039	0	998	2,560	3,330
43,400	43,450	0	11	1,258	2,029	0	990	2,549	3,320
43,450	43,500	0	*	1,248	2,018	0	982	2,539	3,309
43,500	43,550	0	0	1,237	2,008	0	974	2,528	3,298
43,550	43,600	0	0	1,226	1,997	0	966	2,517	3,288
43,600	43,650	0	0	1,216	1,986	0	958	2,507	3,277
43,650	43,700	0	0	1,205	1,976	0	950	2,496	3,267
43,700	43,750	0	0	1,195	1,965	0	942	2,486	3,256
43,750	43,800	0	0	1,184	1,955	0	934	2,475	3,246
43,800	43,850	0	0	1,174	1,944	0	926	2,465	3,235
43,850	43,900	0	0	1,163	1,934	0	918	2,454	3,225
43,900	43,950	0	0	1,153	1,923	0	910	2,444	3,214
43,950	44,000	0	0	1,142	1,913	0	902	2,433	3,204

★   Use this column if your filing status is married filing separately and you qualify to claim the EIC. See the instructions for line 27.

•   If the amount you are looking up from the worksheet is at least $43,450 but less than $43,492, and you have one qualifying child who has a valid SSN, your credit is $3.

If the amount you are looking up from the worksheet is $43,492 or more, and you have one qualifying child who has a valid SSN, you can't take the credit.

Draft as of October 12, 2022.

(Continued)

Earned Income Credit (EIC) Table - *Continued*　　　　(**Caution.** This is **not** a tax table.)

If the amount you are looking up from the worksheet is–		Single, head of household, or qualifying surviving spouse★ and you have–				Married filing jointly and you have–				If the amount you are looking up from the worksheet is–		Single, head of household, or qualifying surviving spouse★ and you have–				Married filing jointly and you have–			
At least	But less than	0	1	2	3	0	1	2	3	At least	But less than	0	1	2	3	0	1	2	3
		Your credit is–				Your credit is–						Your credit is–				Your credit is–			
44,000	44,050	0	0	1,132	1,902	0	894	2,423	3,193	46,800	46,850	0	0	542	1,313	0	447	1,833	2,604
44,050	44,100	0	0	1,121	1,892	0	886	2,412	3,183	46,850	46,900	0	0	532	1,302	0	439	1,822	2,593
44,100	44,150	0	0	1,111	1,881	0	878	2,402	3,172	46,900	46,950	0	0	521	1,291	0	431	1,812	2,582
44,150	44,200	0	0	1,100	1,871	0	870	2,391	3,162	46,950	47,000	0	0	510	1,281	0	423	1,801	2,572
44,200	44,250	0	0	1,090	1,860	0	862	2,381	3,151	47,000	47,050	0	0	500	1,270	0	415	1,791	2,561
44,250	44,300	0	0	1,079	1,850	0	854	2,370	3,141	47,050	47,100	0	0	489	1,260	0	407	1,780	2,551
44,300	44,350	0	0	1,069	1,839	0	846	2,360	3,130	47,100	47,150	0	0	479	1,249	0	399	1,770	2,540
44,350	44,400	0	0	1,058	1,829	0	838	2,349	3,119	47,150	47,200	0	0	468	1,239	0	391	1,759	2,530
44,400	44,450	0	0	1,047	1,818	0	830	2,338	3,109	47,200	47,250	0	0	458	1,228	0	383	1,749	2,519
44,450	44,500	0	0	1,037	1,807	0	822	2,328	3,098	47,250	47,300	0	0	447	1,218	0	375	1,738	2,509
44,500	44,550	0	0	1,026	1,797	0	814	2,317	3,088	47,300	47,350	0	0	437	1,207	0	367	1,728	2,498
44,550	44,600	0	0	1,016	1,786	0	806	2,307	3,077	47,350	47,400	0	0	426	1,197	0	359	1,717	2,488
44,600	44,650	0	0	1,005	1,776	0	798	2,296	3,067	47,400	47,450	0	0	416	1,186	0	351	1,707	2,477
44,650	44,700	0	0	995	1,765	0	790	2,286	3,056	47,450	47,500	0	0	405	1,176	0	343	1,696	2,467
44,700	44,750	0	0	984	1,755	0	782	2,275	3,046	47,500	47,550	0	0	395	1,165	0	335	1,686	2,456
44,750	44,800	0	0	974	1,744	0	775	2,265	3,035	47,550	47,600	0	0	384	1,155	0	327	1,675	2,446
44,800	44,850	0	0	963	1,734	0	767	2,254	3,025	47,600	47,650	0	0	374	1,144	0	319	1,665	2,435
44,850	44,900	0	0	953	1,723	0	759	2,244	3,014	47,650	47,700	0	0	363	1,134	0	311	1,654	2,425
44,900	44,950	0	0	942	1,713	0	751	2,233	3,004	47,700	47,750	0	0	352	1,123	0	303	1,643	2,414
44,950	45,000	0	0	932	1,702	0	743	2,223	2,993	47,750	47,800	0	0	342	1,112	0	295	1,633	2,403
45,000	45,050	0	0	921	1,692	0	735	2,212	2,983	47,800	47,850	0	0	331	1,102	0	287	1,622	2,393
45,050	45,100	0	0	911	1,681	0	727	2,202	2,972	47,850	47,900	0	0	321	1,091	0	279	1,612	2,382
45,100	45,150	0	0	900	1,671	0	719	2,191	2,962	47,900	47,950	0	0	310	1,081	0	271	1,601	2,372
45,150	45,200	0	0	890	1,660	0	711	2,181	2,951	47,950	48,000	0	0	300	1,070	0	263	1,591	2,361
45,200	45,250	0	0	879	1,649	0	703	2,170	2,940	48,000	48,050	0	0	289	1,060	0	255	1,580	2,351
45,250	45,300	0	0	868	1,639	0	695	2,159	2,930	48,050	48,100	0	0	279	1,049	0	247	1,570	2,340
45,300	45,350	0	0	858	1,628	0	687	2,149	2,919	48,100	48,150	0	0	268	1,039	0	239	1,559	2,330
45,350	45,400	0	0	847	1,618	0	679	2,138	2,909	48,150	48,200	0	0	258	1,028	0	231	1,549	2,319
45,400	45,450	0	0	837	1,607	0	671	2,128	2,898	48,200	48,250	0	0	247	1,018	0	223	1,538	2,309
45,450	45,500	0	0	826	1,597	0	663	2,117	2,888	48,250	48,300	0	0	237	1,007	0	215	1,528	2,298
45,500	45,550	0	0	816	1,586	0	655	2,107	2,877	48,300	48,350	0	0	226	997	0	207	1,517	2,288
45,550	45,600	0	0	805	1,576	0	647	2,096	2,867	48,350	48,400	0	0	216	986	0	199	1,507	2,277
45,600	45,650	0	0	795	1,565	0	639	2,086	2,856	48,400	48,450	0	0	205	976	0	191	1,496	2,267
45,650	45,700	0	0	784	1,555	0	631	2,075	2,846	48,450	48,500	0	0	195	965	0	183	1,486	2,256
45,700	45,750	0	0	774	1,544	0	623	2,065	2,835	48,500	48,550	0	0	184	955	0	175	1,475	2,245
45,750	45,800	0	0	763	1,534	0	615	2,054	2,825	48,550	48,600	0	0	173	944	0	167	1,464	2,235
45,800	45,850	0	0	753	1,523	0	607	2,044	2,814	48,600	48,650	0	0	163	933	0	159	1,454	2,224
45,850	45,900	0	0	742	1,513	0	599	2,033	2,804	48,650	48,700	0	0	152	923	0	151	1,443	2,214
45,900	45,950	0	0	732	1,502	0	591	2,023	2,793	48,700	48,750	0	0	142	912	0	143	1,433	2,203
45,950	46,000	0	0	721	1,492	0	583	2,012	2,783	48,750	48,800	0	0	131	902	0	135	1,422	2,193
46,000	46,050	0	0	711	1,481	0	575	2,001	2,772	48,800	48,850	0	0	121	891	0	127	1,412	2,182
46,050	46,100	0	0	700	1,470	0	567	1,991	2,761	48,850	48,900	0	0	110	881	0	119	1,401	2,172
46,100	46,150	0	0	689	1,460	0	559	1,980	2,751	48,900	48,950	0	0	100	870	0	111	1,391	2,161
46,150	46,200	0	0	679	1,449	0	551	1,970	2,740	48,950	49,000	0	0	89	860	0	103	1,380	2,151
46,200	46,250	0	0	668	1,439	0	543	1,959	2,730	49,000	49,050	0	0	79	849	0	95	1,370	2,140
46,250	46,300	0	0	658	1,428	0	535	1,949	2,719	49,050	49,100	0	0	68	839	0	87	1,359	2,130
46,300	46,350	0	0	647	1,418	0	527	1,938	2,709	49,100	49,150	0	0	58	828	0	79	1,349	2,119
46,350	46,400	0	0	637	1,407	0	519	1,928	2,698	49,150	49,200	0	0	47	818	0	71	1,338	2,109
46,400	46,450	0	0	626	1,397	0	511	1,917	2,688	49,200	49,250	0	0	37	807	0	63	1,328	2,098
46,450	46,500	0	0	616	1,386	0	503	1,907	2,677	49,250	49,300	0	0	26	797	0	55	1,317	2,088
46,500	46,550	0	0	605	1,376	0	495	1,896	2,667	49,300	49,350	0	0	16	786	0	47	1,307	2,077
46,550	46,600	0	0	595	1,365	0	487	1,886	2,656	49,350	49,400	0	0	*	776	0	39	1,296	2,066
46,600	46,650	0	0	584	1,355	0	479	1,875	2,646	49,400	49,450	0	0	0	765	0	31	1,285	2,056
46,650	46,700	0	0	574	1,344	0	471	1,865	2,635	49,450	49,500	0	0	0	754	0	23	1,275	2,045
46,700	46,750	0	0	563	1,334	0	463	1,854	2,625	49,500	49,550	0	0	0	744	0	15	1,264	2,035
46,750	46,800	0	0	553	1,323	0	455	1,844	2,614	49,550	49,600	0	0	0	733	0	7	1,254	2,024

★ Use this column if your filing status is married filing separately and you qualify to claim the EIC. See the instructions for line 27.

* If the amount you are looking up from the worksheet is at least $49,350 but less than $49,399, and you have two qualifying children who have valid SSNs, your credit is $5.

If the amount you are looking up from the worksheet is $49,399 or more, and you have two qualifying children who have valid SSNs, you can't take the credit.

Draft as of October 12, 2022.　　　　*(Continued)*

Earned Income Credit (EIC) Table - *Continued*

(**Caution.** This is **not** a tax table.)

If the amount you are looking up from the worksheet is–		And your filing status is–								If the amount you are looking up from the worksheet is–		And your filing status is–							
		Single, head of household, or qualifying surviving spouse★ and you have–				Married filing jointly and you have–						Single, head of household, or qualifying surviving spouse★ and you have–				Married filing jointly and you have–			
At least	But less than	0	1	2	3	0	1	2	3	At least	But less than	0	1	2	3	0	1	2	3
		Your credit is–				Your credit is–						Your credit is–				Your credit is–			
49,600	49,650	0	0	0	723	0	*	1,243	2,014	52,000	52,050	0	0	0	217	0	0	738	1,508
49,650	49,700	0	0	0	712	0	0	1,233	2,003	52,050	52,100	0	0	0	207	0	0	727	1,498
49,700	49,750	0	0	0	702	0	0	1,222	1,993	52,100	52,150	0	0	0	196	0	0	717	1,487
49,750	49,800	0	0	0	691	0	0	1,212	1,982	52,150	52,200	0	0	0	186	0	0	706	1,477
49,800	49,850	0	0	0	681	0	0	1,201	1,972	52,200	52,250	0	0	0	175	0	0	696	1,466
49,850	49,900	0	0	0	670	0	0	1,191	1,961	52,250	52,300	0	0	0	165	0	0	685	1,456
49,900	49,950	0	0	0	660	0	0	1,180	1,951	52,300	52,350	0	0	0	154	0	0	675	1,445
49,950	50,000	0	0	0	649	0	0	1,170	1,940	52,350	52,400	0	0	0	144	0	0	664	1,435
50,000	50,050	0	0	0	639	0	0	1,159	1,930	52,400	52,450	0	0	0	133	0	0	654	1,424
50,050	50,100	0	0	0	628	0	0	1,149	1,919	52,450	52,500	0	0	0	123	0	0	643	1,414
50,100	50,150	0	0	0	618	0	0	1,138	1,909	52,500	52,550	0	0	0	112	0	0	633	1,403
50,150	50,200	0	0	0	607	0	0	1,128	1,898	52,550	52,600	0	0	0	102	0	0	622	1,393
50,200	50,250	0	0	0	596	0	0	1,117	1,887	52,600	52,650	0	0	0	91	0	0	612	1,382
50,250	50,300	0	0	0	586	0	0	1,106	1,877	52,650	52,700	0	0	0	81	0	0	601	1,372
50,300	50,350	0	0	0	575	0	0	1,096	1,866	52,700	52,750	0	0	0	70	0	0	590	1,361
50,350	50,400	0	0	0	565	0	0	1,085	1,856	52,750	52,800	0	0	0	59	0	0	580	1,350
50,400	50,450	0	0	0	554	0	0	1,075	1,845	52,800	52,850	0	0	0	49	0	0	569	1,340
50,450	50,500	0	0	0	544	0	0	1,064	1,835	52,850	52,900	0	0	0	38	0	0	559	1,329
50,500	50,550	0	0	0	533	0	0	1,054	1,824	52,900	52,950	0	0	0	28	0	0	548	1,319
50,550	50,600	0	0	0	523	0	0	1,043	1,814	52,950	53,000	0	0	0	17	0	0	538	1,308
50,600	50,650	0	0	0	512	0	0	1,033	1,803	53,000	53,050	0	0	0	7	0	0	527	1,298
50,650	50,700	0	0	0	502	0	0	1,022	1,793	53,050	53,100	0	0	0	**	0	0	517	1,287
50,700	50,750	0	0	0	491	0	0	1,012	1,782	53,100	53,150	0	0	0	0	0	0	506	1,277
50,750	50,800	0	0	0	481	0	0	1,001	1,772	53,150	53,200	0	0	0	0	0	0	496	1,266
50,800	50,850	0	0	0	470	0	0	991	1,761	53,200	53,250	0	0	0	0	0	0	485	1,256
50,850	50,900	0	0	0	460	0	0	980	1,751	53,250	53,300	0	0	0	0	0	0	475	1,245
50,900	50,950	0	0	0	449	0	0	970	1,740	53,300	53,350	0	0	0	0	0	0	464	1,235
50,950	51,000	0	0	0	439	0	0	959	1,730	53,350	53,400	0	0	0	0	0	0	454	1,224
51,000	51,050	0	0	0	428	0	0	948	1,719	53,400	53,450	0	0	0	0	0	0	443	1,214
51,050	51,100	0	0	0	417	0	0	938	1,708	53,450	53,500	0	0	0	0	0	0	433	1,203
51,100	51,150	0	0	0	407	0	0	927	1,698	53,500	53,550	0	0	0	0	0	0	422	1,192
51,150	51,200	0	0	0	396	0	0	917	1,687	53,550	53,600	0	0	0	0	0	0	411	1,182
51,200	51,250	0	0	0	386	0	0	906	1,677	53,600	53,650	0	0	0	0	0	0	401	1,171
51,250	51,300	0	0	0	375	0	0	896	1,666	53,650	53,700	0	0	0	0	0	0	390	1,161
51,300	51,350	0	0	0	365	0	0	885	1,656	53,700	53,750	0	0	0	0	0	0	380	1,150
51,350	51,400	0	0	0	354	0	0	875	1,645	53,750	53,800	0	0	0	0	0	0	369	1,140
51,400	51,450	0	0	0	344	0	0	864	1,635	53,800	53,850	0	0	0	0	0	0	359	1,129
51,450	51,500	0	0	0	333	0	0	854	1,624	53,850	53,900	0	0	0	0	0	0	348	1,119
51,500	51,550	0	0	0	323	0	0	843	1,614	53,900	53,950	0	0	0	0	0	0	338	1,108
51,550	51,600	0	0	0	312	0	0	833	1,603	53,950	54,000	0	0	0	0	0	0	327	1,098
51,600	51,650	0	0	0	302	0	0	822	1,593	54,000	54,050	0	0	0	0	0	0	317	1,087
51,650	51,700	0	0	0	291	0	0	812	1,582	54,050	54,100	0	0	0	0	0	0	306	1,077
51,700	51,750	0	0	0	281	0	0	801	1,572	54,100	54,150	0	0	0	0	0	0	296	1,066
51,750	51,800	0	0	0	270	0	0	791	1,561	54,150	54,200	0	0	0	0	0	0	285	1,056
51,800	51,850	0	0	0	260	0	0	780	1,551	54,200	54,250	0	0	0	0	0	0	275	1,045
51,850	51,900	0	0	0	249	0	0	769	1,540	54,250	54,300	0	0	0	0	0	0	264	1,035
51,900	51,950	0	0	0	238	0	0	759	1,529	54,300	54,350	0	0	0	0	0	0	254	1,024
51,950	52,000	0	0	0	228	0	0	748	1,519	54,350	54,400	0	0	0	0	0	0	243	1,013

★ Use this column if your filing status is married filing separately and you qualify to claim the EIC. See the instructions for line 27.

· If the amount you are looking up from the worksheet is at least $49,600 but less than $49,622, and you have one qualifying child who has a valid SSN, your credit is $2.

If the amount you are looking up from the worksheet is $49,622 or more, and you have one qualifying child who has a valid SSN, you can't take the credit.

·· If the amount you are looking up from the worksheet is at least $53,050 but less than $53,057, and you have three qualifying children who have valid SSNs, your credit is $1.

If the amount you are looking up from the worksheet is $53,057 or more, and you have three qualifying children who have valid SSNs, you can't take the credit.

Draft as of October 12, 2022.

(Continued)

Earned Income Credit (EIC) Table - *Continued*

(Caution. This is **not** a tax table.)

If the amount you are looking up from the worksheet is—		Single, head of household, or qualifying surviving spouse★ and you have—				Married filing jointly and you have—			
At least	But less than	0	1	2	3	0	1	2	3
		Your credit is—				Your credit is—			
54,400	54,450	0	0	0	0	0	0	232	1,003
54,450	54,500	0	0	0	0	0	0	222	992
54,500	54,550	0	0	0	0	0	0	211	982
54,550	54,600	0	0	0	0	0	0	201	971
54,600	54,650	0	0	0	0	0	0	190	961
54,650	54,700	0	0	0	0	0	0	180	950
54,700	54,750	0	0	0	0	0	0	169	940
54,750	54,800	0	0	0	0	0	0	159	929
54,800	54,850	0	0	0	0	0	0	148	919
54,850	54,900	0	0	0	0	0	0	138	908
54,900	54,950	0	0	0	0	0	0	127	898
54,950	55,000	0	0	0	0	0	0	117	887
55,000	55,050	0	0	0	0	0	0	106	877
55,050	55,100	0	0	0	0	0	0	96	866
55,100	55,150	0	0	0	0	0	0	85	856
55,150	55,200	0	0	0	0	0	0	75	845
55,200	55,250	0	0	0	0	0	0	64	834
55,250	55,300	0	0	0	0	0	0	53	824
55,300	55,350	0	0	0	0	0	0	43	813
55,350	55,400	0	0	0	0	0	0	32	803
55,400	55,450	0	0	0	0	0	0	22	792
55,450	55,500	0	0	0	0	0	0	11	782
55,500	55,550	0	0	0	0	0	0	*	771
55,550	55,600	0	0	0	0	0	0	0	761
55,600	55,650	0	0	0	0	0	0	0	750
55,650	55,700	0	0	0	0	0	0	0	740
55,700	55,750	0	0	0	0	0	0	0	729
55,750	55,800	0	0	0	0	0	0	0	719
55,800	55,850	0	0	0	0	0	0	0	708
55,850	55,900	0	0	0	0	0	0	0	698
55,900	55,950	0	0	0	0	0	0	0	687
55,950	56,000	0	0	0	0	0	0	0	677
56,000	56,050	0	0	0	0	0	0	0	666
56,050	56,100	0	0	0	0	0	0	0	655
56,100	56,150	0	0	0	0	0	0	0	645
56,150	56,200	0	0	0	0	0	0	0	634
56,200	56,250	0	0	0	0	0	0	0	624
56,250	56,300	0	0	0	0	0	0	0	613
56,300	56,350	0	0	0	0	0	0	0	603
56,350	56,400	0	0	0	0	0	0	0	592
56,400	56,450	0	0	0	0	0	0	0	582
56,450	56,500	0	0	0	0	0	0	0	571
56,500	56,550	0	0	0	0	0	0	0	561
56,550	56,600	0	0	0	0	0	0	0	550
56,600	56,650	0	0	0	0	0	0	0	540
56,650	56,700	0	0	0	0	0	0	0	529
56,700	56,750	0	0	0	0	0	0	0	519
56,750	56,800	0	0	0	0	0	0	0	508

If the amount you are looking up from the worksheet is—		Single, head of household, or qualifying surviving spouse★ and you have—				Married filing jointly and you have—			
At least	But less than	0	1	2	3	0	1	2	3
		Your credit is—				Your credit is—			
56,800	56,850	0	0	0	0	0	0	0	498
56,850	56,900	0	0	0	0	0	0	0	487
56,900	56,950	0	0	0	0	0	0	0	476
56,950	57,000	0	0	0	0	0	0	0	466
57,000	57,050	0	0	0	0	0	0	0	455
57,050	57,100	0	0	0	0	0	0	0	445
57,100	57,150	0	0	0	0	0	0	0	434
57,150	57,200	0	0	0	0	0	0	0	424
57,200	57,250	0	0	0	0	0	0	0	413
57,250	57,300	0	0	0	0	0	0	0	403
57,300	57,350	0	0	0	0	0	0	0	392
57,350	57,400	0	0	0	0	0	0	0	382
57,400	57,450	0	0	0	0	0	0	0	371
57,450	57,500	0	0	0	0	0	0	0	361
57,500	57,550	0	0	0	0	0	0	0	350
57,550	57,600	0	0	0	0	0	0	0	340
57,600	57,650	0	0	0	0	0	0	0	329
57,650	57,700	0	0	0	0	0	0	0	319
57,700	57,750	0	0	0	0	0	0	0	308
57,750	57,800	0	0	0	0	0	0	0	297
57,800	57,850	0	0	0	0	0	0	0	287
57,850	57,900	0	0	0	0	0	0	0	276
57,900	57,950	0	0	0	0	0	0	0	266
57,950	58,000	0	0	0	0	0	0	0	255
58,000	58,050	0	0	0	0	0	0	0	245
58,050	58,100	0	0	0	0	0	0	0	234
58,100	58,150	0	0	0	0	0	0	0	224
58,150	58,200	0	0	0	0	0	0	0	213
58,200	58,250	0	0	0	0	0	0	0	203
58,250	58,300	0	0	0	0	0	0	0	192
58,300	58,350	0	0	0	0	0	0	0	182
58,350	58,400	0	0	0	0	0	0	0	171
58,400	58,450	0	0	0	0	0	0	0	161
58,450	58,500	0	0	0	0	0	0	0	150
58,500	58,550	0	0	0	0	0	0	0	139
58,550	58,600	0	0	0	0	0	0	0	129
58,600	58,650	0	0	0	0	0	0	0	118
58,650	58,700	0	0	0	0	0	0	0	108
58,700	58,750	0	0	0	0	0	0	0	97
58,750	58,800	0	0	0	0	0	0	0	87
58,800	58,850	0	0	0	0	0	0	0	76
58,850	58,900	0	0	0	0	0	0	0	66
58,900	58,950	0	0	0	0	0	0	0	55
58,950	59,000	0	0	0	0	0	0	0	45
59,000	59,050	0	0	0	0	0	0	0	34
59,050	59,100	0	0	0	0	0	0	0	24
59,100	59,150	0	0	0	0	0	0	0	13
59,150	59,187	0	0	0	0	0	0	0	**

★ Use this column if your filing status is married filing separately and you qualify to claim the EIC. See the instructions for line 27.

* If the amount you are looking up from the worksheet is at least $55,500 but less than $55,529, and you have two qualifying children who have valid SSNs, your credit is $3.

If the amount you are looking up from the worksheet is $55,529 or more, and you have two qualifying children who have valid SSNs, you can't take the credit.

** If the amount you are looking up from the worksheet is at least $59,150 but less than $59,187, and you have three qualifying children who have valid SSNs, your credit is $4.

If the amount you are looking up from the worksheet is $59,187 or more, and you have three qualifying children who have valid SSNs, you can't take the credit.

Draft as of October 12, 2022.

¶ 1113   Corporate income tax rates; corporate alternative minimum tax.

The corporate tax rate is a flat 21%, (Code Sec. 11(b)).[7] For tax years beginning after 2022, a 15% corporate alternative minimum tax applies (Code Sec. 55(b)), see ¶3213.

¶ 1114   Gift and estate tax rates (unified rate schedule).

The estate tax is imposed under Code Sec. 2001 on the decedent's taxable estate (gross estate less deductions). For credits against the estate tax, see ¶5028 *et seq.* The gift tax is imposed under Code Sec. 2501, based on the cumulative value of current and prior gifts (after a specified exclusion) after specified deductions, see ¶5040 *et seq.* (Code Sec. 2001, Code Sec. 2501)[8]

The unified rate schedule is as follows (Code Sec. 2001(c), Code Sec. 2502(a)(2)):

Unified Rate Schedule

If the amount with respect to which the tentative tax to be computed is:	The tentative tax is:
Not over $10,000	18% of such amount.
Over $10,000 but not over $20,000	$1,800, plus 20% of the excess over $10,000.
Over $20,000 but not over $40,000	$3,800, plus 22% of the excess over $20,000.
Over $40,000 but not over $60,000	$8,200, plus 24% of the excess over $40,000.
Over $60,000 but not over $80,000	$13,000, plus 26% of the excess over $60,000.
Over $80,000 but not over $100,000	$18,200, plus 28% of the excess over $80,000.
Over $100,000 but not over $150,000	$23,800, plus 30% of the excess over $100,000.
Over $150,000 but not over $250,000	$38,800, plus 32% of the excess over $150,000.
Over $250,000 but not over $500,000	$70,800, plus 34% of the excess over $250,000.
Over $500,000 but not over $750,000	$155,800, plus 37% of the excess over $500,000.
Over $750,000 but not over $1,000,000	$248,300, plus 39% of the excess over $750,000.
Over $1,000,000.	$345,800, plus 40% of the excess over $1,000,000

The top estate and gift tax rate (and the GST tax rate) is 40%.

For the estate tax on non-income distributions from a qualified domestic trust for a surviving spouse who isn't a U.S. citizen, see ¶5026.

For the applicable exclusion amount and applicable credit amount, see ¶5028. For the credit against estate tax imposed on estates of nonresident aliens, see ¶5039.

¶ 1115   Post-2025 sunset provisions.

Unless Congress acts, many provisions in the Tax Cuts and Jobs Act (TCJA, P.L. 115-97), the comprehensive tax reform legislation signed into law on Dec. 22, 2017, won't apply after 2025. The majority of the provisions subject to the 2025 sunset affect individuals.

TCJA provisions with a fixed statutory expiration date include the credit for employer-paid family and medical leave (see ¶2332) and the child tax credit (see ¶2349), among others.

---

7. ¶D-1003 *et seq.*   8. ¶s Q-8003 *et seq.*, R-7000 *et seq.*

¶ 1116   Excise tax rates (nonpenalty).

Here are selected "nonpenalty" excise tax rates. [1]

Retail Excise Taxes

Trucks, trailers, etc.

- auto truck chassis and bodies (for vehicles weighing more than 33,000 lbs)

  12% of first retail sale amount. Tax expires after Sept. 30, 2028.

- truck trailer and semi-trailer chassis and bodies (for vehicles weighing more than 26,000 lbs)

- tractors used chiefly for highway transportation in combination with a trailer or semi-trailer (for tractors weighing more than 19,500 lbs and in combination with trailer or semi-trailer weighing more than 33,000 lbs)

- accessories sold with one of the above or installed within 6 months after one of the above is placed in service

Transportation Fuel Taxes

Gasoline other than aviation gasoline; gasohol

Through Sept. 30, 2028, on removal at terminal: 18.4¢ per gal.; 4.3¢ per gal thereafter.

Aviation gasoline

Through Sept. 30, 2023, on removal at terminal: 19.4¢ per gal.; Oct. 1, 2023–Sept. 30, 2028: 4.4¢ per gal.; 4.3¢ per gal. thereafter.

Diesel fuel[2]; diesohol

Through Sept. 30, 2028, on removal at terminal or retail sale, 24.4¢ per gal.; 4.3¢ per gal. thereafter.

- Diesel-water fuel emulsion

  Through Sept. 30, 2028, on removal at terminal: 19.8¢ per gal.; see diesel fuel rate above, thereafter.

- Dyed diesel fuel, other than for export

  Through Sept. 30, 2028, on removal at terminal or retail sale: .1¢ per gal.

Kerosene

Through Sept. 30, 2028, on removal at terminal or retail sale, generally: 24.4¢ per gal.; 4.3¢ per gal. thereafter.

- Noncommercial aviation use—on removal directly into noncommercial aircraft's fuel tank, or retail sale

  Through Sept. 30, 2028: 21.9¢ per gal.; 21.8¢ per gal. thereafter.

- Commercial aviation use—on removal directly into commercial aircraft's fuel tank, or retail sale

  Through Sept. 30, 2028: 4.4¢ per gal.; 4.3¢ per gal. thereafter.

- Dyed kerosene, other than for export

  Through Sept. 30, 2028, on removal at terminal or retail sale: .1¢ per gal.

Alternative fuels

• Special motor fuels (other than LPG and LNG)	Through Sept. 30, 2028, on retail sale or use, for motor vehicle or motorboat use: 18.4¢ per gal.; 4.3¢ per gal. thereafter.
• Liquefied petroleum gas (LPG) (e.g., propane, butane)	18.3¢ per energy equivalent of a gal. of gasoline (13.2¢ per gal.)
• Liquefied natural gas (LNG)	24.3¢ per energy equivalent of a gal. of diesel fuel (14.1¢ per gal.), thereafter.
• Liquid fuel (other than ethanol or methanol) derived from coal and any liquid hydrocarbons derived from biomass	Through Sept. 30, 2028: 24.4¢ per gal.; 24.3¢ per gal. thereafter.
• Partially exempt ethanol and methanol	Through Sept. 30, 2028, for retail sale or use, of: partially exempt ethanol, 11.4¢ per gal.; partially exempt methanol, 9.25¢ per gal. Thereafter, 4.3¢ per gal., for partially exempt ethanol and 2.15¢ per gal. for partially exempt methanol.

Compressed natural gas (CNG)	18.3¢ per energy equivalent of a gal. of gasoline (126.67 cu. ft.)
Fuel used in commercial transportation on inland waterways	Through Sept. 30, 2028, 29.1¢ per gal.; thereafter 29¢ per gal.
Fuel used in fractional ownership aircraft	Through Sept. 30, 2023, 14.1¢ per gal. surtax.

Environmental Excise Taxes

Ozone depleting chemicals (ODCs) taxes

• ODCs, ODC floor stocks, and imported taxable products, various rates	
Superfund chemical excise taxes	July 1, 2022–Dec. 31, 2031, listed taxable chemicals, rates ranging from 44¢ to $9.74 per ton, and imported taxable substances made of taxable chemicals, rates based on taxable chemicals.
Crude oil and petroleum products tax	25.4¢ per barrel for 2023 (9¢ per barrel Oil Spill Liability Trust Fund financing rate, plus 16.4¢ per barrel Hazardous Substance Superfund financing rate); Hazardous Substance Superfund financing rate adjusted for inflation after 2023; Oil Spill Liability Trust Fund financing rate expires after 2025. Before 2023, 9¢ per barrel.

Selected Manufacturers and Other Excise Taxes

Coal (except lignite)

• From underground mines	Lower of $1.10 per ton or 4.4% of selling price, but for sales for Jan.–Sept. 2022, lower of 50¢ per ton or 2% of selling price.
• From surface mines	Lower of 55¢ per ton or 4.4% of selling price, but for sales for Jan.–Sept. 2022, lower of 25¢ per ton or 2% of selling price.

Tires (of type used in highway vehicles, wholly or in part made of rubber)

9.45¢ (4.725¢ for bias ply or super single tires) for each 10 lbs. by which the tire's maximum rated load capacity exceeds 3,500 lbs. Tax expires after Sept. 30, 2028.

Sport fishing equipment

10% of mfrs. sales price of specified sport fishing equipment (up to max. of $10 on fishing rods and poles); 3% for electric outboard motors and fishing tackle boxes.

Gas guzzling passenger autos, as follows:

If the fuel economy of the model type in which the automobile falls is:	*The tax is:*
At least 22.5	0
At least 21.5 but less than 22.5	$1,000
At least 20.5 but less than 21.5	1,300
At least 19.5 but less than 20.5	1,700
At least 18.5 but less than 19.5	2,100
At least 17.5 but less than 18.5	2,600
At least 16.5 but less than 17.5	3,000
At least 15.5 but less than 16.5	3,700
At least 14.5 but less than 15.5	4,500
At least 13.5 but less than 14.5	5,400
At least 12.5 but less than 13.5	6,400
Less than 12.5	7,700

Indoor tanning

10% of amount paid for services. Phototherapy services by licensed medical professionals, spray tans, and topical creams and tanning lotions are excluded.

Branded prescription drugs

Annual fee on "covered entities."

Specified health insurance policies and applicable self-insured health plans

For each policy or plan year ending before Oct. 1, 2029, fee equal to an applicable dollar amount multiplied by average number of lives covered.

Drug manufacturers noncompliance with pricing agreement rules

Manufacturer, producer, and importer sales of "designated drugs" during a "noncompliance period," earliest period to begin on Oct. 2, 2026; excise tax ranging from 185.71% to 1,900% of the drug's price, depending on how long noncompliance lasts.

[1] Check tax.thomsonreuters.com/federaltaxhandbookupdates for legislative changes to excise taxes.

[2] Special rates apply to diesel fuel used in certain buses and trains.

¶ 1117   Applicable Federal Rates.

The IRS tables below show the Applicable one-month Federal Rates (AFRs). The tables provide short-term (obligations not exceeding three years), mid-term (over three years but not over nine years) and long-term (over nine years) rates (in percentages) based on annual, semiannual, quarterly and monthly compounding assumptions.[9]

Applicable Federal Rate (AFR)	Annual	Semi-annual	Quarterly	Monthly
November 2022				
Short-Term				
AFR	4.10%	4.06%	4.04%	4.03%
110% AFR	4.52%	4.47%	4.45%	4.43%
120% AFR	4.93%	4.87%	4.84%	4.82%
130% AFR	5.35%	5.28%	5.25%	5.22%
Mid-Term				
AFR	3.97%	3.93%	3.91%	3.90%
110% AFR	4.37%	4.32%	4.30%	4.28%
120% AFR	4.78%	4.72%	4.69%	4.67%
130% AFR	5.18%	5.11%	5.08%	5.06%
150% AFR	5.99%	5.90%	5.86%	5.83%
175% AFR	7.00%	6.88%	6.82%	6.78%
Long-Term				
AFR	3.92%	3.88%	3.86%	3.85%
110% AFR	4.32%	4.27%	4.25%	4.23%
120% AFR	4.71%	4.66%	4.63%	4.62%
130% AFR	5.10%	5.04%	5.01%	4.99%
October 2022				
Short-Term				
AFR	3.40%	3.37%	3.36%	3.35%
110% AFR	3.74%	3.71%	3.69%	3.68%
120% AFR	4.08%	4.04%	4.02%	4.01%
130% AFR	4.43%	4.38%	4.36%	4.34%
Mid-Term				
AFR	3.28%	3.25%	3.24%	3.23%
110% AFR	3.61%	3.58%	3.56%	3.55%
120% AFR	3.94%	3.90%	3.88%	3.87%
130% AFR	4.27%	4.23%	4.21%	4.19%
150% AFR	4.94%	4.88%	4.85%	4.83%
175% AFR	5.77%	5.69%	5.65%	5.62%
Long-Term				
AFR	3.43%	3.40%	3.39%	3.38%
110% AFR	3.77%	3.74%	3.72%	3.71%
120% AFR	4.12%	4.08%	4.06%	4.05%
130% AFR	4.47%	4.42%	4.40%	4.38%
September 2022				
Short-Term				
AFR	3.05%	3.03%	3.02%	3.01%
110% AFR	3.36%	3.33%	3.32%	3.31%
120% AFR	3.67%	3.64%	3.62%	3.61%
130% AFR	3.98%	3.94%	3.92%	3.91%
Mid-Term				
AFR	2.93%	2.91%	2.90%	2.89%
110% AFR	3.23%	3.20%	3.19%	3.18%
120% AFR	3.52%	3.49%	3.47%	3.46%
130% AFR	3.82%	3.78%	3.76%	3.75%
150% AFR	4.42%	4.37%	4.35%	4.33%
175% AFR	5.15%	5.09%	5.06%	5.04%
Long-Term				
AFR	3.14%	3.12%	3.11%	3.10%
110% AFR	3.46%	3.43%	3.42%	3.41%
120% AFR	3.77%	3.74%	3.72%	3.71%
130% AFR	4.10%	4.06%	4.04%	4.03%

Applicable Federal Rate (AFR)	Annual	Semi-annual	Quarterly	Monthly
August 2022				
Short-Term				
AFR	2.88%	2.86%	2.85%	2.84%
110% AFR	3.17%	3.15%	3.14%	3.13%
120% AFR	3.46%	3.43%	3.42%	3.41%
130% AFR	3.75%	3.72%	3.70%	3.69%
Mid-Term				
AFR	3.15%	3.13%	3.12%	3.11%
110% AFR	3.47%	3.44%	3.43%	3.42%
120% AFR	3.80%	3.76%	3.74%	3.73%
130% AFR	4.11%	4.07%	4.05%	4.04%
150% AFR	4.76%	4.70%	4.67%	4.65%
175% AFR	5.56%	5.48%	5.44%	5.42%
Long-Term				
AFR	3.35%	3.32%	3.31%	3.30%
110% AFR	3.68%	3.65%	3.63%	3.62%
120% AFR	4.02%	3.98%	3.96%	3.95%
130% AFR	4.37%	4.32%	4.30%	4.28%
July 2022				
Short-Term				
AFR	2.37%	2.36%	2.35%	2.35%
110% AFR	2.62%	2.60%	2.59%	2.59%
120% AFR	2.85%	2.83%	2.82%	2.81%
130% AFR	3.09%	3.07%	3.06%	3.05%
Mid-Term				
AFR	2.99%	2.97%	2.96%	2.95%
110% AFR	3.30%	3.27%	3.26%	3.25%
120% AFR	3.59%	3.56%	3.54%	3.53%
130% AFR	3.90%	3.86%	3.84%	3.83%
150% AFR	4.51%	4.46%	4.44%	4.42%
175% AFR	5.27%	5.20%	5.17%	5.14%
Long-Term				
AFR	3.22%	3.19%	3.18%	3.17%
110% AFR	3.54%	3.51%	3.49%	3.48%
120% AFR	3.87%	3.83%	3.81%	3.80%
130% AFR	4.19%	4.15%	4.13%	4.11%
June 2022				
Short-Term				
AFR	2.21%	2.20%	2.19%	2.19%
110% AFR	2.43%	2.42%	2.41%	2.41%
120% AFR	2.66%	2.64%	2.63%	2.63%
130% AFR	2.88%	2.86%	2.85%	2.84%
Mid-Term				
AFR	2.93%	2.91%	2.90%	2.89%
110% AFR	3.23%	3.20%	3.19%	3.18%
120% AFR	3.52%	3.49%	3.47%	3.46%
130% AFR	3.82%	3.78%	3.76%	3.75%
150% AFR	4.42%	4.37%	4.35%	4.33%
175% AFR	5.15%	5.09%	5.06%	5.04%
Long-Term				
AFR	3.11%	3.09%	3.08%	3.07%
110% AFR	3.43%	3.40%	3.39%	3.38%
120% AFR	3.74%	3.71%	3.69%	3.68%
130% AFR	4.06%	4.02%	4.00%	3.99%

9. ¶J-4192

May 2022

Applicable Federal Rate (AFR)	Annual	Semi-annual	Quarterly	Monthly
Short-Term				
AFR	1.85%	1.84%	1.84%	1.83%
110% AFR	2.03%	2.02%	2.01%	2.01%
120% AFR	2.22%	2.21%	2.20%	2.20%
130% AFR	2.40%	2.39%	2.38%	2.38%
Mid-Term				
AFR	2.51%	2.49%	2.48%	2.48%
110% AFR	2.76%	2.74%	2.73%	2.72%
120% AFR	3.01%	2.99%	2.98%	2.97%
130% AFR	3.27%	3.24%	3.23%	3.22%
150% AFR	3.77%	3.74%	3.72%	3.71%
175% AFR	4.41%	4.36%	4.34%	4.32%
Long-Term				
AFR	2.66%	2.64%	2.63%	2.63%
110% AFR	2.92%	2.90%	2.89%	2.88%
120% AFR	3.20%	3.17%	3.16%	3.15%
130% AFR	3.46%	3.43%	3.42%	3.41%

April 2022

Applicable Federal Rate (AFR)	Annual	Semi-annual	Quarterly	Monthly
Short-Term				
AFR	1.26%	1.26%	1.26%	1.26%
110% AFR	1.39%	1.39%	1.39%	1.39%
120% AFR	1.52%	1.51%	1.51%	1.51%
130% AFR	1.65%	1.64%	1.64%	1.63%
Mid-Term				
AFR	1.87%	1.86%	1.86%	1.85%
110% AFR	2.06%	2.05%	2.04%	2.04%
120% AFR	2.24%	2.23%	2.22%	2.22%
130% AFR	2.43%	2.42%	2.41%	2.41%
150% AFR	2.81%	2.79%	2.78%	2.77%
175% AFR	3.29%	3.26%	3.25%	3.24%
Long-Term				
AFR	2.25%	2.24%	2.23%	2.23%
110% AFR	2.48%	2.46%	2.45%	2.45%
120% AFR	2.71%	2.69%	2.68%	2.68%
130% AFR	2.93%	2.91%	2.90%	2.89%

March 2022

Applicable Federal Rate (AFR)	Annual	Semi-annual	Quarterly	Monthly
Short-Term				
AFR	0.97%	0.97%	0.97%	0.97%
110% AFR	1.07%	1.07%	1.07%	1.07%
120% AFR	1.16%	1.16%	1.16%	1.16%
130% AFR	1.26%	1.26%	1.26%	1.26%
Mid-Term				
AFR	1.74%	1.73%	1.73%	1.72%
110% AFR	1.91%	1.90%	1.90%	1.89%
120% AFR	2.09%	2.08%	2.07%	2.07%
130% AFR	2.26%	2.25%	2.24%	2.24%
150% AFR	2.62%	2.60%	2.59%	2.59%
175% AFR	3.05%	3.03%	3.02%	3.01%
Long-Term				
AFR	2.14%	2.13%	2.12%	2.12%
110% AFR	2.35%	2.34%	2.33%	2.33%
120% AFR	2.58%	2.56%	2.55%	2.55%
130% AFR	2.79%	2.77%	2.76%	2.75%

February 2022

Applicable Federal Rate (AFR)	Annual	Semi-annual	Quarterly	Monthly
Short-Term				
AFR	0.59%	0.59%	0.59%	0.59%
110% AFR	0.65%	0.65%	0.65%	0.65%
120% AFR	0.71%	0.71%	0.71%	0.71%
130% AFR	0.77%	0.77%	0.77%	0.77%
Mid-Term				
AFR	1.40%	1.40%	1.40%	1.40%
110% AFR	1.55%	1.54%	1.54%	1.54%
120% AFR	1.69%	1.68%	1.68%	1.67%
130% AFR	1.83%	1.82%	1.82%	1.81%
150% AFR	2.11%	2.10%	2.09%	2.09%
175% AFR	2.47%	2.45%	2.44%	2.44%
Long-Term				
AFR	1.92%	1.91%	1.91%	1.90%
110% AFR	2.11%	2.10%	2.09%	2.09%
120% AFR	2.30%	2.29%	2.28%	2.28%
130% AFR	2.50%	2.48%	2.47%	2.47%

January 2022

Applicable Federal Rate (AFR)	Annual	Semi-annual	Quarterly	Monthly
Short-Term				
AFR	0.44%	0.44%	0.44%	0.44%
110% AFR	0.48%	0.48%	0.48%	0.48%
120% AFR	0.53%	0.53%	0.53%	0.53%
130% AFR	0.57%	0.57%	0.57%	0.57%
Mid-Term				
AFR	1.30%	1.30%	1.30%	1.30%
110% AFR	1.44%	1.43%	1.43%	1.43%
120% AFR	1.57%	1.56%	1.56%	1.55%
130% AFR	1.70%	1.69%	1.69%	1.68%
150% AFR	1.96%	1.95%	1.95%	1.94%
175% AFR	2.29%	2.28%	2.27%	2.27%
Long-Term				
AFR	1.82%	1.81%	1.81%	1.80%
110% AFR	2.00%	1.99%	1.99%	1.98%
120% AFR	2.18%	2.17%	2.16%	2.16%
130% AFR	2.36%	2.35%	2.34%	2.34%

December 2021

Applicable Federal Rate (AFR)	Annual	Semi-annual	Quarterly	Monthly
Short-Term				
AFR	0.33%	0.33%	0.33%	0.33%
110% AFR	0.36%	0.36%	0.36%	0.36%
120% AFR	0.40%	0.40%	0.40%	0.40%
130% AFR	0.43%	0.43%	0.43%	0.43%
Mid-Term				
AFR	1.26%	1.26%	1.26%	1.26%
110% AFR	1.39%	1.39%	1.39%	1.39%
120% AFR	1.52%	1.51%	1.51%	1.51%
130% AFR	1.65%	1.64%	1.64%	1.63%
150% AFR	1.90%	1.89%	1.89%	1.88%
175% AFR	2.22%	2.21%	2.20%	2.20%
Long-Term				
AFR	1.90%	1.89%	1.89%	1.88%
110% AFR	2.09%	2.08%	2.07%	2.07%
120% AFR	2.28%	2.27%	2.26%	2.26%
130% AFR	2.48%	2.46%	2.45%	2.45%

November 2021

Applicable Federal Rate (AFR)	Annual	Semi-annual	Quarterly	Monthly
Short-Term				
AFR	0.22%	0.22%	0.22%	0.22%
110% AFR	0.24%	0.24%	0.24%	0.24%
120% AFR	0.26%	0.26%	0.26%	0.26%
130% AFR	0.29%	0.29%	0.29%	0.29%
Mid-Term				
AFR	1.08%	1.08%	1.08%	1.08%
110% AFR	1.19%	1.19%	1.19%	1.19%
120% AFR	1.30%	1.30%	1.30%	1.30%
130% AFR	1.40%	1.40%	1.40%	1.40%
150% AFR	1.63%	1.62%	1.62%	1.61%
175% AFR	1.90%	1.89%	1.89%	1.88%
Long-Term				
AFR	1.86%	1.85%	1.85%	1.84%
110% AFR	2.05%	2.04%	2.03%	2.03%
120% AFR	2.23%	2.22%	2.21%	2.21%
130% AFR	2.42%	2.41%	2.40%	2.40%

October 2021

Applicable Federal Rate (AFR)	Annual	Semi-annual	Quarterly	Monthly
Short-Term				
AFR	0.18%	0.18%	0.18%	0.18%
110% AFR	0.20%	0.20%	0.20%	0.20%
120% AFR	0.22%	0.22%	0.22%	0.22%
130% AFR	0.23%	0.23%	0.23%	0.23%

Applicable Federal Rate (AFR)	Annual	Semi-annual	Quarterly	Monthly	Applicable Federal Rate (AFR)	Annual	Semi-annual	Quarterly	Monthly
		Mid-Term					*Long-Term*		
AFR	0.91%	0.91%	0.91%	0.91%	AFR	1.74%	1.73%	1.73%	1.72%
110% AFR	1.00%	1.00%	1.00%	1.00%	110% AFR	1.91%	1.90%	1.90%	1.89%
120% AFR	1.09%	1.09%	1.09%	1.09%	120% AFR	2.09%	2.08%	2.07%	2.07%
130% AFR	1.18%	1.18%	1.18%	1.18%	130% AFR	2.26%	2.25%	2.24%	2.24%
150% AFR	1.37%	1.37%	1.37%	1.37%					
175% AFR	1.60%	1.59%	1.59%	1.58%					

¶ 1118   **MACRS Tables.** ▌▬▬▬▬▬▬▬▬▬▬▬▬▬▬▬▬▬▬▬▬▬

Here are MACRS depreciation (cost recovery) tables.

The tables reproduced are the MACRS tables (general depreciation as well as alternative depreciation system (ADS)), plus the listed property tables used to determine income inclusion amounts by lessees of listed property other than automobiles. The depreciation amounts for automobiles under the luxury auto restrictions are carried at ¶1945; the income inclusion amounts for lessees of automobiles carried at ¶1119 are explained at ¶1948 *et seq.*

Under the general depreciation system (GDS) of MACRS, the table rates are based on: (1) the 200% declining balance method for 3-, 5-, 7-, and 10-year personal property; (2) the 150% declining balance method for 15- and 20-year personal property; and (3) the straight-line method for residential and nonresidential realty. Under the alternative depreciation system (ADS) of MACRS, the table rates for personal and real property are based on the straight-line method. The use of the tables is discussed in ¶1910. (IRS alternative minimum tax tables and the tables for straight line depreciation under the midquarter convention are not reproduced in this Handbook. For those tables, see the Appendix to Federal Tax Coordinator 2d Chapter L-7400.)

Table 1
General Depreciation System
Applicable Depreciation Method: 200 or 150 Percent
Declining Balance Switching to Straight Line
Applicable Recovery Periods: 3, 5, 7, 10, 15, 20 years
Applicable Convention: Half-year

If the Recovery Year is:	and the Recovery Period is:					
	3-year	5-year	7-year	10-year	15-year	20-year
			the Depreciation Rate is:			
1	33.33	20.00	14.29	10.00	5.00	3.750
2	44.45	32.00	24.49	18.00	9.50	7.219
3	14.81	19.20	17.49	14.40	8.55	6.677
4	7.41	11.52	12.49	11.52	7.70	6.177
5		11.52	8.93	9.22	6.93	5.713
6		5.76	8.92	7.37	6.23	5.285
7			8.93	6.55	5.90	4.888
8			4.46	6.55	5.90	4.522
9				6.56	5.91	4.462
10				6.55	5.90	4.461
11				3.28	5.91	4.462
12					5.90	4.461
13					5.91	4.462
14					5.90	4.461
15					5.91	4.462
16					2.95	4.461
17						4.462
18						4.461
19						4.462
20						4.461
21						2.231

Table 2
General Depreciation System
Applicable Depreciation Method: 200 or 150 Percent
Declining Balance Switching to Straight Line
Applicable Recovery Periods: 3, 5, 7, 10, 15, 20 years
Applicable Convention: Mid-quarter
(property placed in service in first quarter)

If the Recovery Year is:	and the Recovery Period is:					
	3-year	**5-year**	**7-year**	**10-year**	**15-year**	**20-year**
			the Depreciation Rate is:			
1	58.33	35.00	25.00	17.50	8.75	6.563
2	27.78	26.00	21.43	16.50	9.13	7.000
3	12.35	15.60	15.31	13.20	8.21	6.482
4	1.54	11.01	10.93	10.56	7.39	5.996
5		11.01	8.75	8.45	6.65	5.546
6		1.38	8.74	6.76	5.99	5.130
7			8.75	6.55	5.90	4.746
8			1.09	6.55	5.91	4.459
9				6.56	5.90	4.459
10				6.55	5.91	4.459
11				0.82	5.90	4.459
12					5.91	4.460
13					5.90	4.459
14					5.91	4.460
15					5.90	4.459
16					0.74	4.460
17						4.459
18						4.460
19						4.459
20						4.460
21						0.557

Table 3
General Depreciation System
Applicable Depreciation Method: 200 or 150 Percent
Declining Balance Switching to Straight Line
Applicable Recovery Periods: 3, 5, 7, 10, 15, 20 years
Applicable Convention: Mid-quarter
(property placed in service in second quarter)

If the Recovery Year is:	and the Recovery Period is:					
	3-year	**5-year**	**7-year**	**10-year**	**15-year**	**20-year**
			the Depreciation Rate is:			
1	41.67	25.00	17.85	12.50	6.25	4.688
2	38.89	30.00	23.47	17.50	9.38	7.148
3	14.14	18.00	16.76	14.00	8.44	6.612
4	5.30	11.37	11.97	11.20	7.59	6.116
5		11.37	8.87	8.96	6.83	5.658
6		4.26	8.87	7.17	6.15	5.233
7			8.87	6.55	5.91	4.841
8			3.33	6.55	5.90	4.478
9				6.56	5.91	4.463
10				6.55	5.90	4.463
11				2.46	5.91	4.463
12					5.90	4.463
13					5.91	4.463
14					5.90	4.463

Table 3

General Depreciation System
Applicable Depreciation Method: 200 or 150 Percent
Declining Balance Switching to Straight Line
Applicable Recovery Periods: 3, 5, 7, 10, 15, 20 years
Applicable Convention: Mid-quarter
(property placed in service in second quarter)
(continued)

If the Recovery Year is:	and the Recovery Period is:					
	3-year	5-year	7-year	10-year	15-year	20-year
			the Depreciation Rate is:			
15					5.91	4.462
16					2.21	4.463
17						4.462
18						4.463
19						4.462
20						4.463
21						1.673

Table 4

General Depreciation System
Applicable Depreciation Method: 200 or 150 Percent
Declining Balance Switching to Straight Line
Applicable Recovery Periods: 3, 5, 7, 10, 15, 20 years
Applicable Convention: Mid-quarter
(property placed in service in third quarter)

If the Recovery Year is:	and the Recovery Period is:					
	3-year	5-year	7-year	10-year	15-year	20-year
			the Depreciation Rate is:			
1	25.00	15.00	10.71	7.50	3.75	2.813
2	50.00	34.00	25.51	18.50	9.63	7.289
3	16.67	20.40	18.22	14.80	8.66	6.742
4	8.33	12.24	13.02	11.84	7.80	6.237
5		11.30	9.30	9.47	7.02	5.769
6		7.06	8.85	7.58	6.31	5.336
7			8.86	6.55	5.90	4.936
8			5.53	6.55	5.90	4.566
9				6.56	5.91	4.460
10				6.55	5.90	4.460
11				4.10	5.91	4.460
12					5.90	4.460
13					5.91	4.461
14					5.90	4.460
15					5.91	4.461
16					3.69	4.460
17						4.461
18						4.460
19						4.461
20						4.460
21						2.788

Table 5
General Depreciation System
Applicable Depreciation Method: 200 or 150 Percent
Declining Balance Switching to Straight Line
Applicable Recovery Periods: 3, 5, 7, 10, 15, 20 years
Applicable Convention: Mid-quarter
(property placed in service in fourth quarter)

If the Recovery Year is:	and the Recovery Period is:					
	3-year	5-year	7-year	10-year	15-year	20-year
			the Depreciation Rate is:			
1	8.33	5.00	3.57	2.50	1.25	0.938
2	61.11	38.00	27.55	19.50	9.88	7.430
3	20.37	22.80	19.68	15.60	8.89	6.872
4	10.19	13.68	14.06	12.48	8.00	6.357
5		10.94	10.04	9.98	7.20	5.880
6		9.58	8.73	7.99	6.48	5.439
7			8.73	6.55	5.90	5.031
8			7.64	6.55	5.90	4.654
9				6.56	5.90	4.458
10				6.55	5.91	4.458
11				5.74	5.90	4.458
12					5.91	4.458
13					5.90	4.458
14					5.91	4.458
15					5.90	4.458
16					5.17	4.458
17						4.458
18						4.459
19						4.458
20						4.459
21						3.901

Table 6
General Depreciation System
Applicable Depreciation Method: Straight Line
Applicable Recovery Period: 27.5 years
Applicable Convention: Mid-month

If the Recovery Year is:	And the Month in the First Recovery Year the Property is Placed in Service is:											
	1	2	3	4	5	6	7	8	9	10	11	12
						the Depreciation Rate is:						
1	3.485	3.182	2.879	2.576	2.273	1.970	1.667	1.364	1.061	0.758	0.455	0.152
2-9	3.636	3.636	3.636	3.636	3.636	3.636	3.636	3.636	3.636	3.636	3.636	3.636
10	3.637	3.637	3.637	3.637	3.637	3.637	3.636	3.636	3.636	3.636	3.636	3.636
11	3.636	3.636	3.636	3.636	3.636	3.636	3.637	3.637	3.637	3.637	3.637	3.637
12	3.637	3.637	3.637	3.637	3.637	3.637	3.636	3.636	3.636	3.636	3.636	3.636
13	3.636	3.636	3.636	3.636	3.636	3.636	3.637	3.637	3.637	3.637	3.637	3.637
14	3.637	3.637	3.637	3.637	3.637	3.637	3.636	3.636	3.636	3.636	3.636	3.636
15	3.636	3.636	3.636	3.636	3.636	3.636	3.637	3.637	3.637	3.637	3.637	3.637
16	3.637	3.637	3.637	3.637	3.637	3.637	3.636	3.636	3.636	3.636	3.636	3.636
17	3.636	3.636	3.636	3.636	3.636	3.636	3.637	3.637	3.637	3.637	3.637	3.637
18	3.637	3.637	3.637	3.637	3.637	3.637	3.636	3.636	3.636	3.636	3.636	3.636
19	3.636	3.636	3.636	3.636	3.636	3.636	3.637	3.637	3.637	3.637	3.637	3.637
20	3.637	3.637	3.637	3.637	3.637	3.637	3.636	3.636	3.636	3.636	3.636	3.636
21	3.636	3.636	3.636	3.636	3.636	3.636	3.637	3.637	3.637	3.637	3.637	3.637
22	3.637	3.637	3.637	3.637	3.637	3.637	3.636	3.636	3.636	3.636	3.636	3.636
23	3.636	3.636	3.636	3.636	3.636	3.636	3.637	3.637	3.637	3.637	3.637	3.637
24	3.637	3.637	3.637	3.637	3.637	3.637	3.636	3.636	3.636	3.636	3.636	3.636
25	3.636	3.636	3.636	3.636	3.636	3.636	3.637	3.637	3.637	3.637	3.637	3.637
26	3.637	3.637	3.637	3.637	3.637	3.637	3.636	3.636	3.636	3.636	3.636	3.636
27	3.636	3.636	3.636	3.636	3.636	3.636	3.637	3.637	3.637	3.637	3.637	3.637
28	1.970	2.273	2.576	2.879	3.182	3.485	3.636	3.636	3.636	3.636	3.636	3.636
29	0.000	0.000	0.000	0.000	0.000	0.000	0.152	0.455	0.758	1.061	1.364	1.667

Table 7

General Depreciation System
Applicable Depreciation Method: Straight Line
Applicable Recovery Period: 31.5 years
Applicable Convention: Mid-month

If the Recovery Year is:	And the Month in the First Recovery Year the Property is Placed in Service is:											
	1	2	3	4	5	6	7	8	9	10	11	12
	the Depreciation Rate is:											
1	3.042	2.778	2.513	2.249	1.984	1.720	1.455	1.190	0.926	0.661	0.397	0.132
2-7	3.175	3.175	3.175	3.175	3.175	3.175	3.175	3.175	3.175	3.175	3.175	3.175
8	3.175	3.174	3.175	3.174	3.175	3.174	3.175	3.175	3.175	3.175	3.175	3.175
9	3.174	3.175	3.174	3.175	3.174	3.175	3.174	3.175	3.174	3.175	3.174	3.175
10	3.175	3.174	3.175	3.174	3.175	3.174	3.175	3.174	3.175	3.174	3.175	3.174
11	3.174	3.175	3.174	3.175	3.174	3.175	3.174	3.175	3.174	3.175	3.174	3.175
12	3.175	3.174	3.175	3.174	3.175	3.174	3.175	3.174	3.175	3.174	3.175	3.174
13	3.174	3.175	3.174	3.175	3.174	3.175	3.174	3.175	3.174	3.175	3.174	3.175
14	3.175	3.174	3.175	3.174	3.175	3.174	3.175	3.174	3.175	3.174	3.175	3.174
15	3.174	3.175	3.174	3.175	3.174	3.175	3.174	3.175	3.174	3.175	3.174	3.175
16	3.175	3.174	3.175	3.174	3.175	3.174	3.175	3.174	3.175	3.174	3.175	3.174
17	3.174	3.175	3.174	3.175	3.174	3.175	3.174	3.175	3.174	3.175	3.174	3.175
18	3.175	3.174	3.175	3.174	3.175	3.174	3.175	3.174	3.175	3.174	3.175	3.174
19	3.174	3.175	3.174	3.175	3.174	3.175	3.174	3.175	3.174	3.175	3.174	3.175
20	3.175	3.174	3.175	3.174	3.175	3.174	3.175	3.174	3.175	3.174	3.175	3.174
21	3.174	3.175	3.174	3.175	3.174	3.175	3.174	3.175	3.174	3.175	3.174	3.175
22	3.175	3.174	3.175	3.174	3.175	3.174	3.175	3.174	3.175	3.174	3.175	3.174
23	3.174	3.175	3.174	3.175	3.174	3.175	3.174	3.175	3.174	3.175	3.174	3.175
24	3.175	3.174	3.175	3.174	3.175	3.174	3.175	3.174	3.175	3.174	3.175	3.174
25	3.174	3.175	3.174	3.175	3.174	3.175	3.174	3.175	3.174	3.175	3.174	3.175
26	3.175	3.174	3.175	3.174	3.175	3.174	3.175	3.174	3.175	3.174	3.175	3.174
27	3.174	3.175	3.174	3.175	3.174	3.175	3.174	3.175	3.174	3.175	3.174	3.175
28	3.175	3.174	3.175	3.174	3.175	3.174	3.175	3.174	3.175	3.174	3.175	3.174
29	3.174	3.175	3.174	3.175	3.174	3.175	3.174	3.175	3.174	3.175	3.174	3.175
30	3.175	3.174	3.175	3.174	3.175	3.174	3.175	3.174	3.175	3.174	3.175	3.174
31	3.174	3.175	3.174	3.175	3.174	3.175	3.174	3.175	3.174	3.175	3.174	3.175
32	1.720	1.984	2.249	2.513	2.778	3.042	3.175	3.174	3.175	3.174	3.175	3.174
33	0.000	0.000	0.000	0.000	0.000	0.000	0.132	0.397	0.661	0.926	1.190	1.455

Table 7a

General Depreciation System
Applicable Depreciation Method: Straight Line
Applicable Recovery Period: 39 years
Applicable Convention: Mid-month

Year	Month property placed in service											
	1	2	3	4	5	6	7	8	9	10	11	12
1	2.461%	2.247%	2.033%	1.819%	1.605%	1.391%	1.177%	0.963%	0.749%	0.535%	0.321%	0.107%
2-39	2.564	2.564	2.564	2.564	2.564	2.564	2.564	2.564	2.564	2.564	2.564	2.564
40	0.107	0.321	0.535	0.749	0.963	1.177	1.391	1.605	1.819	2.033	2.247	2.461

Table 8
General and Alternative Depreciation Systems
Applicable Depreciation Method: Straight Line
Applicable Recovery Periods: 2.5-50 years
Applicable Convention: Half-year

If the Recovery Year is:	2.5	3.0	3.5	4.0	4.5	5.0	5.5	6.0	6.5	7.0	7.5	8.0	8.5	9.0	9.5	10.0
							the Depreciation Rate is:									
1	20.00	16.67	14.29	12.50	11.11	10.00	9.09	8.33	7.69	7.14	6.67	6.25	5.88	5.56	5.26	5.00
2	40.00	33.33	28.57	25.00	22.22	20.00	18.18	16.67	15.39	14.29	13.33	12.50	11.77	11.11	10.53	10.00
3	40.00	33.33	28.57	25.00	22.22	20.00	18.18	16.67	15.38	14.29	13.33	12.50	11.76	11.11	10.53	10.00
4		16.67	28.57	25.00	22.23	20.00	18.18	16.67	15.39	14.28	13.33	12.50	11.77	11.11	10.53	10.00
5				12.50	22.22	20.00	18.19	16.66	15.38	14.29	13.33	12.50	11.77	11.11	10.52	10.00
6						10.00	18.18	16.67	15.39	14.28	13.33	12.50	11.77	11.11	10.53	10.00
7							8.33	15.38	14.29	13.34	12.50	11.76	11.11	10.52	10.00
8								7.14	13.33	12.50	11.77	11.11	10.53	10.00
9									6.25	11.76	11.11	10.52	10.00
10										5.56	10.53	10.00
11											5.00

If the Recovery Year is:	10.5	11.0	11.5	12.0	12.5	13.0	13.5	14.0	14.5	15.0	15.5	16.0	16.5	17.0	17.5	18.0
							the Depreciation Rate is:									
1	4.76	4.55	4.35	4.17	4.00	3.85	3.70	3.57	3.45	3.33	3.23	3.13	3.03	2.94	2.86	2.78
2	9.52	9.09	8.70	8.33	8.00	7.69	7.41	7.14	6.90	6.67	6.45	6.25	6.06	5.88	5.71	5.56
3	9.52	9.09	8.70	8.33	8.00	7.69	7.41	7.14	6.90	6.67	6.45	6.25	6.06	5.88	5.71	5.56
4	9.53	9.09	8.69	8.33	8.00	7.69	7.41	7.14	6.90	6.67	6.45	6.25	6.06	5.88	5.71	5.55
5	9.52	9.09	8.70	8.33	8.00	7.69	7.41	7.14	6.89	6.67	6.45	6.25	6.06	5.88	5.72	5.56
6	9.53	9.09	8.69	8.33	8.00	7.69	7.41	7.14	6.90	6.67	6.45	6.25	6.06	5.88	5.71	5.55
7	9.52	9.09	8.70	8.34	8.00	7.69	7.41	7.14	6.90	6.67	6.45	6.25	6.06	5.88	5.72	5.56
8	9.53	9.09	8.69	8.33	8.00	7.69	7.41	7.15	6.89	6.66	6.45	6.25	6.06	5.88	5.71	5.55
9	9.52	9.09	8.70	8.34	8.00	7.69	7.41	7.14	6.90	6.67	6.45	6.25	6.06	5.88	5.72	5.56
10	9.53	9.09	8.69	8.33	8.00	7.70	7.40	7.15	6.89	6.66	6.45	6.25	6.06	5.88	5.71	5.56
11	9.52	9.09	8.70	8.34	8.00	7.69	7.41	7.14	6.90	6.67	6.45	6.25	6.06	5.89	5.72	5.56
12		4.55	8.69	8.33	8.00	7.70	7.40	7.15	6.89	6.66	6.45	6.25	6.06	5.88	5.71	5.55
13				4.17	8.00	7.69	7.41	7.14	6.90	6.67	6.45	6.25	6.06	5.89	5.72	5.56
14						3.85	7.40	7.15	6.89	6.66	6.46	6.25	6.06	5.88	5.71	5.55
15								3.57	6.90	6.67	6.45	6.25	6.06	5.89	5.72	5.56
16										3.33	6.46	6.25	6.06	5.88	5.71	5.56
17												3.12	6.07	5.89	5.72	5.56
18														2.94	5.71	5.55
19																2.78

Table 8
General and Alternative Depreciation Systems
Applicable Depreciation Method: Straight Line
Applicable Recovery Periods: 2.5-50 years
Applicable Convention: Half-year
(continued)

If the Recovery Year is:	and the Recovery Period is:															
	18.5	19.0	19.5	20.0	20.5	21.0	21.5	22.0	22.5	23.0	23.5	24.0	24.5	25.0	25.5	26.0
	the Depreciation Rate is:															
1	2.70	2.63	2.56	2.500	2.439	2.381	2.326	2.273	2.222	2.174	2.128	2.083	2.041	2.000	1.961	1.923
2	5.41	5.26	5.13	5.000	4.878	4.762	4.651	4.545	4.444	4.348	4.255	4.167	4.082	4.000	3.922	3.846
3	5.41	5.26	5.13	5.000	4.878	4.762	4.651	4.545	4.444	4.348	4.255	4.167	4.082	4.000	3.922	3.846
4	5.41	5.26	5.13	5.000	4.878	4.762	4.651	4.545	4.445	4.348	4.255	4.167	4.082	4.000	3.922	3.846
5	5.40	5.26	5.13	5.000	4.878	4.762	4.651	4.546	4.444	4.348	4.255	4.167	4.082	4.000	3.922	3.846
6	5.41	5.26	5.13	5.000	4.878	4.762	4.651	4.545	4.445	4.348	4.255	4.167	4.082	4.000	3.921	3.846
7	5.40	5.26	5.13	5.000	4.878	4.762	4.651	4.546	4.444	4.348	4.255	4.167	4.082	4.000	3.922	3.846
8	5.41	5.26	5.13	5.000	4.878	4.762	4.651	4.545	4.445	4.348	4.255	4.167	4.082	4.000	3.921	3.846
9	5.40	5.27	5.13	5.000	4.878	4.762	4.651	4.546	4.444	4.348	4.255	4.167	4.081	4.000	3.922	3.846
10	5.41	5.26	5.13	5.000	4.878	4.762	4.651	4.545	4.445	4.348	4.255	4.166	4.082	4.000	3.921	3.846
11	5.40	5.27	5.13	5.000	4.878	4.762	4.651	4.546	4.444	4.348	4.256	4.166	4.081	4.000	3.922	3.846
12	5.41	5.26	5.13	5.000	4.878	4.762	4.651	4.545	4.445	4.348	4.255	4.167	4.082	4.000	3.921	3.846
13	5.40	5.27	5.13	5.000	4.878	4.762	4.651	4.546	4.444	4.348	4.256	4.166	4.081	4.000	3.922	3.846
14	5.41	5.26	5.13	5.000	4.878	4.762	4.651	4.545	4.445	4.348	4.255	4.167	4.082	4.000	3.921	3.846
15	5.40	5.27	5.13	5.000	4.878	4.762	4.651	4.546	4.444	4.348	4.256	4.166	4.081	4.000	3.922	3.846
16	5.41	5.26	5.12	5.000	4.878	4.762	4.651	4.545	4.445	4.348	4.255	4.167	4.082	4.000	3.921	3.846
17	5.40	5.27	5.13	5.000	4.878	4.762	4.652	4.546	4.444	4.347	4.256	4.166	4.081	4.000	3.922	3.846
18	5.41	5.26	5.12	5.000	4.878	4.762	4.651	4.545	4.445	4.348	4.255	4.167	4.082	4.000	3.921	3.846
19	5.40	5.27	5.13	5.000	4.878	4.761	4.652	4.546	4.444	4.347	4.256	4.166	4.081	4.000	3.922	3.846
20		2.63	5.12	5.000	4.879	4.762	4.651	4.545	4.445	4.348	4.255	4.167	4.082	4.000	3.921	3.847
21				2.500	4.878	4.761	4.652	4.546	4.444	4.347	4.256	4.166	4.081	4.000	3.922	3.846
22						2.381	4.651	4.545	4.445	4.348	4.255	4.167	4.082	4.000	3.921	3.847
23								2.273	4.444	4.347	4.256	4.166	4.081	4.000	3.922	3.846
24										2.174	4.255	4.167	4.082	4.000	3.921	3.847
25												2.083	4.081	4.000	3.922	3.846
26													2.000	3.921	3.847	3.846
27																1.923

Table 8
General and Alternative Depreciation Systems
Applicable Depreciation Method: Straight Line
Applicable Recovery Periods: 2.5-50 years
Applicable Convention: Half-year
(continued)

If the Recovery Year is:	26.5	27.0	27.5	28.0	28.5	29.0	29.5	30.0	30.5	31.0	31.5	32.0	32.5	33.0	33.5	34.0
								the Depreciation Rate is:								
1	1.887	1.852	1.818	1.786	1.754	1.724	1.695	1.667	1.639	1.613	1.587	1.563	1.538	1.515	1.493	1.471
2-6	3.774	3.704	3.636	3.571	3.509	3.448	3.390	3.333	3.279	3.226	3.175	3.125	3.077	3.030	2.985	2.941
7	3.773	3.704	3.636	3.572	3.509	3.448	3.390	3.333	3.279	3.226	3.175	3.125	3.077	3.030	2.985	2.941
8	3.774	3.704	3.636	3.571	3.509	3.448	3.390	3.333	3.279	3.226	3.175	3.125	3.077	3.030	2.985	2.941
9	3.773	3.704	3.637	3.572	3.509	3.448	3.390	3.333	3.279	3.226	3.175	3.125	3.077	3.030	2.985	2.941
10	3.774	3.704	3.636	3.571	3.509	3.448	3.390	3.333	3.279	3.226	3.174	3.125	3.077	3.030	2.985	2.941
11	3.773	3.704	3.637	3.572	3.509	3.448	3.390	3.333	3.279	3.226	3.175	3.125	3.077	3.030	2.985	2.941
12	3.774	3.704	3.636	3.571	3.509	3.448	3.390	3.333	3.279	3.226	3.174	3.125	3.077	3.030	2.985	2.941
13	3.773	3.703	3.637	3.572	3.509	3.448	3.390	3.334	3.279	3.226	3.175	3.125	3.077	3.030	2.985	2.941
14	3.773	3.704	3.636	3.571	3.509	3.448	3.390	3.333	3.279	3.226	3.175	3.125	3.077	3.030	2.985	2.941
15	3.774	3.703	3.637	3.572	3.509	3.449	3.390	3.334	3.278	3.226	3.175	3.125	3.077	3.031	2.985	2.941
16	3.773	3.704	3.636	3.571	3.509	3.448	3.390	3.333	3.279	3.226	3.174	3.125	3.077	3.030	2.985	2.941
17	3.774	3.703	3.637	3.572	3.509	3.449	3.390	3.334	3.278	3.226	3.175	3.125	3.077	3.031	2.985	2.941
18	3.773	3.704	3.636	3.571	3.508	3.448	3.390	3.333	3.279	3.226	3.174	3.125	3.077	3.030	2.985	2.941
19	3.774	3.703	3.637	3.572	3.509	3.449	3.390	3.334	3.278	3.226	3.175	3.125	3.077	3.031	2.985	2.941
20	3.773	3.704	3.636	3.571	3.508	3.448	3.390	3.333	3.279	3.226	3.174	3.125	3.077	3.030	2.985	2.941
21	3.774	3.703	3.637	3.572	3.509	3.449	3.389	3.334	3.278	3.225	3.175	3.125	3.077	3.031	2.985	2.941
22	3.773	3.704	3.636	3.571	3.508	3.448	3.390	3.333	3.279	3.226	3.174	3.125	3.077	3.030	2.985	2.941
23	3.774	3.703	3.637	3.572	3.509	3.449	3.389	3.334	3.278	3.225	3.175	3.125	3.077	3.031	2.985	2.941
24	3.773	3.704	3.636	3.571	3.508	3.448	3.390	3.333	3.279	3.226	3.174	3.125	3.077	3.030	2.985	2.942
25	3.774	3.703	3.637	3.572	3.509	3.449	3.389	3.334	3.278	3.225	3.175	3.125	3.077	3.031	2.985	2.942
26	3.773	3.704	3.636	3.571	3.508	3.448	3.390	3.333	3.279	3.226	3.174	3.125	3.077	3.030	2.985	2.941
27	3.774	3.703	3.637	3.572	3.509	3.449	3.389	3.334	3.278	3.225	3.175	3.125	3.077	3.031	2.985	2.942
28		1.852	3.636	3.571	3.508	3.448	3.390	3.333	3.279	3.226	3.174	3.125	3.077	3.030	2.985	2.941
29			3.636	1.786	3.509	3.449	3.389	3.334	3.278	3.225	3.175	3.125	3.077	3.031	2.985	2.942
30				1.786	3.509	1.724	3.390	3.333	3.279	3.226	3.174	3.125	3.077	3.030	2.985	2.941
31						1.724	3.390	1.667	3.278	3.225	3.175	3.125	3.076	3.031	2.986	2.942
32								1.667	3.278	1.613	3.174	3.125	3.077	3.030	2.985	2.941
33										1.613	3.174	1.562	3.076	3.031	2.986	2.942
34												1.562	3.076	1.515	2.985	2.941
35														1.515	2.985	1.471

Table 8

General and Alternative Depreciation Systems
Applicable Depreciation Method: Straight Line
Applicable Recovery Periods: 2.5-50 years
Applicable Convention: Half-year
(continued)

If the Recovery Year is:	and the Recovery Period is:															
	34.5	35.0	35.5	36.0	36.5	37.0	37.5	38.0	38.5	39.0	39.5	40.0	40.5	41.0	41.5	42.0
	the Depreciation Rate is:															
1	1.449	1.429	1.408	1.389	1.370	1.351	1.333	1.316	1.299	1.282	1.266	1.250	1.235	1.220	1.205	1.190
2	2.899	2.857	2.817	2.778	2.740	2.703	2.667	2.632	2.597	2.564	2.532	2.500	2.469	2.439	2.410	2.381
3	2.899	2.857	2.817	2.778	2.740	2.703	2.667	2.632	2.597	2.564	2.532	2.500	2.469	2.439	2.410	2.381
4	2.899	2.857	2.817	2.778	2.740	2.703	2.667	2.632	2.597	2.564	2.532	2.500	2.469	2.439	2.410	2.381
5	2.899	2.857	2.817	2.778	2.740	2.703	2.667	2.632	2.597	2.564	2.532	2.500	2.469	2.439	2.410	2.381
6	2.899	2.857	2.817	2.778	2.740	2.703	2.667	2.632	2.597	2.564	2.532	2.500	2.469	2.439	2.410	2.381
7	2.898	2.857	2.817	2.778	2.740	2.703	2.667	2.632	2.597	2.564	2.532	2.500	2.469	2.439	2.410	2.381
8	2.899	2.857	2.817	2.778	2.740	2.703	2.667	2.631	2.597	2.564	2.532	2.500	2.469	2.439	2.410	2.381
9	2.898	2.857	2.817	2.778	2.740	2.703	2.667	2.632	2.597	2.564	2.532	2.500	2.469	2.439	2.410	2.381
10	2.899	2.857	2.817	2.778	2.740	2.703	2.667	2.631	2.598	2.564	2.532	2.500	2.469	2.439	2.410	2.381
11	2.898	2.857	2.817	2.778	2.740	2.703	2.667	2.632	2.597	2.564	2.532	2.500	2.469	2.439	2.410	2.381
12	2.899	2.857	2.817	2.778	2.740	2.703	2.667	2.631	2.598	2.564	2.532	2.500	2.469	2.439	2.410	2.381
13	2.898	2.857	2.817	2.778	2.740	2.703	2.667	2.632	2.597	2.564	2.532	2.500	2.469	2.439	2.410	2.381
14	2.899	2.857	2.817	2.778	2.740	2.703	2.667	2.631	2.598	2.564	2.531	2.500	2.469	2.439	2.409	2.381
15	2.898	2.857	2.817	2.778	2.740	2.703	2.666	2.632	2.597	2.564	2.532	2.500	2.469	2.439	2.410	2.381
16	2.899	2.857	2.817	2.778	2.740	2.703	2.667	2.631	2.598	2.564	2.531	2.500	2.469	2.439	2.409	2.381
17	2.898	2.857	2.817	2.778	2.740	2.703	2.666	2.632	2.597	2.564	2.532	2.500	2.469	2.439	2.410	2.381
18	2.899	2.857	2.817	2.778	2.740	2.702	2.667	2.631	2.598	2.564	2.531	2.500	2.469	2.439	2.409	2.381
19	2.898	2.857	2.817	2.778	2.739	2.703	2.666	2.632	2.597	2.564	2.532	2.500	2.469	2.439	2.410	2.381
20	2.898	2.857	2.817	2.778	2.740	2.702	2.667	2.631	2.598	2.564	2.531	2.500	2.469	2.439	2.409	2.381
21	2.899	2.857	2.817	2.778	2.739	2.703	2.666	2.632	2.597	2.564	2.532	2.500	2.469	2.439	2.410	2.381
22	2.898	2.857	2.817	2.777	2.740	2.702	2.667	2.631	2.598	2.564	2.531	2.500	2.469	2.439	2.409	2.381
23	2.899	2.857	2.817	2.778	2.739	2.703	2.666	2.632	2.597	2.564	2.532	2.500	2.469	2.439	2.410	2.381
24	2.898	2.857	2.817	2.777	2.740	2.702	2.667	2.631	2.598	2.564	2.531	2.500	2.469	2.439	2.409	2.381
25	2.899	2.857	2.817	2.778	2.739	2.703	2.666	2.632	2.597	2.564	2.532	2.500	2.469	2.439	2.410	2.381
26	2.898	2.857	2.817	2.777	2.740	2.702	2.667	2.631	2.598	2.564	2.531	2.500	2.469	2.439	2.409	2.381
27	2.899	2.857	2.817	2.778	2.739	2.703	2.666	2.632	2.597	2.564	2.532	2.500	2.469	2.439	2.410	2.381
28	2.898	2.858	2.817	2.777	2.740	2.702	2.667	2.631	2.598	2.564	2.531	2.500	2.469	2.439	2.409	2.381
29	2.899	2.857	2.817	2.778	2.739	2.703	2.666	2.632	2.597	2.564	2.532	2.500	2.469	2.439	2.410	2.381
30	2.898	2.858	2.817	2.777	2.740	2.702	2.667	2.631	2.598	2.564	2.531	2.500	2.469	2.439	2.409	2.381
31	2.899	2.857	2.817	2.778	2.739	2.703	2.666	2.632	2.597	2.564	2.532	2.500	2.469	2.439	2.410	2.381
32	2.898	2.858	2.816	2.777	2.740	2.702	2.667	2.631	2.598	2.564	2.531	2.500	2.470	2.439	2.409	2.381
33	2.899	2.857	2.817	2.778	2.739	2.703	2.666	2.632	2.597	2.565	2.532	2.500	2.469	2.439	2.410	2.381
34	2.898	2.858	2.816	2.777	2.740	2.702	2.667	2.631	2.598	2.564	2.531	2.500	2.470	2.439	2.409	2.381
35	2.899	2.857	2.817	2.778	2.739	2.703	2.666	2.632	2.597	2.565	2.532	2.500	2.469	2.439	2.410	2.381
36		1.429	2.816	2.777	2.740	2.702	2.667	2.631	2.598	2.564	2.531	2.500	2.470	2.439	2.409	2.381
37				1.389	2.739	2.703	2.666	2.632	2.597	2.565	2.532	2.500	2.469	2.439	2.410	2.381
38						1.351	2.667	2.631	2.598	2.564	2.531	2.500	2.469	2.439	2.410	2.381
39								1.316	2.597	2.565	2.532	2.500	2.469	2.439	2.410	2.381
40										1.282	2.531	2.500	2.470	2.439	2.409	2.381
41												1.250	2.469	2.439	2.410	2.380
42														1.220	2.409	2.381
43																1.190

Table 8

General and Alternative Depreciation Systems
Applicable Depreciation Method: Straight Line
Applicable Recovery Periods: 2.5-50 years
Applicable Convention: Half-year
(continued)

If the Recovery Year is:	42.5	43.0	43.5	44.0	44.5	45.0	45.5	46.0	46.5	47.0	47.5	48.0	48.5	49.0	49.5	50.0
						the Depreciation Rate is:										
1	1.176	1.163	1.149	1.136	1.124	1.111	1.099	1.087	1.075	1.064	1.053	1.042	1.031	1.020	1.010	1.000
2	2.353	2.326	2.299	2.273	2.247	2.222	2.198	2.174	2.151	2.128	2.105	2.083	2.062	2.041	2.020	2.000
3	2.353	2.326	2.299	2.273	2.247	2.222	2.198	2.174	2.151	2.128	2.105	2.083	2.062	2.041	2.020	2.000
4	2.353	2.326	2.299	2.273	2.247	2.222	2.198	2.174	2.151	2.128	2.105	2.083	2.062	2.041	2.020	2.000
5	2.353	2.326	2.299	2.273	2.247	2.222	2.198	2.174	2.151	2.128	2.105	2.083	2.062	2.041	2.020	2.000
6	2.353	2.326	2.299	2.273	2.247	2.222	2.198	2.174	2.151	2.128	2.105	2.083	2.062	2.041	2.020	2.000
7	2.353	2.326	2.299	2.273	2.247	2.222	2.198	2.174	2.150	2.128	2.105	2.083	2.062	2.041	2.020	2.000
8	2.353	2.326	2.299	2.273	2.247	2.222	2.198	2.174	2.151	2.128	2.105	2.083	2.062	2.041	2.020	2.000
9	2.353	2.325	2.299	2.273	2.247	2.222	2.198	2.174	2.150	2.128	2.105	2.083	2.062	2.041	2.020	2.000
10	2.353	2.326	2.299	2.273	2.247	2.222	2.198	2.174	2.150	2.128	2.105	2.083	2.062	2.041	2.020	2.000
11	2.353	2.325	2.299	2.273	2.247	2.222	2.198	2.174	2.150	2.128	2.105	2.083	2.062	2.041	2.020	2.000
12	2.353	2.326	2.299	2.273	2.247	2.222	2.198	2.174	2.150	2.128	2.105	2.083	2.062	2.041	2.020	2.000
13	2.353	2.325	2.299	2.273	2.247	2.222	2.198	2.174	2.150	2.128	2.105	2.083	2.062	2.041	2.020	2.000
14	2.353	2.326	2.299	2.273	2.247	2.222	2.198	2.174	2.151	2.128	2.105	2.083	2.062	2.041	2.020	2.000
15	2.353	2.325	2.299	2.273	2.247	2.222	2.198	2.174	2.150	2.128	2.105	2.083	2.062	2.041	2.020	2.000
16	2.353	2.326	2.299	2.273	2.247	2.222	2.198	2.174	2.151	2.128	2.105	2.083	2.062	2.041	2.020	2.000
17	2.353	2.325	2.299	2.273	2.247	2.222	2.198	2.174	2.150	2.127	2.105	2.083	2.062	2.041	2.020	2.000
18	2.353	2.326	2.299	2.273	2.247	2.222	2.198	2.174	2.151	2.128	2.105	2.083	2.062	2.041	2.020	2.000
19	2.353	2.325	2.299	2.273	2.247	2.222	2.198	2.174	2.150	2.127	2.105	2.084	2.062	2.041	2.020	2.000
20	2.353	2.326	2.299	2.273	2.247	2.222	2.198	2.174	2.151	2.128	2.105	2.083	2.062	2.041	2.020	2.000
21	2.353	2.325	2.299	2.273	2.247	2.222	2.198	2.174	2.150	2.127	2.105	2.084	2.062	2.041	2.020	2.000
22	2.353	2.326	2.299	2.273	2.247	2.222	2.198	2.174	2.151	2.128	2.105	2.083	2.062	2.041	2.020	2.000
23	2.353	2.325	2.299	2.272	2.247	2.222	2.198	2.174	2.150	2.127	2.105	2.084	2.062	2.041	2.020	2.000
24	2.353	2.326	2.299	2.272	2.247	2.222	2.198	2.174	2.151	2.128	2.105	2.083	2.062	2.041	2.020	2.000
25	2.353	2.325	2.299	2.272	2.247	2.222	2.198	2.174	2.150	2.127	2.105	2.084	2.062	2.041	2.020	2.000
26	2.353	2.326	2.299	2.273	2.247	2.222	2.198	2.174	2.151	2.128	2.106	2.083	2.062	2.041	2.020	2.000
27	2.353	2.325	2.299	2.272	2.247	2.223	2.198	2.174	2.150	2.127	2.105	2.084	2.062	2.041	2.020	2.000
28	2.353	2.326	2.299	2.273	2.247	2.222	2.198	2.174	2.151	2.128	2.106	2.083	2.062	2.041	2.020	2.000
29	2.353	2.325	2.299	2.272	2.247	2.223	2.198	2.174	2.150	2.127	2.105	2.084	2.062	2.041	2.020	2.000
30	2.353	2.326	2.299	2.273	2.248	2.222	2.197	2.174	2.151	2.128	2.106	2.083	2.062	2.041	2.020	2.000
31	2.353	2.325	2.299	2.272	2.247	2.223	2.198	2.174	2.150	2.127	2.105	2.084	2.062	2.041	2.021	2.000
32	2.353	2.326	2.299	2.273	2.248	2.222	2.197	2.174	2.151	2.128	2.106	2.083	2.062	2.041	2.020	2.000
33	2.353	2.325	2.298	2.272	2.247	2.223	2.198	2.174	2.150	2.127	2.105	2.084	2.062	2.041	2.021	2.000
34	2.353	2.326	2.299	2.273	2.248	2.222	2.197	2.174	2.151	2.128	2.106	2.083	2.062	2.040	2.020	2.000
35	2.353	2.325	2.298	2.272	2.247	2.223	2.198	2.174	2.150	2.127	2.105	2.084	2.062	2.041	2.021	2.000
36	2.353	2.326	2.299	2.273	2.248	2.222	2.197	2.174	2.151	2.128	2.106	2.083	2.062	2.040	2.020	2.000
37	2.353	2.325	2.298	2.272	2.247	2.223	2.198	2.174	2.150	2.127	2.105	2.084	2.061	2.041	2.021	2.000
38	2.353	2.326	2.299	2.273	2.248	2.222	2.197	2.174	2.151	2.128	2.106	2.083	2.062	2.040	2.020	2.000
39	2.353	2.325	2.298	2.272	2.247	2.223	2.198	2.174	2.150	2.127	2.105	2.084	2.061	2.041	2.021	2.000
40	2.353	2.326	2.299	2.273	2.248	2.222	2.197	2.173	2.151	2.128	2.106	2.083	2.062	2.040	2.020	2.000
41	2.352	2.325	2.299	2.272	2.247	2.223	2.198	2.174	2.150	2.127	2.105	2.084	2.061	2.041	2.021	2.000
42	2.353	2.326	2.299	2.273	2.248	2.222	2.197	2.173	2.151	2.128	2.106	2.083	2.062	2.040	2.020	2.000
43	2.352	2.325	2.298	2.272	2.247	2.223	2.198	2.174	2.150	2.127	2.105	2.084	2.061	2.041	2.021	2.000
44		1.163	2.299	2.273	2.248	2.222	2.197	2.173	2.151	2.128	2.106	2.083	2.062	2.040	2.020	2.000
45				1.136	2.247	2.223	2.198	2.174	2.150	2.127	2.105	2.084	2.061	2.041	2.021	2.000
46						1.111	2.197	2.173	2.151	2.128	2.106	2.083	2.062	2.040	2.020	2.000
47								1.087	2.150	2.127	2.105	2.084	2.061	2.041	2.020	2.000
48										1.064	2.106	2.083	2.062	2.040	2.020	2.000
49												1.042	2.061	2.041	2.021	2.000
50														1.020	2.020	2.000
51																1.000

Table 9
Alternative Depreciation System
Applicable Depreciation Method: Straight Line
Applicable Recovery Period: 40 years
Applicable Convention: Mid-month

And the Month in the First Recovery Year the Property is Placed in Service is:

If the Recovery Year is:	1	2	3	4	5	6	7	8	9	10	11	12
					the Depreciation Rate is:							
1	2.396	2.188	1.979	1.771	1.563	1.354	1.146	0.938	0.729	0.521	0.313	0.104
2 to 40	2.500	2.500	2.500	2.500	2.500	2.500	2.500	2.500	2.500	2.500	2.500	2.500
41	0.104	0.312	0.521	0.729	0.937	1.146	1.354	1.562	1.771	1.979	2.187	2.396

Table I
Leased MACRS Business Listed Property

Income Inclusion Amounts — Step (1) Computation Rates — for Business Listed Property (Except Autos) Leased After '86 (Reg §1.280F-7(b)(2)(i)(C))

First Taxable Year During Lease in Which Business Use Percentage is 50% or Less

Type of Property	1	2	3	4	5	6	7	8	9	10	11	12 & Later
Property with a Recovery Period of Less Than 7 Years under Alternative Depreciation System (Such as Computers, Trucks and Airplanes)	2.1%	−7.2%	−19.8%	−20.1%	−12.4%	−12.4%	−12.4%	−12.4%	−12.4%	−12.4%	−12.4%	−12.4%
Property with a 7- to 10-Year Recovery Period under the Alternative Depreciation System (Such as Recreation Property)	3.9%	−3.8%	−17.7%	−25.1%	−27.8%	−27.2%	−27.1%	−27.6%	−23.7%	−14.7%	−14.7%	−14.7%
Property with a Recovery Period of More Than 10 Years under the Alternative Depreciation System (Such as Certain Property with No Class Life)	6.6%	−1.6%	−16.9%	−25.6%	−29.9%	−31.1%	−32.8%	−35.1%	−33.3%	−26.7%	−19.7%	−12.2%

Table II
Leased MACRS Business Listed Property

Income Inclusion Amounts — Step (2) Computation Rates — for
Business Listed Property (Except Autos) Leased After '86
(Reg §1.280F-7(b)(2)(ii)(C))

First Taxable Year During Lease in Which Business Use Percentage is 50% or Less

Type of Property	1	2	3	4	5	6	7	8	9	10	11	12 & Later
Property with a Recovery Period of Less Than 7 Years under the Alternative Depreciation System (Such as Computers, Trucks and Airplanes)	0.0%	10.0%	22.0%	21.2%	12.7%	12.7%	12.7%	12.7%	12.7%	12.7%	12.7%	12.7%
Property with a 7- to 10-Year Recovery Period under the Alternative Depreciation System (Such as Recreation Property)	0.0%	9.3%	23.8%	31.3%	33.8%	32.7%	31.6%	30.5%	25.0%	15.0%	15.0%	15.0%
Property with Recovery Period of More Than 10 Years under the Alternative Depreciation System (Such as Certain Property with No Class Life)	0.0%	10.1%	26.3%	35.4%	39.6%	40.2%	40.8%	41.4%	37.5%	29.2%	20.8%	12.5%

¶ 1119 Income Inclusion Amounts for Autos, Trucks and Vans. ▰▰▰▰▰

REV. PROC. 2022-17 TABLE 3

DOLLAR AMOUNTS FOR PASSENGER AUTOMOBILES
WITH A LEASE TERM BEGINNING IN CALENDAR YEAR 2022

Fair Market Value of Passenger Automobile		Tax Year During Lease				
Over	Not Over	1st	2nd	3rd	4th	5th & later
56,000	57,000	1	1	1	2	2
57,000	58,000	2	4	5	7	7
58,000	59,000	3	7	9	11	13
59,000	60,000	4	9	14	16	19
60,000	62,000	6	13	20	23	28
62,000	64,000	9	19	27	34	38
64,000	66,000	11	24	36	43	50
66,000	68,000	14	30	43	53	61
68,000	70,000	16	35	52	63	72
70,000	72,000	19	40	61	72	83
72,000	74,000	21	46	68	82	95
74,000	76,000	24	51	77	91	106
76,000	78,000	26	57	85	101	117
78,000	80,000	29	62	93	111	128
80,000	85,000	33	72	107	128	148
85,000	90,000	39	86	127	152	176
90,000	95,000	45	100	147	177	204
95,000	100,000	52	113	167	201	233
100,000	110,000	61	133	198	238	274
110,000	120,000	73	161	239	286	330
120,000	130,000	86	188	279	335	387
130,000	140,000	98	216	319	384	443
140,000	150,000	111	243	360	432	499
150,000	160,000	123	270	401	481	555
160,000	170,000	135	298	441	529	612
170,000	180,000	148	325	482	578	667
180,000	190,000	160	352	523	626	724
190,000	200,000	173	379	563	676	779
200,000	210,000	185	407	603	724	836
210,000	220,000	198	434	644	773	892
220,000	230,000	210	461	685	821	949
230,000	240,000	222	489	725	870	1,005
240,000	and over	235	516	766	918	1,061

Chapter 2   Income—Taxable and Exempt

¶ 1200   **Gross Income Defined.** ▰▰▰▰▰▰▰▰▰▰▰▰▰▰▰▰▰▰▰▰▰▰▰▰▰▰

Under Code Sec. 61, gross income consists of all income, from all sources, such as compensation for services (¶1208 *et seq.*), business income, dividends (¶1285 *et seq.*), interest (¶1301 *et seq.*), rents (¶1337 *et seq.*) and gains from the sale of property. Only items specifically exempt may be excluded.

Gross income also includes illegal gains and income derived from illegal or criminal activities (e.g., from embezzlement, kickbacks, extortion, fraudulent schemes, shareholder misappropriation, and drug dealing). (Reg § 1.61-14(a))[1] For a listing of various taxable and exempt income items, see ¶1206.

Gross income is the starting point in determining tax liability and is broadly defined. (Code Sec. 61)[2] Revenues from crowdfunding are generally includible in gross income ([3], as is income derived from the gig economy (also known as the sharing, on-demand, or access economy, including services such as Airbnb or Uber).[4]

¶ 1201   **Assignment of income—gross income.**

The person who earns and is entitled to receive income is taxed on it under Code Sec. 61 and can't avoid being taxed by assigning the income (i.e., giving the right to the income) to another person.[5] But if a taxpayer assigns, by gift, income-producing *property* before the income is earned, the assignee is taxed on the income.[6]

¶ 1202   **Income from co-owned property—joint tenancies, tenancies in common, co-owners with survivorship, co-owners without survivorship, etc.— gross income.**

In a tenancy in common (co-owners without survivorship), each co-owner is taxable under Code Sec. 61 on the income attributable to the taxpayer's share.[7] Co-owners who are joint tenants (with survivorship) split income from their property according to their ownership interests.[8]

Similarly, any gain (or loss) from sale of jointly owned property is divided among the co-owners unless the joint ownership was created to save taxes on the sale, in which case the original owner is taxed on the full amount of the gain.[9]

Co-owners who are spouses and who file joint returns report their combined income, gains and losses from the jointly-owned property. If they file separately, the income, etc., from the property is split according to how it's shared under state law.[10]

¶ 1203   **Separately filing marrieds in community property states must report half of total community income; community income defined; exceptions; "traditional" and "equitable" relief from separate-return liability; Form 8958; Form 8857—gross income.**

Federal tax law recognizes the principle of community income, which treats half of community income and expenses as belonging to each spouse, in community property states (AZ, CA, ID, LA, NV, NM, TX, WA and WI) or countries. Thus, marrieds living in

---

1. ¶J-1600 *et seq.*
2. ¶s J-1000 *et seq.*
3. ¶J-1009.1)
4. ¶J-1001)
5. ¶J-8151 *et seq.*

6. ¶J-8172 *et seq.*
7. ¶J-8103
8. ¶s J-8101, J-8102
9. ¶J-8107
10. ¶J-8100 *et seq.*

References beginning with a single letter are to paragraphs in Federal Tax Coordinator 2d and RIA's Analysis of Federal Taxes: Income.

community property states, who don't file a joint return, must report half of the total community income earned by the spouses during the tax year. (Reg § 1.66-1(a))[11] Community income is all income from community property (including business property) and salaries, etc., for the services of either or both spouses. Income from separate property during marriage is community income only in ID, LA, TX and WI.[12]

Under Code Sec. 66, if a married couple lived apart for the entire year, filed separate returns *and* one or both spouses had earned income no part of which was transferred between them, community income for the year is taxed to the spouse who earned it rather than under community property laws. (Code Sec. 66(a), Code Sec. 66(d)(1))[13]

If one spouse acts as if solely entitled to an item of community income and fails to notify the other spouse of the nature and amount of the income before the return due date (with extensions), IRS may deny the first spouse any community property benefit. (Code Sec. 66(b))[14]

Registered domestic partners (RDPs). Individuals in registered domestic partnerships or civil unions that are not marriages under state law are not considered married for federal tax purposes. But if state law extends full community property treatment to RDPs, each partner must report half of the community income on that partner's return, whether received as compensation for personal services or as income from property. An RDP who has income that isn't community income must also report that separate income.[15]

Form 8958 is used to allocate tax amounts between married filing separate spouses or RDPs with community property rights.[16]

"Traditional" and "equitable" relief from separate return liability. A spouse who doesn't file a joint return for the tax year for which "traditional" relief is sought, and omits from gross income the spouse's share of community income, is relieved from tax liability on that omitted income if the spouse establishes lack of knowledge or reason to know of the omitted item and, under all the facts, it's inequitable to include the omitted item in the spouse's gross income. (Code Sec. 66(c); Reg § 1.66-4(a)(1))[17] IRS may grant "equitable" relief to a separately-filing spouse from liability attributable to a community income item for which relief isn't otherwise available. (Code Sec. 66(c); Reg § 1.66-4(b);[18]) Traditional relief applies only to deficiencies arising out of omitted income, but equitable relief includes relief from any tax underpayments or deficiencies, including those arising from disallowed deductions or credits. (Reg § 1.66-4(c)) A spouse requests relief under the above provisions by filing Form 8857. (Reg § 1.66-4(j)(1))[19] For joint filers, see ¶4711.

¶ 1204   Claim of right—income received without restriction—gross income.

Income received without restriction—income the taxpayer has dominion and control over—must be reported in the year received, even if it may have to be repaid in a later year.[20] For deduction in the repayment year, see ¶2847 *et seq.*

¶ 1205   The "tax benefit rule"—recoveries attributable to an earlier year's deduction or credit—gross income.

Under Code Sec. 111, the recovery of an amount deducted or credited in an earlier tax year is included in a taxpayer's income in the current (recovery) year, except to the extent the deduction or credit *didn't* reduce federal income tax (or alternative minimum tax, but not the accumulated earnings or personal holding company "penalty" taxes) imposed in

---

11. ¶A-5000; ¶A-5001
12. ¶A-5008
13. ¶A-5021; ¶A-5022
14. ¶A-5026
15. ¶A-5017

16. ¶A-5001
17. ¶A-5029
18. ¶A-5034
19. ¶A-5033
20. ¶J-8000 *et seq.*

the earlier year. (Code Sec. 111(d)(1))[21] (Code Sec. 111(a))[22]

Similarly, if a downward price adjustment (e.g., price reduction) during the tax year affects an amount paid or incurred on which a credit (other than the investment credit or the foreign tax credit) was allowed in an earlier year, the tax for the adjustment year is increased by the amount of credit attributable to the adjustment, to the extent it reduced tax in the earlier year. (Code Sec. 111(b))[23]

This "tax benefit rule" applies to recoveries of both itemized deductions (i.e., taxes, medical expenses and other items deductible on Form 1040, Schedule A) and non-itemized deductions (e.g., bad debts). A taxpayer who recovers an amount deducted in an earlier year as an itemized deduction is taxed on the *lesser* of the amount recovered or the amount deducted on Schedule A. The taxable amount is limited to the itemized deduction amount that reduced the tax in the earlier year. Thus, a taxpayer who was eligible to take the standard deduction in the earlier year is taxed on the *lesser* of itemized deduction recoveries or the amount by which itemized deductions exceeded the standard deduction in the earlier year.[24]

If a taxpayer had negative taxable income for the year the items were deducted, the otherwise includable amount of the recovery is reduced by the negative amount.[25]

The tax benefit rule applies to state income taxes deducted in an earlier year where there's a refund or credit of taxes paid or the cancellation of taxes accrued.[26] But a refundable credit not based on taxes previously paid isn't protected by the exclusionary effect of the tax benefit rule, even if the state calls it an overpayment.[27] A taxpayer who received a tax benefit from the state and local tax deduction in a prior year and received a refund of that tax in the current year, must include in gross income in the year of receipt the lesser of (1) the difference between total itemized deductions taken in the prior year and the amount of itemized deductions that would have been taken in the prior year had the proper amount of state and local tax been paid, or (2) the difference between itemized deductions taken in the prior year and the standard deduction amount for the prior year, if taxpayer wasn't precluded from taking standard deduction in that year. This applies to the recovery of any state or local tax, including state or local income tax and state or local real or personal property tax subject to the 2018−2025 $10,000 limit (see ¶1747) on the itemized deduction for nonbusiness taxes.[28]

The increase of a carryover that hasn't expired as of the start of the tax year of the recovery (deduction) or adjustment (credit item) is treated as a reduction of tax imposed. (Code Sec. 111(c))[29]

The tax rates for the recovery (or adjustment) year are used to compute the tax on the portion that is includable.[30]

¶ 1206   Miscellaneous taxable and exempt income.

Here are selected miscellaneous items, and whether they're taxable or excludable:

. . . Alaska Permanent Fund Dividend. *Taxable.*[31]

. . . Alcohol fuel credit. *Taxable.* (Code Sec. 87)[32]

. . . Cryptocurrency (e.g., Bitcoin)/virtual currency/digital currency. Receipt in exchange for services is *taxable* as ordinary income.[33] Virtual currency/cryptocurrency is treated

21. ¶J-5526, J-5527
22. ¶J-5500 *et seq.*
23. ¶J-5511
24. ¶J-5512
25. ¶J-5512
26. ¶J-5701 *et seq.*
27. ¶J-5505
28. ¶J-5512
29. ¶J-5524
30. ¶J-5530
31. ¶J-1493
32. ¶L-17505
33. ¶J-1433 *et seq.*

as property, and transactions in it are subject to the tax rules that apply for sales and exchanges of other property, i.e., *taxable*.[34]

... "Difficulty-of-care payments." *Excludable,* unless for more than ten individuals under age 19, or for more than five individuals age 19 or older. (Code Sec. 131)[35] See "Medicaid waiver payments," below.

... Electronic health record incentive payments to health care professionals and hospitals. *Taxable*.[36]

... Energy conservation subsidies provided by a public utility to customers for buying or installing "energy conservation measures" for dwelling units. *Excludable*. (Code Sec. 136)[37]

... Executor's or administrator's fees that are waived. *Excludable,* if executor files a formal waiver within six months after appointment, or if conduct amounts to an implied waiver.[38]

... Financial aid grants (emergency financial aid grants) under the Coronavirus Aid, Relief, and Economic Security ("CARES") Act. *Excludable*.[39]

... Foster care payments by state or licensed/certified placement agency to individual foster care provider for caring for qualified foster individual (child or adult) in care provider's home (where provider resides). *Excludable,* but payments received for more than five qualified foster individuals who are 19 or older must be included.[40]

... Frequent flyer miles earned or received in connection with business travel. *Excludable*.[41]

... Geothermal or mineral interests, qualifying—25% of qualifying gain from conservation sales. *Excludable*.[42]

... Grants in lieu of the Code Sec. 48 energy credit or Code Sec. 45 electricity production credit. *Excludable* from income and alternative minimum taxable income. (Code Sec. 48(d)(3)(A))[43]

... Grants to homeowners under a city program to preserve old neighborhoods. *Taxable*.[44]

... Human trafficking victims, mandatory restitution payments awarded under 18 U.S.C. §1593. *Excludable*.[45]

... Identity protection services provided at no cost before or after a data security breach. *Excludable,* but cash received in lieu of identity protection services, or proceeds received under an identity theft insurance policy, are taxable.[46]

... Insurance reimbursement to homeowner for living expenses incurred due to the loss of use of (or government's denial of access to) principal residence (owned or rented) resulting from a fire, storm or other casualty. *Excludable,* to extent it covers the amount by which additional living expenses due to the casualty exceed normal living expenses (balance is *taxable*). (Code Sec. 123; Reg § 1.123-1)[47]

... Interest received from the federal government, connected with an action to recover property seized by IRS under 31 USC § 5317(c)(2), which allows IRS to seize property involved in transactions that violate 31 USC § 5324 (the Bank Secrecy Act's structuring provisions, which bar transactions structured for the purpose of evading reporting and recordkeeping requirements for currency transactions exceeding $10,000). *Excludable*.

34. ¶I-2150 *et seq.*
35. ¶J-1500 *et seq.*
36. ¶J-1430
37. ¶J-1401 *et seq.*
38. ¶J-1419
39. ¶J-1299
40. ¶J-1500 *et seq.*
41. ¶J-1393
42. ¶I-8851
43. ¶J-1480.1
44. ¶J-1487
45. ¶J-1475A
46. ¶J-1434
47. ¶J-1311; ¶J-1314

(Code Sec. 139H)[48]

. . . Leave donated and deposited in an employer-sponsored leave bank under a major disaster leave-sharing plan. *Excludable,* if plan treats payments made by the employer to leave recipients as wages.[49]

. . . Leave received under employer-sponsored leave-sharing plan that allows employees with a medical emergency to receive leave that other employees surrender or deposit into a leave bank. *Taxable,* as compensation.[50]

. . . Malpractice settlement from accountants for advising taxpayers to participate in abusive tax shelter. *Excludable* (under a Tax Court decision, but IRS disagrees).[1]

. . . Medicaid waiver payments (to recipient for care of person who would otherwise be institutionalized). *Excludable* (as "difficulty-of-care payments," above), even if care provider is related to recipient.[2]

. . . Medicare benefits (Part A and Part B). *Excludable,* except for Part B amounts attributable to medical deductions taken in an earlier year.[3]

. . . Mortgage assistance payments by federal agency to mortgagee on mortgagor's behalf, e.g., Pay-for-Performance Success Payments that reduce principal balance of home mortgage under Home Affordable Modification Program. *Excludable,* unless *not* made for the general welfare.[4]

. . . Pell grants. *Excludable,* but if included in income, can result in an increased education credit.[5]

. . . Payments made to or on behalf of homeowners under state housing finance agency programs (listed at www.treasury.gov/HHF.4) with funds allocated from the Housing Finance Agency's Hardest Hit Fund or under the Homeowner Assistance Fund (HAF).[6] For safe harbor methods under which taxpayers who receive these payments may deduct mortgage interest and real property taxes, see ¶1747.

. . . Property tax rebates. *Taxable,* to extent they exceed the property tax paid. Rebates received after the year of payment are subject to the tax benefit rule (¶1205). Rebates received in the year of payment reduce the amount of tax paid for that year. Where the tax was paid over two years, the rebate is apportioned over them.[7] However, state property tax credits are treated as reducing a taxpayer's property tax liability (so are not treated as income) for the year the credit is claimed or carried forward to.

. . . Rebates of part of purchase price to retail customers, or credit card "points." *Excludable,* generally, as an adjustment to the purchase price of acquiring the property.[8]

. . . Relocation payments and similar gov't subsidies, for moving expenses and actual direct losses of property, due to displacement from residence as part of urban renewal. *Excludable,* to extent made by gov't to compensate (and actually so used) for such expenses,[9] and *taxable,* to extent made by nongov't landlords as part of co-op, condo conversion.[10]

. . . Restaurant revitalization grants, Economic Injury Disaster Loan (EIDL) program grants, targeted EIDL advances, and grants for shuttered venue operators. *Excludable.*[11] The exclusions for all of the just-mentioned grants, which were enacted as COVID-19 economic relief, have no effect on deduction, basis, or tax attributes.[12]

. . . Security deposits. If to guarantee performance of obligation, *excludable* if repayment required on performance, but *taxable* if recipient can keep on default.[13]

---

48. ¶J-3075 *et seq.*
49. ¶H-1013.1
50. ¶H-1013.3
1. ¶J-5827
2. ¶J-1504
3. ¶J-1307
4. ¶J-1489
5. ¶A-4542, A-4543.1
6. ¶J-1489
7. ¶J-1394.1
8. ¶J-1391
9. ¶J-1492
10. ¶J-1492
11. ¶J-1299.1
12. ¶L-1007.1
13. ¶J-1371

... State or local gov't payments (certain tax relief, and certain reimbursements) to volunteer firefighters, emergency responders. *Excludable.*[14]

... Subsidies received from Social Security by sponsors of qualified retiree prescription drug plans under the Medicare Prescription Drug Act of 2003 for certain covered retiree drug costs. *Excludable.* (Code Sec. 139A)[15]

... Terrorism, specified victims of, and astronauts—employer-provided death benefits. *Excludable.* (Code Sec. 101(i)(1))[16]

... Transportation service providers' receipt of grants under the Coronavirus Economic Relief for Transportation Services (CERTS) Act (Division N, Title IV, Subtitle B of the Consolidated Appropriations Act of 2021), for providers that experienced annual revenue losses of at least 25% as a result of COVID-19. (The application deadline was July 19, 2021.) *Taxable.* Grants used to pay compensation and certain other expenses are deductible under the rules discussed at ¶1505 *et seq.*[17]

... Use and occupancy insurance reimbursements for loss of profits if business is suspended. *Taxable.*[18]

... Utility's rate reduction or nonrefundable credit to customer for participation in energy conservation program. *Excludable.*[19]

... Whistleblower awards paid by IRS for information about tax law violations. *Taxable.* (Reg § 301.7623-4(d)(5))[20]

... Whistleblower's settlement under Federal False Claims Act *qui tam* action against former employer. *Taxable* (as ordinary income and not capital gain).[21]

¶ 1207 Exclusion for qualified disaster relief payments and qualified disaster mitigation payments—gross income.

Under Code Sec. 139, a qualified disaster relief payment isn't included in gross income, nor is it earnings for self-employment tax, or wages for employment taxes. (Code Sec. 139) The exclusion doesn't apply to amounts received for the sale or disposition of property, but the involuntary conversion rules may apply to such amounts, see ¶2429.[22]

A qualified disaster relief payment, defined in Code Sec. 139(b), includes amounts paid to individuals to reimburse or pay certain reasonable and necessary expenses, certain payments by common carriers, and certain government payments to promote the general welfare.[23]

A qualified disaster is a one that results from a terroristic or military action, a Federally declared disaster, a disaster resulting from an accident involving a common carrier or from any other event that's determined by IRS to be of a catastrophic nature, or, for government payments, a disaster that's determined by the appropriate governmental authority to warrant assistance from the governmental authority.[24]

Qualified disaster mitigation payments are excluded from gross income. (Code Sec. 139(g)) These include payments under the Flood Mitigation Assistance Program, Pre-Disaster Mitigation Program, and Hazard Mitigation Grant Program.[25]

Coronavirus State and Local Fiscal Recovery Funds (SLFR Funds) may be includible or excludible by recipients, depending on the purpose of the payment.[26]

---

14. ¶J-1480.4
15. ¶J-1480.2
16. ¶C-9674
17. ¶J-1480.1
18. ¶J-5830
19. ¶J-1431
20. ¶J-1485.2

21. ¶J-1485.3
22. ¶J-1291
23. ¶J-1294
24. ¶J-1295
25. ¶J-1296
26. ¶J-1299.2; ¶J-1299.3

¶ 1208 **Compensation Income—Wages, Salary, Fees, Tips, Severance, Vacation Pay, Pensions.** ▮

Under Code Sec. 61(a)(1), all forms of compensation received for personal services are included in gross income.

This includes wages, salaries, fees, tips (¶1210), salesperson's commissions (including on sales to self or family), percentage of profits paid as compensation, commissions on insurance premiums, bonuses (including Christmas bonuses, see ¶1211), termination or severance pay, golden parachute payments (excess golden parachute payments subject the recipient to a 20% excise tax (Code Sec. 4999(a)),[27] rewards, jury duty fees (Code Sec. 61(a)(1); Reg § 1.61-2(a)(1)),[28] and fringe benefits not excluded by statute (see ¶1228 *et seq.*). (Code Sec. 61(a)(1)) Vacation pay also is taxable.[29] For stock- and property-based compensation, see ¶1216 *et seq.* For employment-related stock options, see ¶1219 *et seq.*

Pension or retirement allowances to employees (reported to recipients on Form 1099-R) generally are taxable to the recipient, see ¶4328 *et seq.* (Reg § 1.61-11(a))[30] For rules for certain military pensions, see ¶1284.

Amounts withheld from an employee's pay by the employer for income and social security taxes, savings bonds, union dues, etc., must also be included in income by the employee for the year in which withheld.[31] An employee is taxed on compensation even if the employer can't deduct all or part of the amount because it's "unreasonable" (¶1516). (Reg § 1.162-8)[32]

¶ 1209 **Reporting compensation and self-employment income.**

The amount of wages, salaries, tips, etc., that's includible in income (¶1208), which should be shown on a Form W-2 issued by the employer, is reported on Form 1040.[33]

Income (or loss) subject to self-employment tax (¶3133) from a business operated, or a profession practiced, as a sole proprietor is reported on Form 1040, Schedule C or C-EZ. If an individual operates more than one business as a sole proprietor, a separate Schedule C or C-EZ must be prepared for each business. An individual can't report income earned as an employee on Schedule C or C-EZ.[34] For farm income, see ¶4501.

¶ 1210 **Tips, service charges, and similar payments—compensation income.**

Tips and similar payments for special services are income under Code Sec. 61. (Reg § 1.61-2(a)(1)) Mandatory service charges added to customers' bills in lieu of tipping are part of the employee's wages and are not subject to tip reporting (¶4746).[35]

¶ 1211 **Compensation distinguished from gift—compensation income.**

Although gifts are generally excluded from the recipient's gross income (¶1367), a transfer by or for an employer to or for the benefit of an employee can't be excluded as a gift. (Code Sec. 102(c)(1)) Extraordinary transfers to the natural objects of an employer's bounty (e.g., an employee who is the employer's son) aren't transfers to or for the benefit of the employee if the transfer wasn't made in recognition of employment.[36] For de minimis fringe benefits, see ¶1245. For no-additional-cost services, see ¶1242.

If, as a means of promoting goodwill, an employer makes a general distribution to

---

27. ¶H-3003
28. ¶H-1001 *et seq.*
29. ¶s H-1001, H-1012
30. ¶H-3245
31. ¶H-2152

32. ¶H-1021
33. ¶H-1001.1
34. ¶H-1001.1
35. ¶H-4341
36. ¶H-1027.1 *et seq.*

employees of hams, turkeys or other merchandise of nominal value at Christmas or a comparable holiday, the value of the gifts isn't included in the employees' income. But if an employer distributes cash, gift certificates or similar items of readily convertible cash value, the gifts are additional wages or salary, *regardless* of the amount.[37]

¶ 1212 Below-market interest rate loans from employer—compensation income.

An employee or independent contractor who receives a below-market loan (¶1305) that's compensation-related (except for certain de minimis loans), recognizes compensation income equal to: (i) for a demand loan, the foregone interest (at the applicable federal rate, ¶1117) over actual interest payment; and (ii) for other loans, the excess of the amount borrowed over the present value of the payments required to be made under the terms of the loan. (Code Sec. 7872(a)(1), Code Sec. 7872(b)(1))[38]

Certain employee-relocation loans are exempt from these rules. (Reg § 1.7872-5T(b)(6))[39]

¶ 1213 Noncash compensation—compensation income; compensation in cryptocurrency.

If a taxpayer receives property or services rather than money as payment for services rendered, the fair market value (FMV) of the property or services must be included in income. For example, a salesperson must include in income the FMV of a vacation trip awarded as a prize. Where a price has been specified for the services rendered, that price is considered the FMV of the property or services received if there's no evidence showing a different value. (Code Sec. 83; Reg § 1.61-2(d))[40]

The receipt of cryptocurrency/virtual currency in exchange for services is taxable as ordinary income.[41]

¶ 1214 Notes receivable as compensation—compensation income.

Notes and other evidences of indebtedness received in payment for services or in settlement of a claim for compensation are taxable as compensation in the amount of their fair market value when received. When a taxpayer receives as compensation a non-interest-bearing note regarded as good for its face value at maturity, the note's fair discounted value (computed at the prevailing rate) is included in income. As note payments are received, the taxpayer's income includes that portion of each payment representing the proportionate part of the discount originally taken on the entire note. (Reg § 1.61-2(d)(4))[42]

¶ 1215 Bargain purchase from employer—compensation income.

If an employer transfers property, including stock, to an employee for less than its fair market value, the difference is compensation. (Code Sec. 83(a); Reg § 1.83-1(a))[43] For stock options and employee stock purchase plans, see ¶1219 *et seq.*

If an employee pays for stock acquired from an employer under a nonqualified stock option with a recourse note, and the employer later reduces the amount due on the note, the debt reduction is treated as compensation income.[44]

---

37. ¶H-1033
38. ¶s H-2002, H-2004
39. ¶H-2014
40. ¶H-2500 *et seq.*

41. ¶J-1433 *et seq.*
42. ¶H-2513
43. ¶H-2509
44. ¶H-2535

¶ 1216   **Restricted stock or other property—Section 83 rules, receipt of property for services, substantial risk of forfeiture—compensation income.**

Under Code Sec. 83, a person receiving a beneficial interest in stock or other property for performance of services has compensation income equal to the value of that property at the time of receipt. But if the person's interest in the property is subject to substantial risk of forfeiture (is "restricted") and can't be transferred free of that risk, then income is deferred until the interest in the property either: (1) is no longer subject to that risk, *or* (2) becomes transferable free of the risk, whichever occurs earlier. (Code Sec. 83)[45] For election (Code Sec. 83(b) election) not to defer income, see ¶1217. For election (Code Sec. 83(i) election) to defer income from qualified equity grants, see ¶1218.

But the employee (or other owner of the property) has income from the property if it's sold or disposed of before (1) or (2), above. (Code Sec. 83(a))[46]

The amount included in income (in the year in which (1) or (2) occurs) is the excess of the property's fair market value (FMV) in that year (figured without regard to restrictions other than those that by their terms will never lapse), over the amount, if any, paid for the property. (Code Sec. 83(a))[47]

A substantial risk of forfeiture exists only if a person's rights in property that's transferred is conditioned, directly or indirectly, (a) on the future performance (or refraining from performance) of substantial services, or (b) upon the occurrence of a condition related to a purpose of the transfer, if the possibility of forfeiture is substantial. Property isn't transferred subject to a substantial risk of forfeiture if the forfeiture condition is unlikely to be enforced; the employer is required to pay the FMV of a portion of the property to the employee upon the return of the property; or there's a risk that the value of property will decline during a certain period of time. (Code Sec. 83(c)(1), Reg § 1.83-3(c)(1)) An example of property subject to a substantial risk of forfeiture is where property is transferred subject to a requirement that the property must be returned to the employer if total earnings don't increase. (Reg § 1.83-3(c)(2)),[48]

Restrictions on transfer of the property won't create a substantial risk of forfeiture, except as specifically provided in Reg § 1.83-3(j) (dealing with the SEC "short swing" rule, under which insider must pay over profits if stock is sold within six months of receipt), and Reg § 1.83-3(k) (dealing with the SEC "pooling-of-interests accounting" rule, under which employees are prevented from selling stock while their company is engaged in a merger or acquisition). Transfer restrictions that won't result in a substantial risk of forfeiture include restrictions that, if violated, would result in the forfeiture of some or all of the property or liability for damages, penalties, fees, or other amounts. (Reg § 1.83-3(c)(1))[49]

¶ 1217   **Election (Code Sec. 83(b)) not to defer income from restricted stock or other property; immediate recognition of income—compensation income.**

Under Code Sec. 83(b)(1), an employee or other person who receives restricted stock or other property (¶1216) may elect to recognize the income immediately instead of deferring it. (Code Sec. 83(b)(1))[50]

The amount of compensation income included in the year the property is received is the excess of the property's fair market value at receipt (without regard to restrictions other than those that by their terms will never lapse), over the amount, if any, paid for the

---

45. ¶H-2500, ¶H-2517 *et seq.*   48. ¶H-2521
46. ¶H-2547 *et seq.*   49. ¶H-2526
47. ¶H-2532 *et seq.*   50. ¶H-2540

property. (Code Sec. 83(b)(1))[1]

🖉*recommendation:* Elect if the income taxed at grant would be negligible. This defers tax on any post-grant appreciation until sale, makes it eligible for capital gain rates, and may eliminate additional income tax completely if the property is held until death.

If the stock or other property is forfeited after the election is made, the employee can't get a deduction or refund of tax previously paid on income reported. (Code Sec. 83(b)(1))[2] The employee will have capital loss at the time of forfeiture. (Reg § 1.83-2(a))[3]

Elect within 30 days after the property is transferred to the employee (Code Sec. 83(b)(2)) by filing a statement (specified in the regs) with the IRS office where the person who performs the services files the tax return for that year and submitting a copy to the person for whom the services are performed. (Reg § 1.83-2(c); Reg § 1.83-2(d))[4]

IRS will consent to a revocation only if the election was filed under a mistake of fact in the underlying transaction and the revocation is requested within 60 days of discovering the mistake. However, requests to revoke the election within the 30-day period for making it generally will be granted.[5]

¶ 1218 Election to defer income from qualified equity grants (Code Sec. 83(i) election); restricted stock units—compensation income.

A "qualified employee" who receives stock from an eligible employer on the exercise of a stock option or in settlement of a restricted stock unit (RSU) can elect under Code Sec. 83(i) to defer the inclusion of income from the stock for up to five years from the date that the employee's rights in the stock are transferable or aren't subject to a substantial risk of forfeiture. The election applies only for income tax purposes; FICA and FUTA taxes are not affected. (Code Sec. 83(i))[6]

A qualified employee is an employee who isn't (1) a 1% owner under Code Sec. 416(i)(1)(B)(ii) at any time during the current or preceding 10 calendar years; (2) a current or former CEO, CFO, or an individual acting in either capacity; (3) an individual who bears a relationship described in Code Sec. 318(a)(1) to an individual in (2); or (4) an individual who is, or was for any of the 10 preceding tax years, one of the corporation's four highest compensated officers. (Code Sec. 83(i)(3)(B)) In addition, the employee must agree, in the Code Sec. 83(i) election, to meet the requirements determined by IRS to ensure that the employer correctly withholds income tax on the qualified stock. (Code Sec. 83(i)(3)(A))[7]

A corporation is an eligible corporation for a calendar year if none of its stock is readily tradable on an established securities market during any preceding calendar year, and it has a written plan under which a least 80% of U.S. employees employed at any time during that year are granted stock options or RSUs. (Code Sec. 83(i)(2)(C))[8]

The election is made in a manner similar to an Code Sec. 83(b) election (¶1217). The employee files the election with IRS and provides a copy to the employer. The election must be made no later than 30 days after the first time the employee's right to the stock is substantially vested or is transferable, whichever occurs earlier. (Code Sec. 83(i)(4))[9]

Corporations must notify employees who receive qualified stock of their right to make a Code Sec. 83(i) election and are subject to penalty for failure to provide the notice. (Code Sec. 83(i)(6), Code Sec. 6652(p))[10]

1. ¶H-2541
2. ¶M-3503
3. ¶I-1020
4. ¶H-2542 *et seq.*
5. ¶H-2545

6. ¶H-2900 *et seq.*
7. ¶H-2902
8. ¶H-2904
9. ¶H-2907
10. ¶H-2906, V-1989

¶ 1219 Nonstatutory stock options; readily ascertainable FMV—compensation income.

Under Code Sec. 83, an option—other than an option under an employee stock purchase plan (see ¶1220) or an incentive stock option (ISO, see ¶1221)—that is granted in connection with the performance of services, to buy stock at a bargain, results in compensation income to the employee (or independent contractor) grantee. (Code Sec. 83) If the option has a readily ascertainable fair market value (FMV) at grant, it's subject to the restricted property rules of Code Sec. 83 (¶1216 *et seq.*) when the option is granted. (Code Sec. 83; Reg § 1.83-7(a))[11]

An option "ordinarily" has a readily ascertainable FMV only if it (or a substantially identical option) is actively traded on an established market. If not so traded, it has value only if certain conditions specified in the regs exist. (Reg § 1.83-7(b))[12]

If the option doesn't have a readily ascertainable FMV when granted, the employee doesn't realize compensation until the optioned property is transferred at exercise. The amount of compensation is the FMV of the property at transfer less any amount paid for the property. (Reg § 1.83-7(a))[13] (For the employer's compensation deduction, see ¶1524.)

The above treatment for nonstatutory options without a readily ascertainable FMV doesn't apply where the option is transferred before exercise to a "related person." (Reg § 1.83-7(a))[14]

Under an exception, the exercise of an option is treated as the grant of another option, instead of a transfer of shares, where the amount paid for the exercise is a debt secured by the shares on which there's no personal liability. (Reg § 1.83-3(a)(2)) However, this exception doesn't apply simply because options are exercised through a margin loan, and income will be realized on the exercise of options without a readily ascertainable FMV.[15]

¶ 1220 Employee stock purchase plan (ESPP) options—compensation income.

ESPP options are options issued to employees under an employer plan to buy stock in the employer. Under Code Sec. 423, the employee pays no tax on the option or the stock until the stock is disposed of. If the option price at least equals the stock's fair market value (FMV) at grant, gain is capital gain. But gain is ordinary compensation income (to the extent of the spread between option price and FMV of stock when option is exercised) if the stock is sold within two years after the option was granted or within one year after its exercise. (Code Sec. 423(a), Code Sec. 423(c); Reg § 1.423-1, Reg § 1.423-2)[16]

If the option price is less than 100% (but at least 85%) of the stock's FMV at grant, and the above holding period is met, the amount treated as ordinary income (rather than capital gain) is the *lesser* of: (1) the FMV of the stock when the option was granted, minus the option price, or (2) the excess of the FMV at the time of disposition or optionee's death over the amount paid for the share under the option. (Code Sec. 423(c); Reg § 1.423-2(k))[17]

An executive-branch federal employee (or spouse or dependent child) who acquired stock through the exercise of an ESPP option (or ISO, see ¶1221) and sells the stock in order to comply with Code Sec. 1043 federal conflict-of-interest requirements is deemed to satisfy the Code Sec. 423(a)(1) (or Code Sec. 422(a)(1)) holding period requirement. (Code Sec. 421(d))[18]

11. ¶s H-2853, H-2857
12. ¶H-2872
13. ¶H-2861
14. ¶H-2864.1

15. ¶H-2508.1 *et seq.*
16. ¶H-2952 *et seq.*
17. ¶H-2953
18. ¶I-3808

The plan must be nondiscriminatory, i.e., available to all employees (with certain exceptions). (Code Sec. 423(b)(4))[19]

¶ 1221 Incentive stock options (ISOs); disqualifying dispositions—compensation income.

An ISO is granted to an employee by an employer corporation (or its parent or sub) to buy stock or ownership interests in one of those corporations (a term that takes in S corporations, foreign corporations, and limited liability companies treated as corporations for federal tax purposes). (Reg § 1.421-1(d)(3), Reg § 1.421-1(i)(1)) Under Code Sec. 421(a), there are no regular income tax consequences when an ISO is granted or exercised; the employee has capital gain when the stock is sold at a gain. (Code Sec. 421(a))[20] To qualify, an ISO must meet various requirements. (Code Sec. 422(b))[21]

Stock acquired through the exercise of an ISO generally can't be disposed of within two years after the option is granted or one year after the stock is transferred to the employee. (Code Sec. 422(a)(1)) Also, for the entire time from the date an ISO is granted until three months (one year in case of total and permanent disability) before its exercise, the option holder must be an employee of the option grantor (or its parent or sub or certain successor corporations). (Code Sec. 422(a)(2), Code Sec. 422(c)(6))[22] For special holding-period rules for executive-branch federal employees who acquire stock through the exercise of an ISO and who sell the stock to comply with Code Sec. 1043 federal conflict-of-interest requirements, see ¶1220.

If there's a disqualifying disposition of a share of stock, Code Sec. 421 doesn't apply to the transfer of the share. Instead, the exercise of the option is governed by Code Sec. 83 and its regs. Thus, in the tax year in which the disqualifying disposition occurs, the individual recognizes compensation income (and gets a basis increase) equal to the FMV of the stock on the date the stock is transferred, less the exercise price (determined without reduction for any brokerage fees or other disposition costs). (Reg § 1.421-2(b)) If the disqualifying disposition would trigger an allowable loss (e.g., not a sale to a related taxpayer), then the amount includible in the employee's income (and deductible by the employer, see ¶1524) as a result of that disqualifying disposition can't be more than the amount realized on the sale, minus the employee's adjusted basis in the stock. (Code Sec. 422(c)(2); Reg § 1.422-1(b)(2)(i))[23]

🅡ⓘⓐ*caution:* For alternative minimum tax treatment, see ¶3206.

¶ 1222 Sale or cancellation of employment contract—compensation income.

Proceeds from an employee's sale of rights under an employment contract to be performed are ordinary income. The same is true of amounts received from an employer in cancellation of an employment contract.[24]

¶ 1223 Members of Armed Forces—taxability of pay; exclusion from income of qualified military benefits; military housing allowance; combat/hazardous duty pay.

The pay of Armed Forces members is taxable (Reg § 1.61-2(a)(1)), with exceptions.[25]

Under Code Sec. 134(b), gross income doesn't include any "qualified military benefit,"

---

19. ¶H-2972
20. ¶H-2750
21. ¶H-2767
22. ¶H-2795 *et seq.*

23. ¶H-2799
24. ¶H-1048 *et seq.*
25. ¶H-3101 *et seq.*

which is any allowance or in-kind benefit (other than personal use of an automobile) received by a member or former member of the uniformed services of the U.S., or a dependent, and which was excludable from gross income on Sept. 9, '86 under any provision of law, reg or administrative practice (other than the Code) in effect on that date. (Code Sec. 134(b)) It includes any bonus payment made by a state or political subdivision to any member or former member of the U.S. uniformed services, or a dependent, because of service in a combat zone. (Code Sec. 134(b)(6)) Excludable allowances include (within certain limitations) veteran's benefits (¶1224), medical benefits, disability benefits, dependent care assistance program benefits, professional education, moving and storage, group-term life insurance, survivor and retirement protection plan premiums, subsistence, uniform, housing, overseas cost-of-living, evacuation, family separation allowances, death gratuities, interment allowance, various travel allowances and dependent benefits.[26] Specifically, dislocation allowances, temporary lodging allowances and expenses and move-in housing allowances provided in connection with permanent changes of station are excludible from income. (Reg § 1.61-2(b)(2))[27] For treatment of retirement pay, see ¶1284. A "qualified military base realignment and closure" fringe benefit is excluded and isn't subject to FICA. (Code Sec. 132(a)(8))[28]

The recipient of a tax-free military housing allowance isn't thereby prevented from deducting mortgage interest or real estate taxes on a personal residence. (Code Sec. 265(a)(6)(A))[29]

The Code also excludes combat-zone (and qualified hazardous duty) compensation (limited, for commissioned officers, to the maximum enlisted amount). (Code Sec. 112; Reg § 1.112-1) To date, the Afghanistan area, the Kosovo area, and the Arabian Peninsula have been designated as combat zones. Combat zone tax benefits have been designated by Congress for the Sinai Peninsula of Egypt under certain circumstances. Though the former Yugoslavia is no longer treated as a combat zone, certain benefits may still be available to those who served in that area at that time. (IRS Pub No. 3)[30]

For various deadline extensions for a member of the Armed Forces serving in a designated "combat zone," see ¶4719. For tax relief for military and civilian employees of the U.S. dying in combat or terrorist attacks, see ¶4715.

¶ 1224   VA and state benefits to veterans; amounts received under work therapy program—compensation income.

Benefits under any law, regulation, or practice in effect on Sept. 9, '86 and administered by the Department of Veterans' Affairs are excludable from the recipient's gross income (Code Sec. 140(a)(3)), including interest earned on dividends left on deposit with the VA. Benefits include amounts received under a VA-administered work therapy program.[31] State bonuses to veterans for service rendered to the U.S. are also exempt.[32]

¶ 1225   Government employees' compensation is taxable; payments under the Civil Service Retirement System—compensation income.

Federal, state and municipal employees, including federal judges, are taxable on their salary, wages and other compensation under Code Sec. 61 the same as other employees.[33] Payments under the Civil Service Retirement System are taxed like annuities, see ¶1352 et seq.[34] For relief for U.S. military and civilian employees dying in combat or terrorist

26. ¶H-3102
27. ¶H-3103
28. ¶H-3104
29. ¶K-9009
30. ¶H-3106 et seq.

31. ¶H-3128
32. ¶H-3129
33. ¶H-3130
34. ¶J-5052

attacks, see ¶4715.

¶ 1226   Members of clergy—taxability of salaries, fees, and offerings; exclusion of rental/parsonage allowance—compensation income.

Members of the clergy are taxable on the salaries and fees they receive, and on any offerings they receive for marriages, funerals, masses, etc., *but not* on offerings made to the religious institution. (Reg § 1.61-2(a))[35]

Under Code Sec. 107, a current or retired member of the clergy who is a "minister of the gospel"[36] can exclude:

. . . the rental value of a home (parsonage allowance), including utilities, furnished to the clergyperson as part of compensation; (Code Sec. 107(1); Reg § 1.107-1(a)) or

. . . the rental allowance (parsonage allowance) paid to the clergyperson as compensation, to the extent it's used in the year received to rent or provide a home(s) and to the extent it doesn't exceed the fair rental value of the home, including furnishings and appurtenances such as a garage, plus the cost of utilities. (Code Sec. 107(2)) The employer church or organization must designate the payment as a rental allowance before the payment is made. (Reg § 1.107-1(b))[37] One district court has found parsonage allowances to be unconstitutional.[38]

The rental allowance exclusion doesn't prevent a minister from deducting mortgage interest or real estate taxes on a personal residence. (Code Sec. 265(a)(6)(B))[39]

¶ 1227   Compensation of minors—compensation income.

The income of a minor from compensation earned or received in respect of the performance of services is income to the minor, even if received by the parent. (Code Sec. 73(a))[40] For the "kiddie tax" imposed on certain children's net unearned income, see ¶3128 *et seq.*

¶ 1228   Fringe Benefits—Benefits Received by Employee in Connection with Performance of Services. ■■■■■■■■■■

Unless specifically excluded (¶1241), fringe benefits received by an employee in connection with the performance of services are taxable compensation. (Reg § 1.61-21(a)(3))[41]

Under Code Sec. 61, the benefit is includible in the gross income of the person performing the services, even if it's furnished to someone else. (Code Sec. 61(a)(1); Reg § 1.61-21(a)(4))[42] For special valuation rules for employer-provided travel, transportation, and vehicles, see ¶1230 *et seq.* For excludable fringe benefits, see ¶1241 *et seq.*

¶ 1229   Valuation of taxable fringe benefits—general rule; special valuation rule; amount included in gross income; FMV of fringe benefit.

An employee who is taxed on a fringe benefit (¶1228) must include in gross income under Code Sec. 61 the fair market value (FMV) of the benefit minus: (1) any payment for the benefit, and (2) any amount specifically excluded by a Code provision. (Reg § 1.61-21(b)(1))[43] The FMV of a fringe benefit generally is the amount that an individual would have to pay for the particular benefit in an arm's-length transaction. (Reg § 1.61-

35. ¶H-3151
36. ¶H-3163
37. ¶H-3153 *et seq.*
38. ¶H-3153
39. ¶H-3160

40. ¶H-3180 *et seq.*
41. ¶H-1051
42. ¶H-1051, ¶H-1053
43. ¶H-1055

21(b)(2))[44]

Unless a special valuation rule (¶1231) applies, an employer-provided vehicle is valued at the comparable lease cost (¶1232) (Reg § 1.61-21(b)(4)),[45] and flights on employer-provided aircraft at comparable charter cost. (Reg § 1.61-21(b)(6), Reg § 1.61-21(b)(7))[46]

Chauffeur services are valued separately from vehicle availability, at comparable arm's-length transaction costs or by reference to the chauffeur's compensation (including any nontaxable lodging, see ¶1267). (Reg § 1.61-21(b)(5))[47]

¶ 1230 Transportation furnished because of unsafe conditions—value of fringe benefits.

Transportation or reimbursement for it (e.g., cab fare) furnished by an employer under a written policy solely because of unsafe conditions for an employee commuting is valued at $1.50 per one-way commute (i.e., from home to work, or work to home) for each qualifying employee. (Reg § 1.61-21(k)(3))[48]

¶ 1231 Special valuation rules for fringe benefits, such as autos, other vehicles, air flights.

To determine the amount of income to be included under Code Sec. 61, special valuation rules may be used under certain circumstances for certain commonly provided fringe benefits (e.g., the use of employer-provided automobiles generally,[49] the commuting-value method of valuation (¶1236),[50] flights on employer-provided airplanes,[1] and free or discounted flights on commercial airlines.[2] (Reg § 1.61-21(b), Reg § 1.61-21(c)(1), Reg § 1.61-21(c)(3)) Where the special rules aren't used, either by choice or because they aren't permitted, or where they're improperly applied, the value of the fringe benefit must be determined under the general valuation principles at ¶1229. (Reg § 1.61-21(c)(5))[3]

An employee can't use a special valuation rule to value a fringe benefit unless the employer uses the same rule to value it. (Reg § 1.61-21(c)(2))[4]

¶ 1232 Annual lease value method for employer-provided autos using IRS table; fleet-average value method—value of fringe benefits.

To compute an auto's annual lease value using the below table, first determine fair market value (FMV) as of the first date it's made available to *any* employee for personal use. Under safe harbor rules, where the auto is bought at arm's length by the employer, the FMV is the cost, including sales tax, title fees and other purchase expenses. Where leased, it's the suggested retail price less 8%, the retail value as reported in a nationally recognized publication that regularly reports such values (Reg § 1.61-21(d)(5)), or the manufacturer's invoice price plus 4%.[5] Then, find the dollar range in column (1) of the table below that includes the auto's FMV. The corresponding amount in column (2) is its annual lease value. (Reg § 1.61-21(d)(2)(iii))[6]

---

44. ¶H-1056
45. ¶H-2232
46. ¶H-2302 *et seq.*
47. ¶H-2289 *et seq.*
48. ¶H-2201 *et seq.*
49. ¶H-2231 *et seq.*
50. ¶H-2282

1. ¶H-2301 *et seq.*
2. ¶H-2337 *et seq.*
3. ¶H-1057
4. ¶H-1060
5. ¶H-2240
6. ¶H-2238

Automobile fair market value (1)	Annual lease value (2)	Automobile fair market value (1)	Annual lease value (2)
$0 to 999	$600	22,000 to 22,999	6,100
1,000 to 1,999	850	23,000 to 23,999	6,350
2,000 to 2,999	1,100	24,000 to 24,999	6,600
3,000 to 3,999	1,350	25,000 to 25,999	6,850
4,000 to 4,999	1,600	26,000 to 27,999	7,250
5,000 to 5,999	1,850	28,000 to 29,999	7,750
6,000 to 6,999	2,100	30,000 to 31,999	8,250
7,000 to 7,999	2,350	32,000 to 33,999	8,750
8,000 to 8,999	2,600	34,000 to 35,999	9,250
9,000 to 9,999	2,850	36,000 to 37,999	9,750
10,000 to 10,999	3,100	38,000 to 39,999	10,250
11,000 to 11,999	3,350	40,000 to 41,999	10,750
12,000 to 12,999	3,600	42,000 to 43,999	11,250
13,000 to 13,999	3,850	44,000 to 45,999	11,750
14,000 to 14,999	4,100	46,000 to 47,999	12,250
15,000 to 15,999	4,350	48,000 to 49,999	12,750
16,000 to 16,999	4,600	50,000 to 51,999	13,250
17,000 to 17,999	4,850	52,000 to 53,999	13,750
18,000 to 18,999	5,100	54,000 to 55,999	14,250
19,000 to 19,999	5,350	56,000 to 57,999	14,750
20,000 to 20,999	5,600	58,000 to 59,999	15,250
21,000 to 21,999	5,850		

For autos with a FMV in excess of $59,999, the annual lease value equals (.25 × auto FMV) + $500.[7]

Illustration: On Jan. 1, of Year 1, X Co. provides a car worth $31,000 free to its employee E. None of the fringe benefit exclusions apply. The annual lease value (see chart above) is $8,250. This is the value of E's benefit for Year 1. E must include $8,250 in income.

This method takes into account the value of employer-provided insurance and maintenance but not fuel provided to the employee by the employer, whether in kind, by a reimbursement arrangement, or by charging the cost of the fuel directly to the employer. If an employer provides fuel to an employee by any of those means in connection with the employee's use of an auto, the fuel's fair market value (FMV) is an additional fringe benefit that must be included in the employee's gross income, absent an exclusion. Fuel provided in kind by an employer may be valued at FMV based on all the facts and circumstances. Or, it may be valued at 5.5¢ per mile for all miles driven by the employee in the U.S., U.S. possessions and territories, Canada, or Mexico. If reimbursed by or charged to the employer at FMV, fuel is generally valued at its actual reimbursed or charged amount. (Reg § 1.61-21(d)(3))[8]

The annual lease values computed above are based on an assumed 4-year lease term (beginning the first date this method is used and ending on Dec. 31 of the following fourth full calendar year). The annual lease value for each next 4-year period is based on the FMV on the Jan. 1 after the preceding period, using the lease valuation table. (Reg § 1.61-21(d)(2)(iv))[9]

Fleet-average value method. Subject to certain restrictions, an employer with a fleet of 20 or more autos may determine the annual lease value of each auto in the fleet as if its

7. ¶s H-2238, H-2239
8. ¶H-2253

9. ¶H-2246

FMV were equal to the "fleet-average value." (Reg § 1.61-21(d)(5)) The maximum value of an employer-provided auto (including a van or truck) first made available to an employee for personal use in calendar year 2022 for which the fleet-average valuation rule may apply is $56,100 ($51,100 for 2021).[10]

¶ 1233 Prorated annual lease value for employer-provided autos—value of fringe benefits.

Where an employer-provided auto is continuously available to the employee for periods of 30 or more days, but less than an entire calendar year, the value of the availability of the auto is the prorated annual lease value, computed by multiplying the annual lease value (¶1232) by a fraction where the numerator is the number of days of availability and the denominator is 365. (Reg § 1.61-21(d)(4))[11]

¶ 1234 Daily lease value for employer-provided autos—value of fringe benefits.

Where an employer-provided auto is continuously available to the employee for at least one but less than 30 days, the value of the use of the auto is its daily lease value, calculated by multiplying the auto's annual lease value (¶1232) by a fraction where the numerator is four times the number of days of the auto's availability and the denominator is 365. A 30-day period may be used even if availability is less than 30 days if this produces a lower valuation. (Reg § 1.61-21(d)(4))[12]

¶ 1235 Cents-per-mile valuation method for value of employer-provided auto—value of fringe benefits.

Under the cents-per-mile valuation method, the value of an employer-provided auto equals the total number of miles the employee drove it for personal purposes in the tax year times the optional standard mileage rate (58.5¢ per mile for expenses paid or incurred from Jan. 1, 2022 to June 30, 2022; 62.5¢ per mile after June 30, 2022; 56¢ for 2021), see ¶1553.[13] This method takes into account the value of insuring and maintaining the vehicle, and the value of fuel provided by the employer. If fuel isn't provided, the cents-per-mile rate may be reduced by no more than 5.5¢ per mile. (Reg § 1.61-21(e)(3))[14] The maximum value of an employer-provided car, van, or truck first made available to an employee for personal use in calendar year 2022 for which cents-per-mile valuation may be used is $56,100 ($51,100 for 2021).[15]

¶ 1236 Commuting value method for employer-provided use of vehicle—$1.50 per one-way commute—value of fringe benefits.

Under this method, the value of an employee's use of a vehicle for commuting purposes only is computed as $1.50 per one-way commute (e.g., from home to work, or work to home). If more than one employee commutes in a single vehicle, the commuting benefit is still $1.50 per one-way commute for each employee. (Reg § 1.61-21(f)(3))[16] Various requirements must be satisfied, including that the employee must be required to commute in the auto for bona-fide noncompensatory business reasons. The method can't be used for "control employees" (certain owner-employees, higher-paid employees, and directors) (Reg § 1.61-21(f)(1)), or to value the commuting use of any chauffeur-driven vehicle, except for the commuting use by the chauffeur. (Reg § 1.61-21(f)(2))[17]

10. ¶H-2260
11. ¶H-2243
12. ¶H-2245
13. ¶H-2268
14. ¶H-2277 *et seq.*
15. ¶H-2272
16. ¶H-2282
17. ¶H-2283

¶ 1237   Employer-provided air flights—value of fringe benefits.

Air flights provided by an employer for an employee's personal purposes are fringe benefits includible in the employee's gross income. (Reg § 1.61-21(a)(1))[18]

The value of an employee's flight on an employer-provided piloted aircraft is determined under the general valuation principles in Reg § 1.61-21(b)(6)(i).[19] Special valuation methods are also available to value noncommercial flights on employer-provided aircraft (¶1238 *et seq.*), and "space available" flights on commercial aircraft (¶1240). Use of a special method is optional. But if an employer uses either special rule, that rule generally must be used to value all flights taken by employees in a calendar year. (Reg § 1.61-21(g)(14)(i), Reg § 1.61-21(h)(5)(i))[20]

If an employee takes a trip on an employer-provided aircraft primarily for the employer's business, but the trip includes both personal and business flights, the value of the personal flights is a taxable fringe benefit. The value of the benefit equals the excess of the value of all the flights comprising the trip, over the value of the flights the employee would have taken if all travel had been for business. If the employee combines personal and business flights on a trip that's primarily personal, the amount includible is the value of the personal flights that would have been taken had there been only personal flights. The value of all these flights may be computed under the special valuation rules (¶1238 *et seq.*). (Reg § 1.61-21(g)(4))[21]

¶ 1238   SIFL formula for valuing employer-provided noncommercial flights—value of fringe benefits.

For a flight that may be valued using the special valuation rule for noncommercial employer-provided flights, value is determined by multiplying the "base aircraft valuation formula"—also known as the Standard Industry Fair Level (SIFL) formula (cents-per-mile rates that are revised semi-annually)—in effect at the time of the flight by the "aircraft multiple" (based on the takeoff weight of the plane) and adding the applicable "terminal charge." (Reg § 1.61-21(g)(5))[22]

¶ 1239   "Seating capacity" (zero inclusion) rule for noncommercial flights—value of fringe benefits.

The "seating capacity" rule is available for noncommercial flights on employer-provided aircraft where at least half of the aircraft's passenger seating capacity is occupied by employees whose flights are primarily for the employer's business (and whose flights are excludable as a working condition fringe, see ¶1244). In this situation, the includible value of the flight taken by the employee for personal purposes is zero. (Reg § 1.61-21(g)(12))[23]

¶ 1240   "Space-available" rule for commercial flights—value of fringe benefits.

If an employer provides an employee (as specially defined at Reg § 1.132-1(b)(1)) with a flight on a commercial aircraft for the employee's personal purposes, the flight is a taxable fringe benefit whose value must be included in the employee's gross income (¶1237). If the flight is a "space-available flight" on a commercial airline, its value for certain current or former airline employees may be computed under a special rule: 25% of the actual carrier's highest unrestricted coach fare for the flight taken. (Reg § 1.61-21(h)(1))[24]

---

18. ¶H-2301
19. ¶H-2302
20. ¶H-2335; ¶H-2340
21. ¶s H-2314, H-2315

22. ¶H-2304, ¶H-2307 *et seq.*
23. ¶H-2319
24. ¶H-2337

¶ 1241   Excludable fringe benefits, overview.

Under Code Sec. 132, a fringe benefit isn't included in gross income if it's excluded under a specific Code section (see below) (Code Sec. 61(a)), or qualifies as one of the following: (Code Sec. 132(a))[25]

. . . no-additional-cost service (¶1242);

. . . qualified employee discount (¶1243);

. . . working condition fringe (¶1244);

. . . de minimis fringe (¶1245);

. . . qualified transportation fringe (¶1246);

. . . qualified moving expense reimbursement for certain military personnel (¶1247);

. . . employer-provided retirement advice (¶1249).

For qualified military base realignment and closure fringe benefit, see ¶1223.

A fringe benefit that's expressly provided for in any other Code section can't be excluded from gross income under the Code Sec. 132 rules, except as a de minimis fringe or as a qualified moving expense reimbursement. (Code Sec. 132(l))[26] Fringe benefits excluded under a specific Code section include holiday and other gifts of nominal value (¶1211); certain stock options (¶1219); clergy member's home ("parsonage allowance," ¶1226); employee achievement awards (¶1250); on-premises athletic facilities (¶1251); adoption assistance (¶1253); educational assistance (¶2214); medical care coverage, including accident and health insurance (¶1254 *et seq.*); group-term life insurance (¶1262); meals and lodging (¶1267); qualified campus lodging (¶1268); cafeteria (flexible benefit) plans (¶1269); dependent care assistance programs (¶1270); scholarships (¶2215); and cost of living allowances to certain U.S. government employees (¶4610).[27]

¶ 1242   No-additional-cost services—excludible fringe benefits.

No-additional-cost services are excluded from an employee's gross income (see ¶1241). (Code Sec. 132(a)(1))[28] These are services provided by an employer to an employee for personal use by the employee—or the employee's spouse or dependent children—if:

(1) the services are ordinarily offered for sale to nonemployee customers in the ordinary course of the line of business in which the employee works,

(2) the employer incurs no substantial additional cost (including foregone revenue) in providing the services to the employee—computed without regard to any amounts paid by the employee for the services (Code Sec. 132(b)),[29] and

(3) special nondiscrimination rules are satisfied. (Code Sec. 132(j)(1))[30]

No-additional-cost services include services that would remain unused if the employees didn't use them, e.g., hotel accommodations, transportation by air, train, bus, subway or cruise line, and telephone services. (Reg § 1.132-2(a)(2))[31]

¶ 1243   Qualified employee discounts—excludible fringe benefits.

A qualified employee discount is excluded from an employee's gross income (see ¶1241). (Code Sec. 132(a)(2))[32] This is an "employee discount" allowed with respect to "qualified property or services" provided by an employer to an employee, the employee's spouse or

---

25. ¶H-1051
26. ¶H-1052
27. ¶H-1052
28. ¶H-1871

29. ¶H-1872
30. ¶H-1931 *et seq.*
31. ¶H-1872
32. ¶H-1901

dependent children, to the extent the discount doesn't exceed the limits described below. (Code Sec. 132(c)(1))[33]

An "employee discount" is the excess of: (a) the price at which property or services are offered by an employer for sale to nonemployee customers, over (b) the price at which the employer offers the same property or services to employees for use by those employees. (Code Sec. 132(c)(3))[34]

"Qualified property or services" means any property (other than real property, or personal property of a kind held for investment) or services that are offered for sale to nonemployee customers in the ordinary course of the employer's line of business in which the employee works. (Code Sec. 132(c)(4), Code Sec. 132(k))[35]

Limitations. The excludable amount of a qualified employee discount with respect to property is limited to the gross profit percentage of the price at which that property is offered by the employer to customers. (Code Sec. 132(c)(1)(A)) Gross profit percentage equals the aggregate sales price of the property sold by the employer to all customers, whether employees or nonemployees (Reg § 1.132-3(c)(1)(i)), over the aggregate cost of the property (Code Sec. 132(c)(2)(A)(i)), divided by the aggregate sales price. (Code Sec. 132(c)(2)(A)(ii))[36]

The excludable amount for discounted services is limited to 20% of the price at which the employer offers the service to nonemployees. (Code Sec. 132(c)(1)(B), Code Sec. 132(k))[37]

¶ 1244   Working condition fringes—excludible fringe benefits.

Working condition fringes are excluded from the employee's gross income (see ¶1241). (Code Sec. 132(a)(3))[38] A "working condition fringe" is any property or service provided to an employee by the employer to the extent the cost of the property or service would have been deductible by the employee under either Code Sec. 162 (as trade or business expenses) or Code Sec. 167 (as a depreciation expense) if the employee had paid for the property or service. (Code Sec. 132(d))[39] Examples include employer-paid business travel and the use of employer-provided vehicles for business purposes.[40]

Certain benefits qualify as working condition fringes only if special requirements are satisfied. These include the use of consumer goods manufactured for sale to nonemployee customers and provided to employees for product testing and evaluation outside the employer's work place (Reg § 1.132-5(n)(1));[41] the personal use of vehicles otherwise used in connection with the business of farming (Reg § 1.132-5(g));[42] job placement assistance;[43] employer-paid club dues (Reg § 1.132-5(s));[44] employer-paid expenses of a companion on a business trip (Reg § 1.132-5(t));[45] "qualified automobile demonstration use" by automobile salespersons (Code Sec. 132(j)(3); Reg § 1.132-5(o));[46] the use of employer-owned aircraft for business travel (Reg § 1.132-5(k));[47] certain forms of transportation and other employer-provided security measures provided because of bona fide business-oriented security concerns (Reg § 1.132-5(m));[48] the use of "qualified nonpersonal use vehicles" (Reg § 1.132-5(h));[49] and the use of a cell phone provided to an employee primarily for noncompensatory business reasons.[50]

33. ¶H-1902
34. ¶H-1904
35. ¶H-1903
36. ¶H-1909
37. ¶H-1914
38. ¶H-1701
39. ¶H-1701
40. ¶H-1701
41. ¶H-1712
42. ¶H-2370
43. ¶H-1711
44. ¶H-2153.1
45. ¶H-2153.2
46. ¶H-2364
47. ¶H-2351
48. ¶H-2373 *et seq.*
49. ¶H-2354
50. ¶H-1707.2

¶ 1245   De minimis fringe benefits—excludible fringe benefits.

De minimis fringe benefits are excluded from the recipient's gross income (see ¶1241). (Code Sec. 132(a)(4))[1] A de minimis fringe is any property or service whose value is so small that accounting for it is unreasonable or administratively impracticable, taking into account the frequency with which the employer provides similar fringe benefits to its employees. (Code Sec. 132(e)(1))[2]

Examples of de minimis fringes include occasional meals, supper money, or local transportation provided because of overtime work (Reg § 1.132-6(d)(2)); meals at employer-operated eating facilities (see below); transportation (e.g., taxi fare) where other available means of transportation are unsafe, in excess of value over $1.50 per each one-way commute (¶1230) (Reg § 1.132-6(d)(2)); occasional cocktail parties or picnics; traditional holiday gifts of property (not cash) with a low FMV; flowers, fruit, etc., provided under special circumstances, such as sickness or outstanding performance (Reg § 1.132-6(e)(1)); snacks; low-value clothing bearing the employer's name, which must be worn by the employee; electronically filing the employee's income tax return (but not paying someone to prepare the return); and an employee's personal use of a cell phone provided by the employer primarily for noncompensatory business reasons.[3]

No qualified transportation fringe benefit (¶1246) (including amounts in excess of the dollar limit) may be excluded as a de minimis fringe benefit. (Code Sec. 132(f)(7))[4] However, partners, more-than-2% S corporation shareholders and independent contractors (but not employees) can exclude transit passes, tokens and fare cards if not in excess of $21 per month.[5]

Meals at employer-operated eating facilities are de minimis fringes if the facility's annual revenues normally equal or exceed its direct operating costs and certain nondiscrimination rules are met. Employees who are entitled (under the rules at ¶1267) to exclude the value of a meal provided at the facility are treated as having paid an amount for the meal equal to the direct operating costs of the facility attributable to the meal. (Code Sec. 132(e)(2); Reg § 1.132-7(a)(2), Reg § 1.132-7(c))[6] Direct operating costs are the costs of the food and beverages served and the labor for related services performed primarily on the facility's premises. (Reg § 1.132-7(b)(1))[7]

¶ 1246   Qualified transportation fringe benefits—excludible fringe benefits.

An employee (other than a self-employed person) may exclude from income qualified transportation fringe benefits up to specified dollar amounts (below). (Code Sec. 132(a)(5), Code Sec. 132(f)(5)) These benefits include:

(1) Transportation in a commuter highway vehicle (van pool), if in connection with travel between the employee's residence and place of employment. A commuter highway vehicle has a seating capacity of six adults (excluding the driver) for which 80% of the mileage must be reasonably expected to be for employee commuting and to be for trips where the vehicle is at least 50% full, excluding the driver (known as the 80/50 rule). Different qualification and substantiation rules apply depending on whether the van pool arrangement is employer operated, employee operated, or privately or publicly operated.[8]

---

1. ¶H-1800 *et seq.*
2. ¶H-1802
3. ¶H-1802 *et seq.*
4. ¶H-2205

5. ¶H-1806; ¶H-2207; ¶H-2208
6. ¶H-1821
7. ¶H-1823
8. ¶H-2210

(2) Transit passes for use on a mass transit facility (e.g., rail, bus or ferry) or a commuter highway vehicle.[9]

(3) Qualified parking at or near the employer's business premises or a location from which the employee commutes to work by mass transit or hired commuter vehicle. Any parking at or near the employee's residence isn't qualified parking. (Code Sec. 132(f)(1), Code Sec. 132(f)(5); Reg § 1.132-9(b))[10]

For 2023, an employee can exclude up to $300 a month of qualified parking ($280 a month for 2022), and up to an additional $300 a month ($280 a month for 2022) for the combined value of transit passes and transportation in a commuter highway vehicle. (Code Sec. 132(f)(2))[11]

Cash reimbursements (but *not* cash advances) for transit passes are excludable where vouchers, etc. (which may be exchanged only for transit passes) aren't readily available for direct distribution by the employer to the employee. (Code Sec. 132(f)(3); Reg § 1.132-9(b)) Employers can't provide qualified transportation fringe benefits in the form of cash reimbursements in areas where a terminal-restricted debit card (one that can be used at points of sale where only transit fares may be purchased) is readily available.[12] IRS provided detailed guidance on the use of smartcards, debit or credit cards, and other electronic media to provide qualified transportation fringe benefits. (Rev Rul 2014-32, 2014-50 IRB 917)[13]

No amount is included in an employee's gross income solely because a choice is offered between any qualified transportation fringe and otherwise includible compensation. (Code Sec. 132(f)(4)) But if cash is elected instead of a qualified transportation fringe, the employee is taxed.[14] If fringes are chosen rather than cash, the employee isn't taxed on any exchanged cash if requirements are met. (Reg § 1.132-9(b))[15]

The qualified transportation fringe exclusion doesn't apply to any arrangement that results in the reimbursement of an expense the employee hasn't actually incurred, e.g., where the employee is reimbursed for an item paid for through a tax-free salary reduction.[16]

An employee can't receive a cash refund for a balance remaining on the employee's transit pass after the employee ceased to be a participant in the employer's qualified transportation fringe benefit plan because the employee was no longer commuting to work due to the coronavirus pandemic. (Information Letter 2020-0031).[17]

Partners, 2% S corporation shareholders and independent contractors can't exclude qualified transportation fringes. (Code Sec. 132(f)(5)(E))[18]

¶ 1247 Qualified moving expense reimbursement for armed forces—excludible fringe benefits.

For tax years beginning before Jan. 1, 2026, qualified moving expense reimbursements are excluded from gross income only for members of the U.S. Armed Forces on active duty who move pursuant to a military order and incident to a permanent change of station. (Code Sec. 132(a)(6))[19]

A qualified moving expense reimbursement is any amount received (directly or indirectly) from an employer as a payment of (or reimbursement for) moving expenses that

9. ¶H-2212 *et seq.*
10. ¶H-2213
11. ¶H-2217
12. ¶H-2212; ¶H-2212.1; ¶H-2216
13. ¶H-2216A
14. ¶H-2216.1

15. ¶H-2216.1
16. ¶H-2216
17. ¶H-2216.6
18. ¶H-2206
19. ¶H-1971

would have been deductible had the taxpayer paid them directly (for employee's moving expense deduction, see ¶1626 *et seq.*). Expenses aren't excludable if the taxpayer actually deducted them in an earlier year. (Code Sec. 132(g)) To qualify for the exclusion, the moving expense reimbursement must be made under an accountable plan.[20] Otherwise an employer's payment or reimbursement is income to the employee. (Code Sec. 82)[21] The employer reports moving expense reimbursements (but not qualifying payments to third parties or qualifying services furnished in kind) to the employee on Form W-2.[22]

¶ 1248   Reimbursement of employee in connection with sale of residence—fringe benefits.

An employer's reimbursement for an employee's loss on sale of the employee's home is income to the employee.[23] However, if the employer buys the employee's home at its fair market value (FMV), the employee has no income other than gain on the sale. Where, as an alternative to reimbursing an employee for the loss, the employer buys the home for more than its FMV, that *excess* is taxable to the employee.[24]

¶ 1249   Employer-provided retirement advice—excludible fringe benefits.

Qualified retirement planning services are excluded from the income of the employee receiving the services. (Code Sec. 132(a)(7)) These are any retirement planning services provided to an employee by an employer maintaining a qualified employer plan (as defined in Code Sec. 219(g)(5)). (Code Sec. 132(m))[25]

¶ 1250   Employee achievement awards—limits on exclusion; qualified plan awards—fringe benefits.

Under Code Sec. 74, employee achievement awards are excludable only to the extent the employer can deduct the cost of the award—generally limited to $400 for any one employee, or $1,600 for a "qualified plan award," see ¶1573. (Code Sec. 74(c)(2))[26]

observation: "Employee achievement awards" don't include cash, cash equivalents, gift cards, gift coupons, gift certificates, vacations, meals, lodging, tickets to theater or sporting events, stocks, bonds, other securities, and other similar items. (Code Sec. 274(j)(3)(A)(ii)(I)) See ¶1573.

¶ 1251   On-premises athletic facilities—excludable fringe benefits.

The value of an on-premises athletic facility provided by an employer is excluded from an employee's gross income. (Code Sec. 132(j)(4)(A))[27]

¶ 1252   Employer payment of employee's personal debts, expenses, or taxes—income and exclusions.

Where an employer pays the debts or personal expenses of an employee, or reimburses the employee's payment, the employee must include the payment or reimbursement in income under Code Sec. 61.[28] For medical expenses, see ¶1254.

An employer's payment of an employee's income taxes (federal or state) or other taxes is income to the employee. Pyramiding of income, and of tax, results where the employer

20. ¶H-1971
21. ¶H-4418
22. ¶S-3170
23. ¶H-2161
24. ¶H-2162

25. ¶H-1980 *et seq.*
26. ¶L-2312 *et seq.*
27. ¶H-1951
28. ¶H-2151

agrees to pay all the employee's tax. (Reg § 1.61-14)[29]

¶ 1253 Exclusion of employer-provided adoption assistance—Form 8839; qualified adoption expenses; AGI-based phaseout—exclusions from income.

Under Code Sec. 137, amounts paid or expenses incurred under an employer's adoption assistance program for an employee's qualified adoption expenses (¶2348) are excluded from the employee's gross income. For the adoption of a child with special needs, the exclusion applies regardless of whether the employee actually has qualified adoption expenses. (Code Sec. 137(a), Code Sec. 137(b), Code Sec. 137(f))[30]

The maximum exclusion is $15,950 for 2023 ($14,890 in 2022) per child, for both non-special-needs and special-needs adoptions. (Code Sec. 137(a)(2))[31]

For 2023, the excludable amount is phased out for taxpayers with modified adjusted gross income (MAGI—adjusted gross income, as specially computed) over $239,230 ($223,410 for 2022), and is fully eliminated when MAGI reaches $279,230 ($263,410 in 2022). (Code Sec. 137(b)(2), Code Sec. 137(f)) To compute the excluded employer-provided adoption benefits, use Form 8839.[32]

Amounts are excludable in the year in which the employer pays for qualified adoption expenses of an eligible child who is a U.S. citizen or resident when the adoption commenced. If the eligible child isn't a U.S. citizen or resident, the exclusion is available only for adoptions that become final, and only in the year that they're finalized. Where expenses of a foreign eligible child are paid in a year before the adoption becomes final, the employee includes the employer's assistance in income for that year, and claims the otherwise available exclusion in the year the adoption becomes final. A taxpayer may claim both an adoption expense credit (see ¶2348) and an exclusion for the adoption of an eligible child, but can't claim a credit and an exclusion for the same expense.[33]

¶ 1254 Exclusion of employee's medical expenses and insurance premiums reimbursed or insured by employer—exclusions from income.

Under Code Sec. 105, employees exclude from gross income reimbursements from an employer, directly or indirectly, for expenses for the medical care of self, spouse, and dependents. The exclusion also applies to any child of an employee who hasn't attained age 27 as of the end of the year. (Code Sec. 105(b)) However, reimbursement is includible in the employee's income to the extent it exceeds medical expenses or is attributable to medical expense deductions taken in a previous year. (Code Sec. 105(b); Reg § 1.105-2)[34]

An employee also excludes the cost (i.e., premiums paid) of employer-provided *coverage* under an accident or health plan for the employee; the employee's spouse (partners in registered domestic partnerships, civil unions, or other similar formal relationships that aren't marriages under state law aren't spouses for federal tax purposes); the employee's dependents; and the employee's children who haven't reached age 27 as of the end of the employee's tax year. (Code Sec. 106)[35] But insurance premiums paid for partners and more-than-2% S corporation shareholders (who are treated as partners) aren't excludable.[36]

Highly compensated individuals (as defined in Code Sec. 105(h)(5)) who benefit from an employer's "self-insured" medical reimbursement plan that discriminates in their favor must include "excess reimbursements" (reimbursements for benefits not available to other

---

29. ¶H-2157
30. ¶H-1450 et seq.
31. ¶H-1451
32. ¶H-1453
33. ¶H-1452 , ¶H-1457
34. ¶H-1110 *et seq.*
35. ¶H-1102
36. ¶H-1126

plan participants) in income. (Code Sec. 105(h))[37]

¶ 1255 Employer contributions to Archer medical savings account (Archer MSA)—exclusions from income.

Under Code Sec. 106(b)(1), small-employer contributions to an employee's Archer MSA are treated as excludable employer-provided coverage for medical expenses under an accident or health plan (¶1254) to the extent the amounts don't exceed the applicable statutory limits (see ¶1527). (Code Sec. 106(b)(1))[38] Generally, small employers are those that employed on average no more than 50 employees during either of the two preceding years. An employer that grows past the 50-employee limit in a succeeding year may continue MSA contributions until the year after the first year in which it has more than 200 employees. (Code Sec. 220(c)(4))[39] For treatment of Archer MSA distributions, see ¶1371. An Archer MSA must be established outside a cafeteria plan, because a cafeteria plan (¶1269) may not provide for contributions to an Archer MSA. (Prop Reg. § 1.125-1(q)(1)(ix) ["Taxpayers may rely," Prop Regs 8/6/2007])[40]

¶ 1256 Medicare Advantage Medical Savings Accounts (MSAs); tax treatment of contributions and distributions.

Individuals eligible for Medicare can choose either the traditional Medicare program or a Medicare Advantage MSA, which is an MSA as defined in Code Sec. 220(d) (¶1527), but which is designated as a Medicare Advantage MSA by the individual account holder. (Code Sec. 138(b)(1)) A Medicare Advantage MSA is a tax-exempt trust (or a custodial account), similar to an IRA, created exclusively to pay qualified medical expenses of the account holder. The Health and Human Services Dept. makes contributions directly to the Medicare Advantage MSA designated by the account holder (the only other type of allowed contribution is a trustee-to-trustee transfer from another Medicare Advantage MSA). Contributions and earnings on amounts held in a Medicare Advantage MSA aren't currently includible in income. (Code Sec. 138(a))

Distributions from a Medicare Advantage MSA for purposes other than qualified medical expenses of the account holder are included in income and are subject to a 50% penalty (except if made because of the account holder's disability or death). (Code Sec. 138(c)(2))[41] The 15% penalty on the amount includible in gross income for non-qualified distributions from regular Archer MSAs (¶1371) doesn't apply to any payment or distribution from a Medicare Advantage MSA. (Code Sec. 138(c)(2)(A)) Distributions that are excludable from gross income can't be taken as a medical expense deduction.[42]

¶ 1257 Employer contributions to health savings accounts (HSAs)—exclusions.

Employer contributions to an employee's HSA are treated as employer-provided coverage for medical expenses under an accident or health plan (¶1254) to the extent they don't exceed the statutory limits (see ¶1528) applicable to the employee for the tax year, and are deductible by the employer in the year they're paid. (Code Sec. 106(d)(2)) Employer contributions to an HSA on behalf of an eligible individual are excludable from income.[43] The contributions must be reported on the employee's Form W-2.[44] For HSA distributions, see ¶1372. If an employer contributes amounts to an employee's HSA that exceed the maximum annual contribution allowed (see ¶1528) due to an error, the employer may request that the financial institution return the excess to it. If the employer doesn't recover the

37. ¶H-1138 et seq.
38. ¶H-1101.1 et seq.
39. ¶s H-1333, H-1333.1
40. ¶H-2416

41. ¶H-1348.4
42. ¶H-1348
43. ¶H-1101.5
44. ¶S-3152

excess, though, it must be included on the employee's Form W-2 as gross income. [45]

There's no constructive receipt of income solely because the employee may choose between employer contributions to an HSA and to another health plan. (Code Sec. 106(d)(2); Code Sec. 106(b)(2)) Contributions may be made to an HSA through a cafeteria plan (see ¶1269). [46]

¶ 1258 Employer's payments for employee's loss of limb, disfigurement, etc.— exclusions from income.

Under Code Sec. 105(c), amounts received under an employer plan as payment for permanent loss or loss of use of a member or function of the body, or permanent disfigurement, of the employee—or the employee's spouse or dependent—are tax-free, but only if the payment is based on the nature of the injury without regard to the period the employee is absent from work. (Code Sec. 105(c)) [47]

¶ 1259 Worker's compensation; exclusion of amounts received for personal injuries or sickness.

Under Code Sec. 104(a)(1), amounts received under a worker's compensation act or similar law for personal injuries or sickness are excludable from the employee's (or survivor's) income. This rule doesn't apply to the extent payments are determined by reference to the employee's age or length of service or prior contributions, even if retirement is occasioned by occupational injury. (Reg § 1.104-1(b)) Worker's compensation is includible in income to the extent it's attributable to medical expense deductions taken in an earlier year. (Code Sec. 104(a)(1); Reg § 1.104-1(b)) [48]

¶ 1260 Annuities paid to survivors of public safety officers killed in line of duty—exclusions from income.

Under Code Sec. 101(h), survivor annuity benefits paid on account of the death of a public safety officer (including law enforcement officers, firefighters, rescue squad workers and ambulance crew members) killed in the line of duty are excluded: (1) if provided under a governmental plan that meets the requirements of Code Sec. 401(a) to the officer's spouse, former spouse, or child; and (2) to the extent attributable to the officer's service as a public safety officer. (Code Sec. 101(h)(1)) The exclusion doesn't apply under certain circumstances (e.g., if the death was caused by the officer's intentional misconduct). (Code Sec. 101(h)(2)) [49]

¶ 1261 Employer-paid premiums on life insurance policies on employee's life— gross income and exclusions.

Except for group-term insurance, see ¶1262, premiums paid by an employer for policies on the life of an employee are taxable to the employee if the proceeds are payable to the employee's beneficiary, but not where the employer is the beneficiary. (Reg § 1.61-2(d)(2)(ii)) [50]

¶ 1262 Group-term life insurance premiums—exclusions from income.

Under Code Sec. 79(a), an employee isn't taxed on premiums paid by the employer on insurance covering the employee's life under a group-term life insurance policy to the

---

45. ¶H-1350.8D
46. ¶H-2423.9
47. ¶H-1201

48. ¶H-1351
49. ¶H-1650 *et seq.*
50. ¶H-1501 *et seq.*

extent the employee's total coverage provided by all employers doesn't exceed $50,000. If total coverage exceeds $50,000, the employee is taxed on the "cost" (¶1263) of coverage over $50,000 minus the amount paid by the employee. (Code Sec. 79(a))[1] For coverage of employee's spouse and dependents, see ¶1264.

An employee whose total coverage exceeds $50,000 for only part of the year includes the employer's payments for that part of the year's coverage, even if the average coverage for the year is under this ceiling. (Code Sec. 79(a))[2]

But a disabled terminated employee isn't taxable on group term coverage even if it exceeds $50,000. (Code Sec. 79(b)(1))[3] Retired employees are generally treated the same as other employees. (Code Sec. 79(e))[4]

The exclusion doesn't apply to any insurance protection in excess of the maximum allowed by state law for employee group insurance. (Reg § 1.79-1(e))[5]

The exclusion is available to a key employee only if the plan doesn't discriminate in favor of key employees (at any time in the key employee's tax year) (Reg § 1.79-4T, Q&A-11) as to eligibility to participate and in the type and amount of benefits available. (Code Sec. 79(d))[6] If the plan is discriminatory, each key employee must include the *greater of* (a) the actual cost of the insurance (determined by apportioning the net premium allocable to the group-term coverage during the key employee's tax year among the covered employees (Reg § 1.79-4T, Q&A-6(b)), *or* (b) the cost determined from IRS's premium table. (Code Sec. 79(d)(1)(B))[7]

¶ 1263   "Cost" of taxable group-term insurance—IRS uniform premium table—exclusions from income.

An employer providing group-term life insurance must compute the "cost" of taxable group-term coverage (¶1262) and notify the employee on Form W-2 of the amount included in income. The employee must compute the cost if coverage is provided by two or more employers.[8]

The cost of group-term life insurance is determined on the basis of uniform premiums (computed on the basis of five-year age brackets) prescribed by IRS. (Code Sec. 79(c)) The cost for each month of coverage is the number of thousands of dollars of coverage over $50,000 (to the nearest tenth) times the amount in IRS's table for the employee's attained age on the last day of the employee's tax year. (Reg § 1.79-3(d)(2))[9] If the employee contributes to the plan, all the employee's contributions for the tax year are considered made for that part of coverage over $50,000. (Code Sec. 79(a)(2))[10]

¶ 1264   Group-term life insurance coverage of employee's spouse and dependents, determining cost—exclusions from income.

The cost (as determined at ¶1263) of group-term life insurance on the life of an individual other than an employee (e.g., the employee's spouse or dependent) provided in connection with the performance of services by the employee is includible in the employee's gross income. (Reg § 1.61-2(d)(2)(ii)(b)) If, however, the face amount of employer-provided group-term insurance payable on the death of an employee's spouse or dependent doesn't exceed $2,000, it's an excludable de minimis fringe (¶1245).[11]

---

1. ¶H-1518
2. ¶H-1520
3. ¶H-1552
4. ¶H-1555
5. ¶H-1537
6. ¶H-1564

7. ¶H-1565
8. ¶H-1518 *et seq.*; ¶S-3176 *et seq.*
9. ¶H-1521
10. ¶H-1522
11. ¶H-1560 *et seq.*

¶ **1265** **Permanent benefits provided by employer providing group-term life insurance—exclusions from income.**

An employer provides a "permanent benefit" —such as paid-up or cash surrender value—when it provides a benefit under a life insurance policy whose value extends beyond one policy year. When a life insurance policy covering a group of employees provides both term life insurance and permanent benefits, the employee is taxed on the cost of the permanent benefits, and must include in income the cost of the permanent benefits, reduced by the amount the employee paid for the permanent benefits. The amount included in income is computed under a complex formula. (Reg § 1.79-1(d))[12]

¶ **1266** **Split-dollar life insurance—economic benefit regime, loan regime—inclusion of income.**

Under a "split-dollar" insurance arrangement, the employer pays part of the premium for a life insurance policy on the life of the employee (to the extent of the annual increase in cash surrender value) and the employee pays the rest. Out of the insurance proceeds, the employer gets either the cash surrender value or the amount it paid; the employee can designate the beneficiary of the balance.[13] For arrangements entered into (or materially modified) after Sept. 17, 2003, there are two mutually exclusive regimes for taxing split-dollar life insurance arrangements.[14]

Under the Reg § 1.61-22 economic benefit regime, the policy owner is treated as providing economic benefits to the non-owner (as valued in the regs). This regime governs the taxation of what are known as endorsement split-dollar arrangements (e.g., the employer owns the policy and employee's rights are derived from the employer's endorsement in the contract of those rights). This regime automatically applies if the arrangement is (1) entered into in connection with the performance of services, and the employee or other service provider isn't the contract owner, or (2) a gift situation, and the donee isn't the contract owner. (Reg § 1.61-22)[15]

Under the Reg § 1.7872-15 loan regime, the non-owner of the contract is treated as loaning premium payments to the contract owner. Unless specifically excepted, the loan regime applies to any split-dollar loan. The loan regime also governs what are known as collateral assignment split-dollar life insurance arrangements (e.g., employee owns the policy, which is used as collateral for employer's right to recover the premiums it pays). (Reg § 1.7872-15)[16]

The employer (or donor in a gift arrangement) is treated as the owner of a split-dollar life insurance contract if the only economic benefit that the employee (or donee) has under the arrangement is current life insurance protection. (Reg § 1.61-22(c)(1))[17]

If a split-dollar loan is waived, cancelled, or forgiven at any time, then the parties must take the amount waived, cancelled, or forgiven into account in accordance with the relationships between the parties (e.g., as compensation in the case of an employee-employer relationship). (Reg § 1.61-22(b)(6))[18]

In a split-dollar life insurance arrangement taxed under the economic benefit regime, the policy owner is treated as providing economic benefits to the non-owner, and those benefits have to be accounted for fully and consistently by both the owner and the non-owner. The value of the economic benefits, less any consideration paid by the non-owner, is

---

12. ¶H-1544 *et seq.*
13. ¶H-1601
14. ¶H-1604 *et seq.*
15. ¶H-1605 *et seq.*

16. ¶H-1625 *et seq.*
17. ¶H-1602 *et seq.*
18. ¶H-1604

treated as transferred from the owner to the non-owner. The tax consequences of that transfer depend on the relationship between the owner and the non-owner. Thus, depending on the circumstances, it might be treated as compensation, a dividend, or a gift. (Reg § 1.61-22(d)(1))[19]

A payment made under a split-dollar arrangement is a split-dollar loan, and the policy owner and non-owner are treated, respectively, as borrower and lender, if the payment is made directly or indirectly by the non-owner to the owner; the payment either is a loan under general tax law principles or if a reasonable person would expect the payment to be repaid in full to the non-owner; and repayment is to be made from, or secured by, the policy's death benefit or cash surrender value, or both. (Reg § 1.7872-15(a)(2))[20]

Because split-dollar life insurance arrangements typically provide for deferred compensation, Code Sec. 409A (¶1275) generally applies. But Code Sec. 409A doesn't apply for earnings on amounts deferred under a split-dollar life insurance arrangement in tax years beginning before 2005 (unless the plan was materially modified after Oct. 3, 2004), including increases in the policy cash value—but not including increases attributable to continued services performed, compensation earned, or premium payments or other contributions made after Dec. 31, 2004.[21]

Special rules apply to certain split-dollar life insurance arrangements entered into before Sept. 18, 2003[22] and before Jan. 28, 2002.[23]

¶ 1267 Meals and lodging furnished by or on behalf of employer for the convenience of the employer; lodging accepted as a condition of employment—exclusions from income.

Meals or lodging (including utilities) furnished to an employee and family (spouse and dependents) is nontaxable to the employee if (Code Sec. 119):

(1) the meals and lodging are furnished by or on behalf of the employer for the convenience of the employer (e.g., meals supplied because eating places near work are scarce, or because employees must for valid business reasons remain on-premises until their shifts end) (Reg § 1.119-1(a)(2)), and

(2) (a) in the case of *meals,* they're furnished on the employer's business premises, or (b) in the case of *lodging,* the employee is required to accept the lodging as a condition of employment (i.e., to properly perform job duties). (Reg § 1.119-1(b))[24] This means the employee's presence must be required from a business standpoint—e.g., ranches, hotels, motels and resorts.[25] For faculty housing, see ¶1268.

The value (not the cost) of meals or lodging that fails to meet these tests generally is income to the employee. (Reg § 1.61-2(d)(3), Reg § 1.119-1(a)(1))[26] However, all meals furnished on the employer's business premises to its employees are treated as furnished for the employer's convenience—and so are excludable from the employees' income—if *more than half* of the employees to whom the meals are furnished on the premises are furnished the meals for the convenience of the employer. (Code Sec. 119(b)(4))[27]

observation: In other words, if the more-than-half test is met, all employees may exclude the value of meals provided on premises, even those who weren't supplied the meals for the convenience of the employer.

19. ¶H-1608
20. ¶H-1603
21. ¶H-3200.6
22. ¶H-1647 *et seq.*
23. ¶H-1647.11

24. ¶H-1751
25. ¶H-1776
26. ¶s H-1751, H-1785
27. ¶H-1754

Cash allowances for meals are taxable.[28] If the employee can take either cash, or meals or lodging furnished in kind, the value of meals or lodging furnished is income. But occasional "supper money" paid to overtime employees is excludable as a de minimis fringe, see ¶1245.[29]

¶ 1268 Faculty housing—qualified campus lodging furnished to an employee of an educational institution—exclusion of income.

The value of qualified campus lodging furnished to an employee of an educational institution is excludable (with limits, below) from gross income. (Code Sec. 119(d))[30]

Qualified campus lodging is lodging that isn't eligible for the exclusion at ¶1267, that's located on or near a campus of a tax-exempt educational institution (or a qualifying academic health center) and is furnished by the institution to an employee, spouse, and dependents for use as a residence. (Code Sec. 119(d)(3), Code Sec. 119(d)(4))[31]

The exclusion isn't a total one. The employee must include the excess of: (1) the lesser of (a) 5% of the appraised value (as of the close of the tax year) of the qualified campus lodging, or (b) the average of the rentals paid by individuals other than employees or students for comparable lodging provided by the institution; over (2) the rent paid by the employee. (Code Sec. 119(d)(2))[32]

¶ 1269 Cafeteria plans/flexible benefit plans (including flexible spending accounts)—exclusion of income; COVID-19/coronavirus relief.

No amount is included in the gross income of the participant in a cafeteria plan solely because, under the plan, the participant may choose among the benefits of the plan. (Code Sec. 125(a))[33] Cafeteria plans (also referred to as flexible benefit plans) are generally the sole method of employers providing nontaxable benefits where employees can elect between taxable compensation and nontaxable benefits. (Prop Reg. § 1.125-1(b)(1) ["Taxpayers may rely"])

A "cafeteria plan" is a written plan under which participants (all employees) may choose their own "menu" of benefits consisting of "cash" and "qualified benefits." (Code Sec. 125(d))[34] For this purpose, cash means cash from current compensation (including salary reduction), payment for annual leave, sick leave, or other paid time off, and severance pay. Other benefits treated as cash are property, benefits attributable to employer contributions that are currently taxable to the employee, and benefits purchased with after-tax employee contributions. Qualified retirement plan distributions aren't cash. (Prop Reg. § 1.125-1(a)(2) ["Taxpayers may rely"]) Qualified benefits, which generally must be excludible from employees' gross income under a specific Code section and must not defer compensation (with some exceptions) (Code Sec. 125(d)(2)), include group-term life insurance on an employee's life (up to the excludable $50,000 amount, see ¶1262); employer-provided accident and health plans (¶1254) (including health flexible spending arrangements (FSAs), and accidental death and dismemberment policies); a dependent care assistance program (¶1270); an adoption assistance program (¶1253); contributions to a Code Sec. 401(k) plan (¶4305); contributions to certain plans maintained by educational organizations; contributions to Health Savings Accounts (HSAs, see ¶1257); and long-term and short-term disability coverage. (Code Sec. 125(f); Prop Reg. § 1.125-1(a)(3) ["Taxpayers may rely"])[35]

A cafeteria plan generally can't allow participants to revoke their benefit elections after

---

28. ¶H-1790
29. ¶H-1791
30. ¶H-1797
31. ¶H-1799

32. ¶H-1797
33. ¶H-2401
34. ¶H-2405
35. ¶H-2413 *et seq.*

the period of coverage has begun, but it may allow an employee to revoke an election during a period of coverage and to make a new election (i.e., to make "election changes") in circumstances specified in Reg § 1.125-4(b) through Reg § 1.125-4(g)—the only election changes a cafeteria plan may allow during a period of coverage.[36]

A qualified health plan (QHP) purchased through a health insurance Exchange generally isn't a "qualified benefit" (see above) unless it meets the requirements of Code Sec. 125(f)(3).[37] Cafeteria plans can, in certain cases, allow employees to revoke their election for coverage under the employer's group health plan (other than an FSA) during a period of coverage in order to purchase a QHP through an Exchange.[38]

For a "highly compensated participant," the exclusion won't apply to any benefit attributable to a plan year for which the plan discriminates in favor of highly compensated participants as to contributions, benefits or eligibility to participate. (Code Sec. 125(b)(1))[39] "Highly compensated participants" include officers, more-than-5% shareholders, highly compensated employees (¶4315) and spouses and dependents of any of those individuals. (Code Sec. 125(e)(1))[40]

For a key employee (defined in Code Sec. 416(i)(1)), the exclusion won't apply to any plan year if the qualified benefits provided to key employees under the plan exceed 25% of the total of such benefits provided for all employees under the plan. (Code Sec. 125(b)(2))[41]

FSAs. A cafeteria plan can include one or more FSAs. An FSA is a benefit designed to reimburse employees for expenses incurred for certain qualified benefits, up to a maximum amount not substantially in excess of the salary reduction and employer flex-credits allocated for the benefit. The maximum amount of reimbursement reasonably available must be less than five times the value of the coverage. (Prop Reg. § 1.125-5(a) ["Taxpayers may rely"]) Employer flex-credits are non-elective contributions that an employer makes available for every employee eligible to participate in the cafeteria plan, to be used at the employee's election only for one or more qualified benefits (but not as cash or other taxable benefits). (Prop Reg. § 1.125-5(b) ["Taxpayers may rely"]) The three types of FSAs are dependent care assistance, adoption assistance and medical care reimbursements (health FSA).

A health FSA may be limited to a subset of permitted Code Sec. 213(d) medical expenses, or it may be an HSA-compatible limited-purpose health FSA or post-deductible health FSA. (Prop Reg. § 1.125-5(m) ["Taxpayers may rely"]) A health FSA may not reimburse premiums for accident and health insurance or long-term care insurance. (Code Sec. 125(f)) For the 2023 cafeteria plan year, an employee can't contribute more than $3,050 ($2,850 for 2022) to a health FSA through salary reduction contributions. (Code Sec. 125(i)) However, for a married couple, each person may contribute up to this maximum. The health FSA cap doesn't limit the amount permitted for reimbursement under other employer-provided coverage, such as an FSA for dependent care assistance.[42]

Use-it-or-lose-it rule. Unused cafeteria plan amounts left over at the end of a plan year must generally be forfeited (use-it-or-lose-it rule). (Code Sec. 125(d)(2)(A))[43] But a cafeteria plan can provide an optional grace period immediately following the end of each plan year, extending the period for incurring expenses for qualified benefits to the 15th day of the third month after the end of the plan year. The grace period may apply to one or more qualified benefits but can't apply to paid time off or elective contributions to Code Sec. 401(k) plans. Benefits or contributions not used as of the end of the grace period are forfeited. (Prop Reg. § 1.125-1(e)(1) ["Taxpayers may rely"]) [44]

---

36. ¶H-2424 *et seq.*
37. ¶H-1165.1, H-2413.2
38. ¶H-2426.6
39. ¶H-2450
40. ¶H-2455

41. ¶H-2456
42. ¶H-2461 *et seq.*
43. ¶H-2417
44. ¶H-2417.1

Under an exception to the use-it-or-lose-it rule that applies for health FSAs, at the plan sponsor's option and instead of any grace period, employees may be allowed to carry over up to 20% of the maximum salary reduction amount for the year—i.e., for 2023, $610 (20% of $3,050, see above) or for 2022, $570 (20% of $2,850, see above)—of unused amounts remaining at year-end in the health FSA.[45]

COVID-19/coronavirus relief for 2020 and 2021 plan years; effect on 2022 amounts. Temporary changes made due to the COVID-19 pandemic—applicable for the 2020 and/or 2021 plan years—gave plan sponsors options for increasing participant flexibility for using amounts deferred under a health FSA or a dependent care assistance FSA. For example, the above grace period could be expanded; and the 2021 cap of $550 (above) that applied to carryovers from health FSAs did not apply for 2020 or 2021, if a plan sponsor chose to adopt these rules and amended the applicable plans. (Sec. 214(d)(1)DivEE, PL 116-260, 12/27/2020) An IRS notice clarified the application of Sec. 214(d)(1)DivEE, PL 116-260. (Notice 2021-15, 2021-10 IRB 898)[46] Dependent care benefits that would have been excluded from income if used during the preceding tax year (i.e., during the tax year ending in 2020 or 2021, as applicable) remained excludable for the tax years ending in 2021 and 2022. (Notice 2021-26, 2021-21 IRB 1157).

Military reservist exception. Another exception to the use-it-or-lose-it rule allows FSAs to distribute all or part of unused health FSA benefits to military reservists who are called to active duty for a period exceeding 179 days (or an indefinite period). (Code Sec. 125(h))[47] If a plan provides a grace period, unused salary reduction contributions to the health FSA that are carried over into the grace period won't count against the annual dollar limit for the later plan year.[48]

¶ 1270 Dependent care assistance payments excluded from employee's gross income—Form 2441.

Payments incurred by an employer for dependent care assistance under a written plan are excluded from an employee's gross income. (Code Sec. 129(a)(1))[49]

The amount an employee can exclude (computed on Form 2441 with Form 1040) can't exceed the employee's earned income (excluding employer dependent care assistance payments) or, for married employees, the earned income of the lower earning spouse. (Code Sec. 129(b))[50] The aggregate exclusion is further limited to $5,000 ($2,500 for a married individual filing separately). Any excess is includible in the tax year the dependent care services are provided. (Code Sec. 129(a)(2)(B))[1]

Dependent care assistance is the payment for or provision of services that if paid for by the employee would be considered employment-related expenses under the child care credit rules (see ¶2347). (Code Sec. 129(e)(1))[2] For eligible dependents, see ¶2347. An employee includes a self-employed individual who can be covered under a self-employed retirement plan. An individual who owns the entire interest in an unincorporated trade or business is treated as both employer and employee. A partnership is treated as the employer of each partner who is eligible to be included in a self-employed retirement plan. (Code Sec. 129(e)(3), Code Sec. 129(e)(4))[3]

To get the exclusion, the employee must provide, on his or her tax return, the name, address and (except for a tax-exempt service-provider) taxpayer identifying number (TIN) of the person providing the dependent care services. Form W-10 can be used to request this

---

45. ¶H-2461.7 *et seq.*
46. ¶H-2426.8
47. ¶H-2459.2A *et seq.*
48. ¶H-2461.4
49. ¶H-1401

50. ¶H-1402
1. ¶H-1402 *et seq.*
2. ¶H-1419
3. ¶H-1413 *et seq.*

information from the service provider. An employee's failure to provide the information is excused if the employee exercised due diligence. (Code Sec. 129(e)(9))[4]

The plan must satisfy specific nondiscrimination rules and certain other requirements. (Code Sec. 129(d))[5] If an otherwise qualified program fails to meet these requirements, the program will be a dependent care assistance program under which expenses are still excludable for nonhighly compensated employees. (Code Sec. 129(d)(1))[6]

For how dependent care assistance affects the dependent care credit, see ¶2347.

¶ 1271   Time for Reporting Compensation.

Compensation income is reported according to the recipient's accounting method, whether cash (¶1272) or accrual (¶1273), subject to constructive receipt, prepaid-income and deferred-income rules.

¶ 1272   Cash basis taxpayers—time for reporting compensation.

Cash basis taxpayers report compensation for the tax year they actually receive it.[7]

Compensation paid by check is reported for the year the check is received, even if the check covers past or future services, or isn't cashed until the following year.[8]

Compensation income must be reported for the year it's constructively received (¶2816), even if it's not actually received until a later year. Income is constructively received for the year it's credited to the taxpayer's account, set apart for the taxpayer, or otherwise made available so the taxpayer can draw upon it at any time, or could have drawn upon it by giving notice of intent to withdraw. (Reg § 1.451-2(a))[9] For advances, see ¶1274.

¶ 1273   Accrual basis taxpayers—time for reporting compensation.

Accrual basis taxpayers report compensation for the tax year in which it accrues. Compensation accrues when all events have occurred that fix the right to receive the income and its amount can be determined with reasonable accuracy. (Reg § 1.451-1(a))[10]

If the right to compensation for services or its amount can't be determined until the services are completed, the amount of compensation ordinarily isn't reported until the tax year the services are completed and the determination can be made. (Reg § 1.451-1(a))[11]

¶ 1274   Advances and drawing accounts—time for reporting compensation.

A cash basis taxpayer who receives advances against commissions that haven't been earned reports the advances as income for the year they're received if not required to repay the amounts received in excess of commissions. If excess drawings are required to be repaid, they aren't income until offset by a credit for commissions earned.[12]

¶ 1275   Deferred compensation plans, time for reporting compensation—Section 409A rules; substantial risk of forfeiture; NQDC plans; acceleration of benefits.

Code Sec. 409A provides that all amounts deferred under a nonqualified deferred compensation (NQDC) plan for all tax years are currently includible in gross income to the extent not subject to a substantial risk of forfeiture and not previously included in gross

---

4. ¶H-1406 *et seq.*
5. ¶H-1428 *et seq.*
6. ¶H-1418
7. ¶H-3501
8. ¶H-3502

9. ¶H-3508
10. ¶G-2471
11. ¶H-3526
12. ¶H-3515

income, unless the plan:

. . . meets specified distribution, acceleration of benefit, and election requirements (see below); and

. . . is operated in accordance with these requirements. (Code Sec. 409A(a)(1)(A)(i))[13]

The amount includible under this rule is also subject to: (1) interest (at the underpayment rate plus one percentage point) on the tax underpayments that would have occurred had the amount been included in income for the tax year when first deferred, or if later, when not subject to a substantial risk of forfeiture; and (2) a penalty of 20% of the compensation required to be included in income. (Code Sec. 409A(a)(1)(B))[14]

Compensation is subject to a substantial risk of forfeiture if it's conditioned on a person's performance of substantial future services or the occurrence of a condition related to the compensation's purpose (e.g., an amount conditioned on involuntary separation from service without cause), and the possibility of forfeiture is substantial. A noncompete clause does not create a substantial risk of forfeiture. (Reg § 1.409A-1(d)(1))[15]

A NQDC plan is any plan that provides for the deferral of compensation, other than: a qualified employer plan; a bona fide vacation leave, sick leave, compensatory time, disability pay, or death benefit plan; and certain tax-free medical reimbursement arrangements, foreign plans and Code Sec. 457 plans. (Code Sec. 409A(d))[16] There's no deferral of compensation for payments that the service provider actually or constructively receives within $2\frac{1}{2}$ months after the end of the service recipient's or service provider's tax year in which the payment vested, whichever is later. (Reg § 1.409A-1(b)(4))[17]

Incentive stock options (¶1221) and options granted under an employee stock purchase plan (¶1220) aren't subject to Code Sec. 409A. Nonqualified stock options and stock appreciation rights (SARs) are similarly excepted if the exercise price may never be less than the fair market value (FMV) of the underlying stock when the option or right is granted, the number of shares subject to the option is fixed on the grant date, and there's no other deferral feature. (Reg § 1.409A-1(b)(5))[18]

The distribution requirement is met if a NQDC plan provides that compensation deferred under the plan can't be distributed earlier than (1) the participant's separation from service; (2) the date the participant becomes disabled; (3) the participant's death; (4) a time specified, or a schedule fixed, under the plan as of the date of the deferral of the compensation (amounts payable on the occurrence of an event aren't treated as payable at a specified time); (5) a change in the corporation's ownership or effective control, or in the ownership of a substantial portion of the corporation's assets; or (6) the occurrence of an unforeseeable emergency, such as a severe financial hardship resulting from illness, casualty, etc. (Code Sec. 409A(a)(2); Reg § 1.409A-3(a); Prop Reg. § 1.409A-3(b) ["Taxpayers may...rely," Preamble to Prop Regs, 6/21/2016])[19]

The acceleration of benefits requirement is met if a NQDC plan doesn't allow the acceleration of the time or schedule of any payment under the plan, except as provided in IRS regs. (Code Sec. 409A(a)(3)) Changes in the form of distribution that accelerate payments generally are subject to this rule. But payments made in accordance with plan provisions for acceleration in the event of a service provider's separation from service, death or disability, or in the event of a change in control don't violate these rules.[20] Nor do payments under a domestic relations order,[21] payments to comply with a conflict-of-interest

---

13. ¶H-3200.1
14. ¶H-3200.1; ¶H-3200.25 *et seq.*
15. ¶H-3200.50
16. ¶H-3200.36
17. ¶H-3200.27

18. ¶H-3200.28 *et seq.*
19. ¶H-3200.56
20. ¶H-3200.66, ¶H-3200.66A
21. ¶H-3200.67

divestiture,[22] or de minimis cash-out payments.[23] (Reg § 1.409A-3(j))

The election requirement is met if the plan provides that compensation for services performed during a tax year can be deferred at the participant's election only if the initial deferral election is made (1) not later than the close of the preceding tax year; or (2) at another time provided in IRS regs. For performance-based compensation (e.g., bonuses), based on services performed over a period of at least 12 months, the initial deferral election must be made no later than six months before the end of the period. The time and form of distributions must be specified at the time of initial deferral. An election made after the initial election (a redeferral election) generally must not take effect until at least 12 months after the date on which the election is made and must require an additional deferral of at least five years. (Code Sec. 409A(a)(4))[24]

Relief provisions. If an unintentional operational failure to comply with specified Code Sec. 409A(a) requirements (e.g., incorrect amount treated as deferred compensation) is corrected within the year, no amount is generally included in income under Code Sec. 409A(a). Relief is conditioned on timely filing and information reporting and taking commercially reasonable steps to avoid a recurrence of the failure. For other specified unintentional operational failures that aren't corrected until a later year, the amount included in income, and the resulting additional tax, is limited.[25]

For inclusion in income of deferred compensation from tax-indifferent corporations and partnerships under Code Sec. 457A, see ¶1277. The Code Sec. 409A rules apply to NQDC plans separately and in addition to the Code Sec. 457A rules. (Prop Reg. § 1.409A-1(a)(4) ["Taxpayers may rely"])

¶ 1276   Rabbi trusts and funding triggers; assets located or transferred outside of U.S.—time for reporting compensation.

Under Code Sec. 409A, amounts deferred under nonqualified deferred compensation (NQDC) plans (¶1275) generally aren't includible in income if the compensation is payable from general corporate funds that are subject to the claims of general creditors. Arrangements known as "rabbi trusts" generally are irrevocable and don't permit the employer to use the assets for purposes other than payment of deferred compensation. However, the trust assets are subject to the claims of the employer's creditors in the case of insolvency or bankruptcy. Because of this feature, rabbi trusts aren't considered to be funded and so compensation is deferred.[26]

Assets directly or indirectly set aside in a trust for purposes of paying nonqualified deferred compensation are treated, for Code Sec. 83 purposes, as property transferred in connection with the performance of services (see ¶1216), whether or not the assets are available to satisfy claims of general creditors (1) at the time set aside, if the assets are located outside of the U.S.; or (2) at the time transferred, if the assets are later transferred outside of the U.S. (Code Sec. 409A(b)(1))[27]

There's also a transfer of property, for Code Sec. 83 purposes, as of the earlier of (1) the date on which a NQDC plan first provides that assets will become restricted to the provision of benefits under the plan in connection with a change in the employer's financial health; or (2) the date on which assets are so restricted. (Code Sec. 409A(b)(2))[28]

Interest and a 20% penalty apply with regard to the off-shore rabbi trust and financial trigger rules. (Code Sec. 409A(b)(5))[29]

22. ¶H-3200.68
23. ¶H-3200.69
24. ¶H-3200.72 *et seq.*
25. ¶H-3200.18 *et seq.*

26. ¶H-3232 *et seq.*
27. ¶H-2503.1
28. ¶H-3233
29. ¶H-2535.1

¶ 1277 Deferred compensation from tax-indifferent corporations and partnerships—time for reporting compensation.

For deferred amounts attributable to services performed after Dec. 31, 2008, any compensation that's deferred under a nonqualified deferred compensation (NQDC) plan of a nonqualified entity is includible in gross income when there's no substantial risk of forfeiture of the rights to the compensation. (Code Sec. 457A(a))[30] A person's rights to compensation are subject to a substantial risk of forfeiture only if those rights are conditioned on the future performance of substantial services by any individual. (Code Sec. 457A(d)(1))[31] A nonqualified entity is: (1) any foreign corporation unless substantially all of its income is either effectively connected with the conduct of a trade or business in the U.S. or subject to a comprehensive foreign income tax; and (2) any partnership (either domestic or foreign), unless substantially all of its income is allocated to persons other than foreign persons for whom that income isn't subject to a comprehensive foreign income tax (as defined in Code Sec. 457A(d)(2)); or organizations that are exempt from U.S. income tax. (Code Sec. 457A(b))[32]

A NQDC plan for this purpose generally is one described in Code Sec. 409A(d) (see ¶1275), subject to certain exceptions. (Code Sec. 457A(d)(3))[33]

For foreign corporations with income that's effectively connected with the conduct of a U.S. trade or business, Code Sec. 457A doesn't apply to compensation that the corporation could have deducted against its effectively connected income if it had been paid in cash on the date that it ceased to be subject to a substantial risk of forfeiture. (Code Sec. 457A(d)(4))[34] Code Sec. 457A doesn't apply to a NQDC plan if the compensation is: (a) payable to an employee of a domestic subsidiary of the entity, and (b) reasonably expected to be deductible by that subsidiary under Code Sec. 404(a)(5) (¶1536) when it's includible in the employee's income.[35]

If an amount of compensation isn't determinable when it's otherwise includible in income under Code Sec. 457A, it's taken into account when it becomes determinable, subject to an additional 20% tax and an interest charge at the Code Sec. 6621 underpayment rate plus one percentage point, from the tax year first deferred or, if later, the first tax year not subject to a substantial risk of forfeiture. (Code Sec. 457A(c)) An amount isn't determinable if, at the time it is no longer subject to a substantial risk of forfeiture, it varies depending on the satisfaction of an objective condition.[36]

To the extent provided in regs, if compensation is determined solely by reference to the amount of gain recognized on the disposition of an investment asset, that compensation is treated as subject to a substantial risk of forfeiture until the date of the disposition. (Code Sec. 457A(d)(1))[37]

Inclusion of pre-2009 amounts. For a deferred amount to which Code Sec. 457A doesn't apply solely because it's attributable to services performed before 2009, to the extent not includible in gross income in a tax year beginning before 2018, it's includible in the later of (1) the last tax year beginning before 2018; or (2) the tax year in which there's no substantial risk of forfeiture of the rights to the compensation.[38]

¶ 1278 Social Security, Unemployment and Certain Disability Payments. ■■■■■■

Social security benefits may be partly taxable. Unemployment benefits are fully

---

30. ¶H-3401
31. ¶H-3419
32. ¶H-3412
33. ¶H-3404
34. ¶H-3416.1

35. ¶H-3401
36. ¶H-3421
37. ¶H-3420
38. ¶H-3401; ¶H-3424

taxable. Payments under military and government disability pensions may be excludible from income.

For voluntary withholding on social security and certain other federal payments, and on unemployment compensation payments, see ¶3010.

¶ 1279   Social security payments—the Tier I and Tier II taxes; Railroad Retirement benefits—taxability.

Under Code Sec. 86, a taxpayer whose "provisional income" —i.e., modified adjusted gross income (MAGI, see below) plus one half of the social security benefits (including Tier 1 Railroad Retirement benefits) received—for a tax year exceeds either of two threshold amounts is taxed on a portion of social security benefits received that year, as follows:

Tier I: If provisional income exceeds a "base amount," include in gross income the *lesser* of:

. . . 50% of the social security benefits received that year; (Code Sec. 86(a)(1)(A)) or

. . . 50% of the excess of provisional income over the "base amount." (Code Sec. 86(a)(1)(B))[39]

MAGI means adjusted gross income: (1) determined without regard to the social security benefits; the deduction for qualified education loan interest (¶2220); the deduction for higher education expenses; the exclusions for foreign earned income and housing costs (¶4605 *et seq.*), savings bond proceeds for education expenses (¶2219), employer-provided adoption assistance (¶1253), and income from sources within U.S. possessions and Puerto Rico, and (2) increased by the amount of tax-exempt interest received or accrued by taxpayer during the tax year. (Code Sec. 86(b)(2))[40]

The "base amount" is $32,000 for married individuals filing a joint return; zero for a married individual filing a separate return who doesn't live apart from the individual's spouse for the entire tax year; and $25,000 for all other individuals (Code Sec. 86(c)(1)), such as those filing as single, head of household or qualifying widow(er).[41]

illustration: G's MAGI for the tax year consists of pension income of $15,000 and $3,000 of taxable interest and dividends. G's social security benefit is $12,000. He's married and files a joint return. His spouse has no income. The sum of their MAGI ($18,000) plus one-half of G's social security benefit ($6,000) is $24,000. This is less than their base amount ($32,000), so no part of G's social security benefit is taxable.

Tier II: If provisional income exceeds an "adjusted base amount," include in gross income the *lesser* of:

. . . 85% of the social security benefits received that year; or

. . . the sum of: (a) the amount included under the above 50% rule or, if less, one-half of the difference between taxpayer's "adjusted base amount" and "base amount," plus (b) 85% of the excess of provisional income over the "adjusted base amount." (Code Sec. 86(a)(2))

The "adjusted base amount" is $44,000 for married individuals filing jointly; zero for a married individual filing separately who doesn't live apart from the individual's spouse for the entire tax year); and $34,000 for all other individuals. (Code Sec. 86(c)(2))

caution: Any spike in income, e.g., from the sale of stock or a mutual fund, or a retirement plan distribution, may subject a taxpayer to an unexpected tax on social security benefits, if the extra income causes the taxpayer to exceed the base or adjusted base amount.

Benefits a taxpayer repays during a tax year reduce the benefits taxed that year, whether the repayment is for overpayments received that repayment year or any earlier year. (Code Sec. 86(d)(2)(A))[42]

If any portion of a lump-sum social security benefit received during a tax year is attributable to an earlier year, the taxpayer can make a lump-sum election to include in gross income, with respect to that portion, the sum of the increases in gross income that would have resulted had the portion been paid in the earlier year. (Code Sec. 86(e)(1))[43]

¶ 1280 Railroad Retirement Act benefits other than Tier 1 benefits—taxability.

Railroad Retirement Act benefits (other than Tier 1 benefits) are treated as benefits provided under an employer plan that meets the requirements of Code Sec. 401(a) (a "qualified plan," see ¶4307 *et seq.*). (Code Sec. 72(r)(1), Code Sec. 72(r)(3)) Lump-sum termination (early retirement) payments have been held to be taxable under these rules.[44]

¶ 1281 Unemployment compensation benefits, and disability benefits paid as substitute for unemployment—taxability.

Except as described below, unemployment compensation (reported to recipients on Form 1099-G) is fully taxable. (Code Sec. 85(a)) Unemployment compensation includes any amount received under a law of the U.S. or a state that's in the nature of unemployment compensation. (Code Sec. 85(b)) It also includes disability benefits paid under federal or state law as a substitute for unemployment benefits to those who are ineligible for unemployment benefits because they're disabled.[45]

¶ 1282 Unemployment benefits paid by employers; guaranteed annual wage plans—taxability.

Unemployment benefits paid directly by an employer (i.e., not those discussed at ¶1281) are includible in the employee's income. Amounts received from an employer under a "guaranteed annual wage plan" during periods of unemployment are taxable as wages. [46]

¶ 1283 Strike and lockout benefits paid by a union—taxability.

Under Code Sec. 61, strike and lockout benefits paid to an employee by a union, from union dues, including both cash and the fair market value of goods received, are included in the employee's income unless the facts clearly show they're intended as a gift. [47]

¶ 1284 Certain military and government disability pensions—taxability.

Under Code Sec. 104(a)(4), eligible members of the armed forces of any country, the National Oceanic and Atmospheric Administration, or the Public Health Service, and recipients of a disability annuity under section 808 of the Foreign Service Act of 1980, exclude from gross income amounts received as pension, annuity or similar allowance for personal injuries or sickness resulting from active service. Those eligible are primarily individuals with combat-related injuries or sickness or entitled to disability compensation

---

42. ¶J-1467
43. ¶J-1469
44. ¶J-1471

45. ¶H-3007 *et seq.*
46. ¶H-3005
47. ¶H-3009

from the Department of Veterans Affairs. (Code Sec. 104(a)(4))[48] While armed forces retirement pay based on length of service is taxable, that pay is excludible to the extent it could be received as a disability pension.[49]

¶ 1285   Dividends.

When a corporation distributes its earnings to its shareholders, the distribution is usually a dividend. If the dividend is "qualified," it's taxable at rates that apply to net capital gain (¶1288); otherwise it's taxable as ordinary income. But not all corporate distributions are dividends. And some transactions that don't appear to be dividends may be taxed as constructive dividends.

For stock dividends, see ¶1295 *et seq.* For RIC, REIT, and co-op dividends, see ¶1298 *et seq.* For stock redemptions, see ¶3515 *et seq.* For liquidations, see ¶3558 *et seq.*

¶ 1286   How dividends and "qualified dividends" are taxed to shareholders; stock sold before or after record ("ex dividend") date; distributions in excess of E&P.

Dividends, to whom taxed; stock sold before "ex-dividend" date. Dividends (defined at ¶1287) are taxable to the person who has the present, enforceable right to receive them, whether or not that person is the owner of the underlying stock.[50] Dividends received by an agent are taxable to the principal.[1] If the stock is sold before a dividend is declared and paid, or between the declaration and record (or "ex dividend") dates, the dividends are taxed to the buyer. Dividends on stock sold on or after the record date are taxed to the seller. (Reg § 1.61-9(c))[2]

When dividends are taxable. Dividends are taxable in the year received or unqualifiedly made subject to the shareholder's demand. This applies to both cash and accrual shareholders. Thus, if a corporation pays a dividend on Dec. 30 last year, and the shareholder receives the check on Jan. 2 this year, the shareholder reports it on this year's return. (Reg § 1.301-1(b))[3] For RIC (mutual fund) dividends, see ¶1298. For REIT dividends, see ¶1299.

"Qualified dividends," how taxed. Dividends are taxed to shareholders at the rates that apply to net capital gain (see ¶2602) if they constitute "qualified dividend income" (¶1288) paid to noncorporate shareholders (Code Sec. 1(h)(11)) and would otherwise be taxed at ordinary income rates to the extent of the distributing corporation's earnings and profits (E&P, ¶3511). (Code Sec. 301(c)(1)) Thus, for dividends received in 2022, the 15% breakpoint is: $83,350 ($89,250 for 2023) for joint returns and surviving spouses (half these amounts for married taxpayers filing separately), $55,800 ($59,750 for 2023) for heads of household, $41,675 ($44,625 for 2023) for single filers, and $2,800 ($3,000 for 2023) for trusts and estates. For 2022, the 20% breakpoint is $517,200 for joint returns and surviving spouses (half these amounts for married taxpayers filing separately), $488,500 for heads of household, $459,750 for single filers, and $13,700 for estates and trusts. (Code Sec. 1(h)(1)) For 2023, these amounts are $553,850, $523,050, $492,300, and $14,650, respectively.

Treatment of distributions in excess of E&P. The part of a distribution in excess of E&P is treated as a tax-free return of capital and is applied against (reduces) the shareholder's basis in the stock. (Code Sec. 301(c)(2)) Any remaining excess (once basis is reduced to zero) is treated as payment for the stock, i.e., as capital gain if the stock is a

---

48. ¶H-3120
49. ¶H-3123
50. ¶J-2401

1. ¶J-2401
2. ¶J-2405
3. ¶J-2451

capital asset in the shareholder's hands. (Code Sec. 301(c)(3))[4]

¶ 1287 Dividend defined; distribution with respect to stock—dividend income.

Under Code Sec. 316(a), a dividend is a distribution of money or property, other than the corporation's own stock or rights to that stock (¶1295), by a corporation to its shareholders with respect to its stock, out of accumulated or current earnings and profits (E&P, see ¶3511). (Code Sec. 316(a)) "Property" also includes any economic benefit the corporation gives its shareholders, in whatever form (Reg § 1.317-1), e.g., paying their debts (see ¶1289).[5] The distribution must be made in the ordinary course of the corporation's business, but it may be extraordinary in amount. (Reg § 1.316-1(a)(1))[6] A dividend needn't be proportionate and needn't be formally declared.[7]

¶ 1288 Qualified dividend income defined; qualified foreign corporations; holding period rules; exclusions—dividend income.

Under Code Sec. 1(h)(11)(B)(i), qualified dividend income—taxed under the capital-gain-taxation rules discussed at ¶1286—is dividend income received from domestic corporations and qualified foreign corporations (see below).[8]

Qualified foreign corporations are (1) U.S. possessions corporations, and (2) corporations eligible for benefits of a comprehensive income tax treaty with the U.S. that includes an exchange-of-information program (which can include controlled foreign corporation (CFC) dividends if not required to be included under Code Sec. 951(a)(1) (¶4611), but not passive foreign investment companies, and not foreign corporations treated as domestic under Code Sec. 7874(b), which first became "surrogate foreign corporations" after Dec. 22, 2017). Dividends paid by other foreign corporations also are qualified if paid on stock (or American Depository Receipts (ADRs)) that is readily tradable on an established U.S. securities market. (Code Sec. 1(h)(11)(C))[9]

Qualified dividend income doesn't include: (1) dividends paid on stock that was not held for more than 60 days during the 121-day period beginning 60 days before the ex-dividend date (more than 90 days during the 181-day period beginning 90 days before the ex-dividend date for preferred stock dividends attributable to a period of more than 366 days) (Code Sec. 1(h)(11)(B)(iii)(I));[10] (2) dividends on stock to the extent that the taxpayer is under an obligation to make related payments with respect to positions in substantially similar or related property (Code Sec. 1(h)(11)(B)(iii)(II)); (3) any amount that the taxpayer elects to treat as investment income to support an investment interest deduction (Code Sec. 1(h)(11)(D)(i)) (see ¶1728); (4) dividends from corporations that for the distribution year or the preceding year are exempt from tax under Code Sec. 501 (see ¶4100) or Code Sec. 521 (exempt farmers' cooperatives, see ¶4206 *et seq.*) (Code Sec. 1(h)(11)(B)(ii)(I)); (5) dividends deductible under Code Sec. 591 by mutual savings banks (Code Sec. 1(h)(11)(B)(ii)(II)); (6) dividends paid on employer securities owned by an employee stock ownership plan (ESOP), which are deductible under Code Sec. 404(k) (Code Sec. 1(h)(11)(B)(ii)(III)); and (7) dividends received as a nominee.[11]

Qualified dividend income doesn't include payments in lieu of dividends (typically made to owners of stock that has been lent in connection with a short sale). However, if a payment in lieu of dividends is reported as dividend income on a Form 1099-DIV, the recipient may treat the payment as a dividend, and not as a payment in lieu of dividends,

---

4. ¶J-2350 *et seq.*
5. ¶J-2353
6. ¶J-2352
7. ¶J-2351

8. ¶I-5115.1
9. ¶I-5115.5
10. ¶I-5115.2
11. ¶I-5115.1

unless the recipient knows, or has reason to know, of the actual character of the payment.[12]

If an individual, trust, or estate receives extraordinary dividends (within the meaning of Code Sec. 1059(c)) that are qualified dividend income, any loss on the dividend-paying stock is a long-term capital loss to the extent of the extraordinary dividends. (Code Sec. 1(h)(11)(D)(ii))[13]

For dividends from RICs, see ¶1298. For dividends from REITs, see ¶1299.

¶ 1289　Constructive or disguised dividends; payments of a shareholder's debts or expenses—dividend income.

When a corporation pays excessive or unreasonably large amounts to a shareholder or a member of the shareholder's family as salary (Reg § 1.162-7(b)(1)) or rent,[14] or for a purchase price,[15] the excess is a constructive dividend (assuming sufficient E&P, see ¶3511). Similarly, constructive dividends include a corporation's payments of a shareholder's debts[16] or personal expenses.[17] A dividend may also result without a direct payment to the shareholder, if the corporation makes a payment to a third party that's for the shareholder's benefit and made with respect to stock owned by the shareholder.[18]

¶ 1290　Loan vs. dividend treatment for shareholder's borrowing from corporation—dividend income.

A shareholder may borrow money from the corporation with or without interest, and with or without security. If the agreement and the genuine intent (at withdrawal) is that the amount be repaid to the corporation, and there's persuasive evidence of both that intent *and* the shareholder's ability to carry it out, the amount received is treated as a loan (i.e., nontaxable), and not as a dividend[19] (unless a below-market interest rate is involved, see ¶1291).

¶ 1291　Dividends from below-market loans between corporation and shareholder; foregone interest—dividend income.

For any below-market interest rate loan (¶1305) (directly or indirectly) between a corporation and a shareholder, the corporation/lender is treated as having paid a dividend, equal to the amount of the foregone interest that's includible in the shareholder/borrower's income. De minimis ($10,000 or less) and certain other loans are excepted. (Code Sec. 7872(a))[20]

¶ 1292　Determining the amount of a dividend (cash and in-kind)—dividend income.

The amount of a dividend is the sum of the cash plus the fair market value (FMV), at distribution, of any other property received (Code Sec. 301(b)(1), Code Sec. 301(b)(3)), reduced (but not below zero) by the amount of any liability of the corporation that the shareholder assumes in connection with the distribution, or to which the property is subject both immediately before and after the distribution. (Code Sec. 301(b)(2))[21] But the amount taxable as a dividend in kind can't exceed the distributing corporation's E&P (¶3511). (Reg § 1.316-1(a)(2))[22]

---

12. ¶I-5115.4
13. ¶I-5104.1
14. ¶J-2726
15. ¶J-2730
16. ¶J-2749
17. ¶J-2757

18. ¶J-2700 *et seq.*
19. ¶J-2707 *et seq.*
20. ¶J-2721 *et seq.*
21. ¶J-2354
22. ¶J-2356

A dividend consisting of the corporation's obligations equals the FMV of the notes. (Reg § 1.301-1(d)) For stock dividends, see ¶1296.

These rules apply to both corporate (U.S. or foreign) and noncorporate shareholders (but a corporate shareholder may get a dividends-received deduction, see ¶3306 *et seq.*), and to dividends from a foreign corporation to its U.S. corporate shareholder. (Code Sec. 301(b)(1))

¶ 1293 Basis of distributed property to shareholder-distributee—dividend income.

The basis to the shareholder (corporate or individual) for property received as a dividend (¶1287) is the property's fair market value at distribution (Code Sec. 301(d)), i.e., the amount treated as a dividend (see ¶1292), but without the reduction for liabilities.[23]

¶ 1294 Holding period for property received as a taxable dividend—dividend income.

The shareholder's holding period for property received as a taxable dividend begins on the date of its receipt (actual or constructive). (Code Sec. 1223(2))[24]

¶ 1295 Stock dividends—distributions of stock or rights to stock (including options and warrants)—dividend income.

Code Sec. 305 provides that, with certain exceptions (see ¶1296), a stock dividend, including a stock split—i.e., a corporation's distribution of its *own* stock, or rights (e.g., options or warrants) to buy its stock, that's made to shareholders with respect to their stock (i.e., not as compensation)—isn't taxable to the shareholder. (Code Sec. 305) But a corporation's distribution of stock, or rights to buy stock, in *another* corporation (even if affiliated) is a regular dividend in kind, taxed under the rules at ¶1286 *et seq.*[25]

For stock (rights) received in connection with corporate organizations, reorganizations or divisions, see ¶3540.

¶ 1296 Taxable stock (or rights) dividends—dividend income.

Where a stock (or rights) dividend is taxable, the dividend amount is the fair market value (FMV) at distribution of the stock (rights), under the "regular" dividend-in-kind rules, see ¶1292.[26] Where the dividend is taxable because of a cash election, the "dividend" equals: (1) the cash received, for shareholders electing cash, and (2) the FMV of the stock (rights) at distribution, for those receiving stock (rights). (Reg § 1.305-1(b))[27]

These stock (or rights) dividends are *not* tax-free:

(1) A distribution in which *any* shareholder has the option to take cash or other property instead of the stock (or rights); (Code Sec. 305(b)(1); Reg § 1.305-2)[28]

(2) A "disproportionate" distribution that results in the receipt of property by some shareholders and, for others, an increase in their proportionate interests in the corporation's assets or earnings and profits; (Code Sec. 305(b)(2); Reg § 1.305-3)[29]

(3) A distribution that results in the receipt of preferred stock by some common shareholders and the receipt of common stock by others; (Code Sec. 305(b)(3); Reg § 1.305-4)[30]

(4) Any distributions on preferred stock, including a redemption premium treated as a

23. ¶P-5401
24. ¶s I-8903, I-8918
25. ¶J-2501
26. ¶J-2504, J-2506
27. ¶J-2507
28. ¶s J-2508 *et seq.*, J-2501
29. ¶J-2510 *et seq.*
30. ¶J-2515

distribution (for preferred stock issued after Oct. 9, '90, the premium is included as OID, see ¶1313 *et seq.*), *other than* an increase in the conversion ratio of convertible preferred stock made solely to take into account a stock dividend or stock split with respect to the stock into which the preferred is convertible; (Code Sec. 305(b)(4); Reg § 1.305-5)[31]

(5) Any distribution of convertible preferred stock unless IRS is satisfied it won't have the result in (2), above; (Code Sec. 305(b)(5); Reg § 1.305-6)[32]

(6) A constructive stock distribution, e.g., a change in conversion ratio or redemption price, or a redemption premium (difference between redemption price and issue price). (Code Sec. 305(c); Reg § 1.305-5(b), Reg § 1.305-7) Proposed regs detail the amount and timing of taxable income from deemed distributions that are, or that result from, adjustments to rights to acquire stock. (Prop Reg. § 1.305-7(c)(4) ["Taxpayers may rely"]) [33]

¶ 1297   Cash for fractional shares—dividend income.

Where a corporation's purpose in distributing cash (instead of scrip or fractional shares) in a distribution that otherwise qualifies as a nontaxable stock dividend (¶1295) is to save trouble, expense and inconvenience, and not to give any shareholder(s) an increased interest, the distribution is treated as if the fractional shares had been issued and then redeemed by the corporation. (Reg § 1.305-3(c)) The cash received is treated as an amount realized on the sale of a fractional share. Gain or loss is the cash received minus the basis of the share sold. (Reg § 1.305-3(c)(2))[34]

¶ 1298   Dividends from regulated investment companies (RICs, or mutual funds); qualified dividend income—dividend income.

Ordinary dividends that a RIC (¶4201) distributes to its shareholders generally are taxed to them just like other corporate dividends. (¶1286, ¶1292) (Code Sec. 852; Reg § 1.852-4(a))[35] However, if the amount of dividends eligible for qualified dividend income treatment (i.e., taxable at the capital gain rates) (¶1286) received by a RIC for a tax year is less than 95% of its gross income (as specially computed), then only the amount of qualified dividend income received by the RIC for the tax year may be distributed to its shareholders as qualified dividend income. (Code Sec. 1(h)(11)(D)(iii), Code Sec. 854(b)(1)(B)) But capital gain dividends, which the RIC need not actually distribute, result in capital gain income (see ¶4201) (Code Sec. 852(b)(3)(D)),[36] and exempt-interest dividends are treated as tax-exempt interest (¶1330). (Code Sec. 852(b)(5)(B))[37] Capital gain dividends aren't treated as qualified dividend income (¶1288). (Code Sec. 854(a)) The amount of RIC dividends that are qualifying dividend income must be reported to RIC shareholders within 60 days after the close of the RIC's tax year. (Code Sec. 854(b)(2))

A dividend the RIC pays after the close of its tax year generally is treated as received by the shareholder in the year actually paid, even if the RIC elects to treat it as paid in the preceding year (see ¶4203). (Code Sec. 855(b))[38] But dividends the RIC declares in Oct., Nov. or Dec. are treated as received by the shareholder on Dec. 31 if the RIC actually pays them during the following Jan. (Code Sec. 852(b)(7))[39]

✔*caution:* Since dividends paid in Jan. may have to be picked up in the preceding year's income, that year's Form 1099, and not the RIC's monthly statements, should be used to determine the dividends to report for that year.

31. ¶J-2501, J-2516 *et seq.*
32. ¶s J-2501, J-2526
33. ¶J-2501, ¶J-2532
34. ¶J-2514
35. ¶E-6150 *et seq.*

36. ¶E-6152
37. ¶E-6160
38. ¶E-6201
39. ¶E-6202

¶ **1299**   **Dividends from real estate investment trusts (REITs); capital gain dividends—dividend income.**

REITs (¶4202) distribute ordinary dividends and capital gain dividends, which (as with RICs, see ¶1298) the beneficiaries or shareholders (investors) treat, respectively, as ordinary income (except there's no dividends-received deduction) (Code Sec. 857(c)) and capital gain. (Code Sec. 857(b)(3)(B))[40] The only REIT dividends that are eligible for qualified dividend income treatment (¶1286) are those that the REIT received as qualified dividend income, such as dividends paid to the REIT from a taxable REIT subsidiary. (Code Sec. 1(h)(11)(D)(iii), Code Sec. 857(c)(2)) For undistributed capital gains of REITs, see ¶4202. A deficiency dividend the REIT pays for any year is taxed to the shareholder in the year it's paid, not the year *for which* it's paid. (Reg § 1.860-2(a)(3)(i))[41] But any dividend declared by the REIT in Oct., Nov. or Dec. and payable to shareholders of record on a specified date in that month is considered received by the shareholder on Dec. 31 if the REIT actually pays it the next Jan. (Code Sec. 857(b)(8)(A))[42]

REITs are subject to the same capital gain designation rules as RICs (see ¶1298).[43]

¶ **1300**   **Dividends to co-op patrons; patronage dividends and per-unit retain allocations—dividend income.**

Distributions made by a co-op (¶4206) on its stock or other proprietary interests are taxed under the "regular" dividend rules (see ¶1286), but the dividends-received deduction doesn't apply if the co-op is exempt. (Code Sec. 246(a)(1))[44]

Patronage dividends and per-unit retain allocations (¶4207) received in money are included in income by the patron in the year received. Qualified written notices of allocation and qualified per-unit retain certificates (¶4207) are included in income at their stated dollar amount when received. Other property (but not nonqualified allocations or nonqualified per-unit retain certificates) is included at its fair market value when received. (Code Sec. 1385)[45]

But the amount of any patronage dividend isn't included in income to the extent it's: (1) properly taken into account as an adjustment to basis of property, or (2) attributable to personal, living or family items. (Code Sec. 1385(b))[46]

¶ **1301**   **Interest Income.** ▰▰▰▰▰▰▰▰▰▰

As a general rule, regardless of the name given to the amounts or the form of the transaction, the receipt or accrual of interest (¶1302) is taxable as ordinary income, unless specifically exempt. (Code Sec. 61(a)(4); Reg § 1.61-7(a))[47]

The interest is taxable even if it's usurious, unless applicable state law automatically converts the illegal portion into a payment of principal. (Reg § 1.61-7(a))[48]

For below-market and imputed interest, see ¶1305 *et seq.* For original issue discount (OID) as interest, see ¶1312 *et seq.* For market discount bonds, see ¶1323 *et seq.* For municipal and private activity bonds, see ¶1330 *et seq.* For inflation-indexed debt instruments, see ¶1332. For U.S. Savings Bond interest, see ¶1333.

40. ¶E-6616
41. ¶E-6304
42. ¶E-6704
43. ¶E-6617.1
44. ¶J-2608

45. ¶J-2609 *et seq.*
46. ¶J-2612
47. ¶J-2801
48. ¶J-2814

¶ 1302   **Interest defined—amounts paid for use of another's money—interest income.**

Interest is the price paid for the use of another's money or for the right to defer payment of money owed to another, regardless of the form of the transaction.[49] Interest generally includes the FMV of gifts or services received for opening or adding to accounts in financial institutions, but not if it's a de minimis premium (for a deposit of less than $5,000, the premium costs the bank $10 or less; for a deposit of $5,000 or more, it costs $20 or less).[50]

To be interest, generally a payment must be made with respect to a bona fide debt.[1] But other "interest" payments imposed by law, e.g., on judgments, tax refunds, installment sales, etc., are also interest.[2] And IRS may use the Code Sec. 482 allocation rules (¶2845) to "create" interest.[3]

¶ 1303   **Interest on defaulted mortgage—interest income.**

Amounts paid to a mortgagee as a result of the sale of property on foreclosure (or voluntary conveyance in lieu of foreclosure) of the mortgage, that represent accrued interest due on the mortgage, are taxable interest.[4] For mortgagee's gain or loss, see ¶1779.

For mortgage interest recipient's reporting requirements, see ¶4744.

¶ 1304   **"Points" and other loan-related fees—interest income.**

Payments made to a bank or other lender to get a loan are interest, to the extent they're made for the use or forbearance of money rather than for services rendered. Thus, "points" (i.e., charges connected with mortgages that the borrower pays in addition to the stated interest) are interest, while commitment and service fees (for escrow, recording, credit inspection, appraisal) aren't.[5] For recipient's reporting requirements, see ¶4744.

¶ 1305   **Foregone interest on below-market interest-rate loans; demand loans and term loans—interest income.**

Under Code Sec. 7872, the forgone interest on a "below-market" loan is taxed to the lender as interest income. (Code Sec. 7872)[6] A "below-market" loan is:

. . . *a demand loan* where interest is payable on the loan at a rate less than the applicable federal rate (AFR, see ¶1309), (Code Sec. 7872(e)(1)(A))[7] or

. . . *a term loan* where the amount loaned exceeds the present value of all payments due under the loan. (Code Sec. 7872(e)(1)(B))[8]

For a below-market demand loan, the "interest" for any period is the excess of: (1) the interest that would have been payable on the loan if it accrued annually at the AFR, over (2) any interest payable on the loan and properly allocable to the period. (Code Sec. 7872(e)(2)) For below-market term loans, the "interest" (treated as original issue discount (OID), see ¶1312 *et seq.*) is the excess of: (a) the amount loaned, over (b) the present value of all payments required to be made under the loan. (Code Sec. 7872(b)(2)(B))[9]

These rules don't apply to certain de minimis ($10,000 or less) loans (Code

---

49. ¶J-2802 *et seq.*
50. ¶J-2820
1. ¶J-2803
2. ¶J-2834 *et seq.*
3. ¶J-2817
4. ¶M-3703

5. ¶J-2818
6. ¶J-2900
7. ¶J-2939 *et seq.*
8. ¶J-2947 *et seq.*
9. ¶s J-2902, J-2904

Sec. 7872(c)(2), Code Sec. 7872(c)(3)),[10] amounts treated as "unstated interest" (see ¶1306) (Code Sec. 7872(f)(8)),[11] or certain loans under a written continuing care contract to a qualified continuing care facility. (Code Sec. 7872(g))[12]

¶ 1306   Unstated (imputed) interest on deferred payment or installment sales—interest income.

Under Code Sec. 483, for certain deferred payment or installment sales (¶1307) where the sales contract fails to provide for interest at a minimum rate specified by the Code or by IRS, part of the payments received is treated as interest ("unstated interest") that's taxable to the seller despite any contrary intention of the parties. (Code Sec. 483)[13]

¶ 1307   Payments subject to unstated interest rules—interest income.

Under Code Sec. 483(c)(1) and Code Sec. 483(d)(2), with certain exceptions (¶1311), the unstated interest rules (¶1306) apply to any payment where *all* the following requirements are met:

(1) The payment must be made on account of the sale or exchange of property.

(2) The payment must be part of the sales price under the contract.

(3) The "sales price" (determined at the time of sale) must be more than $3,000. "Sales price" includes the amount of any down payment, any liability encumbering the property and any amount treated as unstated interest under these rules, but not any *stated* interest payments.

(4) The payment must be due (under the contract) more than six months after the date of the sale or exchange.

(5) At least one payment under the contract must be due more than one year after the date of the sale or exchange.

(6) There must be total unstated interest (¶1308) under the contract. (Code Sec. 483(c)(1), Code Sec. 483(d)(2); Reg § 1.483-1(b)(1))[14]

A debt instrument of the buyer given in exchange for property isn't itself treated as a payment. Rather, any payment due under the instrument is treated as due under the sales contract. (Code Sec. 483(c)(2))[15]

¶ 1308   "Total unstated interest" for unstated interest rules; present value and discount rates—interest income.

Under Code Sec. 483(b), there's "total unstated interest" under the contract (see ¶1307) if the sum of all payments (other than *stated* interest payments) due under it more than six months after the date of the sale or exchange exceeds the sum of: (1) the present value of all those payments, plus (2) the present value of all interest payments due under the contract (regardless of when due). The total unstated interest equals the excess, if any. (Code Sec. 483(b))[16]

The present value of a payment is determined as of the date of the sale, etc., using a "test" rate prescribed by IRS. This test rate, which depends on the type of property sold, is a discount rate equal to the then applicable federal rate (AFR, see ¶1309), compounded semiannually. (Code Sec. 483(b), Code Sec. 1274(b)(2))[17]

These discount rates are used to determine the amount of unstated interest the seller

10. ¶J-2961
11. ¶J-2918
12. ¶J-2988
13. ¶J-3750 *et seq.*

14. ¶J-3800 *et seq.*
15. ¶J-3806
16. ¶J-3814
17. ¶J-3814 *et seq.*

must report as interest income:

(1) For sales or exchanges of property (not described below), the discount rate may not exceed 9% compounded semiannually if the stated principal amount of the debt instrument doesn't exceed a specified amount, as adjusted for inflation ($6,289,500 in 2022; $6,099,500 in 2021).[18]

(2) For sales or exchanges of new investment credit property, the discount rate is 100% of the AFR, compounded semiannually. (Code Sec. 483(b))[19]

(3) For sales or exchanges where part of the sold property is leased back to the seller, the discount rate is 110% of the AFR, compounded semiannually. (Code Sec. 1274(e))[20]

(4) For sales, etc., of land between family members where the aggregate sales price for all land sales between those individuals in that calendar year isn't over $500,000, the discount rate can't exceed 6% compounded semiannually. (Code Sec. 483(e))[21]

¶ 1309 Applicable federal rate (AFR) used to determine unstated interest and OID—interest income.

IRS issues monthly tables (reproduced at ¶1117 for the most recent 12 months available as we went to press) showing the AFRs to be used in determining whether there's unstated interest (¶1308) (or OID in some cases, see ¶1317) on a sale or exchange of property, and if there is, the amount of that unstated interest.[22] Under Code Sec. 1274(d)(1)(A) the rate to use on a particular sale or exchange depends on the term over which the payments are to be made. If the term is three years or less, use the short-term rate (from the tables). If it's more than three years but not more than nine years, use the mid-term rate. If it's more than nine years, use the long-term rate. (Code Sec. 1274(d)(1)(A))[23] The rate to use also depends on whether the contract was made before July 1, 1985. (Code Sec. 1274(d)(2))[24]

¶ 1310 Allocating total unstated interest under the unstated interest rules—interest income.

For any payment subject to the unstated interest rules (¶1306), that part of the total unstated interest under the contract (¶1308) that is properly allocable to that payment is treated as interest. This "interest" amount is determined in a manner consistent with the method used to compute the amount of currently includible OID (¶1320) (Code Sec. 483(a)) so that unstated interest income must be reported on an economic accrual basis.[25]

¶ 1311 Exceptions to unstated interest rules: transactions under $3,000, issue prices figured under OID rules, sales of patent rights, annuity contracts, divorce payments, section 197 intangibles acquisitions, options, assumptions of debt, below-market interest rate loans—interest income.

Under Code Sec. 483(d), even if all the requirements listed at ¶1307 are met, there's no unstated interest on:

(1) sales or exchanges where the sales price (¶1307) is $3,000 or less; (Code Sec. 483(d)(2))[26]

(2) any debt instrument (given in connection with a sale or exchange of property) whose issue price is figured under the OID rules (¶1312 *et seq.*); (Code Sec. 483(d)(1))[27]

18. ¶J-3816
19. ¶J-3818
20. ¶J-3819
21. ¶J-3820
22. ¶J-4181 *et seq.*
23. ¶J-4181
24. ¶J-4190 *et seq.*
25. ¶J-3951
26. ¶J-3901
27. ¶J-3902

(3) any amount received on the sale of patent rights described in Code Sec. 1235(a) that's contingent on the productivity, use or disposition of those rights; (Code Sec. 483(d)(4))[28]

(4) amounts received under certain annuity contracts;[29]

(5) lump-sum divorce payments and property settlements payable in installments;[30]

(6) certain acquisitions of amortizable section 197 intangibles (¶1957); (Reg § 1.197-2(f)(3)(iv)(B)(3))[31]

(7) payments under options to buy or sell property; (Reg § 1.483-1(c)(3)(v))[32]

(8) assumptions of debt in connection with sales or exchanges and acquisitions of property subject to debt; (Code Sec. 1274(c)(4))[33] and

(9) below-market interest rate loans (¶1305) (Code Sec. 7872(f)(8)).[34]

¶ 1312   Current inclusion of original issue discount (OID)—interest income.

Under Code Sec. 1272, if a debt instrument is acquired from an issuer for less than the issuer will have to pay the holder at maturity, the difference is OID (see ¶1313). No matter which method of accounting is used, the holder must report part of the OID as interest income in each tax year the debt instrument is held (¶1320), even though the OID won't be paid until maturity. (Code Sec. 1272)[35]

The OID current inclusion rules apply to all debt instruments issued with OID (Code Sec. 1272)[36] *other than:*

(1) Tax-exempt obligations (unless stripped). (Code Sec. 1272(a)(2)(A), Code Sec. 1286(d))

(2) U.S. savings bonds. (Code Sec. 1272(a)(2)(B))

(3) Short-term obligations (i.e., with a fixed maturity date not more than one year from the date of issue). (Code Sec. 1272(a)(2)(C))

(4) Certain nonbusiness loans of $10,000 or less between natural persons. (Code Sec. 1272(a)(2)(D))

(5) Debt instruments issued by natural persons before Mar. 2, '84. (former Code Sec. 1272(a)(2)(D)[37]

"Debt instruments" are bonds, debentures, notes, certificates or other instruments or contractual arrangements that are "indebtedness" under tax law principles, e.g., certificates of deposit or loans (Code Sec. 1275(a)(1); Reg § 1.1275-1(d)),[38] and REMIC interests and some similar instruments where payment may be accelerated. (Code Sec. 1272(a)(6)(C))[39] A debt instrument doesn't include a life annuity, or certain annuities issued by insurance companies. (Code Sec. 1275(a)(1)(B); Reg § 1.1275-1(j))[40]

The OID current inclusion rules also apply to preferred stock bought (after being stripped) after Apr. 30, 1993. (Code Sec. 305(e), Code Sec. 1286(a))[41] The OID current inclusion rules don't apply to a holder who buys a debt instrument at a premium (Code Sec. 1272(c)(1))[42] (except as described at ¶1322).

For application of the AFS income inclusion rule in Code Sec. 451(b) to OID resulting from specified fees with respect to lending transactions, including certain credit card fees,

---

28. ¶J-3903
29. ¶J-3905
30. ¶J-3906
31. ¶J-3903.1
32. ¶J-3904
33. ¶J-3909
34. ¶J-3910
35. ¶J-4000 *et seq.*

36. ¶J-4051
37. ¶J-4060 *et seq.*
38. ¶s J-4054, J-4055
39. ¶J-4343
40. ¶J-4057
41. ¶J-4400 *et seq.*
42. ¶J-4005

see ¶2819.

¶ 1313   Original issue discount (OID) defined; de minimis rule—interest income.

Code Sec. 1273(a)(1) provides that OID (see ¶1312) is the excess (if any) of: (1) a debt instrument's stated redemption price at maturity (¶1315) over (2) its issue price (¶1316). (Code Sec. 1273(a)(1))[43]

But the OID is treated as zero if that excess is less than 0.25% of the stated redemption price at maturity, times the number of years to maturity. (Code Sec. 1273(a)(3)) In this case, all stated interest (including amounts that would otherwise be OID) is treated as "qualified stated interest" (¶1314). (Reg § 1.1273-1(d)(1))[44]

¶ 1314   "Qualified stated interest" defined for original issue discount (OID) rules—interest income.

"Qualified stated interest," for purposes of the definition of OID (¶1313), is stated interest that's unconditionally payable in cash or property (other than the issuer's debt instruments), or will be constructively received under Code Sec. 451 (¶2816) at least annually at a single fixed rate. (Reg § 1.1273-1(c)(1))[45]

¶ 1315   Stated redemption price at maturity for original issue discount (OID) rules—interest income.

For OID purposes (¶1313), an instrument's *stated redemption price at maturity* is usually its face value. It includes interest payable at maturity *but not* interest payable at a fixed rate at periodic intervals of a year or less during the entire term of the instrument (Code Sec. 1273(a)(2)), or "qualified stated interest" (¶1314). (Reg § 1.1273-1(b))[46]

¶ 1316   Issue price of debt instrument for original issue discount (OID) rules—interest income.

For purposes of the definition of OID (¶1313), a debt instrument's issue price depends on whether it's issued for cash or property, and if issued for property, whether the instrument or property is publicly traded, as follows:

. . . For a *publicly offered debt instrument issued for money,* the issue price is the initial offering price to the public at which a substantial amount of the instruments is sold. (Code Sec. 1273(b)(1); Reg § 1.1232-3(b)(2)(i))[47]

. . . For a *privately offered debt instrument issued for money,* the issue price is the price paid by the first buyer of that instrument (Code Sec. 1273(b)(2)) or the first price at which a substantial amount of instruments in the issue is sold. (Reg § 1.1273-2(a)(1))[48]

. . . For a *debt instrument issued for property where there's public trading,* the issue price is the instrument's fair market value (FMV) as of the issue date, if it's publicly traded. If the instrument itself isn't publicly traded but is issued for property (i.e., stock or securities) that is, its issue price is the FMV of that property. (Code Sec. 1273(b)(3); Reg § 1.1232-3(b)(2)(iii), Reg § 1.1273-2(b)(1))[49]

. . . For a *nonpublicly traded debt instrument issued for nonpublicly traded property,* the issue price is its stated principal amount (total payments due under the instrument, less stated interest payments or payments designated as interest or points) if the instrument

---

43. ¶J-4100 *et seq.*
44. ¶J-4102
45. ¶J-4112
46. ¶J-4111

47. ¶J-4130
48. ¶J-4138
49. ¶J-4140

pays adequate stated interest (¶1317), or its imputed principal amount (¶1318) if it doesn't. (Code Sec. 1274(a); Reg § 1.1274-2(b)(1))[50] For exceptions, see ¶1319.

. . . For *Treasury securities,* the issue price is the average price of the securities sold (price sold at auction, if sold before Mar. 13, 2001). (Reg § 1.1275-2(d))[1]

. . . For a *debt instrument that provides for one or more contingent payments,* issued after Aug. 12, '96, the issue price is the lesser of the instrument's noncontingent principal payments, or the sum of the present values of the noncontingent payments. (Reg § 1.1274-2(g))[2]

. . . For a *tax-exempt obligation* issued after Aug. 12, '96, the issue price is (a) the greater of the obligation's FMV or its stated principal amount, or (b) for contingent obligations, its FMV. (Reg § 1.1274-2(j))[3]

The issue price of a debt instrument issued in a potentially abusive situation (e.g., a tax shelter) is the FMV of the property received in exchange for the instrument, reduced by the sum of the money plus the FMV of any property or rights (other than the instrument) that are given for the sale or exchange. (Reg § 1.1274-2(b)(3))[4]

¶ 1317 Adequate stated interest of debt instrument for original issue discount (OID) rules—interest income.

For a nonpublicly traded debt instrument issued for nonpublicly traded property (¶1316), there's adequate stated interest for a debt instrument if the sum of the present values (using the discount rate at ¶1308) of all payments of principal and interest due under it equals or exceeds its stated principal amount (¶1316) (Code Sec. 1274(c)(2)), or if the instrument has a single fixed rate of interest that's paid or compounded at least annually and is at least equal to the test rate. (Reg § 1.1274-2(c))[5]

¶ 1318 Imputed principal amount of debt instrument for original issue discount (OID) rules—interest income.

For a nonpublicly traded debt instrument issued for nonpublicly traded property (¶1316), the imputed principal amount is the sum of the present values of all payments of principal and interest due under a debt instrument, computed as of the date of the sale or exchange using the discount rates at ¶1308. (Code Sec. 1274(b)(2); Reg § 1.1274-2(c)(1))[6]

The imputed principal amount of a variable rate debt instrument that provides for stated interest at a qualified floating rate(s) generally is determined by assuming that the instrument provides for a fixed rate of interest for each accrual period to which a qualified floating rate applies. (Reg § 1.1274-2(f)(1)(i))[7]

In a potentially abusive situation (e.g., tax shelter), the imputed principal amount of an instrument received in exchange for property is the property's fair market value, adjusted for other considerations in the transaction. (Code Sec. 1274(b)(3)(A); Reg § 1.1274-3(a))[8]

¶ 1319 Exceptions to original issue discount (OID) rules for nonpublicly traded debt instruments—interest income.

The issue price of a nonpublicly traded debt instrument issued for nonpublicly traded property is its stated redemption price at maturity, instead of the amount determined

---

50. ¶J-4151
1. ¶J-4131
2. ¶J-4151.2
3. ¶J-4151.3, J-4151.4
4. ¶J-4151.5

5. ¶J-4153 *et seq.*
6. ¶J-4154 *et seq.*
7. ¶J-4157
8. ¶J-4173 *et seq.*

under the rules at ¶1316—so there's no OID, see ¶1313)—in these cases: (Code Sec. 1273(b)(4))[9]

(1) Debt instruments with adequate stated interest and no OID; (Reg § 1.1274-1(b)(1))[10]

(1) sales or exchanges involving total payments of $250,000 or less; (Code Sec. 1274(c)(3)(C))[11]

(2) sales or exchanges by an individual of a principal residence; (Code Sec. 1274(c)(3)(B))[12]

(3) sales or exchanges of certain farms where the sales price can't exceed $1,000,000; (Code Sec. 1274(c)(3)(A))[13]

(4) certain sales of patents; (Code Sec. 1274(c)(3)(E))[14]

(5) certain transfers of land between family members where the total price for all land sales between them for the year isn't more than $500,000; (Code Sec. 1274(c)(3)(F))[15]

(6) sales or exchanges where, in exchange for property, a nonaccrual method buyer (other than a dealer) issues a "cash method debt instrument," i.e., a debt instrument whose principal amount doesn't exceed a specified amount ($4,492,500 in 2022; $4,356,800 in 2021), if the "regular" issue price rules otherwise would apply *and* buyer and seller jointly elect cash method treatment for the instrument; (Code Sec. 1274A(c))[16]

(7) sales or exchanges of personal use property (to the issuer) that evidence a below-market loan (¶1305); (Reg § 1.1274-1(b)(3)(i))[17]

(8) transactions involving "demand" below-market loans; (Reg § 1.1274-1(b)(3)(ii))[18] or

(9) transfers between spouses or incident to divorce. (Reg § 1.1274-1(b)(3)(iii))[19]

    observation: Even if there's no OID, there may be unstated interest (see ¶1306).

¶ 1320   Determining amount of currently includible original issue discount (OID)—interest income.

A holder of a debt instrument issued with OID (¶1313) who is required to include part of the OID in gross income currently must include in gross income for the tax year, an amount equal to the sum of the daily portions of the OID for each day the instrument was held during that year. (Code Sec. 1272(a)(1))[20] For accrual under the constant yield method, see ¶1321.

To determine the daily OID portion, allocate to each day in any "accrual period" (below) that day's ratable portion of the increase (during that period) in the instrument's adjusted issue price (below). This increase equals the excess of: (1) the adjusted issue price at the start of the accrual period times the yield to maturity (based on compounding at the end of each accrual period), over (2) the sum of the amounts payable as interest on the instrument during that accrual period. (Code Sec. 1272(a)(3))[21]

The adjusted issue price of a debt instrument at the start of any accrual period is the sum of its issue price (¶1316), plus all adjustments (i.e., OID inclusions) in that issue price for all earlier accrual periods. (Code Sec. 1272(a)(4))[22]

9. ¶J-4196
10. ¶J-4197
11. ¶J-4198
12. ¶J-4199
13. ¶J-4200
14. ¶J-4205
15. ¶J-4206

16. ¶J-4207 *et seq.*
17. ¶J-4202
18. ¶J-4203
19. ¶J-4204
20. ¶J-4301
21. ¶J-4301
22. ¶J-4324

Accrual period generally means a 6-month period (or shorter period from date of issuance) ending on a day in the calendar year corresponding to the debt instrument's maturity date, or a date six months before that date. (Code Sec. 1272(a)(5))[23]

For *inflation-indexed debt instruments,* OID is computed using the coupon bond method or the discount bond method (see ¶1332). (Reg § 1.1275-7(a))[24]

¶ 1321 Accrual of original issue discount (OID) using constant yield method—interest income.

Under the constant yield method, the amount of OID includible in the holder's income for a tax year (¶1320) is determined as follows:

(1) Determine the instrument's yield to maturity. This is the discount rate that, when used to compute the present value of all payments under the instrument, produces an amount equal to the instrument's issue price. The yield must be constant over the instrument's term and must be calculated to at least two decimal places. (Reg § 1.1272-1(b)(1)(i))

(2) Determine the accrual period, which may be any length (based on any reasonable accounting convention), but can't exceed one year. Each scheduled payment must occur either on the first or last day of an accrual period. The simplest OID computation is where the accrual periods correspond to the intervals between payment dates set forth by the instrument. (Reg § 1.1272-1(b)(1)(ii))

(3) Determine the OID allocable to each accrual period. This is the instrument's adjusted issue price at the start of the accrual period, times the instrument's yield, less the "qualified stated interest" (¶1314) allocable to the period. (Reg § 1.1272-1(b)(1)(iii))

(4) Determine the daily portions of OID, by allocating to each day in an accrual period the ratable portion of the OID allocable to that period. The holder includes in income the daily portions of OID for each day in the tax year on which the instrument was held. (Reg § 1.1272-1(b)(1)(iv))[25]

The constant yield method may not be used for certain interests held by a REMIC (¶4204), certain instruments with payments subject to acceleration or that provide for contingent payments, or certain variable rate instruments. (Reg § 1.1272-1(b)(2))[26]

¶ 1322 Original issue discount (OID) inclusion reduced where holder paid acquisition premium—interest income.

If the holder of a debt instrument bought it from someone other than the original issuer, paying an acquisition premium (i.e., an amount in excess of the original issue price plus all OID required to be included in the gross income of earlier holders), the holder's current OID inclusion (¶1320) is reduced. This is done by reducing each daily includible OID portion by this constant fraction: the acquisition premium, divided by the total OID (before reduction) allocable to the days after the purchase date and ending on the date of maturity. However, the reduction applies only to the OID inclusion and isn't taken into account in computing the instrument's adjusted issue price at the start of an accrual period. (Code Sec. 1272(a)(7))[27]

---

23. ¶J-4301
24. ¶J-4379 *et seq.*
25. ¶J-4302

26. ¶J-4303
27. ¶J-4349

¶ 1323   Accrued market discount on disposition of "market discount bonds"; computation of discount via ratable accrual method or a constant interest rate method—interest income.

Under Code Sec. 1276(a)(1), gain on the disposition of a market discount bond (¶1325) is ordinary income to the extent of the accrued market discount on the bond (Code Sec. 1276(a)(1)) (unless the holder elects to include the discount currently, see ¶1326). This ordinary income is treated as interest income, with exceptions. (Code Sec. 1276(a)(4))[28] For partial principal payments, see ¶1324.

The accrued market discount interest is computed under a ratable accrual method or, at taxpayer's election, a constant interest rate method. (Code Sec. 1276(b))[29]

Dispositions by gift and transfers to controlled corporations also can result in interest income under this rule. (Code Sec. 1276(d)(1)(A))[30] If the disposition is other than by sale, exchange or involuntary conversion, the amount realized is equal to the bond's fair market value. (Code Sec. 1276(a)(2))[31]

Interest treatment applies even if the gain wouldn't otherwise be recognized. Regs may allow nonrecognition in certain nontaxable transactions. (Code Sec. 1276(a)(1), Code Sec. 1276(d)(1))[32]

¶ 1324   Accrued market discount when partial principal payments are made—interest income.

If the principal on a market discount bond (¶1325) (acquired after Oct. 22, '86) is paid in more than one installment, any partial principal payment is included as ordinary income to the extent of the accrued market discount on the bond (Code Sec. 1276(a)(3)(A))[33] (unless the holder elects to include the discount currently, see ¶1326).

Any amount that has been included in gross income under this rule reduces the amount of any accrued market discount that's included on any later disposition of (¶1323), or further partial principal payments on, the bond. (Code Sec. 1276(a)(3)(B))[34]

If bond principal can be paid in two or more payments, the accrued market discount is to be determined under regs. (Code Sec. 1276(b)(3))[35]

¶ 1325   "Market discount bonds"; excess of bond's stated redemption price at maturity over taxpayer's basis for the bond—interest income.

Under Code Sec. 1278(a)(1)(A), market discount bonds are any "bonds" having a market discount *other than* short-term obligations (one year or less), tax-exempt obligations bought before May 1, '93, U.S. savings bonds and certain installment obligations. (Code Sec. 1278(a)(1)(A), Code Sec. 1278(a)(1)(B))[36]

Market discount is the excess (if any) of the bond's stated redemption price at maturity (¶1315) over the taxpayer's basis for the bond immediately after acquiring it. (Code Sec. 1278(a)(2))[37] The market discount is zero if it's less than 0.25% of the bond's stated redemption price at maturity times the number of years to maturity after the taxpayer acquires the bond. (Code Sec. 1278(a)(2)(C))[38]

28. ¶J-4551
29. ¶J-4560; ¶J-4562
30. ¶J-4570
31. ¶J-4551
32. ¶s J-4551, J-4569
33. ¶J-4566
34. ¶J-4567
35. ¶J-4568
36. ¶s J-4552, J-4556
37. ¶J-4553
38. ¶J-4554

Special rules determine the stated redemption price at maturity for this purpose if the bond was issued with original issue discount (OID). (Code Sec. 1278(a)(4))[39]

¶ 1326 Election to include accrued market discount in income currently—interest income.

Instead of including a bond's accrued market discount on disposition (¶1323) or partial payment of principal (¶1324), a taxpayer may elect to include the discount as interest income for the tax years to which it's attributable, i.e., currently. The taxpayer may use either the ratable accrual method or the constant interest rate method. (Code Sec. 1278(b)(1); Code Sec. 1276(b))[40]

Elect by attaching to a timely filed income tax return, a statement that market discount has been included in gross income under Code Sec. 1278(b), describing the method used to determine the amount attributable to that tax year.[41]

¶ 1327 Acquisition discount on short-term obligations; mandatory accrual; daily portion of the acquisition discount—interest income.

Under Code Sec. 1281(a)(1), certain holders of short-term obligations (not more than one year) are currently taxed on their daily portions of the "acquisition discount" (for government obligations, or nongovernment obligations if the holder so elects) or original issue discount (for nongovernment obligations), for each day during the year that they hold the obligation. (Code Sec. 1281(a)(1), Code Sec. 1283(c)) Any other interest payable on the obligation also must be taken into account as it accrues. (Code Sec. 1281(a)(2))[42]

An obligation's "acquisition discount" is the excess of its stated redemption price at maturity (¶1315) over taxpayer's basis in it. (Code Sec. 1283(a)(2))[43]

The daily portion of the acquisition discount is computed using the ratable accrual method or, if taxpayer so elects, the constant interest method. (Code Sec. 1283(b))[44]

This mandatory accrual rule applies only to these holders of short-term obligations:

(1) Accrual basis taxpayers;

(2) Taxpayers who hold the obligations primarily for sale to customers in the ordinary course of their trade or business. (Code Sec. 1281(b)(1))[45] This doesn't include banks that make short-term loans bearing only stated interest to customers in the ordinary course of business;[46];

(3) Banks (as defined in Code Sec. 581);

(4) Regulated investment companies (mutual funds, ¶4201) or common trust funds (¶4210);

(5) Taxpayers who identify the obligations as part of a Code Sec. 1256 hedging transaction; and

(6) Taxpayers whose short-term obligations are stripped bonds or stripped coupons that taxpayer stripped. (Code Sec. 1281(b)(1))[47]

The mandatory accrual rule doesn't apply to the ordinary investor.[48] Special rules apply to obligations held by pass-through entities. (Code Sec. 1281(b)(2))[49]

◆/observation: The mandatory accrual rule doesn't apply to a cash basis holder who

---

39. ¶J-4553
40. ¶J-4573
41. ¶J-4574
42. ¶s J-4501, J-4506
43. ¶J-4501
44. ¶J-4503; ¶J-4504

45. ¶J-4502
46. ¶J-4501
47. ¶J-4502
48. ¶J-4502
49. ¶J-4502

isn't a dealer in these obligations and isn't subject to the Code Sec. 1256 hedging rules.

¶ 1328   Interest on bonds sold between interest dates—interest income.

When fixed-interest bonds (not in default) are sold between interest dates, the amount the buyer pays that represents interest accrued as of the sale date is taxable interest to the seller. (Reg § 1.61-7(d)) Interest accrued after the sale date is taxable to the buyer on receipt.[50]

Bonds in default are usually traded "flat" (no part of the selling price is allocated between interest and principal). If there's accrued interest, the part of the selling price that represents interest accrued before the sale isn't taxable to the buyer until it exceeds the buyer's basis.[1]

¶ 1329   Interest credited to frozen deposits—interest income.

Interest credited to a frozen deposit (i.e., in a bankrupt or insolvent (actual or threatened) financial institution) during a calendar year, that's includible in the depositor's income for the year, can't exceed the sum of the net withdrawals during the year plus the amount withdrawable at the end of the year. (Code Sec. 451(i)(1))[2]

¶ 1330   Tax-exempt interest—interest on state or local bonds—interest income.

Under Code Sec. 103(a), Code Sec. 103(c), Code Sec. 7871(a)(4), interest on state and local bonds (i.e., obligations of a state, the District of Columbia, a U.S. possession, certain Indian tribal governments or any political subdivision of the foregoing) is exempt from federal income tax (Code Sec. 103(a), Code Sec. 103(c), Code Sec. 7871(a)(4))[3] (with certain exceptions, see ¶1331). For "educational expense" exclusion for certain U.S. savings bonds, see ¶2219 *et seq*. For tax credit bonds, see ¶2359.

observation: Even if interest isn't subject to federal income tax, it may have to be taken into account for certain other purposes.

caution: There's also a bar against deducting interest on debt incurred or continued to buy or carry tax-exempt bonds (¶1723).

Every person required to file a return must report on it all tax-exempt interest received or accrued during the tax year. (Code Sec. 6012(d))[4]

¶ 1331   Taxable interest from private activity bonds, hedge bonds, arbitrage bonds; exemption for exempt facility, mortgage, veterans' mortgage, small issue, scholarship funding, redevelopment, or Code Sec. 501(c)(3) bonds—interest income.

Under Code Sec. 103(b)(1), Code Sec. 141(e), *private activity bonds* aren't eligible for the interest exemption described at ¶1330 unless the bond meets detailed requirements *and* is one of seven specified types of bonds (exempt facility, mortgage, veterans' mortgage, small issue, scholarship funding, redevelopment, or Code Sec. 501(c)(3) bonds). (Code Sec. 103(b)(1), Code Sec. 141(e))[5] Pre-Aug. 16, '86 industrial development bonds are subject to similar "qualification" rules. [6]

Hedge bonds (i.e., issued to "hedge" another bond) aren't exempt unless 85% of the

---

50. ¶J-2827
1. ¶J-2828 *et seq.*
2. ¶J-3711
3. ¶J-3000

4. ¶J-3002
5. ¶s J-3000 *et seq.*, J-3100, J-3252 *et seq.*, J-3600
6. ¶s J-3153 *et seq.*, J-3227 *et seq.*, J-3251

bond's spendable proceeds (i.e., net of issuance expenses and certain reserves) are reasonably expected to be spent within specified periods, and at least 95% of the issuance costs (which can't be contingent) are paid within 180 days after issuance. (Code Sec. 149(g))[7]

Arbitrage bonds aren't exempt. (Code Sec. 103(b)(2)) This means a bond forming part of an issue any part of whose proceeds is reasonably expected to be used, directly or indirectly, to acquire (or refinance) nontemporary investments with a materially higher yield (more than 1/8 of 1 percentage point) than the bond itself, unless a required rebate is paid. (Code Sec. 148(a), Code Sec. 148(f); Reg § 1.148-2(d)(2)) If an issuer enters a transaction for a principal purpose of getting a material financial advantage based on the difference between tax-exempt and taxable rates, IRS has discretion to clearly reflect the economic substance of the transaction. (Reg § 1.148-10(e)) An issuer can't avoid having a bond treated as an arbitrage bond by giving away the prohibited arbitrage bond profit, e.g., by buying investments at other than fair market value ("yield burning"). [8]

¶ 1332 Inflation-indexed debt instruments; Treasury Inflation-Indexed Securities; coupon bond method and discount bond method of accounting—interest income.

Under Reg § 1.1275-7(c)(1) and Reg § 1.1275-7(h), there are two methods of accounting for stated interest and inflation adjustments on inflation-indexed debt instruments (issued after Jan. 1, '97). Inflation-indexed debt instruments are issued for cash, indexed for inflation and deflation using a general price or wage index, and aren't otherwise contingent payment debt instruments. (Reg § 1.1275-7(c)(1), Reg § 1.1275-7(h)) These rules apply to Treasury Inflation-Indexed Securities (TIPS), but not certain debt instruments, e.g., U.S. savings bonds and bonds issued by qualified tuition programs. (Reg § 1.1275-7(b))[9]

(1) The coupon bond method is a simplified method that applies if (a) the debt instrument is issued at par, and (b) all stated interest on it's qualified stated interest (i.e., it's unconditionally payable in cash at least annually, see ¶1314). Under this method, the stated interest is taxable to the holder when received or accrued, in accordance with its accounting method. Any increase in the inflation-adjusted principal amount is treated as OID (¶1313) for the period in which it occurs. (Reg § 1.1275-7(d)) The coupon bond method applies to TIPS that aren't stripped and to TIPS issued with more than a de minimis amount of premiums. (Reg § 1.1275-7(g)(2))[10]

observation: Assuming there's some inflation and principal continues to be adjusted upward, holders will have to include amounts not yet realized as interest income.

A decrease in a bond's inflation-indexed principal first reduces the interest income attributable to the interest payments for the year of the adjustment. If the decrease exceeds that income, the excess generally is an ordinary deduction to the extent taxpayer previously included interest from the bond in income. Any remaining decrease is carried forward to reduce interest income in future years. A taxpayer generally has a capital loss if the bond is sold, or it matures, before all the decrease has been used. (Reg § 1.1275-7(f)(1), Reg § 1.1275-7(d)(4))[11]

(2) The discount bond method is used if the instrument doesn't qualify for the coupon bond method (e.g., because it's issued at a discount). Under this method, taxpayers make current adjustments to their OID accruals to account for changes in the inflation-adjusted principal amount. If the daily portions for an accrual period are positive amounts, they're

---

7. ¶J-3667 *et seq.*
8. ¶J-3400 *et seq.*
9. ¶J-4056.1, J-4379.1 *et seq.*
10. ¶J-4379.1 *et seq.*
11. ¶J-4379.1 *et seq.*

taken into account under Code Sec. 1272 by the holder (¶1312). If the daily portions are negative, they're taken into account under the rules for deflation adjustments described above. (Reg § 1.1275-7(e)) The discount bond method applies to TIPS that are stripped under the Treasury's STRIPS (Separate Trading of Registered Interest and Principal of Securities) program. (Reg § 1.1286-2)[12]

¶ 1333 Interest on U.S. savings bonds—Series HH "face amount" bonds, Series EE "discount" bonds, Series I inflation-indexed face-amount bonds— interest income.

Interest on U.S. savings bonds now being issued is earned in three ways. On Series HH "face amount" bonds (not issued after Aug. 31, 2004), it's paid semiannually by check. On Series EE "discount" bonds, it's reflected as an increase in the bond's value over stated periods. On Series I inflation-indexed face amount bonds, it's credited monthly (at a fixed rate for the 30-year life of the bond and a semiannual variable inflation rate) and paid when the bond is redeemed. The interest on these bonds (and on any unmatured or extended Series E and Series H bonds still outstanding) is fully taxable unless the exclusion at ¶2218 applies.[13]

Cash basis taxpayers report the interest on Series HH (or H) bonds in the year received.[14]

A cash basis owner of Series EE bonds (and outstanding Series E bonds) and Series I bonds may either: (1) defer reporting any interest (i.e., the bond's increase in value) until the year of final maturity, redemption, or other disposition, whichever is earlier, or (2) elect to report the annual increase in value in each year's return.[15]

Some Series E bonds can, at the owner's option, be held up to 30 years beyond their original maturity ("final maturity"). A cash basis owner who hasn't elected to report the interest on a Series E bond annually (under (2), above) must report all of the interest on the bond in the year in which the bond is redeemed or disposed of or, if earlier, the year in which it reaches "final maturity." (Code Sec. 454(a); Reg § 1.454-1(a)(1))[16]

RIA✓*observation:* Series E bonds issued before Dec., '65 reached final maturity 40 years after their issue date. Series E bonds issued after Nov., '65, and before July, '80, and all Series EE bonds, reach final maturity 30 years after their issue dates. (Series E bonds were issued before July, '80, and stopped paying interest in June of 2011.) This means that any accrued interest on Series EE bonds issued in '82 was taxable in 2012. *Accrual basis taxpayers* include the interest on the above bonds as it accrues.[17]

For the exclusion of income earned on qualified U.S. savings bonds by a payor of higher education expenses, see ¶2218 *et seq.*

¶ 1334 When to report interest income (other than original issue discount (OID)).

Cash basis taxpayers report interest in the tax year it's actually or constructively received, regardless of when the interest is accrued on the debtor's books.[18] Generally, interest isn't constructively received if taxpayer's control of its receipt is subject to substantial limits or restrictions. (Reg § 1.451-2(a))[19] Thus, interest on a 6-month certificate that isn't credited or made available before maturity without penalty isn't taxable until the certificate is redeemed or matures.[20]

---

12. ¶J-4379.5
13. ¶J-3719 *et seq.*
14. ¶s J-3720, J-3721
15. ¶J-3719
16. ¶s J-3721, J-3722

17. ¶J-3719 *et seq.*
18. ¶J-3703
19. ¶J-3706
20. ¶J-3710

Savings institution interest, or interest on life insurance dividends left to accumulate, is considered received when credited to the depositor's (policyholder's) account and subject to its withdrawal.[21]

Where a bank charges a penalty for premature withdrawals from a time savings account, the gross amount of interest paid or credited during the withdrawal year is reported as interest that year, even if the penalty partially or completely offsets the interest.[22] For deduction of forfeited interest, see ¶2164.

Matured interest coupons are constructively received in the year they mature unless it can be shown that there are no funds available for payment of the interest during the year.[23]

Accrual basis taxpayers report interest in the tax year in which the right to receive the interest becomes fixed, regardless of when it's received.[24] But if it appears reasonably certain the interest won't be paid because the debtor is insolvent, the creditor can delay reporting the interest until its collection appears reasonably certain.[25]

For cash and accrual taxpayers, there are special rules on when to include "interest" on below-market rate loans (¶1305), (Code Sec. 7872(a)(2), Code Sec. 7872(b)(2)(A))[26] "points" (¶1335), and unstated interest (¶1336).

caution: These rules don't apply to debt issued with OID (¶1312).

¶ 1335 When "points" are included in income—interest income.

"Points" (¶1304) in the form of discount are taken into account under the "principal-reduction method"—i.e., as stated principal payments on the loan are made. "Points" paid out of funds not from the lender are included on receipt.[27]

¶ 1336 When to report unstated interest income.

A cash method seller includes unstated interest allocated to a payment (¶1306) as interest income in the tax year the payment is received. An accrual method seller includes the unstated interest in the tax year the payment is due. (Reg § 1.483-2(a)(1)(ii))[28]

¶ 1337 Rent and Royalty Income.

Rent is the payment for the use of real or tangible personal property (¶1338 *et seq.*). Royalties are payments for the use of certain rights, e.g., intangible rights such as patents (¶1344). Both are includible in gross income.

¶ 1338 Rents paid in cash or property; when rents are reported as income.

Under Code Sec. 61(a)(5), rents are includible in gross income, whether paid in cash or property. (Code Sec. 61(a)(5); Reg § 1.61-1(a)) If paid in property, the property's fair market value (at receipt) is the amount taxed as rent.[29]

Rents are reported by cash basis taxpayers when received, and by accrual basis taxpayers when due unless they're considered uncollectible.[30] For advance rentals, see ¶1340.

Section 501, Division N, of the Consolidated Appropriations Act, 2021 (P.L. 116-260, 12/21/2020) allows states and their political subdivisions, U.S. territories, Indian Tribes, and the Department of Hawaiian Home Lands to use funds allocated by Treasury to

---

21. ¶s J-3709, J-3717
22. ¶J-2822
23. ¶J-3715
24. ¶J-3701
25. ¶J-3702

26. ¶J-3708
27. ¶E-3004 *et seq.*
28. ¶J-3758
29. ¶J-2200 *et seq.*
30. ¶J-2276

provide emergency assistance to households to pay rent, utilities, home energy expenses, and other related expenses. These payments aren't income to household members, regardless of whether the payment is for rent, utilities, or home energy expenses, and regardless of whether the payment is made to the renter or to the landlord or utility company. (https://www.irs.gov/newsroom/emergency-rental-assistance-frequently-asked-questions)[31]

¶ 1339   Bonuses or extra payments by tenants to lessors; lease cancellation payments—rent income.

A bonus or extra payment by the tenant to the lessor or sublessor on the execution of the lease is taxable as rent to the lessor or sublessor.[32]

If the tenant pays the landlord for permission to cancel the lease, the payments are rent to the landlord (whether cash or accrual basis) in the year received. (Reg § 1.61-8(a)) Payments to the landlord for modifying a lease or consenting to a sublease are also considered rent.[33] Where the lessor pays the tenant to cancel the lease, see ¶1580.

¶ 1340   Advance rentals and security deposits—rent income.

An advance rental is currently taxable (Reg § 1.61-8(b)), even if it's refundable or can be applied against the purchase price.[34] But a security deposit (¶1206) isn't taxable rent.[35]

¶ 1341   Rules for deferred-payment leases—rent income.

Under Code Sec. 467, where the rules on deferred payment leases over $250,000 apply (¶1582), the lessor has a "constant accrual" of rental income in the same way that rental expenses are deductible by the lessee. (Code Sec. 467)[36]

¶ 1342   Tenant's payment of landlord's interest, property taxes, mortgage principal, or other expenses—rent income.

Under Reg § 1.61-8(c), where a tenant is required under the lease to pay interest, property taxes, mortgage principal, etc., thus satisfying the *landlord's* own payment obligation, the payments are treated as rent paid by the tenant to the landlord. (Reg § 1.61-8(c))[37]

¶ 1343   Tenant's improvements to the leased property; construction allowances from lessor; improvements as rent substitutes—rent income.

Code Sec. 109 provides that, where a tenant erects a building or makes other improvements to leased property, the resulting increase in the property's value isn't income to the landlord either at the time the improvements are made or at the end of the lease term. (Code Sec. 109) But the landlord does have rental income if the improvements are made as rent substitutes.[38]

A lessee may exclude any amount received in cash (or as a rent reduction) from a lessor under a short-term lease (15 years or less) of retail space, that's for the purpose of the lessee's constructing or improving qualified long-term real property for use in the lessee's trade or business at the leased space. The construction allowance is excludible to the extent the lessee uses it for that purpose, within 8½ months after the end of the tax year it was received. Qualified long-term real property is nonresidential real property that's part

---

31. ¶J-1486.1
32. ¶J-2278
33. ¶J-2215 *et seq.*
34. ¶J-2218

35. ¶J-2277
36. ¶L-6800 *et seq.*
37. ¶J-2210 *et seq.*
38. ¶J-2250 *et seq.*

of or otherwise present at the retail space and reverts to the lessor at lease termination. The lessor treats any qualified long-term real property that's constructed or improved with an allowance excluded under these rules as its own nonresidential real property (¶1919). (Code Sec. 110; Reg § 1.110-1)[39]

¶ 1344 Royalties for the use of copyrights, patents, trademarks, secret processes and similar intangibles, and for the right to exploit mineral or other natural resources—royalty income.

Under Code Sec. 61(a)(6), royalties (payments received for the use of copyrights, patents, trademarks, secret processes and similar intangibles, and for the right to exploit mineral or other natural resources) are taxable as ordinary income (Code Sec. 61(a)(6)), regardless of the name given to them by the parties or the form of payment (e.g., lump sum or property such as stock).[40]

Royalties are included by cash basis taxpayers on receipt (actual or constructive), and by accrual basis taxpayers when their rights to them are fixed.[41]

¶ 1345 Life Insurance Proceeds, Taxability.

In general, life insurance proceeds payable by reason of the insured's death are fully excludable (Code Sec. 101(a)) or, if paid later than death under an interest option (¶1347) or in installments (¶1346), partially excludable, from the recipient's gross income.

To qualify for the full exclusion, the amounts must be received under a "life insurance contract" (see below) and paid by reason of the insured's death. The exclusion applies to lump sum payments made at the time of the insured's death, and to amounts paid later to the extent the payment doesn't exceed the amount payable at death. (Reg § 1.101-1(a)(1))[42] The exclusion is limited if the policy was transferred for value (¶1350). For contracts that don't qualify as life insurance contracts, the exclusion is limited to the excess of death benefits over the contract's net surrender value. (Code Sec. 7702(g)(2))[43] For dividends and other lifetime payments, see ¶1348. For accelerated death benefits, see ¶1349.

To qualify as a life insurance contract, a contract must be a life insurance (or endowment) contract under local law *and* satisfy either (a) a cash value accumulation test, or (b) a combined guideline premium requirement/cash value corridor test. (Code Sec. 101(f), Code Sec. 7702(a), Code Sec. 7702(h))[44] Pre-'85 contracts must entail risk shifting and risk distribution.[45]

¶ 1346 Life insurance proceeds paid in installments or for life; excludable portion.

Under Code Sec. 101(d)(1), if the life insurance proceeds payable on the insured's death are paid in installments or for life, only part of each payment is excluded. Any amount that exceeds the excluded portion is taxable when received. But if the amount of the total anticipated payments can't exceed the total amount payable at the insured's death, then each payment is fully excludable, whenever it's made. (Code Sec. 101(d)(1); Reg § 1.101-4(a)(1)(i))[46]

The excludable portion of each payment is: (1) the excludable amount held by the insurer with respect to the particular beneficiary, divided by (2) the number of payments to be

---

39. ¶J-2261 *et seq.*
40. ¶J-2300 *et seq.*
41. ¶s J-2305, J-2306
42. ¶J-4700 *et seq.*
43. ¶J-4900 *et seq.*
44. ¶J-4800 *et seq.*
45. ¶J-4950 *et seq.*
46. ¶J-4718

made or, if payments are for life, the number of payments anticipated over the life expectancy of the beneficiary. This same prorated amount of each payment is excludable, regardless of how many payments are made (Reg § 1.101-4) (i.e., even if the beneficiary exceeds anticipated life expectancy). The excludable amount is the present value to the beneficiary (as of the date of death) of the settlement.[47]

¶ 1347 Life insurance proceeds left as interest—taxability.

Under Code Sec. 101(c), where excludable life insurance proceeds are held by the insurer under an agreement to pay interest, the interest is taxable to the recipient, whether the interest option was chosen by the insured or by the insured's beneficiaries or estate. No part of this interest may be excluded under the proration rules (¶1346). (Code Sec. 101(c); Reg § 1.101-3(a))[48]

¶ 1348 Proceeds paid before death of insured—loans, refunds, dividends, policy surrenders, redemption or maturity of a contract—taxability.

Under Code Sec. 72(a), payments made under life insurance or endowment contracts before the death of the insured (e.g., loans, refunds, dividends, and amounts received on surrender, redemption or maturity of a contract) generally are treated as amounts "not received as an annuity (¶1363). (Code Sec. 72(a))[49]

Thus, a transferee generally recognizes ordinary income in the amount received on the surrender of a life insurance policy (cash surrender value) less the adjusted basis in the contract (aggregate premiums paid).[50]

For accelerated death benefits received by terminally or chronically ill individuals, see ¶1349.

¶ 1349 Accelerated death benefits—terminally or chronically ill insureds—viatical settlements—taxability.

Code Sec. 101(g)(1) provides that amounts received under a life insurance contract on the life of individuals who are certified terminally or chronically ill are excluded from gross income as amounts paid by reason of the death of an insured (¶1345). (Code Sec. 101(g)(1)) A similar exclusion applies to amounts received for the sale or assignment of any portion of a death benefit under a life insurance contract to a viatical settlement provider (one that regularly buys or takes assignments of life insurance contracts on the lives of the terminally ill and meets detailed standards) if the insured under the life insurance contract is either terminally or chronically ill. (Code Sec. 101(g)(2)(A))[1] In the case of chronically ill individuals, the exclusions apply only if detailed requirements are met. (Code Sec. 101(g)(3))[2]

¶ 1350 Life insurance proceeds exclusion limited where policy was transferred for value.

Under Code Sec. 101(a)(2), if a transfer of a life insurance policy is made for valuable consideration, the death benefits paid on the life insurance contract are excludable (¶1345) only to the extent of the actual value of the consideration paid by the transferee to acquire the contract (or interest), plus any premiums or 'other amounts' paid by the transferee after the transfer. Thus, for a transfer of an interest in a life insurance policy for valuable

---

47. ¶J-4720
48. ¶J-4717
49. ¶J-5055 *et seq.*

50. ¶J-5058
1. ¶J-4750 *et seq.*, ¶J-4818
2. ¶J-4754 *et seq.*

consideration, including a 'reportable policy sale' (see below) for valuable consideration, the amount of the proceeds from that policy or interest that's excludable from the transferee's gross income is generally limited to the sum of: (1) the actual value of the consideration for the transfer, and (2) the premiums and other amounts later paid by the transferee for that interest. (Reg § 1.101-1(b)(1)(i)) 'Other amounts' includes interest paid or accrued by the transferee on debt relating to the insurance contract/interest if the interest is not deductible under Code Sec. 264(a)(4) (see ¶1720). (Code Sec. 101(a)(2))[3] For gain or loss on sale or exchange of policy, see ¶2415. If only an interest in the contract is transferred, the limit applies only to the part of the proceeds attributable to the transferred interest.[4]

The above limitation doesn't apply if: (a) the transfer is to the insured, a partner or partnership of the insured, or a corporation in which the insured is a shareholder or officer; (Code Sec. 101(a)(2)(B)) or (b) the transferee's basis for the contract (or interest) is determined in whole or in part by reference to the transferor's basis (Code Sec. 101(a)(2)(A)),[5]. However, the exceptions at (a) and (b), above, don't apply to a transfer of a life insurance contract, or any interest in one, in a "reportable policy sale," (Code Sec. 101(a)(3)(A)) which generally is the direct or indirect acquisition of an interest in a life insurance contract by one with no substantial family, business, or financial relationship with the insured apart from the interest in the life insurance contract. (Code Sec. 101(a)(3)(B))[6]

Where the transfer is a gift, including a reportable policy sale that's not for valuable consideration, the amount of the proceeds attributable to the interest that is excludable from gross income is limited to the sum of the amount of the proceeds attributable to the gratuitously transferred interest that would have been excludable by the transferor if the transfer had not occurred and the premiums and other amounts subsequently paid by the transferee with respect to the interest.(Reg § 1.101-1(b)(2))[7]

¶ 1351   Employer-owned life insurance—Form 8925—taxability.

Under Code Sec. 101(j)(1), for contracts issued after Aug. 17, 2006 (except for tax-free Code Sec. 1035 exchanges), an employer in a trade or businesses owning an employer-owned life insurance contract on an employee (reportable annually on Form 8925 (Code Sec. 6039I)) treats proceeds payable to it from such a policy as income, excluding as a death benefit only the premiums and other amounts it paid for the contract. (Code Sec. 101(j)(1))[8] This rule doesn't apply for a contract for which notice and consent requirements are met, if: (1) the insured was an individual who was an employee within 12 months of death; (2) at the time the contract was issued, the insured was a director; a 'highly compensated employee,' (¶4315); or a 'highly compensated individual,' i.e., one of the five highest paid officers, a shareholder owning more than 10%, or anyone else in the top 35% of employees ranked by pay; (3) the amount is paid to a family member of the insured (under Code Sec. 267(c)(4)), an individual who is a designated beneficiary under the contract (other than the policyholder), a trust established for either the family member's or beneficiary's benefit, or the insured's estate; or (4) the amount is used to buy an equity (or partnership capital or profits) interest in the policyholder from the family member, beneficiary, trust or estate. (Code Sec. 101(j)(2)) It's intended that this amount be paid or used by the due date of the tax return for the policyholder's tax year in which the proceeds are received as a death benefit under the insurance contract, so that who is paid and what purchases are made with proceeds are known in the tax year in which the

---

3. ¶J-4729
4. ¶J-4730
5. ¶J-4732

6. ¶J-4729, ¶J-4732
7. ¶J-4731
8. ¶J-4744

exception from the income inclusion rule is claimed.[9]

¶ 1352   **Taxation of Annuity Payments.** ■■■■■■■■■■■■■■■■■■■

Annuity payments consist generally of two parts: nontaxable return of investment based on an exclusion ratio (¶1353), and taxable interest. Other amounts (e.g., withdrawals, dividends) are taxable to the extent they exceed the contract's cost.

Code Sec. 72(a) provides that gross income includes any amount received 'as an annuity' that's paid under an annuity, life insurance or endowment contract. (Code Sec. 72(a))[10] For exclusion under the 'annuity rule,' see ¶1353. For 'nonannuity' payments under the contract (e.g., loans, dividends), see ¶1363. For private annuities, see ¶1366. For annuities paid to survivors of certain public safety officers, see ¶1260. For the partial annuitization rule, see ¶1361.

¶ 1353   **The annuity rule—'exclusion ratio' for amounts received 'as an annuity.'**

Under Code Sec. 72(b)(1), if a payment under an annuity, life insurance or endowment contract is received 'as an annuity' (i.e., a sum of money (or property) payable at regular intervals over a period of more than one full year from the starting date (¶1360) (Reg § 1.72-2(b)), all or part of it may be tax-free (for 'natural person' holders, see ¶1354). The part of each 'annuity' payment that represents return of investment (e.g., premiums paid) is excludable from the recipient's income until the entire investment is recovered. Excess receipts are fully taxable. (Code Sec. 72(b)(1); Reg § 1.72-4(a))[11]

The excludable portion is computed by multiplying each payment received by an 'exclusion ratio,' determined by dividing the investment in the contract (¶1358) by the contract's expected return (¶1359) as of the annuity starting date, and rounding to the nearest tenth. (Code Sec. 72(b); Reg § 1.72-4(a)) But the excludable portion of any payment can't exceed the amount of investment in the contract that's unrecovered immediately before the payment is received. (Code Sec. 72(b)(2))[12] (For employee annuities, see ¶1362.)

Once computed, the exclusion ratio is applied to each 'annuity' payment received under the contract, until the total investment has been recovered tax-free. (Code Sec. 72(b); Reg § 1.72-4(a))[13] But the ratio must be recomputed if the contract is transferred for valuable consideration, matures, is surrendered, or is exchanged. (Reg § 1.72-4(a)(4))[14]

If there was no investment in the contract, all payments are taxable in full. If investment exceeds total expected return, all payments are tax-free. (Reg § 1.72-4(d))[15]

Where the annuitant's death causes the annuity payments (starting after Jan. 1, '86) to stop, the amount of any investment in the contract that the annuitant hasn't yet recovered tax-free may be deducted on the final income tax return. (Code Sec. 72(b)(3)(A))[16] For after-death distribution requirements, see ¶1355.

¶ 1354   **Annuity rule exclusion available only to natural persons—taxation of annuities.**

Code Sec. 72(u)(1) provides that, if an annuity contract is held by a person who isn't a natural person, the annuity rule (¶1353) doesn't apply. The income on the contract (for the holder's tax year) must be treated as ordinary income received or accrued by the holder

---

9. ¶J-4744
10. ¶J-5001
11. ¶J-5100 *et seq.*
12. ¶J-5105

13. ¶J-5104
14. ¶J-5106
15. ¶J-5104
16. ¶J-5109

during that year. (Code Sec. 72(u)(1))[17] A natural person doesn't include a trust or corporation. But holding by a trust, etc., *as agent* for a natural person is disregarded. (Code Sec. 72(u)(1))[18]

However, an *employer* that's the nominal owner (agent) of an annuity contract whose beneficial owners are (the employer's) employees is considered to hold the contract.[19]

The natural person rule *doesn't apply* to contracts acquired by an estate by reason of the decedent's death, held by a qualified plan or IRA, that are 'qualified funding assets' (¶1375); bought by an employer on termination of a qualified plan and held until all amounts under the contract are distributed to the employee (or a beneficiary) for whom the contract was bought; or that are immediate annuities. (Code Sec. 72(u)(3))[20]

¶ 1355 After-death distribution requirements for annuity contracts—taxation of annuities.

Payments under a contract aren't entitled to the partial exclusion under the annuity rule *unless* the contract provides that: (1) if any holder ('primary annuitant' for contracts not held by an individual) dies on or after the annuity starting date (¶1360) (and before the entire interest in the contract has been distributed), the balance will be distributed at least as rapidly as it was at the date of death, and (2) if any holder dies before the starting date, the entire interest must be distributed within five years of death. (Code Sec. 72(s)(1))[21]

However, distributions that are payable to (or for) a designated beneficiary can be made for the beneficiary's life or a period not ending past the beneficiary's life expectancy. As long as the payments begin within one year of the holder's death, they'll be considered distributed on that starting date. (Code Sec. 72(s)(2)) A beneficiary who is the holder's surviving spouse will be considered the holder. (Code Sec. 72(s)(3))[22]

✔️observation: Treating the surviving spouse/beneficiary as the holder means that the after-death distribution provisions must be satisfied with respect to the *spouse's* death.

The after-death distribution rules *don't apply to* contracts provided under qualified pension, profit-sharing, stock bonus or annuity plans; tax-sheltered annuities; individual retirement annuities (or contracts provided under IRAs); qualified funding assets (¶1375), regardless of any qualified assignment (Code Sec. 72(s)(5));[23] or contracts issued before Jan. 19, '85.[24]

¶ 1356 Variable annuities; excludable amount, investment in the contract, anticipated payments—taxation of annuities.

Under Reg § 1.72-2(b)(3) and Reg § 1.72-4(d)(3), a variable annuity contract is one where the amount paid varies depending on investment experience, cost of living indexes, market fluctuations, etc. The excludable portion of each payment is computed by dividing the investment in the contract (¶1358) by the total number of anticipated payments. (Reg § 1.72-2(b)(3), Reg § 1.72-4(d)(3))[25]

The excludable amount stays the same regardless of changes in the amount received. (Reg § 1.72-2(b)(3))[26] But if the amount received in a tax year is *less* than the excludable amount, taxpayer may elect (attach a specified statement to the return) to recompute the exclusion ratio for later years' payments. (Reg § 1.72-4(d)(3)(ii), Reg § 1.72-4(d)(3)(iv))[27]

17. ¶s J-5005, J-5006
18. ¶J-5005
19. ¶J-5005
20. ¶J-5007
21. ¶s J-5014, J-5015
22. ¶J-5014

23. ¶J-5016
24. ¶J-5014
25. ¶J-5143
26. ¶J-5143
27. ¶J-5145

¶ 1357   Joint and survivor annuity contracts—taxation of annuities.

Under a joint and survivor annuity contract, payments are made during the lives of two annuitants and, after the death of one, during the life of the survivor. A single exclusion ratio (¶1353), based on the aggregate expected return to both annuitants, is applied to the payments received by both annuitants. (Reg § 1.72-2(a)(2))[28]

¶ 1358   Investment in the contract—taxation of annuities.

For annuity rule purposes (¶1353), the 'investment in the contract' is, in general, the net cost of the contract as of the annuity starting date (¶1360) or, if later, the date of the first contract payment. It equals the aggregate amount of premiums and other considera-tion paid (as of that date) for the contract, minus the aggregate amount previously received under the contract that was excluded from income. (Code Sec. 72(c)(1))[29] It must also be reduced to account for any refund feature. (Code Sec. 72(c)(2))[30] Separate computations may be required for pre-July '86 and post-June '86 investments. (Reg § 1.72-6(d))[31]

For an employee annuity, investment in the contract includes certain employer contribu-tions that were taxable to the owner (employee). (Reg § 1.72-8(a))[32]

¶ 1359   Expected return from the contract—taxation of annuities.

For annuity rule purposes (¶1353), the 'expected return from the contract' is the total amount to be received (or estimated to be received) under the contract. It's computed as of the annuity starting date (¶1360) (Code Sec. 72(b)(1)) and doesn't take into account any amount for dividends or other payments *not* received as an annuity (¶1363). (Code Sec. 72(c)(3); Reg § 1.72-7(a))[33]

If the annuity is for a fixed term and doesn't depend on any life expectancy, the expected return is the amount of the payment specified for each period multiplied by the number of periods. (Reg § 1.72-5(c))[34]

If the annuity is payable for life or for joint lives, the expected return is the amount of the *annual* payment multiplied by the number of years of life expectancy using IRS actuarial tables. (Code Sec. 72(c)(3)(A); Reg § 1.72-5(a))[35]

If the annuity is for an amount certain payable in periodic installments, the expected return is the total amount guaranteed. (Reg § 1.72-5(d))[36]

¶ 1360   Annuity starting date—taxation of annuities.

The 'annuity starting date' is the first day of the first period for which an amount is received *as an annuity* (¶1353) under the contract. This is the date the contractual obliga-tion becomes fixed or, if later, the first day of the period (year, quarter, etc., depending on whether the payments are to be made annually, quarterly, etc.) that ends on the date of the first annuity payment. (Code Sec. 72(c)(4); Reg § 1.72-4(b)(1))[37] Special rules apply if the contract is transferred or exchanged. (Code Sec. 72(g)(3))[38]

---

28. ¶J-5132 *et seq.*
29. ¶J-5113
30. ¶J-5122
31. ¶J-5117 *et seq.*
32. ¶H-11032 *et seq.*
33. ¶J-5124 *et seq.*

34. ¶J-5130
35. ¶J-5126 *et seq.*
36. ¶J-5131
37. ¶J-5110
38. ¶J-5112

¶ 1361 Partial annuitization of nonqualified annuities, endowments, or life insurance contracts—taxation of annuities.

Under Code Sec. 72(a)(2), taxpayers may partially annuitize a nonqualified annuity, endowment, or life insurance contract. (Code Sec. 72(a)(2)) If any amount is received as an annuity for a period of 10 years or more, or during one or more lives, under any portion of an annuity, endowment, or life insurance contract:[39]

(1) that portion will be treated as a separate contract for annuity taxation purposes;

(2) for purposes of applying Code Sec. 72(b) (calculation of the exclusion ratio for annuity distributions, ¶1353), Code Sec. 72(c) (investment in contract, expected return, and annuity starting date, ¶1358– ¶1360), and Code Sec. 72(e) (taxation of distributions from an annuity, endowment, or life insurance contract, that aren't received as an annuity, ¶1363), the investment in the contract is allocated pro rata between each portion of the contract from which amounts are received as an annuity, and the portion of the contract from which amounts aren't received as an annuity, and

(3) a separate annuity starting date under Code Sec. 72(c)(4) (annuity starting date) is determined for each portion of the contract from which amounts are received as an annuity. (Code Sec. 72(a)(2))

¶ 1362 Employee annuities under a qualified employee plan, a qualified employee annuity, or a tax-sheltered annuity—simplified method for computing nontaxable portion.

Under Code Sec. 72(d)(1)(B), the nontaxable portion of amounts received as an annuity (¶1353) under a Code Sec. 401(a) qualified employee plan, a Code Sec. 403(a) qualified employee annuity or a Code Sec. 403(b) tax-sheltered annuity is computed under a simplified method, by dividing the investment in the contract (¶1358) as of the annuity starting date (¶1360) by a designated number of monthly payments. (Code Sec. 72(d)(1)(B))

For an annuity payable over the life of a single individual, the number of payments is 360 if the age of the annuitant on the annuity starting date isn't more than 55; 310 payments if the age is more than 55 but not more than 60; 260 payments if more than 60 but not more than 65; 210 payments if more than 65 but not more than 70; and 160 payments if more than 70. (Code Sec. 72(d)(1)(B)(iii))[40]

For an annuity payable over the lives of more than one individual, the number of payments is 410 if the combined age of the annuitants on the annuity starting date isn't more than 110; 360 payments if more than 110 but not more than 120; 310 payments if more than 120 but not more than 130; 260 payments if more than 130 but not more than 140; and 210 payments if more than 140. (Code Sec. 72(d)(1)(B)(iv))[41]

Appropriate adjustments must be made if payments aren't made on a monthly basis. (Code Sec. 72(d)(1)(F))[42]

The simplified method doesn't apply if the primary annuitant is 75 or older on the annuity starting date, unless there are fewer than five years of guaranteed payments under the annuity. (Code Sec. 72(d)(1)(E))[43]

A lump-sum payment received in connection with the start of annuity payments is taxable under Code Sec. 72(e) as if received before the annuity starting date (see ¶1363),

---

39. ¶J-5019
40. ¶H-11012
41. ¶H-11012
42. ¶H-11012
43. ¶H-11012

and the investment in the contract is determined by taking into consideration the receipt of this lump-sum payment. (Code Sec. 72(d)(1)(D))[44]

For annuity starting dates after Nov. 18, '96 and before Jan. 1, '98, the designated number of payments is based on the age of the primary annuitant, and there's no separate table for annuities based on the life of more than one individual.[45]

For annuity starting dates before Nov. 19, '96, the general-rule regular annuity rules (¶1352 *et seq.*) apply, unless the employee elects a simplified safe-harbor method.[46]

For treatment of payments from a qualified plan during phased retirement, see ¶1363.

¶ 1363   Amounts under life insurance, endowment and annuity contracts not received as an annuity—cash withdrawals, dividends, etc.—taxation of annuities.

Under Code Sec. 72(e)(2)(A) and Code Sec. 72(e)(3)(A), payments under life insurance, endowment and annuity contracts (other than modified endowment contracts, see ¶1365) that aren't "annuities" (e.g., cash withdrawals, loans, dividends, etc.) are fully taxable if received *on or after* the annuity starting date (¶1360). (Code Sec. 72(e)(2)(A), Code Sec. 72(e)(3)(A))[47]

"Nonannuity" amounts received *before* the annuity starting date are: (1) *not taxable,* to the extent that, as of the date of distribution, they don't exceed the cost of the contract (i.e., accumulated net premiums paid) and (2) *taxable,* to the extent allocable to income (i.e., excess of the contract's cash value over the owner's investment) at that time. (Code Sec. 72(e)(2)(B), Code Sec. 72(e)(3)(B))[48] (Veteran's insurance dividends are tax-free, regardless of cost.)[49]

✔ caution: The pre-annuity starting date withdrawal may be subject to the premature distribution penalty (¶1364).

Receipts less than an insurance or endowment contract's cost don't give rise to a deductible loss.[50]

The contract's cost is reduced by the nontaxable amount of the dividend, etc., for purposes of computing the taxable portion of later payments. (Code Sec. 72(e)(6)(B))[1] For these purposes, all contracts (other than immediate annuities or qualified plan annuities) issued by the same company (or its affiliates) to the same policyholder during any one calendar year are treated as a single contract. (Code Sec. 72(e)(11))[2]

Payments during phased retirement. Payments received by an employee from a qualified retirement plan during phased retirement are "not received as an annuity" if: (i) the employee begins to receive partial retirement benefits when entering phased retirement and beginning part-time employment, and won't begin receiving entire plan benefits until ceasing employment and commencing full retirement at an indeterminate future time (including the possibility that a set date could change); (ii) the plan's obligations to the employee are based in part on the employee's continued part-time employment; and (iii) the employee doesn't have an election under the plan as to the form of the phased retirement benefit, but elects a distribution option at full retirement that applies to the employee's entire retirement benefit, including the portion that commenced as phased benefits. When an employee commences full retirement, the employee's investment in the contract (¶1358) as of the annuity starting date will take into account the investment in

---

44. ¶H-11012
45. ¶H-11016
46. ¶H-11018 *et seq.*
47. ¶J-5053
48. ¶J-5053

49. ¶J-5055
50. ¶J-5308
1. ¶J-5063
2. ¶J-5064

the contract recovered during the period of part-time employment and any additional employee contributions made during that period.[3]

¶ 1364 10% penalty on premature distributions from annuity contracts—nonannuity distributions—Form 5329.

Code Sec. 72(q)(1) imposes a penalty (except as noted below) on a person who receives any nonannuity distribution (¶1363) before the annuity starting date (¶1360) in the tax year the distribution is received. The penalty equals 10% of the taxable portion of the distribution. (Code Sec. 72(q)(1))[4] Calculate and pay the penalty on Form 5329.[5]

This 10% penalty *doesn't apply* to any distribution:

(1) made on or after the date taxpayer (recipient) reaches age 59$\frac{1}{2}$;

(2) made on or after the death of the holder (or the primary annuitant, where the holder isn't an individual);

(3) attributable to recipient's total and indefinite disability;

(4) that's part of a series of substantially equal periodic payments (not less frequently than annually) made for the life (or life expectancy) of taxpayer or the joint lives (or joint life expectancies) of taxpayer and a designated beneficiary;

(5) made from a Code Sec. 401(a) qualified employee plan, a Code Sec. 403(a) qualified annuity plan, a Code Sec. 403(b) tax-sheltered annuity plan or a Code Sec. 818(a)(3) retirement plan for life insurance company employees (but for the separate penalty on premature distributions from these plans, see ¶4334);

(6) made from an individual retirement account or annuity (but for the separate penalty on premature distributions from these plans, see ¶4334);

(7) made under an annuity contract which is purchased by an employer on termination of a qualified plan (bonus, pension, profit-sharing or annuity) and which is held by the employer until the employee separates from service;

(8) under an immediate annuity;

(9) under a "qualified funding asset" (¶1375), regardless of any qualified assignment;

(10) to which the Code Sec. 72(t) tax on premature distributions from qualified plans applies (without regard to the Code Sec. 72(t)(2) exceptions), see ¶4334; or

(11) allocable to pre-Aug. 14, '82 investment in the contract. (Code Sec. 72(q)(2))[6]

¶ 1365 Modified endowment contracts—"7-pay test"—taxation.

Under Code Sec. 7702A(a) and Code Sec. 7702(b), a modified endowment contract is a life insurance contract (entered into after June 20, '88) that fails to meet a "7-pay test" (or that's exchanged for such a contract). The test is failed if the accumulated amount paid under the contract during the first seven years exceeds the net level premiums that would have been paid as paid-up future benefits. (Code Sec. 7702A(a), Code Sec. 7702(b))[7]

Payments under a modified endowment contract that are received before the annuity starting date (¶1360) are includible in gross income to the extent allocable to income on the contract, as described at ¶1363. (Code Sec. 72(e)(10)(A)(i))[8] This applies to any amount received as a loan, or assigned or pledged on the value of the contract, unless the loan, etc., is made solely to cover burial expenses or prearranged funeral expenses where the maximum death benefit under the contract doesn't exceed $25,000. (Code Sec. 72(e)(10)(B))

---

3. ¶H-11030.1
4. ¶J-5017
5. ¶S-2510
6. ¶J-5018
7. ¶J-5066 *et seq.*
8. ¶J-5065

However, taxpayer's investment in the contract (¶1358) is increased by the amount included in income (as a loan or assignment). (Code Sec. 72(e)(4)(A))[9]

Certain amounts received under a modified endowment contract that are includible in income are subject to a 10% penalty tax (Code Sec. 72(v)(1), Code Sec. 72(v)(2))[10] (use Form 5329).[11]

¶ 1366   Private annuities—secured arrangements and unsecured arrangements; lifetime payments—taxation.

A private annuity subject to the rules of Code Sec. 72 generally involves the transfer of money or property to an individual or organization in exchange for the transferee's promise to make lifetime payments to the transferor. These transfers typically are made to family members, controlled entities, or unrelated purchasers; to charitable organizations; and in settlement of a will contest.[12]

Transfer of an "unsecured" private annuity arrangement doesn't result in immediate taxable gain (or loss). Instead, any gain is reportable ratably over the lifetime of the transferor (i.e., annuitant). The gain equals the excess of the present value of the annuity (determined under regs) over the transferor's adjusted basis in the transferred property. Any loss may be disallowed if the arrangement is between related parties (¶2442 *et seq.*).[13]

If the arrangement is "secured" (i.e., the property transferred also is collateral for the payments), it's taxed (except for gift tax aspects) under the rules for commercial annuities, (¶1352 *et seq.*).[14] In applying those rules, the annuitant's basis in the property transferred for the annuity is used as the annuitant's investment in the contract.[15]

The value of annuities issued by charities is determined under IRS tables.[16]

¶ 1367   Gifts and Inheritances—Taxation. ▰▰▰▰▰▰▰▰▰▰▰

Property received as a gift, bequest, devise or inheritance is generally exempt from income tax.

Under Code Sec. 102, a gift of property isn't taxable to a recipient (Code Sec. 102; Reg § 1.102-1)[17] other than an employee, see ¶1211. For gifts, etc. of income, see below. For employee awards, see ¶1250. For gift tax, see ¶5040 *et seq.*

Gifts, devises, bequests, and inheritances (i.e., money and any property that pass on the death of a person by the person's will or under intestacy, including amounts received in settlement of a will contest) are excluded from gross income. (Code Sec. 102; Reg § 1.102-1)[18] However, this exclusion doesn't apply where the source of a devise, bequest or inheritance is income that a decedent had a right to receive at death but hadn't yet actually or constructively received or accrued (known as "income in respect of a decedent," see ¶3961 *et seq.*). For estate tax, see ¶5000 *et seq.*

The above exclusion applies only to the property transferred. Income from the property itself is taxable to the recipient, whether paid periodically or in a lump sum. (Code Sec. 102(b); Reg § 1.102-1(c))[19] For an exception for income paid or credited as a gift or bequest of specific property or money, see ¶3944.

¶ 1368   Prizes and Awards—Taxation. ▰▰▰▰▰▰▰▰▰▰▰

In general, prizes and awards are taxable. (Code Sec. 74(a); Reg § 1.74-1(b))

9. ¶J-5063
10. ¶J-5076
11. ¶S-2510
12. ¶J-5252
13. ¶J-5256 *et seq.*
14. ¶J-5257

15. ¶J-5254
16. ¶P-6615, ¶P-6674 *et seq.*
17. ¶J-6000 *et seq.*
18. ¶J-6000 *et seq.*
19. ¶J-6004, ¶J-6005

However, under Code Sec. 74, qualified scholarships (¶2215) and Olympic prizes (below) may be excludible in full or in part. A prize may also be excludible if it's primarily for religious, charitable, scientific, educational, artistic, literary, etc., achievement; the recipient was selected without any action on the recipient's part, and isn't required to render substantial future services; *and* it's transferred by the payor to a governmental unit or charity the recipient designated (Code Sec. 74(b))[20] before getting any benefit from it.[21] IRS specifies the requirements of the designation (including model language).[22] For employee awards, see ¶1250. The value of medals, and prizes awarded by the United States Olympic Committee, for participation in Olympic and Paralympic games, are excludable from income for athletes with AGI up to $1 million ($500,000 for married separate return filers). (Code Sec. 74(d))[23]

For a prize paid in property or services, the taxable amount is the prize's current fair market (resale) value. (Reg § 1.74-1(a)(2))[24]

¶ 1369 Accident and Health Insurance Benefits, Excludability. ▰▰▰▰

Benefits received from accident and health insurance (or through an arrangement having the effect of accident or health insurance) are excluded from gross income unless the benefits compensate for medical expense deductions from an earlier year.

However, under Code Sec. 104(a)(3), this exclusion doesn't apply to amounts received by an employee to the extent the amounts are (1) attributable to employer contributions that weren't includible in the employee's gross income, or (2) are paid by the employer. (Code Sec. 104(a)(3))[25]

Where an employer-provided disability plan allows employees to elect annually to pay for coverage out of pre- or post-tax dollars, disability benefits paid to an employee who elected the post-tax option for the plan year in which the employee became disabled are excludable from gross income.[26]

Benefits from long-term care insurance policies (¶1370) are subject to special rules.

¶ 1370 Exclusion for benefits from long-term care insurance—per diem limit; qualified long-term care insurance contracts.

Under Code Sec. 7702B(a)(1), qualified long-term care insurance contracts (see ¶2145) issued after '96 are treated as accident and health insurance contracts. (Code Sec. 7702B(a)(1)) Pre-'97 contracts that met applicable state long-term care insurance requirements also qualify. (Reg § 1.7702B-2) Amounts (other than policyholder dividends, as defined in Code Sec. 808 or premium refunds) received from such contracts are treated as amounts received for personal injury or sickness and as reimbursement for expenses actually incurred for medical care, and are excludable (see ¶1369), subject to a per diem limit, below.[27] For deduction of premiums for long-term care, see ¶2145.

If the total of (1) the periodic payments received for any period under all qualified long-term care insurance contracts treated as made for qualified long-term care services for an insured and (2) the periodic payments received for the period which are treated under Code Sec. 101(g) (see ¶1349) as paid by reason of the death of the insured, exceeds the per diem limit for the period, the excess is includible in gross income. A payment isn't taken into account under (2) if the insured is a terminally ill individual at the time the payment

---

20. ¶J-1201 *et seq.*
21. ¶J-1208
22. ¶J-1210
23. ¶J-1220
24. ¶J-1218
25. ¶J-1301
26. ¶H-1115 *et seq.*
27. ¶J-1308

is received. (Code Sec. 7702B(d)(1))[28]

The per diem limit for any period is the excess (if any) of: (a) the greater of (i) $390 for 2022 ($420 for 2023), or the equivalent amount when payments are made on another periodic basis, or (ii) the costs incurred for qualified long-term care services provided for the insured for the period, over (b) the total payments received as reimbursement (by insurance or otherwise) for qualified long-term care services provided for the insured during the period. (Code Sec. 7702B(d)(2)) If payments exceed this limit, the excess is excludible only to the extent of actual costs incurred for long-term care services; amounts with respect to which no such actual costs are incurred are fully includible.[29]

¶ 1371 Exclusion for Archer medical savings account (MSA) distributions; additional tax of 20% for distributions reported on Form 8853.

Under Code Sec. 220(f)(1), distributions from an Archer MSA (see ¶1527 for limitations) are excludable from gross income if used exclusively to pay the qualified medical expenses of the individual (account holder) or the account holder's spouse or dependents. (Code Sec. 220(f)(1))[30] Otherwise, they're (1) included in gross income (Code Sec. 220(f)(2)) and (2) subject to an additional tax of 20% for distributions reported on Form 8853 unless made after the individual attains age 65, dies, or becomes disabled. (Code Sec. 220(f)(4))[31]

Qualified medical expenses are for medical care as defined under the medical expense deduction rules (see ¶2144), but only to the extent not reimbursed by insurance or otherwise. Amounts paid for "menstrual care products," as defined in Code Sec. 223(d)(2)(D), must be treated as paid for medical care. (Code Sec. 220(d)(2)(A)) Qualified medical expenses don't include insurance premiums other than premiums for qualified long-term care insurance (¶2145), health care continuation coverage (COBRA), and coverage while receiving unemployment compensation. (Code Sec. 220(d)(2)(B))[32]

In any year for which an MSA contribution is made, distributions from that MSA to pay medical expenses are included in gross income if, for the month in which the expense was incurred, the individual for whom the expense was incurred wasn't covered under a "high deductible health plan" or had ineligible coverage. (Code Sec. 220(d)(2)(C))[33]

¶ 1372 Exclusion for health savings account (HSA) distributions to pay qualified medical expenses of eligible individuals; when distributions are subject to tax and additional 20% for distributions reported on Form 8889.

Under Code Sec. 223(f), distributions from an HSA (see ¶1528) that are used exclusively to pay the qualified medical expenses of an eligible individual (account holder) or the account holder's spouse or dependents are excludable from gross income. (Code Sec. 223(f)) For this purpose, an individual may qualify as a dependent without regard to whether the individual: (1) is subject to the general rule that a dependent of a taxpayer must be treated as him- or herself having no dependents; (2) is married and files a joint return; and (3) has gross income that exceeds an otherwise applicable gross income limitation. (Code Sec. 223(d)(2)(A))[34]

Qualified medical expenses are expenses paid for medical care as defined under the medical expense deduction rules (see ¶2144), but only to the extent they're not reimbursed by insurance or otherwise. (Code Sec. 223(d)(2)) Amounts paid for "menstrual care products," as defined in Code Sec. 223(d)(2)(D), must be treated as paid for medical care. (Code

---

28. ¶J-1308
29. ¶J-1308
30. ¶H-1337 *et seq.*
31. ¶H-1338 *et seq.*

32. ¶H-1337.1 *et seq.*
33. ¶H-1337.2
34. ¶H-1350 *et seq.*

Sec. 220(d)(2)(A)) Qualified medical expenses, which must be incurred after the HSA is established, don't include insurance premiums other than premiums for qualified long-term care insurance (¶2145), health care continuation coverage (COBRA) (see ¶1529), and coverage while the eligible individual is receiving unemployment compensation. (Code Sec. 223(d)(2)(B))[35]

Distributions not used for qualified medical expenses are subject to tax, they also are subject to an additional 20% for distributions reported on Form 8889 unless made after the individual attains age 65, dies, or becomes disabled. (Code Sec. 223(f))[36]

Contributions for a year exceeding the deduction limit (see ¶1528) can be withdrawn tax-free if the distribution is: (1) completed by the extended tax return due date; and (2) accompanied by the net income (includible in the individual's income) attributable to the excess contribution. (Code Sec. 223(f)(3)(A))[37]

¶ 1373 Exclusion for benefits received through health reimbursement arrangements (HRAs); medical care reimbursements.

Under Code Sec. 106, except as provided below, amounts received by an employee under an HRA are excluded from gross income as amounts received under an accident and health plan (¶1369). This exclusion doesn't apply if *any* person may receive cash or any benefit from the HRA other than a medical care reimbursement. An HRA is a type of employee benefit plan reimbursing employees for medical expenses not covered by other forms of insurance. Medicine or drugs are qualified medical expenses only if prescribed (whether or not available over-the-counter) or insulin. (Code Sec. 105(b), Code Sec. 223(d)(2), Code Sec. 213(b)) Benefits are paid up to a specific dollar amount from funds provided exclusively by the employer (and not through a salary reduction or otherwise under a cafeteria plan (¶1269)). Balances remaining in the employee's account at the end of a coverage period may be carried forward if the plan so provides. An HRA may use debit cards, credit cards, or other electronic media to support and document the tax-free reimbursement of an employee's claimed medical or dental expenses if proper safeguards and substantiation methods are used.[38]

Payments or reimbursements from a "qualified small employer HRA" (as defined in Code Sec. 9831(d)(2)) are excluded if, for the month in which medical care giving rise to the reimbursement is provided, the individual has minimum essential coverage under Code Sec. 5000A(f) (¶4879).[39]

Generally, individual HRAs may be integrated with individual health insurance coverage and Medicare. (Reg § 54.9802-4)[40]

observation: Thus, an employer that does not provide group health insurance to its employees may offer an individual HRA that can satisfy the requirement of minimum essential coverage if it meets certain conditions.

¶ 1374 Damages; Compensatory Nonbusiness damages; Punitive and Non-punitive—Taxation.

Under Code Sec. 104, compensatory nonbusiness damages received on account of personal physical injuries or personal physical sickness are tax-free, but punitive damages generally aren't excludable.

Non-punitive damages to compensate for personal *physical* injury or personal *physical* sickness, whether received by suit or agreement, in a lump sum or as periodic payments,

---

35. ¶H-1350.1 *et seq.*
36. ¶H-1350.11 *et seq.*
37. ¶H-1350.10

38. ¶H-1349 *et seq.*
39. ¶H-1349.18
40. ¶H-1349.16A *et seq.*

are excluded from income. (Code Sec. 104(a)(2); Reg § 1.104-1) If an action has its origin in a physical injury or physical sickness, then all non-punitive damages from that injury or sickness are excluded, whether or not the recipient is the injured party. Emotional distress isn't considered a physical injury or physical sickness, but the exclusion does apply to damages received up to the amount paid for medical care attributable to emotional distress. (Code Sec. 104(a)) Thus, the exclusion doesn't apply to damages (other than for medical expenses attributable to emotional distress) based on a claim of employment discrimination or injury to reputation accompanied by a claim of emotional distress and does apply to non-punitive damages received based on a claim of emotional distress, that are attributable to a physical injury or physical sickness.[41] The exclusion doesn't apply to "delay damages," i.e., damages awarded due to the delay in payment, which have been held to be in the nature of interest.[42]

Punitive damages generally are taxable, regardless of the nature of the claim. (Code Sec. 104(a)(2)) But under an exception, punitive damages received in connection with a physical injury or sickness are tax-free if the are awarded: (i) in a civil wrongful death action, and (ii) under applicable state law (as in effect on Sept. 13, '95, and without regard to later modification) which provides (or has been construed by a court to provide) that only punitive damages may be awarded in the action. (Code Sec. 104(c))[43]

Where a lump-sum award is specifically allocated by the parties between compensatory and punitive damages, or between personal and business injury, that allocation generally controls. But if no allocation is made, the courts look to the nature of the claims (e.g., primary nature of the harm inflicted) and the payor's intent.[44]

¶ 1375   Amounts received for accepting assignment of personal injury liability under structured settlement arrangements—taxation of damages.

Amounts received by an assignee (e.g., insurance company) for accepting assignment of a liability to make periodic payments as damages for personal injury or sickness (in a case involving *physical* injury or sickness), including a liability to pay workers' compensation, are excludable from the assignee's gross income, up to the aggregate cost of any "qualified funding asset" used to satisfy the liability. A "qualified funding asset" is a commercial annuity contract, or a U.S. obligation, having payment periods corresponding to those of the liability, which the assignee: (1) purchased within 60 days before or after the date of the assignment, and (2) uses to satisfy that liability. (Code Sec. 130(c))[45]

¶ 1376   Business damages; compensation for lost profits, business interruption, breach of employment contract; awards for breach of contract or business slander; injury to capital; punitive damages—taxation of damages.

Damages received for injury to business that represent compensation for lost profits (including business interruption insurance proceeds) are taxable as ordinary income. This applies to awards for breach of contract of sale, breach of employment contract, and business slander. Amounts received for injury to capital (e.g., injury to good will, fraudulent stock sale) are tax-free to the extent of basis; any excess is capital gain.[46] Punitive damages (e.g., insiders' profits, treble damages under antitrust laws) are taxable. (Reg § 1.61-14(a))[47]

There's a special deduction for certain expired net operating losses that resulted from the same injury. (Code Sec. 186(d))[48]

---

41. ¶J-5801
42. ¶J-5817
43. ¶J-5816.1 *et seq.*
44. ¶J-5810
45. ¶J-5833 *et seq.*
46. ¶J-5819 *et seq.*
47. ¶J-5829
48. ¶K-8501 *et seq.*

¶ 1377 Attorney's fees payable out of judgment—taxation of damages.

When a litigant's (taxpayer's) recovery—money judgment or settlement—constitutes income, the taxpayer must include in income the portion of the recovery paid to the attorney as a contingent fee (a fee that's paid to the attorney only in the case of a successful recovery; generally computed as a percentage of the recovery). In general, attorney's fees payable from the award are deductible only as a miscellaneous itemized deduction, regardless of whether the fees are contingent or noncontingent.[49] However, certain attorney's fees related to qualifying civil rights suits and whistleblower awards are deductible from gross income; see ¶3108.

¶ 1378 Civil, compensatory, or statutory damages for wrongful incarceration—taxation of damages.

Under Code Sec. 139F, gross income doesn't include civil damages, restitution, or other monetary awards (including compensatory or statutory damages) that an individual receives as compensation for a wrongful incarceration. A wrongfully incarcerated individual is either: (1) an individual who was convicted of a criminal offense under Federal or state law, who served all or part of a sentence of imprisonment relating to such offense, and who was pardoned, granted clemency, or granted amnesty because of actual innocence of the offense; or (2) an individual for whom the conviction for such offense was reversed or vacated and for whom the indictment, information, or other accusatory instrument for such offense was dismissed or who was found not guilty at a new trial after the conviction was reversed or vacated. (Code Sec. 139F) The exclusion doesn't apply to amounts received by (1) an individual wrongfully incarcerated but released before trial and not convicted of any crime, or (2) anyone other than the incarcerated individual, such as a family member.[50]

¶ 1379 Income Realized on Discharge or Cancellation of Debt (COD). ▬▬▬▬▬

Under Code Sec. 61(a)(11), gross income includes income from discharge of indebtedness, whether the debt was reduced or cancelled altogether, and whether the debt was recourse or nonrecourse. (Code Sec. 61(a)(11))[1]

COD income thus can result where a creditor accepts less than full payment as a complete discharge of the debt, or where events or circumstances make its collection unlikely.[2] But if the debtor's payment of the liability would have given rise to a deduction, the debtor won't have income from the discharge. (Code Sec. 108(e)(2))[3]

For information reporting by banks, etc., that discharge indebtedness, see ¶4746.

¶ 1380 Forgiveness for Paycheck Protection Program (PPP) loans made before July 1, 2022 (COVID-19/coronavirus relief); exclusion; expenses paid with forgiven PPP loans are deductible; lenders need not file Form 1099-C.

An "eligible recipient" (i.e., the borrower of a "covered loan") qualifies for forgiveness of debt on a "covered loan" (Paycheck Protection Program or "PPP" loan), in an amount equal to the sum of the payroll, mortgage interest, and certain other costs incurred (as listed in Sec. 7A(a), PL 96-354, 9/19/1980)—and payments made—during the "covered period." (Sec. 7A(b), PL 96-354, 9/19/1980, as redesignated and transferred by Sec. 304(b)(1)(A)DivN, PL 116-260, 12/27/2020 and amended by Sec. 304(b)(2)(B)DivN, PL 116-

---

49. ¶J-8258
50. ¶J-5850
1. ¶J-7001

2. ¶J-7001 *et seq.*
3. ¶J-7503

260, 12/27/2020)

The amount of forgiven PPP loans is not included in gross income. (Sec. 7A(i)(1), PL 96-354, 9/19/1980, as redesignated and transferred by Sec. 304(b)(1)(A)DivN, PL 116-260, 12/27/2020 and amended by Sec. 276(a)(1)DivN, PL 116-260, 12/27/2020; Sec. 276(b)(1)DivN, PL 116-260, 12/27/2020)

But if a taxpayer who doesn't satisfy the conditions for a qualifying forgiveness (e.g., because the taxpayer didn't use the loan for the payroll and other costs referred to above) causes the lender to forgive the PPP loan by wrongly representing that the taxpayer satisfies the conditions, the taxpayer may not exclude the amount of the forgiven loan from gross income. (CCA 202237010)[4]

A covered loan's covered period begins on the date of the origination of the covered loan, and ends on a date selected by the eligible recipient of the covered loan that occurs during the period (1) beginning on the date that is 8 weeks after the date of origination; and (2) ending on the date that is 24 weeks after the date of origination. (Sec. 7A(a)(4), PL 96-354, 9/19/1980, as redesignated and transferred by Sec. 304(b)(1)(A)DivN, PL 116-260, 12/27/2020, further redesignated by Sec. 304(b)(2)(A)(iv)DivN, PL 116-260, 12/27/2020 and amended by Sec. 306DivN, PL 116-260, 12/27/2020)[5]

Debt forgiveness isn't available for loans made after June 30, 2021. (Sec. 7(a)(36)(A)(iii), PL 96-354, 9/19/1980 as amended by Sec. 1102(a)(2)DivA, PL 116-136, 3/27/2020, Sec. 3(a), PL 116-142, 6/5/2020, Sec. 343(a)DivN, PL 116-260, 12/27/2020, and Sec. 2(a), PL 117-6, 3/30/2021)[6]

Lenders who make PPP loans that are later partly or wholly forgiven under the above rule need not file Forms 1099-C or furnish payee statements to report the forgiveness. (Notice 2021-6, 2021-6 IRB 822; Sec. 279DivN, PL 116-260, 12/27/2020)[7]

Expenses paid with a PPP loan are deductible, even if the loan is forgiven. (Sec. 7A(i)(2), PL 96-354, 9/19/1980, as redesignated and transferred by Sec. 304(b)(1)(A)DivN, PL 116-260, 12/27/2020 and amended by Sec. 276(a)(1)DivN, PL 116-260, 12/27/2020; Sec. 276(b)(2)DivN, PL 116-260, 12/27/2020)[8]

Taxpayers may treat tax-exempt income resulting from the forgiveness of certain PPP loans as received or accrued: (1) as eligible expenses are paid or incurred, (2) when the taxpayer files an application for forgiveness of the PPP loan, or (3) when PPP Loan forgiveness is granted. (Rev Proc 2021-48, 2021-49 IRB 835)

IRS provided guidance for partners and partnerships regarding: (a) allocations under Code Sec. 704(b) of certain amounts excluded from gross income, arising from the forgiveness of PPP Loans, certain grant proceeds, or the subsidized payment of certain principal, interest, and fees; (b) allocations under Code Sec. 704(b) of deductions resulting from expenditures attributable to the use of forgiven PPP Loans, certain grant proceeds, or the subsidized payments of certain interest and fees described in Rev Proc 2021-49, 2021-49 IRB 838; and (c) the corresponding adjustments to be made with respect to the partners' bases in their partnership interests under Code Sec. 705. (Rev Proc 2021-49, 2021-49 IRB 838)

---

4. ¶J-7509
5. ¶J-7509
6. ¶J-7509

7. ¶S-4251.9
8. ¶L-1007.1

¶ **1381**   **Cancellation/discharge of student loans: programs requiring public service work; discharges from 2021 through 2025; Public Health Service Act, etc., programs; "Defense to Repayment"/"Closed School" programs.**

Exclusion where cancellation requires work in certain professions. Under Code Sec. 108(f)(1), there's no COD income (¶1379) from the cancellation of all or part of certain government student loans (or certain loans made by tax-exempt educational organizations), or loans made by exempt educational organizations or other exempt organizations to refinance any student loan, if the debtor is required to perform public service work for a period of time in certain professions for any of a broad range of employers. (Code Sec. 108(f)(1))[9]

Exclusion for discharges from 2021 through 2025. Also, for discharges after 2020 and before 2026, under Code Sec. 108(f)(5), there's no COD income from the cancellation of all or part of (1) certain loans for post-secondary educational expenses made, insured, or guaranteed by the U.S., a state, a territory, a U.S. possession, or D.C., or any instrumentality of those governmental entities; or an "eligible educational institution;" (2) "private education loans;" (3) certain loans made by tax-exempt educational organizations, or loans made by exempt educational organizations to encourage students to serve in occupations with unmet needs, etc.; or (4) loans made by other exempt organizations to refinance loans (described in item (3)). The exclusion doesn't apply if the discharge is on account of services performed for the exempt organization (described in item (3)) or the private education lender. (Code Sec. 108(f)(5))[10] When all or a portion of a student loan described in Code Sec. 108(f)(5) is discharged after 2020 and before 2026, an applicable entity isn't required to, and shouldn't, file a Form 1099-C information return with IRS or furnish a payee statement to the borrower under Code Sec. 6050P as a result of the discharge. (Notice 2022-1, 2022-2 IRB 304)[11]

Public Health Service Act, etc., programs. Nor does gross income include any amount received under: (a) Sec. 338B(g) of the Public Health Service Act (relating to the National Health Service Corps Loan Repayment Program); (b) a state program described in Sec. 338I of that Act; or (c) any State loan repayment or loan forgiveness program intended to provide for the increased availability of health care services in underserved or health professional shortage areas (as determined by the State). (Code Sec. 108(f)(4))[12]

"Defense to Repayment" or "Closed School" programs. Taxpayers whose federal student loans are discharged under the Department of Education's Defense to Repayment or Closed School process can exclude the discharged amount from gross income.[13] Lenders need not file a Form 1099-C in this case.[14]

¶ **1382**   **Cancellation of debt (COD) of solvent debtors outside bankruptcy—COD income.**

Any COD of a debtor, other than in a bankruptcy case (¶1384), or where the debtor is insolvent (¶1383), results in the current (i.e., year of discharge) recognition of COD income (¶1379) in the amount of the discharge (Reg § 1.61-12(a))[15] except for certain farm (¶1385) or real property (¶1386) indebtedness.

---

9. ¶J-7506
10. ¶J-7506
11. ¶S-4251.9
12. ¶J-7506

13. ¶J-7001
14. ¶S-4251.9
15. ¶J-7001, ¶J-7200 *et seq.*

¶ 1383　　**Insolvent debtor outside bankruptcy—"insolvency exception"—Form 982—COD income.**

If the indebtedness is discharged when the debtor is insolvent (but not in a bankruptcy case), the discharge is excluded from the debtor's gross income up to the amount of the insolvency. (Code Sec. 108(a)(1)(B), Code Sec. 108(a)(2)(A), Code Sec. 108(a)(3))[16]

The amount excluded under this "insolvency exception" must be applied to reduce the debtor's tax attributes such as loss or credit carryovers or basis in assets. (Credit carryovers are reduced 33⅓¢ per dollar of debt discharge amount; other tax attributes are reduced dollar for dollar.) (Code Sec. 108(b)(3)) (Use Form 982 to report the reduction of tax attributes.) Or the debtor can elect (on Form 982) to apply any or all of the excluded amount *first* to reduce basis in *depreciable* assets (or real property held as inventory). (Code Sec. 108(b)(5)(A), Code Sec. 1017(b)(3); Reg § 1.108-4(b))[17]

Any balance of the discharged debt (excess over the amount the debtor is insolvent) is cancellation of debt (COD) income, as for a wholly solvent debtor (¶1382). (Code Sec. 108(a)(3))[18]

A debtor is insolvent for this purpose if, immediately before the debt is discharged, its liabilities exceed the fair market value of its assets. (Code Sec. 108(d)(3))[19]

If a reorganization or other transaction described in Code Sec. 381(a) ends a year in which the distributor or transferor corporation excludes COD income under Code Sec. 108(a), any tax attributes to which the acquiring corporation succeeds and the basis of property acquired by the acquiring corporation must reflect the reductions required by Code Sec. 108 and Code Sec. 1017. (Reg § 1.108-7(c), Reg § 1.1017-1(b)(4))

In applying the insolvency exception to grantor trusts and disregarded entities, the "taxpayer" for purposes of defining insolvency, etc., is the owner of the trust or entity, not the grantor trust or disregarded entity itself.[20]

For partners and S corporations, see ¶1387.

¶ 1384　　**Cancellation of debt (COD) of bankrupt debtor—Form 982—COD income.**

No amount is included in a debtor's gross income by reason of a discharge of indebtedness in a bankruptcy case (Code Sec. 108(a)(1)(A)), even if the debtor is solvent after the discharge. (Code Sec. 108(a)(2))[21]

The amount of discharged debt that's excluded under this rule must be applied to reduce certain of the debtor's tax attributes (Code Sec. 108(b)(1)) (use Form 982) unless the debtor elects (on Form 982) to apply any or all of the excluded amount *first* to reduce basis in depreciable assets (or real property held as inventory). (Code Sec. 108(b)(5)(A), Code Sec. 1017(b)(3); Reg § 1.1017-1(c))[22] In applying the bankruptcy exception to grantor trusts and disregarded entities, the "taxpayer" for purposes of defining insolvency, etc., is the owner of the trust or entity.[23] For partners and S corporations, see ¶1387.

---

16. ¶J-7401
17. ¶J-7404
18. ¶J-7403
19. ¶J-7403

20. ¶J-7403.2
21. ¶J-7402
22. ¶J-7404
23. ¶J-7403.2

¶ 1385 Cancellation of "qualified farm indebtedness" of solvent farmers—COD income.

A solvent taxpayer whose "qualified farm indebtedness" is discharged (outside bankruptcy) by certain unrelated lenders doesn't have cancellation of debt (COD) income (¶1379), to the extent the discharge doesn't exceed the sum of its adjusted tax attributes plus the aggregate adjusted bases (as of the start of the year after discharge) of its business or income-producing property. (Code Sec. 108(a)(1)(C), Code Sec. 108(g)(1), Code Sec. 108(g)(3)) Any excess is COD income (but the insolvency (¶1383) or bankruptcy (¶1384) rules have precedence). (Code Sec. 108(a)(2))[24]

"Qualified farm indebtedness" is debt incurred directly in connection with taxpayer's farm business if at least 50% of taxpayer's total gross receipts for the three tax years preceding the tax year of the discharge is attributable to farming. (Code Sec. 108(g)(2))[25] For partners and S corporations, see ¶1387.

¶ 1386 Discharge of "qualified real property business indebtedness" (QRPBI)— Form 982—COD income.

A solvent taxpayer other than a C corporation whose QRPBI is discharged (outside bankruptcy) can elect to exclude the discharged amount from income, to the extent of the excess (if any) of (1) the outstanding principal amount of the QRPBI immediately before the discharge, over (2) the fair market value immediately before the discharge of the real property securing the QRPBI (i.e., the single item of real property to which the discharged debt is QRPBI), less the outstanding principal amount of any other QRPBI secured by the property at that time. (Code Sec. 108(a)(1)(D), Code Sec. 108(c)(2)(A), Code Sec. 108(c)(3)(C); Reg § 1.108-6(a)) The only property to be taken into consideration for this purpose is the property that qualified the indebtedness as QRPBI.[26] The excluded amount must be applied (on Form 982) to reduce the basis of taxpayer's depreciable real property. (Code Sec. 108(c)(1)(A))[27]

QRPBI is indebtedness (other than qualified farm indebtedness, ¶1385) incurred or assumed by taxpayer in connection with real property used in a trade or business and secured by the real property (Code Sec. 108(c)(3)(A)) that:

. . . if incurred or assumed by the taxpayer after '92, is "qualified acquisition indebtedness" (Code Sec. 108(c)(3)(B))—i.e., indebtedness incurred or assumed to acquire, construct, reconstruct, or substantially improve the property (Code Sec. 108(c)(4)); *and*

. . . taxpayer elects to treat as "qualified real property business indebtedness" (Code Sec. 108(c)(3)(C))[28] on Form 982 attached to the return for the tax year of discharge. (Code Sec. 108(d)(9)(A); Reg § 1.108-5)[29]

QRPBI also includes indebtedness incurred to refinance QRPBI, but only to the extent it doesn't exceed the amount of the indebtedness being refinanced. (Code Sec. 108(c)(3))[30]

Under a safe harbor, IRS will treat certain debt secured by 100% of the ownership interest in a disregarded entity that holds real property as secured by real property. However, a taxpayer that doesn't qualify for the safe harbor requirements can still argue that the debt meets the "secured by" requirement based on the facts and circumstances. [31]

QRPBI doesn't include debt secured by property that's inventory or held by a taxpayer

---

24. ¶J-7405 *et seq.*
25. ¶J-7406
26. ¶J-7409
27. ¶P-3006.1

28. ¶J-7410
29. ¶J-7412
30. ¶J-7410
31. ¶J-7410

primarily for sale to customers in the ordinary course of its trade or business.[32]

¶ 1387 How cancellation of debt (COD) income exclusions apply to partnership or S corporation debt.

For partnership debt, the insolvency (¶1383), bankruptcy (¶1384), qualified farm indebtedness (¶1385), and qualified real property indebtedness (¶1386) exclusions are applied at the *partner* level, not at the partnership level. (Code Sec. 108(d)(6)) In measuring a partner's insolvency for purposes of the insolvency exclusion, each partner treats as a liability an amount of the partnership's discharged excess nonrecourse debt (i.e., nonrecourse debt in excess of the fair market value of the property securing the debt) based on the allocation of COD income to that partner under Code Sec. 704(b) (¶3717).[33] IRS disagrees with a number of Tax Court cases holding that partners may exclude their share of partnership COD income because the partnership debt was discharged "in a Title 11 case" within the meaning of Code Sec. 108(d)(2).[34]

For an S corporation's debt, the exclusions are applied at the corporate level, not at the shareholder level. (Code Sec. 108(d)(7)(A))[35]

¶ 1388 Discounted purchase of debtor's own obligations—COD income.

When a debtor buys or otherwise acquires its own obligations for less than face value (i.e., at a discount), it usually realizes taxable income to the extent of the discount. (Reg § 1.61-12(a))[36] This also applies if a party related to the debtor acquires the debtor's indebtedness from an unrelated party. (Code Sec. 108(e)(4)(A); Reg § 1.108-2)[37]

A corporation that repurchases its own bonds (directly or indirectly) has cancellation of debt (COD) income (¶1379) to the extent of the excess of the adjusted issue price over the repurchase price. (Reg § 1.61-12(c)(2))[38]

For the debtor to be taxed, the obligation must require the unconditional payment of a fixed amount. If the obligation really represents an equity interest, a corporate debtor will be, in effect, acquiring its own stock and thus won't be taxed on the "discount." [39]

¶ 1389 Satisfaction of debt with property or services (including "stock for debt")—COD income.

If a debtor transfers property (other than debt) to, or performs services for, a creditor (or third party) in full satisfaction of the debt, and the property or services are worth the amount owed, there's no *cancellation* of debt (COD) or accompanying COD income since it was actually paid. But a debtor who satisfies debt with services has taxable *compensation* equal to the debt. (Reg § 1.61-12(a))[40]

A debtor who transfers property (other than debt) in satisfaction of the debt has gain (or loss) to the extent the fair market value (FMV) of the property transferred exceeds (or is less than) its basis in the property. The type of gain (or loss), or whether any loss is deductible, is determined under the regular sale or exchange rules (¶2400 *et seq.*). If the property transferred is worth less than the face amount of the debt, the difference is COD income to the debtor.[41]

If a debtor corporation transfers stock, or a debtor partnership transfers a capital or

32. ¶J-7410
33. ¶J-7415
34. ¶J-7402
35. ¶J-7416
36. ¶J-7011
37. ¶J-7016 *et seq.*
38. ¶J-7204.1
39. ¶J-7007
40. ¶J-7040
41. ¶J-7206

profits interest in that partnership, to a creditor in satisfaction of its recourse or nonrecourse debt, the corporation or partnership is treated as having satisfied the debt with an amount of money equal to the FMV of the stock or the interest. In the case of a partnership, Under a safe harbor, the FMV of the partnership interest in a debt-for-equity exchange will be its liquidation value. Any discharge of debt income recognized under this rule is included in the distributive shares of taxpayers that were partners in the partnership immediately before the discharge. (Code Sec. 108(e)(8), Reg § 1.108-8) So the debtor has taxable income to the extent the principal of the debt exceeds the value of the stock or interest.[42]

¶ **1390** **Exclusion for pre-2026 discharge of "qualified principal residence indebtedness" (home mortgage debt); debt-for-debt exchanges, exclusion—COD income.**

Exclusion for pre-2026 discharge of "qualified principal residence indebtedness." For debt discharged before 2026, any discharge of debt income by reason of a discharge (in whole or in part) of "qualified principal residence indebtedness" (defined in Code Sec. 108(h)(2)) is excluded from the taxpayer's gross income. (Code Sec. 108(a)(1)(E); Code Sec. 108(h)(2))[43]

Debt-for-debt exchanges. Under Code Sec. 108(e)(10)(A), a debtor may satisfy an outstanding "old" debt by issuing a "new" debt. The old debt is treated as having been satisfied with an amount of money equal to the issue price of the new debt. (Code Sec. 108(e)(10)(A)) The excess (if any) of the "old" adjusted issue price over the "new" issue price is cancellation of debt (COD) income (¶1379) to the debtor.[44] For this purpose, "issue price" is generally determined under the OID rules (¶1316). (Code Sec. 108(e)(10)(B))[45]

---

42. ¶J-7015
43. ¶J-7417

44. ¶J-7205
45. ¶J-7205

Chapter 3   Deductions—Expenses of a Business

¶ 1500   Tax Treatment of Start-Up Expenditures. ▬▬▬▬▬▬▬

Under Code Sec. 195, start-up expenditures (below) must be amortized and can't be deducted unless the taxpayer elects (¶1501) to expense up to $5,000 of these costs with that amount reduced by the excess of total start-up expenditures over $50,000 in the tax year in which the trade or business begins.

The remainder of the start-up expenditures may be amortized (deducted ratably) over a 180-month period. (Code Sec. 195(b)(1))[1]

Start-up expenditures are amounts paid or incurred in connection with:

. . . investigating the creation, acquisition, or establishment of an active trade or business, (Code Sec. 195(c)(1)(A)(i)) but not costs incurred after a taxpayer decides whether to enter a new business, and which new business it will enter or acquire;[2]

. . . creating an active trade or business (Code Sec. 195(c)(1)(A)(ii)); or

. . . any activity engaged in for profit and for the production of income before the day the active trade or business begins, in anticipation of that activity becoming an active trade or business. (Code Sec. 195(c)(1)(A)(iii))

The expenditure must be one that, if paid or incurred in connection with the operation of an existing active trade or business (in the same field as the taxpayer's new business), would be deductible for the year in which paid or incurred. (Code Sec. 195(c)(1)(B))[3]

Start-up expenses don't include any amounts deductible under Code Sec. 163(a) (i.e., as interest expenses); Code Sec. 164 (i.e., as taxes); or Code Sec. 174 (i.e., as research and experimental expenses). (Code Sec. 195(c)(1))[4]

¶ 1501   Deemed election to expense/amortize start-up expenditures.

A taxpayer (1) is deemed to have elected to expense/amortize start-up costs under Code Sec. 195(b) (¶1500) for the tax year in which the active trade or business begins, but (2) may forgo the deemed election by clearly electing to capitalize start-up expenditures on a timely filed (including extensions) Federal income tax return for the tax year in which the active trade or business begins. The choice of expensing/amortizing or capitalizing start-up expenditures is irrevocable and applies to all start-up expenditures related to the active trade or business. (Reg § 1.195-1(b))[5]

¶ 1502   Treatment of deferred start-up expenses on disposition of business.

Under Code Sec. 195(b)(2), if the trade or business is disposed of before the end of the amortization period, any deferred expenses not yet deducted may be deducted to the extent the disposition results in a loss under Code Sec. 165. (Code Sec. 195(b)(2))[6]

¶ 1503   Fruitless searches for, or investigations of, new ventures—start-up expenses.

A corporation (but not a noncorporate taxpayer not engaged in the business of locating or promoting new ventures) may deduct as a loss under Code Sec. 165 expenditures made in fruitlessly searching for or investigating a new venture when it abandons the effort.[7] A noncorporate taxpayer that has focused on the acquisition of a specific business or investment can deduct, as business or investment losses under Code Sec. 165, unsuccessful start-

---

1. ¶L-5001
2. ¶L-5013
3. ¶L-5011
4. ¶L-5011
5. ¶L-5002
6. ¶L-5021
7. ¶L-5017

References beginning with a single letter are to paragraphs in Federal Tax Coordinator 2d and RIA's Analysis of Federal Taxes: Income.

up expenses related to an attempt to acquire that business or investment. (¶1765).[8]

¶ 1504   Deduction of expenditures to expand an existing business.

A taxpayer can deduct expenditures made to expand an existing business under Code Sec. 165. The taxpayer must show that the business contemplated and the one already conducted are closely related or "intramural," *and* that the expenditures are ordinary and necessary expenses of the business conducted when the expenses were incurred, and not capital expenditures.

Expansion costs must be capitalized if they provide the taxpayer with long-term benefits, or create separate and distinct assets, or relate to a change in the nature of the taxpayer's activities (e.g., wholesaler opening retail outlet). (Code Sec. 162(a), Reg § 1.162-1(a))[9]

¶ 1505   Ordinary and Necessary Business Expenses. ▬▬▬

Individuals, corporations, and other taxpayers generally can deduct ordinary and necessary (¶1506) expenses paid or incurred during the tax year in carrying on any trade or business (¶1507) under Code Sec. 162. Various limits (e.g., percentage limit on meal and entertainment deductions, see ¶1556) may apply.[10]

¶ 1506   "Ordinary and necessary" requirement for deduction of business expenses.

Under Code Sec. 162, a deductible business expense must be both ordinary and necessary in relation to the taxpayer's industry. (Code Sec. 162(a))[11]

An expense is *ordinary* if it's customary or usual in the taxpayer's business.[12] But an unusual expense may be ordinary if it's reasonably related to the taxpayer's trade or business.[13] A *necessary* expense is one that's appropriate and helpful in developing and maintaining the taxpayer's business. It need not be essential or indispensable. Usually, the taxpayer's judgment as to what's necessary will be accepted.[14]

Some courts have held that to be deductible under Code Sec. 162, an expense must not only be ordinary and necessary, but also reasonable in amount and reasonable in relation to its purpose.[15]

¶ 1507   Deductible business expenses must be directly connected to taxpayer's trade or business—ordinary and necessary expenses.

To be deductible as a business expense under Code Sec. 162, an item must be directly connected with or pertain to a trade or business carried on by the taxpayer. (Code Sec. 162(a); Reg § 1.162-1(a))[16]

Serving as an employee is a business (see ¶1615 for deduction limitations).[17] A trade or business need not be the taxpayer's principal occupation.[18]

¶ 1508   Business expense must benefit person claiming deduction—ordinary and necessary expenses.

A deductible expense under Code Sec. 165 must be an expense of *the taxpayer's* business. Expenses incurred on another's behalf aren't deductible.[19]

8. ¶L-5019
9. ¶L-5101
10. ¶L-1200 *et seq.*
11. ¶L-1200 *et seq.*
12. ¶L-1201
13. ¶s L-1201, L-1209

14. ¶L-1201
15. ¶L-1202
16. ¶L-1002
17. ¶L-3900
18. ¶L-1100 *et seq.*
19. ¶L-4400 *et seq.*

A corporation can't deduct payment of the personal expenses of its shareholders[20] or payment of the personal expenses of its officers and employees, except to the extent the payment represents reasonable compensation (¶1516) or is made for business reasons to provide benefits to employees in general.[21]

A corporate officer can't deduct an expenditure made to pay an expense of the corporation.[22]

If a taxpayer pays the debts or other obligations of another, the payment may sometimes qualify as a business expense.[23] Deductions have been allowed where such a payment is made for a good business reason, e.g., to preserve sales-force morale and customer goodwill, reestablish or protect credit standing, or avoid loss of business patronage, etc.[24]

¶ 1509   Right to business expense deduction—*Cohan* rule—ordinary and necessary expenses.

Where a taxpayer's records or other proof aren't adequate to substantiate expense deductions under Code Sec. 165, he or she may be allowed to deduct an estimated amount under the *Cohan* rule. But a court may allow a much smaller deduction than claimed, bearing heavily against a taxpayer whose inexactitude is of his or her own making.[25] The *Cohan* rule doesn't apply to travel or entertainment expenses, listed property, or business gifts, see ¶1563.

¶ 1510   Expenses of membership organizations—ordinary and necessary business expenses.

Under Code Sec. 277(a), organizations that aren't exempt from tax under the rules discussed at ¶ 4100 *et seq.*, which are operated primarily to furnish services or goods to members, can deduct expenses of furnishing services, insurance, goods, or other items to members only to the extent of income derived during the year from members or transactions with members. (Code Sec. 277(a))[26] Any excess of expenses over income isn't deductible, but may be carried over to the following tax year. (Code Sec. 277(a))[27]

¶ 1511   Deduction of advertising and business promotion costs—ordinary and necessary expenses.

Advertising and promotion costs that relate to an existing business are generally deductible unless they fall into a particular class of nondeductible outlays, such as capital expenditures. So publisher's circulation costs are deductible, though capital in nature, except where an election is made to capitalize them.[28]

Production costs of a business catalog that will remain unchanged for several years must be capitalized according to IRS, but some courts disagree.[29] Display equipment (cabinets, signs, etc.) must be capitalized if it has a useful life beyond the tax year.[30] Package design costs (e.g., physical construction of a package containing a consumer product) do not have to be capitalized. (Reg § 1.263(a)-4(b)(3)(v))[31]

¶ 1512   Costs of determining or contesting tax liability of a business—ordinary and necessary expenses.

Costs relating to tax matters that are ordinary and necessary in the course of the conduct of taxpayer's trade or business, including costs of tax advice, are deductible. The

---

20. ¶L-1214
21. ¶L-4414
22. ¶L-4405
23. ¶L-1214
24. ¶L-1214 *et seq.*
25. ¶L-4509 *et seq.*

26. ¶L-4301
27. ¶L-4301
28. ¶L-2200 *et seq.*
29. ¶L-2205
30. ¶L-2206
31. ¶L-5629

deduction applies to expenses incurred in: (1) preparing tax returns, (2) determining tax liability, (3) contesting tax liability, (4) securing tax counsel. (Code Sec. 62(a)(1); Reg § 1.62-1T(d)) This includes expenses incurred by an individual taxpayer in:[32]

- preparing that portion of the individual's tax return that relates to the taxpayer's business as sole proprietor,
- preparing schedules relating to income or loss from rentals or royalties, or farm income and expenses, and
- resolving asserted tax deficiencies relating to a business, to rental or royalty income, or to a farm.

From 2018 through 2025, *nonbusiness* tax determination costs are nondeductible because they are subject to the suspension of miscellaneous itemized deductions subject to the 2%-of-AGI floor; see ¶2162. For deductibility of interest on taxes, see ¶1708.

¶ 1513 Cost of materials and supplies, license and regulatory fees, and other deductible costs of carrying on a trade or business—ordinary and necessary expenses.

These include:[33]

... cost of materials and supplies (see ¶1630 for timing of deduction);[34]

... annual license and regulatory fees;[35]

... amounts paid to cancel burdensome contracts;[36]

... cost of moving business equipment and machinery;[37]

... current membership fees (but not admission fees), dues (other than certain social club dues) and assessments paid for business association, etc.;[38]

... training costs;[39]

... certain education expenses, see ¶2222 *et seq.*; and

... charitable contributions made in return for state or local tax credits.[40]

¶ 1514 Compensation Deduction. ▮▮▮▮▮▮▮▮▮▮▮▮▮▮▮▮

Reasonable amounts (¶1516 *et seq.*) that are paid or incurred in connection with a trade or business as compensation for personal services actually rendered (¶1515) are deductible under Code Sec. 162, subject to a limit for top officers (¶1518). Payments for fringe benefits (¶1523) are deductible as compensation, subject to some limits.

¶ 1515 Compensation paid for personal services (including severance pay)—deductibility.

Under Code Sec. 162, compensation (including severance pay) paid or incurred for personal services rendered is deductible as a trade or business expense. (Code Sec. 162(a)(1)) Deductible compensation includes amounts paid to independent contractors, as well as employees.[41]

A parent can deduct reasonable wages paid to an unemancipated minor child for personal services actually rendered as a bona fide employee in the business.[42]

For deductibility of amounts paid for fringe benefits, see ¶1523 *et seq.* For when compensation can be deducted, see ¶1535 *et seq.*

---

32. ¶L-3000 *et seq.*
33. ¶L-4200 *et seq.*
34. ¶L-4207 *et seq.*
35. ¶L-4216 *et seq.*
36. ¶L-4213 *et seq.*
37. ¶L-4209 *et seq.*
38. ¶L-4231
39. ¶L-4232.4
40. ¶K-3032.1 *et seq.*
41. ¶H-3600 *et seq.*
42. ¶H-3755

¶ 1516   Compensation only deductible to extent it's "reasonable compensation."

Under Code Sec. 162, compensation is deductible only to the extent it's *reasonable*. Compensation paid to employee-shareholders also must be paid purely for services, or have a purely compensatory purpose, to be deductible. (Code Sec. 162(a)(1)) The question of reasonableness rarely arises unless the payments are made to a person "related" to the taxpayer—that is, to the members of an employer's family, or to stockholders of the employer, or to members of a stockholder's family.[43]

The unreasonable portion of compensation is nondeductible. If the recipient is a shareholder, the unreasonable portion may be treated as a dividend. (Reg § 1.162-7(b)(1))[44]

While reasonableness of compensation normally arises in determining whether a business is trying to deduct too high an amount of compensation, IRS finds the concept equally applicable to employment tax cases (e.g., where S corporation shareholder-employees pay themselves a low salary to reduce Medicare and Social Security taxes).[45]

¶ 1517   Factors determining whether compensation is reasonable for deductibility.

Reasonable compensation deductible under Code Sec. 162 is the amount that would ordinarily be paid for like services by like enterprises under like circumstances. (Reg § 1.162-7(b)(3))[46] Factors determining reasonableness include: (1) duties performed by the employee; (2) character and amount of responsibility; (3) amount of time required; (4) ability and achievements of the employee; (5) volume of business handled by the employee; (6) complexities of the business; (7) relationship of compensation to gross and net income of the business; (8) living conditions in locality; (9) compensation history of the employee; and (10) salary policy as to all employees.[47]

The Seventh Circuit applies a single independent-investor test in evaluating if a stockholder-employee's pay is reasonable (i.e., would an outside investor have paid the compensation amount based on performance). Other courts employ the independent-investor test in conjunction with an analysis of the above factors.[48]

The test of whether compensation is reasonable is normally applied to the compensation paid to the particular individual and not to the total compensation paid to a group of employees.[49] Services rendered in earlier years can be taken into account in determining the reasonableness of compensation paid during the current year.[50] Reasonableness of compensation for part-time services is determined under the usual reasonableness rules.[1]

¶ 1518 $1 million deduction limit for "applicable employee compensation" paid to "covered employees" of publicly held corporations; $500,000 limit for "covered health insurance provider's" compensation deduction.

Under Code Sec. 162(m)(1), a "publicly held corporation" can't deduct applicable employee remuneration (defined below) in excess of $1 million per year paid to a "covered employee." (Code Sec. 162(m)(1); Reg § 1.162-27(b); Reg § 1.162-33(b))[2] The $1 million limit is reduced (but not below zero) by the amount, if any, paid to the executive but not deductible under the golden parachute rules (¶1533). (Code Sec. 162(m)(4)(D); Reg § 1.162-33(e))[3]

Publicly held corporation. A "publicly held corporation" is any corporation that's an

---

43. ¶s H-3725 *et seq.*, H-3752 *et seq.*
44. ¶H-3607
45. ¶H-4329
46. ¶H-3701
47. ¶H-3706
48. ¶H-3721

49. ¶H-3705
50. ¶H-3745
1. ¶H-3715
2. ¶H-3776
3. ¶H-3807

issuer, as defined in section 3 (15 USC §78c) of the Securities Exchange Act of 1934 (Exchange Act): (i) whose securities must be registered under section 12 of the Exchange Act (15 USC §78l); or (ii) that must file reports under section 15(d) of the Exchange Act (15 USC §78o(d)). (Code Sec. 162(m)(2); Reg § 1.162-33(c)(1)(i))[4]

Covered employee. A "covered employee" is any employee of the taxpayer: (1) who was the taxpayer's principal executive officer (PEO) or principal financial officer (PFO), or was acting as such, at any time during the tax year; (2) whose total compensation for the tax year (i) must be reported to shareholders under the Exchange Act because the employee is one of the three most highly compensated officers for the tax year other than the PEO or PFO, or (ii) would have to be reported to shareholders if reporting were required under the Exchange Act; or (3) who was a covered employee of the taxpayer (or any predecessor) for any earlier tax year that began after Dec. 31, 2016. (Code Sec. 162(m)(3)) Regs provide additional guidance as to who is a covered employee. (Code Sec. 162(m)(2); Reg § 1.162-33(c)(2)(i))[5]

Applicable employee remuneration. Applicable employee remuneration means a covered employee's aggregate remuneration for services performed (either during the deduction year or during another tax year) that would be deductible entirely for the tax year if the $1 million limit didn't apply. (Code Sec. 162(m)(4)(A)) Applicable employee remuneration includes performance-based compensation and commissions. It doesn't include certain items excluded, e.g., under Code Sec. 162(m)(4)(B) or Code Sec. 162(m)(4)(C).[6]

Deduction limit for "covered health insurance providers." For services performed during a tax year in which an employer is a "covered health insurance provider," the employer can't claim a compensation deduction over $500,000 for an "applicable individual." A health insurance provider is a covered health insurance provider if at least 25% of the gross premiums it receives in the tax year from providing health insurance coverage is from minimum essential coverage (as defined in Code Sec. 5000A(f)). (Code Sec. 162(m)(6); Reg § 1.162-31(b)(4)(i)(A))[7]

¶ 1519 No deduction of payments for services rendered to another—compensation deduction.

A taxpayer can't deduct, under Code Sec. 162 payments for services rendered to someone other than the taxpayer—for example, payments by a shareholder to employees of the corporation for services to the corporation, or by a corporation to its officers for services to subsidiaries and related corporations, or by a corporation to employees of a sub. But salary paid by a parent corporation to its own executives for supervising the operations of a sub is deductible by the parent as an expense of the parent's business.[8]

¶ 1520 Employer's deduction for payment of employee debts or expenses—compensation deduction.

An employer's payment of an employee's debts or personal expenses is deductible by the employer under Code Sec. 162 as compensation paid (if reasonable, see ¶1516), just as if the employee had been paid directly and had used the money to pay his or her debts or expenses.[9]

¶ 1521 Employer's deduction of contingent compensation.

An employer can deduct contingent compensation under Code Sec. 162, where it's freely bargained for between the employer and the individual before the services are rendered, and not influenced by any consideration on the part of the employer other than that of

---

4. ¶H-3777
5. ¶H-3780
6. ¶H-3781 *et seq.*
7. ¶H-3810 *et seq.*
8. ¶H-3613
9. ¶H-4014

151

securing the individual's services on fair and advantageous terms. This is so even though the arrangement results in higher compensation than would otherwise be allowed as a deduction. The reasonableness of the amount is determined by the circumstances at the date the contract for services is made, not when the contract is questioned. (Reg § 1.162-7(b)(2), Reg § 1.162-7(b)(3))[10]

¶ 1522 Deduction for compensation paid in property other than cash; deemed inclusion rule where reporting requirements met—Form 1099-MISC.

Under Code Sec. 83, the deduction for compensation paid in property, including a bargain sale and including restricted property, is the amount included in the income of the person who performed the services, to the extent the compensation is reasonable. (Code Sec. 83(h))[11] The "amount included" in income is the amount reported by the service provider on an original or amended return, or included in income as a result of an IRS audit. It includes excluded group-term life insurance and foreign income. (Reg § 1.83-6(a)(1))

Under a "deemed inclusion rule," however, a deduction may be taken by an employer (service recipient) if the employer timely complies with the applicable information reporting requirements. Thus, an employee is *deemed* to have included the property received in income, and a deduction can be claimed by the employer if the employer timely satisfies the Code Sec. 6041 or Code Sec. 6041A reporting requirements (Reg § 1.83-6(a)(2)), i.e., by timely reporting the transaction to the service provider and federal government on Form W-2 or Form 1099-MISC, whichever applies. If this rule isn't satisfied, an employer must demonstrate that the compensation amount deducted was actually included in the service provider's income. [12]

The deemed inclusion rule can be used where the service provider is a corporation by issuing Form 1099-MISC even though there would otherwise be a general reporting exemption for a service provider that's a corporation. (Reg § 1.83-6(a)(2))

If a transfer is less than $600 in any tax year (in which case the reporting requirements don't apply), or if the transfer is eligible for any other reporting exemption (applicable to a noncorporate service provider), no Form 1099 reporting is required for the service recipient to rely on the deemed inclusion rule. [13]

In addition, to be deductible, a transfer can't be a capital expenditure, a deferred expense, or part of inventory. (Reg § 1.83-6(a)(4))[14]

If payment is in employer stock, no gain or loss results. (Code Sec. 1032)[15] If payment is in property other than the employer's stock, and the value of the property exceeds the employer's basis for the property, the excess is income to the employer (capital gain or ordinary income, depending on the character of the property used). (Reg § 1.83-6(b)) The employer has a loss deduction where the basis of the property exceeds its fair market value[16] (subject to related-taxpayer restrictions on losses).[17]

The deduction is allowed for the tax year of the employer in which, or with which, the employee's tax year ends. (Code Sec. 83(h))[18]

For restricted property, see ¶1216; for noncash fringe benefits, see ¶1523.

¶ 1523 Deductibility of compensation paid as noncash fringe benefits; nondeductibility of "qualified transportation fringe" (QTF) or commuting expense.

---

10. ¶H-3732
11. ¶H-3650 *et seq.*
12. ¶H-3650 *et seq.*
13. ¶H-3654
14. ¶H-3655 *et seq.*

15. ¶H-3659
16. ¶H-3659
17. ¶H-3659
18. ¶H-3653

If an employer furnishes a noncash fringe benefit to an employee as compensation, the employer may deduct under Code Sec. 162 only the costs it incurs in providing the property to its employees, not the property's value. The employer may claim a depreciation deduction if it owns the property or a deduction for leasing costs if it rents the property. (Reg § 1.162-25T(a))[19]

Employers may not deduct the expense of a QTF, defined in Code Sec. 132(f) (¶1246), provided to an employee. (Code Sec. 274(a)(4)) And, no deduction is allowed for any expense incurred for providing any transportation (or any payment or reimbursement) to an employee for travel between the employee's residence and place of employment, except as necessary to ensure the employee's safety. (Code Sec. 274(l)(1)) Regs provide guidance on the disallowance provisions in Code Sec. 274(a)(4) and Code Sec. 274(l)(1), including how to calculate the disallowed amount. (Reg § 1.274-13; Reg § 1.274-14)[20]

¶ 1524 Employer's deduction for nonstatutory stock options, incentive stock options, or stock transferred under an employee stock purchase plan—compensation deduction.

An employer's deduction for a nonstatutory stock option is determined under the Code Sec. 83 payment-in-property rules at ¶1522 (and thus, the employer would deduct the amount the employee must include in income on exercise of the option, where the option has no readily ascertainable value at grant, see ¶1219).[21] The employer isn't allowed a compensation deduction for stock transferred under an incentive stock option or an employee stock purchase plan, unless the employee has income by reason of a disqualified (premature) disposition of the stock (¶1220 *et seq.*). (Code Sec. 421(a), Code Sec. 421(b))[22]

¶ 1525 Deduction of premiums on company-owned life insurance, endowment or annuity contracts—compensation deduction.

Under Code Sec. 264(a)(1), a taxpayer can't deduct premiums on any life insurance policy, or endowment or annuity contract if it is directly or indirectly a beneficiary under the policy or contract. (Code Sec. 264(a)(1)) But this rule doesn't apply to Code Sec. 72(s)(5) annuity contracts (certain qualified pension plans, retirement annuities, individual retirement annuities and qualified funding assets) or to any annuity contract to which Code Sec. 72(u) (annuity contracts held by other than natural persons) applies. (Code Sec. 264(b)(2)) Premiums are deductible as a noncash fringe benefit where only the insured employee or his or her beneficiaries will get the proceeds. For contracts issued before June 9, '97, the deduction disallowance only applies to premiums on the life of an officer, employee or any person financially interested in any trade or business carried on by the taxpayer if the taxpayer is directly or indirectly a beneficiary of any part of the policy.[23]

Premiums on group term life insurance are deductible (if the employer isn't directly or indirectly a beneficiary) even though the employee isn't taxed (¶1262) on group term coverage of $50,000 or less.[24]

For interest on business life insurance loans, see ¶1720.

¶ 1526 Deduction of health and accident insurance premiums and direct payment or reimbursement of medical expenses under a plan for employees.

The employer's payment of health and accident insurance premiums for employees and their families, or the employer's direct payment or reimbursement of actual expenses if under a plan, is deductible under Code Sec. 162. (Reg § 1.162-10(a))[25] Reimbursements are

19. ¶H-4002
20. ¶L-1620 *et seq.*; ¶L-1628
21. ¶H-2883
22. ¶H-2960

23. ¶H-4035
24. ¶H-4037
25. ¶s H-4071, H-4073

deductible even where the employee is the spouse of a sole proprietor and the medical expenses incurred on behalf of the employee's family include those of the sole proprietor (as the employee's spouse).[26]

¶ 1527 Deduction for contributions to Archer medical savings account (MSA)— Form 8853—deduction.

Eligible small employers (see ¶1255), their employees, and self-employed individuals may deduct contributions to an Archer medical savings account (MSA). (Code Sec. 106, Code Sec. 220) An eligible self-employed claims deductions (as calculated on Form 8853) for MSAs above the line, to arrive at adjusted gross income. (Code Sec. 62(a)(16)) Although no new Archer MSAs may be established after 2007, contributions to and distributions from established Archer MSAs may continue to made. (Code Sec. 220(i))[27]

MSAs are available to employees covered under a high deductible health plan (HDHP) of a small employer (¶1255) and to self-employed individuals covered by a HDHP. An individual isn't eligible for an MSA if he's entitled to benefits under Medicare or covered under any other health plan, unless the other coverage is permitted insurance (e.g., insurance for a specified disease or illness, or fixed payment for hospitalization) or coverage for accidents, disability, dental care, vision care, or long-term care. For employees, contributions can be made by the employee or the employer, but not by both for the same year. An MSA is a tax-exempt entity but is subject to the tax on unrelated business income. (Code Sec. 220(c), Code Sec. 220(d))[28]

For 2022, an HDHP for MSA purposes is a health plan with an annual deductible of at least $2,450 and not more than $3,700 for individual coverage (at least $4,950 and not more than $7,400 for family coverage); in addition, the maximum out-of-pocket expenses can't exceed $4,950 for individual coverage ($9,050 for family coverage). For 2023, an HDHP for MSA purposes is a health plan with an annual deductible of at least $2,650 and not more than $3,950, in the case of self-only coverage (at least $5,300 and not more than $7,900 for family coverage); in addition, the maximum out-of-pocket expenses can't exceed $5,300 for individual coverage ($9,650 for family coverage).Code Sec. 220(c)(2))[29]

The maximum annual contribution for individual coverage is 65% of the HDHP premium (75% for family coverage). The annual contribution limit is the sum of the limits determined separately for each month the individual is MSA-eligible. (Code Sec. 220(b)(1))[30] A self-employed's deduction for contributions to an MSA can't exceed the earned income from the trade or business that established the HDHP (Code Sec. 220(b)(4)(B)),[31] and an employee's contributions to an MSA can't exceed the compensation from the employer that set up the plan. (Code Sec. 220(b)(4)(A))[32] Excess contributions are subject to a 6% penalty tax (on Form 5329). (Code Sec. 4973(a)(2), Code Sec. 4973(d))[33]

For treatment of MSA distributions, see ¶1371.

¶ 1528 Deduction for contributions to health savings accounts (HSAs); comparability rule for employer contributions; excise tax on excess contributions—Form 5329.

Eligible individuals may, subject to statutory limits, make "above-the-line" deductible contributions to a health savings account (HSA). Other persons (e.g., family members) also may contribute on behalf of eligible individuals, as may employers (see ¶1257). (Code Sec. 106, Code Sec. 223) An account holder may deduct contributions to an HSA even if another (e.g., family member) makes the contributions. (Code Sec. 62(a)(19)) An HSA is a tax-exempt entity but is subject to the tax on unrelated business income. (Code

---

26. ¶L-3510
27. ¶H-1326 *et seq.*
28. ¶H-1331.1 *et seq.*, ¶H-1335.4
29. ¶H-1332

30. ¶s H-1335, H-1335.1
31. ¶H-1335.3
32. ¶H-1335.3
33. ¶H-1336.1 *et seq.*

Sec. 223(e)(1))[34]

For tax-free HSA distributions for qualifying medical expenses, see ¶1372.

Eligible individuals. These are individuals who are covered under a high deductible health plan (HDHP) (see below) and are not covered under any other health plan that isn't an HDHP, unless the other coverage is permitted insurance (insurance for worker's compensation, torts, ownership and use of property such as auto insurance, insurance for a specified disease or illness, or providing a fixed payment for hospitalization) or coverage for accidents, disability, dental care, vision care, or long-term care. An individual won't fail to be treated as an eligible individual solely due to receiving hospital care or medical services under any law administered by the Veterans Administration for a service-connected disability. (Code Sec. 223(c))[35]

HSA contributions aren't deductible for an individual who is claimed as a dependent by another taxpayer for the year. (Code Sec. 223(b)(6)) There's no deduction for an HSA contribution for any month an individual is eligible for and enrolled in Medicare. (Code Sec. 223(b)(7))

HDHP. An HDHP is a health plan with an annual deductible of not less than $1,400 for 2022 for individual coverage ($1,500 for 2023), and $2,800 for 2022 ($3,000 for 2023) for family coverage. But an HDHP may have a zero preventive care deductible or a preventive care deductible below the minimum annual deductible. (Code Sec. 223(c)(2)(C))[36] Preventive care does not generally include any service or benefit intended to treat an existing illness, injury, or condition.[37] Maximum out-of-pocket expenses for an HDHP for 2022 can't exceed $7,050 for individual coverage and $14,100 for family coverage (for 2023, $7,500 and $15,000, respectively). (Code Sec. 223(c)(2))[38]

Other coverage. Health flexible spending accounts (FSAs, see ¶1269) and health reimbursement arrangements (HRAs, see ¶1373) are "other coverage" that will generally preclude HSA eligibility. However, exceptions apply for: limited purpose FSAs and HRAs (those providing only certain benefits, e.g., dental and vision); suspended HRAs (where the employee elects to forgo reimbursements for the coverage period); FSAs and HRAs imposing annual deductibles, and HRAs providing benefits only after retirement. An otherwise eligible individual may be covered by an HRA which pays and reimburses expenses for (1) vision, dental and preventive care, and (2) premiums for coverage by an accident and health plan.[39] Coverage under a health FSA during the "grace period" (i.e., the period immediately following the end of a plan year during which unused benefits or contributions remaining may be paid or reimbursed to plan participants for qualified expenses) is disregarded coverage for HSA purposes if the balance in the health FSA at the end of the plan year is zero. (Code Sec. 223(c)(1)(B))

Limit on deductible contributions; due date; inclusion and penalty tax for ineligible taxpayers. The maximum annual HSA deductible contribution is the sum of the monthly contribution limits, based on eligibility and health plan coverage on the first day of the month. The monthly limit is 1/12 of the indexed amount for self-only coverage ($3,650 for 2022; $3,850 for 2023) and for family coverage ($7,300 for 2022; $7,750 for 2023). The maximum HSA contribution is increased by an additional catch-up contribution amount (computed on a monthly basis) for individuals age 55 or older as of the last day of the calendar year who are not enrolled in Medicare. The catch-up contribution amount is $1,000. There is no requirement that the individual have earnings. (Code Sec. 223(b))[40] Contributions for a year can be made until the account holder's tax return due date (without extensions) for that year. Excess contributions are subject to a 6% penalty tax (on Form 5329). (Code Sec. 4973(a)(5), Code Sec. 223(f)(3)) IRS has listed situations in which

---

34. ¶H-1350 *et seq.*
35. ¶H-1350.3 *et seq.*
36. ¶H-1350.6
37. ¶H-1350.6D

38. ¶H-1350.6
39. ¶H-1350.4A
40. ¶H-1350, H-1350.7

an employer can recoup amounts incorrectly contributed to an employee's HSA. (Information Letter 2018-0033)[41] Maximum annual HSA contributions are reduced by Archer MSA (¶1527) contributions for that year. (Code Sec. 223(b)(4))

For computing the annual HSA contribution, a taxpayer who is an eligible individual in the last month of a tax year is "deemed eligible" during every month of that year. (Code Sec. 223(b)(8)) Thus, the taxpayer can make contributions for months before enrollment in an HDHP. But if the taxpayer does not remain an eligible individual (except because of disability) during the testing period (from the last month of the tax year to the last day of the 12th month following that month), contributions for months in which the taxpayer was "deemed eligible" are includible in gross income for the tax year of the first day during the testing period that the taxpayer is not an eligible individual, and are subject to a 10% penalty tax. (Code Sec. 223(b)(8)(B))

HSA rollovers and carryover of HSA funds. Amounts in an HSA can be rolled over tax-free from an HSA, or from an Archer MSA (¶1527) to an HSA. The rollover must be completed within 60 days after the date on which the account holder receives the amounts from the HSA or Archer MSA and is not taken into account in determining the annual contribution limits for the recipient HSA. Only one tax-free rollover into an HSA is permitted per 1-year period. (Code Sec. 223(f)(5), Code Sec. 220(f)(5))[42]

For one-time rollovers from IRAs, see ¶4354.

Comparability rule for employer contributions. In general, employer contributions to employee HSAs must be the same amount or the same percentage of the HDHP deductible for all employees with the same category of HDHP coverage (self-only, or family coverage, i.e., any coverage other than self-only). But employers may make larger HSA contributions for nonhighly compensated employees than for highly compensated employees (as defined in Code Sec. 414(q), see ¶4315). (Code Sec. 4980G(d)) Employers that provide self + 1, self + 2 and self + 3 family coverage apply the comparability rules separately to each category. The comparability rules apply separately to full time, part-time, and former employees (except for former employees under COBRA continuation coverage). An employer that fails the comparability rule is subject to a 35% penalty tax. The comparability rules do not apply to HSA contributions made through a cafeteria plan. Instead, the Code Sec. 125 discrimination rules apply. (Code Sec. 4980G; Reg § 54.4980G-1 - Reg § 54.4980G-5)[43]

¶ 1529   Group-health plan continuation coverage (COBRA), requirements.

Under Code Sec. 4980B(f)(1), with limited exceptions (including one for small employers), a group health plan of, or contributed to by, an employer must provide that each qualified beneficiary who would lose coverage under the plan because of a qualifying event may elect continuation coverage under the plan within a specified at-least-60-day election period. (Code Sec. 4980B(f)(1))[44]

"Qualified beneficiaries" are the covered employee, spouse or dependent child, a deceased employee's surviving spouse in certain cases, and a child born to or placed for adoption with the covered employee during the COBRA coverage period. (Code Sec. 4980B(g)(1))[45]

"Qualifying events" include: death of the covered employee; termination or reduction of hours of employment; divorce or legal separation from the covered employee; cessation of a child's dependency; and the employee's entitlement to certain Medicare benefits. (Code Sec. 4980B(f)(3))[46]

Continuation coverage must be identical to coverage provided under the plan to similarly

---

41. ¶H-1350.8D
42. ¶H-1350.9
43. ¶H-1350.20

44. ¶H-1250 *et seq.*
45. ¶H-1271
46. ¶H-1306

situated beneficiaries who haven't had a qualifying event. (Code Sec. 4980B(f)(2)(A))[47] Coverage for a qualified beneficiary must begin on the date of the qualifying event and end not earlier than the earliest of: a statutory maximum period, the end of the plan, the failure to pay a premium, or the eligibility for group health plan coverage or Medicare.[48] Coverage of the cost of pediatric vaccines can't be reduced below the coverage provided by the plan as of May 1, '93. (Code Sec. 4980B(f)(1))[49]

Employers (or for a multiemployer plan, the plan) and certain responsible persons are liable for an excise tax (Code Sec. 4980B(e))[50] if, with certain exceptions, a group health plan fails to provide the above coverage. (Code Sec. 4980B(a))[1]

¶ 1530   Sole proprietor or self-employed's deduction for health insurance costs.

Under Code Sec. 162(l), a self-employed individual (or a partner or a more-than-2%-shareholder of an S corporation) can deduct as a business expense 100% of the amount paid during the tax year for medical insurance on self, spouse, dependents, and to any child of the taxpayer who has not attained age 27 as of the end of the year. (Code Sec. 162(l)(1)) Medicare premiums can be used in figuring the self-employed's deduction for health insurance costs.[2]

The deduction is limited to the amount of the individual's earned income as defined in Code Sec. 401(c) (net earnings from self-employment) derived from the trade or business for which the plan providing the coverage is established. (Code Sec. 162(l)(2)(A))[3] For purposes of applying the earned income limit to the deduction of a more-than-2% S corporation shareholder, that shareholder's wages from the S corporation are treated as earned income. (Code Sec. 162(l)(5)(A))[4]

No deduction is available for any month in which the self-employed individual is eligible to participate in a subsidized health plan maintained by an employer of the taxpayer, the taxpayer's spouse, any dependent, or any child of the taxpayer who hasn't attained age 27 as of the end of the tax year. This test for eligibility is made for each calendar month. This rule is applied separately to (1) plans that provide coverage for qualified long-term care services (¶2144), or are qualified long-term care insurance contracts (¶2145) and (2) plans which don't include such coverage and aren't such contracts. (Code Sec. 162(l)(2)(B)) Thus, an individual eligible for employer-subsidized health insurance may still be able to deduct long-term care insurance premiums, so long as he or she isn't eligible for employer-subsidized long-term care insurance.[5]

IRS has provided special rules for taxpayers who qualify for both this deduction and the Code Sec. 36B premium tax credit (¶2343).[6]

¶ 1531   Deduction for contributions to funded welfare benefit plans.

Under Code Sec. 419, an employer's contribution to a "welfare benefit fund" is deductible only for the tax year paid, and only to the extent the contribution doesn't exceed the "qualified cost" of the plan for its tax year that relates to (ends with or within) the employer's tax year. (Code Sec. 419(a), Code Sec. 419(b))[7] Contributions for independent contractors are also subject to this rule. (Code Sec. 419(g))[8] The rule, however, doesn't apply to a ten-or-more employer plan if no employer (or related employer) normally contributes more than 10% of total contributions, unless the plan uses experience ratings to determine each employer's contribution. (Code Sec. 419A(f)(6); Reg § 1.419A(f)(6)-1(b)(1))[9]

A welfare benefit fund is a fund that is part of an employer's plan through which the

47. ¶H-1277
48. ¶H-1301
49. ¶H-1250 *et seq.*
50. ¶H-1316
1. ¶H-1315
2. ¶L-3510
3. ¶L-3507

4. ¶L-3511
5. ¶L-3508
6. ¶L-3512
7. ¶s H-4101, H-4113 *et seq.*
8. ¶H-4104
9. ¶H-4154

employer provides welfare benefits to employees or their beneficiaries, but doesn't include amounts held under certain kinds of insurance contracts. (Code Sec. 419(e); Reg § 1.419A(f)(6)-1(b)(4))[10]

¶ 1532 Death benefits to deceased employee's widow(er) or other beneficiaries—employer's deduction.

Payments to the widow(er) or other beneficiaries of a deceased employee, i.e., continuing the decedent's salary for a reasonable period, are deductible by the employer under Code Sec. 162 to the extent they qualify as a business expense. A benefit paid as a gift based on the beneficiary's need doesn't qualify as a business expense. (Reg § 1.404(a)-12(b)(2))[11]

¶ 1533 "Golden parachute" or excess parachute payments—no deduction for employer; excise tax on employee.

No deduction is allowed for an "excess parachute payment." (Code Sec. 280G)[12] In addition, Code Sec. 4999 imposes a nondeductible 20% excise tax on the recipient of an excess parachute payment. An excess parachute payment is the amount by which a parachute payment (below) exceeds the base amount (below) allocated to it. (Code Sec. 280G(b)(1)) If there's only one parachute payment, the entire base amount is allocated to it.[13]

A parachute payment is any payment in the nature of compensation to (or for the benefit of) a disqualified individual (described below) *if*:

(1) the payment is contingent on a change (a) in the ownership or effective control of the corporation, *or* (b) in the ownership of a substantial part of the corporation's assets, *and*

(2) the aggregate present value of all such contingent compensation payments equals, or exceeds, three times the base amount. (Code Sec. 280G(b))[14] This base amount is the average annualized compensation income includible in a disqualified individual's gross income in the 5-tax-year period preceding the tax year in which the change of ownership or control of the corporation occurs. (Code Sec. 280G(b), Code Sec. 280G(d))[15]

A disqualified individual is one who is: (1) an employee, independent contractor, or other person specified in regs who performs personal services for a corporation, *and* (2) is an officer, shareholder or "highly compensated individual." (Code Sec. 280G(c); Reg § 1.280G-1, Q&As 15 to 20)[16] Highly compensated individual means a member of the highest paid 1% of employees or, if less, the highest paid 250 employees. (Code Sec. 280G(c))[17]

A parachute payment doesn't include an amount that the taxpayer can establish, by clear and convincing evidence, is reasonable compensation for services to be rendered on, or after, the date of change in ownership or control. (Code Sec. 280G(b)(4)(A)) The amount of an excess parachute payment can be reduced to the extent that the taxpayer can establish by clear and convincing evidence that the payment is reasonable compensation for personal services actually rendered before the date of change of ownership or control. (Code Sec. 280G(b)(4)(B))[18]

The parachute payment rules don't apply to a corporation (1) that was (immediately before the change in control or assets) a "small business corporation," without regard to whether it has a nonresident alien shareholder (¶3351) or (2) whose stock isn't readily tradeable if shareholder approval has been obtained. (Code Sec. 280G(b)(5)) A corporation that meets the requirements to elect to be treated as an S corporation, but does not elect S

---

10. ¶H-4105 *et seq.*
11. ¶H-4050 *et seq.*
12. ¶H-3826
13. ¶H-3874
14. ¶H-3830

15. ¶H-3871
16. ¶H-3840
17. ¶H-3843
18. ¶H-3876

status, may nevertheless use the small business exemption. (Reg § 1.280G-1, Q&A 6(a)(1))[19]

Payments to or from a qualified pension or profit-sharing plan, Code Sec. 403(a) annuity, simplified employee pension or SIMPLE plan (¶4369 *et seq.*) aren't parachute payments. (Code Sec. 280G(b)(6); Reg § 1.280G-1, Q&A 8)[20]

¶ 1534   Compensation payments that are actually capital outlays—deductibility.

Payments otherwise designated as compensation may actually be payments for property. For example, where a partnership sells out to a corporation and the former partners agree to continue to work for the corporation, the salaries of the former partners may be in part payment for the transfer of their business. (Reg § 1.162-7(b)(1))[21]

¶ 1535   Year for deducting compensation, overview.

An employer deducts compensation under Code Sec. 162 in the year allowed under its accounting method (¶2812 *et seq.*) with special rules for compensation in property and bargain sales (¶1213 *et seq.*), deferred compensation (¶1536), and contributions to employee benefit plans (¶4324).

If salary is paid or accrued in one year for services to be rendered in a later year, the deduction is allowed only over the period during which the services are rendered. This applies to both cash and accrual-basis employers.[22]

For limitations on accrual-basis taxpayers' deductions for compensation paid to related cash-basis taxpayers, see ¶2826.

¶ 1536   When to deduct deferred compensation.

An employer's contributions to a nonqualified deferred compensation plan are deductible in the tax year in which an amount attributable to the contribution is includible in the gross income of employees participating in the plan (Code Sec. 404(a)(5)), even if the employer is an accrual basis taxpayer.[23]

Benefits provided under a welfare benefit fund (Code Sec. 404(b)(2)(B)), and payments of bonuses or other amounts within 2½ months after the close of the tax year in which significant services required for payment have been performed (Reg § 1.404(b)-1T, Ex 2(c)), aren't treated as deferred compensation.[24]

To determine if compensation is deferred compensation, and when deferred compensation is paid, no amount is treated as paid or received until it's actually received by the employee. (Code Sec. 404(a)(11))[25]

If the all events test (¶2823) and recurring item exception (¶2824) are otherwise met, an accrual basis taxpayer may treat its payroll tax liability as incurred in Year 1, regardless of whether the compensation to which the liability relates is deferred compensation deductible under Code Sec. 404 in Year 2.[26]

¶ 1537   When to deduct bonuses paid to employees.

A cash basis employer deducts bonuses under Code Sec. 162 only for the year in which the bonuses are actually paid (¶1536).[27]

Bonuses by an accrual basis taxpayer are deductible in the tax year when all the events have occurred that establish the fact of liability to pay the bonus, the amount can be

---

19. ¶H-3835
20. ¶H-3839
21. ¶H-3604
22. ¶H-3934
23. ¶H-3677

24. ¶s H-3673, H-3674
25. ¶H-3674
26. ¶H-3670
27. ¶s H-3901, H-3916

determined with reasonable accuracy, and economic performance has occurred for the liability (¶2824). (Reg § 1.461-1(a)(2)(i))[28]

To deduct a year-end bonus in the accrual year rather than the actual payment year an employer must pay the bonus within a brief period of time after the close of the employer's tax year. If an employer pays bonuses within 2 ½ months after the close of the tax year, then a deduction for the bonuses won't be subject to the deferred compensation rules (¶1536), which would otherwise bar the deduction until the bonus is included in the employee's income. (Reg § 1.404(b)-1T)[29] Payment after 2 ½ months is presumed to be deferred compensation, and that presumption can only be rebutted by showing that: (1) it was either administratively or economically impossible to avoid a later payment, and (2) as of the end of the employer's tax year, the impracticability was unforeseeable. (Reg § 1.404(b)-1T)[30]

For limitations on accrual-basis taxpayers' deductions for compensation paid to related cash-basis taxpayers, see ¶2826.

¶ 1538   When to deduct vacation pay.

Cash basis employers take a deduction under Code Sec. 162 when the vacation pay is paid (¶1536) in accordance with the general rules for cash basis employers.[31]

For an accrual basis employer, vacation pay earned during any tax year but not paid on or before 2 ½ months after the end of the tax year is deductible for the tax year of the employer in which it's paid. (Code Sec. 404(a)(5))[32]

¶ 1539   Deductible Travel Expenses.

Ordinary and necessary expenses incurred by *self-employed taxpayers* while traveling "away from home" (¶1540) in pursuit of a trade or business are deductible. But unreimbursed expenses of employees and investors for travel away from home are miscellaneous itemized deductions that are disallowed for tax years 2018–2025 (see ¶2162).

Deductible expenses include amounts (other than amounts that are lavish or extravagant) paid for meals and lodging—subject to the restrictions and percentage limits for meals discussed at ¶1556, the substantiation requirements for expenses of travel and meals at ¶1563 *et seq.*, and the limits on travel expenses discussed at ¶1546, ¶2223, and ¶1545. (Code Sec. 162(a)(2); Reg § 1.274-12(a)(4)(i)[33]

A taxpayer isn't away from home unless he or she is away *overnight*, or at least long enough to require rest or sleep.[34]

Deductible business travel expenses include baggage charges, air, rail and bus fares, cost of transporting sample cases or display materials, expenses for sample rooms, cost of maintaining or operating a car, house trailer or airplane, telephone expenses, laundry and dry cleaning costs, taxi fares, etc., from the airport or station to the hotel and back, from one customer to another, transportation from where meals and lodging are obtained to the temporary work assignment, and reasonable tips for any of these expenses. (Reg § 1.162-2(a))[35]

¶ 1540   Home defined for travel expense deduction purposes—taxpayer's "tax home."

A taxpayer's home for travel expense deduction (¶1539) purposes under Code Sec. 162 is his or her "tax home" —the taxpayer's principal place of business, employment station, or

---

28. ¶H-3916
29. ¶H-3919
30. ¶H-3919
31. ¶H-3922

32. ¶H-3922
33. ¶L-1701
34. ¶L-1710
35. ¶L-1705

post of duty, regardless of where his or her family lives.[36]

Where an individual has no principal place of business or employment but continually changes work locations (e.g., a traveling salesperson), the taxpayer's regular residence is his or her tax "home." [37] If such a taxpayer has no regular place of abode in a real and substantial sense, then the taxpayer has no "home" and can't deduct travel expenses. [38]

The tax home of a taxpayer who regularly works at two or more separate locations is the general area where his or her *principal* employment or business is, determined by taking into account (1) time spent, (2) business activity, and (3) financial return. Income is the most significant factor.[39]

Costs of traveling to and from the minor place of employment, 50% of the cost of meals (but see ¶1556 for special rule for 2021 and 2022), and the cost of lodging at the minor post are deductible travel expenses.[40]

An indefinite assignment away from home shifts the "tax home" and a taxpayer can't deduct the expenses of travel, meals and lodging while in the location of the "indefinite" assignment.[41] Employment is indefinite if it lasts for more than one year, or there is no realistic expectation that the employment will last for one year or less.[42]

¶ 1541 Expenses for lodging while not away from home (local lodging)—self-employed taxpayers' deductions.

Under Code Sec. 162, local lodging expenses of *self-employed* taxpayers may be deductible as ordinary and necessary business expenses if certain requirements are met. From 2018–2025, the unreimbursed local lodging expenses of employees aren't deductible (¶1539).

Under a safe harbor, local lodging expenses are ordinary and necessary business expenses if: (1) the lodging is necessary for the individual to participate fully in or be available for a bona fide business meeting, conference, training activity, or other business function; (2) the lodging is for a period not exceeding five calendar days and does not recur more frequently than once per calendar quarter; (3) if the individual is an employee, the employer requires him or her to remain at the activity or function overnight; and (4) the lodging is not lavish or extravagant under the circumstances and does not provide any significant element of personal pleasure, recreation, or benefit. (Reg § 1.162-32(b))[43]

¶ 1542 U.S. travel for both business and pleasure—deduction of expenses.

A travel expense deduction under Code Sec. 162 (¶1539) may be claimed for transportation costs to and from the destination, but only if the trip is related primarily to the taxpayer's business. Expenses at the destination allocable to the taxpayer's business are deductible even if the round-trip travel expenses are disallowed because the trip was primarily for pleasure.[44] If the trip is primarily for business, but the taxpayer extends his or her stay for personal reasons, makes side trips, or engages in other nonbusiness activities, the taxpayer may deduct only the expenses, such as lodging and 50% of the cost of meals, that he or she would have incurred if the trip had been totally for business. But no allocation is required for travel costs to and from the business destination. (Reg § 1.162-2(b)(1))[45]

---

36. ¶L-1801
37. ¶L-1802
38. ¶L-2025
39. ¶L-1805
40. ¶L-1804, L-2102

41. ¶L-1809
42. ¶L-1809
43. ¶L-1631
44. ¶L-1702
45. ¶L-1702

¶ 1543   **Foreign travel for both business and pleasure—deduction of expenses.**

If travel is primarily for pleasure, the rules at ¶1542 apply, so that only the amount of nontransportation expenses directly allocable to business is deductible under Code Sec. 162 (see ¶1539). But under special rules for foreign travel, even where travel is primarily for business, a portion of the transportation cost is nondeductible if the travel has a pleasure element. The nondeductible part is computed on a time ratio, usually in the proportion of nonbusiness days to all travel days.

This allocation and denial of deduction isn't made if: (1) travel is for one week or less; or (2) less than 25% of the time is spent on nonbusiness activity; or (3) the individual traveling had no substantial control over the arranging of the trip; or (4) a personal vacation wasn't a major consideration in making the trip. (Code Sec. 274(c); Reg § 1.162-2(b), Reg § 1.274-4(f)(5))[46] For foreign conventions, see ¶1544.

¶ 1544   **Convention expenses, deductibility—travel to domestic conventions or conventions held outside the "North American area."**

Travel expenses incurred in attending a domestic convention are subject to the regular business trip rules (see ¶1539 et seq) if attendance will benefit or advance the taxpayer's business as distinguished from serving some social, political, or other nonbusiness function. (Reg § 1.162-2(d))[47]

No business expense deduction is allowed for expenses allocable to a convention, seminar, or similar meeting held outside the "North American area" (defined below) unless the taxpayer establishes that the meeting is directly related to the active conduct of his or her trade or business and that after taking specified factors into account, it's as reasonable for the meeting to be held outside the North American area as within it. (Code Sec. 274(h)(1))[48]

North American area means the U.S., its possessions, the Trust Territory of the Pacific Islands, Canada and Mexico. (Code Sec. 274(h)(3)(A)) U.S. possessions include Puerto Rico and the U.S. Virgin Islands.[49] "North American area" also includes Aruba, Antigua, Bahamas, Barbados, Barbuda, Bermuda, Costa Rica, Curacao, Dominica, the Dominican Republic, Grenada, Guyana, Honduras, Jamaica, Panama, Saint Lucia, Trinidad and Tobago.[50]

For business conventions held aboard a cruise ship, a $2,000 per-individual, per-year deduction limit applies, and the deduction is allowable only if the ship is registered in the U.S. and all ports of call of the cruise ship are located in the U.S. or its possessions. (Code Sec. 274(h)(2))[1] A taxpayer claiming the deduction must attach to the return two specified written substantiation statements (including one signed by the sponsor). (Code Sec. 274(h)(5))[2]

¶ 1545   **Travel expense deduction for a spouse, dependent, or other companion.**

No deduction is allowed under Code Sec. 162 (other than moving expenses under very limited circumstances, see ¶1626) for travel expenses paid or incurred for a spouse, dependent, or other individual accompanying the taxpayer (or an officer or employee of the taxpayer) unless: (1) the spouse, etc., is an employee of the taxpayer; (2) the travel of the spouse, etc., is for a bona fide business purpose; and (3) the expenses would otherwise be deductible by the spouse, etc. (Code Sec. 274(m)(3); Reg § 1.274-12(a)(4)(iii)[3]

The limits on deductions for travel companions don't apply to a companion who (1) is a

---

46. ¶L-1726 *et seq.*
47. ¶L-1716
48. ¶L-1744
49. ¶ L-1745
50. ¶L-1746
1. ¶L-1721
2. ¶L-1722
3. ¶L-1739

business associate, (2) comes along for a bona-fide business purpose, and (3) could otherwise deduct the expense if he or she incurred it. (Reg § 1.274-2(g))

If a taxpayer is accompanied by a spouse on a business trip and the spouse's expenses aren't deductible, the deductible expense for transportation and lodging is the single rate cost of similar accommodations for the taxpayer, but the full rental for a car in which both spouses travel is deductible.[4]

¶ 1546 Deduction for travel by ocean liner, cruise ship, or other form of "luxury" water transportation travel is limited.

The travel expense deduction (¶1539) for travel by ocean liner, cruise ship, or other form of "luxury" water transportation is limited to twice the highest domestic per diem allowance of executive branch U.S. government employees (other than high-ranking executive personnel) multiplied by the number of days of luxury water travel. (Code Sec. 274(m)(1)(A)) If the cost includes separately stated amounts for meals, these amounts must be reduced by 50% (¶1556) before applying the per-diem limit. The per diem rule doesn't apply to expenses of a cruise-ship convention or seminar to which the rules at ¶1544 apply (Code Sec. 274(m)(1)(B)(i)), or to the items listed in Code Sec. 274(m)(1)(B)(ii).[5]

¶ 1547 Above-the-line deduction for overnight travel of reservists.

Under Code Sec. 62(a)(2)(E), a member of the Armed Forces reserves who travels over 100 miles from home for an overnight stay connected with the performance of services (e.g., to attend meetings) can deduct travel expenses as an above-the-line adjustment to gross income. The amount deductible is limited to the regular federal per diem rate for lodging, meals, and incidental expenses, and the standard mileage rate for car expenses plus parking fees and tolls. (Code Sec. 62(a)(2)(E)) Expenses for travel that don't take the taxpayer more than 100 miles from home are miscellaneous itemized deductions, not an adjustment to gross income, so they're nondeductible in tax years 2018–2025.[6]

¶ 1548 Transportation Expenses. ███████████████████████

Local transportation expenses (but not commuting expenses; see ¶1549) directly attributable to the conduct of a *self-employed* taxpayer's business are deductible even though he or she isn't away from home overnight. (Reg § 1.162-1(a)) But, unreimbursed local transportation expenses of employees are miscellaneous itemized deductions that are disallowed for tax years 2018–2025 (see ¶2162).

These so-called "local travel expenses" include air, train, bus and cab fares and costs of operating automobiles.[7] If a self-employed taxpayer works at two or more places each day, he or she can deduct the cost of getting from one to the other.[8]

¶ 1549 Expenses of daily transportation between home and work site (commuting expenses)—deductibility.

Expenses of commuting between a taxpayer's residence and regular business location, wherever situated, aren't deductible under Code Sec. 162(Reg § 1.162-2(e), Reg § 1.162-2(f)).[9] But a taxpayer may deduct daily transportation expenses incurred in going between the taxpayer's residence and a temporary (¶1550) work location *outside* the metropolitan area where the taxpayer lives and normally works.[10]

Daily transportation expenses incurred in going between the taxpayer's residence and a

---

4. ¶L-1740 *et seq.*
5. ¶L-1708
6. ¶A-2610
7. ¶L-1601

8. ¶L-1602
9. ¶L-1608 *et seq.*
10. ¶L-1605

temporary (¶1550) work location *within* the same metropolitan area is business transportation if: (1) the taxpayer has one or more regular work locations away from his or her residence; or (2) the taxpayer's residence is his or her principal place of business (¶1619 *et seq.*).[11]

¶ 1550　One-year temporary workplace rule—temporary assignment doesn't shift a taxpayer's "tax home"—deductibility of transportation expenses.

A temporary assignment away from home doesn't shift a taxpayer's "tax home." A work location is temporary for purposes of deducting daily transportation costs under Code Sec. 162 (¶1549) if employment at the location is realistically expected to last (and in fact does last) for one year or less. If the employment initially is realistically expected to last for one year or less, but at some later date it is realistically expected to exceed one year, that employment is considered temporary (absent facts and circumstances indicating otherwise) only until the date that the taxpayer's realistic expectation changes.[12]

A taxpayer generally isn't treated as being temporarily away from home if the period of employment exceeds one year. (Code Sec. 162(a)) However, where an assignment at a work location is expected to last for more than one year, but the taxpayer is realistically expected to be present at that location *for no more than 35 workdays (partial or complete)* during each of the calendar years in that period, the location is temporary for a calendar year in which he or she actually works there for no more than 35 partial or complete workdays.[13]

A *self-employed* taxpayer may deduct the necessary traveling expenses in getting to the temporary assignment and also for the return trip to the tax home after the temporary assignment is completed, plus the expenses for lodging and 50% of the cost of meals (but see ¶1556 for special rule for 2021 and 2022) while in the place to which temporarily assigned.[14] If the taxpayer returns home on nonworking days, he or she may deduct travel expenses to his or her home, but the travel expenses deduction is limited to the amount he or she would have spent to stay at the temporary location.[15] For an employee, these expenses are miscellaneous itemized deductions that are disallowed for tax years 2018–2025 (see ¶2162).

¶ 1551　Unreimbursed employee business expenses (including employee auto expenses); auto expenses of self-employeds; reporting auto expenses—Form 2106, Form 1040 (Schedule C), Form 1040 (Schedule C-EZ).

Unreimbursed employee business expenses (including employee auto expenses) and investment-related expenses (including investment-related auto expenses) are miscellaneous itemized deductions, and so not deductible from 2018–2025 (¶2162). The auto expenses of self-employed taxpayers are deductible as ordinary and necessary business expenses.[16] A taxpayer who makes both personal and business use of a car must apportion expenses between business (deductible) and personal (nondeductible) transportation.[17] Report business auto expenses on Form 2106 (employees, post-2025), or on Form 1040, Schedule C or Form 1040, Schedule C-EZ (self-employeds).[18]

¶ 1552　Transporting tools to work—transportation expenses.

A taxpayer may deduct under Code Sec. 162 only *additional* expenses incurred because of the need to transport tools, etc., to work *and* only if the additional expenses can be determined accurately. The deduction is only for that portion of the cost of transporting the tools, etc., that exceeds the cost of commuting *by the same mode of transportation* without

11. ¶L-1605
12. ¶L-1606
13. ¶L-1606.4
14. ¶L-1806, L-2102
15. ¶L-1825
16. ¶L-1901 *et seq.*
17. ¶L-1907
18. ¶L-1901

the tools, etc.[19]

¶ 1553   Optional business standard mileage rate used to compute the deductible costs of operating passenger automobiles.

Taxpayers may use the optional business standard mileage rate in computing the deductible costs of operating passenger automobiles owned or leased by them (including vans and pickup or panel trucks) for business purposes under Code Sec. 162. A taxpayer who uses this method multiplies the number of business miles by 56¢ per mile for travel during 2021, 58.5¢ per mile for travel from Jan. 1, 2022 through June 30, 2022, and 62.5¢ per mile for travel after June 30, 2022.[20]

A deduction using the standard mileage rate is in lieu of deducting operating and fixed costs, including for depreciation (or leasing costs), maintenance and repairs, tires, gasoline (including taxes), oil, insurance, and registration fees. But deductions for parking fees and tolls are still available.[21]

observation: If operating expenses are high, the standard mileage rate method may produce a smaller deduction than would be obtained by claiming actual expenses plus depreciation or lease payments. However, the standard mileage rate method may yield bigger deductions than the actual expense method if the driver's business mileage is high and his or her auto is a thrifty, high-mileage model.

In general, the standard mileage rate is used by a taxpayer who owned the vehicle and began applying the standard mileage rate for the first year that the taxpayer placed the vehicle in service, or by a taxpayer who leased the vehicle and is using the standard mileage rate for the entire lease period. However, the mileage allowance method can potentially be used after the placed in service year if, in earlier years, the taxpayer deducted actual expenses for the auto. Use of the business standard rate is *not* available for five or more autos that are used simultaneously (e.g., fleet operations) or purchased autos for which the taxpayer has claimed in prior years accelerated depreciation, Code Sec. 179 expensing, or additional first-year depreciation.[22]

A taxpayer may use the optional business standard mileage rate in substantiating reimbursed expenses paid by another.[23] For consequences if the reimbursement is made under an accountable plan, or under a nonaccountable plan, see ¶3104.

¶ 1554   Restrictions and Percentage Limit for Meal Expenses; Nondeductibility of Entertainment Costs. ▬▬▬▬▬▬▬▬

Restrictions apply to the deduction of meal expenses, including a 50% deduction limit, see ¶1556. (But a full deduction is allowed for food and beverages provided by a restaurant in calendar years 2021 and 2022, see ¶1556.)

Except as provided at ¶1555, no business deduction is allowed for entertainment expenses.

¶ 1555   Exceptions to the non-deductibility of entertainment expenses.

No deduction is allowed for any item for any activity of a type that is generally considered to be entertainment, amusement, or recreation. (Code Sec. 274(a)(1)(A)) There are numerous, sometimes highly technical, exceptions to these prohibitions and limits. (Code Sec. 274(e); Code Sec. 274(n)(2))[24]

The exceptions to the nondeductibility rule include the following non-exhaustive list (Code Sec. 274(e); Reg § 1.274-2(f)(2)):

---

19. ¶L-1611
20. ¶L-1903
21. ¶L-1905

22. ¶L-1903 *et seq.*
23. ¶L-4715
24. ¶L-2120

(1) Employee meals on company premises.[25]

(2) Employee recreational and social expenditures.[26]

(3) Expenditures treated as employee compensation.[27]

(4) Expenditures directly related to bona fide business meetings of a employees, shareholders, agents or directors.[28]

(5) Expenditures for items made available to the general public.[29]

(6) Expenditures for items sold to customers.[30]

(7) Certain reimbursements.[31]

¶ 1556   **Restrictions on deduction for meal (food and beverage) expenses; the 50% limit; 100% deduction allowed for food, beverages provided by restaurants in 2021 and 2022; 80% deduction for certain transport workers.**

Taxpayers may deduct food and beverage expenses associated with operating the taxpayer's trade or business, such as meals consumed by employees on work travel. But no deduction is allowed for the expense of any food or beverages provided by the taxpayer (or an employee of the taxpayer) unless (Code Sec. 274(k)(1); Reg § 1.274-12(a)(1)):

(1) the expense isn't lavish or extravagant under the circumstances;

(2) the taxpayer, or an employee of the taxpayer, is present at the furnishing of the food or beverages; and

(3) the food or beverages are provided to the taxpayer or a business associate (defined in Reg § 1.274-12(b)(3)).[32]

The above three limitations on deducting food or beverage expenses are subject to the exceptions in Reg § 1.274-12(c)(2). Expenses that fall within these exceptions are deductible to the extent allowable under the Code. (Reg § 1.274-12(c)(1))[33]

Food and beverages provided at or during an entertainment activity are considered entertainment unless:

. . . they are purchased separately from the entertainment *or*

. . . their cost is stated separately from the cost of the entertainment on one or more bills, invoices, or receipts. The amount charged for food or beverages on a bill, invoice, or receipt must reflect the venue's usual selling cost for those items if purchased separately from the entertainment or must approximate the reasonable value of those items. (Reg § 1.274-11(b)(1)(ii))[34]

The deduction for food or beverage expenses is limited to 50% of the otherwise deductible amount (Code Sec. 274(n)(1)), but this 50% limit is subject to certain exceptions (Code Sec. 274(n)(2)).[35]

100% deduction for food, beverages, provided by restaurant in 2021 and 2022. The 50% limit doesn't apply to food and beverages provided by a restaurant in calendar years 2021 and 2022 (Code Sec. 274(n)(2)(D)). For this purpose, "restaurant" means a business that prepares and sells food or beverages to retail customers for immediate consumption, regardless of whether the food or beverages are consumed on the business's premises, but not a grocery store, specialty food store, beer, wine, or liquor store, drug store, convenience store, newsstand, or a vending machine or kiosk. And an employer can't treat as a restaurant for Code Sec. 274(n)(2)(D) (above): (1) an eating facility located on the business premises of the employer and used in furnishing meals excluded from an employee's gross

25. ¶L-2129
26. ¶L-2131
27. ¶L-2135; ¶L-2137; ¶L-2138 *et seq.*
28. ¶L-2130
29. ¶L-2132
30. ¶L-2133

31. ¶L-2150 *et seq.*
32. ¶L-2101 *et seq.*
33. ¶L-2101 *et seq.*
34. ¶L-2111 *et seq.*
35. ¶L-2101 *et seq.*; ¶L-2115

income under Code Sec. 119 (¶1267), or (2) any employer-operated eating facility treated as a de minimis fringe under Code Sec. 132(e)(2) (¶1245). Solely for these purposes, deduction, a taxpayer that properly applies the per diem rate rules in Rev Proc 2019-48, 2019-52 IRB 1392, may treat the meal portion of a per diem rate or allowance paid or incurred after Dec. 31, 2020, and before Jan. 1, 2023, as attributable to food or beverages provided by a restaurant. (Notice 2021-63, 2021-49 IRB)[36]

For the deduction of reimbursed food or beverage expenses under the regs, see Reg § 1.274-2(f)(2)(iv)(A) and Reg § 1.274-12(c)(2)(ii)(A).[37]

80% deduction for certain transport workers. The deductible percentage of meals for certain transport workers (e.g., air transport employees, truck and bus drivers, railroad employees) while away from home during or incident to the period of duty is 80%. (Code Sec. 274(n)(3))[38]

¶ 1557 Expense Reimbursements—Accountable Plan. ▬▬▬▬▬▬▬

An employee doesn't pay tax on an advance, reimbursement or other expense allowance received under an "accountable plan" (defined below). The tax treatment of an advance or reimbursement to an independent contractor depends on whether the independent contractor accounts to his or her principal for the expense.

An employee doesn't pay tax on an advance, reimbursement or other expense allowance received from the employer (or from a third party) under an "accountable plan." (Reg § 1.62-2(c)(4)) By contrast, an advance, etc., made under a "nonaccountable plan" is fully taxable to the employee and subject to FICA and income tax withholding. (Reg § 1.62-2(c)(5))[39]

An advance, etc., is treated as made under an "accountable plan" if the employee:

(1) meets the business connection requirement—receives the advance, etc., for a deductible business expense that he or she paid or incurred while performing services as an employee of the employer (¶1558),

(2) meets the substantiation requirement—must adequately account to the employer for the expense within a reasonable period of time (¶1559), and

(3) must return any excess reimbursement or allowance within a reasonable period of time (¶1560).

An advance, etc., that doesn't satisfy all three conditions is treated as paid under a nonaccountable plan—i.e., it is taxed to the employee and is subject to FICA and income tax withholding. (Code Sec. 62(c); Reg § 1.62-2(c)(5))[40] An arrangement that recharacterizes taxable wages as nontaxable reimbursements or allowances (e.g., to provide a tool reimbursement for employees), won't satisfy the deductible business expense requirement (condition (1), above).[41] If an employee does not timely return advances or reimbursements in excess of those that are substantiated, only the excess is treated as made under a nonaccountable plan. (Reg § 1.62-2(c)(3)(ii))[42]

An arrangement that would in part be an accountable plan and in part be a nonaccountable plan if both parts were viewed separately is treated as two expense allowance arrangements.[43] But the entire reimbursement for business-travel meals and incidental expenses (M&IE) is deemed paid under a nonaccountable plan if an employer routinely doesn't track expenses and doesn't require employees either to substantiate actual expenses or pay back amounts exceeding the deemed substantiated amount (¶1559).[44]

---

36. ¶L-2115
37. ¶L-2150 *et seq.*
38. ¶L-2114
39. ¶J-1050
40. ¶L-4703

41. ¶L-4703.1A
42. ¶L-4703
43. ¶L-4744
44. ¶L-4704

Reimbursement of employee expenses for reasonable employment-related cell phone usage is nontaxable in most instances.[45]

¶ 1558   Business connection requirement for employee business expenses—accountable plan requirements.

Under Reg § 1.62-2(d), an arrangement satisfies the "business connection" requirement for accountable plans (¶1557) if it provides advances, allowances (including per diem or mileage allowances, or allowances for meals and incidental expenses only), or reimbursements only for business expenses that are (i) allowable as deductions, and (ii) paid or incurred by the employee in connection with performing services as an employee. (Reg § 1.62-2(d))[46] An advance, reimbursement or allowance that would be treated as made partially under a nonaccountable plan solely because the expense is subject to the 50% deduction limit for business meals (¶1556) is treated as made under an accountable plan. (Reg § 1.62-2(h)(1))[47]

¶ 1559   Accounting to employer for expenses of travel, business gifts, or listed property—accountable plan requirements.

To the extent an employee business expense—e.g., travel, or use of auto or other listed property—aren't deductible unless the substantiation requirements of Code Sec. 274(d) are met (¶1563 *et seq.*), the employee must meet those requirements within a reasonable period of time (¶1560), i.e., submit to the payor information sufficient to substantiate the requisite elements of each expense or use.[48]

For all other business expenses, sufficient information must be submitted to enable the one making the reimbursement to identify the specific nature of each expense and to conclude that the expense is attributable to the employer's business activities. (Reg § 1.62-2(e)(3))

For accounting via per diem allowances and other simplified methods, see ¶1565.

¶ 1560   Returning amounts in excess of expenses; when to substantiate—accountable plan requirements.

Under an accountable plan (¶1557), an employee must be required to return to the payor within a reasonable period of time any reimbursement in excess of substantiated business expenses. (Reg § 1.62-2(f)(1)) The definition of reasonable period of time depends on the facts and circumstances. However, under a safe-harbor rule, (1) an advance within 30 days of the time the employee has the expense, (2) an expense adequately accounted for within 60 days after it was paid or incurred, or (3) an amount returned to the employer within 120 days after the expense was paid or incurred, will be treated as having occurred within a reasonable period of time. (Reg § 1.62-2(g)(2)(i)) If the employee is given a periodic statement (at least quarterly) that asks the employee to either return or adequately account for outstanding reimbursements and he or she complies within 120 days of the statement, the amount is adequately accounted for or returned within a reasonable period of time. (Reg § 1.62-2(g)(2))[49]

¶ 1561   Reporting reimbursed employee business expenses.

Under Code Sec. 62(a)(2), if an employee's expenses equal advances or reimbursements made under an accountable plan (¶1557), he or she reports no income from the expenses and claims no deductions. However, if the employee's actual business expenses exceed nontaxable accountable-plan advances or reimbursements, and he or she wishes to deduct

---

45. ¶L-4701
46. ¶L-4703.1
47. ¶L-4703.1

48. ¶L-4705
49. ¶L-4746

the excess, he or she can do so under the rules that follow for deductions under nonaccountable plan reimbursements. (Code Sec. 62(a)(2))[50]

An employee who pays for employment-related business expenses but receives a nonaccountable plan advance or reimbursement (e.g., isn't required to account to the employer) reports the advance or reimbursement as income and claims otherwise allowable deductions on Form 2106 or Form 2106EZ, and on Form 1040, Schedule A as miscellaneous itemized deductions (suspended for 2018–2025; see ¶2162). The employee's meal expenses are subject to the 50% limit (¶1556), and total miscellaneous itemized deductions aren't deductible in tax years 2018–2025. The employee must be able to substantiate each element of the business expenditures. (Reg § 1.274-5T(f)(3))[1] For listed property, see ¶1567.

¶ 1562 Reimbursed expenses of a self-employed person; substantiation requirement.

Expenses of a self-employed person incurred on behalf of and reimbursed by a client or customer aren't included in the self-employed's gross income if the self-employed substantiates the expenses to his or her principal under the rules at ¶1563. But if he or she doesn't substantiate those reimbursed expenses as required, the reimbursements must be included in gross income, and are deductible, subject to the usual limitations (e.g., 50% limit on business meals), if the self-employed has kept the necessary records and receipts. (Reg § 1.274-5T(h)(1), Reg § 1.274-5T(h)(2))[2]

The client or customer must substantiate the expenses if the self-employed accounts for those expenses to the client or customer and is reimbursed. However, if the self-employed person doesn't account for the expenses, the client or customer doesn't have to substantiate reimbursed expenses (and isn't subject to the 50% limit). (Reg § 1.274-5T(h)(2), Reg § 1.274-5T(h)(4))[3]

¶ 1563 Substantiating Travel and "Listed Property" Expenses.

Under Code Sec. 274(d), to deduct travel expenses (including meals and lodging while away from home), each expense must be substantiated. For listed property, certain elements of each expenditure or business use must be proved.

Taxpayers must substantiate each element of every travel expense for which a deduction is claimed. (Code Sec. 274(d)(1), Code Sec. 274(d)(3)) The elements of away-from-home travel expenses are explained at ¶1564. For substantiation of business gifts, see ¶1574.

Taxpayers can't claim deductions or credits for "listed property" (¶1940), such as a passenger auto, unless they substantiate every element of each expenditure and use of the listed property (¶1567) for business or investment purposes. (Code Sec. 274(d)) For depreciation of "listed property," see ¶1939 *et seq.*

Generally, proper substantiation requires "adequate records" (¶1568 *et seq.*), or a taxpayer statement supported by sufficient corroborating evidence (¶1570), plus documentary evidence where required (¶1569). (Code Sec. 274(d))[4] Approximations or estimates aren't sufficient. (Reg § 1.274-5T(a))[5] However, statistical sampling may be used in some cases to establish the amount of meal expenses that isn't subject to the 50% limit (¶1556).[6] All elements of an expenditure or use must be proved. Failure to prove any one will bar the deduction. (Reg § 1.274-5T(c)(1))[7]

In the usual instance, an employee who substantiates expenses to the employer need not account for them to IRS. However, an employee who is "related" to the employer (certain close relatives of an individual employer, or a more than 10% shareholder of a corporate employer) may be asked by IRS to substantiate his or her expense accounts even though he

---

50. ¶L-4701 *et seq.*
1. ¶L-4710
2. ¶L-4757
3. ¶L-4758

4. ¶L-4600 *et seq.*
5. ¶L-4601
6. ¶L-4641
7. ¶s L-4644, L-4608

or she has accounted to the employer. (Reg § 1.274-5T(f)(5)(ii))[8]

Simplified substantiation procedures apply to expenses of certain federal employees.[9]

¶ 1564   Proving travel and transportation expenses.

Under Code Sec. 274, the taxpayer must prove all of the following elements by adequate records or by a sufficiently corroborated statement:

(1) The amount of each separate expenditure for traveling away from home, such as the cost of transportation or lodging. The daily cost of breakfast, lunch, and dinner and other incidental travel elements may be aggregated if they are set forth in reasonable categories, such as for meals, oil and gas, taxi fares, etc.

(2) The dates of the departure and return home for each trip, and the number of days spent on business away from home.

(3) The destinations or locality of the travel.

(4) The business reason for the travel or the nature of the business benefit derived or expected to be derived as a result of the travel. (Code Sec. 274, Reg § 1.274-5T(b)(2))[10]

Incidental travel expenses, e.g., tips, aren't subject to these rules. Where records are incomplete and documentary proof is unavailable, the taxpayer may establish the amount of incidental travel expenses by reasonable approximations. (Reg § 1.162-17(d)(3))[11]

¶ 1565   Substantiation of travel expenses by use of optional meal or incidental expenses allowance.

For purposes of the Code Sec. 274 substantiation requirements, if a payor (i.e., the employer, its agent, or a third party) pays a per diem allowance in lieu of reimbursing actual expenses for lodging, meal and incidental expenses (M&IE) incurred or to be incurred by an employee for travel away from home, the amount of the expenses treated as substantiated for each calendar day (or part of that day) is the lesser of the per diem allowance or the appropriate IRS-approved maximums. Additionally, the employee must provide simplified substantiation (time, place and business purpose). Where these tests are met, the reimbursement is treated as made under an accountable plan—it isn't subject to income- or payroll-tax withholding and isn't reported on the employee's Form W-2. Receipts of expenses aren't required.[12]

Incidental expenses include fees and tips given to porters, hotel staff, etc.

An employee who is "related" to the employer (¶1563) *isn't* considered to have accounted to the employer for the full federal per diem allowances for lodging and M&IE, and must substantiate any deductions claimed, but may use the meals-only per diem and the business standard mileage rate (¶1553).

The following simplified substantiation rules apply to per diems paid under an arrangement that otherwise qualifies as an accountable plan (¶1557):

. . . *Regular federal per diem allowance.* In general, the IRS-approved per-diem maximum is the GSA per-diem rate paid by the federal government to its workers on travel status. This rate varies from locality to locality.[13] For travel outside the continental U.S. (CONUS), a separate lodging expense rate and M&IE rate is available for each locality outside the continental U.S. (OCONUS).[14]

. . . *Simplified (high-low) method for substantiating travel allowances.* A simplified method can be used for per diem amounts paid for lodging plus M&IE during travel within CONUS. If the regular federal per diem option (above) isn't used, for travel on or

8. ¶L-4713
9. ¶L-4714.1 *et seq.*
10. ¶L-4630
11. ¶L-4633

12. ¶L-4717.1
13. ¶L-4717
14. ¶L-4717

after Oct. 1, 2021, the payor may reimburse up to $296 for high-cost localities ($222 for lodging and $74 for M&IE) and $202 for other localities ($138 for lodging and $64 for M&IE). For travel on or after Oct. 1, 2022, the payor may reimburse up to $297 for high-cost localities ($223 for lodging and $74 for M&IE) and $204 for other localities ($140 for lodging and $64 for M&IE).[15]

. . . Transportation industry per diem. Employees or self-employeds whose work directly involves moving people or goods (e.g., by plane, bus, truck, ship) and regularly involves travel to different localities with different M&IE rates may, for travel on or after Oct. 1, 2021, the rates are $69 for any locality in CONUS and $74 for any locality OCONUS. For travel on or after Oct. 1, 2022, the rates are also $69 for any locality in CONUS and $74 for any locality OCONUS. This method also can be used by payors of a per diem allowance only for M&IE away-from-home expenses to an employee in the transportation industry, if the payment qualifies as a regular meals-only allowance.[16]

. . . Optional method for incidental expenses only. Employees and self-employed individuals who don't pay or incur meal expenses for a calendar day (or partial day) of travel away from home may deduct $5 per day as incidental expenses for each away-from-home calendar (or partial) day.[17]

A self-employed individual deducts the amount in determining adjusted gross income. The deduction is subject to the percentage limit on meal expenses (¶1556).[18]

¶ 1566   Substantiation of travel expenses via optional auto allowances.

The following simplified substantiation rules apply to allowances paid under an arrangement that otherwise qualifies as an accountable plan under Code Sec. 274 (¶1557):

. . . Mileage allowance. An employee who receives a fixed mileage allowance of not more than the optional business standard mileage rate (¶1553) to cover transportation expenses while traveling away from home or for transportation expenses is considered to have made an adequate accounting to the employer if the elements of time, place, and business purpose of the travel are substantiated. (Reg § 1.274-5T(f))[19]

. . . Fixed and variable rate (FAVR) allowances for autos. Where an employer provides a mileage allowance under a reimbursement or other expense allowance arrangement for an employee-owned or leased car, the substantiation requirement is satisfied (as to the amount of expense) if the employer reimburses in accordance with a FAVR allowance. A FAVR allowance is periodic fixed payments to cover fixed costs such as depreciation, coupled with periodic variable payments to cover operating costs such as gasoline. Among other things, a FAVR allowance may be paid only to an employee who substantiates at least 5,000 miles driven in connection with the performance of services as an employee, and at least five employees must be covered by the FAVR allowance.[20]

¶ 1567   Substantiating costs of listed property.

Under Code Sec. 274, for listed property (¶1563), all the relevant elements from the following list must be proved for each expenditure or business use of the property:

(1) The amount and date of each separate expenditure (for example, the cost and date of acquisition or leasing, the cost and date of maintenance and repairs, etc.).

(2) The amount and date of each use of the item of listed property for business or investment, based on an appropriate measure (mileage for automobiles and other property used for transportation, time for other types of property, unless IRS approves an alternative method), and the total use of the item of listed property for the tax period.

(3) The business purpose for each expenditure or use with respect to the listed property.

---

15. ¶L-4718
16. ¶L-4721
17. ¶L-4632.1

18. ¶L-4632
19. ¶L-4715
20. ¶L-4725 *et seq.*

(Code Sec. 274, Reg § 1.274-5T(b)(6))[21]

For optional business standard mileage rate, see ¶1553.

¶ 1568   Adequate records of travel expenses and listed-property expenses.

Under Code Sec. 274, adequate records of travel expenses and of listed property (¶1563) expenditures and uses consist of a currently maintained account book, diary, log, statement of expenses, trip sheet, or similar record and, where necessary (¶1569), documentary evidence such as receipts and paid bills, which together are sufficient to establish each element of every expenditure or use that must be substantiated. Information reflected on a receipt need not be duplicated in an account book or other record so long as the account book or other record and the receipt complement each other in an orderly fashion. (Code Sec. 274, Reg § 1.274-5T(c)(2)(i))[22] Both written and computer records are acceptable. (Reg § 1.274-5T(c)(2)(ii)(C)(2))[23]

Where the business purpose of an expenditure is evident from the surrounding facts and circumstances, a written explanation isn't required. (Reg § 1.274-5T(c)(2)(ii)(B))[24]

¶ 1569   Adequate documentary evidence to support lodging expenditures and other expenditures of $75 or more.

Under Code Sec. 274, documentary evidence, such as receipts or bills marked paid is required to support all expenditures for (1) lodging while away from home and (2) for any other expenses of $75 or more (except for transportation charges for which documentary evidence is not readily available). (Code Sec. 274, Reg § 1.274-5(c)(2)(iii))[25]

Receipts or other documentary evidence (original documents, faxes, e-mail printouts)[26] must disclose the amount, date, place, and essential character of the expenditure. A canceled check, together with a bill from the payee, ordinarily will establish the cost but may not alone show business purpose. (Reg § 1.274-5(c)(2)(iii))[27]

¶ 1570   Sufficiently corroborated statements used to substantiate expenses.

Under Code Sec. 274(d), taxpayers may substantiate the elements of their expenditures and uses not only by adequate records, but also by their own statements, written or oral, if those statements are supported by sufficient corroborating evidence. (Code Sec. 274(d))[28]

Corroborating evidence may be oral if from a disinterested, unrelated party who has knowledge of the expenditure or use in question. Written evidence has greater probative value, especially if its contemporaneous. (Reg § 1.274-5T(c)(1)) A taxpayer's written or oral statement must contain specific, detailed information about the element being substantiated, and the taxpayer must present other corroborative evidence sufficient to establish that element. (Reg § 1.274-5T(c)(3)(i))[29]

¶ 1571   Inadequate substantiation of expenditures under Code Sec. 274(d)— remedies.

If a taxpayer hasn't fully substantiated a particular element of an expenditure or use under Code Sec. 274, but does establish to IRS's satisfaction that he or she has substantially complied with the adequate records requirements, IRS may permit the taxpayer to establish the missing element by other evidence that it considers adequate. (Reg § 1.274-5T(c)(2)(v))

---

21. ¶L-4644
22. ¶L-4616 *et seq.*
23. ¶L-4616
24. ¶L-4609
25. ¶s L-4603, L-4619

26. ¶L-4616
27. ¶L-4619
28. ¶L-4626 *et seq.*
29. ¶L-4626

Taxpayers who establish that, by reason of "the inherent nature of the situation," they were unable to get either fully adequate records, or fully sufficient corroborating evidence, will be treated as satisfying the substantiation requirements if they present other evidence that possesses the highest degree of probative value under the circumstances. (Reg § 1.274-5T(c)(4))[30]

A taxpayer who establishes that he or she has maintained adequate records of an expenditure or use, but can't produce them because they've been lost through circumstances beyond his or her control (e.g., damage by fire, flood, etc.), may prove entitlement to a deduction by a reasonable reconstruction of the expenditure or use in question. (Reg § 1.274-5T(c)(5))[31] Destruction of records in marital disputes has been held to fall within this rule.[32]

¶ 1572 Business Gifts and Employee Awards. ▬▬▬▬▬

The costs of ordinary and necessary business gifts to individuals other than employees are deductible, subject to a $25 per-year per-person limit.

"Gift" means any item excludable from gross income by the recipient under Code Sec. 102 (¶1211), but not excludable under any other income tax provision. (Code Sec. 274(b))[33] However, any item for general distribution having a cost of not more than $4 and on which the giver's name is clearly and permanently imprinted, and signs, display racks, or other promotional material donated to a retailer to be used on his or her business premises, aren't classified as gifts. (Code Sec. 274(b)(1); Reg § 1.274-3(b)(2))[34]

Since no amount transferred by or for an employer to or for the benefit of an employee is excludable as a gift (under Code Sec. 102) no such amount is deductible as a gift, though it may be deductible under other rules (e.g., as compensation).[35] Certain noncash awards to employees may also be deductible (¶1573).

¶ 1573 Employer deduction for employee achievement awards.

An employer can deduct the cost of employee achievement awards (defined below). (Code Sec. 274(j)) The maximum deduction for awards made to one employee is $400 per year ($1,600 if the award is a qualified plan award, including the cost of awards that aren't qualified plan awards). (Code Sec. 274(j)(2)) The award must be given as part of a meaningful presentation under conditions and circumstances that don't create a likelihood that the payment is disguised compensation. (Code Sec. 274(j)(3))[36]

An employee achievement award is an item of tangible personal property awarded to an employee because of length of service achievement or safety achievement. (Code Sec. 274(j)(3))[37] Tangible personal property does not include cash, cash equivalents, gifts cards, gift coupons, gift certificates (other than where from the employer pre-selected or pre-approved a limited selection), vacations, meals, lodging, tickets for theatre or sporting events, stock, bonds or similar items. (Code Sec. 274(j)(3)(A)(ii))[38]

A qualified plan award is an item awarded as part of a permanent, written, nondiscriminatory plan of the employer. (Code Sec. 274(j)(3)(B); Reg § 1.274-3(d))[39]

A length-of-service award won't qualify for deduction under these rules if given during an employee's first five years of employment, or if a length-of-service award was given to the same employee during the same year or any of the earlier four years. (Code Sec. 274(j)(4)(B))[40]

Safety achievement awards don't qualify if given to managerial, administrative, professional or clerical employees, or if such awards previously have been given to more than

---

30. ¶L-4628
31. ¶L-4623
32. ¶L-4624
33. ¶L-2306
34. ¶L-2306
35. ¶H-4009

36. ¶L-2312
37. ¶L-2313
38. ¶L-2316
39. ¶L-2317
40. ¶L-2314

10% of other employees during the year. (Code Sec. 274(j)(4)(C))[41]

No deduction is allowed for an employee achievement award (under the normal Code Sec. 162 ordinary and necessary rules or the Code Sec. 212 production of income rules) except under the above rules. (Code Sec. 274(j)(1))[42]

¶ 1574   Substantiating business gift expenses—adequate records or sufficiently corroborated statement.

To substantiate business gift expenses under Code Sec. 274, adequate records or a sufficiently corroborated statement must show: (1) a description of the gift, (2) the taxpayer's cost, (3) when the gift was made, (4) the occupation of or other information about the gift's recipient, including his or her name, title, or other designation sufficient to establish a business relationship to the taxpayer, and (5) the reason for making the gift or the nature of business benefit derived or expected. (Reg § 1.274-5T(b)(5))[43]

¶ 1575   Rent Expense. ▬▬▬▬▬▬▬▬▬▬▬▬▬▬▬▬▬▬

Rent is deductible if paid for the use of property in the taxpayer's trade or business. Rent expense for the production of income is not deductible from 2018–2025 due to the suspension of miscellaneous itemized deductions (¶2162).

Rent for the use of real or personal property in the taxpayer's trade, business, or profession, is deductible. (Code Sec. 162(a)(3)) But rent for personal-use property isn't. (Code Sec. 262(a); Reg § 1.262-1(b)(3))[44]

Besides normal cash rent payable periodically, rent deductible under Code Sec. 162(a)(3) includes a lump sum paid as advance rental, bonus, etc.; a percentage of the tenant's receipts or profits; the tenant's payment of the expenses of maintaining the rented property (taxes, insurance, etc.), and payment in property other than money (deductible to the extent of the property's fair market value).[45]

¶ 1576   Rent paid to related lessor—rent expense.

Rentals paid between parties who are related either as members of a family or by stock ownership may not be deductible under Code Sec. 162(a)(3) to the extent that they exceed the rent that would have been paid in an arm's-length transaction.

A corporation may deduct fair and reasonable rentals paid to corporate shareholders or their relatives. But excessive rentals can be treated as nondeductible dividends.[46] Reasonable rental payments by a shareholder for use of corporate property are deductible.[47]

¶ 1577   Rent under leaseback arrangements—rent expense.

A transfer by sale or gift coupled with a leaseback may be more advantageous than a mortgage loan and can create tax benefits for the transferor. Tax advantages (including rent deduction under Code Sec. 162(a)(3)) of a sale and leaseback arrangement may be lost if IRS treats it as a mortgage loan, a tax-free exchange, or a sham transaction.[48]

A gift in trust with a leaseback of the property to the grantor will generally be upheld as a valid rental or royalty arrangement by the courts if: (1) the transfer is complete and irrevocable, (2) the trustee is independent, and (3) the rent is reasonable. Reasonableness of rent and the independence of the trustee are questions of fact.[49]

---

41. ¶L-2315
42. ¶L-2313 *et seq.*
43. ¶L-4643
44. ¶L-6604
45. ¶L-6605 *et seq.*

46. ¶L-6702
47. ¶L-6710
48. ¶L-6300 *et seq.*
49. ¶L-6317

¶ 1578   Rent or purchase; lease with purchase options—rent expense.

Code Sec. 162(a)(3) provides that a payment is deductible as rent only if the taxpayer-lessee hasn't taken or isn't taking title to the property and has no equity interest in it. (Code Sec. 162(a)(3)) Thus, amounts paid ostensibly as rent which are actually part of the purchase price of the property aren't deductible as rent.[50]

A lease with an option permitting the lessee to buy the property may be construed as a sale so that none of the payments is deductible as rent. This depends essentially on the intent of the parties, per the agreement, read in light of the facts and circumstances existing at the time the agreement was made.[1] Factors indicating sale instead of lease include nominal option price, excessive rent, designating part of the payment as interest, rental plus option price equal to the property's value plus interest, and application of rent payments to the lessee's equity in the property.[2]

¶ 1579   Business lease acquisition costs—rent expense.

Payments made by a lessee to get a business lease aren't currently deductible but must be amortized over the term of the lease. (Reg § 1.162-11(a)) This rule applies whether the tenant is on the cash or accrual basis and even though he has an option to buy the property.[3]

The term of the lease includes all renewal options (and any other period for which the parties reasonably expect the lease to be renewed) if less than 75% of the acquisition cost is attributable to the remaining lease period on the date of acquisition. In determining the term of the lease remaining on the date of acquisition, any period for which the lease may be renewed, extended or continued under an option exercisable by the lessee is not taken into account. (Code Sec. 178)[4]

¶ 1580   Lessor's costs in leasing property; lessee's costs in subletting.

Costs incurred by a lessor in leasing property, or by a lessee in subletting, aren't currently deductible under Code Sec. 162 but must be amortized ratably over the term of the lease.[5] For tax treatment of construction allowances, see ¶1343.

The cost of MACRS improvements made by lessors are recoverable over the cost recovery period applicable to the leasehold improvements—regardless of the period of time the property is leased. (Code Sec. 168(i)(8))[6]

A lessor's payments for cancellation of a lease must be amortized and deducted over the remaining term of the *cancelled* lease,[7] except that if the payment is made in order to enter a lease with a new tenant, the payment must be amortized over the term of the *new* lease.[8]

¶ 1581   Year of deduction for rent; advance rent.

The tax year in which the rent is paid by a cash basis taxpayer or incurred by an accrual basis taxpayer is generally the proper year for deduction under Code Sec. 162(a)(3).[9] Advance rent paid by accrual basis taxpayers must be apportioned and deducted over the term of the lease or other rental period. For application of the 12-month rule to advance payments by cash basis taxpayers, see ¶1637. For deferred rental agreements, see ¶1582.[10]

---

50. ¶L-6201
1. ¶L-6209 *et seq.*
2. ¶L-6210 *et seq.*
3. ¶L-6501
4. ¶L-6501 *et seq.*
5. ¶L-6401

6. ¶L-6404
7. ¶L-6405
8. ¶L-6407
9. ¶L-6616
10. ¶L-6617

¶ 1582　Deferred payments for the use of property or services—rent expense.

Code Sec. 467 provides that rent and interest attributable to a deferred rental agreement must be both reported and deducted as if both parties are accrual basis taxpayers. This rule applies to leases of over $250,000 that require either: (1) at least one payment for the use of property to be paid after the close of the calendar year following the calendar year of the use of the property, or (2) increases (or decreases) in the amounts to be paid as rent. (Code Sec. 467)[11]

For lessees, the deductible rental amount for the tax year is the sum of:

(1) rent deemed accrued by allocating rents in accordance with the rental agreement, taking into account the present value of rent to be paid after the close of the period, and

(2) interest for the year on amounts taken into account for earlier tax years (under (1), above), but which are as yet unpaid. (Code Sec. 467(b)(1))[12]

Present value and interest are computed using a rate equal to 110% of the applicable federal rate (¶1117). (Code Sec. 467(e)(4))[13]

If the agreement is silent as to rent allocation or the agreement is a disqualified leaseback or long-term agreement, then constant rental accrual applies. (Code Sec. 467(b)(2), Code Sec. 467(b)(3)) The constant rental amount is an amount paid as of the close of each lease period which would result in a total present value equal to the present value of the total payments required under the lease. (Code Sec. 467(e)(1))[14]

A rental agreement is a disqualified leaseback or long-term agreement if:

(1) it is part of a leaseback transaction to any person who had an interest in the leased property within two years before the leaseback (Code Sec. 467(e)(2)), or the term of the agreement exceeds 75% of a prescribed recovery period (Code Sec. 467(b)(4)), *and*

(2) a principal purpose of the increased rents provided in the agreement is tax avoidance. (Code Sec. 467(b)(4))[15]

An agreement isn't a disqualified leaseback or long-term agreement if it qualifies for any of the various safe harbors, including the uneven rent test, which is met if the rent allocated to each calendar year does not vary from the average rent allocated to all calendar years by more than 10%. (Reg § 1.467-3(c))

Under regs to be issued, similar rules will apply to certain deferred payments for services. (Code Sec. 467(g))[16]

A reasonable rent holiday won't cause an agreement to be treated as a disqualified leaseback or long-term agreement. (Code Sec. 467(b)(5)) A rent holiday of 3 months or less at the beginning of the lease term is disregarded in determining if the rental agreement has increasing or decreasing rent (Reg § 1.467-1(c)(2)(i)(B)), but longer periods have been upheld where reasonable under the circumstances.[17]

¶ 1583　Research and Experimental (R&E) Expenditures—Form 4562. ■■■■■

Under Code Sec. 174(a)(1), for amounts paid or incurred in tax years beginning after Dec. 31, 2021, taxpayers must charge specified R & E expenditures to capital account, and are allowed an amortization deduction of the expenditures ratably over the five-year period beginning with the midpoint of the tax year in which the expenditures are paid or incurred. For amounts paid or incurred in tax years beginning before Jan. 1, 2022, taxpayers could choose whether to immediately deduct or to capitalize R&E expenditures. (Code Sec. 174(a)(1))

---

11. ¶s L-6800, L-6801.13
12. ¶L-6801
13. ¶L-6804
14. ¶L-6805
15. ¶L-6808
16. ¶G-3451
17. ¶L-6812

For amounts paid or incurred in tax years beginning after Dec. 31, 2021, for a taxpayer's specified R&E expenditures (i.e., for any tax year, R&E expenditures paid or incurred by the taxpayer during the tax year in connection with the taxpayer's trade or business): (1) except for the amortization deduction described in item (2), no deduction is allowed for the R&E expenditures, and (2) the taxpayer must charge the expenditures to capital account, and is allowed an amortization deduction of the expenditures ratably over the five-year period beginning with the midpoint of the tax year in which the expenditures are paid or incurred. (Code Sec. 174(a))[18]

Specified R&E expenditures are R & E expenditures that are paid or incurred by the taxpayer during the tax year in connection with the taxpayer's trade or business. (Code Sec. 174(b))[19]

✍ observation: Presumably, specified R & E expenditures encompass the same type of expenses that were subject to Code Sec. 174 under the definition that applied for amounts paid or incurred in tax years beginning before Jan. 1, 2022, see below.

For amounts paid or incurred in tax years beginning before 2022, if the taxpayer adopted current expense treatment, this had to be used for all qualifying expenses for the year it was adopted and for all later years, unless the taxpayer got IRS permission to switch. Former Code Sec. 174(a)(3).[20] For R&E expenditures that weren't chargeable to depreciable or depletable property, instead of current deduction or capitalizing, the taxpayer could elect (on Form 4562) to deduct the expenditures ratably over 60 months or longer, beginning with the month the taxpayer first realized benefits from the expenditures. (Former Code Sec. 174(b)(1); Reg § 1.174-4(b)(1))[21]

For this purpose, in general, expenditures that qualified as R&E costs were research and development costs in the experimental or laboratory sense. This included all costs incident to the development or improvement of a product, including a pilot model, process, formula, invention, technique, patent or similar property. (Reg § 1.174-2(a))[22]

Under Code Sec. 59(e)(1), a taxpayer subject to the alternative minimum tax (¶3201) could elect to deduct ratably over ten years certain qualified expenditures for which a current deduction otherwise would have been allowed—including research and experimental expenditures deductible under pre-2022 law. (Code Sec. 59(e)(1); Reg § 1.59-1)[23]

For the research credit, see ¶2319. For limitations on deductions for R&E expenses that also qualify for the research credit or the orphan drug credit, see ¶ 2319 and ¶2326, respectively. For alternative minimum tax treatment of R&E expenditures, see ¶ 3206.

¶ 1584   Legal Fees and Accounting Expenses—May Be Deductible. ▪▪▪▪▪▪

Under Code Sec. 162, legal expenses and accounting and related expenses may be deductible.

Attorney's fees, court costs and other legal expenses can qualify as deductible business expenses. Legal expenses aren't deductible if they are either capital expenditures or a personal expense of the taxpayer. (Code Sec. 162, Code Sec. 262(a), Code Sec. 263)[24] Qualified legal expenses can include expenses incurred in litigation, for legal advice, and for the drafting of instruments,[25] but not to acquire, perfect or defend title to property. (Reg § 1.212-1(k))[26] A legal retainer must be capitalized if it is applied to legal expenses associated with the acquisition of a business.[27] No deduction is allowed for attorney fees paid in connection with a sexual harassment suit subject to a nondisclosure agreement. (Code Sec. 162(q))[28]

Fees for bookkeeping and accounting work incurred in the operation of the taxpayer's

---

18. ¶L-3130.1 *et seq.*
19. ¶L-3130.3
20. ¶L-3117
21. ¶L-3121 *et seq.*
22. ¶L-3101
23. ¶A-8194

24. ¶s L-2901, L-2969
25. ¶L-2902
26. ¶L-2908
27. ¶L-2901.1
28. ¶L-2511

business are deductible.[29]

For expenses of determining or contesting tax liability, see ¶1512.

¶ 1585 Insurance Premiums.

Certain premiums that qualify as trade or business expenses, or as investment expenses, are deductible. See ¶1586 for premiums on nonlife policies, ¶1587 for life insurance premiums, and ¶1588 for when to deduct.

¶ 1586 Insurance premiums on nonlife policies—residential and other property insurance—deductibility.

Premiums for insurance against various types of risks, such as property damage, are generally deductible as business expenses (Code Sec. 162; Reg § 1.162-1(a)), but premiums on policies on taxpayer's residence, or for other personal use, aren't. (Code Sec. 262(a); Reg § 1.262-1(b))[30]

Self-insurance reserve funds aren't deductible even if taxpayer can't get business insurance coverage for certain business risks.[31] Neither are payments to "captive" insurance subsidiaries or other similar arrangements where there's no true risk shifting.[32] But a limited deduction is allowed for certain payments made to a medical malpractice self-insurance pool.[33]

Premiums are nondeductible capital expenditures where paid for property insurance during construction. So are premiums for title insurance and for public liability and worker's compensation insurance paid in connection with the construction of a building.[34]

¶ 1587 Life insurance premiums—deductibility.

Code Sec. 264(a)(1) bars a deduction for life insurance premiums if the taxpayer is directly or indirectly a beneficiary. (Code Sec. 264(a)(1); Reg § 1.264-1) See ¶1525. For example, the cost of a corporation's key person insurance isn't deductible.[35] Premiums paid by an individual for personal life insurance aren't deductible. (Reg § 1.262-1(b)(1))[36] For group-term premiums, see ¶1525.

¶ 1588 Time for deducting insurance premiums.

If a cash basis taxpayer pays an otherwise deductible premium for one year's coverage which applies in part to the following tax year, the entire premium is deductible in the year paid. But if premiums for several years are paid in advance, IRS and most courts require the premium to be amortized and deducted over the life of the policy, though one court has allowed a full deduction to a cash basis taxpayer in the year of payment where the taxpayer had consistently deducted premiums in the year of payment.[37]

For an accrual basis taxpayer, deductibility of an accrued liability for insurance expense is determined under the economic performance rules—that is, when the premium is paid. But where prepaid premiums cover more than one year, an accrual basis taxpayer must prorate the premium paid in advance over the life of the policy.[38]

For the "12-month rule" exception to capitalization of certain intangibles, see ¶1629.

¶ 1589 Bribes, Kickbacks, Fines and Penalties—Deductibility.

Certain illegal bribes, kickbacks, rebates and other payments aren't deductible. Nor are fines and penalties for violation of a law, including tax penalties.

---

29. ¶L-2959
30. ¶L-3500 *et seq.*
31. ¶L-3514
32. ¶L-3514
33. ¶L-3504
34. ¶L-3520
35. ¶L-3407
36. ¶L-3401
37. ¶L-3518
38. ¶L-3518 *et seq.*

Public policy isn't a ground for denying a deduction. Unless a payment is nondeductible by law, it's deductible if ordinary and necessary. (Reg § 1.162-1)[39]

¶ 1590 Bribes, kickbacks and other illegal payments—deductibility.

Under Code Sec. 162(c)(2), no deduction is allowed for any illegal bribe, kickback or other illegal payment under any law of the U.S., or of a state (if the state law is generally enforced), that subjects the payor to a criminal penalty or the loss of license or privilege to engage in business, whether or not that penalty or loss of license actually occurs. A kickback includes a payment in consideration of the referral of a client, patient, or customer. (Code Sec. 162(c)(2))[40]

No deduction is allowed for any kickback, rebate, or bribe made by any provider of services, supplier, physician, or other person who furnishes Medicare or Medicaid items or services, if made in connection with the furnishing of such items or services or the making or receiving of such payments. A kickback includes a payment for the referral of a client, patient, or customer. For these payments, deduction is denied regardless of legality. (Code Sec. 162(c)(3))[41]

No business expense deduction is allowed for any illegal bribe or kickback made directly or indirectly to any federal, state, or local public official or employee. If the payment is to an official or an employee of a foreign government, no deduction is allowed if the payment violates the U.S. Foreign Corrupt Practices Act. (Code Sec. 162(c)(1))[42]

Business kickbacks, fee-splitting, etc., that aren't specifically disallowed are deductible if they qualify as ordinary and necessary.[43]

¶ 1591 Illegal businesses and drug trafficking—deductibility of costs.

The ordinary and necessary expenses incurred in operating an illegal business are deductible under Code Sec. 162, even though payment of the expense and the acts performed by the employees of the business are illegal (e.g., a bookmaker's expenses).[44]

But there's no deduction or credit for amounts (including wages) paid or incurred in trafficking in "controlled substances" (Code Sec. 280E), whether or not such trafficking is legal under state law.[45] However, the gross receipts of controlled substance traffickers may be reduced by cost of goods sold.[46]

¶ 1592 No deduction for fines, penalties, other payments, paid to gov't; gov't must report—Form 1098-F.

Under Code Sec. 162(f), subject to certain exceptions—e.g., for amounts that are "restitution," and certain court-ordered amounts—no otherwise-allowable deduction is allowed under Code Sec. 1 – Code Sec. 1400Z-2, for any amount paid or incurred (whether by suit, agreement, or otherwise) to, or at the direction of, a government or governmental entity in relation to the violation of any law or the investigation or inquiry by the government or governmental entity into the potential violation of any law. This rule applies only where a government (or other governmental entity, or nongovernmental entity treated as a governmental entity under Code Sec. 162(f)(5)) is a complainant or investigator with respect to the violation or potential violation of any law. Various exceptions apply, including for certain amounts that are restitution (including certain amounts for taxes due) or that are spent to come into compliance. (Code Sec. 162(f)) Regs provide guidance on the Code Sec. 162(f) disallowance. (Reg § 1.162-21)[47]

---

39. ¶L-2610
40. ¶L-2606
41. ¶L-2608
42. ¶L-2601
43. ¶L-2601

44. ¶L-2631
45. ¶L-2632 *et seq.*
46. ¶L-2632
47. ¶L-2700 *et seq.*

For requirement that government agencies, etc., report (on Form 1098-F) to IRS and the taxpayer the amount of each settlement agreement or order where the aggregate amount required to be paid is at least $50,000, see ¶4746.

¶ 1593 Qualified Business Income (Code Sec. 199A "Pass-Through") Deduction—Form 8995 or 8995-A. ▰▰▰▰▰▰▰▰▰▰▰

Noncorporate taxpayers may deduct 20% of "qualified business income" (QBI; ¶1594) from a partnership, S corporation, or sole proprietorship, generally defined as the net amount of items of income, gain, deduction, and loss with respect to the trade or business to the extent that these are: (i) effectively connected with the conduct of a trade or business within the U.S. (and from Puerto Rico, if certain requirements are met); and (ii) included or allowed in determining taxable income for the tax year. (Code Sec. 199A) The deduction (computed on Form 8995 or Form 8995-A) reduces taxable income, rather than adjusted gross income, but is available whether or not the taxpayer itemizes.

The allowable deduction for any tax year is an amount equal to the lesser of:

(1) the "combined QBI amount" (¶1596) of the taxpayer; or

(2) an amount equal to 20% of the excess (if any) of (a) the taxable income of the taxpayer for the tax year, over (b) the net capital gain (as defined in Code Sec. 1(h)) of the taxpayer for such tax year. (Code Sec. 199A(a))[48]

For the Code Sec. 199A(a) deduction for patrons who receive qualified payments from agricultural or horticultural cooperatives, see ¶1599. For the Code Sec. 199A(g) deduction for qualified production activities income (QPAI) of specified agricultural or horticultural cooperatives, see ¶1600. IRS has provided additional guidance on the Code Sec. 199A deduction. (https://www.irs.gov/newsroom/tax-cuts-and-jobs-act-provision-11011-section-199a-qualified-business-income-deduction-faqs)

¶ 1594 "Qualified business income" (QBI) defined for the Code Sec. 199A pass-through deduction; carryover.

For the Code Sec. 199A deduction (¶1593), QBI for a tax year is the net amount of qualified items of income, gain, deduction, and loss relating to any "qualified trade or business" (¶1595) of the taxpayer. Items excluded from being taken into account as a qualified item of income, gain, deduction or loss (e.g., items of capital gain, dividends, or interest), are set forth in Code Sec. 199A(c)(3)(B), Code Sec. 199A(c)(4), and Reg § 1.199A-3(b). Qualified items of income, gain, deduction, and loss are items of income, gain, deduction, and loss to the extent these items are: (1) effectively connected with the conduct of a trade or business within the U.S. under Code Sec. 864(c) (applied by substituting "qualified trade or business" for "nonresident alien individual or a foreign corporation" or for a "foreign corporation" each place it appears), and (2) are included or allowed in determining taxable income for the tax year. (Code Sec. 199A(c)(3)(A))[49]

QBI from Puerto Rico sources. For a taxpayer with QBI from sources within Puerto Rico, if all the income is taxable in the U.S. under Code Sec. 1 for the tax year, then the taxpayer's QBI for the tax is determined by treating Puerto Rico as part of the U.S. (Code Sec. 199A(f)(1)(C)(i)) For a taxpayer subject to this rule, the W-2 wages of the taxpayer relating to any qualified trade or business conducted in Puerto Rico are determined without regard to the Code Sec. 3401(a)(8) exclusion for remuneration paid for services in Puerto Rico. (Code Sec. 199A(f)(1)(C)(ii))[50]

If the net amount of qualified income, gain, deduction, and loss relating to qualified trade or businesses of the taxpayer for any tax year is less than zero, the amount is carried

---

48. ¶L-4306
49. ¶L-4307 *et seq.*

50. ¶L-4307.7

over as a loss from a qualified trade or business in the succeeding tax year. (Code Sec. 199A(c)(2))[1]

¶ 1595 "Qualified trade or business"; exclusions; income-based exception to "specified service trade or business" exclusion—Code Sec. 199A pass-through deduction.

For the Code Sec. 199A deduction (¶1593), a qualified trade or business is any trade or business *other than:* (1) a specified service trade or business (SSTB, below), (2) performing services as an employee (Code Sec. 199A(d)(1)), or (3) a trade or business conducted by a C corporation.[2] There's a safe harbor to determine when a rental real estate enterprise is a Code Sec. 199A trade or business. (Rev Proc 2019-38, 2019-42 IRB 942)[3]

SSTB exclusion. An SSTB is any trade or business involving the performance of services: (A) described in Code Sec. 1202(e)(3)(A)—other than engineering or architecture—or that would be so described if the term "employees or owners" were substituted for "employees" in Code Sec. 1202(e)(3)(A); or (B) consisting of investing and investment management, trading, or dealing in securities described in Code Sec. 475(c)(2), partnership interests, or commodities described in Code Sec. 475(e)(2). (Code Sec. 199A(d)(2))[4] Regs list fields in which a trade or business involving the performance of services is an SSTB. (Reg § 1.199A-5)[5]

Threshold exception to SSTB exclusion. Although an SSTB generally isn't a qualified trade or business that's eligible for the pass-through deduction, there's an exception to the SSTB exclusion, based on a taxpayer's income. For 2023, if the taxable income of any taxpayer is less than $364,200 for joint filers for married filing joint returns, $182,100 for married filing separate returns, and $182,100 for single returns and head of household returns, the exclusion for SSTBs does not apply, and the deduction is available to the taxpayer, for that year. For 2022, the threshold begins at $340,100 for married filing joint returns, and $170,050 for married filing separate returns, single returns, and head of household returns. If, for any tax year, the taxable income of any taxpayer is less than the sum of the beginning threshold amount plus $50,000 ($100,000 in the case of a joint return), a phaseout rule applies to SSTBs. (Code Sec. 199A(d)(3)(A)(i))[6]

De minimis rule for business with multiple sources of income. If a single business has multiple sources of income, including SSTBs and others, a de minimis rule applies. If a trade or business has gross receipts of $25 million or less, and less than 10% of its gross receipts are attributable to SSTB activities, or if it has gross receipts of more than $25 million, and less than 5% of its gross receipts are attributable to SSTB activities, the business as a whole is not an SSTB. But if the gross receipts from SSTB activities exceed the percentages just mentioned, the entire business is treated as an SSTB. (Reg § 1.199A-5(c)(1))[7]

¶ 1596 "Combined qualified business income amount" for Code Sec. 199A pass-though deduction.

For the Code Sec. 199A deduction (¶1593), a taxpayer's combined qualified business income amount (combined QBI amount, defined in Reg § 1.199A-3(b)) for a tax year is equal to: (1) the sum of the deductible amounts determined for each qualified trade or business (¶1595) carried on by the taxpayer (Code Sec. 199A(b)(1)(A)), plus (2) 20% of the aggregate amount of the taxpayer's qualified real estate investment trust (REIT) dividends and qualified publicly traded partnership (PTP) income for the tax year (Code Sec. 199A(b)(1)(B)), including taxpayer's share of qualified REIT dividends and qualified

---

1. ¶L-4307.8
2. ¶L-4307.1
3. ¶L-4307.1A
4. ¶L-4311

5. ¶L-4311
6. ¶L-4311
7. ¶L-4311.16

181

PTP income from relevant pass-through entities. (Reg § 1.199A-1(d)(3)(i))[8]

A qualified REIT dividend is any dividend from a real estate investment trust received during the tax year that is not a Code Sec. 857(b)(3) capital gain dividend (Code Sec. 199A(e)(3)(A)) and is not Code Sec. 1(h)(11) qualified dividend income. (Code Sec. 199A(e)(3)(B))[9]

Qualified PTP income for any qualified trade or business of the taxpayer is the sum of:

. . . the net amount of the taxpayer's allocable share of each qualified item of income, gain, deduction and loss (determined after excluding reasonable compensation, guaranteed payments and other payments for services) from a Code Sec. 7704 PTP that is not treated as a corporation for tax purposes; (Code Sec. 199A(e)(4)(A)) and

. . . any gain recognized by the taxpayer upon the disposition of its interest in a PTP to the extent the gain is treated as amount realized from a sale or exchange of property other than a capital asset under Code Sec. 751(a). (Code Sec. 199A(e)(4)(B))[10]

¶ 1597　Limit on Code Sec. 199A pass-through deduction—W-2 wages or basis of qualified property.

For the Code Sec. 199A deduction (¶1593), unless the taxpayer is below a threshold amount (see below), the deductible amount for a qualified trade or business is limited, i.e., it is the lesser of:

(1) 20% of the taxpayer's qualified business income (QBI) from the qualified trade or business (Code Sec. 199A(b)(2)(A)) or

(2) the greater of (I) 50% of the W-2 wages relating to the qualified trade or business or (II) the sum of (i) 25% of the W-2 wages relating to the qualified trade or business and (ii) 2.5% percent of the unadjusted basis immediately after acquisition (UBIA) of all qualified property. (Code Sec. 199A(b)(2)(B))[11]

W-2 wages. A person's W-2 wages for a tax year is the total of the wages described in Code Sec. 6051(a)(3) and the Code Sec. 6051(a)(8) elective deferrals paid by the person for employment of employees during the calendar year ending during the tax year, but only for amounts properly allocable to QBI. W-2 wages means W-2 wages of a trade or business (or aggregated trade or business) properly allocable to QBI as determined under Reg § 1.199A-2(b). Amounts not properly included in a return filed with the Social Security Administration on or before the 60th day after the due date (including extensions) for such return are excluded. (Code Sec. 199A(b)(4)) Regs provide guidance on calculating W-2 wages. (Reg § 1.199A-2(b))[12]

Qualified property. Qualified property relating to a qualified trade or business for a tax year is tangible property of a character subject to a Code Sec. 167 depreciation allowance that is: (A) held by, and available for use in, the qualified trade or business at the close of the tax year; (B) used at any point during the tax year in the production of QBI; and (C) the depreciable period for which has not ended before the close of the tax year. (Code Sec. 199A(b)(6)(A))[13]

UBIA. Regs provide guidance on determining the UBIA of all qualified property. (Reg § 1.199A-2(a)(3))[14]

Threshold amount exception. The wage/property limitation doesn't apply for taxpayers with taxable income below the threshold amount discussed at ¶1595. (Code Sec. 199A(b)(3)(A))[15] The limit phases in where taxable income is above the threshold amount, under a formula in the statute. (Code Sec. 199A(b)(3)(B)) Taxpayers can, but

---

8. ¶L-4308
9. ¶L-4307.3
10. ¶L-4307.5
11. ¶L-4309

12. ¶L-4309.3; ¶L-4309.3A *et seq.*
13. ¶L-4309.1; ¶L-4309.3M
14. ¶L-4309.3K
15. ¶L-4309.4 *et seq.*

aren't required to, aggregate separate trades or business in applying these limitations. (Reg § 1.199A-4(a))[16]

Anti-abuse rule. Regs provide that a trust formed or funded with a principal purpose of avoiding, or of using more than one, threshold amount for purposes of calculating the deduction under Code Sec. 199A won't be respected as a separate trust entity for determining the threshold amount for Code Sec. 199A. (Reg § 1.199A-6(d)(3)(vii))[17]

¶ 1598 Code Sec. 199A pass-through deduction for partnerships and S corporations.

Code Sec. 199A(f)(1)(A)(i) provides that the qualified business income deduction for noncorporate taxpayers (¶1593) is applied to partnerships and S corporations at the partner or shareholder level. (Code Sec. 199A(f)(1)(A)(i)) Thus, each partner or shareholder must take into account his or her allocable share of each qualified item of income, gain, deduction, and loss (Code Sec. 199A(f)(1)(A)(ii)), and each partner/shareholder takes his or her allocable share of W-2 wages and unadjusted basis immediately after acquisition (UBIA) of qualified property (¶1597) into account for calculating the combined QBI amount. (Code Sec. 199A(f)(1)(A)(iii)) A partner's or shareholder's allocable share of W-2 wages is determined in the same way as the partner's or shareholder's allocable share of wage expenses, and a partner's or shareholder's allocable share of the UBIA of qualified property is determined in the same way as the partner's or shareholder's allocable share of depreciation. For an S corporation, an allocable share is the shareholder's pro rata share of an item. (Code Sec. 199A(f)(1)(A)) The Code Sec. 199A deduction has no effect on an S corporation shareholder's adjusted basis in its S corporation stock, or a partner's adjusted basis in its partnership interest. (Reg § 1.199A-1(e)(1))[18]

¶ 1599 Code Sec. 199A(a) deduction for patrons of cooperatives

Unless otherwise provided in Reg § 1.199A-7, all the rules in Reg § 1.199A-1 through Reg § 1.199A-6 (on calculating the QBI deduction) apply to patrons and cooperatives. (Reg § 1.199A-7(a)(1))

Cooperatives are C corporations, and not eligible for the Code Sec. 199A deduction. So the Code Sec. 199A(a) deduction applies at the patron level, and patrons who are individuals—as well as trusts and estates—can take the Code Sec. 199A(a) deduction. (Reg § 1.199A-7(a)(2); Reg § 1.199A-7(a)(3)(i))[19]

The regs provide special rules for patrons relating to trades or businesses, for patrons and cooperatives relating to the definition of QBI, for W-2 wages and UBIA of a cooperative patron, and for patrons and cooperatives relating to specified service trades or businesses (SSTBs). (Reg § 1.199A-7)

¶ 1600 Code Sec. 199A(g) deduction (2018–2025) for qualified production activities income (QPAI) of specified agricultural or horticultural cooperatives.

A specified agricultural or horticultural cooperative is allowed a deduction for a tax year under Code Sec. 199A(g), which is similar to the pre-2018 domestic production activities deduction (DPAD) under repealed Code Sec. 199. The Code Sec. 199A(g) deduction equals 9% of the lesser of:

(1) the QPAI of the taxpayer for the tax year, or

(2) the taxable income of the taxpayer for the tax year, computed without any deductions allowable for patronage dividends and per-unit retain allocations under Code Sec. 1382(b) or for nonpatronage distributions under Code Sec. 1382(c). (Code

---

16. ¶L-4308.6
17. ¶L-4314

18. ¶L-4313
19. ¶L-4314.2 *et seq.*

Sec. 199A(g)(1)(A); Code Sec. 199A(g)(1)(C))

The deduction is limited to 50% of the taxpayer's W-2 wages for the tax year (Code Sec. 199A(g)(1)(B)(i)), i.e., W-2 wages that the cooperative paid during the calendar year that ends in its tax year. Only items attributable to the actual conduct of a trade or business are taken into account under Code Sec. 199A(g). (Code Sec. 199A(g)(5)(C))[20]

Reg § 1.199A-8 provides rules for the Code Sec. 199A(g) deduction for income attributable to domestic production activities of a specified agricultural or horticultural cooperative.[21]

¶ 1601   Miscellaneous Business Expenses. ▬▬▬▬▬

Royalty payments (¶1602), circulation costs (¶1603), mine exploration (¶1610) and development (¶1611) costs, and other miscellaneous business costs are deductible subject to certain conditions and limits. A taxpayer may elect to capitalize some deductible expenses, and elect to deduct other expenses that are normally capitalized.

¶ 1602   Royalty payments for the right to use patents, copyrights and similar rights—deductibility.

Royalty payments made for the right to use patents, copyrights and similar rights are deductible.[22] Payments to acquire the property itself are capital expenditures.[23] One court has held that a manufacturer may currently deduct sales-based royalties paid under trademark licensing agreements, but IRS disagrees and says such royalties must be capitalized under Code Sec. 263A (¶1639).[24]

¶ 1603   Circulation costs of periodical publishers—Form 4562—deductibility.

Publishers of periodicals can currently deduct (Code Sec. 173)[25] or elect to capitalize (Reg § 1.173-1(c))[26] their expenditures to establish, maintain and increase circulation. A taxpayer may elect (use Form 4562) to amortize circulation costs over three years beginning with the year the expenditure is made. (Code Sec. 59(e)(1); Reg § 1.59-1) For alternative minimum tax treatment of circulation costs, see ¶3211.

¶ 1604   Taxes, interest, and carrying charges—election to capitalize, Code Sec. 266.

Some taxes and carrying charges that would normally be deducted currently or amortized may be capitalized if the taxpayer so elects under Code Sec. 266. For depreciable property, this has the effect of deferring the deduction to later years as depreciation. For nondepreciable property, such as unimproved real estate, the capitalized expenses increase basis and reduce gain (or increase loss) on a later sale of the property. (Code Sec. 266; Reg § 1.212-1(n), Reg § 1.266-1)[27]

The capitalization election may be made:

. . . for taxes, mortgage interest (subject to the interest capitalization rules at ¶1641) and deductible carrying charges on unimproved and unproductive real property. (Reg § 1.266-1(b))[28]

. . . by a taxpayer engaged in the development of real estate or the construction of an improvement to real estate, for the following items relating to the project: loan interest; taxes measured by compensation paid to employees and taxes imposed on the purchase

---

20. ¶L-4315 *et seq.*
21. ¶L-4315 *et seq.*
22. ¶L-3201
23. ¶L-3203
24. ¶G-5494.1

25. ¶L-2213
26. ¶L-2215 *et seq.*
27. ¶L-5850 *et seq.*
28. ¶L-5852

of materials, or on the storage, use, or other consumption of materials; and other necessary charges, including fire insurance premiums. (Reg § 1.266-1(b)(1))[29]

... for interest on a loan to finance the purchase, transportation, and installation of machinery and other assets, state and local taxes imposed on the taxpayer, transportation, storage, use or other consumption of the property, and state and local taxes, including sales and use taxes, and state and federal unemployment taxes, and the taxpayer's share of federal social security taxes on the wages of employees engaged in transportation and installation of the assets. (Reg § 1.266-1)[30]

¶ 1605 Architectural and transportation barrier removal expenses— deductibility.

Under Code Sec. 190, a taxpayer can elect to treat up to $15,000 of qualified architectural and transportation barrier removal expenses as a deduction rather than as a charge to capital account. (Code Sec. 190(a), Code Sec. 190(c)) To elect, claim the deduction as a separate item identified as such on the timely filed (including extension) return for the tax year for which the election is to apply. (Reg § 1.190-3(a))[31] For the credit for eligible access expenditures, see ¶2323.

¶ 1606 Serial contingent payments for franchises, trademarks, or trade names— deductibility.

Under Code Sec. 1253(d)(1), in the case of a transfer of a franchise, trademark or trade name, a deduction is allowed to the transferee for serial payments contingent on the productivity, use, or disposition of the franchise, trademark or trade name transferred. (Code Sec. 1253(d)(1))[32]

¶ 1607 Computer software—purchased, licensed and self-developed— deductibility.

The tax treatment of computer software depends on whether it is bought, licensed, or self-developed.

Purchased software. The cost of software bought by itself, rather than being bundled into hardware costs, is capitalized and amortized over 36 months using the straight-line method. This rule *doesn't* apply to any software that's a Code Sec. 197 intangible (see ¶1958). (Reg § 1.167(a)-14(b)(1))[33] However, the cost of software included or bundled, without being separately stated, in the cost of hardware is capitalized and depreciated as a part of the hardware cost. (Reg § 1.167(a)-14(b)(2))

Licensed software. For computer software costs to which Rev Proc 2000-50 applies, where a taxpayer leases or licenses software for use in a trade or business, IRS won't disturb a deduction properly allowable under the provisions of Reg § 1.162-11 for rental.

Self-developed software. For tax years beginning after 2021, generally the only allowable treatment is to amortize the costs over the five-year period beginning with the midpoint of the tax year in which the expenditures are paid or incurred.[34]

For amounts paid or incurred in tax years beginning before Jan. 1, 2022, among multiple former treatment options,[35] the costs of developing computer software were eligible for treatment as research or experimental expenditures under former Code Sec. 174 (see ¶1583). To be eligible for that treatment, however, the software development costs had to fall within the definition of "research or experimental expenditures" as set forth by former Code Sec. 174 and its regs.[36] Not all software development costs qualified.

---

29. ¶L-5853
30. ¶L-5854
31. ¶L-3151 *et seq.*
32. ¶I-8415 *et seq.*

33. ¶L-7935
34. ¶L-3130.4
35. ¶L-5613
36. ¶L-3101

¶ 1608   Stock reacquisition expenses; greenmail—deductibility.

Under Code Sec. 162(k), no deduction is allowed for any amount paid or incurred by a corporation in connection with the reacquisition of its stock (e.g., greenmail) or of the stock of any related person as specially defined in Code Sec. 465(b)(3)(C). Amounts deductible as interest under Code Sec. 163 or as dividends paid under Code Sec. 561 are among expenses not subject to this rule. (Code Sec. 162(k)) The no-deduction rule doesn't apply to deductions for amounts properly allocable to indebtedness (e.g., loan commitment fees) and amortized over the term of the indebtedness. (Code Sec. 162(k)(2)(A)(ii))[37]

For 1% excise tax, post-2022, on repurchase (valued over $1 million) of corporate stock, see ¶3318.

¶ 1609   Co-op housing maintenance and lease expenses—deductibility.

Code Sec. 216(d) provides that cooperative housing maintenance and lease expenses are deductible if the cooperative unit is used in a trade or business or for the production of income. However, no deduction is allowed to the co-op stockholder for any payment to the co-op (in excess of the stockholder's share of taxes and interest) to the extent the payment is properly allocable to amounts chargeable to the co-op's capital account. The basis of the stockholder's stock is increased by the amount of any deduction disallowed under this rule. (Code Sec. 216(d))[38]

¶ 1610   Domestic mine exploration costs—Form 4562—deductibility.

Under Code Sec. 617, domestic mine exploration costs incurred before a mine has reached the development stage are nondeductible capital expenditures. However, taxpayers may elect to deduct mining exploration expenditures for minerals (other than oil and gas) that qualify for percentage depletion. (Code Sec. 617)[39]

Deducted exploration costs are subject to recapture when the mine reaches the producing stage, when taxpayer receives a bonus or royalty, or when the taxpayer disposes of all or part of the property, whichever happens first (except where IRS allows recapture to be postponed on disposition of a *part* interest). (Code Sec. 617(b)(1), Code Sec. 1254(a)(1); Reg § 1.1254-1(b))[40]

All taxpayers, including partners and S corporation shareholders, may elect (use Form 4562) to deduct all or any portion of their deductible mine exploration costs ratably over ten years. (Code Sec. 59(e); Reg § 1.59-1)[41]

Corporations' deductions for exploration costs are cut back 30% if they elect to write off the costs in the year they are incurred. (Code Sec. 291(b)(1)) The amount cut back is amortized over 60 months. (Code Sec. 291(b))[42]

¶ 1611   Mine development costs—Form 4562—deductibility.

Code Sec. 616(a) provides that a taxpayer who incurs expenditures to develop minerals other than oil or gas may: (1) deduct those expenditures in the year they were paid or incurred (Code Sec. 616(a));[43] (2) elect to treat them as deferred expenses and deduct them ratably as the units of produced minerals benefited by the expense are sold (Code Sec. 616(b); Reg § 1.616-2(a));[44] or (3) treat them as deferred expenses and elect (use Form 4562) to amortize them ratably over ten years. (Code Sec. 59(e); Reg § 1.59-1)[45]

Corporations' deductions for mine development costs are cut back 30% if the corporation

37. ¶s L-5305, L-5411
38. ¶K-5900 *et seq.*
39. ¶N-3103
40. ¶N-3601 *et seq.*
41. ¶N-3114

42. ¶N-3104
43. ¶N-3116
44. ¶N-3123
45. ¶N-3124

elects to write off the costs in the year incurred. (Code Sec. 291(b)(1)(B)) The amount cutback is amortized over 60 months. (Code Sec. 291(b))[46]

Deducted mine development costs are recaptured (on Form 4797) as ordinary income on disposition of the property. (Code Sec. 1254(a)(1); Reg § 1.1254-1(b))[47]

¶ 1612 Oil and gas geological and geophysical exploration costs; intangible drilling and development costs—deductibility.

Any geological and geophysical expenses paid or incurred in connection with the exploration for, or development of, oil or gas in the U.S. are deductible ratably over the 24-month period beginning on the date that the expenses were paid or incurred. (Code Sec. 167(h)(1))[48] The 24-month amortization period is extended to 7 years for expenses paid or incurred by major integrated oil companies. (Code Sec. 167(h)(5))[49]

Taxpayers have an option to capitalize, amortize or expense certain so-called intangible drilling and development costs (IDCs) of oil and gas wells, or of geothermal wells. (Code Sec. 59(e); Code Sec. 263(c); Reg § 1.263(c)-1; Reg § 1.612-5)[50] For alternative minimum tax treatment of IDCs, see ¶3210.

Deducted IDCs are recaptured (on Form 4797) as ordinary income on disposition of the oil or gas wells. (Code Sec. 1254(a)(1)(A); Reg § 1.1254-1(b))[1]

¶ 1613 Lobbying costs, influencing public on legislation—deductibility.

Code Sec. 162(e) provides that deductible business expenses don't include:

... Any amount paid or incurred (1) in influencing legislation; (2) in connection with participation in or intervention in any political campaign or any attempt to influence the general public with respect to elections, legislative matters, or referendums; or (3) in communicating directly with a covered executive branch official on official matters (Code Sec. 162(e)(1)).

... The portion of dues paid to a tax-exempt organization allocable to lobbying by the organization for which no deduction is allowed, if the organization informs taxpayer of the nondeductible portion. (Code Sec. 162(e)(3))[2]

Taxpayers must allocate costs to legislative-branch lobbying and executive-branch lobbying in determining the nondeductible amount by consistently using a reasonable method. (Reg § 1.162-28(a)(1), Reg § 1.162-29(c)(2))[3]

In-house expenditures of $2,000 or less per year aren't subject to these rules. (Code Sec. 162(e)(4)(B)(i))

¶ 1614 Civil damages— judgments and out-of-court settlements—deductibility.

Civil damages paid under judgments and out-of-court settlements arising out of normal business operations generally are deductible as business expenses under Code Sec. 162[4] if the litigation is directly connected with the taxpayer's business.[5]

No deduction is allowed for two-thirds of treble damage or settlement payments to private parties where the taxpayer (payor) in a criminal proceeding for violation of federal anti-trust law is convicted or pleads guilty or no contest. (Code Sec. 162(g); Reg § 1.162-22)[6] No deduction is allowed for any settlement, payout, or attorneys fees relate to sexual harassment or sexual abuse if such payments are subject to a nondisclosure agreement.

---

46. ¶N-3104
47. ¶N-3309 *et seq.*
48. ¶N-3201
49. ¶N-3201
50. ¶N-3202 *et seq.*
1. ¶N-3406

2. ¶L-2401 *et seq.*
3. ¶L-2400 *et seq.*
4. ¶L-2500 *et seq.*
5. ¶L-2502
6. ¶L-2714

(Code Sec. 162(q))[7]

¶ 1615   Business Expenses of Employees and Self-Employeds. ▆▆▆▆▆▆

From 2018–2025, unreimbursed employee business expenses, such as travel expenses, job-search expenses, union dues, work clothes, etc., are generally nondeductible due to the suspension of miscellaneous itemized deductions (¶2162). Expenses of self-employed individuals may, however, be deductible (¶1616).

¶ 1616   Deductions for expenses of self-employed professionals.

Self-employed individuals can deduct the expenses of their business or profession under Code Sec. 162, such as supplies, rent, transportation, business, travel, telephone, etc. But a professional who is an employee cannot deduct unreimbursed employee expenses from 2018–2025 (see ¶1615).

Self-employed professionals can also deduct expenses peculiar to their professions such as dues to professional organizations, continuing professional education, subscriptions to professional journals, malpractice insurance, and payments to assistants. The cost of professional books, furniture, instruments and equipment are deductible if their useful lives are short.[8] But expenses incurred by business or professional people to build up their reputations are capital expenditures to develop or enhance goodwill, unless the expenses can be tied directly to the production of added income.[9] The following material highlights the rules on deductions for certain types of professionals:

Accountants can't deduct costs of a CPA review course or the CPA exam.[10]

Lawyers have been allowed to deduct bar association dues, but not costs of securing admission to practice (including bar examination fees, expenses to be admitted to second state bar, travel) (Reg § 1.162-5, Reg § 1.212-1(f)), which must be amortized over taxpayer's remaining life expectancy. The cost of bar review courses can't be amortized.[11]

Doctors and dentists can't deduct costs of securing the right to practice, fees on their initial licensing, etc. (Reg § 1.212-1(f))[12] Fees paid to a hospital for staff privileges are amortizable over taxpayer's useful life, or the useful life of the hospital privilege if shorter.[13]

Costs of entering a profession or securing the right to practice are nondeductible. (Reg § 1.212-1(f))[14]

¶ 1617   Impairment-related work expenses, including attendant care services—deductibility.

Under Code Sec. 67(d), impairment-related work expenses are deductible (on Form 2106 or Form 2106-EZ). They are ordinary and necessary expenses, including attendant care services (e.g., a blind taxpayer's use of a reader) at the place of employment, to enable an individual who has a handicap to work. (Code Sec. 67(d)) Impairment-related work expenses are not miscellaneous itemized deductions subject to the 2%-of-AGI floor. (Code Sec. 67(b)(6))[15]

¶ 1618   Residence Used in Part for Business—Home Office Deduction. ▆▆▆▆▆▆

Self-employed individuals may take home office deductions if tough tests are met. From 2018–2025, employees cannot claim home office expense deductions due to the suspension of miscellaneous itemized deductions (¶2162).

---

7. ¶L-2511
8. ¶L-4101
9. ¶L-4100 *et seq.*
10. ¶L-3719
11. ¶L-4102

12. ¶s L-4100, L-4101
13. ¶L-4107
14. ¶L-4101
15. ¶L-3906 *et seq.*

The general rule is that no deduction is allowed for the business use of a dwelling unit that's also used by the taxpayer as a residence during the tax year. But exceptions, discussed below, allow deductions under certain circumstances. (Code Sec. 280A(a)) The disallowance rule applies to individuals, trusts, estates, partnerships, and S corporations. However, disallowance doesn't apply to any deduction allowable without regard to its connection with either a business or income-producing activity. (Code Sec. 280A(b)) For example, the deductions allowed under Code Sec. 163 for interest, Code Sec. 164 for certain taxes, and Code Sec. 165 for casualty losses may be claimed without regard to their connection with the taxpayer's trade or business or income-producing activities. In other words, this disallowance applies only to otherwise deductible *business* expenses (Code Sec. 162) and depreciation.[16]

The home office deduction isn't allowed for expenses of an income-producing activity, unless the activity is a trade or business.[17]

In situations described in ¶1619 *et seq.*, otherwise allowable business expenses are deductible (subject to the limits discussed at ¶1622 and ¶1623) even though they are incurred in connection with the business use of a portion of a taxpayer's residence. In addition, the cost of capital improvements made to the entire residence may be recovered through depreciation to the extent allocable to the portion of the residence used for the taxpayer's business.[18]

Charges (including taxes) for basic local telephone services for the first telephone line for any residence are treated as personal expenses. (Code Sec. 262(b))[19]

¶ 1619 Residence used as principal place of business—home office deduction; Form 1040, schedules C and F.

Under Code Sec. 280A(c)(1)(A), a home office deduction (¶1618) is allowed to the extent allocable to a portion of a residence *used exclusively* and *on a regular basis* (¶1622) as the taxpayer's principal place of business for *any* trade or business of the taxpayer. (Code Sec. 280A(c)(1)(A))[20]

Allowable home-office expenses are deducted on Form 1040, Schedule C (most self-employed persons), and Form 1040, Schedule F (farmers).

Following are the two ways to meet the principal place of business requirement:

(1) Under the statutory administrative/management activities test, the principal place of business test is met if a portion of the home is used for the administrative or management activities of any trade or business of the taxpayer, but only if there is no other fixed location where the taxpayer conducts substantial administrative or management activities of that trade or business. (Code Sec. 280A(c)(1)) Examples of administrative or management activities are: billing customers, clients or patients; keeping books and records; ordering supplies; setting up appointments; and forwarding orders or writing reports. A taxpayer's administrative or management activities at sites that aren't fixed locations of the business (e.g., car or hotel room), don't count. Moreover, if a taxpayer conducts some administrative or management activities at a fixed location of the business outside the home, he or she can still claim a home-office deduction as long as those activities aren't substantial (e.g., the taxpayer occasionally does minimal paperwork at another fixed location of the business). A taxpayer's eligibility to claim a home office deduction under the above rules won't be affected by the fact that he or she conducts substantial non-administrative or non-management business activities at a fixed location outside the home (e.g., meeting with, or providing services to, customers, clients, or patients at a fixed location outside of the home).[21]

illustration: Most of a self-employed plumber's time is spent at customers' homes and

---

16. ¶L-1301 *et seq.*
17. ¶L-1305
18. ¶L-1306 *et seq.*

19. ¶L-1307 *et seq.*
20. ¶s L-1317, L-1324
21. ¶L-1335

offices installing and repairing plumbing. His sole office is in his home and he uses it exclusively and regularly for the administrative or management details of his business (phoning customers, ordering supplies, and keeping his books). The plumber's home office qualifies as a principal place of business.

(2) Under the comparative analysis test, set forth in the Supreme Court's *Soliman* decision, the determination of a taxpayer's principal place of business requires a comparative analysis of: (1) the relative importance of the activities performed at each business location, and (2) the time spent at each place, i.e., time spent at the home compared with time spent in each of the other places where business activities occur. If the nature of the trade or profession requires the taxpayer to meet or confer with clients or patients or to deliver goods or services to a customer, the place where that contact occurs, particularly where that place is a facility with unique or special characteristics, is often important.[22]

¶ 1620   Residence used to meet clients—home office deduction.

Under Code Sec. 280A(c)(1)(B), a home office deduction is allowed to the extent allocable to a portion of a residence that's *used exclusively* and *on a regular basis* (¶1622) as a place of business (even if not a principal place of business) that is used by patients, clients, or customers in meeting or dealing with the taxpayer in the normal course of the trade or business. (Code Sec. 280A(c)(1)(B)) This permits a doctor, lawyer, sales rep, insurance agent, claims adjuster, etc., to deduct home office expenses even though he or she operates the business or profession primarily from an office away from the residence. Telephone conversations alone aren't enough; patients, customers, etc., must be physically present for deductions to be claimed under this rule.[23]

¶ 1621   Specialized rules for business use of home under home office deduction rules.

Under Code Sec. 280A(c), a home office deduction (¶1618) is allowed:

• For costs allocable to a portion of a separate structure (e.g., artist's studio) not attached to the residence if it's used *exclusively* and *on a regular basis* (¶1622) in connection with the taxpayer's business. (Code Sec. 280A(c)(1)(C))[24]

• To the extent allocable to space in a residence that the taxpayer uses *on a regular basis* to store inventory and/or product samples in the business of selling products at retail or wholesale, if the residence is the sole fixed location of the trade or business. (Code Sec. 280A(c)(2))[25]

• If a residence is used regularly to provide day care services for compensation to children, handicapped individuals, or persons 65 or over. If there is only part-time use of a portion of the residence, allocation must be made first on the basis of the proportion of total space used to furnish services and then on the basis of the amount of time that space is used for those services compared to the total time the space is available for all uses. The deduction is allowed only if the day care services aren't primarily educational and comply with any applicable state licensing, certification, or approval requirements. (Code Sec. 280A(c)(4))[26]

¶ 1622   "Exclusive" use on a "regular" basis required for home office deduction.

For purposes of the home office rules (¶1618 *et seq.*), exclusive use means that the taxpayer must use a specific portion of a residence or detached structure for carrying on his or her business. For example, using a den to write legal briefs and prepare tax returns as well as for personal purposes doesn't meet the exclusive use test.[27] Part of a room used

---

22. ¶L-1330 *et seq.*
23. ¶L-1344 *et seq.*
24. ¶L-1347

25. ¶L-1355 *et seq.*
26. ¶L-1359
27. ¶L-1317 *et seq.*

exclusively for business can qualify for the deduction, even though the room isn't divided.[28] Expenses attributable to the exclusive but incidental or occasional trade or business use of a portion of a dwelling unit aren't deductible because the space isn't used on a regular basis.[29]

¶ 1623 Gross income limit on home office deduction.

Under Code Sec. 280A(c)(5), the home office deduction (¶1618) is limited to the activity's gross income reduced by all other deductible expenses that are allowable regardless of qualified use and by the business deductions that aren't allocable to the use of the home itself. (Code Sec. 280A(c)(5)(A), Code Sec. 280A(c)(5)(B)) Expenses disallowed solely because they exceed business income can be carried forward (Code Sec. 280A(c)(5)), subject to this gross income limitation in the later year.[30]

¶ 1624 Allocation of home office expenses for the home office deduction.

Allocation of expenses and depreciation on a house for purposes of the home office deduction (¶1618) is generally based on a comparison of space used for business and personal purposes.[31]

A safe harbor method ($5 per square foot, up to a maximum of 300 square feet) may be used as an alternative to the calculation, allocation, and substantiation of actual home office expenses.[32]

¶ 1625 Rental by employer of space in employee's home—no home office deduction allowed.

Under Code Sec. 280A(c)(6), no home office deduction is allowed for expenses attributable to the rental by an employee of all or part of his or her home to the employer if the employee uses the rented portion to perform services as an employee of the employer. (Code Sec. 280A(c)(6))[33]

¶ 1626 Moving Expense Deduction for Active Duty Armed Forces Members. ▬▬▬▬

An active duty member of the armed forces who move under a military order and incident to a permanent change of station (¶1627) can deduct certain moving expenses regardless of the distance moved or the length of time worked at the new station.

¶ 1627 Moving expenses of active duty members of the armed forces.

Under Code Sec. 217(g), a move by an active duty member of the armed forces under a military order and incident to a permanent change of station can qualify for deduction regardless of the distance moved or the length of time worked at the new station. Cash reimbursements or allowances are excludable to the extent of moving and storage expenses actually paid or incurred, as are all in-kind moving and storage services provided by the military. This exclusion also applies to a spouse and dependents when they don't accompany an armed forces member and move to a location different from that *to* which he or she moves or different from that *from* which he or she moves. Where the military moves the member and family to or from separate locations and they incur unreimbursed expenses, their moves are treated as a single move to the member's new principal place of work. (Code Sec. 217(g)) No deduction is permitted for any moving or storage expense reimbursed by an excluded allowance. (Reg § 1.217-2(g)(6))[34]

---

28. ¶L-1317
29. ¶L-1324
30. ¶L-1365 *et seq.*
31. ¶L-1313

32. ¶L-1310 *et seq.*; ¶L-1316.1
33. ¶L-1354
34. ¶L-3600 *et seq.*

¶ 1628   Deduction vs Capitalization of Tangible Property Costs. ▄▄▄▄▄▄▄▄

In general, repairs and maintenance are deductible currently (¶1629), and materials and supplies are deductible either when used or consumed (if non-incidental), or when paid (if incidental, and other conditions are met) (¶1630). Capitalized expenses generally can't be deducted except through depreciation, expensing, depletion, or amortization deductions.

¶ 1629   Deductible repairs and maintenance costs; routine maintenance safe harbors—tangible property costs.

In general, amounts paid for repairs and maintenance to tangible property are currently deductible if they are not otherwise required to be capitalized. (Reg § 1.162-4(a)) Repair costs that don't directly benefit, and are not incurred because of, an improvement do not have to be capitalized, even if made at the same time as a capitalized improvement. (Reg § 1.263(a)-3(g)(1)(i))[35]

⬤*Illustration:* A business may currently deduct as a repair the cost of replacing a truck's broken headlights and mending the driver's seat, even if the work takes place when the truck is taken out of service to overhaul its engine (a capitalized expense).

Taxpayers may elect to capitalize amounts paid for repair and maintenance consistent with their books and records. (Reg § 1.263(a)-3(n)(1))[36]

Regulated taxpayers (e.g., telecommunications companies) may use an optional simplified method to distinguish between repairs and capitalized costs. (Reg § 1.263(a)-3(m))

Routine maintenance safe harbors. Regs provide for a routine maintenance safe harbor for property other than buildings. (Reg § 1.263(a)-3(i)(1)(ii)) Regs also provide for a routine maintenance safe harbor for buildings. (Reg § 1.263(a)-3(i)(1)(i)) For both of these safe harbors, routine maintenance is treated as not improving the unit of property (UOP, see ¶1633) and therefore is currently deductible. (Reg § 1.263(a)-3(i)(1))

Expenses not treated as routine maintenance include amounts paid to return a UOP to its former ordinarily efficient operating condition, if the property has deteriorated to a state of disrepair and is no longer functional for its intended use. (Reg § 1.263(a)-3(i)(3))[37]

Effect of uniform capitalization rules. All of the above rules apply only to the extent they don't conflict with the uniform capitalization rules (¶1639 *et seq.*). (Reg § 1.263(a)-3(c)(1))

¶ 1630   When to deduct incidental and non-incidental materials and supplies— tangible property costs.

Under Reg § 1.162-3(a), the costs of buying or producing *non-incidental* materials and supplies are deductible in the tax year in which they are used or consumed. But *incidental* materials and supplies that are carried on hand, and for which no record of consumption is kept or physical inventories at the beginning and end of the year are not taken, generally are deductible in the tax year in which they are paid for, if taxable income is clearly reflected. (Reg § 1.162-3(a))[38]

"Materials and supplies" means tangible property used or consumed in the taxpayer's business that is not inventory and that falls within *any* of the following categories:

(1) It is a component acquired to maintain, repair, or improve a unit of tangible property owned, leased, or serviced by the taxpayer and that is not acquired as part of any single unit of tangible property; or

(2) It consists of fuel, lubricants, water, and similar items that are reasonably expected

---

35. ¶L-5601.6   37. ¶L-5601.6
36. ¶L-5601.14B   38. ¶L-4207

to be consumed in 12 months or less, beginning when used in taxpayer's operations; or

(3) It is a unit of property (UOP, see ¶1633) with an economic useful life of 12 months or less, beginning when the property is used or consumed in the taxpayer's operations; or

(4) It is a UOP with an acquisition cost or production cost (as determined under Code Sec. 263A) of $200 or less (or other amount identified in published guidance); or

(5) It is identified in published IRS guidance as materials and supplies. (Reg § 1.162-3(c))[39]

If a taxpayer elects to apply the de minimis safe harbor (¶1633) to amounts paid for the production or acquisition of tangible property, then the taxpayer must, with limited exceptions, apply the de minimis safe harbor to amounts paid for all materials and supplies that meet the de minimis safe harbor requirements. (Reg § 1.162-3(f))[40]

⚡️*caution:* Materials and supplies may have to be capitalized under Code Sec. 263A (¶1639) to property produced or acquired for resale, and Code Sec. 471 (¶2850) may require certain materials and supplies to be included in inventory.

¶ 1631 Rotable, temporary and standby emergency spare parts—tangible property costs.

Rotable and temporary spare parts. Rotable spare parts are materials and supplies (see ¶1630) acquired for installation on a unit of property (UOP, ¶1633), removable from that UOP, generally repaired or improved, and either reinstalled on the same or other property or stored for later installation. Temporary spare parts are materials and supplies that are used temporarily until a new or repaired part can be installed and then are removed and stored for later installation. (Reg § 1.162-3(c)(2))[41]

Rotable and temporary spare parts can be handled in one of four ways:

(1) Deduct the costs when the parts are disposed of. (Reg § 1.162-3(a)(1), Reg § 1.162-3(a)(3))[42]

(2) Adopt an optional method for such costs. (Reg § 1.162-3(a)(3), Reg § 1.162-3(e))[43]

(3) Deduct the costs under the elective *de minimis* rule explained at ¶1633. (Reg § 1.162-3(a)(3), Reg § 1.162-3(f))[44]

(4) Elect to capitalize and depreciate the costs. (Reg § 1.162-3(a)(3), Reg § 1.162-3(d))[45]

Standby emergency spare parts. Standby emergency spare parts are materials and supplies (see ¶1630) that meet a list of 11 criteria including that they are: (a) acquired when particular machinery or equipment is acquired (or later acquired and set aside for use in particular machinery or equipment); (b) set aside for use as replacements to avoid substantial operational time loss caused by emergencies due to particular machinery or equipment failure; and (c) located at or near the site of the installed related machinery or equipment so as to be readily available when needed. (Reg § 1.162-3(c)(3)) Options (1), (3) and (4), above, are available for standby emergency spare parts. (Reg § 1.162-3(a)(1), Reg § 1.162-3(a)(3), Reg § 1.162-3(d))[46]

¶ 1632 General rules for capital expenditures.

Under Code Sec. 263(a), a taxpayer must capitalize amounts paid: (a) for new buildings or for permanent improvements or betterments made to increase the value of any property or estate; or (b) for restoring property or in making good the exhaustion of the property for which an allowance (e.g., depreciation) is or has been made. (Code Sec. 263(a), Reg § 1.263(a)-1(a))

---

39. ¶G-2453
40. ¶G-2453.4
41. ¶G-2453.5
42. ¶G-2453.5

43. ¶G-2453.6
44. ¶G-2453.4
45. ¶G-2453.3
46. ¶G-2453.3

Examples of expenses that must be capitalized include:

- An amount paid or incurred to facilitate the acquisition of a trade or business, a change in capital structure of a business entity, and certain other transactions. (Reg § 1.263(a)-1(d)) There's a rebuttable presumption that success-based fees (i.e., payments contingent on successfully closing a deal) facilitate the transaction. For success-based fees, taxpayers may elect to (a) allocate 70% to deductible fees paid in business acquisitions or reorganizations to activities that don't facilitate the transaction and deduct such fees currently; and (b) treat the remaining 30% as capitalized activities facilitating the transaction.[47]

- An amount paid to acquire or create interests in land, such as easements, life estates, mineral interests, timber rights, or zoning variances.

- An amount assessed and paid under an agreement between bondholders or shareholders of a corporation to be used in a reorganization of the entity or voluntary contributions by shareholders to the capital of the corporation for any corporate purpose. (Reg § 1.263(a)-1(d))[48]

For the Code Sec. 263A rules requiring direct and indirect costs to be capitalized to property produced by the taxpayer and to property acquired for resale, see ¶1639.

¶ 1633   Amounts paid to acquire or produce tangible property—capitalization.

Under Reg § 1.263(a)-2(d)(1), unless the materials and supplies rule applies (see ¶1630) or the de minimis rule (discussed below) applies, a taxpayer must capitalize amounts paid to acquire or produce a unit of property (UOP), including leasehold improvement property, land and land improvements, buildings, machinery and equipment, and furniture and fixtures. The taxpayer also must capitalize costs for work (e.g., to make necessary repairs) performed before the date that the UOP is placed in service by the taxpayer. (Reg § 1.263(a)-2(d)(1))[49]

UOP defined. For purposes of the tangible property capitalization rules, the UOP for assets other than buildings generally consists of all the components that are functionally interdependent (i.e., where placing in service of one component is dependent on the placing in service of other component(s)). The UOP for a building generally is the building and its structural components. (Reg § 1.263(a)-3(e)(2)(i), Reg § 1.263(a)-3(e)(3)(i))[50]

Transaction costs. Amounts paid to facilitate the acquisition (or production) of real or personal property—i.e., paid in the process of investigating or otherwise pursuing the acquisition—must be capitalized and added to the basis of property acquired or produced. (Reg § 1.263(a)-2(f)(3)(i))[1]

ℝ𝕀𝔸 *observation:* Some facilitative expenses may qualify as amortizable start-up expenses under Code Sec. 195; see ¶1500.

Facilitative costs include "inherently facilitative" expenses made up of eleven categories. These include the costs of items such as shipping, moving or appraising property, application fees, sales and transfer taxes, finder's fees, and architectural, engineering, environmental or inspection services related to specific properties, brokers' fees, and services provided by a qualified intermediary in a Code Sec. 1031 exchange. (Reg § 1.263(a)-2(f)(2)(ii))[2]

Costs relating to the process of determining *whether* to acquire realty and *which* realty to acquire generally aren't facilitative expenses (and therefore may be currently deductible), unless they are "inherently facilitative" expenses (e.g., the cost of an engineering study or a broker's fee). (Reg § 1.263(a)-2(f)(2)(iii)) Employee compensation or overhead *doesn't* facilitate the acquisition of real or personal property (but, under Code Sec. 263A,

---

47. ¶L-5762.1
48. ¶L-5601
49. ¶L-5601.1

50. ¶L-5601.12; ¶L-5601.13
1. ¶L-5601.4
2. ¶L-5601.4

may have to be capitalized to property produced by the taxpayer or acquired for resale). However, the taxpayer may elect to capitalize employee compensation or overhead expenses, or both, related to each acquisition. (Reg § 1.263(a)-2(f)(2)(iv)(B))[3]

For commissions paid on the transfer of property, see ¶1635.

De minimis rules. Under a de minimis safe harbor rule (also known as a book-tax conformity rule), amounts paid to acquire or produce a unit of tangible property, including materials and supplies (but not inventory or land), don't have to be capitalized and may be deducted currently, if the taxpayer so elects and:

- the taxpayer has an applicable financial statement (AFS), such as one required to be filed with the Securities and Exchange Commission, or a certified audited financial statement accompanied by an independent CPA's report and used for credit or reporting purposes;

- the taxpayer has written accounting procedures in place at the beginning of the tax year for expensing amounts paid for such property if it costs less than a specified dollar amount or it has an economic useful life of 12 months or less;

- the taxpayer treats such amounts as expenses on its AFS in accordance with its written accounting procedures; and

- the amount paid for the property does not exceed $5,000 per invoice (or per item as substantiated by the invoice) or other amount identified by IRS in published guidance. (Reg § 1.263(a)-1(f)(1)(i))[4]

A similar rule, but with a $2,500-per-item limit, applies to taxpayers that don't have an AFS. (Reg § 1.263(a)-1(f)(1)(ii))

If the taxpayer elects the de minimis safe harbor, that safe harbor must be applied to all eligible materials and supplies (other than rotable, temporary, and standby emergency spare parts that the taxpayer elects to capitalize, and rotable and temporary spare parts subject to the optional method of accounting for these parts, see ¶1631). (Reg § 1.263(a)-1(f)(1), Reg § 1.263(a)-1(f)(2))

The cost of property to which the de minimis rule applies may be subject to capitalization under Code Sec. 263A (see ¶1639 if the amounts paid for tangible property comprise the direct or allocable indirect costs of other property produced by the taxpayer or property acquired for resale. (Reg § 1.263(a)-1(f)(3)(v))

The existence of the de minimis safe harbor does not mean that a taxpayer cannot establish a de minimis deduction threshold in excess of the safe harbor amount, provided the taxpayer can demonstrate that a higher threshold clearly reflects the taxpayer's income.[5]

¶ 1634   Amounts paid to improve tangible property; capitalized betterment costs and capitalized restoration costs.

An expense must be capitalized if it betters or improves a unit of property (UOP, ¶1633), restores it, or adapts it to a new and different use.

Capitalized betterment costs. Capitalized betterment costs consist of amounts paid that:

. . . ameliorate a material condition or defect that either existed prior to the taxpayer's acquisition of the UOP or arose during the production of the UOP, whether or not the taxpayer was aware of the condition or defect at the time of acquisition or production; or

. . . is for a material addition, including a physical enlargement, expansion, extension, or addition of a major component) to the UOP or a material increase in the capacity of the UOP; or

---

3. ¶L-5601.4
4. ¶L-5601.5

5. ¶L-5601.5

... is reasonably expected to materially increase the productivity, efficiency, strength, quality, or output of the UOP. (Reg § 1.263(a)-3(j)(1))[6]

Here are two examples of particular costs and whether they must be capitalized as betterments:

- Costs of cleaning up contamination caused by leaking of underground storage tanks installed by prior owner of property are capitalized. (Reg § 1.263(a)-3(j)(3), Ex. 1)
- Removal and replacement of asbestos installed by a taxpayer in a building before its health hazards were known don't result in a betterment. (Reg § 1.263(a)-3(j)(3), Ex. 2)[7]

Capitalized restoration costs. Costs to restore a UOP are capitalized. An amount is treated as a restoration cost only if it:

(1) Replaces a component of a UOP where the taxpayer has (i) properly deducted a loss for that component (other than a casualty loss under Reg § 1.165-7) or (ii) properly taken into account the adjusted basis of the component in realizing gain or loss resulting from the sale or exchange of the component;

(2) Repairs damage to a UOP for which the taxpayer is required to take a basis adjustment as a result of a casualty loss or casualty event under Code Sec. 165;

(3) Returns the UOP to its ordinarily efficient operating condition if the property has deteriorated to a state of disrepair and is no longer functional for its intended use;

(4) Results in the rebuilding of the UOP to a like-new condition after the end of its class life under Code Sec. 168 for alternative depreciation system (ADS) purposes; or

(5) Replaces a part or a combination of parts that comprise a major component or a substantial structural part of a UOP. (Reg § 1.263(a)-3(k)(1)) All the facts and circumstances are to be considered when determining if this condition is met. (Reg § 1.263(a)-3(k)(6)(i))[8]

Capitalized amounts to adapt property to a new or different use. A taxpayer must capitalize as an improvement an amount paid to adapt a UOP to a new or different use. In general, a "new or different use" means a situation where the adaptation isn't consistent with the taxpayer's intended ordinary use of the property when placed in service. (Reg § 1.263(a)-3(l)(1)) For example, the cost of converting a company's manufacturing facility into a showroom facility must be capitalized. (Reg § 1.263(a)-3(l)(3), Ex 1)[9]

Retail/restaurant safe harbor. Under the "remodel-refresh" safe harbor for taxpayers in the retail and restaurant industries, 75% of qualified costs are deductible and 25% are capitalized.[10]

Per-building safe harbor for qualifying small taxpayers. A safe harbor permits qualifying small taxpayers (those with $10 million or less average annual gross receipts in the three preceding tax years (Reg § 1.263(a)-3(h)(3)(i))) to elect to currently deduct improvements made to an eligible building property (one with an unadjusted basis of $1 million or less (Reg § 1.263(a)-3(h)(4))). (Reg § 1.263(a)-3(h)(1)) This safe harbor election applies only if the total amount paid during the tax year for repairs, maintenance, improvements, and similar activities performed on the eligible building does not exceed the lesser of $10,000 or 2% of the building's unadjusted basis. (Reg § 1.263(a)-3(h)(1))[11]

¶ 1635   Commissions paid on transfers (purchase or sale) of real or other property—deduction vs. capitalization.

Commissions paid for the *purchase* of real estate or other property aren't deductible as expenses but must be capitalized and added to the cost of the property, whether or not the

---

6. ¶L-5601.8   9. ¶L-5601.10
7. ¶L-5601.8   10. ¶L-5635
8. ¶L-5601.9   11. ¶L-5601.13A

taxpayer is engaged in the real estate business.[12]

Commissions paid for the *sale* of real estate or other property by a taxpayer who is not engaged in the real estate business must be capitalized but are not added to the property's basis and are not treated as an intangible. Instead, commissions are offset against the selling price to determine the gain or loss realized on a sale. If the seller is in the real estate business, commissions on property sales are deductible business expenses. (Reg § 1.263(a)-1(e))[13]

¶ 1636   Capitalization Rules for Intangible Assets.

Taxpayers generally must capitalize amounts paid to acquire or create intangible assets or facilitate the acquisition or creation of such assets.

This includes amounts paid or incurred to (i) acquire or create an intangible asset, (ii) create or enhance a separate, distinct intangible asset, (iii) create or enhance a "future benefit" identified in published guidance as capitalizable, or (iv) "facilitate" the acquisition or creation of an intangible in (i) through (iii) (e.g., transaction costs). (Reg § 1.263(a)-4(b)(1)) Capitalizable costs cannot be deducted and are generally added to the basis of the intangible. (Reg § 1.263(a)-4) Compensation (including bonuses and commissions) and overhead costs do not facilitate the acquisition, creation or enhancement of an intangible asset. (Reg § 1.263(a)-4(e)(4)(i))[14] These rules do not affect the treatment of amounts specifically provided for in a Code Section other than Code Sec. 162 or Code Sec. 212 (e.g., Code Sec. 174 research expenses). (Reg § 1.263(a)-4(b)(4))

observation: Capitalized costs may be amortizable (e.g., payment to a departing employee for a 3-year noncompete covenant may be deducted ratably over the 3 years).

For the "12-month" and de minimis exceptions to these requirements, see ¶1637. For 15-year amortization of certain intangibles, see ¶1902.

¶ 1637   De minimis and 12-month rule exceptions to capitalization rules for intangibles.

The following are exceptions to the capitalization rules for intangibles discussed at ¶1636.

De minimis costs—i.e., costs that don't exceed $5,000—paid to another party to create, originate, enter into, renew, or renegotiate an agreement (Reg § 1.263(a)-4(d)(6)(v)), or paid in the process of investigating a transaction (Reg § 1.263(a)-4(e)(4)(iii)), don't have to be capitalized even if they facilitate a capital transaction and otherwise would be subject to the capitalization rules. Payments made in the form of property are valued at fair market value at the time of payment. The de minimis rule applies on a transaction-by-transaction basis. If transaction costs (other than compensation and overhead) exceed $5,000, none of the costs are treated as de minimis. A pooling method may be used for de minimis transaction costs. Commissions paid to facilitate the acquisition of an intangible aren't treated as de minimis costs (and therefore must be capitalized).[15]

12-month rule. Capitalization is not required for amounts paid to create or facilitate the creation of any right or benefit that does not extend beyond the earlier of (1) 12 months after the first date on which the taxpayer realizes the right or benefit; or (2) the end of the tax year following the tax year in which the payment is made. (Reg § 1.263(a)-4(f)) Amounts paid to terminate an agreement before its expiration date create a benefit for the taxpayer that lasts for the unexpired term of the agreement immediately before the termination date. (Reg § 1.263(a)-4(f)(2)) The 12-month rule doesn't apply to amounts paid to create (or facilitate the creation of) financial interests or amortizable Code Sec. 197 intangibles or to amounts paid to create or enhance a right of indefinite duration.

---

12. ¶I-2526
13. ¶I-2527

14. ¶L-5751
15. ¶L-5757.1, ¶L-5760.2D

(Reg § 1.263(a)-4(f)(3), Reg § 1.263(a)-4(f)(4)) The 12-month rule does not affect the determination of whether a liability is incurred during the tax year, including the determination of whether economic performance has occurred. (Reg § 1.263(a)-4(f)(6))[16]

¶ 1638 Capitalization of amounts paid or incurred to facilitate certain transactions—expenditures to acquire or create intangible assets or benefits.

A taxpayer must capitalize an amount paid to facilitate the following transactions, whether the transaction is a single step or a series of steps carried out as part of a single plan and without regard to whether gain or loss is recognized:

. . . acquisition of assets that constitute a trade or business (whether the taxpayer is the acquirer or the target).

. . . acquisition by the taxpayer of an ownership interest in a business entity if, immediately after the acquisition, the taxpayer and the business entity are related within the meaning of Code Sec. 267(b).

. . . acquisition by a person other than the taxpayer of an ownership interest in the taxpayer.

. . . restructuring, recapitalization, or reorganization of the capital structure of a business entity, including Code Sec. 368 reorganizations and distributions of stock by the taxpayer under Code Sec. 355.

. . . Code Sec. 351 or Code Sec. 721 transfer (whether the taxpayer is the transferor or transferee).

. . . formation or organization of a disregarded entity.

. . . acquisition of capital.

. . . stock issuance.

. . . borrowing, i.e., any issuance of debt, including in an acquisition of capital or a recapitalization. A borrowing also includes debt issued in a debt-for-debt exchange.

. . . writing an option. (Reg § 1.263(a)-5(a))[17]

¶ 1639 Uniform Capitalization (UNICAP) Rules; Small Business Exception ▰▰▰▰▰

Subject to exceptions, under the Code Sec. 263A UNICAP rules, manufacturers and certain retailers and wholesalers must use the UNICAP method under Code Sec. 263A to account for property they produce and for property they buy for resale. Under this method, the taxpayer must capitalize all direct and indirect costs properly allocable to such property. The regs provide rules for determining which direct and indirect costs are allocable to particular items of property. Then, once the total capitalizable costs of items of property subject to the rules are calculated, the taxpayer must allocate those costs between (a) ending inventory and other property on hand at the end of the year, and (b) property sold during the year. (Code Sec. 263A(a); Reg § 1.263A-1)[18]

The *allocable costs* are:

. . . the direct costs of the property (Code Sec. 263A(a)(2)(A));

. . . the indirect costs, to the extent of the property's proper share of that part (or all) of the costs allocable to that property. (Code Sec. 263A(a)(2)(B))[19]

Allocable costs include all depreciation deductions for the taxpayer's assets, and interest, but only where the underlying debt was incurred or continued to finance certain produced

---

16. ¶L-5760.5 *et seq.*   18. ¶G-5450 *et seq.*; ¶G-5458 *et seq.*
17. ¶L-5761   19. ¶G-5453

property, see ¶1641.[20] Taxes are allocable indirect costs. (Code Sec. 263A(a)(2)(B))[21] Environmental remediation costs incurred by a manufacturer (e.g., to clean land it contaminated with hazardous waste) must be included in inventory costs under these rules.[22]

Allocable costs don't include:

. . . selling, marketing, advertising and distribution expenses (Reg § 1.263A-1(e)(3)(iii)(A));[23]

. . . any amounts allowable as a deduction under Code Sec. 174 for research and experimental expenditures (Code Sec. 263A(c)(2));[24]

. . . any cost to the extent allowable as a deduction under Code Sec. 263(c) (intangible drilling and development costs), Code Sec. 616(a) (mining development expenses) or Code Sec. 617(a) (mining exploration expenses) (Code Sec. 263A(c)(3));[25]

. . . any qualified creative expense incurred by a "writer," "photographer" or "artist" that would otherwise be deductible. Expenses related to printing photographic plates, motion picture films, or similar items aren't qualified creative expenses (Code Sec. 263A(h));[26]

. . . "deductible service costs." (Reg § 1.263A-1(e)(3)(iii)(K))[27]

Which property is subject to the UNICAP rules? Under the UNICAP rules, a taxpayer must include in inventory or capitalize the allocable costs for:

. . . real or tangible personal property (defined below) that the taxpayer *produced* (defined below) (Code Sec. 263A(b)(1))[28];

. . . real or personal Code Sec. 1221(a)(1) property—inventory and property held primarily for sale to customers in the ordinary course of the taxpayer's trade or business—that the taxpayer acquired for resale. (Code Sec. 263A(b)(2))[29]

Tangible personal property includes a film, sound recording, book, or similar property. (Code Sec. 263A(b))

A taxpayer "produces" tangible property if the taxpayer constructs, builds, installs, manufactures, develops or improves it. (Code Sec. 263A(g)(1)) Where a taxpayer makes progress or advance payments to a contractor, the taxpayer is treated as producing any property the contractor produces for the taxpayer under the contract, to the extent of those payments (whether paid or incurred by the taxpayer under the contract or otherwise). (Code Sec. 263A(g)(2))

Property acquired for resale includes intangible as well as tangible property. Resellers must capitalize the acquisition cost of property acquired for resale, as well as certain indirect costs properly allocable to property acquired for resale. (Reg § 1.263A-1(e)) However, a reseller isn't required to capitalize handling and storage costs incurred at a retail sales facility. (Reg § 1.263A-3(c))

"Property" doesn't include (and so allocable costs don't have to be capitalized for):

. . . Any property produced by the taxpayer for use by the taxpayer other than in a trade or business or an activity conducted for profit. (Code Sec. 263A(c)(1))[30]

. . . Any property produced by the taxpayer under a long-term contract (Code Sec. 263A(c)(4)) except for certain home construction contracts. (Code Sec. 460(e)(1))[31]

. . . Timber and certain ornamental trees. (Code Sec. 263A(c)(5)(A))[32]

Small business exception (gross receipts test) from UNICAP rules. The UNICAP rules

---

20. ¶G-5453
21. ¶G-5495
22. ¶G-5500.1
23. ¶G-5561
24. ¶G-5519
25. ¶G-5518
26. ¶G-5803

27. ¶G-5493
28. ¶G-5461 *et seq.*
29. ¶G-5476
30. ¶G-5466
31. ¶G-5467
32. ¶G-5469

don't apply to any taxpayer (other than a tax shelter prohibited from using the cash receipts and disbursements method of accounting) which meets the Code Sec. 448(c) gross receipts test (¶2814) for any tax year. This is so whether the taxpayer is a producer of tangible property or, for property described in Code Sec. 1221(a)(1), a re-seller of tangible property. The Code Sec. 448(c) test applies even if the taxpayer isn't otherwise subject to Code Sec. 448(a); thus, it applies to individuals. (Code Sec. 263A(i); Reg § 1.263A-1(j))[33]

Simplified method, election; qualifying motor vehicle dealers. Taxpayers who acquire and hold property for resale (such as retailers and wholesalers) may elect a simplified resale method to determine the additional costs properly allocable to the resale property. (Reg § 1.263A-3(d))[34] Qualifying motor vehicle dealerships may (1) treat certain sales facilities as retail sales facilities for purposes of Code Sec. 263A and/or (2) be treated as resellers without production activities for Code Sec. 263A purposes.[35]

For the application of the UNICAP rules to farmers and ranchers, see ¶4519.

¶ 1640 Allocating costs to property under the Uniform Capitalization (UNICAP) rules.

Allocable costs (¶1639) must be allocated to inventory or capitalized as follows:

. . . Direct labor costs are generally allocated by using a specific identification ("tracing") method (Reg § 1.263A-1(g)(2)), but any reasonable method may be used. (Reg § 1.263A-1(f)(4))

. . . Indirect costs should be allocated to particular production, resale, etc., activities using either a specific identification method, the standard cost method, or a method using burden rates, such as ratios based on direct costs, hours, or other items, or similar formulas, so long as the method employed reasonably allocates indirect costs among production, resale, etc., activities. (Reg § 1.263A-1(g)(3)) Taxpayers may be able to use simplified methods such as the simplified production method (Reg § 1.263A-2) and the simplified resale method. (Reg § 1.263A-3)[36]

¶ 1641 Interest capitalization rules—Uniform Capitalization (UNICAP) Rules.

A taxpayer must capitalize interest paid or incurred during a production period that is allocable to property he or she produces if that property (1) has a long useful life (it is real property or property with a class life of 20 years or more); (2) has an estimated production period exceeding two years; or (3) has an estimated production period exceeding one year and a cost exceeding $1 million. (Code Sec. 263A(f)(1); Reg § 1.263A-8(b)(1))[37]

The taxpayer must also capitalize any interest on debt allocable to an asset needed to produce the above property. (Code Sec. 263A(f)(3); Reg § 1.263A-8(a)(2)) A taxpayer must capitalize interest whether he or she produces the property for his or her own use or for sale.

The "production period" begins on the date production of the property begins and ends on the date it is ready to be placed in service or is ready to be held for sale. (Code Sec. 263A(f)(5)(B))[38]

Interest isn't capitalized for real or personal property acquired solely for resale.[39]

A taxpayer doesn't capitalize interest allocable to property that's not subject to the capitalization rules, such as property produced under a long-term contract (see the discussion of this and other exceptions at ¶1639). (Reg § 1.263A-8(d)(2)(v)(A)) Thus, a taxpayer who produces property under a long term contract capitalizes interest only to the extent he or she doesn't report income under the percentage of completion method.[40]

33. ¶G-5479 *et seq.*
34. ¶G-5701 *et seq.*
35. ¶G-5526.1
36. ¶G-5458

37. ¶L-5920
38. ¶L-5922
39. ¶L-5901
40. ¶L-5904

Allocating interest to produced property. Interest is allocable to property a taxpayer produces if the taxpayer incurred or continued the underlying debt to finance the construction or production of the property.

A taxpayer is treated as having incurred or continued debt to finance the production of income: (1) where the debt can be specifically traced to production expenditures, and (2) where the debt can't be so traced, but where production or construction expenditures exceed the debt that is directly traceable. (Reg § 1.263A-9(a)(2))[41]

The interest on the debt incurred or continued to finance production is allocated to the property produced as follows:[42]

(1) interest (other than qualified residence interest) on a debt that is directly attributable to production expenditures for the produced property is assigned to that property (Code Sec. 263A(f)(2)(A)(i); Reg § 1.263A-9(a)(2)(i)(A)); and

(2) interest on any other debt is assigned to the produced property to the extent that the taxpayer's interest costs could have been reduced if production expenditures (not attributable to the debt in (1), above) had not been incurred (Code Sec. 263A(f)(2)(A)(ii); Reg § 1.263A-9(a)(2)(i)(B)) (that is, had the expenditures that were incurred for construction been used instead to repay the debt).

Except as provided in regs, a flow-through entity applies the interest allocation rules at the entity level and then, to the extent the entity has insufficient debt to support the production or construction expenditures, at the beneficiary level. (Code Sec. 263A(f)(2)(C))[43]

---

41. ¶L-5914
42. ¶L-5914
43. ¶L-5918

Chapter 4   Interest Expense—Taxes—Losses—Bad Debts

¶ 1700   Deduction for Interest. ▰▰▰▰▰▰▰▰▰▰▰▰▰▰▰▰▰▰▰▰▰▰▰▰▰

Interest paid or accrued during the tax year is generally deductible whether or not incurred in a trade or business. But personal interest is nondeductible (¶1717 *et seq.*), and deductions are limited for business interest (¶1710), investment interest (¶1726 *et seq.*), qualified residence interest (¶1729 *et seq.*), passive activity interest (¶1797 *et seq.*) and qualified education loan interest (¶2220 *et seq.*).

¶ 1701   What is deductible interest? Valid underlying debt; definitely ascertainable interest.

For purposes of Code Sec. 163, interest is "the compensation allowed by law or fixed by the parties for use, or forbearance, or detention of money." Whether the payment is designated as interest is not controlling. To be deductible, there must be a valid underlying debt, and the amount of interest must be definitely ascertainable.[1]

¶ 1702   Deducting interest on a mortgage on real property.

Under Reg § 1.163-1(b), interest on a mortgage on real property (including a condominium or co-op, ¶1716) is deductible, subject to limitations. (Reg § 1.163-1(b))[2] For "points," see ¶1703. For deductibility of prepayment penalties and late payment charges, see ¶1705. For who deducts mortgage interest, see ¶1715.

Ⓡ*caution:* Interest on a home mortgage must be "qualified residence interest" (¶1729 *et seq.*) to be deductible.

¶ 1703   "Points"—interest deduction.

For purposes of the deduction of mortgage interest under Reg § 1.163-1(b) (see ¶1702), deductible "points" (loan fees that are a specified percentage of the amount borrowed) paid to a lender out of a borrower's own funds to get a loan are deductible as interest *only* if they are *solely* for the use or forbearance of money and not a charge for services. Points paid in lieu of service charges (e.g., a one-point charge for appraisal, etc.) and "commitment fees" for the lender's agreement to make a future loan are not deductible as interest.[3]

For when to deduct points, see ¶1738; for home mortgage points, see ¶1739.

¶ 1704   Finance charges and credit card fees as deductible interest.

For purposes of Code Sec. 163, subject to the bar on deducting personal interest (¶1717), finance charges on credit cards, revolving charge accounts, and similar credit arrangements are deductible as interest, since these amounts are based on the amount deferred and the length of the deferral. Credit card fees imposed for cash, check, or overdraft advances are deductible as interest if the payment isn't a service charge.[4]

¶ 1705   Prepayment penalties and late payment charges as deductible interest.

For purposes of Code Sec. 163, a penalty paid for prepaying a debt (including a mortgage) is deductible as interest, as is a late payment charge that isn't a service charge.[5]

---

1. ¶K-5020 *et seq.*, ¶K-5060 *et seq.*
2. ¶K-5043
3. ¶K-5026

4. ¶K-5029
5. ¶K-5033, K-5034

References beginning with a single letter are to paragraphs in Federal Tax Coordinator 2d and RIA's Analysis of Federal Taxes: Income.

¶ 1706 Deductibility of interest and carrying charges on installment purchases and deferred tuition; 6% rule.

For purposes of Code Sec. 163, interest on installment purchases that is separately stated or definitely determinable and provable is deductible as interest, subject to the rules for credit cards (¶1704). For deduction of "unstated interest," see ¶1707.

If carrying charges (including finance charges, service charges, etc.) on an installment purchase of personal property or educational services are *separately stated*, but the amount of *interest* included in the charges can't be ascertained, the installment payments are considered to include a 6% interest charge based on the average unpaid balance under the contract during the tax year. (Code Sec. 163(b); Reg § 1.163-2)[6]

¶ 1707 Deductibility of unstated interest on deferred payment sales.

For purposes of Code Sec. 163, if property is sold in a deferred payment sale and the parties don't provide for an adequate interest charge on the deferred payments, part of each payment made by the buyer may be treated as "unstated interest" and may be deducted under certain rules, see ¶1306 *et seq.* (Code Sec. 483(a); Reg § 1.483-1)[7]

The unstated interest rules don't apply to (1) purchases of personal use property (Code Sec. 1275(b)(1)) or (2) payments made on account of an installment purchase of personal property where payments include separately-stated carrying charges otherwise treated as interest (¶1706). (Code Sec. 483(d)(3))[8]

¶ 1708 Deductibility of interest on taxes; nondeductibility of interest on tax underpayments attributable to undisclosed "listed" or "reportable" transactions.

Interest on delinquent tax payments is deductible as interest under Code Sec. 163 to the extent allowable.[9] Thus, interest on sales, excise and similar taxes incurred in connection with a taxpayer's business or investment activities may be deducted. But interest paid by a noncorporate taxpayer on income tax underpayments, or on debt used to pay those taxes, is nondeductible personal interest (¶1717). (Reg § 1.163-9T(b)(2))[10]

No deduction is allowed for interest on tax underpayments attributable to certain "listed" or "reportable" transactions that the taxpayer hasn't adequately disclosed. (Code Sec. 163(m))[11]

¶ 1709 Corporate debt or equity; "thin" capitalization—interest deduction.

Under Code Sec. 385(c), the corporate issuer's characterization (at issuance) of a corporate instrument as stock or debt is binding on the issuer and all holders (unless the holder discloses inconsistent treatment on his or her return), but is not binding on IRS. (Code Sec. 385(c))[12] If IRS determines that a corporation's debt obligations should be treated as equity (stock), it will treat "interest" paid on the securities as nondeductible dividends, see ¶1711. Under Code Sec. 385(a) and Code Sec. 385(b), IRS is authorized to prescribe regs for determining whether an interest in a corporation is treated as stock or debt, based on factors such as whether the corporation is thinly capitalized.[13]

IRS and the courts have developed tests for determining whether corporate debt should be treated as stock for tax purposes, particularly for purposes of the interest deduction.[14]

---

6. ¶K-5151
7. ¶K-5280 *et seq.*; ¶K-5283
8. ¶K-5281 *et seq.*
9. ¶K-5048
10. ¶K-5513
11. ¶K-5506.1
12. ¶K-5791.1 *et seq.*
13. ¶K-5790 *et seq.*
14. ¶K-5800 *et seq.*

¶ 1710 Interest deduction limited to 30% of adjusted taxable income for businesses with average gross receipts over $27 million—Form 8990.

Code Sec. 163(j) limits the deduction for net business interest expense to 30% of the adjusted taxable income of the business. (Code Sec. 163(j)(1); Reg § 1.163(j)-2(b)(1); Code Sec. 163(j)(10)(A)(i); Reg § 1.163(j)-2(b)(2)(i)) Disallowed business interest may be carried forward indefinitely, see below.

Exceptions. The Code Sec. 163(j) limitation doesn't apply to a taxpayer that meets the Code Sec. 448(c) gross receipts test (i.e., has average annual gross receipts for the 3-tax-year period before the testing year of no more than *$27 million* for testing years beginning in 2022 and no more than *$29 million* for testing years beginning in 2023, see ¶2814). (Code Sec. 163(j)(3); Reg § 1.163(j)-2(d)(1))[15]

Real property trades or businesses can elect out of Code Sec. 163(j), but must then use the alternative depreciation system (ADS) to depreciate certain real property held by the trade or business, see ¶1927. (Code Sec. 163(j)(7)(A)(ii); Reg § 1.163(j)-9(b)(1))[16]

Farming businesses can also elect out, but must use ADS to depreciate any property used in the farming business with a recovery period of ten years or more, see ¶1927. (Code Sec. 163(j)(7)(A)(iii))[17]

The limitation doesn't apply to interest on "floor plan financing," defined as financing to acquire motor vehicles, boats, or farm machinery for sale or lease that is secured by that inventory. (Code Sec. 163(j)(1)(C); Reg § 1.163(j)-2(b)(1)(iii); Code Sec. 163(j)(9)(A); Reg § 1.163(j)-1(b)(19))[18]

Performing services as an employee isn't considered a "trade or business" for the business interest limitation. (Code Sec. 163(j)(7))[19]

Regs. IRS has issued regs on the business interest limitation. (Reg § 1.163(j)-1 through Reg § 1.163(j)-11; Prop Reg. § 1.163(j)-8)

Adjusted taxable income is the taxpayer's taxable income, computed without regard to any: (i) items of non-business income, gain, deduction, or loss; (ii) business interest or business interest income; (iii) net operating loss deduction (¶1815); and (iv) qualified business income deduction (¶1593). (Code Sec. 163(j)(8); Reg § 1.163(j)-1(b)(1))[20]

Carryover. Any interest that isn't deductible because of the business interest limitation may be carried forward indefinitely and is treated as business interest in the year to which it is carried. (Code Sec. 163(j)(2); Reg § 1.163(j)-2(c)(1))[21]

Partnerships and S corporations. The business interest limitation applies to partnerships at the partnership level. Any deduction for business interest is taken into account in determining the partnership's nonseparately stated taxable income or loss. Each partner's adjusted taxable income is determined without regard to the partner's distributive share of any of the partnership's items of income, gain, deduction, or loss. (Code Sec. 163(j)(4)(A)) Special carryover rules apply. (Code Sec. 163(j)(4)(B)) Similar rules apply to S corporations, but without the special carryover rules. (Code Sec. 163(j)(4)(D))[22]

¶ 1711 No deduction for interest on corporate debt payable in issuer's stock/equity; disqualified debt instrument.

Under Code Sec. 163(l)(1), no deduction is allowed for interest paid or accrued or original issue discount (OID, ¶1742) on a disqualified debt instrument. (Code Sec. 163(l)(1))

---

15. ¶K-5429
16. ¶K-5431 *et seq.*
17. ¶K-5432 *et seq.*
18. ¶K-5421; ¶K-5426

19. ¶K-5430
20. ¶K-5425
21. ¶K-5427, K-5444
22. ¶K-5440 *et seq.*

A *disqualified debt instrument* is any corporate debt (or debt issued by a partnership to the extent of its corporate partners) payable in (1) equity (stock) of the issuer or a related party (under Code Sec. 267(b), ¶2444, or Code Sec. 707(b), ¶3723), or (2) equity held by the issuer (or any related party) in any other person. (Code Sec. 163(l)(2), Code Sec. 163(l)(6)) But it doesn't include certain debt issued by dealers in securities. (Code Sec. 163(l)(5))[23]

A debt instrument is treated as payable in equity if it is required that, or if at the issuer's or related party's option, (i) a substantial amount of the principal or interest is convertible into equity, (ii) a substantial amount of the principal or interest is determined by reference to the value of the equity, or (iii) the indebtedness is part of an arrangement that is reasonably expected to result in a conversion or determination as described in (i) or (ii). (Code Sec. 163(l)(3))[24]

¶ 1712 Deduction barred for disqualified related party interest or royalties paid or accrued in hybrid transactions or with hybrid entities.

Under Code Sec. 267A(a), taxpayers can't deduct any "disqualified related party amount" paid or accrued under a hybrid transaction or by, or to, a hybrid entity (an entity treated as fiscally transparent for U.S. tax law purposes but not the tax law of the foreign country in which it is resident, or vice versa). (Code Sec. 267A(a)) A disqualified related party amount is, in general, any interest or royalty paid or accrued to a related party to the extent that (a) the amount isn't included in the related party's income under the tax law of the country of which the related party is a resident for tax purposes or is subject to tax, or (b) the related party is allowed a deduction for that amount under the tax law of that country. (Code Sec. 267A(b))[25]

¶ 1713 Who may deduct interest? Treatment of guarantors, endorsers, indemnitors, and other secondary obligors.

Generally, a taxpayer's interest deduction is limited to interest the taxpayer pays or accrues on his or her *own* indebtedness, and is not allowed for interest the taxpayer pays or accrues on debts of others.[26] Joint obligors may each deduct the amount of interest each actually pays on the debt.[27]

A taxpayer who pays interest on a debt as a guarantor, endorser, indemnitor, or other type of secondary obligor is not entitled to an interest deduction. But under limited circumstances, the guarantor may be treated as primarily liable for the debt, and allowed an interest deduction.[28]

¶ 1714 Interest paid by a person other than the taxpayer; taxpayer's agent—interest deduction.

A taxpayer can deduct interest on the taxpayer's debt that was paid by another person if the payor is acting (or is treated as acting) as the taxpayer's agent (e.g., where a tenant pays the interest on his or her landlord's mortgage) or if the taxpayer has given some consideration for the payor's payment.[29]

¶ 1715 Who can deduct mortgage interest; joint owners.

Under Reg § 1.163-1(b), a taxpayer can deduct mortgage interest payments that he or she actually makes on property of which the taxpayer is the legal or equitable owner (subject to the "qualified residence interest" limits, ¶1729), even if the taxpayer isn't directly liable for the mortgage debt. (Reg § 1.163-1(b)) A taxpayer who is personally liable

---

23. ¶K-5507 *et seq.*
24. ¶K-5508
25. ¶O-3700
26. ¶K-5120 *et seq.*
27. ¶K-5130
28. ¶K-5133
29. ¶K-5129

for a mortgage debt is entitled to a deduction for otherwise deductible mortgage interest payments actually made, even if the taxpayer no longer owns the mortgaged property.[30]

Where joint owners of mortgaged property are jointly liable on the mortgage, each owner may deduct the mortgage interest actually paid out of separate funds. If the mortgage interest is paid from a joint bank account in which each has an equal interest, each is presumed to have paid an equal amount, absent evidence to the contrary.[31]

¶ 1716 Cooperative housing corporation's (co-op's) mortgage payments; treatment of tenant-stockholders—interest deduction.

Under Code Sec. 216, tenant-stockholders of co-ops deduct their share of the co-op's mortgage interest payments (subject to the "qualified residence interest" limits, ¶1729). (Code Sec. 216)[32]

¶ 1717 No deduction for personal interest of noncorporate taxpayers.

Under Code Sec. 163(h)(1), noncorporate taxpayers can't deduct "personal interest." (Code Sec. 163(h)(1)) Personal interest is all interest *other than* (1) interest on trade or business debt; (2) qualified education loan interest (¶2220 *et seq.*); (3) qualified residence interest (¶1729 *et seq.*); (4) passive activity interest (¶1797 *et seq.*); (5) investment interest (¶1727); and (6) interest on certain deferred estate tax payments. (Code Sec. 163(h)(2))[33]

¶ 1718 Net direct interest expense—market discount bonds—interest deduction.

Under Code Sec. 1277(a), a taxpayer's "net direct interest expense" with respect to any taxable market discount bond (¶1325) is deductible in a tax year only to the extent the expense exceeds the market discount allocable to the days during the year that the taxpayer held the bond. (Code Sec. 1277(a); Code Sec. 1278(a)(1)(C))[34] The disallowed interest expenses are deductible the year the bond is disposed of (Code Sec. 1277(b)(2)(A)), or earlier if the taxpayer so elects, to the extent that the taxpayer has net interest income from the bond. (Code Sec. 1277(b)(1))[35]

"Net direct interest expense" is any excess of (1) interest paid or accrued on debt incurred or continued to buy or carry a market discount bond, over (2) interest (including OID, ¶1313) includible in income for the tax year with respect to the bond. (Code Sec. 1277(c))[36]

¶ 1719 Net direct interest expense—short-term government obligations—interest deduction.

Under Code Sec. 1282(a), the "net direct interest expense" (¶1718) for a short-term government obligation is deductible in a tax year only to the extent the expense exceeds the total of (1) the daily portions of the acquisition discount for each day during the year that the taxpayer held the obligation, plus (2) the amount of any other (stated) interest payable on the obligation that accrued during the tax year while the taxpayer held the obligation and that, because of the taxpayer's accounting method, wasn't included in his or her gross income. (Code Sec. 1282(a))[37]

A deduction for disallowed interest expense generally is deferred until the taxpayer disposes of the obligation, or earlier if the taxpayer so elects where there is "net interest

30. ¶K-5135, K-5136
31. ¶K-5130, K-5138
32. ¶K-5140, K-5900 *et seq.*
33. ¶K-5510, K-5511

34. ¶K-5341
35. ¶K-5343
36. ¶K-5342
37. ¶K-5344

income" from the bond. (Code Sec. 1282(c))[38]

A "short-term obligation" is any bond, debenture, note, certificate, or other evidence of indebtedness that has a fixed maturity date not more than 1 year from the date of issue. (Code Sec. 1283(a)(1))

¶ 1720   Interest on business life insurance, annuity or endowment contract loans; policy covering "key person"—interest deduction.

In general, under Code Sec. 264(a)(4), no deduction is allowed for interest paid or accrued on debt for a life insurance policy owned by the taxpayer covering the life of any individual, or any annuity or endowment contract owned by the taxpayer covering any individual. (Code Sec. 264(a)(4))

A taxpayer *may*, however, deduct a limited amount of interest (if not barred by the rules at ¶1721), subject to certain rate limitations, paid or accrued with respect to policies or contracts covering a "key person" (an officer or 20% owner) to the extent that the aggregate amount of the debt doesn't exceed $50,000. The number of a taxpayer's key persons may not exceed the greater of (1) five individuals or (2) the lesser of 20 individuals or 5% of the taxpayer's officers and employees. (Code Sec. 264(e))[39]

¶ 1721   Single premium life insurance, endowment and annuity contracts; borrowing against life insurance contracts; inside buildup; plan-of-purchase borrowing—interest deduction.

Single premium life insurance, endowment and annuity contracts. Under Code Sec. 264(a)(2), no deduction is allowed for interest on debt incurred or continued to buy or carry single premium life insurance, endowment or annuity contracts. (Code Sec. 264(a)(2); Reg § 1.264-2) A contract is "single premium" if "substantially all" the premiums are paid within four years from the purchase date, or if an amount is deposited with the insurer for payment of a "substantial" number of future premiums on the contract. (Code Sec. 264(c))[40]

Plan-of-purchase borrowing against life insurance contracts. No deduction is allowed for interest on debt incurred or continued to buy or carry a life insurance, endowment or annuity contract under a plan of purchase that contemplates the systematic direct or indirect borrowing of part or all of the increases in the contract's cash value from the insurer or another party (e.g., a bank). (Code Sec. 264(a)(3))[41] Borrowing for more than three years is presumed to be a plan. (Reg § 1.264-4(c)(1)) However, under exceptions to this rule, interest is deductible, among other circumstances, if the debt is incurred because of an unforeseen loss of income or a substantial increase in financial obligations, or in connection with a taxpayer's trade or business. (Code Sec. 264(d); Reg § 1.264-4(d))[42]

Inside buildup—denial of interest deduction for policies held by non-individuals. Generally, no deduction is allowed for the portion of the interest expense allocable to unborrowed policy cash values (i.e., the cash surrender value of all life insurance, annuity, or endowment policies issued after June 8, '97, less loans on the policies). Total interest expense (not just that related to life insurance debt) is allocated to the policy cash values in a pro rata manner according to the average adjusted basis for all assets. The disallowance rule doesn't apply to policies held by individuals. (Code Sec. 264(f))[43]

---

38. ¶K-5343
39. ¶K-5351 *et seq.*
40. ¶K-5570 *et seq.*

41. ¶K-5581 *et seq.*
42. ¶K-5582, K-5584
43. ¶K-5601, ¶K-5604

¶ 1722 Loans from qualified employer plans to plan participants or beneficiaries—interest deduction.

Under Code Sec. 72(p)(3), no deduction is allowed for interest paid on a loan from a qualified employer plan to a plan participant, or to a beneficiary of the participant, that isn't treated as a distribution, for the period (1) on or after the first day the individual to whom the loan is made is a key employee (defined in Code Sec. 416(i)), or (2) during which the loan is secured by amounts attributable to elective deferrals under a Code Sec. 401(k) plan (¶4305) or a Code Sec. 403(b) annuity (¶4375 *et seq.*). (Code Sec. 72(p)(3))[44]

¶ 1723 Loans to buy or carry tax-exempt securities—interest deduction.

Under Code Sec. 265(a), no deduction is allowed for interest on debt incurred or continued to buy or carry tax-exempt securities (e.g., state or local bonds, ¶1330) (Code Sec. 265(a)(2)), or stock of a mutual fund (¶4201) distributing exempt interest. (Code Sec. 265(a)(4))[45]

¶ 1724 Registration-required obligations—interest deduction.

Code Sec. 163(f)(1) bars a deduction for interest on "registration-required obligations" (defined in Code Sec. 163(f)(2)) that are not in registered form. (Code Sec. 163(f)(1))[46]

¶ 1725 Corporate acquisition indebtedness—interest deduction.

Code Sec. 279 limits the amount of a corporation's deductions for interest paid or accrued on indebtedness incurred to acquire the stock or assets of other corporations. The maximum annual deduction for such interest is $5 million, less the amount of interest paid or incurred by the corporation during the year on debt incurred to fund an acquisition, but that is not corporate acquisition indebtedness. "Corporate acquisition indebtedness" is debt that meets the tests for acquisition purpose, subordination, convertibility, and debt-equity or interest coverage. (Code Sec. 279)[47]

¶ 1726 Investment Interest Deduction Limitation—Form 4952. ■■■■■■■■■■

The amount of investment interest (¶1727) that a noncorporate taxpayer may deduct in any tax year generally is limited to the taxpayer's "net investment income" (¶1728) for the year. (Code Sec. 163(d)(1)) Form 4952 is used to compute the limitation.[48]

Interest that is disallowed because of this limit can be carried over and deducted in later years, subject to the later year's investment income limit. (Code Sec. 163(d)(2))[49]

¶ 1727 "Investment interest" defined—Form 4952.

Code Sec. 163(d)(3)(A) defines "investment interest" as interest paid or accrued on indebtedness properly allocable to property held for investment. (Code Sec. 163(d)(3)(A)) The deduction limit on investment interest (¶1726) doesn't apply to interest expense that must be capitalized (e.g., construction interest) or that is disallowed under Code Sec. 265 (¶1723).[50]

Property held for investment is (1) any property that produces income properly allocable to portfolio income under the passive activity rules (¶1802); and (2) any interest in an activity involving a trade or business in which taxpayer doesn't materially participate, if

---

44. ¶K-5506, H-11065 *et seq.*
45. ¶K-5520 *et seq.*, ¶K-5546
46. ¶K-5550 *et seq.*
47. ¶K-5405 *et seq.*

48. ¶K-5310 *et seq.*
49. ¶K-5321
50. ¶K-5312 *et seq.*

that activity isn't "passive" (see ¶1798). (Code Sec. 163(d)(5)(A))[1]

¶ 1728 "Net investment income" defined—Form 4952—investment interest limitation.

Code Sec. 163(d)(4)(A) defines a taxpayer's "net investment income" (¶1726) for a tax year is the excess of "investment income" over "investment expenses" for the year. (Code Sec. 163(d)(4)(A))[2] (For the definition of net investment income for alternative minimum tax purposes, see ¶3206.)

"Investment income" is gross income from property held for investment (¶1727) including *net gain* on the disposition of that property. *Net capital gain* is not treated as investment income, unless the taxpayer elects (on Form 4952) to include it in investment income. For the effect of such an election on net capital gain, see ¶2603. Qualified dividend income (defined at ¶1288) is included in investment income only to the extent the taxpayer so elects on Form 4952. (Code Sec. 163(d)(4)(B); Reg § 1.163(d)-1)[3]

"Investment expenses" are deductible expenses, other than interest, that are directly connected with the production of investment income, such as depreciation or depletion on assets that produce investment income. Nonbusiness bad debts (¶1827) directly connected with the production of income are taken into account to the extent they are currently deductible.[4]

Investment income and expenses don't include any amounts taken into account in computing income or loss from a passive activity (¶1797 *et seq.*). (Code Sec. 163(d)(4)(D))[5]

¶ 1729 Qualified Residence Interest.

A taxpayer may claim an itemized deduction for qualified residence interest. "Qualified residence interest" is interest (subject to dollar limits) paid or accrued during the tax year on acquisition indebtedness (¶1730) with respect to any qualified residence (¶1732) of the taxpayer. Home equity indebtedness (¶1731) is nondeductible from 2018 to 2025, though interest on certain loans *labeled* home equity loans may be deductible based on the use of the proceeds. (Code Sec. 163(h)(3)(A))[6]

¶ 1730 "Acquisition debt" defined.

Code Sec. 163(h)(3)(B)(i) defines "acquisition indebtedness" (¶1729) as debt that is incurred in acquiring, constructing or substantially improving a taxpayer's "qualified residence" (¶1732) (or adjoining land) and is secured by that qualified residence. Debt that a taxpayer incurs to refinance his or her acquisition indebtedness also qualifies, but only up to the amount of the refinanced debt. (Code Sec. 163(h)(3)(B)(i))[7]

Generally, the aggregate amount of debt for any period that may be treated as acquisition indebtedness can't exceed $750,000 ($375,000 for a married individual filing a separate return). (Code Sec. 163(h)(3)(F)(i)(II))[8] But a $1 million limitation ($500,000 for a married separate filer) applies (Code Sec. 163(h)(3)(B)(ii)) to: (i) debt incurred on or before Dec. 15, 2017; (Code Sec. 163(h)(3)(F)(i)(III)) (ii) binding contracts entered into before Dec. 15, 2017, to close on the purchase of a principal residence before Jan. 1, 2018, where the purchase was completed before Apr. 1, 2018; (Code Sec. 163(h)(3)(F)(i)(IV)) and (iii) refinancing of qualified residence debt that was incurred on or before Dec. 15, 2017, up to the amount of the refinanced debt. (Code Sec. 163(h)(3)(F)(iii))[9]

1. ¶K-5322
2. ¶K-5311
3. ¶K-5315 *et seq.*
4. ¶K-5320
5. ¶s K-5315, K-5320

6. ¶K-5471
7. ¶K-5484
8. ¶K-5485
9. ¶K-5486

Where unmarried taxpayers are co-owners of a qualified residence, the acquisition indebtedness limit applies on a per-taxpayer basis, not a per-residence basis.[10]

For where debt exceeds these limits, see ¶1735.

Qualified mortgage insurance means mortgage insurance provided by the Veterans Administration (VA), the Federal Housing Administration (FHA), or the Rural Housing Administration (RHA), and private mortgage insurance. (Code Sec. 163(h)(4)(E)(ii))

¶ 1731　Home equity indebtedness—qualified residence interest (QRI).

Code Sec. 163(h)(3)(C)(i) defines home equity indebtedness (¶1729) as any debt (other than acquisition indebtedness, ¶1730) secured by taxpayer's qualified residence (¶1732), to the extent the aggregate amount of the debt doesn't exceed the residence's fair market value reduced by any acquisition debt on the residence. (Code Sec. 163(h)(3)(C)(i))

Interest on home equity indebtedness is nondeductible from 2018 to 2025. (Code Sec. 163(h)(3)(F)(i)(I)) However, taxpayers can still deduct interest on a loan that is *labeled* a home equity loan, home equity line of credit (HELOC), or second mortgage, if the loan is used to buy, build or substantially improve the taxpayer's home that secures the loan, to the extent the loan doesn't exceed the limitation on acquisition indebtedness (¶1730).[11]

¶ 1732　Qualified residence—qualified residence interest (QRI).

Code Sec. 163(h)(4)(A) defines a qualified residence (¶1729) as a taxpayer's principal residence and/or any other residence (second residence) the taxpayer elects to treat as qualified for the tax year, even if the taxpayer didn't use it as a residence that year. But a second residence that a taxpayer rents out to others can't qualify unless the taxpayer also uses it as a residence during the year for more than the greater of 14 days or 10% of the number of days it is rented out for a fair rental. (Code Sec. 163(h)(4)(A); Reg § 1.163-10T(p)(3)(iii))

A taxpayer may elect a different residence for each tax year to be the taxpayer's second residence. (Code Sec. 163(h)(4)(A)(i); Reg § 1.163-10T(p)(3)(iv))[12]

A residence for this purpose includes a condominium, cooperative housing corporation (co-op) and a time-share. (Code Sec. 163(h)(4)(B); Reg § 1.163-10T(p)(3)(ii); Reg § 1.163-10T(p)(6))[13] A residence under construction may be treated as a qualified residence for a period of up to 24 months, but only if it otherwise qualifies as of the time it's ready for occupancy. (Reg § 1.163-10T(p)(5))[14]

Spouses filing a joint return may treat their common principal residence, as well as property that otherwise qualifies as a second residence and that is owned either jointly or by one spouse only, as a qualified residence. For spouses filing separately, each spouse can treat only one residence as a qualified residence, unless both spouses consent in writing to permit one spouse to elect both the principal residence and one other residence as qualified residences. (Code Sec. 163(h)(4)(A)(ii))[15]

¶ 1733　Allocation Rules for Interest and Debt. ▰▰▰▰▰

All taxpayers (other than widely-held C corporations) must allocate interest expense for purposes of applying the passive activity loss limitation (¶1798), investment interest limitation (¶1726) and personal interest limitation (¶1717). Interest expense is allocated in the same manner as the debt on which the interest is paid. Debt is allocated by tracing the use of the borrowed money. (Reg § 1.163-8T(a)(3), Reg § 1.163-8T(c)(1), Reg § 1.163-8T(a)(4)(i))[16]

---

10. ¶K-5485
11. ¶K-5491
12. ¶K-5475 *et seq.*
13. ¶K-5480, K-5481
14. ¶K-5482
15. ¶K-5479
16. ¶K-5231, K-5232

¶ 1734   How debt and interest expense are allocated—interest allocation rules.

Under Reg § 1.163-8T(a)(3) and Reg § 1.163-8T(c)(1), where the proceeds of a single debt are used for multiple purposes—e.g., to make investments *and* to buy "personal" items—the debt is allocated by tracing disbursements of the debt proceeds to specific expenditures. (Reg § 1.163-8T(a)(3), Reg § 1.163-8T(c)(1))[17]

Debt is allocated to an expenditure for the period (1) beginning on the date the proceeds of the debt are used or treated as used to make the expenditure, and (2) ending on the date the debt is repaid or reallocated, whichever is earlier. (Reg § 1.163-8T(c)(2)(i))[18]

Interest expense that accrues on a debt is generally allocated in the same manner as the debt is allocated, regardless of when the interest is actually paid. (Reg § 1.163-8T(c)(2)(ii)(A))[19]

Where there has been a change in the use of debt proceeds or of assets bought with debt proceeds, the interest on the debt must be reallocated to the new use. The interest so reallocated will be subject to any appropriate deduction limits (¶1733). (Reg § 1.163-8T(j)(1))[20]

¶ 1735   Qualified residence interest not subject to allocation rules.

Qualified residence interest (¶1729 *et seq.*) is deductible without regard to how that interest expense or the underlying debt is allocated under the allocation rules (¶1734).[21]

But, where the debt exceeds the qualified residence interest limits (¶1730, ¶1731), allocation is required for the excess. (Reg § 1.163-10T(e))[22]

¶ 1736   When Interest May Be Deducted. ▐▬▬▬▬▬▬▬▬▬▬

The proper time for deducting interest is generally determined by the taxpayer's accounting method. Special rules govern when mortgage "points" (¶1738 *et seq.*), unstated interest (¶1707), and original issue discount (OID; ¶1742 *et seq.*) must be deducted.

¶ 1737   Cash method taxpayer's interest deduction.

Under Code Sec. 163(a), a cash method taxpayer may deduct interest only if it is actually *paid* during the tax year. (Code Sec. 163(a)) (For accrual taxpayers, see ¶1740.) No deduction is allowed if the interest payment is made with funds obtained from the original creditor through a second loan, advance, or any arrangement similar to a loan.[23]

Interest that is contested (i.e., interest the debtor claims not to owe) isn't deductible. But if a cash method taxpayer transfers money or other property to provide for the satisfaction of the asserted (and otherwise deductible) liability, it's deductible in the year of the transfer. (Code Sec. 461(f))[24] For when prepaid interest (including "points") is deductible, see ¶1738.

¶ 1738   Prepaid interest (including "points")—when to deduct interest.

Code Sec. 461(g)(1) provides that, generally, interest that is prepaid, including "points," is deductible only in the tax year to which the interest is allocable. (Code Sec. 461(g)(1)) Cash method taxpayers thus generally deduct points ratably over the term of the loan.[25]

A taxpayer who "pays" points by receiving discounted loan proceeds gets no current

---

17. ¶K-5231
18. ¶K-5233
19. ¶K-5233
20. ¶K-5254 *et seq.*
21. ¶K-5238

22. ¶K-5498 *et seq.*
23. ¶K-5170 *et seq.*
24. ¶G-2442 *et seq.*
25. ¶K-5177

deduction. Instead, the discount is treated as original issue discount (OID), deductible by the borrower under the OID rules (¶1742). Discounts *not* subject to the OID rules may be deducted ratably as the underlying debt is repaid.[26]

For special rules for home mortgage points and points on refinancing, see ¶1739.

¶ 1739 "Points" on a home mortgage—cash method taxpayer's deduction in year of payment or ratably over the life of the mortgage.

Code Sec. 461(g)(2) provides that a cash method taxpayer may currently deduct points paid on indebtedness incurred in connection with the purchase or improvement of (and secured by) a principal residence in the tax year of actual payment or may deduct points ratably over the life of the mortgage (¶1738). The charging of points must reflect an established business practice in the geographical area where the loan is made, and the deduction allowed can't exceed the amount generally charged there. (Code Sec. 461(g)(2))[27]

Under a safe harbor, for loans to acquire a principal residence, cash method taxpayers may currently deduct amounts paid as points that meet the above tests *and* are (1) clearly designated on Form HUD-1 as points incurred in connection with the loan; (2) computed as a percentage of the stated principal amount of the debt; *and* (3) paid directly by taxpayer to the lender (or mortgage broker).[28]

Points paid to refinance an existing mortgage are not incurred in connection with the purchase or improvement of a residence, and thus are not currently deductible.[29]

Points paid by (or charged to) the seller of a residence in connection with a loan to the buyer (taxpayer) are deductible by the buyer if the buyer subtracted them from the purchase price in computing the basis of the residence.[30]

If the mortgage ends early (e.g., because of a prepayment, refinancing, foreclosure or similar event), the amount of capitalized and unamortized points remaining in the year in which the loan ends is deductible.[31]

¶ 1740 Accrual basis taxpayer's interest deduction.

An accrual basis taxpayer deducts interest in the year it accrues (see ¶2823 *et seq.*), without regard to when the taxpayer pays the interest. (For cash basis taxpayers, see ¶1737.)

Interest that is contingent on events other than the creditor's demand for payment does not accrue until the contingency occurs.[32]

A contested liability is not accrued or deductible. But if the accrual basis taxpayer transfers money or other property to provide for the satisfaction of the asserted liability, a deduction is allowed in the year of the transfer. (Code Sec. 461(f))[33]

¶ 1741 Allocation of interest under the "Rule of 78's" method—when to deduct interest.

The Rule of 78's is a method of allocating interest on a loan among time periods during the term of the loan. However, even where a loan agreement provides that interest is earned under the Rule of 78's, no deduction is allowed for interest in excess of the economic accrual of interest.[34]

---

26. ¶K-5176
27. ¶K-5178 *et seq.*
28. ¶K-5179
29. ¶K-5180
30. ¶K-5179, P-1720

31. ¶K-5183
32. ¶s K-5200, K-5201
33. ¶G-2643 *et seq.*
34. ¶K-5153

¶ 1742   Original issue discount (OID)—when to deduct interest.

Under Code Sec. 163(e)(1), an issuer of a debt instrument issued with OID (¶1312 *et seq.*) may, regardless of its accounting method, deduct part of the OID (¶1743) in each tax year the instrument is outstanding, even though the OID isn't paid until maturity. (Code Sec. 163(e)(1); Reg § 1.163-3(a)(1), Reg § 1.163-4(a)(1); Reg § 1.163-7(a)) However, a cash method obligor of a *short-term obligation* can only deduct OID (and other interest payable) when it is paid. (Code Sec. 163(e)(2)(C))[35]

"OID" has the same meaning for this purpose as it does for purposes of requiring the holder to include OID in gross income currently (¶1313), except that the de minimis exception (¶1313) and the offset for acquisition premium (¶1322) don't apply (Code Sec. 163(e)(2)(B))[36] and a special rule applies for certain non-publicly traded debt instruments. (Code Sec. 1275(b)(1))[37]

¶ 1743   Amount of original issue discount (OID) deductible currently—when to deduct interest.

Under Code Sec. 163(e)(2)(B), the amount of OID the issuer of a debt instrument deducts currently (¶1742) is generally determined in the same way as the amount of OID the holder includes in gross income currently using the constant yield method (¶1320). (Code Sec. 163(e)(2)(B); Reg § 1.163-7(a)) An issuer of a debt instrument with a *de minimis* amount of OID may choose to deduct the OID at maturity, on a straight-line basis over the term of the debt instrument, or in proportion to stated interest payments. (Reg § 1.163-7(b)(2)).[38]

¶ 1744   Limits on original issue discount (OID) deduction for applicable high yield debt obligations (AHYDOs)—when to deduct interest.

Code Sec. 163(e)(5) provides that, for certain AHYDOs (with yields at least five percentage points over the applicable federal rate for month of issue) issued after July 10, '89, a C corporation can't deduct a portion of the OID, and the remainder is not deductible until actually paid. However, these rules were suspended for qualified obligations issued after Aug. 31, 2008, and before Jan. 1, 2011. (Code Sec. 163(e)(5))[39]

¶ 1745   Deduction for Taxes. ▆▆▆▆▆▆▆▆▆▆▆▆▆▆

Certain state, local, U.S. possessions and foreign taxes are deductible whether or not connected with a trade or business. Most federal taxes, including federal income tax, are nondeductible. For individuals, the aggregate deduction for nonbusiness taxes is limited to $10,000 ($5,000 for marrieds filing separately).

Only payments that are really taxes (regardless of what they are called) are deductible as taxes. Taxes are charges imposed on persons or property by governmental authority to raise funds for the support of government or for public purposes. Fees imposed primarily as charges for government services, such as fees for a driver's license, car inspection, or passport, aren't deductible as taxes.[40] Penalties paid to a government for violation of a law aren't taxes. (Code Sec. 162(f))[41]

¶ 1746   Deductible and nondeductible taxes.

The following taxes are deductible (subject to the limits on deductions by individuals at ¶1747):

---

35. ¶K-5712, ¶K-5745
36. ¶K-5727, K-5746
37. ¶K-5724
38. ¶K-5745 *et seq.*, ¶K-5748

39. ¶K-5754, K-5755.2
40. ¶K-4003 *et seq.*
41. ¶K-4009

. . . State, local and foreign real property taxes (but individuals may not deduct foreign real property taxes, see ¶1747); (Code Sec. 164(a)(1), Code Sec. 164(b)(6)(A))

. . . State and local personal property taxes (¶1752); (Code Sec. 164(a)(2))

. . . State, local and foreign income, war profits and excess profits taxes; (Code Sec. 164(a)(3))

. . . State and local general sales taxes, if elected in lieu of deducting state and local income taxes (¶1748); (Code Sec. 164(b)(5))

. . . Federal and state generation-skipping transfer (GST) tax imposed on income distributions; (¶5058 *et seq.*) (Code Sec. 164(a)(4), Code Sec. 164(b)(4))

. . . Federal estate tax attributable to income in respect of a decedent; (¶3965)

. . . 50% of the Code Sec. 1401 self-employment tax other than the additional 0.9% Medicare (HI) self-employment tax. (Code Sec. 164(f)(1))[42]

observation: Although the Medicare tax rate on self-employment income in excess of the applicable threshold is 3.8% (¶1109), the deduction for one-half of self-employment taxes is computed based on a 2.9% rate. The additional 0.9% tax will not generate an income tax deduction.

Although taxes not included above (e.g., gasoline, diesel and other motor fuel taxes, Social Security (FICA) and unemployment (FUTA) taxes on employers, motor vehicle registration fees) aren't deductible as *taxes,* they may be deductible as *business expenses* or *expenses for the production of income* (¶1505 et seq.). (Code Sec. 164(a); Reg § 1.164-2(f))[43]

For state unemployment and disability taxes, see ¶1750.

caution: For the deductibility of taxes for alternative minimum tax purposes, see ¶3206.

The following taxes are not deductible, even if incurred with respect to a trade or business or investment-related activity:

(1) Federal income taxes (including amounts withheld from wages, and the alternative minimum tax). (Code Sec. 275(a)(1); Reg § 1.164-2(a))

(2) Social Security (FICA) tax on employees, and Railroad Retirement tax on employees and employee representatives. (Code Sec. 275(a)(1); Reg § 1.164-2(a))

(3) Federal war profits and excess profits taxes. (Code Sec. 275(a)(2); Reg § 1.164-2(b))

(4) Federal estate, inheritance, legacy, succession and gift tax (other than GST). (Code Sec. 275(a)(3); Reg § 1.164-2(c))

(5) Income, war profits and excess profits taxes of any foreign country or U.S. possession for which the taxpayer takes the foreign tax credit (¶2360 *et seq.*). (Code Sec. 275(a)(4); Reg § 1.164-2(d))

(6) Excise taxes imposed on: charities, private foundations, qualified pension plans, REITs and RICs, excess golden parachute payments and greenmail gains (Code Sec. 275(a)(6); Code Sec. 170(f)(10)(F)(iv))[44]

¶ 1747   Limit on itemized deductions of nonbusiness state, local, and foreign taxes by individuals—Schedule A (Form 1040 or 1040-SR).

Code Sec. 164(b)(6) provides that, for individual taxpayers, from 2018 through 2025, the deduction allowed for nonbusiness state, local, and foreign taxes is subject to the following limits:

. . . the aggregate deduction for any tax year for state and local real property, personal

---

42. ¶K-4001; ¶K-4403 *et seq.*   44. ¶L-2358, L-2359
43. ¶K-4000, L-2350 *et seq.*

property, and general sales taxes (if elected, see ¶1748), and state, local, and foreign income, war profits, and excess profits taxes, is limited to $10,000 ($5,000 for marrieds filing separately) (Code Sec. 164(b)(6)(B)); and

. . . foreign real property taxes are nondeductible. (Code Sec. 164(b)(6)(A))

The above limits do not apply to state and local, and foreign, real property taxes; state and local personal property taxes; and foreign income, war profits, and excess profits taxes, if those taxes are paid or accrued in carrying on a trade or business or a Code Sec. 212 activity. (Code Sec. 164(b)(6)) The limit has been found to be constitutional. (State of New York v. Janet Yellen, (2021, CA2), cert den (2022, S Ct))[45]

Some states have implemented workarounds to the $10,000 limit under which taxpayers can make a deductible contribution to a charitable fund and claim a state tax credit for the donation. Regs issued in response to these workarounds require taxpayers that contribute money or property to or for the use of a Code Sec. 170(c) charitable entity to reduce their charitable deduction by the amount of any state or local tax credit received or expected in return for the contribution. (Reg § 1.170A-1(h)(3)(i))

However, the charitable deduction is not reduced if the total amount of the state or local tax credits received or expected to be received is 15% or less of the taxpayer's payment or of the fair market value of the transferred property. (Reg § 1.170A-1(h)(3)(vi)) The reduction also does not apply where the taxpayer receives a state or local tax *deduction*, rather than a *credit*, in return for the contribution. (Reg § 1.170A-1(h)(3)(ii)(A))[46]

Homeowners who have received, or benefited from, a Homeowner Assistance Fund (HAF) payment for tax years 2021 through 2025 can use a safe harbor to calculate their deduction for qualified residence interest and/or real property tax expenses. (Rev. Proc. 2021-47, 2021-48 IRB 775)[47]

The above taxes are deductible for individual taxpayers who itemize. For deduction of taxes by individuals who don't itemize, see ¶1749.

¶ 1748 State and local sales taxes deductible instead of income tax—Schedule A (Form 1040 or 1040-SR).

Under Code Sec. 164(b)(5), individual taxpayers can elect (on Schedule A of Form 1040 or 1040-SR) to deduct state and local *general sales and use* taxes instead of state and local *income* taxes (subject to the dollar limitation described at ¶1747). With limited exceptions, a sales or use tax is *general* if imposed at one rate with respect to the retail sale of a broad range of classes of items. (Code Sec. 164(b)(5); Reg § 1.164-3)[48]

Electing taxpayers can deduct either:

(1) the amount of state and local general sales taxes paid, by accumulating receipts; or

(2) the amount determined under IRS tables, plus the actual amount of sales taxes paid on motor vehicles, boats and other IRS-specified items (e.g., aircraft, homes). (Code Sec. 164(b)(5)(H))[49]

Foreign sales taxes are not deductible under the above rules. (Reg § 1.164-3(f)) The elective sales tax deduction doesn't apply to sales taxes paid on items used in a taxpayer's trade or business.[50]

State or local sales or use taxes paid or incurred in connection with the acquisition or disposition of property, and taxes on the transfer of property (e.g., securities, real estate), aren't deductible. The buyer treats them as part of the cost, the seller as a reduction in the amount realized. (Code Sec. 164(a))[1]

---

45. ¶K-4001
46. ¶K-3032.1 *et seq.*
47. ¶K-4504.2
48. ¶K-4510 *et seq.*

49. ¶K-4511
50. ¶K-4510 *et seq.*
1. ¶I-2502, K-4500, L-2352.1, P-1174.1

¶ 1749 **Taxes deductible by non-itemizers—above-the-line deductions on Form 1040 or 1040-SR.**

Code Sec. 63(d) provides that an individual taxpayer generally may deduct taxes only if the taxpayer itemizes (on Schedule A of Form 1040 or 1040-SR). (Code Sec. 63(d))[2]

The only taxes that are deductible "above the line" (in arriving at adjusted gross income, ¶3102) by individuals who don't itemize are: (1) taxes attributable to a trade or business (Code Sec. 62(a)(1)) or to property held for the production of rents or royalties (Code Sec. 62(a)(4)) and (2) 50% of self-employment taxes (see ¶1746). (Code Sec. 164(f))[3]

¶ 1750 **Deduction of state unemployment and disability taxes.**

Employers' and employees' contributions to state unemployment insurance funds may be deductible under Code Sec. 164(a). Whether contributions to a state unemployment insurance fund or disability plan are deductible as taxes is determined on a state-by-state basis.[4]

¶ 1751 **Local benefit assessments as deductible taxes.**

Under Code Sec. 164(c)(1), the deductibility as taxes of assessments for public improvements, such as sewers, streets, etc., depends on the purpose of the assessment. Taxes assessed against local benefits of a kind tending to increase the value of the property assessed are deductible by proper owners as taxes only to the extent the taxes are properly allocable to repairs, maintenance or interest charges. If it can't be determined what part of the tax is for maintenance, repair or interest, the taxes are not deductible, but may be capitalized (¶1628 *et seq.*). (Code Sec. 164(c)(1); Reg § 1.164-4(b)(1))[5]

¶ 1752 **Personal property taxes imposed by a state or local government— deductibility.**

Under Code Sec. 164, personal property taxes imposed by a state or local government are deductible (subject to the dollar limitation at ¶1747). (Code Sec. 164(a)(2), Code Sec. 164(b)(6)) The tax must be imposed annually on personal property on an ad valorem basis (i.e., based on the property's value). (Code Sec. 164(b)(1))[6]

¶ 1753 **Who deducts the tax? State and local taxes, real property taxes.**

State and local taxes generally are deductible only by the person on whom they are imposed. (Reg § 1.164-1(a))[7]

One who voluntarily pays a tax imposed on another generally isn't entitled to a deduction. But where a corporation pays a tax imposed on a shareholder on his or her interest as a shareholder, and the shareholder does not reimburse the corporation, the deduction is allowed to the corporation and not to the shareholder. (Code Sec. 164(e))[8]

Real property taxes are deductible by the property owner. (For apportionment of real property tax in year of sale, see ¶1762.) A person who owns a beneficial interest in real property may deduct property taxes paid to protect that interest.[9]

Taxes on property that is leased are deductible by the landlord, even if the tenant makes the payment (which the tenant treats as additional rent expense, ¶1575). (Reg § 1.162-11(a)) But a tenant deducts taxes paid on improvements the tenant makes where the

---

2. ¶A-2701
3. ¶L-2351; ¶K-4401
4. ¶K-4003 *et seq.*; ¶L-2353 *et seq.*
5. ¶K-4600 *et seq.*

6. ¶K-4502
7. ¶K-4100 *et seq.*
8. ¶K-4114
9. ¶K-4103

useful life of the improvements will terminate before the end of the lease.[10]

¶ 1754 Married couple's deduction of taxes.

Spouses filing a joint federal return may deduct all deductible taxes paid by either spouse, whether or not they file joint *state* returns.[11]

If the spouses file separate federal and separate state returns, each spouse may deduct only the state income taxes imposed on and actually paid by that spouse. If a joint state return and separate federal returns are filed, then for federal tax purposes, each spouse is entitled to deduct his or her share of the joint state tax, prorated according to each spouse's gross income, but not to exceed the amount actually paid by the spouse.[12]

¶ 1755 Property taxes on co-owned property: tenants in common, tenants by the entirety, and joint tenants with right of survivorship.

An individual's deduction for taxes on property owned with other persons as tenants in common may be limited to the individual's pro rata part of the taxes, i.e., the amount attributable to his or her interest, even if the individual pays *all* the taxes on the property. This pro rata share limit applies where the tenant is only assessed for his or her share or has a right to contribution from the other tenants.[13]

Tenants by the entirety (i.e., spouses) and joint tenants with right of survivorship are entitled to deduct in full the taxes they pay on the jointly-owned property.[14]

¶ 1756 Cooperative and condominium housing realty taxes, deductibility; treatment of tenant-stockholders and condominium owners.

Code Sec. 216 provides that tenant-stockholders of cooperative housing corporations (co-ops) deduct their share of the co-op's real property taxes. (Code Sec. 216)[15] Condominium owners deduct the real property taxes on their individual interests, subject to the dollar limitation (¶1747).[16]

¶ 1757 When cash basis taxpayers deduct taxes.

A cash basis taxpayer's taxes are deductible for the tax year the taxes are paid. State and local taxes withheld from the taxpayer's wages are deductible in the year they are withheld.[17]

Taxes are deductible in the year of payment even if the taxpayer contests the liability and seeks to recover the payment (¶1760).[18]

For estimated tax payments and prepaid taxes, see ¶1758. For accrual basis taxpayers, see ¶1759.

¶ 1758 When prepaid taxes and estimated tax payments are deductible.

A cash basis taxpayer may deduct an advance payment of tax in the year of payment if it's an actual good faith payment and not a mere deposit. But the advance payment of state taxes that are later refunded won't be deductible unless taxpayer had a reasonable basis, at the time of payment, for believing the taxes were owed.[19]

A deduction in the year of payment is also allowed for advance estimated tax payments

---

10. ¶K-4104
11. ¶s K-4105, K-4107
12. ¶s K-4106, K-4108
13. ¶K-4112
14. ¶K-4112

15. ¶K-5900 *et seq.*
16. ¶K-4103
17. ¶K-4201 *et seq.*
18. ¶K-4201
19. ¶K-4203

made under a pay-as-you-go tax collection system.[20]

¶ 1759   When accrual basis taxpayers deduct taxes.

An accrual basis taxpayer deducts a tax liability in the tax year in which all events have occurred that determine the liability, the amount of the liability can be determined with reasonable accuracy, and economic performance (¶2824) has occurred. (Code Sec. 461(h); Reg § 1.461-1(a)(2), Reg § 1.461-4(g)(6))[21] For ratable accrual of real property taxes, see ¶1761.

An accrual basis taxpayer who pays an additional state tax for prior years without protest or appeal must deduct that tax for federal tax purposes in the year the tax was originally due, and not when it is later assessed or paid.[22] For when to deduct a contested tax, see ¶1760.

For cash basis taxpayers, see ¶1757.

¶ 1760   When to deduct contested tax.

An accrual basis taxpayer who contests an assessment through an overt act of protest or suit can't deduct the contested portion of the tax until the contest is ended and the amount determined.[23]

A cash or accrual basis taxpayer who pays a contested liability without giving up the contest may deduct the tax in the year of payment, if otherwise deductible in that (or an earlier) year. (Code Sec. 461(f))[24] But foreign or U.S. possession income, war profits and excess profits tax can't be deducted until the contest is finally determined. (Code Sec. 461(f))[25]

¶ 1761   Election by accrual basis taxpayers to accrue realty taxes ratably—Form 3115.

An accrual basis taxpayer generally deducts real property taxes when paid. Code Sec. 461(c)(1) provides an exception to this rule, under which an accrual basis taxpayer can elect to accrue any real property tax that is related to a definite time period ratably over that period (ratable accrual election). (Code Sec. 461(c)(1); Reg § 1.461-4(g)(6)(iii)(A))[26]

A taxpayer can make the ratable accrual election without IRS consent for the first tax year in which the taxpayer incurs real property taxes. The election must be made by the due date of the return for the election year (including extensions). (Code Sec. 461(c)(2)(A); Reg § 1.461-1(c)(1))

After the first tax year, a taxpayer may make the election to accrue real property taxes ratably at any time, with IRS consent. (Code Sec. 461(c)(2)(B)) Although a written request for IRS consent must be filed within 90 days after the beginning of the first tax year to which the election applies, taxpayers can get an automatic extension that permits an application on Form 3115 at any time during the first tax year.[27] The election is binding unless IRS consents to its revocation. (Reg § 1.461-1(c)(4))[28]

¶ 1762   Apportionment of real property taxes between seller and buyer for year of sale.

Under Code Sec. 164(d), for both cash and accrual taxpayers, the real property tax on property that is sold during the tax year is considered to be imposed:

20. ¶K-4204
21. ¶G-2673, K-4300 *et seq.*
22. ¶K-4320
23. ¶K-4319 *et seq.*
24. ¶s G-2445, G-2645

25. ¶K-4322
26. ¶K-4327 *et seq.*
27. ¶s K-4329, K-4330
28. ¶K-4334

... *on the seller* to the extent properly allocable to that part of the real property tax year (period to which the tax relates) ending on the day before the date of sale; and

... *on the buyer* to the extent properly allocable to that part of the real property tax year beginning on the date of sale. (Code Sec. 164(d); Reg § 1.164-6)[29]

For when the seller or buyer deducts the sale-year realty tax, see ¶1763. For where seller took an excessive deduction, see ¶1764.

¶ 1763   When seller or buyer deducts real property tax.

Under Code Sec. 164(d)(2)(B), an *accrual basis* taxpayer (seller or buyer) deducts his or her share of sale-year realty tax (as apportioned, ¶1762) in the income tax year in which the accrual date (date of sale) falls. If an election to accrue realty taxes ratably (¶1761) is in effect for that year, the share of the tax is deductible in the year it accrues under the election. (Code Sec. 164(d)(2)(B); Reg § 1.164-6(d)(6))[30]

A *cash basis* taxpayer (seller or buyer) deducts his or her portion of the sale-year realty tax in the income tax year he or she pays it. But where the tax isn't payable until after the sale date, or where the other party is liable for the tax under local law, the taxpayer may, as an option, deduct the tax either in the year of sale (whether or not actually paid) or in the year of payment, if later. (Reg § 1.164-6(d)(1); Reg § 1.164-6(d)(2))[31]

¶ 1764   Excessive deduction of real property tax before sale.

Under Reg § 1.164-6(d)(5), if the seller (cash or accrual) deducted more than his or her share of realty taxes on property sold in a later year, and that "excess" tax payment is allocable to and deductible by the buyer (¶1762), the seller is treated as receiving a recovery in the sale year. The seller must include this "recovery" in gross income for the sale year, to the extent a tax benefit (i.e., the excess deduction) was obtained in that earlier year (¶1205). (Reg § 1.164-6(d)(5))[32]

¶ 1765   Deduction for Losses. ▬▬▬▬▬▬▬▬▬▬▬▬▬▬▬▬▬▬▬▬

Taxpayers may sustain a loss when their property is transferred, stolen, destroyed, confiscated, abandoned, taken by foreclosure or becomes worthless, and they receive less than adequate compensation for it. This loss may be deductible (¶1766 *et seq.*).

Taxpayers may deduct losses they sustain that aren't compensated for by insurance or otherwise, subject to the at-risk rules (¶1790 *et seq.*), the passive loss rules (¶1797 *et seq.*), and the other limits discussed in the following paragraphs. (Code Sec. 165(a))[33]

For losses from a sale or exchange, see ¶ 2400 *et seq.*

¶ 1766   What is a deductible loss? Closed and completed transaction requirement.

Under Code Sec. 165, a deductible loss arises when a taxpayer loses or gives up money, property or rights, or when these items lose value as a result of an identifiable event.[34] It must be shown that the taxpayer sustained a loss of a type that is deductible and that the loss was sustained in the tax year. The amount of the loss also must be shown.

To be deductible, a loss must be evidenced by a closed and completed transaction fixed by identifiable events (Reg § 1.165-1(b)), such as a sale, exchange, foreclosure, stock redemption, abandonment, governmental condemnation or seizure. Mere fluctuations in an

---

29. ¶K-4117
30. ¶s K-4129, K-4130
31. ¶K-4127 *et seq.*

32. ¶K-4131
33. ¶M-1000
34. ¶M-1000 *et seq.*

asset's value don't result in deductible losses.[35]

¶ 1767   How much loss is deductible on disposition of property?

Under Code Sec. 165(b), the amount of a loss sustained on disposition of property is its adjusted basis (¶2468) minus the amount of money and the fair market value of property received in exchange for it. (Code Sec. 165(b); Reg § 1.165-1(c))[36]

No loss is deductible to the extent the taxpayer was reimbursed or compensated for it (¶1781) or the property has salvage value. (Code Sec. 165(a); Reg § 1.165-1(c))[37] For limit on tax-exempt use losses, see ¶1773. For casualty and theft losses, see ¶1782 *et seq.* and ¶1787 *et seq.*

¶ 1768   Limits on losses of individuals; losses incurred in trade or business or transaction entered into for profit; casualty losses; theft losses.

Under Code Sec. 165(c), individuals may deduct losses incurred in a trade or business (¶1769) or a transaction entered into for profit (¶1770). (Code Sec. 165(c)(1), Code Sec. 165(c)(2))[38]

An individual's losses on personal transactions are deductible only if they qualify as casualty (¶1782) or theft (¶1787) losses. From 2018 to 2025, personal casualty and theft losses of an individual are deductible only to the extent they're attributable to a Federally declared disaster. However, where a taxpayer has personal casualty gains (¶1783), a personal casualty loss is deductible to the extent that it doesn't exceed the gains. (Code Sec. 165(h)(5))[39]

Also from 2018 to 2025, deductions attributable to an activity not entered into for profit—so-called "hobby losses" —are not allowed due to the suspension of miscellaneous itemized deductions subject to the 2%-of-AGI floor (¶2162).[40]

Losses on property a taxpayer holds partly for personal use and partly for business or income-producing use are allocated to the uses. Loss on the personal part isn't deductible except as discussed above.[41]

¶ 1769   What is a trade or business for loss deduction rules?

For purposes of loss deductions under Code Sec. 165, a trade or business is a pursuit or occupation carried on for profit, whether or not profit actually results. An isolated transaction isn't a business.[42]

¶ 1770   When a transaction is entered into for profit for loss deduction purposes—Form 5213.

For purposes of loss deductions under Code Sec. 165, a transaction is entered into for profit (¶1768) if a taxpayer intends to receive income from it overall. If the transaction involves property, the taxpayer's primary motive must be to receive income from it or to profit from disposing of it. The presence of a secondary nonprofit motive will not bar a loss deduction if the profit motive predominates.[43]

An activity is presumed to be engaged in for profit for a tax year if it shows a profit for three or more years during the five-year period ending in the current tax year (or two out of seven years for breeding, showing or racing of horses). (Code Sec. 183(d); Reg § 1.183-1(c))[44] A taxpayer who hasn't engaged in an activity for more than five years (seven, for

35. ¶M-1101, M-1305 *et seq.*
36. ¶M-1401
37. ¶M-1401; ¶M-1408
38. ¶M-1501, M-1510
39. ¶M-1524, M-1900A
40. ¶A-2711, A-2729
41. ¶M-1420
42. ¶L-1100 *et seq.*
43. ¶M-1510 *et seq.*
44. ¶M-5818

220

horse breeding, etc.) can elect (on Form 5213) to postpone the determination as to whether these presumptions apply until the close of the fourth tax year (sixth, for horse breeding, etc.) after the first year of the activity. (Code Sec. 183(e); Reg § 12.9)[45]

Whether an activity is engaged in for profit is determined on the corporate level for S corporations, and on the partnership level for partners. (Reg § 1.183-1(f))[46]

¶ 1771   "Vacation home" limits for deducting expenses; no deductions, no inclusion, for less-than-15-day rentals.

Under Code Sec. 280A(a), if an individual, trust, estate, partnership or S corporation owns a vacation home or a dwelling unit and uses it for both personal and rental purposes, deductible expenses are limited, except for those expenses that are deductible without regard to business use of the property—e.g., mortgage interest and real estate taxes. (Code Sec. 280A)[47]

The owner's personal use of the home (or portion of it) for even one day in the tax year triggers these "vacation home" limits. (Code Sec. 280A(e)(1))[48]

Subject to a de minimis rule (below), for any tax year in which the owner uses the (rented) property for personal purposes, or rents it out for less than a fair rental, the owner's deduction for maintenance, utilities, depreciation, etc., can't exceed the percentage of the total expenses for the year "attributable" to the period the unit is rented at a fair rental. (Code Sec. 280A(e)(1))[49] Rental-related deductions, other than otherwise deductible expenses such as mortgage interest and real estate taxes, are limited to net income from the rental. Any rental expenses not allowable because of this limit are carried forward, subject to the income limit in the next year. (Code Sec. 280A(c)(5))[50]

A home is used as a residence in any tax year the owner's personal use exceeds the longer of (1) 14 days, or (2) 10% of the period of rental use. (Code Sec. 280A(d)(1))[1]

Under a de minimis rule, if a home is rented for less than 15 days in a year, the owner can't deduct *any* of the rental expenses, but isn't taxed on any of the rental income. (Code Sec. 280A(g))[2]

¶ 1772   Worthless stock or securities—losses; totally worthless stock vs. partial worthlessness.

Under Code Sec. 165(g)(1), a taxpayer may take a loss deduction for totally worthless stock or other securities, but not for partial worthlessness or mere decline in value. (Code Sec. 165(g)(1); Reg § 1.165-4, Reg § 1.165-5)[3]

The taxpayer must show that the security had value at the end of the year preceding the deduction year and that an identifiable event caused a loss in the deduction year.[4]

The amount of the loss is the security's adjusted basis for determining loss on a sale (¶2468), to the extent the loss is not compensated for (e.g., by insurance). (Code Sec. 165(b); Reg § 1.165-1(c))[5]

The loss is capital if the security is a capital asset to the taxpayer. It is treated as a loss from the sale or exchange of a capital asset on the last day of the tax year. (Code Sec. 165(g)(1))[6]

The loss is ordinary if the security (i) is not a capital asset (Reg § 1.165-5(b)); (ii) is small business corporation stock (¶2634 *et seq.*); or (iii) for corporate taxpayers, is stock in an

45. ¶M-5821
46. ¶M-5802
47. ¶M-6001, M-6006
48. ¶M-6005
49. ¶M-6005, M-6028, ¶ M-6006, *et seq.*
50. ¶M-6018, M-6022

1. ¶M-6024
2. ¶M-6023
3. ¶M-3301, M-3304
4. ¶M-3400 *et seq.*
5. ¶M-3305
6. ¶M-3308

"affiliated" corporation (at least 80%-owned by taxpayer), where more than 90% of the affiliate's gross receipts was from sources other than passive income (e.g., royalties, dividends). (Code Sec. 165(g)(3))[7]

No loss deduction is allowed on a shareholder's surrender of some of his or her stock to the corporation, whether or not the surrender is pro rata. Instead, the shareholder's basis for stock surrendered is added to the basis of stock retained.[8]

¶ 1773　Limits on "tax-exempt use losses."

Generally, under Code Sec. 168(h) and Code Sec. 470, if a taxpayer (i) leases property to a tax-exempt entity or (ii) is a partner in a partnership that owns depreciable property, and the partnership also includes partners that are exempt organizations, subject to some exceptions, the taxpayer cannot claim deductions from the lease transaction in excess of the taxpayer's gross income from the lease or partnership for that tax year. The property subject to the Code Sec. 470 limitations is referred to as "tax-exempt use property." (Code Sec. 168(h), Code Sec. 470) A tax-exempt use loss in excess of gross income may be carried forward to the next tax year, subject to that year's limit. (Code Sec. 470(b))[9]

¶ 1774　Disallowance of "excess business loss" for noncorporate taxpayers— tax years beginning before 2029—Form 461.

Under Code Sec. 461(l), for tax years beginning before Jan. 1, 2029, a noncorporate taxpayer's "excess business loss" (figured on Form 461) is disallowed and carried forward and treated as part of the taxpayer's net operating loss (NOL) carryforward (¶1818) in later tax years. The Code Sec. 461(l) limitation applies after the application of the passive loss rules (¶1797).

An excess business loss for the tax year is the excess of a taxpayer's aggregate deductions attributable to the taxpayer's trades and businesses, over the sum of the taxpayer's aggregate gross income or gain plus an inflation-adjusted threshold amount. For 2022, the threshold amount is $540,000 for married individuals filing jointly and $270,000 for other individuals. For 2023, the threshold amount is $578,000 for married individuals filing jointly and $289,000 for other individuals.[10]

¶ 1775　Demolition losses.

Generally, under Code Sec. 280B, no deduction is allowed to the owner or lessee of a building for any loss on demolition of the building, or for any demolition expenses. The loss or expenses must be capitalized and added to the basis of the land. (Code Sec. 280B)[11]

¶ 1776　Abandonment loss; loss of usefulness or for obsolescence of nondepreciable property.

Under Reg § 1.165-2, a loss deduction is allowed for loss of usefulness or for obsolescence of nondepreciable property, both tangible and intangible (e.g., land, goodwill), *if* (1) the loss is incurred in a business or for-profit transaction; (2) it arises from the sudden termination of usefulness; *and* (3) the property is permanently discarded from use, or the business or transaction is discontinued. (Reg § 1.165-2)[12]

The loss is an ordinary loss not subject to capital loss limitations. (Reg § 1.165-2(b))[13] The loss can't exceed the property's adjusted basis (¶ 2468) for determining loss on a disposition. (Reg § 1.165-1(c))[14] For loss on an abandoned security, see ¶1772. For losses

---

7. ¶M-3308; ¶I-9501; ¶M-3310 *et seq.*
8. ¶M-3501
9. ¶L-6901 *et seq.*
10. ¶M-4450 *et seq.*

11. ¶M-2200 *et seq.*
12. ¶M-2301
13. ¶M-2353
14. ¶M-2351

on mortgaged property, see ¶1779 and ¶1780.

¶ 1777 Costs of unsuccessful investigation of proposed venture—losses.

A corporation that pays or incurs expenses in *unsuccessfully* searching for or investigating a new venture may deduct those costs as a business loss when it abandons the search or investigation (¶1503). For a noncorporate taxpayer, these expenses are personal and nondeductible.[15] For expenses of a *successful* investigation, see ¶1500 *et seq.*

¶ 1778 Gambling losses—Form 1040 or 1040-SR.

Under Code Sec. 165(d), a taxpayer may deduct gambling losses suffered in the tax year, but only to the extent of that year's gambling gains. (Code Sec. 165(d); Reg § 1.165-10)

Gains include "comps" (i.e., complimentary goods and services received from a casino). Losses from one kind of gambling (e.g., horse bets) are deductible against gains from another kind (e.g., keno).[16]

The gambling loss limitation applies to expenses incurred by the individual in connection with the gambling activity, such as transportation to the casino, as well as to the actual costs of wagers.[17]

Individuals not engaged in the gambling business deduct gambling losses (to extent of gambling gains) only as itemized deductions, and must report gambling gains on Form 1040 even if they are exceeded by gambling losses. Individuals in the business of gambling report their gambling losses, to the extent of gambling gains, on Form 1040, Schedule C.[18]

¶ 1779 Mortgagee's loss (or gain) on mortgaged property; loss on compromise or settlement; loss on mortgage foreclosure.

A mortgagee (mortgage lender) treats a loss on *compromise or settlement* of the debt of an insolvent debtor as a bad debt (¶1823 *et seq.*).[19]

A mortgagee to whom mortgaged or pledged property is surrendered has a bad debt deduction if the fair market value (FMV) of the property received is less than the debt. The mortgagee has a gain if the FMV of the surrendered property is greater than the debt's basis.[20] For where the surrender is a repossession by the seller, see ¶ 2461.

A mortgagee's loss on a *mortgage foreclosure* is treated as a bad debt equal to the sum of (1) the excess of the debt's basis over the net proceeds from the property foreclosure; (2) accrued interest previously reported as income; plus (3) legal and other expenses. This is true whether the property is sold to the creditor or another purchaser. (Reg § 1.166-6(a))[21]

¶ 1780 Owner's loss on foreclosure or surrender of mortgaged property; loss on tax sales.

The owner of mortgaged property, whether or not he or she is the mortgagor and whether or not he or she is personally liable for the mortgage debt, realizes a loss (occasionally a gain) on foreclosure of the mortgage or surrender of the property, which is considered a sale or exchange.[22]

The owner-borrower's gain or loss is the difference between adjusted basis of the transferred property and the amount realized. If the owner-borrower isn't personally liable for repaying the mortgage debt, the amount realized includes the full amount of the canceled

---

15. ¶L-5017 *et seq.*
16. ¶M-6100 *et seq.*
17. ¶M-6102.1
18. ¶J-1651, M-6105

19. ¶M-3709
20. ¶M-3710
21. ¶M-3701
22. ¶M-3801

debt. If the borrower is personally liable, the amount realized doesn't include any cancellation of debt income (¶1379) arising from the debt. But if the FMV of the property is less than the canceled debt, the amount realized includes canceled debt up to the FMV.[23]

The tax treatment of an owner whose property is sold for delinquent taxes is similar to the tax treatment for foreclosure, i.e., the tax sale is a sale or exchange.[24]

¶ 1781   When to deduct loss.

A loss is deductible only for the tax year it's sustained. (Code Sec. 165(a)) This is the year the loss occurs, as evidenced by closed and completed transactions and as fixed by identifiable events in that year. (Reg § 1.165-1(d))[25] For casualty or theft losses, see ¶1784 and ¶1789.

If taxpayer has a claim for reimbursement on which there is a reasonable prospect of recovery, the loss can't be deducted until it's reasonably certain whether or not the reimbursement will be made. This may be ascertained by, among other things, settlement, adjudication or abandonment of the claim. (Reg § 1.165-1(d)(2))[26]

¶ 1782   Casualty, Disaster, and Theft Losses—Form 4684. ▬▬▬▬▬

For 2018 through 2025, personal casualty and theft losses of an individual are deductible only to the extent they're attributable to a Federally declared disaster, and to the extent the $100-per-casualty/10%-of-AGI limits (¶1783) are met. (Code Sec. 165(h)(5))[27]

For the amount of casualty loss, see ¶1783. For when to deduct casualty losses, see ¶1784 *et seq.*

A *casualty* is the complete or partial destruction of property resulting from an identifiable event of a sudden, unexpected or unusual nature, such as a fire, storm, shipwreck, car crash or similar event. Progressive deterioration from a steadily operating cause isn't a casualty. The property must suffer physical damage and not just a decline in value, even if that decline resulted from being in or near an area where casualties have occurred and might occur again.[28]

¶ 1783   Casualty loss deduction; amount of casualty loss—Form 4684; personal use property vs. business property.

Under Code Sec. 165 and the regs thereunder, the amount treated as a loss from a casualty depends on whether the taxpayer held the property for personal or business purposes, as follows:

Personal-use property. The deduction for personal casualty losses is suspended through 2025, except for personal casualty losses incurred in a Federally declared disaster. For taxpayers with personal casualty gains, nondisaster personal casualty losses are allowed to the extent of the personal casualty gains. (Code Sec. 165(h)(5))[29]

For property held for personal use, the amount of the casualty loss is the *lesser* of (1) the property's adjusted basis (¶2468), or (2) its decline in value (i.e., its fair market value (FMV) immediately before the casualty *minus* its FMV immediately afterward). (Reg § 1.165-7(b)(1))[30]

Business property. For property used in business or held for the production of income, the amount of the casualty loss is determined under the same rules as for personal-use property, except that if the property is *totally* destroyed, the amount of the loss is the

---

23. ¶M-3803
24. ¶M-3806
25. ¶M-1301
26. ¶M-2136

27. ¶M-1601
28. ¶M-1701
29. ¶M-1900A
30. ¶M-1801 *et seq.*

property's adjusted basis in all cases. (Reg § 1.165-7(b)(1)(ii))[31]

Measuring decline in value. The decline in a property's value should be ascertained by competent appraisal where possible. (Reg § 1.165-7(a)(2)(i))[32]

Costs of repairing, replacing, or cleaning up property after a casualty can be used to measure the amount of the loss (decline in value) if: the repair, etc., is necessary to restore the property to its pre-casualty condition; the amount spent isn't excessive; the repairs do no more than take care of the damage suffered; and the post-repair value is no greater than the pre-casualty value. (Reg § 1.165-7(a)(2)) IRS has provided optional safe harbor methods for individuals to determine the amount of deductions for casualty losses to personal residential property and personal belongings that occur due to natural disasters.[33]

Limits to personal-use property losses. An individual can deduct a casualty loss on personal-use property (where the deduction is available) to the extent that (1) the casualty loss exceeds $100 and (2) all of the individual's casualty losses for the tax year exceed 10% of adjusted gross income for the year. (Code Sec. 165(h))[34]

The casualty loss deduction isn't allowed to the extent the loss is compensated by insurance or otherwise. (Code Sec. 165(a))[35]

¶ 1784 When to deduct casualty losses.

Under Code Sec. 165(a), a casualty loss is considered "sustained" only during the tax year the loss occurs, as fixed by identifiable events occurring in that year. (Code Sec. 165(a); Reg § 1.165-1(d)(1)) A loss may be sustained in the tax year even though repairs or replacements aren't made until a later year. And a loss may be sustained in a year *after* the casualty occurs.[36] For the election to deduct disaster losses early, see ¶1785.

¶ 1785 Early deduction election for disaster losses—Form 4684, Section D.

Under Code Sec. 165(i), a taxpayer may *elect* to deduct a disaster loss for the tax year *before* the year the loss occurred, instead of for the year the loss occurred (¶1784). (Code Sec. 165(i))[37]

A *disaster loss* is an otherwise deductible loss from a disaster occurring in a Federally declared disaster area. (Code Sec. 165(i)(1), Reg § 1.165-11(b)(3))[38] A non-casualty loss may be a disaster loss if incurred in the course of a trade or business or profit-seeking transaction, such as farming losses due to severe drought declared to be a disaster. For casualty losses, any other limitations (e.g., the regular $100 floor for personal use property described at ¶1783) continue to apply. (Code Sec. 165(i))[39]

Election. A taxpayer must generally elect to deduct a disaster loss in the preceding tax year by filing a return, an amended return, or a refund claim within six months after the due date for filing the taxpayer's federal income tax return for the year of the disaster (determined without regard to any extension of time to file). (Reg § 1.165-11(f)) The election may be revoked on or before the date that is 90 days after the due date for making the election. (Reg § 1.165-11(g)) Form 4684, Section D, can be used to make the election or revoke a prior election.[40]

¶ 1786 Losses on deposits in insolvent financial institutions—Form 4684.

Losses on deposits in insolvent financial institutions are nonbusiness bad debts, deductible as short-term capital loss when the deposit becomes worthless. A "qualified individual" can elect, on Form 4684, to treat these losses as casualty losses, but the loss is

---

31. ¶M-1802
32. ¶M-1809
33. ¶M-1815, ¶M-1833 *et seq.*
34. ¶M-1900 *et seq.*
35. ¶M-1408, M-1411, M-1421

36. ¶M-1610
37. ¶M-2001
38. ¶M-2002
39. ¶M-2009
40. ¶M-2011 *et seq.*

deductible only to the extent of the individual's personal casualty gains (¶1783).[41]

¶ 1787   Theft losses—Form 4684.

Theft losses (reported on Form 4684) are deductible under rules that closely follow those for casualty losses, including the $100/10%-of-AGI floors. Personal theft losses of an individual are disallowed through 2025 except where attributable to a Federally declared disaster or where the taxpayer has personal casualty gains (¶1783). (Code Sec. 165(a), Code Sec. 165(h)(1), Code Sec. 165(h)(2))[42]

A theft is the unlawful taking and removing of money or property with the intent to deprive the owner of it, and includes larceny, robbery, embezzlement, burglary, extortion, kidnapping for ransom, blackmail and false representation. (Reg § 1.165-8(d))[43] For determining the amount of a theft loss, see ¶1788.

A theft loss deduction is not allowed for the decline in market value of stock purchased on the open market, where the decline is caused by the disclosure of accounting fraud or other illegal conduct by officers or directors of the issuing corporation.[44]

¶ 1788   Amount of theft loss.

For theft of business or investment property, the amount of the *deductible loss* is the adjusted basis of the property minus insurance or other compensation received or recoverable. (Reg § 1.165-8(c))[45]

For theft of personal-use property (the deduction for which is limited through 2025, see ¶1787), the amount of the *loss* is (1) the lesser of the property's fair market value (FMV) immediately before theft or its adjusted basis, reduced by (2) insurance or other compensation received or recoverable. (Reg § 1.165-8(c)) The $100/10%-of-AGI floors (¶1783) are then applied to determine the amount of the loss that is *deductible*. (Code Sec. 165(c)(3))[46]

If stolen personal-use property is recovered in the deduction year, the amount of the loss is the lesser of (1) the property's adjusted basis, or (2) the decline in its FMV between theft and recovery.[47]

¶ 1789   When to deduct theft loss.

Code Sec. 165(e) provides that a theft loss (¶1787) is deductible in the year the loss is *discovered,* regardless of when the theft actually occurred. (Code Sec. 165(e)) But the deduction is postponed to the extent the taxpayer, in the year of discovery, had a reimbursement claim on which there was a reasonable prospect of recovery. (Reg § 1.165-8(a))[48]

¶ 1790   At-Risk Limitations. ▆▆▆▆▆▆▆▆▆▆▆▆▆▆▆▆

The "at risk" rules limit the deductions of individuals, estates, trusts, and certain C corporations from specified leveraged investment activities (¶1792) to the amount the taxpayer-investor has "at risk" (¶1794).

¶ 1791   Taxpayers subject to "at-risk" rules.

Under Code Sec. 465(a)(1), the at-risk rules (¶1793) apply to individuals, estates and trusts, and closely-held C corporations (more than 50% of the value of the corporation's stock is owned by five or fewer individuals at any time during the last half of its tax year).[49] The at-risk rules *don't apply* to C corporations that: (i) are not personal holding

---

41. ¶M-1761, M-1762, M-1765, M-1766
42. ¶M-2125
43. ¶M-2100 *et seq.*
44. ¶M-2111
45. ¶M-2125
46. ¶M-2126
47. ¶M-2129
48. ¶M-2132
49. ¶M-4511, M-4512, M-4515

companies or personal service corporations (determined by substituting 5% for 10% in Code Sec. 269A(b)(2)); and (ii) are engaged in qualifying active businesses. (Code Sec. 465(c)(7)) The at-risk rules also do not apply to closely-held C corporations engaged in equipment leasing (Code Sec. 465(c)(4)).[50] Although the at-risk rules do not apply to partnerships and S corporations, they do apply to partners and S corporation shareholders.[1]

¶ 1792 "At-risk" activities for at-risk limitation rules.

Code Sec. 465(c) provides that the at-risk rules (¶1793) apply to these specified activities: (i) holding, producing or distributing motion pictures or video tapes; (ii) farming; (iii) equipment leasing; (iv) exploring for, or exploiting, oil and gas resources; or (v) exploring for, or exploiting, geothermal resources; (Code Sec. 465(c)(1)), and to a "catch-all" group of activities other than those specified above (e.g., real estate activities, ¶1796) engaged in by the taxpayer in carrying on a trade or business or in the production of income. (Code Sec. 465(c)(3))[2]

Specified activities and those in the catch-all group are subject to different aggregation rules. (Code Sec. 465(c)(3)(B))[3]

¶ 1793 How the at-risk rules work—Form 6198.

Code Sec. 465(a) provides that a loss from an at-risk activity (¶1792) is deductible in the loss year only to the extent that the taxpayer is at risk (¶1794) with respect to the activity at the end of the year. (Code Sec. 465(a)) The losses so limited are the excess of the otherwise allowable deductions allocable to the activity for the year over the income (other than recapture, ¶1795) from that same activity. (Code Sec. 465(d))[4]

A disallowed loss is treated as allocable to the same activity in the next tax year, and may then be deducted subject to that year's at-risk limit for the activity. (Code Sec. 465(a)(2))[5]

caution: In addition to the at-risk rules, losses and credits from an activity may also be subject to the passive activity rules, discussed at ¶1797 *et seq.*

Form 6198 is used to compute the deductible loss from an at-risk activity.[6]

For the at-risk rules otherwise applicable to real property, see ¶1796.

¶ 1794 Amounts considered "at risk" for at-risk limitation rules.

Code Sec. 465(b) provides that at-risk amounts (¶1793) are: (1) money and the adjusted basis of other property the taxpayer contributed to the activity, plus (2) amounts borrowed for the activity for which taxpayer is personally liable or has pledged property, other than property used in the activity, as security for the borrowed amount. The borrowings can't exceed the fair market value of the taxpayer's interest in the pledged property. No property is treated as security if it is directly or indirectly financed by indebtedness secured by property in (1), above. (Code Sec. 465(b)(1), Code Sec. 465(b)(2))[7]

A taxpayer engaged in the activity of holding real property is considered at risk for his or her share of any "qualified nonrecourse financing" secured by the real property. (Code Sec. 465(b)(6)(A))[8]

The taxpayer's amount at risk isn't increased for amounts borrowed from a person who has an interest in the activity other than as a creditor or from a person considered "related" to such interested parties. (Code Sec. 465(b)(3))[9]

---

50. ¶M-4516 *et seq.*
1. ¶M-4513 *et seq.*
2. ¶M-4521
3. ¶M-4522 *et seq.*
4. ¶M-4502

5. ¶M-4502
6. ¶M-4501
7. ¶M-4541 *et seq.*
8. ¶M-4534
9. ¶M-4557 *et seq.*

Amounts protected against loss by nonrecourse financing, guarantees, stop loss agreements, etc., aren't at-risk. (Code Sec. 465(b)(4))[10]

The at-risk amount for a year is reduced by any losses allowed under the at-risk limitation in earlier years. (Code Sec. 465(b)(5))[11]

¶ 1795   Recapture of losses where amount at risk is less than zero.

Code Sec. 465(e)(1)(A) provides that, if a taxpayer's amount at risk (¶1794) is less than zero (e.g., due to distributions to the taxpayer or by debt changing from recourse to nonrecourse), the taxpayer recognizes income to the extent of that negative amount. (Code Sec. 465(e)(1)(A)) But, the amount recaptured is limited to the excess of the losses previously allowed in that activity over any amounts previously recaptured. (Code Sec. 465(e)(2)) The amount added to income under this recapture rule is treated as a deduction allocable to the activity in the first succeeding year, and is allowed if and to the extent the taxpayer's at-risk basis is increased. (Code Sec. 465(e)(1)(B))[12]

¶ 1796   At-risk rules for real property.

A taxpayer engaged in holding real property is subject to the at-risk rules (¶1790) for losses on property placed in service after '86. The at-risk rules also apply to a taxpayer's losses from real estate attributable to an interest in a pass-through entity that is acquired after '86, without regard to when the entity placed the real property in service. (Code Sec. 465(c)(3)(A))[13]

A taxpayer is considered at risk for his or her share of any "qualified nonrecourse financing" secured by the real property. (Code Sec. 465(b)(6); Reg § 1.465-27(b))[14]

¶ 1797   "Passive Activity" Losses and Credits. ▬▬▬▬▬▬

Losses and credits from passive activities (¶1798) may only be used to offset passive activity income (¶1802). Thus, they can't be used to offset income from, for example, compensation, interest or dividends. Any losses or credits that are unused in a tax year because of this rule are carried forward until used (¶1798), or until the taxpayer disposes of the interest (¶1814).

Although real estate activities are generally subject to the passive activity loss rules, individuals who actively participate in rental real estate activities may use up to $25,000 of losses from those activities to offset nonpassive income; and rental real estate activities are not treated as a passive activity for real estate professionals who materially participate in the activity (¶1811 *et seq.*).

¶ 1798   Disallowance of passive activity losses and credits—Form 8582; Form 8582-CR; Form 8810

Generally, under Code Sec. 469(a)(1), a taxpayer subject to the passive activity loss rules (¶1799) cannot currently deduct a "passive activity loss" or use a "passive activity credit" (both defined at ¶1800). (Code Sec. 469(a)(1); Reg § 1.469-1T(a)(2))[15]

Carryover loss or credit. The disallowed (or suspended) passive activity losses and credits are carried over and allocated among the taxpayer's activities for the following year in a way that reasonably reflects the extent to which each activity continues the loss activity. (Code Sec. 469(b); Reg § 1.469-1(f)(4)(i))[16] Suspended passive activity losses are allowed in full on a taxable disposition of the activity (¶1814).

---

10. ¶M-4568 *et seq.*
11. ¶M-4507
12. ¶M-4509
13. ¶M-4533

14. ¶M-4534 *et seq.*
15. ¶M-4600 *et seq.*
16. ¶M-5504, ¶M-5604

A *passive activity* is an activity that involves the conduct of a trade or business in which the taxpayer does not materially participate (¶1806). Any rental activity (other than a rental real estate activity of a real estate professional) is passive, regardless of whether the taxpayer materially participates (¶1810).

A *trade or business* includes any activity connected with a trade or business for which expenses are allowable as a deduction under Code Sec. 212, or which involves research or experimental expenditures deductible under Code Sec. 174. (Code Sec. 469(c)(5); Code Sec. 469(c)(6))[17]

Whether a loss is disallowed under these rules is determined *after* the application of the at-risk rules (¶1790 *et seq.*) and the partner (¶3726) and S corporation shareholder (¶3368) basis limitation rules. (Reg § 1.469-2T(d))[18]

The passive activity limits are calculated on Form 8582 (for individuals, estates, and trusts); Form 8582-CR (credits for individuals, estates, and trusts); or Form 8810 (closely held corporations and personal service corporations).

For passive activity losses for alternative minimum tax purposes, see ¶3211.

¶ 1799   Who is subject to the passive activity rules?

Under Code Sec. 469, the passive activity limits (¶1798) apply to any individual, estate, trust (other than a grantor trust), a personal service corporation (PSC) as specially defined, and a closely held C corporation (subject to special rules). (Code Sec. 469(a)(2), Code Sec. 469(j), Reg § 1.469-1T(b)(2))[19]

Partnerships (unless publicly traded) and S corporations are not subject to the passive activity rules (¶1798). (Code Sec. 469(a)(2)) But the rules *do* apply to the losses and credits passed through to the partners and shareholders.[20]

Spouses filing a joint return are treated as one taxpayer, with certain exceptions. (Reg § 1.469-1T(j)(1))[21]

¶ 1800   Passive activity loss and credits defined—passive activity loss rules.

Under Code Sec. 469(d)(1), a *passive activity loss* for a tax year is the amount by which the aggregate losses from all passive activities (¶1798) for the tax year exceed the aggregate income from all passive activities for that year. (Code Sec. 469(d)(1); Reg § 1.469-2T(b)(1))[22]

For a closely held C corporation, the passive activity loss is determined as above, except the loss is further reduced by the corporation's net active income. (Code Sec. 469(e)(2)(A); Reg § 1.469-1T(g)(4))[23]

A *passive activity credit* is the excess of specified credits attributable to passive activities over the regular tax liability allocable to those activities. (Reg § 1.469-3T(a)) The credits subject to the passive activity loss rules include general business credits and the credit for new qualified plug-in electric vehicles. (Code Sec. 469(d)(2)(A))[24]

¶ 1801   Passive activity deductions; loss on disposition.

Under Reg § 1.469-2T(d)(5)(i), any loss recognized on the sale, exchange, or other disposition of an interest in property used in an activity at the time of disposition, or of an interest in an activity held through a pass-through entity, is a passive activity deduction if the activity is a passive activity (¶1798) of the taxpayer for the tax year of the disposition. Likewise, any deduction allowed on account of the abandonment or worthlessness of an

---

17. ¶M-4802
18. ¶M-4603 *et seq.*
19. ¶M-4700 *et seq.*
20. ¶s M-4709, M-5302

21. ¶M-4702
22. ¶M-4601
23. ¶M-5507 *et seq.*
24. ¶M-5600 *et seq.*

interest in property or in an activity is treated as a deduction from the activity if the activity is a passive activity of the taxpayer for the tax year of the disposition. (Reg § 1.469-2T(d)(5)(i))[25]

If the interest in property disposed of was used in more than one activity during the 12-month period ending on the date of disposition, the amount realized from the disposition (as well as the adjusted basis of the interest) must be allocated among the activities (with a de minimis exception) on a basis that reasonably reflects those uses. (Reg § 1.469-2T(d)(5)(ii)) A partnership interest or S corporation stock is not property used in an activity for purposes of the above rule. (Reg § 1.469-2T(d)(5)(ii))[26]

¶ 1802   Passive activity gross income—passive activity loss rules.

For taxpayers other than closely held corporations, the passive activity loss for the tax year is the amount by which passive activity deductions exceed passive activity gross income. Passive activity gross income is, in general, gross income from a passive activity (¶1798). (Reg § 1.469-2T(b)(1); Reg § 1.469-2T(c)(1))[27]

The character of a partner's or S corporation shareholder's allocable items of gross income as passive activity gross income is determined, in general, by reference to the partner's or shareholder's participation in the activities that generated the items for the entity's tax year. (Reg § 1.469-2T(e)(1))[28] Passive activity gross income does not include portfolio income (e.g., interest, dividends, annuities, or royalties not derived in the ordinary course of a trade or business) (Code Sec. 469(e)(1)(A)(i)(I); Reg § 1.469-2T(c)(3)(i)), compensation for personal services (as specially defined) (Code Sec. 469(e)(3); Reg § 1.469-2T(c)(4)), certain income from intangible property if a taxpayer's personal efforts contributed significantly to the property's creation, a tax refund, or reimbursement of a casualty or theft loss (Reg § 1.469-2T(c)(7)), and certain income from oil and gas properties (Code Sec. 469(c)(3)(B); Reg § 1.469-2(c)(6)).[29]

For when gain on the disposition of a property interest is passive activity gross income, see ¶1803.

¶ 1803   Gain on dispositions of property used in a passive activity—substantially appreciated property exception.

Generally, any gain recognized on the sale, exchange, or other disposition of an interest in property used in a passive activity at the time of disposition, or of an interest in a passive activity held through a pass-through entity, is passive activity gross income (¶1802) for the tax year in which the gain is recognized. Reg § 1.469-2T(c)(2)(i)(A))[30]

Exception for substantially appreciated property. Gain from the disposition of an interest in property that is substantially appreciated (fair market value exceeds 120% of adjusted basis) is not treated as gain from a passive activity unless used in a passive activity for either: (i) 20% of the period the taxpayer held the interest, or (ii) the entire 24-month period ending on the date of disposition. (Reg § 1.469-2(c)(2)(iii))[31] This exception, however, does not apply to dispositions of partnership interests or of S corporation stock. Regs provide special rules for disposition of interests in pass-through entities. (Reg § 1.469-2T(e)(3)(ii)(A), Reg § 1.469-2T(e)(3)(iii))[32]

For disposition of an *entire* interest in (or substantially all of) a passive activity, see ¶1814.

---

25. ¶M-5406
26. ¶M-5406
27. ¶M-5301
28. ¶M-5302

29. ¶M-5325, ¶M-5332 *et seq.*
30. ¶M-5304
31. ¶M-5306
32. ¶M-5708, ¶M-5343

¶ 1804   Recharacterization of passive income as nonpassive income—passive activity loss rules.

Reg § 1.469-2T(f) minimizes opportunities for taxpayers to create passive income that can be used to offset passive losses by recharacterizing passive income as nonpassive income in various situations. Income from the following passive activities is not treated as income from a passive activity: (i) income from significant participation activities (i.e., activities in which the taxpayer participates for more than 100 hours during the tax year, but does not materially participate (defined at ¶1806 *et seq.*); (ii) income from rental of nondepreciable property; (iii) net interest income from an equity-financed lending activity or certain rental property; and (iv) certain royalty income. (Reg § 1.469-2T(f))[33]

¶ 1805   Rules for grouping passive activities as a single activity—passive activity loss rules.

Reg § 1.469-4 allows taxpayers to group their trade or business activities (¶1798) and rental activities (¶1810) as a single activity for purposes of the passive activity loss and credit limitations if the activities are an appropriate economic unit for measuring gain or loss for purposes of the passive activity rules based on all the relevant facts and circumstances. (Reg § 1.469-4(a); Reg § 1.469-4(c))[34]

A rental activity (¶1810) can't be grouped with a trade or business activity unless the activities being grouped together are an appropriate economic unit *and*

. . . the rental activity is insubstantial in relation to the trade or business activity;

. . . the trade or business activity is insubstantial in relation to the rental activity; or

. . . each owner of the trade or business activity has the same proportionate ownership interest in the rental activity, in which case the part of the rental activity that involves the rental of items of property for use in the trade or business may be grouped with the trade or business activity. (Reg § 1.469-4(b)(2); Reg § 1.469-4(d)(1))[35]

Real property rentals and personal property rentals (other than personal property rentals provided in connection with the real property, or vice versa) can't be grouped together. (Reg § 1.469-4(d)(2))[36]

A taxpayer can't regroup activities in later years unless the original grouping was or has become clearly inappropriate, in which case the taxpayer must regroup the activities. IRS may regroup activities to prevent tax avoidance. (Reg § 1.469-4(e), Reg § 1.469-4(f))[37] Taxpayers must report to IRS their groupings and regroupings of activities and the addition of specific activities within their existing groupings. (Reg § 1.469-4(e)(1))[38]

In a year when there is a disposition of substantially all of an activity, the taxpayer may under specified conditions treat the part disposed of as a separate activity. (Reg § 1.469-4(g))[39]

¶ 1806   What is "material participation" under passive activity loss rules?

Code Sec. 469(h) provides that a taxpayer materially participates (¶1798) in an activity only if he or she is involved in the activity's operations on a regular, continuous and substantial basis (¶1807 *et seq.*). (Code Sec. 469(h)) A trust materially participates in an activity if a fiduciary, in his or her capacity as such, so participates. A closely held C corporation or personal service corporation materially participates, in general, only if one or more of its shareholders who own more than 50% of its stock (by value) themselves

---

33. ¶M-5335
34. ¶M-4803, M-4804, M-4807.2
35. ¶M-4805
36. ¶M-4806

37. ¶M-4808, M-4809
38. ¶M-4808.1
39. ¶M-5701.3

materially participate. (Code Sec. 469(h)(4))[40]

¶ 1807 Material participation and participation by individuals under passive activity loss rules.

Under Reg § 1.469-5T(a), an individual taxpayer materially participates in an activity for a tax year if the taxpayer (or the taxpayer's spouse, whether or not they file jointly) meets one of seven material participation tests:

(1) The individual participates (see below) in the activity for more than 500 hours during the year. (Reg § 1.469-5T(a)(1))

(2) The individual's participation in the activity for the tax year constitutes substantially all of the participation in the activity for the tax year by all individuals (including non-owners). (Reg § 1.469-5T(a)(2))

(3) The individual participates in the activity for more than 100 hours during the tax year and that participation isn't less than the participation in the activity of any other individual (including non-owners) for that year. (Reg § 1.469-5T(a)(3))

(4) The activity is a "significant participation activity" ("SPA") for the tax year, and the individual's aggregate participation in all significant participation activities that year exceeds 500 hours. An SPA is a trade or business (¶1798) in which the individual significantly participates (for more than 100 hours), but in which he or she doesn't otherwise materially participate. (Reg § 1.469-5T(a)(4), Reg § 1.469-5T(c))

(5) The individual materially participated in the activity for any five tax years (consecutive or not) during the 10 immediately preceding tax years. (Reg § 1.469-5T(a)(5))

(6) The activity is a personal service activity, and the individual materially participated in the activity for any three tax years (consecutive or not) before the tax year. (Reg § 1.469-5T(a)(6), Reg § 1.469-5T(d))

(7) The individual meets a facts and circumstances test (¶1808). (Reg § 1.469-5T(a)(7))[41]

Reg § 1.469-5T(c)(1)(ii) provides that an activity is an SPA only if the activity would be an activity in which the individual doesn't materially participate for the tax year if material participation is determined without regard to the SPA test in Reg § 1.469-5T(a)(4) (item (4), above). Under this rule, where an activity satisfies one of the other six tests for material participation under Reg § 1.469-5T(a) (items (1) through (3) and (5) through (7) above) (excluding Reg § 1.469-5T(a)(4)), the activity doesn't satisfy the requirements to qualify as an SPA under Reg § 1.469-5T(c)(1), even though the remaining requirements (trade or business and hours) are met. (IRS Letter Ruling 202229036)[42]

Participation means any work done by an individual in connection with an activity in which he or she owns an interest at the time the work is done, regardless of the capacity in which he or she does the work. (Reg § 1.469-5(f)(1))[43] However, work done in connection with an activity is disregarded if the work isn't of a type that is customarily done by an owner of that type of activity, and one of the principal purposes for the performance of the work is to avoid the passive loss/credit restrictions. (Reg § 1.469-5T(f)(2))[44]

¶ 1808 Facts-and-circumstances test for material participation under passive activity loss rules.

Under Reg § 1.469-5T(a)(7), for purposes of the passive activity loss rules, an individual materially participates (¶1807) in an activity if he or she participates on a regular, continuous and substantial basis during the year, based on all the facts and circumstances. (Reg § 1.469-5T(a)(7)) An individual who participates in the activity for 100 hours or less

---

40. ¶M-4901 *et seq.*, ¶M-5005, ¶M-5006
41. ¶M-4901 *et seq.*
42. ¶M-4908

43. ¶M-4902
44. ¶M-4903

during the year does not meet this test. (Reg § 1.469-5T(b)(2)(iii))[45]

¶ 1809   Limited partner's material participation under passive activity loss rules.

Under Code Sec. 469(h)(2), for purposes of the passive activity loss rules, an individual limited partner is not treated as materially participating (¶1807) in any activity of a limited partnership with respect to his or her interest in that partnership (or to any gain or loss from the activity recognized on a sale or exchange of that interest) *unless* the individual would be treated as materially participating under the 500-hour, five-tax-years-out-of-ten, or three-year-personal-service-activity tests at ¶1807 (items (1), (5) or (6), respectively), if he or she were not a limited partner. (Code Sec. 469(h)(2); Reg § 1.469-5T(e)(2))[46] This rule does not apply if the individual owning the limited partner interest is also the general partner. (Reg § 1.469-5T(e)(3)(ii))[47]

¶ 1810   Rental activities as passive activities—passive activity loss rules.

Code Sec. 469(c)(2) provides that, for purposes of the passive activity loss rules, rental activities are generally treated as passive activities. (Code Sec. 469(c)(2)) This general rule, however, does not apply to individuals who actively participate in rental real estate activities (¶1811) and to certain real estate professionals (¶1813).[48] In addition, under the self-rental rule, taxpayers are prohibited from using net income from the rental of property to offset other passive losses if the property is rented for use in a trade or business in which the taxpayer materially participates. (Reg § 1.469-2(f)(6))[49]

A rental activity is any activity where payments are principally for the use of tangible property (Code Sec. 469(j)(8)), without regard to whether a lease, service contract, or other arrangement is involved. (Reg § 1.469-1T(e)(3)(i)(B)) But, a rental activity does not include an activity involving the use of tangible property if:

(1) The average period the customer uses the property is 7 days or less (Reg § 1.469-1T(e)(3)(ii)(A)), or 30 days or less *and* the owner (or someone on the owner's behalf) provides significant personal services (as defined in the regs). (Reg § 1.469-1T(e)(3)(ii)(B))

(2) The owner (or someone on the owner's behalf) provides extraordinary personal services (as defined in the regs), without regard to the average period the customer uses the property. (Reg § 1.469-1T(e)(3)(ii)(C))

(3) The rental of the tangible property is incidental to a nonrental activity of the taxpayer (Reg § 1.469-1T(e)(3)(ii)(D)) (as measured by certain percentage and other tests). (Reg § 1.469-1T(e)(3)(vi))

(4) The taxpayer customarily makes the property available during defined business hours for nonexclusive use by various customers (e.g., a golf course). (Reg § 1.469-1T(e)(3)(ii)(E))

(5) The property is provided for use in an activity conducted by a partnership, S corporation, or joint venture in which the taxpayer owns an interest. (Reg § 1.469-1T(e)(3)(ii)(F))[50]

¶ 1811   Individuals' active participation rental real estate losses up to $25,000 may be used against nonpassive income.

Under Code Sec. 469(i)(1), an individual who (1) has at least a 10% interest (by value) in any rental real estate activity (including any interest held by a spouse), and (2) otherwise "actively participates" in that activity (¶1812), may offset up to $25,000 of nonpassive

---

45. ¶M-4912
46. ¶M-5003 *et seq.*
47. ¶M-5002.1

48. ¶M-5100 *et seq.*
49. ¶M-5341
50. ¶M-5101 *et seq.*

income ($25,000 offset) with that portion of the passive activity loss, or of the deduction equivalent of the passive activity credit, attributable to that activity. (Code Sec. 469(i)(1), Code Sec. 469(i)(2), Code Sec. 469(i)(6)(A), Code Sec. 469(j)(5))[1]

The allowance is $12,500 for a married person filing a separate return who lived apart from his or her spouse at all times during the tax year. (Code Sec. 469(i)(5)(A)(i)) Otherwise, the allowance on a separate return is zero. (Code Sec. 469(i)(5)(B))[2]

The $25,000 allowance ($12,500 for marrieds filing separately) is reduced (but not below zero) by 50% of the amount by which taxpayer's adjusted gross income (AGI) as specially computed exceeds (1) $100,000 ($50,000 for marrieds filing separately), or (2) $200,000 ($100,000 for marrieds filing separately) in the case of rehabilitation investment credits (¶2307). There's no AGI-based phaseout of the $25,000 ($12,500) offset for low-income housing credits (¶2320). (Code Sec. 469(i)(3), Code Sec. 469(i)(5))[3]

¶ 1812 What is "active participation" for the passive activity loss rules $25,000 offset?

Under Code Sec. 469, to actively participate in a rental real estate activity for purposes of the $25,000 offset (¶1811), a taxpayer must participate (¶1807) in the activity in a significant and bona fide sense. A taxpayer participates if he or she makes management decisions, e.g., approves new tenants, decides on rental terms, approves capital or repair expenditures or arranges for others to provide services (such as repairs). The taxpayer need not have regular, continuous and substantial involvement in operations. But, a merely formal and nominal participation in management, without a genuine exercise of independent discretion and judgment, is insufficient. The active participation test is less stringent than the material participation requirement (¶1806).[4] Active participation is not required to take low-income housing (¶2320) or rehabilitation investment (¶2307) credits. (Code Sec. 469(i)(6)(B))[5]

The participation of a taxpayer's spouse is taken into account in determining whether the taxpayer actively participates. (Code Sec. 469(i)(6)(D))[6]

A taxpayer is not treated as actively participating (except as regs may provide) with respect to any interest as a limited partner. (Code Sec. 469(i)(6)(C))[7]

¶ 1813 Rental real estate activities of real estate professionals not treated as automatically passive.

Code Sec. 469(c)(7)(A)(i) provides that, although rental real estate activities generally are subject to the passive activity loss limitations (¶1798), real estate professionals who materially participate in a rental real estate activity are not subject to the passive activity loss rules (¶1806). (Code Sec. 469(c)(7)(A)(i)) (Reg § 1.469-9(e)(1))[8]

A taxpayer qualifies as a real estate professional for a particular tax year if (1) more than half of the personal services (defined below) the taxpayer performs during that year are performed in real property trades or businesses (defined below) in which the taxpayer materially participates, and (2) the taxpayer performs more than 750 hours of services during that year in real property trades or businesses in which he or she materially participates. (Reg § 1.469-9(b)(6), Code Sec. 469(c)(7)(B))[9] The activities of spouses can't be combined in determining real estate professional status. (Code Sec. 469(c)(7)(B); Reg § 1.469-9(c)(4))[10]

In determining whether a taxpayer is a real estate professional, each interest in the

1. ¶M-5131, ¶M-5135
2. ¶M-5131
3. ¶M-5136 *et seq.*
4. ¶M-5135
5. ¶L-12702, ¶M-5135

6. ¶M-5135
7. ¶M-5135
8. ¶M-5161
9. ¶M-5168
10. ¶M-5171

rental real estate is treated as a separate activity, unless the taxpayer elects (by filing a specified statement with the original income tax return) to treat all interests in rental real estate as one activity. (Code Sec. 469(c)(7)(A); Reg § 1.469-9(g)) The election is binding for the tax year it's made and for all future years in which the taxpayer qualifies. [11]

A closely-held C corporation qualifies as a real estate professional if more than 50% of its gross receipts for the tax year are derived from real property trades or businesses in which it materially participates. (Code Sec. 469(c)(7)(D)(i))[12] The Tax Court has held that a trust may qualify as a real estate professional.[13]

Personal services means any work performed by an individual in connection with a trade or business, but not as an investor. (Reg § 1.469-9(b)(4)) Services performed as an employee do not count, unless the individual is a more-than-5%-owner of the employer. (Code Sec. 469(c)(7)(D)(ii))[14]

A real property trade or business is any real property development, redevelopment, construction, reconstruction, acquisition, conversion, rental, operation, management, leasing or brokerage trade or business. (Code Sec. 469(c)(7)(C)) The determination of a taxpayer's real property trades or businesses is based on all relevant facts and circumstances. (Reg § 1.469-9(d)(1))[15]

¶ 1814 Disposition of entire interest or substantially all of the passive activity— suspended passive activity losses.

Code Sec. 469(g)(1) provides that suspended passive activity losses (¶1798) are deductible in full in the year in which the taxpayer disposes of the taxpayer's entire interest in the passive activity to an unrelated party, in a fully taxable transaction (i.e., a transaction in which all gain or loss on the disposition is recognized). (Code Sec. 469(g)(1))[16]

A taxpayer who disposes of "substantially all" of an activity can deduct the losses associated with the disposed portion. (Reg § 1.469-4(g))[17]

If a taxpayer disposes of an entire interest in a passive activity under the installment method, suspended passive activity losses that exceed the gain are recognized over the term of the installment obligation as the gain on the sale is recognized. (Code Sec. 469(g)(3))[18]

Unlike passive activity losses, unused credits are not allowed on disposition of the activity (Code Sec. 469(g)(1)(A)), but the taxpayer may elect to increase basis of property immediately before the transfer by the amount of unused passive credits that previously reduced the property's basis. (Code Sec. 469(j)(9)).[19]

Special rules apply where the interest in the activity is transferred by reason of death (Code Sec. 469(g)(2)), or where the disposition is by gift. (Code Sec. 469(j)(6))[20]

¶ 1815 Net Operating Losses (NOLs). ■■■■■■■■

Under Code Sec. 172, an NOL (¶1816) sustained in one year may be used to reduce the taxable income for another year. This is done by taking a deduction (the "NOL deduction") equal to the aggregate of NOL carryovers (carryforwards) and, in certain cases (e.g., farming losses), NOL carrybacks to a particular year, see ¶1818. The NOL deduction is subject to an 80%-of-taxable-income limit, see ¶1816. A taxpayer entitled to an NOL carryback can elect not to use it (¶1819).

11. ¶M-5163 *et seq.*, ¶S-4827.2
12. ¶M-5172
13. ¶M-5172.1
14. ¶M-5169, M-5170
15. ¶M-5175

16. ¶M-5701, ¶M-5704
17. ¶s M-5701, M-5701.3
18. ¶M-5701.2
19. ¶M-5701, ¶M-5703
20. ¶M-5705 *et seq.*

¶ 1816 Net operating loss (NOL) deduction—overview; amount of NOL deduction; 80%-of-taxable-income limit.

Under Code Sec. 172(a), a taxpayer's business's NOL (generally, the excess of business deductions, computed with certain modifications, over gross income in a particular tax year) sustained in one year may be used to reduce the taxpayer's taxable income in another year(s). This is done by taking a deduction (the "NOL deduction," summarized below) for that loss—comprised of NOL carryovers and, in certain cases (e.g., farming losses, see ¶1818), carrybacks—to the other tax year(s) in which the taxpayer has gross income that exceeds its business deductions.[21]

The NOL deduction is subject to an 80%-of-taxable-income limitation, under which the NOL deduction equals the sum of: (1) the aggregate amount of NOLs arising in tax years beginning before Jan. 1, 2018 ("pre-2018 NOLs") carried to that tax year, plus (2) the lesser of (i) the aggregate amount of NOLs arising in tax years beginning after Dec. 31, 2017, carried to that tax year; or (ii) 80% of the excess (if any) of taxable income over the aggregate amount of pre-2018 NOLs carried to that tax year.

Taxable income for purposes of the 80% limitation is computed without regard to the NOL deduction and the deductions under Code Sec. 199A (qualified business income, see ¶1593 *et seq.*) and Code Sec. 250 (foreign-derived intangible income (FDII) and global intangible low-taxed income (GILTI) deductions, see ¶3315). (Code Sec. 172(a)(1); Code Sec. 172(a)(2))[22]

¶ 1817 Which taxpayers can use net operating loss (NOL) deduction.

An NOL deduction is allowed to individuals, corporations (Code Sec. 172), estates and trusts (Code Sec. 642(d)), and charitable organizations (for the unrelated business income tax). (Code Sec. 512(b)(6))

An NOL deduction is not allowed to partnerships or common trust funds, but the deduction is allowed to the partners and participants. (Code Sec. 703(a)(2)(D); Code Sec. 584(g)) An NOL deduction is not allowed to regulated investment companies (Code Sec. 852(b)(2)(B)) or S corporations, but losses are passed through to shareholders. (Code Sec. 1366(a))[23]

¶ 1818 Net operating loss (NOL) carryforwards/carryovers and carrybacks; farming losses; insurance companies.

Under Code Sec. 172(b), an NOL (¶1816) for any tax year is carried back to earlier years and carried forward to later years as follows:

(1) Carried back: 2 years for farming losses (Code Sec. 172(b)(1)(B)) and property and casualty insurance company losses. (Code Sec. 172(b)(1)(C))[24]

(2) Carried over (carried forward): to each tax year following the year of the loss (i.e., indefinitely), for NOLs arising in tax years beginning after 2017 ("post-2017 NOLs"); and 20 years for pre-2018 NOLs. (Code Sec. 172(b)(1)(A)(ii))[25] However, property and casualty insurance company NOLs for any tax year can only be carried forward for 20 years. (Code Sec. 172(b)(1)(C))[26]

For the 80%-of-taxable income limitation on NOL deductions, see ¶1816.

So, there are three general categories of NOLs: pre-2018 NOLs, which may be carried forward 20 years; 2018, 2019, and 2020 NOLs, which may be carried forward indefinitely;

---

21. ¶M-4001
22. ¶M-4001 *et seq.*
23. ¶M-4003 *et seq.*

24. ¶M-4301
25. ¶M-4301
26. ¶ M-4313.1

and post-2020 NOLs, which may not be carried back, but may be carried forward indefinitely. Post-2020 farming losses may be carried back 2 years and carried forward indefinitely.[27]

A "farming loss" is the lesser of: (1) the amount that would be the NOL for the tax year taking into account only income and deductions attributable to farming businesses, or (2) the NOL for that tax year. A "farming business" is defined as in Code Sec. 263A(e)(4) under the uniform capitalization rules (¶4521). (Code Sec. 172(b)(1))[28]

¶ 1819   Election to forgo net operating loss (NOL) carryback.

Under Code Sec. 172(b)(3), a taxpayer entitled to an NOL carryback (¶1818) may irrevocably elect to forgo it and instead only carry over (forward) the NOL. The election must be made by the due date (including extensions) for filing the taxpayer's return for the tax year in which the NOL was incurred, by attaching a statement to that year's return (or amended return). (Code Sec. 172(b)(3)) The election also applies to alternative minimum tax NOLs (ATNOLs, ¶3208).[29]

¶ 1820   Computing the net operating loss (NOL) for noncorporate taxpayers.

A noncorporate taxpayer has an NOL in a tax year if allowable deductions exceed gross income, see ¶1816. Under Code Sec. 172(d), in arriving at the NOL for the year, NOL carryback (where allowed, see ¶1818) or carryover deductions from other years, personal exemptions (suspended through 2025), any deduction under Code Sec. 199A (the pass-through deduction, ¶1593), and exclusion of gain from qualified small business stock (¶2638) are not allowed. Moreover, capital loss and nonbusiness deductions are allowed only to a limited extent. (Code Sec. 172(d); Reg § 1.172-3(a))[30]

Where spouses who make a joint return for the deduction year made a joint return for all other tax years involved in computing the NOL deduction, that deduction is computed on the basis of their joint NOLs and combined taxable incomes. (Reg § 1.172-7(c)) Special rules apply if they did not make joint returns for all applicable years. (Reg § 1.172-7)[31]

¶ 1821   Computing the net operating loss (NOL) for corporate taxpayers.

Under Code Sec. 172(d), a corporation's NOL is figured by subtracting its deductions from its gross income, except that, in arriving at the NOL for the year: (1) NOL carrybacks (where allowed, see ¶1818) and carryovers from other years are not deducted; (2) the deduction for dividends received is taken without limiting it by a percentage of the corporation's taxable income; and (3) the deduction for foreign-derived intangible income and global intangible low-taxed income (¶3315) is not taken. (Code Sec. 172(d); Reg § 1.172-2(a))[32]

¶ 1822   Net operating loss (NOL) intervening year modifications.

Under Code Sec. 172(b)(2), if an NOL (¶1816) is not absorbed in the first year to which it is carried, then the amount of loss carried to a second year must be reduced not only by the first carryover year's taxable income but also by certain modifications or adjustments attributable to that first year. If the loss is carried to more than two years, then modifications must be made to each of the years to which it is carried ("intervening years") other than the last one. (Code Sec. 172(b)(2); Reg § 1.172-5)[33]

If the adjusted gross income (AGI) or taxable income of an intervening year is otherwise changed because of the modifications, deductions for that year that are based on, or limited

27. ¶M-4301 ¶M-4401
28. ¶M-4301 *et seq.*
29. ¶M-4304, M-4305
30. ¶M-4109 *et seq.*
31. ¶M-4405 *et seq.*
32. ¶M-4105 *et seq.*
33. ¶M-4200 *et seq.*

to, a percentage of AGI or taxable income must be recomputed. (Reg § 1.172-5(a)(2)(ii))[34]

¶ 1823   Deduction for Bad Debts. ████████████████

Bad debts are deductible whether or not connected with a taxpayer's business. A deduction is allowed for total worthlessness (¶1825) and, in some cases, for partial worthlessness (¶1826).

An item can't be deductible as both a bad debt and a loss. If it could be treated as either, it must be treated as a bad debt.[35] For deducting a loss for worthless stock or securities, see ¶1772.

¶ 1824   Time for deducting wholly worthless debt—bad debts.

Under Code Sec. 166(a)(1), a deduction is allowed for the tax year the debt becomes wholly worthless. (Code Sec. 166(a)(1))[36] (For *partial* worthlessness of *business* debts, see ¶1826.) The taxpayer must show the debt had value at the beginning of the year and no value at the end.[37] Worthlessness is a question of fact requiring consideration of all pertinent evidence, including the debtor's financial condition and the value of any security. (Reg § 1.166-2(a))[38]

¶ 1825   Amount of bad debt deduction; wholly worthless debt.

The amount deductible under Code Sec. 166(b) for a wholly worthless debt (¶1824) is its adjusted basis for determining loss on a sale or exchange (¶2400 *et seq.*), regardless of its face value. (Code Sec. 166(b); Reg § 1.166-1(d))[39] Payments received on the debt and prior deductions taken for a debt's partial worthlessness reduce the adjusted basis.[40]

If the creditor (the taxpayer) has no basis in the debt, the taxpayer is not entitled to a bad debt deduction.[41] Worthless debts arising from unpaid wages, salaries, fees, rents, and similar items of taxable income are not deductible as bad debts unless the income that these items represent has been included in the taxpayer's income. (Reg § 1.166-1(e))[42] Where a taxpayer reports receivables at fair market value (FMV) rather than face, the deduction can't exceed FMV. (Reg § 1.166-1(d)(2))[43]

Where a taxpayer fails to prove a debt's exact basis, it may be estimated by a court if the taxpayer proves the right to *some* deduction.[44]

If a debt is compromised because of inability to pay the full amount, the taxpayer deducts the debt's adjusted basis minus any cash and the value of any property received. If the debt is compromised for some other reason, the taxpayer does not have a bad debt (but may have a loss).[45]

¶ 1826   Deduction for partially worthless business debts.

A bad debt deduction is allowed for partially worthless debts (Code Sec. 166(a)(2)) *only if* (1) the debt is a business debt (¶1827); (2) IRS is satisfied that the debt is recoverable only in part; (3) the amount deducted was *charged off* on the books during the tax year; *and* (4) the debt is not evidenced by a security. (Code Sec. 166(e); Reg § 1.166-5(b))[46]

A taxpayer can charge off and deduct a debt for partial worthlessness as the worthlessness occurs, can defer charge-off and deduction to a later year when partial worthlessness is greater, or can defer deduction until (but not beyond) the year of total worthlessness.

---

34. ¶M-4207
35. ¶M-2503
36. ¶M-2401
37. ¶M-2701
38. ¶M-2702
39. ¶M-2402
40. ¶M-2405

41. ¶M-2404
42. ¶M-2506
43. ¶M-2402
44. ¶M-2404
45. ¶M-2406
46. ¶M-2801 *et seq.*

(Reg § 1.166-3(a)(2)(ii); Reg § 1.166-3(b))[47] For deducting "worthless securities" as losses, see ¶1772.

¶ 1827 Effect of classification as business or nonbusiness bad debt.

Code Sec. 166(a) provides that all debts held by corporations and business debts held by individuals and noncorporate taxpayers are business debts deductible against ordinary income. (Code Sec. 166(a)) Nonbusiness bad debts are deductible as short-term capital losses. (Code Sec. 166(d)(1)(B))[48] Both business and nonbusiness debts can be deducted when wholly worthless (¶1824), but only business debts are deductible when partly worthless (¶1826). (Code Sec. 166(a), Code Sec. 166(d)(1)(A))[49]

A *business debt* is either (1) a debt created or acquired in the course of the taxpayer's trade or business, or (2) a debt the loss from the worthlessness of which is incurred in the taxpayer's trade or business. Whether the loss from the worthlessness was incurred in the taxpayer's trade or business depends on the relation the loss bears to the taxpayer's business. If, at the time of the worthlessness, the relation is a "proximate" one to the conduct of the trade or business, the debt qualifies as a business bad debt. The borrower's use of the funds is irrelevant. (Reg § 1.166-5(b))[50]

A *nonbusiness debt* is a debt other than a business debt. (Code Sec. 166(d)(2); Reg § 1.166-5(b))[1]

For the limitation on deduction of capital losses for noncorporate taxpayers, see ¶2608.

¶ 1828 Bad debts of guarantors, shareholders, and shareholder/employees.

Guarantors. Under Reg § 1.166-9(a), a taxpayer who makes a guarantee agreement in the course of his or her trade or business is entitled to a business bad debt deduction for any payment made as guarantor of principal or interest. (Reg § 1.166-9(a))[2]

If a taxpayer (other than a corporation) makes a guarantee agreement in a transaction for profit (but not in the course of his or her business), and makes a payment of principal or interest, the taxpayer is entitled to a nonbusiness bad debt deduction in the year his or her right of subrogation becomes totally worthless. (Reg § 1.166-9(b), Reg § 1.166-9(e)(2))[3] For time for deducting worthless debt, see ¶1824.

Shareholders. An individual shareholder's loan to his or her corporation generally is not a business debt (¶1827).[4] But a shareholder's loan to his or her corporation can be a business debt if the shareholder is in the business of promoting, financing, and selling corporations.[5]

Shareholder/employee. A loan made by a shareholder/employee to his or her employer may be treated as a business debt if the loan is related to the trade or business of being an employee, required to be made by the employee, or the dominant motive for making the loan was to protect the employee's job.[6]

---

47. ¶M-2412, M-2801
48. ¶s M-2401, M-2901
49. ¶s M-2401, M-2800
50. ¶M-2902
1. ¶M-2902

2. ¶M-3207
3. ¶M-3210, M-3214
4. ¶M-2904
5. ¶M-2911
6. ¶M-2911 *et seq.*

Chapter 5 Depreciation, Amortization, Property Expensing and Depletion

¶ 1900 Depreciation and Other Cost Recovery. ▉

The Code, primarily under Code Sec. 167, Code Sec. 168, Code Sec. 197, Code Sec. 611 or Code Sec. 613A, allows an annual deduction of a portion of the cost of business or income-producing property (not held for sale) with a useful life of more than one year. This deduction (cost recovery) may be for depreciation, amortization or depletion (cost recovery deductions).

For most tangible property, a depreciation deduction is provided under the Modified Accelerated Cost Recovery System (MACRS), see ¶1906 *et seq.*, or under useful-life depreciation, see ¶1950. For general depreciation principles. see ¶1901 *et seq.*

For cost recovery for intangibles, see ¶1902, ¶1949, ¶1951 and ¶1957 *et seq.* For depletion deductions for natural resources, see ¶1960 *et seq.* For specialized amortization provisions, see ¶1954 *et seq.*

An enhanced first-year depreciation allowance of as high as 100% (80% in many situations), commonly referred to as bonus depreciation, may be claimed for qualified property, see ¶1929 *et seq.* For certain property, in lieu of all or part of the depreciation or amortization allowed, cost recovery can take the form of an election under Code Sec. 179 to deduct all or part of the cost in the year the property is placed in service ("expensing"), see ¶1935 *et seq.*, ¶1953 *et seq.*

¶ 1901 Claiming the depreciation deduction—Form 4562.

Generally, depreciation (e.g., under Code Sec. 167 or Code Sec. 168) is claimed using Form 4562. Instructions to Form 4562 specify that taxpayers other than C corporations don't have to complete or attach Form 4562 if (1) the only depreciation (or amortization) claimed is for assets (other than listed property, see ¶1940) placed in service before the tax year, (2) no Code Sec. 179 expense deduction (¶1935) is claimed, and (3) deductions are not claimed for a vehicle on a form other than Form 1040, Schedule C or Form 1040-SR, Schedule C.

Failure to claim depreciation doesn't allow a larger deduction in later years (Reg § 1.167(a)-10(a)) unless, where permitted, the failure is treated as an impermissible accounting method; which is corrected by following the procedures for changing to a permissible method of accounting in a later year, see ¶2827 *et seq.* For changes in computations as changes in method of accounting, see ¶2829. An amended return also can be used to correct depreciation for (1) a mathematical or posting error, or (2) an improper method used for no more than one tax year.[1]

¶ 1902 What property is depreciable? Depreciation of tangible and intangible property.

Under the requirements imposed by Code Sec. 167, most items of tangible property, (Reg § 1.167(a)-2) and certain intangibles (Reg § 1.167(a)-3) (see below), are depreciable if they:

(1) are used in a trade or business or held for the production of income, (Code Sec. 167(a))[2]

(2) have an exhaustible useful life that can be determined with reasonable accuracy, (Reg § 1.167(a)-1(a); Reg § 1.167(a)-1(b); Reg § 1.167(a)-2; Reg § 1.167(a)-3))[3] and

---

1. ¶G-2103, ¶G-2106.1, ¶G-2109, ¶G-2207.1
2. ¶L-7901

3. ¶L-7501, ¶L-7901

References beginning with a single letter are to paragraphs in Federal Tax Coordinator 2d and RIA's Analysis of Federal Taxes: Income.

(3) aren't inventory or stock in trade. (Reg § 1.167(a)-2)[4]

Land (as distinct from buildings and other land improvements) isn't depreciable.[5]

The cost of a life estate or other term interest can be amortized over the term if (1) the interest is acquired by purchase and isn't created by the taxpayer's division of a larger interest, and (2) the remainder interest isn't held by a person related to the taxpayer.[6]

Natural resources such as oil, gas, other minerals in the ground and timber qualify for *depletion* (¶1960 *et seq.*), not depreciation. (Reg § 1.167(a)-2)[7]

An intangible asset is depreciable (but not under MACRS, see ¶1906) if it's used in a trade or business or for production of income, has a limited, ascertainable useful life (with exceptions), and the taxpayer can show the cost of that asset. (Reg § 1.167(a)-3(a))

🅡🅘🅐**observation:** Some intangibles (like goodwill) can be depreciated or amortized, even though they don't have a limited, ascertainable useful life. For how to depreciate or amortize most depreciable intangibles, see ¶1949, ¶1951, and ¶1957 *et seq.*

Property used solely for personal purposes isn't depreciable (Reg § 1.167(a)-2), but property used only partially for personal purposes (mixed-use) is partially depreciable.[8]

Amounts paid for repairs and maintenance of tangible property may be deducted currently instead of depreciated under certain circumstances, see ¶1629 *et seq.*

¶ 1903 Who is entitled to depreciation deductions? Owners; life tenants; tenant-stockholders of cooperative housing corporations.

Ordinarily the property owner is the person entitled to deduct depreciation under Code Sec. 167, Code Sec. 168, or other Code sections.[9] This is the person that has the benefits and burdens of ownership, not necessarily legal title.[10] For depreciation of leased property and leasehold improvements, see ¶1919.

If a life tenancy is in depreciable property, the life tenant deducts depreciation as if he or she were the absolute owner of the property. (Code Sec. 167(d)) After the life tenant's death, the depreciation deduction, if any, is allowed to the remainderman. (Reg § 1.167(h)-1)[11] For rules that limit the depreciation or amortization of life estates and other limited interests in property, see ¶1902.

A tenant-stockholder of a cooperative housing corporation using a proprietary lease in a trade or business or for the production of income can, generally, depreciate the portion of the cost of the cooperative stock allocable to depreciable property. (Code Sec. 216(c))[12]

¶ 1904 When depreciation begins and ends—property placed in service or retired from service.

Under the rule provided under Code Sec. 167, depreciation begins when an asset is placed in service, (Reg § 1.167(a)-10(b)) (i.e., when it's in a condition or state of readiness and availability for a specifically defined function).[13]

Depreciation ends when the asset is retired from service, its cost or other basis is fully recovered, or it's sold or otherwise disposed of, whichever occurs first. (Reg § 1.167(a)-10(b); Reg § 1.167(b)-0(a); Reg § 1.168(i)-8(h))[14] For what are dispositions of MACRS assets, see ¶1905.

For MACRS property (¶1906 *et seq.*), computations for the years in which depreciation

---

4. ¶L-7905
5. ¶L-7912
6. ¶L-7831 *et seq.*
7. ¶L-7929, ¶N-2250 *et seq.*
8. ¶L-7908
9. ¶L-7802
10. ¶L-7803 *et seq.*
11. ¶L-7830
12. ¶K-5921 *et seq.*, ¶L-7828
13. ¶L-7601 *et seq.*
14. ¶L-7701 *et seq.*

begins and ends are subject to depreciation conventions (see ¶1923). For useful-life property (¶1950 *et seq.*), a proportionate part of a year's depreciation is allowed for the part of the year in which an asset is placed in service, but only if no depreciation convention is adopted for the asset. (Reg § 1.167(a)-10(b)) No depreciation deduction is allowed for MACRS property placed in service and disposed of in the same year. (Reg § 1.168(d)-1(b)(3)(ii))

¶ 1905 Dispositions of MACRS assets—transfer of ownership, withdrawal from use, partial dispositions, election of partial disposition treatment.

Regulations under Code Sec. 168 provide rules for the dispositions of MACRS (¶1906 *et seq.*) assets. (Reg § 1.168(i)-8)[15] For separate rules for dispositions from general asset accounts, see ¶1907.

A disposition of an asset depreciable under MACRS occurs when ownership is transferred or when the asset is permanently withdrawn from use either in a trade or business or in the production of income. A disposition includes a sale, exchange, retirement, physical abandonment, destruction, or transfer to a supplies, scrap, or similar account. A disposition doesn't include disposition of a structural component of a building unless the disposition qualifies as a "partial disposition." (Reg § 1.168(i)-8(b)(2))[16]

Partial dispositions include: (A) a disposition of a portion of an asset as a result of a casualty event (¶1782 *et seq.*); (B) a disposition of a portion of an asset for which gain, determined without regard to depreciation recapture (¶2672), isn't recognized in whole or in part under Code Sec. 1031 (like-kind exchanges, ¶2416) or Code Sec. 1033 (involuntary conversions, ¶2429); (C) a transfer of a portion of an asset in a transaction described in Code Sec. 168(i)(7)(B) (corporate or partnership step-in-the-shoes, see ¶1909; or between consolidated return group members, see ¶3338 *et seq.*); (D) *any disposition* of a portion of an asset for which the taxpayer *elects* partial disposition treatment; or (E) a sale of a portion of an asset, even if no partial-disposition-election is made. (Reg § 1.168(i)-8(d)(1))[17] The regulations describe when and how to make the election. (Reg § 1.168(i)-8(d)(2))[18]

The regulations provide additional guidance addressing whether or not, for disposition purposes, an asset is a separate asset or merely part of a larger asset. (Reg § 1.168(i)-8(c)(4))[19] The regulations also provide guidance on the identification of which asset has been disposed of. (Reg § 1.168(i)-8(g))[20]

¶ 1906 The Modified Accelerated Cost Recovery System (MACRS). ■■■■■■■

Modified Accelerated Cost Recovery System (MACRS) depreciation under Code Sec. 168 is determined under: (1) the general depreciation system (GDS), or (2) the alternative depreciation system (ADS), which is mandatory for some MACRS property and elective for all other MACRS property; see ¶1926 *et seq.*

In both systems, the depreciation deduction is determined by applying the depreciation method (¶1921) to the depreciable basis (below) of the property over the applicable recovery period (¶1920), subject to the applicable placed-in-service conventions (¶1923).[21] For "bonus depreciation," see ¶1929 *et seq.*

If the taxpayer doesn't choose to apply the optional IRS depreciation tables (¶1910), MACRS depreciation deductions are computed on the property's adjusted basis (also referred to by IRS as the "unrecovered basis"), except that salvage value is considered to be zero, i.e., is disregarded. (Code Sec. 168(b)(4)) This "unrecovered basis" is adjusted (i.e., ordinarily reduced) by depreciation previously allowed or allowable.[22] For the basis used under the optional IRS depreciation tables, see ¶1910. For mixed-use property, see ¶1902.

---

15. ¶L-10610 *et seq.*
16. ¶L-10612
17. ¶L-10612.1
18. ¶L-10612.2 *et seq.*

19. ¶L-10615
20. ¶L-10616
21. ¶L-8100 *et seq.*
22. ¶L-8601

Subject to certain exclusions (below), expensing rules (¶1935 *et seq.*), and amortization rules (¶1953 *et seq.*), most tangible depreciable property (see ¶1902) must be depreciated under MACRS. (Code Sec. 168(a))[23]

The following property isn't depreciable under MACRS: intangible property (see Code Sec. 168(a)); property ineligible for MACRS under "anti-churning" rules; property that the taxpayer elects to depreciate under a method not expressed in a term of years (e.g., the income-forecast method (¶1949)); public utility property for which the taxpayer doesn't use the MACRS normalization method of accounting; motion picture films or video tapes; and master sound recordings. (Code Sec. 168(f))[24]

¶ 1907 General asset accounts (GAAs) for MACRS property—Form 4562; mixed use property; assets generating foreign income; qualifying dispositions.

Under Code Sec. 168, taxpayers can elect to maintain one or more general asset accounts (GAAs) for eligible MACRS property. (Code Sec. 168(i)(4))[25] The election is made on a Form 4562 that is included in a timely filed return (including extensions) for the tax year in which the assets are placed in service. (Reg § 1.168(i)-1(l)(2)) For partnerships and S corporations, the election is made at the entity level. (Reg § 1.168(i)-1(l)(1))[26]

Assets grouped in a GAA. Each GAA must include only assets with the same depreciation method, recovery period, and convention that are placed in service in the same tax year (and if the assets are subject to the mid-quarter convention or mid-month convention, see ¶1923, then within the same calendar quarter or month, respectively). Also, in addition to being segregated by those common characteristics, regulations specify types of assets that must be further segregated into separate GAAs. For example, an asset for which bonus depreciation is allowed can be grouped only with assets for which the taxpayer claimed the same percentage of bonus depreciation (e.g., 50%, 80%, or 100%, see ¶1929 *et seq.*). (Reg § 1.168(i)-1(c)(2))[27]

Mixed use property (i.e., used both for business or income producing use and personal use), and property bought and disposed of during the same tax year can't be in a GAA.[28] Additionally, special rules apply for assets generating foreign source income. (Reg § 1.168(i)-1(c)(1))[29]

Each GAA is depreciated as a single asset, and the depreciation for each GAA is recorded in a separate depreciation reserve account. (Reg § 1.168(i)-1(d))[30]

General rules for dispositions. A disposition from a GAA occurs when ownership of an asset is transferred or the asset is permanently withdrawn from use in the taxpayer's trade or business or in the production of income. A disposition includes the sale, exchange, retirement, physical abandonment, or destruction of an asset or its transfer to a supplies, scrap, or similar account. A disposition doesn't include disposition of a structural component of a building unless the disposition qualifies as a "partial disposition." (Reg § 1.168(i)-1(e)(1)(i))[31] For dispositions of MACRS assets not held in GAAs, see ¶1905.

Partial dispositions are as defined for purposes of the MACRS disposition rules discussed at ¶1905 except that (1) they also include a disposition in an abusive transaction, and (2) instead of including dispositions of a portion of an asset made under the election discussed at ¶1905, they include partial disposition treatment for a portion of an asset included in a transaction for which an election described in *Qualifying dispositions* or *Optional termination of entire GAA* below is made. (Reg § 1.168(i)-1(e)(1)(ii))[32]

The consequences for dispositions, under the above general rules, from a GAA are that:

---

23. ¶L-8201
24. ¶L-8201
25. ¶L-8922 *et seq.*
26. ¶L-8931
27. ¶L-8922A *et seq.*

28. ¶L-8922
29. ¶L-8922.1
30. ¶L-8922.2
31. ¶L-8930
32. ¶L-8930A

(1) The asset that's disposed of is treated as having an adjusted basis of zero, so a loss can't be realized on the disposition.

(2) Any amount realized on the disposition is ordinary income to the extent that the sum of the GAA's unadjusted depreciable basis and any "expensed cost" (as defined in Reg § 1.168(i)-1(b)(5)) for assets in the account exceeds any amounts previously recognized as ordinary income upon the disposition of other assets in the account. The recognition and character of any excess amount is determined under other applicable Code provisions (other than the recapture rules).

(3) The disposition does not affect how the GAA is depreciated. Thus, depreciation continues as if the disposed-of asset(s) were still in the GAA. (Reg § 1.168(i)-1(e)(2))[33]

Qualifying dispositions. A taxpayer can elect to terminate GAA treatment for a "qualifying disposition" of an asset. Recognition, amount, and character of gain or loss is determined under the rules generally applicable under the Code (rather than under the rules discussed immediately above), except that Code Sec. 1245/Code Sec. 1250 recapture is limited to the excess of the depreciation (and any expensing) allowed or allowable for the GAA over any amounts previously recognized as ordinary income under the general GAA rules. Adjustments are made to the GAA and its depreciation reserve to reflect the removal of the asset. (Reg § 1.168(i)-1(e)(3)(iii))[34]

A qualifying disposition is: (1) a direct result of a casualty or theft; (2) a deductible charitable contribution; (3) a direct result of a cessation, termination, or disposition of a business, manufacturing, or other income-producing process, operation, facility, plant, or other unit (other than by transfer to a supplies, scrap, or similar account); or (4) a nonrecognition transaction other than (i) a Code Sec. 168(i)(7)(B) "step in the shoes" transaction (¶1909), (ii) a Code Sec. 1031 like-kind exchange or a Code Sec. 1033 involuntary conversion, or (iii) an abusive transaction as defined in Reg § 1.168(i)-1(e)(3)(vii). (Reg § 1.168(i)-1(e)(3)(iii)(B))[35]

Optional termination of entire GAA. Generally, a taxpayer continues to recover the cost of a GAA over its normal recovery period even though all of its assets have been disposed of. Alternatively, a taxpayer can elect to end GAA treatment, and recover the GAA's adjusted depreciable basis, when it sells the remaining assets in a GAA. Recognition, amount, and character of gain or loss are determined as described above for qualifying dispositions. (Reg § 1.168(i)-1(e)(3)(ii))[36]

Mandatory termination. A GAA must be terminated when all of its remaining assets are transferred in a Code Sec. 168(i)(7)(B), Code Sec. 1031, or Code Sec. 1033 transaction. If less than all of the assets in the GAA are transferred in any of those transactions, GAA treatment terminates only for transferred assets. Additionally, if the taxpayer disposes of an asset from a GAA in certain recapture transactions and abusive transactions, or if the asset is no longer exclusively used for business or income production, GAA treatment for that asset terminates. (Reg § 1.168(i)-1(e)(3); Reg § 1.168(i)-1(g); Reg § 1.168(i)-1(h)(1))[37]

¶ 1908   Multiple asset accounts (MAAs) for MACRS property.

Under Code Sec. 168, taxpayers can account for depreciation of MACRS assets using multiple-asset accounts (MAAs). In general, the only effects of accounting for MACRS assets in MAAs are that (1) annual calculations of depreciation are simplified, and (2) where specific identification of which asset, among similar assets, is being disposed of is impracticable, a taxpayer can alternatively use (A) in most instances, another reasonable method to determine the basis of the disposed of asset, and (B) one of several methods prescribed by IRS to identify the asset and the year that it was placed in service.

---

33. ¶L-8924
34. ¶L-8925
35. ¶L-8930

36. ¶L-8926
37. ¶L-8922, L-8925.1, L-8925.2, L-8926.1, L-8926.2

(Reg § 1.168(i)-7)[38] For other rules for dispositions of MACRS assets, including dispositions of assets from MAAs, see ¶1905.

¶ 1909 "Step into the shoes" rule for certain carryover-basis property—property acquired in nontaxable transfers.

Under Code Sec. 168, if property is acquired in certain nontaxable transfers (such as transactions described in Code Sec. 332 (¶3560), Code Sec. 351 (¶3500), or Code Sec. 361 (¶3541), the transferee "steps into the shoes" of the transferor for the depreciation period and method of the transferred property. This applies to the extent that the transferee's basis in the property equals the transferor's adjusted basis. (Code Sec. 168(i)(7)(B); Code Sec. 168(i)(7)(C))[39]

¶ 1910 IRS optional MACRS rate tables; "unadjusted depreciable basis" defined.

Under Code Sec. 168, instead of making the MACRS computations described at ¶1906 and ¶1921 for either the general or alternate depreciation systems, a taxpayer can, with no notice to IRS, instead rely on tables provided by IRS (reproduced at ¶1118[40]), subject to the following rules:

(1) All the tables' rates (accelerated or straight-line) are applied to the property's *unadjusted depreciable basis* (or to the *remaining adjusted depreciable basis* when bonus depreciation is claimed, see ¶1929 *et seq.*). For that purpose, unadjusted depreciable basis is the basis for determining gain or loss, not reduced by prior depreciation, and reflecting reductions in basis for: (a) personal-use percentage of the asset for the tax year; (b) any portion of the asset that is expensed under Code Sec. 179 (¶1935) and similar provisions; and (c) other initial basis adjustments—e.g., for the Code Sec. 44 disabled-access credit (¶2323). (Reg § 1.168(k)-1(a)(2)(iii); Reg § 1.168(b)-1(a)(3); Reg § 1.168(k)-2(e)(2)(i))[41]

(2) The taxpayer must use the tables to compute the annual depreciation allowances for the entire recovery period of the property. However, a taxpayer may not continue to use the tables if there are any adjustments to the basis of the property for reasons other than: (a) depreciation allowed or allowable, or (b) an addition or an improvement to such property that is subject to depreciation as a separate item of property.

(3) Use of the tables is denied for a short tax year and for later tax years for personal property not fully depreciated by the end of the short tax year (¶1922).[42]

⚫ *illustration:* T bought an item of 7-year property (P) for $50,000, placed P in service on Aug. 11, Year 1, and used P exclusively in T's business. For Year 1, bonus depreciation for P is 80%. None of the adjustments described in (1) above apply. After the bonus depreciation allowance of $40,000 (unadjusted depreciable basis of $50,000 x 80%), the remaining adjusted depreciable basis of the property is $10,000. The depreciation rates (percentages) for 7-year property using the 200% declining balance method and the half-year convention are found in Table 1, see ¶1118. Based on those rates, the resulting depreciation deductions during the recovery period are as follows (with Year 1 to be added to the bonus depreciation allowance):

Year	Basis	Percentage	Deduction
1	$10,000	14.29%	$1,429
2	10,000	24.49%	2,449
3	10,000	17.49%	1,749

38. ¶L-8932 *et seq.*, ¶L-10614, L-10616
39. ¶L-10401
40. ¶L-8904 *et seq.*
41. ¶L-8602, ¶L-9331.2
42. ¶L-8905

4	10,000	12.49%	1,249
5	10,000	8.93%	893
6	10,000	8.92%	892
7	10,000	8.93%	893
8	10,000	4.46%	446

¶ 1911 Determining the MACRS recovery class for an asset; class life of property.

Under Code Sec. 168, the assignment of MACRS property to a category with a designated recovery class is generally made by reference to that property's "class life" as of Jan. 1, 1986. (Code Sec. 168(i)(1)) The class life of many types of assets is carried in Rev Proc 87-56. The assignment to a MACRS recovery class is determined as follows (Code Sec. 168(e)(1)):

MACRS Recovery Class	Property With a Class Life (in Years) of:
3-Year	4 or less
5-Year	5 or more but less than 10
7-Year	10 or more but less than 16
10-Year	16 or more but less than 20
15-Year	20 or more but less than 25
20-Year	25 or more

Also, MACRS assigns specified property to the recovery classes described above (see ¶1912 *et seq.*) and as follows: water utility property to a 25-year class; residential rental property to a 27.5-year class; nonresidential real property placed in service before May 13, 1993 to a 31.5-year class; nonresidential real property placed in service after May 12, 1993 to the 39-year class; any railroad grading and tunnel bore to a 50-year class. (Code Sec. 168(c))[43]

¶ 1912 MACRS 3-year property—personal property with a class life of four years or less, rent-to-own property, racehorses.

Under Code Sec. 168, MACRS 3-year property includes:

... Depreciable personal property with a class life of four years or less (Code Sec. 168(e)(1)), such as: tractor units for use over-the-road; breeding hogs; special handling devices used in the manufacture of food and beverages; and special tools used in the manufacture of motor vehicles, rubber products, and finished plastic products.

... Qualified rent-to-own (RTO) property (certain consumer durables held for rent). (Code Sec. 168(e)(3)(A); Code Sec. 168(i)(14))

... Racehorses (any age) placed in service before 2022; racehorses over two years old placed in service after 2021; and other (non-race) horses over 12 years old when placed in service. (Code Sec. 168(e)(3)(A))[44]

¶ 1913 MACRS 5-year property—generally personal property with a class life of five to nine years, automobiles, farm machinery and equipment, etc.

Under Code Sec. 168, MACRS 5-year property includes:

... Depreciable personal property with a class life of more than four years and less than 10 years (Code Sec. 168(e)(1)), such as: office machinery (e.g., copiers); information systems (computers); heavy general purpose trucks; trailers and trailer-mounted containers; breeding or dairy cattle; support vessels used in offshore oil and gas operations (whether or not used in connection with drilling); and certain assets used in the drilling

---

43. ¶L-8203   44. ¶L-8206

of oil and gas wells, in construction, in the manufacture of textile yarns, apparel, and other finished goods, and in the cutting of timber.[45]

... Any automobiles or light-general purpose trucks. (Code Sec. 168(e)(3)(B)(i))

... Semiconductor manufacturing equipment in ADR class 36.0. (Code Sec. 168(e)(3)(B)(ii))

... Computer-based telephone central office switching equipment. (Code Sec. 168(e)(3)(B)(iii))

... Qualified technological equipment. (Code Sec. 168(e)(3)(B)(iv))

... Code Sec. 1245 property used in connection with research and experimentation. (Code Sec. 168(e)(3)(B)(v))

... Certain energy-related property. (Code Sec. 168(e)(3)(B)(vi); Code Sec. 48(a)(3)(A))

... Most farm machinery and equipment placed in service after 2017. (Code Sec. 168(e)(3)(B)(vii))[46]

¶ 1914   MACRS 7-year MACRS property—generally property with a class life of 10 to 15 years, office furniture, property without a class life, etc.

Under Code Sec. 168, MACRS 7-year property includes:

... Property with a class life of 10 years or more, but less than 16 years (Code Sec. 168(e)(1)), such as: office furniture, fixtures, and certain other equipment; certain assets (except helicopters) used in air transport; certain assets used in the exploration and production of petroleum and natural gas products, in manufacture of wood products and furniture, and in theme parks, amusement parks and recreation facilities; and farm machinery and equipment (including vineyard trellising) placed in service before 2018.[47]

... Property that doesn't have a class life and isn't specifically assigned to any other MACRS class. (Code Sec. 168(e)(3)(C)(v))

... Any horse not assigned to the three-year class (see ¶1912).[48]

... Railroad tracks. (Code Sec. 168(e)(3)(C)(i))

... Certain Alaska natural gas pipeline property. (Code Sec. 168(e)(3)(C)(iii); Code Sec. 168(i)(16))

... "Natural gas gathering lines" if the taxpayer is the original user. (Code Sec. 168(e)(3)(C)(iv))

... Assets used to convert corn to fuel grade ethanol.[49]

¶ 1915   MACRS 10-year property—property with a class life of 16 to 19 years, fruit-or-nut-bearing trees or vines, qualified smart electric meters, etc.

Under Code Sec. 168, MACRS 10-year property includes:

... Property with a class life of 16 years or more but less than 20 (Code Sec. 168(e)(1)), such as: water transport equipment not used in marine construction; assets used in petroleum refining, and in the manufacture of grain and grain mill products, sugar and sugar products, and vegetable oils and vegetable oil products.[50]

... A single purpose agricultural or horticultural structure (Code Sec. 168(e)(3)(D)(i))

... Any tree or vine bearing fruit or nuts (Code Sec. 168(e)(3)(D)(ii))

... Qualified smart electric meters or qualified smart electric grid systems. (Code Sec. 168(e)(3)(D)(iii); Code Sec. 168(e)(3)(D)(iv); Code Sec. 168(i)(18); Code Sec. 168(i)(19))[1]

45. ¶L-8207
46. ¶L-8207
47. ¶L-8209, ¶N-1361
48. ¶L-8209
49. ¶L-8209
50. ¶L-8213
1. ¶L-8213

¶ 1916   MACRS 15-year property—generally property with a class life of 20 to 24 years, land improvements, gas stations, etc.

Under Code Sec. 168, MACRS 15-year property includes:

(1) Property with a class life of 20 years or more but less than 25 years, (Code Sec. 168(e)(1)) such as: land improvements (e.g., sidewalks and roads) that aren't explicitly included in another class and aren't buildings or structural improvements; "modern" golf-course greens; assets such as service-station and car-wash buildings; and concrete footings used to anchor gas station pump canopies.

(2) Municipal wastewater treatment plants. (Code Sec. 168(e)(3)(E)(i))

(3) Telephone distribution plants and comparable equipment used for two-way exchange of voice and data communications. (Code Sec. 168(e)(3)(E)(ii))

(4) Any Code Sec. 1250 property (generally, depreciable real property) that is a retail motor fuels outlet (many gas stations qualify, even if they include convenience stores). (Code Sec. 168(e)(3)(E)(iii))[2]

(5) Initial clearing and grading land improvements relating to gas utility property. (Code Sec. 168(e)(3)(E)(iv))[3]

(6) Certain new electrical transmission property. (Code Sec. 168(e)(3)(E)(v))

(7) Certain new "natural gas distribution lines" placed in service before Jan. 1, 2011. (Code Sec. 168(e)(3)(E)(vi))[4]

(8) Any qualified improvement property, also discussed at ¶1918. (Code Sec. 168(e)(3)(E)(vii))[5]

¶ 1917   MACRS 20-year property—property with a class life of 25 years or more, farm buildings and gas utility distribution facilities.

Under Code Sec. 168, MACRS 20-year property includes property with a class life of 25 years or more (Code Sec. 168(e)(1)), such as farm buildings (other than single purpose agricultural or horticultural structures, see ¶1915) and gas utility distribution facilities.[6]

¶ 1918   Residential and nonresidential buildings under MACRS—residential rental property, multiple structures, manufactured homes, mobile homes.

Under Code Sec. 168, residential rental property is assigned to a 27.5-year MACRS recovery class. (Code Sec. 168(c)) Residential real property is defined as a building or structure for which 80% or more of the gross rental income is from dwelling units. A dwelling unit is a house or apartment that provides living accommodations in a building or structure, but doesn't include a unit in a hotel, motel, or other establishment more than half of the units in which are used on a transient basis. (Code Sec. 168(e)(2)(A))[7] In applying the 80% test, multiple structures that are on the same tract or parcel (or contiguous tracts or parcels) and operated as a single integrated unit are treated as a single building or structure. For example, an apartment building and a hotel were treated as a single building where located on the same tract and operated as a single integrated unit.[8] Otherwise-qualifying residential rental property can include manufactured homes, and, if permanently anchored, mobile homes. Also, housing in a senior citizens' community isn't barred from qualifying merely because services that include assisted living and nursing care are provided.[9]

2. ¶L-8214, ¶L-8804.1
3. ¶L-8214
4. ¶L-8218, ¶L-8219
5. ¶L-8208, ¶L-8215

6. ¶L-8221
7. ¶L-8226
8. ¶L-8227
9. ¶L-8226

Nonresidential real property is assigned to a 39-year MACRS recovery class, (Code Sec. 168(c)) which includes, generally, buildings or structures that aren't residential rental property. (Code Sec. 168(e)(2)(B))[10]

Elevators and escalators are treated as part of a building or structure. Assets that are viewed by IRS as buildings include floating casinos, if intended to remain permanently in place, and open-air parking garages.[11]

Whether an asset is part of a building or structure—and, thus, depreciated over a longer period than if it were treated as a separate asset—may depend on whether the asset would not have qualified as tangible personal property for purposes of prior law's investment tax credit.[12]

observation: Whether an asset is a structural component of a building (depreciated over 27.5 years or 39 years on a straight-line method, see ¶1921) or is personal property (usually depreciated on an accelerated basis, see ¶1921; over 5 years, see ¶1913; or over 7 years, see ¶1914), significantly changes the tax benefit derived from depreciation of the asset. Thus, it is common for taxpayers to engage tax professionals, usually working with architects, builders or engineers, to produce "cost segregation studies" that, although not binding on IRS, substantiate (1) the taxpayer's treatment of some items of property associated with a building as structural components and some as belonging to various classes of personal property, and (2) the taxpayer's allocation of costs between the building structural components and various classes of personal property.

The depreciation for any additions to, or improvement of, any real property (whether or not recovery property) is determined in the same manner as the depreciation deduction for the real property would be determined if the real property were placed in service at the same time as the addition or improvement. (Code Sec. 168(i)(6)(A))[13]

QIP. Qualified improvement property (QIP) is an improvement made by the taxpayer to an interior portion of a building which is nonresidential real property if it is placed in service after the date the building was first placed in service. However, improvements for the enlargement of the building, any elevator or escalator, or the internal structural framework of the building are not QIP. (Code Sec. 168(e)(6))[14] QIP has a 15-year MACRS recovery period (¶1916), and is eligible for bonus depreciation (¶1929). (Code Sec. 168(k)(2)(A)(i))

¶ 1919 Depreciation of property that is leased and leasehold improvements by lessees or lessors.

Under Code Sec. 167, if property is acquired subject to a lease (e.g., a retail building leased to a tenant), no portion of its adjusted basis can be allocated to the leasehold interest, and the entire adjusted basis is taken into account in determining any depreciation for the property subject to the lease. (Code Sec. 167(c)(2))[15]

A lessor (landlord) deducts depreciation on property that is already on the leased premises when it leases out the property and on any improvements it constructs during the term of the lease. (Reg § 1.167(a)-4) But the lessor can't deduct depreciation where the lease requires the lessee to replace property at the lessee's expense. In that case, the lessor suffers no "depreciable" loss, i.e., wear and tear, etc. [16]

Under Code Sec. 168, if improvements are made by the lessor for the lessee (e.g., to customize the space) and are irrevocably disposed of or abandoned by the lessor at the termination of the lease, then in determining gain or loss, the improvement is treated as disposed of by the lessor when disposed or abandoned. (Code Sec. 168(i)(8)(B))[17]

10. ¶L-8223
11. ¶L-8223
12. ¶L-8223
13. ¶L-9105

14. ¶L-8215
15. ¶L-7911.1; ¶L-6506
16. ¶L-7808, ¶L-7809
17. ¶L-9106

A lessee (tenant) ordinarily depreciates the cost of improvements it makes,[18] and the depreciation deductions are determined without regard to the lease term. (Code Sec. 168(i)(8)) The costs of acquiring a lease are amortizable, not depreciable, see ¶1579.

Where the lease ends and the lessee doesn't retain the improvement, the lessee has a gain or loss, determined with reference to any remaining unrecovered basis of the property.[19]

observation: A gain could arise if, for example, the tenant is paid to terminate the lease, and the amount paid exceeds the basis of the leasehold improvements, and lease acquisition costs, if any.

If a lessee excludes from income advance construction funds received from the lessor (¶1343), the lessor treats the improvements as its own nonresidential real property, including for purposes of the disposition-of-improvements rule (see above). (Code Sec. 110(b))[20]

¶ 1920 MACRS depreciation recovery periods; property classes.

Code Sec. 168 provides MACRS depreciation recovery periods according to depreciable property classifications. For the 3-year, 5-year, 7-year, 10-year, 15-year and 20-year classifications, which are based on asset class life, the depreciation recovery period is the same as the name of the class (e.g., 5 years for 5-year property). The water utility property class has a recovery period of 25 years. The residential rental property class has a recovery period of 27.5 years. The nonresidential real property class has a recovery period of 39 years (but 31.5 years for property is placed in service before May 13, 1993). The railroad grading or tunnel bore class has a recovery period of 50 years. (Code Sec. 168(c))[21]

¶ 1921 MACRS depreciation methods—200% and 150% declining balance methods, straight-line method.

Under Code Sec. 168, there are three depreciation methods used for MACRS property: the 200% and 150% declining balance methods with an appropriate switch to straight-line to maximize deductions, and the straight-line method. (Code Sec. 168(b)) Under the declining balance methods, the depreciation rate (in percentage terms) generally is determined by dividing the declining balance percentage (200% or 150%) by the applicable recovery period and applying that percentage to the property's depreciable basis.[22]

observation: Taxpayer's usually choose to use the optional depreciation tables for ease of computation. For each recovery year, a percentage is provided which has been adjusted for each year to reflect the use of unadjusted depreciable basis within the table rather than the declining adjusted depreciable basis. For discussion and an illustration, see ¶1910.

The 200% declining balance method can be used for MACRS property except where the 150% declining balance method or the straight-line method is required (or elected) as discussed below. (Code Sec. 168(b)(1))

Except where the straight-line method applies, the 150% declining balance method is used for MACRS property that is (1) in the 15-year class (¶1916) or 20-year class (¶1917), (2) a qualified smart electric meter or qualified smart electric grid system, or (3) property for which the taxpayer elects to use this method (see below). (Code Sec. 168(b)(2))[23]

The straight-line method must be used for: residential rental property; nonresidential real property; any railroad grading or tunnel bore; any tree or vine bearing fruit or nuts; water utility property; and qualified improvement property. (Code Sec. 168(b)(3))[24] For

---

18. ¶L-7809
19. ¶L-9106
20. ¶J-2265
21. ¶L-8802

22. ¶L-8902 *et seq.*
23. ¶L-8912
24. ¶L-8917

property not required to use the straight-line method, a taxpayer can elect this method. (Code Sec. 168(b)(3))[25]

The elections to use the 150% declining balance method, or the straight-line method, are made on a class-by-class basis and are irrevocable. (Code Sec. 168(b)(5))

For an alternative depreciation system (ADS) election that changes the depreciation method from accelerated to straight-line, see ¶1926 *et seq.* For computing depreciation for alternative minimum tax purposes, see ¶3207 *et seq.*

¶ 1922 Effect of short tax years on MACRS depreciation; "allocation method" or "simplified method."

Under Code Sec. 168, the depreciation allowance for MACRS personal property placed in service or disposed of in a short tax year (short year) can't be determined by using the IRS optional MACRS rate tables (discussed at ¶1910). The allowance for the short year is instead determined by: (1) multiplying the property's depreciable basis by the applicable depreciation rate, and (2) multiplying that product by a fraction, the numerator of which is the number of months (including fractions of months) the property is deemed in service during the short year under the applicable convention, and the denominator of which is 12.[26] Depreciation for any year following the short year is determined by consistently using either a prescribed "allocation method" or "simplified method." [27] For a short year other than the first year in the recovery period, the allowance must account for the difference between recovery years and tax years.[28]

¶ 1923 MACRS depreciation conventions—mid-month convention, mid-quarter convention, and half-year convention.

Under Code Sec. 168, the mid-month depreciation convention applies in determining MACRS depreciation deductions for the year that the following property is placed in service or disposed of: residential rental property (see ¶1918), nonresidential real property (see ¶1918), and railroad gradings or tunnel bores. Under this rule, property placed in service (or disposed of) during any month is treated as placed in service (or disposed of) at the mid-point of that month in computing MACRS depreciation deductions for the acquisition and disposition years. (Code Sec. 168(d)(2); Code Sec. 168(d)(4)(B))[29]

For all other MACRS property (referred to below as MACRS personal property), the half-year depreciation convention generally applies. It treats all MACRS personal property placed in service or disposed of during a tax year as placed in service or disposed of on the mid-point of that tax year. (Code Sec. 168(d)(1); Code Sec. 168(d)(4)(A))

Except as noted below, the mid-quarter convention applies to all MACRS personal property placed in service during a tax year if more than 40% of the total depreciable basis of all of that property placed in service during the year is placed in service during the year's last three months. (Code Sec. 168(d)(3))[30] Under the mid-quarter convention, property is treated as placed in service or disposed of on the mid-point of the applicable quarter. (Code Sec. 168(d)(4)(C))

When determining if the mid-quarter convention applies, the taxpayer excludes:

. . . Amounts expensed under Code Sec. 179, see ¶1935. (Reg § 1.168(d)-1(b)(4)(i))

. . . Nonresidential real property, residential rental property, and any railroad grading or tunnel bore. (Code Sec. 168(d)(3)(B)(i))

. . . Property placed in service and disposed of in the same tax year. (Code Sec. 168(d)(3)(B)(ii))

---

25. ¶L-8920 *et seq.*
26. ¶L-9002
27. ¶L-9003 *et seq.*
28. ¶L-9007
29. ¶L-8713
30. ¶L-8707 *et seq.*

. . . Property excluded from MACRS under Code Sec. 168(f), (Reg § 1.168(d)-1(b)(1)) such as films, videotapes and sound recordings.

. . . The basis of a business car, if the taxpayer elects for the placed-in-service year to claim deductions using the standard mileage allowance method (¶1553).

. . . That portion of basis attributable to the personal-use of mixed-use assets (e.g., a self-employed's car used for business and personal use). (Reg § 1.168(d)-1(b)(4)(iii))[31]

Additionally, when determining whether the mid-quarter convention applies, the depreciable basis of "qualified property" (property eligible for bonus depreciation, ¶1930) placed in service during the tax year isn't reduced by the bonus depreciation allowed or allowable for the tax year. (Reg § 1.168(k)-2(g)(11))

¶ 1924 MACRS deductions for property after use change—personal-use property converted to or from business or income-producing use.

Under Code Sec. 168, certain depreciation rules apply when there is a change in the use of property.[32]

Personal-use property converted to business or income-producing use (e.g., personal residence converted to rental property) is treated as placed in service on the conversion date, and is subject to the Code Sec. 168 depreciation method, recovery period, and placed-in-service convention applicable to the property beginning in the tax year of the conversion. The property's depreciable basis in the change year is the lesser of its fair market value or adjusted depreciable basis when it is converted. This rule doesn't apply when other rules (e.g., rules under Code Sec. 280F(b)(2)(A)) prescribe the depreciation treatment for a change to business use. (Reg § 1.168(i)-4(b))[33]

MACRS property converted from business or income-producing use to personal use generally is treated as a disposition, with depreciation for the conversion year computed by applying the applicable convention (¶1923). However, the conversion doesn't result in gain, loss, or depreciation recapture. (Reg § 1.168(i)-4(c))[34]

For changes in the primary use of an asset after the placed-in-service year, where the asset continues to be MACRS property in the taxpayer's hands (e.g., commercial property converted to residential rental property), MACRS depreciation for the change year is determined as though the change occurred on the first day of that year. (Reg § 1.168(i)-4(d)(2)(iii))[35]

If a use-change results in:

. . . A shorter recovery period and/or a faster depreciation method, adjusted depreciable basis as of the beginning of the change year is depreciated over the shorter recovery period and/or by the faster method beginning with the year of change as though the property were first placed in service in that year. (Reg § 1.168(i)-4(d)(3)(i)) Taxpayers may elect to continue to depreciate the property as though the change in use had not occurred. (Reg § 1.168(i)-4(d)(3)(ii))[36]

. . . A longer recovery period and/or slower depreciation method, adjusted depreciable basis is depreciated over the longer recovery period and/or by the slower method beginning with the year of change as if the property had been originally placed in service with the longer recovery period and/or slower depreciation method. (Reg § 1.168(i)-4(d)(4))[37]

Where use changes during placed-in-service year, the depreciation allowance generally is established by the primary use of the property during that tax year, determined in a consistently applied and reasonable manner. In determining whether property is used

31. ¶L-8707
32. ¶L-8108, ¶L-9122 *et seq.*, ¶L-9206.1
33. ¶L-8108
34. ¶L-9202, ¶L-9206.1

35. ¶L-9122
36. ¶L-9123
37. ¶L-9124

within or outside the U.S. during the placed-in-service year, the predominant use of the property governs. (Reg § 1.168(i)-4(e))

General asset accounts. A change in use (other than a change to any personal use) doesn't cause or permit the revocation of a general asset account election (¶1907), but, in some cases the property is removed from its existing general asset account and placed in a separate general asset account. (Reg § 1.168(i)-1(h))[38]

¶ 1925 Depreciating MACRS property acquired in a like-kind exchange or involuntary conversion; depreciable exchanged basis and depreciable excess basis.

MACRS property, depreciable under Code Sec. 168, may be acquired (1) in exchange for MACRS property in a Code Sec. 1031 like-kind property exchange (¶2416 *et seq.*), or (2) to replace involuntarily converted MACRS property in a Code Sec. 1033 involuntary conversion (¶2429 *et seq.*). (Reg § 1.168(i)-6(c)(1))

⚓/caution: The Code Sec. 1031 non-recognition rules (see ¶2416) apply only to like-kind exchanges of real property. Thus, exchanges of non-realty assets (even if of like kind) are treated as a sale of the relinquished asset and purchase of the acquired asset, requiring no complex MACRS depreciation calculations.

The replacement property is, for depreciation purposes, divided into the depreciable exchanged basis (i.e., remaining basis of the relinquished property carried over to the replacement property), and the depreciable excess basis (i.e., additional consideration to acquire the replacement property). Where the properties share the same recovery class and depreciation method, the depreciable exchanged basis is written off over what's left of the relinquished property's recovery period; and the depreciable excess basis is in effect treated as a separate property with a recovery period that begins anew. (Reg § 1.168(i)-6(c)(3)(ii))[39]

Complex rules apply if the exchanged properties aren't depreciated with the same period and/or method. (Reg § 1.168(i)-6(c)(3)(iii); Reg § 1.168(i)-6(c)(4))[40]

Under certain circumstances, some or all of the tax basis for replacement MACRS property can be eligible for additional first-year depreciation (bonus depreciation, ¶1929 *et seq.*). The requirements are contained in Reg § 1.168(k)-2(g)(5) and Reg § 1.168(k)-1(f)(5)[41]

Election out. A taxpayer may elect not to apply the above "split basis" approach to exchanged properties, and, instead, treat the exchanged basis and excess basis, if any, in the replacement property as placed in service at the time of replacement and the adjusted depreciable basis of the relinquished MACRS property as being disposed of. (Reg § 1.168(i)-6(i))[42]

¶ 1926 The straight-line "alternative depreciation system" (ADS) of MACRS.

Under Code Sec. 168, the alternative depreciation system (ADS) for MACRS property is a straight-line depreciation system, with generally longer depreciation periods than under the general depreciation system (GDS, see ¶1906). (Code Sec. 168(g)(2)(A), Code Sec. 168(g)(3)(B)) ADS uses the same depreciation conventions as GDS (discussed at ¶1923), (Code Sec. 168(g)(2)(B)) and, like GDS, disregards salvage value. (Code Sec. 168(g)(2)(A))

Depreciation deductions must be computed under ADS only for certain specified properties, see ¶1927. However, ADS may be elected for all other properties—on a class by class

---

38. ¶L-8923
39. ¶L-10600 *et seq.*
40. ¶L-10601.2A

41. ¶L-10602 *et seq.*
42. ¶L-10601.8

basis for personal property and on an individual basis for residential rental and nonresidential real properties. (Code Sec. 168(g)(7)(A)) An ADS election is an irrevocable year-by-year election. (Code Sec. 168(g)(7)(B)) This election is in addition to the straight-line MACRS election (discussed at ¶1921).

For computing earnings and profits of corporations, ADS must be used for all properties, including properties depreciated under GDS (Code Sec. 312(k)(3)(A)). ADS also applies for purposes of computing the depreciation tax preference under the alternative minimum tax, under the rules explained at ¶3207.[43]

¶ 1927   MACRS property required to be depreciated under ADS—including autos and other "Listed" property, property used outside the U.S., tax-exempt use property, certain imported business equipment.

Under Code Sec. 168, the following MACRS property *must* be depreciated under the ADS (¶1926):

(a) "Listed" property (see ¶1939), which includes passenger automobiles, used 50% or more for personal purposes. (Code Sec. 280F(b)(1))

(b) Tangible property used predominantly outside the U.S., but with certain exceptions specified by the Code. (Code Sec. 168(g)(1)(A); Code Sec. 168(g)(4))[44]

(c) Tax-exempt use property (generally, certain property leased to tax-exempt organizations, governmental units or foreign persons or entities). (Code Sec. 168(g)(1)(B); Code Sec. 168(h)(1))[45]

(d) Tax-exempt bond financed property. (Code Sec. 168(g)(1)(C))[46]

(e) Imported business equipment from countries that discriminate against U.S. goods from the date the equipment is placed on a restricted list by Presidential Executive Order. (Code Sec. 168(g)(1)(D); Code Sec. 168(g)(6))[47]

(f) The following categories of property, if held by an electing real property trade or business, as defined in Code Sec. 163(j)(7) (generally, a real property trade or business that elects to not apply limitations on interest deductions, see ¶1710): nonresidential real property (¶1918), residential rental property (¶1918), and qualified improvement property (¶1918). (Code Sec. 168(g)(1)(F); Code Sec. 168(g)(8)) Also, any property with a recovery period of 10 years or more that is held by a farm business that makes a similar Code Sec. 163(j)(7) election. (Code Sec. 168(g)(1)(G); Code Sec. 168(g)(8))[48] For both sets of property, the requirement to use ADS applies even if the property was placed in service before the election year is made. If bonus depreciation (¶1929 *et seq.*) was allowed for the property before the election year, the bonus depreciation is not redetermined.

(g) Pre-production costs of farming property excluded from the UNICAP inventory-capitalization rule (discussed in ¶1639 *et seq.*). (Code Sec. 263A(e)(2))[49]

(h) Intermodal cargo containers not used predominantly in the direct transportation of property to or from the U.S.[50]

(i) Any property for which an election to apply ADS is made (see ¶1926). (Code Sec. 168(g)(1)(E); Code Sec. 168(g)(7))

¶ 1928   ADS depreciation periods; prescribed ADS straight-line periods.

Under Code Sec. 168, the prescribed ADS straight-line recovery periods are:

. . . except as discussed below, the property's "class-life" (see ¶1911). (Code Sec. 168(g)(2)(C); Code Sec. 168(g)(3)(B))

---

43. ¶A-8220
44. ¶L-9406
45. ¶L-9600 *et seq.*
46. ¶L-9500 *et seq.*

47. ¶L-9405
48. ¶L-9402.1, ¶L-9402.2
49. ¶L-9402
50. ¶s L-9402, L-9407

254

... four years—qualified rent-to-own property (¶1912). (Code Sec. 168(g)(3)(B))

... five years—automobiles, light-purpose trucks, (Code Sec. 168(g)(3)(D)) qualified technological equipment, (Code Sec. 168(g)(3)(C)) and semi-conductor manufacturing equipment (¶1913). (Code Sec. 168(g)(3)(B))

... 9.5 years—computer-based telephone central office switching equipment (¶1913). (Code Sec. 168(g)(3)(B))

... 10 years—most new farming equipment and machinery (¶1913) and railroad track (¶1914). (Code Sec. 168(g)(3)(B))

... 12 years—personal property with no class life and not governed by any other rule discussed in this list. (Code Sec. 168(g)(2)(C))

... 14 years—new natural gas gathering lines (¶1914). (Code Sec. 168(g)(3)(B))

... 15 years—any single purpose agricultural or horticultural structure (¶1915). (Code Sec. 168(g)(3)(B))

... 20 years—trees or vines bearing fruit (¶1915), any Code Sec. 1250 property (generally depreciable real property) which is a retail motor fuels outlet (¶1916), gas utility initial clearing and grading land improvements (¶1916), and qualified improvement property (¶1916). (Code Sec. 168(g)(3)(B))

... 22 years—certain Alaska natural gas pipeline property (¶1914). (Code Sec. 168(g)(3)(B))

... 24 years—any municipal wastewater treatment plant; telephone distribution plants for 2-way communications (¶1916). (Code Sec. 168(g)(3)(B))

... 25 years—electric utility initial clearing and grading land improvements (¶1917). (Code Sec. 168(g)(3)(B))

... 30 years—residential rental property (¶1918) placed in service after 2017, (Code Sec. 168(g)(2)(C)) and certain new electrical transmission property (¶1916). (Code Sec. 168(g)(3)(B)) For special treatment for a particular subset of residential rental property placed in service before 2018, see below.

... 35 years—certain new natural gas distribution lines placed in service before Jan. 1, 2011 (¶1916). (Code Sec. 168(g)(3)(B))

... 40 years—nonresidential real property (¶1918); (Code Sec. 168(g)(2)(C) any Code Sec. 1245 real property with no class life; (Code Sec. 168(g)(3)(E)) and if placed in service before 2018, residential rental property (¶1918).[1]

... 50 years for railroad gradings, tunnel bores, or water utility property. (Code Sec. 168(g)(2)(C))[2]

An electing real property trade or business under Code Sec. 163(j)(7)(B) (an "electing taxpayer," see ¶1710), must use the ADS for residential rental property (see ¶1927). As above, prior to 2018 (the TCJA), the ADS recovery period for residential rental property was 40 years instead of 30 years. Thus, an electing taxpayer that held residential rental property placed in service before 2018 (pre-2018 property), and that was forced to switch to the ADS by Code Sec. 168(g)(1)(F), had to use a 40-year recovery period for that pre-2018 property. In Dec. 2020, the ADS recovery period for pre-2018 property was retroactively changed from 40 to 30 years for electing taxpayers changing to the ADS. For applicable electing taxpayers that had started reporting depreciation under the 40-year period prior to the retroactive change, they must correct their method of computation. This may be done by following specific rules and filing either an amended Federal income tax return or information return; an administrative adjustment request (AAR); or a Form 3115 (for a change in accounting method). And if pre-2018 property was included in a general asset account (GAA), taxpayers may use those remedies to change their GAA treatment to comply with Reg § 1.168(i)-1(h)(2) (for when there is a change in use of property). (Rev

---

1. ¶L-9403   2. ¶L-9403

Proc 2021-28)[3]

For "tax-exempt use property" (¶1927) subject to a lease, the above depreciation periods can't be less than 125% of the lease term. (Code Sec. 168(g)(1)(B); Code Sec. 168(g)(3)(A))[4]

¶ 1929   Bonus first-year depreciation allowance for qualified property.

Code Sec. 168(k) provides an additional first-year depreciation deduction allowance (bonus depreciation) for "qualified property" (¶1930). Bonus depreciation is claimed in the year the property is placed in service by the taxpayer for use in its trade or business or for the production of income. Generally, it is equal to the applicable percentage of the "unadjusted depreciable basis" (¶1910) of qualified property. That applicable percentage can be as high as 100%, but is being phased down over time. The applicable percentages to be used for qualified property are as follows:

. . . 100% if *acquired* and placed in service after Sept. 27, 2017, and before Jan. 1, 2023 (before Jan. 1, 2024 for certain long-production-period property and certain aircraft ("k6B Property")).

. . . 80%, if placed in service in 2023 (in 2024 for k6B Property).

. . . 60%, if placed in service in 2024 (in 2025 for k6B Property).

. . . 40%, if placed in service in 2025 (in 2026 for k6B Property).

. . . 20%, if placed in service in 2026 (in 2027 for k6B Property). (Code Sec. 168(k)(1); Code Sec. 168(k)(6)); Code Sec. 168(k)(2)(B); Code Sec. 168(k)(2)(C); Code Sec. 168(k)(6)(B))[5]

Under the Code, the "adjusted basis" of "qualified property" is reduced by the amount of the bonus depreciation allowance before computing the amount otherwise allowable as a depreciation deduction for the tax year and any later tax year. (Code Sec. 168(k)(1)(B)) Regulations use the term "unadjusted depreciable basis" (¶1910) instead of "adjusted basis" for purposes of determining the amount otherwise allowable as a depreciation deduction for the property for the placed-in-service year, or any later year. Under the regulations, the taxpayer (1) reduces the unadjusted depreciable basis by the amount of bonus depreciation allowed or allowable, whichever is greater, to arrive at a "remaining adjusted depreciable basis," and (2) depreciates the remaining adjusted depreciable basis of the property using the applicable depreciation provisions of the Code. (Reg § 1.168(k)-2(e)(2)(i)) If the qualified property is MACRS property (¶1906), the remaining adjusted depreciable basis of the qualified property is also the basis to which the annual depreciation rates in the optional depreciation tables (see ¶1910) apply. (Reg § 1.168(k)-2(e)(2)(i))

Separate, elective, bonus depreciation rules apply for certain plants bearing fruit or nuts. (Code Sec. 168(k)(5))[6]

There's no AMT depreciation adjustment (¶3207) for qualified property for its entire recovery period. (Code Sec. 168(k)(2)(G); Reg § 1.168(k)-2(e)(1)(iv)(A)) There also is no AMT adjustment when a taxpayer elects out of bonus depreciation for a class of property (see ¶1934), or makes an election for a specified plant (above). (Reg § 1.168(k)-2(f)(4))[7]

¶ 1930   "Qualified property" and other property eligible for bonus first-year depreciation—including tangible property with recovery periods up to 20 years, computer software, water utility property, etc.

Under Code Sec. 168(k)(2)(A), "qualified property" eligible for bonus depreciation (¶1929) includes, subject to exclusions (see below), tangible property depreciated under MACRS with a recovery period of 20 years or less, most computer software (but see ¶1607),

---

3. ¶L-9402.1; ¶L-9402.4
4. ¶L-9602
5. ¶L-9311.0

6. ¶L-9311.1A *et seq.*
7. ¶L-9310 *et seq.*; ¶A-8115.1; ¶A-8221.1

water utility property, and certain television productions, film productions, and live theatrical productions. (Code Sec. 168(k)(2)(A)(i))[8]

In addition to being of a qualifying type, the property must meet an original-use-or-qualifying-acquisition requirement (¶1931), a timely acquisition requirement (¶1932, but now applicable mostly in the case of certain aircraft or long-production-period property), and a timely placed-in-service requirement (¶1933).[9]

Exclusions. Property isn't qualified property if it must be depreciated under the alternative depreciation system (see ¶1927). (Code Sec. 168(k)(2)(D)) Also excluded is property primarily used by (1) most regulated public utilities, and (2) certain businesses that have "floor plan financing indebtedness." (Code Sec. 168(k)(9))[10] Furthermore, (a) "primarily used" for this exclusion has the same meaning as in Reg § 1.167(a)-11(b)(4)(iii)(B); and (b) property leased to both of those types of businesses may be eligible for an exception to the exclusion. (Reg § 1.168(k)-2(b)(2)(ii)(F) and Reg § 1.168(k)-2(b)(2)(ii)(G))[11]

Qualified reuse and recycling property. 50% bonus first-year depreciation applies for "qualified reuse and recycling property" that is purchased new by the taxpayer, isn't qualified property, and meets other detailed requirements. (Code Sec. 168(m))[12]

¶ 1931　Original-use or qualifying-acquisition requirement for bonus first-year depreciation for "qualified property."

Under Code Sec. 168(k)(2)(A)(ii), one requirement for being qualified property (¶1930) for bonus depreciation (¶1929) is that depreciable property must meet either an original use requirement (generally, for new property), or an alternative qualifying acquisition requirement (generally, for used property).[13]

Original use (new property). The original use of depreciable property must begin with the taxpayer that claims bonus depreciation. (Code Sec. 168(k)(2)(A)(ii)) Except for property converted to business or income-producing use (see below), and for fractional interests in property, "original use" means the first use to which the property is put, whether or not that use corresponds to the use of the property *by the taxpayer*. (Reg § 1.168(k)-2(b)(3)(ii)(A)) New property first used by a taxpayer for personal use or as inventory and later used by the taxpayer in a trade or business meets the original-use requirement. (Reg § 1.168(k)-2(b)(3)(ii)(B)) There are special rules for reconditioned or rebuilt property, syndication transactions, and fractional interests.[14]

Qualifying-acquisition (used property). Used property satisfies the qualifying-acquisition requirement if (1) the property wasn't used by the taxpayer at any time before the acquisition (the no-prior-use rule) and (2) the acquisition of the property meets the requirements of Code Sec. 179(d)(2)(A), Code Sec. 179(d)(2)(B), Code Sec. 179(d)(2)(C) (related party prohibitions, and carryover-basis prohibitions), and Code Sec. 179(d)(3) (substituted-basis prohibitions). (Code Sec. 168(k)(2)(A)(ii); Code Sec. 168(k)(2)(E)(ii))

For the no-prior-use rule, property is treated as used by a taxpayer or a predecessor before acquisition if the taxpayer or a predecessor had a depreciable interest in the property before the acquisition, whether or not depreciation deductions were claimed. To determine if a taxpayer or a predecessor had a prior depreciable interest, only the 5 calendar years immediately before the taxpayer's current placed-in-service year of the property (as well as the current year) are taken into account. There also is a 90-day de minimis rule for when property is disposed of shortly after it was placed in service. Special rules apply to substantial renovations, and acquisition of a portion of property. (Reg § 1.168(k)-2(b)(3)(iii))[15]

---

8. ¶L-9312, L-9312.1, L-9312.2
9. ¶L-9312
10. ¶L-9313 *et seq.*
11. ¶L-9313.1; ¶L-9313.2

12. ¶L-9361
13. ¶L-9314 *et seq.*
14. ¶L-9314A.2 *et seq.*
15. ¶L-9314B; ¶L-9314B.1

For consolidated groups (¶3338 *et seq.*), a prior depreciable interest of one member of a consolidated group generally is attributed to all other members. Additionally, special rules are provided for a series of related transactions, and for when a member joins or leaves the consolidated group. (Reg § 1.1502-68)[16]

Partnership-specific rules. Partnership-specific rules relating to the original-use or qualifying-acquisition requirement are contained in Reg § 1.168(k)-2(b)(3)(iv).[17]

¶ 1932 Time-of-acquisition deadline for long-production-period property and aircraft for bonus first-year depreciation for "qualified property."

Under Code Sec. 168(k)(2)(B)(i)(III) for certain long-production-period property, and under Code Sec. 168(k)(2)(C)(i) for certain aircraft, one of the requirements for being qualified property (¶1930) eligible for bonus depreciation (¶1929) is that the property must be acquired by the taxpayer either (1) before Jan. 1, 2027 or (2) under a written contract entered into before Jan. 1, 2027. This acquisition deadline is in addition to the post-Sept. 27, 2017 acquisition requirement (see ¶1929) that must be satisfied if property is to qualify for bonus depreciation. (Reg § 1.168(k)-2(d)(1))[18]

Whether the above acquisition rules are met when a taxpayer for its own use, or another person, manufactures, constructs or produces property is determined under Code Sec. 168(k)(2)(E)(i), Reg § 1.168(k)-2(d)(3)(i), and Reg § 1.168(k)-2(d)(3)(ii)(A).[19]

¶ 1933 Placed-in-service date requirements for bonus first-year depreciation for "qualified property" including limitation for long-production-period property.

One requirement for bonus depreciation under Code Sec. 168 (¶1929) is that otherwise eligible property must be placed in service before Jan. 1, 2027. (Code Sec. 168(k)(2)(A)(iii)) The placement into service must be for use in the taxpayer's trade or business or for the production of income (and occur after Sept. 27, 2017). (Reg § 1.168(k)-2(b)(4)(i)) However, certain property with a longer production period, and certain aircraft, can be placed in service as late as Dec. 31, 2027. (Code Sec. 168(k)(2)(B)(i)(II); Code Sec. 168(k)(2)(C)(ii))[20] If property is qualified property (¶1930) only because it qualifies as long-production-period property, the property is eligible for bonus depreciation only to the extent of the adjusted basis of the property attributable to manufacture, construction, or production before Jan. 1, 2027. (Code Sec. 168(k)(2)(B)(ii))[21]

Rules specific to certain television productions, film productions, and live theatrical productions apply to determine when the production is placed in service. (Code Sec. 168(k)(2)(H); Reg § 1.168(k)-2(B)(4)(iii))[22]

Also, there are special placed-in-service rules for syndication transactions and certain non-recognition transactions. (Reg § 1.168(k)-2(b)(4))[23]

¶ 1934 Election-out of bonus first-year depreciation for "qualified property"— Form 4562.

Under Code Sec. 168(k)(7), for qualified property (¶1930), a taxpayer can make an election to (1) not claim bonus depreciation (¶1929); and (2) not claim the increase in the usual cap on first-year depreciation for passenger automobiles, including small trucks and vans (see ¶1946). An "election-out" can be made for all property in a class (or multiple classes) of property placed in service in the tax year.[24]

---

16. ¶L-9314C *et seq.*
17. ¶L-9314.1B
18. ¶L-9315
19. ¶L-9315
20. ¶L-9316 *et seq.*

21. ¶L-9316 *et seq.*
22. ¶L-9312.2
23. ¶L-9316
24. ¶L-9318 *et seq.*

The election-out must be made on Form 4562, generally by the due date (including extensions) of the return for the tax year in which the taxpayer places the property in service. (Reg § 1.168(k)-2(f)(1)(iii))[25] An election-out can be revoked only with IRS consent, but, if certain conditions are met, taxpayers are granted an automatic extension of 6 months to revoke, which runs from the due date of the relevant tax return (without extensions). (Reg § 1.168(k)-2(f)(5))[26]

¶ 1935   Code Sec. 179 Expense Election—Form 4562. ▰▰▰▰▰▰

Under Code Sec. 179, many taxpayers are eligible to deduct the cost of most tangible personal property, and certain other property, used in the active conduct of a trade or business.

This expensing deduction is in lieu of depreciation, and is subject to dollar limits. Furthermore, it is not available for property held merely for the production of income.[27]

Thus, taxpayers, except trusts, estates, and most noncorporate lessors, (Code Sec. 179(d)(4), Code Sec. 179(d)(5)) can elect on Form 4562 to expense the cost (or a portion) of "section 179 property" (see ¶1937), subject to the dollar limits discussed below, for the year the property is placed in service. (Code Sec. 179(a); Code Sec. 179(b)(1); Reg § 1.179-1(a))

The maximum annual amount that can be expensed is $1,080,000 for property placed in service in tax years beginning in 2022 ($1,160,000 in tax years beginning in 2023).[28]

The maximum annual amount is reduced dollar-for-dollar by the amount of section 179 property placed in service during the tax year in excess of the "investment ceiling" (Code Sec. 179(b)(2))—which is $2,700,000 for tax years beginning in calendar year 2022 ($2,890,000 for tax years beginning in 2023).[29]

The deduction amount is further limited to the aggregate amount of taxable income from the taxpayer's active trades or businesses, including from being an employee, (Reg § 1.179-2(c)(6)(iv)) computed without regard to the cost of qualified expense property, the deduction for one-half of self-employment tax, NOL carrybacks or carryforwards, and deductions suspended under other Code sections (e.g., the passive activity rules of Code Sec. 469). (Code Sec. 179(b)(3); Reg § 1.179-2(c)(1)) An amount that can't be deducted due to the taxable income limitation is carried over indefinitely until it can be deducted. (Code Sec. 179(b)(3)(B))[30]

For a partner or S corporation shareholder, the deduction limitation, the investment ceiling limitation, and the taxable income limitation are applied at both the partnership (or S corporation) level and the taxpayer level. (Code Sec. 179(d)(8)) However, for purposes of the investment limitation, the cost of qualifying property that a partnership or S corporation placed in service isn't attributed and allocated to the partner or shareholder. (Reg § 1.179-2(b)(3))[31]

A controlled group is treated as a single taxpayer for purposes of all of the limits on the expense deduction. (Code Sec. 179(d)(6); Reg § 1.179-2(b)(1)) However, the single-taxpayer rule doesn't apply to S corporations that are members of a controlled group.[32]

Married taxpayers are treated as one taxpayer in applying the dollar and investment limits. (Reg § 1.179-2(b)(5)) Married taxpayers filing separately may elect other than a 50-50 allocation of the expense deduction. (Code Sec. 179(b)(4); Reg § 1.179-2(b)(6))[33]

An expensing election or specification of property to be expensed is made on Form 4562.[34] That election can be revoked without IRS consent, but once revoked, can't be re-elected. (Code Sec. 179(c)(2)) Regulations as supplemented by later guidance provide that a

25. ¶L-9318.1
26. ¶L-9318A
27. ¶L-9900 *et seq.*
28. ¶L-9907, ¶L-9907.1
29. ¶L-9907, ¶L-9907.1

30. ¶L-9911 *et seq.*
31. ¶L-9909 *et seq.*
32. ¶L-9908
33. ¶L-9907.01
34. ¶L-9932 *et seq.*

taxpayer can make or revoke an expensing election on an amended return filed within the time for filing an amended return for the election year. (Reg § 1.179-5(c)(1)) A taxpayer that elected to expense only part of the cost basis of property for a particular tax year (or didn't make any expensing election) can file an amended return and expense any part of the cost basis of property that was not expensed under a prior Code Sec. 179 election. (Reg § 1.179-5(c)(2))[35]

For a limit on the election for SUVs (that aren't passenger autos), see ¶1936. For a dollar cap on the election for passenger autos, see ¶1944. For prohibition of the election for certain "listed property," see ¶1941.

¶ 1936   Restricted expensing deduction for heavy SUVs; per-vehicle dollar limit/SUV limit.

In addition to being subject to the overall annual dollar limit on Code Sec. 179 expensing (¶1935), the amount of the cost of a heavy SUV (sport utility vehicle) that can be expensed under Code Sec. 179 is subject to a per-vehicle dollar limit (the SUV limit). (Code Sec. 179(b)(5); Code Sec. 179(b)(6)) The SUV limit is $27,000 for vehicles placed in service in tax years beginning in 2022 ($28,900 in tax years beginning in 2023).[36]

The SUV limit applies to any 4-wheeled vehicle that (1) is primarily designed (or can be used) to carry passengers on public streets, roads and highways (except for rail vehicles), and (2) has a GVWR (gross, or loaded, vehicle weight rating) of more than 6,000 pounds but not more than 14,000 pounds. (Code Sec. 179(b)(5)(B)(i); Code Sec. 280F(d)(5)(A)(ii))

A vehicle is *not* subject to the SUV limit if it (1) is designed for more than nine individuals in seating rearward of the driver's seat; (2) is equipped with an open cargo area, or a covered box not readily accessible from the passenger compartment, of at least six feet in interior length; or (3) has an integral enclosure, fully enclosing the driver compartment and load carrying device, does not have seating rearward of the drivers seat, and has no body section protruding more than 30 inches ahead of the leading edge of the windshield. (Code Sec. 179(b)(5)(B)(ii))[37]

For prohibition of the expensing election for passenger autos and other "listed property" not predominantly used in business, see ¶1941.

> **observation:** The portion of the cost of a heavy SUV that isn't expensed under Code Sec. 179 can be depreciated over the 5-year MACRS recovery period (¶1913) *without regard to* the depreciation dollar caps for luxury autos (¶1944). Furthermore, the cost of a heavy SUV also may be eligible for an additional first-year depreciation allowance (bonus depreciation, see ¶1929).

¶ 1937   Property eligible and ineligible for expense election: tangible MACRS property; off-the-shelf computer software; qualified real property, including qualified improvement property.

Subject to the overall maximum dollar amount and investment ceiling discussed at ¶1935, property eligible for the Code Sec. 179 expense election consists of the following assets if "purchased" (see below) for use in the active trade or business of the taxpayer:

(1) tangible MACRS property that's Code Sec. 1245 property (generally, most depreciable property other than buildings and other land improvements),

(2) off-the-shelf computer software, and

(3) by election of the taxpayer, qualified real property (see below). (Code Sec. 179(d)(1)).[38]

---

35. ¶L-9932 *et seq.*
36. ¶L-9907.2

37. ¶L-9907.2
38. ¶L-9901.1; ¶L-9922 *et seq.*

Code Sec. 179 property doesn't include property held in the production of income (Code Sec. 212 property), and specifically excluded is property used outside the U.S., property used by certain tax-exempt organizations, and property used by governmental units or foreign persons or entities. (Code Sec. 179(d)(1))[39] For prohibition of the expensing election for passenger autos and other "listed property" not predominantly used in business, see ¶1941.

Qualified real property. Qualified real property for the election, above, is property that is either (1) qualified improvement property (described in Code Sec. 168(e)(6), ¶1918) or (2) the following improvements to nonresidential real property after the date such property was first placed in service: roofs; heating, ventilation, and air-conditioning property; fire protection and alarm systems; and security systems. (Code Sec. 179(e)).[40] The election to expense qualified real property is made on an original or amended tax return in accordance with procedures specified by IRS (see ¶1935).[41]

Purchase. Purchase is any acquisition of property *except* property (1) acquired from certain individuals or entities related to the taxpayer (or from a decedent), or (2) whose basis is determined by reference to the adjusted basis of the person from whom acquired (e.g., gifts).[42]

¶ 1938   Recapture of amount expensed under Code Sec. 179—Form 4797; reduction in business use of property.

Code Sec. 179 recapture is triggered when the business use of property placed in service in an earlier year is reduced to 50% or less during the recovery period (under MACRS) of the expensed property. (Code Sec. 179(d)(10); Reg § 1.179-1(e)(1))

The recapture amount (reported on Form 4797) is the expense deduction taken minus the MACRS depreciation amount that would have been allowed on the expensed amount up to and through the recapture year. (Reg § 1.179-1(e)(1))[43]

For the application of the general depreciation recapture rules to Code Sec. 179 expensing, see ¶2672 *et seq.*

¶ 1939   "Luxury" Automobiles and "Listed Property." ▄▄▄▄▄▄▄▄▄▄▄▄▄▄▄▄

Code Sec. 280F addresses depreciation for "luxury" automobiles, and for certain types of property designated as "listed property" (defined as discussed at ¶1940) when there is substantial use for personal purposes. Certain (most) passenger automobiles used for business are included in listed property (see ¶1944). Code Sec. 280F imposes restrictions on deductions for listed property, and limitations on Code Sec. 168 MACRS depreciation deductions (¶1906 *et seq.*) and Code Sec. 179 expense election deductions (¶1935 *et seq.*) for passenger automobiles. Code Sec. 280F also provides special rules for lessees of listed property.

☜observation: While "luxury automobiles" appears in the title of Code Sec. 280F, it is not a statutorily defined term. However, the amounts of the limitations make them mostly consequential to expensive automobiles.

The following restrictions on depreciation (and the Code Sec. 179 expense election, as applicable) apply to listed property:

. . . Depreciation of certain passenger automobiles is subject to maximum ceiling limitations, see ¶1944 *et seq.*

. . . A taxpayer who leases a luxury automobile (lessee) for business must add into income an "inclusion amount," see ¶1948.

---

39. ¶L-9922.1
40. ¶L-8215; ¶L-9901.1; ¶L-9922 *et seq.*
41. ¶L-9932.1

42. ¶L-9925
43. ¶L-9935

. . . A taxpayer who leases listed property (lessee), other than a luxury automobile, must take into income an "inclusion amount" when the property is no longer used more than 50% for business, see ¶1948.

. . . If listed property is not used more than 50% for business, depreciation is under the straight-line method, and, generally, over longer recovery periods (see ¶1941 *et seq.*); and the property is ineligible for both bonus depreciation (¶1929 *et seq.*) and elective expensing (¶1935 *et seq.*).

. . . Specific recapture rules apply to listed property, see ¶2680.

. . . Strict substantiation rules apply to listed property expenses, see ¶1563 and ¶1567.

Lessors of listed property who are regularly engaged in the business of leasing that property aren't subject to the limitations for owners, described above, for any listed property they lease or hold for leasing. (Code Sec. 280F(c)(1))[44]

¶ 1940 Code Sec. 280F "Listed property" defined—passenger autos; other transportation property; property used for entertainment, recreation or amusement.

Under Code Sec. 280F, "listed property" consists of:

. . . passenger autos (defined as discussed at ¶1944);

. . . any other property used as a means of transportation (e.g., trucks, buses, trains, boats, airplanes), except for "qualified nonpersonal use vehicles" (defined below);

. . . any property of a type generally used for entertainment, recreation or amusement; this includes photographic, phonographic, communication and video recording equipment, unless that property is used either exclusively at the taxpayer's regular business establishment, or in connection with the taxpayer's principal trade or business; and

. . . any other property specified by regulations. (Code Sec. 280F(d)(4); Reg § 1.280F-6(b))[45]

observation: Cellular telephones previously were a category of listed property, but they have been omitted from the definition for several years.

"Qualified nonpersonal use vehicles" (QNPUVs) are vehicles that by their nature aren't likely to be used more than a *de minimis* amount for personal purposes. (Code Sec. 274(i)) QNPUVs include, but aren't limited to, various uniformed services vehicles. (Reg § 1.274-5(k))[46]

¶ 1941 Depreciation and expensing restrictions for listed property used no more than 50% for business—post-acquisition recapture—Form 4797.

Code Sec. 280F provides limitations for "listed property" (¶1940) that, for the year it is placed in service, is not used predominantly (not more than 50%) in a qualified business use (generally, in a trade or business, see ¶1942 for the definition and exceptions). (Code Sec. 280F(d)(6)) The limitations are that the listed property: (1) doesn't qualify for the Code Sec. 179 expense election (¶1935), (Reg § 1.280F-3T(c)(1)) (2) is depreciable for all years only under the straight-line method and the "ADS" recovery periods (¶1928), and (3) is ineligible for the bonus first-year depreciation allowance (¶1929). (Code Sec. 168(k)(2)(D)(ii); Code Sec. 280F(b)(1))[47]

Actual deduction amounts for property subject to the above rule are computed by using the "business/investment use" percentage (defined at ¶1943). (Reg § 1.280F-6(d)(3)(i))[48]

---

44. ¶L-10201
45. ¶L-10002
46. ¶L-10002, ¶L-4658 *et seq.*

47. ¶L-10023
48. ¶L-10004

Any MACRS depreciation and Code Sec. 179 expense election deduction disallowed because of non-business/investment use is lost for all later years. (Code Sec. 280F(d)(2))[49]

If the more-than-50% requirement isn't met in a post-acquisition year (during the property's normal recovery period), beginning with that year the property is depreciated under straight-line/ADS and in that year depreciation previously taken in excess of that allowed straight-line ADS property (including amounts expensed, ¶1935, and bonus depreciation, ¶1929) is recaptured (on Form 4797). (Code Sec. 280F(b)(2)(A); Reg § 1.280F-3T(b)(2); Reg § 1.280F-3T(c)(2); Reg § 1.280F-3T(d)(2))[50]

¶ 1942 "Qualified business use" defined for listed property rules; exclusions for production-of-income deductible use, leasing to related parties, use as compensation.

Under Code Sec. 280F, for purposes of the depreciation and expensing restrictions discussed at ¶1941 and the income inclusion discussed at ¶1948, "qualified business use" generally is any use in a trade or business of the taxpayer. (Code Sec. 280F(d)(6)(B))[1]

The following are excluded from qualified business use:

(1) Code Sec. 212 production-of-income deductible use; (Reg § 1.280F-6(d)(2))

(2) leasing property to any 5% owner of the taxpayer or to any person related to the taxpayer; and

(3) the use of listed property as compensation (A) by a 5% owner or a related person, or (B) if the provider fails to include the value of the compensation in the recipient's gross income, properly report it, and, where necessary, treat it as wages subject to withholding. (Code Sec. 280F(d)(6)(C))[2]

The exclusions of items (2) and (3) don't apply to an aircraft if at least 25% of the aircraft's total use during the tax year is qualified business use not described at (2) or (3). (Code Sec. 280F(d)(6)(C)(ii))

¶ 1943 "Business/investment use" for listed property defined for depreciation purposes.

Under Code Sec. 280F, "business/investment use" (see ¶1941 and ¶1948) is the total of business use and investment use of any listed property for the tax year. For example, if an item of listed property is used 70% in a trade or business and 20% for the production of income, the taxpayer may claim, if the property otherwise qualifies, accelerated depreciation deductions (including the expense election deduction) based on 90% business/investment use. Business or investment use (with an exception concerning automobiles, below) is determined under the normal rules of Code Sec. 162 and Code Sec. 212. (Reg § 1.280F-6(d)(3)(i); Reg § 1.280F-6(d)(5), Ex 2)[3]

The use of a taxpayer's automobile by another person (even if that other person is a 5% owner or a related person) is treated as business/investment use of the taxpayer if:

(1) its use is directly connected with the taxpayer's business,

(2) the value of that use is properly reported by the taxpayer as income to the other person, and where required, tax is withheld on that income, or

(3) the use of the taxpayer's automobile by that other person results in payment of fair market rent. (Reg § 1.280F-6(d)(3)(iv))

---

49. ¶L-10023
50. ¶L-10023, ¶L-10026
1. ¶L-10004 *et seq.*

2. ¶L-10004, ¶L-10006
3. ¶L-10004

¶ 1944   **Depreciation and expensing of business automobiles—"luxury" auto dollar cap rules.**

Under Code Sec. 168, automobiles used in a trade or business typically are depreciated as 5-year MACRS property (¶1913). (Code Sec. 168(e)(3)(B)) However, under Code Sec. 280F, the deduction normally obtained for an automobile by applying the MACRS 5-year property rules, the bonus depreciation allowance (¶1929), and the Code Sec. 179 expensing rules (¶1935), is limited by the so-called "luxury" automobile dollar caps. (Code Sec. 280F(a)(1); Code Sec. 280F(d)(1)) The dollar caps (see ¶1945 and ¶1946 for the amounts) are adjusted for inflation, based on the placed-in-service year. (Code Sec. 280F(d)(7))

The dollar caps apply to passenger autos, i.e., four-wheeled vehicles manufactured primarily for use on public streets, roads, and highways, and rated at an unloaded gross vehicle weight of 6,000 pounds or less. For a truck or van, the 6,000-pound test is applied to the truck's or van's gross (loaded) vehicle weight. (Code Sec. 280F(d)(5)(A)) Excepted from the dollar caps are ambulances or hearses used directly in a trade or business, taxis and other vehicles used directly in the trade or business of transporting people or property for pay, and trucks or vans specified by regulations. (Code Sec. 280F(d)(5)(B)) Thus, qualified non-personal use vehicles (discussed at ¶1940) are excepted. (Reg § 1.280F-6(c)(3)(iii))[4]

observation: Sport-utility vehicles (SUVs) are trucks. Thus, SUVs rated at more than 6,000 pounds gross (loaded) vehicle weight are exempt from the dollar caps because they fall outside of the Code Sec. 280F(d)(5) definition of a passenger auto. For the restricted expensing deduction for heavy SUVs, see ¶1936.

¶ 1945   **Regular "luxury" automobile depreciation and expensing dollar cap amounts.**

The "regular" Code Sec. 280F "luxury" automobile dollar caps on depreciation and Code Sec. 179 expense allowances (¶1935), discussed at ¶1944, are utilized for applicable vehicles when no additional first-year depreciation (bonus depreciation, ¶1929) applies. Most passenger autos are eligible for bonus depreciation (see ¶1930), and when it is properly claimed for a passenger auto, and certain other requirements are satisfied, an increased automobile dollar cap for the placed in service year is available, see ¶1946. For additional restrictions on depreciation and expensing that apply to most vehicles not predominantly used in a qualifying business use, see ¶1941. For the income inclusion amounts instead of dollar caps that apply to leased automobiles and other listed property, see ¶1948.

The regular caps for vehicles first placed in service in 2022, and used 100% for business, are as follows: $11,200 for the year in which the vehicle is placed in service, $18,000 for the second year, $10,800 for the third year, and $6,460 for the fourth and later years. (Code Sec. 280F).[5]

Where the auto is not used 100% for business (see ¶1943), the above dollar limits are proportionately reduced.[6] Moreover, depreciation after the normal 5-year recovery period (actually six years because of the operation of the applicable convention) is based on unrecovered basis, i.e., adjusted basis determined as if the auto had been used 100% for business, so that the disallowed MACRS depreciation for the earlier years allocable to personal use is lost forever. (Code Sec. 280F(a)(1)(B); Code Sec. 280F(d)(8))

A taxpayer that uses the optional IRS standard mileage allowance method (discussed at ¶1553) for a tax year isn't subject to the above dollar caps for that year.[7]

---

4. ¶L-10003
5. ¶L-10009, ¶L-10011

6. ¶L-10008
7. ¶L-10021

¶ 1946 "Luxury" automobile depreciation dollar cap amounts when additional first-year depreciation applies.

Under Code Sec. 168(k)(2)(F)(i), the deduction dollar caps for "luxury" automobiles (¶1945) are increased when additional first-year depreciation (bonus depreciation, ¶1929) applies. When this is the case, the "regular" first-year (placed-in-service year) dollar cap amount (¶1945) is increased by a static $8,000. (Code Sec. 168(k)(2)(F)) The dollar cap increase doesn't apply if the taxpayer elects out of bonus depreciation.[8]

Thus, the maximum depreciation deduction for a "luxury" automobile for which bonus depreciation applies and is placed in service in 2022 is: $19,200 for the placed-in-service year; $18,000 for the second tax year; $10,800 for the third tax year; and $6,460 for each succeeding year. (Code Sec. 168(k)(2)(F)(iii))[9]

Under an IRS safe harbor for applying the "luxury" automobile caps to vehicles for which bonus depreciation applies, the taxpayer deducts the increased first-year dollar cap above in the placed-in-service year. In the following years, the remaining basis is depreciated according to the rates provided by the applicable optional depreciation table (¶1910), subject to the applicable dollar cap for each year. (Rev Proc 2019-13)[10]

¶ 1947 Reporting auto depreciation (Schedule C, Form 4562, etc.).

Self-employed individuals and sole proprietors report their vehicle expenses, including Code Sec. 168 depreciation, on Form 1040, Schedule C or Form 1040-SR, Schedule C, or if they are farmers on Form 1040, Schedule F or Form 1040-SR, Schedule F. In each case, a Form 4562 is attached (¶1901). However, depreciation and other vehicle expenses aren't separately deductible if the standard mileage rate is being used, see ¶1553.

Expense reimbursements made to an employee under an accountable plan are excluded from the employee's income, with no offsetting deduction to report, see ¶1557 and ¶1561.

Expense reimbursements made to an employee under a non-accountable plan are reported as employee income. For tax years 2018 through 2025, unreimbursed employee business expenses are nondeductible, see ¶2162. Thus, reimbursements for vehicle expenses under a non-accountable plan are employee income with no offsetting deduction allowed, see ¶1561.

¶ 1948 Listed property "inclusion amount" for lessees.

Code Sec. 280F requires that taxpayers entering leases of listed property (¶1940) of 30 days or more be subject to limitations on deductions similar to the depreciation limits for owners of "luxury" automobiles (¶1944 *et seq.*). The statute imposes a limitation on the amount of a rental payment a lessee may deduct. (Code Sec. 280F(c)(2), Code Sec. 280F(c)(3)) However, as discussed below, IRS implements this rule by imposing an income inclusion instead of a rental deduction modification.

Autos that are listed property. Lessees of business vehicles that are subject to the "luxury" automobile limits (¶1944) must include in gross income an "inclusion amount," figured from IRS's tables. (Reg § 1.280F-7(a)(1))[11]

For vehicles first rented in 2022, the inclusion amount for each tax year of the lease is computed as follows (but there's no inclusion amount unless the fair market value (FMV) of the vehicle is more than $56,000):

(1) Find the line from the appropriate table at ¶1119, which includes the FMV of the leased vehicle.

---

8. ¶L-10010
9. ¶L-10010, ¶L-10012

10. ¶L-10014
11. ¶L-10200 *et seq.*

(2) Prorate, with rounding to the nearest dollar, the dollar amount for the number of days in the lease term included in the tax year at issue.

(3) Multiply the prorated dollar amount by the "business/investment use" (¶1943) percentage for the vehicle for that tax year. The resulting amount is the inclusion amount. (Reg § 1.280F-7(a)(2))

For the last tax year of a lease that doesn't begin and end in the same tax year, the inclusion dollar amount for the preceding year is used. (Reg § 1.280F-7(a)(2)(i))[12]

illustration: On Apr. 1, 2022 a calendar year taxpayer leased and placed in service a vehicle with a FMV of $67,000. The lease is for three years, and the business/investment use is 100% in each year. The taxpayer must include the following "inclusion amounts" (from Rev. Proc. 2022-17, sec. 4.01(2), Table 3 reproduced at ¶1119) in gross income: for 2022, $11 ($14 inclusion amount × 275/365 rounded); for 2023, $30 (full inclusion amount); for 2024, $43 (full inclusion amount); and for 2025, $11 ($43 inclusion amount for preceding year × 90/365 rounded).

Listed property other than autos. For listed property other than autos, the inclusion amount isn't annual. Instead, it is taken into income in the first year the property ceases to be used predominantly (i.e., more than 50%) in a qualified business use (¶1942). (Reg § 1.280F-7(b)(1))[13]

The amount is the sum of the amounts computed under Steps (1) and (2), below.

STEP (1): Multiply the following three items: (a) the FMV of the property, (b) the business/investment use (¶1943) of the property for the year that use is 50% or less, and (c) the applicable percentage from Table I reproduced at ¶1118.

STEP (2): Multiply the following three items: (a) the FMV of the property, (b) the average of the business/investment use for all tax years (in which the property is leased) that precede the year the business/investment use is 50% or less, and (c) the applicable percentage from Table II reproduced at ¶1118. (Reg § 1.280F-7(b)(2))

Special rules apply when a lease term begins within nine months of the end of the lessee's tax year or when the lease term is less than one year. (Reg § 1.280F-5T(g))[14]

¶ 1949   Depreciation Deduction Under the Income Forecast Method—Form 8866. ■■■

Under Code Sec. 167, depreciation deductions under the income forecast method are figured by multiplying (a) the cost of the property (but only amounts that satisfy the Code Sec. 461(h) economic performance standard, ¶2824) less estimated salvage value, by (b) a fraction, the numerator of which is the year's income generated by the property, and the denominator of which is the total estimated income to be earned before the close of the tenth tax year following the year in which the property was placed in service. (Code Sec. 167(g))[15]

Under the income forecast method, the depreciation deduction for the tenth tax year after the tax year in which the property was placed in service is equal to the taxpayer's entire remaining basis in the property. (Code Sec. 167(g)(1)(C)) Taxpayers using the income forecast method pay (or receive) interest in recomputation years (generally in the third and tenth years after the property was placed in service, unless income earned by the property is within 10% of original estimates; use Form 8866 to compute) based on the recalculation of depreciation under a look-back method (but there's no look-back for property that had a cost basis of $100,000 or less). (Code Sec. 167(g))[16]

The income forecast (or similar) method (A) can be used only for (1) motion picture films, video tapes, and sound recordings; (2) copyrights; (3) books; (4) patents; and (5) any other

---

12. ¶L-10204, ¶L-10204.2   15. ¶L-10704; ¶L-10705.1
13. ¶L-10205   16. ¶L-10707.4
14. ¶L-10206 *et seq.*

property specified in regulations, and (B) can't be used to depreciate amortizable section 197 intangibles (see ¶1957). (Code Sec. 167(g)(6))[17] However, see ¶1958 for a special section 197 intangible rule applicable to films, video tapes, and sound recordings.

Specific rules are provided for calculating depreciation for "participations and residuals" (costs that, by contract, vary with the amount of income earned from property) under the income forecast method. (Code Sec. 167(g)(7))[18]

¶ 1950   Depreciation of Some Tangible Property Under the "Useful-Life" Rules. ▬▬

Tangible property not depreciable under MACRS (¶1906) or that was placed in service before 1981 is usually depreciable under the Code Sec. 167 useful-life rules. The asset is depreciated (usually not below salvage value) over the period during which a depreciable asset, or group of similar assets, may reasonably be expected to be useful to the taxpayer in its trade or business or in income production.[19] Under the useful-life rules, a permissible method of depreciation is one prescribed by Code Sec. 167, or a method that results in a reasonable allowance. (Code Sec. 167(a); Reg § 1.167(b)-0; Reg § 1.167(a)-1(c); Reg § 1.167(b)-2(a))[20]

The basis on which depreciation is taken is the adjusted basis under Code Sec. 1011 for the purpose of gain or loss on a sale or other disposition. (Code Sec. 167(c)(1))[21] For specialized useful life depreciation methods, see ¶1952.

¶ 1951   Cost recovery for intangibles excluded from 15-year amortization—computer software; debt servicing rights; patents and copyrights; 15-year and 25-year safe harbors.

Under Code Sec. 167, when certain property is excluded from Code Sec. 197 15-year amortization for goodwill and certain other intangibles, discussed at ¶1959 (e.g., specified property when not acquired as part of the purchase of a trade or business), it is depreciated as follows:

(1) Computer software generally is depreciated using the straight-line method with a useful life of 36 months beginning on the first day of the month that it is placed in service, see ¶1607 for exceptions. (Code Sec. 167(f)(1); Reg § 1.167(a)-14(b)(1))

(2) A right to service debts secured by residential realty is depreciated using the straight-line method with a useful life of 108 months. (Code Sec. 167(f)(3); Code Sec. 197(e)(6); Reg § 1.167(a)-14(d)(1))

(3) A right fixed as to amount, or a right to receive a fixed amount of any property or services, under a contract or granted by a governmental unit has its basis amortized by multiplying the basis by a fraction (the numerator being the amount received during the year and the denominator being the total amount received or to be received). (Code Sec. 167(f)(2); Reg § 1.167(a)-14(c)(1)(i); Reg § 1.167(a)-14(c)(2)(i)) A right to receive an unspecified amount of tangible property or services over a fixed period has its cost or other basis amortized ratably over the period of the right. (Code Sec. 167(f)(2); Reg § 1.167(a)-14(c)(1)(ii)) A right to receive an unspecified amount (other than tangible property or services) over a fixed duration of less than 15 years has its basis amortized ratably over the period of the right. (Code Sec. 167(f)(2); Reg § 1.167(a)-14(c)(2)(ii))

(4) A patent or copyright, where the purchase price is payable at least annually as either a fixed amount per use or a fixed percentage of revenue derived, has a depreciation deduction for a given year equal to the purchase price paid or incurred during that year. Otherwise, basis is depreciated either ratably over the remaining useful life, or by the income forecast method discussed at ¶1949. (Code Sec. 167(f)(2); Reg § 1.167(a)-14(c)(4))

---

17. ¶L-10704A
18. ¶L-10707.1, ¶L-10707.1A
19. ¶L-11711; ¶L-11800 *et seq.*

20. ¶L-11901
21. ¶P-1701

If the property described above, other than in (2), would be "tax-exempt use property" (see ¶1927) if the Code Sec. 168 rules applied to those types of property, then the useful life of the property can't be less than 125% of the lease term for the property. (Code Sec. 167(f)(1)(C); Code Sec. 167(f)(2); Code Sec. 168(h); Code Sec. 168(i)(3))[22]

Also, under a safe harbor taxpayers may treat an intangible asset as having a useful life of 15 years unless:

. . . an amortization period or useful life for the intangible asset is specifically prescribed or prohibited by other rules (e.g., off-the-shelf computer software under item (1) above);

. . . the intangible asset is described in Reg § 1.263(a)-4(c) (intangibles acquired from another person in a purchase or similar transaction) or Reg § 1.263(a)-4(d)(2) (relating to created financial interests);

. . . the useful life of the intangible asset can be estimated with reasonable accuracy; or

. . . the intangible asset is described in Reg § 1.263(a)-4(d)(8) (relating to certain benefits arising from the provision, production, or improvement of realty), in which case the taxpayer may treat the intangible asset as having a useful life equal to 25 years solely for purposes of Reg § 1.167(a)-3(a). (Reg § 1.167(a)-3(b)(1))

The 15-year (or 25-year) safe harbor doesn't apply to amounts that must be capitalized by Reg § 1.263(a)-5 (i.e., paid to facilitate an acquisition of a trade or business, a change in the capital structure of an entity, and certain other transactions). (Reg § 1.167(a)-3(b)(2))

Under the safe harbor, the basis of the intangible (determined without regard to salvage value) is amortized ratably over 15 (or 25) years beginning on the first day of the month in which the intangible asset is placed in service by the taxpayer. The intangible asset is not eligible for amortization in the month of disposition. (Reg § 1.167(a)-3(b)(3))[23]

¶ 1952 Specialized "useful-life" depreciation methods—operating day method, sinking fund method, and unit-of-production method.

Alternative depreciation methods, allowable under Code Sec. 167, based on useful life include:

. . . Operating day method used for equipment affected chiefly by wear and tear rather than obsolescence, such as rotary oil drills.[24]

. . . Sinking fund method (Reg § 1.167(b)-4(a)).[25]

. . . Unit-of-production method used for property, based on estimates of total output before property is worn out. (Reg § 1.167(b)-0(b); Reg § 1.611-5(a); Reg § 1.611-5(b)(2))[26]

¶ 1953 Special Expensing and Amortization Provisions. ▬▬▬▬▬▬

Instead of being subject to the ordinary depreciation or expensing rules, certain property is expensed or amortized as described below or at ¶1954 *et seq.*

For example, Code Sec. 181 provides an election to expense, up to an aggregate dollar limit (usually $15 million), the costs of qualified film, television, and theatrical productions that commence before Jan. 1, 2026.[27] For taxpayers who take the specified actions, Rev Proc 2022-23 provides late election relief for tax years ending in 2018 and 2019.[28]

Research and experimental expenditures connected with a trade or business must be amortized over a 60-month period (but were eligible for a variety of treatments before 2022, see ¶1583). Also, start-up expenditures (¶1500), organization costs of a corporation (¶3510), and organization costs of a partnership (¶3705), generally, can be amortized over a 180-month period. Bond premium (¶2165 *et seq.*) and lease acquisition costs also are

---

22. ¶L-7935, ¶L-8018, ¶L-8025, ¶L-8030
23. ¶L-8001
24. ¶L-10709
25. ¶L-10711

26. ¶L-10702
27. ¶3140 *et seq.*
28. ¶3146

amortized (¶1579).

¶ 1954 Amortization elections for pollution control facilities (60-month); certain air pollution control facilities (84-month).

Under Code Sec. 169, taxpayers may elect to amortize, over 60 months, part or all of the cost of new identifiable pollution control treatment facilities used in connection with a plant or other property in operation before 1976. (Code Sec. 169(a), Code Sec. 169(d)) MACRS depreciation can be taken on any portion that doesn't qualify. (Code Sec. 169(g)) An *air* pollution control facility used in connection with an electric generation plant or other property that is primarily coal fired is subject to different operation date requirements, but in some circumstances may be eligible for 84-month amortization. (Code Sec. 169(d)(5)) For both 60-month amortization and 84-month amortization, certain limits apply. (Code Sec. 169(f); Code Sec. 291(a)(4); Code Sec. 1363(b)(4))[29]

¶ 1955 Amortization and expense elections for reforestation expenditures— Forms 4562 and Form T (Timber); recapture after disposition of timber property; separate accounts for qualified timber property.

Under Code Sec. 194, taxpayers may elect to amortize reforestation costs over 84 months. Taxpayers other than trusts also may make a separate election to immediately deduct up to $10,000 ($5,000 if married filing separately) of reforestation costs. (Code Sec. 194(b)(1))[30] These elections are made by claiming the deductions on Form 4562, or if the taxpayer is required to file Form T (Timber) on Part IV for reforestation activities.[31]

Individuals claim deductions under Code Sec. 194 as adjustments to arrive at adjusted gross income. (Code Sec. 62(a)(11))[32] Costs expensed or amortized under Code Sec. 194 are recaptured as ordinary income (to the extent of gain) if there's a disposition of the timber property within ten years. (Code Sec. 1245(a)(2)(C))[33]

Taxpayers must create and maintain separate accounts for each qualified timber property. Elected-for property can't be included in any other timber account (e.g., a depletion block) for which depletion is allowed under Code Sec. 611 (¶1960 *et seq.*). An amortizable timber account can't become part of a depletable account for purposes of deduction under Code Sec. 165(a).[34]

¶ 1956 24-month amortization for certain oil or gas costs (G&G); 7-year amortization for major integrated oil companies.

Under Code Sec. 167, geological and geophysical ("G&G") expenses in connection with exploring or developing oil and gas within the "United States" (which includes offshore, and is defined in Code Sec. 638) are amortized over the 24-month period—7-year period for a major integrated oil company—beginning on the date that the expenses are paid or incurred. (Code Sec. 167(h)(1); Code Sec. 167(h)(5)) However, any payment during a tax year is treated as made on the mid-point of the year. (Code Sec. 167(h)(2))

Amortization continues over the applicable period even if the underlying property is abandoned or retired. (Code Sec. 167(h)(4)) So, upon abandonment or retirement, unamortized expenses can't be immediately deducted; neither can they be included in basis for purposes of determining gain or loss. Retirements include sales, exchanges, and other withdrawals from service.[35]

Rulings and cases define G&G expenses.[36]

29. ¶L-12600 *et seq.*
30. ¶N-6301
31. ¶N-6317
32. ¶A-2601
33. ¶I-10203; ¶I-10204
34. ¶N-6314.1
35. ¶N-3201 *et seq.*
36. ¶N-3201.1

¶ 1957   Amortization of Intangibles under Code Sec. 197—Form 4562. ▬▬▬

Under Code Sec. 197, the costs of many intangibles, including most intangibles acquired in a business acquisition, are amortized over a 15-year period.

Taxpayers claim deductions for *amortizable Code Sec. 197 intangibles* ("197 intangibles," described in detail at ¶1958) on Form 4562. The deductions are determined by amortizing the adjusted basis (for purposes of determining gain) of that intangible ratably over a 15-year period beginning on the *later* of: the first day of the month in which the 197 intangible is acquired, or, for property held in connection with the conduct of a trade or business or a production-of-income activity, the first day of the month in which the conduct of the trade or business or the activity begins. (Code Sec. 197(a); Reg § 1.197-2(f)(1)(i)))[37] For depreciation of intangibles generally and of many intangibles that aren't 197 intangibles, see ¶1902, ¶1949, and ¶1951.

No loss deduction is permitted on the disposition of a 197 intangible if the taxpayer retains one or more other 197 intangibles acquired in the same transaction or series of related transactions as the 197 intangible disposed of. (Code Sec. 197(f)(1)(A)) On the disposition of that 197 intangible, the bases of the other 197 intangibles acquired in the same transaction or series of related transactions are increased, under a formula, by the amount of the loss barred. (Code Sec. 197(f)(1)(A)(ii))[38]

Anti-churning rules keep taxpayers from converting existing intangibles, for which a depreciation or amortization deduction wasn't allowable under prior law (in effect for assets acquired before Aug. 11, 1993), into 197 intangibles. (Code Sec. 197(f)(9))[39]

The amortization period of any 197 intangible that if it were tangible property would be "tax-exempt use property" (see ¶1927), can't be less than 125% of the lease term. (Code Sec. 197(f)(10))[40] If more than one 197 intangible is disposed of in one transaction, or a series of related transactions, all of the 197 intangibles in the transaction (or transactions)—except for any 197 intangible with an adjusted basis greater than its fair market value—are treated as a single asset for Code Sec. 1245 recapture purposes (see ¶2674). (Code Sec. 1245(b)(8))[41]

¶ 1958   Amortizable section 197 intangibles—goodwill, going concern value, workforce in place, books and records, patents and copyrights, customer-or supplier-based intangibles, government-granted licenses, franchises, trademarks and trade names.

An *amortizable section 197 intangible* is any Code Sec. 197 intangible acquired by the taxpayer and held in connection with the conduct of a trade or business or a Code Sec. 212 production-of-income activity. (Code Sec. 197(c)(1))[42] Assets can't qualify as amortizable section 197 intangibles before the commencement of a trade or business.[43] Amortizable section 197 intangibles include:

. . . Goodwill. (Code Sec. 197(d)(1)(A); Reg § 1.197-2(b)(1))[44]

. . . Going concern value. (Code Sec. 197(d)(1)(B); Reg § 1.197-2(b)(2))[45]

. . . Workforce in place. (Code Sec. 197(d)(1)(C)(i); Reg § 1.197-2(b)(3))[46]

. . . Business books and records, operating systems, or any other information base (including lists or other information with respect to current or prospective customers). (Code Sec. 197(d)(1)(C)(ii); Reg § 1.197-2(b)(4))[47]

---

37. ¶L-7951
38. ¶L-7977
39. ¶L-7983 *et seq.*
40. ¶L-7951.6
41. ¶I-10219.1
42. ¶L-7951.1

43. ¶L-7951.1
44. ¶L-7953
45. ¶L-7953
46. ¶L-7954
47. ¶L-7955

. . . Any patent or copyright (but see the caution below), process, design, pattern, know-how, format or similar item. (Code Sec. 197(d)(1)(C)(iii); Reg § 1.197-2(b)(5))[48]

. . . Customer-based intangibles (Code Sec. 197(d)(1)(C)(iv); Reg § 1.197-2(b)(6)) - which means the value of the composition of market, market share, and any other value resulting from the future provision of goods or services out of relationships with customers (contractual or otherwise) in the ordinary course of business. (Code Sec. 197(d)(2)(A)) This includes certain generic or non-generic website domain names;[49] and in the case of a financial institution, the deposit base and any similar asset. (Code Sec. 197(d)(2)(B)) However, accounts receivable are excluded. (Reg § 1.197-2(b)(6))

. . . Supplier-based intangibles (Code Sec. 197(d)(1)(C)(v)) - which means the value resulting from the future acquisitions of goods or services out of relationships (contractual or otherwise) in the ordinary course of business with suppliers of goods or services to be used or sold by the taxpayer. (Code Sec. 197(d)(3); Reg § 1.197-2(b)(7))[50]

. . . Government granted licenses, permits or other rights (but see the caution below). (Code Sec. 197(d)(1)(D); Reg § 1.197-2(b)(8))[1]

. . . Franchises, trademarks, and trade names. (Code Sec. 197(d)(1)(F); Reg § 1.197-2(b)(10))[2]

⚠️caution: Certain patents, copyrights, and government granted rights qualify only if acquired with the acquisition of a business.

Amortizable section 197 intangibles also include any other item that is similar to workforce in place, information base, know-how, customer-based intangibles, or supplier-based intangibles. (Code Sec. 197(d)(1)(C)(vi))[3]

The following are amortizable section 197 intangibles *only if acquired in connection with the acquisition of assets constituting a trade or business or a substantial portion of one:*[4]

. . . Computer software. (Code Sec. 197(e)(3))[5] For the exclusion of "off-the-shelf" computer software from 15-year amortization, see ¶1959. For software developed by the taxpayer, see ¶1607.

. . . Films, sound recordings, video tapes and books. (Code Sec. 197(e)(4)(A); Reg § 1.197-2(c)(4))[6]

. . . Copyrights and patents. (Code Sec. 197(e)(4)(C))[7]

. . . Mortgage servicing rights secured by residential real property. (Code Sec. 197(e)(6))

. . . Rights to receive tangible property or services under a contract or granted by the government. (Code Sec. 197(e)(4)(B))[8]

. . . Contract rights and government grants if the right has a fixed duration of less than 15 years, or is fixed in amount and, without regard to Code Sec. 197 would be recoverable under a method similar to the unit of production method. (Code Sec. 197(e)(4)(D); Reg § 1.197-2(c)(13))[9]

Covenants not to compete or similar arrangements are amortizable section 197 intangibles if entered into in connection with the acquisition of an interest in a trade or business or a substantial portion of one. The acquisition of that interest can be made in the form of an asset acquisition (including a stock purchase treated as an asset purchase under Code Sec. 338), or a stock or partnership interest acquisition or redemption. (Code Sec. 197(d)(1)(E); Reg § 1.197-2(b)(9))[10] A covenant not to compete agreed to by the seller in connection with an acquisition of an interest (e.g., stock) in a trade or business (as

48. ¶L-7957
49. ¶L-7961
50. ¶L-7964
1. ¶L-7967
2. ¶L-7968
3. ¶L-7952
4. ¶L-7976

5. ¶L-7958.3
6. ¶L-7959
7. ¶L-7960
8. ¶L-7965
9. ¶L-7970
10. ¶L-7966

distinct from an acquisition of assets) was held to be not subject to the substantial portion requirement.[11]

¶ 1959 Intangibles excluded from section 197 intangibles—interests in corporations, partnerships, trusts, and estates; off-the-shelf computer software; futures and foreign currency contracts; land; leases of tangible property; debt instruments.

Code Sec. 197 provides that the following are never treated as section 197 intangibles regardless of how acquired:[12]

. . . Interests in corporations, partnerships, trusts and estates. (Code Sec. 197(e)(1)(A))

. . . Computer software that's readily available for purchase by the general public, is subject to a non-exclusive license, and hasn't been substantially modified (i.e., off-the-shelf). (Code Sec. 197(e)(3)(A)) But, for 36-month straight line depreciation, see ¶1951.

. . . Futures contracts, foreign currency contracts, and notional principal contracts. (Code Sec. 197(e)(1)(B))

. . . Land. (Code Sec. 197(e)(2)) But the right for a wine-maker to use an American viticultural area (AVA) designation isn't an interest in land, and, thus, *is* an amortizable section 197 intangible as a government-granted license, permit or other right (see ¶1958).[13]

. . . Leases of tangible property. (Code Sec. 197(e)(5)(A))

. . . Debt instruments, except for financial institution deposit bases and similar items. (Code Sec. 197(e)(5)(B); Code Sec. 197(d)(2)(B))

. . . Any fees for professional services or transaction costs incurred by parties to a transaction where any part of the gain or loss on the transaction isn't recognized under the rules for corporate organizations and reorganizations. (Code Sec. 197(e)(7))

Certain types of property excluded from being a section 197 intangible when not part of the acquisition of a trade or business (or substantial portion) are described in ¶1958.

Also, amortizable section 197 intangibles exclude intangibles created by the taxpayer (e.g., customer relationships), or for the taxpayer by contract, if they are: (1) neither (a) licenses, permits, or other rights granted by a governmental unit, (b) covenants not to compete (or substantially similar arrangements) made related to the acquisition of an interest in a trade or business (or substantial portion), nor (c) franchises, trademarks, or trade names; and (2) not created in connection with a transaction (or a series of related transactions) that involves the acquisition of assets that constitute all, or a substantial portion of, a trade or business. (Code Sec. 197(c)(2); Reg § 1.197-2(d)(2)) The exclusion doesn't apply to self-created intangibles sold and repurchased in an unrelated transaction.[14]

¶ 1960 Depletion Deduction.

Under Code Sec. 611, all exhaustible natural deposits and timber qualify for deduction of a reasonable allowance for depletion. The deductions are based on the taxpayer's cost or other basis of the resources (cost depletion, see ¶1961). (Code Sec. 611; Code Sec. 612) However, for certain mines, wells (with significant limitations for oil and gas wells), and other natural deposits, depletion deductions may be computed as a specified percentage of gross income if those amounts are greater than cost depletion (percentage depletion, see ¶1962, ¶1963). (Code Sec. 613; Code Sec. 613A)

A taxpayer may take a depletion deduction only if it owns an "economic interest" in the

---

11. ¶L-7966
12. ¶L-7952.1;¶L-7958 *et seq.*

13. ¶L-7967
14. ¶L-7975

mineral deposit or the timber. Generally, what is required is that the taxpayer: (1) look to income from the extraction of the mineral or severance of the timber for a return of capital, and (2) have an interest in the mineral in place or standing timber that was acquired by investment. (Reg § 1.611-1(b))[15]

A taxpayer can claim (1) percentage depletion on one property and cost depletion on another, or (2) for the same property, cost depletion for one year and percentage depletion for another.[16]

Percentage depletion for oil and gas well production (other than gas from certain domestic geothermal deposits or geopressured brine) is limited to "independent producers and royalty owners," see ¶1963. There's no official form for computing depletion, but Form T (Timber) must be attached to the income tax return if a deduction for depletion of timber is taken.[17] The basis of the property must be reduced by the depletion deduction allowed or allowable, whichever is larger.[18]

Cost or percentage depletion must be computed separately for each property. (Code Sec. 612, Code Sec. 613)[19] A "property" is each separate interest owned by the taxpayer in each separate tract or parcel of land. (Code Sec. 614(a)) For that definition, "interest" means economic interest. It includes working or operating interests, royalties, overriding royalties, and net profits interests. It also includes production payments to the extent they aren't treated as loans. (Reg § 1.614-1(a)(2)) Separate properties can be aggregated and treated as a single property. (Code Sec. 614(b); Code Sec. 614(c); Code Sec. 614(e)) An interest in a "mine" may be electively treated as two or more separate properties. (Code Sec. 614(c)(2); Reg § 1.614-3(b))

Specific depletion rules for timber are provided at Reg § 1.611-3.

¶ 1961 Cost depletion for mines, oil and gas wells, and other natural deposits; safe harbor for oil and gas.

The cost depletion deduction for mines, oil and gas wells, and other natural deposits provided by Code Sec. 611 is based on the property's adjusted basis, the number of recoverable units of mineral at the beginning of the year, and the units sold (per the taxpayer's cash or accrual reporting method) during the year. It is computed by dividing the property's adjusted basis by the number of units remaining for the year, and then multiplying by the units sold. (Reg § 1.611-2(a)) An elective safe harbor is available to determine recoverable oil and gas reserves for cost depletion.[20] Total cost depletion deductions can't exceed the basis for the mineral property[21] (which is *only the mineral property's* cost or other basis plus or minus basis adjustments). (Code Sec. 612; Reg § 1.612-1(b)(1); Code Sec. 1016(a))[22]

¶ 1962 Percentage depletion for mines, oil and gas wells, and other natural deposits.

Code Sec. 613 provides percentage depletion for certain mines, wells, and other natural deposits. (Code Sec. 613(a))[23] The allowance is a specified percentage, based on the type of resource, of the "gross income from the property" for the tax year. It can never exceed 50% (100% for oil and gas properties) of the property's taxable income, (Code Sec. 613(a)) which, with some exceptions, is the excess of gross income from the property over the allowable deductions (exclusive of depletion) attributable to the mineral processes (including transportation) on which depletion is claimed. (Reg § 1.613-5(a))[24]

---

15. ¶N-2051 *et seq.*
16. ¶N-2003 *et seq.*; ¶N-2013
17. ¶N-6107
18. ¶N-3009
19. ¶N-2901
20. ¶N-2255.2
21. ¶N-2250 *et seq.*
22. ¶N-3000 *et seq.*
23. ¶N-2311
24. ¶N-2702

The depletion percentages for most minerals are provided in the Code and regulations. (Code Sec. 613(b); Reg § 1.613-2(a)).[25] For oil, gas, and geothermal deposits, see ¶1963. If percentage depletion is lower than cost depletion, then cost depletion must be used. (Code Sec. 613(a))[26]

Percentage depletion reduces basis, but, even if basis is reduced to zero, continues to be deductible as long as there is gross income from the property. A corporation's deductible percentage depletion allowance for iron ore or coal (including lignite) is cut back by 20% of the otherwise allowable deduction that is in excess of the adjusted basis of the property at the close of the tax year (exclusive of the depletion deduction for the tax year). (Code Sec. 291(a)(2))

Natural resources that don't qualify for percentage depletion include timber, (Reg § 1.611-1(a)) and minerals from sea water, the air, or other inexhaustible sources. (Code Sec. 613(b)(7)) Certain coal or iron ore disposed of by contract but with a retained economic interest also doesn't qualify for any depletion. (Reg § 1.611-1(b)(2))[27] For alternative minimum tax treatment of percentage depletion, see ¶3210.

¶ 1963   Percentage depletion for oil and gas claimed by independent producers, and for geothermal deposits; maximum depletable amount.

 Code Sec. 613A allow 15% percentage depletion to oil and gas independent producers (taxpayers that are not retailers or refiners) subject to prescribed limitations. (Code Sec. 613A(c)(1)(A)) Otherwise, percentage depletion for oil and gas wells is not allowed. (Code Sec. 613(d)) Generally, the allowance for independent producers is for so much of the "average daily production" of domestic crude oil and domestic natural gas as doesn't exceed the "depletable oil quantity" or "depletable natural gas quantity." (Code Sec. 613A(c)(1)(A)) Production from "marginal" wells may qualify for a higher percentage depletion rate (never exceeding 25%) where the average price for crude oil for a year was below $20 per barrel ("bbl"). (Code Sec. 613A(c)(6)) The depletable oil quantity (ceiling) is 1,000 bbl per day, and the depletable natural gas quantity (ceiling) is 6,000,000 cubic feet ("cf" where 1,000 equals 1 mcf) of gas per day. A taxpayer who has both types of production must allocate the unified ceiling amount at the rate of 6 mcf of gas per 1 bbl of oil. Over-ceiling production isn't entitled to any depletion. (Code Sec. 613(d); Code Sec. 613A) The deduction can't exceed 65% of the taxpayer's taxable income from all sources. (Code Sec. 613A(d)) The deduction for any costs for which taxpayer claims the 15% enhanced oil recovery credit (¶2322) must be reduced by that credit amount. (Code Sec. 43(d)(1))[28]

Percentage depletion is also available for production of natural heat from geothermal deposits (at a 15% rate) and natural gas production from geopressured brine (at a 10% rate) located in the U.S. or its possession. (Code Sec. 613(e); Code Sec. 613A(b)(2))[29]

Percentage depletion isn't available for any lease bonus, advance royalty or other amount payable without regard to production from any oil, gas, or geothermal property. (Code Sec. 613(e)(3); Code Sec. 613A(d)(5))[30] This restriction applies only to oil and natural gas, but not other minerals, from oil and gas wells.[31]

The maximum depletable quantities for independent producers or royalty owners who are related or are under common control are allocated among them. (Code Sec. 613A(c)(8))[32]

---

25. ¶N-2311
26. ¶N-2300 *et seq.*
27. ¶N-2314
28. ¶N-2400 *et seq.*; ¶N-2425

29. ¶N-2316
30. ¶N-2105 *et seq.*
31. ¶N-2400 *et seq.*
32. ¶N-2420

Chapter 6 Charitable Contributions—Medical Expenses—Alimony—Other Nonbusiness Deductions

¶ 2100   **Charitable Contribution Deduction—Form 1040, Schedule A.** ▄▄▄▄▄▄▄

An individual who itemizes can deduct charitable contributions up to 60% (for cash contributions made in tax years beginning after Dec. 31, 2017 and before Jan. 1, 2026), 30%, or 20% of adjusted gross income, depending on the type of property contributed and the type of donee (¶2123 *et seq.*). A corporation generally can deduct charitable contributions up to 10% of its taxable income (¶2131). Amounts that exceed the ceilings can be carried forward for five years by both individuals (¶2129) and corporations (¶2131). The deduction allowed for property contributions is usually the property's fair market value, but is reduced for gifts of certain types of property (¶2106 *et seq.*).

For individuals, charitable contributions are deductible only as an itemized deduction on Form 1040, Schedule A. (Reg § 1.170A-1(a))[1]

For a charity's requirement to disclose the deductibility of contributions to it, see ¶4120.

¶ 2101   **What is a deductible charitable contribution?**

Under Code Sec. 170, a deductible charitable contribution generally is one that:

. . . is to or for the use of a qualified charitable organization (¶2102) (Code Sec. 170(c));

. . . is paid within taxpayer's tax year, regardless of taxpayer's accounting method (¶2132) (except for certain accrual basis corporations, see ¶2133) (Code Sec. 170(a));

. . . is within the applicable statutory ceilings for individuals (¶2123 *et seq.*), and corporations (¶2131) (Code Sec. 170(b)); *and*

. . . meets certain substantiation requirements (¶2134 *et seq.*). (Reg § 1.170A-13)[2]

¶ 2102   **Qualified charitable organizations; donees eligible to receive deductible contributions.**

Under Code Sec. 170, a qualified charitable organization is one that fits into one of the specified categories *and* which IRS has ruled (or the donor establishes) is eligible to receive deductible contributions.[3] IRS maintains on its website a list of organizations that are eligible to receive tax-deductible charitable contributions, as well information concerning tax-exempt organizations (i.e., in addition to those eligible to receive tax-deductible contributions).[4] Qualified charitable organizations include:

. . . a corporation, trust, community chest, fund or foundation (including a private foundation) that's organized *and* operated exclusively for charitable, religious, educational, scientific or literary purposes, or for the prevention of cruelty to children or animals, or to foster and conduct national or international amateur sports competition (but only if none of the activities involves providing athletic facilities or equipment); *and* that's organized or created in the U.S. or its possessions, or under their laws; *and* none of whose net earnings inures to the benefit of any private shareholder or individual. Corporate contributions to noncorporate donees must be used in the U.S. or its possessions. (Code Sec. 170(c)(2));[5] Additionally, contributions to disregarded single-member LLCs wholly owned and controlled by a U.S. charity are treated as made to the charity;[6]

. . . U.S. states or possessions, their political subdivisions, the U.S., and the District of

---

1. ¶A-2701
2. ¶K-2803
3. ¶K-2850 *et seq.*
4. ¶K-2945
5. ¶K-2862 *et seq.*
6. ¶K-2854

References beginning with a single letter are to paragraphs in Federal Tax Coordinator 2d and RIA's Analysis of Federal Taxes: Income.

Columbia, *but only* if the gift is exclusively for public purposes (Code Sec. 170(c)(1));[7]

... certain war veterans' organizations (Code Sec. 170(c)(3)),[8] certain domestic fraternal societies, orders or associations (Code Sec. 170(c)(4)),[9] and certain nonprofit cemetery companies. (Code Sec. 170(c)(5)).[10]

¶ 2103   Charitable deductions barred for certain contributions: lobbying activities; influencing legislation; contributions to an individual; economic benefit to donor ("quid pro quo").

Under Code Sec. 170(f), no charitable deduction is allowed for the following types of contributions:

... To a charity that conducts lobbying activities on matters of direct financial interest to the donor's trade or business, if a principal purpose was to avoid income tax by getting a charitable deduction for expenses for which a business expense deduction would be disallowed (¶1613) had the donor conducted the activities directly. (Code Sec. 170(f)(9))[11]

... To an organization disqualified from tax exemption because a substantial part of its activities involves trying to influence legislation, or it participates in any political campaign (Reg § 1.170A-1(j)(5)), see ¶4102 *et seq.*[12]

... Made to or for an individual (except for certain students, see ¶2122), unless the individual is an agent for a qualified organization (¶2102).[13]

... By church members and earmarked for a specific individual, e.g., to cover the minister's medical expenses. The church must have control over the funds' use for the donation to be deductible.[14]

... To a charity to the extent the donor derives an economic benefit (for exception, see ¶2104). Thus, no charitable deduction is allowed for: tuition (or required "donation" of excess "tuition" payment), even for parochial school, [15] or a payment in connection with a person's admission to a senior living or retirement home operated by a charity, to the extent allocable to care to be given (may be partly a *medical* expense, see ¶2146) or the privilege of being admitted.[16] Contributions to state programs that entitled taxpayer to state tax credits may not be deductible.[17]

... Subject to a 15% exception (see Reg § 1.170A-1(h)(3)(vi)), taxpayers who make a payment or transfer property to or for the use of a Code Sec. 170(c) entity must reduce their charitable contribution deduction by the amount of any state or local tax credit that the taxpayer receives, or expects to receive, in consideration for the taxpayer's payment or transfer. (Reg § 1.170A-1(h)(3))[18]

... Clothing and household items that aren't in good used condition or better (but deduction may be allowed if amount claimed for the item exceeds $500 and taxpayer includes a qualified appraisal with his or her return, see ¶2137). IRS may also deny a deduction for any contribution of clothing or a household item with minimal monetary value (e.g., used socks or undergarments). IRS says the price a buyer actually pays for a used item in a store such as a thrift shop is an indication of value, but dismissed as inaccurate "standard value listings" supplied by organizations like the Salvation Army. It also says valuation under a fixed formula or method (e.g., percentage of replacement cost), doesn't work well for used clothing. (Code Sec. 170(f)(16))[19]

---

7. ¶K-2899
8. ¶K-2915
9. ¶K-2921
10. ¶K-2925
11. ¶K-2804
12. ¶K-2871
13. ¶K-2953

14. ¶K-2970
15. ¶K-3110, K-3111
16. ¶K-3047
17. ¶K-3059
18. ¶K-3032.1 *et seq.*
19. ¶K-3177.6

¶ 2104   Fundraising events, lotteries, entertainment, etc., for charity; no deduction where taxpayer receives consideration; insubstantial benefits.

Under Code Sec. 170, where amounts are paid in connection with admission to fundraising events for charity (e.g., shows, lotteries, and athletic events), the receipt of tickets or other privileges raises a presumption that the payment isn't a gift. Taxpayer must show that a clearly identifiable part of the payment is a gift. Only the part made with the intention of making a gift *and* for which taxpayer receives no consideration qualifies as a contribution.[20] The charity must show (in its solicitation, tickets, receipts or other related documents) the value (or reasonable estimate) of the event, and how much of the contribution is deductible.[21] For an organization's fundraising disclosure requirements, see ¶4121 *et seq.*

However, the donor may deduct a contribution in full if the benefit is inconsequential or insubstantial. This applies if the charity informs patrons how much is deductible *and* any of these tests is met: (1) the fair market value (FMV) of all benefits received in connection with the payment isn't more than 2% of the payment, or the following dollar figures: $117 for 2022 ($125 for 2023), if less; or (2) the payment is at least $58.50 for 2022 ($62.50 for 2023), and in connection with it the donor receives only token benefits (bookmarks, calendars, mugs, posters, tee shirts, etc.) generally costing no more than $11.70 for 2022 ($12.50 for 2023), or (3) the charity mails or otherwise distributes free, unordered items to patrons.[22]

A taxpayer may rely on either a contemporaneous written acknowledgment (for contributions of $250 or more, see ¶2136) or a written disclosure statement (for quid pro quo contributions of more than $75, see ¶4121) for the FMV of any goods or services he or she receives from the charity. A taxpayer can't treat an estimate as the FMV where he or she knows, or has reason to know, it's unreasonable. (Reg § 1.170A-1(h)(6))[23]

No deduction is allowed for a contribution to a college or university where the donor receives a *right to buy* seating at an athletic event, and the ticket cost itself is nondeductible (Code Sec. 170(l))[24], regardless of whether taxpayer uses it.[25] Amounts paid for raffle tickets, to play bingo, etc., aren't contributions[26] (for deduction as a gambling loss, see ¶1778).

¶ 2105   When a transfer to a charity qualifies as a business expense; sole proprietors may not deduct charitable contributions on Schedule C.

Under Code Sec. 162(b), no Code Sec. 162 deduction is allowed for a contribution that would be allowable as a charitable deduction under Code Sec. 170 if not for the percentage limitations (¶2123 *et seq.*) and other limitations in Code Sec. 170. But under Reg § 1.162-15(a)(1), transfers to a charity that are: (1) directly related to a taxpayer's business, and (2) made with a reasonable expectation of financial return commensurate with the amount transferred, may be deductible as business expenses (on Schedule C) under Code Sec. 162, rather than as a charitable contribution.[27]

A sole proprietor can't deduct charitable contributions on Schedule C (Form 1040 or 1040-SR). Instead, the sole proprietor must itemize deductions to deduct contributions made by the business, and the deduction is subject to the percentage limitations that apply to individuals.[28]

---

20. ¶K-3089
21. ¶K-3105
22. ¶K-3106
23. ¶K-3087.2
24. ¶K-3100

25. ¶K-3094
26. ¶K-3090
27. ¶K-3068 *et seq.*
28. ¶K-2802

¶ 2106   Charitable gift of property (including ordinary income-type property); FMV of donated property; gifts of tangible personal property or capital-gain property.

Under Code Sec. 170, a gift of property to a qualified charitable donee (¶2102) is a contribution to the extent of the property's fair market value (FMV) at the time of the gift, whether or not it has appreciated (Reg § 1.170A-1(c)), except for gifts of ordinary income-type property (¶2107), and certain gifts of tangible personal property or capital gain property (¶2110).[29] For substantiation requirements, see ¶2134 *et seq.* The property's FMV is reduced for donor-placed restrictions on marketability or use (e.g., 3-year bar on transfer or license of donated patent).[30] No gain is realized on a contribution of appreciated property (for certain bargain sales, see ¶2112).[31]

Taxpayer's charitable deduction for the gift can't exceed the property's FMV (at contribution), even if it's less than his or her basis.[32] Nor is taxpayer allowed a loss deduction on the difference between the property's basis and FMV.[33] Special rules apply to gifts of patents[34] and taxidermy property.[35]

¶ 2107   Charitable gift of ordinary-income-type appreciated property—deduction reduced; noncorporate donations of "apparently wholesome food."

Under Code Sec. 170(e), for charitable gifts of ordinary income-type property (below), the amount contributed (property's fair market value (FMV), ¶2106) must be reduced by the amount which would have been recognized as gain other than long-term capital gain if the property had been sold by the donor for its then FMV. (Code Sec. 170(e)(1))[36] However, the reduction does not apply to any gain of a corporation that would not be treated as long-term capital gain under the rules of Code Sec. 291 (¶2677). For exceptions for certain gifts of C corporations, see ¶2108.

Ordinary-income-type property is property which, if sold by taxpayer (donor) at its FMV on the date it was contributed, would have resulted in *some* amount of gain other than long-term capital gain. (Code Sec. 170(e)(1)) This includes: inventory or other property held for sale to customers; Code Sec. 306 stock (¶3524 *et seq.*); capital assets held for less than the long-term holding period as of the date contributed; property subject to depreciation, recapture, etc.; property used in taxpayer's trade or business; and art works, letters, memoranda, and similar property created by or for taxpayer. (Reg § 1.170A-4(b))[37]

Taxpayers that aren't C corporations that donate "apparently wholesome food" (i.e., meant for human consumption, and meeting certain quality and labeling standards) inventory to eligible charities, are entitled to the same enhanced deduction available to C corporations (¶2108), except that the deduction can't exceed 15% of aggregate net income for that tax year from all trades or businesses from which those contributions were made, computed without regard to the taxpayer's charitable deductions for the year. (Code Sec. 170(e)(3)(C)(i)(I))[38]

¶ 2108   Enhanced deductions for C corporation charitable gifts for specified purposes—donations of scientific property, food inventory (COVID-19/coronavirus relief), and inventory for care of the ill, needy, or infants—Form 8283.

---

29. ¶K-3150 *et seq.*
30. ¶K-3151
31. ¶K-3208 *et seq.*, ¶K-3179 *et seq.*
32. ¶K-3151
33. ¶M-1015

34. ¶K-3177.1
35. ¶K-3171.1
36. ¶K-3160 *et seq.*
37. ¶K-3161
38. ¶K-3201.1

Under Code Sec. 170(e)(3) and Code Sec. 170(e)(4), a C corporation may claim an enhanced ("above-basis") deduction equal to the lesser of (a) basis plus half of the property's appreciation, or (b) twice the property's basis, for:

(1) Contributions of inventory, property held primarily for sale to customers in the ordinary course of its trade or business, or depreciable real property used in its trade or business, if the contribution is to an exempt Code Sec. 501(c)(3) organization (see ¶4102) (other than certain private foundations) that uses the property solely for the care of the ill, the needy or infants, and meets other specified requirements. (Code Sec. 170(e)(3)(A))[39]

(2) Certain contributions of scientific equipment or apparatus constructed by taxpayer to a higher education institution or a tax-exempt organization (but not a private foundation) organized and operated primarily to conduct scientific research. (Code Sec. 170(e)(4))[40]

(3) Contributions of food inventory that are "apparently wholesome food" (i.e., meant for human consumption, and meeting certain quality and labeling standards), limited to 15% of taxable income (as specially computed). (Code Sec. 170(e)(3)(C))

¶ 2109 Property contribution where taxpayer realizes income (ordinary income or capital gain) on charitable gift.

If a taxpayer realizes income (ordinary income or capital gain) on a gift of property, the charitable deduction isn't subject to the reduction described at ¶2107. Thus, the taxpayer may deduct the full fair market value of donated installment obligations, obligations issued at a discount, or other receivables. (Reg § 1.170A-4(a))[41]

¶ 2110 Limits on charitable contributions of tangible personal property; gifts of capital-gain property to certain private foundations.

Under Code Sec. 170(e), for certain gifts, the amount treated as contributed and deductible (subject to deduction ceilings, see ¶2123 *et seq.*) is the property's fair market value (FMV) *reduced* by the total amount of the gain that would have been long-term capital gain (determined without regard to Code Sec. 1221(b)(3), see ¶2615) if the property were sold for its then FMV. (Code Sec. 170(e)(1)(B))[42] The donor's deduction is thus limited to his or her basis for these contributions:

. . . tangible personal property that's unrelated to the donee's exempt function (e.g., art to a church that then sells it) (Code Sec. 170(e)(1)(B)(i)); and

. . . any capital gain property except for publicly traded stock (limited to aggregate contributions of not more than 10% of the value of a corporation's outstanding stock by a donor and family) given to a private foundation that isn't an operating foundation or community foundation and that doesn't make timely qualifying distributions. (Code Sec. 170(e)(1)(B)(ii), Code Sec. 170(e)(5))[43]

For contributions of tangible personal property for which a FMV deduction is claimed, but which isn't used for exempt purposes, if the donee sells or disposes of tangible personal property with a claimed value of at least $5,000: (1) in the year of contribution, the deduction is limited to taxpayer's basis; or (2) after the year of contribution, but within the 3-year period beginning on the contribution date, the donor includes in income the amount of the claimed deduction in excess of his or her basis in the property. These rules don't apply if the organization makes a proper certification to IRS. A $10,000 penalty applies for fraudulent identifications of property (i.e., stating it's exempt-use property while knowing

---

39. ¶K-3201 *et seq.*
40. ¶K-3221 *et seq.*
41. ¶K-3178

42. ¶K-3160 *et seq.*
43. ¶K-3175 *et seq.*

it was not intended for such use). (Code Sec. 170(e)(1)(B)(i)(II), Code Sec. 170(e)(7), Code Sec. 6720B)[44]

¶ 2111   Liabilities transferred as part of charitable contribution; deduction for prepayment of interest.

Under Code Sec. 170, the donor's charitable contribution must be reduced by any liability that's assumed (e.g., by the donee) in connection with the gift. (Reg § 1.170A-3(d)) Where the donor transfers property subject to a liability, the amount of that debt is treated as an amount realized for purposes of the bargain sale rules, see ¶2112 (but not for the rule at ¶2109).[45] A reduction also must be made for the prepayment of any interest on the liability attributable to any period after the contribution was made if the donor takes a deduction for interest expense on the same payment. (Code Sec. 170(f)(5))[46]

observation: A taxpayer who can't deduct the prepayment as interest, e.g., because it's personal interest, should be able to get a charitable deduction for that payment since the charity has the obligation to make the interest payment after the contribution.

¶ 2112   Bargain sale to (or exchange with) charity.

Under Code Sec. 1011(b), a taxpayer who sells property to (or exchanges it with) a charity and receives less than its fair market value (FMV) may treat the "bargain" element as a charitable contribution. (Code Sec. 1011(b); Reg § 1.170A-4(c)(2)) In computing the deduction, the amount considered contributed (excess of FMV over selling price) must be reduced by the amount of any required adjustment for ordinary income-type appreciated property (¶2107) for the contribution portion. (Reg § 1.170A-4(c), Reg § 1.1011-2(a))[47]

But the donor generally also realizes taxable gain on the sale. His or her basis for measuring gain is only the portion of his or her total cost or other basis for the property that the bargain selling price (amount realized) bears to its FMV. (Code Sec. 1011(b); Reg § 1.1011-2) This is basis times the selling price, divided by FMV. (Reg § 1.170A-4(c)(2)(i))[48]

illustration: J owns long-term stock that cost $12,000 and is worth $20,000 when he sells it to charity for $12,000. A contribution deduction of $8,000 ($20,000 – $12,000) is allowable. J's basis for the stock is reduced to $7,200 ($12,000 cost × [$12,000 selling price ÷ $20,000 FMV]) which, applied against his $12,000 selling price, gives J a $4,800 taxable gain.

¶ 2113   Gift of stock of closely held corporation to charity followed by redemption ("charitable bail-out").

Owners of closely held corporations may effectively withdraw earnings from their firms tax-free by making a charitable contribution of their corporate stock, which the corporation then redeems. As long as the charity isn't obligated to sell back the stock, the donor can claim a deduction, even if the redemption was preplanned.[49] But, a contribution of stock which is then redeemed from a private foundation may be subject to penalty excise taxes (¶4129).

¶ 2114   Charitable contributions of partial interests in property; transfers in trust or not in trust.

Under Code Sec. 170(f)(2), *for transfers in trust,* a contribution of a partial interest in

---

44. ¶K-3167 *et seq.*; ¶V-2712
45. ¶K-3155, K-3198
46. ¶K-3157

47. ¶K-3190
48. ¶K-3194
49. ¶K-3186

property (e.g., where the donor transfers only his or her right to use the property, or his or her income interest in it) qualifies for a charitable deduction if the interest is:

- a remainder interest transferred to a charitable remainder trust (CRT, ¶2116), or a pooled income fund (¶2117), (Code Sec. 170(f)(2)(A)); or

- an income interest in a charitable lead trust (¶2119). (Code Sec. 170(f)(2)(B))[50]

Under Code Sec. 170(f)(3), *for transfers not in trust,* no charitable deduction is allowed for a contribution of less than the donor's entire interest in the donated property, except to the extent the deduction would have been allowed had the transfer been in trust. (Code Sec. 170(f)(3)(A))[1] Thus, a taxpayer who gives a charity the *right to use* property (e.g., rent-free use of office space), while retaining the property itself, can't take a charitable deduction for the rental or other value of this right.[2] The bar on deductions for transfers not in trust doesn't apply to contributions of:

- A remainder interest in a personal residence or a farm. (Code Sec. 170(f)(3)(B)(i));[3]

- An undivided part of taxpayer's entire interest (even if partial) in property (Code Sec. 170(f)(3)(B)(ii)), such as a remainder or income interest.[4] No deduction is allowed for a contribution of an undivided part of a taxpayer's entire interest in tangible personal property unless, immediately before the contribution, all interests in the property are held by taxpayer or taxpayer and the donee. Additionally, the fair market value (FMV) of any additional contribution of a fractional interest in property is the lesser of: (1) its FMV at the time of the initial fractional contribution, or (2) its FMV at the time of the additional contribution. (Code Sec. 170(o)(1)(A), Code Sec. 170(o)(2)) The deduction is recaptured under certain circumstances. (Code Sec. 170(o)(3)(A), Code Sec. 2522(e)(2)(A));

- A partial interest in property where *all* of taxpayer's interests in the property are given to one or more charities (e.g., income interest to one charity and remainder interest to another charity). (Reg § 1.170A-6(a));[5]

- A partial interest in real property (including remainders and perpetual restrictions) exclusively for "conservation purposes," including a qualifying facade easement. (Code Sec. 170(f)(3)(B)(iii), Code Sec. 170(h)) A facade easement must satisfy a number of requirements, including that it preserve in perpetuity the building's entire exterior and prohibit any change inconsistent with its historical character. No deduction is allowed for a charitable donation of an interest in property which is subject to a mortgage unless the mortgagee subordinates its rights in the property to the right of the charitable donee to enforce the conservation purposes of the gift in perpetuity. (Reg § 1.170A-14(g)(2)) The subordination agreement must be in effect when the easement is granted. And an easement isn't considered to be granted until it's enforceable under state law.[6] The perpetuity requirement is not met if other property can be substituted for the property originally transferred subject to the easement, if the taxpayer retains the right to modify the boundary lines of the donated interest (although the taxpayer may retain the right to modify the boundary lines of tracts *within* the donated interest), if the term of the easement is limited under state law, or if a long-term lessee of a building doesn't have a fee interest in it. But, the Tax Court has held that the right to build a water tower and some hunting blinds didn't affect an easement's qualification as a perpetual conservation restriction.[7] Additionally, the easement is held to have no value, and thus no deduction is allowed, if the facade is already subject to restrictions similar to the easement by virtue of being located in a historic district.[8]

50. ¶K-3250 *et seq.*
1. ¶K-3440.1 *et seq.*
2. ¶K-3440.2
3. ¶K-3440.4 *et seq.*
4. ¶K-3451 *et seq.*

5. ¶K-3473
6. ¶K-3520
7. ¶K-3504 *et seq.*
8. ¶K-3527

¶ 2115   "Personal benefit contract" transactions—Form 8870—charitable contributions.

Under Code Sec. 170(f)(10), no charitable deduction is allowed for a transfer to or for the use of a charity if the charity directly or indirectly pays or paid any premium on any personal benefit contract (e.g., split-dollar life insurance, see ¶1266) for the transferor. Also, no deduction is allowed if there is an understanding or expectation that any person will directly or indirectly pay any premium on any such contract for the transferor. A charity must pay an excise tax (use Form 8870) if it or any such person pays such premiums. (Code Sec. 170(f)(10))[9]

¶ 2116   Charitable remainder trusts (CRTs)—CRATs and CRUTs.

Code Sec. 664(d) provides that a CRT is a trust formed to make current distributions to one or more noncharitable income beneficiaries and to pay the entire remainder to charity or use it for a charitable purpose, that's *either* a "charitable remainder annuity trust" (CRAT) or a "charitable remainder unitrust" (CRUT). (Code Sec. 664(d); Reg § 1.664-1)[10]

¶ 2117   Pooled income funds; trusts; noncharitable beneficiaries—charitable contributions.

Code Sec. 642(c)(5) provides that a pooled income fund is a trust formed to pay income to one or more noncharitable beneficiaries and the remainder to charity. It must be maintained by the donee charity (no donor or income beneficiary may be a trustee) and meet certain other requirements. (Code Sec. 642(c)(5); Reg § 1.642(c)-5)[11]

¶ 2118   Charitable contributions to donor advised funds (DAFs); sponsoring organization.

Under Code Sec. 170(f)(18), DAFs are charitable accounts set up and sponsored by an organization to which donors contribute and provide advice on the account's distributions and investments, although the sponsoring organization must have final say on the actual distributions and investments. Contributions are deductible if: (1) the sponsoring organization isn't listed in Code Sec. 170(f)(18)(A) (e.g., a war veteran's organization or domestic fraternal lodge); and (2) the donor obtains contemporaneous written acknowledgment from the sponsoring organization certifying it has legal control over the contribution. (Code Sec. 170(f)(18)(B))[12]

¶ 2119   Contribution of income interest in trust—charitable lead trusts—"guaranteed annuity" or "unitrust interest."

Under Code Sec. 170(f)(2)(B), a charitable deduction is allowed for a contribution of an income interest in trust (remainder to a noncharity) *only* if: (1) the donor is taxable on the trust income, and (2) the donated income interest is either a "guaranteed annuity" or a "unitrust interest." (Code Sec. 170(f)(2)(B); Reg § 1.170A-6) This type of trust is a "charitable lead trust."[13]

---

9. ¶K-3661, K-3667, S-4928.2
10. ¶K-3261 *et seq.*, ¶K-3291 *et seq.*
11. ¶K-3363 *et seq.*

12. ¶K-3987
13. ¶K-3345 *et seq.*

¶ 2120   Services for charity and related deductible transportation expenses; unreimbursed out-of-pocket expenses.

Under Code Sec. 170, no deduction is allowed for the value of services a taxpayer renders to charity. (Reg § 1.170A-1(g))[14] However, taxpayer is allowed a deduction for his or her unreimbursed out-of-pocket expenses (for travel expenses, see ¶2121) necessarily incurred in performing services (other than lobbying) free for a charity. (Code Sec. 170(f)(6); Reg § 1.170A-1(g))[15]

A taxpayer who uses his or her car in performing these services may deduct 14¢ per mile as a contribution (Code Sec. 170(i)) or his or her actual (unreimbursed) expenses for gas and oil. Parking fees and tolls are deductible in either case, as are deductions otherwise allowable for interest or taxes connected with the car, but not depreciation, insurance, and repairs.[16]

¶ 2121   Charitable travel expenses; requirement of no significant element of personal pleasure.

Under Code Sec. 170(j), no charitable deduction is allowed for taxpayer's travel expenses (including meals and lodging), whether or not reimbursed, while away from home, unless there is no significant element of personal pleasure, recreation or vacation in the travel. (Code Sec. 170(j)) Even then, deduction is limited to amounts necessarily incurred for meals and lodging while away from home overnight in rendering these services.[17]

¶ 2122   Maintaining student in taxpayer's home—charitable contributions.

Under Code Sec. 170(g), a charitable deduction is allowed to a taxpayer who, under a written agreement with a charity and without compensation, maintains a student in the 12th grade or lower (not a dependent or relative) in his or her home. (Code Sec. 170(g); Reg § 1.170A-2)[18] The contribution in any year is the amount so contributed, but not more than $50 times the number of full calendar months (15 days or more is a "month") during the year for which the individual was a member of taxpayer's household and a full-time student. (Code Sec. 170(g)(2); Reg § 1.170A-2(b))[19]

¶ 2123   Annual charitable deduction ceilings for individuals; contributions for disaster relief; COVID-19/coronavirus relief.

Under Code Sec. 170(b)(1), there's a ceiling on the amount an individual may deduct each year as a charitable contribution, based both on the type of property contributed and the type of charity to which the contribution is made. The ceilings (below) for any tax year are a percentage of taxpayer's "contribution base" (below) for the year, subject to an overall 60% ceiling for all charitable gifts. (Code Sec. 170(b)(1))[20] For carryover of excess contributions, see ¶2129.

If the contributions are all to "50% charities" (see ¶2124), the year's ceiling is 60% of the taxpayer's contribution base for cash contributions made in 2018 through 2025 tax years, except for contributions of appreciated capital gain property (¶2126). (Code Sec. 170(b)(1)(A))

> **◆ observation:** Charities, contributions to which are subject to a 60% ceiling, are referred to as "50% charities" because the ceiling on the deductibility of contributions to those charities was 50% in tax years beginning before 2018.

---

14. ¶K-3551
15. ¶K-3601 *et seq.*
16. ¶K-3614 *et seq.*
17. ¶K-3620 *et seq.*

18. ¶K-3650 *et seq.*
19. ¶K-3651
20. ¶K-3670

21

Contributions to 30% charities. If the contributions are all to "30% charities" (see ¶2125), or are "for the use" of *any* charities, the ceiling is 30% of taxpayer's contribution base (except for gifts of appreciated capital gain property, see ¶2128) or, if less, 50% of his or her contribution base minus contributions to 50% charities. (Code Sec. 170(b)(1)(B))[22] Cash contributions that are taken into account under the 60% contribution base limit in effect from 2018 through 2025 tax years aren't taken into account for purposes of applying the 50% contribution base limit. (Code Sec. 170(b)(1)(G)(iii)(I))

Contribution base. An individual's "contribution base" for a year is his or her adjusted gross income (¶3102) for the year, but without deducting any net operating loss carryback to that year. (Code Sec. 170(b)(1)(G))[23] For spouses filing joint returns, these ceilings apply to the couple's combined contributions and their combined contribution base. (Reg § 1.170A-8(a)(1))[24]

Disaster relief efforts. An individual may elect to deduct certain recent disaster relief efforts up to his or her entire contribution base less other contributions. Qualified contributions exceeding this amount are carried forward for five years as contributions to which the 50%/60% limit applies. A qualified contribution is any cash charitable contribution paid to an organization described in Code Sec. 170(b)(1)(A) (see ¶2124). Taxpayers must satisfy substantiation requirements. (Code Sec. 170(b)(1))[25]

Qualified conservation contributions. For qualified conservation contributions (i.e., contribution of a qualified real property interest to a qualified organization exclusively for conservation), a 50% (rather than 30%) limit on the contribution base, less all other contributions, applies, and the carryforward period (¶2129) is 15 years.[26] For qualified farmers and ranchers (more than 50% of gross income from farming as defined at Code Sec. 2032A(e)(5)), this limit is 100% of the contribution base less all other contributions. For property in agriculture or livestock production to be eligible for the 100% limit, the qualified real property interest has to include a restriction that the property remains generally available for such production. A 15-year carryover is allowed. (Code Sec. 170(b)(1)(E)).[27]

¶ 2124   50% charities: churches and synagogues, schools, hospitals, U.S. states or possessions, certain private foundations and membership organizations—charitable contributions.

> **observation:** Charities, contributions to which are subject to a 60% ceiling (see ¶2123), are referred to as "50% charities" because the ceiling on the deductibility of contributions to them was 50% in tax years beginning before 2018.

Under Code Sec. 170(b)(1)(A), for purposes of the deduction ceilings for individuals (¶2123), "50% charities" are (1) churches and synagogues (or church or synagogue conventions or associations); (2) tax-exempt educational organizations; (3) tax-exempt hospitals and certain medical research organizations; (4) certain organizations holding property for state and local colleges and universities; (5) a U.S. state or possession, or any political subdivision of any of these, or the U.S. or the District of Columbia, if the contribution is for exclusively public purposes; (6) organizations organized and operated exclusively for charitable, religious, educational, scientific or literary purposes, or for the prevention of cruelty to children or animals, or to foster national or international amateur sports competition if they normally get a substantial part of their support from the government or general public; (7) certain private foundations; (8) certain membership organizations more than

---

21. ¶K-3671
22. ¶s K-3671, K-3674, K-3684 *et seq.*
23. ¶K-3672
24. ¶K-3673

25. ¶K-3670 *et seq.*
26. ¶K-3694.1, ¶K-3701.1
27. ¶K-3694.2

one-third of whose support comes from the public; and (9) agricultural research organizations. (Code Sec. 170(b)(1)(A))[28]

¶ 2125 30% charities—veterans' organizations, fraternal orders, cemetery companies, certain private nonoperating foundations—charitable contributions.

Under Code Sec. 170(b)(1)(B), for purposes of the ceilings on an individual's charitable deduction (¶2123), "30% charities" are qualifying charitable organizations (¶2102) that aren't 50% charities (¶2124), e.g., war veterans' organizations, fraternal orders, cemetery companies, and certain private nonoperating foundations. (Code Sec. 170(b)(1)(B);[29]

¶ 2126 Gifts of appreciated capital gain property to 50% charities—30% ceiling.

Under Code Sec. 170(b)(1)(C), an individual's deduction ceiling in the tax year for gifts of certain appreciated capital gain property (below) to 50% charities is 30% of his or her contribution base (¶2123), unless he or she makes an election to reduce the amount of his or her contribution (in which case, the 50% ceiling applies, see ¶2127). (Code Sec. 170(b)(1)(C))[30] For ceiling on gifts to 30% charities, see ¶2128.

This rule applies to any capital asset which, if sold for fair market value at contribution, would have given rise to long-term capital gain, *other than* property subject to the reduction at ¶2110. (Code Sec. 170(b)(1)(C))[31]

¶ 2127 Individual's election of 50% ceiling for appreciated property contributions—charitable gifts of capital gain property.

Under Code Sec. 170(b)(1)(C)(iii), an individual donor whose gift of capital gain property to a 50% charity is otherwise subject to the 30% ceiling (¶2126) may elect the 50% ceiling for the gift, *but only* if he or she reduces the amount of his or her contribution (as described at ¶2107)—i.e., the donor's contribution is limited to his or her basis in the property. (Code Sec. 170(b)(1)(C)(iii)[32]

recommendation: Elect where the appreciation is small (value of increased current deduction is greater than loss of eventual deduction of appreciation) or where the 30% limit will prevent deduction of the appreciation even over the carryover period (¶2129).

Once made, the election applies to all gifts of capital gain property (¶2126) to 50% charities made by the donor in the tax year. In computing carryovers to this year, contributions of this property in an earlier year for which the election was *not* made are reduced as if they were subject to the reduction when made. (Code Sec. 170(b)(1)(C)(iii); Reg § 1.170A-8(d)(2))[33] The election is made by attaching a statement specified in the regs, to the original income tax return for the election year. (Reg § 1.170A-8(d)(2)(iii))[34]

¶ 2128 Gifts of appreciated long-term capital gain property to 30% charities— 20% ceiling.

Under Code Sec. 170(b)(1)(D), an individual's deduction ceiling for gifts of appreciated long-term capital gain property to 30% charities is 20% of his or her contribution base (¶2123) (and there's no election like the one for gifts to 50% charities, see ¶2127). (Code Sec. 170(b)(1)(D))[35]

---

28. ¶K-3720 *et seq.*
29. ¶K-3684 *et seq.*
30. ¶K-3686, K-3687
31. ¶K-3687

32. ¶K-3689
33. ¶K-3706
34. ¶K-3690
35. ¶K-3694

¶ 2129   Carryover of excess charitable contributions by individuals; gifts in excess of annual percentage ceilings; coronavirus/COVID-19 relief.

Code Sec. 170(d)(1) provides that, if an individual's charitable gifts for a tax year exceed the percentage ceilings for the year (¶2123), the excess may generally be carried forward and deducted for up to five years (subject to the later year's ceiling). (Code Sec. 170(d)(1)) A statement must be filed with the return for the year the carryover is deducted. The carryforward is available even if the individual didn't itemize deductions in the contribution year. (Reg § 1.170A-10(a)(2))[36]

Contributions are deductible in the following order, up to 50% of the contribution base:

(1) Contributions qualifying for the 50% charity limit (¶2124).

(2) Contributions qualifying for the 30% charity limit (¶2125) up to the lesser of:

. . . 30% of the contribution base, or

. . . (a) 50% of the contribution base minus (b) contributions to 50% limit organizations. For this purpose, (b) includes contributions of capital gain property subject to the 30% limit (¶2126).

(3) Contributions of capital gain property subject to the 30% limit (up to the lesser of 30% of the contribution base or 50% of the contribution base minus other contributions to 50% organizations).

(4) Contributions qualifying for the 20% limit (¶2128) up to the lesser of:

. . . 20% of the contribution base,

. . . 30% of the contribution base minus contributions subject to the 30% limit,

. . . 30% of the contribution base minus contributions of capital gain property subject to the special 30% limit, or

. . . 50% of the contribution base minus the total of contributions to 50% and 30% limit organizations. (Code Sec. 170(b)(1))[37]

Where charitable contributions in more than one limitation category are carried over, the ordering rules determine the deduction limits for each category of contribution. Starting with the first (50% limitation) category, the allowable deduction limit is determined. Current contributions in that category are deducted first. Next, within that category, amounts carried over are deducted, up to the limitation amount for the category. Then, the same process is applied to the next limitation category according to the ordering rules. (Reg § 1.170A-10(b), Reg § 1.170A-10(c)) If there are carryovers from two or more years in any category, the carryover from the earlier year is considered first.[38]

¶ 2130   Excess charitable contributions on decedent's final return.

If an individual dies, any charitable contribution that can't be used on the decedent's final return (under the normal ceilings, see ¶2123) is lost. (Reg § 1.170A-10(d)(4)(iii))[39]

¶ 2131   Corporation's charitable deduction ceiling and carryover period; treatment of qualified conservation contributions; COVID-19/coronavirus relief; elective 100% limit for certain disaster relief contributions.

Under Code Sec. 170(b)(2), a corporation's charitable deduction for a tax year can't exceed 10% of its taxable income for the year. Taxable income for this purpose is computed without deductions for charitable contributions or dividends received, net operating loss

---

36. ¶K-3701 *et seq.*, ¶K-3711
37. ¶K-3701 *et seq.*

38. ¶K-3701 *et seq.*
39. ¶K-3710

carrybacks or capital loss carrybacks to the year, (Code Sec. 170(b)(2); Reg § 1.170A-11(a))[40] or adjustments for excess inclusion income stemming from the corporation's residual interest in a REMIC (¶4204) under Code Sec. 860E.[41] To the extent contributions in any year exceed this limit, the excess can be carried forward and deducted for five years. (Code Sec. 170(d)(2))[42]

A corporation that is a qualified farmer or rancher can make a qualified conservation contribution equal to 100% of its taxable income after taking into account other allowable charitable contributions. To be eligible, the corporation's stock can't be readily tradable on an established securities market at any time during the tax year the contribution is made. To be a qualified rancher or farmer, more than 50% of the corporation's gross income for the tax year has to come from the trade or business of farming. A 15-year carryover is allowed. (Code Sec. 170(b)(2)(B))[43] Alaska Native Corporations are allowed to deduct donations of conservation easements up to 100% of taxable income. (Code Sec. 170(b)(2)(C))[44]

¶ 2132 When to deduct charitable contributions; contributions by check or credit card.

Under Reg § 1.170A-1(a), a charitable contribution is deductible in the tax year it's paid (subject to percentage ceilings, see ¶2123, ¶2131) (Code Sec. 170(a)), regardless of the donor's accounting method (except for accrual method corporations, see ¶2133) or when the gift was pledged. (Reg § 1.170A-1(a))[45] A contribution is "paid" when it's unconditionally delivered to the donee. A contribution by check that's delivered unconditionally is paid when delivered, if it clears in due course. If the check is mailed unconditionally and clears in due course, the contribution is paid when mailed. (Reg § 1.170A-1(b))[46] A contribution charged on a credit card is deductible by a cash basis donor in the year the charge is made, *not* in any later year when the credit card company is paid.[47]

¶ 2133 Corporate election to deduct post-year-end charitable contribution.

Under Code Sec. 170(a)(2), an accrual method corporation, other than an S corporation (¶3358), whose board of directors has authorized a charitable contribution during the tax year may elect to deduct all or part of the contribution in that (authorization) year, if the contribution is paid by the 15th day of the fourth month following the close of the year (for tax years beginning before 2026, for C corporations using a tax year ending on June 30, if the contribution is paid by the 15th day of the *third* month following the close of the year). (Code Sec. 170(a)(2))[48] The election is made by reporting the contribution in the return and attaching a declaration signed by a principal officer, together with a copy of the directors' resolution authorizing the contribution. (Code Sec. 170(a)(2); Reg § 1.170A-11(b))[49]

¶ 2134 Specialized Rules for Claiming Charitable Contributions. ■■■■■■■

Taxpayers (donors) must substantiate their charitable deductions (¶2135), and supply appraisals and other information for certain property contributions. No charitable deduction is allowed for a contribution of $250 or more unless taxpayer substantiates it by a contemporaneous written acknowledgment from the donee (¶2136), and noncash contributions exceeding $500 are also subject to heightened substantiation requirements (¶2137). Special rules apply for contributions of cars, boats, and planes (¶2138), and for gifts of art appraised at $50,000 or more (¶2139).

---

40. ¶K-3830 *et seq.*
41. ¶K-3832
42. ¶K-3833
43. ¶K-3831.1 *et seq.*
44. ¶K-3831.1 *et seq.*

45. ¶K-3851
46. ¶K-3858 *et seq.*
47. ¶K-3861
48. ¶K-3882 *et seq.*
49. ¶K-3883

¶ 2135   Charitable contributions must be substantiated; donor's receipt; Form W-2 for contributions by payroll deduction.

Under Code Sec. 170(a)(1), a charitable deduction isn't allowed unless taxpayer can prove the right to it. (Code Sec. 170(a)(1))[50] For *donee's* information return requirement, see ¶4746.

For cash contributions, taxpayer must keep either a cancelled check, receipt or other reliable evidence. (Reg § 1.170A-13(a)(1))[1] A taxpayer can't deduct *any* contribution of a cash, check, or other monetary gift unless he or she maintains as a record of the contribution a bank record (e.g., a statement from a financial institution or cancelled check) or a written communication from the donee organization showing its name, plus the date and amount of the contribution. (Code Sec. 170(f)(17)) For contributions of property (other than cash), taxpayer must have a receipt from the donee and keep records showing the donee's name and describing the gift. (Reg § 1.170A-13(b)(1))[2] For contributions made via payroll deductions, taxpayer must retain a pay stub, Form W-2, or other employer document showing the amount withheld for the purpose of payment to the donee, plus a pledge card or similar donee document showing the donee's name.[3] For contributions made through the Combined Federal Campaign or a similar program (e.g., United Way), the organization receiving the donation may be treated as the donee for substantiation purposes even if it distributes the funds to another organization. The written communication must contain the ultimate recipient's name.[4] Additional substantiation is required for: contributions of $250 or more (¶2136); noncash contributions exceeding $500 (¶2137); and contributions of cars, boats, and planes (¶2138).

¶ 2136   Substantiation requirement for charitable contributions of $250 or more—contemporaneous written acknowledgment (CWA).

Under Code Sec. 170(f)(8)(A), no charitable deduction is allowed for any (cash or property) contribution of $250 or more unless taxpayer substantiates it by a CWA (not just a cancelled check) from the donee (or its agent). (Code Sec. 170(f)(8)(A); Reg § 1.170A-13(f)(1))[5]

In general, the CWA must state: (1) the amount of cash and a description (but not the value) of any property other than cash contributed; (2) whether the donee provided any goods or services in consideration for the contribution, and if it did, a description and good-faith estimate of their value; and (3) if the goods or services consist entirely of intangible religious benefits (e.g., admission to a religious ceremony, but not religious school tuition or fees), a statement to that effect. (Code Sec. 170(f)(8)(B); Reg § 1.170A-13(f)(2)) Special requirements apply for gifts to a pooled income fund (¶2117). (Reg § 1.170A-13(f)(13))[6]

The donation of virtual currency/cryptocurrency (e.g., Bitcoin) is treated as a noncash contribution for this purpose.[7]

The CWA requirement doesn't apply to transfers to a charitable lead trust (¶2119), charitable remainder annuity trust, or charitable remainder unitrust (¶2116). (Reg § 1.170A-13(f)(13))[8]

Goods or services that have insubstantial value (¶2104), and certain annual membership benefits the charity provides to taxpayer, taxpayer's employees, or the partners of a partnership donor in exchange for the contribution are disregarded in determining the $250 threshold. (Reg § 1.170A-13(f)(8)(i), Reg § 1.170A-13(f)(9)(i))[9] And, separate payments are

50. ¶K-3901 *et seq.*
1. ¶K-3919
2. ¶s K-3926, K-3927
3. ¶K-3939
4. ¶K-3941

5. ¶K-3933
6. ¶K-3933 *et seq.*
7. ¶I-2151.1
8. ¶K-3940.3
9. ¶K-3934

generally treated as separate contributions. (Reg § 1.170A-13(f)(1))[10]

An employer's payment to a charity of $250 or more withheld from taxpayer's paycheck (the amount withheld from each single paycheck is treated as a separate contribution), may be substantiated by a combination of (1) a pay stub, Form W-2, or other employer-provided document showing the amount withheld for this purpose, and (2) a pledge card or other donee document which states it doesn't provide any consideration for the payroll contributions. (Reg § 1.170A-13(f)(11))[11]

¶ 2137 Proving noncash charitable contributions exceeding $500—when taxpayer must have a contemporaneous written acknowledgment (CWA), qualified appraisal, and/or a Form 8283.

Under Code Sec. 170(f)(11), for noncash contributions that are:

(1) more than $500 but not more than $5,000, the donor must substantiate the contribution with a CWA of the gift and attach to its return a description of the contributed property, on Form 8283. This requirement doesn't apply to a C corporation. (Code Sec. 170(f)(11)(B), Reg § 1.170A-16(c))

(2) more than $5,000 but not more than $500,000, the donor must obtain a "qualified appraisal" (one meeting specified IRS requirements) and attach to its return (using Form 8283) information about the property and appraisal (i.e., appraisal summary) as required by IRS. (Code Sec. 170(f)(11)(C))

(3) more than $500,000, the donor must obtain a CWA from the donee, attach a qualified appraisal to its return, and complete a Form 8283. (Code Sec. 170(f)(11)(D), Reg § 1.170A-16(e))

The donation of virtual currency/cryptocurrency (e.g., Bitcoin) is treated as a noncash contribution for this purpose.[12] The requirements in (2) and (3), above, don't apply to: patents, copyrights, etc., as described in Code Sec. 170(e)(1)(B)(iii) (¶2106); property described in Code Sec. 1221(a)(1) (e.g., stock in trade, inventory); publicly traded securities; and "qualified vehicle donations" (¶2138). (Code Sec. 170(f)(11)(A)(ii)(I)) IRS disallows a deduction if the above reporting requirements aren't met, unless the failure was due to reasonable cause. (Code Sec. 170(f)(11)(A))[13]

¶ 2138 Qualified vehicle donations; charitable contributions of cars, boats, and planes—Form 1098-C.

Under Code Sec. 170(f)(12), special rules apply for contributions of motor vehicles, boats, and airplanes that aren't in taxpayer's inventory or held for sale in the ordinary course of business ("qualified vehicle donations"), if the donation's claimed value exceeds $500. (Code Sec. 170(f)(12)) The donor's deduction can't exceed the gross proceeds from the charity's sale proceeds unless:

(1) there's a "significant intervening use" of the vehicle by the charity (actual, significant use to substantially further the charity's regularly conducted activities) before its sale;

(2) the charity materially improves the vehicle (significantly increases its value) before its sale (minor repairs or routine maintenance aren't enough); or

(3) the charity sells it at a price significantly below fair market value (FMV) (or gives it away) to a needy individual, in direct furtherance of its charitable purpose of relieving the poor and distressed or the underprivileged who need vehicles.

If (1), (2), or (3) applies, the donor may claim a deduction for the vehicle's FMV, using

---

10. ¶K-3934
11. ¶K-3940
12. ¶I-2151.1
13. ¶K-3942 *et seq.*

the "blue book" value for a similar vehicle (or private party sale amount, until regs are issued).

A deduction for donated vehicles whose claimed value exceeds $500 isn't allowed unless taxpayer substantiates the contribution by a contemporaneous written acknowledgment (CWA) from the donee (on Form 1098-C) and attach it to the Form 8283. (Code Sec. 170(f)(12)(A); Reg § 1.170A-16(c)(4)) It must:

. . . contain the donor's name and taxpayer identification number (TIN), the vehicle identification number (or similar number), and if exception (1), (2), or (3), above, applies, supporting details;

. . . indicate whether the donee provided goods or services in consideration of the vehicle (and, if so, describe them and estimate their value, or, if they consist solely of intangible religious benefits, a statement to that effect);

. . . generally be made within 30 days after the vehicle's sale (within 30 days of the contribution if exception (1), (2) or (3) applies); and

. . . if the charity sells the vehicle and none of the three above exceptions applies, state that the vehicle was sold in an arm's length transaction between unrelated parties, show the gross proceeds, and declare that the deductible amount can't exceed the gross proceeds.[14]

¶ 2139 IRS "Statement of Value" to substantiate charitable gifts of art appraised at $50,000 or more.

At taxpayer's request, IRS will issue a Statement of Value that taxpayer may rely on to substantiate the value of an item of art (paintings, sculpture, antique furniture, carpets, rare manuscripts, historical memorabilia, and similar objects) that has been appraised at $50,000 or more and transferred as a charitable gift. Taxpayer must request the statement before filing the return that first reports the gift, and must attach a copy of the statement (or of the request, if the statement hasn't been received yet) to that return.[15]

¶ 2140 Medical Expenses.

An individual who itemizes can deduct the amount by which certain unreimbursed medical and dental expenses (¶2144 through ¶2149) paid during the year (see ¶2150) for the taxpayer, spouse, and dependents (¶2142) exceed 7.5% of adjusted gross income (AGI, see ¶2141). But medical expenses aren't deductible if compensated for by insurance or otherwise, see ¶2151.

For whether and when expenses for a decedent's medical care that are paid out of the decedent's estate are treated as paid by him or her (and may be deducted), see ¶2143.

¶ 2141 Medical expense deduction—how much is deductible (7.5% of adjusted gross income (AGI) floor)—Form 1040, Schedule A.

Under Code Sec. 213, the amount of medical expenses (¶2144) an individual can deduct (on Form 1040, Schedule A) is the amount by which unreimbursed payments for those expenses exceed 7.5% of adjusted gross income (AGI, ¶3102). (There's no ceiling on the deduction.) (Code Sec. 213(a); Code Sec. 213(f))[16]

Any expense allowed as a Code Sec. 21 dependent care credit (¶2354), Code Sec. 35 credit for health insurance costs (¶2348), or Code Sec. 162(l) self-employed medical insurance deduction (¶1530) can't be treated as a medical expense. (Code Sec. 213(e), Code Sec. 35(g)(2), Code Sec. 162(l)(3))[17]

14. ¶K-3948.1 *et seq.*
15. ¶T-10080 *et seq.*
16. ¶K-2002
17. ¶K-2003

¶ 2142 Whose medical expenses may taxpayer deduct? Expenses of taxpayer's spouse and dependents.

Under Code Sec. 213(a), a taxpayer may deduct his or her own medical expenses, and those of a spouse and dependents if the status as spouse, etc., exists either when the medical care was rendered or when the expenses were paid. (Code Sec. 213(a); Reg § 1.213-1(e)(3)) For this purpose, "dependent" is defined in Code Sec. 152 (see ¶3113) and is determined without the gross income test for qualifying relatives, the rule that a joint return filer can't be a dependent, and the rule that a dependent is ineligible to have dependents. (Code Sec. 213(a); Reg § 1.213-1(a)(3)(i)) A child of divorced parents is considered a dependent of both if Code Sec. 152(e) applies (see ¶3120), so that each parent may deduct the medical expenses he or she pays for the child. (Code Sec. 213(d)(5))[18] An organ donor's medical expenses are deductible by the payor, whether donor or recipient.[19]

¶ 2143 Decedent's medical expenses paid out of the decedent's estate.

Under Code Sec. 213(c), expenses for a decedent's medical care that are paid out of his or her estate are treated as paid by him or her (and may be deducted) in the year incurred if: (1) they're paid within one year after death, (2) they aren't deducted for federal estate tax purposes, and (3) a statement is filed with the income tax return (or amended return) showing that the expenses weren't allowed for estate tax purposes and that the estate tax deduction is waived. (Code Sec. 213(c))[20]

observation: The choice of an income tax or estate tax deduction depends primarily on the extent to which the expense is deductible for income tax purposes, the decedent's top income tax rate, and the top effective estate tax rate.

¶ 2144 What kinds of medical expenses are deductible? Amounts paid for the diagnosis, mitigation, treatment, prevention of disease.

Under Code Sec. 213(d)(1), deductible medical expenses are amounts paid for the diagnosis, mitigation, treatment, prevention of disease or for the purpose of affecting the body's structure or function (Code Sec. 213(d)(1)),[21] and the costs of nursing services (Reg § 1.213-1(e)(1)(ii))[22] (and related insurance payments, ¶2135, and transportation, ¶2148). Deductible expenses include the costs of:

... Eyeglasses, artificial teeth or limbs (Reg § 1.213-1(e)(1)(ii)), hearing aids, and similar items, as well as breast pumps and supplies that assist lactation.[23]

... Eye surgery to correct defective vision, including laser procedures (e.g., LASIK).[24]

... Discretionary medical procedures affecting the body's structure or function, including legal abortions and procedures to prevent or facilitate pregnancy (e.g., egg donor fees; but in vitro fertilization costs for a taxpayer who wasn't infertile weren't deductible).[25]

... Smoking cessation programs[26] and prescribed drugs designed to alleviate nicotine withdrawal, but not non-prescription nicotine gum and nicotine patches.[27]

... Attending a medical conference on a chronic disease suffered by an individual, spouse, or dependent (but not meal and lodging costs, ¶2149).[28]

... Legally procured prescription drugs (e.g., not aspirin) and insulin. (Code Sec. 213(b), Code Sec. 213(d)(3)) A controlled substance (such as marijuana) obtained for medical

---

18. ¶K-2300 *et seq.*
19. ¶K-2144
20. ¶C-9556
21. ¶K-2100 *et seq.*
22. ¶K-2114
23. ¶K-2103
24. ¶K-2103
25. ¶K-2113
26. ¶K-2118
27. ¶K-2124
28. ¶K-2145

purposes, in violation of the federal Controlled Substances Act, isn't legally procured and is nondeductible, even if state law permits its doctor-prescribed use.[29]

. . . Weight-loss program for treatment of a specific disease (e.g., obesity, hypertension), but not the cost of diet food.[30]

. . . Diagnostic tests aiding in the detection of heart attack, diabetes, cancer, and other diseases (but not the collection and storage of DNA, absent a showing of how the DNA will be used for medical diagnosis). These include pregnancy tests, tests on healthy individuals, and tests taken not at the direction of a physician. Such a test will not fail to qualify due to high cost or if a less expensive alternative may be available.[31]

. . . The price of a DNA testing kit must be allocated between nondeductible ancestry services and deductible medical services (e.g., DNA testing used for medical diagnosis), using a reasonable method to value and allocate the cost of the related deductible and nondeductible services.[32]

. . . Service animals used in mental health therapy.[33]

. . . Sex-change costs (except for breast augmentation undertaken to improve appearance).[34]

. . . Nonlicensed healthcare providers that provided physician-ordered assistance and supervision to a patient suffering from dementia.[35]

. . . Nontraditional or alternative medical practices, treatments or services.[36]

. . . Personal protective equipment, such as masks, hand sanitizer and sanitizing wipes, for the primary purpose of preventing the spread of coronavirus/COVID-19.[37]

Expenses that aren't deductible as medical care include:

. . . Expenses merely beneficial to the individual's general health. (Reg § 1.213-1(e)(1)(ii))[38]

. . . Costs of cosmetic surgery or similar procedure (e.g., teeth whitening), unless necessary to ameliorate a deformity arising from, or directly related to, a congenital abnormality, a personal injury resulting from an accident or trauma or a disfiguring disease (Code Sec. 213(d)(9))—e.g., breast reconstruction surgery after cancer mastectomy.[39]

. . . Payments for illegal operations or treatments. (Reg § 1.213-1(e)(1)(ii))[40]

. . . Insurance premiums paid by an employer-sponsored health insurance plan (cafeteria plan), unless the amounts paid are taxed to the employee (included in taxable compensation box 1 of Form W-2).[41]

A male couple could deduct, as medical expenses, only those costs incurred to have a baby directly related to their own medical care. (PLR 202114001)[42]

Qualified long-term care services are treated as medical care (Code Sec. 213(d)(1)(C)) (unless provided by a relative who isn't a licensed professional, or by a related corporation or partnership. (Code Sec. 213(d)(11))) These services include necessary diagnostic, preventive, therapeutic, curing, treating, mitigating, and rehabilitative services, and maintenance or personal care services, which are required by a chronically ill individual and provided under a plan of care prescribed by a licensed health care practitioner. (Code Sec. 7702B(c)(1))[43]

29. ¶K-2124
30. ¶K-2117
31. ¶K-2108
32. ¶K-2108
33. ¶K-2103
34. ¶K-2101, K-2112
35. ¶K-2123
36. ¶K-2115

37. ¶K-2101
38. ¶K-2105
39. ¶K-2112
40. ¶K-2109
41. ¶K-2127
42. ¶K-2113
43. ¶K-2151

¶ **2145** **Accident and health insurance; Medicare; annual limits on deductibility of premiums paid for qualified long-term care (LTC) insurance—medical expense deduction.**

Under Code Sec. 213(d)(1)(D), the cost of insurance that's deductible as a medical expense is limited to amounts paid for insurance that covers *medical care* as defined at ¶2144. (Code Sec. 213(d)(1)(D))[44]

Amounts paid as *voluntary* premiums under Part B of Medicare (supplementary medical insurance benefits for the aged and disabled) are deductible as medical care, as are voluntary premiums under Medicare Part A (basic Medicare) (Code Sec. 213(d)(1)(D)), and Medicare Part D premiums, but not the *mandatory* employment or self-employment taxes paid for basic coverage under Medicare A. (Reg § 1.213-1(e)(4)(i)(a))[45] IRS has stated that all Medicare parts are insurance that constitutes medical care under Code Sec. 162(l) (see ¶1530).[46] For the business expense deduction for medical care insurance of sole proprietors, partners or 2%-or-more S corporation shareholders who pay Medicare premiums, see ¶1530.

When an insurance contract covers both medical care and other items (e.g., loss of income), no amount is treated as for medical care *unless:* the charge for medical insurance is separately stated, the amount treated as paid for medical insurance doesn't exceed the separately-stated charge, *and* the charge isn't unreasonably large in relation to the total premium for the contract. (Code Sec. 213(d)(6))[47]

Medical expenses include premiums paid for qualified long-term care (LTC) insurance, up to annual limits. For an individual who attained the following age before the close of the tax year the limit is):

... 40 or less, the limit is $450 for 2022 ($480 for 2023);

... more than 40, but not more than 50, the limit is $850 for 2022 ($890 for 2023);

... more than 50, but not more than 60, the limit is $1,690 for 2022 ($1,790 in 2023);

... more than 60, but not more than 70, the limit is $4,510 for 2022 ($4,770 for 2023); and

... more than 70, the limit is $5,640 for 2022 ($5,960 for 2023). (Code Sec. 213(d)(10))[48]

Code Sec. 7702B(b) provides that qualified LTC insurance contracts must provide only coverage of qualified LTC services, must not pay or reimburse expenses to the extent the expenses are reimbursable under Medicare (or would be but for a deductible or coinsurance amount), must be guaranteed renewable, and must meet other detailed requirements. (Code Sec. 7702B(b))[49]

¶ **2146** **Deductible costs of care at hospitals and other institutions; in-patient care (including meals and lodging)—medical expense deduction.**

Under Reg § 1.213-1(e)(1)(v), the cost of in-patient care (including meals and lodging, see ¶2149) furnished by a hospital is a deductible medical expense. (Reg § 1.213-1(e)(1)(v))[50] The cost of in-patient care (including meals and lodging) at a medical-care institution that *isn't* a hospital qualifies if the individual is there primarily for the availability of medical care (as defined at ¶2144), and the meals and lodging are a necessity incident to that care. If this test isn't met, only that part of the cost attributable to medical care qualifies. Medical care status depends on the patient's condition and the nature of the services he or she receives—not on the nature of the institution (e.g., federal, state, local

---

44. ¶K-2140 *et seq.*
45. ¶K-2140
46. ¶L-3509
47. ¶K-2141

48. ¶K-2153
49. ¶K-2154
50. ¶K-2142

or private). The deduction is allowed for:

> . . . costs (including tuition, meals, and lodging) of a mentally or physically handicapped person at a special school (Reg § 1.213-1(e)(1)(v)), e.g., a school for children with learning disabilities like dyslexia. Costs allocable to medical care at a regular school qualify if the school supplies a cost breakdown;[1]

> . . . costs of a nursing home or home for the aged. But if the person isn't there principally for medical reasons, only the cost of medical care qualifies. (Reg § 1.213-1(e)(1)(v))[2] A deduction may be available for advance payments for lifetime care if certain requirements are met, and only for the part of the payment allocable to medical care.[3]

¶ 2147 "Medical" capital expenses for equipment or improvements; elevators, swimming pools, and other permanent improvements to taxpayer's property.

Under Reg § 1.213-1(e)(1)(iii), amounts incurred for elevators, swimming pools, and other permanent improvements to taxpayer's property (including capital expenditures to accommodate a residence to a physically handicapped individual) may be deductible medical expenses (¶2144) if the primary purpose is for the medical care of taxpayer, spouse, or dependents. But the medical deduction is limited to that part of the expenses that exceeds the amount by which the improvement increases the value of taxpayer's property. (Reg § 1.213-1(e)(1)(iii))[4]

Some expenses incurred by or for a physically handicapped individual to remove structural barriers in a residence to accommodate a physical condition (e.g., constructing access ramps, widening doorways, installing support bars) are presumed not to increase the value of the residence and may be deductible in full. (Reg § 1.213-1(e)(1)(iii))[5] Capital expenditures that are related only to the sick person and are detachable from the property aren't permanent improvements, so their full cost can be a medical expense (e.g., detachable inclinators and air conditioners). (Reg § 1.213-1(e)(1)(iii))[6] All the costs of operating or maintaining a medical capital asset are deductible, even if none or only a part of the cost of the asset itself qualifies. (Reg § 1.213-1(e)(1)(iii))[7]

¶ 2148 Transportation expenses (including food and lodging) for medical care.

Under Code Sec. 213(d)(1)(B), the costs of transportation primarily for and essential to medical care (¶2144) qualify as medical expenses. (Code Sec. 213(d)(1)(B)) This includes food and lodging expense (¶2149) while en route to the place of medical treatment (Reg § 1.213-1(e)(1)(iv)), as well as taxi, train, plane, and bus fares and the cost of ambulance services.[8] Deductible medical expenses also include certain out-of-pocket car expenses, e.g., for gas, oil, parking fees, and tolls, but not depreciation, repair, insurance or maintenance. Instead of claiming the actual costs of gas and oil, a taxpayer who uses a car for qualified medical transportation may deduct a flat 18¢ a mile for expenses paid or incurred from Jan. 1, 2022 through June 30, 2022, and 22¢ a mile for expenses after June 30, 2022.[9] However, no medical expense deduction is permitted for the cost of commuting to and from work, even if taxpayer's illness or disability requires a special method of transportation.[10]

---

1. ¶K-2143 *et seq.*
2. ¶K-2136
3. ¶K-2403
4. ¶K-2180 *et seq.*
5. ¶K-2181
6. ¶K-2192
7. ¶K-2182
8. ¶K-2201
9. ¶K-2214 *et seq.*
10. ¶K-2202

¶ 2149 "Away from home" expenses for medical care (meals and lodging)—$50 per night rule.

Under Code Sec. 213(d)(2), expenses for meals and lodging away from home aren't medical expenses unless they're part of the cost of care in a hospital or other institution (¶2146) or medical travel (¶2148).[11] Taxpayer may deduct as a medical expense amounts paid for lodging (not food) while away from home, that's primarily for and essential to medical care in a hospital or equivalent, up to $50 per night for each individual. (Code Sec. 213(d)(2)) No deduction is allowed for lavish or extravagant lodging or where the travel has any significant element of personal pleasure, recreation or vacation. (Code Sec. 213(d)(2)(B))[12]

¶ 2150 When to deduct medical expenses; payments by credit card; advance payment of anticipated medical expenses; prepaid insurance.

Code Sec. 213(a) provides that only medical expenses actually paid during the tax year are deductible. (Code Sec. 213(a)) Deduction is thus allowed for payments in the year even though the expenses were incurred in an earlier year. (Reg § 1.213-1(a)(1)) If the payment is made by credit card, the amount is deductible in the year the charge is made, regardless of when the credit card bill is paid.[13] Advance payment of anticipated medical expenses doesn't qualify for a current deduction unless there is a contractual obligation to pay in the current year.[14] Certain insurance premiums paid by a taxpayer who is under age 65 during the payment year, for medical care for the taxpayer, spouse, and dependents for the period *after* he or she reaches age 65, are deductible in the year paid. (Reg § 1.213-1(e)(4)(i)(b))[15]

¶ 2151 Medical expenses compensated for by insurance or otherwise; compensation for loss of earnings or as damages for personal injuries.

Code Sec. 213(a) provides that medical expenses aren't deductible if they have been compensated for by insurance or otherwise. (Code Sec. 213(a)) Taxpayer must reduce medical expenses by amounts so compensated before applying the percentage of adjusted gross income floor (¶2141). But no reduction is required for amounts received as compensation for loss of earnings or as damages for personal injuries.[16] If reimbursements in a tax year exceed medical expenses in that year, no medical deduction is allowed.[17] Any part of the excess that's attributable to an employer's contribution is taxable; the rest is tax-free.[18] If taxpayer is reimbursed for medical expenses in a year after he or she paid (and deducted) them, the taxpayer must report the reimbursement as income to the extent attributable to the earlier deduction (Reg § 1.213-1(g))—i.e., to the extent the taxpayer got a "tax benefit," see ¶1205.[19]

¶ 2152 Alimony Under Post-2018 and Pre-2019 Instruments— Deductibility/Taxability. ▬▬▬▬▬▬▬▬▬

For any divorce or separation instrument that's: (1) executed after Dec. 31, 2018, or (2) executed on or before Dec. 31, 2018, and modified after Dec. 31, 2018, if the modification expressly provides for such treatment, a deduction for the payment of alimony won't apply (repealed Code Sec. 215, repealed Code Sec. 62(a)(10)), and an inclusion in gross income for the receipt of alimony payments won't apply. So, the alimony-paying spouse won't be able to deduct the payments, and the alimony-

---

11. ¶K-2217
12. ¶K-2218
13. ¶K-2401
14. ¶K-2403
15. ¶K-2404

16. ¶K-2601 *et seq.*
17. ¶K-2605
18. ¶H-1114
19. ¶K-2604

receiving spouse (or the beneficiary of an alimony trust (Code Sec. 682)) won't include them in gross income or pay federal income tax on them. Instead, income used for alimony payments will be taxed at the rates that apply to the payor spouse, rather than those that apply to the recipient spouse. But, IRS intends to issue regs clarifying that Code Sec. 682 will generally continue to apply with regard to trust income payable to a former spouse who was divorced or legally separated under a divorce or separation instrument executed on or before Dec. 31, 2018, unless such instrument is modified after that date and the modification provides that the repeal applies to the modification.[20]

For any divorce or separation instruments executed *before Jan. 1, 2019,* payments of alimony or separate maintenance (¶2153) made under a divorce or separation instrument are taxable to the payee spouse in the year received (repealed Code Sec. 71(a); Reg § 1.71-1(b)(5)), and are deductible by the payor spouse in the year paid, as a deduction from gross income. (repealed Code Sec. 62(a)(10), repealed Code Sec. 215(a))[21] Thus, the payor doesn't have to itemize to be allowed the deduction.[22]

These rules don't apply if the spouses file a joint return with each other. (repealed Code Sec. 71(e))[23] For the requirement that the spouses live apart, see ¶2155.

For the requirement that alimony payments be under a divorce or separation instrument, see ¶2154. For child support payments made under a divorce or separation agreement, see ¶2158.

Cash payments by the payor spouse to a third party on behalf of the payee spouse can be alimony, see ¶2156, as can premiums that one spouse pays for insurance on his or her life if the other (payee) spouse owns the policy, see ¶2157. However, a payment isn't alimony if the divorce or separation instrument designates that a payment that would otherwise qualify as alimony is not to be treated as alimony, see ¶2159. And a payor spouse can't deduct payments the payee spouse receives from an alimony trust which aren't includible in the payor's income under the Code Sec. 682 trust rules, see ¶2160.

For the requirement that "excess" (front-loaded) alimony payments be recaptured by the payor spouse, see ¶2161.

¶ 2153　Alimony requirements—pre-2019 divorce or separation instruments—transfer of property other than cash; payments due after payee spouse's death.

Repealed Code Sec. 71(b)(1) provided that, to qualify as alimony under a pre-2019 divorce or separation instrument, a payment must be made in cash, under a divorce or separation instrument (¶2154). (repealed Code Sec. 71(b)(1)) A transfer of property other than cash can't be alimony,[24] but cash payments can be designated as "nonalimony" (¶2159). There must be no requirement that payments continue beyond the death of the payee spouse (e.g., to the estate) or that any substitute payment (in cash or property) be made after the death of the payee spouse, i.e., the payments must end at the payee spouse's death. (repealed Code Sec. 71(b)(1)(D)) If this rule isn't satisfied, *none* of the payments (even those made during the payee-spouse's life) are alimony. (Reg § 1.71-1T(b), Q&A 10) If it isn't clear from the divorce or separation agreement whether payments cease at the payee spouse's death, local law controls. A lump sum payment in lieu of future alimony payments makes the payments nondeductible.[25] See ¶2158 for the difference between alimony and child support payments.

---

20. ¶C-5433
21. ¶J-1413, K-6001
22. ¶A-2621, K-6002

23. ¶K-6001
24. ¶K-6005
25. ¶K-6036 *et seq.*

¶ 2154 Alimony payment, to be deductible, must be made under a pre-2019 "divorce or separation instrument."

Repealed Code Sec. 71(b)(2) provided that, to be alimony, a payment must be made under a divorce or separation instrument (repealed Code Sec. 71(b)(1)(A)), i.e., a (1) decree of divorce or separate maintenance or a written instrument issued incident to the decree (e.g., a pretrial order), (2) written separation agreement, or (3) decree not described in (1) (e.g., a temporary support order). (repealed Code Sec. 71(b)(2))[26] If made under a divorce or separate maintenance decree (or a written instrument incident to the decree), the payment must be made after the decree. (Reg § 1.71-1(b)(1)(i)) If made under a separation agreement, the payment must be made after execution of that agreement. (Reg § 1.71-1(b)(2))[27]

¶ 2155 Separate household requirement for alimony—pre-2019 divorce or separation instruments.

Repealed Code Sec. 71(b)(1)(C) provided that spouses who are legally separated (but not divorced) under a divorce or separate maintenance decree must not live in the same household when the payment is made, or it won't be alimony (¶2153). (repealed Code Sec. 71(b)(1)(C)) But if the spouses aren't legally separated, a payment under a written separation agreement or temporary support order may be alimony even if they are members of the same household. (Reg § 1.71-1T(b), Q&A 9)[28] The spouses aren't treated as members of the same household if one spouse is preparing to leave it, and does leave within one month after the payment.[29]

¶ 2156 "Alimony" payments to a third party on behalf of the payee spouse— pre-2019 divorce or separation instruments; payments made to maintain property.

Repealed Code Sec. 71(b)(1)(A) provided that payments made in cash by the payor spouse to a third party on behalf of the payee spouse under the terms of the divorce or separation instrument can be alimony (¶2153). (repealed Code Sec. 71(b)(1)(A)) Payments are on behalf of the payee spouse if they satisfy an obligation to that spouse. Thus, cash payments of the payee spouse's rent, mortgage, tax or tuition liabilities that the payor spouse makes as required by the instrument can qualify as alimony, as can payments made to a third party (e.g., a charity) at the payee spouse's written request, if the spouses intend them to be alimony.[30] But payments made to maintain property *owned by the payor spouse* but used by the payee spouse (including mortgage payments, realty taxes, and insurance premiums) *aren't* payments on behalf of the payee spouse (i.e., not alimony), even if made under the terms of the divorce or separation instrument. (Reg § 1.71-1T(b), Q&A 8)[31] A payor spouse who is required by the divorce or separation instrument to pay the mortgage on a home he or she owns jointly with the payee spouse may deduct one-half of those payments as alimony, if they otherwise qualify (the rest may be deductible as qualified residence interest if paid on a qualified home, see ¶1729 *et seq.*).[32]

¶ 2157 Premiums on life insurance contracts as alimony—pre-2019 divorce or separation instruments.

Under Reg § 1.71-1T(b), Q&A 6, premiums that one spouse pays for insurance on his or her life as required by the divorce or separation instrument are alimony if the other (payee) spouse owns the policy. (Reg § 1.71-1T(b), Q&A 6)[33]

26. ¶K-6013
27. ¶K-6018
28. ¶K-6035
29. ¶K-6035
30. ¶K-6006
31. ¶K-6007
32. ¶K-6008
33. ¶K-6010

¶ 2158   Child support payments aren't deductible alimony under rules for pre-2019 divorce or separation instruments.

Repealed Code Sec. 71(c)(1) provides that a payment under a divorce or separation instrument that's "fixed" (or treated as fixed) as support for a child of the payor spouse *isn't* alimony. (repealed Code Sec. 71(c)(1))[34] This applies if the instrument designates a specified amount of money or a part of a payment to be child support. The actual amount may fluctuate. (Reg § 1.71-1T(c), Q&A 16)[35] A part of a payment may be *treated* as fixed if the payment is to be reduced on the happening of a specified contingency relating to the child (repealed Code Sec. 71(c)(2)), e.g., on the child's 18th birthday, or when he or she dies, marries or leaves school.[36] A payment may also be treated as fixed if it ends or is reduced at a time that can clearly be associated with the contingency. (Reg § 1.71-1T(c))[37] If a divorce or separation instrument provides specified amounts for alimony and child support, and the payor spouse pays the payee spouse less than the amount designated for child support, then the *entire* payment is child support; no part is alimony. (repealed Code Sec. 71(c)(3))[38] However, if a fixed amount is paid for family support to a separated spouse, and there is no provision for reduction, e.g., when a child reaches a certain age or graduates from school, the entire amount may be treated as alimony.[39]

> ⓡ*observation:* The tax rules for child support—i.e., that payers of child support don't get a deduction, and recipients of child support don't have to pay tax on those amounts—weren't changed by the Tax Cuts and Jobs Act (PL 115-97, 12/22/2017) that changed the post-2018 alimony rules (¶2152).

¶ 2159   Designating that payments aren't to be treated as alimony—pre-2019 instruments.

Under repealed Code Sec. 71(b)(1)(B), if a divorce or separation instrument designates a payment that would otherwise qualify as alimony as *not* to be treated as alimony (e.g., as a property settlement), the payment won't qualify as alimony. (repealed Code Sec. 71(b)(1)(B); Reg § 1.71-1T, Q&A 8)[40]

¶ 2160   Alimony trusts—pre-2019 divorce or separation instruments.

Under repealed Code Sec. 215(d), a payor spouse can't deduct payments the payee spouse receives from an alimony trust which aren't includible in the payor's income under the Code Sec. 682 trust rules. (repealed Code Sec. 215(d))[41] A payee spouse/beneficiary who's divorced or legally separated, or separated under a written separation agreement, includes in gross income the share of trust income that (without this rule) would be includible in the payor spouse's income—effectively shifting liability for tax on the income. But amounts payable for support of the payor spouse's minor children are taxable to the payor spouse. (repealed Code Sec. 682(a))[42]

Generally, for amounts received after 2018 (see ¶2152 for effective dates), the beneficiary of an alimony trust won't include such amounts in gross income or pay federal income tax on them. (repealed Code Sec. 682)) But, IRS has stated that it intends to provide regs that Code Sec. 682 will continue to apply with regard to trust income payable to a former spouse who was divorced or legally separated under a divorce or separation instrument executed on or before 2019, unless such instrument is modified after that date and the modification provides that the revocation applies to the modification.

34. ¶K-6046
35. ¶K-6047
36. ¶K-6049
37. ¶K-6049
38. ¶K-6048

39. ¶K-6047
40. ¶K-6033
41. ¶K-6009
42. ¶C-5432 *et seq.*

¶ 2161 Recapture rules—excess front-loading of alimony—pre-2019 divorce or separation instruments.

Under repealed Code Sec. 71(f)(1)(A), if there are "excess" alimony payments ("front-loading"), the payor spouse must "recapture" the "excess" by including it in gross income for the third post-separation year (below) (repealed Code Sec. 71(f)(1)(A)).[43] The same amount is deducted by the payee spouse in computing adjusted gross income for *the payee's* third post-separation year . (repealed Code Sec. 71(f)(1)(B))[44] The "recapture" amount is the sum of:

(1) the excess of (a) the alimony or separate maintenance payments in the second post-separation year, over (b) the sum of the payments in the third year, plus $15,000; *plus*

(2) the excess of (a) the payments in the first post-separation year, over (b) the sum of the average of the payments in the second year (minus any excess payment in (1), above) and third year, plus $15,000. (repealed Code Sec. 71(f))[45]

The first post-separation year is the first calendar year in which the payor spouse paid alimony, etc., to the payee spouse. The second and third post-separation years are the succeeding calendar years. (repealed Code Sec. 71(f)(6))[46] There's no recapture if payments cease because either spouse dies or the payee spouse remarries before the close of the third post-separation year. Nor does recapture apply to temporary support payments or payments that fluctuate because of a continuing liability to pay, for at least three years, a fixed portion of income from business, property or services (including self-employment). (repealed Code Sec. 71(f)(5))[47]

¶ 2162 "Nonbusiness" Expenses; Miscellaneous Itemized Deductions. ▬▬▬▬▬▬▬

From 2018 to 2025, miscellaneous itemized deductions subject to the 2%-of-AGI floor are not allowed, including most "nonbusiness" expense deductions —e.g., ordinary and necessary expenses that, though not connected with a taxpayer's trade or business, are paid or incurred for the collection or production of income; the management, conservation or maintenance of property held for the production of income; or the determination, collection or refund of any tax. (Code Sec. 67(g))

Taxpayers may not deduct expenses attributable to tax-exempt income, ¶2163. (Code Sec. 265)

Individuals may deduct penalties for premature withdrawal from a savings accounts, etc., ¶2164(Code Sec. 62(a)(9))

¶ 2163 Expenses for production of tax-exempt income, deductibility.

Under Code Sec. 265(a)(1), a taxpayer may not deduct costs incurred in the production of tax-exempt income (Code Sec. 265(a)(1))[48] (e.g., interest on indebtedness incurred or continued to buy or carry tax-exempt securities, see ¶1723). Expenses attributable to both taxable and tax-exempt income that can't be specifically identified must be prorated. (Reg § 1.265-1(c))[49]

¶ 2164 Penalties for premature withdrawal of interest or principal from a bank or other financial institution—deductibility.

An individual may deduct any interest or principal he or she forfeits to a bank or other

---

43. ¶K-6043, K-6044
44. ¶K-6044
45. ¶K-6044
46. ¶K-6045
47. ¶K-6043
48. ¶K-9000 *et seq.*
49. ¶K-9002

financial institution as a penalty for premature withdrawal from a time savings account, certificate of deposit or similar deposit. The penalty is deductible from gross income in computing adjusted gross income (Code Sec. 62(a)(9)), see ¶3102.[50]

¶ 2165 Bond Premium Amortization.

Under Code Sec. 171(a), any premium on tax-exempt bonds must be amortized (Code Sec. 171(a)(2); Reg § 1.171-1(c)(1)), but premium on *taxable* bonds is amortized only if the holder so elects (see ¶2166), using the procedure discussed in ¶2168. (Code Sec. 171(a)(1), Code Sec. 171(c); Reg § 1.171-1(c)(2)) The amortized amount reduces basis and, for taxable bonds, is treated as an offset to the interest received.[1]

"Bonds" include a bond, debenture, note, or certificate or other evidence of indebtedness. (Code Sec. 171(d); Reg § 1.171-1(b)) These rules don't apply to certain specified debt obligations. (Reg § 1.171-1(b)(2))[2] Bond premium generally arises when the stated interest rate on the bond is higher than its market yield when purchased. The premium is the excess of the holder's basis in the bond immediately after acquisition over the sum of all amounts payable on the bond after the acquisition date (other than payments of qualified stated interest, see ¶1314). (Reg § 1.171-1(d)(1))[3] Basis for this purpose is the holder's basis for determining loss on sale. (Code Sec. 171(b)(1)(A); Reg § 1.171-1(e)(1)(i))[4] If a convertible bond is purchased at a premium, any amount attributable to the conversion feature is excluded from amortizable bond premium. (Code Sec. 171(b)(1))[5] Regs provide special rules for variable rate debt instruments, inflation-indexed debt instruments, and bonds subject to contingencies. (Reg § 1.171-3)[6] For amortization of callable bonds, see ¶2167. For securities dealers, see ¶2169.

¶ 2166 Amortization deduction, basis reduction—tax-exempt bonds and taxable bonds; treatment of bond premium.

Under Code Sec. 171(a)(2), for *tax-exempt* bonds, no deduction is allowed for the amortizable bond premium for a tax year. (Code Sec. 171(a)(2))[7] The bond's basis is reduced by the amortizable bond premium barred as a deduction. (Code Sec. 1016(a)(5)); Reg § 1.1016-5(b)(3))[8] For *taxable* bonds, a taxpayer can elect (¶2168) to deduct amortizable bond premium (Code Sec. 171(a)(1)). The bond premium (computed under a constant-yield method based on yield to maturity (Code Sec. 171(b)(3)(A); Reg § 1.171-1(a)(1))) allocable to an accrual period is deducted as an offset to the qualified stated interest (¶1314) allocable to the period. (Code Sec. 171(e); Reg § 1.171-2(a)(1))[9] Basis is reduced by the offset amount. (Code Sec. 1016(a)(5))[10]

observation: If the holder of a taxable bond doesn't elect to amortize bond premium, the basis of the bond remains the original basis in the holder's hands for determining gain or loss on sale or redemption.

¶ 2167 Amortization of callable bonds; treatment of unamortized bond premium of a called bond.

Under Code Sec. 171(b)(1)(B)(ii), the holder of a taxable bond generally amortizes bond premium by reference to the bond's stated maturity date (see ¶2166), even if the bond is likely to be called. (Code Sec. 171(b)(1)(B)(ii); Reg § 1.171-3(c)(4)(ii)(A), Reg § 1.171-3(e), Ex. 2)[11] The holder can deduct the unamortized bond premium of a called bond (excess of

50. ¶A-2618
1. ¶K-5611
2. ¶K-5614
3. ¶K-5616
4. ¶K-5611
5. ¶K-5622

6. ¶K-5624 *et seq.*
7. ¶K-5611
8. ¶P-5043
9. ¶K-5611
10. ¶P-5043
11. ¶K-5627

adjusted basis at start of the year over the greater of the amount (a) received on early redemption or (b) due on maturity). (Code Sec. 171(b)(2); Reg § 1.171-3(c)(5)(ii), Reg § 1.171-3(e), Ex 2)[12]

¶ 2168   Election to amortize bond premium.

Under Code Sec. 171(c)(2), the election to amortize bond premium on taxable bonds (¶2165) is made by (a) offsetting interest income with bond premium in the holder's timely filed return for the first tax year to which the election applies, and (b) attaching an election statement to the return. (Code Sec. 171(c)(2); Reg § 1.171-4(a)(1)) IRS consent isn't needed. (Reg § 1.171-5(c)(1)) The election (unless revoked with IRS consent) is binding for the year made and later years, and applies to all taxable bonds (1) held by taxpayer at the beginning of the first tax year to which the election applies, and (2) those acquired after that year by taxpayer. (Code Sec. 171(c)(2); Reg § 1.171-4(b)) A holder who has elected to treat all interest on the bond as original issue discount (¶1313) is treated as having elected to amortize bond premium. (Reg § 1.171-4(a)(2))[13]

⬥*recommendation:* The election provides a current interest income offset, which is preferable to a future capital loss deduction.

¶ 2169   Dealers in securities—bond premium amortization—taxable bonds, tax-exempt bonds.

Code Sec. 171(d) provides that taxable bonds that are stock in trade, held primarily for sale to customers, or includable in inventory if on hand at tax year-end aren't subject to the bond amortization rules (Code Sec. 171(d); Reg § 1.171-1(b)(2)(iv)), but tax-exempt bonds held primarily for sale to customers are. (Code Sec. 75(a))[14]

---

12. ¶K-5628
13. ¶K-5633

14. ¶K-5651

Chapter 7   Education—Tax Credits, Exclusions, Deductions—ABLE Accounts

¶ 2200   **Education—Tax Credits, Exclusions, Deductions.** ▬▬▬▬▬▬▬▬

There are several tax breaks designed specifically to help defray the costs of saving and paying for higher education and some pre-college costs.

The three main categories of education tax breaks are:

(1) Tax credits, see ¶2201 *et seq.*,

(2) Exclusions, see ¶2205 *et seq.*, and

(3) Deductions, see ¶2220 *et seq.*

Other tax breaks. Pre-age-59½ distributions from traditional IRAs and Roth IRAs are excepted from the 10% premature distribution penalty tax to the extent they don't exceed qualified higher education expenses for the distribution year (¶4334). Also, there's an unlimited gift-tax exclusion for gifts made on behalf of another individual directly to a qualifying educational organization (¶5049).

¶ 2201   **Tax Credits for Higher Education.** ▬▬▬▬▬▬▬▬▬▬

Under Code Sec. 25A, individual taxpayers may claim an income tax credit for the sum of the American opportunity tax credit (AOTC; formerly the Hope scholarship credit, ¶2202), and the Lifetime Learning credit (LLC, ¶2203) for higher education expenses at accredited post-secondary educational institutions paid for themselves, their spouses, and their dependents. The AOTC is available for qualified expenses of the first four years of undergraduate education; and the LLC is available for qualified expenses of any post-high school education at "eligible educational institutions." The AOTC can't be claimed in the same tax year as the LLC for expenses of any one student (see ¶2203). The credits phase out for higher-income taxpayers (see ¶2202).

¶ 2202   **American opportunity tax credit (AOTC) for qualified higher-education tuition and related (QT&R) expenses; AGI phaseout amounts—Form 8863.**

Under Code Sec. 25A(a)(1), individuals may elect (on Form 8863) a personal, partially refundable AOTC equal to 100% of up to $2,000 of QT&R expenses (¶2204) plus 25% of the next $2,000 of expenses paid for education furnished to an eligible student in an academic period. So, the maximum AOTC is $2,500 a year for *each* eligible student. (Code Sec. 25A(a)(1); Code Sec. 25A(b)(1); Code Sec. 25A(b)(3); Code Sec. 25A(e); Code Sec. 25A(i))[1]

The AOTC (and the Lifetime Learning Credit, LLC, ¶2203) both phase out ratably for taxpayers with modified AGI (MAGI, i.e., AGI increased by foreign, possessions, and Puerto Rico income exclusions) of $80,000 to $90,000 ($160,000 to $180,000 for joint filers). (Code Sec. 25A(d))[2]

The AOTC may be claimed for four tax years for each eligible student, and only for students who haven't completed the first four years of post-secondary education as of the beginning of the tax year. (Code Sec. 25A(b)(2)(A); Code Sec. 25A(b)(2)(C); Reg § 1.25A-3(d)(1)(iii)) Also, for at least one academic period during the year, the student must be enrolled for at least half of the normal full-time workload for the student's course of study

---

1. ¶A-4500 *et seq.*   2. ¶A-4517

References beginning with a single letter are to paragraphs in Federal Tax Coordinator 2d and RIA's Analysis of Federal Taxes: Income.

302

(Code Sec. 25A(b)(2)(B); Code Sec. 25A(b)(3)(B); Reg § 1.25A-3(d)(1)(ii)), and the student can't have been convicted of a federal or state felony drug offense at the end of the tax year. (Code Sec. 25A(b)(2)(D))

The AOTC (or the LLC) and tax-free Coverdell education savings account (CESA) distributions (¶2205) are allowed for the same student for the same year, as long as the credit isn't claimed for education expenses used to generate the tax-free CESA distributions. (Code Sec. 530(d)(2)(C)(i))

If a dependency deduction for an individual is allowed to another taxpayer, the dependent can't claim the AOTC, and QT&R expenses paid by the dependent are treated as paid by the person who is allowed the deduction. (Code Sec. 25A(g)(3))

⊘observation: Although the dependency exemption is suspended for 2018 through 2025, that suspension isn't taken into account in determining whether a deduction for personal exemptions is "allowed" or "allowable" (see ¶3112). So, a student who pays their own QT&R expenses, for whom a taxpayer could (but for the suspension) claim a dependency exemption, can't claim the AOTC.

If a third party (not the taxpayer, spouse, or dependent) pays a student's QT&R expenses directly to an educational institution, the student is treated as receiving the payment and then paying the expenses. (Reg § 1.25A-5(b))

If QT&R expenses are prepaid during one tax year for an academic period that begins during the first three months of the next tax year, the academic period is treated as beginning in the earlier year (Code Sec. 25A(g)(4)), and the credit is allowed only in the tax year in which the expenses are paid. (Reg § 1.25A-3(e)) Special rules apply for tuition refunds and excludable tuition assistance received after the tax year in which QT&R expenses are paid. (Reg § 1.25A-5(c), Reg § 1.25A-5(f))

Subject to an exception, 40% of a taxpayer's otherwise allowable AOTC is refundable. None of the credit is refundable if the taxpayer claiming the credit is a child subject to the kiddie tax. (Code Sec. 25A(i)) A resident of a U.S. possession claims the refundable part of the AOTC in that possession.[3]

To claim any education credit (¶2201): the student's name and taxpayer identification number (TIN) must be included on the taxpayer's return (Code Sec. 25A(g)(1)); QT&R expenses must be adjusted for qualified scholarships, etc. (Code Sec. 25A(g)(2)) (¶2204); there can't be a double benefit under the Code (Code Sec. 25A(g)(5)); married taxpayers must file jointly (Code Sec. 25A(g)(6)); nonresident aliens must be treated as a resident alien under a Code Sec. 6013(g) or Code Sec. 6013(h) election (Code Sec. 25A(g)(7)); and the taxpayer must receive a payee statement (Form 1098-T) from the educational institution containing all required information. (Code Sec. 25A(g)(8)) And, the AOTC (but not the LLC) is barred: (1) unless the taxpayer's and the student's TIN was issued before the return's due date, and the taxpayer includes the employer identification number (EIN) of any institution to which QT&R expenses were paid for the student (Code Sec. 25A(g)(1)); and (2) in certain cases where the AOTC was improperly claimed in a prior year. (Code Sec. 25A(b)(4))

¶ 2203 Lifetime Learning Credit (LLC) for qualified tuition and related expenses (QT&R)—Form 8863.

Under Code Sec. 25A(a)(2), taxpayers may elect (on Form 8863) an LLC equal to 20% of up to $10,000 of QT&R expenses (¶2204) paid during the tax year. So, the maximum credit is $2,000. (Code Sec. 25A(a)(2), Code Sec. 25A(c)(1), Code Sec. 25A(e), Code Sec. 25A(f))[4]

---

3. ¶A-4525.2

4. ¶A-4500 *et seq.*; ¶A-4533 *et seq.*

Unlike the American opportunity tax credit (AOTC, ¶2202), which is available on a per-student basis, the LLC is available on a per-family basis, and the maximum amount doesn't vary with the number of students in the family. So, a joint-filing couple with two children could claim no more than a $2,000 LLC, even if each child is a qualifying student with qualifying expenses.[5]

For AGI phaseout amounts for the LLC and the AOTC, see ¶2202.

The same treatment of expenses paid by a dependent and of certain prepayments, and the general requirements for claiming an education credit (e.g., the bar to credit unless marrieds file jointly) that apply for the AOTC as described at ¶2202, also apply to the LLC. (Code Sec. 25A(g))

Expenses for a student for whom an AOTC is allowed for the tax year don't qualify for the LLC. (Code Sec. 25A(c)(2))

¶ 2204　Qualified tuition and related (QT&R) expenses for the education credit (AOTC and LLC).

Under Code Sec. 25A(f), QT&R expenses for the American opportunity tax credit (AOTC, ¶2202) and Lifetime Learning credit (LLC, ¶2203) are tuition and fees (and for the AOTC only, expenses for course materials) required for the enrollment or attendance of the taxpayer, spouse, or a dependent, at a post-secondary educational institution eligible to participate in the federal student loan program. (Code Sec. 25A(f)(1)(A), Code Sec. 25A(f)(2))[6]

QT&R expenses don't include room and board, transportation, insurance, medical expenses, other similar personal, living, or family expenses, or student fees (unless required for enrollment or attendance). Nor do they include expenses for any course or other education involving sports, games, or hobbies, or noncredit course, unless part of the student's degree program (Code Sec. 25A(f)(1)(B); Code Sec. 25A(f)(1)(C); Reg § 1.25A-2(d)(2), Reg § 1.25A-2(d)(3)) or (LLC only) to help the student acquire or improve job skills. (Code Sec. 25A(c)(2)(B); Reg § 1.25A-2(d)(5))

As to expenses for books, supplies and equipment—for the AOTC, they qualify as QT&R expenses if they're needed for a course of study, whether or not they're purchased from the educational institution as a condition of enrollment[7]—but for the LLC, they qualify as QT&R expenses *only if* required to be paid to the institution as a condition of enrollment or attendance. (Reg § 1.25A-2(d)(2)(ii))

QT&R expenses must be reduced by scholarship amounts excludable from income under Code Sec. 117 (¶2215), educational assistance under chapter 30 through 35 of title 38 U.S. Code or under chapter 1606 of title 10 U.S. Code, and other tax-free payments. But, qualified amounts aren't reduced by amounts paid by gift, bequest, devise, or inheritance. (Code Sec. 25A(g)(2)) No credit is allowed for any expense for which an income tax deduction is allowed. (Code Sec. 25A(g)(5)) Special rules apply for tuition refunds and excludable tuition assistance received after the tax year in which QT&R expenses are paid. (Reg § 1.25A-5(f))

¶ 2205　Coverdell Education Savings Accounts (CESAs). ▄▄▄▄▄▄

Under Code Sec. 530, taxpayers can contribute up to $2,000 per year to CESAs (formerly "education IRAs") for beneficiaries under age 18 and special needs beneficiaries of any age (¶2207). The account is exempt from income tax (¶2206), and distributions of earnings are tax-free if used for qualified education expenses

---

5. ¶A-4534
6. ¶A-4537

7. ¶A-4537

(¶2208).

¶ 2206 Coverdell Education Savings Accounts (CESAs)—Forms 5305-E and 5305-EA.

A CESA is a trust (Form 5305-E) or custodial account (Form 5305-EA) created exclusively for paying an individual beneficiary's qualified education expenses. (Code Sec. 530(b)(1), Code Sec. 530(g)) CESAs are exempt from tax except for the unrelated business income tax. (Code Sec. 530(a)) Allowable annual contributions to CESAs (¶2207) aren't deductible and aren't taxable when withdrawn. Distributions of earnings from CESAs for qualified education expenses are tax-free (¶2208).

CESAs can't invest in life insurance contracts, and, except for common trust or investment funds, trust assets can't be commingled. The account balance must be distributed to the beneficiary within 30 days after the beneficiary turns age 30 (unless the beneficiary has special needs), or, if sooner, to the beneficiary's estate within 30 days after the beneficiary's death (Code Sec. 530(b)(1), Code Sec. 530(d)(8)),[8] unless transferred to a family member's CESA (¶2208).

¶ 2207 Contributions to Coverdell Education Savings Accounts (CESAs); rollovers to CESAs.

Annual contributions to CESAs for any beneficiary can't exceed $2,000, must be made in cash, and can't be made after the beneficiary turns age 18 (except for special needs beneficiaries). (Code Sec. 530(b)(1)(A)) CESA contributions for a year generally may be made as late as the unextended tax return due date for that year. (Code Sec. 530(b)(4))[9]

For individual contributors, the $2,000 limit phases out ratably between $95,000 and $110,000 ($190,000 and $220,000 for joint filers) of modified AGI (MAGI, i.e., AGI plus income excluded under Code Sec. 911, Code Sec. 931, and Code Sec. 933). (Code Sec. 530(c))[10]

observation: A corporation may, without regard to any MAGI limits, contribute to a CESA that has an employee's child as beneficiary. But the contribution is taxed to the employee.

An individual who has received a military death gratuity or Servicemembers' Group Life Insurance (SGLI) payment can roll it over to one or more CESAs, without regard to the annual contribution limit (Code Sec. 530(d)(9)(A)) or the AGI phase-out limit. The contribution must be made before the end of the one-year period beginning on the date on which the contributor received the payment. (Code Sec. 530(d)(9)(A))[11] The rule allowing only one rollover contribution to a CESA during any 12-month period (¶2208) doesn't apply to this rollover. (Code Sec. 530(d)(9)(B))

Excess contributions are subject to a 6% excise tax in the contribution year and each year that an excess amount is in the account (report on Form 5329, Part V). But the excise tax doesn't apply to rollover contributions, or contributions (with net earnings attributable to the excess contributions) returned before June 1 of the year following the contribution year. (Code Sec. 4973(e))[12]

For the gift tax treatment of CESAs, see ¶5049.

---

8. ¶A-4615; ¶A-4628
9. ¶A-4606
10. ¶A-4604

11. ¶A-4619.1
12. ¶A-4607

¶ 2208   Distributions from Coverdell Education Savings Accounts (CESAs).

A distribution from a CESA is included in the distributee's income generally as provided under the Code Sec. 72 annuity rules. (Code Sec. 530(d)(1)) So, distributions consist of a pro-rata share of principal (recovered tax-free) and accumulated earnings (which *may* be excludable under the CESA rules). CESA distributions are entirely excluded if the beneficiary's qualified education expenses (QEEs) equal or exceed total CESA distributions for the year. (Code Sec. 530(d)(2)(A))

QEEs include:

. . . higher education tuition, fees, books, and supplies, and, for half-time or greater students, certain room and board charges (Code Sec. 530(b)(2)(A)(i));

. . . elementary and secondary (K−12) public, private or religious school tuition and expenses, including tutoring, room and board, transportation, uniforms, and extended day programs (Code Sec. 530(b)(2)(A)(ii); Code Sec. 530(b)(3));

. . . special needs services for special needs beneficiaries enrolled in any of the above types of schools (Code Sec. 530(b)(3)(A)); and

. . . contributions to a qualified tuition program (QTP, see ¶2209) on behalf of a designated beneficiary (DB) (Code Sec. 530(b)(2)(B)),[13] but in applying the Code Sec. 72 annuity rules to a CESA distribution that's contributed to a QTP (¶2209) for a DB, any part of the contribution not includible in gross income (because it doesn't exceed the DB's QEEs) won't result in an increase in the investment in the contract (Code Sec. 530(b)(2)(B)).

QEEs are reduced by the same tax-free scholarships and similar payments that reduce qualified tuition and related expenses for education credit purposes (¶2204) (Code Sec. 530(d)(2)(C)(i)(I)), and by the expenses taken into account in determining the education credit (¶2201).[14]

Distributions aren't taxed if rolled over within 60 days (limited to once in a 12-month period) into a CESA for the same beneficiary or a member of the beneficiary's family (as defined at ¶2211) who is under age 30. (Code Sec. 530(d)(5), Code Sec. 530(d)(6))[15] IRS says only one rollover for a CESA is allowed per individual, per year.[16] A CESA transfer to a beneficiary's family member under a divorce decree or after the beneficiary's death also isn't taxable. (Code Sec. 530(d)(7))

If CESA distributions exceed QEEs in a year, the excludable part of the distributions is the earnings portion of the distributions times a fraction with the year's QEEs as the numerator and the year's total distributions as the denominator. The balance of the earnings portion of the distributions is taxable. (Code Sec. 530(d)(2)(B))[17] Any savings bond redemption proceeds transferred to a CESA in a tax-free transfer under Code Sec. 135 (see ¶2219) *don't* increase the investment in the contract in applying the Code Sec. 72 annuity rules to the CESA distributions. (Code Sec. 135(c)(2)(C))

Any taxable amount also is subject to a 10% additional tax, but not: (1) if made on or after the beneficiary's death or disability; (2) to the extent the taxable amount doesn't exceed (a) the amount of a tax-free scholarship received by the beneficiary, or (b) the "advanced education costs" received by the beneficiary at a U.S. service academy (e.g., U.S. Military Academy); (3) if the distribution is taxable solely because of the rule (see above) reducing the total amount of QEEs by the expenses taken into account in determining the education credit for the year; or (4) if the tax is attributable to income on a

---

13. ¶A-4610 *et seq.*
14. ¶A-4612
15. ¶A-4619

16. ¶A-4619
17. ¶A-4609

contribution withdrawn (with associated income) before June 1 of the year after the contribution year. (Code Sec. 530(d)(4))[18]

If aggregate distributions from CESAs and QTPs (¶2209) in a year exceed an individual's QEEs, the expenses must be allocated among the distributions. (Code Sec. 530(d)(2)(C)) No deduction, credit, or exclusion is allowed under any other Code provision for an education expense used in determining the CESA exclusion. (Code Sec. 530(d)(2)(D))[19]

¶ 2209 Qualified Tuition Programs (QTPs)—529 Plans. ▄▄▄▄▄

Under Code Sec. 529, a person can make nondeductible cash contributions to a QTP (or "529 plan") on behalf of a designated beneficiary. The earnings on contributions build up tax-free, and distributions from a QTP are excludable if used to pay for qualified higher education expenses (QHEEs), including some elementary and secondary school tuition.

A QTP (529 plan) is a tax-exempt program established and maintained by a state (including a state agency or instrumentality), or one or more eligible educational institutions (including private ones) under which a taxpayer may:

(1) buy tuition credits or certificates on behalf of a designated beneficiary (DB, ¶2211) which entitle the DB to a waiver or payment of QHEEs (¶2210)—i.e., *a prepaid educational services account,* or

(2) make contributions to an account set up to meet the DB's QHEEs—i.e., *an educational savings account.* This option is available only for state (or state agency or instrumentality) programs. (Code Sec. 529(b)(1)(A); Prop Reg. § 1.529-2(c) ["Taxpayers may rely"])[20]

A QTP must: require all purchases or contributions be made in cash (with no dollar limit on contributions); provide separate accounting for each designated beneficiary; prohibit pledging an interest in the program as security; provide adequate safeguards to prevent contributions exceeding amounts necessary for the DB's qualified higher education expenses; and, for QTP maintained by a private educational institution, generally, get a ruling that it meets applicable requirements. (Code Sec. 529(b)(1))[21].

A QTP must provide that any contributor or DB may, directly or indirectly, direct the investment of any contributions or earnings no more than two times in any calendar year. (Code Sec. 529(b)(4))[22].

For gift-tax treatment of contributions to a QTP, see ¶5049.

¶ 2210 Tax treatment of distributions from qualified tuition programs (QTPs); payments of qualified higher education expenses (QHEEs).

Distributions from a QTP are includible in the distributee's income under the Code Sec. 72 annuity rules, if not excluded under any other Code provision. (Code Sec. 529(c)(3)(A))[23]

In-kind distributions (e.g., tuition credits or waivers, payment vouchers) from state-sponsored QTPs aren't includible in gross income if the benefit, if paid for by the distributee, would have been a payment of a qualified higher education expense (QHEE). (Code Sec. 529(c)(3)(B)(i); Prop Reg. § 1.529-1(c), ["Taxpayers may rely"])[24]

---

18. ¶A-4618
19. ¶A-4609 *et seq.*
20. ¶A-4700 *et seq.*; ¶A-4727
21. ¶A-4700 *et seq.*; ¶A-4703; ¶A-4727

22. ¶A-4707
23. ¶A-4709 *et seq.*
24. ¶A-4712

Cash distributions are fully excludable if they don't exceed QHEEs, reduced by expenses for which in-kind distributions were received. If cash distributions exceed QHEEs, the amount otherwise includible under the Code Sec. 72 annuity rules is reduced by the ratio of QHEEs to distributions. (Code Sec. 529(c)(3)(B)(ii))[25]

QHEEs for QTP purposes are: (1) tuition, fees and expenses for books, supplies, equipment required for the enrollment or attendance of a designated beneficiary (DB, ¶2211) at an eligible educational institution (plus up to $10,000 per DB per tax year for expenses for tuition in connection with enrollment or attendance at an elementary or secondary public, private, or religious school); (2) certain expenses for the purchase of computer or peripheral equipment, computer software, or internet access and related services; (3) expenses for special needs services; (4) room and board costs (subject to a limit) for students who are at least half-time; (5) fees, books, supplies, and equipment required for a DB's participation in a qualified apprenticeship program; and (6) subject to a lifetime limit of $10,000, principal or interest on a qualified education loan (see ¶2221) of the DB or a sibling of the DB. (Code Sec. 529(e)(3); Code Sec. 529(c))[26]

For QTP exclusion purposes, total annual QHEEs are reduced by excludable scholarships or educational assistance received, and by any QHEEs taken into account in determining the American opportunity tax credit and Lifetime Learning credit (¶2201 *et seq.*) allowed to the taxpayer or any other person. (Code Sec. 529(c)(3)(B)(v))[27]

Distributions from a QTP aren't taxed if rolled over within 60 days (limited to once in 12 months) to another QTP (or, for distributions after Dec. 22, 2017 and before Jan. 1, 2026, to an ABLE account up to the ABLE annual contribution limit (see ¶2225)) for the same DB or a family member of the DB (¶2211). (Code Sec. 529(c)(3)(C)(iii))[28] A change in the DB isn't a distribution if the new DB is a member of the old DB's family; see ¶2211. (Code Sec. 529(c)(3)(C)(ii))[29]

A 10% additional tax applies to QTP distributions includible in gross income, in the same way, and with the same exceptions, as for Coverdell education savings account (CESA) distributions (see ¶2208). (Code Sec. 529(c)(6))[30]

If total distributions from a QTP and from a CESA (see ¶2205 *et seq.*) exceed QHEEs otherwise taken into account under the QTP rules (after the above reductions), the taxpayer must allocate the expenses among the distributions for purposes of determining the QTP exclusion. (Code Sec. 529(c)(3)(B)(vi))[31]

¶ 2211   Designated beneficiary (DB) of a qualified tuition program (QTP).

Under Code Sec. 529(e)(1), the DB of a QTP (¶2209) is:

(1) the individual so designated at the start of participation in the QTP; (Code Sec. 529(e)(1)(A))

(2) the new DB, if DBs are changed and the new one is a member of the same family (spouses, individuals meeting the relationship tests at ¶3113, spouses of these individuals, and first cousins of the DB); (Code Sec. 529(e)(1)(B); Code Sec. 529(e)(2); Code Sec. 529(c)(3)(C)) and

(3) the individual receiving the interest in a scholarship, if an interest in a QTP is purchased by a state or eligible educational institution as part of a scholarship program it operates. (Code Sec. 529(e)(1)(C))[32]

---

25. ¶A-4710
26. ¶A-4714
27. ¶A-4714
28. ¶A-4723

29. ¶A-4724, ¶A-4725
30. ¶A-4722
31. ¶A-4719
32. ¶A-4701

¶ 2212 **Employer-Provided Educational Benefits; Scholarships and Fellowships.** ■■

An employee may exclude the value of educational benefits provided by an employer if the benefit qualifies as a working condition fringe (¶2213) or is provided under an educational assistance program (¶2214). Qualified tuition reductions for employees of educational institutions (¶2216) and qualifying scholarships and fellowships (¶2215) also are excludable.

¶ 2213 **When education benefits are excluded as working condition fringes.**

Employer-provided educational expenses are excludable from an employee's income as a working condition fringe to the extent that, if the employee paid for the benefit, the amount paid would have been deducted as an employee business expense. For the criteria for determining if education is a deductible employee business expense, see ¶2222. (Reg § 1.132-1(f), Reg § 1.132-5(a)(2))[33]

🖊 *observation:* Unreimbursed employee business expenses, which are miscellaneous itemized deductions, aren't deductible from 2018 through 2025. But these types of working condition fringe benefits presumably remain excludible.[34]

¶ 2214 **Exclusion for employer-provided educational assistance under qualified educational assistance program; COVID-19/coronavirus relief excludes employer's pre-2026 student loan payments.**

Under Code Sec. 127, educational assistance provided under an employer's qualified educational assistance program, up to an annual maximum of $5,250, is excluded from the employees income. (Code Sec. 127(a)(2)) The education received need not be job-related. (Reg § 1.127-2(c)(4))

Expenses paid by an employer for education or training provided to the employee that aren't excludable under this provision can only be excluded from income if they qualify as a working condition fringe (¶2213). (Code Sec. 132(j)(8))

"Educational assistance" means the employer's payment for or provision of tuition, fees, books, supplies and equipment under an educational assistance program, including amounts for graduate-level courses. It doesn't include meals, lodging, transportation, or tools or supplies (other than textbooks) that may be retained after the course ends. (Code Sec. 127(c)(1); Reg § 1.127-2(c)(3))[35]

Eligibility requirements can't discriminate in favor of "highly compensated employees" (see ¶4315). (Code Sec. 127(b)(2); Reg § 1.127-2(e)(1))[36] No deduction or credit can be taken by the employee for any amount excluded from income. (Code Sec. 127(c)(7))[37]

COVID-19/coronavirus relief. Under the Coronavirus Aid, Relief, and Economic Security Act (CARES Act, PL 116-136, 3/27/2020), "eligible student loan repayments" (below) made after Mar. 27, 2020, and before Jan. 1, 2026, are also excluded from employee gross income, subject to the overall $5,250 per employee limit for all educational payments. Eligible student loan repayments are payments by the employer, whether paid to the employee or a lender, of principle or interest on any qualified higher education loan as defined in Code Sec. 221(d)(1) for the education of the employee (but not of a spouse or dependent). (Code Sec. 127(c)(1)(B)) To prevent a double benefit, student loan repayments for which the exclusion is allowable can't be deducted under Code Sec. 221 (the deduction for student loan interest, see ¶2220). (Code Sec. 221(e)(1))[38]

---

33. ¶H-2052
34. ¶H-1701
35. ¶H-2065

36. ¶H-2069
37. ¶H-2064
38. ¶H-2065

¶ 2215   Exclusion for qualified scholarships and fellowships.

Under Code Sec. 117, a scholarship or fellowship isn't taxable to the extent it's a "qualified scholarship" granted to a degree candidate at an educational organization, and isn't a stipend (¶2217). (Code Sec. 117(a), Code Sec. 117(c))[39] A "qualified scholarship" is any amount received as a scholarship and used for tuition and fees required for enrollment at an educational organization, and for required fees, books, supplies and equipment. (Code Sec. 117(b)(2))[40] An "educational organization" is one that normally maintains a regular faculty, curriculum and regularly enrolled student body in attendance. (Code Sec. 117(b)(2)(A))[41]

¶ 2216   Exclusion for qualified tuition reductions for employees of educational institutions (school employees).

Code Sec. 117(d) provides that qualified tuition reductions for employees of educational institutions are excluded from the recipient's gross income. (Code Sec. 117(d)) A "qualified tuition reduction" is the amount of tuition reduction provided to an employee of an educational organization for below-graduate-level education (not services, see ¶2217) at that or a similar institution, for the employee (whether active, retired, or disabled), or the employee's spouse or dependent children. (Code Sec. 117(d)(2)) But, a tuition reduction for a graduate student engaged in teaching or research can be tax-free. (Code Sec. 117(d)(5))[42]

A qualified tuition reduction provided with respect to a highly compensated employee (¶4315) is excludable only if it's available to all employees on a nondiscriminatory basis. (Code Sec. 117(d)(3))[43]

¶ 2217   Payments for teaching or research not excluded as qualified scholarships or tuition reductions; exceptions for health professions scholarship programs and work-learning-service programs.

The exclusions for qualified scholarships (¶2215) and qualified tuition reductions (¶2216) don't apply to any amount received that represents payment for teaching, research or other services performed by the student as a condition for receiving the qualified benefit. (Code Sec. 117(c)(1))[44] This payment-for-services rule doesn't apply to amounts received under certain health professions scholarship programs (i.e., the National Health Service Corps (NHSC) Scholarship Program and the Armed Forces Health Professions Scholarship and Financial Assistance Program) and, any payments from certain work-learning-service programs that are operated by a work college. (Code Sec. 117(c)(2)).[45]

¶ 2218   Higher Education Exclusion for Savings Bond Income—Form 8815. ▰▰▰

Under Code Sec. 135, subject to a phaseout (below), an individual who pays qualified higher education expenses (QHEEs, ¶2219) during a tax year excludes from that year's gross income any amount of income from the redemption, that year, of any "qualified U.S. savings bond" (Series EE bond issued after '89, or Series I bond). (Code Sec. 135(a), Code Sec. 135(c)(1))[46]

Use Form 8815 to compute the exclusion. Form 8818 (one per bond) may be used to keep a record of the redemptions.[47]

---

39. ¶J-1230
40. ¶J-1232
41. ¶J-1244
42. ¶J-1252 *et seq.*
43. ¶J-1255

44. ¶J-1258
45. ¶J-1258.1
46. ¶J-3051 *et seq.*; ¶J-3055
47. ¶J-3051; ¶J-3062

If taxpayer's aggregate redemption proceeds (principal plus interest) for a tax year exceed the QHEEs paid that year, the excluded interest is limited to the otherwise excludable amount times this fraction: the QHEEs paid that year, divided by the year's aggregate redemption proceeds. (Code Sec. 135(b)(1))[48]

Illustration: Taxpayer redeems $8,000 of qualified U.S. savings bonds ($4,000 interest, $4,000 principal) and pays QHEEs of $6,000. The exclusion ratio is 75% ($6,000 ÷ $8,000), so $3,000 of the interest (75% × $4,000) (and the $4,000 principal) is excludable.[49]

The individual must have bought the bond(s) after reaching age 24 (Code Sec. 135(c)(1)(B)) and must be the sole owner (or joint owner with spouse). The exclusion isn't available to the owner of a bond that was bought by another individual (other than a spouse). Nor is it available to a parent who buys the bonds and puts them in the name of a child or other dependent. But the owner may designate an individual (including a child) as the beneficiary for amounts payable at death without losing the exclusion.[50] A married individual must file jointly to get the exclusion. (Code Sec. 135(d)(3))[1]

For 2022, the exclusion phases out for a taxpayer whose modified AGI (MAGI) for the year exceeds $85,800 ($128,650 for joint filers), and is completely phased out when MAGI reaches $100,800 ($158,650 for joint filers). For 2023, the exclusion phases out for a taxpayer whose modified AGI (MAGI) for the year exceeds $91,850 ($137,800 for joint filers), and is completely phased out when MAGI reaches $106,850 ($167,800 for joint filers).[2]

The exclusion generally applies only if the owner redeems the bonds (Code Sec. 135(a)), i.e., not if the owner transfers them to the educational institution (see ¶2219 for exceptions).[3]

MAGI is AGI determined without the savings bond interest exclusion (see above), the Code Sec. 137 exclusion for employer-provided adoption assistance (¶1253), the Code Sec. 221 deduction for interest on a qualified education loan (¶2220), the pre-2021 former Code Sec. 222 deduction for higher education expenses, or the Code Sec. 911, Code Sec. 931, and Code Sec. 933 exclusions for income earned abroad (¶4605, ¶4603); but after the application of Code Sec. 86, Code Sec. 469 and Code Sec. 219. (Code Sec. 135(c)(4))[4]

¶ 2219   Qualified higher education expenses (QHEEs) for savings bond exclusion; transfers of redemption proceeds to a QTP or CESA as a QHEE.

For the savings bond exclusion (¶2218), QHEEs are tuition and fees required for the enrollment or attendance of a taxpayer, spouse, or a dependent (¶3113) at an eligible educational institution, (Code Sec. 135(c)(2)(A)), e.g., most colleges, junior colleges, nursing schools and vocational schools. (Code Sec. 135(c)(3)) Expenses for any course or other education involving sports, games or hobbies, unless part of a degree program, don't count. (Code Sec. 135(c)(2)(B))[5] The transfer of redemption proceeds to a qualified tuition program (QTP, ¶2209) or to a Coverdell education savings account (CESA, ¶2207) for the taxpayer, spouse, or dependent also is a QHEE. (Code Sec. 135(c)(2)(C))[6]

Expenses otherwise taken into account must be reduced by amounts received for excludable qualified scholarships (¶2215), certain educational assistance allowances and other tax-exempt payments (other than gifts, bequests, devises or inheritances), and a payment, waiver, or reimbursement of qualified higher education expenses under a QTP. (Code

---

48. ¶J-3052
49. ¶J-3052
50. ¶s J-3055, J-3056
1. ¶J-3051
2. ¶J-3053

3. ¶J-3051
4. ¶J-3054
5. ¶s J-3057, J-3061
6. ¶J-3059

Sec. 135(d)(1))[7] The amount of QHEEs also must be reduced by the amount of such expenses taken into account in figuring the exclusions for distributions from CESA (¶2213) and QTPs (¶2209), and by expenses taken into account in determining the education credits (¶2201) allowed to the taxpayer or any other person for those expenses. This reduction is made before applying the rules reducing the excluded amount where redemption proceeds exceed higher education expenses and where taxpayer's modified AGI exceeds specified dollar amounts) (see ¶2218). (Code Sec. 135(d)(2))[8]

¶ 2220   Deduction for Interest Paid on Qualified Education Loans. ▪▪▪▪▪▪

Student loan interest generally is treated as personal interest and so isn't deductible. But, qualifying individuals may, subject to a phaseout, deduct up to $2,500 annually for interest paid on qualified higher education loans. (Code Sec. 221)[9]

The deduction is claimed as an adjustment to gross income to arrive at AGI. (Code Sec. 62(a)(17))[10] There's no deduction for any amount for which a deduction is allowable under any other Code provision; and the deduction is disallowed to the extent the interest was paid from a tax-free distribution from a QTP (see ¶2210). (Code Sec. 221(e)(1))[11]

For 2022, the deduction phases out ratably for taxpayers with modified AGI (MAGI) between $70,000 and $85,000 ($145,000 and $175,000 for joint filers). For 2023, the deduction phases out ratably for taxpayers with modified AGI (MAGI) between $75,000 and $90,000 ($155,000 and $185,000 for joint filers). (Code Sec. 221(b)(2)(B)) MAGI is AGI figured without regard to the deduction for qualified education loan interest, and the exclusions for foreign, possession, and Puerto Rico income. (Code Sec. 221(b)(2)(C)(i))[12]

While the dependency exemption is suspended (for 2018−2025, ¶3112), a person who would otherwise not be allowed to claim this deduction on account of being claimed as a dependent on another taxpayer's return under Code Sec. 221(c) is presumably allowed to claim the deduction. The deduction may be claimed only by a person legally obligated to make the interest payments. (Reg § 1.221-1(b))[13] Married couples must file jointly to take the deduction. (Code Sec. 221(e)(2))[14]

For information reporting requirements for interest payments received on qualified education loans, see ¶4746.

¶ 2221   Qualified education loan defined for purposes of interest deduction.

A qualified education loan for the interest deduction (¶2220) is any debt incurred by the taxpayer solely to pay qualified higher education expenses that are: (1) incurred on behalf of the taxpayer, spouse, or any dependents as of the time the debt was incurred; (2) paid or incurred within a reasonable period of time before or after the debt is incurred; and (3) attributable to education furnished during a period when the recipient was an eligible student (as defined for the American opportunity tax credit, i.e., at least a half-time student, see ¶2202). (Code Sec. 221(d)(1); Code Sec. 221(d)(3))

Revolving lines of credit generally aren't qualified education loans unless the borrower agreed to use the line of credit to pay only qualifying higher education expenses. A qualified education loan includes debt used to refinance debt that qualifies as a qualified education loan, but doesn't include certain debt owed to a related person or a loan under a qualified employer plan. (Code Sec. 221(d)(1))[15]

Qualified higher education expenses include tuition, fees, room and board, and related

---

7. ¶J-3060
8. ¶J-3060
9. ¶K-5500 *et seq.*
10. ¶A-2626; ¶K-5501
11. ¶K-5503.2
12. ¶K-5502; ¶K-5502.1
13. ¶K-5501.1
14. ¶K-5501
15. ¶K-5504; ¶K-5504.2

expenses, but must be reduced by the amount excluded by reason of such expenses under the rules for: employer-provided educational assistance benefits (¶2214), income from U.S. Savings Bonds used to pay higher education expenses (¶2218), Coverdell education savings accounts (¶2205), qualified tuition plans (¶2209), and scholarship or fellowship grants (¶2215). (Code Sec. 221(d)(2)) They also must be reduced by veterans' and armed forces' educational assistance allowances and any other educational assistance excludable from the student's gross income (other than as a gift, bequest, devise or inheritance). (Reg § 1.221-1(e)(2)(ii))[16]

¶ 2222　　Education Expenses Related to Business. ▆▆▆▆▆▆▆

Self-employeds can deduct educational expenses if the education (1) maintains or improves the skills used in the taxpayer's trade or business, or (2) meets the requirements of applicable law or regs, and, under those requirements, is necessary to keep a job, status, or rate of pay. These expenses may be deducted as ordinary and necessary business expenses under Code Sec. 162. But a taxpayer can't deduct costs incurred to meet minimum requirements for a trade or profession or to qualify for a new trade or profession. (Reg § 1.162-5)[17]

A lawyer who has actually practiced law may generally deduct the expenses of any further legal education on the grounds that it maintains or improves required skills even though the education qualifies the lawyer to practice as a specialist.[18] But a non-lawyer employed in allied fields where a legal education is helpful or customary can't deduct legal education costs. (Reg § 1.162-5(b)(3))[19]

Deductions aren't allowed if the education is:

. . . needed to meet the minimum requirements for taxpayer's present or intended trade, business or profession (Reg § 1.162-5(b)(2))[20] or

. . . undertaken to fulfill general education goals or for other personal reasons,[21] or

. . . part of a program of study that will qualify the individual in a new trade or business. (Reg § 1.162-5(b)(3)(i))[22]

Self-employed taxpayers claim education deductions on Form 1040, Schedule C or F.[23]

¶ 2223　　Travel and transportation expenses of education—deductibility; local transportation expenses.

The expenses of travel as a form of education aren't deductible. (Code Sec. 274(m)(2))[24] But travel expenses necessary to other deductible education expenses are deductible by self-employeds.[25]

Local transportation expenses for deductible education are deductible by self-employeds. These are expenses incurred in going directly from work to school, and, if the taxpayer is regularly employed and goes to school on a strictly temporary basis (e.g., expected to last, and in fact lasts, for one year or less), the costs of returning from school to home, or the round-trip costs of going from home to school and back.[26]

Costs of seminar cruises or tours are disallowed if taken primarily for personal purposes even if part of the time is devoted to qualifying professional education.[27] Even if not for personal purposes, the deduction is limited under the rules at ¶1544.

---

16. ¶K-5504.3
17. ¶L-3701 *et seq.*, ¶A-2711 *et seq.*
18. ¶s L-3724, L-3722
19. ¶L-3705; ¶L-3720 *et seq.*
20. ¶L-3713
21. ¶L-3704

22. ¶L-3715
23. ¶L-3741
24. ¶L-3734
25. ¶L-3732 *et seq.*, ¶L-3741, ¶A-2710 *et seq.*
26. ¶L-3730
27. ¶L-3733

¶ 2224　Limited above-the-line deduction for educator expenses; professional development courses, trade or business expenses, books, supplies, classroom materials and equipment, and COVID-related expenses.

Code Sec. 62(a)(2)(D) allows a grade K–12 teacher, instructor, counselor, principal, or aide in a school for at least 900 hours during a school year ("eligible educator," Code Sec. 62(d)(1)) to claim an "above the line deduction" (i.e., an adjustment to gross income to arrive at AGI) for up to $300 for 2022 and 2023) for business expenses paid: (1) for participation in professional development courses that are either related to the subject taught or the students, and (2) for trade or business expenses paid or incurred for books, supplies (other than nonathletic supplies for courses of instruction in health or physical education), computer equipment (including related software and services) and other equipment, and supplementary materials used in the classroom. (Code Sec. 62(a)(2)(D))

For unreimbursed expenses after March 12, 2020, category (2) above includes business expenses paid for COVID-19 protective items used to prevent the spread of COVID-19 in the classroom, including but not limited to: face masks; disinfectant; hand soap; hand sanitizer; disposable gloves; tape, paint or chalk to guide social distancing; physical barriers (e.g., clear plexiglass); air purifiers; and other items recommended by the Centers for Disease Control and Prevention (CDC) to be used for prevention of the spread of COVID-19. (Rev Proc 2021-15, 2021-8 IRB 891)

A deduction is allowed only to the extent the amount of expenses exceeds the amount excludable from income under Code Sec. 135 (education savings bonds), Code Sec. 529(c)(1) (qualified tuition programs), or Code Sec. 530(d)(2) (Coverdell education savings accounts). (Code Sec. 62(d)(2))[28]

¶ 2225　ABLE Accounts for the Disabled or Blind (Form 5329). ■■■■■■■

Code Sec. 529A allows states to establish tax-exempt "Achieving a Better Life Experience" (ABLE) programs that feature accounts that assist persons with disabilities.

General tax rules. A qualified ABLE account is generally exempt from income tax but is subject to the tax imposed by Code Sec. 511 on the unrelated business income of tax-exempt organizations. (Code Sec. 529A(a))[29] Contributions to an ABLE account aren't deductible for income tax purposes.[30] IRS has issued final regs that provide guidance on ABLE accounts. (TD 9923, 10/1/2020)[31]

Qualified ABLE program defined. A qualified ABLE program is a program established and maintained by a state or state agency or instrumentality that (Code Sec. 529A(b)(1)):

. . . limits the aggregate contributions from all contributors (including rollover contributions from a 529 plan, see ¶2210) for a tax year to the amount of the annual gift tax exclusion under Code Sec. 2503(b) for the calendar year in which that tax year begins ($16,000 for 2022, $17,000 for 2023) (Code Sec. 529A(b)(2)); *plus* an- additional contribution during tax years 2018 through 2025 (see below);

. . . provides separate accounting for each designated beneficiary (DB, Code Sec. 529A(b)(3));

. . . limits the DB's investment direction to no more than two times in a calendar year (Code Sec. 529A(b)(4));

. . . prohibits the use of any interest or any portion of an interest in the program as

28. ¶A-2608
29. ¶A-4740 *et seq.*

30. ¶A-4744
31. ¶A-4740 *et seq.*

security for a loan (Code Sec. 529A(b)(5)); and

. . . provides adequate safeguards to prevent excess aggregate contributions. (Code Sec. 529A(b)(6))

Additional contribution for tax years 2018-2025. For tax years 2018 through 2025, in addition to contributions in an amount up to the annual gift tax exclusion, an ABLE account's DB may contribute, subject to a number of limitations, an additional amount up to the lesser of (a) the DB's compensation for the tax year, or (b) the federal poverty line for a one-person household for the calendar year before the calendar year ($13,590 for 2022 and $12,880 for 2021) in which the tax year begins. (Code Sec. 529A(b)(2)(B)(ii)) To qualify to make this additional contribution, a DB must be an employee, including a self-employed individual under Code Sec. 401(c), for whom no contribution is made for the tax year to (i) a defined contribution plan under Code Sec. 414(i), (ii) an annuity contract described in Code Sec. 403(b), or (iii) an eligible deferred compensation plan described in Code Sec. 457(b).[32]

Eligible beneficiaries. The DB of an ABLE account is an eligible individual who established the account and is its owner. (Code Sec. 529A(e)(3)) An individual is an eligible individual for a tax year if, during that tax year:

. . . the individual is entitled to benefits based on blindness or disability under the Social Security disability insurance program or the SSI program, and that blindness or disability occurred before the individual's 26th birthday, (Code Sec. 529A(e)(1)(A)) or

. . . a "disability certification" for the individual has been filed with IRS for the tax year. (Code Sec. 529A(e)(1)(B))

Distributions; rollovers. No amount of a distribution from an ABLE account is includible in gross income if distributions from the account don't exceed the DB's "qualified disability expenses" (Code Sec. 529A(c)(1)(B)(i)), which are any expenses related to the eligible individual's blindness or disability that are made for the benefit of an eligible individual who is the DB. (Code Sec. 529A(e)(5))

A taxpayer who receives a distribution from a qualified ABLE program that's includible in gross income is generally subject to an additional 10% tax on the includible part (Code Sec. 529A(c)(3)(A)), reportable on Form 5329.[33]

A payment or distribution from an ABLE account isn't taxable to the extent the amount received is paid, no later than the 60th day after the date of the payment or distribution, into another ABLE account for the benefit of the DB or an eligible individual who's a family member of the DB. (Code Sec. 529A(c)(1)(C)(i)) Through 2025, tax-free 60-day rollovers may also be made from a qualified tuition program (QTP, or 529 plan, see ¶2209) to an ABLE account. (Code Sec. 529(c)(3)(C)(i)(III))[34]

On the death of a DB, amounts remaining in the account (after Medicaid reimbursements) go to the DB's estate or beneficiary, and are subject to income tax on investment earnings, but not the 10% penalty. (Code Sec. 529A(c)(3)(B))[35]

Returns of qualified ABLE programs. Qualified ABLE programs must file annual information returns with IRS reporting contributions to, and distributions from, an ABLE account, and furnish a copy of the return to the account's DB. (Code Sec. 529A(d)(1))[36]

For Saver's Credit for ABLE program contributions, see ¶2356.

---

32. ¶A-4744.2
33. ¶A-4747.1
34. ¶A-4746.1

35. ¶A-4748
36. ¶S-3424.2

Chapter 8   Tax Credits

¶ 2300   **Tax Credits.** ■■■■■■■■■■■■■■■■■■■■■■■■■■■■■■■■■■■■

Tax credits are either business credits intended to provide special incentives for the achievement of certain economic objectives, or personal credits, which provide tax benefits to certain taxpayers (e.g., the elderly or disabled, etc.). The foreign tax credit, however, may apply to both business and nonbusiness taxpayers.

The three main categories of tax credits are:

(1) The business incentive credits, see ¶2301 *et seq.*

(2) The personal (refundable and nonrefundable) credits, see ¶2336 *et seq.*

(3) The foreign tax credit, see ¶2360 *et seq.*

For credit for alternative minimum tax (AMT), see ¶2358.

For tax credits attributable to certain "passive" activities, see ¶1797 *et seq.*

For treatment, under the post-2022 corporate AMT, of the foreign tax credit and the general business credit, see ¶3213.

For the credit, under the post-2022 corporate AMT, for prior-year minimum tax liability, see ¶3213.

¶ 2301   **Business Incentive Credits—General Business Credit (GBC)—Form 3800.** ■

Certain business incentive credits are combined into one GBC for purposes of determining each credit's allowance limitation for the tax year.

A GBC (Code Sec. 38(a), claimed on Form 3800) is allowed against income tax for a particular tax year and equals the sum of: (1) the business credit carry*forwards* carried to the tax year, (2) the *current-year* GBC, and (3) the business credit carry*backs* carried to the tax year. (Code Sec. 38(a))[1]

The current-year GBC is (subject to certain exceptions) comprised of the credits listed in Code Sec. 38(b), and includes the following credits:[2]

. . . investment credit (Code Sec. 38(b)(1)) (¶2306 *et seq.*) (including the rehabilitation credit (¶2307), the energy credit (¶2310 *et seq.*), the qualifying advanced coal and gasification project credits (¶2312), the qualifying advanced energy project credit (¶2313); and the advanced manufacturing tax credit (manufacturing of semiconductors or semiconductor manufacturing equipment, ¶2314);

. . . work opportunity credit (Code Sec. 38(b)(2)), see ¶2317;

. . . tax-exempt employers' payroll-tax credit for hiring qualified veterans (Code Sec. 52(c)(2) and Code Sec. 3111(e)), see ¶2318;

. . . research credit (Code Sec. 38(b)(4)), see ¶2319;

. . . low-income housing credit (Code Sec. 38(b)(5)), see ¶2320 *et seq.*;

. . . enhanced oil recovery (EOR) credit (Code Sec. 38(b)(6)), see ¶2322;

. . . disabled access credit (DAC) (Code Sec. 38(b)(7)), see ¶2323;

. . . credit for producing electricity from renewable resources; credit for producing Indian coal (Code Sec. 38(b)(8)), see ¶2324;

. . . FICA tip credit (Code Sec. 38(b)(11)), see ¶2325;

. . . orphan drug credit (Code Sec. 38(b)(12)), see ¶2326;

. . . new markets credit (Code Sec. 38(b)(13)), see ¶2327;

---

1. ¶L-15200 *et seq.*   2. ¶L-15201

References beginning with a single letter are to paragraphs in Federal Tax Coordinator 2d and RIA's Analysis of Federal Taxes: Income.

... the new energy-efficient home credit (Code Sec. 45L), see ¶2342;

... small employer pension plan startup credit (Code Sec. 38(b)(14)), see ¶2329;

... employer-provided child care credit (Code Sec. 38(b)(15)), see ¶2328;

... differential wage payment credit (Code Sec. 38(b)(28)), see ¶2331;

... carbon oxide sequestration credit (Code Sec. 38(b)(29)), see ¶2316;

... applicable portion (attributable to depreciable property) of the qualified plug-in electric drive motor vehicle credit/post-2022 new clean vehicle credit (Code Sec. 38(b)(30)), see ¶2354;

... small employer health insurance credit (Code Sec. 38(b)(31)), see ¶2330;

... employer-paid family and medical leave credit (Code Sec. 38(b)(32)), see ¶2332;

... small employer pension plan auto-enrollment credit (Code Sec. 38(b)(33)), see ¶2333; and

... qualified commercial clean vehicle credit (Code Sec. 38(b)(37)), see ¶2334.

In addition, the employee retention tax credit for employers affected by certain federally declared disasters, is treated as a credit under Code Sec. 38(b). Certain credits aren't included in the above Code Sec. 38(b) list, but are also part of the current-year business credit.

¶ 2302 Limitation on general business credits (GBCs) based on tax liability.

Under Code Sec. 38(c)(1), the GBC allowed for any tax year—except for special rules for the empowerment zone employment credit, the New York Liberty Zone business employee credit, eligible small business credits, and "specified credits" —is subject to a limitation (Code Sec. 38(c)(1)) based on the taxpayer's tax liability.

For noncorporate taxpayers, the credit may not exceed the excess (if any) of the taxpayer's "net income tax" (below) over the greater of: (a) the taxpayer's "tentative minimum tax" for the tax year, or (b) 25% of so much of the taxpayer's "net regular tax liability" (below) as exceeds $25,000. (Code Sec. 38(c)(1)(B)) For this purpose, "net income tax" is the sum of the regular tax liability and the alternative minimum tax (AMT) (¶3200 *et seq.*), reduced by the credits allowable under Code Sec. 21 through Code Sec. 30D, and the term "net regular tax liability" means the regular tax liability reduced by the credits allowable under Code Sec. 21 through Code Sec. 30D. (Code Sec. 38(c)(1)) Tentative minimum tax is the AMT increased by the "regular tax" that was subtracted in arriving at the AMT, see ¶3201.

For corporations, *for tax years beginning before 2023,* the limitation is computed under the formula for noncorporate taxpayers (above) by treating the corporation as having a tentative minimum tax of zero. *For tax years beginning after 2022,* a corporation's credit may not exceed the excess (if any) of the taxpayer's net income tax (defined above) over 25% of the taxpayer's net income tax as exceeds $25,000. (Code Sec. 38(c)(6)(E)(i))[3]

Spouses who file separate returns are each limited to $12,500 instead of $25,000, but if the taxpayer's spouse has no carryforward, carryback or current year GBC in the tax year that ends within or with the taxpayer's tax year, the taxpayer gets the full amount of $25,000. (Code Sec. 38(c)(6)(A))[4]

For estates and trusts, the $25,000 amount is reduced to an amount equal to $25,000 multiplied by a fraction (numerator is the estate's or trust's total income not allocated to beneficiaries, denominator is the estate's or trust's total income). (Code Sec. 38(c)(6)(D))[5]

3. ¶L-15202
4. ¶L-15204

5. ¶L-15207

The empowerment zone employment credit is limited as provided in Code Sec. 38(c)(2).[6]

"Specified credits" may offset 100% of a taxpayer's AMT. These credits are listed in Code Sec. 38(c)(4)(B). (Code Sec. 38(c)(4))[7]

¶ 2303   Carryback or carryforward of general business credit (GBC).

Under Code Sec. 39(a), a 1-year carryback (except for a 5-year carryback for the marginal well production credit under Code Sec. 39(a)(3)), and a 20-year carryforward, applies to the GBC. (Code Sec. 39(a)) No portion of the unused business credit for any tax year that is attributable to a credit listed under Code Sec. 38(b) (see ¶2301) or to a portion of that listed credit, can be carried back to any tax year before the first tax year for which that listed credit or portion is, without regard to the carryback/carryforward rules, allowable. (Code Sec. 39(d))[8]

¶ 2304   Deduction for unused qualified business credits after the carryover period.

Under Code Sec. 196(a) and Code Sec. 196(b), if any portion of a qualified business credit (defined in Code Sec. 196(c)), i.e. the: investment credit (¶2306 *et seq.*), work opportunity credit (¶2317), alcohol fuel credit, research credit (¶2319), enhanced oil recovery credit (¶2322), empowerment zone employment credit, Indian employment credit, FICA tip credit (¶2325), new markets tax credit (¶2327), small employer pension plan startup credit (¶2329), small employer health insurance credit (¶2330), biodiesel fuels credit, low sulfur diesel fuel production credit, and new energy-efficient home credit (¶2342), hasn't been allowed after the carryover period expires, the taxpayer can deduct the unused portion in the first tax year after the last tax year of the carryover period (or in the tax year of the taxpayer's death or cessation if earlier). (Code Sec. 196(a), Code Sec. 196(b)) But, for the investment tax credit (other than the rehabilitation credit), the deduction is 50% of the unused amount. (Code Sec. 196(d))[9]

¶ 2305   Ordering rules for the use, carryback or carryforward of general business credits (GBCs).

Under Code Sec. 38(d)(1), the order in which the credits of the GBC (listed at ¶2301) are used in a tax year or as a carryback or carryforward is based on the order they are listed in Code Sec. 38(b) (¶2301) as of the close of the tax year in which the credit is used. (Code Sec. 38(d)(1)) The order in which the credits that make up the business investment credit are used is determined on the basis of the order they are listed in Code Sec. 46 as of the close of the tax year in which the credit is used. (Code Sec. 38(d)(2))[10]

¶ 2306   The investment tax credits: rehabilitation, energy, qualifying advanced coal and gasification project, qualifying advanced energy project, and (pre-2027/post-2022) advanced manufacturing (semiconductors)—Form 3468.

The Code Sec. 46 investment tax credit (claimed on Form 3468)[11] consists of: (1) the rehabilitation investment credit (Code Sec. 47), see ¶2307 *et seq.*;[12] (2) the energy credit (Code Sec. 48(a)), see ¶2310 *et seq.*;[13] (3) the qualifying advanced coal project credit (Code

---

6. ¶L-15202.1
7. ¶L-15202.3
8. ¶L-15209 *et seq.*
9. ¶L-15212

10. ¶L-15208
11. ¶L-16500 *et seq.*
12. ¶L-16100
13. ¶L-16400

Sec. 48A), see ¶2312;[14] (4) the qualifying gasification project credit (Code Sec. 48B), see ¶2312;[15] (5) the qualifying advanced energy project credit (Code Sec. 48C), see ¶2313; and the (pre-2027/post-2022) advanced manufacturing tax credit (Code Sec. 48D) (manufacturing of semiconductors or semiconductor manufacturing equipment, ¶2314).[16]

Property qualifying for the investment credit (depreciable or amortizable property) is treated as investment credit property. (Code Sec. 50(a)(5)) But certain otherwise qualified property is denied the applicable credit if it's used:

. . . predominantly outside the U.S., except for property listed in Code Sec. 168(g)(4)—dealing with rolling stock, spacecraft, satellites, etc. (Code Sec. 50(b)(1))

. . . predominantly to furnish, or in connection with the furnishing of, permanent lodging, except for certain nonlodging commercial facilities, lodging facilities used by transients, certified historic structures, and energy property. (Code Sec. 50(b)(2))

. . . by certain tax-exempt organizations. (Code Sec. 50(b)(3)) If property is leased to a partnership or other pass-through entity, a proportionate share of the property is treated as leased to each tax-exempt entity partner (under the rules of Code Sec. 168(h)(5) and (6)) in determining whether any portion of the property is tax-exempt use property. (Code Sec. 50(b)(4))

. . . by the U.S. or other governmental units, except for short-lease property. (Code Sec. 50(b)(4))[17]

A *lessee* of new investment credit property can take the investment credit on the property if the lessor elects to pass it to him or her. (Code Sec. 50(d)(5); Reg § 1.48-4) The election statement is described in the regs. (Reg § 1.48-4(f), Reg § 1.48-4(g)) The effect is to treat the lessee as having acquired the property for its FMV, but the lessor's basis is used instead when the lessor and lessee are members of a controlled group. The lessee uses the same investment credit life for the property as the lessor.[18] In lieu of a basis adjustment, the lessee must ratably include in gross income an amount equal to the amount of the credit (50% for the energy credit) over the shortest recovery period. (Reg § 1.50-1(b)(2))[19] But a lessor's election to pass the credit from property with an over-14-year ADR depreciation "class life" to a lessee results in only a partial transfer of the credit if the lease is for a period that is less than 80% of the property's "class life" and isn't a "net lease." (Reg § 1.48-4(a)(2))[20]

If there is a net decrease in the amount of nonqualified nonrecourse financing (under the *at-risk* rules, ¶1790 *et seq.*) as of the close of a tax year following that in which property was placed in service, the net decrease is treated as an increase in the credit base for the property. Thus, an increase in the taxpayer's at-risk amount for an investment credit property is additional qualified investment. (Code Sec. 49(a)(2))[21]

¶ 2307 Rehabilitation investment credits—Form 3468; qualified rehabilitation expenditures (QREs); coordination with bonus depreciation.

The rehabilitation credit (Code Sec. 47(a), claimed on Form 3468) for any tax year during the 5-year period beginning in the tax year in which a qualified rehabilitation building (QRB, see ¶2308) is placed in service, is an amount equal to the ratable share for that year. The ratable share for any tax year during the 5-year period is the amount equal to 20% of the qualified rehabilitation expenditures (QREs) for the QRB, as allocated ratably to each year during that period. The rehabilitation credit is properly determined in the year the QRB is placed in service, but allocated ratably over the 5-year period, rather than

14. ¶L-16450
15. ¶L-16470
16. ¶L-16460 *et seq.*
17. ¶L-16501
18. ¶s L-16506, L-17010 *et seq.*
19. ¶L-17048 *et seq.*
20. ¶L-17015
21. ¶L-16505

319

resulting in the determination of five separate rehabilitation credits. (Code Sec. 47(a); Reg § 1.47-7(b)[22]

A QRE is any amount charged to the capital account and incurred in connection with the rehabilitation (including reconstruction, or an addition or improvement) of a QRB (¶2308) that's depreciable under Code Sec. 168, and is nonresidential real property, residential rental property, real property with a class life of more than 12.5 years, or an addition or improvement to the property just listed. (Code Sec. 47(c)(2)(A))[23]

If QREs for a QRB are property eligible for bonus first-year depreciation (¶1929), the rehabilitation credit may be claimed (assuming other requirements are met): (1) for the part of the basis of the QRB attributable to the QREs, if the taxpayer elects (see ¶1934) not to deduct any bonus depreciation for the class of property that includes the QRE (Reg § 1.168(k)-2(g)(9)(i)(A); Reg § 1.168(k)-1(f)(10)(i)(A)); or (2) for the part of the "remaining rehabilitated basis" (i.e., the "unadjusted depreciable basis," as defined in Reg § 1.168(b)-1(a)(3), of the QREs that are property eligible for bonus depreciation, reduced by the bonus depreciation allowed or allowable, whichever is greater) of the QRB that is attributable to the QREs, if the taxpayer claims the bonus depreciation on the "unadjusted depreciable basis" of the QREs, and depreciates the "remaining adjusted depreciable basis" (see Reg § 1.168(k)-2(e)(2)(i)) of those QREs using straight line cost recovery under Code Sec. 47(c)(2)(B)(i) and Reg § 1.48-12(c)(7)(i). (Reg § 1.168(k)-2(g)(9)(i)(A); Reg § 1.168(k)-1(f)(10)(i)(A)) If the taxpayer claims the bonus depreciation for the QREs under Reg § 1.168(k)-2(g)(9)(i) (above), the term "rehabilitation credit determined" equals 20% of the remaining rehabilitated basis of the QRB for the tax year in which the building is placed in service. (Reg § 1.47-7(c))[24]

QREs don't include the costs listed in Code Sec. 47(c)(2)(B) or S Rept No. 97-144 (PL 97-34) p. 72 (e.g., expenditures for which straight-line depreciation isn't used). (Code Sec. 47(c)(2)(B))[25]

In addition to owner-taxpayers of qualified property, the rehabilitation credits are available to lessees for qualified expenditures incurred by them, but only if, on the rehabilitation's completion date, the remaining term of the lease (without regard to renewal) is at least the recovery period under Code Sec. 168(c). (Code Sec. 47(c)(2)(B)(vi))[26]

IRS has provided a safe harbor under which, if certain requirements are met, it will respect allocations of the rehabilitation credits by a partnership to its partners.[27]

Transition rule. A transition rule applied both to QREs for certified historic structures and for pre-1936 buildings (i.e., buildings other than certified historic structures) that qualified for the rehabilitation credit under the pre-2018 rules. (Sec. 13402(c)(2), PL 115-97, 12/22/2017)[28]

¶ 2308   Which buildings qualify for the rehabilitation credit? Qualified rehabilitated buildings.

A "qualified rehabilitated building" (Code Sec. 47(c)(1)) is any building (and its structural components) that:

(1) has been substantially rehabilitated. A substantial rehabilitation is one in which the qualified rehabilitation expenditures (QREs) during the 24-month period selected by the taxpayer (as prescribed in regs) and ending with or within the year exceed the greater of: (a) $5,000; or (b) the adjusted basis of the building and its structural components as of

---

22. ¶L-16101
23. ¶L-16102
24. ¶L-16102.1
25. ¶L-16102; ¶L-16115

26. ¶L-16102
27. ¶B-2903B
28. ¶L-16101

the first day of the 24-month period, or of the holding period (without regard to reconstruction), whichever is later. (Code Sec. 47(c)(1)(B)(i)) Rehabilitation includes reconstruction; (Code Sec. 47(c)(1)(C))[29]

(2) was placed in service before the beginning of the rehabilitation;

(3) is a certified historic structure; *and*

(4) is depreciable or amortizable. (Code Sec. 47(c)(1)(A))[30]

For any rehabilitation that may reasonably be expected to be completed in phases set forth in architectural plans and specifications completed before the rehabilitation begins, a 60-month (instead of 24-month) period applies. (Code Sec. 47(c)(1)(B)(ii))[31]

¶ 2309 Progress expenditure rehabilitation credit; qualified rehabilitated buildings; Form 3468.

Instead of claiming a rehabilitation credit when the qualified rehabilitated property is placed in service, under Code Sec. 47(d), if any building being rehabilitated by or for the taxpayer has a normal rehabilitation period of 2 years or more, and it's reasonable to expect the building to be a qualified rehabilitated building (¶2308) in the taxpayer's hands when placed in service (Code Sec. 47(d)(2)), the taxpayer may irrevocably elect (on Form 3468) to account for qualified rehabilitation expenditures (QREs) made for that property as follows:

(1) where it's reasonable to believe that *more* than half these expenditures will be made directly by the taxpayer, any QRE is taken into account for the tax year it's properly chargeable to the capital account (i.e., includible in computing the property's basis), and

(2) where it's reasonable to believe that *no more than* half of the qualified expenditures will be made directly by the taxpayer, any QRE is taken into account in the tax year it's paid. (Code Sec. 47(d)(1); Reg § 1.46-5(g)(1))[32]

¶ 2310 Business energy credit—Form 3468; qualified fuel cell, solar energy, and other types of eligible energy property.

Subject to limits on the credit amount for certain energy property, the business energy investment credit for a tax year is the energy percentage (see below) times the basis of each energy property (see below) placed in service during the tax year. (Code Sec. 48(a)(1))[33]

"Energy percentage" and "energy property." The energy percentage is generally either 6% or 2%, depending on the type of energy property. However, phaseouts (see **"6% energy percentage. . ."** below) apply for non fiber-optic solar energy property, qualified fuel cell property, qualified small wind energy property, fiber-optic solar energy property and geothermal heat pump systems. And the credit can be increased up to five times (30% or 10%) if certain requirements are satisfied, see below.

⚓️*observation:* The Inflation Reduction Act of 2022 (PL 117-169, 8/16/2022) reduced the energy credit available for most energy properties that do not meet prevailing wages/apprenticeship requirements (see below) from 30% and 10% to 6% and 2%, eliminated previous phase-down and phase-out rules, extended beginning-of-construction deadlines, and added new categories of energy property.

No credit is allowed for property unless it's depreciable or amortizable; its construction,

29. ¶L-16106
30. ¶ L-16103
31. ¶L-16113

32. ¶L-16200 *et seq.*
33. ¶L-16400 *et seq.*

reconstruction or erection is completed by the taxpayer or, if acquired by the taxpayer, its original use begins with the taxpayer; and it meets the official quality and performance standards in effect at the time of acquisition. (Code Sec. 48(a)(3))[34]

6% energy percentage—property placed in service after 2021; beginning-of-construction deadlines; limits on credit for certain property. Except as provided in Code Sec. 48(a)(6) and Code Sec. 48(a)(7) (phased-down percentage amounts, as noted for applicable property types, below) the energy percentage is 6% (Code Sec. 48(a)(2)(A)(i))[35] for the type of energy property listed below that is placed in service after 2021.

To be eligible for the credit, construction of each type of property listed must begin **before Jan. 1, 2025.**

. . . Qualified fuel cell property (defined in Code Sec. 48(c)(1)) (Code Sec. 48(a)(3)(A)(iv)).[36] *Limit on credit.* The credit can't exceed $1,500 for each 0.5 KW of capacity.[37] *Property placed in service before 2022:* The phased-down percentage for qualified fuel cell property, the construction of which began after Dec. 31, 2019 and that was placed in service before Jan. 1, 2022, is 26%. (Code Sec. 48(a)(6))[38]

. . . Solar energy equipment property (including non fiber-optic solar, defined in Code Sec. 48(a)(3)(A)(i), and fiber-optic solar, defined in Code Sec. 48(a)(3)(A)(ii)),[39] and geothermal property (defined in Code Sec. 48(a)(3)(A)(iii)).[40] *Property placed in service before 2022:* The phased-down percentage for both types of solar, the construction of which began after Dec. 31, 2019 and that was placed in service before 2022, is 26%. (Code Sec. 48(a)(6)) The percentage for geothermal property placed in service before 2022 is 10%.[41]

. . . Qualified small wind energy property (defined in Code Sec. 48(c)(4)). (Code Sec. 48(a)(3)(A)(vi))[42] *Property placed in service before 2022:* The phased-down percentage for small wind energy property, the construction of which began after Dec. 31, 2019 and that was placed in service before 2022, is 26%. (Code Sec. 48(a)(6))[43]

. . . Waste energy recovery property (defined in Code Sec. 48(c)(4)). (Code Sec. 48(a)(3)(A)(viii))[44] *Property placed in service before 2022:* The prior-law percentage 30% was reduced under a prior-law phase-down rule.[45]

For the following type of property *placed in service after Dec. 31, 2022,* the energy percentage is also 6%. To be eligible for the credit, construction of the property must begin **before Jan. 1, 2025.**

. . . Combined heat and power system (CHP) property (defined in Code Sec. 48(c)(3)). (Code Sec. 48(a)(3)(A)(v))[46] *Limit on credit.* For CHP property with an electrical capacity in excess of the "applicable capacity" placed in service during the tax year, the credit (determined without regard to the Code Sec. 48(c)(3)(B) limitation) for the year equals the amount that bears the same ratio to the credit as the applicable capacity bears to the capacity of the property. (Code Sec. 48(c)(3)(B))[47] *For property placed in service before 2023,* the credit amount for CHP property is 10%.[48]

For the following listed types of property *placed in service after Dec. 31, 2022,* the energy percentage is also 6%. To be eligible for the credit, construction of each type of property

34. ¶L-16402
35. ¶L-16401A
36. ¶L-16436
37. ¶L-16436
38. ¶ L-16401A
39. ¶L-16424
40. ¶L-16426
41. ¶ L-16401A

42. ¶L-16436.4
43. ¶ L-16401A
44. ¶L-16436.5
45. ¶ L-16401A
46. ¶L-16436.3 *et seq.*
47. ¶L-16436.3B *et seq.*
48. ¶L-16436.3; ¶ L-16401A

must begin **before Jan. 1, 2035.** The first three property types were added by the Inflation Reduction Act.

. . . Energy storage technology (defined in Code Sec. 48(c)(6)). (Code Sec. 48(a)(3)(A)(ix))[49]

. . . Qualified biogas property (defined in Code Sec. 48(c)(7)). (Code Sec. 48(a)(3)(A)(x))[50]

. . . Microgrid controllers (defined in Code Sec. 48(c)(8)). (Code Sec. 48(a)(3)(A)(xi))[1]

. . . Geothermal heat pump systems (defined in Code Sec. 48(a)(3)(A)(vii)). (Code Sec. 48(a)(3)(A)(vii))[2] A phase-down of the credit applies, see Code Sec. 48(a)(7). *For property placed in service before 2023,* the credit amount for CHP property is 10%.[3]

2% energy percentage—property placed in service after 2021; beginning-of-construction deadlines; limits on credit for certain property. The energy percentage is 2% for the basis of any energy property not listed above under **"6% energy percentage. . ."** that is placed in service during the tax year. (Code Sec. 48(a)(2)(A)(ii)) To be eligible for the credit, construction of each type of property must begin **before Jan. 1, 2025.**

2% property includes:

. . . Qualified microturbine property (defined in Code Sec. 48(c)(2)). (Code Sec. 48(a)(3)(A)(iv))[4] *Limit on credit.* The credit can't exceed an amount equal to $200 for each kilowatt of capacity for the property. Thus, the credit is limited to the lesser of [2]% of the basis of the property or $200 for each kilowatt of capacity. (Code Sec. 48(c)(2)(B))[5] *Property placed in service before 2022:* The percentage for microturbine property placed in service before 2022 is 10%.[6]

. . . Qualified interconnection property (defined in Code Sec. 48(a)(8)). This property, which is eligible for the investment tax credit, is certain property used by a regulated utility in connection with other credit-eligible property (other than microgrid controllers).[7]

Increase of credits to 30% or 10% if requirements are satisfied. The energy credit can be increased in several ways. It can be increased 5 times (6% to 30% and 2% to 10%) under the "small project requirements," "recently begun construction," or "prevailing wage/apprenticeship" rules (see below). Other provisions, which apply for property placed in service after 2022, allow an increase of 10% (or 2%) if the properties involve domestic content, are in certain energy communities, or environmental justice facilities (see below).[8]

5 times multiplier increase—for property placed in service after Dec. 31, 2021. The percentage of 6% or 2% is multiplied five times (30% or 10%) for an "energy project" (a project consisting of one or more energy properties that are part of a single project), if the project meets one of the following requirements:

(1) Small project increase—the facility has a maximum net output of electrical (alternating current) or thermal energy less than 1 megawatt. (Code Sec. 48(a)(9)(B)(i))

(2) Increase for recently begun construction—property is placed in service before IRS issues guidance—i.e., where the construction of a project begins before 60 days after IRS publishes guidance with respect to the requirements of the prevailing wage and apprenticeship rules (see (3), below). (Code Sec. 48(a)(9)(B)(ii))

(3) Prevailing wage and apprenticeship-compliant increase—laborers or mechanics employed by the taxpayer, contractor, or subcontractor must be paid wages at least at prevailing rates in the locality in which the project is located, during construction, renovation and

49. ¶L-16436.6
50. ¶L-16436.7
1. ¶L-16436.8
2. ¶L-16438
3. ¶ L-16401A

4. ¶ L-16401A; ¶L-16437
5. ¶ L-16401A; ¶L-16437
6. ¶ L-16401A
7. ¶L-16436.9
8. ¶L-16401B

alteration of the project, for a five-year period after placement in service of an energy project. (Code Sec. 48(a)(10))

Credit increase for domestic content—for property placed in service after Dec. 31, 2022. The energy credit is increased if the taxpayer certifies to IRS that any steel, iron, or manufactured product that is a component of the facility (upon completion) was produced in the U.S. The increase is 10 percentage points for a project that is eligible for the 5 times multiplier credit increase but only two percentage points for projects that is not. (Code Sec. 48(a)(12))

Credit increase in energy communities—for property placed in service after Dec. 31, 2022. The energy credit is increased for projects in certain brownfield sites, areas in which certain coal, oil, or natural gas activities take place and that have an increase in unemployment, and areas where a coal mine has closed after 1999 or a coal-fired electric generating unit retired after 2009 (energy communities). The increase is 10 points for a project that is eligible for the 5 times multiplier credit increase, but only two points for projects that is not. (Code Sec. 48(a)(14))

For increased energy credit (for 2023 and 2024) for solar and wind facilities in certain low-income communities, see ¶2311.

Election (post-2022) by certain entities to be treated as paying income tax equal to amount of credit. For tax years beginning after 2022, an "applicable entity" (Code Sec. 6417(d)(1)(A)) can make this election with regard to the Code Sec. 48 credit. (Code Sec. 6417(b))[9]

Election (post-2022) by taxpayers that are not "applicable entities" (see above) to transfer the credit to other taxpayers. For tax years beginning after 2022, taxpayers, other than "applicable entities" (above), can make this election with regard to the Code Sec. 48 credit. (Code Sec. 6418(a))[10]

For the increased energy credit for solar and wind facilities in certain low-income communities, see ¶2311.

For the Code Sec. 48(a)(5) election to have "qualified property" that's part of certain "qualified investment facilities" (under Code Sec. 45) treated as energy property eligible for a credit under Code Sec. 48, see ¶2324.

¶ 2311   Increased energy credit (2023 and 2024) for solar and wind facilities in certain low-income communities.

Under Code Sec. 48(e) (added by the 2022 Inflation Reduction Act, P.L. 117-169, 8/16/2022), a taxpayer can claim an added credit of either 10% or 20% for any qualified solar or wind facility for which IRS makes an allocation of "environmental justice solar and wind capacity." (Code Sec. 48(e)(4))[11]

The allocation provision applies for calendar years 2023 and 2024. (Code Sec. 48(e)(4)(C)) No allocation of additional credit may be made after 2024. (Code Sec. 48(e)(4)(C))

To qualify for the allocation, a qualified solar or wind facility must be located in a low-income community or on Indian land, or must be part of a qualified low-income residential building project or a qualified low-income economic benefit project. (Code Sec. 48(e)(2)(A)) A recapture provision applies for property that ceases to be eligible for the increased amount. (Code Sec. 48(e)(5)))

9. ¶L-17980 *et seq.*   11. ¶L-16439
10. ¶L-17990 *et seq.*

¶ **2312**   **Credits for qualifying advanced coal projects and gasification projects—Form 3468.**

Advanced coal projects. A credit (under Code Sec. 48A(a)) can be claimed for investments in qualifying advanced coal projects. (Code Sec. 48A(a)) The overall $2.55 billion of allocable credits are allocated among qualifying projects certified by IRS in consultation with the Dept. of Energy (DOE). The credit is 30% of the qualified investment for advanced coal-based generation technology projects; 20% of the qualified investment for the tax year in integrated gasification combined cycle projects; and 15% of the qualified investment for the tax year in projects that use other advanced coal-based generation technologies.[12]

Gasification projects. A separate investment credit can also be claimed for qualified investment in qualifying gasification projects. An IRS program considers and awards certifications to qualifying gasification project sponsors. The credit is 20% or 30% of the qualified investment for the tax year. (Code Sec. 48B(a)) The Code Sec. 48B credit is not allowed for any qualified investment for which the Code Sec. 48A credit is allowed. (Code Sec. 48B(e))[13] (Code Sec. 48(d)(2))[14]

¶ **2313**   **Qualifying advanced energy project credit—Form 3468.**

Under Code Sec. 48C, a taxpayer can claim a 30% credit for investment in qualified property used in a qualifying advanced energy project, i.e., a project that re-equips, expands, or establishes a manufacturing facility for the production of property designed to: (1) be used to produce energy from the sun, wind, or geothermal deposits or other renewable resources; (2) manufacture fuel cells, microturbines, or an energy storage system for use with electric or hybrid-electric motor vehicles; (3) manufacture electric grids to support the transmission of intermittent sources of renewable energy, including storage of that energy; (4) manufacture equipment for use for carbon capture or sequestration; or (5) refine or blend renewable fuels (but not fossil fuels), to produce energy conservation technologies (including energy-conserving lighting technologies and smart grid technologies). It also includes a facility for the production of new qualified plug-in electric drive motor vehicles (¶2354), components designed specifically for these vehicles; or other advanced energy property designed to reduce greenhouse gas emissions. The credits are allocated among qualifying projects certified by IRS in consultation with the Dept. of Energy (DOE). (Code Sec. 48C(c)(1))[15] Qualified property must be depreciable (tangible) property used in a qualifying advanced energy project and doesn't include property designed to manufacture equipment for use in the refining or blending of any transportation fuel (other than renewable fuels). (Code Sec. 48C(c)(1)) The property's basis is reduced by the amount of credit received.[16] The Code Sec. 48C credit is not allowed for any qualified investment for which the Code Sec. 48, Code Sec. 48A, or Code Sec. 48B credits are allowed. (Code Sec. 48C(e))

Effective Jan. 1, 2023, Code Sec. 48C will be expanded and extended by the Inflation Reduction Act of 2022 (P.L. 117-169, 8/16/2022) to include a range of industrial or manufacturing facilities that focus on energy conservation and renewable energy. The amount of credits available may not exceed $10 billion (of which no more than $6 billion may be allocated to investments that aren't located in certain census tracts). The credit will have a base amount of 6% (which can go up to 30%, if certain prevailing-wage and apprenticeship requirements are met). The Code Sec. 48C credit won't be available for an investment if a credit is allowed for such investment under Code Sec. 48, Code Sec. 48A, Code Sec. 48B, Code Sec. 48E, Code Sec. 45Q, or Code Sec. 45V.

---

12. ¶L-16450 *et seq.*
13. ¶L-16470 *et seq.*
14. ¶L-16476.16

15. ¶L-16463
16. ¶L-16460 *et seq.*

Election (post-2022) by certain entities to be treated as paying income tax equal to amount of credit. For tax years beginning after 2022, an "applicable entity" (Code Sec. 6417(d)(1)(A)) can make this election with regard to the Code Sec. 48C credit. (Code Sec. 6417(b))[17]

Election (post-2022) by taxpayers that are not "applicable entities" (see above) to transfer the credit to other taxpayers. For tax years beginning after 2022, taxpayers, other than "applicable entities" (above), can make this election with regard to the Code Sec. 48C credit. (Code Sec. 6418(a))[18]

¶ 2314 "Advanced manufacturing tax credit" (manufacturing of semiconductors or semiconductor manufacturing equipment) will apply—property placed in service after Dec. 31, 2022.

Code Sec. 48D provides for the advanced manufacturing credit, a component of the business investment tax credit. The credit will be 25% of a qualified investment in qualified property (Code Sec. 48D(a)), which is generally tangible depreciable property that is either constructed, re-constructed or erected by the taxpayer, or is new property acquired by the taxpayer. The tangible property can include, in addition to equipment, buildings or building portions if they are not used for office space, administrative functions or other functions not related to manufacturing. (Code Sec. 48D(b))[19]

The investment will have to be made in a facility whose primary purpose is the manufacture of semiconductors or semiconductor manufacturing equipment. (Code Sec. 48D(b)(3))[20]

The taxpayer will be able to elect to treat the amount of the credit earned as a payment of taxes, thus avoiding the provisions that require aggregate business credits to be carried back and then forward because they are allowed to offset only a portion of regular tax liability. (Code Sec. 48D(d)(1))[21] Rules show how to apply the election to partnerships and S corporations. (Code Sec. 48D(d)(2))[22]

The credit will be effective for property placed in service after Dec. 31, 2022. For property whose construction, reconstruction or erection begins before Jan. 1, 2023, the credit will be allowed only to the extent of the basis of that property that's attributable to the construction, reconstruction, or erection after Aug. 9, 2022. (CHIPS Act, Sec. 107) The credit won't be allowed for property whose construction begins after Dec. 31, 2026. (Code Sec. 48D(e))[23]

¶ 2315 Recapture of investment credits—Form 4255; investment credit property disposed of or no longer used as investment credit property.

Under Code Sec. 50(a), if investment credit property is disposed of or ceases to be investment credit property for the taxpayer before the end of the recapture period, the credit taken for all earlier years is recaptured on Form 4255 (i.e., added to the tax liability for the recapture year). (Code Sec. 50(a)(1)) The recapture percentage is 100% during the first full year after the property is placed in service. This percentage decreases by 20 percentage points every succeeding full year. There's no recapture after the fifth full year. (Code Sec. 50(a)(1))[24] Recapture applies only to credit used to reduce tax liability. If any part of it isn't used, carrybacks and carryovers of the credit must be appropriately adjusted. (Code Sec. 50(a)(3))

No recapture applies to a transfer by reason of death (Code Sec. 50(a)(4)(A)), a mere

17. ¶L-17980 *et seq.*
18. ¶L-17990 *et seq.*
19. ¶L-17961
20. ¶L-17961

21. ¶L-17962
22. ¶L-17963
23. ¶L-17961
24. ¶L-17312

change in form of doing business (Code Sec. 50(a)(4)(B)), or a transfer between spouses or incident to divorce (under the rules of Code Sec. 1041(a)). (Code Sec. 50(a)(5)(B))[25]

Different recapture computation methods apply to the progress expenditures credit (¶2309) depending on whether the recapture year occurs before or after the progress expenditure property is placed in service. (Code Sec. 50(a)(2))[26]

If the amount of nonqualified nonrecourse financing (¶1796) for at-risk property increases as of the close of the tax year, then the tax for the tax year is increased by the total decrease in credits allowed in earlier tax years that would result if the credit base for the earlier credits had been reduced by the amount of the increase in the nonqualified nonrecourse financing. For purposes of computing recapture, the increase in nonqualified nonrecourse financing is treated as reducing the credit base and correspondingly reducing the qualified investment in the year the property was placed in service. (Code Sec. 49(b)(1)) The transfer of (or an agreement to transfer) any evidence of indebtedness won't be treated as an increase in nonqualified nonrecourse financing, if the transfer occurs (or the agreement is entered into) more than one year after the indebtedness was incurred. (Code Sec. 49(b)(2))[27]

If a taxpayer fails to pay the principal on a level payment nonqualified nonrecourse loan (¶1796) used for qualified energy property, the taxpayer is treated as increasing the amount of nonqualified nonrecourse financing to the extent of the recapture. (Code Sec. 49(b)(3))[28]

¶ 2316   Carbon oxide/carbon dioxide sequestration credit—Form 8933.

A carbon oxide sequestration credit (Code Sec. 45Q, as amended by the Inflation Reduction Act of 2022 (P.L. 117-169, 8/16/2022); also called the carbon dioxide sequestration credit) is allowed for carbon oxide captured. (Code Sec. 45Q)

Amount of credit; applicable amount. The credit equals the sum of: (1) $20 (as adjusted for inflation, see below) per metric ton of qualified carbon oxide that's (a) captured by the taxpayer using carbon capture equipment originally placed in service at a qualified facility *before* Feb. 9, 2018 and (b) disposed of by the taxpayer in secure geological storage and not used as described at (2)(b), below (Code Sec. 45Q(a)(1)); (2) $10 (as adjusted for inflation, see below) per metric ton of qualified carbon oxide that's (a) captured by the taxpayer using carbon capture equipment originally placed in service at a qualified facility *before* Feb. 9, 2018 and (b) *used* by the taxpayer as a tertiary injectant in a qualified enhanced oil or natural gas recovery project and *disposed of* by the taxpayer in secure geological storage or utilized in another specified manner (see Code Sec. 45Q(f)(5)) (Code Sec. 45Q(a)(2)); (3) the applicable dollar amount, for facilities or equipment placed in service before 2023, as determined under Code Sec. 45Q(b)(1)(A) and Code Sec. 45Q(b)(1)(B), and for facilities or equipment placed in service after 2022, as determined under Code Sec. 45Q(b)(1)(A) through Code Sec. 45Q(b)(1)(D), as amended by the Inflation Reduction Act of 2022 (P.L. 117-169, 8/16/2022) (Code Sec. 45Q(a)(3))[29] per metric ton of qualified carbon oxide that's (a) *captured* by the taxpayer using carbon capture equipment originally placed in service at a qualified facility *after* Feb. 8, 2018, during the 12-year period beginning on the date the equipment was originally placed in service, and (b) *disposed of* by the taxpayer in secure geological storage (Code Sec. 45Q(a)(3)); and (4) the applicable dollar amount, for facilities or equipment placed in service before 2023, as determined under Code Sec. 45Q(b)(1)(A) and Code Sec. 45Q(b)(1)(B), and for facilities or equipment placed in service after 2022, as determined under Code Sec. 45Q(b)(1)(A)

---

25. ¶L-17301
26. ¶L-17314
27. ¶L-17307

28. ¶L-16419
29. ¶L-18401.1

through Code Sec. 45Q(b)(1)(D), as amended by the Inflation Reduction Act of 2022 (P.L. 117-169, 8/16/2022) (Code Sec. 45Q(a)(4))[30] per metric ton of qualified carbon oxide that's (a) *captured* by the taxpayer using carbon capture equipment originally placed in service at a qualified facility *after* Feb. 8, 2018, during the 12-year period beginning on the date the equipment was originally placed in service, and (b) *used* by the taxpayer in the manner described at (2)(b), above (Code Sec. 45Q(a)(4)).[31]

The final calendar year for which taxpayers may claim the credit under (1) and (2), above, is 2022. (Code Sec. 45Q(g))

Direct air capture facilities, post-2022. For direct air capture facilities (Code Sec. 45Q(d)(2)(A), Code Sec. 45Q(e)(3)) placed in service after Dec. 31, 2022, a special rule applies for determining the applicable amount. (Code Sec. 45Q(b)(1)(B)).

5-time increase, post-2022, for meeting prevailing-wage and apprenticeship requirements. For facilities or equipment placed in service after 2022, if the requirements of Code Sec. 45Q(h) are met, taxpayers will be entitled to a 5-time increase in the amount of credit available if prevailing wage and apprentice requirements are satisfied. (Code Sec. 45Q(h))[32]

2022 and 2021 credit amounts. The credit under (1) above for calendar year 2022 is $25.07 per metric ton of qualified carbon oxide, above, and the credit under (2) above for 2022 is $12.53 per metric ton of qualified carbon oxide. The credit for calendar year 2021 was $24.10 per metric ton of qualified carbon oxide under (1), above, and $12.05 per metric ton of qualified carbon oxide under (2), above.[33]

The 2022 credit under (3) above is $37.85 per metric ton; the 2021 credit under (3) above is $34.81 per metric ton. The 2022 credit under (4) above is $25.15 per metric ton; the 2021 credit under (4) above is $22.68 per metric ton. (Code Sec. 45Q(b)(1)(A), Code Sec. 45Q(b)(1)(B))[34]

Qualified carbon dioxide/oxide. For the credit, qualified carbon oxide is defined as any carbon dioxide or carbon oxide that meets certain requirements. (Code Sec. 45Q(c))[35]

Regs. Regs provide guidance for claiming the credit, including a reduction of the credit recapture period to three years. (Reg § 1.45Q-1, Reg § 1.45Q-2, Reg § 1.45Q-3, Reg § 1.45Q-4, Reg § 1.45Q-5)[36]

Qualified facility; beginning-of-construction deadline. The construction of a qualified facility (an industrial facility, Code Sec. 45Q(d), or direct air capture facility, Code Sec. 45Q(e)(3)) must begin before Jan. 1, 2033. (Code Sec. 45Q(d)(1)).[37]

Recapture. If any qualified carbon oxide ceases to be used in a required manner, the benefit of the credit can be recaptured. (Code Sec. 45Q(f)(4))[38]

Form 8933. Form 8933 is used to claim the credit. Form 3800 is used to figure the extent to which the credit is limited by overall limits on the general business credit (see ¶2302).

Election (post-2022) by certain entities to be treated as paying income tax equal to amount of credit. For tax years beginning after 2022, an "applicable entity" (Code Sec. 6417(d)(1)(A)) can make this election with regard to so much of the Code Sec. 45Q(a) as is attributable to carbon capture equipment originally placed in service after 2022. (Code Sec. 6417(b))[39]

Election (post-2022) by taxpayers that are not "applicable entities" (see above)

---

30. ¶L-18401.1
31. ¶L-18401 *et seq.*
32. ¶L-18403.2
33. ¶L-18412
34. ¶L-18401.1

35. ¶L-18402
36. ¶L-18401 *et seq.*
37. ¶L-18403
38. ¶L-18417 *et seq.*
39. ¶L-17980 *et seq.*

to transfer the credit to other taxpayers. For tax years beginning after 2022, taxpayers, other than "applicable entities" (above), can make this election with regard to the Code Sec. 45Q(a) credit. (Code Sec. 6418(a))[40]

¶ 2317 Work opportunity tax credit (WOTC) for hiring members of targeted groups before 2026—Forms 5884, 8850.

Generally, the WOTC (Code Sec. 51) allows employers who hire members of certain "targeted groups" (see below) before Jan. 1, 2026, and obtain a certification from the relevant state agency on the individual's status as a member of a targeted group, to get a credit against income tax (using Form 5884) of 40% of first-year wages up to a maximum amount. (Code Sec. 51) Subject to the special rules for summer youth employees, long-term family assistance recipients, and certain qualified veterans, no more than $6,000 of qualified first-year wages may be taken into account for any individual. (Code Sec. 51(b)(3))[41] The credit percentage is 25% for employees who have completed at least 120, but less than 400, hours of service for the employer. (Code Sec. 51(i))[42]

To be eligible for the WOTC, a new employee has to be certified as a member of a targeted group by a "designated local agency" (DLA). The employer can either get the certification by the day the prospective employee begins work, or complete (and have the applicant complete) a pre-screening notice (using Form 8850) for the employee *on or before* the day he or she is offered employment, and submit it to the DLA (not to IRS) as part of a request for certification *within 28 days* after the employee begins work (but see the transitional relief discussed below). (Code Sec. 51(d)(13))[43] Special rules apply for the certification of certain veterans.[44]

The targeted groups are: (1) qualified IV-A recipients (qualified recipients of aid to families with dependent children or successor program); (2) qualified veterans; (3) qualified ex-felons; (4) designated community residents (i.e., the former "high-risk youths" targeted group but with the maximum age requirement raised and the residency requirement expanded to include rural renewal residents); (5) vocational rehabilitation referrals; (6) qualified summer youth employees; (7) qualified supplemental nutrition assistance benefits recipients; (8) qualified SSI recipients; (9) long-term family assistance recipients, i.e., members of a family that receives or received assistance under a IV-A program for a minimum period of time; and (10) qualified long-term unemployment recipients (i.e., those who have had a period of unemployment that is not less than 27 consecutive weeks, and includes a period in which the individual was receiving unemployment compensation under State or Federal law). (Code Sec. 51(d))[45]

No WOTC is allowed for employees who are related to the employer or to certain owners of the employer. (Code Sec. 51(i))[46]

Wages paid (a) for federally funded on-the-job training, (Code Sec. 51(c)(2)(A))[47] and (b) to an individual who performed the same or substantially similar services as those of employees participating in or affected by a strike or lockout at the employer's plant do not qualify for the credit. (Code Sec. 51(c)(3))[48] Creditable wages are reduced by any supplementation payments made to the employer for an employee under Social Security Act §482(e). (Code Sec. 51(c)(2)(B))[49] Wages paid or incurred in carrying on a business of trafficking in marijuana don't qualify for the WOTC. (Chief Counsel Memorandum 202205024)[50]

---

40. ¶L-17990 *et seq.*
41. ¶L-17775 *et seq.*
42. ¶L-17778
43. ¶L-17784.1
44. ¶L-17784.1D
45. ¶L-17776 *et seq.*

46. ¶L-17784.2
47. ¶L-17784.2
48. ¶L-17783.3
49. ¶L-17783
50. ¶L-17784.2

The WOTC reduces the employer's wage deduction dollar-for-dollar. (Code Sec. 280C(a); Reg § 1.280C-1)[1] But the taxpayer can elect not to take the WOTC by not claiming the credit. (Code Sec. 51(j))[2]

¶ 2318　Tax-exempt employers' payroll-tax WOTC credit for hiring qualified veterans before 2026—Form 5884-C.

Under Code Sec. 52(c)(2) and Code Sec. 3111(e), for veterans hired before 2026, a tax-exempt employer (one described in Code Sec. 501(c) and exempt from tax under Code Sec. 501(a)) can claim (on Form 5884-C) a credit for the work opportunity tax credit (WOTC, see ¶2317) that it could have claimed for hiring qualified veterans if it were not tax-exempt (¶2317). (Code Sec. 52(c)(2), Code Sec. 3111(e)) The credit is allowed against the OASDI (Social Security) tax (¶3024). The credit, which can't exceed the OASDI tax otherwise payable for employment of all the tax-exempt's employees during the applicable employment period, is calculated as it would be under Code Sec. 51, but with a number modifications. The general credit percentage of qualifying first-year wages is 26% (instead of 40%); the credit percentage of qualifying wages is 16.25% (instead of 25%) for a qualified veteran who has completed at least 120, but less than 400, hours of service for the employer; and the tax-exempt employer can only take into account wages paid to a qualified veteran for services in furtherance of the activities related to the purposes or function constituting the basis of the organization's exemption under Code Sec. 501. (Code Sec. 3111(e)(2), Code Sec. 3111(e)(3))[3]

Any credit that exceeds the employer Social Security tax for the period the credit is claimed is carried forward.[4]

¶ 2319　Research credit—Form 6765; qualified research expenses, university basic research credit, energy research consortium; offset against payroll tax for qualified small businesses.

The research credit (Code Sec. 41(a)), claimed on Form 6765, equals the sum of:

(1) 20% of the excess (if any) of the qualified research expenses (QREs) for the tax year over a base amount, or, instead of that amount, if elected by the taxpayer, the alternative simplified research credit (see below).

(2) The university basic research credit, i.e., 20% of the basic research payments determined under Code Sec. 41(e)(1)(A).

(3) 20% of the amounts paid or incurred by the taxpayer to a research consortium for energy research. (Code Sec. 41(a))[5]

The base amount is a fixed-base percentage of taxpayer's average annual gross receipts from a U.S. trade or business, net of returns and allowances, for the 4 tax years before the credit year; it can't be less than 50% of the year's QREs. The fixed-base percentage for a non-startup company is the percentage (not exceeding 16%) that taxpayer's total QREs are of total gross receipts for tax years beginning after '83 and before '89. (Code Sec. 41(c))[6]

For a start-up company, except when a taxpayer elects the alternative simplified research credit (below), for each of its first five tax years in which the start-up has QREs, the fixed-base percentage is 3% (instead of the fixed-base percentage discussed above). (Code Sec. 41(c)(3)(B)(ii)(I)) For the second 5 tax years in which a startup company has QREs, the fixed-base percentage is determined under special rules. (Code Sec. 41(c)(3)(B)(ii)(II))[7]

---

1. ¶L-17780
2. ¶L-17781
3. ¶H-4687.8, ¶H-4687.8A
4. ¶H-4687.8

5. ¶L-15300 *et seq.*
6. ¶L-15309 *et seq.*
7. ¶L-15310 *et seq.*

To qualify for the research credit, research must be conducted within the U.S. (including Puerto Rico and U.S. possessions). (Code Sec. 41(d)(4), Code Sec. 41(f)(6)(C)) The following must also be met:

(a) the expenditures for the research must be able to be treated as specified research or experimental expenditures under the provisions of Code Sec. 174;

(b) the research must be undertaken for purposes of discovering information that (1) is technological in nature, and (2) the application of which is intended to be useful in the development of a new or improved business component of the taxpayer; and

(c) substantially all of the activities of the research are elements of a process of experimentation that relate to a new or improved function, performance, reliability or quality. (Code Sec. 41(d)(1); Reg § 1.41-4(a)(2))[8]

Under Code Sec. 41(d)(4)(E), research for computer software developed by a taxpayer for internal use—other than for use in an activity that's qualified research, or a production process for which the requirements for the research credit are met—is not considered "qualified research," except as provided in regs. The regs provide tests that must be met for internal use software to be eligible for the research credit. (Reg § 1.41-4(c)(6))[9] Certain activities (e.g., marketing, surveys, duplication of existing business components, post-commercial-production activities) aren't qualified expenses. (Code Sec. 41(d)(4)) To pass test (b), above, research has to be intended to eliminate uncertainty about the development or improvement of a business component, and the process of experimentation has to fundamentally rely on principles of the physical or biological sciences, engineering, or computer science. Courts generally apply these tests strictly.[10] The issuance of certain patents is conclusive evidence that a taxpayer has discovered technological-in-nature information that is intended to eliminate uncertainty about the development or improvement of a business component. (Reg § 1.41-4(a)(3)(iii))[11]

QREs are amounts the taxpayer paid or incurred during the tax year "in carrying on any trade or business" (including certain start-up costs) of the taxpayer for: in-house research expenses, which consists of certain wages and supplies; and contract research expenses, i.e., 65% of amounts paid to certain nonemployees, and 100% of the taxpayer's expenditures to eligible small businesses, universities, and federal laboratories for qualified energy research. (Code Sec. 41(b); Reg § 1.41-2)[12]

For calculating the allowable research credit for persons that acquired the major portion of either a trade or business or a separate unit of a trade or business of another person, the QREs paid or incurred by the acquiring person during the "measurement period" (Code Sec. 41(f)(3)(A)(vi)) is increased by certain of the predecessor's expenses, and the acquiring person's gross receipts for the period is increased by certain of the predecessor's gross receipts. (Code Sec. 41(f)(3)(A), Code Sec. 41(f)(3)(B))[13]

The credit for each member of a controlled group is determined on a proportionate basis to its share of the aggregate of the QREs, basic research payments, and amounts paid or incurred to research consortiums (discussed above), taken into account by the controlled group for purposes of the research credit. (Code Sec. 41(f)(1)(A)(ii)) A similar rule applies to members of a group of commonly controlled trades or businesses. (Code Sec. 41(f)(1)(B)(ii)) Regs provide further guidance on how the research credit is allocated in controlled groups.[14]

Any expense taken into account in computing the orphan drug credit (¶2326) for a tax year can't be taken into account in computing the credit. (Code Sec. 45C(c)(1)) But, any

---

8. ¶L-15406 *et seq.*
9. ¶L-15437
10. ¶L-15408; ¶L-15411
11. ¶L-15410

12. ¶L-15401 *et seq.*
13. ¶L-15321 *et seq.*
14. ¶L-15317

orphan drug expenses for any tax year that are QREs can be taken into account in determining base period research expenses in later tax years. (Code Sec. 45C(c)(2))[15]

If the amount of the research credit determined for the tax year under Code Sec. 41(a)(1) exceeds the amount allowable as a deduction for the tax year for QREs or basic research expenses, the amount chargeable to capital account for the tax year for the expenses is reduced by the amount of the excess. Code Sec. 280C(c)(1))[16]

A taxpayer can elect an *alternative simplified research credit* equal to 14% of the excess of the QREs for the tax year over 50% of the average QREs for the three tax years preceding the tax year for which the credit was being determined. (Code Sec. 41(c)(4)(A), Reg § 1.41-9(a)) If a taxpayer has no QREs in any one of the three preceding tax years, the alternative simplified research credit is 6% of the QREs for the tax year for which the credit is being determined. (Code Sec. 41(c)(4)(B)) The election applies to the tax year for which it is made and all following tax years unless revoked with IRS's consent. The election can't be made on an amended return if both the Code Sec. 41(a)(1) credit was previously claimed on an original or amended return and the tax year was closed by the period of limitations on assessments. (Code Sec. 41(c)(4)(C); Reg § 1.41-9(b))[17]

The 20% *university basic research credit* component applies to 100% of cash expenditures by corporations (except S corporations, personal holding companies, or service organizations) for basic research over the sum of: (1) the minimum basic research amount, plus (2) the maintenance-of-effort amount. (Code Sec. 41(e); Reg § 1.41-7)[18] The minimum basic research amount (Code Sec. 41(e)(4); Reg § 1.41-7) is the greatest of: (1) 1% of the average amount paid for in-house and contract research expenses during the base period (the three tax years before the first tax year beginning after 1983); (Code Sec. 41(e)(7)(B)) (2) the contract research expense for the base period; or (3) 50% of the basic research payments if the taxpayer wasn't in existence for a full year in the base period.[19] The maintenance-of-effort amount is: (a) the average charitable contribution to all educational institutions during the base period (see above) multiplied by the cost-of-living adjustment (Code Sec. 41(e)(5)(C)), *minus* (b) the charitable contributions to educational institutions for the year. (Code Sec. 41(e)(5)(A))[20]

Offset against AMT. Eligible small businesses ($50 million or less of gross receipts) may claim the credit against their alternative minimum tax (AMT) liability. (Code Sec. 38(c)(4)(B)(ii))[21]

Offset against payroll tax. Qualified small businesses (QSBs) may elect to claim up to $250,000 of their research credit as a credit against their employer OASDI payroll tax liability, rather than against their income tax liability, and for tax years beginning after 2022—under Code Sec. 41(h) as amended by the Inflation Reduction Act of 2022 (P.L. 117-169, 8/16/2022)—up to an additional $250,000 against their Hospital Insurance (Medicare) payroll tax liability. (Code Sec. 41(h)(4)(B)(i)(II))[22] The credit against OASDI liability can't exceed the tax imposed for any calendar quarter, and the credit against the employer share of Medicare can't exceed the Hospital Insurance (Medicare) payroll tax liability for any calendar quarter. Credits that exceed these limits may be carried forward to the following calendar quarter. (Code Sec. 41(h), Code Sec. 3111(f))[23] A QSB is one that, in the case of a corporation or partnership, for any tax year, has gross receipts of less than $5 million, and did not have gross receipts for any tax year preceding the 5-tax-year period ending with the tax year. (Code Sec. 41(h)(3)(A)(i)) Individuals can qualify if they meet the two conditions above, taking into account the aggregate gross receipts received by them in carrying

15. ¶L-15621
16. ¶L-3131.1
17. ¶L-15302.2
18. ¶L-15501 *et seq.*
19. ¶s L-15508, L-15507

20. ¶L-15509
21. ¶L-15202.3
22. ¶L-15528.1 *et seq.*
23. ¶L-15526 *et seq.*

on all their trades or businesses. (Code Sec. 41(h)(3)(A)(ii)) Special aggregation rules apply. An exempt organization can't be a QSB. (Code Sec. 41(h)(3)(B)) The election may be made for no more than five tax years. (Code Sec. 41(h)(4)(B)(ii))

Claims for refund. IRS has listed the information taxpayers must include for a valid Code Sec. 41 research credit claim for refund. (LAFA 20214101F; IR 2021-203 (10/15/2021)) IRS provided a grace period until Jan. 10, 2022 before requiring the inclusion of the required information with timely filed research credit claims for refund. On expiration of the grace period, there is a one-year transition period, during which taxpayers have 45 days to perfect a research credit claim for refund before IRS's final determination on the claim. IRS announced that taxpayers can continue to use the 45-day perfection period until Jan. 10, 2024. (https://www.irs.gov/businesses/corporations/research-credit-claims-section-41-on-amended-returns-frequently-asked-questions (1/24/2022))[24]

¶ 2320   Low-income housing credit for qualified buildings—Forms 8609, 8586.

Under Code Sec. 42, the low-income housing credit is allowed annually over a 10-year credit period beginning with the tax year the qualified building is placed in service, or, under an irrevocable election (on Form 8609), the next tax year. (Code Sec. 42(f)(1)) The credit period for an existing building can't begin before the first tax year of the tax period for rehabilitation expenses for the building. (Code Sec. 42(f)(5)(A))[25]

The credit equals the qualified building's qualified basis times the applicable percentage (see below) (Code Sec. 42(a)) prescribed by IRS for the month placed in service or elected in agreement with the housing credit agency. (Code Sec. 42(b)(2)(A)) The building owner can't claim a credit amount in excess of the allocation received from the state or housing credit agency for that year. (Reg § 1.42-1T(e)(1))[26]

IRS prescribes percentages that will yield, over a 10-year period, credit amounts that will have a present value equal to 70% of the qualified basis of new buildings (not federally subsidized) and 30% of the qualified basis of existing buildings and federally subsidized new buildings, see following table; however, for any new building that is placed in service by the taxpayer after July 30, 2008 and that is not federally subsidized for the tax year, the applicable percentage can't be less than 9%. (Code Sec. 42(b))[27]

Month	Year	70% present value credit	30% present value credit
Nov.	2022	7.91%	3.39%
Oct.	2022	7.78%	3.33%
Sept.	2022	7.70%	3.30%
Aug.	2022	7.75%	3.32%
July	2022	7.72%	3.31%
June	2022	7.70%	3.30%
May	2022	7.60%	3.26%
Apr.	2022	7.47%	3.20%
Mar.	2022	7.44%	3.19%
Feb.	2022	7.38%	3.16%
Jan.	2022	7.36%	3.15%
Dec.	2021	7.36%	3.15%
Nov.	2021	7.34%	3.14%

A credit for rehabilitation expenditures (treated as a separate building (Code Sec. 42(e)(1))) is allowed only if during any 24-month period they are the greater of: 20% of the building's adjusted basis or, for 2023, $7,900 ($7,400 for 2022) per low-income unit. (Code Sec. 42(e)(3)(A)) Under IRS-provided COVID-19-related relief, if a qualified low-income

---

24. ¶T-5601.1   26. ¶L-15702
25. ¶L-15700 *et seq.*   27. ¶L-15718

building's 24-month MRE period originally ended on or after on or after Jan. 1, 2022, and on or before June 30, 2022, the deadline is extended to June 30, 2023. If the original deadline is on or after July 1, 2022, and on or before Dec. 31, 2022, then that deadline is extended to the original date plus 12 months. If the original deadline is on or after Jan. 1, 2023, and on or before Dec. 31, 2023, then that deadline is extended to Dec. 31, 2023. (Notice 2022-52, 2022-43 IRB)[28]

To claim the credit, taxpayers must file Form 8586 for each tax year in the 10-year credit period. (Reg § 1.42-1(h))[29] Form 8609 is filed once with the taxpayer's tax return.[30]

A qualified low-income building is a building that at all times during the "compliance period" of 15 tax years beginning with the first tax year of the credit period, is part of a qualified low-income housing project. (Code Sec. 42(c)(2), Code Sec. 42(g), Code Sec. 42(i)(1)) In addition, no credit is allowed unless an extended low income housing commitment (for an additional 15-year period) between the taxpayer and the housing credit agency is in effect at the end of the tax year. (Code Sec. 42(h)(6))[31]

¶ 2321   Recapture of low-income housing credit—Form 8611.

Under Code Sec. 42(j), if, at the close of any year in the compliance period (¶2320), the building's qualified basis is less than it was at the close of the earlier tax year, the taxpayer's tax for the year is increased (Code Sec. 42(j)(1), Code Sec. 42(j)(4)(B)) by the sum of:

(1) the total decrease in taxpayer's general business credits for all earlier tax years that would have resulted if the accelerated portion of the credit (below) allowable for the earlier tax years wasn't allowed for all earlier tax years for the decrease in qualified basis, plus

(2) an amount of nondeductible interest on (1), above, computed at the rate charged for overpayment of tax, see ¶4837. (Code Sec. 42(j)(2))

The accelerated portion of the credit for the earlier tax years is the excess of the total credit allowed for the earlier tax years over the total credit that would have been allowable for those years if the total credit that would have been allowable for the entire compliance period were allowable ratably over 15 years. (Code Sec. 42(j)(3))[32]

The disposition of a building (or interest in it) won't result in an increase in tax from credit recapture if it's reasonably expected that the building will continue to be operated as a qualified low-income building for the remaining compliance period for that building. The otherwise applicable statute of limitations is extended until three years after IRS is notified (as specified in guidance) of noncompliance with the low-income housing tax credit rules. (Code Sec. 42(j)(6))[33]

¶ 2322   Enhanced oil recovery (EOR) credit.

The EOR credit (Code Sec. 43(a)) for any tax year is 15% of the taxpayer's qualified EOR costs (under Code Sec. 43(c)(1)) for the tax year. (Code Sec. 43(a))[34] The credit is phased out under a formula that's based both on oil prices for the previous calendar year, and on an inflation-adjusted figure. (Code Sec. 43(b)) For 2022, because the reference price for the 2021 calendar year ($65.90) exceeds $28 multiplied by the inflation adjustment factor for the 2022 calendar year ($28 multiplied by 1.8607 = $52.10) by $13.80, the enhanced oil recovery credit for qualified costs paid or incurred in 2022 is phased out completely. For

28. ¶L-15727
29. ¶L-15701 *et seq.*
30. ¶S-3456
31. ¶L-15719 *et seq.*

32. ¶L-16050 *et seq.*
33. ¶L-16050 *et seq.*
34. ¶L-17600 *et seq.*

2021, because the reference price for the 2020 calendar year ($37.07) didn't exceed $28 multiplied by the inflation adjustment factor for the 2020 calendar year ($49.9772), the EOR credit for qualified costs paid or incurred in 2021 was determined without regard to the phase-out for crude oil price increases.[35]

¶ 2323 Disabled access credit (DAC) for eligible small businesses (ESBs)— Form 8826; eligible access expenditures.

An "eligible small business" (ESB) may elect (on Form 8826) to apply against income tax a DAC (Code Sec. 44(a)) of 50% of the amount of "eligible access expenditures" for the tax year that's over $250 and not more than $10,250. (Code Sec. 44(a))[36]

For partnerships and S corporations, the limitation applies at the entity and the individual partner or shareholder levels. (Code Sec. 44(d)(3))[37]

An ESB for any tax year is any person who either: (1) has gross receipts of $1 million or less for the past tax year, net of returns and allowances, or (2) employed 30 or fewer full-time employees (a full-time employee is employed at least 30 hours a week for 20 or more calendar weeks in the tax year) in the past tax year. (Code Sec. 44(b), Code Sec. 44(d)(5))[38]

Eligible access expenditures are amounts paid or incurred so a business can comply with the Americans With Disabilities Act of '90 (ADA, as in effect on Nov. 5, '90). (Code Sec. 44(c)(1)) These expenses include *only* expenses that are necessary to comply with ADA, that are paid or incurred: (1) for the purpose of removing architectural, communication, physical or transportation barriers in connection with any facility first placed in service before Nov. 6, '90, which prevent a business from being accessible to, or usable by, disabled individuals; (2) to provide qualified interpreters or other effective methods of making aurally delivered materials available to hearing impaired individuals; (3) to provide qualified readers, taped texts and other effective methods of making visually delivered materials available to visually impaired individuals; (4) to acquire or modify equipment or devices for disabled individuals; or (5) to provide other similar services, modifications, materials or equipment. (Code Sec. 44(c))[39]

¶ 2324 Credit for producing electricity from renewable resources; Form 8835; Code Sec. 48 election (Form 3468).

Code Sec. 45 provides for a credit for electricity produced from certain renewable resources. The credit (claimed on Form 8835) is available for electricity produced from qualified energy resources, which is produced at a qualified facility during the ten-year period beginning on the date the facility was originally placed in service. The electricity must be sold by the taxpayer to an unrelated person during the tax year. (Code Sec. 45(a)) Qualified energy resources include (1) wind, (2) closed-loop biomass, (3) open-loop biomass, (4) geothermal or solar energy, (5) small irrigation power, (6) municipal solid waste (landfill gas), (7) trash, (8) qualified hydropower production, and (9) marine and hydrokinetic renewables (e.g., waves and tides). (Code Sec. 45(c)) Qualified facility status generally requires construction on a facility to begin before Jan. 1, 2025. (Qualified small irrigation power facilities had to be placed in service before Oct. 3, 2008, but small irrigation power facilities placed in service after that date continue to qualify for the credit as marine and hydrokinetic renewable energy facilities.) (Code Sec. 45(d))[40]

Base credit rate. The base credit rate, for facilities placed in service after Dec. 31, 2021, is 0.3¢ 1.1 per kilowatt hour (KWH) of electricity. (Code Sec. 45(a)(1)) The base credit

---

35. ¶L-17615
36. ¶L-17901
37. ¶L-17905

38. ¶L-17903
39. ¶L-17902 *et seq.*
40. ¶L-17750 *et seq.*

rate is subject to an inflation adjustment. (Code Sec. 45(b)(2))[41] For increase in credit rate for meeting prevailing-wage and other requirements, see below.

For facilities placed in service before 2022, the credit is 1.5¢, as adjusted for inflation, or 2.6¢ per KWH for 2022. For 2021, the rate is 2.5¢ per KWH.[42]

50% reduction for certain facilities. For facilities placed in service before 2023, for electricity produced in qualified facilities discussed at (3), (5), (6), (7), (8), or (9) above, the credit amount is reduced by one-half. For facilities placed in service after 2022, there is no 50% reduction in the credit for facilities in (8) and (9), above. (Code Sec. 45(b)(4)(A)).[43]

Increased credit for meeting prevailing-wage and certain other requirements. For facilities placed in service after 2021, a facility that meets one of the requirements in (i) through (iii) is entitled to an increased credit (i.e., 1.5%, as adjusted for inflation): (i) the facility has a maximum net output of less than 1 megawatt (as measured in alternating current); (ii) the facility's construction begins before the date that is 60 days after IRS publishes guidance on the prevailing wage and apprenticeship requirements; (iii) the facility satisfies the prevailing-wage and apprenticeship requirements. (Code Sec. 45(b)(6))[44]

Increased credit, post-2022, for domestic content requirement, and for location in energy community. For facilities placed in service after Dec. 31, 2022: (1) a domestic content bonus will allow taxpayers to increase their credit if a certain percentage of the steel, iron, or manufactured products that are components of the facility are produced in the U.S.; and (2) the credit will be increased if facilities are located in "energy communities." (Code Sec. 45(b)(9), Code Sec. 45(b)(11))[45]

Phase-out for wind facilities where construction began after 2016. Facilities producing electricity from wind qualify for the credit are subject to a phaseout in certain years. For a facility the construction of which began in 2017, the credit is reduced by 20%; for a facility the construction of which began in 2018, the credit is reduced by 40%; for a facility the construction of which began in 2019, the credit is reduced by 60%; and for a facility, the construction of which began in 2020 or 2021, the credit is reduced by 40%. (Code Sec. 45(b)(5))[46]

Allocation of credit. The credit is allocated to a taxpayer in proportion to his or her ownership interest in the gross sales from the qualifying facility. (Code Sec. 45(e)(3))[47] The safe harbor under which partnership allocations of wind energy production credits are respected (¶3717) does *not* apply to partnership allocations of Code Sec. 48 energy credits.[48]

Phaseout when applicable reference price exceeds threshold. The credit is proportionately phased out when the national average price of electricity produced from the applicable renewable resource exceeds a specified, inflation-adjusted threshold price per KWH. (Code Sec. 45(b)(1)) There is no phaseout for 2022.[49]

Election under Code Sec. 48. Taxpayers can elect to have "qualified property" that's part of certain "qualified investment facilities" treated as energy property eligible for a 30% investment credit under Code Sec. 48 (¶2310). (Code Sec. 48(a)(5), Code Sec. 48(a)(5)(C))

The irrevocable election (on Form 3468) is made on a timely filed return (including extensions) for the tax year in which the facility is placed in service.[50]

Election (post-2022) by certain entities to be treated as paying income tax equal to amount of credit. For tax years beginning after 2022, an "applicable entity" (Code Sec. 6417(d)(1)(A)) can make this election with regard to so much of the Code

41. ¶L-17751
42. ¶L-17761
43. ¶L-17751
44. ¶L-17766 *et seq.*
45. ¶L-17769 *et seq.*
46. ¶L-17771.5
47. ¶L-17755
48. ¶B-2903A
49. ¶L-17760 *et seq.*
50. ¶L-16401.1 *et seq.*

Sec. 45(a) credit as is attributable to qualified facilities originally placed in service after 2022. (Code Sec. 6417(b))[1]

Election (post-2022) by taxpayers that are not "applicable entities" (see above) to transfer the credit to other taxpayers. For tax years beginning after 2022, taxpayers, other than "applicable entities" (above), can make this election with regard to the Code Sec. 45(a) credit. (Code Sec. 6418(a))[2]

¶ 2325 FICA tip credit for food and beverage establishments—Form 8846.

Under Code Sec. 45B, a food and beverage establishment is allowed a credit (on Form 8846) for the amount of the employer's FICA tax obligation (7.65%) attributable to employee tips received for providing, delivering, or serving food or beverages (whether or not the tips are reported as required by Code Sec. 6053). (Code Sec. 45B) However, no credit is given for tips used to meet the federal minimum wage rate. (Code Sec. 45B) Employers determine their Code Sec. 45B credit using the minimum wage in effect on Jan. 1, 2007 (Code Sec. 45B(b)(1)) (i.e., $5.15).[3] No deduction is allowed for any amount taken into account in determining the FICA tip credit. (Code Sec. 45B(c)) A taxpayer can elect out of the credit for any tax year. (Code Sec. 45B(d))[4]

¶ 2326 Qualified clinical testing expense ("orphan drug") credit—Form 8820; drugs for rare diseases.

Under Code Sec. 45C, a taxpayer that incurs qualified clinical testing expenses (QCTEs) for drugs for rare diseases may claim (on Form 8820) a credit equal to 25% of those expenses for the tax year. (Code Sec. 45C)[5] QCTEs are amounts which, with certain modifications, would qualify as qualified research expenses for the research credit (¶2319). (Code Sec. 45C(b)(1))

Deductions (or amounts chargeable to capital account) for QCTEs are reduced by the amount of the allowable orphan drug credit. (Code Sec. 280C(b)(1), Code Sec. 280C(b)(2))

Taxpayers can elect to take a reduced orphan drug credit instead of reducing allowable deductions. (Code Sec. 280C(b)(3))

¶ 2327 New markets tax credit, before 2026—Form 8874; qualified equity investments to acquire stock in a community development entity (CDE).

Before 2026, a "new markets tax credit" (Code Sec. 45D) applies for qualified equity investments to acquire stock in a community development entity (CDE).[6] Nationally, the maximum annual amount of qualifying equity investments is capped at $3.5 billion each calendar year from 2010 through 2019, and at $5 billion for each of tax years 2020 through 2025; but no amount can be carried over to any calendar year after 2030.[7] A CDE is any domestic corporation or partnership (1) whose primary mission is serving or providing investment capital for low-income communities or low-income persons, (2) that maintains accountability to residents of low-income communities through representation on governing or advisory boards of the CDE, and (3) is certified by Treasury as an eligible CDE.[8] A qualified equity investment is stock or a similar equity interest acquired directly from a CDE for cash. Substantially all (at least 85%, reduced to 75% for the final year of the 7-year credit period) of the cash has to be used by the CDE to make investments in, or loans

---

1. ¶L-17980 *et seq.*
2. ¶L-17980 *et seq.*
3. ¶L-17860 *et seq.*
4. ¶L-17860 *et seq.*

5. ¶L-15615 *et seq.*
6. ¶L-17920 *et seq.*
7. ¶L-17927
8. ¶L-17923

337

to, qualified active businesses located in low-income communities or certain financial services to businesses and residents in low-income communities. A qualified equity investment made by an LLC (classified as a partnership) can include cash from a nonrecourse loan or a recourse loan to the LLC that the LLC invests as equity in a qualified CDE, where the loan is indebtedness for federal income tax purposes. (Code Sec. 45D; Reg § 1.45D-1(c)(5))[9]

The new markets tax credit (claimed on Form 8874) is: (a) 5% for the year in which the equity interest is purchased from the CDE and for the first two anniversary dates after the purchase (for a total credit of 15%), *plus* (b) 6% on each anniversary date thereafter for the following four years (for a total of 24%).[10] The credit is recaptured if the entity fails to continue to be a CDE or the interest is redeemed within seven years, unless it is allowed to, and does, correct its failure. (Code Sec. 45D(g); Reg § 1.45D-1(e))[11]

¶ 2328   Employer's credit for employer-provided child care—Form 8882; qualified child care expenses, qualified child care resource and referral expenses.

A tax credit for "employer-provided child care" (Code Sec. 45F(a)) is allowed an employer for the sum of the following expenses (up to $150,000) for the tax year Code Sec. 45F(b)):[12]

(1) *25% of qualified child care expenses,* which are expenses to buy, build, rehabilitate, or expand property to be used as part of an employer's qualified child care facility, for which a deduction for depreciation (or amortization) is allowable, and which isn't part of the taxpayer's (or an employee's) principal residence. Qualifying child care expenses also include operating costs of a taxpayer's qualified child care facility (including costs related to employee training, scholarship programs, and to providing increased compensation to employees with higher levels of child care training), and amounts paid under a contract with a qualified child care facility to provide child care services to the taxpayer's employees. (Code Sec. 45F(c)(1)(A)) Qualified child care expenses don't include expenses in excess of the FMV of the care; *and* (Code Sec. 45F(c)(1)(B))

(2) *10% of qualified child care resource and referral expenses* (i.e., amounts paid or incurred under a contract to provide child care resource and referral services to an employee).[13]

Generally, a qualified child care facility is one principally used to provide child care assistance, and which meets the requirements of the state or local government in which it is located, including its licensing as a child care facility. (Code Sec. 45F(c)(2)(A)) The facility must be open to the taxpayer's employees during the tax year, and, if it is the taxpayer's principal trade or business, at least 30% of its enrollees must be the dependents of the taxpayer's employees.[14]

The provision of child care resource and referral services or facilities can't discriminate in favor of highly compensated employees (within the meaning of Code Sec. 414(q)) (see ¶4315). (Code Sec. 45F(c)(2)(B), Code Sec. 45F(c)(3))[15]

A taxpayer claiming a Code Sec. 45F credit for acquiring, constructing, rehabilitating, or expanding a qualified child care facility must reduce its basis in the facility by the amount of the credit. (Code Sec. 45F(f)(1)(A))[16] No deduction or credit is allowed for any amount taken into account in determining Code Sec. 45F credit. (Code Sec. 45F(f)(2))[17]

---

9. ¶L-17924
10. ¶L-17922
11. ¶L-17928
12. ¶L-17871; ¶L-17872
13. ¶L-17870 *et seq.*

14. ¶L-17874
15. ¶L-17875
16. ¶L-17876
17. ¶L-17877

338

Recapture rules apply for the first 10 years after the facility is placed in service. (Code Sec. 45F(d))[18]

For the credit, all persons treated as one employer under Code Sec. 52(a) or Code Sec. 52(b) are treated as one taxpayer.[19] Regs are to address credit allocations between an estate or trust and its beneficiaries, and among partners of a partnership. (Code Sec. 45F(e))[20]

¶ 2329 Small employer pension plan startup credit—Form 8881; eligible small employers, qualified startup costs.

Under Code Sec. 45E, eligible small employers that adopt a new qualified defined benefit or defined contribution plan (e.g., pension plan, Code Sec. 401(k) plan, SIMPLE plan, SEP) may claim a credit. (Code Sec. 45E) The credit equals 50% of "qualified startup costs" in each of the first three plan years, subject to a dollar limit. The dollar limit is generally $250 per employee per year, but no less than $500 and no more than $5,000. Before 2020, the dollar limit was $500 for the first credit year and for each of the two following tax years. (Code Sec. 45E(a), Code Sec. 45E(b), Code Sec. 45E(d)(3))[21]

The pension plan startup credit is available only to an employer that employs 100 or fewer employees who received at least $5,000 of "compensation" from the employer for the preceding year. But, an employer isn't an eligible employer if, during the 3-tax-year period immediately before the first tax year for which the credit is otherwise allowable, it or any member of any controlled group including the employer (or any predecessor of either) established or maintained a qualified employer plan to which contributions were made, or benefits were accrued, for substantially the same employees that are in the qualified employer plan. (Code Sec. 45E(c))[22] For Code Sec. 45E, all persons treated as a single employer under Code Sec. 52(a) or Code Sec. 52(b) or Code Sec. 414(m) or Code Sec. 414(o) are treated as one taxpayer. (Code Sec. 45E(e)(1))[23] To be eligible for the credit, the plan must cover at least one nonhighly compensated employee. (Code Sec. 45E(d)(1)) If the credit is for the cost of a payroll-deduction IRA plan, it must be made available to all employees who have worked with the employer for at least three months.[24]

No deduction is allowed for that portion of the qualified startup costs paid or incurred for the tax year that are equal to the credit. (Code Sec. 45E(e)(2))[25] An eligible employer may elect not to have the credit apply for any tax year. (Code Sec. 45E(e)(3))[26]

¶ 2330 Small employer health insurance credit—Form 8941; Form 990-T; eligible small employer.

Under Code Sec. 45R, an eligible small employer (ESE) may claim, subject to a phaseout, a credit equal to 50% of nonelective contributions for health insurance for its employees. (Code Sec. 45R) The credit is allowed for the "credit period" —the 2-consecutive-tax-year period beginning with the first tax year for which the ESE files an income tax return with an attached Form 8941. (Code Sec. 45R(e)(2), Reg § 1.45R-1(a)(3)) The credit reduces the ESE's Code Sec. 162 deduction. (Code Sec. 45R(e)(5))[27]

Eligible employers. An ESE is generally an employer that: (1) has no more than 25 full-time equivalent employees (FTEs) employed during its tax year; (2) has employees who have average annual wages of no more than an indexed dollar amount ($57,400 for 2022; $61,400 for 2023); and (3) has in effect a qualifying arrangement in which the employer

18. ¶L-17878
19. ¶L-17879
20. ¶L-17879.1
21. ¶L-15690 *et seq.*
22. ¶L-15691

23. ¶L-15694
24. ¶L-15692
25. ¶L-15693.1
26. ¶L-15691
27. ¶L-15681, ¶L-15689.11

has to contribute at least 50% of the premiums. (Code Sec. 45R(d)(1), Reg § 1.45R-2(a))[28]

The FTEs of an ESE are determined by dividing (a) the total hours of service (up to 2,080 hours, determined using either an employee's actual hours of service, a days-worked equivalency method, or a weeks-worked equivalency method) by (b) 2,080. (Code Sec. 45R(d), Reg § 1.45R-2(a))[29] The average annual wages of an ESE for any tax year is the amount determined by dividing the aggregate amount of wages that were paid by the ESE to employees during the tax year by the number of the ESE's FTEs and rounding that amount to the next lowest multiple of $1,000. (Code Sec. 45R(d)(3))[30]

Regarding self-employed individuals, including partners and sole proprietors, 2% S corporation shareholders, and 5% owners of the employer (within the meaning of Code Sec. 416(i)(1)(B)(i)): (1) they aren't treated as employees; (2) their wages or hours are not counted in determining either the number of FTEs or the amount of average annual wages; and (3) premiums paid on their behalf are not counted in determining the credit. (Code Sec. 45R(e)) Similarly, an employee-spouse of any of the following isn't taken into account: (1) a more-than-2% S shareholder; (2) a more-than-5% owner of a business; (3) a partner owning more than a 5% interest in a partnership; and (4) a sole proprietor.[31]

Credit amount. The credit equals 50% (35% for a tax-exempt ESE, see below) of the lesser of:

(1) the aggregate amount of nonelective contributions (i.e., an employer contribution other than one under a Code Sec. 125 salary reduction arrangement) the ESE made on behalf of its employees during the tax year under a contribution arrangement for premiums for qualified health plans offered by the employer to its employees through a Small Business Health Options Program (SHOP) exchange; (Code Sec. 45R(b)(1)) or

(2) the aggregate amount of nonelective contributions which the ESE would have paid if each employee were enrolled in a plan with a premium equal to the average premium for the small group market in the state (or in an area in the state) in which the employer is offering health insurance coverage. (Code Sec. 45R(b)(2))[32]

The above credit amount is reduced for an ESE if: (i) it has more than 10 FTEs; or (ii) the average annual full-time equivalent wages per employee are more than $28,700 for 2022 ($30,700 for 2023). The otherwise applicable credit is reduced (but not below zero) by the sum of: (1) that credit amount multiplied by a fraction, the numerator of which is the total number of the employer's FTEs in excess of 10, and the denominator of which is 15; and (2) the credit amount multiplied by a fraction, the numerator of which is the average annual wages in excess of $28,700 for 2022 ($30,700 for 2023) and the denominator of which is $28,700 for 2022 ($30,700 for 2023). (Code Sec. 45R(c)(1), Code Sec. 45R(c)(2))[33]

❖ observation: The phaseout of the credit amount under Code Sec. 45R(c) operates in such a way that an employer with exactly 25 FTEs, or with average annual wages exactly equal to twice the inflation-adjusted wage amount, is not eligible for the credit.

Qualifying arrangement. A ESE must generally make premium payments on behalf of its employees for qualified health plans offered by the employer to its employees through a SHOP Exchange. (Code Sec. 45R(d)(4), Reg § 1.45R-2(a), Reg § 1.45R-1(a)(15)) Employer contributions to, or amounts made available under, a health reimbursement arrangement (HRA), health flexible spending arrangement (health FSA), or a health savings account (HSA) are not taken into account in determining the premium payments by the employer for a tax year. (Reg § 1.45R-3(g)(2)(ii))[34]

---

28. ¶L-15682
29. ¶L-15682 *et seq.*
30. ¶L-15689
31. ¶L-15688

32. ¶L-15689.7
33. ¶L-15689.2
34. ¶L-15689.4A; ¶L-15689.5M

Tax-exempt ESEs. The applicable percentage for an eligible small tax-exempt employer (tax-exempt ESE) is 35%. For tax-exempt ESEs, the credit is a refundable tax credit (claimed on Form 990-T) limited to the amount of the employer's payroll taxes (income tax and Medicare tax withheld from employees' wages and the employer share of Medicare tax on employees' wages) during the calendar year in which the tax year begins. (Code Sec. 45R(b); Code Sec. 45R(f), Reg § 1.45R-3(e))[35]

observation: Employers can deduct employee health insurance expenses not qualifying for the small employer health insurance credit as ordinary and necessary business expenses for employee compensation.

¶ 2331 Differential wage payment credit—Form 8932; employees called to active duty; members of the armed services.

Under Code Sec. 45P, employers that pay differential wages (i.e., payments for periods that employees are called to active duty with the U.S. uniformed services, see ¶3005) to a qualified employee can claim a credit (on Form 8932) equal to 20% of up to $20,000 of differential pay made to a qualified employee during the tax year. (Code Sec. 45P) A qualified employee is one who was an employee for the 91-day period immediately before the period for which any differential wage payment was made. (Code Sec. 45P(b)(2))[36]

The credit can't be claimed by a taxpayer that has failed to comply with the employment and reemployment rights of members of the armed services (as provided under Chapter 43 of Title 38 of the United States Code). (Code Sec. 45P(d)) No deduction can be taken for that part of compensation that equals the credit, and the amount of any otherwise allowable income tax credit for compensation paid to an employee must be reduced by the differential wage payment credit allowed for the employee. (Code Sec. 280C(a), Code Sec. 45P(c))[37]

¶ 2332 Employer-paid family and medical leave credit—wages paid before 2026—Form 8994.

For wages paid in tax years beginning after 2017 and before 2026, under Code Sec. 45S, a general business credit may be claimed (on Form 8994) equal to 12.5% of the amount of wages paid to qualifying employees during any period in which the employees are on family and medical leave if the rate of payment is at least 50% of the wages normally paid to an employee, up to a maximum of 12 weeks of leave for any employee for the tax year. (Code Sec. 45S(b)(3)) The credit is increased by 0.25 percentage points (but not above 25%) for each percentage point by which the rate of payment exceeds 50%.[38]

To qualify for the credit, an employer must have a written policy containing certain requirements, and all "qualifying" full-time employees must be given at least two weeks of annual paid family and medical leave (all less-than-full-time qualifying employees must be given a commensurate amount of leave on a pro rata basis). (Code Sec. 45S) A qualifying employee must have been employed by the employer for one year or more, and, for the preceding year, had compensation not in excess of an amount equal to 60% of the "highly compensated employee" threshold under Code Sec. 414(q)(1)(B)(i) (see ¶4315). A taxpayer can't take both a credit and a deduction for amounts for which the paid family and medical leave credit is claimed. (Code Sec. 280C(a))[39]

---

35. ¶L-15689.14 *et seq.*
36. ¶L-15675 *et seq.*
37. ¶L-15678.2, ¶L-15678

38. ¶L-17881.1
39. ¶L-17880 *et seq.*

¶ 2333   Small employer pension plan auto-enrollment credit; eligible automatic contribution arrangements (EACAs).

Under Code Sec. 45T, an "eligible employer" (Code Sec. 45T(c)) can claim a general business credit of $500 for any tax year in the credit period (generally 3 tax years, beginning with the first tax year for which the employer includes an eligible automatic contribution arrangement (EACA) in its qualified employer plan). The credit is in addition to the small employer pension plan start-up credit (¶2329). (Code Sec. 45T(a))[40]

¶ 2334   Qualified commercial clean vehicle credit—after 2022.

Under Code Sec. 45W(a), added by the Inflation Reduction Act of 2022 (P.L. 117-169, 8/16/2022), a credit for qualified commercial clean vehicles will be available for vehicles acquired and placed in service after Dec. 31, 2022, and before 2033. The credit is a component of the Code Sec. 38 general business credit. (Code Sec. 45W(a); Code Sec. 45W(g))[41]

Credit amount. The credit per vehicle will be the lesser of: (1) 15% of the vehicle's basis (30% for a vehicle not powered by a gasoline or diesel engine), or (2) the "incremental cost" of the vehicle over the cost of a comparable vehicle in size and use powered solely by a gasoline or diesel engine. The maximum credit per vehicle will $7,500 for vehicles with gross vehicle weight ratings of less than 14,000 pounds, or $40,000 for other vehicles. (Code Sec. 45W(b))[42]

Qualified commercial clean vehicle. A qualified commercial clean vehicle must be acquired for use or lease by the taxpayer, and not for resale. It must be manufactured for use on public streets, roads, and highways, or be "mobile machinery" as defined in Code Sec. 4053(8) (vehicles with construction, manufacturing, farming, mining, etc. machinery or equipment permanently attached). The vehicle must be propelled to a significant extent by an electric motor powered by a battery with a capacity of not less than 15 kilowatt hours (7 kilowatt hours for vehicles with gross vehicle weight ratings less than 14,000 pounds) capable of being recharged by an external electricity source. Qualified commercial fuel cell vehicles will also be eligible for the credit. Qualifying vehicles must be depreciable property. Only vehicles made by qualified manufacturers that have written agreements with IRS, and provide periodic reports to IRS, can qualify. (Code Sec. 45W(c))[43]

Technical requirements. Special rules will apply to vehicles placed in service by tax-exempt entities. This credit will not be allowed if a credit was allowed under Code Sec. 30D (¶2354), the general clean vehicle credit. (Code Sec. 45W(d)) A vehicle identification number (VIN) will be required on returns claiming the credit. (Code Sec. 45W(d))[44]

IRS regs. IRS will issue regs or other guidance deemed necessary to carry out Code Sec. 45W, including determination of the incremental cost of a qualified commercial clean vehicle. (Code Sec. 45W(f))[45]

Election (post-2022) by certain entities to be treated as paying income tax equal to amount of credit. For tax years beginning after 2022, a tax-exempt entity described in Code Sec. 168(h)(2)(A)(i), Code Sec. 168(h)(2)(A)(ii), or Code Sec. 168(h)(2)(A)(iv), can make this election for qualified commercial vehicles determined under Code Sec. 45W by reason of Code Sec. 45W(d)(3). (Code Sec. 6417(b))[46]

40. ¶L-15695 *et seq.*
41. ¶L-18035 *et seq.*
42. ¶L-18037
43. ¶L-18038

44. ¶L-18038
45. ¶L-18036
46. ¶L-17980 *et seq.*

¶ 2335   Qualified advanced production credit—after 2022.

For components produced and sold after Dec. 31, 2022, Code Sec. 45X provides, as one of the credits that makes up the Code Sec. 38 general business credit, the advanced manufacturing production credit (the AMPC). (Code Sec. 45X(a)(1))[47]

Credit amount generally. This amount is equal to the sum of the credit amounts determined (see **Credit amount—specific computations** below) for each eligible component (see below), that is produced by the taxpayer and, during the tax year, sold by the taxpayer to an unrelated person. (Code Sec. 45X(a)(1)) The production and sale must be in a trade or business of the taxpayer (Code Sec. 45X(a)(2)) and sales are included only if they are sales of eligible components produced in the U.S. or its possessions. (Code Sec. 45X(d)(2))[48]

Related persons. Persons are treated as related if they would be treated as a single employer under Code Sec. 52(b). (Code Sec. 45X(d)(1)) But a taxpayer can elect not to apply the unrelated person requirement if beforehand the taxpayer provides, to the extent required by IRS, any information and registration necessary to prevent duplication, fraud, or an improper or excessive amount of credit. (Code Sec. 45X(a)(3)(B))[49]

Eligible components. Eligible components include: (1) solar energy components, (2) wind energy components, (3) inverters (products used to convert certain solar and wind energy from direct current to alternating current), (4) qualifying battery components, and (5) applicable critical minerals (certain minerals that are processed by the taxpayer). (Code Sec. 45X(c)(1)(A)) Eligible components do not include any property produced in a facility if the basis of any property that is part of the facility is taken account of for purposes of the credit allowed under Code Sec. 48C (the advanced energy project credit) after August 16, 2022. (Code Sec. 45X(c)(1)(B)) Detailed definitions of the types, and often subtypes, of eligible components are provided. (Code Sec. 45X(c)(2) through Code Sec. 45X(c)(6))[50]

Credit amount—specific computations. The formulas that determine how much credit is earned for each sale of a unit of an eligible component are not the same for all five types of eligible components and different formulas can apply to different subtypes. (Code Sec. 45X(b)(1)) For example, the credit amount for solar grade polysilicon, a type of solar energy component, is $3 per kilogram while the credit amount for a polymeric backsheet, another type of solar component, is 40 cents per square meter. (Code Sec. 45X(b)(1)(C); Code Sec. 45X(b)(1)(D))[1]

Election (post-2022) to be treated as paying income tax equal to amount of credit. For tax years beginning after 2022, a taxpayer can make this election with regard to the Code Sec. 45X credit. (Code Sec. 6417(b)(7); Code Sec. 6417(d)(1)(D))[2]

Election (post-2022) to transfer the credit to unrelated taxpayers. For tax years beginning after 2022, most taxpayers can make this election with regard to the Code Sec. 45X credit. (Code Sec. 6418(a); Code Sec. 6418(f)(1)(A)(vi)); Code Sec. 6418(f)(2))[3]

¶ 2336   Personal (Refundable and Nonrefundable) Credits. ■■■■■■■■■■■■

Taxpayers, whether or not in business, may qualify for one or more personal credits. Some credits are refundable—i.e., the excess of the credit over tax liability is refunded to the taxpayer—others are partly refundable, and some are nonrefundable.

---

47. ¶L-17520 *et seq.*
48. ¶L-17521
49. ¶L-17521
50. ¶L-17521

1. ¶L-17522 *et seq.*
2. ¶L-17980 *et seq.*
3. ¶L-17990 *et seq.*

The *refundable* credits are the:

. . . Earned income tax credit (EITC), see ¶2337 *et seq.*;

. . . Pre-2033 new energy-efficient home credit for eligible contractors, see ¶2342;

. . . Premium tax credit (PTC) for health insurance purchased on Exchange, see ¶2343;

. . . Credit for income tax withheld, see ¶2344;

. . . Credit for excess social security tax withheld, see ¶2345;

. . . Credit for child and dependent care expenses, see ¶2347;

. . . Child tax credit (CTC), partly refundable, see ¶2350;

. . . American opportunity tax credit (AOTC), partly refundable, see ¶2202;

. . . Credit for capital gain tax paid by a regulated investment company (RIC), see ¶4201; and

. . . Credit for excise tax on certain nontaxable uses of fuels (see Code Sec. 6420, Code Sec. 6421, Code Sec. 6427).

The *nonrefundable* credits are the:

• Credit for the elderly and disabled, see ¶2346;

• Credit for child and dependent care expenses, nonrefundable for years other than 2021, see ¶2347;

• Credit for adoption expenses, see ¶2348;

• CTC (but see above), see ¶2349 *et seq.*;

• Credit for certain mortgage interest under qualified MCC program, see ¶2351;

• AOTC credit (but see above for partial refundability) and Lifetime Learning Credit (LLC), see ¶2201 *et seq.*;

• Pre-2023 nonbusiness energy property credit/post-2022 energy efficient home improvement credit, see ¶2352;

• Pre-2035 residential clean energy credit, formerly known as the residential energy efficient property (REEP) credit, see ¶2353;

• Vehicle credits: qualified plug-in electric drive motor vehicle (Form 8936), (new) clean vehicle credit (vehicles placed in service post-2022), pre-2022 two-wheeled plug-in electric (Form 8834) credits; see ¶2354; post-2022 previously owned clean vehicle credit, see ¶2355;

• "Saver's" credit for elective deferrals and IRA contributions, see ¶2356;

• Minimum tax credit (MTC) for alternative minimum tax (AMT), see ¶2358; and

• Credit for qualified tax credit bonds (QTCBs) issued before 2018, see ¶2359.

For the limit on the combined amount of certain personal nonrefundable credits, see ¶2357.

For the treatment of a refund or advance payment of a refundable credit, see ¶4841.

¶ 2337   Earned income tax credit (EITC)—overview; Schedule EIC.

Under Code Sec. 32, an eligible individual (¶2339) is allowed an EITC equal to the credit percentage of earned income (up to an "earned income amount") for the tax year. (Code Sec. 32(a)(1)) The EITC for a tax year (determined under IRS tables) can't be more than the excess (if any) of (1) the credit percentage of the earned income amount, over (2) the phaseout percentage of AGI (or earned income, if greater) over a phaseout amount. (Code Sec. 32(a)(2)) The tables below show the 2022 and 2023 amounts for the credit percentage, earned income amount, phaseout percentage, and phaseout amounts. Also, note that the phaseout amounts in both tables below are for filers *other than* joint returns.[4]

FOR 2022

Qualifying Children:	The Credit % is:	The Earned Income Amount is:	The Phaseout % is:	The Phaseout Amount is:
No qualifying children	7.65%	$7,320	7.65%	$9,160
1 qualifying child	34%	$10,980	15.98%	$20,130
2 qualifying children	40%	$15,410	21.06%	$20,130
3 or more qualifying children	45%	$15,410	21.06%	$20,130

The 2022 phaseout amounts for joint filers are $15,290 for no qualifying children, and $26,260 for one or more qualifying children.[5]

The EITC for 2022 is completely phased out at the following amounts of earned income (or AGI, if greater):

... no qualifying children, $16,480 ($22,610 for joint filers),

... one qualifying child, $43,492 ($49,622 for joint filers),

... two qualifying children, $49,399 ($55,529 for joint filers), and

... three or more qualifying children, $53,057 ($59,187 for joint filers).[6]

The maximum EITC for 2022 is $560 (no qualifying children), $3,733 (one qualifying child), $6,164 (two qualifying children), and $6,935 (three or more qualifying children).[7]

FOR 2023

Qualifying Children:	The Credit % is:	The Earned Income Amount is:	The Phaseout % is:	The Phaseout Amount is:
No qualifying children	7.65%	$7,840	15.3%	$9,800
1 qualifying child	34%	$11,750	15.98%	$21,560
2 qualifying children	40%	$16,510	21.06%	$21,560
3 or more qualifying children	45%	$16,510	21.06%	$21,560

The 2023 phaseout amounts for joint filers are $16,370 for no qualifying children, and $28,120 for one or more qualifying children.[8] The EITC for 2023 is completely phased out at the following amounts of earned income (or AGI, if greater):

... no qualifying children, $17,640 ($24,210 for joint filers),

... one qualifying child, $46,560 ($53,120 for joint filers),

... two qualifying children, $52,918 ($59,478 for joint filers), and

... three or more qualifying children, $56,838 ($63,398 for joint filers).[9]

The maximum EITC for 2023 is $600 (no qualifying children), $3,995 (one qualifying

4. ¶A-4201 *et seq.*
5. ¶A-4202
6. ¶A-4202
7. ¶A-4201
8. ¶A-4202
9. ¶A-4202

child), $6,604 (two qualifying children), and $7,430 (three or more qualifying children).[10]

To claim the credit, taxpayers generally must file Schedule EIC with Form 1040.[11]

No EITC is allowed if the taxpayer has excess disqualified income, see ¶2340.

The EITC is refundable.[12]

No EITC is allowed for 10 years after a year in which the credit was claimed fraudulently (2 years for erroneously claimed credit due to reckless or intentional disregard of the rules). If the EITC is denied under deficiency procedures, including administrative procedures (but not mathematical or clerical errors), no credit is allowed for any later tax year unless the taxpayer provides information IRS requires to demonstrate eligibility (Code Sec. 32(k); Reg § 1.32-3(b)) (use Form 8862). (Reg § 1.32-3(c))[13] For due diligence requirements for return preparers, see ¶4871.

¶ 2338 Earned income defined for earned income tax credit (EITC).

Under Code Sec. 32(c)(2)(A), earned income for the EITC (¶2337) includes wages, salaries, tips, and other employee compensation, but only if those amounts are includible in gross income for the tax year; plus net earnings from self-employment less the Code Sec. 164(f) deduction for half of self-employment tax (¶1746), for the year. (Code Sec. 32(c)(2)(A)) Nontaxable pay (e.g. dependent care benefits and adoption benefits) isn't earned income. (Information Release 2022-46, 3/2/2022) Taxpayers may elect to treat nontaxable combat pay (¶1223) as earned income. (Code Sec. 32(c)(2)(B)(vi))[14]

Earned income is reduced by any net loss in earnings from self-employment (Reg § 1.32-2(c)(2)) and *doesn't* include any amount received as a pension or an annuity (including social security or VA benefits), any amount subject to the 30% withholding tax on a nonresident alien individual's U.S. income (not connected with U.S. business) (Code Sec. 32(c)(2)(B)), unemployment or worker's compensation (Reg § 1.32-2(c)(2)), amounts earned while an inmate in a penal institution, or amounts received for "workfare" services to the extent subsidized by a state program. (Code Sec. 32(c)(2)(B)(iv)) Earned income is determined without regard to community property laws. (Code Sec. 32(c)(2))[15]

¶ 2339 Eligible individual defined for earned income tax credit (EITC); qualifying child.

Under Code Sec. 32(c)(1)(A)(i), an individual who has a "qualifying child" (¶2341) for the tax year is an eligible individual for the EITC (¶2337). (Code Sec. 32(c)(1)(A)(i))

For tax years beginning in years other than 2021 (when special rules applied), an individual who doesn't have a qualifying child for the tax year is an eligible individual *if*:

. . . the individual's principal place of abode is in the U.S. for more than half the tax year (U.S. Armed Forces personnel are considered to have a U.S. abode while stationed outside the U.S. on extended active duty, Code Sec. 32(c)(4)),

. . . the individual or spouse (if any) is older than 24 but younger than 65 before the tax year end, *and*

. . . the individual can't be claimed as another's dependent for a tax year beginning in the same calendar year as the individual's tax year. (Code Sec. 32(c)(1)(A)(ii))[16]

An individual can't be an eligible individual for a tax year if the individual: is another's qualifying child (¶2341) (Code Sec. 32(c)(1)(B)); elects to exclude foreign earned income

---

10. ¶A-4201
11. ¶A-4201
12. ¶A-4201
13. ¶A-4206 *et seq.*

14. ¶A-4222 *et seq.*
15. ¶A-4222 *et seq.*
16. ¶A-4209, A-4217

(¶4605) (Code Sec. 32(c)(1)(C)); or is a nonresident alien (unless they elect under Code Sec. 6013(g) or Code Sec. 6013(h) to be treated as a U.S. resident). (Code Sec. 32(c)(1)(D))[17]

Married individuals are eligible for only one EITC on their combined earned income and must file a joint return to claim the credit. (Code Sec. 32(d)) Certain married individuals who are separated and meet other requirements need not file jointly to claim the EITC. (Code Sec. 32(d); IR 2022-46, 3/20/2022, Q&A 12) IRS won't follow a Tax Court decision which, contrary to the Code, allowed the credit to a married taxpayer filing separately.[18]

Except for short-period returns due to an individual's death, only individuals filing a return for a full 12-month year can claim the credit. (Code Sec. 32(e))[19]

No EITC is allowed to an eligible individual who doesn't include the individual's taxpayer identification number (TIN—social security number, not an individual taxpayer identification number (ITIN) or adoption taxpayer identification number (ATIN)) and, if married, the TIN of the individual's spouse on the return. And a qualifying child (¶2341) isn't taken into account in computing the EITC unless the taxpayer includes the name, age, and TIN of each qualifying child on the return. However, if an otherwise eligible individual has qualifying children, but cannot provide proper identification for them, then the individual can still claim the EITC that applies for individuals that have no qualifying children. (Code Sec. 32(m), Code Sec. 32(c)(1)(E), Code Sec. 32(c)(3)(D))[20]

¶ 2340   No earned income tax credit (EITC) for individuals with investment income ("disqualified income") over $10,300 for 2022 ($11,000 for 2023).

Code Sec. 32(i)(1) provides that a taxpayer with "disqualified income" over $11,000 for 2023 ($10,300 for 2022), can't claim the EITC. (¶2337). (Code Sec. 32(i)(1))[21]

Disqualified income means:

(1) interest or dividends to the extent includible in gross income for the year (Code Sec. 32(i)(2)(A));

(2) tax-exempt interest (as defined for return disclosure) received or accrued in the year (Code Sec. 32(i)(2)(B));

(3) the excess (if any) of (a) gross income from nonbusiness rents or royalties, over (b) the sum of noninterest deductions clearly and directly allocable to that gross income plus properly allocable interest deductions (Code Sec. 32(i)(2)(C));

(4) capital gain net income for the year (but not gain treated as long-term capital gain under Code Sec. 1231(a)(1), ¶2666) (Code Sec. 32(i)(2)(D)); and

(5) the excess, if any, of total income from all passive activities for the year (without regard to amounts otherwise included in earned income, or other disqualified income) over total losses from all passive activities for the year (as so determined). (Code Sec. 32(i)(2)(E))[22]

¶ 2341   Qualifying child defined for earned income tax credit (EITC).

Code Sec. 32(c)(3)(A) provides that a "qualifying child" for the EITC (¶2337) means a qualifying child of the taxpayer, as defined for the dependency exemption in Code Sec. 152(c) (¶3114) but without the requirement that the child not have provided more than half of the child's own support, and without regard to a custodial parent's release of the dependency exemption (¶3120). (Code Sec. 32(c)(3)(A))[23]

---

17. ¶A-4209
18. ¶A-4221
19. ¶A-4209
20. ¶A-4219

21. ¶A-4204
22. ¶A-4205
23. ¶A-4210 *et seq.*

347

¶ 2342   Pre-2033 new energy-efficient home credit for eligible contractors—Form 8908; manufactured homes.

Under Code Sec. 45L, for homes acquired before 2033, eligible contractors that construct new energy-efficient homes meeting certain requirements can qualify for a credit (claimed on Form 8908). For homes acquired in 2022, the credit is $2,000 for a "50% home" or a "50% manufactured home," or $1,000 for certain manufactured homes. For homes acquired after 2022, under changes made by the Inflation Reduction Act of 2022 (P.L. 117-169, 8/16/20220), the credit will be $500, $1,000, $2,500, or $5,000, depending on which energy-efficiency requirements (as revised by the Act) the home satisfies, and whether the construction of the home meets prevailing wage requirements set forth in Code Sec. 45L(g). (Code Sec. 45L(a), Code Sec. 45L(g))[24]

A property's basis is reduced by the amount of credit. However, for homes acquired after 2022, the basis reduction won't apply in determining the adjusted basis of any property under Code Sec. 42 (the low-income housing credit, ¶2320). (Code Sec. 45L(e))[25]

¶ 2343   Premium tax credit (PTC) for health insurance purchased on Health Benefit Exchange; Form 8962.

Under Code Sec. 36B, a refundable PTC is available on a sliding-scale basis for individuals and families with household income of at least 100% (and, for years after 2025, no more than 400%) of the federal poverty line (FPL) who are enrolled in an Exchange-purchased qualified health plan (QHP), and who aren't eligible for other qualifying coverage or "affordable" employer-sponsored health insurance plans providing "minimum value." (Code Sec. 36B(a); Code Sec. 36B(c)(1); Reg § 1.36B-1(k))[26]

The PTC equals the lesser of (1) the premiums for the plan or plans in which the taxpayer or one or more members of the taxpayer's family enroll, or (2) the excess of the premiums for the applicable second lowest cost "silver plan" (the applicable "benchmark plan") covering the taxpayer's family offered by the Exchange, *over* the taxpayer's contribution amount (required share). The taxpayer's required share equals the taxpayer's household income multiplied by an "applicable percentage" for the tax year.

The applicable percentage for a tax year is based on the taxpayer's income level relative to the FPL for the year, and is subject to inflation adjustments and a failsafe provision.

Table of applicable percentages for 2021 – 2025. A temporary table of applicable percentages, with no inflation adjustment, applies from 2021 through 2025, (as extended by the Inflation Reduction Act of 2022 (P.L. 117-169, 8/16/2022)). The percentages in this table are lower than those that would otherwise have applied, resulting in a smaller required share and a greater PTC. The temporary table includes a tier for taxpayers with household income of 400% of FPL or higher, because those taxpayers are eligible for the PTC in 2021 through 2025. (Code Sec. 36B(b)(2), Code Sec. 36B(b)(3)(A)(iii)(II))[27]

Eligibility for the credit is based on the FPL for the preceding year, so eligibility for a 2022 credit is determined based on 2021 household income and FPL guidelines, e.g., for the 48 contiguous states and Washington, D.C., household income of $12,880 for one individual; $17,420 for a family of two; and $26,500 for a family of four. The 2023 credit is determined based on 2022 household income and FPL guidelines, e.g., for the 48 contiguous states and Washington, D.C., household income of $13,590 for one individual; $18,310 for a family of two; and $27,750 for a family of four.

---

24. ¶L-17941; ¶L-17949; ¶L-17947
25. ¶L-17949.14

26. ¶A-4240 *et seq.*
27. ¶A-4243.5 *et seq.*; ¶A-4245

For the PTC to apply, taxpayers who are married must file jointly. An exception to the joint-filing rule applies for taxpayers who are victims of domestic violence or spousal abandonment and who file married filing separately. (Reg § 1.36B-2(b)(2))

The PTC doesn't apply to an individual for whom a dependency deduction is allowable to another taxpayer for a tax year beginning in the calendar year in which the individual's tax year begins. (Code Sec. 36B(c)(1)(D))[28]

Household income is an individual's modified adjusted gross income (MAGI) plus the aggregate MAGIs of all other individuals who: (a) are counted in determining the taxpayer's family size (i.e., taxpayer, spouse, and dependents); and (b) are required to file an income tax return for the tax year. MAGI doesn't include Supplemental Security Income (SSI) (Code Sec. 36B(d)(2); Reg § 1.36B-1(e)(1)), but does include all social security benefits received during the tax year, even if a Code Sec. 86(e) election is made to treat a portion as received in an earlier year. (IR 2022-44, 2/24/2022, Fact Sheet 2022-13, Q&A 42 (Feb. 2022)[29]

An employee who is provided a "qualified small employer health reimbursement arrangement" (QSEHRA, or small employer HRA, as defined in Code Sec. 9831(d)(2)) that qualifies as "affordable coverage" for any given coverage month isn't eligible for a PTC for that month. (Code Sec. 36B(c)(4)(A)) But, if the QSEHRA doesn't constitute affordable coverage, the employee is eligible for a PTC for a coverage month, although the PTC is reduced under Code Sec. 36B(c)(4)(C).[30]

An eligible employer-sponsored plan is "affordable" for an *employee* if the portion of the annual premium the employee must pay for self-only coverage doesn't exceed 9.61% of the taxpayer's household income for the 2022 plan year (9.12% for the 2023 plan year). An eligible employer-sponsored plan is affordable for a *related individual* (any individual eligible to enroll in the plan because of his or her relationship to the employee) if the portion of the annual premium the employee must pay for family coverage under the plan doesn't exceed the percentages just mentioned of the taxpayer's household income for the tax year. (Code Sec. 36B(c)(2)(C); Reg § 1.36B-2(c)(3)(v))[31]

Employers must provide employees with a summary of benefits and coverage that indicates whether the plan provides minimum value.[32]

The PTC is generally payable in advance directly to the insurer, with the taxpayer reconciling, on a timely filed return, the actual credit due to the taxpayer. Or, individuals can elect to purchase health insurance out-of-pocket and apply to IRS for the credit at the end of the tax year. Either way, an individual must file an income tax return with Form 8962 attached to claim the credit. If the advance payment exceeds the credit amount, the taxpayer owes the excess as an additional tax liability, but a repayment cap applies if household income is under 400% of the FPL. (Code Sec. 36B(f)(2)(B); Reg § 1.36B-4(a)(3))[33]

¶ 2344 Credit for income tax withheld; backup withholding.

Code Sec. 31 allows the recipient of wages, pensions, annuities, gambling winnings, etc., a credit for the amount of income tax withheld from those amounts in a calendar year, for the last tax year beginning in that calendar year. (Code Sec. 31(a); Reg § 1.31-1(a))[34] For amounts withheld under the backup withholding rules (¶3043 *et seq.*), the credit is allowed for the tax year in which the income is received. (Code Sec. 31(c))[35]

If spouses file separate returns, each must claim credit for the actual amount of tax withheld from salary or wages. In a community property state, each spouse may claim a

---

28. ¶A-4243.2 *et seq.*
29. ¶A-4247.1
30. ¶A-4246
31. ¶A-4246.2B *et seq.*

32. ¶A-4246.2B *et seq.*
33. ¶A-4241 *et seq.*; ¶A-4248.1
34. ¶A-4005 *et seq.*
35. ¶J-9009

credit for half the tax withheld on community wages. (Code Sec. 31(a); Reg § 1.31-1(a))[36]

¶ 2345 Credit for excess social security tax withheld.

Under Code Sec. 31(b)(1) and Code Sec. 6413(c)(1), if more than the maximum social security tax (¶1108) is withheld from an employee's wages for a calendar year because the employee worked for two or more employers, the excess is a credit against income tax on the employee's return for the year. (Code Sec. 31(b)(1), Code Sec. 6413(c)(1); Reg § 1.31-2(a)(2), Reg § 31.6413(c)-1) If two spouses both work, the ceiling is applied separately to each. If more than the maximum was withheld by one employer, the employee can't claim the credit; the employer must refund the over-collection.[37]

¶ 2346 Credit for the elderly and permanently and totally disabled—Schedule R.

A credit under Code Sec. 22 is available to a "qualified individual" —i.e., one who: (1) is 65 or older at the end of the tax year, or (2) is under 65 at the end of the tax year, retired on permanent and total disability, received taxable disability income during the tax year, and hasn't reached mandatory retirement age on the first day of the tax year. (Code Sec. 22(b))[38]

Permanently and totally disabled means the individual is unable to engage in any substantial gainful activity because of a medically determinable physical or mental impairment that can be expected to result in death, or that has lasted or can be expected to last for a continuous period of at least 12 months. (Code Sec. 22(e)(3))[39] IRS requires a physician's statement (part of Form 1040, Schedule R) certifying the disability to be kept as part of taxpayer's records (but not filed). For joint returns, the statement is required for each spouse under 65 who is retired on permanent and total disability.[40]

Disability income is gross income from amounts received as (or in lieu of) wages while out of work due to a permanent and total disability. (Code Sec. 22(c)(2))[41]

Married individuals must file jointly to claim the credit unless they qualify as married living apart, ¶3126. (Code Sec. 22(e)(1)) A nonresident alien (NRA) isn't eligible for the credit (Code Sec. 22(f)), unless the NRA has a U.S. spouse and elects under Code Sec. 6013(g) or Code Sec. 6013(h) to be treated as a U.S. resident. (Reg § 1.37-1(d))[42]

The credit is 15% of an "initial amount" (Step 1 below), reduced by amounts based on the taxpayer's AGI (Step 2) and on the taxpayer's income from tax-free pensions and annuities (Step 3) (use Schedule R, with Form 1040):

Step (1): The "initial amount" is:

. . . $5,000 for a single person, 65 or over;

. . . $5,000 for spouses filing jointly, one spouse is a qualified individual, 65 or over;

. . . $7,500 for spouses filing jointly, both spouses are qualified individuals, 65 or over;

. . . $3,750 for a married person, 65 or over, filing separately. (Code Sec. 22(c)(2)(A))

For *individuals under 65,* the "initial amount" is the *lesser* of the above initial amount, or:

• single persons/married filing separately: taxpayer's disability income for the year;

• joint returns, both spouses under 65 and disabled: spouses' combined disability incomes;

---

36. ¶A-4006
37. ¶A-4002
38. ¶A-4101
39. ¶A-4102

40. ¶A-4102
41. ¶A-4103
42. ¶A-4101

- joint returns, one spouse under 65 and disabled, other spouse 65 or older: sum of $5,000 plus disabled spouse's disability income;

- joint returns, both spouses under 65, one spouse disabled: disabled spouse's disability income. (Code Sec. 22(c)(2)(B))

Step (2): If AGI exceeds a threshold amount ($7,500 for single persons; $10,000 for joint returns; $5,000 for married filing separately), the "initial amount" must be reduced by one-half of the excess. (Code Sec. 22(d)) The reduction applies regardless of the taxpayer's age.

🅡️observation: Step (2) eliminates the credit for joint filers at AGI of $25,000 (both spouses 65 or over) or $20,000 (if one is), and for a single person at AGI of $17,500.

Step (3): The initial amount as adjusted under Step (2) must be further reduced by the sum of the amounts received by the individual (for a joint return, by either spouse) as a pension or annuity or as a disability benefit that's: (a) excluded from gross income and payable under title II of the Social Security Act, the Railroad Retirement Act, or a law administered by the VA; or (b) excluded from gross income under any non-Code provision of law. (Code Sec. 22(c)(3)(A))[43] Social security benefits (¶1279) (Code Sec. 86(f)(1)) and worker's compensation that reduces such benefits (Code Sec. 22(c)(3)(B)) are received as a pension or annuity.[44]

¶ 2347 Credit for household and dependent care expenses; Form 2441; employment-related expenses.

A credit under Code Sec. 21 may be claimed by an individual taxpayer (use Form 2441 with Form 1040) who: (1) has one or more qualifying individuals, and (2) incurs employment-related expenses enabling the taxpayer to be gainfully employed. (Code Sec. 21(a)(1); Reg § 1.21-1(a))[45]

For years other than 2021 (when a special rule applied), the credit is nonrefundable. (Code Sec. 21(g)(1))[46]

For years other than 2021 (when special rules applied), the credit is equal to 35% of employment-related expenses, for taxpayers with AGI of $15,000 or less. The percentage decreases by 1 percentage point for each $2,000 (or fraction) of AGI over $15,000, but not below 20%. (Code Sec. 21(a)(1), Code Sec. 21(a)(2); Reg § 1.21-1(a))[47]

For years other than 2021 (when special rules applied), the maximum amount of employment-related expenses that may be used to compute the credit is $3,000 for one qualifying individual, or $6,000 for two or more qualifying individuals. (Code Sec. 21(c); Reg § 1.21-2(a)(1))[48]

An otherwise eligible taxpayer may claim the credit for a qualifying individual who lives with the taxpayer for more than half the year, even if the taxpayer doesn't provide more than half the household maintenance costs. (Code Sec. 21(a); Reg § 1.21-1(b))[49]

Qualifying individuals for a taxpayer's dependent care credit are:

. . . a taxpayer's under-age-13 dependent (as defined in Code Sec. 152(a)(1) for the dependency exemption, ¶3114) (Code Sec. 21(b)(1)(A), Reg § 1.21-1(b)(1));

. . . a taxpayer's dependent who is physically or mentally incapable of self care and who has the same principal place of abode as the taxpayer for more than half the tax year. For this purpose, "dependent" is defined in Code Sec. 152 (¶3113), but without the gross

---

43. ¶A-4105, A-4106
44. ¶A-4107
45. ¶A-4301 *et seq.*
46. ¶A-4301

47. ¶A-4301
48. ¶A-4302, ¶A-4303
49. ¶A-4301

income test for qualifying relatives, the rule that a joint filer can't be a dependent, and the rule that a dependent can't have dependents (Code Sec. 21(b)(1)(B); Reg § 1.21-1(b)(1)); or

. . . the taxpayer's spouse, if the spouse is physically or mentally incapable of self care and has the same principal place of abode as the taxpayer for more than half the tax year. (Code Sec. 21(b)(1)(C); Reg § 1.21-1(b)(1))[50]

Employment-related expenses qualifying for the credit are expenses for household services or for the care of qualifying individuals that are incurred to enable the taxpayer to be gainfully employed (for earned income limit, see below). Costs of a housekeeper, maid, babysitter, or cook ordinarily qualify. (Code Sec. 21(b)(2)(B); Reg § 1.21-1(d))[1]

Payments for services provided outside the taxpayer's household count only if incurred for a qualifying individual who either is a dependent under age 13, or regularly spends at least 8 hours each day in taxpayer's household. (Code Sec. 21(b)(2)(B); Reg § 1.21-1(e)(1))[2] Also, for services performed by a *dependent care center*, the center must comply with all applicable state or local laws and regs. (Code Sec. 21(b)(2)(C); Reg § 1.21-1(e)(2))[3]

observation: The credit isn't available for expenses of full institutional care unless incurred for a dependent under age 13.

Payments to taxpayer's relatives or household members don't qualify if the person paid is: a dependent (under Code Sec. 151(c)) of the taxpayer or spouse, a child of the taxpayer (under Code Sec. 152(f)(1)) under 19 at the end of the tax year, taxpayer's spouse, or the parent of taxpayer's child who's a qualifying individual. (Code Sec. 21(e)(6); Reg § 1.21-4(a))[4]

The amount of employment-related expenses that may be taken into account can't exceed: (1) for an individual who isn't married at the end of the tax year, the individual's earned income, or (2) for an individual who is married at the end of the tax year, the lesser of individual's, or spouse's, earned income for the year (even if married for only part of the year). (Code Sec. 21(d)(1); Reg § 1.21-2(b))[5]

A spouse who is a full-time student or who is a qualifying individual because incapable of self-care is deemed to have earned income of $250 per month if there's one qualifying individual in the household, and $500 a month if there are two or more qualifying individuals. But this deemed earned income rule applies to only one spouse for any given month. (Code Sec. 21(d)(2); Reg § 1.21-2(b)(4))[6]

The credit is available to married couples only on a joint return. (Code Sec. 21(e)(2); Reg § 1.21-3(a))[7] A married individual living apart from a spouse may claim the credit on a separate return if the individual maintains a household for which the individual furnishes over half the maintenance costs for the tax year, the household is a qualifying individual's principal place of abode for more than half the tax year, and the other spouse is absent for the last six months of the tax year. (Code Sec. 21(e)(4), Reg § 1.21-3(b))[8]

Divorced or legally separated parents claim the credit for a child under age 13 or physically or mentally incapable of self-care as follows: if the child receives more than half the child's support during the year from the child's parents, and is in the custody of one or both of the parents for more than half the calendar year, the child is a qualifying individual for the parent with longer custody. That parent may claim the credit even if that

50. ¶A-4312
1. ¶A-4319 *et seq.*
2. ¶A-4325
3. ¶A-4327
4. ¶A-4331

5. ¶A-4304, A-4305
6. ¶A-4306
7. ¶ A-4310
8. ¶A-4311

parent can't claim the child as a dependent and even if that parent released the dependency exemption (¶3120) to the other parent. (Code Sec. 21(e)(5); Reg § 1.21-1(b)(5))[9]

The care provider's name, address, and taxpayer identification number (TIN) must be included on taxpayer's return. The TIN isn't required for tax-exempt care providers (write "tax-exempt" instead). (Code Sec. 21(e)(9)) The care provider should give this information and certify the TIN on Form W-10. If the care provider doesn't comply with a request, the taxpayer should furnish whatever information is available, and include a statement that the other required information was requested but wasn't given. (Code Sec. 21(e)(9))[10]

No credit is permitted for a qualifying individual unless the individual's TIN is included on the return claiming the credit. (Code Sec. 21(e)(10))[11]

¶ 2348   Adoption expense credit rules—Form 8839; adoption fees, court costs, attorney fees, and other adoption-related expenses.

An individual may claim a credit under Code Sec. 23 (use Form 8839 with Form 1040) for qualified adoption expenses (Code Sec. 23(a)(1)), which are reasonable and necessary adoption fees, court costs, attorney fees, and other expenses that are directly related to and the principal purpose of which is for the taxpayer's legal adoption of an eligible child (an individual under age 18, or physically or mentally incapable of self-care.) (Code Sec. 23(d)) The credit is a nonrefundable personal credit allowed against the income tax and alternative minimum tax. The total amount that may be taken as a credit for all tax years for the adoption of a child is $14,890 for 2022 ($15,950 for 2023). (Code Sec. 23(b)(1))[12]

For 2022, phaseout begins with amounts over $223,410 and the credit is fully eliminated at $263,410 (for 2023, credit phases out over $239,230 to $279,230). (Code Sec. 23(b)(2))[13]

If the expenses are paid or incurred before the tax year the adoption becomes final, the credit is allowed for the year after the year when they're paid or incurred. For expenses paid or incurred during or after the tax year the adoption becomes final, the credit is allowed for the year they're paid or incurred. (Code Sec. 23(a)(2))[14]

For an adoption of a child with special needs (defined in Code Sec. 23(d)(3)), the taxpayer is treated as having paid (in the tax year the adoption becomes final) the maximum credit amount regardless of actual expenses. (Code Sec. 23(a)(3))[15]

The credit isn't allowed for a foreign adoption unless it becomes final. Expenses paid or incurred in the tax year the adoption is finalized or in earlier years are allowed in the year finalized. Expenses paid or incurred after that year are taken into account when paid or incurred. (Code Sec. 23(e)) Taxpayers may treat certain adoptions as final if the competent authority enters a decree of adoption or a home state enters a decree of re-adoption. Under a safe harbor, IRS won't challenge another country's treatment of an adoption as final if it enters a final decree of adoption, or the Secretary of State issues a specified certificate.[16]

No adoption expense credit is allowed if a deduction or credit (or exclusion, ¶1253) is otherwise allowed, or government funds are received, for the expense. (Code Sec. 23(b)(3)).[17]

To get the credit, married individuals must file jointly (unless legally separated or living apart). (Code Sec. 23(f)(1))[18] The taxpayer's return must include (if known) the name, age and taxpayer identification number (TIN) of the child. (Code Sec. 23(f)(2))[19]

---

9. ¶A-4314
10. ¶A-4334
11. ¶A-4333
12. ¶A-4401, A-4407, A-4410
13. ¶A-4404
14. ¶A-4402
15. ¶A-4401
16. ¶A-4402, A-4403
17. ¶A-4409
18. ¶A-4412, A-4413
19. ¶A-4414

If the adoption expense credit exceeds the "applicable limitation" (i.e., the limit imposed by Code Sec. 26(a), ¶2357), for the tax year, reduced by nonrefundable personal credits other than the adoption expense credit, the residential energy efficient property credit, and the prior-law D.C. first-time homebuyer's credit) for the year, the excess is carried over to each of the next five years. (Code Sec. 23(c)(1))[20]

¶ 2349   Child tax credit (CTC) for a qualifying child; partial credit for certain other dependents; advance CTC payments.

Under Code Sec. 24, a taxpayer may claim (on Form 1040) a CTC for each "qualifying child." (Code Sec. 24(a)) Enhanced CTC rules apply for tax years 2018–2025. (Code Sec. 24(a), Code Sec. 24(h))[21]

Generally, for the CTC, a qualifying child is as defined in Code Sec. 152(c) (child related to taxpayer, who, generally, lived with taxpayer for at least 6 months during the year, and who was a U.S. citizen or national, or U.S. resident)—who hasn't turned 17 by year-end. (Code Sec. 24(c))[22] A child can be a qualifying child of more than one person, but only one person can claim the CTC for the same qualifying child. (IR 2022-96, 04/27/2022, FS-2022-28, Apr., 2022, Q&A F5)

For 2018–2025 (other than 2021, for which special rules applied), the CTC is $2,000 per qualifying child. (Code Sec. 24(h)(2)) (After 2025, the credit drops to $1,000 per qualifying child.) (Code Sec. 24(a))[23]

The CTC is phased out for taxpayers with modified adjusted gross income (MAGI) above certain levels. For 2018–2025, the $2,000 CTC (and the $500 ODC, see below) is phased out for taxpayers with MAGI above $400,000 for joint filers and $200,000 for all others. (After 2025, the credit is phased out at lower MAGIs.) (Code Sec. 24(b))[24]

No CTC is allowed for a child for a tax year unless the taxpayer's return includes the child's name and social security number (SSN). (Code Sec. 24(e))[25]

In addition to the CTC for qualifying children, for 2018–2025, a $500 nonrefundable credit is allowed for each of the taxpayer's dependents (as defined in Code Sec. 152) who isn't a qualifying child for CTC purposes (called the "ODC" or "family credit"). The ODC can be claimed for a qualifying child for whom the regular CTC isn't allowed because the taxpayer didn't include an SSN for the child. (Code Sec. 24(h)(4))[26]

For refundability of the CTC, see ¶2350.

For limits on combined amount of nonrefundable personal credits, see ¶2357.

For the requirement to use ID.me to sign in to IRS online accounts and verify identity to check enrollment for advance payments, unenroll from advance payments, update bank account information and mailing address, and view payments, see ¶4757.

No credit is allowed for a short tax year unless due to the taxpayer's death. (Code Sec. 24(f))[27]

Special rules apply for residents of Guam, the Commonwealth of the Northern Mariana Islands, and the U.S. Virgin Islands (the so-called "Mirror Code territories"), Puerto Rico, and American Samoa. Code Sec. 24(k))[28]

---

20. ¶A-4406
21. ¶A-4052
22. ¶A-4054
23. ¶A-4052
24. ¶A-4053

25. ¶A-4062
26. ¶A-4061
27. ¶A-4052
28. ¶A-4071 *et seq.*

¶ 2350   Refundability of the child tax credit (CTC)—Form 8812.

The Code Sec. 24 CTC (¶2349) is, generally, a partially refundable credit (claimed on Schedule 8812 filed with Form 1040) (commonly called the "additional child tax credit" or "ACTC"). (Code Sec. 24(d); Code Sec. 24(h))[29]

The $500 credit for dependents other than qualifying children (the "family credit" or "ODC," ¶2349) is nonrefundable. (Code Sec. 24(h)(5)(A))[30]

Other than for 2021, when special rules applied, the CTC is refundable only to the extent of the *greater of*: (1) 15% of taxable earned income above $2,500 (after 2025, above $3,000), or (2) for a taxpayer with three or more qualifying children, the excess of the taxpayer's social security taxes for the tax year over the taxpayer's earned income tax credit (¶2337) for the year. For 2022, the maximum refundable credit for any qualifying child is limited to $1,500 (for 2023, $1600,). After 2025, no maximum limit applies. (Code Sec. 24(d) , Code Sec. 24(h)(5), Code Sec. 24(h)(6)))[31]

A taxpayer who elects to exclude any amount from gross income under the Code Sec. 911 foreign earned income/foreign housing exclusions (¶4605, ¶4606) can't claim the partially refundable credit for that tax year. (Code Sec. 24(d)(3))

Earned income is defined in Code Sec. 32 (¶2338), and includes amounts excluded from gross income under Code Sec. 112 (combat zone pay, see ¶1223). (Code Sec. 24(d)(1))

¶ 2351   Credit for mortgage interest under the qualified mortgage credit certificate (MCC) program—Form 8396, Form 8828.

Code Sec. 25 allows holders of state and local government revocable mortgage credit certificates issued under qualified MCC programs to claim a credit (on Form 8396) equal to the credit certificate rate (the MCC rate) multiplied by the interest paid or accrued by the taxpayer during the tax year on a mortgage. (Code Sec. 25(a)(1)) If the MCC rate exceeds 20%, the credit is limited to $2,000. (Code Sec. 25(a)(2), Code Sec. 25(b)(1))[32] The credit is subject to recapture (on Form 8828) if the taxpayer sells or otherwise disposes of any interest in the residence within nine years after the mortgage was provided. (Code Sec. 143(m))[33] If the credit exceeds the applicable limitation for the year, the excess is carried over to each of the next three years. The applicable limitation is the Code Sec. 26(a) limitation (¶2357) for the tax year, reduced by the nonrefundable personal credits (other than the MCC credit, the adoption expense credit, the residential energy efficient property credit, and the D.C. first-time homebuyer credit) for the year. (Code Sec. 25(e)(1))[34]

¶ 2352   Pre-2023 nonbusiness energy property credit/post-2022 energy efficient home improvement credit—Form 5695; energy efficiency improvements and residential energy property expenses before 2033.

Pre-2023 credit. For property placed in service before 2023, under Code Sec. 25C (which was amended by the Inflation Reduction Act of 2022, PL 117-169, 8/16/2022, for property placed in service after 2022, see below), for qualifying energy efficient improvements, individual taxpayers are allowed the nonbusiness energy property credit (Code Sec. 25C(a)).[35] The credit equals the sum of: (1) 10% of the amount paid or incurred by the taxpayer for qualified energy efficiency improvements (i.e., energy-efficient building envelope components[36]) installed during the tax year; and (2) the amount of residential energy

29. ¶A-4056
30. ¶A-4061
31. ¶A-4056
32. ¶A-4008 *et seq.*

33. ¶I-4901 *et seq.*
34. ¶A-4010
35. ¶A-4751 *et seq.*
36. ¶A-4754

property expenditures (REPES, i.e., expenditures for advanced main air circulating fans, for qualified natural gas, propane, or oil furnace or hot water boilers, and for "energy-efficient building property," including heat pumps, water heaters, and central air conditioners[37]) paid or incurred by the taxpayer during the tax year. (Code Sec. 25C(a)(2))[38]

Pre-2023 credit: dollar limits. Dollar limits apply to the overall credit. Generally, the credit can't exceed the excess of $500 over the aggregate credits allowed to that taxpayer for all previous tax years ending after Dec. 31, 2005. (Code Sec. 25C(b))[39] Specific dollar limits apply on the REPES component of the credit. (Code Sec. 25C(c)(1)(A). Code Sec. 25C(d)(1)(A))[40]

Pre-2023 credit: other rules. The credit is available only for property installed in or on the taxpayer's main home located in the U.S. (Code Sec. 25C(d))[41] The nonbusiness energy property credit is nonrefundable, and is subject to the tax-liability-based limit on aggregate nonrefundable personal tax credits (¶2357). A taxpayer who's subject to the alternative minimum tax (AMT) can claim the nonbusiness energy property credit and may offset the AMT with the credit. The nonbusiness energy property credit is claimed on Form 5695, which must be attached to Form 1040 and 1040-SR.[42]

Post-2022 credit. Under Code Sec. 25C for property placed in service after 2022 but before 2033, a taxpayer will be able to claim a nonrefundable personal tax credit equal to 30% of the sum of the cost/amount of (1) "qualified energy efficiency improvements" (under Code Sec. 25C(c)), and (2) REPEs (under Code Sec. 25C(d)), paid/incurred in that year. The credit will be increased for amounts spent for a home energy audit (under Code Sec. 25C(a)(3)), limited to a $150 increase. (Code Sec. 25C(a); Code Sec. 25C(b)(6)(A)). The following annual credit limits will apply: (a) $1,200 per taxpayer per year; (b) $600 for credits for REPEs, windows, and skylights; and (c) $250 for any exterior door ($500 total for all exterior doors). Notwithstanding these limits, a $2,000 annual limit will apply to the cost of specified heat pumps, heat pump water heaters, and biomass stoves and boilers. (Code Sec. 25C(b)) The expenses must be for property originally placed in service by the taxpayer and made on or in connection with a dwelling unit located in the U.S. and used by the taxpayer as a residence. (Code Sec. 25C(d)(1))[43]

Post-2022 credit: property placed in service after 2024. Property placed in service after 2024 must be produced by a qualified manufacturer, and taxpayers will have to provide IRS with a qualified product identification number to qualify for the credit. (Code Sec. 25C(h))[44]

Code Sec. 25C credit, in general. CleanEnergy.gov, part of the White House's website, provides consumer-oriented information on incentives (including the nonbusiness energy property credit) for home energy conservation upgrades.

¶ 2353 Clean energy credit (formerly known as residential energy efficient property or REEP credit)—Form 5695.

Under Code Sec. 25D, as amended by the Inflation Reduction Act of 2022 (P.L. 117-169, 8/16/2022), individuals are allowed a nonrefundable personal tax credit (on Form 5695) for the purchase of: qualified solar electric property (that uses solar power to generate electricity in a home), qualified solar water heating property (i.e., property to heat water for use in a home if at least half of the energy it uses is derived from the sun), qualified fuel cell property (as defined in Code Sec. 48(c)(1), up to a maximum $500 credit for each 0.5 kilowatt (kw) of capacity), qualified small wind energy property (wind turbine to generate

37. ¶A-4759
38. ¶A-4751
39. ¶A-4752
40. ¶A-4759

41. ¶A-4753
42. ¶A-4751
43. ¶A-4751 *et seq.*
44. ¶A-4759

electricity for a home), qualified geothermal heat pump property (to heat water for use in a residence if at least half of the energy used is derived from the sun), biomass fuel property (in 2021 or 2022), and (post-2022) qualified battery storage technology. (Code Sec. 25D(a), Code Sec. 25D(d), Code Sec. 25D(g)) The credit rate for property placed in service: (1) before 2022 was 26%; (2) after 2021 and before 2033 is 30%; (3) after 2031 and before 2034 is 26%; and (4) after 2033 and before 2035 is 22%. (Code Sec. 25D(g))[45]

The property must be installed for use in a dwelling that's located in the U.S. and used as the taxpayer's residence (Code Sec. 25D(d)), and can't be used to heat a swimming pool or hot tub. (Code Sec. 25D(e)(3)) The credit can be claimed for either an existing home or a newly constructed home. A taxpayer can claim the credit for property described above that is installed on or in a second or vacation home. IRS has allowed the credit for the cost of solar panels (and a partial ownership interest in related equipment) installed in an off-site community-shared solar project.[46]

Taxpayers can rely on an appropriate manufacturer's certification that a component meets energy requirements, unless IRS withdraws the manufacturer's right to certify before taxpayer's purchase.[47]

The credit covers installation and labor costs (Code Sec. 25D(e)(1)) and includes sales tax. An expense is treated as made when the original installation is completed, except an expense for the construction or reconstruction of a structure is treated as made when the taxpayer's original use of the constructed or reconstructed structure begins. (Code Sec. 25D(e)(8))[48] If the equipment is used less than 80% for nonbusiness purposes, only the expenses properly allocable to nonbusiness use are taken into account. (Code Sec. 25D(e)(7))[49]

For the limit on the combined amount of certain personal nonrefundable credits, see ¶2357.

If the credit is allowed for an expense for a property, the basis increase is reduced by the credit allowed (¶2472). (Code Sec. 25D(f), Code Sec. 1016(a)(34))[50]

CleanEnergy.gov, part of the White House's website, provides consumer-oriented information on incentives (including the above credit) for home energy conservation upgrades.

¶ 2354 Vehicle credits: qualified plug-in electric drive motor vehicle credit (Form 8936); (new) clean vehicle credit (vehicles placed in service post-2022); pre-2022 two-wheeled plug-in electric (Form 8834) credits.

A taxpayer can claim a credit under Code Sec. 30D (on Form 8936) for each electric vehicle placed in service during the tax year that meets certain criteria. For vehicles placed in service before Jan. 1, 2023, this credit was called the new qualified plug-in electric drive motor vehicle (NQPEDMV) credit. For vehicles placed in service after Dec. 31, 2022, the credit is called the "clean vehicle credit." (Code Sec. 30D(a))[1]

Definition of a NQPEDMV/new clean vehicle. To qualify for the Code Sec. 30D credit, a vehicle must meet the requirements of Code Sec. 30D(d)(1). (Code Sec. 30D(d)(1)) The taxpayer must be the original user of the vehicle, and must have acquired it for use or lease and not for resale. The vehicle must qualify as a motor vehicle under title II of the Clean Air Act and have a gross vehicle weight of less than 14,000 pounds. (Code Sec. 30D(d)(1))[2]

For vehicles sold after Aug. 16, 2022, final assembly of the vehicle must take place in

45. ¶A-4781, A-4782
46. ¶A-4783
47. ¶A-4784
48. ¶A-4785

49. ¶A-4786
50. ¶A-4781
1. ¶L-18001, L-18031
2. ¶L-18009, L-18032.3

North America. (Code Sec. 30D(d)(1)(G)) New qualified fuel cell motor vehicles (as defined in Code Sec. 30B(b)(3)) placed in service after Dec. 31, 2022, are considered new clean vehicles that qualify for the credit (Code Sec. 30D(d)(6)).[3]

Minimum battery capacity. Vehicles placed in service before Jan. 1, 2023, must have a battery capacity of not less than four kilowatt hours to qualify for the NQPEDMV credit. For vehicles placed in service after Dec. 31, 2022, the minimum battery capacity increases to seven kilowatt hours for the clean vehicle credit. (Code Sec. 30D(d)(1)(F))[4]

Foreign entities of concern. An excluded entity (foreign entity of concern) prohibition will apply with respect to the critical minerals requirement (for vehicles placed in service after Dec. 31, 2024) and the battery component requirement (for vehicles placed in service after Dec. 31, 2023). A car containing either critical minerals or battery components from foreign entities of concern will be completely disqualified from the credit. (Code Sec. 30D(d)(7))[5]

Amount of the credit. For vehicles placed in service on or before the date the IRS issues proposed guidance under the Inflation Reduction Act of 2022 (P.L. 117-169, 8/16/2022), the amount of the NQPEDMV credit is the sum of: (1) $2,500; plus (2) for a vehicle that draws propulsion energy from a battery with not less than five kw hours of capacity, $417 for each kw hour of capacity in excess of 5 kw hours, but not in excess of $5,000. Thus, the maximum credit is $7,500, regardless of weight. (Code Sec. 30D(b))[6]

For vehicles placed in service after the IRS issues proposed guidance under the Inflation Reduction Act, which it is required to do before Jan. 1, 2023, the taxpayer gets a $3,750 credit for meeting the critical minerals requirement and a $3,750 credit for meeting the battery component requirement ($7,500 total clean vehicle credit) (Code Sec. 30D(b)) Under the critical minerals requirement, a certain percentage of critical minerals have to be extracted or processed in the U.S. or a country with which the U.S. has a free trade agreement, or must be recycled in North America. For vehicles placed in service before Jan. 1, 2014, this percentage is 40%. (Code Sec. 30D(e)(1)) Under the battery component requirement, a certain percentage of the value of the components of the vehicle's battery must be manufactured or assembled in North America. For vehicles placed in service before Jan. 1, 2014, this percentage is 50%. (Code Sec. 30D(e)(2))[7]

Manufacturer limitation. The NQPEDMV credit phases out beginning in the second calendar quarter after that in which a manufacturer sells its 200,000th plug-in electric drive motor vehicle for use in the U.S. after 2009. (Code Sec. 30D(e)) Phase-outs apply for vehicles manufactured by Tesla (beginning Jan. 2019), and GM (beginning Apr. 2019).

The manufacturer limitation has been eliminated for vehicles sold after Dec. 31, 2022, for the (new) clean vehicle credit. (Sec. 13401(d) of the Inflation Reduction Act, striking Code Sec. 30D(e))[8]

MAGI limitation. For vehicles placed in service after Dec. 31, 2022, a modified adjusted gross income (MAGI) limitation applies. Taxpayers can only claim the (new) clean vehicle credit if their MAGI for the current or previous tax year (whichever is lower) does not exceed the MAGI limit, which is $300,000 for married taxpayers filing joint returns or surviving spouses, $225,000 for heads of household, and $150,000 for other taxpayers (single taxpayers, married taxpayers filing separate returns). (Code Sec. 30D(f)(10))[9]

MSRP limitation. For vehicles placed in service after Dec. 31, 2022, a manufacturer's suggested retail price (MSRP) limitation applies. The (new) clean vehicle credit is not allowed for vans, pickup trucks, or sport utility vehicles (SUVs) with an MSRP greater than $80,000. The credit is not allowed for other vehicles with an MSRP greater than

---

3. ¶L-18009
4. ¶L-18009, L-18032
5. ¶L-18009
6. ¶L-18031.2

7. ¶L-18002 *et seq.*
8. ¶L-18031.2
9. ¶L-18011

$55,000. (Code Sec. 30D(f)(11))[10]

Other rules. Any portion of the credit attributable to depreciable property is treated as part of the general business credit (¶2301). The remaining portion is a nonrefundable personal credit. (Code Sec. 30D(c)(1))[11] For limits on combined amount of nonrefundable personal credits, see ¶2357.

The vehicle's basis, and any other allowable deduction or credit, must be reduced by the amount of the NQPEDMV credit allowed. The vehicle must be used predominantly in the U.S. (Code Sec. 30D(f)(4)) and meet certain provisions of the Clean Air Act (Code Sec. 30D(f)(7)). (Code Sec. 30D(f)(1), Code Sec. 30D(f)(2))[12]

Claiming the credit at time of purchase. For vehicles placed in service after Dec. 31, 2023, the taxpayer will be allowed to claim the credit through the dealership at the time of purchase (by "transferring" the credit to it). (Code Sec. 30D(g))

¶ 2355 Vehicle credits: previously owned clean vehicle credit—after 2022.

Under Code Sec. 25E(a), added by the Inflation Reduction Act of 2022 (P.L. 117-169, 8/16/2022), a qualified buyer who acquires and places in service a previously owned clean vehicle after 2022 and before 2033 will be allowed an income tax credit equal to the lesser of $4,000 or 30% of the vehicle's sale price. (Code Sec. 25E(a); Code Sec. 25E(g))[13]

Adjusted gross income limit. No credit will be allowed if the lesser of the taxpayer's modified adjusted gross income (as defined for the new clean vehicle credit, see ¶2354) for the year of purchase or the preceding year exceeds $150,000 for a joint return or surviving spouse, $112,500 for a head of household, or $75,000 for others. (Code Sec. 25E(b))[14]

Qualified buyer. A qualified buyer is an individual who (1) purchases the vehicle for use and not for resale, (2) is not a tax dependent of another taxpayer, and (3) has not been allowed a credit for a previously owned clean vehicle during the three year period ending on the sale date. (Code Sec. 25E(c)(3))[15]

Previously owned clean vehicle. A previously owned clean vehicle is a motor vehicle (1) with a model year at least two years earlier than the calendar year in which the taxpayer acquires it, the original use of which starts with a person other than the taxpayer, that is acquired in a qualified sale, and generally meets the definition of a clean vehicle eligible for the credit for new clean vehicles, other than the original owner requirement (see ¶2354); or (2) that is a clean fuel-cell vehicle with a gross weight rating of less than 14,000 pounds. (Code Sec. 25E(c)(1)) A motor vehicle for this purpose is a vehicle with at least four wheels manufactured primarily for use on public streets, roads, and highways. (Code Sec. 25E(c)(4)) The vehicle's VIN number must be included on the return claiming the credit. (Code Sec. 25E(d)) This credit is allowed only once for any vehicle's VIN number. (Code Sec. 25E(e); Code Sec. 30D(f)(8))[16]

Qualified sale. A qualified sale is a dealer sale of a motor vehicle for $25,000 or less that is the first transfer since enactment of the Inflation Adjustment Act of 2022 (P.L. 117-169, 8/16/2022)—i.e., since Aug. 16, 2022—to a qualified buyer other than the vehicle's original buyer. (Code Sec. 25E(c)(2))[17]

Election to transfer credit to dealer. For vehicles acquired after 2023, purchasers of previously owned clean vehicles will be able, up to the time of sale, to elect to transfer the credit to the selling dealer for cash or a partial down payment, under rules similar to those for transfers of the new clean vehicle credit. (Code Sec. 25E(f), see ¶2354)[18]

---

10. ¶L-18012
11. ¶L-18013, L-18034, L-18034.1
12. ¶L-18001, L-18032.1, L-18033.2, L-18033.3
13. ¶A-4790 *et seq.*
14. ¶A-4792

15. ¶A-4792
16. ¶A-4793
17. ¶A-4793
18. ¶A-4794

CleanEnergy.gov, part of the White House's website, provides consumer-oriented information on tax incentives, including the above vehicle credit.

¶ 2356 "Saver's" credit for elective deferrals and IRA contributions—Form 8880; qualified retirement savings contributions.

An eligible lower-income taxpayer can claim a nonrefundable credit under Code Sec. 25B (use Form 8880 with Form 1040) for a percentage of up to $2,000 of qualified retirement savings contributions—"the saver's credit." (Code Sec. 25B(a)) The applicable percentage (50%, 20%, or 10%) depends on filing status and AGI. (Code Sec. 25B(b))[19]

For tax years beginning in 2022, the amounts are:

. . . Joint filers: $0 to $41,000, 50%; $41,000 to $44,000, 20%; and $44,000 to $68,000, 10% (no credit if AGI is above $68,000).

. . . Heads of household: $0 to $30,750, 50%; $30,750 to $33,000, 20%; and $33,000 to $51,000, 10% (no credit if AGI is above $51,000).

. . . All other filers: $0 to $20,500, 50%; $20,500 to $22,000, 20%; and $22,000 to $34,000, 10% (no credit if AGI is above $34,000).

For tax years beginning in 2023, the amounts are:

. . . Joint filers: $0 to $43,500, 50%; over $43,500 but not over $47,500, 20%; over $47,500 but not over $73,000, 10% (no credit if AGI is above $73,000).

. . . Heads of household: $0 to $32,625, 50%; over $32,625 but not over $35,625, 20%; over $35,625 but not over $54,750, 10% (no credit if AGI is above $54,750).

. . . All other filers: $0 to $21,750, 50%; over $21,750 but not over $23,750, 20%; over $23,750 but not over $36,500, 10% (no credit if AGI is above $36,500).

The taxpayer's AGI is determined without regard to the foreign, possessions, and Puerto Rico income exclusions. (Code Sec. 25B(e))

To be eligible, an individual must have reached age 18 by the end of the tax year, and can't be either a full-time student or claimed by another as a dependent for the tax year beginning in the calendar year the individual's tax year begins. (Code Sec. 25B(c))[20]

The credit is available for: elective contributions to a Code Sec. 401(k) plan (including SIMPLE 401(k)s), Code Sec. 403(b) annuity, Code Sec. 457 plan, SIMPLE IRA plan, or salary reduction SEP; contributions to traditional or Roth IRAs; voluntary after-tax employee contributions to qualified retirement plan or Code Sec. 403(b) annuity; and (for 2018−2025) a designated beneficiary's contributions to an ABLE account (¶2225). (Code Sec. 25B(d)(1))[21] The credit is in addition to any otherwise applicable deduction or exclusion.[22]

The amount of any credit-eligible contribution is reduced (not below zero) by distributions received by the individual (and spouse, for joint returns) from any of the above savings arrangements during a testing period (i.e., the tax year for which the credit is claimed, the two preceding tax years, and the period after the end of the tax year and before the due date (including extensions) for filing the taxpayer's return for that year) to the extent they're either taxable or are Roth IRA distributions that aren't rolled over. (Code Sec. 25B(d)(2)) Distributions listed in Code Sec. 25B(d)(2)(C), such as qualified plan loans not treated as distributions, don't reduce a credit-eligible contribution.[23]

---

19. ¶A-4451
20. ¶A-4452
21. ¶A-4453

22. ¶A-4451
23. ¶A-4454

For limits on the combined amount of nonrefundable personal credits, see ¶2357.

¶ 2357   Limit on combined amount of nonrefundable personal credits.

Under Code Sec. 26(a), the total amount of nonrefundable personal credits (below) allowed for the tax year can't exceed the sum of: (a) the taxpayer's regular tax liability (below) for the tax year reduced by the foreign tax credit (¶2360), (Code Sec. 26(a)(1)) plus (b) the tax imposed by Code Sec. 55(a) (i.e., the alternative minimum tax (AMT), ¶3200) for the year (Code Sec. 26(a)(2)).[24]

> ⓇⒾⒶ *observation:* Thus, all otherwise allowable nonrefundable personal credits can be used to reduce AMT (as well as regular tax). Under this rule, the taxpayer can claim up to the amount of the sum of the regular tax and the AMT as nonrefundable personal credits.

The Code Sec. 26(a) limitation applies to the: dependent care credit (¶2347); credit for the elderly and disabled (¶2346); adoption expense credit (¶2348); child tax credit, nonrefundable portion (CTC, ¶2349, ¶2350); mortgage credit certificate (MCC) credit (¶2351); American Opportunity Tax Credit (AOTC), nonrefundable portion (¶2202) and Lifetime Learning credit (¶2203); saver's credit (¶2356); pre-2023 nonbusiness energy property credit/post-2022 energy efficient home improvement credit (¶2352); the residential clean energy credit, formerly known as the residential energy efficient property (REEP) credit (¶2353); nonbusiness portions of: qualified plug-in electric drive motor vehicle credit (Form 8936), (new) clean vehicle credit (vehicles placed in service post-2022), pre-2022 two-wheeled plug-in electric (Form 8834) credit (¶2354); and new qualified fuel cell motor vehicle credit/alternative motor vehicle credit.[25]

> ⓇⒾⒶ *observation:* The limitation under Code Sec. 26(a) is the starting point for determining the credit carryover for the adoption expense, MCC, AOTC, and residential clean energy credit (former REEP).

Regular tax liability means the tax imposed by Chapter 1 *except* for the taxes listed in Code Sec. 26(b)(2).[26]

¶ 2358   Minimum tax credit (MTC)/"AMT credit"—Forms 8801, 8827.

A taxpayer incurring an AMT liability (see ¶3200 *et seq.*, ¶3213) may be entitled under Code Sec. 53 to carry forward a minimum tax credit (MTC, sometimes called the "AMT credit"). The MTC can be used to offset regular tax liability in a later year for which the tentative minimum tax (see ¶3201, ¶3213) is less than the regular tax liability. The MTC is computed on Form 8801 (Form 8827 for corporations). The MTC for any tax year is the excess, if any, of (1) the adjusted net minimum tax (ANMT), (Code Sec. 53(d)(1)(B)(i))) imposed for all earlier tax years beginning after 1986, over (2) the amount allowable as an MTC credit for those earlier years. For computation for purposes of the post-2022 corporate minimum tax, see below. (Code Sec. 53(a), Code Sec. 53(b))[27]

The MTC for a tax year can't exceed the excess of: taxpayer's regular tax liability (¶2357) reduced by the sum of allowable nonrefundable credits, *over* the tentative minimum tax (¶3201, ¶3213) for the tax year. (But see modification of this rule for post-2022 corporate AMT, below. (Code Sec. 53(c))[28]

For purposes of the post-2022 corporate minimum tax,[29] the MTC is the excess, if any, of the net minimum tax (Code Sec. 53(d)(1)(A)) for all prior tax years beginning after 2022

---

24. ¶A-4901
25. ¶A-4902
26. ¶A-4905

27. ¶A-8801
28. ¶A-8801
29. ¶A-8900 *et seq.*

over the amount allowable as MTCs for those prior years. (Code Sec. 53(e)(1)) And for purposes of the limitation under Code Sec. 53(c), the regular tax includes the base erosion anti-abuse tax (¶3316) for the tax year. (Code Sec. 53(e)(2))[30]

¶ 2359　Credit for qualified tax credit bonds (QTCBs) issued before 2018.

The Code provisions authorizing issuance of, and credit for, tax credit bonds and the provision allowing direct-pay bonds (Former Code Secs. 54A, 54B, 54C, 54D, 54E, 54F, and 6431), were repealed, effective for bonds issued after 2017.[31]

caution: Although Former Code Sec. 54A below allowing holders of QTCBs a credit, is repealed for bonds issued after 2017, its provisions continue to apply to QTCBs issued before 2018.

Credit for holders of QTCBs issued before 2018. Taxpayers holding QTCBs on specified "credit allowance dates" are entitled to a nonrefundable credit (rather than interest payments) against regular income tax and alternative minimum tax (AMT) liability. The credit accrues quarterly and is includible in gross income as interest paid on the bond. The amount of the credit is determined by multiplying the bond's credit rate by its face amount. The credit rate is determined by IRS and is a rate that allows the bonds to be issued without discount and interest cost to the issuer. (Former Code Sec. 54A)[32]

QTCBs could be: (1) *Qualified forestry conservation bonds (QFCBs)* (Former Code Sec. 54A(d)(1)(A); Former Code Sec. 54B)[33], (2) *New clean renewable energy bonds (New CREBs).* (Former Code Sec. 54A(d)(1)(B); Former Code Sec. 54C)[34], (3) *Qualified energy conservation bonds (QECBs).* (Former Code Sec. 54A(d)(1)(C); Former Code Sec. 54D)[35], (4) *Qualified zone academy bonds (QZABs).* (Former Code Sec. 54A(d)(1)(D); Former Code Sec. 54E)[36], and (5) *Qualified school construction bonds (QSCBs).* (Former Code Sec. 54A(d)(1)(E); Former Code Sec. 54F)[37]

Direct Pay Tax Credit Bonds. For New CREBs, QECBs, QZABs (with certain exceptions), and QSCBs issued before 2018, the issuer could have made an irrevocable election to treat the bond as a "Direct Pay Tax Credit Bond," entitling issuer to receive a direct payment from IRS based on a market-determined interest rate, on the bond's interest payment dates (special limits applied to new CREBs and QECBs). If the issuer made this election, the bond holder can't claim any otherwise available QTCB credit for the bond, and is, instead, taxed on any bond interest paid. Any income tax deduction otherwise allowed to the issuer is reduced by the amount of the payment made under former Code Sec. 6431 for the interest. (Former Code Sec. 6431(f))[38]

¶ 2360　Foreign Tax Credit. ▰▰▰▰▰▰▰

Under Code Sec. 901, U.S. taxpayers who pay income taxes to foreign governments may generally credit them dollar-for-dollar against their U.S. tax liability on their worldwide income.

Taxpayers may elect to either take a foreign tax credit against U.S. income tax for income tax paid to a foreign country or U.S. possession, or deduct the tax. (Code Sec. 901, Code Sec. 27, Code Sec. 164)[39] Foreign income taxes can't, however, be deducted in the same year that a credit is claimed for any foreign income tax, and excess foreign taxes eligible for carryover can't be claimed in a year in which a deduction for current foreign taxes is taken. The deduction of other foreign taxes doesn't affect the creditability of

30. ¶A-8801
31. ¶L-15530 *et seq.*
32. ¶L-15530 *et seq.*
33. ¶L-15550 *et seq.*
34. ¶L-15560 *et seq.*

35. ¶L-15570 *et seq.*
36. ¶L-15580 *et seq.*
37. ¶L-15590 *et seq.*
38. ¶L-15547 *et seq.*
39. ¶K-4700; ¶O-4001

foreign income taxes. (Code Sec. 164(a)(3), Code Sec. 275(a)(4), Code Sec. 904(c); Reg § 1.901-1(c), Reg § 1.901-1(h)(2))[40]

On a joint return, the credit is based on total taxes paid or accrued by both spouses. (Reg § 1.901-1(e))[41]

The credit is allowed to U.S. citizens, domestic corporations, U.S. residents and bona fide residents of Puerto Rico, for the entire tax year as to foreign or possessions taxes paid or accrued during the tax year. (Code Sec. 901(b)(1), Code Sec. 901(b)(2), Code Sec. 901(b)(3)) Nonresident aliens and foreign corporations can claim the credit for foreign or possessions tax only on certain income effectively connected with a U.S. business (¶4630). (Code Sec. 901(b)(4), Code Sec. 906)[42]

A person described above who is a member of a partnership or S corporation, a beneficiary of an estate or trust, or a shareholder of an electing regulated investment company (RIC, ¶4201), may credit his or her share of foreign tax paid or accrued by the partnership, estate, trust or RIC. (Code Sec. 901(b)(5), Code Sec. 853(a), Code Sec. 1373(a)) Trusts and estates are allowed the foreign tax credit for taxes not allocable to beneficiaries. (Code Sec. 642(a), Code Sec. 901(n)(3))[43]

A foreign tax is only creditable by the taxpayer upon whom foreign law imposes legal liability for the tax, even if another person pays the tax. (Reg § 1.901-2(f)) In addition, foreign tax credits may be suspended under a matching rule to prevent the separation of creditable foreign taxes from the associated foreign income when certain related persons account for the associated income in another tax period (a tax credit splitting event). IRS provides an exclusive list of arrangements that qualify as splitting events. (Code Sec. 909)[44]

¶ 2361 When and how to claim foreign tax credit—Forms 1116, 1118.

The foreign tax credit is claimed on Form 1116 by an individual, trust or estate, and on Form 1118 by a corporation. (Reg § 1.905-2(a)(1))[45] A cash basis taxpayer may elect to credit *all* qualified foreign taxes on an accrual basis, but the election is binding with respect to all taxes for that year, whenever paid. (Code Sec. 905(a); Reg § 1.905-1(a))[46]

¶ 2362 Which taxes qualify for a foreign tax credit? Income taxes, war profits taxes and excess profits taxes.

Under Code Sec. 901, income taxes, war profits taxes and excess profits taxes paid or accrued during the tax year to a foreign country or a U.S. possession qualify for the foreign tax credit. (Code Sec. 901) However, a tax conditioned on its eligibility for the credit (a soak up tax) or used by the foreign country to provide a subsidy doesn't qualify. (Reg § 1.901-2(c), Reg § 1.901-2(e)(3)) A payment also qualifies if it is *in lieu* of taxes on income. (Code Sec. 903) Taxes on wages, dividends, interest and royalties generally qualify. (Reg § 1.901-2)[47] In the case of certain elections and transactions that create additional asset basis for cost recovery in the U.S. (e.g., qualified stock purchases, acquisitions of partnership interests with a Code Sec. 754 election in place), a portion of the foreign income tax paid on the income or gain attributable to the underlying foreign assets is disqualified. (Code Sec. 901(m))[48]

Taxes imposed by and paid to certain countries that the U.S. doesn't recognize or have diplomatic relations with or that have been designated as a country supporting acts of

---

40. ¶K-4701; ¶O-4002; ¶O-4601
41. ¶O-4001
42. ¶O-4101 *et seq.*
43. ¶E-6165; ¶O-4101
44. ¶O-4104; ¶O-4113 *et seq.*

45. ¶O-5501
46. ¶O-5504
47. ¶O-4200 *et seq.*
48. ¶O-4013 *et seq.*

international terrorism may not be credited; but these taxes may be taken as itemized deductions. (Code Sec. 901(j)) The credit is also reduced or denied to international boycott participants (see ¶4623). (Code Sec. 908)[49]

The credit is generally denied for a foreign withholding tax if the underlying property wasn't held for a minimum holding period, or to the extent that the recipient is obligated to make related payments with respect to positions in substantially similar or related property. (Code Sec. 901(l))[50]

¶ 2363   Limitations on the foreign tax credit (FTC); carryback and carryforward of FTC.

Under Code Sec. 904(a), the total credit for foreign taxes for a year is limited to the amount of U.S. tax that would be imposed on the taxpayer's foreign source income. (Code Sec. 904(a))[1] Separate calculations are required for different categories of income (see ¶2364).

An individual may elect an exemption from the limitation (by not filing the Form 1116) on *de minimis* amounts if the individual has $300 or less ($600 in the case of joint filers) of creditable foreign taxes and no foreign source income other than qualified passive income, so long as the amounts are shown on Form 1099 or other statement. However, there is no carryover of excess foreign taxes to or from a tax year for which the election is made. (Code Sec. 904(j))[2]

Special rules apply in determining the foreign tax credit limitation where there is a capital gain rate differential. (Code Sec. 904(b)(2), Code Sec. 904(b)(3); Reg § 1.904(b)-1) In certain cases, noncorporate taxpayers may elect not to apply the adjustment for rate differentials. (Reg § 1.904(b)-1(b)(3))[3]

If foreign income taxes paid or accrued exceed the amount that may be credited for the tax year, the excess may be carried back one year and forward 10 years. (Code Sec. 904(c)) The carryback and carryover rule does not apply to foreign taxes on global intangible low-taxed income (GILTI, see ¶4614). (Code Sec. 904(c); Reg § 1.904-2)[4]

Additional limitations apply to foreign taxes on foreign mineral income (Code Sec. 901(e); Reg § 1.901-3)[5] and foreign oil and gas extraction income. (Code Sec. 907)[6]

¶ 2364   Separate foreign tax credit (FTC) limitations for separate income categories.

Under Code Sec. 904(d), the foreign tax credit limitation (see ¶2363) is computed separately for (1) global intangible low-taxed income (GILTI, see ¶4614), (2) foreign branch income (i.e., the business profits of a U.S. person which are attributable to one or more qualified business units outside the U.S.), (3) passive category income (i.e., generally any income which would be foreign personal holding company (FPHC) income (¶4613) but not export financing interest, high-taxed income, financial services income, or active rents and royalties), and (4) general category income (i.e., income other than amounts included in the previous three categories). Additional categories may be mandated by other Code provisions. (Code Sec. 904(d); Reg § 1.904-1; Reg § 1.904-4)[7]

Dividends, interest, rents, and royalties received by a U.S. shareholder from a controlled

---

49. ¶K-4701; ¶O-4004; ¶O-4005
50. ¶O-4009 *et seq.*
1. ¶O-4300 *et seq.*
2. ¶O-4334
3. ¶O-4404 *et seq.*

4. ¶O-4601 *et seq.*
5. ¶O-5100 *et seq.*
6. ¶O-5200 *et seq.*
7. ¶O-4300 *et seq.*

foreign corporation (CFC) receive look-through treatment and so are characterized according to the source of the income to the CFC. Similarly, subpart F inclusions and GILTI inclusions are only treated as passive category income to the extent the amount included is attributable to passive category income of the CFC. Look-through treatment also applies to dividends from noncontrolled 10% owned foreign corporations (¶2367). CFC and U.S. shareholder status is determined for these purposes without attribution of stock from a non-U.S. person down to a U.S. entity (Code Sec. 904(d)(3), Code Sec. 904(d)(4); Reg § 1.904-4; Reg § 1.904-5; Reg § 1.904-5(a)(4))[8]

¶ 2365 Re-sourcing of certain foreign-source income as U.S. source, and recapture of overall foreign and domestic losses (Form 1118, Schedule J)— foreign tax credit limitation rules.

Under Code Sec. 904(h), certain income items that are derived from U.S.-owned foreign corporations (Code Sec. 904(h)(6)) that would otherwise be treated as derived from non-U.S. sources, are treated as derived from U.S. sources for purposes of the foreign tax credit limitation rules (see ¶2363). The items are: interest and dividends (subject to exceptions), and amounts included in gross income under Code Sec. 951(a)(1)(A) (¶4611, ¶4613), Code Sec. 951A(a) (¶4614), or Code Sec. 1293 (¶4619). (Code Sec. 904(h)(1))[9]

An overall foreign loss (OFL) is created whenever a taxpayer's foreign losses exceed foreign gross income (disregarding any NOLs, foreign expropriation losses, and losses arising from fire, storm, shipwreck, other casualty, or theft). OFLs are recaptured by recharacterizing a portion of the taxpayer's foreign source taxable income for each succeeding tax year as U.S. source income. This portion is generally the lesser of the unrecaptured OFL and 50% of the taxpayer's taxable foreign source income for that succeeding tax year. This recharacterization reduces the credit limitation until the OFL is completely offset. Ordering rules apply to match OFLs to the various separate income categories (¶2364). A taxpayer who disposes of property used in a trade or business predominantly outside the U.S., or of stock of certain CFCs, recognizes the gain as foreign-source income to the extent of any unrecaptured OFLs. (Code Sec. 904(f)) Corporations track these amounts on Form 1118, Schedule J.[10]

An equivalent rule recharacterizes the U.S.-source income of a taxpayer as foreign-source income for the foreign tax credit limitation to the extent of the taxpayer's prior overall domestic loss (ODL). (Code Sec. 904(g))[11]

¶ 2366 Currency exchange rate for translating foreign tax payments—foreign tax credit.

In determining the foreign tax credit, under Code Sec. 986(a)(1), an accrual-basis taxpayer must (subject to exceptions) translate foreign income taxes into dollars by using the weighted average exchange rate (Reg § 1.989(b)-1) for the tax year to which the taxes relate. (Code Sec. 986(a)(1); Reg § 1.986(a)-1(a)) For a cash-basis taxpayer, foreign income tax is translated into dollars using the spot rate on the date of payment of the taxes. Foreign income taxes withheld in foreign currency are translated into dollars using the spot rate on the date on which those taxes were withheld. (Code Sec. 986(a)(2)(A); Code Sec. 986(a)(2)(B)(i); Reg § 1.986(a)-1(b))[12]

---

8. ¶O-4325 *et seq.*
9. ¶O-4501 *et seq.*
10. ¶O-4700 *et seq.*

11. ¶O-4720 *et seq.*
12. ¶G-6972

¶ 2367   Deemed-paid foreign tax credit for subpart F and GILTI inclusions.

Under Code Sec. 960(a), a domestic corporation that is a U.S. shareholder (¶4612) of a controlled foreign corporation (CFC, ¶4612), and that includes in gross income any item of income under Code Sec. 951(a)(1) with respect to that CFC (see ¶4611) is treated as having paid so much of the foreign corporation's foreign income taxes (Code Sec. 960(e)) as are properly attributable to that item of income. Qualified electing fund (QEF, ¶4619) inclusions are treated as amounts included under Code Sec. 951(a)(1) for this purpose. (Code Sec. 960(a), Code Sec. 1293(f))

A deemed-paid foreign tax credit is also allowed for amounts includible in the gross income of a domestic corporation as global intangible low-taxed income (GILTI, see ¶4614), but it is limited to 80% of the attributable foreign taxes. (Code Sec. 960(d))

If an individual U.S. shareholder makes the election (under Code Sec. 962) to be taxed on amounts included in his or her gross income under Code Sec. 951(a) at the corporate rates, then, for the deemed-paid credit rules, these amounts are treated as if they were received by a domestic corporation. (Code Sec. 962(a)(2); Reg § 1.962-1(a)(2))[13]

If any portion of a distribution from a CFC to a U.S. corporate shareholder is excluded from gross income as previously taxed income (PTI), the shareholder is deemed to have paid so much of the foreign CFC's foreign income taxes as are properly attributable to that portion, and have not previously been deemed paid by the shareholder under these rules. (Code Sec. 960(b)) The foreign tax credit limitation (see ¶2363) is increased for additional taxes paid or deemed paid on distributions of PTI. (Code Sec. 960(c))

A holding period requirement applies for purposes of qualifying for the credit, except in the case of certain securities dealers. (Code Sec. 901(k)(2))

If a domestic corporation chooses to claim a foreign tax credit for any tax year, an amount equal to the taxes deemed paid by that corporation under the above rules (determined without regard to the 80% limitation for GILTI-related taxes) for the tax year is treated for income tax purposes (other than for purposes of the deduction of U.S.-source dividends from foreign corporations and the deduction for foreign source dividends from foreign corporations (see ¶3314)) as a dividend received by that domestic corporation from the foreign corporation. (Code Sec. 78)[14]

---

13. ¶O-2457   14. ¶O-4900 *et seq.*

Chapter 9 Sales and Exchanges—Tax-Free Exchanges—Basis

¶ 2400 Gain or Loss on Sales or Exchanges. ▆▆▆▆▆▆▆

Taxpayers realize gain to the extent the amount realized from a sale or exchange exceeds their adjusted basis (usually cost, increased for improvements and decreased for depreciation or amortization). If the adjusted basis of the property disposed of exceeds the amount realized (¶2401), the difference is a loss. (Code Sec. 1001(a))[1] With limited exceptions (e.g., when property is subject to the mark-to-market rules discussed at ¶2643), a taxpayer doesn't realize gain or loss when property merely goes up or down in value.

⦿️observation: Whether realized gain or loss is recognized in the tax year of sale or exchange depends on whether it was realized in a taxable or tax-deferred transaction.

¶ 2401 Amount realized on a sale or other disposition of property; property sold subject to a mortgage or other debt—sales or exchanges.

Under Code Sec. 1001, the amount realized on a sale or other disposition of property is the amount of money plus the fair market value (FMV) of any property received by the seller. (Code Sec. 1001(b))[2] Where the buyer of property assumes a seller's debt, or pays one (e.g., pays seller's taxes or legal fees), the amount of the debt is added to the amount realized by the seller. (Reg § 1.1001-2(a))[3] If property is sold subject to a mortgage or other debt, the amount of the liability is included in the sales price whether or not the seller is personally liable on the debt. This is so whether or not the buyer assumes the debt.[4]

FMV is the price at which the property would change hands between a willing buyer and a willing seller, neither being under any compulsion to buy or sell and both having reasonable knowledge of relevant facts. (Reg § 1.170A-1(c)(2), Reg § 1.412(c)(2)-1(c)(1), Reg § 1.1445-1(g)(7))[5] In determining gain or loss on property, fair market value is treated as being not less than the amount of the nonrecourse debt to which it's subject. (Code Sec. 7701(g))[6]

If a taxpayer sells an asset, selling expenses (e.g., brokers' commissions) ordinarily reduce the amount realized, thus reducing any realized gain or increasing any loss realized on the sale.(Reg § 1.263(a)-1(e))[7]

For the effect of unstated interest on a deferred payment or installment sales, see ¶1306.

¶ 2402 Virtual currency (e.g., cryptocurrency) treated as property for tax gain/loss; transactions in virtual currency; charitable donations; reporting requirements (Form 8949; Schedule D)—sales or exchanges.

When virtual currency/cryptocurrency is sold, a taxpayer must recognize gain or loss. If the fair market value (FMV) of property received in exchange for virtual currency exceeds the taxpayer's adjusted basis in it, the taxpayer has taxable gain. If the FMV of the property received is less than the adjusted basis of the virtual currency, the taxpayer has a loss. When virtual currency is sold for real currency, the gain or loss equals the difference between the adjusted basis in the virtual currency and the amount received in exchange for the virtual currency; this amount should be reported on the taxpayer's income tax return in U.S. dollars.[8]

---

1. ¶I-2501
2. ¶I-2502
3. ¶I-2510
4. ¶I-2510

5. ¶P-6002
6. ¶I-2515
7. ¶I-2527
8. ¶I-2151

References beginning with a single letter are to paragraphs in Federal Tax Coordinator 2d and RIA's Analysis of Federal Taxes: Income.

Generally, gain or loss is capital if the virtual currency is a capital asset in the hands of the taxpayer.[9]

If a taxpayer owns multiple units of one kind of virtual currency, acquired at different times, the taxpayer may choose which specific units are deemed to be sold or exchanged in a transaction if the taxpayer can specifically identify which units are involved, and can substantiate the basis in those units.[10]

A taxpayer that pays for a service using virtual currency held as a capital asset has an exchange of a capital asset for that service, and has a capital gain or loss. A taxpayer that exchanges virtual currency held as a capital asset for other property, including goods or other virtual currency, must recognize gain or loss. In both of these situations, the gain or loss is the difference between the FMV of the services or property received, and the adjusted basis in the virtual currency exchanged.[11]

A taxpayer that donates virtual currency to a charitable organization doesn't recognize income, gain, or loss from the donation. The amount of the charitable deduction is generally equal to the virtual currency FMV at the time of the donation if the virtual currency has been held for more than one year. If held for one year or less, the deduction is the lesser of basis or FMV at the time of the donation.[12]

A taxpayer must report income, gain, or loss from all taxable transactions involving virtual currency for the tax year of the transaction, regardless of the amount and regardless of whether the taxpayer received a payee statement or information return. Sales and other capital transactions, and calculation of capital gain or loss, are reported, e.g., on Form 8949; capital gains and deductible capital losses are then summarized on Form 1040, Schedule D. Ordinary income from virtual currency is reported on Form 1040, Form 1040-SS, Form 1040-NR, or Form 1040, Schedule 1. Taxpayers must maintain records sufficient to establish the positions taken on returns, documenting receipts, sales, exchanges, or other dispositions, and FMV.[13]

A taxpayer that sells or exchanges property (other than U.S. dollars) held as a capital asset for virtual currency recognizes capital gain or loss on the property. If the exchanged or sold property is not held as a capital asset, the taxpayer recognizes ordinary gain or loss.[14]

¶ 2403   Open transactions—payment in the form of a property right or obligation whose value depends on future events—sales or exchanges.

When a seller receives payment in the form of a property right or obligation whose value depends on future events, if the seller can prove that the right or obligation has no ascertainable value, he or she reports gain only when the proceeds from the obligation exceed basis, and loss is fixed only when further payments can't reasonably be expected.[15] For contingent payment sales and open sales under the installment sale rules, see ¶ 2450.

¶ 2404   Repossession of real estate by a secured seller—sales or exchanges.

Under Code Sec. 1038, when real property is sold and the sale gives rise to a debt to the seller secured by the real property (a purchase-money mortgage or similar lien), and the seller later repossesses the property (through voluntary transfer or foreclosure) because of actual or imminent default by the buyer, then (1) no loss results to the seller from the repossession or reacquisition, nor does the mortgage debt become worthless; and (2) the

---

9. ¶I-2151
10. ¶I-2151
11. ¶I-2151.1
12. ¶I-2151.1

13. ¶I-2151.1
14. ¶I-2151.2
15. ¶G-6567 *et seq.*

seller's gain on repossession is limited to the money and the value of property (other than the repossessed property) received by the seller with respect to the original sale to the extent these amounts haven't already been reported as income. The resulting gain can't exceed the gain on the original sale. (Code Sec. 1038)[16]

If gain isn't recognized under the Code Sec. 121 exclusion rules (¶ 2439) and the seller repossesses the home and then resells it within 1 year after the date of the repossession, the above rules don't apply and the resale of the home is treated as part of the original sale of the residence. (Code Sec. 1038(e))[17] If the resale isn't made within 1 year, the regular repossession rules apply, and the seller recognizes gain, including gain previously excluded under the exclusion rules (¶2439 *et seq.*).[18]

¶ 2405 Gain or loss to the seller when personal property is repossessed—sales or exchanges.

Gain or loss to the seller on repossession of personal property sold in a deferred payment transaction, not reported on the installment method, is the difference between the fair market value of the property when repossessed and the basis of the defaulted obligation, with that basis decreased by amounts paid on the note and increased for costs incurred in connection with the repossession. Gain or loss is reported in the year of repossession.[19]

¶ 2406 When sellers report gain or loss—sales or exchanges.

Under Code Sec. 451, a *cash basis* seller reports gain on a sale or exchange in the tax year the sales proceeds are received, actually or constructively. A loss is reported in the tax year the transaction is completed by a fixed, identifiable event. (Code Sec. 451(a); Reg § 1.451-1(a))[20]

An *accrual basis* seller reports gain or loss in the tax year a sale is completed and an unqualified right to the purchase price arises, usually when title passes to the buyer but, generally not later than the tax year in which the income is taken into account for financial accounting purposes (Code Sec. 451(b)), see ¶2818.[21] For securities sales, see ¶2408.

¶ 2407 Delivery of deed or title in escrow—effect on recognition of gain—sales or exchanges.

Where both the deed (or other evidence of title) and the purchase price are placed in escrow pending examination and the buyer's approval of the title, a sale isn't completed (and gain or loss isn't realized) until the buyer signifies approval. Until then, the seller doesn't have an unqualified right to payment. Once the buyer approves title, the seller can't postpone reporting gain by directing the escrow agent to hold the payment. But if the deed is delivered in escrow as security for the performance of an unconditional obligation of the buyer (usually payment of the purchase price), the sale is completed when the deed is delivered and the buyer enters into possession of the property.[22]

¶ 2408 Sales and exchanges of securities.

Under Code Sec. 1001, gain or loss on the sale of securities arises when the seller has sold or committed to sell specific shares.[23] Gain or loss on the exchange of securities arises

---

16. ¶G-6851 *et seq.*
17. ¶G-6877 *et seq.*
18. ¶G-6877
19. ¶G-6801

20. ¶I-2601
21. ¶I-2602
22. ¶I-1112
23. ¶I-2615

when the taxpayer acquires a right to specific securities.[24]

In stock exchange transactions, cash and accrual basis taxpayers realize gain or loss on the trade date, and not on the later settlement date.[25] For short sales, see ¶ 2629.

No gain or loss is recognized by owners of securities when they loan the securities in return for the agreement of the borrower to return identical securities, but the agreement must not reduce the transferor's risk of loss or opportunity for gain in the transferred securities. (Code Sec. 1058(a))[26]

Transactions structured to appear to be loans are sometimes found to be sales where they have the practical effect of sales, e.g., certain forward share and/or lending agreements where the taxpayer no longer has any substantial risk of loss.[27]

¶ 2409   Sales of load mutual funds with reinvestment right—sales or exchanges.

Under Code Sec. 852, a load charge incurred in buying mutual fund shares is disregarded (in whole or in part) in computing gain or loss on the disposition of those shares within 90 days, if the buyer was given a reinvestment right under which shares in the same (or another) mutual fund could be bought at less than the usual load charge. The load charge is disregarded to the extent of the reduction in the load charge on the later purchase. (Code Sec. 852(f))[28]

¶ 2410   Significant modification of debt instrument treated as an exchange— sales or exchanges.

For purposes of Code Sec. 1001, a significant modification of a debt instrument results in an exchange of the original debt instrument for a modified instrument that differs materially either in kind or in extent. (Reg § 1.1001-3(b))[29]

RIA *observation:* Exchanges of corporate bonds, but not of government bonds, can be tax-free under the reorganization provisions (¶3534), but only to the extent the principal amount isn't increased. Thus, in most cases, an exchange (or modification, which is considered an exchange for tax purposes) results in the holder's recognizing gain or loss. For example, if a modification of a debt instrument results in a reduction of the debt, the debtor has cancellation of debt income. (¶1379)

Examples of significant modifications in the terms of a debt instrument include certain changes in the yield of a debt instrument and certain changes to the timing of payments (including any resulting change in the amount of payments). (Reg § 1.1001-3(e))[30]

A modification of a debt instrument can sometimes cause it to be recharacterized as an instrument or property right that isn't debt, but a deterioration in the debtor's financial condition isn't taken into account in making that determination unless there is a substitution of a new obligor or the addition or deletion of a co-obligor. (Reg § 1.1001-3(f)(7)(ii))[31]

Qualifying taxpayers can make a debt restructuring election to treat a substitution of certain publicly traded debt instruments for new ones as a realization event even if the substitution isn't an exchange under the above rules. Electing taxpayers don't recognize any realized gain or loss on the date of the substitution. Instead, gain or loss generally is taken into account as income or deductions over the term of the new debt instruments.[32]

---

24. ¶I-2616
25. ¶I-2615.1
26. ¶I-1311, I-3802
27. ¶I-1311 *et seq.*
28. ¶P-5038 *et seq.*

29. ¶I-1050 *et seq.*
30. ¶I-1058 *et seq.*
31. ¶I-1075.1
32. ¶I-1081.8

¶ 2411   **Tax-Free Exchanges of Stock, Other Assets.** ▬▬▬▬▬▬▬

A taxpayer doesn't recognize gain or loss on exchanges of common or preferred stock for other common or preferred stock of the same corporation (¶2412). A corporation doesn't recognize gain or loss when it sells or exchanges its own stock for property or services (¶2413). Certain U.S. obligations can be exchanged tax-free (¶2414), as well as certain insurance policies and annuities (¶2415).

¶ 2412   **Stock exchanged for stock of same corporation—tax-free exchanges of stock, other assets.**

Under Code Sec. 1036, no gain or loss is recognized on the exchange of common stock for other common, or preferred stock for other preferred, of the same corporation. (Code Sec. 1036(a)) It's tax-free whether between a shareholder and the corporation or between 2 shareholders, and even if voting stock is exchanged for nonvoting stock. (Reg § 1.1036-1(a))[33] But, nonqualified preferred stock (¶3542) is treated as property other than stock for this purpose. (Code Sec. 1036(b))[34]

Although an exchange of common stock for preferred stock in the same corporation isn't tax-free, if this type of exchange occurs as part of a corporate reorganization it may be tax-free under the reorganization rules (¶3527 *et seq*. (Reg § 1.1036-1(a)))[35]

¶ 2413   **Corporation's sale or exchange of its own stock for property or services—tax-free exchanges of stock, other assets.**

Under Code Sec. 1032, a corporation doesn't recognize gain or loss on the sale or exchange of its stock (including treasury stock) for money, other property, or services. (Code Sec. 1032(a); Reg § 1.1032-1)[36] It also doesn't recognize gain or loss on the lapse of an option (warrant) to buy or sell its stock (including treasury stock). (Code Sec. 1032(a); Reg § 1.1032-3(d))[37]

¶ 2414   **Tax-free exchanges of U.S. obligations—tax-free exchanges of stock, other assets.**

Under Code Sec. 1037, IRS regs can provide for the tax-free exchange of one U.S. obligation (bond, note, etc.) for another. (Code Sec. 1037(a); Reg § 1.1037-1) The Treasury designates the specific obligations it will exchange for the previously issued obligations without recognition of gain or loss.[38]

¶ 2415   **Tax-free exchanges of insurance policies, annuities, endowments and/or qualified long-term care contracts; gain or loss on taxable sale or exchange of policy.**

Under Code Sec. 1035, no gain or loss is recognized on the exchange by the owner (or by a beneficiary on the death of the owner) of (1) a life insurance contract for another or for an endowment or annuity contract or a qualified long-term care contract (QLTCC); (2) an endowment contract for an annuity or another endowment contract providing for regular payments beginning at a date not later than the beginning date under the old contract, or a QLTCC; (3) an annuity contract for another or a QLTCC; or (4) a QLTCC for another QLTCC. To qualify for tax-free exchange treatment, the insured or annuitant must remain

---

33. ¶I-3301
34. ¶I-3301.1
35. ¶I-3301
36. ¶I-3201, I-3208
37. ¶I-6517
38. ¶I-3400 *et seq*.

the same. (Code Sec. 1035; Reg § 1.1035-1(c)) The direct transfer of a part of funds from 1 annuity contract to another annuity contract can qualify as a nontaxable exchange if certain conditions are met.[39]

To the extent provided in regs, the rules allowing a tax-free exchange of insurance policies and annuities don't apply to any exchange having the effect of transferring property to a non-U.S. person. (Code Sec. 1035(c))[40]

If the sale or exchange of a policy is taxable, under Code Sec. 1001(a), the taxable gain is the amount by which the consideration a taxpayer receives on the sale (or surrender), exceeds his or her "adjusted basis" in the contract (i.e., aggregate premiums paid minus cost of insurance already provided). Where the insured (seller) sells a term life insurance contract to an unrelated investor, the seller's gain is determined by subtracting the basis in the contract from the amount realized (the sum of money received from the sale). The seller's basis in the contract is the total premiums paid under the contract.[41] For a sale or assignment of any portion of a death benefit in a viatical settlement, see ¶1349.

¶ 2416   **Like-Kind (Code Sec. 1031) Real Property Exchanges—Forms 8824, 8949.** ■

Under Code Sec. 1031, no gain or loss is recognized on the exchange of real property held for productive use in a trade or business or for investment if the real property is exchanged solely for like-kind (¶2417) real property that is to be held either for productive use in a trade or business or for investment. Whether real property is trade or business or investment property is determined by the taxpayer's intent at the time of the exchange (¶2418). Multi-party exchanges and deferred exchanges can qualify. However, gain, but not loss, is recognized if boot (¶2420) is also received.

This nonrecognition provision doesn't apply to any exchange of real property held primarily for sale. (Code Sec. 1031(a)(2))[42]

Nonrecognition under Code Sec. 1031 is mandatory if the conditions are met.[43]

Report a like-kind exchange on Form 8824. If gain is recognized on the exchange because boot (money and/or non-like-kind property) is received, also report the transaction on Form 8949 (sales and other dispositions of capital assets) and Schedule D of the applicable tax form (e.g., Form 1040, Form 1041, Form 1065, or Form 1120), Form 4797, or Form 6252 (whichever applies).[44]

¶ 2417   **Like-kind property defined under like-kind real property exchange rules; real property defined.**

Under Code Sec. 1031, "like-kind" refers to the nature or character the property, not to its grade or quality. Thus, an exchange of real estate for real estate is an exchange of "like-kind" property. (Reg § 1.1031(a)-1(b))[45] "Real property" under Reg § 1.1031(a)-3 is property that is real property under the law of the state or local jurisdiction in which that property is located.[46] It doesn't matter where the real estate is located or whether it's improved or not, but foreign and U.S. real property can't be like-kind. (Code Sec. 1031(h))[47] State law classification of property as real or personal isn't determinative for determining whether properties are like-kind.[48] While the exchange of a leasehold in real property for real property is generally not a like-kind exchange, under safe harbor rules, an exchange of real property for a 30-year leasehold on real property is a like-kind exchange.

39. ¶J-5301 *et seq.*
40. ¶J-5306.1
41. ¶J-5307
42. ¶I-3050 *et seq.*
43. ¶I-3053

44. ¶I-3051
45. ¶I-3069
46. ¶I-3063*et seq.*, ¶I-3068
47. ¶I-3072
48. ¶I-3068

(Reg § 1.1031(a)-1(c))[49] Also, an undivided fractional interest in real property can qualify as like-kind replacement property for other real property.[50] Development rights that a corporation intended to acquire as replacement property were like-kind to a fee interest in relinquished property.[1]

Reg § 1.1031(a)-1 (above) applies only to qualifying exchanges of real property (under Reg § 1.1031(a)-3) that's held for productive use in a trade or business or for investment, and that's not held primarily for sale. (Reg § 1.1031(a)-1(a)(3))[2]

¶ 2418 Property held for productive use in a trade or business or for investment—like-kind real property exchanges.

In a Code Sec. 1031 exchange, both the real property exchanged ("relinquished property") and the property received in the exchange ("replacement property") must be primarily held either for productive use in a trade or business or for investment ("productive use" test). (Code Sec. 1031(a)(1))[3] Whether real property is trade or business or investment property is determined by the taxpayer's intent at the time of the exchange.[4]

Property held for productive use in a trade or business can be exchanged for property held for investment. Similarly, property held for investment can be exchanged for property held for productive use in a trade or business. (Reg § 1.1031(a)-1(a)(1))[5] Reg § 1.1031(a)-1 applies only to qualifying exchanges of real property (under Reg § 1.1031(a)-3) that's held for productive use in a trade or business or for investment, and that's not held primarily for sale. (Reg § 1.1031(a)-1(a)(3))[6]

Under a safe harbor, IRS won't challenge whether a dwelling unit (e.g., a vacation home) meets the productive use test if the unit (whether relinquished property or replacement property) meets certain ownership, rental, and personal use tests. (Rev Proc 2008-16, 2008-1 CB 547)[7] Also, property used for business and personal purposes can't be treated as 2 separate assets for purposes of determining whether the productive use test is satisfied.[8]

¶ 2419 Multi-party (including deferred) nontaxable like-kind exchanges—like-kind real property exchanges.

If a taxpayer wants to engage in a Code Sec. 1031 exchange, but the party who wants taxpayer's property (the relinquished property) doesn't own any like-kind property, the taxpayer can still set up a tax-free exchange if the other party acquires the like-kind replacement property and taxpayer then exchanges the relinquished property for that like-kind property. A multi-party transaction won't qualify as a tax-free exchange if it is viewed for tax purposes as a sale followed by reinvestment of the proceeds in like-kind property.[9]

illustration: A holds Whiteacre for investment. A doesn't want to sell it if that would result in tax, but would exchange it for Blackacre. B wants Whiteacre. C owns Blackacre and is willing to sell, but doesn't want Whiteacre. B buys Blackacre from C for cash. A transfers Whiteacre to B for Blackacre. The exchange is nontaxable to A.

An exchange can be nontaxable (if the time limits at ¶2422 are met) even where a taxpayer transfers the relinquished property in exchange for a written promise by the transferee to deliver like-kind replacement property to the taxpayer in the future, i.e., a deferred or non-simultaneous exchange.[10]

---

49. ¶I-3080
50. ¶I-3077
1. ¶I-3077
2. ¶I-3051
3. ¶I-3086
4. ¶I-3086

5. ¶I-3086
6. ¶I-3052
7. ¶I-3088 *et seq.*
8. ¶I-3100
9. ¶I-3059
10. ¶I-3104

A multiparty tax-free exchange can be set up by using a qualified intermediary (QI) (someone other than the taxpayer or a "disqualified person," e.g., taxpayer's agent) to facilitate the transaction. (Reg § 1.1031(k)-1(g)(4))[11] Reg § 1.1031(k)-1 (above) applies only to qualifying exchanges of real property (under Reg § 1.1031(a)-3) that's held for productive use in a trade or business or for investment, and that's not held primarily for sale. (Reg § 1.1031(a)-1(a)(3))[12] Reverse exchanges (replacement property is acquired before the relinquished property is transferred) can be implemented using qualified exchange accommodation arrangements (QEAAs) under IRS-approved safe-harbor rules. However, the safe-harbor rules don't apply to replacement property owned by the taxpayer within the 180-day period ending on the date of transfer of ownership of the property to an exchange accommodation titleholder (EAT). IRS recognizes, however, that under case law, some reverse exchanges can still qualify even if they don't meet the safe-harbor requirements.[13]

Where property or cash is set aside in a qualified escrow account, qualified trust, or similar account ("exchange funds") pending completion of a deferred like-kind exchange, the exchange funds are generally treated as an exchange facilitator loan, i.e., a demand loan from the taxpayer to the exchange facilitator (i.e., the QI, transferee, escrow holder, trustee, or other party holding exchange funds for the taxpayer in the deferred exchange), and all items of income, deduction, and credit (including capital gains and losses) attributable to the exchange funds are taken into account by the exchange facilitator. (Reg § 1.468B-6(c)(1))[14] If all earnings attributable to the exchange funds are paid to the taxpayer under the terms of the agreement, then the taxpayer takes all items of income, deduction, and credit into account. (Reg § 1.468B-6(c)(2))[15]

¶ 2420 Taxing "boot" in otherwise tax-free exchange—like-kind real property exchanges.

Under Code Sec. 1031(c), if a taxpayer receives boot (money or any other property that doesn't qualify for nonrecognition) in an otherwise nontaxable exchange of stock under Code Sec. 1032 (¶2412), insurance policies under Code Sec. 1035 (¶2415), like-kind real property under Code Sec. 1031 (¶2416), or U.S. obligations under Code Sec. 1037 (¶2414), then, gain to the taxpayer is recognized (is taxable) in an amount not exceeding the value of the boot received (Code Sec. 1031(b)), but loss to the taxpayer isn't recognized (isn't deductible). (Code Sec. 1031(c))[16]

illustration: In a like-kind exchange, T exchanges business real estate worth $500,000 and having an adjusted basis of $200,000 for business real estate worth $400,000 plus $100,000 cash. T's realized gain is $300,000 ($400,000 + $100,000 − $200,000 basis), but the gain recognized is limited to the boot ($100,000). The tax on the remaining $200,000 of realized gain is deferred.

Where a taxpayer gives money in a nontaxable exchange, no gain is recognized. But, if the boot given is property other than money, gain or loss can be recognized. Thus, where stock that has depreciated in value is given in connection with a nontaxable exchange of real estate, loss on the stock is recognized to the extent the stock's adjusted basis exceeds its fair market value. (Reg § 1.1031(d)-1(e))[17]

¶ 2421 Assumption of liabilities treated as boot in a tax-free exchange—like-kind real property exchanges.

Under Code Sec. 1031, liabilities assumed are treated as boot (¶2420) in a nontaxable

---

11. ¶I-3104, ¶I-3118
12. ¶I-3052
13. ¶I-3128 *et seq.*
14. ¶J-1379.1 *et seq.*

15. ¶J-1379.1J *et seq.*
16. ¶I-3160
17. ¶I-3163

exchange. Whether a liability is "assumed" in the exchange is determined under Code Sec. 357(d) (¶3506). (Code Sec. 1031(d)) A taxpayer who assumes the liability is the one giving the boot, while a taxpayer whose liability is assumed *receives* the boot.[18] If each party assumes a liability of the other, only the net liability is boot given or received. (Reg § 1.1031(b)-1(c))

> *illustration:* In a like-kind exchange, A exchanges real property worth $700,000 (basis of $200,000) that is subject to a $200,000 mortgage, with B for replacement real property that is worth $600,000 (basis of $300,000) that is subject to a $100,000 mortgage. A recognizes gain of $100,000 since the mortgage on A's replacement property is $100,000 less than the mortgage on the relinquished property. B recognizes no gain on the transaction.

¶ 2422 Time limits for receipt of replacement property in deferred like-kind real property exchanges.

Like-kind exchange treatment (¶2416) is barred under Code Sec. 1031 if the replacement property isn't identified (e.g., unambiguously described in a written document) on or before 45 days after the transfer, or isn't received within 180 days after the transfer or by the due date (with extensions) of the return for the year of transfer, if earlier. (Code Sec. 1031(a)(3); Reg § 1.1031(k)-1(b))[19] Reg § 1.1031(k)-1 (above) applies only to qualifying exchanges of real property (under Reg § 1.1031(a)-3) that's held for productive use in a trade or business or for investment, and that's not held primarily for sale. (Reg § 1.1031(a)-1(a)(3))[20] There's no good faith exception to these deadlines,[21] but IRS can extend the deadlines for exchanges affected by disasters.[22] A safe harbor provides a method for reporting gain or loss for certain taxpayers who initiate deferred exchanges but fail to complete the exchange because of a default by a qualified intermediary (QI). (Rev Proc 2010-14, 2010-12 IRB 456.)[23]

¶ 2423 Related-party like-kind exchanges—Form 8824—like-kind real property exchanges.

Where a taxpayer exchanges like-kind property with a related taxpayer under Code Sec. 267(b) (¶2444) or Code Sec. 707(b)(1) (¶3723) and, within 2 years of the date of the last transfer that was part of the exchange, either party disposes of the property received in the exchange, then gain or loss not recognized in the Code Sec. 1031 exchange is recognized on the date the later disposition occurs. A disposition includes indirect transfers. Exceptions are made for death, certain involuntary conversions, and non-tax-avoidance transactions. (Code Sec. 1031(f))[24] Form 8824 must be filed for the year of the exchange and also for the 2 years following the exchange.[25]

A qualified intermediary (QI; ¶2419) can't be used to circumvent the limitations that would have applied to a direct exchange between related parties. For example, an exchange was part of a transaction structured to avoid the related party rules (and didn't qualify for nonrecognition treatment) where: (1) a taxpayer (T) transferred appreciated property to a QI, which (2) sold it to an unrelated party and used the proceeds to purchase like-kind property from a party related to T, then (3) transferred that property to T.[26]

---

18. ¶I-3165
19. ¶I-3105
20. ¶I-3052
21. ¶I-3110
22. ¶S-8012

23. ¶I-3119 *et seq.*
24. ¶I-3132 *et seq.*
25. ¶I-3137
26. ¶I-3142

¶ 2424   Rollover of Gain from Certain Sales.

Eligible taxpayers can elect to roll over gain from (1) the sale of qualified empowerment zone assets (¶2425), (2) the sale of qualified small business stock (QSBS; ¶2426), and (3) certain gain from the sale of property that is invested in a Qualified Opportunity Fund (QOF, see ¶2427).

¶ 2425   Election to roll over (and defer recognition of) gain from qualified empowerment zone (QEZ) assets—rollover of gain from certain sales.

Under Code Sec. 1397B, a taxpayer can elect to defer recognition of capital gain on the sale of a QEZ asset held for more than 1 year where replacement QEZ assets are purchased within 60 days. (Code Sec. 1397B(a), Code Sec. 1391(d)(1)(A)(i))[27]

Under Code Sec. 1397B(b)(1)(A) and Code Sec. 1391(d)(1)(A)(i), QEZ assets include qualified community stock, qualified community partnership interests, or qualified community tangible property acquired by the taxpayer after Dec. 31, 2001 and before Jan. 1, 2021.[28]

The rollover rules don't apply to any gain treated as ordinary income or any gain attributable to real property, or an intangible asset, which isn't an integral part of an enterprise zone business. (Code Sec. 1397B(b)(2))[29]

If the rollover is elected, capital gain from the sale of a QEZ asset is recognized only to the extent that the amount realized from the sale exceeds the cost of any QEZ asset (with respect to the same zone as the asset sold) purchased during the 60-day period beginning on the sale date, reduced by any part of the cost previously taken into account under the rollover rule. (Code Sec. 1397B(a))[30]

The basis of the replacement zone asset is reduced by gain not recognized on the rollover, but this rule doesn't apply for purposes of Code Sec. 1202 (exclusion for gain on the sale of small business stock; see ¶2638). (Code Sec. 1397B(b)(4))[31]

¶ 2426   Rollover election for gain from sale of qualified small business stock (QSBS)—rollover of gain from certain sales.

Under Code Sec. 1045, taxpayers other than corporations can elect to roll over capital gain from the sale of QSBS (¶2639) held for more than 6 months, so that gain is recognized only to the extent that the amount realized exceeds (1) the cost of QSBS bought during the 60-day period beginning on the sale date, reduced by (2) any part of the cost previously taken into account under the rule. (Code Sec. 1045(a))

Rules similar to those under Code Sec. 1202(g) (for determining which holders of interests in pass-through entities are eligible for the 50% exclusion of gain from the sale of QSBS, see ¶2638) apply to the rollover of gain from the sale of QSBS by a pass-through entity. (Code Sec. 1045(b)(5))[32]

The replacement stock's holding period includes the holding period of the stock sold, but not for purposes of determining whether the 6-month holding period required for rollovers is met. To qualify as QSBS, the issuing corporation must meet an active business test during substantially all of the taxpayer's holding period for the stock. For purposes of the rollover rules, the replacement stock must meet the active business requirement for the 6-month period following the purchase. (Code Sec. 1045(b)(4))[33]

---

27. ¶I-3431
28. ¶I-3432
29. ¶I-3435 *et seq.*
30. ¶I-3431 *et seq.*

31. ¶I-3433
32. ¶I-9201
33. ¶I-9204

For adjustments to basis of the replacement QSBS, see ¶2501.

¶ 2427 Deferral and exclusion of gains invested in Qualified Opportunity Fund (QOF)—Forms 8949, 8996, 8997; investments in Qualified Opportunity Zone (QOZ) property.

Under Code Sec. 1400Z-2, at a taxpayer's election on the sale or exchange of any property to an unrelated person:

(1) gross income for the tax year doesn't include eligible gain (limited to capital gain, and as otherwise defined under Reg § 1.1400Z2(a)-1(b)(11)(i)(A)(1)), up to the aggregate amount invested by the taxpayer in a QOF during the 180-day period beginning on the date of the sale or exchange (the temporary deferral election);

(2) gain excluded under (1) is included in gross income when an inclusion event occurs or on Dec. 31, 2026 under Code Sec. 1400Z-2(b) (see below); and

(3) the permanent exclusion of certain gain from the investment in the QOF is determined under Code Sec. 1400Z-2(c) (the permanent exclusion/basis adjustment election). (Code Sec. 1400Z-2(a)(1); Reg § 1.1400Z2(a)-1(a)(1))[34]

The election to defer capital gain invested in a QOF is made on Form 8949; Form 8997 is used to inform IRS of the QOF investments and deferred gains held at the beginning and end of the current tax year, as well as any capital gains deferred by investing in a QOF and QOF investments disposed of during the current tax year.

No elections can be made for a sale or exchange if a Code Sec. 1400Z-2 election previously made for the sale or exchange is in effect. (Code Sec. 1400Z-2(a)(2))[35] For how to elect, and annual reporting requirement, see Reg § 1.1400Z2(a)-1(a)(2) and Reg § 1.1400Z2(a)-1(d).[36]

A QOF is, in general, any investment vehicle organized as a corporation or partnership for the purpose of investing in Qualified Opportunity Zone (QOZ) property that holds at least 90% of its assets (90% Asset Test) in QOZ property (as defined in Code Sec. 1400Z-2(d); Reg § 1.1400Z2(d)-1). A QOF must file Form 8996 annually with its income tax return.[37]

A QOZ is a low-income community population census tract that was nominated by the CEO of a state and certified by IRS. Each population census tract in Puerto Rico that is a low-income community is considered to be certified and designated as a QOZ. A designation ends at the close of the 10th calendar year beginning on or after the date of designation. (Code Sec. 1400Z-1(b)) IRS issued a complete list of all population census tracts it has designated as QOZs.[38]

Gain temporarily deferred under item (1) above is included in income in the tax year that includes the *earlier* of: the date on which the investment is sold or exchanged (i.e., the date of an inclusion event), or Dec. 31, 2026. The amount of gain included is the lesser of (a) the deferred gain or the FMV of the investment, over (b) the basis in the investment (¶2502). (Code Sec. 1400Z-2(b)(1); Reg § 1.1400Z2(c)-1(b)(1)(i))[39]

Basis adjustment/permanent exclusion. At the taxpayer's election for an investment held for at least 10 years, the basis of the property equals the FMV of the investment on the date it is sold or exchanged, (Code Sec. 1400Z-2(c); Reg § 1.1400Z2(b)-1(c)(1)) thereby excluding from income any post-acquisition capital gains on QOF investments held for at least 10 years.[40]

---

34. ¶I-8821 *et seq.*
35. ¶I-8823
36. ¶I-8823.2
37. ¶I-8828 *et seq.*

38. ¶I-8838
39. ¶I-8824
40. ¶I-8827

For basis of a QOF investment, see ¶2502.

¶ 2428   **Election of nonrecognition of gain on sale of employer stock to ESOP or EWOC.** ▬▬▬▬▬▬▬▬▬▬▬▬▬▬▬▬▬▬▬▬▬▬▬▬

Under Code Sec. 1042, a taxpayer (but not a C corporation) or taxpayer's executor who sells qualified securities (certain common stock) to an employee stock ownership plan (ESOP) or eligible worker-owned cooperative (EWOC) that holds specified percentages of the securities, can elect nonrecognition of gain if the seller buys "qualified replacement property" (QRP) or securities of another corporation (that doesn't exceed certain passive income limits) within a specified period of time. The seller's gain is recognized only to the extent the sale proceeds exceed the cost of the QRP. Nonrecognition treatment applies only if the gain on the sale of the stock would otherwise have been long-term capital gain. (Code Sec. 1042)[41] However, with some exceptions (e.g., for gifts), gain not recognized on the sale to the ESOP is recognized on the disposition of the QRP. (Code Sec. 1042(e))[42]

Code Sec. 1042 can also apply to the sale of stock of a qualified refiner or processor to an eligible farmers' cooperative. (Code Sec. 1042(g)(1))

¶ 2429   **Involuntary Conversions—Forms 4797 and 8949.** ▬▬▬▬▬▬▬▬▬▬▬▬▬▬▬▬▬▬

No gain is recognized when property is compulsorily or involuntarily converted (¶2431) into property similar or related in service or use. (Code Sec. 1033(a)(1)) Where property is involuntarily converted into money (e.g., insurance proceeds for the property or disaster relief grants) or into property that isn't similar or related in service or use, the taxpayer can defer tax on any gain, if the election is made and replacement property is bought (¶2435) or acquires control of a corporation that owns the replacement property (or acquires the property within a specified time).

The cost of the replacement property must be equal to or more than the net proceeds from the converted property, and the replacement must generally be made within 2 years after the close of the first tax year in which any part of the gain is realized. (Code Sec. 1033) A loss on an involuntary conversion is recognized or not recognized without regard to the involuntary conversion rules. (Reg § 1.1033(a)-1(a))[43] Use Form 8949 to report gain or loss from an involuntary conversion. Form 4797 is used to report an involuntary conversion of assets used in a trade or business.[44]

¶ 2430   **Nonrecognition of gain on involuntary conversions; replacement property.**

No gain is recognized under Code Sec. 1033 where property is involuntarily converted (¶2431) into other property similar or related in service or use to the converted property. (Code Sec. 1033(a)(1)) But, if the taxpayer receives dissimilar property or cash when his or her property is involuntarily converted, the taxpayer must buy "replacement" property (¶2435)[45] or acquire 80% control of a corporation owning or acquiring replacement property within a specified time.[46] Gain is recognized only to the extent the amount realized on the conversion exceeds the cost of the replacement property. (Code Sec. 1033(a)(2)(A))[47]

If a principal residence is involuntarily converted and gain is excluded under Code Sec. 121 (¶2439), then the amount realized under Code Sec. 1033 is the amount realized

41. ¶H-12103 *et seq.*
42. ¶H-12111
43. ¶I-3701
44. ¶I-3773

45. ¶I-3700 *et seq.*
46. ¶I-3743
47. ¶I-3701

less the excluded gain. (Code Sec. 121(d)(5)(B))[48]

Insurance proceeds that compensate for the loss of the right to use property due to loss or destruction can qualify for nonrecognition as involuntary conversion proceeds, but the proceeds of a use and occupancy insurance contract that expressly insures against actual lost profits don't qualify and are included in gross income. (Reg § 1.1033(a)-2(c)(8))[49]

¶ 2431 Involuntary conversion of property defined.

Under Code Sec. 1033, an involuntary conversion is the compulsory or involuntary conversion of property into similar property (¶2435), dissimilar property, or money due to the property's destruction, theft, seizure, requisition or condemnation (actual or threatened). (Code Sec. 1033(a))[50]

Involuntary conversions include the following: sales in actual or threatened condemnation (¶2433); certain sales (or the destruction) of livestock due to disease (Code Sec. 1033(d)); the sale or exchange of livestock (in excess of the number taxpayer would sell under usual business practices) solely on account of drought, flood, or other weather-related conditions (Code Sec. 1033(e)(1));[1] the sale or transfer of property to the federal government, a state or local government, or an Indian tribal government to implement hazard mitigation (Code Sec. 1033(j));[2] and the sale of publicly traded stock under a state escheat law.[3] However, payments for the temporary use of a taxpayer's property by the government where the taxpayer continues to own the property are treated as rental income and not payments in exchange for the property.[4]

¶ 2432 Principal residence or contents converted in a federally declared disaster—involuntary conversions.

Under Code Sec. 1033(h), if the taxpayer's principal residence, or any of its contents, is located in a disaster area and is compulsorily or involuntarily converted because of a "federally declared disaster" (as defined in Code Sec. 165(i)(5)) any gain resulting from the receipt of insurance proceeds for personal property that was part of the contents of the residence and wasn't "scheduled property" for insurance purposes isn't recognized, regardless of the use to which the taxpayer puts those proceeds. (Code Sec. 1033(h)(1); Code Sec. 1033(h)(3))[5] Insurance proceeds received for the home or its "separately scheduled" contents are treated as received for a single item of property, and any property which is similar or related in service or use to the residence so converted (or its contents) is treated for purposes of the involuntary conversion rules as property similar or related in service or use to that single item of property.[6]

For when an extended replacement period applies, see ¶2438.

¶ 2433 Disposition under the threat or imminence of condemnation as an involuntary conversion.

Under Code Sec. 1033, a disposition under the threat or imminence of condemnation is treated as an involuntary conversion (¶2431). (Code Sec. 1033(a)(2)(E)(ii)) Threat or imminence of condemnation exists (1) when taxpayer is informed, orally or in writing, by a representative of a governmental body or an authorized public official, that the body or official has decided to acquire the property, and taxpayer has reasonable grounds to believe that condemnation proceedings will be initiated if he or she doesn't voluntarily sell,

---

48. ¶I-4565
49. ¶I-3724
50. ¶I-3702
1. ¶N-1216 *et seq.*
2. ¶I-3716.1

3. ¶I-3712
4. ¶I-9021
5. ¶I-3772.1 *et seq.*
6. ¶I-3772.2

or (2) where the taxpayer gets information as to a decision to acquire the property for public use through a report in the news media, if a representative of the governmental body or public official involved confirms the published report and taxpayer has reasonable grounds to believe that the necessary steps to condemn will be taken if he or she doesn't sell.[7] Sales to third parties (as distinguished from the condemning agency) also qualify as involuntary conversions if made under the threat or imminence of condemnation.[8]

Condemnation proceeds can't be greater than the amount specifically awarded for the requisitioned property. It may, however, be less if there are any legal or other expenses or special assessments which must be deducted. Sums withheld from the award to pay liens on the property don't reduce the amount realized.[9]

¶ 2434 Severance damages for partial condemnations—involuntary conversions.

Where only part of a property is condemned, the owner may be paid severance damages as compensation for a loss of value in the part of the property retained. Severance damages may be paid, for example, because of impairment of access to the property retained. Payments are considered severance damages only if specifically agreed to in the condemnation proceeding; otherwise, the entire award is considered made for the condemned property. Where severance damage proceeds are used to acquire replacement property, the taxpayer can elect not to recognize any gain from the receipt of the severance damages.[10]

¶ 2435 Similar or related in service or use—replacement property—involuntary conversions.

Under Code Sec. 1033, the replacement property must be similar or related in service or use to the property replaced. (Code Sec. 1033(a)(1)) "Similar or related in service or use" means the use of the replacement property must be substantially similar to the use of the replaced property. But, the replacement property doesn't have to duplicate the converted property.[11]

Alternatively, the taxpayer can acquire control of a corporation owning replacement property. (Code Sec. 1033(a)(2)(A)) In that case, the "like-kind" replacement rule for real property (¶2437) isn't available. The replacement property must qualify under the "similar use" rule. (Code Sec. 1033(g)(2))[12]

If leased property is replaced with other leased property, the similarity of the replacement property is determined on the basis of the nature of the owner's (lessor's) relation to the properties rather than the actual end use made of the properties by the lessee. If the replacement property involves similar business risks, management and landlord services, etc., it is similar even if the lessee's use of the replacement property differs from the lessee's use of the old.[13]

Tangible property acquired and held for productive use in a trade or business is treated as similar or related in service or use to property that (a) was held for investment or for productive use on a trade or business (including inventory), and (b) was involuntarily converted as a result of a federally declared disaster. (Code Sec. 1033(h)(2))[14]

illustration: If a business loses its delivery truck in a federally declared disaster, it can defer tax on any gain realized by timely (¶2438) reinvesting the insurance proceeds in a production machine.

---

7. ¶I-3703
8. ¶I-3706
9. ¶I-3764
10. ¶I-3768 *et seq.*

11. ¶I-3725
12. ¶I-3743
13. ¶I-3730
14. ¶I-3772.6

If, because of drought, flood, or other weather-related conditions or soil contamination or other environmental contamination, it isn't feasible for a taxpayer to reinvest the proceeds from compulsorily or involuntarily converted livestock (¶2431) in property similar or related in use to the old livestock, he or she can reinvest the proceeds in other property (including real property in the case of soil contamination or other environmental contamination) used for farming purposes. (Code Sec. 1033(f))[15]

¶ 2436 Related party exception to nonrecognition rule for involuntary conversions.

Nonrecognition of gain in an involuntary conversion under Code Sec. 1033 isn't permitted if a taxpayer described below acquires replacement property or stock from a related party (under Code Sec. 267(b) (¶2444), or Code Sec. 707(b)(1) (¶3723)):

. . . C corporations.

. . . A partnership if 1 or more C corporations own, directly or indirectly under Code Sec. 707(b)(3) (¶3725), more than 50% of the capital interest or the profits interest of the partnership at the time of the involuntary conversion.

. . . Any other taxpayer (including an individual) if, with respect to property which is involuntarily converted during the tax year, the aggregate realized gain on property on which there is realized gain exceeds $100,000. (Code Sec. 1033(i))[16]

But, nonrecognition applies if the related party acquired the replacement property or stock from an unrelated party, within the replacement period (¶2438). (Code Sec. 1033(i)(1))[17]

For a partnership (or S corporation), this denial of nonrecognition rule applies to a partnership (or S corporation) and to each partner (or S shareholder). Thus, the annual $100,000 limit applies to both the entity and each partner (or S shareholder).[18]

¶ 2437 Replacement of condemned real estate—qualification for nonrecognition treatment—involuntary conversions.

Under Code Sec. 1033, a replacement of condemned real estate held for productive business use or for rental or investment qualifies for nonrecognition treatment if the replacement property is property of a like-kind. (Code Sec. 1033(g)(1)) Determination of whether replacement property is of like-kind is made under the rules at ¶2416, rather than the "similar use" rule. For example, improved realty isn't similar in use to unimproved realty (Reg § 1.1033(a)-2(c)(9)(i)), but the 2 properties are of like-kind, see ¶2417.[19] But, this rule doesn't apply to real estate held primarily for sale (Code Sec. 1033(g)(1)) or where control of a corporation owning replacement property is acquired. (Code Sec. 1033(g)(2))[20]

¶ 2438 Replacement period for involuntarily converted property.

Under Code Sec. 1033, converted property must be replaced within a period:

(1) beginning with the earlier of (a) the date the property was destroyed, stolen, condemned, etc., or (b) the date condemnation or requisition was first threatened or became imminent, (Code Sec. 1033(a)(2)(B)), and

(2) ending (a) 2 years after the close of the first tax year in which any part of the gain is realized (3 years in the case of condemnation or threat of condemnation of real property described at ¶2437; 4 years for principal residences converted due to federally declared

15. ¶N-1220
16. ¶I-3733.1, I-3733.2
17. ¶I-3733.1
18. ¶I-3733.2
19. ¶I-3727*et seq.*
20. ¶I-3727

disasters, see ¶2432, and for certain livestock converted on account of drought, flood, or other weather-related conditions, see ¶2431), or (b) at a later date allowed by IRS on application by the taxpayer, or as extended by IRS for livestock sales in regions with persistent droughts. (Code Sec. 1033(a)(2)(B), Code Sec. 1033(g)(4), Code Sec. 1033(h)(1)(B), Code Sec. 1033(e)(2))[21]

¶ 2439   Exclusion of Gain on Principal Residence. ▮▮▮▮▮▮▮▮▮▮

Under Code Sec. 121, a taxpayer can exclude up to $250,000 ($500,000 for certain joint filers) of gain from the sale of his or her principal residence owned and used by the taxpayer as a principal residence for at least 2 of the 5 years before the sale. (Code Sec. 121(a))[22]

The exclusion doesn't apply if, during the 2-year period ending on the sale date, the exclusion applied to another sale by the taxpayer. (Code Sec. 121(b)(3); Reg § 1.121-2(b)(1))[23]

Married joint filers (¶4705) for the year of sale can exclude up to $500,000 of gain if (1) either spouse met the ownership test (¶2441), (2) both spouses meet the use test (¶2441), and (3) neither spouse is ineligible for a full exclusion because of the once-every-2-year limit. (Code Sec. 121(b)(2)(A); Reg § 1.121-2(a)(3))[24] A surviving spouse can qualify for the up-to-$500,000 exclusion if the sale occurs not later than 2 years after the other spouse's death, if the requirements for the $500,000 exclusion were met immediately before the spouse's death, and the survivor hasn't remarried before the sale. (Code Sec. 121(b)(4))[25]

If joint filers aren't eligible for the $500,000 exclusion, the amount of the exclusion that they can claim is the sum of each spouse's maximum exclusion determined on a separate basis as if they had not been married. For this purpose, each spouse is treated as owning the house during the period that either spouse owned the house. (Code Sec. 121(b)(2)(B))[26]

Gain from the sale or exchange of property that is attributable to periods of "nonqualified use' isn't eligible for the exclusion. (Code Sec. 121(b)(5)(A))[27] Nonqualified use refers to any period after 2008 during which the property isn't used as the principal residence of the taxpayer, or spouse or former spouse. (Code Sec. 121(b)(5)(C)(i))[28] Exceptions to the definition of 'period of nonqualified use' include (1) use occurring in the 5-year testing period after the date the residence was last used as a principal residence, (2) temporary absence (not to exceed an aggregate period of 2 years), and (3) any period during which the taxpayer or spouse is serving on qualified official extended duty (not to exceed an aggregate period of 10 years), see ¶2441. (Code Sec. 121(b)(5)(C)(ii))[29]

The gain allocated to periods of nonqualified use is the total amount of gain, multiplied by a fraction, the numerator of which is the aggregate periods of nonqualified use during the period the taxpayer owned the property, and the denominator of which is the period the taxpayer owned the property. (Code Sec. 121(b)(5)(B))[30]

The exclusion also doesn't apply to gain attributable to post-May 6, '97 depreciation (Code Sec. 121(d)(6)),[31] and that gain isn't taken into account in determining the amount of gain allocated to nonqualified use. (Code Sec. 121(b)(5)(D))[32]

The exchange or involuntary conversion (destruction (but only if the residence is totally destroyed), as well as condemnation) of a principal residence is treated as a sale for purposes of the exclusion. (Code Sec. 121(d)(5)(A))[33]

---

21. ¶I-3734; ¶N-1216.2 *et seq.*
22. ¶I-4520 *et seq.*
23. ¶I-4539*et seq.*
24. ¶I-4536
25. ¶I-4538.1
26. ¶I-4537
27. ¶I-4568.1

28. ¶I-4568.3
29. ¶I-4568.4
30. ¶I-4568.2
31. ¶I-4568
32. ¶I-4568.7
33. ¶I-4565

If property is used for both residential and business (or investment) purposes, no allocation of gain is required if both the residential and non-residential portions of the property are within the same dwelling unit, but gain isn't excludable to the extent of any post-May 6, '97, depreciation. However, gain is allocated if the part of the home for which the use requirement isn't met is separate from the dwelling unit. (Reg § 1.121-1(e)(1))[34]

Individuals subject to the expatriate tax rules (¶4639) can't claim the exclusion. (Code Sec. 121(e))[35]

For a taxpayer who acquired a home in a like-kind exchange (¶2416 *et seq.*) in which any gain wasn't recognized, or a donee of that taxpayer, the exclusion doesn't apply for the 5-year period beginning with the date of the acquisition. (Code Sec. 121(d)(10))[36]

A taxpayer can elect out of the exclusion. (Code Sec. 121(f))[37]

If all of the homesale gain is excluded, the transaction isn't reported on the return. But, entries on Form 8949 are necessary if there is taxable gain on the homesale (e.g., realized gain exceeds the excludable amount).[38]

¶ 2440 Reduced exclusion for partially qualifying principal residence sales or exchanges.

A reduced maximum Code Sec. 121 exclusion can apply to taxpayers who sell or exchange their principal residence but (1) fail to qualify for the 2-out-of-5-year ownership and use test, or (2) previously sold another home within the 2-year period ending on the sale date of the current home in a transaction to which the exclusion applied (¶2439). If a taxpayer's failure to meet either rule occurs because he or she must sell the home due to a change of place of employment, health or, certain unforeseen circumstances, then the taxpayer can claim a reduced exclusion. Under these circumstances, the maximum gain that can be excluded is equal to the full $250,000 or $500,000 exclusion times a fraction having as its numerator the shorter of (a) aggregate periods of ownership and use of the home by the taxpayer as a principal residence during the 5 years ending on the sale date, or (b) the period of time after the last sale to which the exclusion applied, and before the date of the current sale, and having 2 years (or its equivalent in months) as its denominator. (Code Sec. 121(c); Reg § 1.121-3(g))[39]

Illustration: S, a single taxpayer, owned and used a home as a principal residence for the last 18 months. S sells the home because S has a new job in another city. S realizes $50,000 on the sale. Since S doesn't meet the 2-year ownership and use tests and the sale is due to a change in place of employment, S qualifies for the reduced exclusion. The amount of gain excluded by S can't exceed $187,500 ($250,000 × 1.5 ÷ 2). S can exclude all of the gain ($50,000) from the sale.

The up-to-10-year suspension for qualifying military services or Foreign Service members or intelligence community employees (¶2441) can be elected to determine the amount of the reduced exclusion. (Code Sec. 121(d)(9)(A))[40]

To claim a reduced exclusion, the sale or exchange must be due to a change of place of employment, health, or unforeseen circumstances. If a safe harbor applies, a sale is deemed to be made for a qualifying reason. If a safe harbor doesn't apply, a sale or exchange is by reason of a change in place of employment, health, or unforeseen circumstances only if the primary reason for the sale or exchange is one of those reasons. (Reg § 1.121-3(b))[41]

---

34. ¶I-4532 *et seq.*
35. ¶I-4569
36. ¶I-4561.1
37. ¶I-4570
38. ¶I-4521
39. ¶I-4557
40. ¶I-4557.1
41. ¶I-4541

A sale or exchange is due to a change in place of employment, if, in the case of a qualified individual (taxpayer, spouse, co-owner, or a person living in the taxpayer's household), the primary reason for the sale or exchange is a change in the location of the individual's employment (including self-employment). A distance safe harbor can apply if the new place of employment is at least 50 miles farther from the residence sold or exchanged than was the former place of employment (for the formerly unemployed, 50 miles between the new place of employment and the residence sold or exchanged).(Reg § 1.121-3(c))[42]

The health condition is met if the primary reason for the sale is to (1) obtain, provide, or facilitate the diagnosis, cure, mitigation, or treatment of disease, illness, or injury of a qualified individual (defined in Reg § 1.121-3(f)), or (2) obtain or provide medical or personal care for a qualified individual suffering from a disease, illness, or injury. The health condition isn't satisfied if the sale is merely beneficial to the individual's general health or well-being. If a doctor recommends a change of residence for the health reasons listed above in (1) or (2), a safe harbor can apply. (Reg § 1.121-3(d); Reg § 1.121-3(f))[43]

A sale, etc. is caused by unforeseen circumstances if the primary reason for it is an event that the taxpayer couldn't reasonably have anticipated before buying and occupying the residence. A sale, etc. by reason of unforeseen circumstances (other than a circumstance covered by a safe harbor, or an event designated by IRS as an unforeseen circumstance) doesn't qualify for the reduced exclusion if the primary reason for the sale, etc. is a preference for a different residence or an improvement in financial circumstances. (Reg § 1.121-3(e))[44]

¶ 2441 Ownership and use tests to qualify for homesale exclusion of gain on sale of principal residence.

The maximum Code Sec. 121 exclusion (¶2439) applies only if a taxpayer owned the home and used it as a principal residence for at least 2 of the 5 years ending on the date of the sale. (Code Sec. 121(a))

A taxpayer is treated as the owner and seller of a residence held by a trust during the period that he or she is treated as the owner of a grantor trust (¶3951 *et seq.*) or the part of the trust that includes the residence. Similar treatment applies to certain disregarded entities (e.g., single member LLCs, see ¶3701). (Reg § 1.121-1(c)(3))[45]

Each unmarried taxpayer who jointly owns a principal residence can exclude up to $250,000 of gain that is attributable to that taxpayer's interest in the residence. (Reg § 1.121-2(a)(2))[46]

Gain from the sale or exchange of partial interests (other than interests remaining after the sale or exchange of a remainder interest) in the taxpayer's principal residence is excludable if the interest sold, etc. includes an interest in the dwelling unit. Only 1 maximum limitation amount of $250,000 ($500,000 for certain joint returns) applies to the combined sales or exchanges of partial interests. (Reg § 1.121-4(e))[47]

An individual's bankruptcy estate (¶3968) in a chapter 7 or 11 bankruptcy case under title 11 of the U.S. Code succeeds to and takes into account the exclusion if the individual (debtor) otherwise satisfies the requirements. (Reg § 1.1398-3)[48]

Under the following circumstances, a taxpayer can 'tack on' someone else's ownership and/or use period to his or her own period.

. . . An unmarried individual whose spouse (¶4705) was deceased on the sale date can

---

42. ¶I-4542 *et seq.*
43. ¶I-4543 *et seq.*
44. ¶I-4547 *et seq.*
45. ¶I-4529 *et seq.*

46. ¶I-4535
47. ¶I-4567
48. ¶C-9718.01

tack on the decedent's ownership and use period to his or her own period. (Code Sec. 121(d)(2))[49]

... An individual who receives a home in a Code Sec. 1041(a) transaction (¶2443), such as a tax-free transfer from a spouse (or former spouse), can tack on the transferor's ownership period to his or her own ownership period. (Code Sec. 121(d)(3)(A))[50]

... An individual is treated as using a home as his or her principal residence during any period of ownership that the individual's spouse (see ¶4705) or former spouse is granted use of the property under a divorce or separation instrument. (Code Sec. 121(d)(3)(B))[1]

However, if a taxpayer voluntarily demolishes the principal residence and builds a new residence on the same land, the period that the taxpayer owned and used the demolished principal residence isn't taken into account in determining qualification for the exclusion on the sale of the new residence.[2]

If a taxpayer becomes physically or mentally incapable of self-care and, during the 5-year period ending on the home's sale date, owns and uses the home as a principal residence for periods aggregating at least 1 year, the taxpayer is treated as using the home as a principal residence during any time in the 5-year period in which he or she owns the home and lives in a facility (including a nursing home) licensed by a state or political subdivision to care for someone in the taxpayer's condition. (Code Sec. 121(d)(7))[3]

A member of the uniformed services or the Foreign Service, and intelligence community employees can elect to suspend the 5-year period for measuring ownership and use during any period that service member and his or her spouse (¶4705) is serving on extended duty at least 50 miles from the residence or while residing under orders in government quarters. (Code Sec. 121(d)(9)(A)) The suspension can't last more than 10 years. (Code Sec. 121(d)(9)(B))[4] A Peace Corps volunteer or his or her spouse serving outside the U.S. can also make the election. (Code Sec. 121(d)(12))[5]

¶ 2442 Sales and Exchanges Between Related Taxpayers. ▬▬▬▬▬

No gain or loss is recognized on a transfer of property between spouses (or former spouses incident to divorce; ¶2443). No deduction is allowed for any loss from the sale or exchange of property between specified related taxpayers (¶2444). A loss from a transfer between members of the same controlled group is generally deferred until the property is transferred outside the group (¶2446).

¶ 2443 Gain or loss not recognized on transfer to spouse—related taxpayer sales and exchanges.

Under Code Sec. 1041, no gain or loss is recognized on a transfer of property to (or in trust for the benefit of) the transferor's spouse, or to a former spouse incident to a divorce. (Code Sec. 1041(a))[6] Certain transfers to third parties on behalf of (i.e., in satisfaction of an obligation or liability of) the spouse or former spouse qualify for nonrecognition. (Reg § 1.1041-1T(c), Q&A-9)[7] However, nonrecognition doesn't apply to transfers in trust where liability exceeds basis (Code Sec. 1041(e)),[8] to transfers in trust of installment obligations (Code Sec. 453B(g)),[9] or where the transferee spouse is a nonresident alien. (Code Sec. 1041(d))[10]

A transfer of property is incident to divorce if it occurs within 1 year after the date the

---

49. ¶I-4559
50. ¶I-4558
1. ¶I-4558
2. ¶I-4527
3. ¶I-4563
4. ¶I-4528.1

5. ¶I-4528.7
6. ¶I-3601
7. ¶I-3604
8. ¶I-3608
9. ¶I-3609
10. ¶I-3611

marriage ceases (Code Sec. 1041(c)(1)) or the transfer is related to the cessation of the marriage. (Code Sec. 1041(c)(2)) A transfer is related to the cessation if the transfer is under a divorce or separation instrument and the transfer occurs not more than 6 years after the date the marriage ceases. For later transfers, there's a presumption that the transfer isn't related to the cessation. (Reg § 1.1041-1T(b), Q&A-7)[11]

¶ 2444 Losses from sales and exchanges between related taxpayers—family members, controlled corporations, controlled group members, corporations and partnerships.

Under Code Sec. 267, no deduction is allowed for losses from sales or exchanges between certain related taxpayers. (Code Sec. 267(a)) The following are related taxpayers:

Members of the seller's family, but only brothers and sisters (whole or half blood), spouse, ancestors, and lineal descendants. (Code Sec. 267(a), Code Sec. 267(b)(1), Code Sec. 267(c)(4))[12] In-laws aren't considered members of the seller's family. [13]

Controlled corporations. A taxpayer and a controlled corporation, and a fiduciary and a corporation controlled by the trust or grantor. "Control" is direct or indirect ownership of more than 50% in value of the outstanding stock. (Code Sec. 267(b)(2), Code Sec. 267(b)(8))[14]

Controlled group member. Corporations that are members of the same controlled group of corporations. (Code Sec. 267(b)(3))[15] For deferral of losses on sales, etc. between controlled group members, see ¶2446.

A corporation and a partnership, if the same persons own more than 50% in value of the corporation's outstanding stock, and more than 50% of the capital interest, or the profits interest, in the partnership. (Code Sec. 267(b)(10))[16]

An S corporation and another S corporation, if the same persons own more than 50% in value of each corporation's outstanding stock. (Code Sec. 267(b)(11))[17]

An S corporation and a C corporation, if the same persons own more than 50% in value of each corporation's outstanding stock. (Code Sec. 267(b)(12))[18]

An estate and a beneficiary of that estate, except in the case of a sale or exchange in satisfaction of a pecuniary bequest. (Code Sec. 267(b)(13))[19]

Trustees, grantors, and beneficiaries, that is, a trust's grantor and the fiduciary; the trust's fiduciary and its beneficiary; the fiduciaries of 2 different trusts with the same grantor; a fiduciary of one trust and the beneficiary of another trust with the same grantor; and a trust fiduciary and a corporation if the trust or its grantor owns more than 50% in value of the corporation's outstanding stock directly or indirectly. (Code Sec. 267(b)(4), Code Sec. 267(b)(5), Code Sec. 267(b)(6), Code Sec. 267(b)(7), Code Sec. 267(b)(8))[20]

Exempt organizations. A person and an exempt organization controlled, directly or indirectly, by that person or the family members. (Code Sec. 267(b)(9))[21]

For this purpose, ownership of stock is attributed to a taxpayer as follows:

(1) A shareholder is considered to own a proportionate share of the stock owned by the corporation.

(2) A partner is considered to own a proportionate share of the stock owned by the

11. ¶I-3613
12. ¶I-3512
13. ¶I-3515
14. ¶I-3519
15. ¶I-3522
16. ¶I-3532

17. ¶I-3531
18. ¶I-3531
19. ¶I-3533
20. ¶I-3527
21. ¶I-3530

partnership.

(3) An individual owning some stock in a corporation is considered the owner of stock owned by his or her partner.

(4) A beneficiary is considered to own a proportionate share of the stock owned by the trust or estate.

(5) An individual is considered to own stock owned by family members (as defined above) whether or not he or she is the actual owner of stock in the same corporation. (Code Sec. 267(c); Reg § 1.267(c)-1)[22]

¶ 2445 Disallowed loss can reduce gain on a later sale by related buyer—related taxpayer sales and exchanges.

Under Code Sec. 267, a related buyer (¶2444) can reduce gain on property he or she resells at a gain by the loss disallowed to the seller under these conditions: (1) a loss deduction was barred under Code Sec. 267; (2) the resale or exchange is at a gain, and the property is either the property on which the loss was disallowed or property the basis of which is determined by reference to the basis of that property; (3) the loss deduction on the original sale to the taxpayer wasn't barred under the wash sale rules (¶2456); and, for sales and exchanges of property acquired after Dec. 31, 2015, loss with respect to the property that has been sold or exchanged is subject to federal income tax in the transferor's hands immediately before the transfer. (Code Sec. 267(d); Reg § 1.267(d)-1)[23]

Illustration: H sells farmland (basis: $80,000) to his wife (W) for $55,000. H can't deduct the realized loss of $25,000. W exchanges the farmland, held for investment purposes, with an unrelated individual for 2 city lots, also held for investment purposes. W's basis in the city lots ($55,000) is a substituted basis determined by reference to the farmland's basis. Later, W sells the city lots for $100,000. Although W's realized gain is $45,000 ($100,000 – $55,000), W's recognized gain is only $20,000, the excess of the realized gain ($45,000) over the loss ($25,000) not allowable to H. (Reg § 1.267(d)-1(a)(4), Ex (4))

¶ 2446 Loss between members of controlled group are deferred—related taxpayer sales and exchanges.

Under Code Sec. 267, with some exceptions, a loss from a transfer between controlled group members is deferred (rather than denied). The loss is recognized when the property is transferred outside the group if the loss would be recognized under consolidated return principles. (Code Sec. 267(f)(2))[24]

For purposes of any Code section other than Code Sec. 267 which refers to a relationship which would result in a disallowance of losses under Code Sec. 267, deferral under Code Sec. 267(f)(2) is treated as a disallowance. (Code Sec. 267(f)(4); Reg § 1.267(f)-1)[25]

¶ 2447 Installment Sales and Other Deferred Payment Sales. ▰▰▰▰▰▰▰▰

Under the installment method in Code Sec. 453, a nondealer (unless he or she elects out, see ¶2451) reports gain on a sale as payments are received, instead of reporting all the gain in the year of sale (¶2448).

For sales that don't qualify for installment reporting, see ¶2449. For contingent payment sales, see ¶2450. For character of gain when depreciable property is sold, see ¶2452. For sales and other dispositions of installment notes, see ¶2453. For an installment sale to a related person who resells the property, see ¶2454. For pledge and interest rule, see ¶2455.

---

22. ¶I-3516
23. ¶I-3538

24. ¶s E-8250, I-3524 *et seq.*
25. ¶I-3505

For unstated interest on installment sales, see ¶1306 *et seq.*

¶ 2448 Reporting gain elect nonrecognition of gain under the installment sale rules—Form 6252.

Under Code Sec. 453, both cash-method and accrual-method taxpayers can use the installment sale rules to report gain on the disposition of non-dealer property where at least 1 payment is to be received after the close of the tax year of the disposition unless the taxpayer elects not to use the installment method (see ¶2451) or the transaction is one for which the installment method can't be used (see ¶2449). (Code Sec. 453)[26] The amount of a payment included in the seller's income is that part of the payments received in the year that the gross profit realized or to be realized bears to the total contract price (the "gross profit ratio"). (Code Sec. 453(c); Reg § 15A.453-1(b)(2)(i))[27]

illustration: Taxpayer sells personal-use property for a gross profit of $20,000 at a contract price of $80,000. The gross profit ratio is 25% ($20,000 ÷ $80,000). Therefore, 25% of each payment collected on the sale (including the down payment) is gain that is included in gross income for that tax year. The ratio remains constant for all installment payments received on the sale.

Payments include:

(a) amounts actually received by the seller, e.g., cash, other property, foreign currency, marketable securities, or evidences of indebtedness of persons other than the buyer. (Reg § 15A.453-1(b)(3)(i))[28] Evidences of indebtedness of the buyer are treated as payment if they are payable on demand or readily tradable; (Code Sec. 453(f)(4))[29]

(b) the buyer's payments of the seller's selling expenses;[30] and

(c) the amount by which qualifying debt assumed or taken subject to by the buyer exceeds the seller's basis. (Reg § 15A.453-1(b)(3)(i))[31]

Gross profit is the selling price less the property's adjusted basis (as increased by selling expenses). (Reg § 15A.453-1(b)(2)(v)) The selling price is the gross selling price without reduction to reflect any existing mortgage or other encumbrance on the property (whether assumed or taken subject to by the buyer) and without reduction to reflect any selling expenses. Neither interest (whether stated or unstated) nor OID is part of the selling price. (Reg § 15A.453-1(b)(2)(ii))[32] The *total contract price* is the selling price, reduced by debt on the property that the buyer assumes (or takes subject to), but only to the extent of the seller's basis in the property. (Reg § 15A.453-1(b)(2)(iii))[33]

Gain recaptured under Code Sec. 1245 (¶2674) or Code Sec. 1250 (¶2676), including gain attributable to the Code Sec. 179 expense election (¶1935 *et seq.*), or so much of the unrealized receivables under Code Sec. 751 (¶3747) as relates to Code Sec. 1245 or Code Sec. 1250, is ordinary income in the year of sale. Only gain that isn't recapture income is taken into account under the installment method. (Code Sec. 453(i))[34] The recaptured amount is added to the adjusted basis of the property for purposes of determining basis recovered and gain recognized from each installment.[35]

While gain on the sale of a partnership interest qualifies for installment reporting, gain attributable to inventories and unrealized receivables held by the partnership does not.[36]

---

26. ¶G-6000 *et seq.*
27. ¶G-6052 *et seq.*
28. ¶G-6151 *et seq.*
29. ¶G-6163
30. ¶G-6151
31. ¶G-6155

32. ¶G-6053 *et seq.*
33. ¶G-6060
34. ¶G-6097 *et seq.*
35. ¶G-6097
36. ¶G-6010

¶ 2449 When the installment method can't be used; dealers in property.

Code Sec. 453(b)(2) provides that the installment method (¶2447) can't be used by dealers in property, real or personal. (Code Sec. 453(b)(2))[37] However, the installment method can be used for:

- dispositions by farmers (not merchants) of any property used or produced in the trade or business of farming (Code Sec. 453(l)(2)(A)); and
- dispositions to an individual in the ordinary course of a taxpayer's trade or business of the following, but only if interest is paid on the tax deferred when the installment method is used: (Code Sec. 453(l)(2)(B))

. . . a timeshare right to use, or a timeshare right to an ownership interest in, residential real property for not more than 6 weeks per year, or a right to use specified campgrounds for recreational purposes (timeshare rights or ownership interests held by the spouse, children, grandchildren or parents of an individual are treated as held by the individual), or

. . . any residential lots, but only if the taxpayer (or any related person) isn't to make any improvements with respect to the lots.[38]

The installment method can't be used for:

. . . sales of stock or securities traded on an established securities market (Code Sec. 453(k)(2)(A)), but it can be used for unregistered restricted stock sold in a private placement;[39]

. . . sales at a loss;[40]

. . . sales of depreciable property between persons related within the Code Sec. 1239(b) rules (¶2671), and between controlled partnerships (as defined in Code Sec. 707(b)(1)(B), ¶3723 *et seq.*), unless it's established to IRS's satisfaction that the sale didn't have as 1 of its principal purposes the avoidance of federal tax. (Code Sec. 453(g))[41]

¶ 2450 Contingent payment installment sales.

The installment method (¶2447) is used to report contingent payment sales (sales or other dispositions of property in a tax year in which the total selling price can't be determined at the close of that tax year), unless the taxpayer elects out of the installment method (¶2451). (Reg § 15A.453-1(c)(1)) In general, basis is allocated to payments received and to be received by treating the stated maximum selling price as the selling price. (Reg § 15A.453-1(c)(2)(i)) However, if:

. . . the maximum selling price can't be determined, but the maximum period over which payments may be received is fixed, the seller's basis is allocated to the tax years in which payments may be received in equal annual increments. (Reg § 15A.453-1(c)(3)(i))

. . . the agreement neither specifies a maximum selling price nor limits payments to a fixed period, the transaction can be a sale or payments under the agreement may be rent or royalty income. If the transaction is a sale, basis (including selling expenses) generally is recovered in equal annual increments over a period of 15 years starting with the date of sale. (Reg § 15A.453-1(c)(4))[42]

A seller may (if IRS grants permission) use an alternative basis recovery method if it's able to demonstrate that applying the normal basis recovery rule would substantially and

---

37. ¶G-6601;
38. ¶G-6603 *et seq.*
39. ¶G-6016 *et seq.*

40. ¶G-6015
41. ¶G-6201 *et seq.*
42. ¶G-6250 *et seq.*

inappropriately defer recovery of basis and the alternative method would likely result in basis recovery at a rate at least twice as fast. (Reg § 15A.453-1(c)(7))[43]

¶ 2451　Electing out of the installment method—Form 8949.

Under Code Sec. 453(d), an election out of the installment method for a sale is made by reporting an amount realized equal to the selling price (including the full face amount of any installment obligation), on the return filed for the year of the sale. The full amount is reported on Form 8949, the totals from which are carried to Schedule D. The election out must be made on or before the due date (including extensions) for filing the return for the year of sale. A late election is allowed only if IRS concludes taxpayer had good cause. An election out may be revoked only with IRS's consent. (Code Sec. 453(d); Reg § 15A.453-1(d)(3))[44]

recommendation: Consider electing out if the seller will be in a much higher tax bracket in post-sale years than in the sale year, or if he or she is selling a property with large suspended passive activity losses so these losses can be used immediately to offset nonpassive income (¶1814).

A taxpayer who elects out of the installment method recognizes gain on the sale under his or her accounting method. The amount realized attributable to a debt instrument received is the debt instrument's issue price as determined under the OID rules (¶1316). (Reg § 1.1001-1(g))[45]

¶ 2452　Character of installment gain on sale of depreciable realty.

When a noncorporate taxpayer sells depreciable real property, the gain may be partially 25%-rate gain (unrecaptured section 1250, see ¶2604), and partially adjusted net capital gain (taxed at a lower rate, see ¶2603). If there are both types of gain, the 25%-rate gain is taken into account as payments are received before any adjusted net capital gain is included. (Reg § 1.453-12(a)) See ¶2600 *et seq.* for the taxation of capital gains.[46]

illustration: T sells depreciable real property for a total price of $150,000. T's total gain is $30,000, $20,000 of which is 25%-rate gain, and $10,000 of which is adjusted net capital gain. The sales price is payable in 5 equal annual installments of $30,000, with the 1st installment due in the year of sale. T takes $6,000 of gain into account for each installment. The entire gain ($6,000 on the 1st 3 installments, and $2,000 on the 4th installment), is taxed as 25%-rate gain. The remaining $4,000 of gain on the 4th installment and the entire $6,000 of gain on the 5th installment is taxed at the applicable rate for adjusted net capital gain.

Net Code Sec. 1231 gain that would otherwise be taxed as long-term capital gain, is taxed as ordinary income to the extent of non-recaptured net Code Sec. 1231 losses for the preceding 5 years (¶2666). If net Code Sec. 1231 gain for a tax year consists of both 25%-rate gain and adjusted net capital gain, the 25%-rate gain is recharacterized as ordinary income first. This rule also applies to installment payments. (Reg § 1.453-12(d), Ex. 3)[47]

¶ 2453　Sale, exchange, or satisfaction of installment obligations.

For installment obligations satisfied at face value, gain or loss is computed under the general rules (¶2448) for computing income on the installment method.[48]

If an installment obligation is satisfied at other than face or is sold or exchanged, gain or

---

43. ¶G-6279 *et seq.*
44. ¶G-6350 *et seq.*
45. ¶G-6550 *et seq.*

46. ¶G-6102
47. ¶G-6105
48. ¶G-6052

loss is the difference between the basis of the obligation and the amount realized. If it's distributed, transmitted, or disposed of other than by sale or exchange, gain or loss is the difference between its basis and its fair market value (FMV) (Code Sec. 453B(a)),[49] except that if it's distributed in a complete liquidation of a subsidiary to which Code Sec. 337(a) applies (¶3560), no gain or loss is recognized. (Code Sec. 453B(d))[50] If there's a repossession by the seller of the personal property sold following the buyer's default (i.e., a disposition of the installment obligation by the seller),[1] the seller's gain or loss is: (1) the FMV of the property, plus anything received from the buyer in addition to the repossessed property; *minus* (2) the seller's basis in the installment obligation, plus any expense in connection with the repossession.[2] Transmission of an installment obligation at death doesn't result in gain or loss to the decedent. (Code Sec. 453B(c); Reg § 1.451-1(d)(2))[3]

A reduction of the purchase price, or a modification of an installment obligation by changing the payment terms (e.g., reducing the purchase price and interest rate, and deferring or increasing the payment dates) isn't a disposition of the obligation.[4]

The basis of an obligation is the excess of its face value over the amount equal to the income that would be returnable if the obligation were fully satisfied. (Code Sec. 453B(b))[5]

🅡ꞮA observation: Thus, an installment obligation's basis is the adjusted basis of the property sold less any part of that basis allocated to a payment made at the time of sale.

¶ 2454   Installment sale to related person who then resells.

Under Code Sec. 453(e), if a person disposes of property in an installment sale (1st disposition) to a related person (see below) who then disposes of the property (2nd disposition) within 2 years of the 1st disposition, and before all payments are made on the 1st disposition, the amount the related person (i.e., the buyer in the 1st disposition) realizes as a result of the 2nd disposition is treated as being received by the original seller at the time of the 2nd disposition. (Code Sec. 453(e)(1), Code Sec. 453(e)(2))

The amount treated as received by the person making the 1st disposition because of the 2nd disposition can't be more than:

. . . the lesser of the total amount realized on any 2nd disposition of the property occurring in the tax year, or the total contract price for the 1st disposition; minus

. . . the sum of the aggregate amount of payments received with respect to the 1st disposition before the close of the tax year in which the 2nd disposition occurs, and the aggregate amount treated as received with respect to the 1st disposition because of earlier dispositions of installment obligations by related persons. (Code Sec. 453(e)(3))[6]

For this purpose, if the 2nd disposition isn't a sale or exchange, the property's fair market value is treated as the amount realized. (Code Sec. 453(e)(4))[7]

A "related person" is someone whose stock would be attributed to the initial seller under Code Sec. 318(a) (¶3523), other than under the option attribution rules, or a person who is related to the initial seller under Code Sec. 267(b) (disallowance of loss on sales between related parties, ¶2444). (Code Sec. 453(f)(1))[8]

Exceptions include involuntary conversions, deaths, corporations' reacquisition of their own stock, and where IRS rules out tax avoidance. (Code Sec. 453(e)(6), Code Sec. 453(e)(7))[9]

---

49. ¶G-6454 *et seq.*
50. ¶G-6489
1. ¶G-6476
2. ¶G-6481
3. ¶G-6507
4. ¶G-6486

5. ¶G-6456
6. ¶G-6401 *et seq.*
7. ¶G-6403
8. ¶G-6416
9. ¶G-6411 *et seq.*

Except for marketable securities, the 2-year period stops running when puts, options, or short sales, etc., are involved. (Code Sec. 453(e)(2))[10]

¶ 2455   Installment sales of certain property for more than $150,000—"pledge and interest" rule.

Under Code Sec. 453A, the following rules apply to an installment sale of "any" property (except personal use or farm property, and dealer sales of timeshares or residential lots) where the selling price is over $150,000: (Code Sec. 453A)[11]

(1) If an installment obligation from the sale plus all other installment obligations that arose from dispositions during the tax year and are still outstanding at the close of the tax year total over $5 million, the seller must pay, as additional tax, interest at the underpayment rate (¶4849) on the deferred tax attributable to those installment obligations. Once interest is required on an obligation that arises during any year, interest must be paid for any later tax year if any of the obligation is still outstanding at the close of that later year.

(2) If an installment obligation from the sale becomes security for any indebtedness, the net proceeds of the indebtedness are treated as a payment of the obligation as of the later of the time the indebtedness becomes secured or the proceeds of the indebtedness are received by the seller. (Code Sec. 453A(d)(1)) Payment of indebtedness is treated as secured by an interest in an installment obligation to the extent that an arrangement allows the taxpayer to satisfy all or part of the debt with the installment obligation (i.e., gives the taxpayer the *right* to repay the loan by transferring the installment note to his or her creditor). (Code Sec. 453A(d)(4))

¶ 2456   Wash Sales; Loss Disallowance Rule. ▬▬▬▬▬▬▬▬

No loss deduction is allowed under Code Sec. 1091 for any loss from any sale or other disposition of stock or securities (including contracts or options to acquire or sell stock or securities) if, within a period beginning 30 days before and ending 30 days after the sale, the taxpayer acquires, or has entered into a contract or option to acquire, substantially identical stock or securities. (Code Sec. 1091(a); Reg § 1.1091-1(a))[12]

illustration: June 1: T buys 100 shares of Corp A stock for $15 per share. Dec. 1: T buys 100 shares of Corp A stock for $10 per share. Dec. 31: T sells the 100 shares of Corp A stock bought on June 1 for $10 per share realizing a $500 loss. T can't deduct the loss because he bought substantially identical stock within 30 days before the sale. The same result would occur if the 2nd purchase had been made on the following Jan. 30.

caution: The wash sale rule can ensnare investors (e.g., mutual fund investors) who participate in automatic dividend reinvestment plans since the reinvestment of dividends within the prohibited period is a purchase of substantially identical securities.

Loss is also disallowed where the repurchase is made either by an IRA (¶4341) or by a Roth IRA (¶4357), established for the exclusive benefit of the original purchasing taxpayer or his or her beneficiaries.[13]

"Substantially identical securities" requires something less than precise correspondence. Stock or securities of different issuers or obligors aren't substantially identical. Stock or securities of the same issuer are substantially identical if they are substantially the same in all important particulars.[14]

---

10. ¶G-6408, G-6409
11. ¶G-6300 *et seq.*
12. ¶I-3901

13. ¶I-3906
14. ¶I-3914 *et seq.*

🄡*observation:* It is often possible to recognize losses by selling a security and investing the proceeds in a similar but not substantially identical security (e.g., sell common stock in one drug company and buy stock in another drug company, or sell stock in one exchange-traded fund (ETF) and buy stock in another ETF that invests in the same types of securities).

The wash sale rule also disallows a loss on the closing of a short sale of stock or securities, or the sale, exchange, or termination of a securities futures contract to sell, if, within the period beginning 30 days before the date the short sale is closed and ending 30 days after that date: (1) substantially identical stock or securities are sold, or (2) another short sale of (or securities futures contracts to sell) substantially identical stock or securities is entered. (Code Sec. 1091(e))[15]

Special rules apply to residual interests in REMICs (Code Sec. 860F(d)),[16] and to tax straddles. (Reg § 1.1092(b)-1T, Reg § 1.1092(b)-5T)[17]

The wash sale rules don't apply to: (a) any losses on shares in a floating net asset value money market fund.[18], or (b) a dealer in stocks or securities if the loss is sustained in a transaction made in the ordinary course of that business. (Code Sec. 1091(a))[19]

For the basis and holding period of the acquired stock, see ¶2495 and ¶2655.

¶ 2457   **Basis of Property.** ▄▄▄▄▄▄▄▄▄▄▄▄▄▄▄▄▄

Under Code Sec. 1012, basis is generally the cost (¶2458) of property, subject to certain adjustments (¶2468), for tax purposes. It is the point of departure for determining gain or loss on the disposition of the property, for computing annual deductions for depreciation, amortization, depletion, casualty losses, bad debts, and losses from "at-risk" activities, and for many other tax computations.

In general, basis for computing loss and gain is the same, whatever the transaction may be. But, the basis for computing loss can differ from the basis for computing gain for (1) property converted from personal use to business or income-producing use (¶2467), and (2) property acquired by gift (¶2504).

For basis in corporate transactions and in nontaxable exchanges, see ¶2476 *et seq.*

For basis of property acquired by gift, or from a decedent or a spouse, see ¶2503 *et seq.*

¶ 2458   **Cost as basis of property; basis of virtual currency/cryptocurrency.**

Under Code Sec. 1012, a property's original basis is the taxpayer's cost, except where otherwise specifically provided (Code Sec. 1012) (¶2491 *et seq.*) or where a transaction isn't made at arm's length (in which case its basis is its fair market value). Cost is the amount paid in cash or other property, and liabilities incurred (¶2459). (Reg § 1.1012-1(a))[20] Payments made in connection with the acquisition of property, e.g., commissions and legal fees, are included in basis as part of the property's cost.[21]

IRS and most courts say that the cost basis of property received in an arm's-length taxable exchange is the fair market value (FMV) of the property *received* in the exchange, at the time of the exchange, unless the FMV of the property received can't be determined with a fair degree of certainty. Then, the FMV of the property given up will be used as a way of valuing the property received. However, some courts say the cost basis of property received in an arm's-length taxable exchange is the FMV of the property given up, not the property received.[22]

---

15. ¶I-3904, I-3905
16. ¶I-3902, I-3903
17. ¶I-7540 *et seq.*
18. ¶I-3916

19. ¶I-3917
20. ¶P-1119; ¶P-1108
21. ¶P-1102
22. ¶P-1114

Generally, basis in virtual currency/cryptocurrency is the amount spent to acquire it, including fees, commissions, etc., in U.S. dollars.[23] For virtual currency received in an arm's length transaction in exchange for property or services, basis is the virtual currency's FMV when received.[24] For virtual currency received in an airdrop following a hard fork, basis is the amount the recipient included in income.[25] When virtual currency received as a bona fide gift is disposed of, for determining whether there is a gain, the basis is the donor's basis, plus any gift tax paid by the donor for the gift. For determining whether there is a loss, the basis is the lesser of the donor's basis, or the FMV of the virtual currency at the time the gift was received. If there's no documentation to substantiate the donor's basis, then the recipient's basis for the virtual currency is zero.[26] Basis in property received in an arm's length transaction in exchange for virtual currency/cryptocurrency is the FMV of the property at the time it is received.[27]

¶ 2459   Mortgages and other liabilities as part of basis.

Taxpayer's cost (¶2458) of property (basis) includes the amount of a mortgage or other liability assumed in connection with the purchase, plus the amount of any liabilities that the purchased property is subject to (whether or not the taxpayer assumes the liabilities).[28] Under Code Sec. 1055, redeemable ground rents are treated as mortgages. (Code Sec. 1055)[29]

✐ illustration: J buys a building for $20,000 and an $80,000 mortgage. J's basis is $100,000. It would also be $100,000 if J assumed an existing $80,000 mortgage. Also, the basis would be $100,000 if, J paid $20,000 cash and J acquired the building subject to a mortgage without assuming it, or if J agreed to pay a seller's debt of $80,000.

Mortgages or other liabilities aren't part of the cost if they are contingent *and* there's a clear indication they would never have to be paid or that taxpayer doesn't intend to pay.[30]

¶ 2460   Effect of original issue discount (OID) and unstated interest on basis.

Under Code Sec. 483, if the OID rules (¶1742 *et seq.*) or the unstated interest rules (¶1707) apply so that a part of a debt included in the buyer's cost for the property is treated as OID or unstated interest, the basis doesn't include any OID or unstated interest. (Reg § 1.483-1(a)(2))[31]

¶ 2461   Basis of repossessed mortgaged real estate.

Under Code Sec. 1038(c), a seller's basis in repossessed property is equal to the adjusted basis of the mortgage debt (determined under Code Sec. 453 and Code Sec. 1011) to the seller (as of the date of repossession), *plus* the sum of: (1) the repossession gain, and (2) the amount of money and the fair market value of other property (other than the buyer's obligations) which the seller transfers in connection with the repossession. If the mortgage debt isn't discharged on repossession, the seller's basis in the mortgage debt is zero. (Code Sec. 1038(c))[32]

¶ 2462   Basis of property received in satisfaction of debt or claim.

Under Code Sec. 1012, the cost basis of property received in whole or partial satisfaction of a debt or claim is the amount of the debt, etc. satisfied, but not more than the property's

23. ¶P-1181
24. ¶P-1181; ¶J-1433A
25. ¶P-1181; ¶J-1433B
26. ¶P-1181
27. ¶P-1181

28. ¶P-1104 *et seq.*
29. ¶P-1175
30. ¶P-1134
31. ¶s P-1138, P-1139
32. ¶G-6872 *et seq.*

fair market value.[33]

¶ 2463 Property acquired through exercise of options—basis.

Under Code Sec. 1012, the basis of property acquired by exercising an option or warrant other than an option granted for services is (a) the basis of the option, plus (b) the option price. For the cost of the option to be included in the basis, the option must be bought in a bona fide sale.[34]

¶ 2464 Holder's basis in certain debt instruments acquired at a discount.

Under Code Sec. 1272, a holder's basis in a debt instrument issued with original issue discount (OID) is increased by the OID currently included in gross income (¶1312 *et seq.*). (Code Sec. 1272(c)(2))[35] This rule also applies for inflation-indexed debt instruments (¶1332); however, the basis of the instruments is reduced for deflation adjustments. (Reg § 1.1275-7(f)(2))[36]

Short-term debt instruments. If the holder includes the daily portions of acquisition discount (or OID) in gross income, that holder increases basis in the debt instrument by the amount so included. (Code Sec. 1283(d)(1))[37]

Tax-exempt obligations issued with OID. A holder's basis is increased by the amount of OID that the holder would have included in gross income currently if the obligation had not been tax-exempt. (Code Sec. 1288(a)(2), Code Sec. 1288(b)(3))[38]

Market-discount bonds. Where an election is made to include accrued market discount in income currently (see ¶1326), the bond's basis is increased by the amount of income included. (Code Sec. 1278(b)(4))[39]

For determining cost of, and original basis in, property received in exchange for an OID debt instrument, see ¶2460.

¶ 2465 Intangible assets (goodwill, patents, copyrights, and covenants not to compete)—cost basis.

Under Code Sec. 1012, the basis of goodwill, a patent, a copyright, or a covenant not to compete is the amount taxpayer paid for it.[40]

Where a patent is obtained from the government, its basis is the cost of development, such as research and experimental expenditures (but not if deducted currently), drawings, attorneys' and governmental fees, etc. The value of any time spent on an invention isn't part of an inventor's basis. The basis of a copyright acquired from the government is the cost of securing the copyright, including the cost of producing the work covered by the copyright, but not including the value of the author's time.[41]

Accounts receivable in the hands of a cash basis taxpayer have a zero basis.[42]

¶ 2466 Basis allocation, including "applicable asset acquisitions"—Form 8594.

If a single transaction involves a number of separate properties, the total cost is allocated to establish the cost of the individual properties under Code Sec. 1012. The total basis is allocated to each item in proportion to the fair market value (FMV) of each item at

---

33. ¶P-1116
34. ¶P-1165 *et seq.*
35. ¶P-5044
36. ¶P-5044.1
37. ¶P-5047
38. ¶P-5048
39. ¶J-4573 *et seq.*
40. ¶P-1178, P-1179, P-1180
41. ¶P-1178
42. ¶P-1121

the time of acquisition.[43]

However, for an applicable asset acquisition (defined below) that is subject to Code Sec. 1060, the residual method is used to allocate the purchase price among 7 classes of assets. Under the residual method, the purchase price is reduced first by the amount of cash and cash equivalents (Class I). The amount remaining is allocated among the following assets in proportion to (but not in excess of) their FMV on the purchase date, in the following order: actively traded personal property (Class II); certain mark-to-market assets and debt instruments (Class III); stock in trade, inventory (Class IV); all assets not in any other class (Class V); all Code Sec. 197 intangibles (¶1958) except those in the nature of goodwill and going concern value (Class VI); and Code Sec. 197 intangibles in the nature of goodwill and going concern value (Class VII). (Reg § 1.1060-1(c)(2))[44]

The parties to an applicable asset acquisition can agree in writing to an allocation of consideration for, or a determination of the FMV of, any asset in the acquisition. The agreement is generally binding on the parties. But, the existence of a written agreement doesn't restrict IRS from challenging those allocations or values. (Code Sec. 1060(a); Reg § 1.1060-1(c)(4), Reg § 1.1060-1(e))[45] A party to the agreement can challenge the terms of the agreement only by showing fraud, mistake, undue influence, etc.[46]

An *applicable asset acquisition* is any direct or indirect transfer of a group of assets that is a trade or business in the hands of either the seller or buyer if (except for certain like-kind exchanges) the buyer's basis in the transferred assets is determined wholly by reference to the buyer's consideration. (Code Sec. 1060(c); Reg § 1.1060-1(b)(1))[47]

The buyer and seller have to provide IRS with specified information about the assets on Form 8594. (Code Sec. 1060(b); Reg § 1.1060-1(e)(1))[48]

¶ 2467   Basis of personal use property converted to business use.

Under Reg § 1.167(g)-1, when a residence or other nonbusiness property is converted from personal use to business or income-producing use, for purposes of calculating losses or depreciation (but not gain) under Code Sec. 167, the basis for the property on the date of its conversion is the *lower* of its adjusted basis or fair market value on that date. This basis is thereafter adjusted for depreciation, etc., after conversion. (Reg § 1.167(g)-1)[49]

¶ 2468   Adjusted basis.

Basis is increased or decreased under Code Sec. 1016 to reflect events, such as capital improvements or depreciation, whether the original basis was cost or something else.[50]

The basis of property is adjusted (increased) to include the amount of the capital expenditures with respect to the property. (Code Sec. 1016(a)(1))[1] A lessee's basis for a leasehold is increased by capital expenditures.[2] However, a lessee's capital improvements don't increase or diminish the lessor's basis of the leased property. (Code Sec. 1019)[3]

Basis can be increased for items that are ordinarily deductible as expenses if the taxpayer has capitalized those items, e.g., taxes and carrying charges, see ¶1629.

For information reporting of organizational actions such as stock splits that affect the basis of specified securities, see ¶4746.

For adjusted basis for AMT purposes, see ¶3209.

---

43. ¶P-1300 *et seq.*
44. ¶P-1406.1
45. ¶P-1400 *et seq.*
46. ¶I-8612
47. ¶P-1402 *et seq.*
48. ¶S-4301

49. ¶P-1908
50. ¶P-1700 *et seq.*
1. ¶P-1801
2. ¶L-6507
3. ¶P-1809

For basis adjustments for a Qualified Opportunity Fund (QOF) investment, see ¶2502.

In determining the basis of a life insurance or annuity contract (entered into after Aug. 25, 2009), no basis adjustment is made for mortality, expense, or other reasonable charges incurred under the contracts (known as "cost of insurance"). (Code Sec. 1016(a)(1)) This reverses the position of IRS in Rev. Rul. 2009-13 that, on the sale of a cash value life insurance contract, the insured's (seller's) basis is reduced by the cost of insurance. [4]

¶ 2469 Contributions and returns of capital—effect on basis.

Under Code Sec. 118, a shareholder's contribution to the capital of a corporation is an additional price paid for the stock and thus, increases the basis in the stock.[5] A partner's contribution of cash or other property to the partnership increases the basis in a partnership interest[6] (¶3729 *et seq.*).

Basis is also reduced for receipts representing a return of capital (Code Sec. 1016(a)(1); Reg § 1.1016-2(a)), such as damages taxpayer received for injury to property.[7]

¶ 2470 Depreciation, amortization, etc.—adjustments to basis.

Under Code Sec. 1016, basis is reduced for depreciation, cost recovery, Code Sec. 179 expensing, pre-2010 commercial revitalization deductions under former Code Sec. 1400I, or amortization deductions with respect to the property. The amount of the reduction is the larger of (1) the amount of the depreciation, cost recovery, amortization, or depletion deductions *allowable* under the law, or (2) the amount that was actually *allowed* and resulted in a reduction of tax. (Code Sec. 1016(a)(2))[8]

Basis is reduced for the Code Sec. 179D energy efficient commercial building property deduction . (Code Sec. 1016(a)(31))[9]

Allowable depreciation (or cost recovery) is the amount the taxpayer was legally entitled to deduct, whether or not the taxpayer actually took more or less and whether or not a tax benefit results. Where a taxpayer didn't adopt a depreciation method under Code Sec. 167, the amount allowable is figured under the straight-line method. (Code Sec. 1016(a))[10]

The depreciation (or cost recovery) *allowed* is the amount claimed on a tax return and allowed by IRS.[11]

In the case of business autos for which the optional business standard mileage rate (see ¶1553) is used, depreciation is considered to have been allowed at a rate of 24¢ for 2015 and 2016, 25¢ for 2017 and 2018, 26¢ for 2019, 27¢ for 2020, and 26¢ for 2021 and 2022.[12]

¶ 2471 Effect on basis of partial losses due to casualty or theft.

If property is partly lost or destroyed through casualty or theft under Code Sec. 165, basis is reduced by (1) the amount of insurance or other reimbursement received, and (2) the amount of deductible loss. But a nondeductible loss (¶1782 *et seq.*) does *not* reduce basis.[13]

Expenses with respect to that property, e.g., to remove debris and to restore the property to pre-casualty condition, increase basis, unless they are deducted as repairs.[14]

4. ¶J-5058
5. ¶F-1916
6. ¶B-1502;
7. ¶P-1821
8. ¶P-1901
9. ¶L-3176
10. ¶P-1902
11. ¶P-1903
12. ¶P-1909
13. ¶P-1811
14. ¶P-1811

¶ 2472 Basis of credit property reduced by certain credits allowed.

Under Code Sec. 50, the basis of investment credit property (¶2306), for purposes of computing depreciation or cost recovery deductions and gain or loss, is reduced by 100% of the amount of the credit so determined. (Code Sec. 50(c)(1))[15] The basis of energy credit property (¶2310) is reduced by 50% of the allowed credit.Code Sec. 50(c)(3)(A))[16]

The basis of property is also reduced for certain other credits, such as: the pre-2033 Code Sec. 25C nonbusiness energy property credit (¶2352) (Code Sec. 1016(a)(33))[17]; the pre-2035 Code Sec. 25D residential clean energy credit, formerly known as the residential energy efficient property (REEP) credit (¶2353) (Code Sec. 1016(a)(34))[18]; the Code Sec. 30B alternative motor vehicle credit (Code Sec. 1016(a)(35))[19]; the Code Sec. 30D credit for certain electric vehicles (¶2354) (Code Sec. 1016(a)(37))[20]; the Code Sec. 45F credit for employer-provided child care assistance (¶2328) (Code Sec. 1016(a)(28))[21]; and the Code Sec. 45L energy efficient homes credit (¶2342). (Code Sec. 1016(a)(32))[22]

¶ 2473 Recaptured tax credits—effect on basis.

Under Code Sec. 50(c), where certain tax credits are recaptured, a percentage of the recapture amount is added back to basis immediately before the event causing the recapture. A "recapture amount" is any increase in tax (or adjustment in carrybacks or carryovers) due to the credit recapture provision. (Code Sec. 50(c)(2), Code Sec. 50(c)(3)(B))[23]

¶ 2474 Special lessor-lessee rule doesn't require basis-reduction adjustment.

Under Code Sec. 50(d)(5), a lessor of certain credit property who elects to pass the credit for the leased property to the lessee isn't required to make the basis-reduction adjustment (¶2472). (Code Sec. 50(d)(5), Reg § 1.50-1(b)(1))[24]

¶ 2475 How credits affect basis in partnership interest or S corporation stock.

Under Code Sec. 50(c)(5), the basis of a partner's interest in a partnership or of an S corporation shareholder's stock is adjusted to reflect a partner's or shareholder's share of the required adjustments to the basis of partnership or S corporation property when credits are either allowed or recaptured. (Code Sec. 50(c)(5))[25]

¶ 2476 Property Acquired in Nontaxable Exchanges. ▮▮▮▮▮▮▮▮▮▮▮▮

The basis of property received (replacement property) in a nontaxable exchange, depending on the type of transaction, generally is the same as its basis in the hands of the transferor or is the same as the basis of the property transferred (relinquished property) by the recipient in the exchange. If gain is recognized in part on the transaction, the basis of the property received may have to be adjusted.

For corporate transactions that affect basis, see ¶2477 *et seq.* For other nontaxable transactions, see ¶2496 *et seq.* For basis of replacement property after an involuntary conversion, see ¶2498.

---

15. ¶P-2000 *et seq.*
16. ¶P-2005
17. ¶P-1710.4
18. ¶P-1710.5
19. ¶L-18023
20. ¶P-1710.6
21. ¶P-1710.1
22. ¶P-1710.01
23. ¶P-2007
24. ¶L-17048
25. ¶P-2009

¶ 2477 Controlled corporation's basis in property received in a tax-free transfer.

Under Code Sec. 362, the basis of property received by a controlled corporation in a tax-free transfer, whether upon the incorporation of the corporation (¶3500 *et seq.*) or otherwise (such as paid-in surplus or as a contribution to capital), is equal to the basis of the property in the transferor's hands increased by any gain recognized by the transferor on the transfer. (Code Sec. 362(a))[26]

For limitations on an increase in basis due to the assumption of a liability and/or a built-in loss, see ¶2479.

¶ 2478 Acquiring corporation's basis in property received in a tax-free reorganization.

Under Code Sec. 362(b), the basis of property received by the acquiring corporation in a tax-free reorganization (¶3527), is the transferor's (target's) basis increased by any gain recognized to the target. However, if the property consists of stock or securities of the target, this rule applies only if the property was acquired in exchange for stock or securities of the acquirer or the acquirer's parent corporation. (Code Sec. 362(b))[27]

For when an acquirer must reduce basis in assets received in a tax-free reorganization if the transferor has cancellation of debt income in connection with the transfer, see ¶1383.

For limitations on basis increase due to the assumption of a liability, see ¶2479.

¶ 2479 Limit on basis increase due to assumption of liability or built-in loss— basis of property acquired in nontaxable exchange.

For purposes of the basis increase for a tax-free transfer to a controlled corporation (¶2477) or a reorganization exchange (¶2478), the property's basis can't be increased above its fair market value (FMV) due to gain recognized by the transferor as a result of a liability assumed by the transferee under Code Sec. 362. For this purpose, FMV is determined without regard to Code Sec. 7701(g) (providing that a property's FMV isn't less than the amount of nonrecourse debt to which it is subject). (Code Sec. 362(d)(1))[28]

The basis of certain built-in loss property transferred in a tax-free reorganization is its fair market value (instead of the transferor's pre-transaction basis in property) if the transaction would result in an importation of a net built-in loss. (Code Sec. 362(e)(1); Reg § 1.362-3) If this rule doesn't apply, a second carryover basis limitation rule (not limited to property as to which the transferor would not have recognized gain or loss) limits the total basis for property transferred by any transferor to its FMV, with the basis of each property transferred reduced by its allocable part of the transferor's net built-in loss. (Code Sec. 362(e)(2); Reg § 1.362-4(b)) However, the transferor and transferee can jointly elect to reduce the basis of the stock received by the transferor instead of the basis of the assets transferred. (Code Sec. 362(e)(2)(C); Reg § 1.362-4(d)) IRS has prescribed how to make the election. (Reg § 1.362-4(d))[29]

¶ 2480 Target corporation's basis in property received in a tax-free reorganization.

Under Code Sec. 358, the basis of property (other than stock and securities of another corporation that is a party to the reorganization, see ¶3541 *et seq.*) received under a plan of

---

26. ¶F-1851
27. ¶F-4305

28. ¶F-1852
29. ¶F-1857 *et seq.*

reorganization by the target equals the fair market value of the property on the exchange date. (Code Sec. 358(a)(2), Code Sec. 358(f))[30]

¶ 2481 Corporation's basis in property acquired in a taxable acquisition of property for its stocks or bonds.

In cases other than tax-free contributions or reorganizations, the basis of property a corporation acquires in exchange for its stock is the stock's fair market value at the time of the exchange under Code Sec. 1012.[31] The cost to a corporation of property it acquires in exchange for its bonds is the face amount of the bonds.[32] For bonds with OID or unstated interest, see ¶2460.

¶ 2482 Basis of property to distributee shareholders or security holders—basis of property acquired in nontaxable exchange.

For purposes of determining basis under Code Sec. 358, property received by a distributee in connection with a transfer to a controlled corporation, a reorganization, or a corporate division (¶3500 *et seq.*) is either nonrecognition property or other property (i.e., property other than nonrecognition property or money). Nonrecognition property is property received without recognition of gain or loss to the recipient (stock in the transferee corporation in the case of a transfer to a controlled corporation, and stock or securities in the distributing corporation in tax-free reorganizations and corporate divisions). (Code Sec. 358(a)(1))

The basis of nonrecognition property is the same as the basis of the property given up in the exchange, except that basis is (1) decreased by any money received, by the fair market value of any other property received, and by any loss recognized by the distributee on the exchange; and (2) increased by any part of the distribution that is treated as a dividend, and by any other gain recognized by the distributee on the exchange. (Code Sec. 358(a)(1))[33] The basis is allocated among the nonrecognition property received in the transaction without recognition of gain or loss. If no stock or securities of the issuing corporation are issued and distributed in the transaction, shareholders that own actual shares in the issuing corporation can designate the shares of stock of the issuing corporation to which the basis, if any, of the stock or securities surrendered will attach. (Reg § 1.358-2(a)(2))[34]

Where, as part of the consideration for the transfer of the distributee corporation's property to the acquirer, another party to the deal assumes a liability of the distributee, the assumption of that liability is treated as though it were money received by the distributee on the reorganization exchange (for basis purposes only). (Code Sec. 358(d)(1))[35]

observation: Thus, the basis of the nonrecognition property received by the distributee on the exchange is reduced by an amount equal to the liabilities assumed.

IRS can provide adjustments for divisive reorganization transactions (¶3545) among affiliated group members. (Code Sec. 358(g))[36]

¶ 2483 Basis of other property received in tax-free transfer or reorganization.

Under Code Sec. 358, the basis of property, other than stock or securities, received by a shareholder on a tax-free transfer to a controlled corporation, a reorganization, or a corporate division (¶3500 *et seq.*) is its fair market value as of the date of the transaction. (Code

---

30. ¶F-4304
31. ¶P-1158
32. ¶P-1160
33. ¶F-4034

34. ¶F-4036
35. ¶F-4035
36. ¶F-4632

Sec. 358(a)(2))[37]

¶ 2484   Basis of property received in complete liquidation of corporation.

Under Code Sec. 334(a), if property is received in a complete liquidation and any gain or loss is recognized on the receipt of the property, its basis, in the hands of the shareholder-distributee is its fair market value at the time of the distribution. (Code Sec. 334(a))[38]

¶ 2485   Incorporation of a partnership—basis in stock.

If a partnership incorporates, the basis of the corporation in the partnership's assets and the basis of the former partners in their stock in the corporation depends on the method used to incorporate.[39]

If the partnership transfers all of its assets subject to its liabilities to a newly formed corporation in return for all its stock, then distributes the stock to the partners, the corporation's basis in the partnership's assets is equal to the partnership's basis in the assets before the transaction, and each partner's basis in the stock of the corporation (¶3740) is equal to the adjusted basis of that partner's interest in the partnership.[40]

If the partnership distributes all of its assets subject to liabilities to the partners, who in turn transfer them to the new corporation for its stock, the corporation's basis in its assets is the same as the partners' basis in the assets before their contribution to the corporation, and the partners' basis in the stock of the corporation is the same as their basis in the assets distributed in liquidation reduced by liabilities assumed by the corporation.[41]

If the partners transfer their partnership interests to the new corporation in exchange for its stock and the corporation then liquidates the partnership, the corporation's basis in its assets is equal to the partners' basis in their partnership interests before the transaction, and the partners' basis in their stock is equal to their basis in their partnership interests reduced by the liabilities assumed by the corporation.[42]

¶ 2486   Basis of property received as a dividend.

Under Code Sec. 301, the basis for property received as a dividend, including stock or stock rights received as a taxable stock dividend, is its fair market value on the date of distribution. (Code Sec. 301(d))[43] For basis of nontaxable stock dividends, see ¶2487.

¶ 2487   Basis allocation for nontaxable stock dividend.

Under Code Sec. 307, if a shareholder gets a nontaxable dividend of stock or stock rights, the (adjusted) basis of the old stock (that is, of the stock on which the dividend was distributed) is allocated between the old and new stock (or rights) in proportion to the fair market value (FMV) of each on the date of distribution. (Code Sec. 307(a)) Where only part of the stock dividend is nontaxable, the basis of the old stock is allocated between the old stock and that part of the new stock (or rights) which isn't taxable, in proportion to the FMV of each on the date of distribution. The date of distribution is, in both cases, the date on which the new stock (or the stock rights) was distributed, not the record date. (Reg § 1.307-1(a))[44]

✐illustration: S bought 1 share of voting common for $45. The corporation distributed 2 new shares of voting common for each share held. This gave S 3 shares of voting common

---

37. ¶F-1804, F-4034, F-5003
38. ¶F-13101
39. Rev Rul 84-111, 1984-2 CB 88,¶s F-1011, F-1851
40. Rev Rul 84-111, 1984-2 CB 88, ¶s F-1011, F-1851

41. Rev Rul 84-111, 1984-2 CB 88, ¶s F-1011, F-1851
42. Rev Rul 84-111, 1984-2 CB 88, ¶s F-1011, F-1851
43. ¶P-5400 *et seq.*
44. ¶P-5301

with a basis of $15 each. If S had owned 2 shares before the distribution, one purchased for $30 and the other for $45, S would have 6 shares: 3 with a basis of $10 each, and 3 with a basis of $15 each.

If the FMV of stock rights at the time of distribution is less than 15% of the FMV of the stock on which they were distributed, the basis for the rights received is zero unless the taxpayer elects to allocate basis to the rights. (Code Sec. 307(b)(1); Reg § 1.307-2)[45]

¶ 2488   Basis of stock acquired through dividend reinvestment plans (DRPs).

If a corporation allows shareholders to receive dividends in either cash or stock, then, depending on the situation, the receipt of stock is treated either as the receipt of a taxable stock dividend, because the shareholder has the choice of receiving either cash or stock, or as the receipt of a cash dividend which the shareholder used to buy stock (in some cases, at a discount). If the transaction is treated as a stock dividend, the shareholder's basis is equal to the value of the shares received at the time of the receipt. But, if the transaction is treated as a cash dividend, the shareholder's basis in the shares is equal to the amount of cash the shareholder could have received.[46]

The basis of stock acquired after 2011 in connection with a DRP, while held as part of the DRP, is determined using 1 of the methods available for determining the basis of mutual fund stock. (Code Sec. 1012(d)(1)) Thus, the average basis method for mutual fund shareholders (¶2493) is available for shares of stock acquired after 2011 in connection with a DRP, but only if the shares are identical (i.e., have the same CUSIP number, or other acceptable security identifier number). (Reg § 1.1012-1(e)(1))[47]

¶ 2489   Effect of extraordinary dividends on corporate shareholder's basis.

Under Code Sec. 1059, if a corporation receives an extraordinary dividend with respect to a share of stock that it hasn't held for more than 2 years before the dividend announcement date, the basis of the stock, is reduced (but not below zero) by the non-taxed portion (i.e., the excess (if any) of: (a) the distribution amount over (b) the taxable part of the dividend that is included in gross income, reduced by the amount of any dividend received deduction allowable under Code Sec. 243, or Code Sec. 245). (Code Sec. 1059) Where a redemption is treated as an extraordinary dividend, the basis in the nonredeemed shares is also reduced if the redemption is part of a partial liquidation of the redeeming corporation, or isn't pro rata as to all shareholders, but not if the redemption wouldn't have been treated (in whole or in part) as a dividend if an option hadn't been taken into account under the Code Sec. 318(a)(4) option attribution rules or the Code Sec. 304(a) related-party stock purchase rules.[48]

¶ 2490   Effect of Sec. 245A dividends-received deduction on corporate shareholder's basis.

If a corporation that is a "U.S. shareholder" of a 10% owned specified foreign corporation receives a dividend from that foreign corporation, a deduction is allowed for the foreign-source portion of the dividend under Code Sec. 245A (see ¶3314). A domestic corporation that receives that dividend in any tax year, solely for purposes of determining loss on any disposition of stock of that foreign corporation in that tax year or any later tax year, must reduce its basis in that stock (but not below zero) by the amount of the Code Sec. 245A deduction allowable to the domestic corporation on that stock. (Code Sec. 961(d)) However, no reduction in basis is required to the extent the basis in the specified 10%

---

45. ¶P-5303
46. ¶P-5201.4

47. ¶P-5201.4
48. ¶P-5100 *et seq.*

owned foreign corporation's stock was already reduced under Code Sec. 1059 (¶2489).[49]

¶ 2491 Identifying shares or bonds transferred—effect on basis.

Under Reg § 1.1012-1(c), where a taxpayer can adequately identify which shares of stock or which bonds are transferred, the basis used is the basis of that stock or those bonds (specific identification). Shares of stock or bonds are adequately identified where it can be shown that the shares or bonds that were delivered to the transferee are from a lot acquired on a certain date or for a certain price. (Reg § 1.1012-1(c)(1); Reg § 1.1012-1(c)(2); Reg § 1.1012-1(c)(6))[50]

If a number of lots were acquired and the ones sold can't be adequately identified, a first-in, first-out (FIFO) rule applies. If the earliest lot purchased or acquired is held in a stock certificate that represents multiple lots of stock, and the taxpayer doesn't adequately identify the lot from which the stock is sold or transferred, the stock sold or transferred is charged against the earliest lot included in the certificate. (Reg § 1.1012-1(c)(1)(i)) Where shares are held in more than 1 account, the FIFO rule applies only to the particular account from which the shares were transferred.[1]

¶ 2492 Adequate identification of shares vs. wrong delivery—effect on basis.

In certain situations, if a taxpayer specifically identifies certain shares of stock or bonds as the ones to be transferred (¶2491), and certain other conditions are met, these will be treated as the ones transferred even though some other lot is actually delivered. This rule applies (1) for sales of stock or bonds held by a broker or agent (Reg § 1.1012-1(c)(3)(i)), (2) where a single certificate represents different lots of stock (Reg § 1.1012-1(c)(3)(ii)), and (3) for certain transfers by a trustee, executor, or administrator. (Reg § 1.1012-1(c)(4))[2]

¶ 2493 Mutual fund shares—election to use average basis.

Under Code Sec. 1012, a mutual fund investor can use the average basis method to determine the cost of shares left in the custody of a broker. (Reg § 1.1012-1(e)(1)) The average basis method applies on an account by account basis. A taxpayer can use the average basis method for shares in one account but use a different basis determination method for identical stock in a different account. The election average basis election applies to all identical stock within the same account. A taxpayer must make separate elections for stock held in separate accounts. (Reg § 1.1012-1(e)(10)) Unless a single-account election is in effect, a taxpayer can not average together the basis of identical stock held in separate accounts. (Reg § 1.1012-1(e)(7)(i))[3]

¶ 2494 Determining basis for "specified securities" held in brokerage accounts.

Under Code Sec. 1012(c)(1), in the case of a sale, exchange or other disposition, the broker reported basis in a "specified security" (defined below) is determined under the conventions prescribed in existing regs and applied to each separate account, on an account-by-account basis. (Code Sec. 1012(c)(1)) Reported basis is computed using a first-in-first-out (FIFO) method, the specific-identification method, or the average-basis convention (Reg § 1.1012-1) (¶2491, ¶2493).[4]

A "specified security" is stocks, notes and other debt, certain commodity contracts and derivatives, as well as other financial instruments determined by IRS. For returns required to be filed after 2023 (i.e., beginning with 2023 transactions), the term also includes

---

49. ¶O-2423.1
50. ¶P-5202 *et seq.*
1. ¶P-5212 *et seq.*

2. ¶P-5200 *et seq.*
3. ¶P-5214 *et seq.*
4. ¶P-5201.1

digital assets (as defined in Code Sec. 6045(g)(3)(D)—including cryptocurrency). (Code Sec. 6045(g)(3)(B))[5]

¶ 2495   Basis of stock acquired in wash sale.

Under Code Sec. 1091(d), where a loss is disallowed under the wash sale rule (¶2456), under Code Sec. 1091, the basis of the acquired stock takes account of the unrecognized loss in the following manner: (Code Sec. 1091(d))

(1) If the sales price is less than the repurchase price, the basis of the new stock is the basis of the stock sold plus the difference between the repurchase and the sales prices.

Illustration (1): T owns 100 shares of X Corp stock which cost $100 per share. On May 1, T sells the 100 shares at $80 per share. On May 20, T buys 100 shares of X at $90 per share. No loss is allowed on the May 1 sale. The basis of each share acquired May 20 is $110, i.e., the basis of the shares sold ($100) plus the $10 difference between the repurchase and sale prices ($90 − $80). (Reg § 1.1091-2(a))

(2) If the sales price is more than the repurchase price, the basis of the new stock is the basis of the stock sold minus the difference between the sale and the repurchase prices.[6]

Illustration (2): If, in Illustration (1), the May 1 sale price had been $90 per share and the May 20 repurchase price was $80 per share, the basis of each share acquired May 20 would be $90, i.e., the basis of shares sold ($100) minus the difference between the sale and repurchase prices ($90 − $80). (Reg § 1.1091-2(a))

¶ 2496   Basis of replacement properties received in a nontaxable exchange.

Under (Code Sec. 1031(d), the basis of replacement property received in a like-kind exchange and nontaxable exchanges of stock in the same corporation (¶2412), U.S. obligations (¶2414), and life insurance and annuity contracts (¶2415) where no part of the gain is recognized is the adjusted basis of the relinquished property. (Code Sec. 1031(d))

If money is received as part of the exchange and some gain is recognized, the replacement property's basis is decreased by the money received and increased by any gain recognized. Reg § 1.1031(d)-1(b)) Basis is increased by the amount of any money paid. (Reg § 1.1031(d)-1(a))

In determining the basis, liabilities assumed by the other party are treated as money (boot) received by the taxpayer. (Reg § 1.1031(d)-2)

If other property (boot) is received and some gain is recognized, basis is allocated (based on fair market value) to all the properties received. (Reg § 1.1031(d)-1(c))

If boot is given as part of the exchange, and gain or loss is recognized on transfer of the boot, the basis of the nonrecognition property received is the total basis of all the properties given, increased by any recognized gain on the boot, or decreased by any recognized loss on the boot. (Reg § 1.1031(d)-1(e))[7]

¶ 2497   Basis after tax-free exchange of multiple properties.

In a nontaxable exchange of multiple properties, the aggregate basis of properties received in each of the "exchange groups" is allocated proportionately to each property in the group based on its fair market value. (Reg § 1.1031(j)-1(c))[8]

⊘bservation: For exchanges completed after Dec. 31, 2017, like-kind exchanges are

---

5. ¶P-5201.3; ¶S-3743
6. ¶P-5019

7. ¶I-3176 *et seq.*
8. ¶I-3193

limited to exchanges of real property and all real property are included in the same exchange group.

¶ 2498   Basis of replacement property after involuntary conversion.

Under Code Sec. 1033(b)(1), if property is involuntarily converted directly into similar property and gain on the conversion isn't recognized under Code Sec. 1033(a)(1) (¶2430), the basis of the replacement property is the basis of the converted property (1) decreased by the amount of any money received that wasn't reinvested in similar property (¶2435), and (2) increased by the amount of gain recognized, or decreased by the amount of loss recognized. (Code Sec. 1033(b)(1)) Where a taxpayer's property is involuntarily converted into money or other property that isn't similar or related in use and, within the prescribed period (¶2438), the taxpayer buys replacement property that is similar or related in service or use to the converted property and elects not to recognize any part of the gain, the basis of the replacement property is its cost, reduced by the amount of unrecognized gain. If more than 1 piece of replacement property is bought, the basis (cost less nonrecognized gain) is allocated to each piece in proportion to its cost. (Code Sec. 1033(b)(2))[9] If a taxpayer satisfies the replacement property requirement by buying a controlling stock interest in a corporation (¶2430), the corporation reduces its basis in its assets by the amount by which the taxpayer reduces its basis in the stock. (Code Sec. 1033(b)(3))[10]

¶ 2499   Basis of replacement for stock sold to ESOP or EWOC.

Under Code Sec. 1042(d), if the seller of qualified securities to an employee stock ownership plan (ESOP) or eligible worker-owned cooperative (EWOC) reinvests in qualified replacement property and elects gain nonrecognition (¶2428), basis is reduced by the unrecognized gain. If more than 1 item of replacement property is bought, basis reduction is allocated among each item (as the cost of that item bears to the cost of all items). (Code Sec. 1042(d))[11]

¶ 2500   Basis for Specialized Small Business Investment Company (SSBIC) rollovers.

Any gain not recognized under the now-repealed SSBIC rollover rules (that applied to gain from certain pre-2018 sales of publicly traded securities rolled over into SSBICs) reduced the taxpayer's basis in any SSBIC investment made during the 60-day rollover period. If taxpayer made more than one SSBIC investment during this period, the bases of those other investments were reduced in the order they were acquired.[12]

¶ 2501   Basis for Qualified Small Business Stock (QSBS) rollovers.

Code Sec. 1045(b)(3) provides that gain from the sale of QSBS that isn't recognized because of the Code Sec. 1045(a) rollover election (see ¶2426) reduces (in the order acquired) the basis for determining gain or loss of any QSBS that's purchased by the taxpayer within the 60-day rollover period beginning on the sale date. (Code Sec. 1045(b)(3))[13]

¶ 2502   Basis of investments in Qualified Opportunity (QO) Funds.

Under Code Sec. 1400Z-2(b)(2)(B), except for the increases to basis described below, a taxpayer's basis in the investment in a QO Fund (¶2427) is zero. For an investment held for at least 5 years, the basis of the investment is increased by 10% of the amount of gain

---

9. ¶P-1154
10. ¶P-1154.1
11. ¶H-12110

12. ¶I-3791
13. ¶I-9206

temporarily deferred. For an investment held for at least 7 years, basis is increased by an additional 5% of the amount of gain deferred. The basis is also increased by the amount of gain recognized at the end of the temporary deferral period. (Code Sec. 1400Z-2(b)(2)(B))[14]

¶ 2503   Property Acquired by Gift, from a Decedent, or from a Spouse—Basis. ▬▬

Special rules apply to determine the basis of property acquired by gift, from a decedent, or from a spouse. Property acquired by gift or certain transfers in trust generally has a carryover basis, see ¶2504 *et seq.* Property acquired from a decedent generally has a fair market value basis, see ¶2508 *et seq.* Property acquired from a spouse (or former spouse) generally has a carryover basis, see ¶2514.

¶ 2504   Basis of property acquired by gift or transfer in trust—carryover basis.

Under Code Sec. 1015, a donee's original or unadjusted basis (that is, the basis before adjustments made while the donee owned it) for property the donee acquires by gift is the same as the property's adjusted basis in the donor's hands, or in the hands of the last preceding owner who didn't acquire the property by gift. But if the property's fair market value (FMV) at the date of the gift is lower than that adjusted basis, then the property's basis for determining *loss* is its FMV on that date. (Code Sec. 1015(a))[15]

Because two different methods exist to determine the basis of property acquired as a gift, it's possible that neither gain nor loss determined in reference to basis will be realized when the donee sells or exchanges the property. (Reg § 1.1015-1(a)(2))[16]

Illustration: T acquires by gift income-producing property with an adjusted basis of $100,000 at the date of gift. The FMV on the date of gift is $90,000. T later sells the property for $95,000. T has neither gain nor loss since the basis for determining gain is $100,000 and the basis for determining loss is $90,000.

If a transfer in trust is made for consideration (whether full and adequate, or less), the basis is the same as it would be in the grantor's hands, increased by the amount of gain or decreased by the amount of loss recognized to the grantor upon the transfer under the law applicable to the year in which the transfer was made. (Code Sec. 1015(b))[17]

For part sales and part gifts, see ¶2505.

¶ 2505   Basis after transfer that is part purchase, part gift.

Where a transfer of property is part purchase and part gift, the transferee's basis is the greater of cost or the transferor's adjusted basis for the property at the time of the transfer under Code Sec. 1015. And, the taxpayer is required to establish the transferor's donative intent. In either event, basis is increased to the extent of any gift tax paid (¶2507). However, for determining loss, the basis can't exceed the property's fair market value at the time of transfer. (Reg § 1.1015-4)[18]

¶ 2506   Basis rules for donees of partial interests.

Under Reg § 1.1015-1(b), if 2 or more donees receive gifts of partial interests in the same property, the basis of each interest is its proportionate part of the donor's basis. To determine the part of total basis allowable to life tenants and remaindermen, see ¶2513. (Reg § 1.1015-1(b))[19]

---

14. ¶I-8826
15. ¶P-3103; ¶P-3104
16. ¶P-3105

17. ¶P-3112
18. ¶P-1113
19. ¶P-3131

¶ 2507 Increase in basis for gift tax paid by donor.

Under Code Sec. 1015(d)(6), if the property's fair market value at the date of the gift is greater than the donor's adjusted basis, the donee's basis (i.e., the donor's basis) is increased by any gift tax paid that is attributable to the net appreciation in the gift's value under Code Sec. 1015. This part is determined by multiplying the gift tax paid by a fraction whose numerator is the net appreciation in value of the gift and whose denominator is the amount of the gift. (Code Sec. 1015(d)(6))

If a gift consists of more than 1 item of property, the gift tax paid with respect to each item is computed by allocating to each item a proportionate part of the gift tax paid. If more than 1 gift was made during the calendar year, the total tax paid is apportioned to each gift to determine the amount paid on each gift. (Code Sec. 1015(d)(2))

The gift tax paid on a split gift (¶5055) is the sum of the taxes, computed separately, paid with respect to each spouse's half of the gift. (Code Sec. 1015(d)(3); Reg § 1.1015-5(b)(3))[20]

¶ 2508 Basis of property acquired from a decedent—stepped-up basis.

Under Code Sec. 1014, the basis of property acquired from a decedent by inheritance, bequest, devise, etc. (¶2511), that hasn't been sold, exchanged, or otherwise disposed of before the decedent's death, is generally equal to its fair market value (FMV) at the date of the decedent's death (i.e., a stepped-up basis). (Code Sec. 1014(a)(1)) However, if:

(1) the fiduciary elects to value the decedent's gross estate at the alternate valuation date (¶5016), the basis of the property is its FMV at that date (Code Sec. 1014(a)(2)).

(2) the fiduciary elects for estate tax purposes the special use valuation method of valuing farm or other closely held business real property included in the decedent's gross estate (¶5017), the basis of the real property is its value determined for purposes of the special use valuation election (rather than its FMV). (Code Sec. 1014(a)(3))[21]

(3) land acquired at death is subject to a qualified conservation easement, it is excluded from the decedent's gross estate (see ¶5016), and its basis (to the extent that it's subject to the easement) is the basis in the decedent's hands. (Code Sec. 1014(a)(4))[22]

FMV on the date of the decedent's death (or the alternate valuation date, if applicable) doesn't apply to determine the basis of property that's:

. . . appreciated property acquired by a decedent by gift in the 1-year period ending on death, and that is reacquired by the donor (or the donor's spouse) from the decedent, see ¶2510;

. . . included in the decedent's estate but disposed of by the taxpayer before the decedent's death, see ¶2511;

. . . stock in a domestic international sales corporation (DISC) or former DISC (Code Sec. 1014(d)), or of certain foreign entities; or

. . . a right to receive income in respect of a decedent (Code Sec. 1014(c)), see ¶3961.[23]

. . . acquired from a decedent who died in 2010 if the executor elected the modified carryover basis rules (and exemption from the estate tax).[24]

FMV of property at the decedent's death or at the alternate valuation date is the FMV as determined by an appraisal for federal estate tax purposes. If no federal estate tax

20. ¶P-3107 *et seq.*
21. ¶P-4001 *et seq.*
22. ¶P-4021.1
23. ¶P-4003 *et seq.*
24. ¶P-4060

return is required to be filed, the FMV of the property appraised as of the date of death for purposes of state inheritance or other transmission taxes (e.g., legacy taxes) is used to determine FMV. However, if no federal estate tax return is filed, the alternate valuation date can't be used to determine FMV. (Reg § 1.1014-3(a))[25]

¶ 2509 When estate tax value is also income tax basis—Form 8971.

Under Code Sec. 1014(f), for property with respect to which an estate tax return is filed after July 31, 2015 and whose inclusion in the decedent's estate increases the estate's estate tax liability (reduced by allowable credits), the basis of that property for income tax purposes can't exceed: (A) in the case of property, the final value of which has been determined for purposes of the estate tax, that value; and (B) in the case of property not described in (A) and with respect to which a statement (Form 8971) has been furnished under Code Sec. 6035(a) (see ¶4746), the value on Form 8971. (Code Sec. 1014(f); Prop Reg. § 1.1014-10 ["Taxpayers may rely"]) [26] If the final estate tax value is later determined and that value is different from the value reported on Form 8971, the taxpayer can't rely on the Form 8971 initially furnished for the value of the property. Before the determination of final estate value, the recipient of property can't claim an initial basis in excess of the value on Form 8971. Final estate value is considered to occur when IRS doesn't contest the value shown on the return, the executor doesn't contest a value specified by IRS, or a court order or settlement agreement with IRS specifies value. (Prop Reg. § 1.1014-10(c) ["Taxpayers may rely"]) [27]

For property with respect to which an estate tax return was filed before Aug. 1, 2015, or whose inclusion in the decedent's estate doesn't increase the estate's estate tax liability (reduced by credits allowable against the tax), the value for estate tax purposes is only presumptively correct for basis purposes. Except where facts have been misrepresented, neither taxpayer nor IRS is barred from using a value for basis purposes that differs from the value accepted for estate tax purposes. However, where a discount is allowed in valuing property (e.g., artwork) for estate tax purposes, full value generally won't be allowed in valuing the same property for income tax purposes.[28]

¶ 2510 Appreciated property reacquired by donor from donee-decedent—basis.

Code Sec. 1014(e)(1) provides that, if: (1) appreciated property was acquired by the decedent by gift during the 1-year period ending at death, and (2) that property is acquired from the decedent by (or passes from the decedent to) the donor of the property (or the donor's spouse), the basis of the property in the hands of the donor (or spouse) is the adjusted basis of the property in the decedent's hands immediately before death. (Code Sec. 1014(e)(1))[29]

¶ 2511 When is property considered "acquired from a decedent"—basis.

Under Code Sec. 1014(b)(1), property is "acquired from a decedent" (for the fair-market-value-basis-determination rules at ¶2508), only if it fits into one of the following categories:

Property acquired by bequest, devise, or inheritance, or by the decedent's estate from the decedent. (Code Sec. 1014(b)(1); Reg § 1.1014-2(a)(1))[30] Property included in decedent's estate includes: (1) property acquired as a surviving joint tenant or tenant by the entireties

25. ¶P-4022
26. ¶P-4022
27. ¶P-4022.1

28. ¶P-4022, P-4023, P-4024
29. ¶P-4002
30. ¶P-4101

408

(¶2513), and (2) certain gifts within 3 years of the decedent's death, which must be included in the decedent's gross estate (¶5002). (Reg § 1.1014-2(b))[31] For the basis of property acquired before the death of the decedent that's included in the decedent's gross estate, see Code Sec. 1014(b)(9) and Reg § 1.1014-6(a)(1).[32]

Property transferred to an inter vivos trust with power to revoke, alter, amend, or terminate. Property is treated as acquired from a decedent if transferred by the decedent-grantor during his or her lifetime, in trust, to pay the income for life to the decedent or under the decedent's direction to others, with the right reserved to the decedent at all times before death to revoke, alter, amend or terminate the trust. (Code Sec. 1014(b)(2); Code Sec. 1014(b)(3); Reg § 1.1014-2(a)(2))[33]

Property passing under a general power of appointment. Property is treated as acquired from a decedent if it passes without full and adequate consideration under a general power of appointment (¶5009) exercised by will. (Code Sec. 1014(b)(2); Code Sec. 1014(b)(4))[34]

Property passing under community property laws. A surviving spouse's share in community property is treated as property acquired from the decedent spouse if at least one-half of the community property was includible in the deceased spouse's estate (Code Sec. 1014(b)(6)), even if an estate tax return for the estate of the decedent wasn't required, or if required, no estate tax was payable. (Reg § 1.1014-2(a)(5))[35]

Qualified terminable interest property. Qualified terminable interest property (QTIP) that's includible in a surviving spouse's estate (¶5008), is treated as passing from that surviving spouse for determining a remainderman's basis. (Code Sec. 1014(b)(10)) Thus, the basis of the remainderman in the QTIP property is the fair market value of the QTIP property at the surviving spouse's death.[36]

The following (among others) are not considered received from a decedent:

. . . property acquired after the death of the decedent by the fiduciary as an investment. (Reg § 1.1014-3(c))[37]

. . . property bought from a decedent's estate. Its basis to the buyer is its cost or other basis with appropriate adjustments.[38]

. . . income in respect of a decedent (IRD, see ¶3961). (Code Sec. 1014(c)) Its basis is equal to the decedent's basis (if any).[39]

. . . property transferred by the executor, administrator or trustee to a beneficiary in discharge of a specific pecuniary bequest. The beneficiary's basis is the fair market value of the property on the date of the transfer. (Reg § 1.1014-4(a)(3))[40]

¶ 2512   Basis of postponed or contingent remainder interests—basis.

Under Code Sec. 1014, taxpayer's basis for property acquired from a decedent (¶2511) is determined on the date of the decedent's death under the rules at ¶2508 *et seq.*, whether or not, at the decedent's death, the taxpayer's interest was conditional or contingent, and whether or not the taxpayer can immediately possess and enjoy the property. (Reg § 1.1014-4(a)(2))[41]

observation: If an estate tax return is filed, and the alternate valuation date (¶2508) is elected, the value would be determined as of the alternate valuation date.

---

31. ¶P-4101
32. ¶P-3123
33. ¶P-4101
34. ¶P-4101
35. ¶P-4101
36. ¶P-4101
37. ¶P-4101; ¶P-4054
38. ¶P-4101
39. ¶P-4003
40. ¶P-4055
41. ¶P-4018

¶ 2513   Multiple interests in one property acquired from a decedent—basis of property.

Under Reg § 1.1014-4(b), where more than 1 person has an interest in property acquired from a decedent (¶2511), the basis in the property is determined under Code Sec. 1014 and adjusted without regard to the multiple interests. Therefore, a life tenant (LT) adjusts basis for depreciation as if LT were the absolute owner. LT's basis adjustments are an adjustment in the hands of every person who receives an interest by reason of the decedent's death. (Reg § 1.1014-4(b))[42]

¶ 2514   Basis of property transferred between spouses or incident to a divorce—carryover basis.

Under Code Sec. 1041, a transferee-spouse is treated as acquiring the property by gift; the transferee's basis in the property received is the transferor-spouse's adjusted basis in the property. (Code Sec. 1041(b)) This rule applies even where the transaction is a sale between the spouses or where the transferee-spouse pays the transferor-spouse (as required under the divorce settlement) for the transfer of title to the property to the transferee-spouse. (Reg § 1.1041-1T(a), Q&A-2) This carryover basis rule applies whether the adjusted basis of the transferred property is less than, equal to, or greater than its fair market value at the time of transfer and applies for purposes of determining loss as well as gain, upon later sale by the transferee. (Reg § 1.1041-1T(d), Q&A-11)[43] Exceptions apply to certain transfers in trust (where liabilities assumed by the trust exceed the transferor's adjusted basis) (Code Sec. 1041(e)), and to transfers of installment obligations into a trust (Code Sec. 453B(g)).[44] The transferor must, at the time of the transfer, give the transferee records sufficient to determine the adjusted basis and holding period of the property at the date of transfer. (Reg § 1.1041-1T(e), Q&A-14)[45]

---

42. ¶P-4014 *et seq.*
43. ¶P-1146

44. ¶P-1147
45. ¶P-1153

Chapter 10 Capital Gains and Losses—Section 1231— Depreciation Recapture

¶ 2600   **Capital Gains and Losses.** �â–ˆâ–ˆâ–ˆâ–ˆâ–ˆâ–ˆâ–ˆ

The tax treatment of capital gains and losses depends on whether the gains and losses are long-term or short-term and on whether the taxpayer is a corporation or not. For noncorporate taxpayers, the maximum tax rate on net long-term capital gains is lower than the top rate on ordinary income. That maximum tax depends on the type of capital asset sold, and the taxpayer's marginal tax rate (the top rate on the taxpayer's ordinary income). Corporate long-term capital gains, and short-term gains of both corporations and noncorporate taxpayers, are taxed at the same rates as their ordinary income. The deduction for capital losses is limited, see ¶2609 (noncorporate) and ¶2611 (corporate).

The main features of the income tax treatment of capital gains and losses are:

. . . Short-term capital gains and losses are netted, long-term capital gains and losses are netted, and then long- and short-term are netted with each other (¶2601 *et seq.*). Further netting may be required if a noncorporate taxpayer has capital losses and long-term capital gain subject to differing maximum tax rates. (¶2606)

. . . A net capital gain (excess of net long-term capital gain over net short-term capital loss) of a noncorporate taxpayer is generally taxed more favorably than ordinary income. The maximum tax rate depends on whether the net capital gain is adjusted net capital gain (¶2602), unrecaptured section 1250 gain (¶2604), collectibles gain (¶2605) or section 1202 gain (¶2605).

. . . Section 1231 nets gains and losses to arrive at a net of long-term capital gain or ordinary loss (¶2607 and ¶2666 *et seq.*).

. . . Recapture provisions restrict the possibility of converting ordinary income into capital gains via cost recovery or depreciation (¶2672 *et seq.*).

Capital gains and losses are gains and losses from sales or exchanges (¶2661) of capital assets (¶2612). Capital gain treatment also applies to gains in certain transactions involving assets that aren't capital assets, e.g., depreciable property used in business (¶2667).[1]

⊘observation: Not all losses (capital or ordinary) are deductible. Individuals can only deduct losses incurred in business or transactions for profit, or resulting from certain federally declared disasters (in tax years beginning after 2017 and before 2026, ¶1782). So, a loss on a sale of a personal residence is a nondeductible capital loss.

With limited exceptions, report capital gains and losses on Form 8949, and then carry the totals over to Schedule D of the applicable form (e.g., Form 1040 for individuals, Form 1041 for trusts and estates, Form 1065 for partnerships, Form 1120 for corporations and Form 1120-S for S corporations) where the net short-term and long-term capital gain or loss is computed. Taxpayers may report the total of their capital gains and losses transactions on the applicable schedule and provide details on attachments such as brokers' statements. Individuals whose only capital gains are capital gains distributions (other than unrecaptured section 1250 gain (¶2604), collectibles gain (¶2605), or section 1202 gain (¶2605)) reported on Form 1099-DIV don't have to file a Form 8949 or Schedule D. They enter capital gains on Form 1040 and complete a capital gain tax worksheet in the instructions.

For the deduction when stock or securities become worthless, see ¶1772.

---

1. ¶I-5100 *et seq.*

References beginning with a single letter are to paragraphs in Federal Tax Coordinator 2d and RIA's Analysis of Federal Taxes: Income.

¶ 2601   Tax effect of capital asset sales and exchanges; short-term and long-term capital gains and losses.

Under Code Sec. 1222, if a capital asset is held for not more than the short-term holding period (¶2652), the gain or loss from its sale or exchange is short-term. If held for more than the short-term holding period, gain or loss is long-term. (Code Sec. 1222)[2]

Short-term capital gains and losses are netted to get net short-term capital gain or net short-term capital loss. (Code Sec. 1222(5), Code Sec. 1222(6))

Long-term capital gains and losses are netted to get net long-term capital gain or net long-term capital loss. (Code Sec. 1222(7), Code Sec. 1222(8))

There's a further netting if 1 group shows a loss and the other a gain:

If capital losses exceed capital gains, see ¶2608 *et seq.* (noncorporate) or ¶2611 (corporate).

If net long-term capital gains exceed net short-term capital losses, the excess is net capital gain (Code Sec. 1222(11)), taxed under the rules at ¶2602 to ¶2608 (individuals and other noncorporate taxpayers) or at ¶2610 *et seq.* (corporate taxpayers). *If net short-term capital gains exceed net long-term capital losses,* the excess is taxed (both for noncorporate and corporate taxpayers) at the same rate as ordinary income.[3]

A taxpayer who has an excess of capital gains over capital losses (whether long-term or short-term) for the tax year, has "capital gain net income" (Code Sec. 1222(9)), which is included in gross income.[4]

¶ 2602   Noncorporate taxpayer's tax on net capital gain—joint filers, surviving spouses, heads of household, singles, marrieds filing separately, estates and trusts.

Here's a summary of the application of the 0%, 15%, and 20% rates to a noncorporate taxpayer's net capital gain (¶2603) under Code Sec. 1(j)(5):[5]

0% rate: For 2022, the 0% tax rate applies to adjusted net capital gain up to:

. . . $83,350 for joint filers and surviving spouses ($89,250 for 2023),

. . . $55,800 for heads of household ($59,750 for 2023),

. . . $41,675 for single filers and married taxpayers filing separately ($44,625 for 2023),

. . . $2,800 for estates and trusts ($3,000 for 2023).

15% rate: For 2022, the 15% tax rate applies to adjusted net capital gain over the amount subject to the 0% rate, and up to:

. . . $517,200 for joint filers and surviving spouses ($553,850 for 2023),

. . . $488,500 for heads of household ($523,050 for 2023),

. . . $459,750 for single filers ($492,300 for 2023),

. . . $258,600 for married taxpayers filing separately ($276,900 for 2023),

. . . $13,700 for estates and trusts ($14,650 for 2023).

The 20% capital gains tax rate applies to adjusted net capital gain over the maximum amounts subject to the 15% rate (see immediately above).

Under Code Sec. 1(h)(1), unrecaptured section 1250 gain continues to be taxed at a

---

2. ¶I-5103, I-5104
3. ¶I-5100
4. ¶I-5106
5. ¶I-5110 *et seq.*

maximum rate of 25%, and 28% rate gain at a maximum rate of 28%. (Code Sec. 1(h)(1))

Sellers of interests in S corporations, partnerships, and trusts held for more than 1 year recognize collectibles gain if the entity owns the appreciated assets at the time of sale. (Code Sec. 1(h)(5)(B)) Regs explain how to figure the seller's deemed collectibles gain and his or her residual long-term gain or loss and use the same approach for sales of interests in various entities. (Reg § 1.1(h)-1) See ¶3755 for the regs' approach in the context of sales of partnership interests, which also may cause a partner to recognize unrecaptured section 1250 gain. But, sales of interests in S corporations and trusts don't trigger unrecaptured section 1250 gain—only collectibles gain and residual long-term capital gain or loss.[6]

The 3.8% surtax on net investment income of noncorporate taxpayers whose modified adjusted gross income is over specified thresholds includes capital gains, see ¶3143.

For netting rules where a noncorporate taxpayer has capital losses, see ¶2606.

¶ 2603 Adjusted net capital gain defined—capital gains and losses.

Under Code Sec. 1(h)(3), adjusted net capital gain is net capital gain (¶2601) determined without taking qualified dividend income (see ¶1288) into account less the amount that the taxpayer takes into account as investment income under Code Sec. 163(d)(4)(B)(iii) (see ¶1728), reduced (but not below zero) by the sum of:

. . . unrecaptured Code Sec. 1250 gain (¶2604), and

. . . 28% rate gain (as defined at ¶2605), and increased by

the amount of qualified dividend income. (Code Sec. 1(h)(3))[7]

observation: Effectively, adjusted net capital gain is the sum of that part of a taxpayer's net capital gain, if any, that is eligible to be taxed at a maximum rate of 20% or less (see ¶2602), plus the amount of qualified dividend income.

¶ 2604 Noncorporate taxpayer's unrecaptured section 1250 gain—capital gains and losses.

Under Code Sec. 1(h)(6), unrecaptured Code Sec. 1250 gain is taxed at a maximum rate of 25%. It is the excess (if any) of:

(1) the amount of long-term capital gain (¶2601) not otherwise treated as ordinary income, and which would be treated as ordinary income if Code Sec. 1250(b)(1) recapture applied to all depreciation (rather than only to depreciation in excess of straight line), and the applicable percentage under Code Sec. 1250(a) (¶2676) were 100%, over

(2) the excess (if any) of the amount of losses taken into account in computing 28% rate gain (¶2605) over the amount of gains taken into account in computing 28% rate gain. (Code Sec. 1(h)(6))[8]

The amount in (1), above, from sales exchanges and conversions described in Code Sec. 1231(a)(3)(A) (i.e., section 1231 gain) for any tax year can't exceed the net section 1231 gain (¶2666) for that tax year. (Code Sec. 1(h)(6)(B))

observation: Under MACRS, real property must be depreciated using the straight-line method (¶1921), so any gain on the sale or exchange of such property attributable to depreciation will be unrecaptured Code Sec. 1250 gain if held for more than 1 year.

illustration: Y, an individual, sells nonresidential real property on Aug. 15 for $200,000, realizing a gain of $50,000. This is Y's only transaction involving a capital asset for the year. Y held the property for more than 1 year. Y depreciated the property using MACRS, and claimed $25,000 of depreciation during Y's ownership. There is no depreciation recapture under Code Sec. 1250(b)(1) because Y didn't claim accelerated depreciation. But, $25,000 of Y's gain, representing depreciation deductions claimed by Y, is unrecaptured section 1250 gain.

For how to handle unrecaptured Code Sec. 1250 gain where a sale of real property is reported on the installment method, see ¶2452. For how unrecaptured Code Sec. 1250 gain can arise on sale of a partnership interest, see ¶3755.

¶ 2605 Noncorporate taxpayer's 28% rate gain; collectibles gain and losses and section 1202 gain—capital gains and losses.

Under Code Sec. 1(h)(4), the 28% rate gain is the sum of collectibles gain and losses and section 1202 gain less the sum of collectibles loss, the net short-term capital loss for the tax year, and the long-term capital loss carryover to the tax year. (Code Sec. 1(h)(4))[9]

⚫*observation:* The way 28% rate gain is defined causes a long-term capital loss carryover from an earlier tax year to always be used first to offset 28% rate gain, see ¶2606.

Collectibles gain or loss is gain or loss from the sale or exchange of a collectible which is a capital asset held for more than 1 year, but only to the extent such gain or loss is taken into account in computing gross income. (Code Sec. 1(h)(5)) Any work of art, rug or antique, metal or gem, stamp or coin, alcoholic beverage, or any other tangible personal property specified by IRS for this purpose is a collectible.[10]

For how collectibles gain can arise on the sale of interests in a partnership, S corporation, or trust, see ¶2602.

Section 1202 gain is the excess of (1) the gain that would be excluded from gross income on the sale of certain qualified small business stock (QSBS) under Code Sec. 1202, if the percentage limitations of Code Sec. 1202(a) (see ¶2638) didn't apply, over (2) the gain actually excluded under Code Sec. 1202. (Code Sec. 1(h)(7))[11]

⚫*observation:* If any portion of the gain on the sale of QSBS is excluded from gross income, the part includible in gross income is taxed at a maximum rate of 28%.

See ¶3206 for AMT treatment of section 1202 gain.

¶ 2606 Netting and ordering rules where taxpayer has short-term and/or long-term capital losses.

Under Code Sec. 1222, the following netting and ordering rules apply where the taxpayer has capital losses:

(1) Short-term capital losses are applied first to reduce short-term capital gains, if any. If there's a net short-term capital loss, it first reduces any net long-term gain from the 28% group, then gain from the 25% group, and finally reduces adjusted net capital gain.

(2) Long-term capital losses are handled as follows:

. . . A net loss from the 28% group (including long-term capital loss carryovers from prior years) first reduces gain from the 25% group, then reduces adjusted net capital gain.

. . . A net loss from a group in which net gain would be treated as adjusted net capital gain first reduces net gain from the 28% group, then from the 25% group.[12]

9. ¶I-5110.11
10. ¶I-5110.12
11. ¶I-5110.13
12. ¶I-5107

✏️*illustration:* T has a loss of $40,000 from the sale of stock, collectibles gain of $25,000, and unrecaptured section 1250 gain of $25,000. T's net capital gain is $10,000 (total gain of $50,000 less $40,000 loss). T's $40,000 loss from the sale of stock completely offsets the collectibles gain of $25,000, and offsets $15,000 of the $25,000 of unrecaptured section 1250 gain. T has unrecaptured section 1250 gain of $10,000.

¶ 2607 Noncorporate taxpayer's nonrecaptured net section 1231 losses; allocation of amount treated as ordinary income—capital gains and losses.

Under Code Sec. 1(h)(8), if any Code Sec. 1231 gain is treated as ordinary income under Code Sec. 1231(c) (i.e., Section 1231 gain treated as ordinary income to the extent of nonrecaptured Section 1231 losses, see ¶2666), the amount to be treated as ordinary income is allocated first to any net section 1231 gain in the 28% group, then to any section 1231 gain in the 25% group, and then to any net section 1231 gain in the 0%/15%/20% group.[13]

¶ 2608 Capital losses of noncorporate taxpayers.

Under Code Sec. 1211, a noncorporate taxpayer may deduct capital losses only to the extent of capital gains plus (if the losses exceed the gains) the lower of:

(1) $3,000 ($1,500 for married individuals filing separate returns), or

(2) the excess of the losses over the gains. (Code Sec. 1211(b))[14]

✏️*illustration:* B has a short-term capital loss of $100 and a long-term capital loss of $3,600 for the tax year. B's total capital loss for the tax year is $3,700. This capital loss is deductible from ordinary income up to a maximum of $3,000. See ¶2609 for carrying over the excess capital loss.

A noncorporate taxpayer's capital losses for a tax year consist of the capital losses sustained during the year plus the total of all capital losses sustained in other years that are carried to that tax year (¶2609). (Code Sec. 1212(b); Reg § 1.1211-1(b)(1))[15]

¶ 2609 Noncorporate capital loss carryovers; individuals (including decedents), trusts, and estates—capital gains and losses.

Under Code Sec. 1212, if an individual, trust or estate has a net capital loss that exceeds the maximum deductible in the current year (¶2608), the excess is carried forward to later years indefinitely until used. (Code Sec. 1212(b)) Carrybacks aren't allowed.[16] A decedent's capital loss that can't be used on his or her final income tax return is lost; it can't be carried over.[17]

The capital loss keeps its original character as long- or short-term when carried over. For purposes of determining the amount of excess long- or short-term capital loss that is carried over, short-term capital loss is applied first to offset ordinary income, and long-term capital loss is applied only to the extent that the amount that can be offset exceeds the total short-term capital loss for the year (including any short-term capital loss carried over from an earlier year). (Code Sec. 1212(b))[18]

---

13. ¶I-9003.1
14. ¶I-5112
15. ¶I-5113

16. ¶I-5122
17. ¶I-5133
18. ¶I-5123

¶ 2610   Capital gains of corporate taxpayers.

Under Code Sec. 1211, corporate taxpayers must include capital gains in full in gross income but only to the extent that they exceed capital losses.[19]

¶ 2611   Corporation's capital losses; carryback and carryforward of excess capital losses.

Under Code Sec. 1211, corporations may deduct capital losses only to the extent of their capital gains. Excess capital losses can't be deducted from a corporation's ordinary income. (Code Sec. 1211(a))[20]

Under Code Sec. 1212, a corporation's capital losses in excess of its capital gains for the current year are carried back 3 years, but only to the extent the loss isn't attributable to a foreign expropriation capital loss and to the extent that the carryback doesn't increase or produce an NOL for the tax year to which it's carried back. (Code Sec. 1212(a)(1)(A)) A net capital loss can't be carried back to a tax year in which the corporation was either a regulated investment company (RIC) or a real estate investment trust (REIT). (Code Sec. 1212(a)(4))

The carryforward period is 5 years (10 years for foreign expropriation capital losses, and there is no limit on how long a RIC may carry forward capital losses). (Code Sec. 1212(a)(1)(B); Code Sec. 1212(a)(1)(C); Code Sec. 1212(a)(3))[21]

A capital loss carryback or carryover is treated as a short-term capital loss whether or not it was short-term when sustained (Code Sec. 1212(a)(1)) except that the capital losses of a RIC retain their character as short-term or long-term when carried over. (Code Sec. 1212(a)(3)(A)) A carryover from 1 year can't be included in computing a new net capital loss for another year. (Code Sec. 1222(10))[22]

¶ 2612   Assets to Which Capital Gain and Loss Rules Apply. ▬▬▬▬▬▬

The capital gain or loss rules apply to assets that are capital in nature. An asset's character depends upon what it is and what use it has in the taxpayer's hands.

Under Code Sec. 1221, capital assets include all assets held by the taxpayer *except*:

(1) Stock in trade of the taxpayer or other property of a kind that would properly be included in the inventory of the taxpayer if on hand at the close of the tax year, or property held by the taxpayer primarily for sale to customers in the ordinary course of his or her trade or business. (Code Sec. 1221(a)(1))[23]

(2) Depreciable property, amortizable Code Sec. 197 intangibles, and real property used in the taxpayer's trade or business, see ¶2666 *et seq.* (Code Sec. 1221(a)(2))[24]

(3) Copyrights, literary, artistic, or musical works (unless, for musical works or copyrights in them, the election discussed at ¶2615 is made); certain letters, memoranda, or similar property; and, patents, inventions, models or designs (whether or not patented), secret formulas or processes. (Code Sec. 1221(a)(3))[25]

(4) Accounts or notes receivable acquired in the ordinary course of a trade or business for services rendered or from the sale of any properties described in (1) or (2), above. (Code Sec. 1221(a)(4))[26]

(5) U.S. government publications (e.g., Congressional Record) received from the government without charge or below the price sold to the public, in the hands of the recipient

---

19. ¶I-5116
20. ¶I-5121
21. ¶I-5125 *et seq.*
22. ¶I-5125

23. ¶I-6100 *et seq.*
24. ¶I-6006
25. ¶I-6601 *et seq.*
26. ¶I-6127 *et seq.*

and carryover-basis transferees. (Code Sec. 1221(a)(5))[27]

(6) Commodities derivative financial instruments held by a commodities derivatives dealer (except for certain instruments not connected to the dealing activity). (Code Sec. 1221(a)(6))[28]

(7) Any hedging transaction, see ¶2616. (Code Sec. 1221(a)(7))[29]

(8) Supplies of a type regularly used or consumed by the taxpayer in the ordinary course of the taxpayer's trade or business. (Code Sec. 1221(a)(8))[30]

Property held for personal use is a capital asset, as is property used for the production of income. (Reg § 1.1221-1(b)) Examples of capital assets include stock and securities held for investment,[31] including tax-exempt bonds[32] (¶2621). A payment received in exchange for the right to ordinary income isn't a capital asset.[33] Depending on the circumstances, a contractual right to purchase land can be a capital asset.[34]

For the sale of: real property, see ¶2613 *et seq.*; SBIC and RIC stock, see ¶2619 *et seq.*; debt instruments, see ¶2621; investments by a dealer in securities, see ¶2622; a business, see ¶2625; and life estates, terms for years, etc., see ¶2626.

For options and straddles, see ¶2617 *et seq.* For transfers of patents, trademarks, etc., see ¶2623 *et seq.*

¶ 2613 Sale of real property held for sale in the ordinary course of the taxpayer's trade or business—capital assets.

Under Code Sec. 1221, real property held primarily for sale in the ordinary course of the taxpayer's trade or business doesn't qualify as a capital asset. Whether particular real estate sold is a capital asset is decided on a case by case basis taking into consideration many factors including the number and taxpayer's frequency of sales, subdividing and promotional activities.[35]

¶ 2614 5-year land subdivision rule for taxpayers other than C corporations; when land is held primarily for sale to customers—capital assets.

Under Code Sec. 1237, a taxpayer other than a C corporation isn't treated as holding land primarily for sale to customers merely because the taxpayer subdivided a tract of land into lots or parcels and engaged in advertising, promotion, selling activities, or the use of sales agents in selling lots in the subdivision, if the taxpayer:

. . . hasn't previously held any part of the same land primarily for sale to customers in the ordinary course of business, and, in the year of sale doesn't hold any other real estate for sale to customers;

. . . doesn't (while he or she holds the land or as part of a contract of sale with the buyer) make "substantial improvements" on the land that substantially increase the value of the lot sold (except, if elected, improvements needed to make marketable land that has been held for 10 years or more); and

. . . either has owned the land for 5 years or more, or acquired it by inheritance or devise. (Code Sec. 1237(a); Reg § 1.1237-1(a)(2), Reg § 1.1237-1(a)(5), Reg § 1.1237-1(b)(1))[36]

But, if more than 5 lots or parcels in the same tract are sold or exchanged, gain from any sale or exchange (which occurs in or after the tax year in which the 6th lot or parcel is sold

27. ¶I-6002
28. ¶I-6291
29. ¶I-6231*et seq.*
30. ¶I-6140
31. ¶I-6201
32. ¶I-7801
33. ¶I-6824.1
34. ¶I-6317
35. ¶I-6300 *et seq.*
36. ¶I-6400 *et seq.*

or exchanged) of any lot or parcel covered by the above 5-year rule will be treated as ordinary income to the extent that 5% of the selling price exceeds the expenses of the sale. (Code Sec. 1237(b)(1); Reg § 1.1237-1(e)(2))[37]

illustration: T divides a tract covered by the 5-year rule into 6 parcels. If T sells all 6 parcels in Year 1, gain from the sale of each parcel is treated as ordinary income to the extent that 5% of the selling price exceeds the expenses of the sale. But, if T doesn't sell the 6th parcel until Year 2, the 5% rule applies only to the gain from the sale of that parcel.

The rules discussed above don't apply to the sale or exchange of otherwise qualifying subdivided land that is business property, and the capital gain-ordinary loss rules of Code Sec. 1231 (see ¶2666) apply. (Reg § 1.1237-1(f))[38]

¶ 2615   Patents, copyrights, literary, musical, artistic compositions, etc.—capital assets.

Under Code Sec. 1221, a patent, invention, model or design (whether or not patented), secret formula or process, copyright, literary, artistic, and (except as noted below) musical composition, etc., aren't capital assets or Code Sec. 1231 assets if the taxpayer is either (1) the author or creator of property through his or her own personal efforts, or (2) the donee of the author or creator, or one who otherwise has a basis for the property determined in whole or in part by reference to the basis in the donor's hands.

A letter, memorandum or similar property prepared or produced for a taxpayer isn't a capital asset to the taxpayer (or the taxpayer's donee or other carryover-basis transferee). (Code Sec. 1221(a)(3))[39]

A taxpayer may elect to treat a sale or exchange of musical compositions or copyrights in musical works created by the taxpayer's personal efforts (or having a basis determined by reference to the basis in the hands of a taxpayer whose personal efforts created them) as the sale or exchange of a capital asset. (Code Sec. 1221(b)(3)) A taxpayer must make the election on Form 8949 and Schedule D (Form 1040) by treating the sale or exchange as the sale or exchange of a capital asset on or before the due date (including extensions) of his or her return for the tax year of the sale or exchange. (Reg § 1.1221-3(b)) The election is revocable with IRS consent. IRS automatically grants taxpayers a 6-month extension from the due date of the taxpayer's income tax return (excluding extensions) to revoke an election, if the taxpayer timely filed the income tax return and, within the 6-month extension period, files an amended return that treats the sale or exchange as the sale or exchange of property that isn't a capital asset. (Reg § 1.1221-3(c))[40]

¶ 2616   Hedging transactions—capital assets.

Under Code Sec. 1221, the term "capital asset" doesn't include property that's part of a hedging transaction. (Code Sec. 1221(a)(7); Reg § 1.1221-2(a)) A hedging transaction is a transaction that a taxpayer enters into in the normal course of the taxpayer's trade or business, primarily to reduce the risk of price changes or currency fluctuations with respect to ordinary property, or to reduce the risk of interest rate or price changes or currency fluctuations with respect to borrowings or ordinary obligations. (Reg § 1.1221-2(b)) Property is ordinary property only if its sale or exchange by the taxpayer couldn't produce capital gain or loss regardless of the holding period. An obligation is an ordinary

37. ¶I-6420
38. ¶I-6424

39. ¶I-6601 *et seq.*
40. ¶I-6601

obligation if performance or termination of the obligation by the taxpayer could not produce capital gain or loss. (Reg § 1.1221-2(c)(2))[41] Thus, hedging in corn futures (to stabilize the cost of corn inventory) as an integral part of a taxpayer's inventory-purchase system produces ordinary income and loss.[42]

A taxpayer must identify a transaction (including recycling an existing hedge) as a hedging transaction before the close of the day he or she enters it. (Reg § 1.1221-2(f)(1))[43]

The accounting method used for a hedging transaction must clearly reflect income and reasonably match the transaction's timing with the timing of the item(s) being hedged. Special rules give the accounting methods for various transactions. (Reg § 1.446-4)[44]

¶ 2617   Noncompensatory options to buy or sell—capital assets.

Under Code Sec. 1234, gain or loss from the sale or exchange of a noncompensatory option to buy or sell property is considered a gain or loss from the sale or exchange of a capital asset if the optioned property is (or would be if acquired) a capital asset in the taxpayer's hands. (Code Sec. 1234(a)(1); Reg § 1.1234-1(a))[45] If the holder of an option incurs a loss because he or she fails to exercise the option, the option is considered to have been sold or exchanged on the date it expires. (Code Sec. 1234(a)(2); Reg § 1.1234-1(b))[46]

A dealer in options is considered a dealer in the property subject to the option, and any gain or loss received from sale or exchange of the option is ordinary. (Reg § 1.1234-1(d))[47]

¶ 2618   Tax treatment of transactions involving "put" and "call" options; straddles.

Under Code Sec. 1234, there are no tax consequences to the buyer or writer of an option until the option is exercised, otherwise closed out, or lapses. The holder treats the premium paid as a nondeductible capital expenditure at the time of payment. The premium isn't included in income of the writer at the time of receipt.[48] The premium received by the writer for granting a "put" or "call" option that's not exercised ("lapses"), so that the writer simply keeps the money, is generally treated as ordinary income, and gain or loss to the writer on repurchase of an option ("closing transaction") is also generally ordinary. (Reg § 1.1234-1(b)) But, gain or loss to a nondealer from a lapse or closing transaction involving options in stocks, securities, commodities or commodity futures is treated as short-term capital gain or loss. (Code Sec. 1234(b); Reg § 1.1234-3)[49]

Where a put is exercised, the premium received by the writer for granting the option is deducted from the option price for the property in determining the net basis to the writer of the property purchased. The holder deducts the premium from the amount received from the writer, in computing the gain or loss realized on the sale. Where a call is exercised, the premium received by the writer (i.e., seller) for granting the option is added to the sale proceeds received. This is included in the holder's (buyer's) basis for the property.[50]

⊘illustration: A bought a 180-day put from B for $5,000 that gave A the right to sell 1,000 shares of stock to B for $50,000. The stock originally cost A $25,000. The put was timely exercised. A has a gain of $20,000 on the sale ($50,000, less $30,000 ($5,000 paid for put and $25,000 original cost of stock). B's basis in the stock is $45,000 ($50,000 paid to A on the exercise of the put, less $5,000 received by B from A for the put).

---

41. ¶I-6231 *et seq.*
42. ¶I-6268
43. ¶I-6250
44. ¶G-2519 *et seq.*
45. ¶I-6504
46. ¶I-6510
47. ¶I-6509
48. ¶s I-6521, I-6522
49. ¶I-6515
50. ¶s I-6530, I-6531

When the put or call is bought from the original holder (or the original holder's assignee), the buyer is treated as a holder, and the amount paid by him or her to the original holder is likewise treated as a premium. But, the original holder isn't treated as a writer, and must include that premium in his or her amount realized upon disposition of the option, see ¶2617.[1]

✒observation: Thus, if a holder (other than a dealer) of a put or call option on publicly traded stock closes out a position by selling the option on an exchange, the gain or loss is a capital gain or loss.

A "straddle" option combines a put and a call. (Reg § 1.1234-3(b)(4))[2] The allocation of a premium received for a straddle or multiple option between or among the component options is made on the basis of the relative market value of the component options at the time of their issuance or on any other reasonable and consistently applied basis acceptable to IRS. (Reg § 1.1234-3(e))[3]

¶ 2619 Sale of small business investment company (SBIC) stock—tax treatment of losses and gains.

Under Code Sec. 1242, losses from the sale, exchange or worthlessness of SBIC (¶4205) stock are deductible by a shareholder as an ordinary loss attributable to the shareholder's business. (Code Sec. 1242; Reg § 1.1242-1) Gains on the sale or exchange of SBIC stock are capital gains.[4]

¶ 2620 Sale of regulated investment company (RIC) stock—tax treatment of losses.

Under Code Sec. 852, a loss realized on the sale or exchange of stock in a RIC is a long-term capital loss to the extent of any long-term capital gain realized via a distribution made with respect to the stock, if the taxpayer held the stock for 6 months or less. Also, the loss of a shareholder who receives an exempt-interest dividend on stock which is held for 6 months or less is disallowed to the extent of the exempt interest dividend received by the shareholder. Rules for periodic liquidations differ. (Code Sec. 852(b)(4))[5]

¶ 2621 Type of gain on a sale or exchange of debt instruments; instruments issued with original issue discount (OID); sale or exchange of short-term government or nongovernment obligations or tax-exempt bonds.

Debt instruments issued with original issue discount (OID). Under Code Sec. 1271, if a debt instrument is issued with OID (¶1313) and, if at the time of original issue there was an intention to call the debt instrument before maturity, any gain realized on the sale or exchange of the instrument is treated as ordinary income to the extent the gain doesn't exceed the OID reduced by the part of the OID previously included in the income of any holder. For purposes of this rule, any part of the OID that would have been included in the income of the holder had there been no acquisition premium is treated as if it had been included. (Code Sec. 1271(a)(2)(A)) This rule doesn't apply to tax-exempt obligations or to the sale or exchange by a holder who purchased the debt instrument at a premium. (Code Sec. 1271(a)(2)(B))[6]

Sale or exchange of short-term government obligations. On the sale or exchange of any short-term government obligation, any gain realized that doesn't exceed an amount equal

---

1. ¶I-6523
2. ¶I-6526
3. ¶I-6528

4. ¶I-9543
5. ¶E-6162
6. ¶I-8001

to the ratable share of the acquisition discount is treated as ordinary income (Code Sec. 1271(a)(3)(A)) unless the seller was required to include the discount in gross income currently under the rules at ¶1327. (Code Sec. 1283(d)(3))[7]

Sale or exchange of short-term nongovernment obligations. On the sale or exchange of any short-term nongovernment obligation, any gain realized that doesn't exceed an amount equal to the ratable share of OID is treated as ordinary income (Code Sec. 1271(a)(4)(A)), unless the seller was required to include the discount in gross income currently under the rules at ¶1327. (Code Sec. 1283(d)(3))[8]

Sale or exchange of tax-exempt bonds. The sale or exchange of tax-exempt obligations is a taxable event, even if the interest on the bonds is exempt. The seller has gain to the extent that the amount realized exceeds adjusted basis (¶2468) in the bonds. The seller's basis for this purpose means the price paid, even if the bonds were purchased at a discount. But, the holder of a tax-exempt bond issued with OID can increase the adjusted basis in the bond by the amount of OID accrued during the period the bond is held. If the bond is bought at a premium over face value, the holder must reduce the adjusted basis in the bond by the amount by which the premium is amortized under the rules discussed at ¶2165.[9]

¶ 2622 Investments by dealer in securities: treatment of gain or loss on transactions.

Under Code Sec. 1236, a securities dealer who buys securities for resale to customers may also hold securities purchased as investments for the dealer's own account. But gain from the sale or exchange of those securities won't be capital gain unless (1) the security is clearly identified in the dealer's records as a security held for investment on the day it is acquired, and (2) the security isn't held by the dealer primarily for sale to customers in the ordinary course of a trade or business at any time after the acquisition date. (Code Sec. 1236(a))[10]

A loss is a capital loss if the security has ever been clearly identified in the dealer's records as held for investment, even though held primarily for sale at the time of its disposition. (Code Sec. 1236(b); Reg § 1.1236-1(b))[11]

¶ 2623 Transfer of patents by an individual inventor—sale or exchange of capital assets.

Under Code Sec. 1235, if an individual inventor or financial backer transfers (other than by gift, inheritance or devise) all substantial rights to a patent, or an undivided interest (e.g., a half, a third) in those rights, the transfer is considered a sale or exchange of a long-term capital asset, even though the transferor hasn't held the patent rights for the period required for long-term treatment (see ¶2652), and even though the payments to the seller are: (1) made periodically during the buyer's use of the property; or (2) contingent on the productivity, use or disposition of the buyer's rights in the property (i.e., are like royalties). (Code Sec. 1235(a); Reg § 1.1235-1(a))[12] But, effective control of the transferee would prevent treatment as a transfer of all substantial rights.[13]

It's not necessary that the patent or patent application be in existence at the time of that transfer for long-term capital gain treatment to apply. (Reg § 1.1235-2(a))[14]

This treatment doesn't apply to a transfer by the inventor's employer (Code

---

7. ¶I-8004
8. ¶I-8005
9. ¶I-4001 *et seq.*
10. ¶I-6209

11. ¶I-6215
12. ¶I-8301
13. ¶I-8325
14. ¶I-8307

Sec. 1235(b)(2)(A)),[15] or to transfers made (directly or indirectly) to or by certain persons related to the inventor. (Code Sec. 1235(b)(2)(B); Reg § 1.1235-2(f))[16]

¶ 2624 Franchise, trademark, or trade name transfers—sale or exchange of capital assets.

Under Code Sec. 1253, the transfer of a franchise, trademark, or trade name isn't a sale or exchange of a capital asset if the transferor retains any significant power, right or continuing interest (such as the right to terminate at will, prescribe standards of quality, or require the transferee to sell only the transferor's products). (Code Sec. 1253(a), Code Sec. 1253(b)(2))[17] Thus, ordinary income treatment applies to payments received by a transferor that are contingent on production, use, or disposition of a franchise, etc. (Code Sec. 1253(c))[18]

For deduction and amortization of these payments, see ¶1606 and ¶1958.

¶ 2625 Sale of businesses—sole proprietorship; allocation of selling price; goodwill and covenants not to compete.

Sole proprietorship. If a sole proprietorship is sold, there isn't a sale of just 1 asset (i.e., the business), rather, there's a sale of the individual assets that *comprise* the business. So, gain or loss on some assets is ordinary while on others it is capital.[19]

Allocation of selling price on sale of business. If assets of a going business are sold, the selling price is allocated among the assets (including goodwill) for purposes of determining gain or loss (and the type of gain or loss, e.g., capital gain or ordinary income) separately for each. Allocation is made under the rules for determining the buyer's basis in each of them, see ¶2466.[20]

Goodwill and covenants not to compete. Goodwill is a capital asset, unless it is treated as an amortizable section 197 intangible (see ¶1957 *et seq.*). If the Code Sec. 197 rules don't apply, proceeds from the sale of a business that are allocable to goodwill are taxed under the capital gain and loss rules,[21] and payments for a covenant not to compete that is severable from the sale of goodwill results in ordinary income.[22]

¶ 2626 Life estates, term of years, income beneficiaries of a trust, etc.—capital gain treatment.

A life tenant, a tenant for a term of years, or an income beneficiary of a trust is generally entitled to capital gain on the sale of that interest.[23] But, under Code Sec. 1001(e), where the interest was acquired by gift, from a decedent, by a transfer in trust, or by a transfer from a spouse (or a former spouse incident to divorce), that part of the basis that's determined under the Code rules for those types of acquisitions (e.g., fair market value basis where acquired from a decedent) isn't taken into account in computing gain or loss on the sale or exchange of the interest, unless the entire interest in the underlying property is transferred in the same transaction. (Code Sec. 1001(e); Reg § 1.1001-1(f))[24]

¶ 2627 Constructive Sales of Appreciated Financial Positions. ▮▮▮▮▮▮▮▮

The constructive sale rules restrict a taxpayer's ability to defer recognition of gain

---

15. ¶I-8322
16. ¶s I-8301, I-8325
17. ¶I-8401
18. ¶I-8412
19. ¶I-8501

20. ¶I-8506 *et seq.*
21. ¶I-8601
22. ¶I-8603
23. ¶I-7014
24. ¶P-3129

on appreciated property the taxpayer owns even though the taxpayer locks in his or her gain and limits risk of loss through the use of "short sales against the box" and similar transactions. In general, the taxpayer is treated as constructively selling property if he or she borrows and sells the same or substantially identical property.

Under Code Sec. 1259, a taxpayer must recognize gain upon entering into a constructive sale of any appreciated financial position in stock, a partnership interest, or certain debt instruments. (Code Sec. 1259) In general, an appreciated financial position is any position with respect to any stock, debt instrument, or partnership interest if there would be gain if the position were sold, assigned, or otherwise terminated at its fair market value (FMV). (Code Sec. 1259(b)(1)) Except as provided at ¶2628, a constructive sale of an appreciated position occurs when the taxpayer (or a related person):

(1) enters into a short sale of the same or substantially identical property,

(2) enters into an offsetting notional principal contract with respect to the same or substantially identical property,

(3) enters into a futures or forward contract to deliver the same or substantially identical property,

(4) in the case of an appreciated financial position that's a short sale or a contract described in (2) or (3) above with respect to any property, acquires the same or substantially identical property, or

(5) to the extent provided in regs, enters into 1 or more other transactions (or acquires 1 or more positions) that have substantially the same effect as a transaction described in (1), (2), (3), or (4) above. (Code Sec. 1259(c)(1))[25]

Persons are "related" with respect to a transaction if their relationship is described in Code Sec. 267(b) (¶2444) or Code Sec. 707(b) (¶3723), and the transaction is entered into with a view toward avoiding the purposes of the constructive sale rules. (Code Sec. 1259(c)(4))[26]

The constructive sale rules don't apply to a short sale of stock that the seller borrows if he or she doesn't hold substantially identical property at the time of the sale. But, if the taxpayer acquires the same stock that the taxpayer borrowed and sold, and has a gain, the constructive sale rules apply on the acquisition date even if the acquired stock isn't delivered to the lender.[27]

As a result of a constructive sale,

. . . the taxpayer recognizes gain as if the position were sold, assigned, or otherwise terminated at its FMV value on the constructive sale date (Code Sec. 1259(a)(1)), and

. . . for purposes of applying the Code for periods after the constructive sale, (1) an appropriate adjustment is made in the amount of gain or loss later realized on the position for the gain taken into account because of the constructive sale rule, and (2) a new holding period for the position begins as if the taxpayer had acquired the position on the date of the constructive sale. (Code Sec. 1259(a)(2))[28]

illustration: On May 1, 2021, S bought 100 shares of ABC stock for $10,000. On Sept. 3, 2021, S sold short 100 shares of ABC stock for $16,000. S made no other transactions involving ABC stock for the rest of 2021 and the first 30 days of 2022. S's short sale is treated as a constructive sale of an appreciated financial position because a sale of the ABC stock on the date of the short sale would have resulted in a gain. S recognizes a $6,000 short-term capital gain from the constructive sale and has a new holding period in the ABC stock that begins on Sept. 3, 2021.

The term "appreciated financial position" does *not* include (1) certain positions with respect to nonconvertible debt if the holder is unconditionally entitled to receive a specified principal amount and certain specified conditions with respect to interest are met (Code Sec. 1259(b)(2)(A)); (2) any hedge with respect to a position described in (1), above (Code Sec. 1259(b)(2)(B)); and (3) any position which is marked to market under any Code section or the regs thereunder. (Code Sec. 1259(b)(2)(C))[29]

¶ 2628 Exceptions to rules for constructive sales of appreciated financial positions.

Under Code Sec. 1259, a taxpayer isn't treated as having made a constructive sale solely because the taxpayer enters a contract for the sale of any stock, debt instrument, or partnership interest which isn't a marketable security if the contract settles within 1 year after the date the contract is entered. (Code Sec. 1259(c)(2))[30] In addition, any transaction which would otherwise cause a constructive sale during the tax year is disregarded if:

(1) it's closed on or before the 30th day after the close of the tax year it was entered,

(2) the taxpayer holds the appreciated financial position to which the transaction relates (e.g., the stock where the transaction is a short sale) throughout the 60-day period beginning on the date the transaction is closed, and

(3) at no time during that 60-day period is the taxpayer's risk of loss reduced with respect to the position (applying the principles of Code Sec. 246(c)(4), relating to suspension of the holding period where the risk of loss is diminished for purposes of the dividends received deduction, see ¶3310). (Code Sec. 1259(c)(3)(A))[31]

observation: If a taxpayer meets the above requirements, a "short sale against the box" isn't a constructive sale as long as he or she remains at risk with respect to the appreciated financial position for 60 days after the closing.

¶ 2629 Short Sales.

In a short sale, an investor sells a security for delivery in the future. The short seller may meet his or her obligation to deliver by buying the security on the delivery ("closing") date. If the security has declined in value by the time the short seller closes or covers the sale, he or she has a gain equal to the sale price minus cost; if the value has increased, the purchase price is higher than the sale price, and the short seller has a loss. The nature of the gain or loss on a short sale depends upon the nature of the property used to close the short transaction.

Under Code Sec. 1233, if the property used to close the short sale is a capital asset in the hands of the short seller, the gain or loss on the transaction is capital gain or loss. (Code Sec. 1233(a); Reg § 1.1233-1(a)(1)),[32] and the period the taxpayer held the property determines whether the gain or loss is long or short term, unless the limits at ¶2630 *et seq.* apply. (Reg § 1.1233-1(a)(3))[33]

caution: Entering into certain short sales may result in a taxpayer recognizing gain under the constructive sale rules (¶2627 *et seq.*).

Entering into a securities futures contract (¶2648) to sell is treated as a short sale and the settlement of the contract is treated as the closing of the short sale for determining whether gain or loss is long- or short-term and for the holding period rules at ¶2655. (Code

29. ¶I-7741 *et seq.*
30. ¶I-7736
31. ¶I-7737

32. ¶I-7704
33. ¶I-7708

Sec. 1233(e)(2)(E))[34]

For the effect of the wash sale rules on short sales, see ¶2456.

¶ 2630　Limits on long-term capital gains on short sales; substantially identical property.

Under Code Sec. 1233, capital gain realized in a short sale is short-term, regardless of the actual holding period, where the seller either: (1) as of the date of the short sale, has owned for not more than 1 year (determined without regard to the effect of the short sale on the holding period, see ¶2655) property that's "substantially identical" (¶2456) to that which he or she used to close the sale, or (2) after the short sale and on or before its closing, he or she acquires substantially identical property. (Code Sec. 1233(b); Reg § 1.1233-1(c)(2)) This doesn't apply to any capital gain on property in excess of the amount of substantially identical property. This keeps the taxpayer from turning what would normally be a short-term capital gain into a long-term capital gain.[35]

The above rule applies only to stocks, securities, and commodity futures, but doesn't include any position subject to the straddle rules of Code Sec. 1092(b). (Code Sec. 1233(e)(2)(A))[36]

¶ 2631　Capital loss limits on short sales; substantially identical property.

Under Code Sec. 1233, if property "substantially identical" (¶2456) to that sold short was held by the taxpayer for more than 1 year as of the sale date, any loss on closing of the short sale is long-term capital loss, regardless of how long he or she held the property used to close the sale. (Code Sec. 1233(d)) This doesn't apply to any capital loss on property used to close the short sale in excess of the amount of substantially identical property. (Code Sec. 1233(e)(1))[37] This rule applies only to stocks, securities and commodity futures, but doesn't include any position to which the straddle rules of Code Sec. 1092(b) apply. (Code Sec. 1233(e)(2)(A))[38]

¶ 2632　Commodity futures and hedging transactions—short sales.

Under Code Sec. 1233, commodity transactions are generally subject to the same rules for short sales as stocks and securities. A commodity future is a contract to buy some fixed amount of a commodity at a future date at a fixed price. Gain or loss from the short sale of a commodity future is capital gain or loss if the future used to close the short sale is a capital asset to the taxpayer. But, the short sale rules don't apply where the sale of the commodity future is a bona fide hedging transaction (¶2616). (Code Sec. 1233(g); Reg § 1.1233-1(b))[39]

¶ 2633　Gain recognition required when property sold short becomes worthless.

Under Code Sec. 1233, if a taxpayer enters into a short sale of property, and that property becomes substantially worthless, the taxpayer recognizes gain in the same manner as if the short sale were closed when the property becomes substantially worthless. (Code Sec. 1233(h)(1))[40]

If property becomes substantially worthless during a tax year and a short sale of the property remains open at that time, the period for assessing any deficiency attributable to any part of the gain on the transaction doesn't expire before the earlier of: (1) the date 3

34. ¶I-7712.2
35. ¶I-7710
36. ¶I-7709
37. ¶I-7714
38. ¶I-7709
39. ¶I-7724
40. ¶I-7707.1

years after the date IRS is notified by the taxpayer (in a manner that IRS prescribes in regs) of the property's substantial worthlessness, or (2) the date 6 years after the date the return for the tax year during which the position became substantially worthless is filed. Also, the deficiency may be assessed before the expiration of the assessment period in spite of any other law that would otherwise prevent the assessment. (Code Sec. 1233(h)(2))[41]

¶ 2634   Section 1244 ("Small Business Corporation") Stock. ▄▄▄▄▄▄

Loss on the sale, exchange or worthlessness of Code Sec. 1244 stock is deductible, within limits, as an ordinary loss, even though gain on the stock is capital gain (¶2635). This ordinary deduction is available only to an individual to whom the stock was issued by a small business corporation (¶2637), or an individual who was a partner in a partnership at the time the stock was issued to a partnership by a small business corporation. Transferees of these original purchasers don't qualify. (Code Sec. 1244(a); Reg § 1.1244(a)-1(b)(2))[42]

Under Code Sec. 1244, the aggregate amount of the ordinary loss is limited to $50,000 on separate returns and $100,000 on joint returns each year. Spouses may deduct the $100,000 maximum in a joint return even if only 1 spouse owned the stock. (Code Sec. 1244(b))[43]

A loss on qualifying Code Sec. 1244 stock is deductible as an ordinary loss attributable to the shareholder's business. So, the loss is deductible in full from gross income and may give rise to a net operating loss. Losses exceeding the limits must be treated as regular capital losses. (Code Sec. 1244(d)(3))[44]

See ¶2636 for how to claim the Code Sec. 1244 ordinary loss.

¶ 2635   Qualifying for Section 1244 ordinary loss treatment.

To qualify as Code Sec. 1244 stock, all of the following tests must be met: (Code Sec. 1244(c))[45]

... The stock must be stock (common or preferred, voting or nonvoting) issued by a domestic "small business" corporation (¶2637).[46]

... The stock must have been issued for money or property (other than stock and securities). Stock issued for the cancellation of corporate debt (not evidenced by a security or issued for services) qualifies, but not stock issued for services rendered or to be rendered to, or for the benefit of, the issuing corporation. (Reg § 1.1244(c)-1(d)(1))[47]

... The issuing corporation must have shown that over 50% of its aggregate gross receipts within the 5 most recent tax years ending before the date of the loss (or within the period before the date of the loss if the corporation was in existence for less than 5 tax years at that time) came from sources other than rents, royalties, dividends, interest, annuities, and sales or exchanges of stock or securities. (Code Sec. 1244(c)(1)(C))[48]

¶ 2636   How to claim the Section 1244 ordinary loss—Form 4797.

Claim the Code Sec. 1244 ordinary loss on Form 4797 (attached to Form 1040). No information statement is required to be filed with the return but records must be maintained to establish a loss and whether the stock qualifies as Code Sec. 1244 stock. (Reg § 1.1244(e)-1(b))[49]

41. ¶T-4221.2
42. ¶I-9503
43. ¶I-9505
44. ¶I-9502
45. ¶I-9508 *et seq.*

46. ¶I-9508 *et seq.*
47. ¶I-9511, I-9512
48. ¶I-9524 *et seq.*
49. ¶I-9537, I-9538

¶ 2637   Small business corporation (SBC) defined; limit on capital receipts— Sec. 1244 stock treatment.

Under Code Sec. 1244, a corporation is an SBC if at the time the stock is issued its "capital receipts" don't exceed $1 million. Capital receipts means the aggregate amount of money and other property received by the corporation for stock, as a contribution to capital, and as paid-in surplus. This includes amounts received for the Code Sec. 1244 stock and for all stock issued previously. The corporation can designate which shares issued in a year capital receipts exceed $1 million are to be treated as Section 1244 stock. The designation must be made by the 15th day after the end of the tax year. If no designation is made, part of the loss on stock issued that year may qualify as ordinary loss under allocation rules contained in the regs. (Code Sec. 1244(c)(3)(A); Reg § 1.1244(c)-2(b))[50]

¶ 2638   Exclusion of Gain from Qualified Small Business Stock (QSBS). ▬▬▬▬

Under Code Sec. 1202, noncorporate taxpayers that hold qualified small business stock (QSBS) for more than five years can potentially exclude all the gain realized on the sale or exchange of that QSBS (¶2639). (Code Sec. 1202(a))

The percentage of gain excluded is determined by the acquisition date of the QSBS, as follows: 100% for QSBS acquired after Sept. 27, 2010; 75% for QSBS acquired before Sept. 28, 2010 and after Feb. 17, 2009; 50% for QSBS acquired before Feb. 18, 2009 and after Aug. 10, '93; 60% of pre-2019 gain on QSBS in a qualified business entity (QBE, defined in Code Sec. 1397C(b), relating to empowerment zones) held more than 5 years and acquired before Feb. 18, 2009. (Code Sec. 1202(a))[1]

The acquisition date is the first day on which the stock was held by the taxpayer, determined after applying the holding period rules in Code Sec. 1223 permitting the tacking of holding periods for substituted basis property, see ¶2659. (Code Sec. 1202(a)(3); Code Sec. 1202(a)(4))

But a taxpayer (or a related party) who takes an offsetting short position before the required 5-year holding period is completed cannot exclude gain from the disposition of QSBS. (Code Sec. 1202(j))[2]

A per-issuer dollar limitation on eligible QSBS gain applies. (Code Sec. 1202(b)(1))[3]

The exclusion is denied where the corporation redeems stock from the taxpayer or a related person during certain periods, or buys its own stock in excess of certain amounts during specified periods. (Code Sec. 1202(c)(3))[4]

Additional rules apply where pass-through entities hold the stock. (Code Sec. 1202(g))[5]

For the rollover of gain from QSBS to other QSBS, see ¶2426.

For alternative minimum tax treatment of the exclusion, see ¶3210.

¶ 2639   Qualified small business stock (QSBS) defined—exclusion of gain.

Under Code Sec. 1202, QSBS is any stock (but not an option to acquire stock) originally issued after Aug. 10, '93 in a C corp., if:

. . . as of the issuance date, the corp. is a qualified small business. (Code Sec. 1202(c)(1)(A)) This means a domestic C corp. whose total gross assets (treating all members of the same parent-subsidiary controlled group as 1 corp.) at all times after

---

50. ¶I-9518 *et seq.*
1. ¶I-9100 *et seq.*
2. ¶I-9126

3. ¶I-9118 *et seq.*
4. ¶I-9108 *et seq.*
5. ¶I-9119

Aug. 10, '93 and before issuance, and immediately after issuance (taking into account amounts received in the issuance), don't exceed $50,000,000, and that meets certain reporting requirements (Code Sec. 1202(d));

. . . the taxpayer claiming the exclusion acquired the stock at its original issuance for money or other property (not stock) or as compensation for services provided to the corp. (other than services performed as an underwriter) (Code Sec. 1202(c)(1)(B)); *and*

. . . during substantially all of taxpayer's holding period for the stock, the corp. is a C corp. (other than certain excluded corporations) *and* meets an active business test. (Code Sec. 1202(c)(2)(A), Code Sec. 1202(e))[6]

¶ 2640   **Tax Straddles and Section 1256 Contracts.** ▬▬▬▬▬▬▬

Losses on certain unregulated straddles (¶2641) are deferred to the extent taxpayer has offsetting unrecognized gain (¶2642). Related interest and carrying charges must be capitalized. Regulated futures contracts and other Code Sec. 1256 contracts (¶2644) are subject to the "mark-to-market" rule (¶2643) which treats unrealized capital gain or loss from the contract for the year as 60% long-term and 40% short-term. Hedging transactions are excepted from these rules (¶2647).

There are a number of rules provided to restrict tax avoidance opportunities in commodity futures straddles and to curb certain tax shelters involving tax straddles.[7]

Under the constructive sale rules (¶2627), a taxpayer must recognize gain (but not loss) upon entering into a constructive sale of any appreciated financial position in stock, a partnership interest, or certain debt instruments. (Code Sec. 1259). The constructive sale rules generally are intended to apply to transactions that are identified as hedging or straddle transactions under other Code provisions such as Code Sec. 1092(a)(2) (dealing with a special rule for straddles that are identified as straddles at the close of a tax year), Code Sec. 1092(b)(2) (dealing with regs with respect to identified mixed straddles, ¶2645), Code Sec. 1092(e) (dealing with an exception for hedging transactions), and Code Sec. 1256(e) (dealing with the nonapplication of the mark-to-market rules to hedging transactions, ¶2647).[8]

The interest and carrying charges properly allocable to personal property that is part of a straddle aren't deductible, but must be charged to the capital account of the property for which they were paid or incurred. (Code Sec. 263(g)(1)) But this requirement doesn't apply to any identified hedging transactions (¶2647). (Code Sec. 263(g)(3))[9]

¶ 2641   **Straddle defined: offsetting positions with respect to personal property—tax straddle rules.**

Under Code Sec. 1092, a straddle is "offsetting positions" with respect to personal property. (Code Sec. 1092(c)(1)) A "position" is an interest, including a futures or forward contract or option, in personal property. (Code Sec. 1092(d)(2)) Personal property includes stock only if the stock is of a type which is actively traded and at least 1 of the positions offsetting the stock is a position with respect to that stock or substantially similar or related property, or the stock is in a corporation formed or used to take positions in personal property which offset positions taken by any shareholder. (Code Sec. 1092(d)(3)(A))

A taxpayer holds "offsetting positions" if he or she has reduced the risk of loss from holding the property by holding 1 (or more) other positions, whether or not the items of personal property involved in the different positions are the same kind. (Code

---

6. ¶I-9105 *et seq.*   8. ¶I-7746
7. ¶I-7500 *et seq.*   9. ¶L-5985

Sec. 1092(c)(2)(A))[10]

If a taxpayer is the obligor under a debt instrument on which 1 or more payments are linked to the value of personal property or a position with respect to personal property, then the taxpayer's obligation under the debt instrument is a position with respect to personal property and may be part of a straddle. (Reg § 1.1092(d)-1(d))[11]

¶ 2642 Recognition of losses postponed on certain nonregulated futures straddles (loss deferral rule).

Under Code Sec. 1092, loss deductions on nonregulated straddles, that is, those straddle positions not on the "mark-to-market" system (see ¶2643), are limited to the amount by which the losses exceed "unrecognized gains" on any offsetting straddle positions. Losses in excess of the limitation (deferred losses) are carried forward to the next year and are subject to the deferral rules in that year. (Code Sec. 1092(a)(1))[12]

¶ 2643 Regulated futures contracts, etc. (Section 1256 contracts), under "mark-to-market" system.

Under Code Sec. 1256, taxpayers must report (on Form 6781) gains and losses from regulated futures contracts and other "Section 1256 contracts" (¶2644) on an annual basis under the "mark-to-market" rule. All Section 1256 contracts must be marked-to-market at year end. Each Section 1256 contract held by a taxpayer is treated as if it were sold for fair market value on the last business day of the tax year. (Code Sec. 1256(a)(1)) If a taxpayer holds Section 1256 contracts at the beginning of a tax year, any gain or loss later realized on the contracts must be adjusted to reflect any gain or loss taken into account with respect to the contracts in an earlier year. (Code Sec. 1256(a)(2))

Any capital gain or loss on a Section 1256 futures contract that is marked-to-market is treated as if 40% of the gain or loss is short-term capital gain or loss, and as if 60% of the gain or loss is long-term capital gain or loss. (Code Sec. 1256(a)(3))[13]

The wash sale rules (¶2456) don't apply to losses taken into account when a Section 1256 contract is marked to market. (Code Sec. 1256(f)(5))[14]

¶ 2644 Section 1256 contracts defined; regulated futures contracts, foreign currency contracts, nonequity options, dealer equity options, and dealer securities futures contracts.

Code Sec. 1256 contracts include: regulated futures contracts, foreign currency contracts, nonequity options, dealer equity options, and dealer securities futures contracts (¶2648). (Code Sec. 1256(b))[15] For a partnership that's a qualified fund, Section 1256 contracts include bank forward contracts, foreign currency futures contracts, and similar instruments prescribed by IRS regs. (Code Sec. 988(c)(1)(E)(iv)(I))[16] A Court of Appeals, disagreeing with IRS and the Tax Court, said a foreign currency option is a foreign currency transaction that is treated as a Section 1256 contract.[17] Proposed regs, on which taxpayers may rely, would define the term "foreign currency contract" under Code Sec. 1256 to include only foreign currency forward contracts. (TD REG-130675-17, 07/06/2022)[18]

Section 1256 contracts don't include (1) any securities futures contract, or option on a

---

10. ¶I-7503 *et seq.*
11. ¶I-7532
12. ¶I-7501
13. ¶I-7602, ¶I-7603.3
14. ¶I-7602

15. ¶I-7604
16. ¶I-7607
17. ¶I-7611
18. ¶I-7611

securities futures contract, unless the contract or option is a dealer securities futures contract, or (2) any interest rate swap, currency swap, basis swap, interest rate cap, interest rate floor, commodity swap, equity swap, equity index swap, credit default swap, or similar agreement. (Code Sec. 1256(b)(2))[19]

¶ 2645 Election for mixed straddles—Form 6781; interests that are (and aren't) in a Section 1256 contract.

If straddles are composed of at least 1 position in a Code Sec. 1256 contract (¶2644) and 1 or more positions in interests in property that aren't Code Sec. 1256 contracts, a taxpayer may elect on Form 6781 to exclude all positions in the mixed straddle (including Code Sec. 1256 contracts) from the mark-to-market rules, in which case they will be subject to the loss deferral, wash sale, and short sale rules, and the straddle won't be a mixed straddle. (Code Sec. 1256(d))[20] If that election isn't made, so that the straddle is a mixed straddle, a taxpayer may elect to offset gains and losses in the mixed straddle by either separately identifying the positions of the mixed straddle or establishing a mixed straddle account. (Reg § 1.1092(b)-4T)[21]

Unrealized gain or loss on a position held before establishing an identified mixed straddle is taken into account at the time, and has the character, provided by the Code provisions that would apply if the identified mixed straddle had not been established. (Reg § 1.1092(b)-6(a))[22]

¶ 2646 Carryback election for losses from Section 1256 contracts—Form 6781—carryforwards.

Taxpayers other than corporations, estates, and trusts can elect to carry net Code Sec. 1256 losses back 3 years and apply them against net Code Sec. 1256 gains for the period. The carryback is available only if, after netting Code Sec. 1256 contracts and other positions subject to the mark-to-market rule with capital gains and losses from other sources, there is a net capital loss for the tax year which, but for the election, would be a capital loss in the succeeding year. The lesser of that net capital loss or the net loss resulting from the application of the mark-to-market rules is the net Code Sec. 1256 loss which may be carried back. Capital losses carried back must be treated as 40% short-term capital losses and 60% long-term capital losses. The losses must be absorbed in the earliest year to which they may be carried back. Any remainder is then carried forward to the next year. The losses may be applied in the carryback year against the lesser of net Code Sec. 1256 contracts gain or capital gain net income for that year. (Code Sec. 1212(c))

Capital losses that are carried forward, to the extent they were determined under the mark-to-market rule, continue to be treated as losses from Code Sec. 1256 contracts in the year to which they are carried. (Code Sec. 1212(c)(6)(B))[23]

¶ 2647 Hedging transactions not covered by the Code Sec. 1256 mark-to-market rules.

Under Code Sec. 1256, the "mark-to-market" rules don't apply to "hedging transactions" as defined in Code Sec. 1256(e)(2). (Code Sec. 1256(e)(1))[24]

¶ 2648 Securities Futures Contracts.

Gain or loss on the sale, exchange, or termination of a securities futures contract

19. ¶I-7604
20. ¶I-7616
21. ¶I-7571 *et seq.*
22. ¶I-7570
23. ¶I-7606
24. ¶I-7620

(as defined in Code Sec. 1234B(c)) generally has the same character as gain or loss from transactions in the underlying security. (Code Sec. 1234B(a)(1))

For example, if the underlying asset would be a capital asset in the taxpayer's hands, gain or loss from the sale of the contract is capital gain or loss. This rule doesn't apply to (1) securities futures contracts that aren't capital assets because they are Code Sec. 1221(a)(1) inventory assets, or are identified as Code Sec. 1221(a)(7) hedging transactions, or (2) any income derived in connection with a contract which would otherwise not be capital gain. (Code Sec. 1234B(a)(2))[25]

Except as provided in regs under Code Sec. 1092(b), or Code Sec. 1234B, or in Code Sec. 1233, capital gain or loss from the sale, exchange, or termination of a securities futures contract to sell property is treated as short-term capital gain or loss. (Code Sec. 1234B(b))

If the security to which a securities futures contract that isn't a Code Sec. 1256 contract (see ¶2644) relates is acquired in satisfaction of that contract, the taxpayer's holding period for the security includes the period for which the taxpayer held the contract if the contract was a capital asset in the taxpayer's hands. (Code Sec. 1223(14))[26]

A dealer securities futures contract is treated as a Code Sec. 1256 contract. (Code Sec. 1256(b)(1)(E)) A dealer securities futures contract is any securities futures contract and any option to enter into such a contract that (1) is entered into by the dealer (or, in the case of an option, is purchased or granted by the dealer) in the normal course of his or her activity of dealing in such contracts or options, as the case may be, and (2) is traded on a qualified board or exchange. (Code Sec. 1256(g)(9)(A))[27]

¶ 2649   Conversion and Constructive Ownership Transactions. ▬▬▬▬▬▬▬

Capital gain on the disposition of property that was part of a conversion transaction (i.e., functionally equivalent to a loan) is treated as ordinary income (¶2650). Certain gains from derivative contracts (constructive ownership transactions) with respect to financial assets are recharacterized as ordinary income (¶2651).

¶ 2650   Gain recharacterized on disposition or other termination of position held as part of conversion transactions similar to loans.

Under Code Sec. 1258, gain recognized on the disposition or other termination of any position held as part of a conversion transaction (defined below), that would otherwise be treated as capital gain, is treated as ordinary income, to the extent it doesn't exceed the applicable imputed income amount. (Code Sec. 1258(a))[28] The applicable imputed income amount equals the excess of (1) taxpayer's net investment in the transaction multiplied by 120% of (a) the applicable federal rate (¶1117), compounded semiannually, for the period covered by the transaction, if the transaction has a definite term, or (b) the federal short-term rates (compounded daily) in effect under Code Sec. 6621(b) for the period of the conversion transaction, if the term of the transaction is indefinite, over (2) the amount already so treated with respect to the same transaction. (Code Sec. 1258(b), Code Sec. 1258(d)(2))[29]

When a taxpayer disposes or terminates all positions of an identified (as part of the same transaction on taxpayer's books and records) netting transaction within a 14-day period in 1 tax year, all gains and losses on those positions realized within that period are netted to determine the amount of gain treated as ordinary income. (Reg § 1.1258-1(b))[30]

---

25. ¶I-6280 *et seq.*
26. ¶I-8924.1
27. ¶I-7615.1

28. ¶I-8200 *et seq.*
29. ¶I-8208
30. ¶I-8209.1 *et seq.*

A conversion transaction is any transaction where substantially all of taxpayer's expected net return is attributable to the time value of his or her net investment, and which is:

... the holding of any property (whether or not actively traded) and substantially contemporaneous making of a contract to sell that or substantially identical property at a price determined in accordance with the contract (Code Sec. 1258(c)(2)(A));

... a straddle (¶2641) of actively traded personal property (Code Sec. 1258(c)(2)(B));

... any other transaction that is marketed or sold as producing capital gains, and substantially all of the expected return from that transaction is attributable to the time value of the taxpayer's net investment in the transaction (Code Sec. 1258(c)(2)(C)); or

... any other transaction specified in regs to be issued. (Code Sec. 1258(c)(2)(D))[31]

Conversion transactions don't include transactions of options dealers and commodities traders in the normal course of their trade or business. (Code Sec. 1258(d)(5)(A))[32]

¶ 2651 Certain long-term capital gains from derivative contracts (constructive ownership transactions) are recharacterized as ordinary income.

Under Code Sec. 1260, the amount of long-term capital gain a taxpayer can recognize from certain derivative contracts (constructive ownership transactions (defined in Code Sec. 1260(d))) for certain financial assets is limited, and an interest charge is imposed on the tax underpayment for each year that the constructive ownership transaction was open. (Code Sec. 1260) If a taxpayer has gain from a constructive ownership transaction with respect to any financial asset and that gain would otherwise be treated as a long-term capital gain, then (1) the gain is treated as ordinary income to the extent it exceeds the net underlying long-term capital gain, and (2) to the extent gain is treated as long-term capital gain, the determination of the capital gain rate (or rates) applicable to the gain under Code Sec. 1(h) (i.e., the individual capital gains rates) is determined on the basis of the respective rate (or rates) that would have applied to the net underlying long-term capital gain. (Code Sec. 1260(a))[33]

¶ 2652 Holding Period of Capital Asset Before Sale or Exchange. ▬▬▬▬▬

The length of time that a capital asset is held before its sale or exchange determines whether the proceeds from the sale or exchange are taxable as long-term capital gain or loss or as short-term capital gain or loss.

The length of time an asset is held is also crucial in qualifying for Code Sec. 1231 (capital gain/ordinary loss) treatment, see ¶2667.

Holding a capital asset for the short-term holding period (1 year or less) results in short-term capital gain or loss on the sale or exchange of that asset. (Code Sec. 1222(1), Code Sec. 1222(2)) Holding a capital asset for the long-term holding period (more than 1 year) results in long-term capital gain or loss on the sale or exchange of that asset. (Code Sec. 1222(3), Code Sec. 1222(4))[34]

The holding period is computed in terms of calendar months, not days.[35] It begins on the day after the day of acquisition and ends on the day of sale, exchange or other disposition. Thus, the taxpayer excludes the day of acquisition but includes the date of disposition.[36]

✒️*illustration:* To meet the more-than-one-year long-term holding period, a capital asset acquired on Feb. 15 must be held until Feb. 16 of the next year.

31. ¶I-8205
32. ¶I-8210 *et seq.*
33. ¶I-8251
34. ¶I-8901
35. ¶I-8904
36. ¶s I-8904, I-8906

For the holding period for:

... a partnership interest, see ¶2653.

... a profits interest (carried interest) in a partnership, see ¶2654

... stocks and securities, see ¶2655.

... property acquired through options, see ¶2656.

... property inherited from a decedent, see ¶2657.

... property acquired by a gift, see ¶2658.

... property received in a tax-free exchange, see ¶2659.

... property received to replace property lost in an involuntary conversion, see ¶2660.

¶ 2653 Divided holding period of partnership interest—holding period of capital asset.

Under Code Sec. 1223, a partner doesn't have a divided holding period in his or her partnership interest unless he or she acquired parts of it at different times or in exchange for property transferred at the same time but resulting in different holding periods. (Reg § 1.1223-3(a)) The holding period of a part of a partnership interest is determined based on a fraction equal to the fair market value (FMV) of the part of the partnership interest received in the transaction to which the holding period relates over the FMV of the entire partnership interest (determined immediately after the transaction). (Reg § 1.1223-3(b))[37]

Illustration: A contributes $50,000 and a nondepreciable capital asset that he's held for 2 years to a partnership for a 50% interest in it. A's basis in the capital asset is $50,000, and its FMV is $100,000. After the exchange, A's basis in his interest in the partnership is $100,000, and the FMV of the interest is $150,000. A's holding period in the one-third of the interest received for cash begins on the day after the contribution. Under Code Sec. 1223(1), A has a 2-year holding period in the two-thirds of the interest received in the partnership for the capital asset.

¶ 2654 Treatment of partners with carried interests—partnership interests held in connection with performance of services in applicable trade or business (ATB)—API holding rule; applicable partnership interest (API)

Under Code Sec. 1061, if a taxpayer holds one or more "applicable partnership interests" (APIs, below, also called "carried interests") at any time during the tax year, then the excess (if any) of (1) the taxpayer's net long-term capital gain for those interests for that tax year, over (2) the taxpayer's net long-term capital gain for those interests for that tax year computed by applying Code Sec. 1222(3) and Code Sec. 1222(4) (¶2655) by substituting "3 years" for "1 year," is treated as short-term capital gain (taxed at the same rates as ordinary income). This rule is the "API holding rule." Thus, there's generally a 3-year holding period for certain net long-term capital gain for any API held by the taxpayer. The amount treated as short-term capital gain under the API holding rule is the "recharacterization amount." (Code Sec. 1061; Reg § 1.1061-4(a)(1)) Except for any portion of a partnership interest that is a capital interest, the API holding rule applies regardless of whether an applicable party has made an election under Code Sec. 83(b) (¶1217) or included amounts in gross income under Code Sec. 83 (¶1216 *et seq.*).[38]

The API holding rule applies to partnership interests transferred or held in connection with the performance of substantial services in an "applicable trade or business" (ATB,

---

37. ¶I-8934.1

38. ¶B-1480

below). (Code Sec. 1061(c)(1))[39]

A provision of the API holding rule causes a gross income inclusion for the transferor on a transfer of an API to a related person. (Code Sec. 1061(d))[40]

Reporting requirements related to the API holding rule apply. (Code Sec. 1061(e);)[41]

Unless an exception applies, an API is any interest in a partnership which, directly or indirectly, is transferred to (or is held by) the taxpayer (which includes an "owner taxpayer" or a "passthrough taxpayer," both defined in the regs) in connection with the performance of substantial services by the taxpayer, or any other related person, in any *applicable trade or business* (ATB, see below). (Code Sec. 1061(c)(1); Reg § 1.1061-1(a))[42]

An ATB is any activity conducted on a regular, continuous, and substantial basis which, regardless of whether the activity is conducted in one or more entities, consists (in whole or part) of raising or returning capital, and either: (A) investing in (or disposing of) specified assets (or identifying specified assets for the investing or disposition), or (B) developing specified assets. (Code Sec. 1061(c)(2)) Under the regs, an ATB is any activity for which the ATB "activity test" regarding "specified actions" is met. It also includes all specified actions taken by related persons, including combining activities occurring in separate partnership tiers or entities as one ATB. (Reg § 1.1061-1(a); Reg § 1.1061-2(b))[43]

¶ 2655   Holding period for stocks and securities on a registered securities exchange or in the "over-the-counter" market.

Under Code Sec. 1223, the holding period for stocks and securities acquired by purchase, whether on a registered securities exchange or in the "over-the-counter" market, is determined by reference to the "trade date" on which the stock or security is acquired and the "trade date" on which it is sold. The "settlement dates" aren't considered.   [44]

The holding period for stock or securities acquired from a corporation by the exercise of rights begins on, and includes, the day the rights are exercised. (Code Sec. 1223(5); Reg § 1.1223-1(f))[45]

The holding period for property "substantially identical" to that sold short in a transaction to which the rule at ¶2630 applies is considered to begin on the day the short sale is closed or, if earlier, on the date the property is sold, given away or otherwise disposed of. (Code Sec. 1233(b)(2))[46]

The holding period for stock, stock rights or other property received as a taxable dividend begins on the date the distribution is actually or constructively received.[47] If the distribution is tax-free, the holding period for the stock, etc., includes the period that the underlying stock was held. (Code Sec. 1223(4); Reg § 1.1223-1(e))[48]

The holding period for restricted stock (or property) begins after it is substantially vested, unless an election (¶1217) is made to include the property in income in the year of transfer, in which case it begins just after the transfer. (Code Sec. 83(f); Reg § 1.83-4(a))[49]

Where the loss on a sale of stock or securities is disallowed under the "wash sale" rules (¶2456), the holding period for the new similar stock includes the holding period for the old stock that was sold. (Code Sec. 1223(3))[50]

The holding period for U.S. Treasury bonds and notes is measured from the acquisition date; for those sold at auction, this is the date the Treasury gives notice of acceptance to

39. ¶B-1480; ¶B-1481C
40. ¶B-1481E
41. ¶B-1481G
42. ¶B-1481B
43. ¶B-1481C *et seq.*
44. ¶I-8914 *et seq.*

45. ¶I-8924
46. ¶I-7720
47. ¶I-8918
48. ¶I-8921
49. ¶I-8916
50. ¶I-8929

bidders; for those sold in a subscription offering at a specified interest rate, it's the date the buyer submits an offer.[1]

If an individual rolls over gain from qualified small business stock (QSBS) by way of the timely acquisition of other QSBS stock (¶2426), the holding period for the acquired QSBS stock includes the holding period for the sold QSBS stock. (Code Sec. 1223(13))[2]

¶ 2656 Holding period for property acquired through exercise of options.

Under Code Sec. 1223, the holding period for property acquired through the exercise of an option begins the day after the option is exercised.[3]

¶ 2657 Holding period for property inherited from a decedent; qualified heir.

Under Code Sec. 1223, the holding period of property acquired from a decedent starts with the date of death.[4] But, property acquired from a decedent which is sold within the short-term capital gain holding period after the decedent's death is considered to be held for the *long*-term capital gain holding period if the person selling the property has a basis that is determined under Code Sec. 1014 (by reference to the property's fair market value on the date of death or the alternate valuation date). (Code Sec. 1223(9))[5]

The long-term holding period is also met where special use valuation property (¶5017) is acquired by a "qualified heir" from the decedent's estate, and is sold within the short-term holding period to another "qualified heir." (Code Sec. 1223(10))[6]

The holding period of the surviving spouse's share of community property that vested at the time of the acquisition by the community (as opposed to the share inherited from the deceased spouse) starts from the date of acquisition.[7]

¶ 2658 Donee's holding period for gifts.

Under Code Sec. 1223, the holding period for property acquired by gift includes the donor's holding period if the property has the same basis for gain or loss (see ¶2457 *et seq.*) in whole or in part in the donee's hands as it would have in the donor's hands. (Code Sec. 1223(2); Reg § 1.1223-1(b)) But if the donee sells the property at a loss based on its market value on the date of the gift (and not the donor's basis), the holding period starts on the day after the date of the gift, i.e., the day after the property is acquired under the rule at ¶2652.[8]

¶ 2659 Holding period for tax-free exchange property; "tacking on."

Under Code Sec. 1223, the holding period for property received in a partially or wholly tax-free exchange (¶2411) includes the holding period for the property surrendered. This "tacking on" applies where the new property has the same basis, in whole or in part, as the old property (Code Sec. 1223(1)), e.g., like-kind exchanges (¶2416), tax-free stock distributions (¶2655), involuntary conversions (¶2660), or incorporations and tax-free corporate reorganizations (¶3500 *et seq.*).[9]

---

1. ¶I-8915
2. ¶I-9207
3. ¶I-8949
4. ¶I-8944
5. ¶I-8942

6. ¶I-8943
7. ¶I-8945
8. ¶I-8966
9. ¶I-8960 *et seq.*

¶ 2660   Holding period for replacements for property lost or damaged in involuntary conversion.

Under Code Sec. 1223, the holding period of the original property is tacked on to that of property acquired to replace property lost or damaged in an involuntary conversion (¶2429 *et seq.*), where gain isn't recognized.[10]

¶ 2661   Sales and Exchanges. ▬▬▬▬▬▬▬▬▬▬▬▬▬▬▬▬▬▬▬▬

Unless a transaction involving a capital asset is treated as a sale or exchange, any resulting gain or loss doesn't qualify as capital gain or loss.

A sale is a transfer of property for money or promise to pay money, while an exchange is a transfer of property for other property. (Reg § 1.1002-1(d))[11]

To qualify as a sale or exchange, the transaction must be complete, and bona fide in all respects. If it's real in substance as well as form, it qualifies as a sale or exchange even though it was designed to reduce taxes.[12] But, it may be treated as a sham for tax purposes if (a) there is no business motive for the transaction other than getting tax benefits, and (b) the transaction has no economic substance. (Code Sec. 7701(o))[13]

Where shareholders deal with their corporation, or family members sell or exchange property among themselves, IRS scrutinizes the deal closely. If a sale or exchange is a sham, IRS can disallow any of the sought-after tax benefits.[14]

Retirement of debt instruments. In general, under Code Sec. 1271, amounts received by a holder on retirement of a debt instrument are treated as received in exchange for the debt instrument. (Code Sec. 1271(a)(1))[15]

observation: Since the retirement is treated as an exchange, see ¶2621 for the effect on gain recognized on retirement when there is an intent to call a debt instrument issued with OID before maturity.

Payment of debt with property. A debtor realizes gain or loss when he or she transfers property to his or her creditor in complete or partial satisfaction of a debt. The transfer is treated as a sale or exchange of the property by the debtor. Gain or loss is the difference between the amount of debt satisfied and the basis of the transferred property.[16]

Conversion of bonds. No gain or loss is realized upon the conversion of bonds into stock of the *same* corporation under a conversion privilege set forth in the terms of the bond.[17] But, if a bond is convertible into the stock of another corporation, the exercise of the conversion privilege results in an exchange on which gain or loss is recognized.[18]

For whether certain terminations are treated as the sale of a capital asset, see ¶2662.

For the cancellation of a lease or distribution agreement as a sale or exchange, see ¶2663.

For whether a sale with a leaseback, reservations, or restrictions is a sale or exchange, see ¶2664.

For transactions that are in part a gift and part a sale, or a conditional gift, see ¶2665.

---

10. ¶I-8963
11. ¶I-1002, I-1104
12. ¶I-1212 *et seq.*
13. ¶M-5901
14. ¶I-1201 *et seq.*

15. ¶I-1901
16. ¶I-1501 *et seq.*
17. ¶I-1909
18. ¶I-1909

¶ 2662 Gain or loss from certain terminations treated as capital gain or loss; rights or obligations with respect to capital assets; Section 1256 contracts.

Under Code Sec. 1234A, gain or loss attributable to the cancellation, lapse, expiration, or other termination of the following is treated as gain or loss from the sale of a capital asset:

(1) A right or obligation (other than a securities futures contract (¶2648)) with respect to property which is (or on acquisition would be) a capital asset in the taxpayer's hands (Code Sec. 1234A(1)), or

(2) A Code Sec. 1256 contract (¶2644) not described in (1) above which is a capital asset in the taxpayer's hands. (Code Sec. 1234A(2))

These rules don't apply to the retirement of any debt instrument (whether or not through a trust or other participation arrangement). (Code Sec. 1234A)[19] Also, they don't apply to a forfeited deposit received on a canceled sale of Code Sec. 1231 property (¶2667).[20]

¶ 2663 Cancellation of lease or distribution agreement as sale or exchange.

Under Code Sec. 1241, amounts received by a lessee or tenant for the cancellation of a lease, or by a distributor of goods for the cancellation of a distributorship agreement, are considered amounts received *in exchange* for the lease or agreement. (Code Sec. 1241)[21]

observation: Thus, capital gain-ordinary loss treatment (¶2666) is available for gain or loss from the cancellation of a business lease or distributorship held long-term. But, if the lease was for the tenant's home, a gain would be taxed as a capital gain, but any loss wouldn't be deductible.

¶ 2664 Sale with leaseback, reservations or restrictions; leaseback of realty; completed sales—treatment as sale or exchange.

The fact that a sale of property is accompanied by a leaseback doesn't bar recognizing the sale as closed for tax purposes.[22] But, a leaseback of realty (including renewal options) extending for 30 years or more may be considered an exchange of like-kind property (¶2417) on which gain or loss isn't recognized.[23] A sale restricting the buyer's use of the property may be recognized as a completed sale, as where stock is sold subject to security-device restrictions,[24] but if the rights retained are significant enough, the seller may be considered as selling only a partial interest or as granting a license to use.[25]

¶ 2665 Part gift, part sale; conditional gifts—treatment as sale or exchange.

Under Code Sec. 1001, if an owner combines a gift with a sale (e.g., to a family member), gain is realized to the extent the price received exceeds the owner's adjusted basis. But, no loss is recognized if the amount received is less than the owner's basis. (Reg § 1.1001-1(e))[26]

If a donor gives appreciated property to a donee on condition the donee pay the donor's gift tax, there's a sale by the donor for the amount of the gift tax. To the extent the gift tax

19. ¶I-6275 *et seq.*
20. ¶I-6276
21. ¶I-1400 *et seq.*
22. ¶I-1122
23. ¶I-3077
24. ¶I-1125
25. ¶I-1602 *et seq.*
26. ¶I-1006

paid by the donee exceeds the donor's basis, the donor has income.[27]

¶ 2666   Capital Gain/Ordinary Loss Rule—Form 4797. ▆▆▆▆▆▆▆▆▆▆▆▆▆▆

Under Code Sec. 1231, if there's a net gain for the tax year from (1) sales and exchanges of property used in a trade or business (Code Sec. 1231 assets as defined at ¶2667), and (2) involuntary or compulsory conversions of certain assets used in the trade or business or held in connection with a trade or business or a transaction entered for profit, it's treated as long-term capital gain, except as discussed below. A net loss is treated as an ordinary loss. (Code Sec. 1231(a); Reg § 1.1231-1(b))[28] Code Sec. 1231 gains and losses are reported and netted on Form 4797.

A net Code Sec. 1231 gain is treated as ordinary income to the extent of nonrecaptured net Code Sec. 1231 losses. (Code Sec. 1231(c)(1))

A nonrecaptured net Code Sec. 1231 loss is the net Code Sec. 1231 loss for the 5 most recent preceding tax years that hasn't been offset by a net Code Sec. 1231 gain in an intervening tax year. (Code Sec. 1231(c)(2)) Net Code Sec. 1231 gain is the excess of the Code Sec. 1231 gains over the Code Sec. 1231 losses. Net Code Sec. 1231 loss is the excess of the Code Sec. 1231 losses over the Code Sec. 1231 gains. (Code Sec. 1231(c)(3), Code Sec. 1231(c)(4))[29]

illustration: In Year 1, X Corp had a net Code Sec. 1231 loss of $10,000. In Year 2 and Year 3, X Corp had net Code Sec. 1231 gains of $7,000 and $5,000 respectively. In Year 2, the corporation recaptured $7,000 of its $10,000 net Code Sec. 1231 loss, thus treating its $7,000 gain as ordinary income. In Year 3, X Corp applied the remaining Code Sec. 1231 loss, $3,000 ($10,000 less $7,000) against its net Code Sec. 1231 gain of $5,000 for Year 3. Thus, in Year 3 the company reported $3,000 as ordinary income and $2,000 ($5,000 less $3,000) as long-term capital gain.

If the recognized losses from involuntary conversions arising from fire, storm, shipwreck or other casualty, or from theft, exceed the recognized gain, they aren't included in the Code Sec. 1231 computations. (Code Sec. 1231(a)(4)(C), Code Sec. 1231(c)(5))[30]

observation: This means that losses from such involuntary conversions will be treated as ordinary losses, but won't reduce the amount of net Code Sec. 1231 gains realized from other transactions eligible for capital gain treatment. But, if there is a net gain from such involuntary conversions, that net gain will be eligible for Code Sec. 1231 treatment. Capital gain treatment under Code Sec. 1231 is also barred to the extent that the depreciation recapture rules apply, see ¶2672 *et seq.*

For the applicability of Code Sec. 1231 treatment to timber cutting, see ¶2668; to timber, coal or U.S. iron ore sold with a retained economic interest, see ¶2669; and to advance payments for timber, coal or domestic iron ore, see ¶2670.

¶ 2667   Section 1231 assets defined—certain assets used in taxpayer's trade or business.

Code Sec. 1231 assets are certain assets used in taxpayer's trade or business that were held for more than 1 year at the time of disposition. Except as explained below, these assets include depreciable tangible and intangible personal property, and real property, whether or not depreciable. They include timber, certain livestock (other than poultry), and unharvested crops that are transferred with land. (Code Sec. 1231(b))

---

27. ¶I-1007
28. ¶I-9001

29. ¶I-9003
30. ¶I-9004

They don't include: (1) inventory, (2) property held primarily for sale to customers in the ordinary course of the taxpayer's business, (3) patents, inventions, models or designs (whether or not patented), secret formulas or processes, copyrights, artistic, literary, or musical compositions (unless, for musical compositions or copyrights in them, the election discussed at ¶2615 is made), letters or memoranda, or similar property, in the hands of the creator or other taxpayer described in Code Sec. 1221(a)(3), and (4) U.S. government publications obtained without charge or below the price sold to the general public. (Code Sec. 1231(b)(1); Reg § 1.1231-1(c))[31]

Property held for rent usually is treated as property used in business, but IRS (with the support of some, but not all, courts) denies this status where rental activity is slight.[32]

¶ 2668 Timber cutting treated as sale or exchange—Form T.

Under Code Sec. 631, a taxpayer who owns timber, or has a contract right to cut it, for more than 1 year before it was cut, may elect to treat the cutting as a sale or exchange qualifying for Section 1231 capital gain-ordinary loss treatment. Taxpayers who elect must file Form T with their returns unless they only have an occasional sale of timber. Once made, the election can be revoked only with IRS's consent, but if it was made for a tax year ending before Oct. 23, 2004, it can be revoked for any later tax year without IRS's consent. (Code Sec. 631(a); Code Sec. 1231(b)(2); ; Reg § 1.631-1)[33]

¶ 2669 When timber, coal or U.S. iron ore sold with a retained economic interest qualifies for Section 1231 treatment.

Under Code Sec. 631, a disposition of timber, coal or U.S. iron ore held more than 1 year qualifies for Section 1231 treatment if disposed of under a contract in which the taxpayer retains an economic interest. (Code Sec. 631(b), Code Sec. 631(c), Code Sec. 1231(b)(2); Reg § 1.631-2(a)(1), Reg § 1.631-3(a)(1))[34] For timber sales, Section 1231 treatment can apply if the owner makes an outright sale of the timber even if no economic interest is retained. (Code Sec. 631(b))[35]

When the disposition qualifies for Code Sec. 1231 treatment, no cost depletion deduction (¶1961) is allowed. (Reg § 1.611-1(b)(2)) And, for dispositions of coal and iron ore, no percentage depletion deduction is allowed if the maximum tax rate for the year on net capital gain is less than the maximum rate for ordinary income. (Code Sec. 631(c))[36]

¶ 2670 Advance payments for timber, coal or domestic iron ore—treated as subject to Code Sec. 1231.

Under Code Sec. 631, advance or minimum royalty payments or other amounts received or accrued before cutting of timber or before the mining of coal or iron ore (disposed of with a retained economic interest) are treated as realized from a sale subject to Code Sec. 1231 if the contract of disposal provides that they are to be applied as payment for timber cut later or coal or iron ore mined later. (Reg § 1.631-2(d)(1), Reg § 1.631-3(c)(1)) But if the right to cut or to mine ends or is abandoned before the timber, coal or iron ore is cut or mined, those advance payments are ordinary income. (Reg § 1.631-2(d)(2), Reg § 1.631-3(c)(2))

If the taxpayer elects to treat the date of payment as the date of disposal of timber (Code Sec. 631(b); Reg § 1.631-2(b)(1)), Code Sec. 1231 applies only if the timber is held for the required period at the time of the advance payment. (Reg § 1.631-2(c)(2)) If the election

---

31. ¶I-9007 *et seq.*
32. ¶I-9013
33. ¶N-6201 *et seq.*

34. ¶N-7001 *et seq.*
35. ¶N-7001
36. ¶N-7021

isn't made, the required holding period is measured as of the time it's cut. (Reg § 1.631-2(d)(1))[37] This election is made by attaching a specified statement to the return (filed not later than the due date, including extensions) for the year payment is received. (Reg § 1.631-2(c))[38]

¶ 2671　Sale of Depreciable Property to Related Parties—Capital Gain Bar. ▬▬▬

Under Code Sec. 1239, in a direct or indirect sale or exchange of property between related persons, any gain recognized is treated as ordinary income if that property is, in the transferee's hands, subject to the Code Sec. 167 allowance for depreciation, or is an amortizable Code Sec. 197 intangible asset. (Code Sec. 197(f)(7), Code Sec. 1239(a))

It also applies to property that would be subject to depreciation except that the buyer has elected amortization instead of depreciation (Reg § 1.1239-1(a)), and to patent applications. (Code Sec. 1239(e))[39]

Related persons are:

(1) a person and all entities that are controlled entities with respect to that person (see below) (Code Sec. 1239(b)(1));

(2) a taxpayer and any trust in which the taxpayer or the taxpayer's spouse is a beneficiary (unless the interest is a remote contingent interest) (Code Sec. 1239(b)(2));

(3) an executor of an estate and a beneficiary of the estate (except in the case of a sale or exchange in satisfaction of a pecuniary bequest) (Code Sec. 1239(b)(3));

(4) an employer and any person related to the employer (within the meaning of (1) through (3) above) (Code Sec. 1239(d)(1)); and

(5) a welfare benefit fund controlled directly or indirectly by anyone in (4), above (Code Sec. 1239(d)(2)).[40]

A controlled entity ((l), above) means, with respect to any person:

. . . a corporation more than 50% of the value of the stock of which is owned (directly or indirectly) by or for the person (Code Sec. 1239(c)(1)(A)),

. . . a partnership more than 50% of the capital interest or profits interest in which is owned (directly or indirectly) by or for the person (Code Sec. 1239(c)(1)(B)), or

. . . any entity that is a related person to the person under Code Sec. 267(b)(3) (controlled group of corporations), Code Sec. 267(b)(10) (certain related corporations and partnerships), Code Sec. 267(b)(11) (S corporations controlled by the same person), or Code Sec. 267(b)(12) (S corporations and C corporations controlled by the same person). (Code Sec. 1239(c)(1)(C))

And, under Code Sec. 267(c), there is attribution for stock owned by children, grandchildren, ancestors and siblings, as well as by the spouse. (Code Sec. 1239(c)(2))[41]

¶ 2672　Depreciation Recapture under Code Sec. 1245 and Code Sec. 1250. ▬▬▬

Two provisions restrict the possibility of converting ordinary income into capital gains by use of depreciation or amortization deductions.

One applies to personal property that is Code Sec. 1245 property (¶2673); the other to real property that is Code Sec. 1250 property (¶2675). (Code Sec. 1245(a)(3), Code Sec. 1250(c)) Recapture applies only to the extent of gain on a sale or other "disposition" (¶2679) of property. (Code Sec. 1245(a)(1), Code Sec. 1250(a)) Compute recapture on Form

4797.

For the treatment of basis reduction for the investment credit, see ¶2678.

For transactions and event that trigger or escape depreciation recapture, see ¶2679.

For recapture rules for listed property, see ¶2680.

¶ 2673 What is Section 1245 property? Certain MACRS property, ACRS property, and property subject to Section 167 depreciation rules or Section 197 amortization rules.

Code Sec. 1245 property includes:

(1) all MACRS property other than residential real property (27.5-year class) and non-residential real property (39-year class; 31.5-year class if placed in service before May 13, '93);

(2) all ACRS property other than 19-year, 18-year or 15-year real property: (a) that is residential rental property, (b) that is foreign-held realty, (c) with respect to which an optional (straight-line) cost recovery period was elected, or (d) that includes any 1 of certain categories of subsidized low-income rental housing;

(3) other property subject to the depreciation rules of Code Sec. 167 or the amortization rules of Code Sec. 197 (¶1958) that's personal property, certain real property (not including buildings) to the extent of certain amortization (or Code Sec. 179) deductions taken.[42]

Code Sec. 1245 property includes property, other than a building or its structural components, used as an integral part of manufacturing, production or extraction, or for furnishing transportation, communication or other public utility services, and research or storage facilities used in connection with any of these activities. It also includes single purpose agricultural or horticultural structures, and storage facilities (except buildings and their structural components) used in distributing petroleum or any primary product of petroleum. (Code Sec. 1245(a)(3); Reg § 1.1245-3))[43]

For recapture rules for Code Sec. 1245 property, see ¶2674.

¶ 2674 Depreciation recapture rules for disposition of Section 1245 property.

A gain on the disposition (¶2679) of Code Sec. 1245 property (¶2673) is treated as ordinary income to the extent of depreciation or amortization allowed or allowable on the property. (Code Sec. 1245(a))[44] The following deductions are treated as amortization for purposes of the Code Sec. 1245 recapture rules: the expense deduction under Code Sec. 179 (¶1935 *et seq.*); the deductions for certain refining costs under Code Sec. 179B and Code Sec. 179C (for property placed in service before 2010 (or before 2014 if constructed under a written binding contract entered into before 2010); the deduction for 50% of the cost of qualified advanced mine safety equipment property under Code Sec. 179E (for property placed in service before 2018); qualified architectural and transportation barrier removal expenses under Code Sec. 190 (¶1605); and reforestation expenses under Code Sec. 194 (¶1955). (Code Sec. 1245(a)(2)(C))[45]

The environmental remediation expensing deduction (that applied to costs paid or incurred before Jan. 1, 2012, see Code Sec. 198(e)),[46] and the amortization of a Section 197 intangible (¶1958) (Code Sec. 197(f)(7)) also are subject to recapture under Code Sec. 1245.[47]

---

42. ¶I-10101 *et seq.*
43. ¶I-10101
44. ¶I-10200 *et seq.*
45. ¶I-10204
46. ¶L-6160.4
47. ¶L-7981.2

The amount of gain treated as ordinary income on the disposition is limited to the lower of:

(1) the recomputed basis of the property minus the adjusted basis of the property. (Code Sec. 1245(a)(1)(A)) Recomputed basis is the adjusted basis of the property increased by the recapturable depreciation and amortization deductions reflected in the adjusted basis (Code Sec. 1245(a)(2)); or

(2) in the case of a sale, exchange or involuntary conversion, the amount realized minus the adjusted basis of the property; or in the case of any other disposition, the fair market value of the property minus the adjusted basis of the property. (Code Sec. 1245(a)(1)(B))[48]

If a taxpayer disposes of more than 1 amortizable Code Sec. 197 intangible (¶1958) in a transaction or a series of related transactions, all of the amortizable intangibles are treated as 1 Code Sec. 1245 property for purposes of the recapture rules. But, this rule doesn't apply to an intangible if its adjusted basis exceeds its fair market value. (Code Sec. 1245(b)(8))[49]

A taxpayer who disposes of qualified real property (¶1937) for which a Code Sec. 179 election has been made (¶1935 *et seq.*) may use any reasonable allocation method to determine the part of the gain that is attributable to Code Sec. 1245 property, i.e., to the part of the unadjusted basis of the property that was reduced by the Code Sec. 179 expense deduction. The remaining unadjusted basis of the property is allocated to Code Sec. 1250 property, see ¶2676.[50]

¶ 2675   What is Section 1250 property? Certain MACRS property, ACRS property, and real property placed in service before '81.

All real property subject to depreciation that isn't Code Sec. 1245 property is Code Sec. 1250 property. (Code Sec. 1250(c)) Thus, Code Sec. 1250 property includes:

(1) MACRS residential real property (in the 27.5-year class) and nonresidential real property (in the 39-year class; 31.5-year class if placed in service before May 13, '93).

(2) The types of ACRS real property that aren't Code Sec. 1245 property, see ¶2673.

(3) The following real property placed in service before '81: (a) depreciable intangible real property; (b) all depreciable buildings and their structural components; and (c) other depreciable real property excluded from the definition of Code Sec. 1245 property (¶2673). (Reg § 1.1250-1(e)(3))[1]

For recapture rules for Code Sec. 1250 property, see ¶2676.

For 20% additional depreciation on dispositions of realty by corporations, see ¶2677.

¶ 2676   Depreciation recapture rules for disposition of Section 1250 property.

Gain on the disposition of Code Sec. 1250 property is treated as ordinary income to the extent of the lower of (1) the "applicable percentage" of the additional depreciation allowed or allowable on the property, or (2) in the case of a sale, exchange or involuntary conversion, the excess of the amount realized over the adjusted basis, or in the case of any other disposition, the fair market value of the property over its adjusted basis. For Code Sec. 1250 property held longer than 1 year, the additional depreciation is the excess of the actual depreciation taken over the depreciation figured using the straight line method. If held less than a year, it's all the depreciation taken. (Code Sec. 1250(a); Code

---

48. ¶I-10200 *et seq.*
49. ¶I-10219.1

50. ¶I-10220.1 *et seq.*
1. ¶I-10112 *et seq.*

Sec. 1250(b))[2] Thus, Code Sec. 1250 recapture doesn't apply to residential rental or non-residential real property depreciated under MACRS since such property is depreciated using the straight line method, see ¶1918. Code Sec. 1250 recapture does apply to the pre-2010 commercial revitalization deduction. (Former Code Sec. 1400I(f)(2))[34]

The applicable percentage is generally 100% for depreciation attributable to periods after '75, but is lower on the disposition of low income housing and other special rental housing property.[5]

For the allocation between Code Sec. 1245 and Code Sec. 1250 of recapture income on the sale of qualified real property (¶1937) for which the Code Sec. 179 election (¶1935 *et seq.*) was made, see ¶2674.

For treatment of a noncorporate taxpayer's unrecaptured Code Sec. 1250 gain, see ¶2604.

¶ 2677 Additional 20% depreciation recapture on sale or other disposition of residential or nonresidential realty by corporations.

Under Code Sec. 291, for sales or other dispositions (of both residential and nonresidential property), 20% of the amount by which the gain recapturable if Code Sec. 1245 rules applied exceeds the gain recaptured under Code Sec. 1250 is treated as ordinary income (to the extent of gain) to a corporation. (Code Sec. 291(a))[6] This rule applies to an S corporation only if it was formerly a C corporation for any of the 3 immediately preceding tax years. (Code Sec. 1363(b)(4))[7]

¶ 2678 Treatment of basis reduction for investment credit; recapturable amount—depreciation recapture.

Under Code Sec. 50, in determining the recapturable amount, the reduction of basis for the investment credit is treated as a deduction allowed for depreciation. (Code Sec. 50(c)(4)(A))[8] But, this basis reduction is disregarded in computing straight-line depreciation for purposes of determining "additional depreciation" subject to recapture for Code Sec. 1250 property. (Code Sec. 50(c)(4)(B))[9]

¶ 2679 Transactions and events that trigger or escape depreciation recapture.

The following is a list of transactions and events that either trigger or escape depreciation recapture under Code Sec. 1245 and Code Sec. 1250:[10]

* A sale in a sale and leaseback transaction, a sale under a conditional sales contract, and a transfer of title back to the seller, creditor, or new purchaser upon foreclosure of a security interest trigger recapture. But, a transfer of legal title to a creditor upon creation of a security interest, or to a debtor upon termination of a security interest, escapes recapture. (Reg § 1.1245-1(a)(3), Reg § 1.1250-1(a)(2)(i))

* For like-kind exchanges and involuntary conversions, Section 1245 depreciation isn't recaptured unless gain is recognized or non-Code Sec. 1245 property is acquired (Code Sec. 1245(b)(4); Reg § 1.1245-4(d)); and Code Sec. 1250 depreciation isn't recaptured except where gain is recognized, stock is bought to acquire control of a corporation owning replacement property, or non-Code Sec. 1250 property is acquired. (Code Sec. 1250(d)(4); Reg § 1.1250-3(d))

---

2. ¶I-10400 *et seq.*
3. ¶L-12709
4.
5. ¶I-10417 *et seq.*
6. ¶I-10422 *et seq.*

7. ¶I-10422
8. ¶I-10204
9. ¶I-10507
10. ¶I-10501 *et seq.*

- Conversion to personal use (except for Code Sec. 179 property, see ¶1938) doesn't trigger recapture, but a later sale will. (¶1924)

- Termination or disposition of a lease where depreciation was taken by the lessee (or sublessee) generally triggers recapture. (Reg § 1.1245-2(a)(3)(i))

- Incorporation of a business triggers recapture only if gain is otherwise recognized. (Code Sec. 1245(b)(3), Code Sec. 1250(d)(3); Reg § 1.1245-4(c), Reg § 1.1250-3(c))

- Corporate distributions in kind (including liquidating distributions) generally trigger recapture, except in a tax-free complete liquidation of a subsidiary with carryover basis, where recapture is triggered upon disposition by the parent-transferee. (Code Sec. 1245(b)(3), Code Sec. 1250(d)(3); Reg § 1.1245-4(c), Reg § 1.1250-3(c))

- Corporate split-ups and reorganizations generally don't trigger recapture, except to the extent that gain is otherwise recognized on transfer of the property. (Code Sec. 1245(b)(3), Code Sec. 1250(d)(3); Reg § 1.1245-4(c), Reg § 1.1250-3(c))

- S corporation elections or termination of S status don't trigger recapture.

- Sale of a partnership interest triggers recapture. Contributions to a partnership generally don't trigger recapture, but may if property is subject to a liability. (Code Sec. 1245(a), Code Sec. 1245(b)(3), Code Sec. 1250(a), Code Sec. 1250(d)(3); Reg § 1.1245-4(c), Reg § 1.1250-3(c))

- Gifts generally don't trigger recapture, but recapturable depreciation carries over to donee. (Code Sec. 1245(b)(1), Code Sec. 1250(d)(1); Reg § 1.1245-4(a), Reg § 1.1250-3(a))

- For transfers by reason of death, recapturable depreciation is neither triggered nor carried over. (Code Sec. 1245(b)(2), Code Sec. 1250(d)(2); Reg § 1.1245-4(b), Reg § 1.1250-3(b))[11]

- When a trust or estate realizes gain from the distribution of depreciable property in satisfaction of a fixed-dollar bequest, or from a distribution property in satisfaction of a bequest of other property, recapture is triggered. (Reg § 1.1245-4(b), Reg § 1.1250-3(b))[12]

For the effect of depreciation recapture on installment sales, see ¶2448.

¶ 2680 Special depreciation recapture rules for listed property; reduction of business use; excess depreciation.

Under Code Sec. 280F, a reduction of business use of listed property (¶1939 *et seq.*) from more-than-50% to 50% or less triggers recapture of excess depreciation previously taken. (Code Sec. 280F(b)(2)(A)) "Excess depreciation" means depreciation allowable for years before the first year in which the property wasn't predominantly used in a qualified business use, over the amount of depreciation which would have been allowable for those years if the property hadn't been predominantly used in a qualified business (¶1941 *et seq.*) for the year it was acquired and if there had been no Code Sec. 179 expense election for the property. (Code Sec. 280F(b)(2)(B))[13]

---

11. ¶I-10002, I-10301 *et seq.*
12. ¶C-7154

13. ¶L-10026

Chapter 11 Tax Accounting—Periods and Methods— Inventories

¶ 2800   **Accounting Periods.** ■■■■■■■■■■■■■■■■■■■■■■■■■■■■■■■■■■

Under Code Sec. 441, each taxpayer must compute taxable income and file a return on the basis of an accounting period called a tax year (¶2801).

¶ 2801   **Tax year—annual accounting period (calendar year or fiscal year).**

Under Code Sec. 441, taxpayers must compute their taxable income on the basis of their tax year. (Code Sec. 441(a); Reg § 1.441-1(a)) "Tax year" is generally the annual accounting period on the basis of which taxpayers regularly compute income in keeping their books, Code Sec. 441(c)) if that's the calendar year or a fiscal year. (Code Sec. 441(b)(1))[1]

The calendar year is the 12-month period ending on Dec. 31. (Code Sec. 441(d)) In general, a taxpayer must use the calendar year if it keeps no books, has no annual accounting period, has an accounting period that doesn't qualify as a fiscal year (Code Sec. 441(b)(2), Code Sec. 441(g)) or hasn't established a fiscal year. (Reg § 1.441-1(b)(4))[2]

A fiscal year is any 12-month period ending on the last day of a month other than December, or the 52-53 week tax year described at ¶2802. (Code Sec. 441(e))[3] If a return is properly made for a period of less than 12 months, the tax year is the "short tax year" (¶2804) for which the return is made. (Code Sec. 441(b)(3))[4]

A sole proprietorship must use the same tax year as the proprietor unless the proprietor gets IRS consent to use a fiscal year.[5]

Restrictive rules apply to trusts and estates, partnerships, S corporations, and certain other entities, see ¶2805 *et seq.*

¶ 2802   **Tax year of 52-53 weeks as alternative to a calendar or fiscal tax year.**

Under Code Sec. 441, a taxpayer, as an alternative to a calendar or fiscal tax year (¶2801), can adopt a tax year that varies from 52 to 53 weeks and always ends on the same day of the week. That day must be either the day of the week that last occurs in a calendar month or the day that falls nearest to the end of the calendar month (in which case the last day of the tax year may fall in the next month). (Code Sec. 441(f)(1); Reg § 1.441-2(a)(1)) A taxpayer may elect a 52-53 week tax year if it otherwise satisfies Code Sec. 441 and its regs; for example, the taxpayer doesn't violate rules in Reg § 1.441-1(b)(2)(i) that require specified tax years in specified situations. (Reg § 1.441-2(a)(3))[6]

If a pass-through entity or its owner, or both, use a 52-53-week tax year and the tax years of both end with reference to the same calendar month, then, for purposes of determining the tax year in which pass-through items are taken into account by its owner, the owner's tax year is deemed to end on the last day of the pass-through's tax year. (Reg § 1.441-2(e)(1)) Similarly, if the tax year of a personal service corporation (PSC) and an employee-owner end with reference to the same calendar month, then for purposes of determining the tax year in which an employee-owner takes into account items that are deductible by the PSC and includible in the owner's income, the employee-owner's tax year is deemed to end on the last day of the PSC's tax year. (Reg § 1.441-2(e)(2))

---

1. ¶G-1001, G-1002
2. ¶s G-1001, G-1003
3. ¶G-1004

4. ¶s G-1001
5. ¶G-1067
6. ¶G-1101

References beginning with a single letter are to paragraphs in Federal Tax Coordinator 2d and RIA's Analysis of Federal Taxes: Income.

¶ 2803   Establishing a tax year for a new taxpayer—Form 1128

A new taxpayer generally may adopt any tax year that satisfies Code Sec. 441 and its regs, see ¶2801, by simply filing its first federal income tax return using that tax year. (Reg § 1.441-1(c)(1)) However, a newly formed partnership, S corporation, or personal service corporation that wants to adopt a tax year other than its required calendar tax year end, a tax year elected under Code Sec. 444 (¶2810), or a 52-53 week tax year (¶2802) that ends with reference to its required tax year or to one elected under Code Sec. 444, must establish a business purpose and get IRS approval. (Reg § 1.441-1(c)(2)) Use Form 1128 following IRS procedures.

A new taxpayer using a 52-53 week tax year (¶2802) must file a statement with the return for its first 52-53 week tax year. (Reg § 1.441-2(b)(1)(ii))[7]

¶ 2804   Short tax years; years of less than 12 months; change of the taxpayer's annual accounting period.

Under Code Sec. 443, a taxpayer must use a tax "year" of less than 12 months if the taxpayer: (1) isn't in existence for what would otherwise be the taxpayer's full tax year (Code Sec. 443(a)(2));[8] or (2) properly changes the annual accounting period (¶2811). (Code Sec. 443(a)(1))[9] But if the short year arises because of the taxpayer's death, the taxpayer's last return may be filed and the tax paid as if the taxpayer had lived to the end of his or her last tax year. (Reg § 1.443-1(a)(2))[10] For filing requirements for short years, see ¶ 4716 and ¶ 4727.

If the short year results from a change of the taxpayer's annual accounting period, the short period's taxable income must be annualized. (Code Sec. 443(b)) Under the general method of annualization, gross income for the short period (less allowable deductions) is multiplied by 12 (months) and divided by the number of months in the short period. The result is the annualized taxable income on which tentative tax is computed. The tax due is arrived at by multiplying the tentative tax by the number of months in the short period and dividing by 12. (Code Sec. 443(b)(1); Reg § 1.443-1(b)(1)(i))[11] Special annualization rules apply to the alternative minimum tax (AMT). (Code Sec. 443(d))[12]

There are exceptions to the annualization requirements for self-employment tax, accumulated earnings tax, personal holding company tax, undistributed foreign personal holding company income, income of regulated investment companies and real estate investment trusts, and a subsidiary changing to conform to the year of the affiliated group filing a consolidated return.[13]

Net operating loss (NOL) carryforwards or carrybacks are applied to the short year and may entirely eliminate the need to annualize income.[14]

The income is *not* annualized if the short year is caused by the taxpayer not being in existence for a full tax year. (Code Sec. 443(b)) In this case, tax is computed as if the short period were a full year. (Reg § 1.443-1(a)(2))[15]

If a taxpayer changes to or from a 52-53 week year, income for the short period must be annualized, with this exception: If the short period is 359 days or more, it is treated as a full tax year; while if it is six days or less, it is added to the following tax year. (Code Sec. 441(f)(2)(B); Reg § 1.443-1(b)(1)(ii))[16]

---

7. ¶G-1054
8. ¶G-1153
9. ¶G-1155
10. ¶G-1154
11. ¶G-1166

12. ¶A-8119
13. ¶G-1163
14. ¶G-1166
15. ¶G-1162
16. ¶G-1108

Annualizing may create a tax hardship for taxpayers who have a disproportionately large amount of taxable income in the short period. To avoid this, taxpayers may use an optional method that computes the tax for the full 12 months starting at the beginning of the short year and prorates the tax according to the amount of income earned in the short period. (Code Sec. 443(b)(2)) This method is available only on a claim for credit or refund, filed no later than the due date (including extensions) of taxpayer's return for the first tax year that ends on or after the day that is 12 months after the first day of the short period. (Reg § 1.443-1(b)(2)(v)(a))[17]

¶ 2805 Tax years of trusts and estates.

Under Code Sec. 644, trusts must use the calendar year, except for trusts exempt from tax under Code Sec. 501(a), wholly charitable trusts described in Code Sec. 4947(a)(1) (Code Sec. 644) and grantor trusts).[18] Estates may adopt either a calendar year or a fiscal year.[19]

¶ 2806 Tax years of Domestic International Sales Corporations (DISCs).

Under Code Sec. 441, DISCs must use the tax year of the shareholder (or group of shareholders with the same 12-month tax year) with the highest percentage of voting power. (Code Sec. 441(h)(1))[20]

¶ 2807 Tax year of S corporation; required year—Form 2553.

Under Code Sec. 1378, an S corporation (¶3349 *et seq.*), unless it makes the election at ¶2810, or elects a 52-53 week tax year (¶2802) ending with reference to its required year or the year elected under the rules at ¶2810, must have a "required year," i.e., a calendar year or any other accounting year for which it shows a business purpose satisfactory to IRS; use Form 2553. (Code Sec. 1378; Reg § 1.441-1(b)(2)(i)(L), Reg § 1.441-1(b)(2)(ii)(B), Reg § 1.1378-1(a))[21]

¶ 2808 Tax year of personal service corporation (PSC).

Under Code Sec. 441, the tax year of a PSC (see below) must be a calendar year unless it makes the election at ¶2810, elects a 52-53 week tax year ending with reference to the calendar year or the year elected under the rules at ¶2810, or can satisfy IRS that there's a business purpose for a different tax year. (Code Sec. 441(i)(1); Reg § 1.441-1(b)(2)(i)(B), Reg § 1.441-3(a))[22]

A PSC is, as defined under the rules permitting IRS to reallocate PSC income and deductions (¶2846), any corporation whose principal activity is the performance of personal services that are substantially performed by employee-owners. But for this purpose, PSC doesn't include S corporations, and the term "owner-employee" includes all employees with *any* stock ownership in the corporation. In determining ownership, attribution from a corporation (under Code Sec. 318(a)(2)(C)) is applied if *any* stock is owned by the shareholder in that corporation. (Code Sec. 441(i)(2))[23] Independent contractors who own stock in the corporation and perform personal services for or on behalf of it are treated as employees. (Reg § 1.441-3(g)(2))[24]

The performance of personal services is considered the corporation's principal activity if the corporation's compensation cost for a testing period for activities that are considered

---

17. ¶G-1170 *et seq.*
18. ¶G-1401
19. ¶C-7008
20. ¶O-2041

21. ¶G-1250
22. ¶G-1300
23. ¶G-1302
24. ¶G-1306

the performance of personal services exceeds 50% of its total compensation cost for the period. (Reg § 1.441-3(e)(1)) The testing period is the preceding tax year (or, for a corporation's first tax year, the period beginning the first day of the first tax year and ending the last day of that tax year or, if earlier, the last day of the calendar year in which that tax year began). (Reg § 1.441-3(c)(2)) Personal services are substantially performed by employee-owners if, during the testing period, more than 20% of the corporation's compensation cost (excluding qualified plan or SEP contributions) attributable to the performance of personal services is attributable to personal services performed by employee-owners. (Reg § 1.441-3(f), Reg § 1.441-3(e)(2)(ii))[25]

¶ 2809 Tax year of partnership—"majority interest tax year," tax year of principal partners, or "least-aggregate-deferral" year.

Under Code Sec. 706, unless a partnership makes an election as described below, or can satisfy IRS that there's a business purpose for a different tax year (Code Sec. 706(b)(1)(B); Code Sec. 706(b)(1)(C); Reg § 1.706-1(b)(2)(ii)),[26] it must adopt:

(1) the "majority interest tax year" (Code Sec. 706(b)(1)(B)(i))—the tax year of one or more of the partners having an aggregate interest in partnership profits and capital of more than 50% on each testing day (the first day of the partnership's tax year as otherwise determined, or days prescribed by IRS) (Code Sec. 706(b)(4)(A));

(2) the tax year of all its principal partners (5%-or-more interest in profits or capital (Code Sec. 706(b)(3))) if there's no majority interest tax year (Code Sec. 706(b)(1)(B)(ii)); or

(3) the "least-aggregate-deferral" year, if there's no majority interest tax year and the principal partners don't have the same tax year. (Code Sec. 706(b)(1)(B)(iii); Reg § 1.706-1(b)(2)(i)(C))[27]

A partnership may have a tax year other than its required year if it makes an election under Code Sec. 444 (¶2810), or elects to use a 52-53-week tax year (¶2802) that ends with reference to its required year or a tax year elected under Code Sec. 444. (Reg § 1.706-1(b)(2)(ii))

A partnership that's required to change to a majority-interest tax year isn't required to change to another tax year for either of the two tax years following the year of change. (Code Sec. 706(b)(4)(B))[28]

A partnership tax year ends as dictated by its accounting period, except that it closes earlier (1) for a partner who sells his or her entire interest or whose interest is completely liquidated (Code Sec. 706(c); Reg § 1.706-1(c)(2)(i)), and (2) for all its partners on the date the partnership terminates for tax purposes. (Reg § 1.706-1(c)(1))[29]

¶ 2810 Section 444 election of tax year other than required tax year for S corporation, personal service corporation, or partnership—Form 8716; Form 8752; Form 1120, Schedule H.

Under Code Sec. 444, an S corporation (¶2807), personal service corporation (PSC) (¶2808), or partnership (¶2809) may elect (on Form 8716) to have a tax year other than the required tax year (Code Sec. 444(a)), but only if the deferral period (i.e., the number of months between the beginning of elected fiscal tax year and the following Dec. 31) for the tax year elected isn't longer than three months. (Code Sec. 444(b)(1); Reg § 1.444-1T(b))[30]

---

25. ¶G-1302.1, G-1304, G-1305
26. ¶G-1200 *et seq.*
27. ¶G-1200 *et seq.*

28. ¶G-1201
29. ¶G-1224, G-1225
30. ¶G-1500 *et seq.*

A partnership or S corporation that elects a different tax year has to make a "required payment," a non-interest earning tax deposit refunded or credited to the partnership in the next year and reported on Form 8752. The payment approximates the tax that the partners or S corporation shareholders would have paid on short-period income if the election hadn't been made. (Code Sec. 444(c)(1); Code Sec. 7519; Reg § 1.444-3T)[31]

A PSC that elects a fiscal tax year but doesn't make required minimum distributions (e.g., payments of compensation) to its employee-owners before the end of the calendar year must postpone part or all of its corresponding deductions to its next fiscal tax year. (Code Sec. 280H) To figure the required minimum distribution and maximum deductible amount, use Form 1120, Schedule H.[32]

¶ 2811 How to change accounting periods—Form 1128; IRS approval to change accounting periods; automatic IRS approval of change.

Under Code Sec. 442, a taxpayer must get prior IRS approval to change accounting periods unless authorized by the Code (e.g., Code Sec. 444, ¶2810) or regs (Reg § 1.441-1(e), Reg § 1.442-1(a))[33]

IRS will approve a request for a change in tax years only if the taxpayer establishes a substantial business purpose for it and agrees to any terms, conditions or adjustments required to effect it, including any that IRS feels are necessary to avoid a substantial distortion of the taxpayer's income. (Reg § 1.442-1(b)(2); Reg § 1.442-1(b)(3))[34]

To request IRS approval, file Form 1128 within the time and in the manner provided in IRS administrative procedures. (Reg § 1.442-1(b)(1), Reg § 1.442-1(b)(3))[35] Fiscal year individuals must follow an exclusive procedure to change to a calendar year.[36]

If a taxpayer changed its annual accounting period within 48 months before the last month of the requested tax year, a copy of the previous change application, the ruling letter, and any related correspondence from IRS, must be attached to the application.[37]

A taxpayer may change his or her annual accounting period without IRS approval, or in many of the cases listed below under procedures that provide for "automatic" IRS approval, where the taxpayer:

. . . changes to a 52-53 week tax year that ends with reference to the same calendar month as the month ending his or her previous tax year (Reg § 1.441-2(b)(2));[38]

. . . marries a person with a different tax year (Reg § 1.442-1(d)(1));[39]

. . . is an individual with a fiscal year tax year who changes to a calendar year tax year;[40]

. . . is a partnership changing its tax year to its required tax year as described at ¶2809;[41]

. . . is a C corporation that meets certain tests;[42]

. . . is an S corporation changing its tax year to meet the tests described at ¶2807;[43]

. . . is a personal service corporation changing to a calendar year or a 52-53 week tax year ending with reference to a calendar year; (Reg § 1.441-3(b)(2))[44] or

. . . is a subsidiary corporation required to change its tax year to that of members of its affiliated group that file a consolidated return. (Reg § 1.442-1(c))

---

31. ¶G-1500, G-1550.1 *et seq.*
32. ¶G-1600 *et seq.*
33. ¶G-1701
34. ¶G-1701.1 *et seq.*
35. ¶G-1701.1 *et seq.*
36. ¶G-1726
37. ¶G-1882

38. ¶G-1101
39. ¶G-1708
40. ¶G-1725
41. ¶G-1222, G-1751 *et seq.*
42. ¶G-1801 *et seq.*
43. ¶G-1751 *et seq.*
44. ¶G-1301, G-1751 *et seq.*

¶ 2812   Accounting Methods. ▰▰▰▰▰

Under Code Sec. 446, taxable income must be computed under the method of accounting on the basis of which the taxpayer regularly computes income in keeping its books. Tax accounting methods are the methods by which taxpayers determine when income items, gains, losses, and deductions are taken into account for tax purposes. Various methods of are permissible, but each must be used consistently and clearly reflect income. See ¶2813 for establishing a method of accounting and ¶2814 for limits on choice of accounting method.

¶ 2813   Establishing a method of tax accounting; permissible accounting methods.

Under Code Sec. 446, a taxpayer's book accounting method determines the taxpayer's accounting method, and a taxpayer establishes a tax accounting method by setting up books, keeping accounts, and preparing income tax returns under any of the permissible methods. The method first used in accounting for business income and deductions in connection with each trade or business, as evidenced in the taxpayer's income tax return in which the income or deductions are first reported, must be followed consistently after that. (Reg § 1.446-1(d)(1))[45]

A taxpayer may use one method of accounting to keep personal books and another to keep the books for a trade or business. (Reg § 1.446-1(c)(1)(iv)(b)) But the two must be strictly separated.[46]

A taxpayer whose only income is wages doesn't have to keep formal books in order to establish an accounting method, but may establish a method of accounting by means of tax returns (or copies) or other records. (Reg § 1.446-1(b)(2))[47]

A new taxpayer may adopt a method of accounting in connection with filing the first income tax return. An existing taxpayer entering into a business that's separate and distinct from any trade or business that the taxpayer previously carried on may adopt a method of accounting for the separate and distinct business in connection with filing the first tax return reporting income from that business. (Reg § 1.446-1(e)(1))[48]

Use of different accounting methods that create or shift profits or losses between the taxpayer's various trades or businesses (e.g., by using inventory adjustments, sales, purchases or expenses) resulting in a distortion of the taxpayer's income isn't allowed. (Reg § 1.446-1(d)(3))[49]

Taxpayers may use any combination of the cash, accrual, and specifically permitted special methods of accounting if the combination is a clear reflection of income and is consistently used. (Reg § 1.446-1(c)(1)(iv))[50]

Generally, a taxpayer filing even only one return reflecting use of an accounting method has adopted the method and must obtain IRS consent to change the method. However, a taxpayer filing a return for only one year reflecting an impermissible method can simply amend the return to change to a permissible method.[1]

¶ 2814   Limits on choice of accounting methods and small business exceptions (gross receipts test)—inventory limits and cash-method limits.

Inventory limits. Under Code Sec. 446 and Code Sec. 471 the accrual method (¶2818

---

45. ¶G-2051
46. ¶G-2052
47. ¶G-2051
48. ¶G-2051

49. ¶G-2052
50. ¶G-2003
1. ¶G-2201.2

et seq.) is mandatory for purchases and sales (unless IRS consents to a change) where inventories must be used. (Code Sec. 471(a), Reg § 1.446-1(c)(2)(i)) Inventories must be used where the production, purchase or sale of merchandise is an income-producing factor. (Reg § 1.446-1(a)(4)(i); Reg § 1.471-1)[2]

Inventory limits—gross receipts test. A major exception to inventory accounting applies for businesses (other than tax shelters) that satisfy a $25 million (adjusted for inflation) "gross receipts test" of Code Sec. 448(c) and Reg § 1.448-2(c)(2) (also discussed under *Cash method limits* below) that requires average annual gross receipts for the three-tax-year period preceding the testing year (or its existence period before that year if less than 3 years (Code Sec. 471(c)(3))) of no more than *$27 million* for a testing year beginning in 2022 (*$29 million* for a testing year beginning in 2023). If a taxpayer meets the gross receipts test and applies one of the alternative required accounting methods—see (1) and (2), below—Code Sec. 471(a) doesn't apply to that taxpayer for that tax year, and the taxpayer's method of accounting for inventory is treated as meeting the clear-reflection-of-income standard for that tax year. (Code Sec. 471(c)(1); Reg § 1.471-1(b))[3] Gross receipts for short tax years must be annualized. (Code Sec. 448(c)(3)) Persons treated as a single employer under the controlled group or affiliated service group rules are treated as one person for purposes of the gross receipts test. (Code Sec. 448(c)(2); Code Sec. 448(c)(3))[4]

For individuals, trusts, and estates, the gross receipts test is applied as if each trade or business of that taxpayer were a corporation or a partnership. (Code Sec. 471(c)(3)) A change in method of accounting made under Code Sec. 471(c) is treated as made with IRS consent. (Code Sec. 471(c)(4))[5]

For a taxpayer who meets the gross receipts test, the taxpayer's method of accounting for inventory won't be treated as failing to clearly reflect income if the method (Code Sec. 471(c)(1)(B) and Reg § 1.471-1(b)(3))[6]:

(1) treats inventory as non-incidental materials and supplies (the Code Sec. 471(c) materials and supplies method); or

(2) conforms to the method reflected in the taxpayer's applicable financial statement (AFS defined in Reg § 1.471-1(b)(5)(ii)) for each tax year for each item; or

(3) if the taxpayer doesn't have any AFS for the tax year, conforms to the method reflected in the taxpayer's books and records prepared in accordance with the taxpayer's accounting procedures, for each item.

Limits on use of cash method. Under Code Sec. 448, C corporations, partnerships with a C corporation partner, and tax shelters generally may not use the cash method of accounting (¶2815 *et seq.*). (Code Sec. 448(a))[7] However, a corporation, or partnership with a C corporation partner, that *isn't a tax shelter* and that meets the gross receipts test described above is exempt from the limitation. (Code Sec. 448(b), Code Sec. 448(c))[8] The Code Sec. 448 restriction doesn't apply to farming businesses and personal service corporations that aren't tax shelters (Code Sec. 448(a), Code Sec. 448(b)), but a separate limitation, that has a gross receipts exception and other exceptions, applies to farming businesses, see ¶4510.[9]

For the cash method limitation, an accounting method that records some but not all items on the cash method (i.e., a hybrid method) is treated as the cash method of accounting. (Reg § 1.448-1T(a)(4))[10] Tax-exempt trusts and tax-exempt C corporations are subject to the above rules for unrelated trade or business income. (Code Sec. 448(d)(6);

2. ¶G-5001 *et seq.*
3. ¶G-5004, ¶G-2069
4. ¶G-2069 *et seq.*
5. ¶G-5004
6. ¶G-5004

7. ¶G-2054
8. ¶G-2069
9. ¶G-2057, ¶G-2058
10. ¶G-2054

Reg § 1.448-1T(a)(3))[11]

¶ 2815   The Cash Method of Accounting. ▬▬▬▬▬▬▬▬▬

The cash method is one of the allowable methods of tax accounting for income and deductions under, respectively, Code Sec. 451 (¶2816) and Code Sec. 461 (¶2817). Under the cash method, income is reported when cash or property is actually or constructively received (¶2816), and deductions are taken in the year cash or property is paid or transferred (¶2817).[12]

For income a taxpayer receives under a claim of right, see ¶1204. For restrictions on use of the cash method by certain taxpayers (and exceptions for small businesses), see ¶2814.

A check issued by a payor is income when received by a cash basis payee, unless there's a restriction on the payee's right to cash the check.[13] Receipt of a check by an agent is considered receipt by the principal.[14] For cash method deduction purposes, a check is considered paid when delivered, not when cashed, if it's honored when it's first presented for payment.[15]

¶ 2816   Constructive receipt of income for cash-basis taxpayers.

In applying Code Sec. 451 to a cash method taxpayer, income not actually received is constructively received and reportable if it's within the taxpayer's control. Cash basis taxpayers must report money unconditionally subject to their demand as income, even if they haven't received it.[16] There's no constructive receipt if the amount is available only on surrender of a valuable right,[17] or if there are substantial limits on the right to receive it. (Reg § 1.451-2(a))[18]

¶ 2817   Timing of deductions under the cash method.

Under Code Sec. 461, cash method taxpayers generally take deductions (if otherwise allowable) in the year the items are paid. (Reg § 1.461-1(a)(1))[19] There's no constructive payment doctrine.[20]

Where an expense (e.g., rent or an insurance premium) relates to a period covering more than 12 months, IRS and most courts agree that the deduction must be spread over the period to which the expense applies.[21] For an exception for points paid on a home mortgage, see ¶1739. For deduction of prepaid taxes, see ¶1758.

¶ 2818   The Accrual Method of Accounting. ▬▬▬▬▬▬▬▬▬

In applying the accrual method of accounting to income inclusion under Code Sec. 451, under the all-events test, income is generally included in the year all events have occurred that determine the taxpayer's right to receive it and the amount can be determined with reasonable accuracy (Reg § 1.451-1(a)).[22] The right to receive the income must not be contingent on a future event; it must be reasonably susceptible of accurate estimate, and reasonably expected to be received in due course.[23] In addition, under the "conformity requirement" rules, a taxpayer using the accrual method to compute taxable income can't treat the all-events test as met any later than when the item is taken into account as revenue in an applicable financial statement (AFS, ¶2819). (Code Sec. 451)[24] For rules

---

11. ¶G-2055
12. ¶G-2410 *et seq.*
13. ¶G-2415
14. ¶G-2419
15. ¶G-2438
16. ¶G-2424
17. ¶G-2426
18. ¶G-2425
19. ¶G-2436 *et seq.*
20. ¶G-2443
21. ¶G-2450 *et seq.*, ¶L-6616 *et seq.*
22. ¶G-2471, G-2472
23. ¶G-2471
24. ¶G-2472.1*et seq.*

relating to advance payments, see ¶2821 and ¶2822. For deductions under the accrual method, see ¶2823.

Under Code Sec. 448(d)(5), a special accrual accounting rule for bad debts known as the Nonaccrual Experience (NAE) method of accounting is available for service entities in the fields of accounting, actuarial science, architecture, consulting, engineering, health, law or the performing arts whose average annual gross receipts meet the requirements under Code Sec. 448(c), (i.e., don't exceed *$27 million* for tax years beginning in 2022; *$29 million* for tax years beginning in 2023). Several safe harbor methods of calculating the NAE exist, but the method is only available if the taxpayer doesn't charge interest or penalties to customers who fail to timely pay. Reg § 1.448-3; Code Sec. 448(d)(5))[25]

¶ 2819 Requirement of accrual method income inclusion for tax purposes no later than for financial reporting—the AFS income inclusion rule.

Under the AFS income inclusion rule in Code Sec. 451(b), if a taxpayer uses an accrual method of accounting for federal income tax purposes and has an AFS (applicable financial statement), the all-events test (¶2818) for an item (or portion of an item) of gross income is met no later than when the item (or portion) is taken into account as AFS revenue.[26] In addition to not applying to taxpayers without an AFS, the rule doesn't apply to (1) mortgage service contracts and (2) items of gross income where the taxpayer uses a special method of accounting. But Code Sec. 451(b)) doesn't treat as special methods the rules inCode Sec. 1271 through Code Sec. 1288 (i.e., the original issue discount [OID] rules and other income timing and character rules for bonds and other debt instruments).[27]

Nevertheless, regs provide that subject to future additions of other items, the only original discount that must be taken into account no later than when the AFS inclusion requires is the OID resulting from specified fees with respect to lending transactions. Certain credit card fees are specifically identified as specified fees.[28]

Regs also provide an additional non-exclusive list of financial accounting treatments not subject to the AFS income inclusion rule; for example, where a taxpayer isn't required to mark a financial instrument to market for tax purposes but does so for financial purposes.[29]

An AFS is, in priority order, (1) a financial statement certified as being GAAP compliant and that is also (A) of a type filed with the SEC (10-K, etc.), (B) an audited financial statement used for certain substantial non-tax purposes, or (C) filed with other federal agencies for nontax purposes if the statements described in (A) and (B) don't exist, or (2) a financial statement prepared in accordance with international financial reporting standards (IFRS) and that is either (A) filed with an agency of a foreign government equivalent to the U.S. SEC and has reporting standards not less stringent, or (B) an audited financial statement used for certain substantial non-tax purposes, or (C) filed with any other regulatory governmental body specified by IRS, or (3) if statements described in (1) and (2) don't exist, financial statements filed with any regulatory or governmental body specified by IRS. (Code Sec. 451(b)(3); Reg § 1.451-3(a)(5)[30]

¶ 2820 Contingent versus non-contingent rights to income for accrual-method taxpayers.

Under Code Sec. 451, subject to the rules for applicable financial statements (¶2819) and advance payments ¶2821, where the right to income is contingent on a future event,

---

25. ¶G-2502 *et seq.*
26. ¶G-2472.2 *et seq.*
27. ¶G-2472.2A

28. ¶G-2472.2C *et seq.*
29. ¶G-2472.2B *et seq.*
30. ¶G-2472.2B

an accrual basis taxpayer doesn't have to recognize the income until that event occurs.[31]

Where litigation is involved and liability to the taxpayer is admitted, the income must be recognized if the taxpayer can accurately estimate the amount of recovery.[32] But if liability isn't admitted, the income accrues when the litigation is concluded or settlement reached, whichever is earlier.[33] An offer in compromise is income when the dispute is settled or the offer is unconditionally accepted.[34]

If an accrual method taxpayer overbills a customer due to clerical error and the customer discovers the error and disputes its liability in the following year, gross income accrues in the year of sale for the correct amount.[35] An accrual method taxpayer does not accrue income in the year of sale if, during that year, the customer disputes its liability because incorrect goods were shipped. However, income does accrue in the year of sale if excess quantities of goods are shipped and the customer agrees to pay for them.[36]

Where a dealer sells at a discount customers' notes to a finance company that keeps a portion of the sales price of the notes as security against possible customer defaults, a dealer that uses the accrual method must include in income when the notes are sold the full sales price (i.e., undiminished by the portion retained by the finance company (the "dealer reserve")). [37]

¶ 2821   Advance payments received by accrual-basis taxpayers; Code 451(c) one-year deferral election.

With some exceptions, an accrual method taxpayer must include advance payments in gross income when received or due, even if they haven't yet been earned.[38]

One exception to this rule is the elective one-year deferral under Code Sec. 451(c) for taxpayers with an AFS (¶2819).[39] (Advance payments, for this purpose, are defined in Code Sec. 451(c)(4)(A) and Reg § 1.451-8(c)(1)).[40]

Although Code Sec. 451(c), read literally, only grants the elective deferral to taxpayers with an AFS, under Reg § 1.451-8(d) taxpayers without an AFS may also elect the one-year deferral. Under that deferral, amounts earned after the year of receipt of the advance payment are recognized in the year after the receipt of the advance payment.[41]

Under the elective one-year deferral for taxpayers with an AFS, an accrual-basis taxpayer who receives an advance payment during the tax year may (1) include in gross income for the year of receipt the portion of the advance payment that must be included in gross income in that year under the AFS income inclusion rule (¶2819); and (2) include the remaining amount of the advance payment in gross income in the next following tax year. (Code Sec. 451(c)(1)(B); Reg § 1.451-8(c)(1).[42]

illustration: On July 1, Year 1, C, in the business of selling and repairing TV sets, receives an advance payment for a two-year contract under which C agrees to repair or replace certain parts in the customer's TV set if those parts fail to function properly. In its AFS, C recognizes 1/4 of the payment in revenues for Year 1, 1/2 of the payment in revenues for Year 2, and 1/4 of the payment in revenues for Year 3. C makes the deferral election. C must include 1/4 of the payment in gross income for Year 1 and the remaining 3/4 of the payment in gross income for Year 2. Reg § 1.451-8(c)(10)(iv), Ex 4

The deferral doesn't apply if the taxpayer ceases to exist during the tax year of receipt.

31. ¶s G-2484, G-2485
32. ¶G-2506
33. ¶G-2506
34. ¶s G-2506, G-2507
35. ¶G-2487
36. ¶G-2511.1

37. ¶G-2513
38. ¶G-2540 *et seq.*
39. ¶G-2548 *et seq.*
40. ¶G-2548.1 *et seq.*
41. ¶G-2548.2
42. ¶G-2548 *et seq.*

(Code Sec. 451(c)(3)) The election must be made at the time, in the form and manner, and with respect to the categories of advance payments, as IRS may provide, and is effective for the tax year for which it is first made and later year years unless IRS consents to its revocation. (Code Sec. 451(c)(2))[43] For taxpayers changing from another method of accounting for advance payments, the deferral election is a change in accounting method for which IRS provides an automatic (streamlined) consent-to-change procedure.[44] Excluded from eligibility for the election are payments listed in Code Sec. 451(c)(4)(B) and Reg § 1.451-8(a)(1)(ii), Ex 4 (e.g., rent, certain insurance premiums, payments for financial instruments, payments for service warranty contracts and guaranty contracts where a third party is the primary obligor and other payments received at least two (2) years before the tax year of the contractual delivery date for "specified goods"). [45]

Alternatively, an accrual-method taxpayer that doesn't make the election can continue to use a "full inclusion" method of accounting for advance payments, under which the taxpayer includes the full amount of advance payments in gross income in the tax year of receipt, regardless of whether the taxpayer recognizes the full amount of advance payments in revenues for that tax year for financial reporting purposes, and regardless of whether the taxpayer earns the full amount of advance payments in that tax year.[46]).

¶ 2822 Advance payments or security deposits under the accrual method; advance trade discounts.

A deposit that guarantees the customer's payment of amounts owed to the creditor isn't a deposit but an advance payment includible in income under Code Sec. 61 (unless, for an accrual method taxpayer deferrable, see ¶2821). But a deposit securing someone's property is a true security deposit and not an advance payment until used.[47]

In line with case authority that treats payments of advance trade discounts as being in the nature of the receipt of a security deposit (not of income),[48] IRS allows taxpayers to adopt an advance trade discount method of accounting in which advance trade discounts aren't recognized as income on receipt by accrual method taxpayers with inventories, but instead are taken into account in the amount and manner that the taxpayer accounts for the discount in its financial statements.[49]

¶ 2823 Timing of accrual of expense deductions.

In applying the accrual method of accounting as permitted under Code Sec. 461, expenses are deductible under the accrual method in the period in which: (1) all events have occurred that determine the fact of the liability; (2) the amount of the liability can be determined with reasonable accuracy; and (3) economic performance (see ¶2824) has occurred. Requirements (1) and (2) are referred to as the "all events" test. (Code Sec. 461(h)(1), Code Sec. 461(h)(4); Reg § 1.461-1(a)(2))

Under requirement (1), no accrual can be made where the liability has not actually been incurred, is contingent upon an uncertain future event, or is contested and not paid. Once the fact of the liability is established, accrual under this requirement is generally not postponed because of later-year events, later-year non-payment of later-year adjustment in the amount of the liability. The fact of a liability—generally, the earlier of the event fixing the liability (e.g., the required performance) or when payment is due—isn't established by executing a contract for services to be provided in the future. The "all events" test isn't satisfied, and a liability isn't established, by a statistical probability, however high, that

43. ¶G-2548
44. ¶G-2207.19C
45. ¶G-2548.1
46. ¶G-2548

47. ¶J-1435 *et seq.*
48. ¶G-2541
49. ¶G-2546.1, G-2546.2

the taxpayer will ultimately pay the expense; rather, the test requires that nothing further be needed to create a fixed liability. For bonuses that are payable to a group of employees that can't revert to the employer, IRS has ruled that the fact of the liability can be shown, even though the employer doesn't know the identity of any particular bonus recipient or the amount payable to that individual recipient until after the end of the tax year. A reasonable estimate of the liability must be accrued for the tax year in which it was incurred; if there is a difference between the estimate and the amount finally determined, the difference must be added to or deducted from income when the final determination is made.[50]

IRS held that a manufacturer's contractual liability to pay certain trade promotion rebates to customers became fixed and determinable under the all events test in the year that the underlying goods were purchased; the later filing of a rebate claim was a mere formality that didn't delay accrual of the liabilities.[1] But, IRS disagreed with (nonacquiesced in) a Third Circuit case holding that discounts against future purchases that were redeemable after the year were currently deductible as unconditionally fixed "near-certain" obligations; IRS reasoned that the future purchase by the customer was a condition precedent to liability for the discount.[2]

Where the accrual doesn't involve a current expense, but results in the creation of an asset having a useful life extending substantially beyond the end of the tax year, the deduction must be taken as depreciation, amortization, etc. (Reg § 1.461-1(a)(2))[3]

An accrual basis taxpayer may deduct a properly accrued expense, regardless of whether it has been paid.[4]

¶ 2824   Economic performance requirement for deductions under the accrual method.

Under Code Sec. 461, accrual basis taxpayers won't be considered to have met the all-events test for deductibility purposes (¶2823) until economic performance has occurred. (Code Sec. 461(h))[5] Economic performance occurs when the property or service to which the accrual relates is actually provided or used. (Code Sec. 461(h)(2))[6] If a liability arises out of the providing of services or property to the taxpayer by another person, economic performance occurs as the services or property are provided. (Code Sec. 461(h)(2)(A)(i), Reg § 1.461-4(d)(2)(i)) Thus, economic performance for a liability to pay compensation generally occurs as the employee renders services.[7] If a taxpayer's liability arises out of the use of property, economic performance occurs ratably over the period of time that the taxpayer is entitled to the use of the property. (Code Sec. 461(h)(2)(A)(iii), Reg § 1.461-4(d)(3)(i)) Payment constitutes economic performance for: (i) liabilities arising under a workers compensation act or out of any tort, breach of contract, or violation of law; (ii) rebates and refunds; (iii) awards, prizes and jackpots; (iv) insurance, warranty and service contracts; and (v) taxes (other than real property taxes for which a Code Sec. 461(c) election (¶1761) has been made and creditable foreign taxes); and (vi) any other liabilities where specific economic performance rules aren't provided in a reg, revenue ruling or revenue procedure. (Code Sec. 461(h)(2)(C), Code Sec. 461(h)(2)(D), Reg § 1.461-4(g)(1) through Reg § 1.461-4(g)(7))

Exceptions. A taxpayer is allowed to treat property or services as provided when they're paid for, but only if the taxpayer can reasonably expect the property or services to be provided by the other person within 3 ½ months after the payment is made. (Reg § 1.461-

---

50. ¶G-2620 *et seq.*
1. ¶G-2628.1
2. ¶G-2742
3. ¶G-2620

4. ¶G-2620
5. ¶G-2653
6. ¶G-2656
7. ¶G-2656

4(d)(6)(ii))[8]

In addition, certain "recurring" expenditures may be treated as incurred in the year the all-events test is otherwise met, even though economic performance doesn't occur until the following year. This applies if:

(1) economic performance occurs on or before the date taxpayer files a timely (including extensions) return for the tax year the expense is accrued or, if shorter, 8 ½ months after the close of that year; and

(2) the item is recurring and taxpayer consistently treats items of that kind as incurred in the tax year the all-events test (excluding the economic performance test) is met; and

(3) the item is either not a material item or its accrual in the year before economic performance results in a more proper match against income than if it were accrued in the year of economic performance. (Code Sec. 461(h)(3)(A); Reg § 1.461-5(b))[9]

Under a safe harbor, the recurring item exception is allowed for payroll taxes on compensation, including bonuses and vacation pay.[10] The recurring item exception doesn't apply to liabilities for interest, for items for which payment is economic performance (above), or for items incurred by a tax shelter. (Code Sec. 461(i)(1); Reg § 1.461-5(c))[11]

Taxpayers who are recipients of services under "Ratable Service Contracts" can treat economic performance as occurring ratably under a safe harbor and deduct the cost of regular and routine services as the services are provided under the contract. A Ratable Service Contract is one where: (a) the contract provides for similar services to be provided on a regular basis (such as daily, weekly, or monthly); (b) each occurrence of the service provides independent value, such that the benefits of receiving each occurrence of the service isn't dependent on the receipt of any previous or subsequent occurrence of the service, and; (c) the term of the contract doesn't exceed 12 months (without regard to contract renewal provisions). If a single contract includes services that satisfy these requirements and services (or other items) that do not, the services (or other items) that do not satisfy the requirements must be separately priced in the contract for the contract to qualify as a Ratable Service Contract.[12]

¶ 2825   Contested liabilities—accrual-method taxpayers.

In applying the accrual method of accounting as permitted under Code Sec. 461, an otherwise deductible expense (¶2823¶2824) isn't allowable, as long as the taxpayer denies and contests the liability, until the contest is resolved by agreement or final court decision.[13] However, a deduction is allowed in the year of transfer (payment) where:

(1) the taxpayer contests an asserted liability;

(2) the taxpayer transfers money or other property to satisfy the liability;

(3) the contest with respect to the asserted liability exists after the transfer; and

(4) but for the contest, a deduction would be allowed for the tax year of the transfer (or an earlier year). (Code Sec. 461(f)) The contest need not involve court proceedings.[14]

Except as provided under Code Sec. 468B (designated settlement funds), economic performance does not occur when a taxpayer transfers money or property to a trust, escrow account, or court to provide for the satisfaction of a contested workers compensation, tort, or a liability that arises out of a breach of contract or violation of law and requires a payment or a series of payments to another person unless the trust, escrow account, or

8. ¶G-2656
9. ¶G-2686
10. ¶K-4302.1
11. ¶G-2458
12. ¶G-2659.1
13. ¶G-2643, G-2644
14. ¶G-2645

court is the claimant, or the taxpayer's payment discharges the taxpayer's liability to the claimant. (Reg § 1.461-2(e)(2)(ii))[15]

¶ 2826   Accrual-basis taxpayer's payables to related cash-basis taxpayer.

Under Code Sec. 267, an accrual basis taxpayer can deduct expenses and interest owed to a related cash basis person only when payment is made and the amount involved is includible in the gross income of the cash basis payee. (Code Sec. 267(a)(2)) In other words, an accrual basis taxpayer is treated as on the cash method for purposes of deducting amounts owed to a related cash basis person.[16]

The rule applies in general to all deductible expenses if the timing of the deduction depends on the taxpayer's method of accounting or on electing to expense the item.[17] But it doesn't apply to defer the deduction of otherwise deductible original issue discount or below-market loan interest. (Reg § 1.267(a)-2T(b), Q&A-2) Nor does it apply to defer the deduction of otherwise deductible depreciation or amortization, except as to amounts owed to a related person for interest, rent, or for the performance or nonperformance of services (which amount the payor capitalized or treated as a deferred expense). (Reg § 1.267(a)-2T(b), Q&A-4)

¶ 2827   Changes of Accounting Methods. ■■■■■■■■■■

Under Code Sec. 446, taxpayers may change (¶2829) their accounting methods only with IRS consent and on IRS-imposed terms (e.g., specifications for required adjustments to income, see ¶2831 *et seq.*). When the streamlined automatic consent procedures (¶2834) don't apply, requirements for a change of accounting method generally include requesting a letter ruling (¶2828).

¶ 2828   IRS permission to change method of accounting—Form 3115—regular procedures and streamlined automatic procedures.

Generally, under Code Sec. 446, a taxpayer who has adopted an accounting method must continue to use it until IRS requires a change in method, or the taxpayer requests, and gets, IRS permission to change. (Code Sec. 446(e); Reg § 1.446-1(e)(2)) This is so even if the taxpayer has been using an incorrect method, or a method that doesn't clearly reflect income.[18] Generally, a taxpayer filing even only one return reflecting use of an accounting method has adopted the method and must obtain IRS consent to change the method. However, a taxpayer filing a return for only one year reflecting an impermissible method can simply amend the return to change to a permissible method.[19]

The regular procedures, and streamlined automatic procedures (¶2834), for obtaining consent, and the effects of consent, are set forth in Rev Proc 2015-13.[20] However, other guidance lists the changes for which automatic consent is available and provides for some of these changes, additional guidance as to how to apply for automatic consent and, the effect of the automatic consent (¶2834). For when to apply for consent, see ¶2830. Consent other than automatic consent generally must be obtained through the issuance of a letter ruling.[21]

Taxpayers that obtain consent to an accounting method change, including consent received under the automatic consent procedures, receive audit protection, subject to some limitations and exclusions, for years before the year of change.[22]

---

15. ¶G-2645
16. ¶G-2700 *et seq.*
17. ¶G-2701
18. ¶G-2201

19. ¶G-2201.2
20. ¶G-2175 *et seq.*
21. ¶G-2187.3
22. ¶G-2190 *et seq.*

Consent to a change generally requires that the taxpayer make Code Sec. 481(a) adjustments to the extent necessary to prevent the omission or duplication of tax items due to the change, see ¶2831.

¶ 2829 What is a change in accounting method? Change of the taxpayer's overall method of accounting or change in the treatment of a material item of income or expense.

Under Code Sec. 446, a change in accounting method is a change of the taxpayer's overall method of accounting or a change in the treatment of a material item of income or expense. Changes in overall methods of accounting include but aren't limited to changes:

. . . from the cash to accrual basis, or vice-versa;

. . . from the long-term contract method to the cash or accrual method, or vice-versa;

. . . from one basis of inventory valuation to another; and

. . . to or from a specialized basis, e.g., the crop basis. (Reg § 1.446-1(e)(2)(ii))[23]

A material item is any item that involves the proper time for the inclusion of the item in income or the taking of a deduction. It doesn't include corrections of mathematical or posting errors, or errors in computing tax liability. (Reg § 1.446-1(e)(2)(ii))[24]

Depreciation changes that aren't accounting method changes include the following: adjustments in the useful life of a depreciable or amortizable asset for which depreciation is determined under Code Sec. 167 (but not under Code Sec. 168 or other Code sections that assign a recovery period to an asset), changes in computing depreciation or amortization allowances in the tax year in which the use of an asset changes in the hands of the same taxpayer, changes in depreciation caused by certain revocations of elections and late elections, and changes in the placed-in service date. (Reg § 1.446-1(e)(2)(ii)[25]

However, most changes in computing depreciation (or amortization) are treated as accounting method changes. Depreciation changes, not excepted above, that are accounting method changes include the following: changes in depreciation or amortization methods, recovery periods or conventions, e.g., half-year to midquarter (but a switch from 200% or 150% declining balance to straight line is allowable without IRS's consent in the first tax year in which it produces a higher allowance), changes from regular MACRS to the alternative depreciation system, changes from treating property as nondepreciable or nonamortizable to depreciable or amortizable (or vice versa), and changes from depreciating or amortizing an item to deducting it as an expense (or vice versa). (Reg § 1.446-1(e)(2)(ii))[26]

¶ 2830 When to apply for a change in accounting method (including automatic consent accounting method change requests)—Form 3115.

Under Code Sec. 446, an application for change generally must be filed with IRS on the latest version of Form 3115 by the end of the tax year of the change. (Reg § 1.446-1(e)(3)(i))[27] However, automatic consent accounting method change requests (¶2834) may be made on a Form 3115 that's either:

(1) attached to the taxpayer's timely filed (including extensions) original return that implements the change for the change year; if required, a copy of the completed Form 3115 must be sent to the address specified in IRS guidance, no earlier than the first day of the change year, and no later than the date the taxpayer files the original Form 3115 with the return; or

---

23. ¶G-2103
24. ¶G-2104, G-2109
25. ¶G-2106.1

26. ¶G-2106.1
27. ¶G-2181.2

(2) filed under the automatic 6-month extension to file a Form 3115, within six months of the original return due date (excluding extensions) for the change year, if the taxpayer: (a) timely filed (including extensions) its return for the change year; (b) files an amended return within the 6-month extension period; (c) attaches the original Form 3115 to the amended return; (d) files a signed copy of the Form 3115 at the address specified in IRS guidance, no later than the date the original Form 3115 is filed with the amended return; (e) provides an additional copy to the appropriate IRS official specified in guidance; and (f) attaches a statement to the Form 3115—the original and any other copy required—that the Form 3115 is being filed under Reg § 301.9100-2(b).[28]

IRS stated that where the original tax return is timely filed without extension and *with* the original Form 3115 attached, the 6-month automatic extension applies to the copy.[29]

Extensions beyond the periods specified above won't be granted except in unusual and compelling circumstances.[30]

¶ 2831 Adjustments required on change of accounting method—Code Sec. 481(a) adjustments.

In any year in which taxpayer uses a different tax accounting method from the method used in the preceding year, Code Sec. 481(a) adjustments must be made to the extent necessary to prevent items of income or expense from being duplicated or entirely omitted. (Reg § 1.446-1(e)(3)(i))[31] The adjustments must take into account inventories, accounts receivable, accounts payable, and any other necessary items. (Reg § 1.481-1(b))[32] The adjustments can be positive (increasing taxable income), or negative (decreasing taxable income). (Reg § 1.481-1(c))[33]

IRS may determine that certain changes in accounting methods must be made without a Code Sec. 481(a) adjustment (for example, on a cut-off basis). Under the cut-off method, only the items arising on or after the beginning of the year of change (or other operative date) are accounted for under the accounting method for which consent is granted. Any items arising before the year of change (or other operative date) continue to be accounted for under the taxpayer's former accounting method.[34]

For when the adjustments are taken into account, see ¶2832.

¶ 2832 When and over what period Code Sec. 481(a) adjustments are taken into account—change of accounting method.

Regs state that Code Sec. 481(a) adjustments required as a result of an accounting method change (¶2831) must be taken into account in the year of change—i.e., the first tax year in which the taxpayer's method of accounting is different from that used in the previous tax year. (Reg § 1.481-1(a)(1)) This applies to both positive adjustments (increases in taxable income) and negative adjustments (decreases in taxable income). (Reg § 1.481-1(c))[35]

However, instead of taking the Code Sec. 481(a) adjustment into account in the year of change, a taxpayer may take the adjustment into account ratably over an appropriate period agreed to (in writing) by IRS or under a period specified in IRS guidance. (Code Sec. 481(c); Reg § 1.481-4(a), Reg § 1.481-4(b))[36]

Thus, IRS guidance provides that the Code Sec. 481(a) adjustment period for voluntary

---

28. ¶G-2181, G-2182
29. ¶G-2182
30. ¶G-2182
31. ¶G-2215
32. ¶G-2290 *et seq.*

33. ¶G-2291.2
34. ¶G-5216.2
35. ¶G-2290
36. ¶G-2291

accounting method changes, including automatic consent changes (¶2834), is one tax year for negative adjustments and four tax years for positive adjustments beginning with the year of change. However, taxpayers can elect to account for a positive adjustment in the year of change if it's less than $50,000. And in some situations positive adjustments must be taken into account in the year of change or are subject to acceleration (shortening) of the four year inclusion period.[37]

The Code in some cases prescribes the Code Sec. 481(a) adjustment period. For example the inclusion period is six years for Code Sec. 481 adjustments attributable to S elections revoked during the 2-year period beginning Dec. 22, 2017 if the corporation's stock is owned by the same shareholders and in the same proportion on the revocation date as it was on Dec. 22, 2017 (¶3375).Code Sec. 481(d))[38]

For a rule that might provide relief as to the amount of the adjustments, see ¶2833.

¶ 2833 Reduction in amount of some Code Sec. 481(a) adjustments—calculation using 3-year spread or allocation to specific years under old method.

Where Code Sec. 481(a) adjustments (¶2831) increase taxable income of the change-over year by more than $3,000, the taxpayer can compute the tax for that year using whichever of these two methods produces the lower tax:

(1) *3-year allocation*—The tax that would have resulted if ⅓ of the increase had been included in taxable income in each of the two preceding years and in the change-over year. (Code Sec. 481(b)(1); Reg § 1.481-2(a))

(2) *Allocation of specific years under new method of accounting*—Where the taxpayer establishes taxable income under the new method of accounting for one or more tax years consecutively preceding the year of change (in which the old method was actually used), the tax is reduced to the amount that would have been paid if:

(a) the tax for the preceding years was figured under the new method, and

(b) the then-remaining adjustments were allocated to the change-over year. (Code Sec. 481(b)(2); Reg § 1.481-2(b))[39]

¶ 2834 Automatic consent procedures for certain accounting method changes— Form 3115.

The streamlined automatic procedures for obtaining the consent to an accounting method change that is generally required under Code Sec. 446, and the effects of that consent, are set forth in Rev Proc 2015-13.[40] However, it is Rev Proc 2022-14 and any later modifications (e.g., Rev Proc 2022-23) that list the many changes for which automatic consent procedures are available. Rev Proc 2022-14 and any later modifications also provide rules for each change that add to, and sometimes modify, the guidance provided by Rev Proc 2015-13.[41]

There are no user fees for automatic-consent accounting method change requests.[42]

For the general deadlines for applying for automatic consent, which can modified for specific changes as discussed above, see ¶2830.

For the general rules for Code Sec. 481(a) adjustments to income, which can be modified for specific changes as discussed above, see ¶2831 *et seq.*

---

37. ¶G-2185 *et seq.*
38. ¶D-1913
39. ¶G-2296
40. ¶G-2175 *et seq.*
41. ¶G-2203.1
42. ¶G-2183.1

¶ 2835   **Reserves for Estimated Expenses and Contingent Liabilities.** ▬▬▬

Taxpayers often maintain accounting reserves for various future liabilities. Generally, Code Sec. 451 bars exclusions from income and Code Sec. 461 prohibits deductions for additions to these reserves, even if they are required by state law or contract.

But income exclusions or deductions for additions to reserves for estimated expenses or contingent liabilities are allowed when expressly authorized by the Code (e.g., depreciation, nuclear decommissioning costs, designated settlement funds).[43] There is allowed a reserve for trading stamps or premium coupons (Reg § 1.451-4(a)) (but hybrid coupons that can either be redeemed for products or used for discounts on product purchases don't qualify as premium coupons)[44] or for container deposits. However, the use of this method for container deposits applies only where the containers are leased or loaned, *not* sold. Thus, container deposits received on the sales of beverages are includible in income at sale and deductible when later refunded.[45]

¶ 2836   **Long-Term Contracts.** ▬▬▬

Under Code Sec. 460, taxpayers must account for long-term contracts (except for certain home and other real property construction contracts, see ¶2837) under the percentage-of-completion method (¶2839), subject to an election to use a modified percentage-of-completion method ("10% method," ¶2840).[46]

A long-term contract is any contract for the manufacture, building, installation, or construction of property, if not completed in the tax year in which entered into. (Code Sec. 460(f)(1); Reg § 1.460-1(b)(1)) Whether the taxpayer reasonably expected that the contract would be completed within the tax year is not relevant.[47] But a manufacturing contract isn't long-term unless it involves manufacture of a unique item (of a type not normally included in inventory), or an item that normally requires more than 12 months to complete. (Code Sec. 460(f)(2))[48]

Rules are provided for allocating costs to a long-term contract (¶2838) and for mid-contract changes in taxpayer (¶2843). And subject to exceptions, interest may have to be paid to or by the taxpayer to account for the difference between estimated and actual contract costs in applying the look-back method (¶2841, ¶2842). For how to account for long-term contracts for alternative minimum tax purposes, see ¶3206.

¶ 2837   **Completed contract method for home and real property construction contracts.**

Under Code Sec. 460, the completed contract method (CCM) may be used instead of the percentage-of-completion method (described at ¶2839) for home construction contracts (defined in Code Sec. 460(e)(5)(A) and Reg § 1.460-6(b)(2)[49]). The CCM is permitted for other real property construction contracts if (a) the taxpayer (other than a tax shelter) estimates at contract inception that it will be completed within two years, and (b) under the three-year gross receipts test described in more detail at ¶2814, the taxpayer's average annual gross receipts don't exceed an annual limit, which is *$27 million* for a testing year beginning in 2022 and *$29 million* for a testing year beginning in 2023. (Code Sec. 460(e); Reg § 1.460-1(a)(2), Reg § 1.460-3(b))[50] Under the completed contract method, a taxpayer

---

43. ¶s G-2733, G-2737
44. ¶G-2742
45. ¶G-2740
46. ¶s G-3100, G-3229

47. ¶G-3103
48. ¶G-3102, G-3106
49. ¶G-3211
50. ¶G-3209

doesn't report income until a contract is complete (Reg § 1.460-4(d)), even though payments are received in years before completion.[1]

¶ 2838 Allocation of costs to long-term contracts.

Under Code Sec. 460, all costs that directly benefit, or are incurred by reason of, a long-term contract (including research and experimental costs) must be allocated to the contract in the same manner as costs were allocated to extended-period long-term contracts entered into before Mar. 1, '86, under (former) Code Sec. 451, except that past service pension costs must be allocated to the contract. Also, in the case of a cost-plus contract or a federal long-term contract or subcontract, any other costs (e.g., general and administrative expenses) must be allocated to the contract if identified by the taxpayer (or a related person) as being attributable to it under the contract, or under federal, state, or local law or regulation. (Code Sec. 460(c)(1), Code Sec. 460(c)(2))[2] Interest costs are allocated to long-term contracts in a way that's similar to the way interest costs are allocated under the uniform capitalization rules (Code Sec. 263A(f)) (¶1639) that apply to property produced by a taxpayer. (Code Sec. 460(c)(3); Reg § 1.460-5(b)(2)(v))[3]

The allocation rules don't apply to any expenses for unsuccessful bids and proposals; marketing, selling, and advertising expenses; or independent research and development (IR&D) expenses. IR&D expenses don't include expenses directly attributable to a long-term contract in existence when the expenses are incurred, or expenses under an agreement to perform research and development. (Code Sec. 460(c)(4), Code Sec. 460(c)(5))[4] Costs of a guaranty, warranty, or maintenance agreement aren't treated as part of a long-term contract. (Reg § 1.460-1(d)(2))

Alternatively, a taxpayer may elect to use the simplified cost-to-cost allocation method (Code Sec. 460(b)(3)(A)) under which a contract's completion factor is determined based upon only direct material costs; direct labor costs; and depreciation, amortization, and cost recovery allowances on equipment and facilities directly used to manufacture or construct the subject matter of the contract. Material or labor costs associated with a subcontractor's activities must be allocated to the contract. Elect the simplified cost-to-cost method for all long-term contracts entered into during the tax year by using it on the original federal income tax return for the election year. The election isn't available if the percentage-of-completion method (¶2839) is not used for all long-term contracts or if the 10% method (¶2840) is used. (Reg § 1.460-5(c)) A taxpayer electing this method must use it to apply the look-back method (¶2841) and to determine alternative minimum taxable income, see ¶3210.[5]

Home construction and real property construction contracts (¶2837) are not required to use the above cost allocation rules other than the interest allocation rules. They can use any permissible method. (Code Sec. 460(e))[6]

¶ 2839 Percentage-of-completion method of accounting for long-term contracts.

Under this method (the PCM) as prescribed by Code Sec. 460, a long-term contract's percentage of completion must be determined by comparing costs allocated to the contract and incurred before the close of the tax year, with estimated total contract costs. (Code Sec. 460(b)(1)(A)) For qualified property described in Code Sec. 168(k)(2) (¶1930) with a recovery period of 7 years or less that's placed in service before 2027 (2028 for long production period property), bonus depreciation (¶1929) isn't taken into account in applying the PCM. (Code Sec. 460(c)(6)) Events that occur after the end of the tax year that are

---

1. ¶G-3245
2. ¶G-3143 *et seq.*
3. ¶G-3150

4. ¶G-3154 *et seq.*
5. ¶G-3138
6. ¶G-3209 *et seq.*

reasonably subject to estimate as of the last day of the tax year are taken into account in applying the PCM.[7]

Gross income recognized in a particular year under the PCM equals total revenue expected from the contract times the cumulative percentage of the contract completed as of the end of the tax year, less the total cumulative amount of contract revenue required to be included in gross income in all preceding tax years. (This can result in a deductible loss for a year if total estimated contract costs increase.) (Reg § 1.460-4(b)(2))[8]

If the total contract price has not been included in gross income by the completion year, the taxpayer must include the remaining portion of the total contract price in gross income for the following tax year. (Code Sec. 460(b)(1); Reg § 1.460-4(b)(3))

When the contract is completed (or, for amounts received or accrued after completion, when those amounts are received or accrued), the taxpayer must either pay (or be entitled to receive) interest computed under the look-back method discussed at ¶2841. (Code Sec. 460(b)(1)(B))[9]

¶ 2840   Modified percentage-of-completion method of accounting for long-term contracts—"the 10% method."

Under Code Sec. 460, for purposes of the percentage-of-completion method (¶2839), a taxpayer may elect not to recognize income under the contract and not to take into account any costs allocable to the long-term contract for any tax year if, as of the end of the tax year, less than 10% of the estimated total contract costs have been incurred. (Code Sec. 460(b)(5)) Elect by using the 10% method for all long-term contracts entered into during the tax year on the original federal income tax return for the election year. If elected, the method is used to apply the look-back method (¶2841) and to determine alternative minimum taxable income. It can't be used if the simplified cost-to-cost method (¶2838) is used. (Reg § 1.460-4(b)(6)(ii))[10]

¶ 2841   Look-back method for interest on tax in year long-term contract is completed—Form 8697.

Under Code Sec. 460, in the tax year a long-term contract (with exceptions, below) is completed, the taxpayer must compare the amount of taxes paid in previous years under the percentage method with the tax that would have been owed if actual, rather than anticipated, costs and contract price had been used to compute gross income. Interest at the "adjusted overpayment rate" (overpayment rate (¶4837) for the calendar quarter in which the "interest accrual period" begins) for any "interest accrual period" (period beginning the day after the return due date, without extensions, and ending on the return due date of the following tax year) is owed by or payable to the taxpayer (use Form 8697) if there is, respectively, an underpayment or overpayment for any tax year. (Code Sec. 460(b)(2), Code Sec. 460(b)(7))[11] For pass-through entities, see ¶2842.

Taxpayers may elect (for all contracts completed in the election year and all future years, revocable only with IRS consent) not to apply the look-back method if, at the close of each contract year before the tax year in which the look-back method would otherwise have to be applied, the cumulative taxable income (or loss) under the contract (using estimated contract price and costs) is within 10% of the cumulative look-back income or loss under the contract. (Code Sec. 460(b)(6)) Elect by attaching a statement to a timely filed (including extensions) original return for the election year. (Reg § 1.460-6(j))[12]

---

7. ¶G-3143
8. ¶G-3126 *et seq.*
9. ¶G-3156

10. ¶G-3229 *et seq.*
11. ¶G-3161 *et seq.*
12. ¶G-3203.1

The look-back method doesn't apply to any contract whose gross price (at completion) doesn't exceed the lesser of $1 million or 1% of taxpayer's average annual gross receipts for the three tax years preceding the tax year the contract was completed if the contract is completed within two years of its start date. (Code Sec. 460(b)(3)(B))[13] Nor does it apply to home construction contracts or others described at ¶2837. (Reg § 1.460-6(b)(2))[14]

¶ 2842 Simplified look-back marginal-impact method for pass-through entities— Form 8697—long-term contracts.

Under Code Sec. 460, for partnerships, S corporations and trusts (where 50% or more of the entity isn't held directly or indirectly by five or fewer persons), a simplified look-back marginal-impact method is applied at the entity level if substantially all the income from the contract is U.S.-source. The amount of taxes treated as overpaid or underpaid under a contract in any year is found by multiplying the amount of contract income over- or under-reported for the year by the top marginal tax rate applicable for the year. (Code Sec. 460(b)(4); Reg § 1.460-6(d)(1))[15] Individuals, C corporations and owners of closely-held pass-through entities may elect to use this method. Also, widely-held pass-through entities may elect to use the method for foreign contracts. (Reg § 1.460-6(d)(4))[16]

¶ 2843 Long-term contract following mid-contract change in taxpayer—"constructive completion transaction" or "step-in-the-shoes transaction."

Under Code Sec. 460, the tax treatment following a mid-contract change in taxpayer of a long-term contract depends on whether the change is a "constructive completion transaction" or a "step-in-the-shoes transaction." In a constructive completion transaction, the old taxpayer is treated as completing the contract and the new taxpayer as entering into a new contract on the transaction date. This approach applies to any transaction not subject to the step-in-the-shoes approach. (Reg § 1.460-4(k)(2)) In general, with a step-in-the-shoes transaction, the old taxpayer's obligation to account for the contract terminates on the transaction date and is assumed by the new taxpayer. The new taxpayer assumes the old taxpayer's methods of accounting for the contract, with both the contract price and allocable contract costs based on amounts taken into account by both parties. Special rules apply to the treatment of certain partnership transactions. (Reg § 1.460-4(k), Reg § 1.460-6(g))[17]

¶ 2844 Reconstruction of Income by IRS.

Under Code Sec. 446, where taxpayer's records are inadequate, IRS can reconstruct taxpayer's income by whatever method will in its opinion clearly reflect the income.[18]

The methods most often used are:

The net worth method. Here, IRS attempts to establish an opening net worth or total value of the taxpayer's assets at the beginning of a given year. It then proves increases in the taxpayer's net worth for each later year during the period under examination and calculates the difference between the adjusted net values of the taxpayer's assets at the beginning and end of each of the years involved. The taxpayer's nondeductible expenditures, including living expenses, are added to these increases and nontaxable receipts are deducted. If the resulting figure for any year is greater than the taxable income reported by the taxpayer for that year, IRS treats the excess as unreported taxable income.[19]

---

13. ¶G-3158
14. ¶G-3159
15. ¶G-3195 *et seq.*
16. ¶G-3201

17. ¶G-3246
18. ¶G-2903
19. ¶G-2912

Bank deposit method. The bank deposit method assumes that all deposits represent income unless the taxpayer can show otherwise.[20]

Percentage markup method. IRS determines taxpayer's net income by applying certain percentages, e.g., gross profit to sales, or net income to gross income, or net income to sales, derived from other taxpayers in the same kind of business.[21]

¶ 2845   Reallocations of Income by IRS.

IRS is authorized, under Code Sec. 482, to distribute, apportion, or allocate gross income, deductions, credits or allowances among two or more organizations, trades, or businesses owned or controlled by the same interests in order to prevent tax evasion or to reflect the true taxable income of any of those entities. A similar rule also allows IRS to reallocate tax items (under Code Sec. 269A) for a personal service corporation.

IRS can reallocate income under Code Sec. 482 regardless of the entities' *motives* for shifting it, and can reallocate even if the shift was unintentional. (Reg § 1.482-1(c))[22]

If an allocation is made for a transaction between controlled taxpayers, IRS will also take into account the effect of any other non-arm's length transaction between the same controlled taxpayers in the same tax year which will result in a setoff against the original allocation. (Reg § 1.482-1(g)(4)(i)) Procedures have been issued for notifying IRS of a proposed setoff.[23]

Regs on the tax treatment of services transactions ensures that valuable intangibles cannot be transferred outside the U.S. for less than arm's length consideration, and update guidance on the transfer pricing methods to determine the arm's-length price in services transactions. (Reg § 1.482-9)[24]

Under advance pricing agreements (APAs) with IRS, taxpayers can prospectively determine and apply transfer pricing methodologies to international transactions by related foreign or domestic taxpayers (and resolve other related issues).[25]

¶ 2846   Reallocation of personal service corporation (PSC) income to prevent tax avoidance or evasion or clearly reflect income.

Under Code Sec. 269A, to prevent tax avoidance or evasion or to clearly reflect income, IRS may allocate all income, deductions, credits, exclusions and other allowances between a PSC and its employee-owner who owns more than 10% of the PSC stock (on any day in the tax year) if: substantially all of its services are performed by or for one other corporation, partnership, or entity (including as one entity related parties (Code Sec. 269A(b)(3))) and are availed of principally to avoid federal income tax by securing for any employee-owner significant tax benefits that he or she wouldn't otherwise have. (Code Sec. 269A(a)) A PSC is a corporation whose principal activity is the performance of personal services, substantially all of which are performed by employee-owners. (Code Sec. 269A(b)(1)) The Code Sec. 318 attribution rules apply for purposes of the 10% test, except that for purposes of applying the Code Sec. 318(a)(2)(C) rules, attribution is triggered by 5% rather than 50% stock ownership. (Code Sec. 269A(b)(2))[26]

¶ 2847   Deduction for Previously Reported Income Repayments.

Taxpayers who must repay amounts previously reported as income may deduct the repayments in the year they are made. But for tax years beginning before 2027,

---

20. ¶G-2941
21. ¶G-2948
22. ¶G-4018
23. ¶G-4108

24. ¶G-4500 *et seq.*; ¶G-4500 *et seq.*
25. ¶G-4740 *et seq.*
26. ¶G-4761 *et seq.*

this deduction is barred by a disallowance, under Code Sec. 67, of miscellaneous itemized deductions (¶2162).[27] But under Code Sec. 1341 (which isn't a provision affected by the ban on miscellaneous itemized deductions), if the amount repaid exceeds $3,000, the taxpayer may recover the tax paid on that amount in the year the income was reported if that provides a greater tax benefit (¶2848).

For a cash basis taxpayer, the year of the deduction, and accordingly the year the special computation might be available, is the year the previously reported income was repaid. If the taxpayer reported the income as constructively received, the year of deduction is the year the taxpayer's claim to the income had to be relinquished. (Reg § 1.1341-1(e))[28]

For an accrual basis taxpayer, the deduction year is the year liability for repayment becomes fixed. If the taxpayer received the income reported, the deduction year is the year it's finally established the taxpayer had no unrestricted right to it. (Reg § 1.1341-1(e))[29]

¶ 2848 Repayments that exceed $3,000—deduction for previously reported income repaymenents.

Under Code Sec. 1341, if the amount of the deduction allowed for a tax year (¶2847) with respect to an item reported as income in an earlier tax year is more than $3,000, and:

. . . that item was included in gross income in the earlier year because it appeared that the taxpayer then had an unrestricted right to it, and

. . . the deduction is allowed (under another Code provision independent of Code Sec. 1341[30]) because it was shown after the close of the earlier year that taxpayer did *not* have an unrestricted right to all or part of that item,

then the tax for the year in which the deduction is allowed is the lesser of:

(1) the tax for that year computed with the deduction, or

(2) the tax for that year computed *without the deduction,* minus the decrease in tax for the earlier year resulting solely from excluding the deductible repayment. (Code Sec. 1341(a))

This relief for repayments exceeding $3,000 doesn't apply:

. . . where repayment is required because of a liability that arose later, as distinguished from absence of an unrestricted right to the income previously reported;[31]

. . . where an item was originally included in gross income by reason of the sale or other disposition of stock-in-trade, or other property includible in inventory if on hand at the close of the earlier tax year, or property held primarily for sale to customers in the ordinary course of business—i.e., it doesn't apply to sales returns and allowances and similar items (Code Sec. 1341(b)(2); Reg § 1.1341-1(f));

. . . to deductions attributable to bad debts or to legal fees and other expenses incurred in contesting the repayment of income previously included. (Reg § 1.1341-1(g), Reg § 1.1341-1(h))[32]

¶ 2849 Inventories. ▬▬▬▬▬▬▬▬▬

Under Code Sec. 471, where producing, buying or selling merchandise is an income-producing factor, inventories are needed to determine the correct cost of goods sold, subject to a major exception for small businesses.

Inventories serve to allocate the expense of buying merchandise to the year in which

---

27. ¶G-3001
28. ¶G-3027
29. ¶G-3028

30. ¶G-3018
31. ¶G-3018.1
32. ¶s G-3032, G-3034, G-3035

that merchandise is sold, (consistent with the financial accounting matching principle).[33] Inventories must be used whenever IRS finds their use is needed to clearly determine a taxpayer's income. (Code Sec. 471) Generally, this is the case where the "production, purchase or sale of merchandise" is an income-producing factor. (Reg § 1.471-1)[34] A taxpayer that must use inventories also must use the accrual method of accounting for its purchases and sales. (Reg § 1.446-1(c)(2)(i))[35] A taxpayer (other than a tax shelter prohibited from using the cash method) is exempted from the inventory use requirement if (1) under the three-year gross receipts test described in more detail at ¶2814, the taxpayer's average annual gross receipts don't exceed an annual limit, which is *$27 million* for a testing year beginning in 2022 (*$29 million* for a testing year beginning in 2023) and (2) the taxpayer's method of accounting either (a) treats inventory as non-incidental materials and supplies, or (b) conforms to the taxpayer's financial accounting treatment of inventories. (Code Sec. 471(c))[36] There is considerable judicial and IRS guidance as to when maintaining inventories is required in specific industries.[37]

caution: Under Code Sec. 263A, the uniform inventory inclusion and capitalization rules (UNICAP), (¶1639 *et seq.*), certain direct and indirect costs are either included in inventory or capitalized.

¶ 2850 What goods are included in inventory? Merchandise held for sale in the ordinary course of business.

Under Code Sec. 471, inventories include all merchandise that is held for sale in the ordinary course of business or that is to become a physical part of merchandise intended for sale. Inventories generally cover finished or partly finished goods as well as raw materials and supplies acquired for sale or that will physically become a part of merchandise intended for sale. For items to be included in inventory, taxpayer must have title. A seller's inventory includes goods the seller has contracted to sell but not yet segregated and applied to the contract, while a buyer's inventory includes merchandise in transit to the buyer or that for other reasons hasn't been reduced to possession but to which the buyer has title A buyer does *not* include in inventory goods ordered for delivery where title hasn't been transferred. (Reg § 1.471-1)

Merchandise shipped on approval or sold on sample is kept in the seller's inventory until its acceptance. Consigned goods or goods in the hands of others for processing (e.g., dyeing) and returnable in kind are kept in the consignor's inventory.[38]

Containers that are to be *sold* with the merchandise they contain should be included in the seller's inventory, regardless of whether they are returnable. If the containers are merely leased or loaned with a deposit received to guarantee their return, they aren't included in inventory since they aren't part of the merchandise held for sale.[39] For ways containers not part of the sold merchandise can or must be treated, see[40] concerning supplies.

¶ 2851 Valuing inventory—cost or lower of cost or market.

Under Code Sec. 471, the two most commonly recognized bases of valuing inventories are: (1) cost, and (2) the lower of cost or market. (Reg § 1.471-2(c))[41] Farmers may use other valuation methods, see ¶4513 *et seq.* For inventories of dealers in securities, see ¶2864. Consistency from year to year in whatever inventory procedure is adopted is of first

---

33. ¶G-5000 *et seq.*
34. ¶G-5001
35. ¶G-2089
36. ¶G-5004
37. ¶G-5001A

38. ¶G-5009
39. ¶G-5010
40. ¶G-2453
41. ¶G-5101

importance. (Reg § 1.471-2(b))[42]

¶ 2852 Valuation of unsalable, slow-moving and traded-in goods—inventories.

Under Code Sec. 471, any goods in inventory that are unsalable at normal prices or in the normal way because of damage, imperfections, style changes, etc., can at the taxpayer's option be written down—that is, valued at selling prices less direct costs of disposition—whether the cost or the lower of cost or market method is used. If the goods consist of raw materials or partly finished goods held for use or consumption, they must be valued upon a reasonable basis, considering the usability and condition of the goods, but in no case at less than scrap value. (Reg § 1.471-2(c))[43] Selling price means the actual price at which goods are offered for sale during a period ending not later than 30 days after the date of inventory. (Reg § 1.472-2(c))[44] Normal but slow-moving inventory (i.e., goods in excess of current demand) can't be written down based on arbitrary cut-off time periods.[45]

¶ 2853 Prohibited valuation methods and practices—inventories.

Under Code Sec. 471, the following aren't permitted in valuing inventory:

(1) Deducting from inventory a reserve for price changes or an estimated depreciation in the value of inventory (but for permissible estimates of inventory shrinkage, see ¶2854).

(2) Valuing work in process, or other parts of the inventory, at a nominal price or at less than its proper value.

(3) Omitting portions of the stock on hand.

(4) Using a constant price or nominal value for so-called normal quantity of material or goods in stock.

(5) Segregating indirect production costs into fixed and variable classifications and allocating only the variable costs to the cost of goods produced while treating fixed costs as currently deductible (the "direct cost" method).

(6) Treating all or substantially all indirect production costs (whether classified as fixed or variable) as currently deductible (the "prime cost" method). (Reg § 1.471-2(f))[46]

¶ 2854 Estimates of inventory shrinkage; retail safe harbor method—inventories.

Under Code Sec. 471, a method of determining inventories doesn't fail to clearly reflect income solely because it uses estimates of inventory shrinkage that are confirmed by a physical count only after the last day of the tax year if the taxpayer: (1) normally does a physical count at each location on a regular and consistent basis, and (2) makes proper adjustments to inventories and to its estimating methods if estimates are greater or less than actual shrinkage. (Code Sec. 471(b)) Taxpayers can adopt at any time a method of estimating shrinkage if it had not used one before if the method clearly reflects income. Also, there is a retail safe harbor method of estimating inventory shrinkage (using a historical ratio of shrinkage-to-sales to estimate the shrinkage between the last physical inventory and the end of the tax year). Taxpayers using a different estimation method can change to the safe harbor under the automatic consent procedure for some accounting method changes (¶2834).[47]

---

42. ¶G-5002
43. ¶G-5159
44. ¶G-5161

45. ¶G-5164
46. ¶G-5124
47. ¶G-5120 *et seq.*

¶ 2855   What is inventory cost? Invoice price, trade discounts, cash discounts.

Under Code Sec. 471, the cost of goods on hand at the start of an accounting period is their inventory value (Reg § 1.471-3(a)), that is, the amount at which they were valued in the closing inventory of the period before.[48]

The cost of the goods purchased ordinarily is the invoice price reduced by trade or other discounts. Strictly cash discounts approximating a fair interest rate may be deducted at the option of the taxpayer if the method is consistently followed. (Reg § 1.471-3(b))[49] To this net invoice price should be added transportation or other necessary charges incurred in acquiring possession of the goods. (Reg § 1.471-3(b))[50]

The costs of goods produced by the taxpayer include, in addition to the opening inventory, costs of raw materials and supplies entering into or consumed in manufacture, regular and overtime direct labor costs, and indirect costs (which include an appropriate portion of management expenses, but not costs of selling or return on capital.(Reg § 1.471-3(c))[1]

For the uniform capitalization rules for including costs in inventory, see ¶1639 *et seq.*

¶ 2856   Valuing inventory using the lower of cost or market method.

Under this method of valuing inventory under Code Sec. 471, market value on the inventory date is compared with the cost of each item. The lower of the two is the inventory value of the item. (Reg § 1.471-4(c)) Total inventory is the aggregate of the inventory values so computed for each item in the inventory. It is *not* the lower of the total cost or total market value of all items. (Reg § 1.471-4(a))[2]

¶ 2857   Market value defined for inventory valuation purposes.

For purposes of the inventory valuation rules under Code Sec. 471, market value normally means the current bid price prevailing at the inventory date for the particular merchandise in the volume usually purchased by the taxpayer. Market price is applied to: (1) goods purchased and on hand, and (2) the basic elements of cost (materials, labor and overhead) of goods in process of manufacture and of finished goods on hand. (Reg § 1.471-4(a))[3]

Market price may not be applied to goods on hand or in process if the merchandise is covered by a firm sales contract at fixed prices (i.e., not legally subject to cancellation by either buyer or seller). If, under the contract, the taxpayer is protected against actual loss, the goods must be inventoried at cost with no deduction for inventory decline. (Reg § 1.471-4(a)) Moreover, goods covered by firm sales contracts at the end of the year must be valued at cost even though the contracts are cancelled after the close of the year at the customer's request.[4] If the contract gives the seller an almost certain loss, IRS says the seller isn't allowed to write the inventory down but must value it at cost, thus taking the loss when actually realized (Reg § 1.471-4(a)), but some courts disagree.[5]

A taxpayer may write down inventory below market if, in the regular course of business, he or she has offered the merchandise for sale at below-market prices. (Reg § 1.471-4(b))

If no market exists in the taxpayer's usual volume, or if quotations are nominal because of an inactive market, the taxpayer must use whatever evidence of a fair market price at

---

48. ¶G-5102
49. ¶G-5107, G-5108
50. ¶G-5103, G-5110
1. ¶G-5402

2. ¶G-5150
3. ¶G-5151
4. ¶G-5154 *et seq.*
5. ¶G-5154 *et seq.*

the date or dates nearest his or her inventory date may be available. (Reg § 1.471-4(b))[6]

¶ 2858 Inventory cost identification methods—specific identification method, "first-in first-out" (FIFO) and "last-in first-out" (LIFO) methods.

Under the specific identification method of identifying inventory for purposes of Code Sec. 471, goods are matched with their invoices (less appropriate discounts) to find the cost of each item. (Reg § 1.471-2(d))[7]

Where it isn't possible or practicable to identify each item of inventory with its cost, an assumption must be made to determine which items were sold and which remain in inventory. Although only two methods of costing intermingled merchandise are specifically approved (the "first-in first-out" (FIFO) and the "last-in first-out" (LIFO) methods), any method that comes within the best accounting practice of the particular business and clearly reflects income is acceptable. Two permissible cost identification methods are averaging the cost of each type or grade of goods in the inventory (¶2860) and mainly relying on the taxpayer's accounting records to arrive at the correct inventory value (¶2862). The base stock method (the assumption that a certain portion of inventory will be maintained from year to year and therefore need not be revalued) isn't permitted.[8]

The FIFO method can be used where the costs of goods are so intermingled they cannot be identified with specific invoices. Under the FIFO method, the goods sold are the goods in inventory that have been purchased or acquired the earliest. (Reg § 1.471-2(d))[9]

Under the LIFO method, to the extent permitted by Code Sec. 472, the newest, most recently purchased, merchandise is treated as sold first. (Code Sec. 472(b)(1))[10] LIFO may generally be used only where inventory is valued at cost. (Reg § 1.472-2(b))[11] When there is a change to LIFO, any difference in value resulting from the required change to cost valuation is taken into account ratably over a 3-year period (beginning with the year of the election to LIFO). (Code Sec. 472(d))[12]

The inventory price index computation (IPIC) method, under which inventory price indexes are computed with reference to consumer or producer price indexes published by the U.S. Bureau of Labor Statistics (BLS) (Code Sec. 472(f); Reg § 1.472-8(e)(3)), is intended to simplify the use of the dollar-value LIFO method (¶2860).[13]

observation: The most tax-favorable inventory valuation method is the LIFO method. Using LIFO results in the lowest tax compared to other inventory valuation methods because the newer, more expensive, items in inventory are used to calculate cost of goods sold, resulting in lower net income.

In order to use LIFO for tax purposes, the enterprise must also use LIFO in its reports to partners, stockholders, etc., and for credit purposes. (Code Sec. 472(c))[14]

Qualifying LIFO or FIFO heavy equipment dealers, like auto dealers, can use replacement cost to determine heavy parts inventory costs under safe harbor rules.[15]

¶ 2859 Electing last-in first-out (LIFO)—Form 970—inventories.

To elect the LIFO method, where permitted under Code Sec. 472, the taxpayer must file Form 970 (or other acceptable statement) with the return for the tax year as of the close of which LIFO is first to be used (Reg § 1.472-3)[16] or re-elected in the fifth or later tax year

---

6. ¶G-5157
7. ¶s G-5121, G-5265
8. ¶G-5125 *et seq.*
9. ¶G-5121
10. ¶G-5200
11. ¶G-5212

12. ¶G-5208
13. ¶G-5253
14. ¶G-5307
15. ¶G-5248.4
16. ¶G-5202

after changing from LIFO (otherwise IRS permission is needed for the change, see ¶2828 *et seq.*). Once made, the election applies to all later years unless IRS grants permission to change. (Reg § 1.472-5)[17] Automatic consent procedures (¶2834) apply to adoption of certain specialized LIFO methods and to changes from LIFO.

¶ 2860 Dollar-value last-in first-out (LIFO) and simplified dollar-value LIFO—inventories.

Under the LIFO method (if permitted under Code Sec. 472), a taxpayer dealing in a large variety of products may elect to value inventory by dollar value rather than natural units. To use the dollar value method, the taxpayer must break up the inventory into natural-business-unit pools or multiple pools. (Reg § 1.472-8)[18] The electing taxpayer can further elect to compute an inventory price index in accordance with the IPIC method (Reg § 1.472-8(e)(3)(ii)), see ¶2858.

An eligible small business can elect a simplified dollar-value method of pricing inventories under LIFO, using average cost of each grade of goods. (Code Sec. 474(a)) An eligible small business is one whose average annual gross receipts (determined under Code Sec. 448(c)(3), see ¶2814, and Code Sec. 474(d)(1)) don't exceed $5 million for the 3-tax-year period ending immediately before the tax year. (Code Sec. 474(c))[19]

¶ 2861 Retailers' inventory; ending inventory and price change adjustments.

Under Code Sec. 471, retailers can convert the retail selling price of ending inventory to an approximation of cost (retail cost method) or an approximation of lower of cost or market (retail LCM method) (instead of valuing inventory at cost or lower of cost or market). (Reg § 1.471-8(a))[20] Price change adjustments are determined by reference generally to U.S. Bureau of Labor Statistics price indexes. (Reg § 1.472-1(k))[21]

¶ 2862 Book (perpetual) inventory method.

Under Code Sec. 471, inventory accounts are charged with the actual cost of goods purchased or produced, and credited with the cost of goods used, transferred or sold. The net amount is considered to be the cost of the goods on hand, if the balances shown on the books are adjusted at reasonable intervals to conform to physical inventories. (Reg § 1.471-2(d))[22]

¶ 2863 Miners' and manufacturers' inventory.

Under Code Sec. 471, miners and manufacturers that use a single process or uniform series of processes, derive a product of two or more kinds, sizes or grades with a unit cost substantially alike, meet other conditions, and get IRS consent can allocate total cost among each kind, size or grade as the cost basis for pricing inventories. (Reg § 1.471-7)[23]

¶ 2864 Mark-to-market rules for securities and commodities dealers' inventories and for their non-inventory securities or commodities.

Under Code Sec. 475, any security that's inventory in the hands of a securities dealer must be included in inventory at its fair market value (FMV). (Code Sec. 475(a)(1)) In the case of a non-inventory security that's held at the close of a tax year, the dealer must recognize gain or loss as if the security were sold for its FMV on the last business day of

---

17. ¶G-5201 ¶G-5227
18. ¶G-5245 *et seq.*
19. ¶G-5302 *et seq.*
20. ¶G-5351

21. ¶G-5362
22. ¶G-5119
23. ¶G-5020

that year, and any gain or loss must be taken into account for that tax year, generally as ordinary income or loss. (Code Sec. 475(a)(2), Code Sec. 475(d)(3)) For this purpose, FMV cannot be less than the amount of nonrecourse debt to which the property is subject.[24] A "security" doesn't include any security held for investment and certain other securities and hedges of any of those securities (but only if the hedge is clearly identified as a hedge in the dealer's records before the close of the business day on which it was acquired, originated or entered into). (Code Sec. 475(b))[25] Also excluded is nonfinancial customer paper arising from the sale of nonfinancial goods or services by sellers or providers of those goods or services that are held by them (or related parties) at all times since issue. (Code Sec. 475(c)(4))[26] Where the Code Sec. 475 rules don't apply, a securities dealer inventories securities at: (1) cost, (2) lower of cost or market, or (3) market value. (Reg § 1.471-5)[27]

A dealer is one who regularly buys and sells securities to customers or regularly offers to enter into, assume, offset, assign or otherwise terminate securities positions with customers in the ordinary course of business. (Code Sec. 475(c)(1))[28]

Commodities dealers may elect (under interim procedures[29]) to apply the mark-to-market rules to commodities held by them in the same way that the rules apply to securities held by securities dealers. (Code Sec. 475(e)(1)) Once made, the election may be revoked only with IRS consent. (Code Sec. 475(e)(3))[30] For the mark-to-market election by persons that are traders but not dealers of securities or commodities, see ¶2865.

¶ 2865 Mark-to-market election for securities and commodities traders—inventories.

Under Code Sec. 475, a securities or commodities trader may elect to have mark-to-market rules apply to the trade or business. In that case, gain or loss is recognized on any security (or commodity) held in connection with the business at the close of any tax year as if it were sold for its fair market value on the last business day of the tax year, and (2) any gain or loss is ordinary income or loss (Code Sec. 475(f)(1)(A), Code Sec. 475(f)(1)(D)), Code Sec. 475(f)(2)) The election may be revoked only with IRS consent. (Code Sec. 475(f)(3)) The rules don't apply to securities or commodities not connected to trading activities if clearly identified as such before the close of the day acquired. (Code Sec. 475(f)(1)(B)) Elected-for securities and commodities aren't subject to the Code Sec. 1259 constructive sale rules (¶2627). (Code Sec. 475(f)(1)(C))[31]

---

24. ¶I-2515
25. ¶I-7657 *et seq.*
26. ¶I-7657.1
27. ¶G-5021

28. ¶I-7656
29. ¶I-7669
30. ¶I-7667 *et seq.*
31. ¶I-7670 *et seq.*

Chapter 12   Withholding Tax on Wages and Other Income Payments

¶ 3000   **Withholding on Wages.** ███████████

Employers must withhold income tax from wages paid to employees (¶3003), but not from amounts paid to independent contractors (¶3004). "Wages" include most forms of taxable compensation (¶3005 *et seq.*). Employees are entitled to a withholding allowance (¶3016). Withheld tax must be paid through electronic funds transfers (¶3028).

Businesses can shift their withholding responsibilities to IRS-certified professional employer organizations (PEOs), see ¶3002.

For withholding on certain federal payments (e.g., social security payments), see ¶3010. For other nonpayroll withholding, see ¶3031. For withholding from U.S. source amounts paid to nonresident aliens and foreign corporations, see ¶4647.

¶ 3001   **Withholding of tax by employers.**

Under Code Sec. 3402(a)(1), employers must withhold tax. (Code Sec. 3402(a)(1); Reg § 31.3402(a)-1(b))[1] An employer is any person or organization for whom an individual performs any service as an employee. (Code Sec. 3401(d)) For purposes of withholding, an employer is any individual, corporation, partnership, trust, estate, joint-stock company, association, syndicate, or other unincorporated organization, group, or entity that pays remuneration for services, whether legal or illegal. (Reg § 31.3401(d)-1(c) An employer includes individuals engaged in a trade or business, any person paying wages to a former employee, (Reg § 31.3401(d)-1(b)), as well as tax-exempt organizations. (Reg § 31.3401(d)-1(d))[2]

If the employer for whom services are performed doesn't control payment of the wages to the employee, then whoever does have control of the payment of the wages is treated as the employer for withholding purposes Examples of entities other than the actual employer controlling the payment of wages are temporary personnel companies and trustees in bankruptcy. (Code Sec. 3401(d)(1))[3]

If a person pays wages on behalf of a nonresident employer not engaged in trade or business in the U.S., that person must withhold. (Code Sec. 3401(d)(2))[4]

¶ 3002   **Professional employer organizations (PEOs); certified PEOs (CPEOs); employee leasing companies.**

An employer can contract with a professional employer organization (PEO— also called an "employee leasing company") to take care of the employer's payroll, withholding, tax deposit, and other functions. Under Code Sec. 3511(a)(1), if a PEO becomes certified under IRS rules, the certified PEO (CPEO) is considered to be the sole employer for purposes of payroll taxes. Thus, the CPEO, not the employer, is liable for payroll taxes. (Code Sec. 3511(a)(1))[5]

To be certified, a PEO must satisfy various requirements intended to ensure that the PEO properly remits wages and employment taxes. (Code Sec. 7705)[6]

---

1. ¶H-4222
2. ¶H-4226
3. ¶H-4229

4. ¶H-4229.2
5. ¶H-4861
6. ¶H-4864; ¶H-4869

References beginning with a single letter are to paragraphs in Federal Tax Coordinator 2d and RIA's Analysis of Federal Taxes: Income.

The CPEO must pay an annual fee of $1,000. (Code Sec. 7528(b)(4))[7]

¶ 3003 "Employees" defined for wage withholding—Form SS-8; managers, supervisors, and directors.

Every individual who performs services subject to the will and control of an employer, both as to what is to be done and how it's to be done, is an employee for withholding purposes. It doesn't matter that the employee has considerable discretion and freedom of action, so long as the employer has the *legal right* to control both the method and the result of the services. (Reg § 31.3401(c)-1(b))[8]

For how IRS determines whether a worker is an employee or independent contractor, see ¶3004.

It doesn't matter that the employee is designated a partner, agent or independent contractor, or how payments are measured or paid or what they're called. (Reg § 31.3401(c)-1(e))[9]

Managers and other supervisory personnel are employees. An officer of a corporation is an employee (Code Sec. 3401(c)), but a director in his or her capacity as director isn't an employee. (Reg § 31.3401(c)-1(f))[10]

Persons in business for themselves aren't employees. For example, self-employed physicians, lawyers, veterinarians, construction contractors and others who offer their services to the public aren't employees. (Reg § 31.3401(c)-1(c))[11]

Qualified real estate agents and direct sellers are treated as independent contractors. (Code Sec. 3508(a))[12]

Statutory employees, such as certain drivers, life insurance salespersons, home workers, and other salespersons are treated as employees for FICA purposes (Code Sec. 3121(d)(3)) but aren't common law employees or employees for income tax purposes.[13]

If a payor isn't sure whether a payee is an employee or independent contractor, the payor may get an IRS ruling by filing Form SS-8.[14] Adverse rulings can be reviewed by the Tax Court (Code Sec. 7436) after IRS sends an adverse notice of determination.[15]

Employees who have been misclassified as independent contractors by an employer use Form 8919 to figure and report the employee's share of uncollected Social Security and Medicare taxes due on their compensation. The worker performing the services must meet one of several criteria supporting the belief that the worker is an employee, e.g., receipt of an SS-8 determination letter.[16]

¶ 3004 How IRS determines employee/independent contractor status of workers—Forms 8952—withholding.

To determine whether a worker is an independent contractor or an employee, IRS examines the relationship between the worker and the business, and considers all evidence of control and independence. The facts that provide this evidence fall into the following three categories:

(1) *Behavioral control* covers facts that show whether the business has a right to direct and control how the work is done through instructions, training, or other means.

(2) *Financial control* covers facts that show whether the business has a right to control

---

7. ¶T-10002
8. ¶H-4251
9. ¶H-4251
10. ¶H-4252
11. ¶H-4258
12. ¶H-4283
13. ¶H-4559
14. ¶H-4282
15. ¶U-2143
16. ¶S-1709.1

the financial and business aspects of the worker's job.

(3) *Type of relationship* which includes written contracts describing the relationship the parties intended to create; the extent to which the worker is available to perform services for other, similar businesses; whether the business provides the worker with employee-type benefits; the permanency of the relationship; and the extent to which services performed by the worker are a key aspect of the company's regular business.

IRS's 3-category approach distills the 20-factor test IRS uses to determine whether a worker is an employee or an independent contractor.[17]

If a taxpayer has a reasonable basis for treating an individual as a non-employee (e.g., judicial precedent, IRS ruling, past audit allowance), a special statutory rule (section 530 of the '78 Revenue Act) may allow non-employee treatment regardless of the above factors.[18]

IRS has two classification programs—the Classification Settlement Program, for those under audit, and the Voluntary Classification Settlement Program, for prospective application.[19]

¶ 3005   "Wages" subject to employer withholding; computational and other rules; year of payment; wages paid in property.

Under Code Sec. 3401(a), "wages" include all types of employee compensation, including salaries, fees, bonuses, commissions, tips (¶3006), fringe benefits (¶3011), amounts includible in an employee's gross income for failure to comply with the Code Sec. 409A deferred compensation rules (¶1275), noncash wages (e.g., goods, lodging, or meals), vacation allowances, back pay, front pay, severance pay, age-discrimination settlement payments, supplemental unemployment compensation benefits (no FICA) (¶3102), differential wage payments (no FICA or FUTA) (¶2331), and qualified stock for which a Code Sec. 83(i) election (¶1216) has been made. It's immaterial whether wage payments are based on the hour, day, week, month, year or on a piecework or percentage plan, or whether they're called wages, salaries, fees, etc. (Code Sec. 3401(a); Reg § 31.3401(a)-1(a)(2), Reg § 31.3401(a)-1(a)(3))[20]

Compensation paid to employees engaged in certain specified occupations, and certain types of compensation, are excluded from the definition of wages subject to withholding (¶3007).

Special rules for withholding on bonuses, commissions, overtime pay or other supplemental wages apply (¶3012).[21]

For withholding, wages are treated as paid in the year they are includable in gross income.[22]

For wages paid in property other than money, such as stocks, bonds, etc., the fair market value (FMV) of the property is the amount to be included as wages. (Reg § 31.3401(a)-1(a)(4)) The FMV of virtual currency/cryptocurrency (¶2402) that is "convertible" (i.e., that has an equivalent value in real currency, or that acts as a substitute for real currency) paid by an employer for services is wages, and subject to withholding.[23]

Withholding is computed on gross wages before any deductions by the employer for social security tax, pensions, union dues, insurance, etc. (Reg § 31.3401(a)-1(b)(5))[24]

Employers must collect the employee's FICA taxes. (¶3024).

17. ¶H-4259
18. ¶H-4303 *et seq.*
19. ¶H-4282.1
20. ¶H-4326 *et seq.*

21. ¶H-4530
22. ¶H-4326, ¶H-4333.1
23. ¶H-4327
24. ¶H-4331

An employer must withhold an additional 0.9% Medicare tax (see ¶1108) on wages, and is liable for the tax it fails to withhold from wages or collect from the employee. The obligation applies only to wages over $200,000 the employee receives from the employer. For this threshold, the employer disregards wages received by the employee's spouse.[25]

¶ 3006 Tips—cash tips; tips other than cash—wage withholding.

Under Code Sec. 3401(f), wages include tips, but withholding isn't required on cash tips of less than $20 a month received by an employee, or for tips paid in any medium other than cash (such as passes, tickets or other goods or commodities). (Code Sec. 3401(f); Code Sec. 3401(a)(16); Reg § 31.3401(a)(16)-1) But, if cash tips amount to $20 or more in a month, none of the cash tips are exempt. The $20 test is applied separately for cash tips received by the employee for services to each employer. (Reg § 31.3401(a)(16)-1)[26] (For the business tax credit for employer FICA tax paid on tips for food and beverage service, see ¶2325.)

¶ 3007 Exempt "wages"—fringes, reimbursed expenses, domestic service, travel expenses, moving expenses, etc.—withholding.

Under Code Sec. 3401, the following aren't wages subject to income tax withholding:

. . . Fringe benefits, if it's reasonable to believe that the employee will be able to exclude them from income as a qualified scholarship, qualified tuition reductions, a no-additional-cost service, a qualified employee discount, a working condition fringe, a de minimis fringe, a qualified transportation fringe, a qualified moving expense reimbursement, an employee achievement award, or medical care reimbursements. (Code Sec. 3401(a)(19))[27] (For the employer's election not to withhold on a vehicle fringe benefit, see ¶3008.)

. . . Amounts specifically advanced or reimbursed to employees for traveling or other ordinary and necessary expenses incurred in the employer's business. If a reimbursement or other expense allowance arrangement meets the requirements of Code Sec. 62(c) (¶3104, i.e., an "accountable plan"), payments that don't exceed the substantiated expenses aren't wages and aren't subject to withholding. Per diem or mileage allowances at a rate over the deemed substantiated amount are subject to withholding. If the arrangement doesn't meet the Code Sec. 62(c) requirements, all amounts paid are wages and subject to withholding. (Reg § 31.3401(a)-4(a), Reg § 31.3401(a)-4(b), Reg § 1.62-2(h)(1), Reg § 1.62-2(h)(2))[28]

. . . Moving expense reimbursements, if a corresponding deduction is allowable under the normal Code Sec. 217 rules (limited to members of the U.S. Armed Forces for 2018–2025), see ¶1627. (Code Sec. 3401(a)(15))[29]

. . . Tips, under the circumstances described at ¶3006.

. . . Benefits paid by a labor union to workers unemployed because of a strike or lockout.[30]

. . . Certain payments for agricultural labor except if during the year: (1) cash payments to an employee are $150 or more (except for certain hand harvest laborers) or (2) the employer pays all such employees $2,500 or more. (Code Sec. 3401(a)(2), Code Sec. 3121(a)(8))[31]

. . . Payments for domestic service in a private home, local college club, or fraternity or sorority chapter. (Code Sec. 3401(a)(3))[32]

. . . Certain payments for services by a U.S. citizen for an employer outside the U.S. if the

---

25. ¶H-4701.1
26. ¶H-4341
27. ¶H-4401 *et seq.*
28. ¶H-4340

29. ¶L-3600 *et seq.*
30. ¶H-4354
31. ¶H-4426
32. ¶H-4450 *et seq.*

U.S. citizen qualifies for the foreign earned income exclusion under Code Sec. 911 described at ¶4605 (Code Sec. 3401(a)(8)(A)(i))[33]

. . . Premiums paid by employer for group term insurance on an employee's life, see ¶1262. (Code Sec. 3401(a)(14))[34]

. . . Payments to or on behalf of an employee or his or her beneficiary to or from a qualified plan (except payments for services rendered by a plan employee) (Code Sec. 3401(a)(12)(A)); to or under a qualified annuity plan (Code Sec. 3401(a)(12)(B)); under a SIMPLE retirement account (Code Sec. 3401(a)(12)(D)); to or under a governmental section 457 plan (Code Sec. 3401(a)(12)(E)); or, for certain contributions to a simplified employee pension for an employee. (Code Sec. 3401(a)(12)(C))[35]

. . . Payments under an educational assistance or dependent care program, if reasonable to believe the employee can exclude them. (Code Sec. 3401(a)(18))[36]

. . . Payment of deceased employee's accrued wages to his or her estate or beneficiaries.[37]

. . . Combat zone compensation excludible under Code Sec. 112. (Code Sec. 3401(a)(1))[38]

. . . Employer contributions to medical savings accounts. (Code Sec. 3401(a)(21), Code Sec. 3401(a)(22))[39]

. . . Benefits/payments excludible under Code Sec. 139B(a) (certain payments to volunteer emergency workers, see ¶1206). (Code Sec. 3401(a)(23))[40]

. . . Qualified adoption expenses under an employer's adoption assistance program.(Code Sec. 137(a)(1))[41]

. . . Disqualifying dispositions of stock acquired through exercise of an incentive stock option or an option under an employee stock purchase plan (ESPP) (Code Sec. 421(b)) or for any amount treated as compensation under the ESPP discount option rule. (Code Sec. 423(c))[42]

¶ 3008 Employer's election not to withhold on employer-provided vehicle fringe benefit.

Under Code Sec. 3402(s), employers may elect not to withhold on an employee's use of an employer-provided vehicle where that use is wages to the employee. The employer must notify the employee of the election and include the amount of the benefit on a timely furnished Form W-2. (Code Sec. 3402(s))[43]

¶ 3009 Withholding on sick pay—Form W-4S; sick pay paid by third party.

Under Code Sec. 3402(o)(1)(C), sick pay paid by an employer to an employee is a wage subject to withholding if the sick pay is includible in the gross income of the employee. Sick pay paid by a third party, such as an insurance company, isn't subject to mandatory income tax withholding. But, the employee may request withholding (on Form W-4S) on third party sick pay. (Code Sec. 3402(o)(1)(C); Reg § 31.3402(o)-3(b))[44]

¶ 3010 Voluntary withholding agreements—Forms W-4, W-4V, and W-4P; voluntary withholding on Social Security benefits, crop disaster payments, Commodity Credit Corporation loans, and unemployment compensation, annuity payments.

33. ¶H-4442; ¶H-4443
34. ¶H-1518 *et seq.*, ¶J-8548
35. ¶H-4480
36. ¶H-4401
37. ¶H-4350
38. ¶H-4447
39. ¶H-4336.1
40. ¶H-4336.2
41. ¶H-1451
42. ¶H-4448.2
43. ¶s H-4411, H-4412
44. ¶H-4337; ¶H-4481 *et seq.*

Under Code Sec. 3402(p), workers can, via Form W-4 (¶3015), voluntarily request income tax withholding on payments that aren't otherwise subject to mandatory withholding; they may also increase the amount of withholding. (Code Sec. 3402(p)) Workers can request to have their withholding increased above the required amount of wage withholding. (Code Sec. 3402(i))[45]

The rules generally applicable to mandatory withholding, including withholding rates and tables, apply to the voluntary withholding. An employee requests voluntary withholding by filing a Form W-4 with his or her employer—unless he or she wants the voluntary withholding to apply for a limited period of time, in which case, he or she must also give the employer a statement that includes the date the voluntary withholding will terminate. A taxpayer can request voluntary withholding at a rate of 7%, 10%, 15%, or 22% on certain federal payments, including Social Security benefits, crop disaster payments, and Commodity Credit Corporation loans (Code Sec. 3402(p)(1)), and at a 10% rate on unemployment compensation payments (¶1281). (Code Sec. 3402(p)(2)) Use Form W-4V.[46]

Similar rules apply to the request for withholding on annuities under Code Sec. 3402(o)(4) except that the request is made on Form W-4P. ([47])

A voluntary withholding agreement may be terminated by the employer or employee by giving advance notice to the other in accordance with the regs. (Reg § 31.3402(p)-1)[48]

¶ 3011 Election to treat fringe benefits as paid quarterly, semiannually, annually, for withholding purposes.

For the Code Sec. 3501 requirement that employers withhold taxes on fringe benefits, an employer may elect to treat fringe benefits as paid quarterly, semiannually, annually, or on another basis. Fringe benefits must be treated as paid at least annually by Dec. 31 of that year. An employer may also treat a fringe benefit as paid in installments, even if the entire benefit is paid at one time. Transfers of either personal property of a kind normally held for investment or real property, however, must be reported when they are actually paid. (Announcement 85-113, 1985-31 IRB 31)[49]

Employers may treat taxable fringe benefits as part of regular wages for the payroll period and compute withholding on the total, or instead treat the fringe benefits as supplemental wages and withhold on the value of fringe benefits at the flat 22% rate (for tax years 2018–2025) that applies to supplemental wages (37% for supplemental wage payments exceeding $1 million for tax years 2018–2025) (¶3012). (Reg § 31.3501(a)-1T, Q&A-10)[50]

For when withholding isn't required on a presumptively tax-free fringe benefit, see ¶3007. For the election to not withhold on the value of a vehicle fringe benefit provided to the employee, see ¶3008.

¶ 3012 Withholding on supplemental wage payments—bonuses, commissions, overtime pay, other supplemental wages.

Under Code Sec. 3402, employers must withhold taxes on supplemental wage payments (i.e., bonuses, commissions, overtime pay or other supplemental wages) paid:

. . . *with regular wages*, as if the total supplemental and regular wages were a single payment for the regular payroll period;

. . . *at a different time*, by adding the supplemental wages either to the regular wages for

---

45. ¶H-4475
46. ¶H-4483 *et seq.*
47. ¶H-4482.2
48. ¶H-4477 *et seq.*
49. ¶H-4403
50. ¶H-4541 *et seq.*

the current payroll period or to the last preceding payroll period within the same calendar year;

. . . *where tax has been withheld on regular wages,* (at the employer's option) by using a flat rate of not less than 22% (for tax years 2018–2025)without regard to the withholding allowance claimed by the employee and without regard to any regular wage payment. (Reg § 31.3402(g)-1(a))[1]

But, for supplemental wage payments totalling more than $1 million for a calendar year, the withholding rate is increased to the maximum tax rate under Code Sec. 1 (i.e., 37% for tax years 2018–2025). (Reg § 31.3402(g)-1(a)(2))[2]

The employer has the option of treating either the entire supplemental payment or just that which brings the total payment over $1 million as subject to this mandatory withholding. (Reg § 31.3402(g)-1(a)(4)(iv))[3]

Where tax isn't withheld from regular wages for employees who receive both regular wages and supplemental wages (e.g., tips), the flat supplemental withholding rate can't be used; the tips are added to the current or preceding regular wage payment and withholding is computed at the regular graduated rates. (Reg § 31.3402(g)-1(a)(5))[4] A payment qualifies as supplemental wages even if no regular wages have been paid to the employee.[5]

¶ 3013 Computing the amount withheld; percentage method, wage bracket method; rules for employers who fail to withhold due to treating worker as non-employee.

Under Code Sec. 3402(a)(1), employers that pay wages must deduct and withhold on those wages a tax determined under tables or computational procedures prescribed by IRS. These tables or procedures must apply to the amount of wages paid during the periods that IRS prescribes; they must also be in such a form, and provide for those amounts to be deducted and withheld in a way, that IRS determines to be most appropriate to carry out the collection of income tax at the source, and to reflect the rules of income tax that apply to those periods. The "amount of wages" means the amount by which the wages exceed the taxpayer's withholding allowance (¶3015), prorated to the payroll period. (Code Sec. 3402(a)(2))[6]

IRS's downloadable, spreadsheet-based tool, the "Income Tax Withholding Assistant for Employers" —geared to smaller employers who might otherwise figure withholding manually—helps in determining the right amount of income tax to withhold from employees' pay.[7]

The two principal systems of withholding for which IRS provides tables are: (1) the percentage method, and (2) the wage bracket method.[8] Whichever method is used, the employer applies the filing status and other entries on the employee's Form W-4, ¶3015 *et seq.* For variations of these two methods, see ¶3014.

If an employer fails to withhold income tax and the employee's portion of FICA taxes because the employer failed to treat the payee as an employee, for prior years the withholding rate is generally reduced to 1.5% of wages for income tax withholding, and only 20% of the regular amount to be withheld for FICA will generally have to be withheld. Certain exceptions apply. (Code Sec. 3509)[9]

---

1. ¶s H-4531, H-4539, H-4544.1
2. ¶H-4542
3. ¶H-4542.1 *et seq.*
4. ¶H-4539
5. ¶H-4532

6. ¶H-4492
7. ¶H-4492
8. ¶H-4493 *et seq.*
9. ¶H-4225; ¶H-4703

¶ 3014 **Alternative withholding methods—withholding based on annualized wages, cumulative wages, part-year employment, or average estimated wages.**

Under Code Sec. 3402(h), IRS authorizes withholding on the basis of: (1) annualized wages, (2) cumulative wages, (3) part-year employment, (4) average estimated wages, and (5) any other method that results in substantially the same amount of withholding as either the percentage or wage bracket method. Methods (2) and (3) are at the employee's request. (Code Sec. 3402(h))[10]

¶ 3015 **Employee's withholding certificate (Form W-4)—wage withholding.**

On or before the date employment begins, employees must furnish the employer with a signed withholding certificate (Form W-4) relating to the withholding allowance claimed. (Code Sec. 3402(f)(2)(A)) A Form W-4 filed by a new employee is effective on the first payment of wages. (Code Sec. 3402(f)(3)) If an employee has no valid Form W-4 in effect with the employer at the time of the payment of wages, and fails to furnish a valid Form W-4 to the employer, the employee is treated as single but having the withholding allowance provided in forms, instructions, publications, and other guidance prescribed by IRS. (Reg § 31.3402(f)(2)-1(a)(4))[11]

An employer can establish a system for its employees to file Form W-4 electronically. (Reg § 31.3402(f)(5)-1(c))[12]

¶ 3016 **Employee's withholding allowance; employee with more than one employer—wage withholding—Form W-4.**

Under Code Sec. 3402(f)(1), an employee's withholding allowance (used in determining the amount to be withheld, ¶3013) and claimed on Form W-4 (¶3015) is based on (Code Sec. 3402(f)(1); Reg § 31.3402(f)(1)-1(b)(2)):

(1) Whether the employee is an individual for whom a dependency deduction could be claimed by another taxpayer;

(2) If the employee is married, whether the employee's spouse is an individual for whom a dependency deduction could be claimed by another taxpayer, but only if the spouse doesn't have in effect a Form W-4 claiming such a deduction;

(3) If the employee is married, whether the employee's spouse is entitled to additional deductions, credits, or other items the employee elects to take into account under Code Sec. 3402(m), or would be so entitled if the employee's spouse were an employee receiving wages, but only if the spouse doesn't have in effect a Form W-4 claiming such an allowance;

(4) Any child tax credit (CTC, ¶2349 *et seq.*) that the employee expects to claim on their return for the calendar year for which the Form W-4 applies, except that the employee may not take into account any CTC if the credit is claimed on another valid Form W-4 in effect for another employer of the employee or of the employee's spouse.

(5) Any additional deductions, credits, or other items the employee elects to take into account under Code Sec. 3402(m) for the calendar year for which the Form W-4 is in effect;

(6) The basic standard deduction (¶3110) relating to the filing status the employee expects to claim on his or her return for the calendar year for which the Form W-4 is in

---

effect; the allowance is based on 1/2 of the standard deduction for an employee who is married and whose spouse is an employee receiving wages subject to withholding; and

(7) Any adjustment resulting from multiple Forms W-4 the employee, the employee's spouse, or both have or expect to have in effect for one or more employers, determined based on the Form W-4 Instructions and other IRS guidance for the calendar year for which the Form W-4 is in effect.[13]

If a Form W-4 is in effect for one employer, an employee isn't entitled under a Form W-4 in effect with another employer to any withholding allowance claimed under the first Form W-4. (Code Sec. 3402(f)(7)) See also (7), above.[14]

¶ 3017   Employees with no tax liability—certificate of nontaxability—wage withholding.

Under Code Sec. 3402(n), an employee with no tax liability can claim an exemption from income tax withholding if the employee certifies on Form W-4 to the employer that the employee expects to have no federal income tax liability for the current year, *and* had no federal income tax liability in the preceding year.[15]

An employee who can be claimed as a dependent on someone else's tax return (whether or not actually claimed) can't claim exemption from withholding if his or her income exceeds $1,150 for 2022 ($1,250 for 2023) and includes more than $400 for 2022 ($400 for 2023) of unearned income, such as interest and dividends. Special calculations must be made by an employee who is 65 or older and/or blind.[16]

¶ 3018   Amending withholding certificate (Form W-4); change in employee's status—wage withholding.

Under Code Sec. 3402(f)(2)(B), during the calendar year, whenever an employee's status changes so that the employee becomes entitled to less of a withholding allowance (¶3016) than is shown on the employee's Form W-4, the employee must give the employer a new Form W-4 within 10 days after the change of status occurs. If the employee's withholding allowance increases, the employee may furnish a new certificate, but isn't required to do so. (Code Sec. 3402(f)(2)(B))[17]

¶ 3019   Employer withholding tax return—Forms 941 and 944—quarterly return.

Every employer (except household employers, see ¶3030) must file with IRS a quarterly return reporting withheld income taxes on Form 941. (Reg § 31.6011(a)-1, Reg § 31.6011(a)-4) Employers must submit copies of W-4s to IRS only when directed to do so by written notice or as directed in published guidance. (Reg § 31.3402(f)(2)-1(g)(1)) Where a serious underwithholding problem is found to exist for a particular employee, IRS will notify the employer to withhold income tax from that employee at a more appropriate rate (i.e., issue a "lock-in letter"). (Reg § 31.3402(f)(2)-1(g)(2))[18]

Form 941 must be filed by Apr. 30, July 31, Oct. 31 and Jan. 31 for the calendar quarters ending Mar. 31, June 30, Sept. 30 and Dec. 31, respectively, unless monthly filing is required. But the returns may be filed ten days later if timely deposits in full payment of the tax are made. (Reg § 31.6071(a)-1(a))[19] Form 941 reflects the 0.9% Medicare surtax (¶1108).[20]

13. ¶H-4505
14. ¶H-4509
15. ¶H-4519
16. ¶H-4519
17. ¶H-4524
18. ¶S-2603
19. ¶S-4918
20. ¶H-4685 *et seq.*

In certain cases (e.g., for taxpayers who must separately account, see ¶3025), IRS can require monthly wage withholding returns. (Reg § 31.6011(a)-5(a)(1))[21]

Employers with annual employment tax liabilities of $1,000 or less who have received written notification from IRS that they qualify for the "Form 944 program" can file Form 944 annually, if they choose, instead of Form 941. (Reg § 31.6011(a)-4(a)(4)(i))[22]

For nonpayroll withholding (backup withholding, withholding for pension, annuities, and gambling winnings, etc.), see ¶3031.

¶ 3020 Errors in withholding and payment of FICA and income tax; correction of underwithholding—Form 941-X.

Where underwithholding of FICA and income tax is ascertained before the return is filed, the employer must report and pay the correct amount of tax by the due date of the return. (Reg § 31.6151-1, Reg § 31.6205-1(b)(1), Reg § 31.6205-1(c)(1))[23]

Rules are provided for making corrections (in some cases on an interest-free basis) after the return is filed. (Reg § 31.6205-1(b)(2))[24] Form 941-X is used to correct errors in a previously filed Form 941.[25]

¶ 3021 Wage and tax statement furnished to employees—Form W-2; Form W-3—withholding.

Employers must furnish to each employee a written statement (described in Code Sec. 6051(a)) on Form W-2 reporting the amount of the wages paid by the employer to the employee and the amount of tax withheld on those wages. (Code Sec. 6051(a))[26]

Form W-3 must be filed with the Social Security Administration (SSA) with copies of all Forms W-2 issued for the year.[27]

If an employer files at least 250 W-2s per year, the W-2s must be filed electronically. (Reg § 301.6037-2(a))[28]

An employer in business must give each employee copies of Form W-2, before Feb. 1 of the year after the calendar year for which the wages were paid. If an employee leaves the job before the end of the calendar year and isn't expected to return within the calendar year, Form W-2 must be given to the employee not later than 30 days after the employer receives a written request for it from the employee, if that 30-day period ends before Jan. 31. (Code Sec. 6051; Reg § 31.6051-1(d))[29]

¶ 3022 Nonreceipt of Form W-2 by employee—Form 4852—withholding.

An employee who doesn't receive a Form W-2 should ask the employer for it. If the employer doesn't provide the form, the taxpayer should contact IRS, which will ask the employer to send a copy or duplicate form. An employee who hasn't received a Form W-2 in time to file his or her return should file a return estimating wages and the income tax withheld on Form 4852. (Internal Revenue Manual 21.3.6.4.7.1 (10/1/2019))[30]

¶ 3023 Earned income credit notice to employees with no tax withheld—Notice 797.

An employer must notify any employee who hasn't had any tax withheld from wages

21. ¶S-2604
22. ¶S-4918
23. ¶S-5525
24. ¶S-5526
25. ¶S-5533

26. ¶S-3152
27. ¶S-3183
28. ¶S-1942
29. ¶S-4930
30. ¶S-3193

(other than an employee who certifies, see ¶3017, that he or she has no tax liability) that the employee may be eligible for a refund because of the earned income credit (¶2337 *et seq.*). IRS Notice 797 or a written statement containing an exact reproduction of the wording in Notice 797 must be used and furnished within one week of the date the employee should receive a timely Form W-2 or, if none is required, before Feb. 8th of the following calendar year. (Reg § 31.6051-1(h))[31]

¶ 3024 Payroll taxes—Federal Insurance Contributions Act (FICA) taxes: the Old Age, Survivors and Disability Insurance (OASDI) tax and the Medicare Hospital Insurance (HI) tax.

The Federal Insurance Contributions Act (FICA) imposes two taxes, the Old Age, Survivors and Disability Insurance (OASDI) tax and the Medicare Hospital Insurance (HI) tax. These taxes are imposed on employers for wages paid with respect to employment, and on employees for wages received with respect to employment. The OASDI tax rate is 6.2% on wages up to an annually-adjusted "wage base" (see ¶1108).

The HI tax rate generally is 1.45% on all wages, regardless of amount. An additional 0.9% Medicare tax applies to certain high wage earners; see ¶1108.

¶ 3025 Separate accounting for employment tax; employer failure to collect, deposit, and/or report income or employment taxes.

Under Code Sec. 7512, IRS can require an employer who fails to collect, account for, deposit, etc., income or related employment taxes or make timely deposits or file returns to make deposits in a special trust account. (Code Sec. 7512; Reg § 301.7512-1(b))[32]

¶ 3026 Deposit of employment taxes (income, FICA (social security and Medicare) taxes); monthly depositors, semi-weekly depositors.

Under Code Sec. 6302, employers must deposit federal income tax withheld, and both the employer and employee social security and Medicare taxes (¶1108). An employer is either a monthly or semi-weekly depositor. (Reg § 31.6302-1(a))[33]

An employer is a monthly depositor for the entire calendar year if the aggregate amount of employment taxes reported for the "lookback period" (i.e., the 12-month period ended the preceding June 30) is $50,000 or less. Monthly depositors must deposit taxes accumulated with respect to payments made during a calendar month on or before the 15th day of the following month. (Reg § 31.6302-1(b)(2)(i), Reg § 31.6302-1(b)(4); Reg § 31.6302-1(c)(1))[34]

An employer is a semi-weekly depositor for the entire calendar year if the aggregate amount of employment taxes reported for the lookback period (i.e., the 12-month period ended the preceding June 30) exceeds $50,000. The employer must deposit taxes on or before the following IRS due dates. If the wage payment date is:

. . . Wednesday, Thursday, and/or Friday, the deposit date is on or before the following Wednesday.

. . . Saturday, Sunday, Monday, and/or Tuesday, the deposit date is on or before the following Friday. (Reg § 31.6302-1(b)(3), Reg § 31.6302-1(b)(4); Reg § 31.6302-1(c)(2))[35]

Notwithstanding the above rules, under the "one-day rule," if on any day an employer

31. ¶H-4851 *et seq.*
32. ¶S-5541 *et seq.*
33. ¶S-5500 *et seq.*
34. ¶S-5503
35. ¶S-5506

has \$100,000 or more of employment taxes accumulated, these taxes must be deposited by the close of the next banking day. (Reg § 31.6302-1(c)(3)) The day after a monthly depositor becomes subject to the one-day rule it becomes a semi-weekly depositor for the remainder of that calendar year and for the following calendar year. (Reg § 31.6302-1(b)(2)(ii))[36]

No taxes are required to be deposited on any day that is a Sat., Sun., or legal holiday; deposits are required only on business days. (Reg § 31.6302-1(c)(4))[37]

Deposits are considered timely if mailed (postmarked, or date marked by a designated delivery service, see ¶4754) at least two days before the due date if the deposit is actually received by the bank. (Code Sec. 7502(e)) But a deposit of \$20,000 or more by a person who is required to make a deposit more than once a month must be actually received by the due date. (Code Sec. 7502(e)(3))[38]

In general, taxpayers must deposit taxes by electronic funds transfer (¶3028).

For failure-to-deposit penalty (Code Sec. 6656), see ¶4881.

For Code Sec. 3511 (which requires certified professional employer organizations (CPEOs) to be treated as employers for employment tax withholding purposes, see ¶3002), for a CPEO (as defined in Code Sec. 7705(a)) that has entered into a service contract described in Code Sec. 7705(e)(2) with a customer, if that customer directed that CPEO to defer payment of any applicable employment taxes during the payroll tax deferral period under these deferral rules, the customer, notwithstanding Code Sec. 3511(a) and Code Sec. 3511(c), was solely liable for the payment of those applicable employment taxes before the applicable date for any wages paid by the CPEO to any worksite employee performing services for that customer during that period. (Sec. 2302(c)(2)DivA, PL 116-136, 3/27/2020)[39]

¶ 3027 Employment tax single deposit safe harbor and de minimis rules.

Under the single deposit safe harbor, an employer will be considered to have satisfied the deposit obligations if:

(1) the amount of any shortfall (the excess of the amount required to be deposited over the amount deposited for the applicable period—monthly, semi-weekly or daily) doesn't exceed the greater of \$100 or 2% of the amount of employment taxes required to be deposited (Reg § 31.6302-1(f)(1)(i), Reg § 31.6302-1(f)(2)), and

(2) the employer deposits the shortfall on or before the shortfall make-up date. (Reg § 31.6302-1(f)(1)(ii)) For a monthly depositor, this is no later than the due date for the quarterly return. For a semi-weekly or a one-day depositor, this is on or before the first Wednesday or Friday (whichever is earlier) falling on or after the 15th day of the month following the month the deposit was required to be made. (Reg § 31.6302-1(f)(3))[40]

An employer with accumulated employment taxes of less than \$2,500 for a return period (quarterly or annual) doesn't have to make deposits and can instead remit the full liability with a timely filed return for the period. (Reg § 31.6302-1(f)(4))[41]

¶ 3028 Employment tax deposits by electronic funds transfer (EFT); use of Electronic Federal Tax Payment System (EFTPS) to make federal tax deposits.

Under Code Sec. 6302(h), unless exempted, all of the following are required to be deposited via EFT:

---

36. ¶S-5510
37. ¶S-5512
38. ¶T-10777 *et seq.*

39. ¶H-4869.23
40. ¶S-5513 *et seq.*
41. ¶S-5516

. . . FICA and FUTA taxes and withheld income taxes;

. . . corporate income and estimated taxes;

. . . unrelated business income taxes of tax-exempt organizations;

. . . private foundation excise taxes;

. . . taxes withheld on nonresident aliens and foreign corporations;

. . . estimated taxes on certain trusts;

. . . railroad retirement taxes;

. . . nonpayroll taxes, including backup withholding; and

. . . certain excise taxes.

(Code Sec. 6302(h); Reg § 31.6302-1(h)(2)(iii))[42]

A taxpayer required to deposit by EFT must use the Electronic Federal Tax Payment System (EFTPS) to make federal tax deposits.[43] Taxpayers must enroll in EFTPS before they can make EFT deposits. Enroll on-line at www.eftps.gov.[44]

Federal income taxes (including estimated taxes) (Reg § 1.6302-4), estate (Reg § 20.6302-1) and gift taxes (Reg § 25.6302-1), and various excise taxes (Reg § 40.6302(a)-1) may be made voluntarily by EFT.[45]

A taxpayer required to deposit taxes by EFT that (without reasonable cause) deposits by other means is subject to the Code Sec. 6656 failure to deposit penalty. (Rev Rul 95-68, 1995-2 CB 272)[46]

¶ 3029 Motion picture industry employment taxes; motion picture project employers; film and television production workers.

Under Code Sec. 3512, motion picture payroll service companies that qualify as "motion picture project employers" are treated as the employer of their film and television production workers for FICA and FUTA purposes. As a result, all remuneration paid by a motion picture project employer to a worker during a calendar year is subject to a single FICA wage base and a single FUTA wage base. (Code Sec. 3512)[47]

¶ 3030 Payment of Domestic Service Employment Tax ("Nanny Tax")—Form 1040, Schedule H, Form 941, Form 943, Form 944. ■■■■■■■■■■■■■■■

An employer of a domestic service employee must file an annual return of "domestic service employment taxes" on a calendar-year basis (Code Sec. 3510(a)(1)) on or before the 15th day of the fourth month following the close of the employer's tax year. (Code Sec. 3510(a)(2))

Household employers report FICA, FUTA, and withheld income tax for their household employees on their individual income tax return (Form 1040, Schedule H). (Reg § 31.6011(a)-1(a)(3); Reg § 31.6011(a)-4(a)(2))[48]

If an employer is required to report wages paid to domestic workers on Form 941, Form 943, or Form 944, the requirement to file Schedule H to report FICA doesn't apply. An employer who reports wages on Form 941, Form 943, or Form 944 also has to file Form 940 to report FUTA tax. (Reg § 31.6011(a)-1(a)(3))[49]

There's no requirement to make deposits of domestic service employment taxes, or to pay installments of these taxes under Code Sec. 6157. (Code Sec. 3510(a)(3))[50]

42. ¶S-5627
43. ¶S-5621
44. ¶S-5630
45. ¶S-5629
46. ¶V-1658

47. ¶H-4685 *et seq.*
48. ¶S-2608
49. ¶S-2608
50. ¶S-5519.1

Domestic service employment taxes are: (1) any FICA and FUTA taxes on remuneration paid for domestic service in a private home of the employer (for dollar threshold see below), and (2) and any income tax on these payments that's withheld under the Code Sec. 3402(p) voluntary withholding agreement rules (¶3010) (for the otherwise applicable exemption from income tax withholding on domestic service employment, see ¶3007). (Code Sec. 3510(c))[1]

Domestic service is service of a household nature performed in and about the private home of the person for whom the services are performed. (Reg § 31.3121(a)(7)-1(a), Reg § 31.3401(a)(3)-1(a))[2]

Non-cash payments for domestic services in an employer's private home are excluded from FICA wages. Cash remuneration paid by an employer for domestic service in the employer's private home isn't FICA wages if the cash remuneration paid during the year is less than the "applicable dollar threshold" —$2,400 in 2022 ($2,600 in 2023). (Code Sec. 3121(a)(7), Code Sec. 3121(x))[3]

🅡observation: The dollar threshold applies separately to each domestic employee. So, for example, if an employer pays just under $2,600 each to a babysitter and a house-keeper in 2023, no FICA tax is due for either.

Domestic service performed in the private home of the employer in any year by an individual under the age of 18 during any portion of the year is excepted from employment for FICA if the service isn't the principal occupation of the employee. (Code Sec. 3121(b)(21))[4]

Form W-2. An employer must furnish Form W-2 to household employees whose wages are subject to Social Security taxes even if they aren't subject to income tax withholding. (Reg § 31.6051-1(b)(1)) Use a Form W-3 transmittal to file even one Form W-2.[5]

¶ 3031 Nonpayroll Withheld Taxes. ▬▬▬▬▬▬▬▬

Income tax on gambling winnings, payments subject to backup withholding, retirement plan payments, IRAs, annuities and certain other deferred compensation is withheld under "nonpayroll withheld taxes" rules.

The employment tax deposit rules of ¶3026 *et seq.* apply to determine the time and manner of making deposits of nonpayroll withheld taxes. (Reg § 31.6302-4(a))[6] Whether a taxpayer is a monthly or a semi-weekly depositor for a calendar year is based on an annual determination and generally depends on the aggregate amount of nonpayroll withheld taxes reported by the taxpayer for the "lookback period" —i.e., the second calendar year preceding the current calendar year. A new taxpayer is treated as having nonpayroll withheld taxes of zero for any calendar year in which the taxpayer didn't exist. (Reg § 31.6302-4(c)(2)(iv))[7]

A taxpayer is a monthly depositor of nonpayroll withheld taxes for a calendar year if the amount of nonpayroll withheld taxes accumulated in the lookback period is $50,000 or less. A taxpayer ceases to be a monthly depositor of nonpayroll withheld taxes on the first day after the taxpayer is subject to the "one-day rule" (¶3026) with respect to nonpayroll withheld taxes. At that time, the taxpayer immediately becomes a semi-weekly depositor of nonpayroll withheld taxes for the remainder of the calendar year and the succeeding calendar year. (Reg § 31.6302-4(c)(2)(ii))[8]

A taxpayer is a semi-weekly depositor of nonpayroll withheld taxes for a calendar year if the amount of nonpayroll withheld taxes accumulated in the lookback period exceeds

---

1. ¶S-2608.3
2. ¶H-4654
3. ¶H-4653.1
4. ¶H-4611.1
5. ¶S-3159
6. ¶S-5582 *et seq.*
7. ¶S-5582
8. ¶S-5582

$50,000. (Reg § 31.6302-4(c)(2)(iii))[9]

Nonpayroll withheld taxes are income taxes withheld from: gambling winnings (¶3033) (Reg § 31.6302-4(b)(1)); retirement pay for services in the Armed Forces under Code Sec. 3402 (Reg § 31.6302-4(b)(2); retirement plan payments, IRAs, annuities and certain other deferred compensation (¶3034) (Reg § 31.6302-4(b)(3)); and under the backup withholding rules (¶3043). (Reg § 31.6302-4(b)(5))[10]

For the requirement that some taxpayers deposit nonpayroll withheld taxes by electronic funds transfer (EFT), see ¶3028.

¶ 3032   Annual nonpayroll tax return—Form 945.

Taxpayers who withhold income tax from nonpayroll payments must report the withholding annually on Form 945. The return must be filed on or before Jan. 31 following the calendar year. But, if timely deposits of tax have been made, the return may be filed by Feb. 10. (Reg § 31.6071(a)-1(a)(1))[11]

¶ 3033   Withholding on gambling or wagering winnings—Form W-2G and Form 5754; withholding on Indian casino profits.

Payors must withhold 24% on proceeds of more than $5,000 (Code Sec. 3402(q)(1)) from:

(1) a wagering transaction in a parimutuel pool with respect to horse races, dog races or jai alai if the amount of the proceeds is at least 300 times as large as the amount wagered; (Code Sec. 3402(q)(3)(C)(ii))

(2) a wager placed in a state-conducted lottery; (Code Sec. 3402(q)(3)(B))

(3) a sweepstakes, wagering pool or lottery (other than a state-conducted lottery); (Code Sec. 3402(q)(3)(C)(i)) or

(4) all other wagering transactions if the amount of the proceeds is at least 300 times as large as the amount wagered. (Code Sec. 3402(q)(3)(A))[12]

"Proceeds" means amount received from the wager reduced by the amount of the wager. (Code Sec. 3402(q)(4)(A))[13] Amounts paid with respect to identical wagers are treated as paid with respect to a single wager. (Reg § 31.3402(q)-1(c)(1)(ii))[14]

A person who receives gambling winnings subject to withholding must provide certain information on Form W-2G or Form 5754 and give it to the payor. (Code Sec. 3402(q)(6); Reg § 31.3402(q)-1(e))[15]

The above withholding rules don't apply to slot machines, keno and bingo winnings. (Code Sec. 3402(q)(5)) But, backup withholding (¶3043) may apply.[16] A payor must file a Form W-2G for every person the payor pays $1,200 or more in winnings from slot machines or bingo, or $1,500 or more from Keno (after deducting the cost of the winning Keno game). (Reg § 1.6041-10(b)(1)(i))[17]

Casinos and other sponsors of poker tournaments must report tournament winnings of more than $5,000. Sponsors who comply with the reporting requirement won't need to withhold. But, if the reporting requirement isn't met, IRS will enforce it and also require the sponsor to pay any tax that should have been withheld. (Rev Proc 2007-57, Sec. 5, 2007-36 IRB 547)[18]

Withholding on Indian casino profits. Withholding equal to a payment's proportionate

---

9. ¶S-5582
10. ¶S-5581
11. ¶S-2609.1 *et seq.*, S-4918
12. ¶J-8601; ¶J-8603
13. ¶J-8606 *et seq.*

14. ¶J-8610
15. ¶J-8614
16. ¶J-8604
17. ¶S-3697.1
18. ¶J-8603

share of annualized tax is required under tables provided by IRS (Reg § 31.3402(r)-1(a)(2)) on payments to Indian tribal members from the net revenue of most gambling activities of the tribe. (Code Sec. 3402(r))[19]

¶ 3034 Pension, Annuity and Other Withholding. ▬▬▬▬▬▬

Withholding of 20% is required on any designated distribution (¶3036) that's an eligible rollover distribution (¶3035), unless there's a direct trustee-to-trustee transfer. Withholding is required on periodic and lump-sum payments from certain employee plans and certain annuities. But, certain recipients may elect not to have tax withheld (¶3038 *et seq.*).

¶ 3035 Mandatory 20% withholding on designated distributions that are eligible rollover distributions.

Unless a distributee elects to have the distribution paid directly to an eligible retirement plan under the Code Sec. 401(a)(31)(A) trustee-to-trustee rules (¶4307), a payor must withhold 20% of any designated distribution that's an "eligible rollover distribution" as defined by Code Sec. 402(f)(2)(A). The Code Sec. 3405(a) and Code Sec. 3405(b) elective withholding rules (¶3036 *et seq.*) don't apply to an eligible rollover distribution. (Code Sec. 3405(c); Reg § 31.3405(c)-1, Q&A-1)[20]

An eligible rollover distribution (reported by the payor on Form 1099-R) (Reg § 31.3405(c)-1, Q&A-16) is any distribution to an employee from a qualified trust (not from an IRA, SEP, or SIMPLE plan) *other than:*

. . . a required distribution under Code Sec. 401(a)(9);

. . . any distribution that's one of a series of substantially equal periodic payments made (a) not less frequently than annually for the life (or life expectancy) of the employee (or joint lives or expectancies of the employee and his or her designated beneficiary), or (b) for a specified period of ten years or more; or

. . . a hardship distribution from a 401(k) or 403(b) plan. (Code Sec. 3405(c)(3), Code Sec. 402(c)(4), Code Sec. 402(f)(2)(A), Code Sec. 403(b)(8)(B); Reg § 1.402(c)-2, Q&A-3[21]

No withholding is required if the total distribution paid to the distributee under the plan within one tax year is expected to be less than $200. (Reg § 31.3405(c)-1, Q&A-14)[22]

¶ 3036 Required withholding for designated distributions (periodic as well as non-periodic (including lump-sum) payments from pension, profit sharing, stock bonus or other employer deferred compensation plans or IRAs).

Withholding is required for designated distributions (Code Sec. 3405(d)(1)),[23] but the recipient generally may elect out (¶3038) unless the distribution is an eligible rollover distribution (¶3035). Designated distributions are periodic as well as non-periodic (including lump-sum) payments from pension, profit sharing, stock bonus or other employer deferred compensation plans, as well as from IRAs (other than Roth IRAs) and commercial annuities, whether or not the contract was purchased under an employer's plan for employees. (Code Sec. 3405(e)) Annuity payments and other distributions under a state or local government deferred compensation plan, other than a Code Sec. 457 plan, including the Civil Service Retirement System are subject to income tax withholding as well.

19. ¶J-8617
20. ¶J-8576 *et seq.*
21. ¶J-8586

22. ¶s J-8584
23. ¶J-8501 *et seq.*

(Reg § 35.3405-1T, Q&A-22 and 23)[24]

A payor must withhold income tax from any designated distribution (without regard to where the payment is sent or any attempt to elect out of withholding) if a payee has a residence address located outside the U.S. Thus, withholding would be required even if a payee with a foreign residence address asks for the payment to be deposited with a financial institution located in the U.S. (Prop Reg. § 31.3405(e)-1(d)(2), Q&A-3)[25]

The payor of a designated distribution must withhold and is liable for the payment of the tax (unless the payee elects out). But, in the case of a qualified pension, profit sharing, stock bonus, annuity, or 457 governmental plan, the plan administrator has the responsibility, unless he or she directs the payor to withhold and provides the payor with the information set out in the regs. In that case, the responsibility reverts to the payor. (Code Sec. 3405(d); Reg § 35.3405-1T, Q&A E-3)[26]

¶ 3037   Amount of withholding from periodic payments that aren't eligible rollover distributions; withholding certificate (Form W-4).

Payors of a periodic payment (¶3036) that isn't an eligible rollover distribution (¶3035) must withhold on the payment as if it were a wage payment (¶3013) unless the payee elects not to have withholding apply (¶3038). A payee's withholding election (or election of no withholding) is made using Form W-4P. Tax is withheld in accordance with a recipient's Form W-4. If no W-4 is in effect, the amount withheld is determined described in IRS forms, instructions, publications, and other guidance. This "default" rate of withholding is based on treating the payee as married and claiming three withholding allowances. (Code Sec. 3405(a)(1); Code Sec. 3405(a)(4); Reg § 31.3405(a)-1(b); IR 2020-223 09/28/2020)[27]

¶ 3038   Election out of withholding on periodic payments—Form W-4P.

Under Code Sec. 3405(a)(2), a recipient of periodic payments (except for certain U.S. citizens and expatriates living abroad, see ¶3042) may elect not to have any tax withheld. The election remains in effect until revoked. (Code Sec. 3405(a)(2))[28] Elect (or revoke) on Form W-4P.[29]

If the recipient doesn't furnish his or her taxpayer identification number (TIN) to the payor or if IRS has notified the payor that the TIN furnished is incorrect, an election out of withholding isn't effective. (Code Sec. 3405(e)(12))[30]

For periodic payments that are "eligible rollover distributions," see ¶3035.

¶ 3039   Withholding from nonperiodic distributions.

The payor of any nonperiodic distribution that isn't an eligible rollover distribution subject to 20% mandatory withholding (¶3035) must withhold an amount equal to 10% of that distribution (Code Sec. 3405(b)(1)),[31] unless the recipient elects out of withholding (¶3040).

¶ 3040   Electing out of withholding on nonperiodic distributions—Form W-4P.

Under Code Sec. 3405(b)(2), a payee (except for recipients of eligible rollover distributions (¶3035), and certain U.S. citizens and expatriates living abroad (¶3042)) may elect exemption from withholding for any nonperiodic distribution. The election is made on

---

24. ¶J-8504 *et seq.*
25. ¶J-8550
26. ¶J-8518 *et seq.*
27. ¶J-8525

28. ¶J-8526
29. ¶J-8528
30. ¶J-8513
31. ¶J-8533

Form W-4P on a distribution-by-distribution basis. (Code Sec. 3405(b)(2))[32]

If the recipient doesn't furnish his or her taxpayer identification number (TIN) to the payor or if IRS has notified the payor that the TIN furnished is incorrect, an election out of withholding isn't effective. (Code Sec. 3405(e)(12))[33]

¶ 3041   Payor must notify payee of right to elect to have no tax withheld.

Under Code Sec. 3405(e)(10)(B), for periodic payments, the notice to make, renew, or revoke the election out of withholding is required no earlier than six months before and no later than the date of the first payment. For nonperiodic payments, the notice should be given not earlier than six months before the distribution and not later than the time that will give the payee reasonable time to elect out. (Code Sec. 3405(e)(10)(B); Reg § 35.3405-1T, Q&A D-4 and D-9)[34] The notice must state that withholding will apply unless the payee elects otherwise, and if the payee elects no withholding, estimated tax may apply. A sample statement is in the regs. (Reg § 35.3405-1T, Q&A D-21 and D-25)[35]

¶ 3042   Electing out of withholding for any periodic or nonperiodic payment where payment is delivered outside the U.S.

An election out of withholding can't be made for any periodic or nonperiodic payment that is to be delivered outside the U.S. and its possessions (Code Sec. 3405(e)(13)(A)) *unless* the recipient certifies to the payor that the recipient is neither a U.S. citizen, a resident alien, nor a nonresident alien who in the last 10 years has lost his or her U.S. citizenship to avoid U.S. taxes and is thus subject to Code Sec. 877. (Code Sec. 3405(e)(13)(B))[36]

¶ 3043   When Backup Withholding Is Required. ▬▬▬▬▬▬▬

A payor of any reportable payment (¶3044) must withhold 24% of the payment if:

(1) The payee has failed to furnish his or her taxpayer identification number (TIN) to the payor (Code Sec. 3406(a)(1)(A)) or furnishes an "obviously incorrect number," (Code Sec. 3406(h)(1)) i.e., one without nine digits or which includes letters of the alphabet. (Reg § 31.3406(h)-1(b))

(2) IRS or a broker has notified (the "B-notice") the payor that the TIN furnished by the payee is incorrect. (Code Sec. 3406(a)(1), Code Sec. 3406(d)(2))

(3) There has been a notified payee underreporting with respect to interest and dividends. (Code Sec. 3406(a)(1)(C))

(4) The payee has failed to make the exemption certification (on Form W-9) with respect to interest and dividends. (Code Sec. 3406(a)(1)(D))[37]

Backup withholding doesn't apply to any payment made to

. . . an organization exempt from tax under Code Sec. 501(a) (with certain exceptions);

. . . the U.S., a state, the District of Columbia, a U.S. possession, or their political subdivisions;

. . . a foreign government or its political subdivisions;

. . . an international organization;

. . . any wholly-owned agency or instrumentality of any of the above political entities; or

. . . any other person specified in regs. (Code Sec. 3406(g)(1))

Payments to a fiduciary or nominee account or to an exempt recipient (Reg § 31.3406(d)-

---

32. ¶J-8539
33. ¶J-8513
34. ¶J-8528 *et seq.*, ¶J-8539 *et seq.*

35. ¶J-8541, J-8543
36. ¶J-8554
37. ¶J-9001

5(b)) aren't subject to backup withholding.[38]

¶ 3044 Reportable payments, including payments for which information returns are required; payments in property—backup withholding.

Reportable payments include most payments for which information returns are required, such as an interest or dividend payment. (Code Sec. 3406(b)(1))[39] Original issue discount (OID) is treated as a payment of interest for backup withholding purposes, but the amount withheld is limited to the cash paid. (Reg § 31.3406(b)(2)-2(a))[40] Code Sec. 6050W reportable payment transactions (¶4746) are subject to backup withholding.[41] For payments made in property, the payor must backup withhold 24% of the fair market value of the property. Payments made using virtual currency/cryptocurrency (¶2402) are subject to backup withholding.[42]

Reportable payments are treated as if they were wages. Amounts deducted and withheld are treated as if they were deducted and withheld from wages. (Code Sec. 3406(h)(10))[43]

¶ 3045 How to stop backup withholding—certification that withholding should stop—stop date.

A payee can stop backup withholding once it has started by showing that there was no underreporting, correcting any underreporting, showing that backup withholding will cause undue hardship and that it's unlikely the payee will underreport again, or showing that a bona fide dispute exists as to whether there has been any underreporting. (Reg § 35a.3406-2(g)(1), Reg § 31.3406(c)-1(g)) If IRS determines that backup withholding should stop, it will give the payee a written certification to that effect and notify payors and brokers to stop withholding. (Reg § 35a.3406-2(h)(1), Reg § 35a.3406-2(d)(1), Reg § 31.3406(c)-1(g)(1))[44]

Withholding must stop as of the close of the day before the "stop date" (generally 30 days after receipt of the stop notice from IRS or a copy of the certification IRS gave the payee, whichever is earlier). (Code Sec. 3406(e)(5)) The payor may elect to shorten or eliminate the 30-day period. (Code Sec. 3406(e)(5)(C); Reg § 35a.3406-2(e)(2)(iii), Reg § 31.3406(c)-1(e)(2)(i)(B)).[45]

---

38. ¶J-9109
39. ¶J-9101
40. ¶J-9111.1
41. ¶J-9126.2

42. ¶J-9013
43. ¶J-9009
44. ¶J-9603
45. ¶J-9607

Chapter 13 Individual's Tax Computation—Kiddie Tax— Self-Employment Tax—Net Investment Income Tax—Estimated Tax

¶ 3100   **How Income Tax on Individuals Is Computed.** ▬▬▬▬▬

An individual's annual income tax liability on taxable income (¶3101) is computed using either the tax rate schedules or (if taxable income is less than $100,000) the tax tables, see ¶1101 *et seq.* This tax liability may be increased by other taxes, e.g., self-employment tax or alternative minimum tax, and is reduced by certain credits.

For taxation of unearned income of children subject to the kiddie tax, see ¶3128 *et seq.*

For the threshold amounts of gross income that must be reached before a tax return must be filed, see ¶4701.

¶ 3101   **Steps in computing individual's taxable income.**

An individual taxpayer first computes gross income—generally all income from all sources (Code Sec. 61), see ¶1200 *et seq.*

From gross income, taxpayer subtracts the deductions specified at ¶3102 to reach adjusted gross income (AGI). (Code Sec. 62)

Finally, taxpayers who itemize reduce AGI by allowable deductions. (Code Sec. 63(a)), see ¶3109 *et seq.* Non-itemizers reduce AGI by the standard deduction (¶3110), the 20% deduction for qualified business income (¶1593*et seq.*), and the Code Sec. 170(p) deduction (the non-itemizers deduction for charitable contributions for 2021 tax years. (Code Sec. 63(b))[1]

¶ 3102   **Deductions taken "above the line" to reach individual's adjusted gross income (AGI).**

Subtract the following deductions from gross income to reach AGI (¶3101): (Code Sec. 62(a), Reg § 1.62-1T)[2]

. . . Trade or business expenses (¶1507), other than unreimbursed employee business expenses (¶3104). For business-related deductions of "statutory employees," see ¶3103.

. . . Employee expenses that are reimbursed by the employer or a third party (¶3104).

. . . One-half of self-employment tax (¶1746), other than the additional 0.9% self-employment tax (¶1108).

. . . Employee business expenses of certain performing artists (¶3105) and of state and local government officials compensated on a fee basis (¶3106).

. . . Deduction of up to $300 for 2022 (and 2023) of qualifying expenses of educators (¶2224).

. . . Certain unreimbursed travel expenses of National Guard and Reserve members (¶1547).

. . . Losses from the sale or exchange of property (¶2400).

. . . Deductions for property held for production of rents or royalties. (Code Sec. 62(a)(4))

. . . Contributions to tax-favored retirement plans for the self-employed (¶4316).

. . . Contributions to individual retirement accounts (IRAs) or annuities (¶4341).

. . . The "total taxable amount" of a retirement plan lump-sum distribution with respect

---

1. ¶A-2600 *et seq.*   2. ¶A-2601

References beginning with a single letter are to paragraphs in Federal Tax Coordinator 2d and RIA's Analysis of Federal Taxes: Income.

to a participant born before '36, to the extent included in recipient's gross income (¶4329).

. . . Amounts forfeited on premature withdrawal of savings accounts or deposits (¶2164).

. . . Alimony and separate maintenance payments, generally for divorce or separation instruments executed before 2019 (¶2152 *et seq.*).

. . . Repayments of supplemental unemployment compensation. (Code Sec. 62(a)(12))

. . . Jury duty pay remitted to an employer (¶3107).

. . . Depreciation and depletion deductions of a life tenant or an income beneficiary of a trust, or of an heir, legatee or devisee of an estate (¶3917).

. . . Amortization or expensing of reforestation expenditures (¶1955).

. . . Certain foreign housing costs of individuals having income earned abroad (¶4607).

. . . Self-employed medical insurance premiums (¶1530).

. . . Moving expense deduction (limited to members of the U.S. armed forces for 2018–2025) (¶1626 *et seq.*).

. . . Contributions to an Archer medical savings account (Archer MSA, ¶1527).

. . . Deduction for interest on qualified education loans (¶2220 *et seq.*).

. . . Contributions to a health savings account (HSA, ¶1528).

. . . Attorney fees and court costs of civil rights suits, whistleblower awards, and awards under section 21F of the Securities Exchange Act of '34 (¶3108).

¶ 3103 Business-related expenses of "statutory employees"—above-the-line deductions.

For purposes of computing adjusted gross income (AGI) (¶3101), the allowable deductions attributable to the services rendered by a statutory employee (drivers, life insurance salespersons, home workers and other salespersons meeting certain conditions) are treated as trade or business expenses (deductible on Schedule C, rather than as itemized deductions).[3]

¶ 3104 Reimbursed and unreimbursed employee expenses—above-the-line deductions.

Under Code Sec. 62(a)(2)(A), in computing adjusted gross income (AGI) (¶3101), an employee can deduct from gross income employee expenses for which the employee is reimbursed by the employer, its agent, or third party (for whom the employee performs services as an employee of the employer) under an express agreement for reimbursement or other expense allowance under an accountable plan. (But there's no normal "deduction," since the reimbursement is excluded from the employee's gross income —i.e., no deduction for the expense to the extent there's no inclusion of the reimbursement.) (Code Sec. 62(a)(2)(A); Reg § 1.62-2(c)(4))[4] The expense must be otherwise allowable as a deduction (i.e., not a personal expense).[5]

If the reimbursement is for less than the total expenses paid or incurred by the employee, employees may not deduct these unreimbursed expenses for 2018–2025 due to suspension of miscellaneous itemized deductions for those years.[6]

A reimbursement or other expense allowance arrangement under an accountable plan is one that meets tests for (1) business connection, (2) substantiation, and (3) return of amounts in excess of expenses. (Reg § 1.62-2(c)(2)) See ¶1557 *et seq.* for details.

A payor can have more than one arrangement as to one employee. (Reg § 1.62-2(c)(1))[7]

---

3. ¶A-2603
4. ¶A-2604
5. ¶A-2602

6. ¶A-2605
7. ¶L-4703.2

For an above-the-line deduction for expenses of educators, see ¶2224.

¶ 3105 Expenses of certain performing artists—Form 2106—above-the-line deductions.

Under Code Sec. 62(a)(2)(B), expenses of certain performing artists are deductible (use Form 2106 or Form 2106-EZ) in arriving at adjusted gross income (AGI) (¶3101), notwithstanding the disallowance of unreimbursed employee business expenses as above-the-line deductions. To qualify, the taxpayer must have earned at least $200 as a performing artist from each of at least two employers during the tax year. (Code Sec. 62(b)(1)(A), Code Sec. 62(b)(2)) Also, the allowable expenses must exceed 10% of gross income from the services, and AGI for the year (before deducting these expenses) can't exceed $16,000. (Code Sec. 62(b)(1)(B), Code Sec. 62(b)(1)(C)) A married performing artist who lives with a spouse at any time during the year must file a joint return to deduct these expenses to reach AGI. (Code Sec. 62(b)(3)(A)) The two-employer requirement and 10%-of-gross-income test are applied separately to each spouse, but the $16,000 test is applied to their combined income. (Code Sec. 62(b)(3)(B))[8]

¶ 3106 Business expenses of state and local officials paid on a fee basis—above-the-line deductions.

Under Code Sec. 62(a)(2)(C), employee business expenses relating to service as an official of a state or local government (or a political subdivision thereof) are deductible in computing AGI, if the official is compensated on a fee basis.[9]

¶ 3107 Jury duty pay remitted to an employer—above-the-line deductions.

Under Code Sec. 62(a)(13), an individual may deduct jury pay from gross income if the individual is required to remit any of the jury pay to the employer in exchange for compensation for the period the individual was performing jury duty.[10]

¶ 3108 Attorney fees & court costs of civil rights suits, whistleblower awards, and false claims under securities laws—above-the-line deductions.

Any deduction allowable under Chapter 1 for attorney fees and court costs paid by, or on behalf of, the taxpayer in connection with the following is deductible from gross income:

. . . an action involving a claim (1) of unlawful discrimination (defined in Code Sec. 62(e)), (2) of a violation of subchapter III of chapter 37 of title 31, United States Code (Claims Against the U.S. Government), or (3) made under Sec. 1862(b)(3)(A) of the Social Security Act (42 U.S.C. 1395y(b)(3)(A)) (private cause of action under the Medicare Secondary Payer statute), but only up to the amount includible in taxpayer's gross income for the tax year on account of the judgment or settlement. (Code Sec. 62(a)(20))[11]

. . . any Code Sec. 7623(b) whistleblower award or award under section 21F of the Securities Exchange Act of '34, a state law false or fraudulent claim meeting requirements of section 1909(b) of the Social Security Act, or section 23 of the Commodity Exchange Act, but only up to the amount includible in taxpayer's gross income for the tax year on account of the award. (Code Sec. 62(a)(21))[12]

---

8. ¶A-2606
9. ¶A-2607
10. ¶A-2624

11. ¶A-2629
12. ¶A-2630

¶ 3109   Itemized deductions defined—computing individual's income tax.

Itemized deductions (Code Sec. 63(d)) are all the allowable Chapter 1 deductions *other than:* (1) the deductions taken from gross income to reach adjusted gross income (AGI) (¶3102); and (2) any deduction listed in Code Sec. 63(b) (for non-itemizers)—i.e., the standard deduction, the post-2025 Code Sec. 151 exemptions, the pass-through deduction for qualified business income (¶1593 *et seq.*), and the Code Sec. 170(p) charitable deduction for non-itemizers for 2021 only.[13]

caution: For itemized deductions under the alternative minimum tax, see ¶3206.

¶ 3110   Standard deduction—computing individual's income tax.

Under Code Sec. 63(c)(1), the standard deduction is the sum of the basic standard deduction, and the additional standard deduction, as adjusted each year for inflation.[14] Here are the basic standard deduction amounts:[15]

Basic Standard Deduction

Filing Status	2022	2023
Joint filers and surviving spouses	$25,900	$27,700
Heads of household	19,400	20,800
Singles	12,950	13,850
Marrieds filing separately	12,950	13,850

The basic standard deduction of individuals who can be claimed as dependents by another taxpayer can't exceed the greater of (a) $1,150 for 2022 ($1,250 for 2023), or (b) $400 for 2022 ($400 for 2023), plus the individual's earned income. But the basic standard deduction can't be more than the regular basic standard deduction amount shown above ($12,950 for 2022; $13,850 for 2023). (Code Sec. 63(c)(5))[16]

The standard deduction is zero for: a married individual filing separately whose spouse itemizes deductions; a nonresident alien individual; an individual filing a short-year return due to an accounting period change; and, an estate or trust, common trust fund, or partnership. (Code Sec. 63(c)(6))[17]

Elderly and blind taxpayers get additional standard deductions. (Code Sec. 63(c)(3)) A taxpayer who is 65 before the end of the tax year, or blind at the end of the tax year, is entitled to an additional standard deduction. An individual is considered to have reached age 65 on the day before the individual's actual 65th birthday.[18] Here are the additional standard deduction amounts: (Code Sec. 63(f)(1), Code Sec. 63(f)(2), Code Sec. 63(f)(3), Code Sec. 63(c)(4))[19]

Additional Standard Deduction

Filing Status	2022	2023
Marrieds and surviving spouses	1400	1500
Heads of household	1,750	1,850
Singles	1,750	1,850

One who is elderly *and* blind gets an additional standard deduction for each status. (Code Sec. 63(c)(3))[20]

A married individual who files a separate return can claim a spouse's additional standard deduction if the spouse has no gross income and isn't the dependent of another

13. ¶A-2700 *et seq.*
14. ¶A-2801
15. ¶A-2803
16. ¶A-2804
17. ¶A-2802
18. ¶A-2806
19. ¶A-2806, A-2807
20. ¶A-2806

taxpayer. (Code Sec. 63(f)(1)(B), Code Sec. 63(f)(2)(B), Code Sec. 151(b))[21]

An individual claiming an additional standard deduction for blindness who isn't totally blind must get (and keep, but not file) a certification from an eye doctor or registered optometrist. If the eye condition will never improve, the statement should state this.[22]

On a decedent's final return, the fiduciary may claim the full amount of the appropriate standard deduction regardless of the date of death.[23]

caution: For the standard deduction under the alternative minimum tax, see ¶3206.

¶ 3111 Election to itemize deductions in computing taxable income—computing individual's income tax.

Under Code Sec. 63(e), no itemized deductions are allowed unless an election to itemize is made on the return. A taxpayer who elected to itemize and wants to switch to the standard deduction, or vice versa, can. But the change isn't allowed unless a separately filing spouse makes a consistent change, and both spouses consent in writing to assessment of any deficiency resulting from the change. (Code Sec. 63(e)(3); Reg § 1.63-1)[24]

¶ 3112 Personal exemptions/dependent deductions, suspended for 2018–2025; inflation-adjusted amount still applies for certain purposes.

Under Code Sec. 151(d)(5)), the Code Sec. 151 deduction for personal exemptions—including deductions for dependents as defined in Code Sec. 152 (¶3113)—is suspended (i.e., reduced to zero) for 2018–2025.

But, for purposes of any Code provision other than Code Sec. 151, the reduction to zero isn't taken into account. So, for tax years 2018–2025, although the personal exemption is zero, if another Code provision refers to a taxpayer being allowed a deduction (or an individual for whom a taxpayer is allowed a deduction) under Code Sec. 151, Code Sec. 151 does apply for that purpose, and annual inflation-adjusted exemption amounts apply, as set forth in IRS guidance. This is the case for, among other provisions: the Code Sec. 24 child tax credit (¶2350), the earned income credit (¶2337), and qualification for head-of-household filing status (¶3127). The amount treated as the exemption amount for these rules is $4,400 for 2022 ($4,700 for 2023). (Reg § 1.152-2(e)(1))[25]

¶ 3113 "Dependent" defined—computing individual's income tax.

Under Code Sec. 152(a), a person qualifies as a taxpayer's dependent (¶3112) if the person is the taxpayer's qualifying child (¶3114) or qualifying relative (¶3116).[26] (From 2018 through 2025, the exemption amount under Code Sec. 151 is zero, but the operation of Code provisions that refer to a taxpayer who is allowed a deduction (or an individual for whom a taxpayer is allowed a deduction) under Code Sec. 151 is unchanged, and two different exemption amounts are provided for 2018–2025 see ¶3112.[27]) An individual who is a taxpayer's dependent for a tax year is treated as having no dependents for the individual's tax year beginning in the calendar year when the taxpayer's tax year begins. (Code Sec. 152(b)(1)) But, for purposes of this rule, the individual isn't considered a dependent of a person if that person isn't required to file an income tax return and either doesn't file a return, or files a return solely to claim a refund of estimated or withheld taxes. (Prop Reg. § 1.152-1(a)(2)(i) ["Taxpayers may apply"]) [28]

Also, an individual isn't treated as a taxpayer's dependent if the individual makes a joint return with the individual's spouse for the tax year beginning in the calendar year

21. ¶A-2806
22. ¶A-2807
23. ¶C-9603
24. ¶A-2702

25. ¶A-3500.1
26. ¶A-3601
27. ¶A-3600.1
28. ¶A-3626

when the taxpayer's tax year begins. (Code Sec. 152(b)(2))[29]

A dependent must be a U.S. citizen, national, or resident, or a resident of Canada or Mexico at some time in the calendar year in which the taxpayer's tax year begins. (Code Sec. 152(b)(3)(A), Reg § 1.152-2(a)(1))[30] But, an adopted child who isn't a U.S. citizen or resident (or a resident of Canada or Mexico) isn't excluded from the definition of dependent if: (i) for the taxpayer's tax year, the child has the same principal place of abode as the taxpayer; (ii) for the taxpayer's tax year, the child is a member of the taxpayer's household; and, (iii) the taxpayer is a U.S. citizen or national. This rule is limited to adopted children, and doesn't apply to stepchildren of a U.S. citizen who have not been adopted or lawfully placed for adoption. (Code Sec. 152(b)(3)(B))[31]

¶ 3114   "Qualifying child" defined—computing individual's income tax.

A taxpayer's "qualifying child" qualifying as a dependent (¶3113) for a tax year is an individual who: (1) bears a relationship to the taxpayer specified below; (2) has the same principal place of abode as the taxpayer for more than half the tax year (except that a child of divorced or separated parents can be treated as the noncustodial parent's qualifying child if the custodial parent has released the claim to the child's dependency exemption to the noncustodial parent under Code Sec. 152(e)); (3) hasn't reached a specified age (see below); (4) hasn't provided over half the child's own support for the calendar year in which the taxpayer's tax year begins; and (5) hasn't filed a joint return (other than for a refund claim) with the individual's spouse for the tax year beginning in the calendar year in which the taxpayer's tax year begins. (Code Sec. 152(c)(1), Code Sec. 152(e)(1))[32] For tie-breaking rules, see ¶3115.

The following relationships of an individual to the taxpayer meet requirement (1), above:

. . . a child (defined below) of the taxpayer, or a child's descendant (Code Sec. 152(c)(2)(A)), or

. . . a brother, sister, stepbrother, stepsister, half-brother, or half-sister of the taxpayer or a descendant of those relatives. (Code Sec. 152(c)(2)(B), Code Sec. 152(f)(4))[33]

For this purpose, the term "child" means an individual who is:

- a son, daughter, stepson, or stepdaughter of the taxpayer (Code Sec. 152(f)(1)(A)(i)), or
- an eligible foster child of the taxpayer (Code Sec. 152(f)(1)(A)(i)), i.e., an individual placed with the taxpayer by an authorized placement agency or by judgment, decree, or other order of any court of competent jurisdiction. (Code Sec. 152(f)(1)(C))

For this purpose, a registered domestic partner (or partner in other formal relationship that isn't a marriage under state law) is the stepparent of the partner's child if so treated under the law of the state in which the partners reside.[34]

In determining if an individual is taxpayer's son, daughter, stepson, stepdaughter, brother, or sister, one who's legally adopted by an individual, or lawfully placed with one for legal adoption by the individual, is treated as a child of that individual by blood. (Code Sec. 152(f)(1)(B))[35]

An individual meets the age requirement in (3), above, if the individual:

. . . is younger than the taxpayer and hasn't reached age 19 as of the end of the calendar year in which the taxpayer's tax year begins;

. . . is younger than the taxpayer and is a student who hasn't reached age 24 as of the end of that calendar year (Code Sec. 152(c)(3)(A)); or

---

29. ¶A-3622
30. ¶A-3623
31. ¶A-3624
32. ¶A-3605.2

33. ¶A-3605.3
34. ¶A-3605.3
35. ¶A-3612

... is permanently and totally disabled, as defined in Code Sec. 22(e)(3) (¶2346), at any time during that calendar year. (Code Sec. 152(c)(3)(B))[36]

✪observation: If a child of the taxpayer doesn't meet the definition of a "qualifying child," for example, because the child doesn't meet the age test, the child may still qualify as a dependent under the "qualifying relative" test, ¶3116.

¶ 3115 "Qualifying child"—tie-breaking rules where two or more taxpayers claim a qualifying child.

If an individual can be claimed as a qualifying child (¶3114) by two or more taxpayers for a tax year beginning in the same calendar year, the following tie-breaking rules apply:

(1) If two or more taxpayers may claim an individual as a qualifying child for a tax year beginning in the same calendar year, the individual will be treated as the qualifying child of the taxpayer who is: (a) a parent of the individual, or (b) if item (a) doesn't apply, the taxpayer with the highest adjusted gross income (AGI) for that tax year. (Code Sec. 152(c)(4)(A)) If more than one taxpayer who can claim an individual as a qualifying child is a parent of the individual, then any one of those parents may claim the individual as a qualifying child. (Prop Reg. § 1.152-2(g)(1)(i) ["Taxpayers may apply"])

(2) If the parents don't file a joint return together, the child will be treated as the qualifying child of: (a) the parent with whom the child resided for the longest period of time during the tax year, or (b) if the child resided with both parents for the same amount of time during the tax year, the parent with the higher AGI. (Code Sec. 152(c)(4)(B)) The same rule will apply where a child is a qualifying child of both parents who are registered domestic partners or partners in a similar formal relationship that isn't a marriage under state law.

(3) If an individual's parents can claim the individual as a qualifying child but no parent does, another taxpayer may claim the individual as a qualifying child, but only if that taxpayer's AGI is higher than the highest AGI of any parent of the individual. (Code Sec. 152(c)(4)(C))[37]

¶ 3116 "Qualifying relative" defined—computing individual's income tax.

Under Code Sec. 152(d)(1), a "qualifying relative" qualifying as a dependent (¶3113) for a tax year is an individual:

(1) who bears a specified relationship to the taxpayer (see below);

(2) whose gross income for the calendar year in which that tax year begins is less than the exemption amount ($4,400 for 2022; $4,700 for 2023);

(3) with respect to whom the taxpayer provides over half of the individual's support (¶3118) for the calendar year in which that tax year begins (for multiple support agreements, see ¶3117); and

(4) who isn't a qualifying child (¶3114) of that taxpayer or of any other taxpayer for any tax year that begins in the calendar year in which that tax year begins.[38]

A registered domestic partner is a dependent of the partner if the requirements of Code Sec. 151 and Code Sec. 152 are met. Registered domestic partners who live in community property states are unlikely to meet the requirements of (2) and (3) above.[39]

The following relationships to the taxpayer meet the relationship test (item (1), above): a child or a descendant of a child, including foster and adopted children who will qualify

---

36. ¶A-3605.4
37. ¶A-3605.5 *et seq.*

38. ¶A-3605.6
39. ¶A-3608.1

under the rules in ¶3114; a brother, sister, half-brother, half-sister, stepbrother, or stepsister; the father or mother, or an ancestor of either; a stepfather or stepmother; a nephew or niece; an uncle or aunt; a son-in-law, daughter-in-law, father-in-law, mother-in-law, brother-in-law, or sister-in-law; and an individual (other than one who, at any time in the tax year, was the taxpayer's spouse, determined without regard to Code Sec. 7703) whose principal place of abode is the taxpayer's home and who is a member of the taxpayer's household for the taxpayer's tax year. (Code Sec. 152(d)(2), Code Sec. 152(f)(4))[40]

¶ 3117   Multiple support agreement—Form 2120—computing individual's income tax.

For purposes of the support test for qualifying relatives (¶3116), over one-half of an individual's support (¶3118) for a calendar year is treated as received from the taxpayer if:

(1) no one person contributed over half of that support;

(2) over half of that support was received from two or more persons each of whom, but for the fact that that person alone didn't contribute over half of that support, would have been entitled to claim the individual as a dependent for a tax year beginning in that calendar year;

(3) the taxpayer contributed over 10% of that support; *and*

(4) each person described in (2), other than the taxpayer, who contributed over 10% of that support files a written declaration that the person won't claim the individual as a dependent for any tax year that begins in that calendar year. (Code Sec. 152(d)(3))[41]

¶ 3118   "Support" of dependent defined—computing individual's income tax.

Support for purposes of determining if an individual is a dependent (see ¶3112 *et seq.*) includes:[42]

. . . food and clothing;

. . . recreation, including toys, summer camp, horseback riding, entertainment, vacations;

. . . medical and dental care, including premiums on accident and health insurance;

. . . child care expenses, even though a credit is also allowed for these expenses;

. . . allowances, gifts;

. . . lodging—when furnished in kind, measured by its fair market value rather than actual cost (Reg § 1.152-1(a)(2));[43]

. . . education—these costs include board, uniforms at military schools, and tuition, even where free schooling is available. Scholarship payments received by a dependent are treated as support furnished by someone other than the taxpayer, but aren't counted in determining if the taxpayer furnished more than half the dependent's support if the dependent is the taxpayer's child (including stepchild, foster child, or child adopted or placed for adoption) who is a full-time student at an educational institution. (Code Sec. 152(f)(5), Reg § 1.152-1(c))[44]

Under proposed regs that taxpayers can apply prior to finalization, a surviving child's social security benefit payment used to support the child is considered as paid by the child for the child's own support (Prop Reg. § 1.152-4(a)(3)(ii)(B) ["Taxpayers may apply"]), [45] and governmental payments and need-based subsidies for an item of support are support provided by a third party, the government. (Prop Reg. § 1.152-4(a)(3)(i), ["Taxpayers may

40. ¶A-3606
41. ¶A-3731
42. ¶A-3701 *et seq.*

43. ¶A-3701 *et seq.*, A-3714 *et seq.*
44. ¶A-3721
45. ¶A-3712

apply"]) But governmental payments that are based on a taxpayer's earnings and contributions into the Social Security system are support provided by the individual for whose benefit the payments are made, to the extent those payments are used for that individual's support. (Prop Reg. § 1.152-4(a)(3)(ii)(A) ["Taxpayers may apply"]) [46]

Armed Forces dependency allotments—the amount contributed by the government *and* the amount withheld from the pay of the member of the Armed Forces—are treated as contributed by the member.[47]

¶ 3119 Allocating support of several contributors to several dependents—computing individual's income tax.

Where more than one member of a household contributes toward expenses that are equally applicable to all members of the household, the contributors are presumed (absent contrary evidence) to have pooled their contributions toward the support (¶3118) of all members. The total contributed is divided equally among the members as amounts paid for their support, unless there is proof of how much was actually spent for particular members.[48]

¶ 3120 Treatment of child as "qualifying child" or "qualifying relative" by noncustodial parent—Form 8332—computing individual's income tax.

A child is treated as being the "qualifying child" (¶3114) or "qualifying relative" (¶3116) of the noncustodial parent for a calendar year, for qualifying as a dependent (see ¶3113) if:

(1) the child receives over half of the child's support during the calendar year from the parents;

(2) the child's parents: (a) are divorced or legally separated under a decree of divorce or separate maintenance; (b) are separated under a written separation agreement; or (c) live apart at all times during the last six months of the calendar year, whether or not they are or were married;

(3) the child is in the custody of one or both parents for over half the calendar year; and

(4) the custodial parent signs a written declaration (on Form 8332) stating that he or she won't claim that child as a dependent for the tax year beginning in that calendar year, which the noncustodial parent attaches to his or her return *or* a pre-'85 decree of divorce or separate maintenance or written separation agreement between the parents provides that the noncustodial parent can claim the child as a dependent, and the noncustodial parent provides at least $600 for support of the child during the year. Code Sec. 152(e)(1), Code Sec. 152(e)(2),Reg § 1.152-4(b))[49]

A child is in the custody of one or both parents for more than one-half of the calendar year (item (3), above) if one or both parents have the right under state law to physical custody of the child for more than one-half of the calendar year. (Reg § 1.152-4(c)) But a child isn't in the custody of either parent for this purpose after the child reaches the age of majority and is emancipated under state law.[50]

The custodial parent is the parent with whom the child resides for the greater number of nights during the calendar year. (Code Sec. 152(e)(4)(A),Reg § 1.152-4(d))[1]

The above rules apply despite: the Code Sec. 152(c)(1)(B) requirement that a qualifying child have the same principal place of abode as the taxpayer for more than half the year, ¶3114; the Code Sec. 152(c)(4) tie-breaking rules, ¶3115; or the Code Sec. 152(d)(1)(C)

---

46. ¶A-3712
47. ¶A-3711
48. ¶A-3708

49. ¶A-3851
50. ¶A-3852
1. ¶A-3853

support test for qualifying relatives, ¶3116. (Code Sec. 152(e)(1),Reg § 1.152-4(b)(1))[2]

In certain cases, IRS treats a child of parents who are divorced, separated, or living apart as the dependent of both parents for purposes of Code Sec. 105(b) (employer-provided medical expense reimbursements, ¶1254), Code Sec. 132(h)(2)(B) (excludable fringe benefits, ¶1241), Code Sec. 213(d)(5) (deductible medical expenses, ¶2142), Code Sec. 220(d)(2) (Archer Medical Savings Accounts (MSAs), ¶1527), and Code Sec. 223(d)(2) (Health Saving Accounts (HSAs), ¶1528) when the custodial parent hasn't released the claim to the exemption for the child under Code Sec. 152(e)(2).[3]

The above rules relating to release don't apply where, under the Code Sec. 152(d)(3) rules for multiple support agreements (¶3117), more than half the child's support is treated as having been received from a taxpayer. (Code Sec. 152(e)(5))[4]

For purposes of these rules, if a parent remarries, support of a child received from this remarried parent's spouse is treated as received from the parent. (Code Sec. 152(e)(6))[5]

¶ 3121 Relationship test—effect of death or divorce—computing individual's income tax.

For purposes of rules that incorporate the definition of "dependent" (see ¶3112), death or divorce doesn't end relationships established by marriage. So, for example, the relationship of son-in-law and father-in-law survives the spouse's death. (Reg § 1.152-2(d))[6]

¶ 3122 Tax status of kidnapped children—computing individual's income tax.

Solely for the purposes listed below, a taxpayer's child who is presumed by law enforcement authorities to have been kidnapped by a non-family member, and who had, for the tax year in which the kidnapping occurred, the same principal place of abode as the taxpayer for more than half of the portion of that year before the kidnapping date, is treated as meeting the requirement in Code Sec. 152(c) that a "qualifying child" have the same principal place of abode as the taxpayer for more than half the tax year for all tax years ending during the period that the individual is kidnapped. (Code Sec. 152(f)(6)(A)) This rule applies for purposes of (i) the child tax credit; (ii) surviving spouse or a head of a household status; and (iii) the earned income credit. (Code Sec. 152(f)(6)(B)) Comparable treatment applies to certain qualifying relatives (¶3116). (Code Sec. 152(f)(6)(C))[7]

¶ 3123 Tax rate schedules for individuals.

There's a tax rate schedule for:

(1) Single persons (not married at year's end), including certain marrieds living apart (¶3126), see ¶1102. These rates are more favorable than those for marrieds filing separate returns, but less favorable than head-of-household and (generally) joint return rates.

(2) Married couples filing joint returns, and certain widows and widowers who qualify as "surviving spouses" (¶3125), see ¶1103. These are often the most favorable rates.

(3) Heads of household (¶3127), see ¶1105—more favorable rates than those for single persons.

(4) Married persons filing separately, see ¶1104—least favorable rates. (Code Sec. 1)[8]

For 2018–2025, the individual tax rates are 10%, 12%, 22%, 24%, 32%, 35%, and 37%. (Code Sec. 1)[9]

---

2. ¶A-3851
3. ¶A-3861
4. ¶A-3851
5. ¶A-3851

6. ¶A-3606
7. ¶A-3601.1
8. ¶A-1101 *et seq.*
9. ¶A-1102

¶ 3124 Tax tables—computing individual's income tax.

IRS has prepared tax tables, based on the tax rates. (Code Sec. 3(a)(1))[10] The 2022 table for Form 1040 filers with taxable income less than $100,000 is reproduced at ¶1111. The tables aren't used by those who file a short-period return because they changed their accounting period. (Code Sec. 3(b)(1))[11]

¶ 3125 When surviving spouse (qualifying widow/er) gets lower joint return rates.

A surviving spouse (qualifying widow/er) whose spouse died during either of the surviving spouse's two tax years immediately preceding the tax year (Code Sec. 2(a)(1)) is taxed at joint return rates (Code Sec. 1(a)(2)) if the surviving spouse:

. . . hasn't remarried at any time before the end of the tax year (Code Sec. 2(a)(2)(A)),

. . . "maintains" (pays over 50% of the costs of) a household as the surviving spouse's home that's the "principal place of abode" of a dependent (a) who is taxpayer's son or daughter (including adopted children, but not foster children), stepson, or stepdaughter, and (b) for whom taxpayer would have been entitled to a dependency deduction (¶3112 et seq) for the tax year (Code Sec. 2(a)(1)(B)), and

. . . could file a joint return with the deceased for the year of death. (Code Sec. 2(a)(2)(B))[12]

observation: The surviving spouse rules *don't* apply for the year the spouse died. For when a joint return can be filed (and joint return rates used) for that year, see ¶4705 and ¶4708.

A special rule applies for spouses of individuals in "missing status" as a result of "combat zone" or "qualified hazardous duty area" service. If an MIA or POW is officially determined to be dead, and so is removed from the missing status rolls, surviving spouse status doesn't depend on the actual date of death. The relevant date is the date of the official determination, or, if earlier, two years after the date of official termination of combat activities in that zone. If a later actual death is established, that date will control. (Code Sec. 2(a)(3))[13]

¶ 3126 Certain married individuals (spouses) living apart treated as unmarried; abandoned spouse filing-status rule.

Under Code Sec. 7703(b), a married taxpayer is considered single for tax purposes if the taxpayer meets all of the following tests (Code Sec. 7703(b); Reg § 1.7703-1(b)):

(1) Files a separate return.

(2) Maintains as the taxpayer's home a household that for more than half the tax year is the principal place of abode of a child (defined in Code Sec. 152(f)(1), ¶3114) for whom the taxpayer is entitled to a dependency deduction for the year, or would be so entitled if the taxpayer hadn't released the exemption to the noncustodial parent (¶3120). (Code Sec. 7703(b)(1))

(3) Furnishes over half the cost of maintaining the household. (Code Sec. 7703(b)(2))

(4) During the last six months of the tax year, the taxpayer's spouse isn't a member of the household. (Code Sec. 7703(b)(3))[14]

observation: Individuals treated as unmarried under this "abandoned spouse" rule

---

10. ¶A-1100*et seq.*
11. ¶A-1181
12. ¶A-1700 *et seq.*

13. ¶A-1703
14. ¶A-1610 *et seq.*

can use the single or head-of-household rates.

Either or both spouses can qualify as "unmarried" by meeting the tests. If only one spouse qualifies, the other spouse must use married-filing-separately rates.[15]

A taxpayer who doesn't meet the above rules is considered married even though living apart from a spouse, unless legally separated under a decree of divorce or separate maintenance. (Reg § 1.7703-1(a))[16]

¶ 3127 Head-of-household filing status.

Under Code Sec. 2(b)(1), to qualify as a head of household for a tax year, a taxpayer must:

(1) be unmarried (or treated as unmarried, ¶3126) at the end of the year;

(2) not be a surviving spouse (Code Sec. 2(b)(1), Reg § 1.2-2(b)(1));

(3) not be a nonresident alien at any time that year (Code Sec. 2(b)(3)(A); *and*

(4) maintain a household: (a) that is the taxpayer's home, and for more than half of the tax year, the principal place of abode of a child or other dependent who is a "member of that household" (Code Sec. 2(b)(1)(A)), or (b) (not necessarily the taxpayer's own) that for the tax year is the principal place of abode for either the taxpayer's father or mother. (Code Sec. 2(b)(1)(B))[17]

The same individual can't be used to qualify more than one taxpayer as head of household during the same tax year. (Reg § 1.2-2(b)(2))[18]

A qualifying child for this purpose is defined in Code Sec. 152(c) (¶3114), but without regard to Code Sec. 152(e) (custodial parent's release of exemption, ¶3120). But a taxpayer isn't eligible for head of household status if the child is married at the end of taxpayer's tax year and isn't taxpayer's dependent because the child filed a joint return and/or isn't a U.S. citizen or resident. (Code Sec. 2(b)(1)(A)(i))[19] If registered domestic partners who reside in a community property state pay all the costs of maintaining a household from community funds, each partner has incurred half the cost, and neither can qualify. Even if one partner pays more than half by contributing separate funds, that partner cannot file as head of household if that partner's only dependent is the other registered domestic partner.[20]

¶ 3128 Tax on Unearned Income of Children—Kiddie Tax. ▬▬▬▬▬

Children to whom the kiddie tax (Code Sec. 1(g)(1)) rules apply (¶3129), who have over the prescribed amount of unearned income (¶3131) for the tax year, are taxed on that excess amount at the parents' tax rates, if the parents' tax rates are higher than the child's rates.

¶ 3129 Children who are subject to the kiddie tax.

Under Code Sec. 1(g)(2), the kiddie tax applies to a child if: (1) the child is under age 19 by the close of the tax year, or is a full-time student age 19 to 23; (2) the child's unearned income (i.e., investment income) exceeds an inflation-adjusted prescribed amount ($2,300 for 2022; $2,500 for 2023); and (3) the child doesn't file a joint return. For a child age 18, or a child age 19 to 23 who is a full-time student, the kiddie tax rules apply only if the child's earned income doesn't exceed one-half of the amount of the child's support. (Code Sec. 1(g)(2))[21]

---

15. ¶A-1502
16. ¶A-1611
17. ¶A-1401.1 *et seq.*
18. ¶A-1401.1
19. ¶A-1406 *et seq.*
20. ¶A-1416 *et seq.*
21. ¶A-1301

Chapter 13 / *Kiddie Tax*

¶ 3130   **Computing the kiddie tax—Form 8615.**

Under Code Sec. 1(g)(1), the tax on the income of a child subject (¶3129) to the kiddie tax rules is computed (on Form 8615) as follows.

The tax equals the greater of: (1) the tax that would be imposed if the kiddie tax rules didn't apply; or (2) the sum of: (a) the tax that would be imposed if the kiddie tax rules didn't apply and if the child's taxable income for the tax year were reduced by the child's net unearned income (¶3131), plus (b) the child's share of the "allocable parental tax." (Code Sec. 1(g)(1))[22]

The "allocable parental tax" is the excess of: (A) the tax that would have been imposed on the parent's taxable income if that income included the net unearned income (¶3131) of all that parent's children subject to the kiddie tax rules, over (B) the tax that would be imposed on the parent's taxable income without regard to the kiddie tax rules. (Code Sec. 1(g)(3)(A); Reg § 1.1(i)-1T, Q&A 4)[23]

Parent's TIN. If a child has investment income that's taxed at the parent's marginal rate under the kiddie tax rules, the parent's taxpayer identification number (TIN) must be included on the child's return, and the parent must furnish the number to the child. (Code Sec. 1(g)(6))[24] If a child can't get the required information from a parent, the child (or legal representative) can request the necessary information from IRS. (Code Sec. 6103(e)(1)(A)(iii); Reg § 1.1(i)-1T)[25]

¶ 3131   **"Net unearned income" for kiddie tax purposes.**

For the kiddie tax rules (¶3130), "net unearned income" (Code Sec. 1(g)(4)(A)) is the portion of the child's "AGI not attributable to earned income" (i.e., the child's investment income), reduced by the sum of the following amounts (collectively, the "reduction amount") (Code Sec. 1(g)(4)(A); Reg § 1.1(i)-1T):

(1) the amount in effect for the tax year under Code Sec. 63(c)(5)(A) (Code Sec. 1(g)(4)(A)(ii)(I); Reg § 1.1(i)-1T, Q&A6), relating to one component of the standard deduction for a child who can be claimed as a dependent—i.e., $1,150 for 2022 ($1,250 for 2023, see ¶3110);

(2) the greater of (a) the amount in (1) or (b) the amount of the itemized deductions directly connected with the production of the unearned income if the child itemizes deductions (Code Sec. 1(g)(4)(A)(ii)(II); Reg § 1.1(i)-1T, Q&A6);

(3) adjustments to income attributable to the unearned income, such as the penalty on early withdrawal of savings.[26]

observation: For children who don't itemize deductions, the "reduction amount" for net unearned income is generally $2,300 for 2022 ($2,500 for 2023).

But a child's net unearned income can't exceed the child's taxable income. (Code Sec. 1(g)(4)(B))[27]

Earned income means earned income as defined in Code Sec. 911(d)(2)—i.e., income attributable to wages, salaries, or other amounts received as compensation for personal services. (Code Sec. 1(g)(4)(A)(i); Reg § 1.1(i)-1T, Q&A6) Distributions from certain qualified disability trusts are treated as earned income. (Code Sec. 1(g)(4)(C)) But the taxable part of social security or pension benefits paid to the child is unearned income. (Reg § 1.1(i)-1T, Q&A9) Unearned income also includes taxable interest, dividends, capital gains (including capital gain distributions), rents, royalties, etc.[28]

---

22. ¶A-1301
23. ¶A-1311
24. ¶S-1544
25. ¶S-6302, ¶S-6403

26. ¶A-1305
27. ¶A-1305
28. ¶A-1301.1, A-1307

¶ 3132   Parents' election to be taxed on child's unearned income—Form 8814—kiddie tax.

Under Code Sec. 1(g)(7)(B)(i), a parent can irrevocably elect (on Form 8814) to include in the parent's gross income for the tax year the child's gross income in excess of $2,300 for 2022 ($2,500 for 2023). (Code Sec. 1(g)(7)(B)(i); Reg § 301.9100-8(a)(4)(i)) The child is then treated as having no gross income for the year and isn't required to file a return. (Code Sec. 1(g)(7)(A))[29]

For 2022, the election applies only if: the child's gross income is only from interest, dividends, and capital gain distributions; is more than $1,150 and less than $11,500 ($1,250 and $12,500 for 2023); the child made no estimated tax payments for, and didn't apply any overpayments to, the year; and backup withholding didn't apply. (Code Sec. 1(g)(7)(A))[30]

For 2022, the electing parent's tax equals the sum of: (1) the tax on the parent's taxable income after taking into account the child's gross income over $2,300, plus (2) 10% of the lesser of (a) $1,150, or (b) the excess of the child's gross income over $1,150. (Code Sec. 1(g)(7)(B)(ii))[31] Any interest income that is a tax preference item of the child is treated as that of the electing parent. (Code Sec. 1(g)(7)(B)(iii)) For 2023, the electing parent's tax equals the sum of: (1) the tax on the parent's taxable income after taking into account the child's gross income over $2,500, plus (2) 10% of the lesser of (a) $1,250, or (b) the excess of the child's gross income over $1,250.[32]

    illustration: S, age 6, receives $5,000 in interest income in 2022. The requirements for making the election to report his income on his parents' return are satisfied, and his parents make the election. So they include $2,700 of S's gross income on their tax return ($5,000 gross income, minus $2,300 (2 × $1,150)). They also must pay an additional tax of $115 (i.e., 10% of the lesser of (a) $1,150, or (b) $3,850 ($5,000 − $1,150)). Assuming a 25% tax bracket applies to the parents, the added tax under the election would be $790, i.e., $675 (25% × $2,700) + $115.

¶ 3133   Self-Employment (SE) Tax—Schedule SE ▬▬▬▬▬▬

Self-employeds pay social security (OASDI) and Medicare (hospital insurance) taxes as part of their income tax.

These taxes are imposed (compute on Form 1040, Schedule SE) on self-employment income (¶3134). (Code Sec. 1401(a), Code Sec. 1401(b)).[33] For contribution bases and rates for the SE tax, including the 0.9% additional Medicare self-employment tax, see ¶1109. For who is subject to the SE tax, see ¶3138.

¶ 3134   Self-employment (SE) income subject to SE tax.

SE income consists of net earnings from self-employment (¶3135). But in computing an individual's SE tax (¶3133), the maximum amount of SE income subject to OASDI tax for a tax year (whether 12 months or less) is the contribution base (¶1109) for the calendar year in which the tax year begins, minus wages received in the same tax year. If net earnings from self-employment are less than $400 ($100 for a church employee (Code Sec. 1402(j)(2)(B))), SE income for that year is zero. (Code Sec. 1402(b); Reg § 1.1402(b)-1)[34]

    observation: Since a 7.65% deduction (¶3135) is allowed from net profits (i.e., net earnings from self-employment before that deduction), an individual can have actual net profits of up to $433.13 (92.35% of $433.13 = $400) without triggering SE tax.

---

29. ¶A-1326
30. ¶A-1327
31. ¶A-1330

32. ¶A-1330
33. ¶A-6001
34. ¶A-6031 *et seq.*

A mitigation provision can come into play where wages were erroneously reported as self-employment income or vice versa. (Code Sec. 6521)[35]

¶ 3135 Net earnings from self employment; computation; exclusions—self-employment (SE) tax.

Under Code Sec. 1402(a), net earnings from self employment is gross income, under the individual's income tax accounting method, from a trade or business carried on by the individual, less allowable deductions for that business, plus the distributive share of partnership taxable income (whether or not distributed) or loss from a partnership of which the individual's a member. (Code Sec. 1402(a); Reg § 1.1402(a)-1)[36] In addition to gross income derived from a trade or business, certain other items, such as directors' fees, are included in determining net earnings from self employment.[37] An independent contractor who receives virtual currency/cryptocurrency (¶2402, e.g., Bitcoin), as payment for services has self-employment income in the amount of the FMV of the virtual currency. If a taxpayer's "mining" of convertible virtual currency is a trade or business and isn't undertaken as an employee, the net earnings from self-employment from that activity is self-employment income.[38]

A deduction is allowed for 7.65% of net earnings from self-employment for the tax year (determined without this deduction), computed without regard to the 0.9% additional Medicare self-employment tax (see ¶1109). (Code Sec. 1402(a)(12))[39]

An individual with more than one business must combine the net earnings from each to determine self-employment income. The gains and loss from the businesses are netted, so a loss in one reduces a gain in another. (Reg § 1.1402(a)-2(c))[40] If an individual has a part-time business and a regular job as an employee, only the income from the part-time business is included in net earnings.[41]

In computing net earnings from self-employment, the following deductions *aren't* allowed:

. . . deduction for a self-employed's health insurance costs (Code Sec. 162(l)(4));

. . . deduction for net operating losses (Code Sec. 1402(a)(4));

. . . nonbusiness deductions.[42]

Net earnings from self-employment *don't include*:

• certain income received by a retired partner under a written plan of the partnership (Code Sec. 1402(a)(10));[43]

• dividends or interest on investments (Code Sec. 1402(a)(2));[44]

• gains (or losses) from disposition of a capital asset or other property that's not inventory or held for sale to customers (Code Sec. 1402(a)(3));[45] but options and commodities dealers must include gains and losses derived from dealing or trading in options and regulated futures subject to mark-to-market rules in SE net earnings (Code Sec. 1402(i));[46]

• gain or loss of a securities or commodities trader that's treated as ordinary solely by reason of the election of mark-to-market treatment (Code Sec. 475(f)(1)(D));[47]

• qualified disaster relief (or mitigation) payments (Code Sec. 139(d));[48]

• rentals from real estate (and personal property leased with it) held for investment. (Code Sec. 1402(a)(1)) The fact that an activity is characterized as a "rental activity"

35. ¶T-3634
36. ¶A-6100 *et seq.*
37. ¶A-6110
38. ¶A-6110.1
39. ¶A-6114
40. ¶A-6103
41. ¶A-6103

42. ¶A-6113
43. ¶A-6166
44. ¶A-6108
45. ¶A-6109
46. ¶A-6112
47. ¶A-6112.1
48. ¶A-6105

under Code Sec. 469(c)(2) (¶1810) does not determine whether the activity is "rentals from real estate" under this exclusion. The exclusion doesn't apply to rents received by real estate dealers in the normal course of business (Reg § 1.1402(a)-4(a)),[49] or if the rent is for living quarters where *services* (e.g., maid service) are also rendered primarily for the occupant's convenience (Reg § 1.1402(a)-4(c)(2)), such as in hotels, boarding houses, tourist camps or homes, parking lots, warehouses and storage garages;[50]

• rents paid in crop shares unless paid under an arrangement where the landowner (or tenant) materially participates in crop production or controls and directs the farming operation and pays the farmer at a fixed rate as an employee (Reg § 1.1402(a)-4(b));[1]

• certain termination payments received by former insurance salesmen (Code Sec. 1402(k));[2]

• a shareholder's share of an S corporation's income (whether distributed or not) or loss.[3]

A passive activity loss that's disallowed for income tax purposes isn't taken into account in computing net earnings from self-employment. (Reg § 1.469-1T(d)(3))[4]

Holding public office isn't an SE trade or business, except for certain state or local officials paid solely on a fee basis (¶3138). (Code Sec. 1402(c)(1))[5]

¶ 3136   Partner's self-employment tax—self-employment (SE) tax.

A partner's net earnings from self-employment (Code Sec. 1402(a)) are, generally, the partner's distributive share of the partnership's taxable income arising out of the trade or business of the partnership plus the partner's guaranteed payments. (Code Sec. 1402(a); Reg § 1.1402(a)-1(a)(2), Reg § 1.1402(a)-1(b))[6]

The distributive share of any item of income or loss of a limited partner is excluded. But this exclusion doesn't apply to guaranteed payments to that partner for services actually rendered to or on behalf of the partnership, to the extent the payments are shown to be remuneration for those services. (Code Sec. 1402(a)(13))[7]

¶ 3137   Married couple's self-employment (SE) tax.

Under Code Sec. 6017, SE tax is computed on the separate self-employment income of each spouse, whether or not they file joint returns. But the spouses are jointly and severally liable for SE tax due on a joint return. (Code Sec. 6017; Reg § 1.6017-1(b))[8]

¶ 3138   Who is subject to self-employment (SE) tax?

Under Code Sec. 1401 and Code Sec. 1402(b), the SE tax (¶3133) is a tax on self-employed individuals (U.S. citizens and resident aliens). Income earned as an employee isn't subject to SE tax (Code Sec. 1402(c)(2)),[9] with these exceptions:

. . . Members of the clergy, see ¶3139.

. . . Persons 18 or older employed to sell magazines and newspapers to the public at a fixed price, whose pay is the excess of the fixed price over their cost. (Code Sec. 1402(c)(2)(A))[10]

. . . U.S. citizens employed by a foreign government, its wholly owned instrumentality, or an international organization (e.g., the U.N.). (Code Sec. 1402(c)(2)(C))[11]

---

49. ¶A-6105, A-6106
50. ¶A-6107
1. ¶A-6202 *et seq.*
2. ¶A-6032.1
3. ¶A-6084
4. ¶M-4603
5. ¶A-6095

6. ¶A-6150 *et seq.*
7. ¶A-6157
8. ¶S-1812
9. ¶A-6092
10. ¶A-6087.1
11. ¶A-6097

... Fishing boat crew who work on a boat that normally has fewer than 10 crew members and who get no fixed remuneration other than a share of the catch and certain small cash payments. (Code Sec. 1402(c)(2)(F))[12]

... Sharecroppers whose earnings depend on production.[13]

... State or local government officials whose pay is *solely* fees, unless the services are covered by social security under a federal-state agreement. (Code Sec. 1402(c)(2)(E))[14]

Statutory employees (¶3103) don't pay SE tax (they pay FICA instead) even if treated as self-employed for income tax purposes. (Code Sec. 1402(d), Code Sec. 3121(d)(3))[15]

Members of certain religious sects who conscientiously oppose social security and file an exemption (Form 4029) are exempt. (Code Sec. 1402(g); Reg § 1.1402(h)-1)[16]

¶ 3139 Clergy members' self-employment (SE) tax.

Members of the clergy, members of religious orders, and Christian Science practitioners are subject to SE tax (¶3133) on services performed in the exercise of their ministry (Code Sec. 1402(c)(4), Code Sec. 1402(c)(5)) *unless* they have taken a vow of poverty (Code Sec. 1402(c))[17] or irrevocably elect (on Form 4361) *not* to be covered. (Code Sec. 1402(e))[18]

¶ 3140 Farmers' self-employment (SE) tax.

Under Code Sec. 1402(a), self-employed persons must pay SE tax (¶3133) on the income from their farming operations. Unless received by an individual who is getting social security retirement or disability payments, IRS holds that conservation reserve program (CRP) payments are includible in SE income. (Code Sec. 1402(a)(1)) Where the payment is to a landlord who doesn't materially participate in production or management of the property, IRS holds the payment is rental and not SE income. But the Eight Circuit holds that CRP payments made to non-farmers are rental income, excludable from the SE self-employment tax; IRS disagrees and will not follow in any circuit for CRP payments after 2007.[19]

Since a farmer has an optional method of computing SE tax on farm income (¶3141), the farmer may have to distinguish farm income from other self-employment income. Farm income comes from an operation on a farm in which more than half the time is devoted to farming activities. (Reg § 1.1402(a)-13)[20]

¶ 3141 Optional methods for computing self-employment (SE) earnings.

The optional method for computing SE earnings—called the "nonfarm optional method" for nonfarming businesses, and the "farm optional method" for farming businesses—is as follows: for 2022, if an individual's gross income from the business is not more than $9,060 (not more than $9,840 for 2023), the individual may elect to treat 66²/₃ % of that gross income as SE net earnings from the business. For 2022, if it's more than $9,060 (more than $9,840 for 2023) and net profits from the business are less than $6,540.34 for 2022 (less than $7,103.41 for 2023), the individual may elect to treat $6,040 ($6,560 for 2023) as SE net earnings from the business. But if net profits are $6,540.34 or more for 2022 ($7,103.41 or more for 2023), the individual must use the net profits. (Code Sec. 1402(a), Code Sec. 1402(l); Reg § 1.1402(a)-15(a)(1))[21]

The optional nonfarm method may be used only if: net profits from the nonfarming business are less than $6,540.34 for 2022 (less than $7,103.41 for 2023) *and* less than 72.189% of gross nonfarm income, SE net earnings were at least $400 in 2 of the prior 3

---

12. ¶A-6090
13. ¶A-6209
14. ¶A-6092
15. ¶A-6081
16. ¶A-6327 *et seq.*

17. ¶A-6301
18. ¶A-6321
19. ¶A-6208 *et seq.*
20. ¶A-6201 *et seq.*
21. ¶A-6117

years, *and* taxpayer has used this method for fewer than 5 years (consecutive or not). (Code Sec. 1402(a), Code Sec. 1402(h))[22]

An individual may use the optional farm method for 2022 if gross farm income isn't more than $9,060 (isn't more than $9,840 for 2023), or net farm profits are less than $6,540.34 (less than $7,103.41 for 2023). (Code Sec. 1402(a), Code Sec. 1402(h))[23]

An individual with both farm and nonfarm incomes may use both methods (if otherwise allowed): the farm optional method for the farm income and the nonfarm optional method for the nonfarm income. For 2022, if both methods are used, the combined total SE net earnings can't be more than $6,040 (can't be more than $6,560 for 2023). (Code Sec. 1402(a); Reg § 1.1402(a)-15)[24]

Elect the optional method by computing (on Schedule SE, Form 1040) SE net earnings under that method. The election may be made or revoked after the return is filed, on an amended return. (Code Sec. 1402(a); Reg § 1.1402(a)-16)[25]

¶ 3142   3.8% Net Investment Income Tax (NIIT)—Form 8960. ■■■■■■■

Under Code Sec. 1411, certain unearned, passive, and trading income, plus certain net gain, of individuals, trusts, and estates is subject to a 3.8% net investment income tax (NIIT).

For individuals, the NIIT, also called the unearned income Medicare contribution tax, is 3.8% of the lesser of:

(1) net investment income (NII), ¶3143); or

(2) the excess of modified adjusted gross income (MAGI) over an unindexed threshold amount ($250,000 for joint filers or surviving spouses, $125,000 for a married individual filing a separate return, and $200,000 in any other case). (Code Sec. 1411(a)(1), Code Sec. 1411(b), Reg § 1.1411-2(b)(1), Reg § 1.1411-2(d)(1))[26]

illustration (1): For 2022, A, an unmarried U.S. citizen, has MAGI of $190,000, which includes $50,000 of NII. A isn't liable for the NIIT because the threshold amount for a single individual is $200,000. (Reg § 1.1411-2(b)(2))

illustration (2): For 2022, B, an unmarried U.S. citizen, has MAGI of $220,000, which includes $50,000 of NII. B pays a NIIT of $760 (3.8% x $20,000). The $20,000 figure is the lesser of the $50,000 NII or the $20,000 excess of MAGI over the $200,000 threshold amount. (Reg § 1.1411-2(b)(2))

MAGI is adjusted gross income (AGI) plus any amount excluded as foreign earned income under Code Sec. 911(a)(1) (net of the deductions and exclusions disallowed with respect to the foreign earned income). (Code Sec. 1411(d), Reg § 1.1411-2(c)(1)(ii))

Any federal income tax credit that may be used to offset a tax imposed by subtitle A of the Code may be used to offset the NIIT, but if a credit is allowed only against income tax, it may not be credited against the NIIT unless specifically provided. (Reg § 1.1411-1(e))[27]

For an estate or trust, the NIIT is 3.8% of the lesser of (1) undistributed NII or (2) the excess of adjusted gross income (AGI, as defined in Code Sec. 67(e)) over the dollar amount at which the highest income tax bracket applicable to an estate or trust begins (see ¶1106). (Code Sec. 1411(a)(2), Reg § 1.1411-3(a)(1))[28]

---

22. ¶A-6121
23. ¶A-6122;
24. ¶A-6119
25. ¶A-6125

26. ¶A-6361 *et seq.*
27. ¶A-6361.1 *et seq.*
28. ¶C-5801; ¶C-9581

¶ 3143   What is net investment income (NII)—net investment income tax.

For net investment income tax (NIIT) purposes (¶3142), NII (Code Sec. 1411(c)) is investment income less deductions properly allocable to NII. Investment income is:

. . . gross income from interest, dividends, annuities, royalties, and rents, unless derived in the ordinary course of a trade or business to which the NIIT *doesn't* apply,

. . . other gross income derived from a trade or business to which the NIIT *does* apply, and

. . . net gain (to the extent taken into account in computing taxable income) attributable to the disposition of property other than property held in a trade or business to which the NIIT *doesn't* apply. (Code Sec. 1411(c), Reg § 1.1411-4(a))[29]

The NIIT applies to a trade or business only if it's a Code Sec. 469 passive activity of the taxpayer, or a trade or business of trading in (a) financial instruments or (b) commodities, as defined in Code Sec. 475(e)(2). (Code Sec. 1411(c)(2))

Gain or loss from a disposition of an interest in a partnership (¶3755) or S corporation (¶3366) is taken into account by the partner or shareholder as NII only to the extent of the net gain or loss that the transferor would take into account if the entity had sold all its property for fair market value immediately before the disposition. (Code Sec. 1411(c)(4))[30]

Deductions taken into account in determining NII include adjustments to income, itemized deductions, and losses. Unless provided elsewhere in the NIIT regs, only the properly allocable deductions listed in Reg § 1.1411-4(f) may be taken into account in determining NII. (Reg § 1.1411-4(f)) If a properly allocable deduction is allocable to both NII and excluded income, taxpayers may use any reasonable method to determine the portion that's properly allocable to NII. (Reg § 1.1411-4(g)(1))[31]

⊘*observation:* To minimize NIIT at year-end, some taxpayers should minimize (e.g., through deferral) additional NII for the rest of the year, others should try to reduce MAGI other than unearned income, and others should minimize both NII and other types of MAGI.

Items excluded from NII. Investment income for NIIT purposes doesn't include any amount subject to the self-employment tax (¶1109) or amounts distributed from retirement plans (¶4347). (Code Sec. 1411(c)(5), Reg § 1.1411-9(a), Code Sec. 1411(c)(6), Reg § 1.1411-8(a)) NII doesn't include items excluded from gross income for income tax purposes. "Excluded income" means items that are: (i) excluded from gross income for income tax purposes, such as interest on state and local bonds (¶1330) and gain from the sale of a principal residence (¶2439); (ii) not included in NII under Reg § 1.1411-4 and Reg § 1.1411-10, such as wages, unemployment compensation, Alaska Permanent Fund Dividends, alimony, and Social Security benefits; (iii) specifically excluded by Code Sec. 1411, its regs, or other IRS guidance, e.g., gains from the disposition of property used in a trade or business that isn't passive activity or trading activity, and distributions from certain qualified plans. So operating income from a nonpassive business, unemployment compensation, social security benefits, alimony, tax-exempt interest, Alaska Permanent Fund Dividends, distributions from certain qualified plans, self-employment income, and wages aren't NII. (Reg § 1.1411-1(d)(4))[32]

Although NII doesn't include income or net gain derived in the ordinary course of a trade or business (other than a passive activity or trading business), any item of gross income from the investment of working capital is treated as not derived in the ordinary course of a trade or business for the NIIT any net gain attributable to the investment of working capital is treated as not derived in the ordinary course of a trade or business. So that gross

---

29. ¶A-6363
30. ¶A-6373
31. ¶A-6367 *et seq.*
32. ¶A-6368 *et seq.*

income and net gain is subject to the NIIT Code Sec. 1411(c)(3), Reg § 1.1411-6(a))[33]

¶ 3144   Who is subject to the net investment income tax (NIIT)?

Under Code Sec. 1411(a), the 3.8% NIIT (¶3142) applies to individuals, trusts, and estates. A bankruptcy estate in which the debtor is an individual is treated as a married taxpayer filing a separate return. (Reg § 1.1411-3(b)(2))

The NIIT doesn't apply to: nonresident aliens (special rules apply to nonresident aliens married to U.S. citizens or residents); bona fide residents of a U.S. territory (but the NIIT does apply if the individual is required to file a U.S. income tax return after application of Code Sec. 931, Code Sec. 932, or Code Sec. 933); trusts, all the unexpired interests in which are devoted to charitable purposes described in Code Sec. 170(c)(2)(B); trusts exempt from tax under Code Sec. 501; charitable remainder trusts (CRTs) exempt from tax under Code Sec. 664 (¶2116); or "grantor trusts" (but the income and deductions of the trusts are taken into account in determining the owners' NII). (Code Sec. 1411(e)) (Reg § 1.1411-2(a), Reg § 1.1411-3(b)) Electing small business trusts (ESBTs), ¶3353) and CRTs are subject to special rules. (Reg § 1.1411-3(c))[34] A taxpayer was subject to NIIT on dividends received from a closely held C corporation of which he was both the majority shareholder and an employee. (CCA 202118009).[35]

¶ 3145   Individual Estimated Tax. ▄▄▄▄▄▄▄▄

Under Code Sec. 6654, an individual must make four quarterly installment payments of estimated tax based on the amount of the "required annual payment" to avoid an underpayment penalty. The required annual payment is the lower of 90% of the tax shown on the current year return or 100% (110%, for high income individuals) of the tax shown on the prior year return. There's no penalty if the tax shown on the return (after withholding) is less than $1,000, or if other specified exceptions or waivers apply.

To avoid the penalty, an individual must: (1) pay each "required installment" (¶3148) by its due date (¶3151), (2) meet an exception (¶3155), *or* (3) get a waiver (¶3156).[36]

caution: The 3.8% net investment income tax (¶3142) isn't subject to withholding, so individuals who are subject to that tax should increase either their withholding or their estimated tax payments to avoid the underpayment penalty.

¶ 3146   How to pay individual estimated tax—Form 1040-ES.

Estimated tax payments can be made by check or money order using payment voucher Form 1040-ES (Form 1040-ES (NR) for nonresident aliens) and phone or online using a credit (MasterCard, VISA, American Express, or Discover) or debit card.[37]

Taxpayers also have the option to pay estimated taxes online under the electronic federal tax payment system (EFTPS). Individuals must first register to use the system online at www.eftps.gov or by calling 1-800-555-4477 and ordering an enrollment kit. (Reg § 301.6311-2)[38]

Estimated tax liability is computed as the expected taxes on expected taxable income for the year, minus the tax withheld (or to be withheld) from the year's wages and the expected tax credits (Code Sec. 6654(f), Code Sec. 6654(g); Reg § 1.6654-5(a)), taking into account the taxes, credits, and other amounts listed in Reg § 1.6654-1(a)(4). (Reg § 1.6654-5(b))[39]

---

33. ¶A-6372
34. ¶C-5802
35. ¶A-6363.2
36. ¶S-5200 *et seq.*

37. ¶S-5756.1A
38. ¶S-5253
39. ¶S-5201

¶ 3147   Married individuals' estimated tax.

A married person determines estimated tax liability based on the married person's separate income. Spouses making joint estimated tax payments apply the rules on a joint basis. Joint estimated tax payments don't affect the choice of joint or separate income tax returns.[40] Joint payments can be apportioned between the spouses' separate returns. (Reg § 1.6654-2(e)(5))[41]

¶ 3148   Amount of individual's required estimated tax installment.

Under Code Sec. 6654(d)(1), unless the annualized income method (¶3149) is used, the amount of each required estimated tax installment is 25% of the "required annual payment." For most individuals, the required annual payment is the lower of: (1) 90% of the tax shown on the current year's return (or, if no return is filed, 90% of the current-year tax), or (2) 100% of the tax shown on the previous year's return, if that tax year was a 12-month year and the taxpayer filed a return (even a late one) for that year.[42]

Different rules apply to high-income individuals. If an individual's previous year's return showed adjusted gross income exceeding $150,000 ($75,000 for marrieds filing separately), the required annual payment is the lower of (1), above, or 110% of the tax shown on the previous year's return. (Code Sec. 6654(d)(1)(C))[43]

¶ 3149   Annualized income method for individuals' estimated tax.

Under Code Sec. 6654(d)(2)(A)(i), for any estimated tax installment for which the taxpayer establishes that the "annualized income installment" (below) is less than the required installment determined under the rules at ¶3148, the annualized income installment becomes the required installment. The annualized income installment is the excess (if any) of:

(1) an amount equal to the "applicable percentage" (below) of the annualized tax (computed by placing taxable income, alternative minimum taxable income (AMTI), and adjusted self-employment income (below) on an annualized basis) for the months in the tax year ending before the due date for the installment, over

(2) the sum of any earlier required installments for the tax year. (Code Sec. 6654(d)(2)(B))[44]

The applicable percentages are 22.5%, 45%, 67.5% and 90%, respectively, for the first, second, third and fourth required installments. (Code Sec. 6654(d)(2)(C)(ii))[45]

Adjusted self-employment income means self-employment income (¶3134) except that wages for calendar months ending before the installment due date must be annualized as in (1), above. (Code Sec. 6654(d)(2)(C)(iii))[46]

If, for an installment, the annualized income installment is the required installment because it is less than the installment determined under the rules at ¶3148, the excess must be recaptured—i.e, added to the next required installment that isn't an annualized income installment. (Code Sec. 6654(d)(2)(A)(ii))[47]

¶ 3150   Withholding as payment of individuals' estimated tax.

Under Code Sec. 6654(g)(1), any withholding is treated as a payment of estimated tax. An equal part of the withheld tax is considered paid on each installment date unless the

---

40. ¶S-5254
41. ¶S-5255
42. ¶S-5204
43. ¶S-5204.1

44. ¶S-5219 *et seq.*
45. ¶S-5235
46. ¶S-5225
47. ¶S-5229

individual establishes the dates the amounts were actually withheld. (Code Sec. 6654(g)(1))[48]

✔*recommendation:* An individual who underpays an early required installment can avoid or reduce the underpayment penalty by increasing withholding for the rest of the year.

¶ 3151 Time for paying individuals' estimated tax installments.

Under Code Sec. 6654(c), calendar year individuals (but not farmers and fishermen, ¶3152, or nonresident aliens, ¶3153) must pay estimated taxes in four installments, due Apr. 15, June 15, Sept. 15 of the current year, and Jan. 15 of the next year. But an individual who first has income subject to the tax after Mar. 31 makes the first payment by the due date for the period in which the individual has the income.[49] The last installment, ordinarily due on Jan. 15, needn't be paid if the individual files a return and pays the tax shown on it by Jan. 31. (Code Sec. 6654(h))[50]

The due dates for fiscal year taxpayers are the 15th day of the 4th, 6th, and 9th month of the fiscal year and the 15th day of the first month of the next tax year. (Code Sec. 6654(k))[1]

¶ 3152 Estimated tax of farmers and fishermen.

Under Code Sec. 6654(i), a farmer or fisherman doesn't have to pay estimated tax for a year if the taxpayer files the return and pays the tax shown on it by Mar. 1 of the next year. Otherwise, the taxpayer must make one estimated tax payment for the year, due Jan. 15 of the next year.[2] The required installment calculation (¶3148) uses 66²/₃% (not 90%) of the current year tax. (Code Sec. 6654(i)(1))[3]

An individual is a farmer or fisherman if at least 66²/₃% of the farmer/fisherman's gross income for the current or preceding tax year is from farming or fishing. (Code Sec. 6654(i)(2))[4]

¶ 3153 Nonresident aliens' estimated tax—Form 1040-ES (NR).

Under Code Sec. 6654(j)(2), nonresident aliens required to file U.S. income tax returns (¶4642) must pay three required estimated tax installments for the year, due on June 15, Sept. 15, and Jan. 15 of the next year.[5] The required installments (compute on Form 1040-ES(NR)) are 50%, 25%, and 25%, respectively, of the required annual payment (¶3148). (Code Sec. 6654(j)(3)(A)) The applicable percentages under the annualized income method (¶3149) are 45%, 67.5%, and 90%, respectively. (Code Sec. 6654(j)(3)(B))[6]

¶ 3154 Estimated tax underpayment penalty—Form 2210, Form 2210F.

The penalty for underpayment equals the product of the interest rate (using simple interest) (Code Sec. 6622(b)) on deficiencies (¶4849), times the amount of the underpayment, for the period of the underpayment. (Code Sec. 6654(a))[7]

The *amount of the underpayment* is the excess of the "required installment" (¶3148) over any amount paid on or before the due date of the installment. (Code Sec. 6654(b)(1))[8] It's adjusted to reflect the number of days the underpayment is outstanding.[9]

The *period of underpayment* runs from that due date to the earlier of: (1) Apr. 15 following the end of the tax year, or (2) the date the underpayment is paid. (Code

48. ¶S-5248
49. ¶S-5241, S-5242
50. ¶S-5260
1. ¶S-5243
2. ¶S-5247
3. ¶S-5237

4. ¶S-5238
5. ¶S-5246
6. ¶S-5236
7. ¶S-5260
8. ¶S-5261, S-5262
9. ¶S-5260

Sec. 6654(b)(2)) For these purposes, a payment is credited against unpaid installments in the order the installments are required to be paid. (Code Sec. 6654(b)(3))[10]

Form 2210 (Form 2210F for farmers and fishermen) may be used to compute the penalty,[11] or IRS will compute it and send a bill.[12] For exceptions, see ¶3155. For waivers, see ¶3156.

¶ 3155   Exceptions to estimated tax underpayment penalty.

The underpayment penalty (¶3154) doesn't apply:

(1) if the tax shown on the return (or the tax due if no return is filed) is less than $1,000 after reduction for withholding tax paid (Code Sec. 6654(e)(1)),[13] or

(2) if the individual was a U.S. citizen or resident for the entire preceding tax year, had no tax liability for that year, and that year was a 12-month year (Code Sec. 6654(e)(2)),[14] or

(3) for the 4th installment, if the individual (not a farmer or fisherman, ¶3152) files the return by the end of the 1st month after the tax year (Jan. 31 for calendar year taxpayers), and pays in full the tax computed on the return (Code Sec. 6654(h)),[15] or

(4) in certain cases while a Title 11 bankruptcy case is pending. (Code Sec. 6658(a))[16]

¶ 3156   Waiver of estimated tax underpayment penalty.

The underpayment penalty (¶3154) may be waived by IRS if:

(1) failure to pay was due to casualty, disaster, or other unusual circumstances where penalty would be inequitable or against good conscience (Code Sec. 6654(e)(3)(A)),[17] or

(2) underpayment was due to reasonable cause (not willful neglect), and the taxpayer retired (after reaching age 62) or became disabled during the year for which the payments in question were required or in the preceding tax year. (Code Sec. 6654(e)(3)(B))[18]

---

10. ¶S-5262, S-5263
11. ¶S-5265
12. ¶S-5260
13. ¶S-5265
14. ¶S-5265

15. ¶S-5260
16. ¶V-7378
17. ¶S-5265
18. ¶S-5265

Chapter 14 Alternative Minimum Tax

¶ 3200   **Alternative Minimum Tax on Noncorporate and Corporate Taxpayers.** ▬▬▬

The alternative minimum tax (AMT) on non-corporate taxpayers equals the excess (if any) of the tentative minimum tax over the regular tax (¶3201). A new 15% corporate alternative minimum tax (effective for tax years beginning after 2022), on the adjusted financial statement income of "applicable corporations," will apply if the minimum tax exceeds the taxpayer's regular tax for the tax year (¶3213).

The noncorporate AMT was designed to prevent a taxpayer from avoiding all tax liability by using exclusions, deductions, and credits. Under it, AMT rates are applied to AMT income determined after the taxpayer "gives back" an assortment of tax benefits. AMT is paid only if, and to the extent, it exceeds the taxpayer's regular tax. A taxpayer's total tax liability for the year will equal the taxpayer's regular tax liability, plus AMT liability. (Code Sec. 55(a))[1]

Any noncorporate taxpayer subject to the regular tax is also subject to the AMT. (Code Sec. 55(a), Code Sec. 55(b)) Partnerships (Code Sec. 701) and S corporations (Code Sec. 1363(a)) aren't subject to the noncorporate AMT, but their partners and shareholders are.[2]

For the minimum tax credit ("MTC" or "AMT credit") against regular tax that applies for the noncorporate AMT, see ¶2358.[3]

¶ 3201   **Computing alternative minimum tax (AMT)—Form 6251; Form 1041, Schedule I—noncorporate AMT.**

The AMT applies to noncorporate taxpayers (Code Sec. 55(a)). It equals the excess (if any) of the tentative minimum tax (below) for the tax year, over the regular tax (below) for the tax year. AMT is computed on Form 6251, Schedule I for individuals, and on Form 1041, Schedule I for fiduciaries (estates and trusts).[4]

For taxpayers other than marrieds filing separately, the tentative minimum tax for 2022 equals 26% of the "taxable excess" (defined below) that doesn't exceed $206,100, plus 28% of the taxable excess above $206,100, reduced by the AMT foreign tax credit (AMTFTC), ¶3212, for the year. (Code Sec. 55(b)(1)(A); Code Sec. 55(d)(4)(B)(i)) For 2023, the tentative minimum tax equals 26% of the taxable excess that doesn't exceed $220,700, plus 28% of the taxable excess above $220,700, reduced by the AMTFTC. For marrieds filing separately, the amount used to compute tentative minimum tax is 50% of the amount used for marrieds filing jointly. (Code Sec. 55(b)(1)(C)) Tentative minimum tax on net capital gain and qualified dividend income is computed using the long-term capital gain rates that apply for regular tax purposes (Code Sec. 55(b)(3)) (¶2602). "Taxable excess" is the excess of alternative minimum taxable income (AMTI, ¶3202) for the tax year over the applicable AMT "exemption amount" (¶3203). (Code Sec. 55(b)(1)(B))[5]

The regular tax for this purpose is the regular tax liability used for determining the limitation on nonrefundable credits for the tax year (¶2357), reduced by the regular (i.e., not the AMT) foreign tax credit (¶2360) and without including any investment credit or low-income housing credit recapture (¶2315, ¶2321), or Code Sec. 45(e)(11)(C) income tax increase for a farmer's cooperative from electricity production credits passed through to patrons. (Code Sec. 55(c)(1))[6]

In computing regular tax liability for AMT purposes, income averaging for farmers and fishermen isn't taken into account. (Code Sec. 55(c)(2))[7]

---

1. ¶A-8100 *et seq.*
2. ¶A-8130 *et seq.*
3. ¶A-8801 *et seq.*
4. ¶A-8101

5. ¶A-8101, ¶A-8102
6. ¶A-8105
7. ¶A-8105

References beginning with a single letter are to paragraphs in Federal Tax Coordinator 2d and RIA's Analysis of Federal Taxes: Income.

⚠️*observation:* I.e., the "regular tax" used to determine if the farmer/fisherman is subject to AMT is computed as if income averaging wasn't used, so use of 3-year income averaging doesn't trigger or increase AMT liability.

¶ 3202 Alternative minimum taxable income (AMTI)—noncorporate AMT.

AMTI (Code Sec. 55(b)(2)) is computed by taking the taxpayer's regular taxable income for the tax year and (i) adding or subtracting AMT "adjustments" (¶3205 *et seq.*) and (ii) adding AMT "preferences" (¶3210).[8] The alternative minimum tax (AMT) (¶3201) can apply if a taxpayer only has adjustment items; a taxpayer without preference items must still compute AMTI with the adjustments.[9]

All Code provisions that apply in determining regular taxable income also apply in determining a taxpayer's AMTI (Reg § 1.55-1(a)), e.g., the limitations on the use of capital losses by noncorporate taxpayers (¶2608, ¶2609) also apply for AMT purposes.[10]

The noncorporate taxpayer's net capital gain and qualified dividend income are included in AMTI, but are taxed at the same capital gains rates that apply for regular tax purposes (¶3201).[11]

The at-risk rules (¶1790), and the partnership (¶3726) and S corporation (¶3368) loss limitation rules, are applied in computing AMTI taking into account all AMT adjustments and preferences. (Code Sec. 59(h))[12]

The Code Sec. 199A(a) pass-through deduction for qualified business income (QBI) (¶1593 *et seq.*) allowed in determining AMTI, is computed without regard to any AMT adjustments. (Reg § 1.199A-1(e)(5))[13]

If a taxpayer's regular tax is determined by reference to an amount other than taxable income (e.g., an exempt org.'s unrelated business taxable income, ¶4124), that amount is treated as taxable income in determining AMTI. (Code Sec. 55(b)(2))[14]

There are rules for the apportionment of items that are treated differently for AMT purposes for holders of interests in regulated investment companies (RICs), real estate investment trusts (REITs), and common trust funds. (Code Sec. 59(d))[15]

¶ 3203 Alternative minimum tax (AMT) exemption amounts—noncorporate AMT.

The Code Sec. 55(d) AMT exemption amounts used in computing AMT (¶3201) are:

. . . *Married individuals filing jointly and surviving spouses: for 2022,* $118,100, less 25% of AMTI exceeding $1,079,800 (zero exemption when AMTI is $1,552,200 or more). *for 2023,* $126,500, less 25% of AMTI exceeding $1,156,300 (zero exemption when AMTI is $1,662,300 or more).

. . . *Unmarried individuals: for 2022,* $75,900, less 25% of AMTI exceeding $539,900 (zero exemption when AMTI is $843,500 or more). *for 2023,* $81,300, less 25% of AMTI exceeding $578,100 (zero exemption when AMTI is $903,300 or more). For a special limitation, applicable after 2025, on the exemption for children subject to the kiddie tax, see ¶3204

. . . *Married individuals filing separately: For 2022,* $59,050, less 25% of AMTI exceeding $539,900 (zero exemption when AMTI is $776,100 or more). But, AMTI for marrieds filing separately must be increased (for 2022) by the lesser of: $59,050 or 25% of the excess of AMTI (determined without this exemption reduction) over $776,100. *For 2023,* $63,250, less 25% of AMTI exceeding $578,150 (zero exemption when AMTI is $831,150 or more). But, AMTI for marrieds filing separately must be increased (for 2023) by the

---

8. ¶A-8101
9. ¶A-8109
10. ¶A-8108
11. ¶A-8102

12. ¶A-8115 *et seq.*
13. ¶A-8103.1
14. ¶A-8107
15. ¶A-8112

lesser of: $63,250 or 25% of the excess of AMTI (determined without this exemption reduction) over $831,150. (Code Sec. 55(d), Code Sec. 55(d)(1), Code Sec. 55(d)(3))[16]

. . . *Estates and trusts: for 2022,* $26,500, less 25% of AMTI exceeding $88,300 (zero exemption when AMTI is $194,300) *for 2023,* $28,400, less 25% of AMTI exceeding $94,600 (zero exemption when AMTI is $208,200). (Code Sec. 55(d)(1)(D), Code Sec. 55(d)(4)(B)(ii))[17]

In no case can the AMT exemption amount be less than zero. (Code Sec. 55(d))[18]

¶ 3204   AMT exemption amount of a child subject to the kiddie tax—post-2025 limitation—noncorporate AMT.

The Code Sec. 59(j) special limit on the AMT exemption for a child subject to the kiddie tax (see below) was made inapplicable, retroactively, to tax years beginning before 2026. (Code Sec. 55(d)(4)(A)(iii)) Under the post-2025 limitation, for a child to whom the kiddie tax rules apply (see ¶3129), the AMT exemption amount computed under the rules at ¶3203 can't exceed the sum of: (a) the child's earned income for the tax year (as defined in Code Sec. 911(d)(2)), plus $5,000, as adjusted for inflation. (Code Sec. 59(j))[19]

¶ 3205   Difference between AMT adjustments and preferences—noncorporate AMT.

Adjustments differ from preferences in computing alternative minimum taxable income (AMTI, ¶3202) for the AMT (¶3201). Adjustments involve *substituting* AMT treatment of an item for the regular tax treatment. Preferences involve *adding* the difference between the AMT treatment and the regular tax treatment. Some (but not all) adjustments can be negative amounts—i.e., they may result in AMTI that's less than taxable income. Preferences can't be negative amounts.[20]

For AMT adjustments, see ¶3206 *et seq.*, for AMT preferences, see ¶3210, and for certain losses denied for the AMT, see ¶3211.

A taxpayer can avoid preference/adjustment treatment for certain costs by electing amortization (use Form 4562), rather than a current deduction. (Code Sec. 59(e); Reg § 1.59-1)[21]

¶ 3206   AMT adjustments for individuals, other noncorporate taxpayers—noncorporate AMT.

The following AMT adjustments (¶3205) apply in computing alternative minimum taxable income (AMTI) (¶3202) of *individual taxpayers:*

(1) *Itemized deductions adjustment.* Itemized deductions for AMT (¶3201) purposes are computed the same as for regular tax purposes, *except:*

(a) Property, income, and state and local general sales taxes that are deductible for regular tax purposes only as itemized deductions (on Form 1040, Schedule A, ¶1749) aren't deductible in computing AMTI. (Code Sec. 56(b)(1)(A)(ii)) But, these taxes, if deductible in computing adjusted gross income for regular tax purposes—i.e., in computing income from a trade or business or farming activity (on Form 1040, Schedule C or Form 1040, Schedule F), or taxes that are an expense of producing income (on Form 1040, Schedule E)—are deductible in computing AMTI. (Code Sec. 56(b)(1)(A))[22]

(b) Qualified housing interest (instead of qualified *residence* interest (QRI), ¶1729) is

16. ¶A-8162
17. ¶A-8164
18. ¶A-8162; ¶A-8164
19. ¶A-8163

20. ¶A-8191
21. ¶A-8194 *et seq.*
22. ¶A-8308

518

deductible in computing AMTI. (Code Sec. 56(b)(1)(B), Code Sec. 56(e)) So, home equity indebtedness isn't allowed for AMT purposes unless it's used to buy, build, or substantially improve the taxpayer's principal residence or one other qualified dwelling.[23] (For 2018–2025, AMT and regular tax treatment of home equity debt are essentially the same.[24])

(c) Net investment income (NII) (for limit on deduction of investment interest) is generally computed the same as for regular tax (¶1728), but qualified housing interest (instead of QRI) is excluded, and AMT adjustments and preferences are taken into account. And, tax-exempt bond interest that's an AMT preference item (¶3210) is included in NII. (Code Sec. 56(b)(1)(B))[25]

(d) Miscellaneous itemized deductions (in effect after 2025), aren't allowed. (Code Sec. 56(b)(1)(A)(i))[26]

(e) The Code Sec. 68 3%/80% reduction in itemized deductions (in effect after 2025), doesn't apply in computing AMT. (Code Sec. 56(b)(1)(E))[27]

(2) *Standard deduction and personal exemptions adjustments.* The standard deduction (¶3110) and the deduction for personal exemptions for individuals (in effect after 2025, ¶3112) *and for trusts and estates* (¶3922), *aren't* allowed for the AMT. (Code Sec. 56(b)(1)(D))[28]

(3) *State, etc., tax recoveries adjustment.* If an itemized deduction for state, etc., taxes paid is permitted for regular tax purposes but denied for AMT purposes ((1)(a), above), and any portion of that tax is refunded, the refund isn't included in AMTI. (Code Sec. 56(b)(1)(C))[29]

(4) *Research and experimental (R&E) expenditures adjustment.* The deduction allowed is the amount that results from capitalizing Code Sec. 174(a) R&E expenditures (¶1583) and amortizing them on a straight-line basis over 10 years. (Code Sec. 56(b)(2)(A)(ii), Code Sec. 59(e)(6)) This doesn't apply to expenses incurred in an activity in which the taxpayer materially participates under Code Sec. 469(h) (¶1806). (Code Sec. 56(b)(2)(C))[30]

(5) *Circulation expenditures.* The AMT circulation expenditures deduction is the amount that results from capitalizing the costs and amortizing them over three years (¶1603). (Code Sec. 56(b)(2))[31]

(6) *Incentive stock option (ISO) adjustment.* The Code Sec. 83 restricted property rules (¶1216)—and not the favorable Code Sec. 421 rules that apply for regular tax (¶1221)—apply in determining AMTI, unless the stock is acquired and disposed of in the same tax year. (Code Sec. 56(b)(3))[32] The amount included in AMTI (but not regular income) equals the excess of the stock's fair market value on the exercise date over the exercise (strike) price. This applies to vested stock, and to nonvested stock for which the taxpayer makes a Code Sec. 83(b) election (¶1217).[33]

Adjustments for these items apply in computing the AMTI of *all taxpayers:*

. . . *Depreciation* adjustment, see ¶3207.

. . . *Alternative tax net operating loss deduction (ATNOLD)* adjustment, see ¶3208.

. . . *Mine exploration and development costs.* The AMT deduction is the amount that results from capitalizing the costs allowed under Code Sec. 616(a) or Code Sec. 617(a) for the tax year without the Code Sec. 291(b)(1) 30% cutback (¶1610, ¶1611), and amortizing them ratably over 10 years. (Code Sec. 56(a)(2)(A), Code Sec. 59(e)(6))[34]

. . . *Certain long-term contracts.* For long-term contracts, except home construction contracts), AMTI is computed using the percentage-of-completion accounting method

23. ¶A-8310 *et seq.*
24. ¶K-5471
25. ¶A-8313
26. ¶A-8314
27. ¶A-8306
28. ¶A-8305, ¶A-8315

29. ¶A-8309
30. ¶A-8316
31. ¶A-8245
32. ¶A-8302, ¶A-8303
33. ¶A-8302, ¶H-2508.2
34. ¶A-8235

(¶2839). For small construction contracts (under Code Sec. 460(e)(1), ¶2837), use the Code Sec. 460(b)(3) simplified cost allocation method (¶2838) to find the percentage of contract completed. (Code Sec. 56(a)(3); Reg § 1.460-4(f))[35]

. . . *Pollution control facilities.* In computing AMTI, the Code Sec. 169 deduction for amortization of pollution control facilities (¶1954) placed in service after '98 is determined under Code Sec. 168 using the straight-line method of depreciation. For facilities placed in service after '86 and before '99, the AMT deduction is the amount allowable under the Alternative Depreciation System (ADS, ¶1926). (Code Sec. 56(a)(5))[36]

. . . *Adjusted basis* adjustment, see ¶3209.

. . . *Alcohol fuel credit* amount that's included in gross income (¶1206) isn't included in AMTI. (Code Sec. 56(a)(7))[37]

¶ 3207   Depreciation adjustment—noncorporate AMT.

Except as provided below, the following Code Sec. 56(a)(1) AMT adjustment (¶3205) rules apply to all noncorporate taxpayers subject to the AMT (¶3201), for depreciable property placed in service after '86 (and after July 31, '86 and before '87, for which the taxpayer elected to have the MACRS rules, ¶1906 *et seq.*, apply):

(1) For property placed in service before '99, AMT depreciation for Code Sec. 1250 property (¶2675) and property depreciated under the straight-line method for regular tax purposes is computed using the Alternative Depreciation System (ADS, ¶1926). For property subject to accelerated depreciation for regular tax purposes, AMT depreciation is computed using ADS recovery periods and the 150% declining balance method (switching to straight-line in the year that method yields a higher allowance).

(2) For property placed in service after '98, AMT depreciation is computed using the 150% declining balance method (switching to straight-line in the year that method yields a higher allowance), except straight-line is used for Code Sec. 1250 property and other property for which straight-line is used for regular tax purposes. (Code Sec. 56(a)(1)(A), Code Sec. 56(a)(1)(C)(ii)) The recovery period is the same as for regular tax purposes.[38]

The AMT adjustment (i.e., the amount to be added or subtracted in computing alternative minimum taxable income (AMTI) (¶3202)) generated by the above calculations is determined by subtracting the amount of AMT depreciation for all property covered by the above rule from the MACRS depreciation for that property.[39]

The above rules don't apply to: (a) certain property to which the MACRS rules don't apply; (b) natural gas gathering lines placed in service after Apr. 11, 2005 (Code Sec. 56(a)(1)(B), Code Sec. 56(a)(1)(C));[40] (Code Sec. 168(m)(2)(D));[41] (c) qualified property that is or was eligible for bonus first-year depreciation under Code Sec. 168(k) (¶1930), repealed Code Sec. 1400L(b) (qualified New York Liberty Zone property), or former Code Sec. 1400N(d) (GO Zone property), (Code Sec. 168(k)(2)(G), repealed Code Sec. 1400L(b)(2)(E), former Code Sec. 1400N(d)(4), Code Sec. 168(l)(6));[42] and (d) qualified Indian reservation property placed in service after '93 and before 2022. (Code Sec. 168(j)(3))[43]

¶ 3208   Alternative tax net operating loss deduction (ATNOLD)—noncorporate AMT.

For the AMT (¶3201), under Code Sec. 56(a)(4), an ATNOLD is allowed instead of the regular tax net operating loss (NOL) deduction (RNOLD, ¶1815 *et seq.*). A taxpayer's

---

35. ¶A-8202 *et seq.*
36. ¶A-8237
37. ¶A-8247
38. ¶A-8220
39. ¶A-8220

40. ¶A-8221 *et seq.*
41. ¶A-8221 *et seq.*
42. ¶A-8221 *et seq.*
43. ¶L-8806

ATNOLD generally can't reduce the taxpayer' alternative minimum taxable income (AMTI, ¶3202) by more than 90%.[44]

In general, the ATNOLD is the same as the RNOLD *except that:*

(1) the amount of the ATNOLD is limited to 90% of AMTI, determined without regard to the ATNOLD and the pre-2018, Code Sec. 199 production activities deduction. But the 90%-of-AMTI limitation doesn't apply to carrybacks and carryovers of amounts attributable to: 2008 or 2009 NOLs for which an extended carryback period was elected under former Code Sec. 172(b)(1)(H) (¶1818), and pre-2010 qualified disaster losses, or certain other disaster losses such as qualified GO Zone losses (Code Sec. 56(d)(1)(A), Code Sec. 56(d)(3), former Code Sec. 1400N(k)(1)(B)), which can offset up to 100% of AMTI[45]; and

(2) the ATNOL is determined with AMT adjustments (¶3206 *et seq.*) and is reduced by AMT preferences (¶3210) (but only to the extent the preference increased the NOL for the year). (Code Sec. 56(d)(2))[46]

An election to forego the regular NOL carryback period (for farming losses, ¶1819) also applies for ATNOLD purposes. (The election must be made for regular tax purposes to get it for AMT purposes.)[47]

The difference between the regular tax basis and AMT basis (¶3209) of stock acquired under an incentive stock option (ISO) isn't an adjustment and doesn't result in an ATNOL.[48]

¶ 3209   Different AMT adjusted basis for some property—noncorporate AMT.

Under Code Sec. 56(a) and Code Sec. 56(b), for the AMT (¶3201), the adjusted bases of the following types of property are computed by taking into consideration the AMT adjustment (¶3205) listed below with the property:

(1) Depreciable property subject to the Code Sec. 56(a)(1) depreciation adjustment (¶3207).

(2) Property subject to the Code Sec. 56(b)(2) adjustment for circulation or research and experimental expenditures (¶3206) paid or incurred after '86.

(3) Property subject to the Code Sec. 56(a)(2) adjustment for mine exploration or development expenditures (¶3206) paid or incurred after '86.

(4) Pollution control facilities subject to the Code Sec. 56(a)(5) adjustment (¶3206), if placed in service after '86. (Code Sec. 56(a)(6))

(5) Stock acquired under an incentive stock option (ISO) (¶3206). Generally, the basis of the stock is determined under the Code Sec. 83 rules rather than the Code Sec. 421 rules. (Code Sec. 56(b)(3)) So, the taxpayer gets a cost basis in the ISO stock for regular tax purposes, and a fair market value basis in the stock for AMT purposes (¶1221).[49]

¶ 3210   AMT preference items—noncorporate AMT.

(1) *Tax-exempt interest* on certain private activity bonds (not certain housing bonds or bonds issued in 2009 or 2010), less related expenses that aren't deductible for regular tax purposes, is an AMT preference item (¶3205). (Code Sec. 57(a)(5))[50]

(2) *Depletion.* Except for independent oil and gas producers and royalty owners, the excess of percentage depletion (¶1962) over the property's adjusted basis (disregarding the current year's depletion) at the end of the year is a preference item. (Code Sec. 57(a)(1))[1]

---

44. ¶A-8210 *et seq.*
45. ¶A-8212, ¶A-8213
46. ¶A-8211
47. ¶A-8216

48. ¶A-8211
49. ¶A-8193 *et seq.*
50. ¶A-8201
1. ¶A-8233

(3) *Excess intangible drilling costs* (IDCs) are a preference item. This is the excess of the allowable Code Sec. 263(c) IDC deduction for the tax year for oil, gas, and geothermal wells (¶1612), over the amount that would have been allowable had the costs been capitalized and amortized ratably over 120 months. For integrated oil companies, the preference equals this excess, reduced by 65% of the net income received from all oil, gas, and geothermal properties. For other taxpayers, the preference applies only to the extent that, had it applied fully, it would have increased alternative minimum taxable income (AMTI, ¶3202) by more than 40% of the AMTI for the tax year (without the IDC preference or the alternative tax NOL deduction, ¶3208). The preference is computed separately for oil and gas properties, and for geothermal properties. (Code Sec. 57(a)(2), Code Sec. 57(b), Code Sec. 59(e)(6))[2]

(4) *Qualified small business stock (QSBS) exclusion.* For gain on the disposition of QSBS that's partly excluded from gross income (¶2638 *et seq.*), 7% is treated as a preference item. (Code Sec. 57(a)(7)) But, for QSBS to which the 100% exclusion applies, the excluded portion of the gain isn't treated as a preference item. (Code Sec. 1202(a)(4)(C))[3]

¶ 3211   Denial of certain losses for noncorporate AMT.

(1) *Farm losses.* For the AMT (¶3201), under Code Sec. 58(a) and Code Sec. 58(c)(1), no loss is permitted from any "tax shelter farm activity" of a noncorporate taxpayer, except to the extent the taxpayer is insolvent at the end of the tax year. A tax shelter farm activity is (a) a farming syndicate (¶4511), or (b) any other "passive activity" (¶1798) consisting of farming unless the taxpayer materially participates in it.[4]

(2) *Passive losses.* The rules limiting the regular tax deduction of losses from passive activities (¶1797 *et seq.*) apply for AMT purposes *except that:*

. . . AMT preferences and adjustments (¶3205 *et seq.*) are taken into account;

. . . qualified housing interest (¶3206) (rather than qualified residence interest) is omitted from the passive loss calculation (Code Sec. 58(b)); and

. . . the amount of losses disallowed under the regular tax limitation is reduced by the amount, if any, by which the taxpayer is insolvent at year end. (Code Sec. 58(c)(1))[5]

¶ 3212   AMT foreign tax credit (AMTFTC)—noncorporate AMT.

Under Code Sec. 55(b)(1)(A), the AMTFTC is subtracted in the computation of a noncorporate taxpayer's AMT (¶3201).[6]

The AMTFTC is computed the same as the regular foreign tax credit (¶2359), *except* that in applying the Code Sec. 904 limitation on the amount of the credit: (1) alternative minimum taxable income (AMTI, ¶3202) is substituted for taxable income (but see below); (2) the "pre-credit tentative minimum tax" is substituted for "the tax against which the foreign tax credit is taken;" and (3) the AMT rate (¶3201) is used in determining "high-taxed" income instead of the regular tax highest tax rate. (Code Sec. 59(a)(1), Code Sec. 59(a)(2); Reg § 1.904-4(k))[7]

If a taxpayer so elects for the first tax year for which the taxpayer claims an AMTFTC (Code Sec. 59(a)(3)(B)(i)), the AMTFTC limitation is figured in a simplified way, based on the proportion that regular taxable income from sources outside the U.S. (but not in excess of the taxpayer's entire AMTI) bears to the entire AMTI for the tax year. (Code Sec. 59(a)(3)(A)) Letting taxpayers use foreign source regular taxable income to compute the limitation eliminates the need to reallocate and reapportion every deduction. Once made, the election applies to all tax years and can be revoked only with IRS consent. (Code

---

2. ¶A-8238 *et seq.*
3. ¶A-8304 *et seq.*
4. ¶A-8242

5. ¶A-8244
6. ¶A-8181
7. ¶A-8181

Sec. 59(a)(3)(B)(ii))[8]

¶ 3213   Corporate alternative minimum tax—tax years beginning after 2022.

The Inflation Reduction Act of 2022, PL 117-169 , 8/16/2022, imposes a new 15% corporate alternative minimum tax on the adjusted financial statement income of "applicable corporations." The corporate AMT will apply if the tentative minimum tax exceeds the taxpayer's regular tax, plus the base erosion and anti-abuse tax (¶3316), for the tax year. (Code Sec. 55(a), Code Sec. 55(b)(2))[9] The corporate AMT is effective for tax years beginning after Dec. 31, 2022. (Inflation Reduction Act, PL 117-169 , 8/16/2022, Sec. 10101(f))

"Applicable corporation" status based on financial statement income. An "applicable corporation" for a tax year is any corporation (other than an S corporation, regulated investment company (RIC), or real estate investment trust (REIT) that meets a 3-tax-year-period average annual adjusted financial statement income test for one or more earlier tax years that end after Dec. 31, 2021. Thus, the tax will apply if the average annual adjusted financial statement income for the 3-tax-year period (determined without regard to loss carryovers) exceeds $1 billion. A special rule will apply to members of a foreign-parented multinational group, under which the average annual adjusted financial statement income for a corporation has to equal or exceed $100 million, if the adjusted financial statement income of all members of the group (as adjusted) exceeds $1 billion. (Code Sec. 59(k))[10]

Adjusted financial statement income. Adjusted financial statement income is the net income or loss of the taxpayer as presented in the taxpayer's applicable financial statements, and is computed by taking the items on the group's applicable financial statement that are allocable to members of that group into account where the corporations file consolidated returns. In addition, adjusted financial statement income of disregarded entities owned by the corporation, and the corporation's distributive share of adjusted financial statement income of partnerships in which the corporation has an interest, are included. Various adjustments are made to determine adjusted financial statement income. For instance, income (but not losses) of controlled foreign corporations (CFCs) are taken into account, but a foreign corporation's income that is not effectively connected with the conduct of a U.S. trade or business is excluded. Notwithstanding the financial-statement-income basis of the tax, certain items are taken into account on a tax basis, rather than on a financial statement (book) income basis. (Code Sec. 56A)[11]

AMT foreign tax credit. A domestic corporation will be able to take a corporate AMT foreign tax credit for the direct foreign or U.S. possessions taxes that are taken into account on the corporation's applicable financial statement and paid or accrued (for tax purposes) by the applicable corporation, and may take a limited indirect credit for foreign or U.S. possessions taxes paid by controlled foreign corporations (CFCs, see ¶4611 *et seq.*) Unused indirect foreign taxes will be carried forward for up to five years. (Code Sec. 59(l))[12]

Treatment of general business credit. The corporate general business credit will generally be limited to 25% of the taxpayer's tentative minimum tax exceeding $25,000. (Code Sec. 38(c)(6)(E))[13]

Credit for prior-year minimum tax liability—minimum tax credit/AMT credit. Where the regular tax is higher than the minimum tax, a corporation will be able to carry forward a minimum tax credit (¶2358) for all prior tax years beginning after 2022 to reduce the taxpayer's regular tax, including the base erosion anti-abuse tax. (Code Sec. 53(e))[14]

---

8. ¶A-8182
9. ¶A-8900 *et seq.*
10. ¶A-8900, ¶A-8901
11. ¶A-8903

12. ¶A-8906
13. ¶L-15202
14. ¶A-8801

Chapter 15   Corporations—Accumulated Earnings Tax— Personal Holding Companies—Consolidated Returns—Estimated Tax—S Corporations

¶ 3300   **Taxation of Corporations.** ▐

A corporation is an entity distinct from its shareholders. How a corporation is taxed depends on whether it is a C corporation (¶3301 *et seq.*) or an S corporation (¶3349 *et seq.*).

¶ 3301   **What is a corporation for tax purposes; "check-the-box" mandatory classification—Form 8832.**

Under regs that set forth a "check-the-box" system of classifying entities for federal tax purposes, the following business entities are mandatorily classified as corporations:

. . . A business entity organized under a federal or state statute, or under a statute of a federally recognized Indian tribe, if the statute describes or refers to the entity as incorporated or as a corporation, body corporate, or body politic.

. . . An association as determined under Reg § 301.7701-3 (see below).

. . . A business entity organized under a state statute, if the statute describes or refers to the entity as a joint-stock company or joint-stock association.

. . . An insurance company.

. . . A state-chartered business entity conducting banking activities, if any of its deposits are insured under the Federal Deposit Insurance Act.

. . . A business entity wholly owned by a state or any of its political subdivisions.

. . . A business entity that's taxable as a corporation under a provision of the Code other than Code Sec. 7701(a)(3), such as a publicly traded partnership (see ¶3302).

. . . Certain foreign business entities and business entities formed under the laws of U.S. territories and possessions ("per se" corporations). (Reg § 301.7701-2(b))[1]

Under the "check-the-box" regs, if a joint undertaking is an entity separate from its owners for federal tax purposes, the entity is a business entity and not a trust, and the business entity is an "eligible entity" (i.e., not mandatorily classified as a corporation), it may elect its classification for federal tax purposes. An eligible entity with at least two members may elect to be classified as a partnership or as an association (i.e., a corporation). An eligible entity with a single owner may elect to be classified as an association or to be disregarded as an entity separate from its owner.[2] An eligible entity that wishes to elect a classification other than its default classification, or any eligible entity that wishes to change its classification, does so by filing Form 8832 with the IRS Service Center designated on the form.[3]

An entity organized in more than one jurisdiction is treated as a corporation for federal tax purposes if it is so treated in any of those jurisdictions. (Reg § 301.7701-2(b)(9))[4]

¶ 3302   **Publicly traded partnerships (PTPs) generally taxed as corporations.**

Under Code Sec. 7704, a PTP is taxable as a corporation (¶3303).[5] A partnership is a PTP if its interests are either: (1) traded on an established securities market (including a

---

1. ¶D-1101 *et seq.*
2. ¶D-1151
3. ¶D-1159

4. ¶D-1101.1
5. ¶D-1321

References beginning with a single letter are to paragraphs in Federal Tax Coordinator 2d and RIA's Analysis of Federal Taxes: Income.

national exchange, a regional or local exchange, certain foreign exchanges, and an interdealer quotation system), or (2) readily tradable on a secondary market or its substantial equivalent. (Code Sec. 7704(b); Reg § 1.7704-1)[6]

However, a PTP won't be treated as a corporation if at least 90% of its gross income for the tax year is specified passive-type "qualifying" income, and certain other requirements are met. (Code Sec. 7704(c))[7]

¶ 3303 How C Corporations Are Taxed.

Under Code Sec. 11, corporations are taxed at a flat 21% rate.[8]

For the post-2022 corporate alternative minimum tax, see ¶3213.

For penalty taxes imposed on corporations with earnings accumulations in excess of the reasonable needs of the business, see ¶3320 *et seq.*

For penalty taxes imposed on corporations with earnings accumulations in excess of the reasonable needs of the business, see ¶3320 *et seq.*

For the post-2022 1% excise tax on repurchases of corporate stock, see ¶3318.

For the personal holding company tax, see ¶3324 *et seq.*

For taxation of corporations making certain outbound transfers, see ¶3568.

¶ 3304 C corporation's taxable income; contributions to capital are not gross income.

Under Code Sec. 63, a C corporation's taxable income equals its gross income less the deductions allowed by the Code.[9] Generally, a C corporation's gross income doesn't include contributions to its capital. (Code Sec. 118) The term "contributions to capital" does not include: (i) any contribution in aid of construction or any other contribution as a customer or potential customer, or (ii) any contribution by any governmental entity or civic group (other than a contribution made by a shareholder as such). (Code Sec. 118(b))[10] For a C corporation's gain or loss from distributing property to its shareholders, see ¶3526.

¶ 3305 Computing a C corporation's tax.

A C corporation's tax is computed by applying the Code Sec. 11 rate(s) in effect for its tax year (¶1113) to its taxable income (¶3304) for that year, and then subtracting any available tax credits (¶2300 *et seq.*).[11]

For the post-2022 corporate alternative minimum tax, see ¶3213.

Special rules apply for computing the tax for years that straddle a rate change (Code Sec. 15(a))[12] and for short tax years, see ¶2804.

¶ 3306 Deduction for Dividends from Domestic and Certain Foreign Corporations. ◼

Under Code Sec. 243(a)(1) and Code Sec. 243(c), subject to specific disallowances, reductions, and limitations (¶3309 *et seq.*), a C corporation may deduct 50% of the dividends received or accrued from *domestic* corporations (65% for dividends received or accrued from a corporation at least 20% of the stock of which, not counting preferred stock described in Code Sec. 1504(a)(4), is owned, by vote and value, by the corporate shareholder).[13]

---

6. ¶D-1321
7. ¶D-1336 *et seq.*
8. ¶D-1000 *et seq.*
9. ¶D-1001

10. ¶F-1901 *et seq.*
11. ¶D-1001 *et seq.*
12. ¶D-1009 *et seq.*
13. ¶D-2201; ¶D-2205 *et seq.*

Members of an affiliated group (as specially defined) that file separate returns may deduct 100% of the dividends received from other group members if certain requirements are met. (Code Sec. 243(a)(3), Code Sec. 243(b))[14]

For a small business investment company's dividends-received deduction, see ¶4205.

The deduction applies to taxable dividends (¶1285 *et seq.*) (Code Sec. 243(a)), "boot" dividends (¶3542), consent dividends (¶3334)[15] and the "dividend equivalent" portion of applicable high yield debt obligations (¶1744). (Code Sec. 163(e)(5)(B))[16] For dividends that aren't deductible, see ¶3313.

For the deduction allowed for dividends received from a specified 10%-owned foreign corporation, see ¶3314.

¶ 3307   Dividends from regulated investment companies (RICs)—dividends-received deduction.

Under Code Sec. 243(d)(2) and Code Sec. 854(b)(3), a corporate shareholder that receives a properly designated dividend (other than capital gain or exempt-interest dividends) from a RIC is eligible for the dividends-received deduction (DRD) to the extent the RIC would have been allowed to deduct the amount as a DRD if it were taxed as a regular corporation.[17]

¶ 3308   Dividends from foreign corporations and possession corporations—dividends-received deduction.

Under Code Sec. 245(a)(1) and Code Sec. 245(a)(2)), a U.S. corporation that owns at least 10% (by vote and value) of the stock of a foreign corporation (other than a passive foreign investment company) may deduct the applicable percentage (50% or 65%) see ¶3306) of the *U.S.-source* portion of the dividends it receives from that foreign corporation.[18]

The U.S.-source portion of any dividend is the amount that bears the same ratio to the dividend that the payor's post-'86 undistributed U.S. earnings bears to its total post-'86 undistributed earnings. (Code Sec. 245(a)(3), Code Sec. 245(a)(4), Code Sec. 245(a)(5))[19] Special rules apply for dividends paid out of pre-'87 earnings.[20]

A 100% dividends-received deduction is allowed (instead of the above percentages) if all the foreign corporation's gross income is effectively connected with its U.S. business in the year the dividends are earned, and all its outstanding stock is owned by the U.S. payee both in that year and in the payee's tax year in which the dividends are received. (Code Sec. 245(b))[21]

For the deduction allowed for dividends received from a specified 10%-owned foreign corporation, see ¶3314.

For domestic international sales corporation (DISC) dividends, see ¶3313.

¶ 3309   Taxable income limit on dividends-received deduction (DRD).

Under Code Sec. 246(b)(1), for dividends that are subject to the 50% or 65% (but not the 100%) rule (¶3306), the DRD may not exceed 50% or 65% of the corporation's "taxable income." For this purpose, taxable income is computed without regard to the deductions for capital loss carrybacks, net operating losses (NOLs), dividends received, and income

---

14. ¶D-2223 *et seq.*
15. ¶D-2209 *et seq.*
16. ¶D-2221
17. ¶D-2216, ¶E-6163
18. ¶D-2244
19. ¶s D-2244, D-2246
20. ¶D-2246
21. ¶D-2247

attributable to domestic production activities, and without any basis reduction for extraordinary dividends (¶2489).[22]

If a taxpayer receives both 65% and 50% dividends, this limitation is applied in two stages. First, the 65% deduction for dividends from 20%-owned corporations is restricted to 65% of taxable income. Second, for dividends qualifying for the 50% deduction, the limitation is 50% of the taxable income reduced by dividends from 20% or greater owned corporations.[23]

A corporation with an NOL for the tax year is not subject to this limitation. (Code Sec. 246(b)(2))[24]

For the deduction allowed for dividends received from a specified 10%-owned foreign corporation, see ¶3314.

¶ 3310 Holding period requirements—dividends-received deduction.

Under Code Sec. 246(c), no dividends-received deduction (DRD) is allowed for any dividend on any share of stock held by the taxpayer for 45 days or less during the 91-day period beginning on the date that is 45 days before the date on which the stock becomes ex-dividend (i.e., the latest purchase date for collecting a dividend) with respect to the dividend (90 days or less out of the relevant 181-day period for any preferred stock with respect to which the taxpayer gets dividends that are attributable to a period or periods aggregating in excess of 366 days). In other words, a DRD is allowed only if the taxpayer's holding period for the dividend paying stock is satisfied over a period immediately before or immediately after the taxpayer becomes entitled to receive the dividend.[25]

In determining how long the shareholder has held the stock, the day of disposition, but not the day of acquisition, is taken into account. (Code Sec. 246(c)(3)(A))[26]

The holding period for the stock is reduced for any period during which the shareholder:

(1) has an option to sell, is under a contractual obligation to sell, has made (and not closed) a short sale of, or is the grantor of an option to buy, substantially identical stock or securities (as defined under the "wash sale" rules, see ¶2456). (Code Sec. 246(c)(4)(A), Code Sec. 246(c)(4)(B); Reg § 1.246-3(c)(2))[27]

(2) has diminished the risk of loss by holding one or more other positions with respect to substantially similar or related property (i.e., the fair market values (FMVs) of the stock and the property primarily reflect a single firm or enterprise, and changes in the stock's FMV are reasonably expected to approximate (directly or indirectly) changes in the property's FMV), where changes in the FMVs of the stock and the positions are reasonably expected to vary inversely. (Code Sec. 246(c)(4)(C); Reg § 1.246-5)[28]

The Code Sec. 245A dividends-received deduction (¶3314) is generally available only to taxpayers who have held shares of the specified 10%-owned foreign corporation for more than 365 days during a 731-day period. (Code Sec. 246(c)(5))[29]

¶ 3311 No dividends-received deduction (DRD) where shareholder is obligated to make certain payments.

Under Code Sec. 246(c)(1)(B), a corporate shareholder gets no DRD for any dividends received on any stock acquired after July 18, 1984 to the extent the shareholder is under an obligation (by a short sale or otherwise) to make related payments with respect to

---

22. ¶D-2251 *et seq.*
23. ¶D-2253
24. ¶s D-2251, D-2252
25. ¶D-2263

26. ¶D-2263
27. ¶s D-2264, D-2266
28. ¶D-2268 *et seq.*
29. ¶O-2953

positions in substantially similar or related property (see ¶3310).[30]

¶ 3312　Deduction reduced for dividends on debt-financed portfolio stock.

Under Code Sec. 246A(a) and Code Sec. 246A(b), the 50% and 65% dividends-received deduction (but not the 100% deduction) (¶3306) is reduced for dividends on debt-financed portfolio stock with a holding period that began after July 18, 1984. As reduced, the applicable percentage for deducting these dividends equals: (1) 50% (65% for dividends from 20%-owned corporations), multiplied by (2) 100% minus the "average indebtedness percentage."[31] The reduction for any dividend may not exceed the interest deduction (including short sale expense) allocable to that dividend. (Code Sec. 246A(e))[32]

¶ 3313　Dividends from certain corporations aren't deductible.

No dividends-received deduction is allowed for dividends from:

. . . a corporation that's exempt from tax as a charitable organization under Code Sec. 501 or as a farmer's cooperative under Code Sec. 521. (Code Sec. 246(a)(1))[33]

. . . a domestic international sales corporation (DISC; ¶4604) or former DISC to the extent paid out of accumulated DISC income or previously taxed income, or amounts considered distributed in the year of qualification as a DISC. (Code Sec. 246(d))[34]

. . . a real estate investment trust (REIT). (Code Sec. 243(d)(3))[35]

. . . a mutual savings bank, savings and loan associations, and other banks allowed a deduction under Code Sec. 591. (Code Sec. 243(d)(1))[36] However, certain dividends from federal home loan banks qualify to the extent set out in a specified formula. (Code Sec. 246(a)(2))[37]

¶ 3314　"Participation exemption" system—deduction for dividends received from a specified 10%-owned foreign corporation.

Under Code Sec. 245A(a), a domestic corporation (not a REIT or RIC) that is a U.S. shareholder of a specified 10%-owned foreign corporation can, if certain requirements are met, take a deduction in an amount equal to the foreign-source portion of any dividend received from the specified 10%-owned foreign corporation. For this purpose, a U.S. shareholder is a U.S. person that owns 10% or more of the total vote or value of shares of all classes of stock of the foreign corporation. (Code Sec. 951(b)) Amounts treated as dividends under Code Sec. 1248 (¶4615) and Code Sec. 964(e) are treated as dividends for purposes of the Code Sec. 245A dividends-received deduction.[38]

The foreign-source portion of a dividend from a specified 10%-owned foreign corporation is the amount that bears the same ratio to the dividend as the undistributed foreign earnings of the specified 10%-owned foreign corporation bears to the total undistributed earnings of such foreign corporation. (Code Sec. 245A(c)) Undistributed earnings are the E&P of the specified 10%-owned foreign corporation as of the close of the tax year without any reduction for dividends distributed during the tax year. (Code Sec. 245A(c)(2)) Undistributed foreign earnings are undistributed earnings reduced by post-'86 undistributed earnings described in Code Sec. 245(a)(5)(A) that are attributable to income effectively connected with the conduct of a trade or business in the U.S., and any dividends received

---

30. ¶D-2261
31. ¶D-2255 *et seq.*
32. ¶D-2255
33. ¶D-2213
34. ¶D-2212

35. ¶D-2215
36. ¶D-2211
37. ¶s D-2214, D-2219
38. ¶O-2950 *et seq.*

from an 80%-owned domestic corporation described in Code Sec. 245(a)(5)(B) (but by treating RICs and REITs as domestic corporations). (Code Sec. 245A(c)(3))[39]

No foreign tax credit (¶2360) or deduction is allowed for any taxes paid or accrued with respect to a dividend that qualifies for the deduction,[40] and the domestic corporation's basis in the 10%-owned foreign corporation's stock is reduced (but not below zero) by the amount of the deduction allowable on that stock. (Code Sec. 961(d))[41]

The Code Sec. 245A(a) deduction doesn't apply to a hybrid dividend received by a U.S. shareholder from a controlled foreign corporation (¶4612) (Code Sec. 245A(e)(1); Reg § 1.245A(e)-1(b)(1)(i)); or to hybrid dividends of tiered corporations (Code Sec. 245A(e)(2); Reg § 1.245A(e)-1(c)(1)). The deduction also doesn't apply to "purging distributions" of a passive foreign investment company (PFIC), ¶4617 *et seq.*), i.e., to any amount that a shareholder of a passive foreign investment company (PFIC), ¶4617 *et seq.*) that has made a qualified electing fund (QEF) election treats as a deemed dividend under Code Sec. 1291(d)(2)(B). (Code Sec. 245A(f))[42]

¶ 3315 Deductions for Foreign-Derived Intangible Income (FDII) and Global Intangible Low-Taxed Income (GILTI). ▄▄▄▄▄▄▄▄▄▄▄▄▄▄▄▄▄▄▄

Under Code Sec. 250, *for tax years that begin after Dec. 31, 2017 and before Jan. 1, 2026,* subject to a limitation based on taxable income (Code Sec. 250(a)(2)), a domestic corporation may deduct an amount equal to the sum of:

(1) 37.5% of the FDII (Code Sec. 250(b)) of the domestic corporation for the tax year, plus

(2) 50% of (i) the GILTI (¶4614) amount (if any) which is included in the gross income of the domestic corporation under Code Sec. 951A for the tax year, and (ii) the amount treated as a dividend received by the corporation under Code Sec. 78 which is attributable to the amount described in item (i). (Code Sec. 250)[43]

For tax years that begin after Dec. 31, 2025, the above percentages decrease to (1) 21.875%; and (2) 37.5%, respectively. (Code Sec. 250(a)(3))[44]

¶ 3316 Base Erosion and Anti-abuse Tax (BEAT)—Payments to Foreign Related Parties—Form 8991. ▄▄▄▄▄▄▄▄▄▄▄▄▄▄▄▄▄▄▄

Under Code Sec. 59A, a tax equal to the "base erosion minimum tax amount" (¶3317) for the tax year is imposed on each "applicable taxpayer" (i.e., with at least $500 million in average annual gross receipts for the previous three years, and that meet other requirements, see ¶3317). The tax (reported on Form 8991) is structured as an alternative minimum tax that applies when a multinational company reduces its regular U.S. tax liability to less than a specified percentage of its taxable income, after adding back deductible base eroding payments and a percentage of tax losses claimed that were carried from another year. It applies to deductible payments to foreign affiliates from domestic corporations, as well as to foreign corporations engaged in a U.S. trade or business in computing the tax on their effectively connected income.

IRS deferred the applicability date of the Form 8991 reporting requirement discussed above for "qualified derivative payments" (which aren't treated as base erosion payments subject to the base erosion tax) until tax years beginning on or after Jan. 1, 2025. (Notice 2022-30, 2022-29 IRB, superseding Notice 2021-36, IRB 2021-26)

---

39. ¶O-2951
40. ¶O-2951
41. ¶O-2423.1

42. ¶O-2952 *et seq.*
43. ¶O-3000 *et seq.*
44. ¶O-3001

¶ 3317   Base Erosion and Anti-abuse Tax (BEAT, Form 8991): "applicable tax-payers"; "base erosion minimum tax amount."

Under Code Sec. 59A, a tax equal to the "base erosion minimum tax amount" (below) for the tax year is imposed on each "applicable taxpayer" (below).

"Applicable taxpayer." Generally, this means corporations—other than regulated investment companies, real estate investment trusts, or S corporations—including foreign corporations as to their effectively connected income, with: (i) at least $500 million in average annual gross receipts for the previous three years, and (ii) base erosion payments (Code Sec. 59A(d)) that account for 3% of their deductions (2% if the affiliate group includes a bank). (Code Sec. 59A(e))[45]

"Base erosion minimum tax amount." An applicable taxpayer who is subject to the tax under Code Sec. 59A must pay a tax equal to the "base erosion minimum tax amount" for the tax year. (Code Sec. 59A(a)) This amount is the excess of 10% of the taxpayer's "modified taxable income" (Code Sec. 59A(c)) over its regular tax liability, reduced (not below zero) by specified credits. (Code Sec. 59A(b)(1))[46]

¶ 3318   Excise Tax (1%) on Repurchase (Valued Over $1 Million) of Corporate Stock.

For repurchases of stock after 2022, Code Sec. 4501 (added by the Inflation Reduction Act of 2022) will impose on each "covered corporation" a tax equal to 1% of the fair market value of any stock of the corporation that is repurchased (as defined in Code Sec. 4501(c)) by the corporation during the tax year. (Code Sec. 4501(a))

For "covered corporation," see ¶3319. For exclusions, see ¶3319. a

¶ 3319   1% excise tax on repurchase (over $1 million) of corporate stock after 2022: "covered corporation"; exclusions.

A "covered corporation" is any domestic corporation the stock of which is traded on an established securities market (within the meaning of Code Sec. 7704(b)(1)). (Code Sec. 4501(b))[47]

The 1% excise tax will not apply: (1) to the extent the repurchase is part of a reorganization (within the meaning of Code Sec. 368(a)) and no gain or loss is recognized on the repurchase by the shareholder because of the reorganization, (2) in any case in which the stock repurchased is, or an amount of stock equal to the value of the stock repurchased is, contributed to an employer-sponsored retirement plan, employee stock ownership plan, or similar plan, (3) in any case in which the total value of the stock repurchased during the tax year doesn't exceed $1 million, (4) under IRS regs, in cases in which the repurchase is by a dealer in securities in the ordinary course of business, (5) to repurchases by a regulated investment company (Code Sec. 851) or a real estate investment trust, or (6) to the extent that the repurchase is treated as a dividend. (Code Sec. 4501(e))[48]

¶ 3320   Accumulated Earnings Tax.

With limited exceptions (see below), every corporation that accumulates earnings and profits, rather than distributing them, in order to avoid the imposition of income tax on its shareholders (¶3321), is subject to an annual accumulated earnings (penalty) tax equal to 20% of its "accumulated taxable income" for the year

---

45. ¶D-1255 *et seq.*   47. ¶F-11920
46. ¶D-1251   48. ¶F-11923

(¶3322). The tax is in addition to the regular corporate tax, but is not self-assessed and arises only on a deficiency assessment.

The tax generally applies to all corporations, regardless of the number of shareholders and regardless of whether the corporation is widely held.[49] It also applies to foreign corporations on their U.S.-source income if *any* of their shareholders is subject to U.S. income tax on distributions. (Reg § 1.532-1(c))[50]

Personal holding companies (¶3324), tax-exempt corporations, passive foreign investment companies, and S corporations are exempt from the accumulated earnings tax. (Code Sec. 532(b), Code Sec. 1363(a))

¶ 3321 "Reasonable needs" of the business—accumulated earnings tax.

Under Code Sec. 533(a), for purposes of the accumulated earnings tax (¶3320), a corporation that accumulates earnings and profits (E&P) beyond the reasonable needs of its business is considered to have done so to avoid tax on its shareholders, *unless* it proves otherwise by the preponderance of the evidence.[1]

An accumulation is in excess of the reasonable needs of a business if it exceeds the amount that a prudent business person would consider appropriate for the present purposes of the business and for its reasonably anticipated future needs. (Code Sec. 537; Reg § 1.537-1(a), Reg § 1.537-1(b)(1))[2] The reasonable needs of a corporation's business include the Code Sec. 303 death tax redemption needs of the business (Code Sec. 537(a)(2)[3] and the excess business holdings redemption needs of the business. (Code Sec. 537(a)(3))[4]

Corporations facing an accumulated earnings tax may use a formula to compute the amount reasonably needed for working capital to test their liability for the penalty. The Tax Court in *Bardahl Manufacturing Corp* held that necessary working capital should be determined by: (1) calculating a corporation's operating cycle percentage (the period of time, expressed as a percentage of a year, needed to convert cash to inventory, inventory to sales and accounts receivable, and accounts receivable to cash), and then (2) multiplying that percentage by the corporation's total operating expenses for the year.[5]

¶ 3322 Accumulated taxable income—accumulated earnings tax.

Under Code Sec. 535(a), for purposes of computing the accumulated earnings tax (¶3320), a corporation's accumulated taxable income is its taxable income, adjusted as described below, *minus:* (1) the dividends-paid deduction (¶3331), and (2) the accumulated earnings credit (¶3323).[6]

The corporation's taxable income is *reduced* by:

... federal income and excess profits taxes accrued during the tax year (not the accumulated earnings tax or the personal holding company tax) (Code Sec. 535(b)(1));

... taxes of foreign countries and U.S. possessions accrued or deemed paid by a domestic corporation and included in the foreign tax credit (¶2360 *et seq.*) (Code Sec. 535(b)(1));[7]

... charitable contributions in excess of the deduction ceiling (¶2131) (Code Sec. 535(b)(2));[8]

... net capital gains (less attributable taxes) (Code Sec. 535(b)(6)(A));[9] and

... net capital losses. (Code Sec. 535(b)(5)(A))[10]

---

49. ¶D-2602
50. ¶D-2607
1. ¶D-2704
2. ¶D-2779, D-2783, D-2792
3. ¶D-2828
4. ¶D-2830

5. ¶D-2848
6. ¶D-2901
7. ¶D-2913
8. ¶D-2906
9. ¶D-2908
10. ¶D-2911

Taxable income is *increased* by:

. . . special corporate deductions (e.g., for dividends received (¶3306 *et seq.*), but not for organizational expenditures) (Code Sec. 535(b)(3));

. . . net operating loss deduction (¶1815 *et seq.*) (Code Sec. 535(b)(4)); and

. . . capital loss carryback or carryover (¶2611). (Code Sec. 535(b)(7)(B))[11]

¶ 3323 Accumulated earnings credit—accumulated earnings tax.

Under Code Sec. 535(c), for purposes of computing accumulated taxable income (¶3322) for a corporation other than a mere holding or investment company, the accumulated earnings credit equals the *greater* of:

(1) $250,000 ($150,000 for a corporation whose principal function is the performance of health, legal, engineering, accounting, or certain other services) *plus* dividends paid during the first 2 ½ months of the tax year *minus* accumulated earnings and profits (E&P) at the end of the preceding tax year (Code Sec. 535(c)(2), Code Sec. 535(c)(4)); or

(2) an amount equal to that part of the E&P for the tax year that is retained for the reasonable needs of the business (i.e., the amount in excess of the dividends-paid deduction (¶3331, Code Sec. 535(c)(4)), *minus* the net capital gains deduction, if any, allowed in adjusting the corporation's taxable income (¶3322). (Code Sec. 535(c)(1); Code Sec. 535(c)(2))[12]

¶ 3324 Personal Holding Company (PHC) Penalty Tax—Form 1120, Schedule PH. ■

For any year in which a corporation is a PHC, it is liable for an additional 20% penalty tax (Code Sec. 541) on its undistributed PHC income (¶3325), reported on Form 1120, Schedule PH. (Reg § 1.6012-2(b))[13] With exceptions (¶3326), a corporation is a PHC for the tax year if the following "PHC tests" are met: (i) it is closely held (i.e., at any time during the last half of the year, more than 50% of the value of its outstanding stock is owned, directly or indirectly, by not more than five individuals, see ¶3327); and (ii) at least 60% of the adjusted gross income of which is "PHC income" (¶3329).[14]

The foreign tax credit isn't allowed against the PHC tax. (Reg § 1.545-2(a)(3))[15]

¶ 3325 Undistributed personal holding company (PHC) income subject to the PHC penalty tax.

A corporation's undistributed PHC income that is subject to the PHC penalty tax (¶3324) is its taxable income (Code Sec. 545(a)),[16] adjusted as described below.

. . . The following amounts are *subtracted* from taxable income:

. . . Federal income tax accrued during the year, and U.S. possession and foreign income taxes not deductible in computing taxable income. (Code Sec. 545(b)(1))[17]

. . . Excess charitable contributions, i.e., amounts over the *corporate* ceiling up to the amount allowed under the *individual* ceiling (¶2123 *et seq.*). (Code Sec. 545(b)(2))[18]

. . . Net capital gain (i.e., excess of net long-term capital gain over net short-term capital loss), minus income taxes attributable to that excess (Code Sec. 545(b)(5)),[19] except in the case of a foreign corporation, only taking into account gains and losses

---

11. ¶D-2907
12. ¶D-2915
13. ¶D-3601
14. ¶D-3203
15. ¶D-3619

16. ¶D-3603
17. ¶D-3606
18. ¶D-3609
19. ¶D-3610

that are effectively connected with a US trade or business and not exempt under a treaty. (Code Sec. 545(b)(7)),[20]

. . . The preceding tax year's net operating loss (NOL) carryforward. (Code Sec. 545(b)(4))[21]

. . . The dividends-paid deduction (¶3330 *et seq.*). (Code Sec. 545(a))[22]

. . . The following amounts are *added* to taxable income:

. . . Special corporate deductions. (¶3306 *et seq.*). (Code Sec. 545(b)(3))[23]

. . . NOL deduction. (Code Sec. 545(b)(4))[24]

. . . Expenses and depreciation exceeding income from property (unless such income was the highest obtainable). (Code Sec. 545(b)(6))[25]

¶ 3326 Corporations exempt from personal holding company (PHC) classification.

Under Code Sec. 542(c), the following are not subject to the PHC penalty tax (¶3324):

. . . S corporations (¶3349 *et seq.*); (Code Sec. 1363(a))

. . . tax-exempt corporations; (Code Sec. 542(c)(1))

. . . banks or domestic building and loan associations; (Code Sec. 542(c)(2))

. . . life insurance companies; (Code Sec. 542(c)(3))

. . . surety companies; (Code Sec. 542(c)(4))

. . . certain active lending or finance companies; (Code Sec. 542(c)(6), Code Sec. 542(d))

. . . small business investment companies (¶2619), provided no shareholders own, directly or indirectly, a 5%-or-more interest in a small business concern to which the investment company provides funds; (Code Sec. 542(c)(7))

. . . corporations subject to the jurisdiction of a court in a bankruptcy case or in a receivership, foreclosure or similar proceeding in a federal or state court, if the proceedings aren't primarily to avoid the PHC tax; (Code Sec. 542(c)(8)) and

. . . foreign corporations. (Code Sec. 542(c)(5))[26]

¶ 3327 Determining stock ownership—personal holding company tax.

For purposes of determining liability for the personal holding company (PHC) penalty tax (¶3324), an individual is the owner of any stock he or she owns directly or indirectly (Code Sec. 542(a)(2)), or constructively under the following rules:

(1) Stock owned by or for a corporation, partnership, estate or trust is considered owned proportionately by its shareholders, partners or beneficiaries. (Code Sec. 544(a)(1))[27]

(2) Stock owned by or for an individual's family or partner is considered owned by the individual. An individual's family includes only his or her brothers and sisters (whether by the whole or half blood), spouse, ancestors and lineal descendants. (Code Sec. 544(a)(2))[28]

(3) If any person has an option to acquire stock, the stock subject to the option is considered owned by that person. An option to acquire the option, and each one of a series of these options, is considered an option to acquire the stock. (Code

20. ¶D-3611
21. ¶D-3614
22. ¶D-3800 *et seq.*
23. ¶D-3613
24. ¶D-3614
25. ¶D-3615
26. ¶D-3301
27. ¶D-3406
28. ¶D-3408

Sec. 544(a)(3))[29]

Stock that may be considered owned by an individual under either rule (2) or rule (3) is considered owned by him or her under rule (3). (Code Sec. 544(a)(6))[30]

Rules (2) and (3) apply only if the result is to make the corporation a PHC or to make income PHC income (¶3329). (Code Sec. 544(a)(4))[31]

Stock *constructively* owned by a person under rule (1) or rule (3) is considered *actually* owned by that person for purposes of again applying rule (1), or applying rule (2), to make *another* person the *constructive* owner of the same stock. (Code Sec. 544(a)(5))[32]

Only outstanding stock (i.e., not Treasury stock) is counted. (Reg § 1.542-3(b))[33] Outstanding securities convertible into stock are considered outstanding stock, *but only if* converting them would make the corporation a PHC or the income PHC income (except where there are differing conversion dates none of the convertibles may be counted as stock unless all outstanding securities having the same or an earlier conversion date are also included). (Code Sec. 544(b))[34]

¶ 3328 Adjusted ordinary gross income used in personal holding company (PHC) tests.

Under Code Sec. 543(b)(2), for determining liability for the PHC penalty tax (¶3324), *adjusted ordinary gross income* is ordinary gross income (below) minus certain interest income, with these adjustments: for each of the separate categories of rents, mineral, oil and gas royalties, working interests in an oil or gas well and property produced by the taxpayer, gross income from the category is reduced (but not below zero) by certain expenses allocated to each category.[35]

Ordinary gross income is gross income minus all gains from the sale or other disposition of capital assets and Code Sec. 1231(b) assets. (Code Sec. 543(b)(1))[36]

¶ 3329 Personal holding company (PHC) income used in PHC tests.

For purposes of determining liability for the PHC penalty tax (¶3324), PHC income is the portion of adjusted ordinary gross income (¶3328) that consists of: dividends; interest; annuities; rents; mineral, oil and gas royalties; copyright, patent, etc., royalties (but not certain "active business computer software royalties"); produced film rents; compensation for more-than-25% shareholder's use of corporate property; amounts received under personal service contracts; and amounts received from estates and trusts.[37]

¶ 3330 Dividend Distributions to Reduce Special Taxes on Corporations. ▬▬▬▬

A deduction for dividends paid is allowed in computing the accumulated earnings penalty tax (¶3320) and personal holding company (PHC) penalty tax (¶3324), and in determining a corporation's qualification as a regulated investment company ¶4201) or real estate investment trust (¶4202). A deduction is also allowed in some cases for undistributed amounts shareholders consent to report as dividends.

Depending on the entity involved, the dividends-paid deduction may consist of:

(1) dividends paid during the tax year (¶3331),

(2) "late paid" dividends (¶3332),

---

29. ¶D-3410
30. ¶D-3411
31. ¶s D-3408, D-3410
32. ¶D-3411
33. ¶D-3402

34. ¶D-3412
35. ¶D-3506
36. ¶D-3505
37. ¶D-3507

(3) liquidating dividends (¶3333),

(4) consent dividends (¶3334),

(5) dividend carryover—only for PHCs (¶3335), and

(6) deficiency dividends (¶3336)—only for PHCs. (Code Sec. 561 *et seq.*; Reg § 1.561-1)[38]

¶ 3331 Dividends paid during the tax year—dividends paid to reduce special corporate taxes.

Under Code Sec. 561(a)(1), the dividends-paid deduction includes dividends (¶1287) paid and actually received by the shareholder during the tax year. (Code Sec. 561(a)(1); Reg § 1.561-2(a)(1))[39]

No deduction is allowed if the dividend is preferential, i.e., it must be pro rata. (Code Sec. 562(c); Reg § 1.562-2(a))[40]

The amount of "dividends" paid is the amount by which the distribution reduces the corporation's earnings and profits (E&P). (Code Sec. 316(a), Code Sec. 562(a))[41]

A personal holding company's (PHC's, ¶3324 *et seq.*) dividends-paid deduction may equal its undistributed PHC income, even if this exceeds its E&P. (Code Sec. 316(b)(2), Code Sec. 562(a))[42]

¶ 3332 Deduction for "late paid" dividends—dividends paid to reduce special corporate taxes.

A corporation (except for corporations with a June 30 tax year, see below) may treat dividends paid after the close of the tax year but within the first 4½ months of the next year as paid on the last day of the earlier year for the accumulated earnings tax (¶3320 *et seq.*) and, if elected (on the earlier year return), personal holding company (PHC) tax (¶3324 *et seq.*). For a C corporation with a tax year ending on June 30, for tax years beginning before 2026, a dividend paid after the close of the tax year but within the first 3½ months of the next year, is considered paid during the tax year. However, for tax years beginning after Dec. 31, 2025, a C corporation with a tax year ending on June 30 may treat dividends paid after the close of the tax year but within the first 4½ months of the next year as paid during the tax year. (Code Sec. 563(a), Code Sec. 563(b))[43]

¶ 3333 Liquidating distributions—dividends paid to reduce special corporate taxes.

Under Code Sec. 562(b)(1)(A), corporations (including mutual funds and real estate investment trusts) other than personal holding companies (PHCs) may include liquidating distributions in their dividends-paid deduction, to the extent the distribution is properly chargeable to earnings and profits (E&P).[44] Where there's a deficit in E&P at the start of the tax year of distribution, no dividends-paid deduction is allowed if current E&P for that year doesn't exceed the deficit. (Reg § 1.562-1(b)(1))[45] A liquidation for this purpose includes a redemption of stock to which Code Sec. 302 applies (¶3515 *et seq.*), other than a redemption by a mere investment or holding company. (Code Sec. 562(b)(1))[46]

If a *complete* liquidation of a corporation other than a PHC occurs within 24 months after the plan of liquidation is adopted, any distribution under the plan within the 24-

38. ¶D-3800 *et seq.*
39. ¶D-3810
40. ¶D-3819 *et seq.*
41. ¶D-3807
42. ¶D-3807

43. ¶D-3825 *et seq.*
44. ¶D-3828
45. ¶D-3835
46. ¶D-3829

month period is treated as a dividend for this purpose, to the extent of the corporation's E&P for the tax year of the distribution, computed without regard to capital losses. (Code Sec. 562(b)(1)(B)) Thus, the dividends-paid deduction is allowed for the amount of the distribution up to current E&P, even if there's an E&P deficit at the start of the year. (Reg § 1.562-1(b)(1))[47]

For PHCs only, distributions made within 24 months after the plan of liquidation is adopted qualify for the dividends-paid deduction.[48] Distributions (in this period) to *corporate* shareholders qualify to the extent the undistributed PHC income for the tax year of the distribution is allocable to corporate shareholders. (Code Sec. 562(b)(2))[49] Distributions to *noncorporate* shareholders qualify if the corporation designates the amount distributed as a dividend and notifies the shareholders that it must be reported as a dividend. (Code Sec. 316(b)(2)(B), Code Sec. 562(b)(2))[50]

¶ 3334   Consent dividends—Form 972 and Form 973—dividends paid to reduce special corporate taxes.

Under Code Sec. 565(a), a corporation may claim a dividends-paid deduction for amounts with respect to "consent" stock (below) that are not actually paid out as dividends, if those who are shareholders on the last day of its tax year consent (on Form 972) to report these hypothetical amounts as dividend income on their tax returns. (Code Sec. 565(a); Reg § 1.565-1(a), Reg § 1.565-1(b))[1]

This amount is treated for all tax purposes as if it had been distributed in money to the consenting shareholder on the last day of the corporation's tax year, and contributed to the corporation's capital by the shareholder on the same day. (Code Sec. 565(c))[2]

Consent stock includes common stock, and preferred stock with unlimited participation rights. (Code Sec. 565(f); Reg § 1.565-6(a)(1))[3]

The corporation must file Form 972 duly executed by each consenting shareholder, and a return on Form 973, with its income tax return not later than the due date (with extensions) of the return. (Reg § 1.565-1(b)(3))[4]

¶ 3335   Dividend carryover for personal holding companies (PHCs)—dividends paid to reduce special corporate taxes.

Under Code Sec. 564, a PHC may increase its dividends-paid deduction for the tax year by the excess of: (1) dividends paid in the two preceding tax years, over (2) its undistributed PHC income for those years. (Code Sec. 564; Reg § 1.564-1)[5]

¶ 3336   Deficiency dividend deduction for personal holding companies (PHCs)—Form 976—dividends paid to reduce special corporate taxes.

If a corporation is "determined" (i.e., by a final court decision, closing agreement, or signed agreement with IRS relating to PHC tax liability (Code Sec. 547(c)))[6] to be liable for a deficiency in PHC tax (¶3324 *et seq.*) for any tax year, it may reduce or eliminate the deficiency (or get a refund of part or all of any deficiency paid) by making a "deficiency dividend" distribution and then claiming a deduction (on Form 976) for it. This deduction is allowed only for purposes of determining the *PHC tax* for that year (but not any interest, additional amounts or assessable penalties computed with respect to the PHC tax). (Code

47. ¶D-3836
48. ¶D-3837
49. ¶D-3844 *et seq.*
50. ¶D-3838 *et seq.*
1. ¶s D-3851, D-3854, D-3861

2. ¶D-3853
3. ¶s D-3859, D-3861
4. ¶D-3867
5. ¶D-3869
6. ¶D-3705

Sec. 547(a))[7]

The deduction isn't allowed if the determination finds that any part of the deficiency is due to fraud or willful failure to file a timely income tax return. (Code Sec. 547(g))[8]

¶ 3337 Limitation on Tax Benefits for Members of "Controlled Groups." ▬▬▬▬

Under Code Sec. 1561(a), if two or more corporations constitute a controlled group of corporations (below), the group is allowed only one credit in computing the accumulated earnings tax (¶3320). This credit is divided equally among the component members of the group. (¶3323)[9]

A controlled group of corporations is a group of two or more corporations connected through stock ownership and may consist of a parent-subsidiary group, a brother-sister group, or a combined group (a combined parent-subsidiary/brother-sister group).

A *parent-subsidiary controlled group* consists of one or more chains of corporations connected through stock ownership with a common parent where:

. . . the common parent owns stock having at least 80% of the total combined voting power of all classes of stock entitled to vote, or at least 80% of the total value of shares of all classes of stock, of at least one other corporation in the chain; *and*

. . . at least 80% of the stock (combined voting power or value) of each corporation in the chain (other than the parent) is owned by one or more of the other corporations in the chain. (Code Sec. 1563(a)(1); Reg § 1.1563-1(a)(2))[10]

A *brother-sister controlled group* consists of two or more corporations if (a) more than 50% of the total combined voting power of all classes of stock, or (b) more than 50% of the value of all shares of stock, of each corporation is owned by five or fewer persons who are individuals, estates, or trusts, taking into account the stock ownership of each person only to the extent the stock ownership is identical for each corporation. (Code Sec. 1563(a)(2), Code Sec. 1563(f)(5); Reg § 1.1563-1(a)(3))[11]

Specific constructive ownership rules apply in determining whether these stock ownership tests are met. (Code Sec. 1563(d))

¶ 3338 Consolidated Returns by Affiliated Groups. ▬▬▬▬

An affiliated group (defined at ¶3339) can elect to file a single consolidated return instead of each group member filing a separate return.

Any affiliated group of one or more chains of "includible" corporations (¶3339) connected through the requisite stock ownership with a common parent may file a consolidated return in place of separate returns by each member. (Code Sec. 1501—Code Sec. 1505)[12] Generally, once this election to file a consolidated return is made, the group must continue to file a consolidated return. (Reg § 1.1502-75(a)(2))[13]

Tax saving considerations usually determine whether to file a consolidated return. Advantages of consolidated returns include:

. . . operating losses of one group member offset operating profits of other members.[14]

. . . capital losses of one group member offset capital gains of other members.[15]

. . . deferral of income on intercompany distributions.[16]

. . . group's ability to use foreign taxes paid by a member in excess of its limitation on

---

7. ¶s D-3703, D-3716
8. ¶D-3719
9. ¶E-10301
10. ¶E-10601
11. ¶E-10604

12. ¶E-7500 *et seq.*
13. ¶E-10000
14. ¶E-7503
15. ¶E-7503
16. ¶E-8300 *et seq.*

foreign tax credits.[17]

. . . the 50% or 65% dividends-received deduction for dividends received from unrelated corporations, that may not be fully usable on a separate return basis because of the income limitation rule, may be fully used in a consolidated return. (¶3306)[18]

Where an affiliated group files a consolidated return, the base erosion and anti-abuse tax (¶3316) is imposed on a consolidated basis.[19]

Regs prescribe detailed rules for the tax treatment of items of income, gain, deduction and loss of members from intercompany transactions. The rules are designed to clearly reflect the group's taxable income (and tax liability) as a whole by preventing intercompany transactions from creating, accelerating, avoiding, or deferring consolidated taxable income or consolidated tax liability. (Reg § 1.1502-13)[20] There is also significant case law preventing the deduction of duplicate losses.[21]

¶ 3339   "Affiliated group" defined—consolidated returns.

Under Code Sec. 1504(a), to qualify as an affiliated group:

(1) the common parent must directly own at least 80% of the total voting power and 80% of the total value of the stock in at least one other "includible" corporation; *and*

(2) one or more of the other includible corporations must directly own at least 80% of the stock (by vote or value) in each of the remaining includible corporations (i.e., not the parent).[22]

All corporations connected through these stock ownership requirements are "includible" corporations *except*:

. . . tax-exempt organizations;

. . . life insurance companies, except (under certain conditions) where two or more insurance companies are themselves an affiliated group;

. . . regulated investment companies (i.e., mutual funds) and real estate investment trusts (¶4201 *et seq.*);

. . . foreign corporations, except for certain Mexican or Canadian subs of a U.S. parent;

. . . domestic international sales corporations (DISCs, ¶4604);

. . . S corporations. (Code Sec. 1504(b), Code Sec. 1504(c))

¶ 3340   Forms for consolidated reporting—Form 851, Form 1120, and Form 1122.

A consolidated return is made by the common parent on Form 1120 with an attached Form 851 (affiliation schedule), and a Form 1122 (consent) signed by each subsidiary unless a consolidated return was filed (or required) for the preceding tax year. (Reg § 1.1502-75(b), Reg § 1.1502-75(h))[23] If a group member fails to file Form 1122, IRS can nonetheless treat that member as having joined in the making of a consolidated return if the facts and circumstances warrant such treatment. (Reg § 1.1502-75(b)(2)) In addition, in Rev Proc 2014-24, Sec. 1.02, 2014-13 IRB 879, IRS provided requirements for obtaining an automatic determination that a subsidiary is to be treated as if it had filed Form 1122.[24]

17. ¶E-9750 *et seq.*
18. ¶E-8905
19. ¶E-9670 *et seq.*
20. ¶E-8250 *et seq.*

21. ¶E-8501 *et seq.*
22. ¶E-7601
23. ¶E-7754 *et seq.*
24. ¶E-7757

¶ 3341　Consolidated groups—unified loss rules.

When a member of a consolidated group claims a loss on the disposition or worthlessness of a share of another member's stock, the unified loss rules determine what portion of that loss is allowable. The unified loss rules apply when a consolidated group member transfers stock of a subsidiary (S), and after taking into account all applicable rules, the share is a loss share (i.e., its basis exceeds its value). In such a case: (1) the members' basis in the transferred S stock is redetermined to reduce any disparity between the members' bases in the S stock; (2) if the transferred share is still a loss share, the transferor members' basis in the transferred loss share is reduced; and (3) if the transferred share is still a loss share, attributes of S and of its lower-tier subsidiaries are reduced. Thus, the selling group is now entitled to claim its stock loss, but the departing member must reduce its tax attributes immediately after it leaves the group, thereby precluding that member (or the consolidated group it joins) from enjoying a second tax benefit. (Reg § 1.1502-36)[25]

Special anti-avoidance rules under Reg § 1.1502-35 bar the circumvention of the basis redetermination and loss suspension rules,[26] including rules that prevent groups from avoiding the loss suspension rule by "reimporting" losses to the group. (Reg § 1.1502-35(g)(3))[27]

Special rules apply when assets are distributed to multiple group members from a liquidating member in a Code Sec. 332 liquidation. (Reg § 1.1502-80(g))[28]

¶ 3342　Dual Consolidated Losses. ■■■■■■■■

A corporation that is subject to tax on its worldwide income in the U.S. and a foreign jurisdiction (e.g. a company incorporated in the U.S. but managed and controlled in another country) is referred to as a "dual resident corporation" (DRC). If a DRC is a resident of a foreign country that permits its losses to offset the income of other commonly controlled foreign corporate residents, then the DRC could use a single loss to offset both foreign and U.S. taxable income. The use of a dual consolidated loss to offset the income of a domestic affiliate is permitted only if the loss does not offset the income of a foreign corporation under foreign law. (Code Sec. 1503(d))[29]

¶ 3343　Corporate Estimated Tax—"Required Annual Payment." ■■■■■■■

Under Code Sec. 6655(f), a corporation owing $500 or more in income tax for the tax year must make estimated tax payments—i.e., installment payments (¶3345) of its "required annual payment" —or be subject to a penalty.

A corporation's required annual payment equals the *lesser* of:

(1) 100% of the tax shown on its return for the year (or if no return is filed, 100% of its tax for that year); or

(2) 100% of the tax shown on its return for the preceding tax year (except as noted below). (Code Sec. 6655(d)(1)(B))[30]

A corporation's required annual payment can't be based on the preceding year's tax if:

. . . it didn't file a return for the preceding tax year showing a liability for tax (Code Sec. 6655(d)(1)) (a return showing zero tax, e.g., because of a net operating loss (NOL), isn't a return showing a liability for tax);

. . . the preceding tax year was less than 12 months (Code Sec. 6655(d)(1)); or

. . . it's a "large corporation" (see below). (Code Sec. 6655(d)(2)(A)) However, a large

---

25. ¶E-8574 *et seq.*
26. ¶E-8566
27. ¶E-8569
28. ¶E-7552.2
29. ¶E-9200 *et seq.*
30. ¶S-5329 *et seq.*

corporation may use its prior year's tax to determine the amount of its first required installment for any tax year, but it must recapture any resulting reduction in that first installment, by increasing its next required installment by the amount of the reduction. (Code Sec. 6655(d)(2)(B))[31]

A corporation is "large" in any tax year if it (or any predecessor corporation) had taxable income of $1,000,000 or more for any of the three immediately preceding tax years. For this purpose, taxable income doesn't include carryback or carryover of NOLs or capital losses. Special rules apply to controlled groups. (Code Sec. 6655(g)(2))[32]

For quick refunds where a corporation pays *too much* in estimated tax, see ¶4835.

¶ 3344 What is "tax" for corporate estimated tax purposes?

Under Code Sec. 6655(g)(1), a corporation's "tax" for estimated tax purposes is the excess of: (1) the sum of its regular corporate income tax (or, if applicable, insurance company tax), base erosion anti-abuse tax (¶3316), and, for foreign corporations, the tax on gross transportation income (¶4637), over (2) the sum of its tax credits.[33]

For S corporations, regular corporate taxes also include: built-in gains tax (¶3361) or tax on net capital gains for certain S corporations (¶3360), tax on excess passive income (¶3364), and tax on recapture of pre-S election investment credit (Code Sec. 6655(g)(4)(A)), but not the last-in, first-out (LIFO) recapture tax (¶3363).[34]

Special rules apply for foreign corporations, insurance companies and tax-exempt organizations (for unrelated business income tax). (Code Sec. 6655(g)(1), Code Sec. 6655(g)(3))[35]

¶ 3345 "Required installments" of corporate estimated tax—Form 1120-W.

Generally, a corporation pays its estimated tax electronically, if required (see ¶3028), otherwise by Electronic Funds Transfer (EFT) in four equal "required installments" of its "required annual payment" (¶3343). Corporations can use Form 1120-W (which is not sent to IRS) as a worksheet for computing estimated tax.[36] (Code Sec. 6655(c)(1), Code Sec. 6655(d)(1)(A), Reg § 31.6302-1(h)(2)(iii)) For a calendar year corporation, the installments are due Apr. 15, June 15, Sept. 15, and Dec. 15, assuming that those days do not fall on a Saturday, Sunday, or legal holiday. (Code Sec. 6655(c)(2)) For a fiscal year corporation, they are due on the 15th day of the corresponding months of the tax year (Code Sec. 6655(i)(1)) (i.e., the fourth, sixth, ninth and twelfth months).[37]

For reduced installments in certain situations, see ¶3346 and ¶3347.

¶ 3346 Use of lower "annualized income installment" as required installment— Form 8842—corporate estimated tax.

Under Code Sec. 6655(e)(1)(A), a corporation may use an "annualized income installment" as its estimated tax installment, if that's less than the "required installment" (¶3345).[38]

The annualized income installment is the excess (if any) of: (1) the applicable percentage of the tax for the year and modified taxable income computed by placing on an annualized basis (as provided by regs) the taxable income for months in the tax year ending before the due date for the installment; *over* (2) the sum of any earlier required installments for the

---

31. ¶S-5329 *et seq.*
32. ¶S-5335 *et seq.*
33. ¶S-5325
34. ¶S-5401 *et seq.*

35. ¶S-5321 *et seq.*, S-5421 *et seq.*
36. ¶S-5334
37. ¶S-5324.1; ¶T-10796
38. ¶S-5329

540

tax year. (Code Sec. 6655(e)(2)(A), Code Sec. 6655(e)(2)(B); Reg § 1.6655-2)[39]

Alternatively, a corporation may elect on Form 8842, by the due date of the first installment (Reg § 1.6655(e)-1(b)), to determine its annualized income based on its income for *either:* (1) the first two months (first installment), first four months (second), first seven months (third) and first ten months (fourth); *or* (2) the first three months (first), first five months (second), first eight months (third), and first eleven months (fourth). (Code Sec. 6655(e)(2)(C))[40]

Any reduction in an installment resulting from using the annualization method must be made up (recaptured) by increasing the amount of the next required installment that *isn't* determined under the annualization method by the amount of the reduction. (Code Sec. 6655(e)(1)(B))[41]

¶ 3347 Use of lower "adjusted seasonal installment" as required installment—corporate estimated tax.

A corporation may use an "adjusted seasonal installment" as its estimated tax installment if it's less than the required installment (¶3345) or the annualized income installment (Code Sec. 6655(e)(1)(A)), but only if the corporation's "base period percentage" (below) for any six consecutive months of the tax year is at least 70%. (Code Sec. 6655(e)(3)(B); Reg § 1.6655-3)[42]

A corporation computes its adjusted seasonal installment by: (1) computing the taxable income for all months during the tax year before the filing month (i.e., the month the installment is required to be paid), (2) dividing this amount by the base period percentage for those preceding months, (3) determining the tax on the result, and (4) multiplying that tax by the base period percentage for the filing month and all preceding months in the tax year (Code Sec. 6655(e)(3)(C), Code Sec. 6655(e)(3)(D)(ii)), and then subtracting from the result of the preceding four steps the aggregate of all earlier required installments. (Code Sec. 6655(e)(3)(A); Reg § 1.6655-3(c))[43]

The "base period percentage" for any specific period of months is the average percentage that the corporation's taxable income for the corresponding months in each of the three preceding tax years bears to its taxable income for those three years. (Code Sec. 6655(e)(3)(D)(i); Reg § 1.6655-3(d))[44]

Any reduction in an installment resulting from the adjusted seasonal method must be made up (recaptured), by increasing the amount of the next required installment that *isn't* determined under the adjusted seasonal method by the amount of the reduction. (Code Sec. 6655(e)(1)(B))[45]

¶ 3348 Penalty for failure to pay corporate estimated tax—Form 2220.

Under Code Sec. 6655(a), a corporation that underpays its estimated tax must add to its income tax an amount equal to the underpayment interest rate (¶4849) multiplied by the amount of the underpayment, for the period of the underpayment. Form 2220 is used to compute and report the underpayment penalty.[46]

The amount of the underpayment is the excess of the required installment (¶3345) over the amount (if any) of the installment paid on or before its due date. (Code Sec. 6655(b)(1))[47]

39. ¶S-5342 *et seq.*
40. ¶S-5342 *et seq.*
41. ¶S-5351.26 *et seq.*
42. ¶S-5351.21 *et seq.*
43. ¶S-5351.21 *et seq.*

44. ¶S-5351.23
45. ¶S-5351.27
46. ¶S-5358
47. ¶S-5323

The period of the underpayment runs from the due date for the installment to the earlier of: (1) the 15th day of the fourth month after the close of the tax year (15th day of the third month for C corporations with June 30 tax-year ends occurring on or before Dec. 31, 2025, after which time the "15th day of the fourth month" rule applies) or (2) with respect to any portion of the underpayment, the date the portion is paid. (Code Sec. 6655(b)(2), Code Sec. 6655(g)(4)(E)) For this purpose, a payment of estimated tax is credited against unpaid required installments in the order those installments were due. (Code Sec. 6655(b)(3))[48]

No estimated tax penalty is imposed for any tax year if the tax shown on the return for that year (or if no return is filed, the tax liability) is less than $500. (Code Sec. 6655(f))[49] Nor is the penalty imposed for a period in which the failure to pay the required installment(s) results from a pending Title 11 bankruptcy case. (Code Sec. 6658(a))[50]

¶ 3349   S Corporations.

An eligible corporation may elect to be taxed as an S corporation which, with limited exceptions, isn't taxed at the corporate level. Instead, its items of income, loss, deduction and credit are passed through to, and taken into account by, its shareholders in computing their individual tax liabilities (¶3366).

For S election eligibility, see ¶3350 *et seq.*

¶ 3350   Rules for eligibility to elect S corporation status.

Under Code Sec. 1361(a)(1), an S corporation is a corporation for which an election to be taxed under Subchapter S of the Code is in effect.[1] Only a small business corporation may elect to be an S corporation. (Code Sec. 1362(a)(1)) A corporation (or an unincorporated entity that's taxable as a corporation) qualifies as a small business corporation if:[2]

(1) It is a domestic corporation (created under the law of the U.S. or of any state). (Code Sec. 1361(b)(1))[3]

(2) It is not *ineligible*. (Code Sec. 1361(b)(1); Reg § 1.1361-1(d))

A corporation is ineligible if it is:

. . . a financial institution that uses a reserve method of accounting for bad debts,

. . . taxable as an insurance company (with certain exceptions),

. . . a domestic international sales corporation (DISC) or former DISC (¶4604) (Code Sec. 1361(b)(2)), or

. . . a taxable mortgage pool. (Reg § 301.7701(i)-4(c)(1))[4]

(3) It doesn't have more than 100 shareholders, see ¶3352. (Code Sec. 1361(b)(1)(A); Reg § 1.1361-1(e))[5]

(4) All shareholders are individuals, decedents' estates, bankruptcy estates, trusts described at ¶3353, or tax-exempt Code Sec. 501(c)(3) charitable organizations (Code Sec. 1361(b)(1)(B); Reg § 1.1361-1(f)), except that an otherwise eligible S corporation can be wholly owned by another S corporation, see ¶3351. A partnership can hold S corporation stock as a nominee for an eligible shareholder. (Reg § 1.1361-1(e)(1))[6] With a very limited exception for certain banks that are S corporations, Individual Retirement Accounts (including one designated as a Roth IRA) may not be shareholders in an S corporation. (Reg § 1.1361-1(h)(1)(vii), Reg § 1.1361-1(h)(3)(i)(G))

---

48. ¶S-5324
49. ¶S-5359
50. ¶V-7378
1. ¶D-1421
2. ¶I-9529

3. ¶D-1432
4. ¶D-1434 *et seq.*
5. ¶D-1441
6. ¶D-1445

(5) No shareholder is a nonresident alien (Code Sec. 1361(b)(1)(C)), or married to a nonresident alien who has a current ownership interest in his or her stock under local law (unless the spouses elect under Code Sec. 6013(g) to be taxed as U.S. residents). (Reg § 1.1361-1(g)(1))[7] A nonresident alien may, however, be a potential current beneficiary of an Electing Small Business Trust (ESBT); see ¶3353.[8]

(6) It has only one class of stock, see ¶3354. (Code Sec. 1361(b)(1)(D); Reg § 1.1361-1(b)(1))[9]

¶ 3351　Treatment of subsidiaries of S corporations; QSub rules—Form 8869.

Under Code Sec. 1361(b), S corporations may have 80%-or-more owned C ("regular") corporation subsidiaries and wholly-owned S corporation subsidiaries.

A C corporation subsidiary is treated as a separate taxpayer. If it operates profitably, it pays tax on its income. If it operates at a loss, it cannot pass the loss through to the S corporation. A C corporation subsidiary may file a consolidated return with other C corporations with which it is affiliated. The S corporation cannot be included in this return (¶3339).

An S corporation cannot have a corporate shareholder. (Code Sec. 1361(b)(1)(B); Reg § 1.1361-1(f)) This rule ordinarily prevents a subsidiary from being an S corporation. However, an S corporation can have an S corporation subsidiary if it owns 100% of the subsidiary's stock, the sub is not an ineligible corporation, and the S corporation parent elects (on Form 8869)[10] to treat the subsidiary as a qualified Subchapter S subsidiary (QSub). (Code Sec. 1361(b)(3)(B); Reg § 1.1361-2, Reg § 1.1361-3)[11]

A QSub isn't treated as a separate corporation for federal tax purposes; rather, its assets, liabilities, and items of income, deduction, and credit are treated as those of the parent S corporation. (Code Sec. 1361(b)(3)(A); Reg § 1.1361-4)[12] However, except to the extent otherwise provided by IRS, QSubs are treated as separate entities for purposes of making information returns. (Code Sec. 1361(b)(3)(E))[13]

If a QSub loses its qualification, it is treated as if it sold an undivided interest in its assets (based on a percentage of the stock sold) and transferred the remaining assets to itself in a tax-free incorporation. Thus, if an S corporation sells 21% of the stock of its QSub to an unrelated party, it will recognize 21% of the gain on the QSub's assets. (Code Sec. 1361(b)(3)(C); Reg § 1.1361-5)[14] If QSub status terminates, the corporation or its successor may not elect QSub status or S corporation status before its fifth year beginning after the first tax year for which the termination was effective, without IRS consent. (Code Sec. 1361(b)(3)(D); Reg § 1.1361-5(c))[15] IRS may waive inadvertent or invalid QSub elections and terminations of elections. (Code Sec. 1362(f))[16] For late election relief, see ¶3357.

A QSub generally uses the parent S corporation's employee identification number (EIN). If the election terminates, the sub must get an EIN; but if the entity either had an EIN before becoming a QSub or got an EIN while it was a QSub, it must use that EIN. (Reg § 301.6109-1(i))[17]

¶ 3352　Determination of number of shareholders—S corporation eligibility.

In applying the 100-shareholder limit (¶3350), everyone who owns stock is counted separately, even if the stock is owned jointly with someone else (e.g., joint tenant, tenant in

7. ¶D-1456 *et seq.*
8. ¶D-1473 *et seq.*
9. ¶D-1495 *et seq.*
10. ¶D-1539
11. ¶D-1540
12. ¶D-1531
13. ¶D-1532
14. ¶D-1536
15. ¶D-1538
16. ¶D-1554; ¶D-1909
17. ¶D-1532

common), except as follows:

(1) Spouses (and their estates) are treated as one shareholder, no matter how the stock is held (separately, jointly, etc.). (Code Sec. 1361(c)(1)(A)(i); Reg § 1.1361-1(e)(2))[18]

(2) Where stock is owned by a grantor trust and also by the grantor directly, they are treated as one shareholder.[19]

(3) All members of a family and their estates are treated as one shareholder. Family members include the common ancestor, lineal descendants of the common ancestor, and the spouses (or former spouses) of the lineal descendants or common ancestor. But, an individual isn't considered a common ancestor if, on the applicable date (see below), the individual was more than six generations removed from the youngest generation of shareholders who would (but for this limitation) be family members. For this purpose, a spouse (or former spouse) is treated as being of the same generation as the individual to which such spouse is (or was) married. Adopted children are treated as children if they are (i) legally adopted, (ii) lawfully placed with an individual for legal adoption, or (iii) eligible foster children (defined under Code Sec. 152(f)(1)(C), ¶3114). (Code Sec. 1361(c)(1)) The applicable date is the latest of: the date the S election was made; the earliest date that a family member holds stock in the S corporation; or Oct. 22, 2004. (Code Sec. 1361(c)(1)(B)(iii))[20]

Each potential current beneficiary (i.e., one who may receive a discretionary distribution of income or principal during the relevant period) of an electing small business trust (ESBT), ¶3353) is treated as a shareholder in applying the limit. The ESBT is treated as the shareholder for periods when there's no potential current beneficiary. (Code Sec. 1361(c)(2)(B)(v); Reg § 1.1361-1(m)(4)) Unexercised powers of appointment are not taken into account in determining potential current beneficiaries. In addition, a person who first becomes a potential current beneficiary during the 1-year period ending with the date of the trust's disposition of all of its stock in an S corporation isn't a potential current beneficiary of that corporation. (Code Sec. 1361(e)(2))[21]

¶ 3353   Trusts that are allowable as shareholders; QSSTs—S corporation eligibility.

Only the following trusts may be S corporation shareholders:

(1) Grantor trusts—domestic trusts that are treated as being owned by an individual ("grantor") who is a U.S. citizen or resident, during the period the trust holds the S corporation stock. The grantor, not the trust, is treated as the shareholder. (Code Sec. 1361(c)(2); Reg § 1.1361-1(h)) But after the grantor dies, the trust may continue as the shareholder for two years. (Code Sec. 1361(c)(2)(A)(ii))[22]

(2) Code Sec. 678 trusts—where a person other than the grantor is treated as the substantial owner of the trust, during the period the trust holds the S corporation stock. The deemed owner, who must be a U.S. citizen or resident, is treated as the shareholder. (Code Sec. 1361(c)(2); Reg § 1.1361-1(h))[23]

(3) Voting trusts, but each beneficiary is counted as a separate shareholder. (Code Sec. 1361(c)(2); Reg § 1.1361-1(h))[24]

(4) Testamentary trusts, for two years beginning with the day when stock was transferred to the trust under the testator's will. (Code Sec. 1361(c)(2)(A)(iii); Reg § 1.1361-1(h)(1)(iv))[25]

18. ¶D-1447
19. ¶D-1461
20. ¶D-1447.1
21. ¶D-1474

22. ¶s D-1460, D-1461
23. ¶D-1461
24. ¶D-1479
25. ¶D-1478

(5) "Qualified Subchapter S trusts" (QSSTs), if the beneficiary elects (on Form 2553, in certain circumstances) to be treated as the owner of the trust so that it is eligible to hold the S stock (as in (1), above), and is treated as the shareholder. (Code Sec. 1361(d); Reg § 1.1361-1(j))[26] For late election relief, see ¶3357.

A QSST can be converted to an electing small business trust (below) if certain conditions are met.[27]

(6) "Electing small business trusts" (ESBTs) —these trusts are subject to fewer restrictions than QSSTs but carry a heavy tax cost, see ¶3907. (Code Sec. 1361(c)(2)(A)(v), Code Sec. 1361(e); Reg § 1.1361-1(m)) To elect, the trustee must sign and file a specified statement with the service center with which the corporation files its income tax return. In the case of a newly electing S corporation, the trustee can attach the ESBT's consent to the Form 2553.[28] An ESBT can be converted to a QSST if certain conditions are met .[29] For late election relief, see ¶3357. Nonresident aliens can potentially be current beneficiaries of an ESBT. (Code Sec. 1361(c)(2)(B)(v))[30]

(7) Tax-exempt Code Sec. 401(a) qualified plan trusts. (Code Sec. 1361(c)(6))[31]

¶ 3354   One class of stock—S corporation eligibility.

A corporation is treated as having only one class of stock (¶3350) if:

. . . all outstanding shares of its stock confer identical rights to distribution and liquidation proceeds, based on certain governing provisions (e.g., corporate charter, by-laws, state law, etc.) (Reg § 1.1361-1(l)(1), Reg § 1.1361-1(l)(2)(i)); and

. . . it hasn't issued any instrument or obligation or entered into any arrangement that's treated as a second class of stock. (Reg § 1.1361-1(l)(4))[32]

The one-class-of-stock rule isn't violated *solely* because of differences in voting rights. Thus, voting and nonvoting common can be issued. (Code Sec. 1361(c)(4))[33]

Buy-sell agreements among shareholders, redemption agreements and agreements restricting the transferability of stock generally won't violate the one-class-of-stock rule *unless:* (1) a principal purpose of the agreement is to circumvent the rule, and (2) it establishes a purchase price for the stock that's significantly above or below its fair market value (FMV). (Reg § 1.1361-1(l)(2)(iii))[34]

A call option, warrant or similar instrument is, with certain exceptions, treated as a second class of stock if it's substantially certain to be exercised and has a strike price substantially below the stock's FMV on the date it's issued, transferred to an ineligible shareholder, or materially modified. (Reg § 1.1361-1(l)(4)(iii)(A))[35]

Straight debt isn't treated as a second class of stock if specified safe harbor rules are met. (Code Sec. 1361(c)(5)(A), Code Sec. 1361(c)(5)(B))[36] However, any instrument, obligation or arrangement is, with certain exceptions, treated as a second class of stock if: (1) it constitutes equity or otherwise results in the holder being treated as the owner of stock under general tax law, and (2) its principal purpose is to circumvent these rules. (Reg § 1.1361-1(l)(4))[37] Restricted bank director stock is not taken into account for the one class of stock requirement. (Code Sec. 1361(f)(1))[38]

---

26. ¶D-1466
27. ¶D-1476
28. ¶D-1475
29. ¶D-1476
30. ¶D-1473 *et seq.*
31. ¶D-1480
32. ¶D-1495 *et seq.*

33. ¶D-1497
34. ¶D-1507 *et seq.*
35. ¶D-1523
36. ¶D-1519
37. ¶D-1516
38. ¶D-1444.1

¶ 3355   How to elect S corporation status—Form 2553.

The S election is made by the corporation (Code Sec. 1362(a)(1)) by filing a Form 2553 signed by its authorized officer, with the required shareholder consents (¶3356) (and IRS user fee), at the IRS Service Center designated on the form. (Reg § 1.1362-6(a)(2))[39]

An S election for a tax year may be made during the preceding tax year, or by the 15th day of the third month of the tax year for which it's to be effective. (Code Sec. 1362(b)(1)) If this first tax year is less than two months and 15 days, the election must be made no later than two months and 15 days after the first day of that year. (Code Sec. 1362(b)(4))[40]

An S election will be effective retroactively to the first day of a tax year *only if:*

. . . on all days in the tax year before the day the election is made, the corporation would have been eligible to elect (Code Sec. 1362(b)(2)(B)(i)), *and*

. . . all persons who were shareholders at any time during the tax year before the day of the election, but who aren't shareholders on that date, consent (along with persons who *are* shareholders, see ¶3356). (Code Sec. 1362(b)(2)(B)(ii))[41]

If either of the above conditions isn't met, the election is treated as made for the next tax year. (Code Sec. 1362(b)(2))[42]

A partnership that converts to a corporation under check-the-box rules (¶3301) or a state law conversion statute may make an S election effective for the corporation's first tax year.[43]

IRS may waive invalid elections (e.g., because of an inadvertent failure to get all the necessary consents (¶3356) or to qualify to elect S status). (Code Sec. 1362(f))[44] For late election relief, see ¶3357.

¶ 3356   Shareholder consents—S corporation election.

Under Code Sec. 1362(a)(2), all shareholders owning stock in the corporation on the day it elects S status must consent to the election. (Code Sec. 1362(a)(2); Reg § 1.1362-6(b)(2)(i))[45] The consents may be given on Form 2553 (¶3355), or on separate statements attached to it. (Reg § 1.1362-6(b))[46]

A shareholder's failure to file a timely consent won't invalidate an otherwise valid timely filed election if consents are filed within an extended period of time as granted by IRS, and IRS is satisfied that: (1) there was reasonable cause for the failure; (2) the extension was requested within a reasonable time; and (3) its interests won't be jeopardized by treating the election as valid. (Reg § 1.1362-6(b)(3)(iii)(A))[47] Special rules apply for requests for automatic relief when a community property spouse fails to timely consent to an S corporation election.[48]

¶ 3357   Relief for late-filed S corporation and related elections.

IRS has provided exclusive simplified methods for taxpayers to request relief for late S corporation elections, electing small business trust (ESBT) elections, qualified Subchapter S trust (QSST) elections, qualified Subchapter S subsidiary (QSub) elections, and late corporate classification elections under Reg § 301.7701-3(c)(1)(v)(C) which the taxpayer intended to take effect on the same date that an S corporation election for the entity was to

---

39. ¶D-1551, ¶D-1552, ¶T-10004
40. ¶D-1553
41. ¶D-1553
42. ¶D-1553
43. ¶D-1481

44. ¶D-1554 *et seq.*; ¶D-1909
45. ¶D-1552
46. ¶D-1552
47. ¶D-1555
48. ¶D-1556

take effect. (Rev Proc 2013-30, 2013-36 IRB 173) If certain requirements are met, a taxpayer can obtain relief without having to obtain a private letter ruling (PLR). However, if the taxpayer doesn't qualify for the simplified method in Rev Proc 2013-30, the taxpayer may still seek relief through a PLR. In considering the taxpayer's PLR request, IRS has the authority to treat an election as timely made if it determines, among other things, that there was reasonable cause for the failure to timely elect.[49]

¶ 3358 "Taxable income" of an S corporation.

Under Code Sec. 1363(b), an S corporation's taxable income is computed in the same manner as an individual's taxable income *except that*:[50]

(1) Items of income (including tax-exempt interest), loss, deduction or credit must be separately stated if their separate treatment by a shareholder could affect his or her tax liability. (Code Sec. 1363(b)(1))

(2) The corporation can't take the following deductions allowed to individuals: personal exemptions; foreign taxes; charitable contributions; net operating loss (NOL) deduction; additional itemized deductions; and oil and gas depletion. (Code Sec. 1363(b)(2))

(3) A deduction is allowed for the amortization of the corporation's organizational expenditures under Code Sec. 248 (¶3510). (Code Sec. 1363(b)(3))[1]

(4) The Code Sec. 291 rules that reduce certain corporate tax benefits apply to an S corporation (or any predecessor) that was a C corporation for any of the three immediately preceding tax years. (Code Sec. 1363(b)(4))[2]

Except as otherwise provided in the Code, or to the extent inconsistent with the Subchapter S rules, the Subchapter C rules (transfers to related corporations, redemptions, reorganizations, liquidations, etc., see ¶3500 *et seq.*) apply to an S corporation and its shareholders. (Code Sec. 1371(a))[3] But there are these modifications:

. . . For liquidating distributions, no gain or loss is recognized on distributions of installment obligations where the shareholders' receipt of them (as part of a 12-month complete liquidation) isn't treated as payment for their stock by reason of Code Sec. 453(h)(1). (Code Sec. 453B(h)(1))[4]

. . . Except for the organizational expenditures deduction (above), Code provisions governing the computation of taxable income which apply only to corporations (e.g., dividends-received deduction, ¶3306) don't apply to S corporations. (Code Sec. 1363(b))[5]

. . . Limitations on the amount allowed for: (1) expensing certain depreciable assets (Code Sec. 179(d)(8)), and (2) writing off reforestation expenses (Code Sec. 194(b)(2)(B)) are determined at both the corporate and shareholder level.[6]

. . . Generally, an item (e.g., an NOL) cannot be carried over from a C corporation year to an S corporation year (except in computing the built-in gains tax, see ¶3361). (Code Sec. 1371(b)(1))[7]

¶ 3359 Deductions for fringe benefits—Form W-2—S corporations.

Under Code Sec. 1372, in applying the Code's fringe benefit rules, an S corporation is treated as a partnership, and its more-than-2% shareholders are treated as partners. Fringe benefits furnished by an S corporation to its more-than-2% shareholder-employees

---

49. ¶D-1557 *et seq.*
50. ¶D-1591
1. ¶D-1594
2. ¶D-1595
3. ¶D-1600

4. ¶s D-1600, D-1601
5. ¶D-1595
6. ¶D-1596
7. ¶D-1603

are treated like partnership guaranteed payments[8] and reported on Form W-2.[9]

¶ 3360   Taxation of S corporations.

Under Code Sec. 1363(a), an S corporation is generally exempt from federal income taxes.[10] Instead, the corporation's income is passed through, and taxed, to its shareholders (¶3366). But some S corporations may be subject to corporate-level taxes on recognized built-in gains (¶3361); excess net passive income (¶3364); last-in, first-out (LIFO) recapture (¶3363); and recapture of investment credit.[11] For an S corporation's liability to make estimated tax payments, see ¶3343 *et seq.*

¶ 3361   Built-in gains tax—Form 1120S, Schedule D—S corporations.

Under Code Sec. 1374(a), an S corporation is subject to a corporate-level built-in gains tax in any tax year beginning in the recognition period in which it has a "net recognized built-in gain" (¶3362). The recognition period is the 5-year period beginning with the first day of the first tax year for which the corporation was an S corporation. (Code Sec. 1374(d)(7))[12] The tax is imposed only on S corporations that were formerly C corporations. (Code Sec. 1374(c)(1))[13]

In addition, the built-in gains tax may be imposed where an S corporation acquires property in a transaction, and its basis in the property is determined by reference to the basis that the property had in the hands of a C corporation (a "§1374(d)(8) transaction"). (Code Sec. 1374(d)(8)(A); Reg § 1.1374-1(e), Reg § 1.1374-8(a))[14]

The built-in gains tax (computed on Form Form 1120S, Schedule D) equals the highest corporate rate (¶1113) multiplied by the net recognized built-in gain. (Code Sec. 1374(b)(1))[15]

In this computation, net recognized built-in gains are taken into account only to the extent of the excess of the net *unrealized* built-in gain over net recognized built-in gains for earlier tax years in the recognition period. (Code Sec. 1374(c)(2); Reg § 1.1374-2(a))[16] Net unrealized built-in gain means the excess (if any) of: (1) the fair market value of the S corporation's assets (including inventory) over (2) the aggregate adjusted basis of the assets, at the start of its first tax year as an S corporation ("S tax year"). (Code Sec. 1374(d)(1))[17]

Regs prevent gain or loss from being counted twice for the built-in gains tax when a C corporation converting to S status owns stock in a subsidiary that's later liquidated. (Reg § 1.1374-3)[18]

¶ 3362   Net recognized built-in gain defined—S corporations.

Under Code Sec. 1374(d)(2)(A), the *net recognized built-in gain* for any tax year in the recognition period (¶3361) is the *lesser of:* (1) the amount that would be the S corporation's taxable income for that year if only recognized built-in gains (below) and recognized built-in losses are taken into account, and (2) the taxable income for that year determined without taking into account net operating loss (NOL) carryovers or special corporate deductions, e.g., for dividends received.[19] However, if (1) exceeds (2), the excess is treated as recognized built-in gain in the next tax year. (Code Sec. 1374(d)(2)(B); Reg § 1.1374-2(c))[20]

8. ¶D-1621
9. ¶S-3178
10. ¶D-1641
11. ¶D-1640
12. ¶D-1655
13. ¶D-1643
14. ¶D-1650

15. ¶D-1657
16. ¶D-1657
17. ¶D-1658
18. ¶D-1651
19. ¶D-1644
20. ¶D-1645

Recognized built-in gain means any gain recognized (and certain related amounts taken into account) during the recognition period on the disposition of any asset held on the first day of the corporation's first S tax year (¶3361), but only to the extent the gain doesn't exceed the excess (if any) of the asset's fair market value over its adjusted basis on that first day. (Code Sec. 1374(d)(3); Reg § 1.1374-4)[21]

Special rules apply to determine an S corporation's recognized built-in gain on the disposition of transferred-basis and exchanged-basis property acquired after it became an S corporation. (Code Sec. 1374(d)(8); Reg § 1.1374-8)[22]

¶ 3363 Last-in, first-out (LIFO) recapture amount—S corporations.

Under Code Sec. 1363(d)(1), a C corporation that maintained its inventory using the LIFO method for its last tax year before the S corporation election is effective must include a "LIFO recapture amount" in its income for that last C corporation year. [23] LIFO recapture also applies to QSub elections (¶3351). (Reg § 1.1363-2(a))[24] In addition, a C corporation that transfers LIFO inventory to an S corporation in a nonrecognition transaction must include a LIFO recapture amount in income the year of the transfer. (Reg § 1.1363-2(a))[25]

The "LIFO recapture amount" is the excess (if any) of the inventory amount under FIFO (first-in, first-out) over the inventory amount under LIFO, at the close of the last C corporation tax year. (Code Sec. 1363(d)(3))[26]

Any resulting increase in tax is payable in four equal installments over four tax years. The first installment must be paid on or before the due date (without regard to extensions) for the tax return for the last year for which the corporation was a C corporation. The other three installments must be paid on or before the due date for the corporation's return for the three succeeding tax years. (Code Sec. 1363(d)(2))[27]

A C corporation holding LIFO inventory indirectly through a partnership must recognize a lookthrough LIFO recapture amount if it either elects to be an S corporation or transfers its partnership interest to an S corporation in a nonrecognition transaction. (Reg § 1.1363-2(b))[28]

¶ 3364 Tax on excess net passive income—S corporations.

Under Code Sec. 1375(a), a corporate-level tax is imposed on an S corporation's "excess net passive income" (below) for any tax year in which it has: (1) accumulated earnings and profits (i.e., E&P from a year it was taxed as a C corporation) at the close of the tax year, and (2) passive investment income (¶3365) that exceeds 25% of gross receipts (¶3365). This tax is imposed at the highest regular corporate rate (¶1113),[29] but IRS can waive the tax if the S corporation shows that its determination of no year-end C corporation E&P was made in good faith, and that within a reasonable time after it was determined otherwise, those E&P were distributed. Code Sec. 1375(d))[30]

Net passive income is passive investment income reduced by deductions directly connected with the production of that income. (Code Sec. 1375(b)(2)) A deduction item that is attributable partly to passive investment income and partly to other income is allocated on a reasonable basis. (Reg § 1.1375-1(b)(3)(ii))[31] But passive investment income may not be

21. ¶D-1646 *et seq.*
22. ¶D-1650 *et seq.*
23. ¶D-1580
24. ¶D-1583
25. ¶D-1583
26. ¶D-1582

27. ¶D-1585
28. ¶D-1582.1
29. ¶D-1690 *et seq.*
30. ¶D-1696
31. ¶D-1693 *et seq.*

reduced by the net operating loss (NOL) deduction or any of the special corporate deductions (e.g., for dividends received). (Code Sec. 1375(b)(2))[32]

Excess net passive income means the amount that bears the same ratio to total net passive income for the year as: (1) the amount by which passive investment income for the tax year exceeds 25% of gross receipts for the year ("excess passive investment income"), bears to (2) total passive investment income for the tax year. However, an S corporation's excess net passive income for the year can't exceed its taxable income for the year computed as though it were a C corporation but without any NOL deduction or any of the special corporate deductions described above. (Code Sec. 1375(b)(1))[33]

¶ 3365 "Passive investment income" and "gross receipts" defined—S corporations.

For purposes of the tax on excess net passive income (¶3364) and in determining whether there has been an involuntary termination (¶3374), passive investment income means gross receipts derived from royalties, rents, dividends, interest, and annuities. (Code Sec. 1362(d)(3)(C); Code Sec. 1375(b)(3))[34]

However, in the case of a bank, a bank holding company, a financial holding company, or a depository institution holding company, passive investment income does not include (1) interest income earned by the bank or holding company or (2) dividends on assets that must be held by the bank or holding company. (Code Sec. 1362(d)(3)(C)(v)(I))[35]

Gross receipts are the total amount received or accrued under the S corporation's accounting method before reduction for returns, allowances, cost, or deductions. But gross receipts don't include amounts received in nontaxable sales or exchanges, except to the extent gain is recognized by the corporation. (Code Sec. 1362(d)(3), Code Sec. 1375(b)(3))[36]

Special rules apply to determine gross receipts from the sale of capital assets other than stock or securities.[37]

¶ 3366 Taxation of S corporation's shareholders; pass-through of items; Form 7203.

Under Code Sec. 1366(a)(1), an S corporation's income is taxed directly to its shareholders by allocating the corporation's items of income, loss, deduction and credit for each day in its tax year pro rata among the persons who were shareholders on that day. (Code Sec. 1366(a)(1); Reg § 1.1366-1(a); Code Sec. 1377(a)(1))[38] Use Form 7203, S Corporation Shareholder Stock and Debt Basis Limitations, to figure potential limitations of the shareholder's share of the S corporation's deductions, credits, and other items that can be deducted on the shareholder's return.

IRS provided relief to qualified farmers and fisherman for the estimated tax payment due Jan. 15, 2022, on account of a third-party software issue affecting qualifying farmers and fishermen attempting to electronically file Form 7203, S Corporation Shareholder Stock and Debt Basis Limitations. Qualifying farmers and fishermen are those who are not subject to an addition to tax for failing to pay the required estimated tax installment payment by that date, if they file their returns and pay the full amount of tax reported on the return as payable by Mar. 1, 2022. (IR 2022-49, 3/3/2022)

Items of income, loss, deduction and credit are separately allocated to each shareholder whenever separate treatment could affect the tax liability of a shareholder. (Code

---

32. ¶D-1693
33. ¶D-1692
34. ¶D-1713 *et seq.*
35. ¶D-1737

36. ¶D-1699, D-1700
37. ¶D-1701 *et seq.*
38. ¶D-1760 *et seq.*

Sec. 1366(a)(1)(A); Reg § 1.1366-1(a)) Under regs, the following S corporation items must be taken into account separately:

. . . The combined net amount of gains and losses from sales or exchanges of capital assets grouped by applicable holding periods, Code Sec. 1(h) tax rates, and by any other classification that may be relevant in determining the shareholder's tax liability.

. . . The combined net amount of gains and losses from sales or exchanges of Code Sec. 1231 property grouped by applicable holding periods, Code Sec. 1(h) tax rates, and by any other classification that may be relevant in determining the shareholder's tax liability.

. . . The charitable contributions, grouped by the Code Sec. 170(b) percentage limitations (see ¶2123 *et seq.*), made by the corporation within its tax year.

. . . The foreign taxes paid (or accrued) by the corporation.

. . . Each of the separate items involved in determining credits, except credits for certain uses of gasoline and special fuels.

. . . Each of these separate items: Code Sec. 165(d) gains and losses from wagering transactions; Code Sec. 175 soil and water conservation expenditures; Code Sec. 179 expense election deductions; Code Sec. 213 medical, dental, etc. expenses; additional itemized deductions for individuals under Code Sec. 212 *et seq.*; and any other deductions subject to the Code Sec. 67 or Code Sec. 68 limitations on itemized deductions.

✐ observation: Miscellaneous itemized deductions under Code Sec. 67(b) are suspended from 2018 through 2025. (¶2162)

. . . Any of the corporation's items of portfolio income or loss, and related expenses, as defined in the regs under Code Sec. 469.

. . . The corporation's tax-exempt income.

. . . Any item identified in IRS guidance (including forms and instructions) as an item required to be separately stated. (Reg § 1.1366-1(a)(2))[39]

The character of any item in the shareholder's hands is determined as if the item had been realized directly from the source from which the corporation realized it, or incurred in the same manner as incurred by the corporation. (Code Sec. 1366(b); Reg § 1.1366-1(b))[40]

A shareholder's share of an S corporation's items is taken into account in his or her tax year that includes the last day of the corporation's tax year (¶2807). (Code Sec. 1366(a)(1); Reg § 1.1366-1(a)(1))[41]

When shareholders perform services for an S corporation, dividends paid to the shareholders in lieu of reasonable compensation for these services can be treated as wages subject to employment taxes, regardless of whether the shareholder also receives a salary.[42]

If a shareholder sells all of his or her S corporation stock during the corporation's tax year and all affected shareholders (all terminating shareholders and their transferees) consent (by attaching a specified statement to Form 1120S for the tax year during which the shareholder's interest is terminated), the corporation's tax year can be split into two tax years, the first of which ends on the date the seller's interest is terminated. Items will be allocated between those tax years according to the corporation's normal method of accounting. (Code Sec. 1377(a)(2); Reg § 1.1377-1(b))[43] This also applies where the S corporation elects to terminate its tax year because of a "qualifying disposition." (Reg § 1.1368-1(g))[44]

---

39. ¶D-1765
40. ¶D-1762
41. ¶D-1764

42. ¶H-4329
43. ¶D-1769
44. ¶D-1771

Any gain or loss from a shareholder's disposition of an interest in an S corporation is taken into account by the shareholder as net investment income for purposes of the 3.8% surtax on unearned income (¶3142 *et seq.*) *only* to the extent of the net gain or loss that the transferor would take into account if the entity had sold all its property for fair market value immediately before the disposition. (Code Sec. 1411(c)(4))

If a shareholder dies (or a trust terminates) before the end of an S corporation tax year, his or her (or its) pro rata part of the corporation's items is reported on his or her (its) final return. (Code Sec. 1366(a)(1))[45]

¶ 3367 Amount passed through to shareholders reduced for corporate-level taxes—S corporations.

Under Code Sec. 1366(f)(2), the amount of any corporate-level built-in gains tax (¶3361) that's imposed on an S corporation is treated as a loss sustained by the corporation during the tax year. The character of the loss is determined by allocating it proportionately among the recognized built-in gains giving rise to the tax. (Code Sec. 1366(f)(2); Reg § 1.1366-4(b)) If a corporate-level tax is imposed on an S corporation's excess net passive income (¶3364), each item of passive investment income that's passed through to a shareholder is reduced by a pro rata part of that tax. (Code Sec. 1366(f)(3); Reg § 1.1366-4(c))[46]

¶ 3368 Shareholders' deductions and losses limited to basis—S corporations.

All deductions and losses of an S corporation (e.g., capital losses and net operating losses) are passed through to and (except as otherwise limited by the Code) deductible by shareholders, see ¶3366. However, under Code Sec. 1366(d)(1), a shareholder may deduct his or her pro rata share of these passed-through items only to the extent of his or her adjusted basis (¶3370) in his or her S corporation stock, determined by taking into account the increases in basis for his or her share of the S corporation income during the year, and the decreases in basis for nondividend distributions for the year, plus any debt owed to him or her by the corporation.[47]

Any deduction or loss that can't be deducted (for lack of basis) is suspended and may be carried over to be used whenever the shareholder has basis to apply against all or part of the amount the shareholder carried over. (Code Sec. 1366(d)(2); Reg § 1.1366-2(a)(3))[48] Special rules apply where the S corporation is in bankruptcy or is insolvent. (Code Sec. 108(d)(7)(B))[49]

If an S corporation's stock, or the debt it owes to a shareholder, becomes worthless in any tax year of the corporation or shareholder, the corporate items for that year will be taken into account by the shareholders, and the adjustments to basis of stock or debt will be made, before the worthlessness is taken into account. (Code Sec. 1367(b)(3))[50]

¶ 3369 Consistent treatment on shareholder's return and S corporation's return—Form 8082.

Under Code Sec. 6037(c)(1), a shareholder must on his or her own return treat a Subchapter S item in a manner that is consistent with the treatment of that item on the corporation's return (Form 1120S). A shareholder that treats a Subchapter S item differently must notify IRS of the inconsistency (Code Sec. 6037) on Form 8082.[1]

---

45. ¶D-1768
46. ¶D-1767
47. ¶D-1775
48. ¶D-1785

49. ¶D-1785, J-7416
50. ¶D-1789
1. ¶D-1801

¶ 3370 Shareholder's basis in S corporation's stock or debt—how computed.

A shareholder's basis in the stock of an S corporation is *increased* by his or her share of the corporation's income items that are passed through to him or her—i.e., its separately and non-separately computed income items (including tax-exempt income) and the excess of the deduction for depletion over the basis of depletable property. (Code Sec. 1367(a)(1); Reg § 1.1367-1(b)) An S corporation shareholder may increase his or her basis of S corporation indebtedness owed to the shareholder for bona fide loans to the S corporation (determined under general tax principles), but gets no basis increase for debts of the S corporation that he or she guarantees. (Code Sec. 1366(d)(1); Reg § 1.1366-2(a)(2))[2] Debt discharge income of an S corporation that is excluded from its income is not income to a shareholder and does not increase shareholder basis in the S corporation's stock.[3] Basis in stock is *decreased* (but not below zero) by: the shareholder's share of the corporation's items of deduction, loss and nondeductible expenses (except those chargeable to the capital account); the shareholder's depletion deduction for oil and gas property; and distributions to the shareholder that aren't taxable as dividends. (Code Sec. 1367(a)(2); Reg § 1.1367-1(c))[4]

For charitable contributions made by an S corporation, shareholders reduce their basis in the S corporation stock by their pro rata shares of the adjusted basis (as opposed to the fair market value) of the contributed property. (Code Sec. 1367(a)(2))

In any tax year of an S corporation when the total of the amount of items (other than distributions) that reduce a shareholder's basis in stock exceeds the amount that would reduce that basis to zero, the balance is applied to reduce the basis (but not below zero) of any shareholder debt in the S corporation. (Code Sec. 1367(b)(2)(A); Reg § 1.1367-2(b))[5]

If the shareholder's basis in S corporation debt in any tax year is reduced below his or her original basis in it, that basis must be increased to (but not above) its original amount, before the shareholder's basis in *stock* is increased. (Code Sec. 1367(b)(2)(B); Reg § 1.1367-2(b))[6] For purposes of the basis adjustment rules, shareholder advances aggregating less than $25,000 and not evidenced by separate written instruments and repayments on the advances are treated as a single indebtedness. (Reg § 1.1367-2(a)(2))[7]

¶ 3371 Tax treatment of S corporation distributions to shareholders; accumulated E&P.

Under Code Sec. 301(c) and Code Sec. 1368(a), the amount of a distribution from an S corporation to a shareholder equals the amount of cash distributed plus the fair market value (at distribution) of any other property distributed.[8]

If an S corporation has no accumulated earnings and profits (E&P), the amount distributed reduces the shareholder's basis in his or her stock (¶3370). If the amount exceeds basis, the excess is treated as payment in exchange for stock, i.e., as capital gain. (Code Sec. 1368(b)(2))[9]

If IRS finds that the salary paid to an S corporation shareholder-employee is unreasonably low, it may reclassify dividend payments made to the shareholder as salary.[10]

If an S corporation has accumulated E&P, its distributions are treated as follows:[11]

(1) The portion of the distribution that doesn't exceed the accumulated adjustments

---

2. ¶D-1775 *et seq.*
3. ¶D-1861
4. ¶D-1862
5. ¶D-1865
6. ¶D-1866

7. ¶D-1865
8. ¶D-1813
9. ¶D-1815
10. ¶H-4329
11. ¶s D-1817, D-1816

account (AAA), see ¶3373) is taxed the same as a distribution from an S corporation with no accumulated E&P (above). If more than one distribution is made in a tax year, and the total amount distributed exceeds the amount in the AAA at the end of that year, the balance in that account is allocated among the distributions in proportion to the size of each distribution. (Code Sec. 1368(c)(1))[12]

(2) The portion of the distribution that remains after applying (1) is treated as a dividend to the extent it doesn't exceed the S corporation's accumulated E&P. (Code Sec. 1368(c)(2))

(3) Any portion of the distribution remaining after applying (2) is treated the same as a distribution by an S corporation with no accumulated E&P. (Code Sec. 1368(c)(3))[13]

The tax effects of an S corporation's distributions to shareholders with respect to stock are determined only after taking into account:

(i) adjustments that increase the basis of the shareholder's stock; and

(ii) adjustments to the AAA, other than for distributions to shareholders and without regard to any net negative adjustments, for the S corporation's tax year. (Code Sec. 1368(d); Reg § 1.1368-1(e)(2))[14]

observation: The effect of taking the basis increases, but not the decreases, into account is that the shareholder may receive more nontaxable distributions, at the cost of a decrease in the amount of loss that he or she may deduct.

An S corporation may elect, with the consent of all affected shareholders (i.e., those to whom distributions are made), to treat distributions as made out of accumulated E&P *before* being made out of the AAA. (Code Sec. 1368(e)(3); Reg § 1.1368-1(f)(2))[15]

¶ 3372   S corporation's earnings and profits (E&P).

An S corporation, unlike a C corporation, generally does not generate E&P.[16] Any E&P carried over from prior C corporation years, or acquired from a C corporation in a reorganization, remains unadjusted while the corporation retains S status, except: (Code Sec. 1371(c)(1))

. . . E&P is reduced to reflect distributions that are taxable to the shareholders as dividends. (Code Sec. 1371(c)(3))

. . . E&P is adjusted (up or down) to reflect the effect of redemptions, liquidations, tax-free reorganizations and corporate divisions. (Code Sec. 1371(c)(2))

. . . E&P is reduced to reflect any tax paid by an S corporation because of the recapture of a pre-S election investment credit. (Code Sec. 1371(d)(3))

. . . E&P is adjusted for LIFO recapture tax. (¶3363) (Code Sec. 1363(d)(5))[17]

For purposes of determining the S corporation's accumulated E&P, all pre –'83 S corporation generated E&P has been eliminated for tax years beginning after May 25, 2007.[18]

¶ 3373   Accumulated adjustments account (AAA)—S corporations.

The AAA is a corporate account consisting of the corporation's income that was previously taxed to its shareholders and not distributed. An S corporation's AAA[19] is increased each tax year by:

---

12. ¶D-1816, D-1819
13. ¶s D-1817, D-1816
14. ¶D-1818
15. ¶D-1835

16. ¶D-1631
17. ¶D-1633
18. ¶D-1632
19. ¶D-1823

(1) Separately computed items of income (other than income that is exempt from tax).

(2) Nonseparately computed income.

(3) The excess of deductions for depletion over the basis of property subject to depletion. (Code Sec. 1368(e)(1); Reg § 1.1368-2(a)(2))[20]

The AAA is decreased each tax year by:

(a) Items of separately computed loss and deduction.

(b) Nonseparately computed loss.

(c) Nondeductible expenses (other than expenses chargeable to capital account) unless related to tax-exempt income.

(d) The amount of the shareholder's deduction for depletion under Code Sec. 611 with respect to oil and gas wells.

(e) Distributions from an S corporation that has no E&P and distributions that are made out of the AAA.

(f) The amount that was treated as paid out of the AAA on redemptions that were treated as payments in exchange for stock under Code Sec. 302(a) or Code Sec. 303(a). This equals the amount in the account before the redemption multiplied by a fraction, the numerator of which is the number of redeemed shares and the denominator of which is the total number of outstanding shares before the redemption. (Code Sec. 1368(e)(1); Reg § 1.1368-2(a)(3))[21]

Special ordering rules apply with regard to the above mentioned increases and decreases. (Reg § 1.1368-2(a)(5))[22]

Where there is a net negative adjustment for the tax year, any net loss for the year is disregarded in adjusting the AAA for purposes of distributions made during the tax year. (Code Sec. 1368(e)(1)(C))[23]

The balance in an S corporation's AAA at the end of a tax year may be reduced below zero if the items that reduce the AAA exceed the sum of the AAA plus the items that increase the AAA (items (1) − (3), above). (Code Sec. 1368(e)(1)(A)) Income in a later year will cause the AAA to become positive only after the negative balance has been restored. (Reg § 1.1368-3)[24]

The AAA isn't to be adjusted (i.e., reduced) for federal taxes attributable to any tax year when the S corporation was a C corporation. (Code Sec. 1368(e)(1))[25]

If distributions made during the year exceed the AAA at the close of the tax year, then the AAA is allocated pro rata among the distributions (Code Sec. 1368(c); Reg § 1.1368-2(b)(1))[26]

Special rules apply to distributions after the S election is terminated. (Code Sec. 1371(e))[27]

¶ 3374 Involuntary termination of S corporation election.

Under Code Sec. 1362(d), a corporation's S election is terminated if either:

(1) The corporation ceases to meet all of the S corporation eligibility requirements discussed at ¶3350. (Code Sec. 1362(d)(2)(A)) The termination is effective as of the day the eligibility requirement is no longer met (Code Sec. 1362(d)(2)(B));[28] or

---

20. ¶D-1824
21. ¶D-1825 *et seq.*
22. ¶D-1829
23. ¶D-1826.1
24. ¶D-1830

25. ¶D-1823
26. ¶D-1819
27. ¶D-1846 *et seq.*
28. ¶D-1903

(2) The S corporation's passive investment income (¶3365) exceeds 25% of its gross receipts for three consecutive tax years and at the end of each of those years, the corporation had accumulated earnings and profits (E&P, ¶3364). The termination is effective as of the first day of the first tax year beginning after the third of these years. (Code Sec. 1362(d)(3)(A))[29]

IRS can waive inadvertent terminations or invalid elections if certain conditions are met. (Code Sec. 1362(f)) Regs explain how to request relief. (Reg § 1.1362-4(c))[30] QSubs are eligible for the same relief (as discussed above) for an inadvertently invalid QSub election or inadvertent termination. (Reg § 1.1362-4)

¶ 3375　Voluntary revocation of the S corporation election; rescission.

Under Code Sec. 1362(d)(1), a corporation's S election may be revoked with the consent of holders of a majority of the corporation's issued and outstanding stock (including non-voting stock). (Code Sec. 1362(d)(1); Reg § 1.1362-2(a)(1))[31]

If no effective date is specified, a revocation is effective for the tax year in which made, if made by the 15th day of the third month of that year. Otherwise, it's effective as of the first day of the next tax year. (Code Sec. 1362(d)(1)(C))[32] But if the revocation specifies that it's to be effective on a date on or after the date it's made, it will be effective on that date even if it causes the corporation's tax year to be split. (Code Sec. 1362(d)(1)(D))[33]

A corporation may *rescind* the revocation at any time before it becomes effective. A rescission may be made only with the consent of each person who consented to the revocation and of each person who became a shareholder during the period from the day after the date the revocation was made through the date the rescission is made. (Reg § 1.1362-2(a)(4))[34]

¶ 3376　When new S corporation election can be made after termination or revocation.

Under Code Sec. 1362(g), after a revocation or termination of its S election, a corporation must wait five years before making a new S election unless IRS consents to an earlier election.[35]

---

29. ¶D-1905
30. ¶D-1909
31. ¶D-1901
32. ¶D-1903

33. ¶D-1901
34. ¶D-1902 *et seq.*
35. ¶s D-1951, D-1953

Chapter 16 Corporate Transactions— Organization—Distributions—Reorganization— Acquisitions—Liquidations

¶ 3500 Incorporations and Transfers to Controlled Corporations—Code Sec. 351. ■

Incorporating a business or transferring property to a controlled corporation can be partly or wholly tax-free under Code Sec. 351(a), if technical requirements are satisfied.[1] No gain or loss is recognized if property (¶3501) is transferred to a corporation solely in exchange for stock (¶3502) of that corporation, if, immediately after the transfer, the transferor or transferors are in control (¶3503) of the corporation. (Code Sec. 351(a))[2] A transfer of property may be respected as a Code Sec. 351 exchange even if followed by later transfers of the property as part of a prearranged, integrated plan.

For exceptions to nonrecognition on transfers to controlled corporations, see ¶3504 (receipt of boot), ¶3505 (assumption of liabilities by transferee corporation), ¶3507 (transfers to investment companies), and ¶3508 (transfers in bankruptcy).

See ¶3509 for gain or loss to a corporation on the issuance of its stock, and ¶3510 for the deductibility of a corporation's organization costs.

For transfers to foreign corporations, see ¶3568.

For the basis of property received in the exchange, see ¶2476 *et seq.*

¶ 3501 Property—incorporations and transfers to controlled corporations (Code Sec. 351).

Property that may be transferred tax-free under Code Sec. 351 includes cash, tangible property and intangible personal property, e.g., stock, partnership interests, patent rights, and working interests in oil and gas properties.[3]

Property doesn't include: (i) services to the transferee corporation (Code Sec. 351(d)(1)); (ii) transferee corporation debt not evidenced by a security (Code Sec. 351(d)(2)); or (iii) unpaid interest on transferee corporation debt accrued during the transferor's holding period for the debt. (Code Sec. 351(d)(3))[4]

¶ 3502 Stock—incorporations and transfers to controlled corporations (Code Sec. 351).

For purposes of transfers to controlled corporations, property must be transferred *solely in exchange for stock* (Code Sec. 351(a)), which doesn't include (1) stock rights or warrants (Reg § 1.351-1(a)), or (2) nonqualified preferred stock. (Code Sec. 351(g)) (¶3542) Shares in an association, joint stock company or insurance company are treated as stock. (Code Sec. 7701(a)(7))[5]

¶ 3503 Control—incorporations and transfers to controlled corporations (Code Sec. 351).

Under Code Sec. 368(c), for purposes of transfers to controlled corporations, *control* means at least 80% of the transferee's combined voting power and at least 80% of the total

1. ¶F-1000 *et seq.*
2. ¶F-1001
3. ¶F-1002
4. ¶F-1002 ; ¶F-1011
5. ¶F-1004

References beginning with a single letter are to paragraphs in Federal Tax Coordinator 2d and RIA's Analysis of Federal Taxes: Income.

number of shares of all other classes of the transferee's stock (¶3539).[6] The transferor group must hold at least 80% of the voting power immediately after the transfer; but not every transferor must hold voting stock.[7]

¶ 3504　Gain on receipt of cash or property ("boot")—incorporations and transfers to controlled corporations (Code Sec. 351).

If transferors receive *boot* (¶3542) as well as stock in a Code Sec. 351 transfer, nonrecognition is limited and the transferor (i) recognizes gain up to the amount or fair market value of the boot, and (ii) doesn't recognize any loss. (Code Sec. 351(b))[8]

¶ 3505　Assumption of liabilities—incorporations and transfers to controlled corporations (Code Sec. 351).

If a corporation assumes liabilities (¶3506) in connection with an otherwise tax-free exchange, it is still tax-free (Code Sec. 357(a))[9] subject to the following exceptions.

- *Tax avoidance rule.* If the principal purpose for the assumption of liabilities is tax avoidance or isn't a bona fide business purpose, the full amount of *all* assumed liabilities are treated as cash received by the transferor (even those assumed for nontax avoidance or valid business purposes) and taxed as boot (¶3504). (Code Sec. 357(b)(1))[10]

- *Excess liabilities rule.* If the total liabilities assumed exceed the transferor's adjusted basis in the transferred property, gain is recognized to the extent of the excess. (Code Sec. 357(c)(1))[11]

Where both anti-abuse rules apply, tax avoidance takes precedence and all liabilities are treated as boot. (Code Sec. 357(c)(2)(A))[12]

The excess liabilities rule doesn't apply to any liability that (i) would give rise to a deduction when paid by the transferor, or (ii) would be a liquidating payment to a partner described in Code Sec. 736(a), see ¶3758. (Code Sec. 357(c)(3)(A))[13]

The excess liabilities rule applies to transfers in a divisive Type D reorganization under Code Sec. 361. It doesn't apply, however, to acquisitive reorganizations in which the transferor corporation goes out of existence (and cannot benefit from the transferee's assumption of liabilities), i.e., Code Sec. 351 transfers that also qualify as either (1) a Type A or Type C reorganization, or (2) a nondivisive Type D or Type G reorganization that meets the requirements of Code Sec. 354(b)(1) (discussed at ¶3530 *et seq.*).[14]

The amount of a liability assumed in a Code Sec. 351 exchange reduces the transferor's basis in the stock received, regardless of whether the transferor recognizes any gain or loss on the exchange. (Code Sec. 358(a), Code Sec. 358(d)(1)) However, the transferor's basis in the stock won't be reduced by the assumption of any liability described in Code Sec. 357(c)(3) that would have been deductible by the transferor had it not been assumed or which would have been a liquidating payment to a partner. (Code Sec. 358(d)(2))[15]

If a transferor's basis in stock received in a Code Sec. 351 exchange exceeds the fair market value (FMV) of the stock, the basis is reduced (but not below FMV) by the amount of any liability that (i) is assumed in exchange for the stock, and (ii) didn't otherwise reduce that basis by reason of the assumption. However, basis isn't reduced if the trade or business with which the liability is associated is transferred as part of the exchange to the

6.　¶s F-1200 *et seq.*, F-5501 *et seq.*
7.　¶F-1202
8.　¶F-1501
9.　¶F-1509
10.　¶F-1511 *et seq.*

11.　¶F-1507 *et seq.*
12.　¶F-1506
13.　¶F-1509
14.　¶F-4203 *et seq.*
15.　¶F-1803; ¶F-1509

person assuming the liability. (Code Sec. 358(h); Reg § 1.358-5)[16]

¶ 3506   When a liability is treated as assumed—incorporations and transfers to controlled corporations (Code Sec. 351).

Except as provided in regs, under Code Sec. 357(d),

(1) A recourse liability is treated as having been assumed by the transferee if, based on all facts and circumstances, the transferee has agreed to and is expected to satisfy it, regardless of whether the transferor has been relieved of the liability. (Code Sec. 357(d)(1)(A))

(2) A nonrecourse liability is treated as having been assumed by the transferee of any asset subject to the liability (Code Sec. 357(d)(1)(B)), except that the amount so treated is reduced by the lesser of:

(i) the amount of the liability that the owner of other untransferred assets subject to the same liability has agreed with the transferee to, and is expected to, satisfy, or

(ii) the FMV of those other untransferred assets determined without regard to Code Sec. 7701(g) (providing generally that the FMV of property subject to nonrecourse debt isn't less than the debt (¶2401)). (Code Sec. 357(d)(2))[17]

🔑 observation: If the owner of untransferred assets securing nonrecourse debt doesn't agree to pay any of it, the amount of the liability treated as assumed by the transferee isn't reduced at all. Thus, liabilities may exceed basis and cause gain recognition.

For the limit on basis increase for assumption of liabilities, see ¶2479.

¶ 3507   Transfers to investment companies (swap funds)—incorporations and transfers to controlled corporations (Code Sec. 351).

The Code Sec. 351 nonrecognition rule doesn't apply to the transfer of property to an investment company in exchange for its stock (Code Sec. 351(e); Reg § 1.351-1(c)(1)).[18] A transfer is to an investment company if the transfer diversifies a transferor's interests, and the transferee is (1) a regulated investment company (RIC), (2) a real estate investment trust (REIT), or (3) a corporation more than 80% of the value of whose total investment assets are marketable securities, interests in RICs or REITs, or stocks and securities (including specified types of property, such as money, that are treated as stocks or securities) (Code Sec. 351(e)(1); Reg § 1.351-1(c)(1)). This rule doesn't apply if each transferor transfers a portfolio of already diversified assets. (Reg § 1.351-1(c)(6))[19]

¶ 3508   Transfer of debtor's property in a bankruptcy or similar proceeding—incorporations and transfers to controlled corporations (Code Sec. 351).

The Code Sec. 351 nonrecognition rule doesn't apply to transfers in a bankruptcy, receivership, foreclosure or similar proceeding (including agency receivership proceedings involving banks), but only to the extent the stock received by the debtor in exchange for assets is used to satisfy the debtor's indebtedness. (Code Sec. 351(e)(2))[20]

---

16. ¶F-1803
17. ¶F-1504
18. ¶F-1301

19. ¶F-1302
20. ¶F-1303

¶ 3509   Gain or loss to corporation on issuance of stock—incorporations and transfers to controlled corporations (Code Sec. 351).

Under Code Sec. 1032(a), a corporation doesn't recognize gain or loss on the exchange of its stock (including treasury stock) for property or money.[21] Similarly, no gain or loss is recognized in otherwise taxable transactions where a corporation acquires stock directly or indirectly from the issuing corporation in what otherwise would be a transferred basis transaction and immediately transfers the stock to acquire money or other property (including services), and no party receiving the issuing corporation stock receives a substituted basis in the stock of the issuing corporation. (Reg § 1.1032-3(b), Reg § 1.1032-3(c))[22] For stock issued to a creditor in satisfaction of a corporation's debt, see ¶1389.

¶ 3510   Deductibility of costs of organizing a corporation—incorporations and transfers to controlled corporations (Code Sec. 351).

Under Code Sec. 248(a), a corporation is deemed to have made an election to deduct up to $5,000 of its organizational expenditures in the tax year it begins business. The $5,000 amount is reduced (but not below zero) by the amount, if any, by which its organizational expenditures exceed $50,000. Remaining organizational expenditures are deductible ratably over the 180-month period beginning with the month it begins business. (Code Sec. 248(a); Reg § 1.248-1(a)) A corporation may irrevocably forgo the deemed election by clearly electing to capitalize *all* organizational expenditures on a timely filed Federal income tax return (including extensions) for the tax year in which it begins business. (Reg § 1.248-1(c))

Such expenses include fees for legal services, incorporation fees, temporary directors' fees and organizational meeting costs. Costs relating to capital structure, e.g., of issuing stock, can't be deducted or otherwise recovered. (Code Sec. 248(b); Reg § 1.248-1(b))[23]

¶ 3511   Corporate Distributions; Earnings and Profits (E&P). ▄▄▄▄▄▄▄▄▄▄▄

Under Code Sec. 301(c) and Code Sec. 316(a), a distribution of property (i.e., money, securities, and any other property except stock of the distributing corporation) by a corporation to its shareholders is treated as a dividend and is taxable as ordinary income to the extent it is made out of current and accumulated E&P (¶1285 *et seq.*). The part of the distribution in excess of E&P is treated as a return of capital to the extent of the shareholder's basis in the stock of the distributing corporation. The remainder of the distribution, if any, is generally taxed as capital gain.[24]

The amount of a distribution is reduced by an associated liability only if it is assumed by the shareholder within the meaning of Code Sec. 357(d). (¶3506) (Reg § 1.301-1(f))[25]

For adjustments in E&P for corporate distributions, see ¶3512, for depreciation, see ¶3513, and for other E&P adjustments, see ¶3514.

For the tax treatment of the distributing corporation, see ¶3526 *et seq.*

¶ 3512   How corporate distributions affect earnings and profits (E&P).

With certain exceptions discussed below, under Code Sec. 312, distributions of property by a corporation with respect to its stock reduce E&P by the following amounts:

---

21. ¶I-3201
22. ¶I-3213
23. ¶L-5201 *et seq.*

24. ¶J-2351 *et seq.*
25. ¶J-2354

(1) The amount of money distributed. (Code Sec. 312(a)(1))[26]

(2) The principal (face) amount of the corporation's obligations (i.e., its own notes, bonds, etc.) distributed without original issue discount (OID) (¶1312 *et seq.*) (or the aggregate issue price of the obligations for distributions of obligations having OID). (Code Sec. 312(a)(2))[27]

(3) The adjusted basis of other distributed property (Code Sec. 312(a)(3)) as determined for purposes of computing E&P. However, since a corporation's distribution of appreciated property (other than its own obligations) increases its E&P by the excess of the property's fair market value (FMV) over its adjusted basis, E&P is decreased by the FMV of the appreciated property. ((Code Sec. 312(b))[28]

However, special rules apply to certain types of distributions, including the following:

(1) Redemption distributions that are treated as payment in exchange for stock (¶3515) reduce E&P by an amount not in excess of the ratable share of the distributing corporation's E&P attributable to the redeemed stock. (Code Sec. 312(n)(7))[29]

(2) Reorganizations and other tax-free distributions don't reduce E&P if the distributee doesn't recognize any gain. (Code Sec. 312(d)(1)(A); Reg § 1.312-11(b), Reg § 1.312-11(c))[30]

(3) The distribution to a distributee by or on behalf of a corporation of its stock or securities, of stock or securities in another corporation, or of property, isn't a distribution of E&P if no gain to the distributee is recognized, or if the distribution isn't subject to tax in the hands of the distributee by reason of Code Sec. 305(a). (Code Sec. 312(d)(1)(B)) But if a distribution of stock is *taxable* to the shareholders (¶1296), E&P is reduced by the FMV of the taxable part of the stock or rights. (Reg § 1.312-1(d))[31]

(4) Distributions to 20% corporate shareholders may require adjustments to E&P solely for purposes of determining the distributee's income and stock basis. (Code Sec. 301(e))[32]

Basis can be different for E&P and taxable income (TI) purposes if the corporation uses different depreciation or cost recovery methods for computing E&P and TI. (¶3513).[33]

¶ 3513 Effect of depreciation on earnings and profits (E&P)—corporate distributions.

Depreciation deductions for E&P purposes (Code Sec. 312(k)(3)) are often lower than the corresponding deductions for computing taxable income. (¶1900 *et seq.*) For modified accelerated cost recovery system (MACRS) property (other than property expensed under Code Sec. 179 and certain other expensing provisions), the E&P deduction is computed under the alternative depreciation system (ADS), even if a different system is used in computing taxable income. (Code Sec. 312(k)(3)(A))[34] For Accelerated Cost Recovery System (ACRS) property placed in service before '87, the E&P deduction is computed by using the straight-line method over the regular or alternative ACRS recovery periods, which may be longer than those used in computing taxable income.[35] The E&P deduction for depreciable property placed in service before '81 is computed by using the straight-line or similar method (e.g., units of production), even if an accelerated method is used in computing taxable income.[36] For property expensed under Code Sec. 179 and certain other expensing provisions, the cost is deducted from E&P ratably over five tax years. (Code Sec. 312(k)(3)(B))[37]

26. ¶F-10502
27. ¶F-10503
28. ¶F-10505 *et seq.*
29. ¶F-10701
30. ¶F-10801
31. ¶F-10509 *et seq.*

32. ¶F-10601 *et seq.*
33. ¶F-10300 *et seq.*
34. ¶F-10303
35. ¶F-10307
36. ¶F-10309
37. ¶F-10304

¶ 3514   Commonly made adjustments to earnings and profits (E&P)—corporate distributions.

Here are some common adjustments (Code Sec. 312) made to E&P to reflect economic gain or loss.

... Circulation expenses must be capitalized and treated as part of the basis of the asset to which they relate, even if they are deducted currently in computing taxable income (TI). (Code Sec. 312(n)(3))[38]

... Completed contract method of accounting can't be used for E&P purposes. The percentage of completion method must be used instead. (Code Sec. 312(n)(6))[39]

... Construction period carrying charges (interest, property taxes, etc.) must be capitalized as part of the assets to which they are allocable. (Code Sec. 312(n)(1)(A)) The capitalized amounts must be written off for E&P purposes, as is the asset itself.[40]

... Depletion is determined on a *cost,* not percentage, basis. (Reg § 1.312-6(c)(1))[41]

... Exempt income (e.g., state or local bond interest) increases E&P. (Reg § 1.312-6(b))[42]

... Income tax liabilities reduce E&P as of the close of the tax year for an accrual basis corporation, and, according to some courts, a cash basis corporation. (IRS and other courts say a cash basis corporation reduces E&P only when the tax (including estimated tax) is *paid*.)[43]

... Installment sales are accounted for without regard to the installment method, i.e., principal amounts must be treated as received in the year of sale. (Code Sec. 312(n)(5))[44]

... Intangible drilling costs that are deductible when paid or incurred for TI purposes (other than costs incurred in connection with a nonproductive well) must be capitalized and deducted ratably over a 60-month period. (Code Sec. 312(n)(2)(A))[45]

... Life insurance proceeds increase E&P if the corporation is the beneficiary, even if not includible in TI.[46]

... E&P is increased or decreased by the amount of any increase or decrease in the LIFO (last-in, first-out) recapture amount as of the close of each tax year. (Code Sec. 312(n)(4))[47]

... Loss carryovers and carrybacks don't reduce E&P of the year to which they are carried and reductions of loss carryovers don't increase E&P in a later carryover year.[48]

... Losses recognized, but not allowed as a deduction (e.g., losses under the related party rules (¶2443), and capital losses (¶2611)) decrease E&P by the disallowed amount. A wash sale loss doesn't reduce E&P since it isn't recognized. (Reg § 1.312-7(b)(1)[49]

... Mineral exploration and development costs that are deductible for taxable income purposes must be capitalized and deducted ratably over a 120-month period. (Code Sec. 312(n)(2)(B))[50]

... Organizational expenses must be capitalized and treated as part of the basis of the asset to which they relate, even if they are amortized in computing TI (as described at ¶3510). (Code Sec. 312(n)(3))[1]

... Premiums paid for life insurance on corporate officers reduce E&P, even if they aren't deductible in computing TI.[2]

38. ¶F-10206
39. ¶F-10003
40. ¶F-10208
41. ¶F-10314
42. ¶F-10101
43. ¶F-10223 *et seq.*
44. ¶F-10405
45. ¶F-10221

46. ¶F-10102
47. ¶F-10212
48. ¶F-10001
49. ¶F-10403
50. ¶F-10220
1. ¶F-10204
2. ¶F-10234

¶ **3515**   **Stock Redemptions.** ∎

Under Code Sec. 317(b), the redemption by a corporation of its own stock from a shareholder in exchange for cash or property is treated as a taxable dividend distribution to the shareholder (¶1285 *et seq.*) unless it qualifies for sale or exchange treatment for which capital gain treatment is allowed (if the stock is a capital asset in the hands of the taxpayer) whether or not the stock acquired is cancelled, retired, or held as treasury stock.[3] The following redemptions will be treated as a sale or exchange of stock:

(1) *Substantially disproportionate redemptions.* (¶3516)

(2) *Complete redemptions of a shareholder's interest.* (¶3517)

(3) *Redemptions not essentially equivalent to a dividend.* (¶3519)

(4) *Redemptions from noncorporate shareholders in partial liquidation.* (¶3520)

(5) *Redemptions of a decedent's stock to pay death taxes.* (¶3521) (Code Sec. 302(a))[4]

For the treatment of stock sales between related corporations as redemptions, see ¶3522.

For constructive ownership rules applicable to redemptions, see ¶3523.

¶ **3516**   **Substantially disproportionate redemptions.**

Under Code Sec. 302(b)(2)(C), a redemption is *substantially disproportionate* if it satisfies both of the following tests:

(1) *80% test.* Immediately after the redemption, the ratio of the shareholder's voting stock to the corporation's total outstanding voting stock is less than 80% of that ratio immediately before the redemption. The same 80% test must also be met with regard to the corporation's *common stock,* voting and nonvoting, based on the fair market value of the aggregate shares of each class of common stock. (Code Sec. 302(b)(2)(C))

(2) *50% test.* Immediately after the redemption, the shareholder owns less than 50%, by vote, of the corporation's voting stock. (Code Sec. 302(b)(2)(B))[5]

A redemption solely of nonvoting stock doesn't qualify as substantially disproportionate. However, if voting stock is redeemed at the same time in a redemption that qualifies as substantially disproportionate, the redemption of the nonvoting stock (other than Code Sec. 306, see ¶3524 *et seq.*) will also be substantially disproportionate. (Reg § 1.302-3(a))[6]

¶ **3517**   **Complete redemptions—termination of a shareholder's interest in the corporation.**

Under Code Sec. 302(b)(3), to qualify as a complete redemption, all stock in the corporation that is owned, or treated as owned under the constructive ownership rules (¶3523) (unless waived (¶3518)), by the shareholder must be redeemed.[7]

A redemption on the installment basis can qualify as a complete redemption if the corporation and the shareholder are bound by a purchase agreement to complete the redemption by a certain date and for a maximum price.[8]

---

3. ¶F-11001
4. ¶F-11101 *et seq.*
5. ¶F-11203 *et seq.*

6. ¶F-11212
7. ¶F-11301 *et seq.*
8. ¶F-11307

¶ 3518   Family attribution rules waived on complete terminations—treatment of redemptions.

Under Code Sec. 302(c)(2), an individual who receives a distribution that is otherwise in complete redemption of all the stock the individual actually owns won't be treated as constructively owning the stock owned by a spouse, child, grandchild or parent if the individual:

(1) has no personal financial interest in the corporation (prohibited interest), other than as a creditor, immediately after the redemption;

(2) no longer serves as director, officer or employee;

(3) doesn't acquire any prohibited interest (except by inheritance) or position within ten (10) years after the redemption;

(4) didn't acquire any of the redeemed stock from close family members, and didn't transfer any stock to them, within ten years before the redemption, except acquisitions or transfers not principally motivated by tax avoidance; *and*

(5) attaches a separate statement (in duplicate) to his or her income tax return for the redemption year stating that he or she hasn't acquired any new prohibited interest (except by inheritance) and will notify the district director within 30 days after acquiring any new interest. (Code Sec. 302(c)(2); Reg § 1.302-4)[9]

Waiver of family attribution allows an individual to completely redeem his or her interest without all related persons redeeming their stock and applies only for purposes of determining that a distribution is a complete redemption. There is no need for the waiver if the redemption would otherwise qualify as payment in exchange for stock. (Code Sec. 302(b)(6))[10]

A partnership, estate, trust or corporation (entity) can waive family attribution if the partner, beneficiary or shareholder (related person) owns stock solely as a function of the family constructive ownership rules. Such ownership isn't reattributed to the entity if both the entity and the related person satisfy the conditions for a waiver and agree to be jointly and severally liable for any tax deficiency resulting from any acquisition of an interest within the 10-year period. (Code Sec. 302(c)(2)(C))[11]

¶ 3519   Redemptions not essentially equivalent to a dividend treated as sale or exchange.

Under Code Sec. 302(b)(1), a redemption is treated as payment in exchange for stock if it isn't essentially equivalent to a dividend.[12] A redemption isn't essentially equivalent to a dividend if it results in a meaningful reduction in the redeemed shareholder's proportionate interest in the distributing corporation, without regard to how it affects the distributing corporation. A redemption of a sole shareholder and a pro rata redemption cannot qualify as not essentially equivalent to a dividend since they don't reduce a shareholders' proportionate interest in the distributing corporation.[13]

A redemption from a shareholder with over 50% of the voting power usually results in a meaningful reduction if that shareholder's voting power is reduced to 50% or less. Additionally, a redemption of voting stock from a substantial minority shareholder results in a meaningful reduction if, after the redemption, the number of shareholders the redeemed

---

9. ¶F-11313 *et seq.*
10. ¶F-11311
11. ¶F-11314

12. ¶F-11401
13. ¶F-11402 *et seq.*

shareholder must act in concert with to control the corporation is increased; and a redemption of voting stock from a low percentage minority shareholder is usually treated as a meaningful reduction so long as there is some reduction in proportionate interest.[14]

Redemptions of nonvoting preferred stock from shareholders who own no common stock and no voting stock always result in a meaningful reduction in interest.[15]

The constructive ownership rules (¶3523) apply in determining the redeemed shareholder's stock ownership before and after the redemption (Code Sec. 302(c)(1)), even if no stock is actually owned after the redemption.[16]

¶ 3520 Redemptions from noncorporate shareholder in a partial liquidation.

Under Code Sec. 302(b)(4) and Code Sec. 302(e)(1), a partial liquidating distribution in redemption of stock of a noncorporate shareholder is treated as a sale or exchange even if it is made pro rata. A redemption distribution is treated as made in partial liquidation if it is (1) made with respect to a noncorporate shareholder, (2) not essentially equivalent to a dividend determined at the corporate level (i.e., it results from a contraction of the corporate business), and (3) made under a plan of liquidation within the tax year in which the plan is adopted or the next tax year.[17]

¶ 3521 Redemption of decedent's stock to pay death taxes.

Under Code Sec. 303(a)), distributions in redemption of stock included in a decedent's gross estate for federal estate tax purposes are treated as payment for stock up to the sum of: (1) all death taxes (federal and state), including interest, and (2) funeral and administration expenses allowable as federal estate tax deductions,[18] *but only if*:

(1) the value of the redeeming corporation's stock included in the estate exceeds 35% of the decedent's adjusted gross estate, with the stock of two or more corporations treated as stock of a single corporation if 20% or more of the value of the outstanding stock of each corporation is included in the decedent's gross estate (Code Sec. 303(b)(2));[19]

(2) the redemption distribution takes place after the decedent's death and within three years and 90 days after the estate tax return is filed (or due, if filed early), or, in some cases, later specified dates (Code Sec. 303(b)(1));[20] and

(3) the redeemed shareholder bears the burden of the taxes or expenses. (Code Sec. 303(b)(3))[21]

¶ 3522 Stock sales between related corporations—treatment of redemptions.

Under Code Sec. 304(a), if shareholders control two corporations and sell stock of one controlled corporation (Issuer) to the other (Acquirer) in return for cash or other property, the sale is treated as a stock redemption, rather than as a sale. The redemption will be treated as a dividend, unless it qualifies for nondividend treatment under one of the exceptions listed at ¶3515.[22] If the Acquirer is a brother corporation (see below) of the Issuer, the sale is treated as a redemption by the Acquirer. (Code Sec. 304(a)(1)) If the Issuer is a parent (see below) of the Acquirer, the sale is treated as a redemption by the Issuer. (Code Sec. 304(a)(2))[23]

If the sale is treated as a dividend, the amount taxable to the shareholder is determined

14. ¶F-11403
15. ¶F-11403
16. ¶F-11408
17. ¶F-11500 *et seq.*; Reg § 1.346-1(a)
18. ¶F-11600 *et seq.*

19. ¶F-11603 *et seq.*
20. ¶F-11613 *et seq.*
21. ¶F-11617
22. ¶F-11704
23. ¶F-11701 *et seq.*

as if it were distributed *first* by the Acquirer to the extent of its earnings and profits (E&P), and *then* by the Issuer to the extent of its E&P. (Code Sec. 304(b)(2))[24] The parties to transactions subject to Code Sec. 304 entered into with a principal purpose of avoiding its application to certain corporations, however, may be recast for purposes of determining the dividend amount. (Reg § 1.304-4)[25] In the case of a *foreign* Acquirer, (a) the amount of E&P that can support a deemed dividend is limited to E&P attributable to stock of a U.S. shareholder accumulated while Acquirer was a controlled foreign corporation (CFC) (¶4611 *et seq.*) and (b) its E&P isn't taken into account if more than 50% of the consequent dividend would be *neither* subject to U.S. tax for the year of the dividend, *nor* includible in the E&P of a CFC. (Code Sec. 304(b)(5))[26]

If a deemed distribution from a stock sale between brother-sister corporations is treated as a dividend, (1) the stock that was sold is deemed to have been transferred by Issuer to Acquirer for stock of Issuer in a tax-free transfer to a controlled corporation, and (2) Acquirer is deemed to have redeemed the stock that is treated as having been issued to it in the constructive transfer, preventing Issuer from using the dividends-received deduction to shelter any part of the deemed distribution. (Code Sec. 304(a)(1))[27]

A corporation is a parent if it controls another corporation. (Code Sec. 304(a)(2)) A brother-sister relationship exists where the same person(s) control(s) each of two corporations. (Code Sec. 304(a)(1)) Control means ownership of stock possessing at least 50% of the total combined voting power of all classes of the voting stock, or at least 50% of the total value of all classes of stock. (Code Sec. 304(c)(1))[28] Constructive ownership rules similar to those at ¶3523 apply with modifications. (Code Sec. 304(c)(3))[29]

The parent-subsidiary redemption rules apply even if, as a result of the constructive ownership rules, a brother-sister relationship also exists, and the brother-sister redemption rules apply where the parent's control over the subsidiary results from constructive and not actual ownership. (Reg § 1.304-2(c))[30]

¶ 3523   Constructive ownership—treatment of redemptions.

For purposes of the stock redemption rules, under Code Sec. 302(c), a person is treated as owning not only his or her own direct holdings, but also those of certain closely related taxpayers:

. . . An individual is considered as owning stock owned, directly or indirectly, by a spouse (unless divorced or legally separated), children (including adopted children), grandchildren and parents. (Code Sec. 318(a)(1))[31]

. . . Stock owned by or for an S corporation, partnership or estate is considered as owned proportionately by its shareholders, partners, or beneficiaries. (Code Sec. 318(a)(2)(A), Code Sec. 318(a)(5)(E)) Stock owned by or for an S corporation shareholder, partner or estate beneficiary is attributed in full to the S corporation, partnership or estate. (Code Sec. 318(a)(3)(A), Code Sec. 318(a)(5)(E))[32]

. . . Stock owned by or for a trust is considered owned by its beneficiaries in proportion to their actuarial interest in the trust. (Code Sec. 318(a)(2)(B)(i)) Stock owned by or for a trust beneficiary is attributed in full to the trust unless the beneficiary's interest in the trust is a remote contingent interest. (Code Sec. 318(a)(3)(B)(i))[33]

. . . A 50%-or-more shareholder in a C corporation is considered as owning his or her proportionate share of stock in other corporations owned by the C corporation. (Code

24. ¶F-11706
25. ¶F-11707
26. ¶F-11719.2; ¶F-11719.3
27. ¶F-11716
28. ¶F-11711

29. ¶F-11720 *et seq.*
30. ¶F-11723
31. ¶F-11803 *et seq.*
32. ¶F-11812 *et seq.*
33. ¶F-11827 *et seq.*

Sec. 318(a)(2)(C)) A C corporation is considered as owning all the stock (except its own) owned by its 50%-or-more shareholder. (Code Sec. 318(a)(3)(C); Reg § 1.318-1(b)(1))[34]

. . . The holder of an option to buy stock is treated as the owner of the stock covered by the option. (Code Sec. 318(a)(4))[35] This includes an option that isn't exercisable until after the lapse of a fixed period of time.[36]

Stock constructively owned is considered to be actually owned for purposes of further attribution (Code Sec. 318(a)(5)(A)),[37] *except* as follows (where so-called double or sidewise attribution is prohibited):

. . . Stock constructively owned by a person under the family attribution rules won't be attributed further to make another family member the constructive owner of that stock. (Code Sec. 318(a)(5)(B))[38]

illustration: If a father and son each own 50 shares in a corporation, each is treated as owning all 100 shares. But the father's constructive ownership of the son's shares can't be further attributed from the father to his daughter.

. . . Stock constructively owned by a partnership, estate, trust or corporation can't be further attributed from the partnership, etc., to make another (partner, heir, beneficiary or shareholder) the constructive owner of that stock. (Code Sec. 318(a)(5)(C))[39]

¶ 3524   Section 306 Stock.

Code Sec. 306 prohibits capital gain treatment on the disposition of certain preferred stock received either as a nontaxable stock dividend or in certain substituted basis transactions when ordinary income treatment would have applied if cash had been distributed instead. Exemptions apply to dispositions that don't ordinarily bail out a corporation's earnings and profits.[40]

Proceeds from a redemption of Code Sec. 306 stock (defined at ¶3525) are treated as a current distribution of property subject to the regular Code Sec. 301 dividend rules (see ¶1285 *et seq.*). (Code Sec. 306(a)(2))[41]

If Code Sec. 306 stock is sold or otherwise disposed of in a transaction other than a redemption, the entire amount realized is treated as ordinary income to the extent the fair market value on the distribution date would have been a dividend had the corporation distributed cash instead of stock. Ordinary income treatment is thus limited to the corporation's E&P at the time of the distribution rather than the sale. (Code Sec. 306(a)(1)(A))[42]

Gain is recognized to the extent the amount received exceeds the sum of the amount treated as ordinary income plus the adjusted basis of the stock, but loss isn't recognized. (Code Sec. 306(a)(1)(B); Code Sec. 306(a)(1)(C))[43] The ordinary income is treated as qualified dividend income for individuals and other noncorporate taxpayers (¶1288).[44]

An amount realized on the disposition of Code Sec. 306 stock won't be treated as a dividend in the case of:

. . . A complete disposition of the shareholder's interest in the corporation, including stock attributed under the Code Sec. 318(a) constructive ownership rules. (Code Sec. 306(b)(1)(A))

---

34. ¶F-11808 *et seq.*
35. ¶F-11834
36. ¶F-11835
37. ¶F-11805
38. ¶F-11804
39. ¶s F-11811, F-11814, F-11824, F-11832

40. ¶F-12100 *et seq.*
41. ¶F-12106
42. ¶ F-12101 *et seq.*
43. ¶F-12103
44. ¶F-12101

. . . A redemption (i) of all of a shareholder's Code Sec. 306 stock terminating the shareholder's corporate ownership, or (ii) from a noncorporate shareholder in partial liquidation of the corporation. (Code Sec. 306(b)(1)(B)).

. . . A redemption in a complete liquidation of the corporation. (Code Sec. 306(b)(2))

. . . A transaction in which gain or loss isn't recognized on the disposition of the Code Sec. 306 stock (in which case the stock retains the Code Sec. 306 taint in the transferee's hands). (Code Sec. 306(b)(3))

. . . A transaction, if the issuance and/or subsequent disposition of the stock wasn't under a plan having one of its principal purposes the avoidance of federal income tax. (Code Sec. 306(b)(4))[45]

For stock treated as Code Sec. 306 stock, see ¶3525.

¶ 3525   Stock treated as Section 306 stock.

Code Sec. 306 stock includes (Code Sec. 306(c)(1)):

(1) Stock received as a stock dividend, other than common stock issued with respect to common stock, if any part wasn't taxable on its receipt; usually preferred stock distributed on common stock. (Code Sec. 306(c)(1)(A))[46]

(2) Stock other than common stock received in a reorganization, spin-off, split-up or split-off, to the extent that (a) the transaction was substantially the same as the receipt of a stock dividend, or (b) the stock was received in exchange for Code Sec. 306 stock. (Code Sec. 306(c)(1)(B))[47]

(3) Stock (unless described in (2) above) whose basis is determined by reference to the basis of Code Sec. 306 stock. (Code Sec. 306(c)(1)(C))[48]

(4) Preferred stock (but not nonqualified preferred stock (see ¶3542)) received in a Code Sec. 351 transfer (except for certain bank transfers) if receipt of cash (in lieu of the stock) would have been treated as a dividend to any extent after applying the related corporation redemption rules (¶3522). (Code Sec. 306(c)(3))[49]

Code Sec. 306 stock doesn't include any stock of any class which, at the time of distribution, wouldn't in any part have been a dividend if cash had been distributed instead because there were no earnings and profits. (Code Sec. 306(c)(2))[50]

¶ 3526   Nonliquidating Distributions, Taxation of Corporation. ■■■■■■■■■■■■■■

In determining the tax effects to a corporation of nonliquidating distributions (dividends or distributions in redemption of the corporation's stock) (Code Sec. 311) to its shareholders, the following rules apply:

. . . A corporation doesn't recognize gain or loss on distributions of its stock or rights to acquire its stock. (Code Sec. 311(a)(1)).[1]

. . . Except as noted below, a corporation doesn't recognize loss on distribution of property to its shareholder. (Code Sec. 311(a)(2))[2]

. . . A corporation recognizes gain when it makes a nonliquidating distribution of appreciated property (other than its own obligations) to its shareholders as if the property had been sold, at the time of the distribution, to the distributee for its then fair market value (FMV). (Code Sec. 311(b)(1))[3]

---

45. ¶F-12108 *et seq.*
46. ¶F-12122
47. ¶F-12124 *et seq.*
48. ¶F-12128
49. ¶F-12123
50. ¶F-12132
1. ¶F-14002 *et seq.*
2. ¶F-14002
3. ¶F-14004 *et seq.*

. . . If distributed property is subject to any debt, or the shareholder assumes any debt in connection with the distribution, the FMV of the property is treated as not less than the amount of that debt. (Code Sec. 311(b)(2))[4] If the liability is unsecured, it is allocated among all the distributed assets (including any asset that secures another liability) according to the assets' relative FMVs.[5]

✓recommendation: Instead of distributing property with a basis in excess of its value to its shareholders, a corporation should consider selling that property to a third party so the loss can be recognized in computing its taxable income.

For how nonliquidating distributions affect earnings and profits (E&P), see ¶3512.

¶ 3527   Corporate Reorganizations. ▬▬▬▬▬

Under Code Sec. 354(a), if one corporation transfers property to another corporation solely in exchange for stock or securities of the other corporation and the exchange is made under a plan of reorganization, neither will recognize gain or loss on the exchange if the transaction complies with strict statutory and regulatory requirements. The following are the different types of reorganizations: Type A: Merger or consolidation (¶3530); Type B: stock for stock (¶3531); Type C: Assets for stock (¶3532); Type D: Transfer of assets to subsidiary (¶3533); Type E: Recapitalization (¶3534); Type F: Change of identity (¶3535); Type G: Bankruptcy (¶3536); and triangular reorganization where the acquirer's parent is a party (¶3537).

For requirements common to all reorganizations, see ¶3528.

For reorganizations involving investment companies, see ¶3529.

For the tax effects of the transfer of property acquired in a reorganization, see ¶3538.

For how shareholders and corporate parties are taxed in a reorganization, see ¶3540 *et seq.*

For the deductibility of reorganization costs, see ¶3544.

¶ 3528   Requirements common to all corporate reorganizations: plan, party, continuity, business purpose.

The following definitions and requirements apply to all reorganization types, with exceptions noted. Failure to meet any requirement may disqualify a reorganization and result in gain recognition and/or dividend treatment.[6]

Plan of reorganization. An exchange must be under a plan of reorganization. (Code Sec. 354(a)(1); Reg § 1.368-2(g))[7] The plan must be adopted by each party to the reorganization (see below) and each party must include a statement on its return pursuant to regs. (Reg § 1.368-3(a))[8]

Party to a reorganization. A corporation whose stock or securities are exchanged must be a party to the reorganization for nonrecognition treatment to apply. (Code Sec. 354(a)(1))[9] This includes any corporation resulting from a reorganization and, in the case of an acquisition by one corporation of the stock or properties of another, both corporations. The parent of the acquiring corporation in a Type B, C, or G reorganization is a party to the reorganization if its stock is the consideration for the acquisition of assets or stock. A parent of the surviving corporation in a statutory merger is a party to the reorganization if

---

4. ¶s F-14005, F-14402   7. ¶F-4009
5. ¶F-14006   8. ¶F-4108
6. ¶F-2000 *et seq.*   9. ¶F-4001

its stock is used as consideration and the transaction qualifies as a Type A reorganization under Code Sec. 368(a)(2)(D) or Code Sec. 368(a)(2)(E). If assets or stock received in a Type A, B, C, or G reorganization are dropped down under Code Sec. 368(a)(2)(C), the corporation controlling the transferee is a party to the reorganization. (Code Sec. 368(b)) (Reg § 1.368-2(f))[10]

Continuity of interest. The regulatory continuity of proprietary interest doctrine incorporates the judicial requirement that the former target shareholders retain a significant equity participation in the target corporation after the reorganization. A proprietary interest in the target is sufficiently preserved if (1) it is exchanged for a proprietary interest in the issuing corporation, (2) it is exchanged by the acquiring corporation for a direct interest in the target corporation enterprise, or (3) it otherwise continues as a proprietary interest in the target corporation. (Reg § 1.368-1(e))[11]

Continuity of business enterprise. An acquiring corporation must either (1) continue the target's historic business (generally, its most recent business unless the most recent business was entered under the plan of reorganization), or (2) use a significant part of the target's historic business assets in a business. The business may be conducted by, or the assets held through, one or more members of the acquiring corporation's qualified group, i.e., one or more chains of corporations connected through stock ownership, if the acquiring corporation has 80% control of at least one of them and each of the other corporations is controlled by one of the other corporations). (Reg § 1.368-1(d))[12]

Business purpose. A transaction that is structured as a reorganization but has no business purpose isn't in the nature of a reorganization and isn't treated as such.[13]

The continuity of interest and continuity of business enterprise requirements don't apply to recapitalizations involving a single corporation (Type E reorganizations, ¶3534) or change-in-identity (Type F) reorganizations (¶3535). (Reg § 1.368-1(b))[14]

¶ 3529   Corporate reorganizations involving investment companies.

If two or more investment companies are parties to a transaction, the transaction cannot qualify as a nonrecognition reorganization with respect to either company or the holders of its stock and securities unless it was a regulated investment company (¶4201), a real estate investment trust (¶4202), or a corporation that meets specific diversified investment company requirements. (Code Sec. 368(a)(2)(F))[15]

¶ 3530   Type A: Merger or consolidation—corporate reorganizations.

A Type A reorganization is a merger or consolidation effected under statutory law (including foreign laws). (Code Sec. 368(a)(1)(A); Reg § 1.368-2(b)(1)(ii))[16] The merger of a disregarded entity into a corporation doesn't qualify as a tax-free statutory merger or consolidation, although the merger of a corporation into a disregarded entity may qualify. (Reg § 1.368-2(b)(1)(iii))[17]

¶ 3531   Type B: Acquisition of stock in exchange for stock—corporate reorganizations.

A Type B reorganization is the acquisition by one corporation of stock in a second (target) corporation in exchange *solely for voting stock* of the acquiring corporation (or voting stock of its parent in the case of a triangular Type B reorganization (¶3537)), if the

---

10. ¶F-4013
11. ¶ F-3600 *et seq.*
12. ¶F-3701 *et seq.*
13. ¶F-3800 *et seq.*

14. ¶F-3626; ¶F-3709
15. ¶F-2100 *et seq.*
16. ¶F-2200 *et seq.*
17. ¶F-2201.2 *et seq.*

acquiring corporation is in *control* (¶3539) of the target immediately after the exchange. (Code Sec. 368(a)(1)(B)) An acquiring corporation that transfers property other than voting stock in connection with a Type B reorganization plan doesn't violate the *solely for voting stock* requirement as long as the target's *stock* is acquired solely for voting stock.[18]

¶ 3532 Type C: Acquisition of a target's assets for stock—corporate reorganizations.

A Type C reorganization is the acquisition by one corporation of *substantially all* of the properties of a target corporation in exchange for voting stock of the acquiring corporation (or the stock of its parent in the case of a triangular C reorganization (¶3537)). Except as noted below, liabilities assumed by the acquiring corporation are disregarded. (Code Sec. 368(a)(1)(C))[19]

There is no definition of *substantially all* of a target's properties or rules on what part of the assets the target can safely retain. However, for purposes of a favorable IRS ruling, the target must transfer at least 90% of the fair market value (FMV) of the net assets and at least 70% of the FMV of the gross assets that it held immediately before the transfer.[20]

A transaction won't qualify as a C reorganization unless the target, under the plan of reorganization, liquidates and distributes to its shareholders all stock, securities and other property received under the plan, as well as its other properties. IRS may waive this distribution requirement under certain conditions. (Code Sec. 368(a)(2)(G))[21]

To satisfy the *solely for voting stock* requirement, at least 80% of the FMV of property received must be acquired solely for voting stock. The remainder of the property may be acquired for cash or other property. If any cash or other property is transferred, liabilities assumed with respect to acquired properties are treated as cash. (Code Sec. 368(a)(2)(B))[22] Preexisting ownership by an acquiring corporation of a part of the target's stock does not, in and of itself, prevent the solely for voting stock requirement from being satisfied. (Reg § 1.368-2(d)(4))[23]

¶ 3533 Type D: Transfer of assets to subsidiary—corporate reorganizations.

A Type D reorganization is the transfer by one corporation of all or part of its assets to a second corporation, if, immediately after the transfer, the transferor and/or its shareholders are in control (¶3539) of the transferee corporation *and* the transferor satisfies a distribution requirement by:

. . . distributing all of the assets (including stock and securities) of the transferee to its shareholders under a plan of reorganization as a part of the transferor's liquidation (*acquisitive* or *nondivisive* D); or

. . . distributing the stock and securities of the transferee in a tax-free spin-off, split-off or split-up (corporate separation, or *divisive* D (¶3545 *et seq.*). (Code Sec. 368(a)(1)(D))[24]

The distribution requirements of Code Sec. 368(a)(1)(D) and Code Sec. 354(b)(1)(B) are deemed satisfied even if no stock is actually distributed in cases where the same person or persons own(s) directly or indirectly all of the stock of the transferor and transferee corporations in the same proportions. Except in certain related party triangular reorganizations, if fair market value (FMV) is paid for the assets, the transferee is deemed to issue a nominal share of stock to the transferor, which is deemed further distributed as necessary to reflect actual ownership. (Reg § 1.368-2(l)(2))[25]

---

18. ¶F-2500 *et seq.*
19. ¶F-2600 *et seq.*
20. ¶F-2618 *et seq.*
21. ¶F-2629 *et seq.*

22. ¶F-2613
23. ¶F-2617
24. ¶ F-2700 *et seq.*; ¶F-4500 *et seq.*
25. ¶F-2707 *et seq.*

An acquiring corporation's transfer of target corporation assets to a controlled subsidiary as part of a plan of reorganization may not disqualify an otherwise qualifying D reorganization. (Reg § 1.368-2(k))[26]

A Type D reorganization may also qualify as a Type C, in which case it will be treated only as a Type D. (Code Sec. 368(a)(2)(A))[27]

¶ 3534   Type E: Recapitalization—corporate reorganizations.

A Type E reorganization is a recapitalization (Code Sec. 368(a)(1)(E)) or change in the capital structure of a single corporation. It may be achieved through an exchange of stock for stock, bonds for bonds, stock for bonds, or bonds for stock. Recapitalizations include:

. . . An issuance of preferred stock in discharge of outstanding bonds;

. . . An exchange of one class of common for another class of common, or preferred for common (provided that new preferred isn't Code Sec. 306 stock (¶3523), and provided that the fair market value of the post-reorganization stock equals that of the pre-reorganization stock), or vice-versa;

. . . An exchange of old bonds for new bonds with a different face value, interest rate, etc.;

. . . Changes in stock or securities effected by a change in the corporate charter. (Reg § 1.368-2(e))[28]

¶ 3535   Type F: Change in Identity—corporate reorganizations.

A Type F reorganization is limited to a change in identity, form or place of organization *of one corporation* and may be accomplished using various methods. (Code Sec. 368(a)(1)(F))[29]

¶ 3536   Type G: Bankruptcy—corporate reorganizations.

A Type G reorganization is the transfer by a corporation of all or part of its assets to another corporation (including a bridge bank) under a court-approved reorganization plan in a Title 11 or similar case (e.g., bankruptcy, receivership, or foreclosure), but only if stock or securities of the corporation to which the assets are transferred are distributed in a transaction that qualifies under Code Sec. 354, Code Sec. 355, or Code Sec. 356. (Code Sec. 368(a)(1)(G), Code Sec. 368(a)(3)(A))[30] The acquirer can use parent stock to acquire the debtor corporation in a triangular Type G reorganization. (Code Sec. 368(a)(2)(D))[31]

¶ 3537   Triangular reorganizations—corporate reorganizations.

Tax-free treatment applies to the following triangular reorganizations in which the acquirer's parent is a party to the transaction:

(1) *Forward triangular merger.* Where the acquirer uses parent stock to acquire *substantially all* of the target's assets (¶3532), the transaction is a forward triangular merger. If certain requirements are met, a forward triangular merger qualifies as a Type A reorganization. (Code Sec. 368(a)(2)(D))[32]

(2) *Triangular C reorganization.* Where the acquiring corporation acquires substantially all the assets of the target corporation solely in exchange for all or a part of the voting stock of the acquirer's parent, the transaction qualifies as a triangular Type C reorganization. (Code Sec. 368(a)(1)(C))[33]

26. ¶F-2702.1
27. ¶F-2710
28. ¶F-3000 *et seq.*
29. ¶F-3100 *et seq.*

30. ¶F-3200 *et seq.*
31. ¶F-3207
32. ¶F-2300 *et seq.*
33. ¶F-2650 *et seq.*

(3) *Triangular B reorganization.* A triangular reorganization qualifies for Type B treatment if the acquirer acquires target stock solely in exchange for parent stock.[34]

(4) *Reverse triangular merger.* Where target shareholders exchange stock of the target constituting control for voting stock of the parent of the merged corporation and the target holds substantially all of its own properties and of those of the merged subsidiary after the merger, the merger is a reverse triangular merger. (Code Sec. 368(a)(2)(E))[35] A reverse triangular merger is tax-free despite a later sale of half of the target's operating assets.[36] If certain requirements are met, a reverse triangular merger that doesn't qualify as a Type A reorganization may qualify as a Type B reorganization. (Reg § 1.368-2(j)(6), Ex 4)[37]

¶ 3538 Later transfer of property acquired in a reorganization—corporate reorganizations.

An otherwise tax-free reorganization isn't disqualified by one or more later (or successive) transfers of assets or stock, provided that (i) there is continuity of business enterprise (¶3528), (ii) target's corporate existence isn't terminated in connection with the drop-down, and (iii) the drop-down doesn't cause the target to cease to be a member of the qualified group. (Reg § 1.368-2(k))[38]

¶ 3539 Control defined—corporate reorganizations.

For purposes of the rules for reorganizations (other than nondivisive Type Ds), *control* is the ownership of: (i) stock possessing at least 80% of the total combined voting power of all voting stock, and (ii) at least 80% of the total number of shares of each class of nonvoting stock. (Code Sec. 368(c))[39] For nondivisive Type Ds, *control* is defined under the related corporation redemption rules (i.e., 50%, rather than 80%, ownership, see ¶3522). If the corporate division requirements of Code Sec. 355 (¶3546) are satisfied, control isn't affected by later transfers by shareholders of the distributed controlled corporation stock or by the issuance by the corporation whose stock was distributed of additional stock. (Code Sec. 368(a)(2)(H))[40]

¶ 3540 How shareholders are taxed; nonqualified preferred stock; stock rights; boot—corporate reorganizations.

Under Code Sec. 354(a), if, under a plan of reorganization, the holder of stock or securities receives only stock in a corporation that's a party to the reorganization, the recipient recognizes no gain or loss. Nonrecognition also applies when securities of a corporate party to the reorganization are received in exchange for other securities, if the principal (face) amount of the securities received isn't more than the face amount given up. (Code Sec. 354(a)(1); Code Sec. 354(a)(2)(A))[41] Nonqualified preferred stock (¶3542) received for stock that isn't nonqualified preferred stock isn't treated as stock or securities unless it's received in a recapitalization (¶3534) of a family-owned corporation. (Code Sec. 354(a)(2)(C))[42] Stock rights (except rights to acquire nonqualified preferred stock not received as part of a family corporation recapitalization) are treated as securities with no principal amount. (Reg § 1.354-1(e), Reg § 1.355-1(c), Reg § 1.356-6(a)(2), Reg § 1.356-6(b)(1))[43] For the treatment of nonqualified preferred stock and excess securities as boot, see ¶3542.

34. ¶F-2550 *et seq.*
35. ¶F-2402 *et seq.*
36. ¶F-2405; ¶F-3250 *et seq.*
37. ¶F-2402
38. ¶F-2308, ¶F-3250 *et seq.*

39. ¶F-4502, ¶F-5500 *et seq.*
40. ¶F-4502
41. ¶F-4001, F-4022
42. ¶F-4001.1, F-4001.2
43. ¶F-4012; ¶F-4012.1

Type D and Type G reorganizations aren't tax-free unless (i) the transferee corporation receives substantially all of the transferor's assets, and (ii) the stock, securities and other property received by the transferor, as well as its remaining assets, are distributed by the transferor under the reorganization plan. (Code Sec. 354(b))[44]

If nonrecognition would apply, but doesn't because property other than stock or securities (i.e., boot (¶3542)) is also received in the exchange, then gain is recognized up to the sum of the boot received. (Code Sec. 356(a)(1))[45] A loss on one block of stock exchanged in a reorganization may not reduce gain on another block.[46] Gain recognized in a reorganization with boot is treated as a dividend if the exchange has the effect of a distribution (see ¶3515). The gain is treated as ordinary income to the extent of the taxpayer's ratable share of the accumulated earnings and profits of the distributing corporation, and the balance is treated as gain from the sale or exchange of property. (Code Sec. 356(a)(2))[47]

For basis of property received in the exchange, see ¶2482.

¶ 3541   How the corporate parties are taxed—corporate reorganizations.

Under Code Sec. 361(a), no gain or loss is recognized by a corporation that is a party to a reorganization (¶3528) and that exchanges property solely for stock or securities of another corporation that is also a party to that reorganization.[48] If the corporation receives other property or money (boot, see ¶3542) in addition to stock or securities, then if the corporation distributes all of the boot, it doesn't recognize gain on the exchange (but may recognize gain on the distribution of appreciated property, see below). However, if the corporation doesn't distribute any part of the boot, gain is recognized on the exchange, but only to the extent of the undistributed boot. (Code Sec. 361(b))[49]

Gain or loss isn't recognized on the distribution of *qualified property* received under the plan of reorganization. Qualified property is stock (or the right to acquire stock) in the distributing corporation, and stock or obligations of another party to the reorganization that are received in the reorganization exchange. Gain (but not loss) is recognized on the distribution of property that isn't qualified property. (Code Sec. 361(c))[50]

For acquirer's basis in property received in the exchange, see ¶2478. For target's basis, see ¶2480.

¶ 3542   Treatment of boot; nonqualified preferred stock, securities in non-parties—corporate reorganizations.

Boot (Code Sec. 356) is money or the fair market value (FMV) of property other than stock or securities of a party to the reorganization (¶3528) that's received by the target in exchange for its property, or by target shareholders in exchange for their stock, under the plan of reorganization.[1] Nonqualified preferred stock received for stock other than nonqualified preferred stock is boot unless received in a recapitalization of a family-owned corporation. (Code Sec. 356(e))[2] Nonqualified preferred stock is generally preferred stock that the issuer is required to redeem, or is more likely than not to redeem, or preferred stock with a dividend rate that varies with changes in interest rates or similar indices. (Code Sec. 351(g)(2))[3] For the effect of liabilities on characterization of property as boot, see ¶3543.

Securities in corporations not parties to the reorganization are always boot and gain is taxable to the extent of the securities' FMV. In the case of securities in corporations that

44. ¶s F-2701, F-3205
45. ¶F-4017
46. ¶F-4018
47. ¶F-4017; ¶F-4025
48. ¶F-4100 *et seq.*

49. ¶F-4101
50. ¶F-4102
1. ¶F-4017
2. ¶F-4001.1; ¶F-4001.2
3. ¶F-1510

are parties to the reorganization, only the excess, if any, of the face amount of securities received over the face amount of securities surrendered is boot. If no securities are surrendered, the FMV of any securities received is boot. (Code Sec. 354(a)(2), Code Sec. 356(d)) A stock right treated as a security having no principal amount (¶3540) isn't boot whether or not securities are surrendered in the exchange. (Reg § 1.356-3(b))[4]

¶ 3543 Treatment of assumption and transfer of liabilities—corporate reorganizations.

Under Code Sec. 357(a), where a party to a reorganization (¶3528) exchanges property for stock or securities in a corporation and the corporation assumes the transferor's liabilities, the assumed liabilities aren't treated as boot (¶3542) for the purpose of *recognizing* gain.[5] However, if the principal purpose for the assumption of the liabilities is tax avoidance, or is something other than a bona fide business purpose, *all the liabilities assumed* are treated as cash (i.e., boot) in both computing *and* recognizing gain. (Code Sec. 357(b))[6]

If, in the case of a Type D reorganization (¶3533) in which stock or securities of the transferee corporation are distributed in a qualifying tax-free separation under Code Sec. 355 (¶3545), the sum of the liabilities assumed exceeds the total adjusted basis of the property transferred, the excess is taxed as a gain from the sale or exchange of property (capital gain or ordinary income, depending on the character of the property in the hands of the transferor). (Code Sec. 357(c))[7]

For what constitutes assumption of a liability, see ¶3506.

¶ 3544 Deductibility of corporate reorganization costs; IRS safe harbor.

Generally, expenses incurred in connection with a corporate reorganization, including borrowing costs, are capital expenditures (¶1636) and not deductible business expenses.[8] If a proposed reorganization is abandoned, the costs are deductible in the year of abandonment.[9]

IRS has provided a safe harbor allowing taxpayers to allocate 70% of the success-based fees (¶1632) paid in business acquisitions or reorganizations to activities that don't facilitate the transaction and deduct such fees currently. The remaining 30% is treated as going to activities that facilitate the transaction and must be capitalized. However, an acquired taxpayer that elects to treat a stock sale as an asset sale under Code Sec. 338(h)(10) (¶3567) can't elect the safe harbor.[10]

¶ 3545 Spin-Offs, Split-Offs and Split-Ups. ■■■■■■■■

If certain requirements are met (¶3546), a corporate division may be accomplished on a tax-free basis in the form of a (1) *spin-off*, i.e., a pro rata distribution of a controlled corporation's stock to the distributing corporation's shareholders without requiring the shareholders to surrender any of their distributing corporation stock; (2) *split-off*, i.e., a pro rata or non pro rata distribution of a controlled corporation's stock to one or more of the distributing corporation's shareholders in exchange for stock held in the distributing corporation; or (3) *split-up*, i.e., a transfer of all the businesses of a distributing corporation to controlled corporations

---

4. ¶F-4021 *et seq.*
5. ¶F-4201
6. ¶F-4202
7. ¶F-4203

8. ¶L-5400 *et seq.*
9. ¶L-5416
10. ¶L-5762.1A

followed by a distribution of the stock of the controlled corporations to the distributing corporation's shareholders and the liquidation of the distributing corporation. The distribution of controlled corporation stock to the distributing corporation's shareholders can be pro rata or non pro rata.[11]

For how boot is taxed to shareholders in a spin-off, split-off, or split-up, see ¶3547.

For how the distributing corporation is taxed, see ¶3548.

¶ 3546 Requirements for a tax-free spin-off, split-off or split-up.

The following requirements (Code Sec. 355) for nonrecognition apply to spin-offs, split-offs, or split-ups.

(1) The distributing corporation (P) must distribute to its shareholders "with respect to" their stock, or to its security holders in exchange for their securities, solely stock or securities in a corporation (S) that it "controls" (¶3539) immediately before the distribution. (Code Sec. 355(a)(1)) Nonqualified preferred stock (¶3542) received in exchange for stock other than nonqualified preferred stock isn't treated as stock or securities for this purpose. (Code Sec. 355(a)(3)(D))[12]

(2) The transaction must not be used principally as a device for distributing earnings and profits (E&P) of either P or S. (Code Sec. 355(a)(1)(B)) The regs identify "device factors" (the presence of which are evidence of a device) and nondevice factors, and certain distributions that aren't ordinarily considered to have been used principally as a device even though device factors are present. (Reg § 1.355-2(d))[13]

(3) One or more of P's pre-distribution shareholders must end up with an amount of stock that establishes a continuity of interest (¶3528) in both P and S, though not necessarily proportionately (see (6), below). (Reg § 1.355-2(c)(1))[14]

(4) Both P and S (or each controlled subsidiary) must be engaged in the active conduct of a trade or business immediately after the distribution. (Code Sec. 355(b)(1)(A), Code Sec. 355(b)(2)(A)) For this purpose, all members of the corporation's separate affiliated group are treated as one corporation. (Code Sec. 355(b)(3)(A))[15] The trades or businesses must have been actively conducted throughout the 5-year period ending on the date S's stock is distributed. (Code Sec. 355(b)(2)(B))[16]

(5) The active trade or business (see (4), above) must not have been acquired during the 5-year period ending on the date S's stock is distributed in a transaction in which gain or loss was recognized in whole or in part. (Code Sec. 355(b)(2)(C))[17]

(6) A distribution doesn't qualify as a tax-free Code Sec. 355 division if immediately after the transaction (including any series of related transactions) (1) either the distributing or controlled corporation is a disqualified investment corporation, and (2) any person that didn't hold 50% or more by vote or value in the disqualified investment corporation immediately before the transaction holds a 50% or greater interest (voting or value). (Code Sec. 355(g))[18]

(7) A distribution generally won't qualify as a tax-free Code Sec. 355 division if either the distributing or controlled corporation (but not both) is a real estate investment trust (¶4202). (Code Sec. 355(h))[19]

(8) P must distribute either all its stock or securities in S, or at least an amount of S stock that's treated as "control" (¶3539). The distributions don't have to be pro rata or under a plan of reorganization. However, if P retains *any* stock or securities in S, tax

---

11. ¶F-4600 *et seq.*
12. ¶F-4602 *et seq.*
13. ¶F-4701 *et seq.*
14. ¶F-4612;
15. ¶F-4800 *et seq.*;

16. ¶F-4818
17. ¶F-4822 *et seq.*
18. ¶F-5400 *et seq.*
19. ¶F-5450 *et seq.*

avoidance must not be a principal purpose for the retention. (Code Sec. 355(a)(1)(D), Code Sec. 355(a)(2))[20]

In addition, one or more corporate business purposes must support the transaction for nonrecognition treatment to apply. (Reg § 1.355-2(b)) IRS has established guidelines for whether a corporate business purpose exists.[21]

If a parent corporation (P) transfers property (including property that is an active trade or business) to its subsidiary (D), and if, under the same plan, D distributes the stock of its controlled subsidiary (C) to P (a "north-south" transaction), whether the transaction is treated for federal income tax purposes as a Code Sec. 351 tax-free exchange followed by a Code Sec. 355 tax-free distribution depends on whether the transactions are treated as separate (tax-free) or integrated (taxable).[22]

¶ 3547   Boot taxed to shareholders in Sec. 355 transactions—spin-off, split-off or split-up.

The receipt of boot in an otherwise tax-free spin-off, split-off or split-up (¶3546) may trigger shareholder tax. Boot includes cash and the fair market value of:

... Any property (including stock warrants, short-term notes, etc.) *except* (and subject to the limitations below) stock or securities (other than nonqualified preferred stock (¶3542) (Code Sec. 356(e)) in the spun-off corporation (S) (Code Sec. 356(a));

... Any excess in the face amount of securities of S received over the face amount of securities in distributing corporation (P) which are surrendered. (Code Sec. 355(a)(3)(A), Code Sec. 356(d)(2)(C)) Stock rights are treated as securities having no principal amounts. (Reg § 1.355-1(c))

... Stock in S that P acquired in a partially or wholly taxable transaction during the five-year period preceding the distribution. (Code Sec. 355(a)(3)(B))[23]

Boot received in a spin-off (where no stock or securities of P are surrendered) is treated like a Code Sec. 301 dividend (¶1286). (Code Sec. 356(b))[24]

Boot received in a split-off or split-up (where stock or securities of P are surrendered) is taxable to the recipient to the extent gain is recognized, but not in excess of the value of the boot received. (Code Sec. 356(a)(1)) If, however, the exchange "has the effect of the distribution of a dividend," it is treated as a dividend to the extent of the taxpayer's ratable share of accumulated earnings and profits. The remainder, if any, of the recognized gain is generally treated as capital gain. (Code Sec. 356(a)(2))[25] In determining whether boot has the effect of a dividend, the transaction is treated as though the shareholder had retained the P stock which he or she actually surrendered in exchange for S stock, and had received the boot in exchange for an amount of P stock with a value equal to the amount of the boot; the redemption rules (¶3515 *et seq.*) are then applied to determine whether the boot is treated as a dividend.[26] No loss is recognized, whether or not boot is received. (Code Sec. 355(a), Code Sec. 356(c))[27]

For shareholders' basis in property received, see ¶2482.

¶ 3548   How distributing corporation is taxed—tax-free spin-off, split-off or split-up.

Except as stated below, no gain or loss is recognized by a distributing corporation (P) on

---

20. ¶F-4602 *et seq.*
21. ¶F-4900 *et seq.*
22. ¶F-4608
23. ¶F-5003 *et seq.*

24. ¶F-4017 *et seq.* ¶F-5003
25. ¶F-4017 *et seq.* ¶F-5003
26. ¶F-4026
27. ¶F-4018

distributions to which the tax-free corporate separation rules of Code Sec. 355 apply (Code Sec. 355(c)(1), Code Sec. 361).

(1) Gain is recognized by P on the distribution of appreciated property other than qualified property (i.e., stock and securities of S) in the same manner as if the property were sold for its fair market value (FMV). The FMV of distributed property is considered to be not less than the amount of any liability to which the property is subject or which is assumed by a shareholder in connection with the distribution. (Code Sec. 355(c)(2))[28]

(2) If the distribution is *disqualified* (as defined below), stock and securities of S aren't treated as qualified property, and P recognizes gain on their distribution in the same manner as gain is recognized in (1), above. (Code Sec. 355(d)(1) *et seq.*)[29]

(3) If, following the distribution, there is an acquisition of an interest greater than or equal to 50% in either S or P (including a predecessor of or successor to S or P (Reg § 1.355-8)[30]) under a plan or in a series of transactions, P generally must recognize gain as if it had sold the stock or securities of S to the distributee for FMV immediately before the distribution. (Code Sec. 355(e)) Regs discuss factors for and against a finding of a plan or a series of related transactions. (Reg § 1.355-7)[31]

Except as provided in regs, tax-free division treatment isn't available for distributions from one affiliated group member to another in a plan under which any person acquires (directly or indirectly) an interest greater than or equal to 50% in either P or S, determined after application of Code Sec. 355(e). (Code Sec. 355(f))[32]

A distribution is disqualified (unless it doesn't violate the purpose of Code Sec. 355(d) (Reg § 1.355-6(b)(3)(i))) if (1) immediately after the distribution, any shareholder (or any two or more shareholders acting under a plan) holds (actually or constructively) at least 50% of the stock of P or S, and (2) that stock was purchased (or acquired) within the immediately preceding 5-year period, or was received as a distribution on P stock purchased (or acquired) during that period. (Code Sec. 355(d))[33]

¶ 3549   Carryovers of Tax Items. ▬▬▬▬▬▬▬▬▬▬▬▬▬▬▬

Under Code Sec. 381(a), a corporation that acquires the assets of another corporation in certain tax-free reorganizations or liquidations also succeeds to and takes into account numerous tax items (¶3550) of the transferor (predecessor) corporation.

Under Code Sec. 381(a), a predecessor's tax items are carried over to the successor corporation in a:

. . . Type A (¶3530), C (¶3532) or F (¶3535) reorganization;

. . . Type D (¶3533) or G (¶3536) reorganization, but only if the transferor transfers substantially all its assets to the acquiring corporation and then (in effect) completely liquidates; or

. . . Complete liquidation of an 80% subsidiary (¶3560).[34]

The carryover rules don't generally apply to divisive reorganizations, but items may be carried over under general principles of corporate succession. (Reg § 1.381(a)-1(b)(3))[35]

---

28. ¶F-5100 *et seq.*
29. ¶F-5200 *et seq.*
30. ¶F-5333 *et seq.*
31. ¶F-5300 *et seq.*

32. ¶F-4630 *et seq.*
33. ¶F-5200 *et seq.*
34. ¶F-7000 *et seq.*
35. ¶F-7005; ¶F-7013

¶ 3550 Tax items carried over in reorganizations or liquidations.

When the Code's carryover provisions apply, the acquiring corporation succeeds to and takes into account the following tax items of the transferor (Code Sec. 381(c)): accounting method; amortization of bond discount or premium; capital loss carryovers; charitable contributions carryover; depreciation allowance and method; earnings and profits (E&P); employee benefit plan contributions; general business credit; installment method; inventory method; involuntary conversions; minimum tax credit; mining development and exploration expenses; net operating loss carryovers; percentage depletion on extraction of ores or minerals from waste or residue of earlier mining; personal holding company (PHC) deficiency dividend; PHC dividend carryover; real estate investment trust (REIT) or regulated investment company (RIC) deficiency dividend; tax benefit items; and items under Subchapter U (Code Sec. 1391 *et seq.*) dealing with enterprise zones, as regs provide.[36]

Tax items to which an acquiring corporation succeeds, including the basis of property acquired, must reflect reductions for cancellation of debt. (Reg § 1.108-7(c))[37]

¶ 3551 Tax Avoidance Acquisition Bar to Tax Benefits.

Under Code Sec. 269, any deduction, credit or other allowance may be disallowed where, for the principal purpose of tax avoidance:

. . . Any person or persons acquire, directly or indirectly, stock having at least 50% of the total combined voting power of all classes of a corporation's voting stock, or at least 50% of the total value of all classes of its stock; or

. . . Any corporation acquires, directly or indirectly, property of another corporation not controlled, directly or indirectly, by the acquirer (or its shareholders) immediately before the acquisition, if the acquirer takes a carryover basis in the property. (Code Sec. 269(a))[38]

IRS may also disallow a deduction, credit, or other allowance where a target that a corporation acquired in a qualified stock purchase (¶3565) *without* making a Code Sec. 338 election (¶3564) is liquidated primarily for tax avoidance or evasion, under a plan of liquidation adopted within two years after the acquisition date. (Code Sec. 269(b))[39]

¶ 3552 Limits on Use of Built-in Gains of One Corporation to Offset Losses of Another.

Under Code Sec. 384(a), if a corporation acquires directly (or through one or more other corporations) control (as defined at ¶3339) of another corporation, or acquires the assets of another corporation in a Type A, C, or D reorganization, and either corporation is a gain corporation, then any income of either corporation attributable to recognized built-in gain within a 5-year period beginning on the date of the ownership change (¶3556) can't be offset by any pre-acquisition loss of the other corporation. (Code Sec. 384(a); Code Sec. 384(c)(5)) Similar rules limit the use of any excess credit or net capital loss. (Code Sec. 384(d))[40]

The above offset prohibition doesn't apply to any pre-acquisition loss of any corporation if that corporation and the gain corporation were members of the same controlled group at all times during the 5-year period ending on the acquisition date (or shorter period of either corporation's existence). (Code Sec. 384(b))[41]

---

36. ¶F-7012, F-7098, F-7099
37. ¶J-7404.2
38. ¶F-7900 *et seq.*

39. ¶F-7912
40. ¶F-7850 *et seq.*
41. ¶F-7860

¶ 3553   The Code Sec. 382 Limitation on Loss Carryovers After Ownership Change. ▪

Under Code Sec. 382, if an ownership change (¶3556) occurs with respect to a "loss corporation," that corporation's taxable income for any post-change year can be offset by pre-change losses and credits (¶3555) only to the extent of a certain percentage of the value of the corporation at the time of the change.

Thus, a loss corporation that is entitled to use a net operating loss (NOL) carryover in, or that has an NOL for, the tax year in which an ownership change (¶3556) occurs, may offset taxable income for any tax year ending after the ownership change by pre-change loss carryforwards only to the extent of the "Code Sec. 382 limitation" for that year (Code Sec. 382(a); Code Sec. 382(k)(1)).[42] The "Code Sec. 382 limitation" is equal to the value of the loss corporation immediately before the ownership change multiplied by the long-term tax-exempt rate (¶3554). (Code Sec. 382(b)(1))[43] Except in the case of redemptions or other corporate contractions, and some capital contributions, that value is the value of its stock immediately before the ownership change. (Code Sec. 382(e)(1), Code Sec. 382(e)(2), Code Sec. 382(l)(1)(A), Code Sec. 382(l)(4))[44]

If a loss corporation has net unrealized built-in gain on assets held immediately before the change date in excess of a defined amount, the Code Sec. 382 limitation may be increased by recognized built-in gains on an asset within the 5-tax-year recognition period (beginning on the date of the ownership change), but only to the extent of the excess of the asset's fair market value over its adjusted basis on that date. Prepaid income isn't treated as built-in gain. The limitation may also be increased by certain recognized Code Sec. 338 gains. (Code Sec. 382(h)(1), Code Sec. 382(h)(6)) The disallowed part of a recognized built-in loss can be carried forward like an NOL subject to the Code Sec. 382 limitation in later years as if it were a pre-change NOL. IRS guidance describes two alternative safe harbors to determine built-in income and deduction items after an ownership change.[45]

The Code Sec. 382 limitation doesn't apply to the loss corporation's taxable income for the part of the change year before the ownership change occurs. (Code Sec. 382(b)(3))[46] Nor does it apply if the loss corporation is under the jurisdiction of a court in a bankruptcy, receivership, foreclosure, or similar proceeding (unless it elects not to have this exception apply). (Code Sec. 382(l)(5); Reg § 1.382-9(i))[47] Special rules apply for consolidated (Reg § 1.1502-90 to Reg § 1.1502-96, Reg § 1.1502-98 to Reg § 1.1502-99),[48] and controlled (Reg § 1.382-8) groups,[49] and for successive ownership changes. (Reg § 1.382-5(d))[50]

¶ 3554   Long-term tax-exempt rate—Code Sec. 382 limitation.

Under Code Sec. 382(f), for the Code Sec. 382 limitation (¶3553), the long-term tax-exempt rate is the highest of the adjusted federal long-term rates for any month in the three-calendar month period ending with the month in which the ownership change occurs.[1] The long-term tax-exempt rate for ownership changes in:

. . . Nov. 2022 is 2.97%.

. . . Oct. 2022 is 2.60%.

. . . Sept. 2022 is 2.54%.

. . . Aug. 2022 is 2.54%.

. . . July 2022 is 2.43%.

. . . June 2022 is 2.36%.

---

42. ¶F-7200 *et seq.*
43. ¶F-7250 *et seq.*
44. ¶F-7300 *et seq.*
45. ¶F-7340 *et seq.*
46. ¶F-7255 *et seq.*
47. ¶F-7700 *et seq.*
48. ¶E-9060 *et seq.*
49. ¶F-7335 *et seq.*
50. ¶F-7257
1. ¶F-7336

... May 2022 is 2.01%.

... Apr. 2022 is 1.71%.

... Mar. 2022 is 1.63%.

... Feb. 2022 is 1.46%.

... Jan. 2022 is 1.45%.

... Dec. 2021 is 1.45%.

... Nov. 2021 is 1.40%.[2]

¶ 3555   Pre-change losses and credits subject to Code Section 382 limitation.

Under Code Sec. 382(d)(1), the Code Sec. 382 limitation applies to (1) any net operating losses (NOLs) of the old loss corporation that are carried forward to the tax year ending with the ownership change or in which the change date occurs; (2) any NOL of the old loss corporation for the tax year in which the ownership change occurs to the extent the loss is allocable to the period in that year on or before the change date; (3) any recognized built-in loss in a recognition period tax year (¶3553); (4) any pre-change capital loss described in (1)–(3); and (5) any pre-change credits (below). (Reg § 1.383-1(c)(2); Code Sec. 382(d)(1); Reg § 1.382-2(a)(2))[3] Pre-change credits are excess foreign taxes under Code Sec. 904(c), unused Code Sec. 38 business credits, and the available Code Sec. 53 minimum tax credit, to the extent attributable to periods ending on or before the change date. (Reg § 1.383-1(c)(3))[4]

For the order in which pre-change losses and credits are absorbed, see ¶3557.

¶ 3556   Ownership change defined—Code Sec. 382 limitation.

Under Code Sec. 382(g)(1) and Code Sec. 382(i)(1), for the Code Sec. 382 limitation (¶3553), there is an ownership change if, immediately after any owner shift involving a 5% shareholder or an equity structure shift, the stock of the loss corporation owned by one or more 5% shareholders has increased by more the 50 percentage points over these shareholders' lowest percentage ownership at any time during a three-year testing period.[5] A 5% shareholder is any person holding 5% or more by value of the stock of the corporation at any time during the testing period. (Code Sec. 382(k)(7)) The percentage of stock owned is determined on the basis of value, and nonvoting preferred stock is generally disregarded. (Code Sec. 382(k)(6))[6] Certain nonstock interests may be treated as stock. (Reg § 1.382-2T(f)(18)(iii))[7] Special aggregation rules apply to treat groups of shareholders as single shareholders. (Reg § 1.382-2T(j))[8]

¶ 3557   Order of loss absorption for Code Section 382 limitation.

A loss corporation must absorb its Code Sec. 382 limitation (¶3553) in the following order for each post-change year: (1) pre-change losses that are built-in capital losses recognized during that year, (2) pre-change losses that are capital loss carryovers, (3) pre-change losses that are built-in ordinary losses recognized during that year, (4) pre-change losses that are net operating loss carryovers, (5) pre-change credits for excess foreign taxes carried forward under Code Sec. 904(c), (6) pre-change credits that are unused general business credits carried over under Code Sec. 39, and (7) pre-change credits that are unused minimum tax credits under Code Sec. 53. (Reg § 1.383-1(d)(2))[9]

---

2. ¶F-7336
3. ¶F-7363; ¶F-7386
4. ¶F-7408
5. ¶F-7441

6. ¶F-7505 *et seq.*
7. ¶F-7603
8. ¶F-7510 *et seq.*
9. ¶F-7360 *et seq.*; ¶F-7405

The losses absorb the Code Sec. 382 limitation on a dollar-for-dollar basis, but the credits must be converted to a "deduction equivalent" for this purpose. (Reg §   1.383-1(e)(2))[10]

¶ 3558   Corporate Liquidations.

Under Code Sec. 336(a), a liquidating corporation recognizes taxable gain or loss on distributions of property as if the property had been sold to the distributee for its fair market value (FMV). If the distributed property is subject to a liability, or if any shareholder assumes a liability of the liquidating corporation in connection with the distribution, the property's FMV is treated as not less than the amount of the liability. (Code Sec. 336(b))[11] The liquidating corporation's shareholders generally recognize capital gain or loss on the receipt of the distributions (¶3559).

Exceptions apply for gain or loss on liquidating distributions made (i) by an 80%-owned subsidiary to its parent (¶3560), and (ii) in connection with tax-free reorganizations (¶3541). (Code Sec. 336(c))[12]

For the taxation of asset transfers to an exempt entity or a change to exempt entity status, see ¶3562. For the deductibility of costs of corporate dissolution and liquidation, see ¶3563.

¶ 3559   Shareholder's tax on corporate liquidating distributions.

Under Code Sec. 331(a), amounts received by a shareholder in a distribution in complete liquidation of a corporation are treated as payment in exchange for the stock (i.e., capital gain or loss).[13] Gain or loss is the total amount distributed minus the shareholder's basis in the stock. (Reg § 1.331-1(b)) The amount of the distribution is the sum of the cash plus the fair market value of any other property (reduced by any liability assumed) received by the shareholder in exchange for the stock. (Code Sec. 1001(b))[14]

A shareholder who receives a series of distributions in complete liquidation of a corporation reports gain only after the cost or other basis of all of the stock has been recovered.[15]

For basis of property received in the distribution, see ¶2484.

¶ 3560   Taxation of parent corporation on liquidation of 80% subsidiaries.

When a parent corporation completely liquidates its 80%-owned subsidiary, the *parent* (as shareholder) doesn't recognize gain or loss on the liquidating distributions (Code Sec. 332(a)), whether *cash* or other property is distributed, if: (i) the parent owns at least 80% of the subsidiary stock by vote and value on the date the plan of liquidation is adopted and until the final liquidating distribution is received (Code Sec. 332(b)(1)); (ii) the distributions are made under a plan of *complete* liquidation, and in complete redemption of all of the subsidiary's stock (Code Sec. 332(b)(2), Code Sec. 332(b)(3)); and (iii) the distributions are made within one tax year of the subsidiary, or within three years from the close of the tax year during which the first of the series of distributions under the plan of liquidation is made. (Code Sec. 332(b); Reg § 1.332-4(a))[16] However, any gain or loss realized by the parent on the satisfaction of the subsidiary's debt to the parent is recognized to the parent at the time of the liquidation.(Reg § 1.332-7)[17]

If the 80% subsidiary liquidation qualifies for nonrecognition treatment, the parent takes a carryover basis in the distributed assets. (Code Sec. 334(b)(1))[18]

---

10. ¶F-7360 *et seq.*; ¶F-7423 *et seq.*
11. ¶F-14400 *et seq.*
12. ¶F-4102, ¶F-14400 *et seq.*
13. ¶F-13101
14. ¶F-13105

15. ¶F-13107 *et seq.*
16. ¶F-13200 *et seq.*
17. ¶F-13202
18. ¶F-13208 *et seq.*

Where a distribution from a regulated investment company (RIC) or a real estate investment trust (REIT) qualifies as a distribution in complete liquidation of the RIC or REIT under Code Sec. 332(b), the corporation receiving the distribution is required to include in income as a dividend from the RIC or REIT an amount equal to the dividends-paid deduction allowable to the RIC or REIT by reason of the distribution. (Code Sec. 332(c))[19]

Minority shareholders of a subsidiary must generally recognize gain or loss under the regular liquidation rules (¶3559). (Reg § 1.332-5)[20]

¶ 3561 How 80% subsidiary corp. is taxed on liquidating distribution.

Under Code Sec. 336(d)(3) and Code Sec. 337(a), a sub doesn't recognize any gain or loss on liquidating distributions to its 80% distributee-parent, but it does recognize gain (not loss) on distributions to minority shareholders.[21]

However, if property of a C corporation becomes the property of a regulated investment company (RIC) or real estate investment trust (REIT) by the qualification of that C corporation as a RIC or REIT or by the transfer of assets of that C corporation to a RIC or REIT, then the RIC or REIT will be subject to tax on the net built-in gain on the sale of that property within the five-year recognition period provided for S corporations under Code Sec. 1374 (¶3361). (Reg § 1.337(d)-7(b)) This rule doesn't apply if the C corporation makes a "deemed sale election" to recognize gain and loss as if it sold the converted property to an unrelated party at its fair market value. (Reg § 1.337(d)-7(c)(1)) Regs provide the deemed sale election is treated as made on certain transactions that occur within 10 years of a Code Sec. 355 distribution (¶3546). (Reg § 1.337(d)-7(c)(6))

The regs contain exceptions to the above rules for the following:

. . . Gain otherwise recognized. (Reg § 1.337(d)-7(d)(1))

. . . Reelection of RIC or REIT status. (Reg § 1.337(d)-7(d)(2))

. . . Like-kind exchanges and involuntary conversions. (Reg § 1.337(d)-7(d)(3))[22]

¶ 3562 Taxation of corporation on asset transfers to exempt entity or change to exempt entity status.

With some exceptions, a corporation recognizes gain or loss on the transfer of its assets to a tax-exempt entity and on a change of its status to tax-exempt. (Reg § 1.337(d)-4)[23]

¶ 3563 Deductibility of costs of corporate dissolution and liquidation.

Filing fees, legal and accounting fees, and other expenditures, including payments for tax advice, incurred in connection with the complete liquidation and dissolution of a corporation are generally deductible in full by the dissolved corporation.[24]

¶ 3564 Code Sec. 338 Election to Treat a Stock Purchase as an Asset Purchase; Form 8023.

A corporate acquirer that makes a qualified stock purchase (¶3565) of the stock of another corporation (target) may be able to get a stepped-up basis for the target's assets by making a Code Sec. 338 election to treat the stock purchase as an asset purchase.

If a Code Sec. 338 election is made, the target is treated (for tax purposes only) as two

---

19. ¶F-13206
20. ¶F-13201
21. ¶F-14402

22. ¶E-6850 *et seq.*
23. ¶F-14609 *et seq.*
24. ¶L-5500 *et seq.*

corporations: an old target and a new target. The old target is treated as if it sold its assets as of the close of the acquisition date for their fair market value (FMV) in a single transaction (Code Sec. 338(a)),[25] and the new target is treated as though it had purchased all of the assets of the old target as of the beginning of the day after the acquisition date (Code Sec. 338(a)(2)) for an amount equal to the sum of: the grossed-up basis of the acquiring corporation's recently purchased stock, the basis of the acquiring corporation's nonrecently purchased stock, the target's liabilities, and other relevant items. This sum (as adjusted) is the target's "adjusted grossed-up basis" for the assets. (Code Sec. 338(b)(1), Code Sec. 338(b)(2); Reg § 1.338-4(a), Reg § 1.338-5(b)(1))[26]

The acquirer may step up its basis in the target's assets by making a "gain recognition election" with respect to its nonrecently purchased stock. (Code Sec. 338(b)(3); Reg § 1.338-5(d)(3))[27] Regs specify how basis is allocated among the target's assets. (Code Sec. 338(b)(5); Reg § 1.338-6)[28]

RIA *observation:* Because a Code Sec. 338 election requires the target to recognize gain from the "sale" of its assets and the seller to recognize gain on the sale of the stock, it can best be used where the target has losses to offset gains, owns predominantly depreciated property, or will benefit from stepped-up basis through deductions for depreciation or amortization.

The acquirer must make the Code Sec. 338 election on Form 8023 on or before the 15th day of the 9th month beginning after the month of the acquisition. (Code Sec. 338(g)(1))[29] Once made, the election is irrevocable. (Code Sec. 338(g)(3))[30]

For the consistency requirement, see ¶3566. For an election where target is a member of a consolidated group, see ¶3567. For the Code Sec. 338(h)(10) and Code Sec. 336(e) elections to treat stock sales as asset transfers, see ¶3567.

¶ 3565   "Qualified stock purchase" (QSP) requirement—Code Sec. 338 election.

Under Code Sec. 338(d)(3), the Code Sec. 338 election may be made only if the acquiring corporation makes a QSP of the target (Code Sec. 338(a)), i.e., the acquiring corporation purchases, in one or more transactions during a 12-month acquisition period, the target's stock, and the shares so purchased have at least 80% of the target's total combined voting power and at least 80% of the value of all the target's stock.[31]

¶ 3566   Consistency rules for purchases from target or target affiliate—Code Sec. 338 election.

Consistency rules prevent acquiring corporations from receiving a basis step-up in only selected assets where (1) a corporation acquires both target stock and target assets, (2) a Code Sec. 338 election isn't made, and (3) the asset acquisition resulted in a stepped-up basis of target stock (or receipt of a dividend eligible for the 100% dividends received deduction) to the seller. The stock consistency rule applies to all qualified stock purchases of members of an affiliated group during the consistency period (generally, the period beginning one year before the 12-month acquisition period and ending one year after the acquisition date). The asset consistency rule applies where the purchasing corporation acquires assets of the target or a target affiliate at any time during the consistency period, unless the acquisition is pursuant to a sale in the ordinary course of the seller's business or if certain other conditions apply. (Code Sec. 338(e), Code Sec. 338(f); Code

---

25. ¶F-8201, F-8202
26. ¶F-8500 *et seq.*
27. ¶F-8511
28. ¶F-8600 *et seq.*

29. ¶F-8700 *et seq.*
30. ¶F-8706
31. ¶F-8100 *et seq.*

Sec. 338(h)(4)(A)), (Reg § 1.338-8)[32]

¶ 3567 Code Sec. 338(h)(10) and Code Sec. 336(e) elections to treat stock acquisitions as asset transfers.

> **✐*observation:*** Although Code Sec. 338(h)(10) elections and Code Sec. 336(e) elections both treat stock acquisitions as asset acquisitions resulting in a single level of tax, the requirements of the elections differ. A transaction can be structured to qualify for either election, but not both.

Under Code Sec. 338(h)(10), for a qualified stock purchase (¶3565) of the stock of a member of a selling consolidated group, or stock sold by a selling affiliate or S corporation shareholders, the acquiring corporation and the sellers can jointly elect to have the sellers recognize (and report) gain or loss as though the target sold all of its assets in a single taxable transaction. (Code Sec. 338(h)(10); Reg § 1.338(h)(10)-1(c))[33]

A Code Sec. 338(h)(10) election results in the following tax consequences:

. . . No gain or loss will be recognized by the sellers on the actual sale of target stock in a qualified stock purchase.

. . . The target is treated as if, at the close of the acquisition date but after the deemed sale, it had distributed all of its assets in complete liquidation under Code Sec. 331 (¶3559), or under the 80% subsidiary liquidation rules (¶3560).

. . . If the acquirer owns nonrecently purchased target stock, it is deemed to have made a "gain recognition election" with respect to that stock.

. . . The acquirer's adjusted gross-up basis in the target is determined under the rules described at ¶3564, with adjustments. (Reg § 1.338(h)(10)-1(d))[34]

A Code Sec. 336(e) election provides for essentially similar asset sale treatment in the case of qualified stock dispositions by selling corporations or S corporation shareholders. (Reg § 1.336-1, Reg § 1.336-2)[35]

¶ 3568 Transfers to Foreign Corporations—Code Sec. 367 Transfers. ■■■■■■■■

Under Code Sec. 367(a)(1) and Code Sec. 367(c), transfers of property to foreign corporations (outbound transfers) that would otherwise be tax-free under the transfer to controlled corporation (¶3500), reorganization (¶3527), or liquidation (¶3558) rules are treated as transfers to non-corporate transferees in determining the extent that gain is recognized on the transfer, unless one of the following exceptions applies:[36]

. . . *Certain transfers of foreign corporation stock or securities.* The transfer of foreign corporation stock or securities by a U.S. person to another foreign corporation isn't taxable under Code Sec. 367(a) if (i) the U.S. person owns less than 5% of the vote and value of the transferee stock immediately after the transfer, or (ii) the U.S. person enters into a gain recognition agreement ("GRA," see below) with respect to the transferred stock or securities. (Code Sec. 367(a)(2); Reg § 1.367(a)-3(b)(1))[37] The transfer of foreign corporation stock as part of a Type E recapitalization qualifies for nonrecognition. (Reg § 1.367(a)-3(a)(2)(i))[38]

. . . *Certain transfers of U.S. corporation stock or securities.* The transfer of U.S. stock or

---

32. ¶F-8900 *et seq.*
33. ¶F-8800 *et seq.*
34. ¶F-8800 *et seq.*
35. ¶F-14450 *et seq.*

36. ¶F-6000 *et seq.*
37. ¶F-6202 *et seq.*
38. ¶F-6201

securities to a foreign corporation isn't taxable under Code Sec. 367(a) if (i) U.S. transferors receive 50% or less of the vote and value of the transferee stock in the transaction; (ii) U.S. persons who are officers or directors of the U.S. target or 5% transferee shareholders don't own more than 50% of the transferee stock; (iii) either the U.S. transferor isn't a 5% transferee shareholder, or, if the U.S. transferor is a 5% transferee shareholder, it enters into a GRA; and (iv) the transferee has been actively engaged in business for at least three years. (Reg § 1.367(a)-3(c))[39]

The above exceptions for transfers of foreign stock don't generally apply to Code Sec. 361(a) and Code Sec. 361(b) outbound transfers incident to a reorganization. (Code Sec. 367(a)(4))[40] However, regs contain an elective exception under which, if five or fewer domestic corporations are in Code Sec. 368(c) control (¶3539) of the transferor corporation and subject to basis adjustment regs, the exceptions may apply to *asset* reorganizations under Code Sec. 361(a) or Code Sec. 361(b). (Reg § 1.367(a)-7)[41]

Transfers of foreign loss branches. If a domestic corporation transfers substantially all of the assets of a foreign branch (within the meaning of Code Sec. 367(a)(3)(C) in effect before Dec. 22, 2017) to a specified 10% owned foreign corporation with respect to which it is a U.S. shareholder (¶3314) after the transfer, the domestic corporation includes in gross income for the tax year which includes the transfer an amount equal to the transferred loss amount (as defined in Code Sec. 91(b)) for the transfer. (Code Sec. 91(a)) The transferred loss amount is reduced (but not below zero) by the amount of gain recognized by the taxpayer on account of the transfer (other than amounts recognized due to the recapture of overall foreign loss (¶2365)). (Code Sec. 91(c)) Under a "transition rule," the amount of gain taken into account under Code Sec. 91(c) must be reduced by the amount of gain which would be recognized under Code Sec. 367(a)(3)(C) (as in effect before Dec. 22, 2017) with respect to losses incurred before Jan. 1, 2018.[42]

Qualification under some exceptions may require a GRA under which the U.S. transferor generally agrees to include in income any gain not recognized on the original transfer of stock or securities to the foreign corporation if the foreign transferee disposes of the stock or securities within five years. Some nonrecognition transactions, however, aren't triggering events when certain requirements are satisfied. (Reg § 1.367(a)-8) The amount of gain recognized under a GRA when a disposition or other event requires recognition under more than one GRA is determined under an ordering rule. (Reg § 1.367(a)-8(c)(1)(ii))[43]

Outbound distributions of subsidiary stock under Code Sec. 355 are generally treated as exchanges and result in recognition of gain (but not loss) unless the distribution is made to a qualified U.S. person, i.e., a domestic corporation or a U.S. citizen or resident. (Code Sec. 367(e)(1); Reg § 1.367(e)-1)[44] Outbound parent-subsidiary liquidation distributions generally result in recognition of both gain and loss to the liquidating subsidiary. (Code Sec. 367(e)(2); Reg § 1.367(e)-2)[45]

The taxable transfer treatment under Code Sec. 367(a) doesn't apply for Code Sec. 351 or Code Sec. 361 transfers of intangibles to foreign corporations. Instead, the transferor is treated as receiving deemed payments over the life of the intangible and a lump sum payment if there is a disposition of the property. For this purpose, intangible property includes goodwill (foreign and domestic), going concern value, and workforce in place (including its composition and terms and conditions (contractual or otherwise) of its employment). (Code Sec. 367(d))[46]

39. ¶F-6209 *et seq.*
40. ¶F-6201
41. ¶F-6239 *et seq.*
42. ¶F-6128.1

43. ¶F-6300 *et seq.*
44. ¶F-6800 *et seq.*
45. ¶F-6900 *et seq.*
46. ¶F-6005; ¶F-6500 *et seq.*

Chapter 17 Partnerships

¶ 3700   **Partnership defined—Form 8832.** ▬▬▬▬▬▬▬

Under Code Sec. 761(a), a "partnership" includes a syndicate, group, pool, joint venture or other unincorporated organization through, or by means of which, any business, financial operation or venture is carried on if it isn't, within the meaning of the Code, a corporation, trust or estate.[1] For tax purposes, a partnership is a business entity with two or more members that has elected, or defaulted to (below), partnership classification under the "check-the-box" entity classification regs. (Reg § 301.7701-2(c))[2]

Under default provisions, unless a domestic eligible entity elects otherwise, it's a partnership if it has two or more members. (Reg § 301.7701-3(b)(1)(i))[3] In general, an eligible entity that wishes to elect a classification other than its default classification, or that wishes to change its classification, does so by filing Form 8832. (Reg § 301.7701-3(c)(1)(i))[4] A partnership that changes to an association is deemed to contribute all of its assets and liabilities to the association in exchange for stock in it. Then, the partnership is deemed to liquidate by distributing the stock to its partners. (Reg § 301.7701-3(g)(1)(i))[5] An eligible entity classified as a partnership becomes disregarded as an entity separate from its owner when the entity's membership is reduced to one member. (Reg § 301.7701-3(f)(2))[6]

For tax years of a partnership, see ¶2809.

For partnership tax returns (including Schedules K-1, K-2, and K-3 (Form 1065)), see ¶4731.

¶ 3701   **Limited liability companies (LLCs); "check the box" rules; election (Form 8832) to be taxed as partnership or corporation; disregarded entity.**

LLCs, which are a creation of state law, are owned (and in some cases managed) by members who aren't personally liable for the LLC's debts or obligations.[7]

Under the "check-the-box" entity classification rules (¶3700), if an LLC isn't mandatorily classified as a corporation, it's an "eligible entity" that may elect (on Form 8832) to be classified for tax purposes either as a partnership or as a corporation (Reg § 301.7701-2(c)), except that a single-member LLC that doesn't elect to be a corporation is treated as a disregarded entity and its activities are treated in the same manner as a sole proprietorship, branch or division. (Reg § 301.7701-2(a), Reg § 301.7701-2(c)(2)(i))[8]

¶ 3702   **Rules for family partnerships.**

If capital isn't a material income-producing factor, a family member is recognized as a partner only if he or she contributes substantial services.[9]

If capital is a material income-producing factor in the enterprise, a valid family partnership may be created by gift of a capital interest. (Code Sec. 761(b))[10]

The donee-partner's distributive share of partnership income is included in the donee-partner's gross income, provided that: (1) it must be determined after allowance of reasonable compensation for services rendered to the partnership by the donor, and (2) the donee's share attributable to donated capital must not be proportionately greater than the

---

1. ¶B-1000 *et seq.*
2. ¶D-1151
3. ¶D-1152
4. ¶D-1159
5. ¶D-1167
6. ¶D-1168
7. ¶D-1150 *et seq.*
8. ¶D-1165
9. ¶B-3422
10. ¶B-3402

References beginning with a single letter are to paragraphs in Federal Tax Coordinator 2d and RIA's Analysis of Federal Taxes: Income.

donor's share attributable to his or her capital. (Code Sec. 704(e)(1))[11]

A capital interest purchased from a partner by the partner's spouse, ancestor, lineal descendant, or any trust for the primary benefit of such persons is considered to be a gift of the partnership interest by the seller to the buyer. (Code Sec. 704(e)(2))[12]

A donee or purchaser of a capital interest in a family partnership isn't recognized as a partner unless the transfer to him or her is bona fide. (Reg § 1.704-1(e)(1)(iii))[13]

A minor child generally won't be recognized as a partner unless either: (1) the child is shown to be competent (despite legal disability under state law) to manage his or her own property, or (2) control of the child's interest is exercised by a fiduciary for the child's sole benefit, subject to any required judicial supervision. (Reg § 1.704-1(e)(2)(viii))[14]

¶ 3703 Election by certain unincorporated organizations to be excluded from partnership rules.

Certain unincorporated organizations can elect under Code Sec. 761 to be excluded from the partnership rules, i.e., exempt from Subchapter K of the Code (or only some of those provisions under a partial exclusion election). The election is available only if the income of each separate member of the partnership can be adequately determined without computation of partnership taxable income. (Code Sec. 761(a); Reg § 1.761-2(a)(1))[15] The election is available for:

... "Investing partnerships" whose members own property as co-owners, reserve the right separately to dispose of their share of property, and aren't engaged in the active conduct of a business; (Reg § 1.761-2(a)(2))[16]

... "Operating agreement groups" under which a number of co-owners engage in the joint production, extraction or use of property, but not for the purpose of selling services or property produced or extracted; and (Reg § 1.761-2(a)(3))[17]

... Syndications formed for a short period by dealers in securities to underwrite, sell or distribute an issue of securities. (Code Sec. 761(a)(3))[18]

¶ 3704 Partnerships vs. other forms of doing business.

As provided by Code Sec. 701, partnerships are "pass-through entities" — that is, their income is subject to tax only once, at the partner level. They share this characteristic with S corporations, but not C corporations (whose income is taxed twice, once at the corporate and again at the shareholder levels). Partnerships offer several advantages over S corporations, including: no limitations on the identity or number of partners; greater flexibility in allocating the enterprise's profits, losses and credits (by means of special allocations, see ¶3717 *et seq.*); and a partner's basis in the partner's partnership interest includes the partner's share of partnership liabilities (see ¶3750 *et seq.*).

¶ 3705 Organization and syndication fees—partnership taxation.

Under Code Sec. 709(a), no deduction is allowed to a partnership or to any partner for any amounts paid or incurred to organize a partnership or to promote the sale of, or to sell, an interest in that partnership, except as described below.[19]

If it so elects, a partnership may deduct, for the tax year in which it begins business, an

---

11. ¶B-3423
12. ¶B-3403
13. ¶B-3408
14. ¶B-3416
15. ¶B-1200 *et seq.*

16. ¶B-1204
17. ¶B-1205
18. ¶B-1210
19. ¶B-1300 *et seq.*

amount equal to the lesser of: (1) the amount of organizational expenses with respect to the partnership, or (2) $5,000, reduced (but not below zero) by the amount by which such organizational expenses exceed $50,000. The remainder of such organizational expenses may be deducted ratably over the 180-month period beginning with the month the partnership begins business. If the partnership liquidates before the end of the 180-month period, any unamortized organization expenses may be deducted then. (Code Sec. 709(b)(2))

Syndication expenses aren't amortizable and must be capitalized. They are expenses connected with the marketing of interests in the partnership. (Reg § 1.709-2(b)) Syndication expenses can't be deducted as a loss when the partnership is liquidated (Reg § 1.709-1(b)(3)) or the syndication effort is abandoned.[20]

For an election to deduct start-up costs, see ¶1500.

¶ 3706 Partnership anti-abuse rules.

Under Reg § 1.701-2, if a partnership is formed or used in connection with a transaction with a principal purpose of substantially reducing the present value of the partners' total tax liability in a manner that is inconsistent with the intent of subchapter K, IRS may recast the transaction as appropriate to achieve a tax result that is consistent with the intent of subchapter K.[21] These anti-abuse rules apply only with respect to federal income taxes. (Reg § 1.701-2(h))[22]

IRS also may treat a partnership as an aggregate of its partners, in whole or in part (except as described below), as appropriate, in order to carry out the purpose of any provision of the Code or regs. (Reg § 1.701-2(e)(1)) But IRS may not treat a partnership as an aggregate to the extent that:

(1) a Code or reg provision prescribes the treatment of a partnership (in whole or in part) as an entity; and

(2) that treatment and the ultimate tax results, taking into account all the relevant facts and circumstances, are clearly contemplated by that provision. (Reg § 1.701-2(e)(2))[23]

¶ 3707 Treatment of Contributions to a Partnership. ▇▇▇▇▇▇▇

In general, no gain or loss is recognized when a partner makes contributions to a partnership's capital, whether on formation of the partnership or later. (Code Sec. 721; Reg § 1.721-1)

However, this rule doesn't apply where: a partner acts in his or her individual capacity (vs. as a partner) in a transaction with the partnership (¶3721); a partner contributes property to a partnership and the partnership assumes a liability of the partner, with the resulting decrease in the partner's liabilities being treated as a distribution of money to the contributing partner (¶3735); disguised sales;[24] or in the situations listed at ¶3708 *et seq.*[25] Also, IRS has regulatory authority (1) to provide for gain recognition in cases where the gain would otherwise be transferred to foreign partners (Code Sec. 721(c)) and (2) to treat intangibles transferred to a foreign partnership as sold. (Code Sec. 721(d)) Tax-free contributions to a partnership will not trigger depreciation recapture. (Code Sec. 1245(b)(3), Code Sec. 1245(b)(6), Code Sec. 1250(d)(3)),[26] Similarly, an investment credit isn't recaptured as long as the transfer is a mere change in the form of conducting the business of the contributing partner. (Reg § 1.47-3(f)(6), Ex (5))[27]

For gain or loss on the distribution of contributed built-in gain or loss property, see

---

20. ¶B-1305
21. ¶B-1251
22. ¶B-1250 *et seq.*
23. ¶B-1255

24. ¶B-2100 *et seq.*
25. ¶B-1401
26. ¶s I-10311, I-10503
27. ¶L-17418

¶3743.

¶ 3708   Partnership investment companies—contributions to partnership.

Under Code Sec. 721(b), gain, but not loss, is recognized where a transfer of appreciated stocks, securities or other property is made to a partnership that would be treated as an investment company under Code Sec. 351 were the partnership a corporation. The partnership is treated as an investment company if, after the exchange, over 80% of the value of its assets (excluding cash and nonconvertible debt) is held for investment and consists of readily marketable stocks or securities (or interests in real estate investment trusts or regulated investment companies). This exception doesn't apply where the transaction doesn't result in a diversification[28] of the transferor's investment.[29]

¶ 3709   Contribution of services to partnership for capital interest or profits interest.

Where a taxpayer receives a capital interest in a partnership in exchange for services, that interest is taxable compensation income to the taxpayer under Reg § 1.721-1. When the income must be recognized depends on the facts and circumstances, including whether there are any restrictions on the taxpayer's right to withdraw from the partnership or otherwise dispose of the partnership interest. (Reg § 1.721-1(b)(1))[30]

Where a taxpayer receives a profits interest in a partnership (even if substantially unvested) in exchange for services, IRS won't treat the transaction as giving rise to compensation income, unless: (1) the profits interest relates to a substantially certain and predictable stream of income from partnership assets; (2) the partner disposes of the profits interest within two years; or (3) the profits interest is a limited partnership interest in a publicly traded partnership. Cases hold that no income is includible where the profit interest has only speculative value.[31]

¶ 3710   Partnership's basis and holding period in property contributed to it.

Under Code Sec. 723, property received by a partnership from a contributing partner takes the same basis in the partnership's hands as it had in the contributing partner's hands at the time of the contribution (increased by any gain recognized if the partnership is an "investment company partnership," see ¶3708). (Code Sec. 723; Reg § 1.723-1)[32]

A partnership tacks the contributing partner's holding period. (Code Sec. 1223(2); Reg § 1.723-1)[33]

¶ 3711   Partnership Income and Deductions.

Under Code Sec. 701, a partnership is essentially a conduit that passes through to each partner his or her share of income and deductions generated by the partnership.

Thus, the partners, not the partnership, are taxed on the partnership's income. (Code Sec. 701) The partnership only files an information return (Form 1065, see ¶4731) showing each partner's distributive share of the partnership income, deductions, gains, losses, etc. Each partner includes his or her share of these items on his or her own return. (Code Sec. 702)[34]

Partnership taxable income is computed the same as an individual's, except that certain

28. ¶F-1302
29. ¶B-1416
30. ¶B-1408 *et seq.*
31. ¶B-1410
32. ¶B-1423
33. ¶B-1424
34. ¶B-1900 *et seq.*

items are separately stated (see ¶3712) and the following deductions aren't allowed: standard deduction (Code Sec. 63(c)(6)(D)); personal exemptions; charitable contributions; nonbusiness expenses, medical expenses, alimony, retirement savings under Code Sec. 219, and taxes and interest paid to cooperative housing corporations; capital loss carryovers; net operating loss deduction; taxes paid to a foreign country or U.S. possession that can be taken as a credit or as a deduction (income and similar taxes); and oil and gas well depletion. (Code Sec. 703(a)(2); Reg § 1.703-1(a)(2))[35]

¶ 3712 "Separately stated" items of income and deductions—partnerships.

Under Code Sec. 702, partnerships are required to "state separately" —that is, to compute as separate items—certain classes of income and deductions. These are then directly "passed through" to the partnership's partners, who take them into account for tax purposes by including their distributive share of each of the classes as separate items on their tax returns. (Code Sec. 702(a))

Key items that must be separately stated include: charitable contributions; certain dividends; foreign and U.S. possession taxes eligible for the foreign tax credit; income, gains and losses from the sale or exchange of unrealized receivables and substantially appreciated inventory; items that are specially allocated under the partnership agreement (¶3717 *et seq.*); long- and short-term capital gains and losses; nonbusiness production of income expenses; recoveries of tax benefit items; and Code Sec. 1231 gains and losses.

Partnerships must also separately state—and partners must separately take into account their distributive share of—any partnership item, if separately stating that item would result in a tax liability for any partner different from that partner's tax liability if the item weren't separately stated. (Reg § 1.702-1(a)(8))[36]

For a discussion of the separately stated items relating to the Code Sec. 199A qualified business income deduction for tax years beginning after 2017 and before 2026, see ¶1593 *et seq.*

For a discussion of the Code Sec. 163(j) business interest deduction limitation as it applies to partnerships, see ¶1710.

¶ 3713 Items not required to be separately stated and character of passed through items—partnership income and deductions.

After determining which of its items of income, gains, losses, deductions and credits must be separately stated under Code Sec. 702, a partnership computes its taxable income or loss based on items that don't have to be separately stated. The partnership's partners, in computing their income tax liabilities, take into account their distributive shares of the partnership's nonseparately stated income or loss, as well as their distributive shares of each separately stated item. (Code Sec. 702(a)(8); Reg § 1.702-1(a)(9))

Each item passed through to the partners and separately stated on their returns has the same character as if realized or incurred directly by the partnership. (Code Sec. 702(b); Reg § 1.702-1(b))[37] Under an exception to this rule certain allocations of long-term capital gain are treated as short-term capital gain in the case of holders of partnerships interests that have rights to receive "carried interest" distributions, see ¶2654.

---

35. ¶B-1901
36. ¶B-1903

37. ¶B-1904 *et seq.*

¶ 3714   Consistent treatment on partner's and partnership's return—Form 8082—partnership income and deductions.

Under Code Sec. 6222(a), a partner must, on his or her own return, treat a partnership item in a manner that's consistent with the treatment of that item on the partnership's return. A partner that treats a partnership item differently must notify IRS of the inconsistency on Form 8082. (Code Sec. 6222(b))[38]

¶ 3715   When partnership income is reported by the partners.

Under Code Sec. 706(a), each partner reports his or her distributive share of the partnership income, deductions and other items (including guaranteed payments, see ¶1593) for a partnership tax year on his or her individual return for his or her tax year with or within which ends the partnership tax year (discussed at ¶2809). (Code Sec. 706(a); Reg § 1.706-1(a))[39]

If two partnership years end within the partner's year, the income for both years is included in that year even though partnership income for a period of more than twelve months is then included in the partner's income.[40]

¶ 3716   Elections—partnership income and deductions.

Elections affecting partnership taxable income must be made by the partnership—except for certain elections involving discharge of indebtedness, foreign tax credits, mining exploration costs, and the election by nonresident alien individuals and foreign corporations regarding income from U.S. real property, which are made at the partner level. (Reg § 1.703-1(b))[41]

¶ 3717   Partnership Allocations. ■

Under Code Sec. 704(a), a partnership's allocations (the partners' distributive shares) of partnership income, gains, losses, deductions and credits are normally determined by the partnership agreement.

The partnership agreement's allocations of partnership items will be respected for tax purposes if:

. . . they have substantial economic effect, see ¶3718; or

. . . they are in accord with the partners' interests in the partnership; or

. . . they are treated as being in accord with the partners' interests in the partnership. (Code Sec. 704(b); Reg § 1.704-1(b)(1))[42]

If, however, the partnership agreement fails to make such allocations, they must be determined in accord with the partners' interests in the partnership. (Code Sec. 704(b)(1))

Retroactive allocations—that is, allocations that give particular partners shares of partnership items of income, expense, etc., that were paid or accrued before these partners joined the partnership—aren't permitted. (Code Sec. 706(d)(1))[43]

Special allocation rules apply for certain items that cannot have economic effect, such as: certain tax preferences relating to pre-MACRS depreciation;[44] income, gains, losses, etc., with respect to property whose book value differs from its adjusted basis;[45] tax credits and

---

38. ¶B-1801
39. ¶B-1701
40. ¶B-1701
41. ¶B-1907

42. ¶B-2401
43. ¶B-3201
44. ¶B-2901
45. ¶B-2902

credit recapture amounts;[46] creditable foreign taxes and amounts relating to foreign tax credits;[47] "excess percentage depletion;" [48] the basis of partnership oil and gas properties;[49] recapture income under Code Sec. 1245 and Code Sec. 1250;[50] and allocations attributable to the partnership's nonrecourse debt.[1] Special safe harbors apply to allocations of the Code Sec. 45 wind energy production credit[2], the Code Sec. 45Q carbon capture tax credit[3], and the Code Sec. 47 rehabilitation credit.[4] For how a partnership can treat tax-exempt income resulting from the forgiveness of Payroll Protection Program (PPP) loans (including allocation rules), see ¶1380.

Subject to exceptions (Reg § 1.706-4(b)), partnership allocations must take into account the varying interests of the partners during the year. (Code Sec. 706(d)(1)) In general, if there is a change in any partner's interest in the partnership during the year, the partnership determines each partner's distributive share of partnership income, gain, loss, deduction or credit for such tax year by using the "interim closing method" or the "proration method," under which a partnership allocates its items among the partners in accordance with either their partnership interests during each segment of the tax year or their pro rata shares of the items for the entire tax year, respectively. (Reg § 1.706-4(d)) A partnership may use different methods for different ownership changes in the same year provided that the overall combination of methods is reasonable.[5] Certain "extraordinary items" are allocated using special rules, as are "allocable cash basis items" under Code Sec. 706(d)(2)(B).[6]

¶ 3718 Determining whether a partnership allocation has substantial economic effect.

Under Reg § 1.704-1(b)(2), an allocation of partnership income, gain, loss, deduction or credit among partners has substantial economic effect if it passes a two-part test applied as of the end of the partnership year to which the allocation relates.

First, the allocation must have economic effect. (Reg § 1.704-1(b)(2)(i)) This means that it must be consistent with the underlying economic arrangement of the partners. An allocation is treated as having economic effect only if, through the full term of the partnership, the partnership agreement states:

(1) the partners' capital accounts are to be determined and maintained according to the capital account maintenance rules set forth in the regs (see ¶3719);

(2) when the partnership liquidates, or a partner's interest is liquidated, liquidating distributions are to be made according to the partners' positive capital account balances; and

(3) a partner with a deficit balance in his or her capital account after the liquidation of his or her partnership interest is unconditionally obligated to restore the amount of the deficit to the partnership. (Reg § 1.704-1(b)(2)(ii))[7]

Second, the economic effect of the allocation must be substantial. (Reg § 1.704-1(b)(2)(i)) The economic effect of an allocation is substantial if there's a reasonable possibility that it will affect substantially the dollar amounts to be received by the partners from the partnership, independent of the tax consequences. (Reg § 1.704-1(b)(2)(iii))[8]

46. ¶B-2903
47. ¶B-2903.1 *et seq.*
48. ¶B-2904
49. ¶B-2905
50. ¶B-2906 *et seq.*
1. ¶B-3001
2. ¶B-2903A

3. ¶B-2903A.1
4. ¶B-2903B
5. ¶B-3201
6. ¶B-3204 *et seq.*
7. ¶B-2503 *et seq.*
8. ¶B-2700 *et seq.*

⊘observation: Generally, the economic effect test tests whether partnership allocations of income and gain correspond to real distributions of money and property, and that allocations of deductions, losses and credits correspond to the partners' actual liabilities for partnership expenses and losses. The substantiality test seeks to ensure that economic effects of an allocation don't arise principally from the allocated item's tax character—e.g., from an income item's tax-exempt or foreign-sourced character—or that a loss is from the sale of partnership property used in its business.

Determining whether the economic effect of an allocation is substantial where partners are look-through entities (e.g., partnerships, S corps, trusts or estates) or members of a consolidated group is done by taking into account the tax consequences that result from the interaction of an allocation with the tax attributes of any person that is an owner (or for a trust or estate, the beneficiary) of an interest in the partner. (Reg § 1.704-1(b)(2)(iii)(d)(1))[9]

¶ 3719 Partner capital account maintenance rules—partnership allocations.

For partner capital accounts to be determined and maintained properly under Reg § 1.704-1(b)(2)(iv) for the economic effect rules (see ¶3718), each partner's account must be increased by cash contributed by the partner (including cash treated as contributed when the partner assumes partnership liabilities), and by the fair market value of property contributed by the partner (net of liabilities secured by the property). The account must also be increased by the partner's allocable share of partnership income and gain, including tax-exempt income, book income (not tax income) for property whose book value differs from basis, and unrealized income with respect to accounts receivable and certain other accrued but unpaid items.

Each account must be decreased by cash distributed to the partner (including cash treated as distributed when the partnership assumes partner liabilities), and by the fair market value of property distributed to the partner (net of liabilities secured by the property). The account must also be decreased by the partner's allocable share of partnership expenditures that are neither deductible nor capitalizable, and partnership loss and deduction, including book (not tax) loss for property whose book value differs from basis, and unrealized deductions for accounts payable and certain other accrued but unpaid items. (Reg § 1.704-1(b)(2)(iv))

Capital account adjustments may also be required when partnership property is revalued or distributed, and on the transfer of a partnership interest. For example, partnership property may be revalued (and capital accounts adjusted) if property is contributed by, or distributed to, a partner in exchange for a partnership interest. Revaluation is also allowed where a partnership interest is granted as payment for services or when a noncompensatory option to acquire a partnership interest is issued. (Reg § 1.704-1(b)(2)(iv))

An adjustment may also be required if an optional basis adjustment election is in effect (see ¶3764) and property is distributed or an interest is transferred. (Reg § 1.704-1(b)(2)(iv))[10]

¶ 3720 Partner's Dealings with Partnership. ▬▬▬▬▬▬▬▬▬

Partners may deal with their partnerships in other than their capacity as partners (¶3721). "Guaranteed payments" to partners are generally treated as made to nonpartners (¶3722). Certain sales between partners and their partnerships establish the character of any gain, and require the deferral of loss (¶3723 *et seq.*).

---

9. ¶B-2702   10. ¶B-2600 *et seq.*

¶ 3721 "Separate entity" transactions between partner and partnership.

If a partner provides services for or transfers property to his or her partnership, he or she may be treated as dealing with the partnership either as a member or as an outsider under the rules in Code Sec. 707. If there's a related allocation and distribution of partnership income (direct or indirect), and the transaction as a whole is properly characterized as a sale or exchange between a partnership and an outsider, it will be treated that way for tax purposes. (Code Sec. 707(a)(2)(A), Code Sec. 707(a)(2)(B))[11] Contribution and distribution transactions that occur within two years of one another are generally presumed to be a sale of property unless the facts and circumstances clearly establish otherwise. (Reg § 1.707-3(c)(1))

¶ 3722 Guaranteed payments—partner's dealings with partnership.

Guaranteed payments are payments to a partner for services or capital *without regard to partnership income*, and their tax consequences are determined under the principles of Code Sec. 707(c).[12] Guaranteed payments for a partner's services or capital are treated like salary payments to employees or interest payments to creditors, not like partnership distributions. (Code Sec. 707(c); Reg § 1.707-1(c))[13]

For a guaranteed payment to be deductible as a business expense by the partnership, it must qualify as a business expense as if the payment had been made to a person who wasn't a partner. In determining whether a partnership may deduct or must capitalize a guaranteed payment, the regular capital expenditure rules apply. (Code Sec. 707(c))[14]

When a partnership makes a guaranteed payment using property other than cash, it is treated as a sale or exchange of that property by the partnership on which gain is recognized, and not a partnership distribution treated as discussed at ¶3734.[15]

¶ 3723 Losses on sales and exchanges with controlled partnership—partner's dealings with partnership.

Code Sec. 707(b) provides that no deduction is allowed for losses from sales or exchanges between:

. . . a partnership and a person owning, directly or indirectly, over 50% of the capital interest, or profits interest, in the partnership; or

. . . two partnerships in which the same persons own over 50% of the capital or profits interests.

For constructive ownership rules, see ¶3725.

If property on which a loss was disallowed under the above rule is later sold by the transferee at a gain, the gain is taxable only to the extent it exceeds the loss previously disallowed. (Code Sec. 707(b)(1); Reg § 1.707-1(b)(1))[16]

¶ 3724 Gain on sale or exchange with controlled partnership—partner's dealings with partnership.

Under Code Sec. 707(b)(2), the character of the property in the hands of the transferee, immediately after the transfer, determines the character of a *gain to the transferor* on a direct or indirect sale or exchange of property between:

---

11. ¶B-2000 *et seq.*
12. ¶B-2005
13. ¶B-2006 *et seq.*
14. ¶B-2009
15. ¶B-2006
16. ¶B-2016

. . . a partnership and a person owning, directly or indirectly, over 50% of the capital interest, or profits interest, in the partnership; or

. . . two partnerships in which the same persons own, directly or indirectly, more than 50% of the capital interest or profits interest in each. (Code Sec. 707(b)(2); Reg § 1.707-1(b)(2))[17]

For constructive ownership rules, see ¶3725.

Thus, if the property is a noncapital asset in the hands of the transferee, the transferor will have ordinary income on the sale. (Code Sec. 707(b)(2); Reg § 1.707-1(b)(2))[18]

¶ 3725 Constructive ownership of partnership interests.

In determining the percentage of ownership of partnership interests for purposes of ¶3723 and ¶3724, the constructive ownership rules for stock under Code Sec. 267(c) (¶2444) apply (substituting "capital or profits interest" for "stock"), except that a partner isn't considered as owning the interest of his or her partners (unless they are relatives, etc.). (Code Sec. 707(b)(3))[19]

¶ 3726 Limitations on a Partner's Deductible Loss. ■■■■■■■■■

A partner's deduction for partnership losses may not exceed the adjusted basis of his or her interest in the partnership (¶3729 *et seq.*) at the end of the partnership's loss year. (Code Sec. 704(d)) However, partners (although not partnerships) are allowed loss carrybacks and carryovers.

Where a partnership has more than one class of losses (e.g., capital losses, Code Sec. 1231 losses, and operating losses) in the same year and a partner's total share of those losses exceeds the adjusted basis of his or her partnership interest, the limitation is allocated proportionately to each type of loss. (Reg § 1.704-1(d))

Excess losses disallowed to a partner in any year are carried over, and are deductible by him or her at the end of the partnership year in which the adjusted basis of the partner's interest at the end of the year exceeds zero (before reduction by that year's loss). (Reg § 1.704-1(d)(4))[20]

For limits on a partner's loss under the at-risk rules, see ¶1791 *et seq.*, and under the passive activity rules, see ¶1799 *et seq.*

¶ 3727 Basis adjustments made before applying partner's loss limitations.

In determining whether a partner's deductible share of partnership loss exceeds (and is thus limited by) his or her basis in the partnership interest (¶3726), the basis adjustments described at ¶3731 are made first. (Reg § 1.704-1(d)(2))[21]

¶ 3728 Loss carrybacks and carryovers—limits on partner's loss.

A carryover or carryback of net operating losses isn't allowed to a partnership, but a partner may carry back or carry over his or her share of the partnership's net business loss for any year to the extent it can't be used by that partner in the year it's passed through to him or her. (Code Sec. 702)[22]

¶ 3729 Partner's Basis in Partnership Interest. ■■■■■■■■■

A partner's basis for his or her interest in a partnership ("outside basis") depends

---

17. ¶B-2017
18. ¶B-2017
19. ¶B-2018

20. ¶B-3500 *et seq.*
21. ¶B-3501 *et seq.*
22. ¶B-3508

on how it was acquired. It may be the amount of cash contributed to the partnership, the adjusted basis of the property contributed, or the amount paid to purchase it.

For the initial basis of partnership interest, see ¶3730. For adjustments to basis, see ¶3731. For alternative adjusted basis computation, see ¶3732.

¶ 3730   Partner's initial basis in partnership interest.

Under Code Sec. 722, a partner's interest acquired by a tax-free contribution of money or property to the partnership has a basis equal to the amount of money plus the partner's adjusted basis in the property when contributed.[23] If the contributed property is subject to indebtedness or if liabilities of the partner are assumed by the partnership, the basis of the contributing partner's interest is reduced by the portion of the indebtedness assumed by the other partners. (Reg § 1.722-1)[24]

A partner's capital interest acquired for services has a basis equal to the value of the capital interest acquired. (Reg § 1.722-1; Reg § 1.721-1(b))[25]

A partner's interest acquired by purchase or inheritance has a basis determined under the general basis rules (¶2457 *et seq.*). (Code Sec. 742; Reg § 1.742-1)[26]

A partner may have a divided holding period in his or her partnership interest, see ¶2653. (Reg § 1.1223-3)[27]

¶ 3731   Adjustments to basis in partner's interest in partnership.

The basis of a partner's interest in a partnership is increased by: further contributions (but not by his or her own personal note given to the partnership);[28] the cost of additional interests purchased or inherited (¶3730) (Code Sec. 742); any increase in his or her share of partnership liabilities (since the increase is treated as a contribution of money to the partnership, see ¶3750);[29] his or her distributive share of partnership income, including tax-exempt income and any excess of net long-term capital gains over losses (Code Sec. 705(a)(1)); and his or her distributive share of the excess of percentage depletion deductions over the basis of the depletable property. (Code Sec. 705(a)(1))[30]

The basis of a partner's interest is reduced (but not below zero) by: the adjusted basis allocable to any part of his or her interest sold or otherwise transferred;[31] the amount of money and the adjusted basis of partnership property distributed to him or her in nonliquidating distributions (Code Sec. 705(a)(2), Code Sec. 733);[32] any decrease in his or her share of partnership liabilities (since the decrease is treated as a distribution of money by the partnership, see ¶3750); his or her distributive share of partnership losses (including capital losses) *and* nondeductible expenditures not chargeable to capital account (Code Sec. 705(a); Reg § 1.705-1(a)) (for the partner's distributive share of losses in excess of his or her adjusted basis, see ¶3726); and his or her percentage depletion deduction for partnership oil and gas property to the extent the deduction doesn't exceed his or her allocated proportionate share of the property's basis. (Code Sec. 705(a)(3))[33] In determining the amount of the partner's loss, the partner's distributive shares under Code Sec. 702(a) of partnership charitable contributions and taxes paid or accrued to foreign countries or U.S. possessions are taken into account. (Code Sec. 704(d)(3)(A)) However, in the case of a charitable contribution of property with a fair market value that exceeds its adjusted

---

23. ¶B-1502
24. ¶B-1501
25. ¶B-1501
26. ¶B-1501
27. ¶I-8934.1
28. ¶B-1501

29. ¶B-1501 *et seq.*
30. ¶B-1514
31. ¶B-3804
32. ¶B-1501
33. ¶B-1514

basis, the partner's distributive share of the excess is not taken into account. (Code Sec. 704(d)(3)(B))[34]

Regs prevent the acceleration or duplication of losses through a partnership's assumption of obligations that are not treated as resulting in a deemed cash contribution or distribution by or to the partner under the rules discussed at ¶3750 *et seq.* These obligations are called "Reg § 1.752-7 liabilities." Where such a liability is assumed by a partnership from a partner in a property contribution by a partner to a partnership in exchange for a partnership interest (a Code Sec. 721(a) contribution), the liability is treated as having a built-in loss (see ¶3743) equal to the amount of the liability as of the date of the partnership's assumption of the liability. (Reg § 1.752-7; Reg § 1.704-3)[35]

Regs prevent inappropriate increases or decreases in the basis of a corporate partner's interest in a partnership resulting from the partnership's disposition of the corporate partner's stock. (Reg § 1.705-2)[36]

¶ 3732 Alternative adjusted basis computation—partner's basis in partnership interest.

The adjusted basis of a partner's interest in a partnership may be determined under a "short-cut" method by reference to what would be his or her proportionate share of the adjusted basis of the partnership property upon a termination of the partnership (Code Sec. 705(b)) where: (1) it isn't practicable to use the regular rule, or (2) IRS is satisfied the result under the alternative method won't vary substantially from that under the regular rule. (Reg § 1.705-1(b))[37]

¶ 3733 Partnership Distributions.

A partnership generally doesn't recognize gain or loss on a distribution to a partner (¶3734), but the partner often will recognize gain or loss (¶3735).

¶ 3734 Partnership's gain or loss on distribution to partner.

Under Code Sec. 731(b), no gain or loss is recognized to a partnership on a current or liquidating distribution to a partner of money or other property, except where a disproportionate distribution is treated as a sale by the partnership, see ¶3746.[38]

¶ 3735 Partner's gain or loss on receipt of distribution from partnership.

Under Code Sec. 731, gain or loss isn't recognized to a partner on receipt of a current or liquidating distribution from a partnership, except as follows:

. . . Gain is recognized to the extent that *money* (defined to include marketable securities, see ¶3736) distributed exceeds the adjusted basis of the partner's interest in the partnership immediately before the distribution. (Code Sec. 731(a))[39] This is treated as a gain from sale or exchange of the partner's interest. (Code Sec. 731(a); Reg § 1.731-1(a)(3))[40] A reduction in a partner's liabilities (due either to the partnership's assumption of them or a reduction in the partner's share of partnership liabilities) is treated as a money distribution. (Code Sec. 752(b))[41]

. . . Loss is recognized to the extent the adjusted basis of the partner's interest exceeds the sum of any money, and the basis to the distributee of any unrealized receivables and inventories received if the distribution is in liquidation of the partner's interest in the

34. ¶B-3506
35. ¶B-1503 *et seq.*
36. ¶B-1502
37. ¶B-1517

38. ¶B-3601
39. ¶B-3602
40. ¶B-3614
41. ¶B-3603

598

partnership *and* no other property is distributed. This is treated as a loss from sale or exchange of the partner's interest in the partnership. (Code Sec. 731(a))[42]

If gain or loss is recognized under one of the above rules, the partnership may elect to, or may have to, adjust the basis of its assets, as explained at ¶3764 *et seq*.

Notwithstanding the above rules, gain or loss may be recognized in the following cases (Code Sec. 731(c); Reg § 1.731-1(c)):[43]

. . . disproportionate distributions involving unrealized receivables and substantially appreciated inventory, see ¶3746;

. . . payments to a retiring partner or a deceased partner's successor in interest, which may be treated in part as regular distributions in liquidation, and in part as distributive shares of partnership income or guaranteed payments, see ¶3758;

. . . distributions to a partner that contributed built-in gain property to the partnership, see ¶3743.

¶ 3736 Distribution of marketable securities treated as cash—distributions to partner.

Subject to exceptions, under Code Sec. 731, a distribution of marketable securities (stock and other equity instruments, evidences of indebtedness, precious metals commodities, options, forward or futures contracts, notional principal contracts and derivatives) is treated as a distribution of money. The securities are taken into account at their fair market value (FMV) as of the date of the distribution. (Code Sec. 731(c); Reg § 1.731-2)

Gain is recognized by a distributee partner to the extent that the cash and the FMV of the marketable securities exceed the basis of the partner's interest in the partnership. But where a partner realizes a loss on a distribution of marketable securities, the loss isn't recognized. These rules are applied after the application of the rules that treat a shift in the partners' interests in accounts receivables and substantially appreciated inventory as a sale. (Code Sec. 731(a))[44]

The amount of marketable securities taken into account under the above rule is reduced (but not below zero) by the excess (if any) of:

(1) the partner's distributive share of the net gain that would be recognized if all marketable securities of the same class and issuer as the distributed securities held by the partnership were sold (immediately before the transaction to which the distribution relates) by the partnership for FMV, over

(2) the partner's distributive share of the net gain attributable to the marketable securities of the same class and issuer as the distributed securities held by the partnership immediately after the transaction, determined using the FMV described in (1) above. (Code Sec. 731(c)(3)(B))

All marketable securities held by the partnership are treated as marketable securities of the same class and issuer as the distributed securities. (Reg § 1.731-2(b))[45]

¶ 3737 Partner's holding period—distributions to partner.

Under Code Sec. 735(b), a partner's holding period for property distributed to him or her in kind includes the period the partnership held the property. If contributed to the partnership by a partner, the recipient partner's holding period also includes the period that

---

42. ¶B-3613
43. ¶B-3602

44. ¶B-3602; ¶B-3607
45. ¶B-3609

the property was held by the contributing partner before contribution. (Reg § 1.735-1(b))[46]

¶ 3738   Character of certain contributed property—distributions to partner.

Under Code Sec. 724(a), when a partner contributes what was an unrealized receivable in his or her hands to a partnership, the partnership's gain or loss on disposition of the item will still be ordinary income or loss. The same rule applies to contributed inventory, but in this case, ordinary income or loss will result only if the assets are disposed of by the partnership within five years of the contribution. (Code Sec. 724(b))[47]

If a partner contributes a capital asset with a basis higher than its fair market value, and the partnership disposes of it within five years of the contribution, the partnership's loss will be capital to the extent of the basis/value variance at contribution. (Code Sec. 724(c))[48]

If any of the above property is disposed of by the partnership in a nontaxable disposition, the above rules apply to the substituted basis property that results. (Code Sec. 724(d)(3))[49]

¶ 3739   Partner's basis for property received in nonliquidating distributions from partnership.

Code Sec. 732(a) provides that the basis to a partner of property distributed to him or her in kind, other than in liquidation of his or her partnership interest, is the same as the property's adjusted basis to the partnership immediately before the distribution. But the basis of the property to the partner may not exceed the adjusted basis of his or her interest in the partnership reduced by any money distributed to him or her in the same transaction. (Code Sec. 732(a); Reg § 1.732-1(a))[50]

¶ 3740   Partner's basis for property distributed in liquidation by partnership.

Under Code Sec. 732, a partner's basis for property distributed in liquidation of his or her partnership interest is the same as the adjusted basis for his or her partnership interest reduced by any money distributed to him or her in the same transaction. However, the partner's basis in inventory and unrealized receivables cannot exceed the basis the partnership had in such items. (Code Sec. 732(b), Code Sec. 732(c); Reg § 1.732-1(b))[1]

¶ 3741   Basis adjustments to assets of corporation whose stock is distributed to corporate partner.

Under Code Sec. 732(f), a corporate partner that receives a distribution of stock in another corporation ("distributed corporation") must, subject to limitations and exceptions, reduce the basis of the distributed corporation's assets if:

. . . the corporate partner "controls" (by 80% vote and value) the distributed corporation immediately after the distribution or at any time thereafter, and

. . . the partnership's adjusted basis in the stock of the distributed corporation immediately before the distribution exceeded the corporate partner's adjusted basis in such stock immediately after the distribution. (Code Sec. 732(f)(1))[2]

The basis reduction equals the excess described above and is applied to the property held by the distributed corporation following the distribution, if the corporate partner then has control of the distributed corporation. (Code Sec. 732(f)(1))[3]

---

46. ¶B-3706
47. ¶B-1425
48. ¶B-1426
49. ¶B-1427

50. ¶B-3701
1. ¶B-3702
2. ¶B-3704
3. ¶B-3704

Regs provide that if (i) two or more corporate partners receive a distribution of stock in another corporation and (ii) the corporation whose stock was distributed by the partnership is or becomes a member of the distributee partners' consolidated group following the distribution, the basis reduction rules apply only to the extent that the partnership's adjusted basis in the distributed stock immediately before the distribution exceeds the aggregate basis of the distributed stock of the corporation in the hands of corporate partners that are members of the same consolidated group (as defined in Reg § 1.1502-1(h)) immediately after the distribution. (Reg § 1.732-3(b))[4]

The basis reduction cannot exceed the lesser of:

(A) the amount by which (i) the sum of the aggregate adjusted bases of the property and the amount of money of the distributed corporation exceeds (ii) the corporate partner's adjusted basis in the stock of the distributed corporation, or

(B) the adjusted basis of any property of the distributed corporation (determined before the reduction). (Code Sec. 732(f)(3))[5]

If, in applying the basis-reduction rule, the amount by which basis is to be reduced exceeds the aggregate adjusted bases of the property of the distributed corporation, then the excess is recognized by the corporate partner as long-term capital gain and increases its basis in the stock of the distributed corporation. (Code Sec. 732(f)(4))[6]

¶ 3742 Allocation of basis to distributed property when limited by basis of partner's interest.

Under Code Sec. 732(c) when a partner receives—

. . . a current distribution in which the partner's basis in his or her partnership interest is less than the partnership's basis in the property distributed, or

. . . a liquidating distribution,

the partner's basis in his or her partnership interest (reduced by any money received) must be allocated among the distributed property in the following manner:

(1) First, to any unrealized receivables and inventory items in an amount equal to the adjusted basis of each such property to the partnership. (Code Sec. 732(c)(1)(A)(i)) If the basis to be allocated is less than the sum of the adjusted bases of these properties in the hands of the partnership, a basis decrease is applied as described below. (Code Sec. 732(c)(1)(A)(ii); Reg § 1.732-1(c)(2)(i))

(2) To the extent any basis isn't allocated under (1), basis is allocated to other distributed properties. This allocation is made by assigning to each property its adjusted basis in the hands of the partnership (Code Sec. 732(c)(1)(B)(i); Reg § 1.732-1(c)(2)(ii)) and then increasing or decreasing the basis to the extent any increase or decrease in basis is required in order for the adjusted bases of the other distributed properties to equal the remaining basis to be allocated under the rules described below. (Code Sec. 732(c)(1)(B)(ii); Reg § 1.732-1(c)(2)(ii))

Any basis *increase* is allocated (i) first to properties with unrealized appreciation in proportion to their respective amounts of unrealized appreciation before such increase to the extent of each property's unrealized appreciation (Code Sec. 732(c)(2)(A); Reg § 1.732-1(c)(2)(ii)) and (ii) to the extent the required increase isn't allocated under (i), in proportion to the respective fair market values of the properties. (Code Sec. 732(c)(2)(B); Reg § 1.732-1(c)(2)(ii))

---

4. ¶B-3704
5. ¶B-3704.1

6. ¶B-3704.1

Any basis *decrease* is allocated (a) first to properties with unrealized depreciation in proportion to their respective amounts of unrealized appreciation before such decrease to the extent of each property's unrealized depreciation (Code Sec. 732(c)(3)(A); Reg § 1.732-1(c)(2)(i)) and (b) to the extent the required decrease isn't allocated under (a), in proportion to the respective bases of the properties (as adjusted under (a)). (Code Sec. 732(c)(3)(B); Reg § 1.732-1(c)(2)(i))[7]

¶ 3743   Built-in gain or loss property contributed to partnership; gain recognition required on distribution (seven-year rule, distribution to contributing or non-contributing partner); allocations required for contributed property—reasonable methods (traditional method, traditional method with "curative allocations," and "remedial allocation" method).

If the basis of property contributed to a partnership by a partner is different from the property's fair market value (FMV) at contribution (i.e., there's built-in gain or loss), then the following rules of Code Sec. 704(c) and Code Sec. 737 apply:

If the partnership distributes the contributed property to a partner or partners *other than the contributing partner* within seven years of the contribution, then the distributed property is treated as sold by the partnership for its FMV at the time of the distribution, and the contributing partner must recognize any gain or loss from this constructive sale in an amount equal to the amount of gain or loss that would have been allocated to him or her if the property had actually been sold. (Code Sec. 704(c)(1)(B); Reg § 1.704-4(a)(5), Ex (1))[8]

Where property is distributed to the partner *who contributed the property,* the partner will recognize as gain the lesser of (a) the excess of the FMV of the property over the adjusted basis of the partner's interest in the partnership immediately before the distribution (reduced, but not below zero, by any money or marketable securities received), or (b) the partner's net precontribution gain, *i.e.,* the gain that would have been recognized by the distributee partner under the rules discussed, above, if all property held by the partnership immediately before the distribution that had been contributed to it by the distributee partner within seven years of the distribution, was distributed to another partner. (Code Sec. 737(a), Code Sec. 737(b))[9] Distributions of property previously contributed by the distributee partner aren't taken into account for purposes of determining (a) and (b), above. (Code Sec. 737(d)(1))[10]

Special rules apply if the partnership distributes to the contributing partner property that's of "like kind" to the contributed property (within the meaning of Code Sec. 1031, see ¶2416) to limit recognition of gain by the contributing partner. (Code Sec. 704(c)(2))[11]

The rules requiring gain recognition on distributions described above do not apply when a partnership transfers all of its assets and liabilities to a partnership in exchange for an interest in the transferee partnership, and distributes the interest to its partners in liquidation as part of the same plan (a merger). With respect to a later distribution of "built-in gain" property that was transferred in the merger, the seven-year period is measured from the date that the property was originally contributed to the transferor partnership, and not from the date of the transfer to the transferee partnership. However, the merger is considered a contribution of assets, so a new seven-year period begins but only with respect to the appreciation in value that occurred while the property was held by the transferor partnership. (Reg § 1.704-4(c)(4))[12]

---

7. ¶B-3703
8. ¶B-3141
9. ¶B-3171 *et seq.*

10. ¶B-3178
11. ¶B-3151 *et seq.*
12. ¶B-3157

Income, gain, loss and deductions for property contributed to the partnership after Mar. 31, 1984 are shared among the partners so as to take into account the difference between the property's FMV and its basis at the time of the contribution. (Code Sec. 704(c)(1)(A)) Built-in gain or loss must be allocated using a reasonable method, i.e., the traditional method following the ceiling rule or with curative allocations, the remedial allocation method or another method appropriate to the circumstances. (Reg § 1.704-3(a)(1)) Under anti-abuse rules, an allocation isn't reasonable if made with a view to shifting the tax consequences of built-in gain or loss among partners (including indirect partners), in a way that substantially reduces the present value of the partners' aggregate tax liability. (Reg § 1.704-3(a)(10))[13]

If any property contributed to a partnership after Oct. 22, 2004 has a built-in loss, then: (1) the built-in loss is taken into account only in determining the amount of items allocated to the contributing partner, and (2) except as provided in regs, in determining the amount of items allocated to other partners, the basis of the contributed property in the hands of the partnership is treated as being equal to its FMV at the time of the contribution. (Code Sec. 704(c)(1)(C))[14]

If a partnership makes an installment sale of built-in gain or loss property, the installment obligation it receives is treated as built-in gain or loss property. (Reg § 1.704-3(a)(8)(ii))[15]

¶ 3744 Character of unrealized receivables and inventory to a distributee-partner.

Under Code Sec. 735(a), gain or loss on disposition of unrealized receivables and inventory by a distributee-partner is:

. . . in the case of *unrealized receivables*, ordinary gain or loss; (Code Sec. 735(a)(1))

. . . in the case of *inventory items* (whether or not substantially appreciated) sold or exchanged within five years from the date of the distribution, ordinary gain or loss. (Code Sec. 735(a)(2)) If disposed of after five years from the date of distribution, the character of the gain or loss depends upon the character of the item in the partner's hands on the date of disposition. (Reg § 1.735-1(a)(2))[16]

¶ 3745 Disproportionate Distributions. ████████████████

Disproportionate distributions (¶3746) of partnership property that include "unrealized receivables" (including recapturable deductions, certain transfers of franchises, trademarks or trade names, see ¶3747) and "substantially appreciated inventory" (see ¶3748) (collectively, "hot assets") may trigger ordinary income, gain or loss to both the partnership and its partners.

¶ 3746 Disproportionate distributions defined—partnerships.

Under Code Sec. 751(b), a disproportionate distribution of partnership assets to a partner is treated as a sale or exchange that may result in recognition of gain or loss to the partner and the partnership. The rule applies to all distributions, both liquidating and nonliquidating, except for: (1) a distribution of contributed property to the same partner who contributed it; and (2) liquidation payments to a retiring or deceased partner that are treated as ordinary income under the rules at ¶3758. (Code Sec. 751(b))[17]

---

13. ¶B-3100 *et seq.*
14. ¶B-3130 *et seq.*
15. ¶ B-3116 *et seq.*

16. ¶B-3705
17. ¶B-3905 *et seq.*

A distribution is "disproportionate" if a partner receives more than his or her proportionate share of "hot assets" (see ¶3745) and less of his or her proportionate share of other property (including money), or vice versa. In such a case, a partner, in effect, sells or exchanges part or all of his or her share in property of one category for property of the other category, see ¶3749. The general rules on partnership distributions apply to the balance of the distribution not treated as a sale or exchange. (Reg § 1.751-1(b))[18]

The partners may agree as to which particular assets in one category are considered to have been sold or exchanged for particular assets in the other category, but absent such an agreement, a proportionate part of each asset relinquished in one category will be considered to have been sold or exchanged for excess assets received in the other. (Reg § 1.751-1(g))[19]

Under proposed regs on which taxpayers may rely, a distribution of partnership property (including money) is a "Code Sec. 751(b) distribution," and may give rise to an income recognition requirement (see ¶3749) if it gives rise to a "Code Sec. 751(b) amount" for any partner. A partner's Code Sec. 751(b) amount is the greatest of: (i) the amount by which the partner's net Code Sec. 751 unrealized gain immediately before the distribution exceeds the partner's net Code Sec. 751 unrealized gain immediately after the distribution; (ii) the amount by which the partner's Code Sec. 751 unrealized loss immediately after the distribution exceeds the partner's net Code Sec. 751 unrealized loss immediately before the distribution; and (iii) the amount of the partner's net Code Sec. 751 unrealized gain immediately before the distribution, increased by the total amount of the partner's net Code Sec. 751 unrealized loss immediately after the distribution (where neither of those numbers equals zero). (Prop Reg. § 1.751-1(b)(2), [Taxpayers may rely])[20]

For this purpose, a partner's interest in the partnership's Code Sec. 751 property would include allocations of tax items under Code Sec. 704(c) principles. (Prop Reg. § 1.751-1(b)(1)(i), [Taxpayers may rely])[21]

¶ 3747 "Unrealized receivables"—partnership disproportionate distributions.

Under Code Sec. 751, unrealized receivables include any contractual or other rights to payment for:

... goods delivered, or to be delivered, to the extent the proceeds would be treated as amounts received from the sale or exchange of noncapital assets;

... services rendered, or to be rendered.

Such receivables are included only to the extent not previously includible in income under the method of accounting used by the partnership. Other items, such as various recapture items and discount on market discount bonds and short-term obligations are also treated as unrealized receivables. (Code Sec. 751(c))[22]

¶ 3748 "Inventory items" and "substantially appreciated" inventory items—partnership disproportionate distributions.

For purposes of the subchapter K partnership rules, inventory items include property properly includible in inventory and property held primarily for sale to customers in the ordinary course of business (Code Sec. 751(d)(1)), as well as:

... any other property that would produce ordinary income on sale or exchange by the partnership (Code Sec. 751(d)(2)), including accounts receivable for goods or services and

---

18. ¶B-3906 *et seq.*
19. ¶B-3912
20. ¶B-3907.1

21. ¶B-3907.1
22. ¶B-3914 *et seq.*

unrealized receivables as described at ¶3747 (Reg § 1.751-1(d)(2)(ii)); and

. . . any other property held by the partnership that would be inventory items, as defined above, if held by the selling or distributee-partner. (Code Sec. 751(d)(3)) However, this rule doesn't apply to property actually distributed to a partner. (Reg § 1.751-1(d)(2)(iii))[23]

Inventory items are "substantially appreciated" in value if the fair market value of *all* such items (including unrealized receivables) exceeds 120% of their adjusted basis to the partnership. (Code Sec. 751(b)(3)(A)) The 120% limit is computed by excluding any item acquired principally to avoid meeting it. (Code Sec. 751(b)(3)(B))

If the test is met on the basis of all inventory items, a distribution of any inventory item is a distribution of a substantially appreciated one, even though the particular item may not have appreciated at all. If the test isn't met on the basis of all items, no distribution of an inventory item is a distribution of a substantially appreciated item. (Reg § 1.751-1(d)(1))[24]

¶ 3749 Gain or loss on disproportionate distribution—partnerships.

If a distributee-partner receives *more* than his or her share of unrealized receivables and substantially appreciated inventory items and *less* than his or her share of other property (including money), he or she is considered to have sold or exchanged the portion of his or her share of the other property relinquished for the excess unrealized receivables and substantially appreciated inventory items received. (Reg § 1.751-1(b)(2)(i), Reg § 1.751-1(b)(2)(iii))

The partnership (as constituted after the distribution) is considered to have sold or exchanged the excess unrealized receivables and substantially appreciated inventory items distributed to the partner in exchange for the other property relinquished. (Reg § 1.751-1(b)(2)(i), Reg § 1.751-1(b)(2)(ii))[25]

Rules analogous to those described above apply where the distributee partner receives a disproportionate distribution of *less* than his or her share of unrealized receivables and substantially appreciated inventory items and *more* than his or her share of other property (including money). (Reg § 1.751-1(b)(3))[26]

Under proposed regs on which taxpayers may rely, in the case of a Code Sec. 751(b) distribution described at ¶3746, the partnership may choose a reasonable approach that is consistent with the purpose of Code Sec. 751 (i.e., to prevent a partner from converting its rights to ordinary income into capital gain) under which each partner with a Code Sec. 751(b) amount would recognize ordinary income (or would take it into account by eliminating a basis adjustment) equal to the Code Sec. 751(b) amount immediately before the Code Sec. 751(b) distribution. However, in certain circumstances, a distributee partner would also be allowed or required to recognize capital gain. (Prop Reg. § 1.751-1(b)(3), [Taxpayers may rely])[27]

¶ 3750 Liabilities of Partnerships and Partners. ▬▬▬▬▬▬

Changes in partners' shares of partnership liabilities are treated as cash contributions to, or distributions by, the partnership. Partners' shares of partnership liabilities depend on whether the liability is recourse (¶3751) or nonrecourse (¶3752).

Specifically, if a partner's share of partnership liabilities increases, or if he or she

---

23. ¶B-3920
24. ¶B-3921
25. ¶B-3909 *et seq.*

26. ¶B-3910
27. ¶B-3907.2

assumes any partnership liabilities, it's treated as a contribution of money from the partner to the partnership. (Code Sec. 752(a); Reg § 1.752-1(b))[28]

If a partner's share of partnership liabilities decreases, or if the partnership assumes any of his or her liabilities, it's treated as a distribution of money to the partner. (Code Sec. 752(b); Reg § 1.752-1(c))[29]

An unassumed liability to which property is subject is considered a liability of the owner of the property (e.g., the partnership) to the extent of its fair market value. (Code Sec. 752(c))[30]

An obligation is a liability that is taken into account under Code Sec. 752 only if incurring the obligation (i) creates or increases the basis of any of the obligor's assets (including cash), (ii) gives rise to an immediate deduction to the obligor, or (iii) gives rise to an expense that is not deductible in computing the obligor's taxable income and is not properly chargeable to capital. Obligations include, but are not limited to, debt obligations, environmental obligations, tort obligations, contract obligations, pension obligations, obligations under a short sale, and obligations under derivative financial instruments such as options, forward contracts, and futures contracts. (Reg § 1.752-1(a)(4))[31]

¶ 3751 Partner's share of partnership's debts that are recourse liabilities.

A partnership debt is a recourse liability under Code Sec. 752 to the extent that any partner bears the economic risk of loss for the liability. A partner's share of a recourse liability is the part of the economic risk of loss for the liability the partner bears. (Reg § 1.752-1(a)(1))[32]

Generally, a partner bears the economic risk of loss for a partnership liability to the extent that the partner (or a related person) would be obligated to pay the creditor or contribute to the partnership (and wouldn't be entitled to reimbursement) in a constructive liquidation. (Reg § 1.752-2(b)(1)) However, IRS may disregard a partner's purported obligation to make a payment under anti-abuse rules. (Reg § 1.752-2(j))[33]

¶ 3752 Share of nonrecourse liabilities—liabilities of partnerships and partners.

If no partner bears the economic risk of loss for a partnership liability (e.g., unassumed mortgages), the liability is nonrecourse. (Reg § 1.752-1(a)(2)) Nonrecourse liabilities of a partnership are first allocated among all the partners to reflect their shares of:

(a) "partnership minimum gain," the excess of partnership nonrecourse liabilities over the basis (or, if the assets are recorded on the books at a value different from basis, the book value of the assets) of the partnership assets those liabilities encumber; and

(b) the gain that would be allocated to the partners under Code Sec. 704(c), or under similar principles in connection with a revaluation of partnership property, if, in a taxable transaction, the partnership disposed of all property subject to a nonrecourse liability in satisfaction of those liabilities and for no other consideration.

Any excess is allocated among the partners in proportion to their interests in partnership profits. The partnership agreement may specify the partners' profit interests as long as those interests are reasonably consistent with allocations (which have substantial economic effect) of some significant item of partnership income or gain among the partners. Alternatively, the excess may be allocated in accordance with the manner in which it's expected that the deductions attributable to the nonrecourse debt will be allocated. In

---

28. ¶B-1601
29. ¶B-1602
30. ¶B-1608

31. ¶B-1607
32. ¶B-1650 *et seq.*
33. ¶B-1654 *et seq.*

addition, the excess may be allocated first to the contributing partner to the extent any built-in-gain with respect to that property exceeds the amount allocated to that partner under (b), and thereafter under one of the other methods described above. (Reg § 1.752-3(a))[34]

¶ 3753   Transfer and Liquidation of Partnership Interest. ▬▬▬▬

The transfer or liquidation (¶3740 *et seq.*) of a partnership interest, while generally resulting in capital gain or loss, is subject to special rules that may turn part of the gain or loss from capital to ordinary (¶3756).

¶ 3754   Liquidation vs. sale of partner's interest in partnership.

Withdrawal of a partner from a partnership ordinarily may be accomplished either by a partner's sale (Code Sec. 741) or liquidation (Code Sec. 736) of his or her interest in the partnership.

Where a partner's interest in a partnership in which capital is not a material factor is liquidated, payments are taxable to that partner as guaranteed payments or income distributions to the extent they exceed the value of his or her interest in the partnership property (¶3758 *et seq.*).[35]

Where a partner *sells* his or her interest, payments to him or her that exceed his or her basis for his or her interest are capital gain except to the extent of payments for unrealized receivables and inventory items (¶3755 *et seq.*). (Code Sec. 741; Reg § 1.741-1)[36]

¶ 3755   Sale or exchange of partnership interest.

If a partner sells or exchanges all or a part of his or her interest in a partnership after holding it for more than one year, he or she may recognize ordinary income, collectibles gain (¶2605), section 1250 gain, or residual long-term capital gain or loss. (Reg § 1.1(h)-1(a)) He or she recognizes ordinary income (¶3756) to the extent his or her gain is attributable to unrealized receivables (¶3747) and inventory (¶3748). (Code Sec. 741, Code Sec. 751(a), Code Sec. 751(c))[37]

The capital gain or loss is the difference between:

. . . the amount realized *reduced* by the portion attributable to unrealized receivables and inventory; and

. . . the transferor-partner's adjusted basis for the partnership interest transferred *reduced* by the portion attributable to unrealized receivables and inventory. (Reg § 1.741-1(a))[38]

Any gain or loss from a partner's disposition of an interest in a partnership is taken into account by the partner as net investment income for purposes of the 3.8% surtax on unearned income (¶3142 *et seq.*) *only* to the extent of the net gain or loss that the transferor would take into account if the entity had sold all its property for fair market value immediately before the disposition. (Code Sec. 1411(c)(4))

The seller's collectibles gain is the amount that would be allocated to him or her if the partnership had sold all of its collectibles for fair market value in a fully taxable transaction immediately before the sale of the interest in the entity. (Reg § 1.1(h)-1(b)(2)(ii)) The seller must take into account under Code Sec. 1(h)(6)(A)(i) in determining his or her unrecaptured section 1250 gain (¶2604) the amount of "section 1250 capital gain" that would

---

34. ¶B-1670
35. ¶B-3807, B-4102
36. ¶B-3800 *et seq.*

37. ¶B-3850 *et seq.*
38. ¶B-3801, B-3901

be allocated to him or her if the partnership had sold all of its section 1250 property in a fully taxable transaction immediately before the transfer of the partnership interest. (Reg § 1.1(h)-1(b)(3)(ii)) The amount of residual long-term capital gain or loss recognized by a selling partner is the amount of long-term capital gain or loss that the partner would recognize under Code Sec. 741 (as explained above) minus (1) the collectibles gain allocable to the sold interest, and (2) the section 1250 gain allocable to the sold interest. (Reg § 1.1(h)-1(c))

¶ 3756　Ordinary gain or loss—transfer or liquidation of partnership interest.

To the extent that money or property received by a partner in exchange for all or part of his or her partnership interest is attributable to his or her share of partnership unrealized receivables or inventory items—collectively Code Sec. 751 property—the gain or loss is ordinary income or loss. (Code Sec. 751(a))

The income or loss realized by a partner on the sale or exchange of his or her interest in Code Sec. 751 property is the amount of income or loss from Code Sec. 751 property (including any remedial allocations) that would have been allocated to the partner (to the extent attributable to the partnership interest sold or exchanged) if the partnership had sold all of its property in a fully taxable transaction for cash in an amount equal to the fair market value (FMV) of such property (taking into account the Code Sec. 7701(g) rule that the FMV must be not less than the amount of the nonrecourse debt to which the property is subject) immediately before the partner's transfer of the interest in the partnership. Gain or loss attributable to Code Sec. 751 property is ordinary. The difference between the amount of capital gain or loss that the partner would realize absent Code Sec. 751 and the amount of ordinary income or loss is capital gain or loss on the sale of his or her partnership interest. (Reg § 1.751-1(a)(2))[39]

The basis for unrealized receivables includes all attributable costs or expenses paid or accrued but not previously taken into account under the partnership's method of accounting. (Reg § 1.751-1(c)(2)) The basis of any potential gain from the following property (treated as unrealized receivables) is zero: (1) mining exploration expenditures recapture under Code Sec. 617; (2) gain from stock of a domestic international sales corporation (DISC) or a former DISC under Code Sec. 995(c); (3) depreciation recapture under Code Sec. 1245 and Code Sec. 1250; (4) gain from stock of a controlled foreign corporation under Code Sec. 1248(a); (5) gain from disposition of farm land under Code Sec. 1252(a)(1); (6) gain from transfers of franchises, trademarks, or trade names under Code Sec. 1253(a); or (7) oil, gas, or geothermal wells intangible drilling and development cost recapture under Code Sec. 1254. (Reg § 1.751-1(c)(5))[40]

¶ 3757　Sale of partnership business vs. sale of partnership assets.

A transaction can be structured either as a sale of assets (see ¶2400 *et seq.*) or as a sale of the partnership interests (with the tax consequences determined under Code Sec. 741 and Code Sec. 751, see ¶3755 *et seq.*). However, where all the assets of the partnership are sold (except for cash or insignificant assets) and the partnership does not engage in business after the transfer, the transaction will be treated as a sale of the partnership interests.[41]

¶ 3758　Payments After Partner's Death or Retirement. ▬▬▬▬▬▬

When a partner either retires or dies and payments are made in liquidation of his or her partnership interest, the payments are broken down into several categories,

---

39. ¶B-3901
40. ¶B-3903

41. ¶B-3809

which are treated as ordinary income or capital gains.

These payments may be for the partner's interest in the fair market value of the partnership assets, his or her interest in unrealized receivables, or payments under an agreement akin to mutual insurance. These amounts have to be separately considered.[42]

Liquidation payments received by a retiring partner, a partner expelled from a partnership, or by a deceased partner's successor in interest are treated as distributions taxable under the rules for regular distributions discussed at ¶3735 if they are for the partner's interest in partnership property, see ¶3759. (Code Sec. 736(b)(1))[43] Payments for *substantially appreciated* inventory (¶3748) may result in ordinary income under the rules governing disproportionate distributions (see ¶3749). (Reg § 1.736-1(b)(1))

Liquidation payments that aren't in exchange for partnership property are treated either as distributive shares of partnership income (if the amount is determined with regard to partnership income) or as guaranteed payments (if the amount is determined without regard to partnership income). (Code Sec. 736(a); Reg § 1.736-1(a)(3))[44]

¶ 3759 Payment for interest in partnership property—payments after partner's death or retirement.

Payments for partnership property don't include payments to a retiring or deceased general partner in a partnership in which capital isn't a material income-producing factor for (i) unrealized receivables (which for this purpose includes only accounts receivable and unbilled amounts) or (ii) goodwill (unless the partnership agreement provides for payments for goodwill). (Code Sec. 736(b)(2), Code Sec. 736(b)(3))[45]

¶ 3760 Allocation of payments between income and property—payments after partner's death or retirement.

The allocation of payments between income and property is an issue that arises when Code Sec. 736 payments liquidating a partner's interest are made over two or more years. Retirement or death payments must be allocated between the portion received in exchange for partnership property and the balance, received in the form of guaranteed payments or as a distributive share of partnership income. This allocation may be made in any manner in which the remaining partners and the withdrawing partner (or a deceased partner's successor in interest) agree. However, the *total* allocated to property must not exceed the fair market value of the property at the date of death or retirement. (Reg § 1.736-1(b)(5)(iii))

In the absence of an allocation agreement, payments will be allocated between income and property as follows:

. . . Payments that aren't fixed in amount are first treated as made in exchange for the partner's interest in partnership property to the extent of the value of that interest. Additional amounts are ordinary income. (Reg § 1.736-1(b)(5)(ii))

. . . Payments fixed in amount and to be received over a fixed number of years are apportioned year by year in accordance with the overall ratio of property payments to total payments. (Reg § 1.736-1(b)(5)(i))[46]

A payment for goodwill is treated as a payment made in exchange for partnership property where payment for goodwill is provided by the partnership agreement. (Reg § 1.736-1(b)(3))[47]

---

42. ¶B-4102 *et seq.*
43. ¶B-4103
44. ¶B-4106

45. ¶B-4104
46. ¶B-4110
47. ¶B-4104

¶ 3761 Withdrawing partner's share of final year's income—payments after partner's death or retirement.

A retiring partner must recognize his or her distributive share of the partnership income under Code Sec. 736 for the partnership year in which he or she retires. His or her share of partnership income for the year is allocable to him or her only for the portion of the year he or she was a member of the partnership. (Reg § 1.706-1(c)(2))[48]

¶ 3762 Deceased partner—partnership items included on decedent's final return.

Under Code Sec. 706, the tax year of a partnership closes with respect to a deceased partner on the date of his or her death. Thus, partnership items for the short partnership tax year that closes on the partner's death are included in his or her final return. (Code Sec. 706(c)(2))[49]

¶ 3763 Continuation of retiring or deceased partner's partner status—payments after partner's death or retirement.

Under the Code Sec. 708 and Code Sec. 736 regs, a retiring partner or a deceased partner's successor in interest who receives retirement or death payments is regarded as a partner until his or her entire interest in the partnership is liquidated. Thus, even a two-person partnership isn't terminated until the retiring or deceased partner's interest is liquidated. (Reg § 1.708-1(b)(1)(i), Reg § 1.736-1(a)(6))[50]

¶ 3764 Special Basis Adjustments to Partnership Property. ▅▅▅▅▅▅▅▅▅

A partnership's basis in its assets ("inside basis") is unaffected by partnership distributions and transfers of partnership interests unless there is a substantial basis reduction or the partnership makes a special basis election (¶3769). Under certain circumstances, the transferee of a partnership interest may elect to adjust the basis of property distributed to him or her as if the partnership had made the special basis election (¶3767).

¶ 3765 Post-transfer adjustments to basis—basis adjustments of partnership property.

A transfer of a partnership interest by reason of a sale or exchange or the death of a partner causes a basis adjustment of the partnership's property if (i) a basis adjustment election under Code Sec. 754 is in effect, or (ii) the partnership has a substantial built-in loss immediately after the transfer. (Code Sec. 743(a)) A partnership is treated as having a substantial built-in loss if (1) the partnership's adjusted basis in the partnership property exceeds by more than $250,000 the fair market value (FMV) of that property or (2) the transferee partner would be allocated a loss of more than $250,000 if the partnership assets were sold for cash equal to their FMV immediately after the transfer. (Code Sec. 743(d)(1))[1]

A contribution of cash or property to the partnership does not cause a basis adjustment to the partnership's property, regardless of whether a basis adjustment election is in effect. (Reg § 1.743-1(a))[2] If the election is in effect, the partnership's basis in its property with

---

48. ¶G-1225 *et seq.*
49. ¶B-4201
50. ¶B-4112

1. ¶B-4011
2. ¶B-4015

respect to the transferee partner is increased by any excess of the partner's basis in his or her interest over his or her share of the basis of partnership property (or decreased if his or her basis in the interest is lower). (Reg § 1.743-1(b))[3] Regs provide rules for allocating the basis adjustment among the partnership's assets. (Reg § 1.755-1)[4]

¶ 3766 Post-distribution adjustments to basis of undistributed partnership property.

The basis of partnership property is not adjusted when the partnership makes a distribution to a partner unless a basis adjustment election under Code Sec. 754 is in effect, or the partnership has a substantial basis reduction with respect to the distribution. (Code Sec. 734(a)) A substantial basis reduction exists where the sum of (i) the amount of the partner's loss on the distribution, and (ii) the basis increase to the distributed properties, is over $250,000. (Code Sec. 734(d))[5] If an adjustment is made on a partnership distribution, the partnership's basis in its retained property (1) is increased by the amount of gain recognized by the distributee partner on the distribution, and the amount by which the basis of the distributed property in the hands of the partnership before the distribution exceeds the basis of the property in the hands of the distributee partner (Code Sec. 734(b)(1)), and (2) is decreased by the amount of loss recognized by the distributee partner on the distribution and the amount by which the basis of the distributed property in the hands of the distributee partner exceeds the basis the partnership had in the property before the distribution. (Code Sec. 734(b)(2)(B))[6] Regs provide rules for allocating the basis adjustment among the partnership's assets. (Reg § 1.755-1)[7]

In allocating any basis reduction in partnership property under Code Sec. 734(b) as a result of a distribution, no allocation may be made to stock in a corporation that is a partner in the partnership, or to the stock of any person related to the corporation, and any amount not allocable to stock is allocated to other partnership property. Where the reduction that must be allocated to other partnership property exceeds the aggregate adjusted basis of the other partnership property immediately before the required allocation, gain is recognized by the partnership to the extent of the excess. (Code Sec. 755(c))[8]

Where the basis of a partnership's recovery property is increased as a result of a distribution of property by the partnership, the increased portion of the basis is taken into account for depreciation purposes as if it were newly purchased recovery property placed in service when the distribution or transfer occurs. Any applicable recovery period and method may be used to determine the recovery (depreciation) deduction for the increased portion of the basis. However, no change is allowed in determining the recovery (depreciation) deduction for the portion of the basis of recovery property for which there is no increase. (Reg § 1.734-1(e)(1))[9]

Where the basis adjustment requires a decrease in the basis of partnership recovery property, the basis decrease must be accounted for over the remaining recovery period of the property beginning with the recovery period in which the basis is decreased. (Reg § 1.734-1(e)(2))[10]

¶ 3767 Partner's basis adjustments—basis adjustments of partnership property.

Where a partnership interest is transferred and the partnership later distributes property, but hasn't made the election described at ¶3765, the transferee-partner may elect under the Code Sec. 732 regs to have the basis of the property distributed to him or her

3. ¶B-4010
4. ¶B-4050 *et seq.*
5. ¶B-4003
6. ¶B-4002

7. ¶B-4055 *et seq.*
8. ¶B-4054.1
9. ¶B-4008
10. ¶B-4008

adjusted as if the partnership had made the election. The election to make the adjustment applies only for purposes of determining the basis of distributed property (other than money) in the partner's hands. It doesn't enable the partner to amend prior income tax returns to recompute income based on an adjusted basis. (Code Sec. 732(d)) Accordingly, in computing the adjustment, there is no reduction for any depletion or depreciation of that portion of the basis of partnership property arising from the basis adjustment, because no depletion or depreciation on the basis adjustment for the period before the distribution is allowed or allowable unless the partnership had an election described at ¶3765 in effect. (Reg § 1.732-1(d)(1)(iv))[11]

The transferee-partner may make this election only with respect to property (other than money) distributed to him or her within two years after he or she acquired his or her interest by transfer. (Code Sec. 732(d))[12]

The adjustment is *required* (without regard to the 2-year limit) if, at the time the transferee-partner acquired the transferred partnership interest, all three of the following conditions existed:

(1) The fair market value of all partnership property (other than money) exceeded 110% of its adjusted basis to the partnership;

(2) Allocation of basis under Code Sec. 732(c) (general rule for allocation of basis of distributed properties) upon a liquidation of his or her interest immediately after the transfer of the interest would have resulted in a shift of basis from property not subject to depreciation, depletion or amortization to property that is so subject; and

(3) The post-transfer adjustment as if the election at ¶3765 had been made would change the basis to the transferee-partner of the property actually distributed. (Code Sec. 732(d); Reg § 1.732-1(d)(4))[13]

¶ 3768   Basis of unrealized receivables and inventory items distributed to a partner.

If unrealized receivables (¶3747) or inventory items (¶3748)—as defined in Code Sec. 751—are distributed to a *transferee partner* who has a special basis adjustment for those assets under either the post-transfer adjustment rule (¶3765) or the distributed property adjustment rule (¶3766), the partnership's adjusted basis, immediately before distribution, of any unrealized receivables or inventory items distributed to such a partner takes into account the following portions of the post-transfer or distributed property basis adjustments that the distributee partner has for those assets:

. . . The entire amount of the post-transfer or distributed property basis adjustments *if* the distributee-partner receives his or her entire share of the fair market value of the unrealized receivables or inventory items of the partnership.

. . . The same proportion of the post-transfer or distributed property basis adjustments as the value of the unrealized receivables or inventory items distributed to him or her bears to his or her entire share of the total value of all those items of the partnership, *if* the distributee-partner gets less than his or her entire share of those items. (Reg § 1.732-2(c))[14]

¶ 3769   Electing basis adjustments—basis adjustments of partnership property; revocation of election on Form 15254.

The election to adjust the basis of the partnership assets on a distribution, sale, or

---

11. ¶B-4032   13. ¶B-4034
12. ¶B-4032   14. ¶B-4021

transfer of a partnership interest (¶3765, ¶3766) is made by the partnership filing a statement of election with the partnership return for the tax year during which the transfer of interest or the distribution of property occurs. (Code Sec. 754; Reg § 1.754-1(b); TD 9963, 8/5/2022) Once made, the election applies to all current and future distributions and transfers until revoked. (Code Sec. 754; Reg § 1.754-1(a))[15] Partnerships can request revocation on Form 15254. (Form 15254 p. 2)[16]

A transferee-partner who wishes to make the distributed property adjustment (¶3767) must elect as follows:

. . . If the distribution includes any depreciable, depletable, or amortizable property, elect with the return for the distribution year.

. . . If it doesn't include any such property, elect not later than the first tax year in which the basis of any of the distributed property is pertinent in determining the transferee-partner's tax. (Reg § 1.732-1(d)(2), Reg § 1.732-1(d)(3))[17]

¶ 3770   Termination of a Partnership. ▰▰▰▰▰▰▰

A partnership terminates for tax purposes (whether or not it has terminated under applicable local law) when it stops doing business as a partnership or it has only one owner. (Code Sec. 708, Code Sec. 761(e); Reg § 1.708-1(b)(1))[18]

The cessation of doing business as a partnership may result from a cessation of the business or because there is only one continuing former partner conducting the business.[19]

¶ 3771   Split-up of partnership—partnership terminations.

If a partnership splits up into two or more partnerships, each resulting partnership is considered a continuation of the old partnership under Code Sec. 708(b)(2)(B) as long as the members of the resulting partnership had more than a 50% interest in the capital and profits of the old partnership. A resulting partnership whose members had an interest of 50% or less in the old partnership is treated as a new partnership.

If the members of none of the resulting partnerships had more than a 50% interest in the old partnership, the old partnership is considered terminated as of the date of the division, and all the resulting partnerships are treated as new partnerships. (Code Sec. 708(b)(2)(B); Reg § 1.708-1(d)(2))[20]

Any members of the original partnership who do not become members of a resulting partnership that is treated as a continuation of the original partnership are considered to have had their partnership interests liquidated as of the date of the division. (Reg § 1.708-1(d)(1))

For divisions, the resulting partnership (referred to as the divided partnership) that is treated as a continuation of the prior partnership must file a return for the entire tax year of the partnership that has been divided and must retain the employer identification number (EIN) of the prior partnership. All other resulting partnerships that are regarded as continuing and new partnerships must file separate returns for the tax year beginning on the day after the date of the division with new EINs for each partnership. (Reg § 1.708-1(d)(2))

15. ¶B-4026 *et seq.*
16. ¶B-4028
17. ¶B-4033
18. ¶B-4301
19. ¶B-4302
20. ¶B-4308

Chapter 18 Trusts—Estates—Decedents

¶ 3900   **Income Taxation of Trusts and Estates—Form 1041.** ▬▬▬▬▬▬▬▬

Trusts and estates are generally treated as separate taxpayers and, with some important qualifications, are taxed in the same way as individuals.

Trust and estate income is normally taxed to the fiduciary (that is, to the trust or estate itself) if retained by the trust, or to the beneficiary if distributed. Thus, if the fiduciary passes on income to the beneficiary, the trust or estate deducts the distributed income which then becomes taxable to the beneficiary. A special yardstick called "distributable net income" (DNI) (see ¶3929 and ¶3931) is used to limit both the amount deducted by the trust or estate as a distribution, and the amount taxed to the beneficiary. (Code Sec. 643, Code Sec. 651, Code Sec. 652, Code Sec. 661, Code Sec. 662)[1]

The income that's passed on to the beneficiary has the same tax attributes in the beneficiary's hands as when received by the fiduciary (¶3940).

Trusts and estates compute their tax under a tightly-compressed, 5-bracket tax rate schedule (¶1106) that quickly reaches the top marginal rate. (Code Sec. 1(e))[2]

Trusts and estates can't use the tax tables for individuals to figure their capital gains tax. (Code Sec. 3(b)(2)) For 2022, the 20% maximum rate for capital gains and qualified dividends applies to estates and trusts with income above $13,700, the 0% rate applies to amounts up to $2,800, while the 15% rate applies to amounts over $2,800 and up to $13,700. For 2023, the 20% maximum rate for capital gains and qualified dividends applies to estates and trusts with income above $14,650, the 0% rate applies to amounts up to $3,000, while the 15% rate applies to amounts over $3,000 and up to $14,650.

⚠ *caution:* For treatment of trusts and estates for AMT purposes, see ¶3200 *et seq.*

A foreign trust or estate is taxed as if it were a nonresident alien individual who isn't present in the U.S. at any time (see ¶4624 *et seq.*), subject to special rules for trusts. (Code Sec. 641(b))[3]

The fact that any organization is technically cast in the trust form won't change the real character of the organization if it is more properly classified as a business entity under Reg § 301.7701-2. (Reg § 301.7701-4(b))[4]

For income tax returns of trusts and estates (Form 1041), see ¶4732 *et seq.* Form 1041 must be e-Filed using Form 8453-FE, U.S. Estate or Trust Declaration for an IRS e-File Return. Beneficiaries must report items consistently with the entity's return or notify IRS (on Form 8082) of the inconsistency. (Code Sec. 6034A(c)).[5]

For the 3.8% surtax on a trust's or estate's unearned income, see ¶3950.

For the tax years of trusts and estates, see ¶2805.

Optional Form 1041-V, Payment Voucher is used to include information about the taxpayer's remittance of the balance due on Form 1041. IRS encourages its use if payment is made by check or money order. Payment may also be made electronically.[6]

¶ 3901   **Election to treat revocable trust as part of estate for income tax purposes—Form 8855.**

Under Code Sec. 645, an election can be made to have an individual's revocable trust

---

1. ¶C-2600 *et seq.*, ¶C-7000 *et seq.*
2. ¶s C-1003 *et seq.*, C-7002 *et seq.*
3. ¶C-1014 *et seq.*.

4. ¶C-5003
5. ¶s C-3081, C-9081
6. ¶S-1654

References beginning with a single letter are to paragraphs in Federal Tax Coordinator 2d and RIA's Analysis of Federal Taxes: Income.

treated as part of his or her estate for income tax purposes. (Code Sec. 645) If there is an executor, the trustee and the executor make the election by filing Form 8855. If there is no executor, the trustee makes the election by filing Form 8855. (Reg § 1.645-1(c))[7]

¶ 3902   Estimated tax payments by trusts and estates—Form 1041-ES.

Under Code Sec. 6654(l)(1), trusts and certain estates must make estimated income tax payments (using Form 1041-ES and vouchers unless the Electronic Federal Tax Payment System (EFTPS) is used) under rules similar to those that apply to individuals, with certain adjustments.[8] Trusts and estates generally have 45 days to compute their estimated tax payments under the annualization rules. (Code Sec. 6654(l)(4))[9]

Estates and grantor trusts that receive the residue of a probate estate are exempt from making estimated tax payments for their first two tax years after the date of decedent's death. (Code Sec. 6654(l)(2))[10] Charitable trusts subject to tax under Code Sec. 511 are subject to corporate, not individual estimated taxes. (Code Sec. 6654(l)(3), Code Sec. 6655(g)(3))[11]

Where an electing small business trust (ESBT) election (see ¶3907) is effective on a date other than the first day of the trust's tax year, the trust is considered one trust for estimated tax purposes. (Reg § 1.1361-1(m)(3)(v))[12]

A trust or estate with a short tax year must pay estimated tax installments on or before the 15th day of the 4th, 6th and 9th month of such tax year, and the 15th day of the first month of the following year. For a short tax year in which the trust or estate terminates, installments due before the last day of the short year must be paid, and a final installment must be paid by the 15th day of the first month following the month the short year ends.[13]

¶ 3903   Election to treat estimated tax payments as paid by beneficiary—Form 1041-T.

Under Code Sec. 643(g)(1), a trustee may elect (on Form 1041-T) to treat any part of the trust's estimated tax payments as paid by a beneficiary. Any amount so treated is considered paid or credited to the beneficiary on the last day of the trust's tax year and is considered an estimated tax payment made by the beneficiary on Jan. 15, following the trust's tax year.[14] The election is also available to an estate for a tax year reasonably expected to be its last tax year. (Code Sec. 643(g)(3))

Elect on or before the *65th day* after the tax year. (Code Sec. 643(g)(2)) Attach Form 1041-T to Form 1041 only if the election is made with Form 1041. Otherwise, file Form 1041-T separately. The election is irrevocable. (Reg § 301.9100-8(a)(4))[15]

observation: Since a trust or estate's return is due 3½ months after the close of its tax year (¶4732), Form 1041-T must be filed before the return due date.

¶ 3904   Trust's termination—income taxation of trusts and estates.

When a trust terminates, it ends as a separate tax entity and no longer reports gross income or claims deductions, credits, etc. (Reg § 1.641(b)-3(d))

Though the duration of a trust may depend on the occurrence of a particular event under the trust instrument—e.g., the life beneficiary reaching a specified age—for tax purposes

---

7. ¶C-1021 *et seq.*
8. ¶S-5300 *et seq.*
9. ¶S-5304
10. ¶s S-5302, S-5203
11. ¶s S-5301, S-5420

12. ¶S-5301
13. ¶S-5311
14. ¶S-5309
15. ¶S-5310

the trust nevertheless continues for a reasonable period beyond this time to allow for the orderly completion of administration. (Reg § 1.641(b)-3(b))[16]

For unused deductions allowed to a beneficiary on a trust's termination, see ¶3945.

¶ 3905　Estate's termination—income taxation of trusts and estates.

Under Code Sec. 641(a)(3), an estate's status as a separate taxpayer exists only during the period of administration or settlement of the estate. This is the period actually required to perform the ordinary duties of administration, such as collecting assets and paying legacies and debts.[17] If estate administration is unduly prolonged, IRS considers the estate terminated for tax purposes after expiration of a reasonable period for performance by the executor of all the duties of administration. (Reg § 1.641(b)-3(a))[18]

For unused deductions allowed to a beneficiary on an estate's termination, see ¶3945.

¶ 3906　Status of liquidating trusts—income taxation of trusts and estates.

Liquidating trusts are ordinary trusts if their primary purpose is to liquidate the assets transferred to them. They are corporations if liquidation is only an incidental or ultimate intention and the primary objective is to continue normal business operations for an indefinite time. (Reg § 301.7701-4(d))[19]

¶ 3907　Electing small business trusts (ESBTs) for holding S stock—income taxation of trusts and estates.

Under Code Sec. 641(c), ESBTs, which may hold stock of an S corporation, are taxed as follows: For the portion of an ESBT consisting of S stock, the normal pass-through rules don't apply; instead, the trust is taxed at a flat rate of 39.6% on its taxable ordinary income as specially computed, and its capital gains are taxed at the preferential rates that apply for individuals. Interest paid or accrued on debt incurred to acquire S stock is taken into account in determining the income of the S portion of an ESBT. A grantor trust may elect to be an ESBT and if it does, the trust consists of a grantor portion, an S portion, and a non-S portion. The items of income, deduction, and credit attributable to the grantor portion are taxed to the deemed owner of that portion. The S portion is taxed under the special rules of Code Sec. 641(c), while the non-S portion is subject to the normal trust rules. (Reg § 1.641(c)-1)[20]

¶ 3908　Qualified funeral trusts—Form 1041-QFT—income taxation of trusts and estates.

Under Code Sec. 685, a trustee of a qualified funeral trust may elect simplified tax treatment for the trust on Form 1041-QFT, if it would otherwise be treated as a grantor trust.[21]

¶ 3909　Multiple trusts—income taxation of trusts and estates.

If a grantor creates multiple trusts, each trust is treated as a separate taxpayer. Separate trusts may be created even though there is only one trust instrument and only one trustee.[22]

Two or more trusts are treated as one if: (1) the trusts have substantially the same

16. ¶C-1012
17. ¶C-7010
18. ¶C-7011 *et seq.*
19. ¶C-5015

20. ¶C-5700 *et seq.*
21. ¶C-1013.1
22. ¶C-5150 *et seq.*

grantor or grantors and substantially the same primary beneficiary or beneficiaries, and (2) a principal purpose of the trusts is avoidance of federal income tax. (Code Sec. 643(f))[23]

¶ 3910   Charitable remainder annuity trusts (CRATs) and charitable remainder unitrusts (CRUTs)—income taxation of trusts and estates.

Under Code Sec. 664(c), if CRATs and CRUTs (¶2116) have unrelated business taxable income (UBTI), they must pay an excise tax equal to 100% of the UBTI. (Code Sec. 664(c); Reg § 1.664-1(a)(1))[24]

¶ 3911   Pooled income fund (PIF)—income taxation of trusts and estates.

A PIF formed to pay income to noncharitable beneficiaries and the remainder to charity (¶2117) generally is taxed under the trust rules[25] even if it isn't a trust under local law. (Reg § 1.642(c)-5(a)(2))[26] However, a PIF is allowed a charitable deduction for long-term capital gain that is, under the terms of its governing instrument, permanently set aside for charitable purposes during the tax year. (Code Sec. 642(c)(3); Reg § 1.642(c)-2(c)) No amount of net long-term capital gain will be considered "permanently set aside for charitable purposes" if, under the terms of the PIF's governing instrument and applicable local law, the trustee has the power, whether or not exercised, to satisfy the income beneficiaries' right to income by the payment of either (1) an amount equal to a fixed percentage of the fair market value of the PIF's assets, whether determined annually or averaged on a multiple year basis; or (2) any amount that takes into account unrealized appreciation in the value of the PIF's assets. (Reg § 1.642(c)-2(c))[27]

¶ 3912   Gross income of trusts and estates.

What would be gross income in the hands of an individual is gross income when received by a trust or estate. (Reg § 1.641(a)-2)[28]

Gross income includes income accumulated or held for future distribution under the terms of a will or trust, income that's currently distributable, income received by a decedent's estate during administration or settlement, and income that, in the fiduciary's discretion, may be either accumulated or distributed. (Code Sec. 641(a))[29]

¶ 3913   Income from real estate passing directly to heirs—income taxation of trusts and estates.

Where, under local law, real property is subject to an estate's administration, the income from it is that of the estate for the period that the estate is under administration.[30]

Where state law vests legal title to decedent's real estate upon death directly in the decedent's heirs, devisees, or other beneficiaries, income from the real estate is taxed to the beneficiaries and not the estate. (Reg § 1.661(a)-2(e))[31]

¶ 3914   Gain or loss on distribution of property; Code Sec. 643(e) election—income taxation of trusts and estates.

Gain or loss is realized by a trust or estate (or by the other beneficiaries) upon a distribution of property, if the distribution is in satisfaction of a right to receive a specific

---

23. ¶C-5153
24. ¶C-5039
25. ¶s C-2312, C-2316
26. ¶C-5040
27. ¶C-2316

28. ¶s C-2100 *et seq.*, C-7100 *et seq.*
29. ¶s C-2101, C-7101
30. ¶C-7105
31. ¶C-7109

dollar amount, specific property other than that distributed, or income, if income is required to be distributed currently. In addition, gain or loss is realized if the trustee or executor makes the Code Sec. 643(e) election to recognize gain or loss. (Reg § 1.661(a)-2(f))[32]

Trusts and estates may not deduct a loss on property to which a Code Sec. 643(e)(3) election applies because of the rule barring losses on sales between related parties (¶2444).

¶ 3915 Estate income from community property—income taxation of trusts and estates.

If a decedent dies leaving community property, the income from one-half of the property is taxable to the estate, and the income from the other half is taxable to the surviving spouse.[33]

¶ 3916 Deductions and credits of trusts and estates.

The deductions and credits of a trust generally follow those of individuals. Exceptions to this rule include the trust's deduction for distributions to beneficiaries (¶3927), and the treatment of a trust's miscellaneous itemized deductions (¶3919) (which are disallowed in years 2018–2025, and are subject to a 2%-of-adjusted-gross-income floor in other years). (Code Sec. 641(b); Reg § 1.641(b)-1)[34] Certain deductions and credits are apportioned between the trust and the beneficiaries, ¶3917.

For treatment of grantor trusts, for which deductions and credits generally pass through to the deemed trust owner, see ¶3951.

¶ 3917 Apportionment of depreciation, depletion, and amortization, and of certain credits, between trusts/estates and beneficiaries—income taxation of trusts and estates.

The right to certain deductions and credits is limited to the portion remaining after allocation to the beneficiaries of their proper share in these deductions and credits. Apportionment is specifically provided for the following:

Depreciation and depletion are deductible by a trust only to the extent they aren't allowable to the beneficiaries (including charitable beneficiaries). (Code Sec. 642(e); Reg § 1.642(e)-1) Apportionment between the trustee and the income beneficiaries is required. (Code Sec. 167(d); Code Sec. 611(b)(3); Reg § 1.167(h)-1(b)) The extent to which depreciation and depletion are allowable to income beneficiaries depends primarily on the provisions of the trust instrument.[35]

Similar rules apply—for trusts or estates—to apportion amortization of pollution control facilities and 15-year amortization of Code Sec. 197 intangibles between the income beneficiaries and the trust. (Code Sec. 642(f); Reg § 1.642(f)-1)[36]

Depreciation and depletion are deductible by the fiduciary of an estate only to the extent they're not allowable to the beneficiaries (including charitable beneficiaries). (Code Sec. 642(e); Reg § 1.642(e)-1) For an estate this requires apportionment between the estate and the heirs, legatees, and devisees. (Code Sec. 167(d); Code Sec. 611(b)(4); Reg § 1.167(h)-1(c))[37]

The following credits are among those subject to apportionment between a trust/estate and beneficiaries: foreign tax credit (Code Sec. 642(a)); investment credit (Code

32. ¶s C-2151, C-7151
33. ¶C-7108
34. ¶s C-2200 *et seq.*, C-7200 *et seq.*

35. ¶C-2202; ¶C-2209
36. ¶C-2209; ¶C-7221
37. ¶C-7220

Sec. 50(d)(6)), as apportioned under former Code Sec. 48(f) (Code Sec. 50(d)(6); Code Sec. 48(f)(1) before repeal by Sec. 11813(a), PL 101-508, 11/5/90); the work opportunity tax credit (Code Sec. 52(d)); biodiesel fuels credit (Code Sec. 40A(d)(4)); renewable diesel fuel credit (Code Sec. 40A(f)(1); Code Sec. 40A(d)(4)); research credit (Code Sec. 41(f)(2)(A)); orphan drug credit (Code Sec. 45C(d)(3)); low-income housing credit (Code Sec. 42(i)(6)); and federal income tax withheld (Code Sec. 31(a)), including backup withholding (Code Sec. 31(c); Code Sec. 643(d)(1)).[38]

¶ 3918 Administration expenses; expenses allocable to exempt income—income taxation of trusts and estates.

The deductibility of business and nonbusiness expenses from trust or estate income follows substantially the same rules that apply to individuals. (Code Sec. 641(b)) Among the expenses common in fiduciary administration and recognized as deductible are reasonable amounts paid or incurred by the fiduciary for administration expenses, including fiduciaries' fees and expenses of litigation, if they are ordinary and necessary in performing the duties of administration, aren't allocable to the production or collection of tax-exempt income (see below), and haven't been allowed for federal estate tax purposes. (Reg § 1.212-1(i))[39] For the election to deduct these expenses against income or estate tax, see ¶3920.

✔️ observation: Where the trust administration expenses aren't trade or business expenses, they are miscellaneous itemized deductions (disallowed 2018–2025, and subject to the 2%-of-AGI floor in other years), see ¶3919.

Under Code Sec. 265, no deduction may be taken for *any* expenses allocable to tax-exempt income. (Code Sec. 265; Reg § 1.212-1(i))[40]

¶ 3919 Trust's/estate's miscellaneous itemized deductions (disallowed 2018–2025, and subject to 2%-of-AGI floor in other years)—income taxation of trusts and estates.

From 2018 - 2025, miscellaneous itemized deductions subject to the 2% floor are suspended (¶2162). But Code Sec. 67(e) deductions—i.e., for costs paid or incurred in connection with the administration of a trust or estate, and that wouldn't be incurred if the property weren't held in trust (Code Sec. 67(e)(1)), as well as the deductions listed in Code Sec. 67(e)(2)—are *not* itemized deductions under Code Sec. 63(d) (¶3109) and are *not* miscellaneous itemized deductions under Code Sec. 67(b) (¶2162). So Code Sec. 67(e) deductions aren't disallowed under Code Sec. 67(g), and aren't subject to the 2% floor. (Reg § 1.67-4(a)(1))[41]

Fees for investment advice (including related services that would be provided to an individual investor as part of an investment advisory fee), incurred by a non-grantor trust or by an estate, and that would be incurred commonly or customarily by an individual investor, are subject to the post-2025 2% floor. But incremental costs of investment advice beyond the amount normally charged to an individual investor, such as an additional charge added solely because the investment advice is rendered to a trust, or is attributable to an unusual investment objective or the need for a specialized balancing of the interests of various parties (beyond the usual balancing of the varying interests of current beneficiaries and remaindermen), aren't subject to the 2% floor. Thus, the amount of the investment advisory fees incurred by a non-grantor trust or by an estate that exceeds the amount of fees that would be charged to an individual investor is the amount not subject to

---

38. ¶C-2202; ¶C-7201
39. ¶C-2208, C-7215

40. ¶C-2208, C-7217
41. ¶C-2204 *et seq.*, C-7202 *et seq.*

the 2% floor (and fully deductible). (Reg § 1.67-4(b)(4))[42]

A "bundled fee" (a single fee, such as a fiduciary's commission, which includes costs subject to the 2% floor and costs (in more than de minimis amounts) not subject to the 2% floor) paid by a non-grantor trust or an estate must be allocated between the costs subject to the 2% floor and the costs that aren't subject to the 2% floor. (Reg § 1.67-4(c)(1))[43]

¶ 3920   Election to take either income tax or estate tax deduction—income taxation of estates.

Under Code Sec. 642(g), administration expenses, including commissions and other selling expenses, and casualty and theft losses during administration, may be taken either: (1) as a deduction (or an offset against the sales price of property in determining gain or loss) in computing the estate's taxable income for *income tax* purposes, or (2) as a deduction in computing the decedent's taxable estate for *estate tax* purposes, but not both. To take the income tax deduction, the executor files in duplicate (a) a statement that the amount involved hasn't already been taken as a deduction for federal estate tax purposes, and (b) a waiver of the right to take it as an estate tax deduction. (Reg § 1.642(g)-1)[44]

Some items or portion of an item can be deducted for income tax purposes if the statement and waiver are filed, while a similar item or different portion of the same item can be taken for estate tax purposes. (Reg § 1.642(g)-2)[45]

Similar rules apply for the GST tax. (Code Sec. 642(g))[46]

¶ 3921   Deductions that can be claimed for both income and estate tax purposes.

The rule barring deductions for *both* income tax and estate tax purposes (¶3920) doesn't apply to obligations of the decedent for interest, taxes and expenses that are allowable as deductions in respect of a decedent (see ¶3964) (Reg § 1.642(g)-2), or items that qualify for deduction on the estate tax return as claims against the estate.[47]

¶ 3922   Estate and trust exemption amounts—income taxation of trusts and estates.

Under Code Sec. 642(b), an estate is entitled to an exemption of $600.[48]

A trust that's required to distribute all of its income currently has a $300 exemption (even for a year in which it makes a corpus distribution or a charitable contribution). All other trusts generally deduct a $100 exemption (other than a qualified disability trust, see below). (Code Sec. 642(b); Reg § 1.642(b)-1)[49]

The exemption amount for a qualified disability trust is $4,400 in 2022 ($4,700 for 2023).[50]

---

42. ¶C-2205, C-7202.3
43. ¶C-2205, C-7202.4
44. ¶C-7226 *et seq.*
45. ¶C-7232
46. ¶C-7227

47. ¶s C-7234, C-7235
48. ¶C-7207
49. ¶C-2206
50. ¶C-2207

¶ 3923   Income taxation of trusts and estates—standard deduction.

Under Code Sec. 63(c)(6)(D), the standard deduction of a trust or estate is zero.[1]

¶ 3924   Net operating loss (NOL)—income taxation of trusts and estates.

Trusts and estates are entitled to the NOL deduction under Code Sec. 172 (¶1815 *et seq.*). (Code Sec. 642(d)) In computing the NOL, the charitable deduction and the deduction for distributions are disregarded. (Reg § 1.642(d)-1)[2]

¶ 3925   Charitable contributions—Form 1041-A—income taxation of trusts and estates.

Under Code Sec. 642(c)(1), an estate or trust may deduct any amount of gross income, without limitation, that, under the terms of the governing instrument, is *paid* during the tax year for a charitable purpose. (Code Sec. 642(c)(1); Reg § 1.642(c)-1(a)) A provision in a governing instrument or local law that specifically provides the source from which amounts are to be paid, permanently set aside, or used for a purpose specified in Code Sec. 642(c), must have economic effect independent of income tax consequences in order to be respected for Federal tax purposes. (Reg § 1.642(c)-3(b)(2), Reg § 1.643(a)-5(b)) A contribution made out of income accumulated in earlier years is deductible, but only if no deduction was allowed for any previous year for the amount currently contributed. However, for a donation of property purchased from income in a prior year, the entity may claim a charitable deduction only for the property's adjusted basis and not its higher fair market value.[3]

File Form 1041-A for a trust that claims a charitable deduction under Code Sec. 642(c). Use Form 8868 for an extension, see ¶4126.

Estates are allowed to deduct any amount of gross income, without limit, which under the terms of the governing instrument is, during the tax year, permanently *set aside* for a charitable purpose. (Code Sec. 642(c)(2); Reg § 1.642(c)-2(a), Reg § 1.642(c)-2(b))[4]

Trusts are denied the set-aside deduction, except for pooled income funds, see ¶3911. (Code Sec. 642(c)(2), Code Sec. 642(c)(3); Reg § 1.642(c)-2(b), Reg § 1.642(c)-2(c))[5]

Contributions made out of tax-exempt income, such as state or municipal bond interest, aren't deductible. (Reg § 1.642(c)-3(b), Reg § 1.643(a)-5(b))[6]

¶ 3926   Election to accelerate charitable deduction—income taxation of trusts and estates.

Under Code Sec. 642(c)(1), a trust or estate can elect to treat a contribution actually paid in one tax year as paid in the preceding tax year. The election must be made not later than the due date (including extensions) of the income tax return for the tax year *following the tax year* to which the deductions are pushed back.[7] The election is made by attaching a statement to the return or amended return for the year to which the deductions are pushed back. (Reg § 1.642(c)-1(b))[8]

---

1. ¶s C-2204, C-7205
2. ¶C-2210, C-7222
3. ¶s C-2301 *et seq.*, C-7301 *et seq.*
4. ¶C-7311
5. ¶C-2312 *et seq.*
6. ¶s C-2308, C-7308
7. ¶s C-2303, C-7304
8. ¶s C-2305, C-7305

¶ 3927   Deduction for distributions to trust and estate beneficiaries—income taxation of trusts and estates.

Under Code Sec. 651(b) and Code Sec. 661(a), distributions to beneficiaries are deductible up to the "distributable net income" (DNI) of the trust or estate for the tax year. [9] The distribution deduction of a trust depends on whether the trust is a simple trust or a complex trust.

A "simple" trust (¶3928) is one that makes no distribution other than of current income and the terms of which require all of its income to be distributed currently and don't provide for charitable or similar contributions. A "complex" trust (¶3930) permits accumulation of income or charitable contributions or distributes principal.[10]

A trust may shift its character from simple to complex and vice versa. (Reg § 1.651(a)-1, Reg § 1.661(a)-1)[11]

¶ 3928   Distributions deduction of a simple trust—income taxation of trusts.

Under Code Sec. 651(b)), this deduction for a simple trust is the amount of its income for the tax year that's required to be distributed currently, up to the ceiling of its distributable net income (DNI) for the year (¶3929). Tax-exempt income is excluded both from accounting income and DNI in figuring the deduction. (Reg § 1.651(b)-1)[12]

¶ 3929   Distributable net income (DNI) of a simple trust—income taxation of trusts.

Under Code Sec. 643(a), the starting point for DNI is *taxable* income, i.e., gross income minus deductions. These adjustments are then made to taxable income:

(1) Add back the deduction for personal exemption and any deduction for distributions. (Code Sec. 643(a)(1), Code Sec. 643(a)(2); Reg § 1.643(a)-1, Reg § 1.643(a)-2)

(2) Subtract any extraordinary dividends (in cash or property) and taxable stock dividends that the trustee doesn't pay or credit because he or she determines they are allocable to principal. (Code Sec. 643(a)(4); Reg § 1.643(a)-4)

(3) Subtract any capital gains that are allocated to principal and aren't paid, credited or required to be distributed during the tax year. Add back any capital losses, except to the extent they are taken into account in computing capital gains that are paid, credited or required to be distributed during the tax year. Add back any gain excluded under Code Sec. 1202 on the sale of qualified small business stock. (Code Sec. 643(a)(3); Reg § 1.643(a)-3(b))[13]

Gains from the sale or exchange of capital assets are included in DNI to the extent they are allocated to: (i) income; (ii) corpus, but treated consistently by the fiduciary on the trust's books, records, and tax returns as part of a distribution to a beneficiary; or (iii) corpus, but actually distributed to the beneficiary or used by the fiduciary in determining the amount that is distributed or required to be distributed to a beneficiary. (Reg § 1.643(a)-3(b))[14]

---

9. ¶s C-2501, C-8001
10. ¶C-2601
11. ¶C-2501

12. ¶C-2603 *et seq.*
13. ¶C-2606 *et seq.*
14. ¶C-2608

¶ 3930 Distributions deduction of a complex trust or estate—trust and estate income taxation.

Under Code Sec. 661(a), a complex trust or estate deducts, up to its distributable net income (DNI) ceiling for the year (¶3931), the sum of:

(1) any income for the tax year required to be distributed currently (¶3932); and

(2) any other amounts, whether income or principal, properly paid or credited or required to be distributed for that tax year (¶3933). (Code Sec. 661(a); Reg § 1.661(a)-2(a))[15]

No distributions deduction may be taken for any portion of DNI that represents an item, such as tax-exempt interest, that isn't included in the gross income of the trust or estate. (Code Sec. 661(c); Reg § 1.661(c)-1) Unless the instrument or local law requires another allocation, the distribution is considered to contain the same proportion of tax-exempt items entering into DNI as the total tax-exempt income bears to total DNI. (Code Sec. 661(b); Reg § 1.661(b)-1)[16]

¶ 3931 Distributable net income (DNI) for a complex trust or estate—income taxation of trusts and estates.

Under Code Sec. 643(a), the DNI of a complex trust or an estate is its taxable income with these adjustments:

(1) No deduction for distributions or personal exemption is allowed. (Code Sec. 643(a)(1))

(2) Capital gains are excluded unless they are: allocated to income; allocated to corpus, but treated consistently by the fiduciary as part of a distribution to a beneficiary; allocated to corpus but actually distributed to the beneficiary or used by the fiduciary in determining the amount that is distributed or required to be distributed to a beneficiary; or allowed as a charitable deduction. Capital losses are excluded except to the extent they enter into a determination of any capital gains paid, credited or required to be distributed to a beneficiary during the tax year. Any gain excluded under Code Sec. 1202 on the sale of qualified small business stock is added back. (Code Sec. 643(a)(3); Reg § 1.643(a)-3(b))

(3) Tax-exempt interest, reduced by allocable, nondeductible expenses, is included except to the extent allocable to the charitable deduction. (Code Sec. 643(a)(5); Reg § 1.643(a)-5)[17]

¶ 3932 "Income required to be distributed currently"—income taxation of trusts and estates.

Under Code Sec. 643(b), income required to be distributed currently means accounting income of the trust or estate determined under the trust instrument or will and applicable local law. It doesn't include items of gross income that the fiduciary allocates to corpus.

An allocation of amounts between income and principal under applicable local law will be respected if local law provides for a reasonable apportionment between the income and remainder beneficiaries of the total return of the trust for the year, including ordinary and tax-exempt income, capital gains, and appreciation. (Reg § 1.643(b)-1)

A distribution required to be made out of income or corpus, such as an annuity, is considered to be out of currently distributable income to the extent it's paid out of income

15. ¶s C-2701, C-8101
16. ¶s C-2707, C-8107

17. ¶s C-2702 *et seq.*, C-8102 *et seq.*

for the tax year. (Code Sec. 661(a)(1); Reg § 1.661(a)-2(b))

Currently distributable income is deductible for the tax year of the trust or estate in which it is received even though, as a matter of practical necessity, it isn't distributed until after the end of that year. (Reg § 1.651(a)-2(a), Reg § 1.651(a)-2(b))[18]

¶ 3933 "Other amounts properly paid or credited or required to be distributed"—income taxation of trusts and estates.

Under Code Sec. 661(a), "other amounts properly paid or credited or required to be distributed" must be actually distributed or at least made available on demand by the beneficiary. Even though designated by the fiduciary as a payment of *principal* of the trust or estate, a distribution actually paid or made available is deductible by the fiduciary as a distribution of "other amounts." It isn't necessary that the distribution actually be made out of income. (Code Sec. 661(a); Reg § 1.661(a)-2(c))[19] An amount that a trust has elected to treat as an estimated tax payment by a beneficiary (¶3903) is a deductible distribution. (Code Sec. 643(g))[20]

¶ 3934 Deduction for distribution of property in kind—income taxation of trusts and estates.

Distributions of property in kind qualify for deduction as other amounts paid. (Reg § 1.661(a)-2(c)) If the trust or estate elects to recognize gain or loss (¶3914), the property distributed is taken into account at its fair market value for purposes of the distribution deduction. If the election isn't made, the property is taken into account only to the extent of the lesser of the basis of the property in the hands of the beneficiary (¶3943) or the fair market value of the property. (Code Sec. 643(e)(2), Code Sec. 643(e)(3))[21]

¶ 3935 Family support allowances—income taxation of trusts and estates.

Family support allowances (for a decedent's widow(er) or dependent) paid by an estate under a court order or decree, or under local law, are treated as distributions deductible by the estate, subject to the regular distributable net income (DNI) deduction ceiling. (Reg § 1.661(a)-2(e), Reg § 1.662(a)-2(c))[22]

¶ 3936 Nondeductible distributions—income taxation of trusts and estates.

No distribution deduction is allowed for:

. . . distributions to charity (Reg § 1.663(a)-2);[23]

. . . the value of any interest in real estate, title to which passes directly from decedent to the decedent's heirs and devisees (Reg § 1.661(a)-2(e));[24]

. . . a gift or bequest of specific property or of a specific sum of money that is paid or credited all at once or in not more than three installments—an amount that can be paid only from income isn't considered a gift or bequest of a specific sum of money and is therefore includible in the distributions deduction (Code Sec. 663(a)(1));[25]

. . . any amount reported as a distribution in an earlier year's return because it was credited or required to be distributed in the earlier year (Code Sec. 663(a)(3); Reg § 1.663(a)-3);[26] or

---

18. ¶s C-2504 *et seq.*, C-8003 *et seq.*
19. ¶s C-2524 *et seq.*, C-8014 *et seq.*
20. ¶C-2530
21. ¶s C-2525, C-8015
22. ¶C-8011

23. ¶s C-2533, C-8026
24. ¶C-8027
25. ¶s C-2531 *et seq.*, C-8022 *et seq.*
26. ¶s C-2534, C-8028

... any amount paid or credited within the first 65 days of the current year which the fiduciary elected to treat as paid or credited in the preceding year, see ¶3937.

¶ 3937 Election to deduct "late paid" distributions—the "65-day rule"—income taxation of trusts and estates.

The fiduciary of a complex trust and the executor of an estate can elect, by checking a box on Form 1041, to treat an amount properly paid or credited within the first 65 days of any tax year of the entity as paid or credited on the last day of the preceding tax year. (Code Sec. 663(b))[27]

The amount to which the election applies can't exceed the greater of: (1) the entity's accounting income for the year for which the election is made, or (2) its distributable net income (DNI) for that year, in each case reduced by any amounts paid, credited, or required to be distributed in that year other than amounts considered paid or credited in a preceding tax year by reason of the "65-day" rule. (Reg § 1.663(b)-1(a))[28]

¶ 3938 Amount taxed to beneficiary of a simple trust.

Under Code Sec. 652, the beneficiary of a simple trust is generally taxed on the *lower* of these two items:

(1) the amount of trust income for the tax year of the trust required to be distributed to the beneficiary currently whether distributed or not; or

(2) the beneficiary's proportionate share of the trust's distributable net income (DNI). (Code Sec. 652(a); Reg § 1.652(a)-1)

DNI is computed as explained at ¶3929, except that for this purpose it includes tax-exempt interest minus allocable deductions. (Code Sec. 643(a)(5)) Tax-exempt income items, however, aren't taxable to the beneficiary because of the character rule explained at ¶3940. Income from sources outside the U.S. is included for foreign trusts. (Code Sec. 643(a)(6))[29]

¶ 3939 Amount taxed to beneficiary of a complex trust or estate.

Under Code Sec. 662, the beneficiary of a complex trust or of an estate includes in gross income the sum of the following amounts, subject to the distributable net income (DNI) ceiling (see below) and the elimination of tax-exempt items under the character rule (¶3940):

(1) income required to be distributed to the beneficiary currently (though not actually distributed), which includes an annuity or other amount required to be paid out of income or corpus, to the extent it is paid out of income for the tax year; and

(2) all other amounts (whether from income or principal) properly paid, credited or required to be distributed to the beneficiary for the tax year (Code Sec. 662(a))[30] including income from property distributed in kind, see ¶3943. (Reg § 1.662(a)-3(b))

A beneficiary of a complex trust or an estate need not report as income more than the beneficiary's share of DNI, so that the total amount of income reported by all beneficiaries cannot exceed the total DNI of the trust or estate for the tax year. For this purpose, the beneficiaries are divided into two groups or "tiers:"

(1) The first tier is composed of beneficiaries entitled to income distributions currently,

27. ¶C-2713, ¶C-8113
28. ¶C-2713, ¶C-8113
29. ¶C-3001
30. ¶s C-3006 *et seq.*, C-9001 *et seq.*

that is "income required to be distributed currently."

(2) The second tier is composed of beneficiaries receiving or entitled to receive other "noncurrent" distributions. (Code Sec. 662(a); Reg § 1.662(a)-3(c))[31]

First-tier beneficiaries report, in the aggregate, the amount of their current distributions, up to the amount of DNI for the tax year of the trust or estate, computed as explained at ¶3931 without any charitable deduction. Thus, if the total of first-tier distributions is equal to or less than DNI (without charitable deduction), each first-tier beneficiary reports his or her full share of the distributions. (Code Sec. 662(a)(1))[32]

But if the total of first-tier distributions exceeds DNI (without charitable deduction) each beneficiary reports an amount equal to his or her pro rata share of DNI (without charitable deduction). (Code Sec. 662(a)(1); Reg § 1.662(a)-2(b))[33]

Second-tier beneficiaries report, in the aggregate, the amount of their second-tier distributions up to the DNI of the trust or estate as reduced for first-tier distributions of current income. For this purpose, DNI is computed *with* allowance of any charitable deduction.

If the total of second-tier distributions equals or is less than the ceiling (DNI as reduced for first-tier distributions), each second-tier beneficiary reports his or her full share of the second-tier distributions. But, if the total of second-tier distributions exceeds the ceiling, each second-tier beneficiary reports only his or her pro rata share of the ceiling amount. (Code Sec. 662(a)(2); Reg § 1.662(a)-3(c))[34]

¶ 3940   Character of trust's and estate's income in beneficiary's hands—income taxation of beneficiaries.

Under Code Sec. 652(b) and Code Sec. 662(b), for simple trusts, complex trusts and estates, the amounts taxable to the beneficiaries have the same character (e.g., as tax-exempt income) in the hands of the beneficiaries as the amounts had when received by the trust or estate. (Code Sec. 652(b), Code Sec. 662(b); Reg § 1.652(b)-1, Reg § 1.662(b)-1)[35]

Unless the instrument specifically allocates different classes of income to different beneficiaries, amounts distributed are treated as consisting of the same proportion of each class of items entering into the computation of distributable net income (DNI) as the total of each class bears to the total DNI of the trust or estate. (Code Sec. 652(b), Code Sec. 662(b); Reg § 1.652(b)-1, Reg § 1.662(b)-1)[36]

Deductions that enter into the computation of DNI are allocated among the classes as follows:

. . . Deductions *directly* attributable to a particular class of income (interest, rents, dividends, capital gains, etc.) are allocated to that class.

. . . If deductions *directly* attributable to a class of income exceed that class, the excess may be allocated to any other class (including capital gains) included in DNI in the manner shown below for deductions not directly attributable, except that excess deductions directly attributable to tax-exempt income cannot be used to reduce any other class of income.

. . . Deductions not directly attributable to a specific class of income can be allocated to any item of income (including capital gains) included in DNI, but a part must be allocated proportionately to tax-exempt income. Examples of these "neutral" deductions are trustees' commissions (both income and corpus), and state income and personal property taxes. (Reg § 1.652(b)-3)[37]

---

31. ¶s C-3010, C-9006
32. ¶s C-3011 *et seq.*, C-9007 *et seq.*
33. ¶s C-3011, C-9008
34. ¶s C-3013, C-9009

35. ¶s C-3002, C-3016, C-9012
36. ¶s C-3003, C-3016, C-9012
37. ¶s C-3004, C-3017, C-9013

A *charitable deduction* by an estate or complex trust is allocated just before the other deductions. Allocation follows the terms of the instrument or local law, or if these are silent, the charitable deduction is allocated to each class of income items in the proportion that the total of each class bears to the total of all classes. (Reg § 1.643(a)-5(b), Reg § 1.662(b)-2)[38]

¶ 3941 Trust or estate beneficiaries' separate shares treated separately for income tax.

If a complex trust or an estate accumulates income for one beneficiary and distributes principal to another beneficiary, the normal tax rules would impose a tax burden on the recipient of principal since that recipient in effect must pay tax on income accumulated for the other beneficiary. To prevent this, the "separate share rule" (Code Sec. 663(c)) treats substantially separate and independent shares of different beneficiaries of a single trust or estate as though each share represented a separate trust or estate. This applies *only* in computing distributable net income (DNI) as a ceiling on the amount deductible by the trust or estate and taxable to the beneficiaries (Code Sec. 663(c); Reg § 1.663(c)-1(b)), and is mandatory. (Reg § 1.663(c)-1(d))[39] Code Sec. 663(c), Reg § 1.663(c)-1(a))[40] A surviving spouse's elective share is a separate share,[41] as is a pecuniary formula bequest unless it's not entitled to income or to share in appreciation or depreciation and can paid or credited in more than three installments. (Reg § 1.663(c)-4(b))[42]

¶ 3942 When a beneficiary of a trust or estate is taxed.

Under Code Sec. 652(a), amounts required to be distributed currently are taxed to the beneficiary when they are required to be distributed even though not actually distributed. Other distributions are taxed to a beneficiary when they are made or credited, or required to be made. (Code Sec. 652(a), Code Sec. 662(a); Reg § 1.662(a)-3(a))[43]

If a beneficiary's tax year is different from that of the estate or trust, the beneficiary includes his or her share of the trust or estate income in the return for the tax year in which the tax year of the trust or estate ends. (Code Sec. 652(c), Code Sec. 662(c))[44]

On termination of an estate, a beneficiary's calendar-year return must include income received from the estate during the estate's fiscal year and final short year where both years end within the beneficiary's calendar year.[45]

Where the 65-day rule is elected (¶3937), the beneficiary is considered as receiving the distribution in his or her tax year that includes the close of the trust's or estate's tax year in which the distribution is considered made. (Reg § 1.663(b)-1(a)(2)(ii))[46]

In *Kaestner*, the Supreme Court found that the presence of in-state beneficiaries alone doesn't allow a state (NC) to tax trust income that hasn't been distributed to those beneficiaries, where the beneficiaries have no right to demand that income and may not ever receive that income.[47]

¶ 3943 Distributions in kind includible in beneficiary's income—income taxation of beneficiaries.

For property distributed in kind, the amount taken into account under Code Sec. 662(a)(2) (¶3939) for determining the amount includible in the beneficiary's income,

38. ¶s C-3018, C-9015
39. ¶C-2711 *et seq.*
40. ¶C-8111
41. ¶C-8112.1
42. ¶C-8112.2

43. ¶s C-3025, C-9017
44. ¶s C-3026, C-9018
45. ¶C-9018
46. ¶C-3028, ¶C-9019
47. ¶C-1007.1

and for determining basis in the property, depends on whether the estate or trust elected to recognize gain or loss on the distribution (see ¶3914).

If the estate or trust elects, the property is taken into account at fair market value (FMV). (Code Sec. 643(e)(3))

If the estate or trust doesn't elect, the property is taken into account only to the extent of the lesser of: (1) the FMV of the property, or (2) its basis in the hands of the beneficiary. (Code Sec. 643(e)(2))[48]

The beneficiary's basis for property distributed in kind is the adjusted basis of the property in the hands of the estate or trust immediately before the distribution, adjusted for any gain or loss recognized by the estate or trust on the distribution. (Code Sec. 643(e)(1))[49]

¶ 3944   Nontaxable gifts and bequests—income taxation of beneficiaries.

Under Code Sec. 663(a)(1), a beneficiary isn't taxable on any amount paid or credited as a gift or bequest of specific property or of a specific sum of money, and that is paid or credited all at once or in not more than three installments.[50]

¶ 3945   Beneficiaries' deductions on estate or trust termination—NOL carryovers, capital loss carryovers, "excess deductions"—income taxation of beneficiaries.

A deduction, under Code Sec. 642(h), is allowed to beneficiaries who, on termination, succeed to trust property, only for the beneficiary's tax year in which the trust or estate terminates. The following deductions (of which the fiduciary could make no use) are allowed: (1) a carryover of a net operating loss (under Code Sec. 172) or of a capital loss (under (Code Sec. 1212); and (2) any deductions for the last tax year of the trust (other than the personal exemption and charitable contributions) in excess of its gross income for that year. A beneficiary may claim all or part of the amount of the deductions discussed above, as determined after taking into consideration Reg § 1.642(h)-2(b), before, after, or together with the same character of deductions separately allowable to the beneficiary for the beneficiary's tax year in which the trust terminated. Each deduction comprising the excess deductions under Code Sec. 642(h)(2) retains, in the hands of the beneficiary, its character (specifically, as allowable in arriving at adjusted gross income, as a non-miscellaneous itemized deduction, or as a miscellaneous itemized deduction) while in the trust. (Miscellaneous itemized deductions aren't allowed for 2018 through 2025, see ¶2162.) A deduction succeeded to by a beneficiary remains subject to any additional applicable limit and must be separately stated if it could be limited, as provided in the instructions to Form 1041 and the Schedule K-1 (Form 1041). (Code Sec. 642(h); Reg § 1.642(h)-2(a))[1]

¶ 3946   Income taxation of beneficiaries of charitable remainder trusts (CRTs).

Under Code Sec. 664, amounts paid to an income beneficiary of a CRT retain the character they had in the hands of the trust, with this qualification: each payment is treated as consisting of (1) ordinary income, to the extent of the trust's ordinary income for that year and undistributed ordinary income for earlier years, (2) capital gain, to the extent of capital gain for that year and undistributed capital gain (determined on a cumulative net basis) for earlier years, (3) other income (e.g., tax-exempt interest), to the extent of that income for that year and undistributed amounts for earlier years, and (4) trust corpus. (Code Sec. 664(a), Code Sec. 664(b); Reg § 1.664-1(d)(1)) Within categories (1) and (2),

---

48. ¶s C-3009, C-9004
49. ¶s C-3009, C-9004

50. ¶s C-2531, C-8022
1. ¶s C-3033 *et seq.*, C-9053 *et seq.*

items are assigned to different classes to reflect rate differences (e.g., qualified dividends and different capital gain classes). (Reg § 1.664-1(d)(1)(i)(b))[2]

¶ 3947 Determining basis in a term interest in a charitable remainder trust (CRT) for sale or other disposition—income taxation of beneficiaries.

The basis of a term interest (an interest, present or future, in the income from property or the right to use property which will terminate or fail on the lapse of time, on the occurrence of an event or contingency, or on the failure of an event or contingency to occur) in a CRT of a taxable beneficiary is the portion of the adjusted uniform basis assignable to that interest, reduced (but not below zero) by an amount determined by applying the same share of that portion to the sum of (1) the amount of the trust's undistributed net ordinary income; and (2) the amount of the trust's undistributed net capital gain. (Reg § 1.1014-5(c))[3]

¶ 3948 Distribution of accumulated trust income—"throwback" rules—income taxation of beneficiaries.

The throwback rules tax beneficiaries on distributions of income accumulated by the trust before the year of distribution, as though the income had been distributed currently to the beneficiaries in the years received by the trust. (Reg § 1.665(a)-0A(a)(1))[4]

The throwback rules apply to foreign trusts, domestic trusts previously treated as foreign trusts (except as provided in regs), and domestic trusts created before Mar. 1, '84, that would be treated as multiple trusts under Code Sec. 643(f). (Code Sec. 665(c))

The throwback rules generally apply only to complex trusts. Estates aren't subject to the throwback rules. (Code Sec. 666; Reg § 1.665(a)-0A(d))[5]

The fiduciary of a trust subject to the throwback rules must complete Schedule J (Form 1041) and attach it to the trust's return.[6]

Distributions of income accumulated before the birth of the beneficiary or before the beneficiary reaches age 21 are exempt from the throwback rules. But this exclusion doesn't apply to distributions from a foreign trust or to certain distributions from multiple trusts. (Code Sec. 665(b))[7] Distributions not exceeding accounting income are also exempt. (Code Sec. 665(b))[8]

¶ 3949 Beneficiary's tax under throwback rules—Form 4970.

The beneficiary includes in his or her income for the current year:

... the amount of the accumulation distribution considered distributed; and

... the trust's income tax considered distributed. (Code Sec. 667(a), Code Sec. 666(b))[9]

The beneficiary's total tax liability for the current year is:

(1) a partial tax on the beneficiary's taxable income *reduced* by the total amounts considered distributed to the beneficiary under the throwback rules; *plus*

(2) a partial tax on the amounts considered distributed under the throwback rules (Code Sec. 667(a)); *plus*

(3) in the case of a foreign trust, a special nondeductible interest charge. (Code

2. ¶C-3051
3. ¶P-3130.1
4. ¶C-4001
5. ¶C-4002

6. ¶C-4001
7. ¶C-4007
8. ¶C-4008
9. ¶C-4101

Sec. 667(b))[10]

The beneficiary's partial tax under (2) is computed (on Form 4970) under a special "shortcut" method and is then reduced by any estate tax or generation-skipping transfer tax attributable to the partial tax. (Code Sec. 667(b)(6))[11]

¶ 3950   3.8% surtax on "unearned income" of estate or trust—Form 8960.

Certain unearned income of individuals (¶3144), estates, and trusts is subject to a surtax on "unearned income" (i.e., it's payable on top of any other tax payable on that income). For an estate or trust, the surtax is 3.8% of the lesser of (1) undistributed net investment income (¶3143) or the excess of adjusted gross income (as defined in Code Sec. 67(e)) over the dollar amount at which the highest income tax bracket applicable to an estate or trust begins. (Code Sec. 1411(a)(2)) The tax doesn't apply to trusts all the unexpired interests in which are devoted to charitable purposes; trusts exempt from tax under Code Sec. 501; or charitable remainder trusts exempt from tax under Code Sec. 664. (Code Sec. 1411(e)) The 3.8% tax is computed on Form 8960 and reflected on and paid with Form 1041.[12]

¶ 3951   Grantor or others taxed as owner of trust—grantor trust rules.

A trust grantor or another person with power over a trust or its property may be taxed on its income as the "owner" of the trust. Under IRS guidance, a grantor trust is ignored as a separate entity apart from the owner for all federal income tax purposes. These grantor trust rules are discussed at ¶3952 *et seq.*[13] These rules don't apply to charitable remainder trusts or pooled income funds. (Reg § 1.671-1(d)[14] These rules generally apply only to the extent they result in amounts being currently taken into account in computing the income of a U.S. citizen, resident or domestic corporation. (Code Sec. 672(f); Reg § 1.672(f)-1, Reg § 1.672(f)-2, Reg § 1.672(f)-3)

observation: Thus, the grantor trust rules generally don't apply where they would treat a foreign person as owner of the trust. This ensures that either the U.S. or the foreign jurisdiction taxes the trust income.

For this purpose, a grantor includes any person who creates a trust, or directly or indirectly makes a gratuitous transfer of property, including cash, to a trust. (Reg § 1.671-2(e))[15]

These rules may be applicable to the entire trust or, where appropriate, to only a specific portion of a trust. (Reg § 1.671-3(a))[16] If a grantor or other person is considered to be the owner of the *entire* trust, he or she computes his or her own personal income tax by taking into account all trust income, deductions and credits, as though the trust didn't exist. (Reg § 1.671-3(a)(1)) But, where a grantor is treated as owner solely because of his or her interest in trust *income*, the grantor takes into account only the share of trust items that would be reported by a current income beneficiary. (Reg § 1.671-3(c))[17]

For purposes of taxing the grantor as the owner of a trust, the grantor is treated as holding any power or interest held by any individual who was the spouse of the grantor at the time of the creation of the power or the interest, or who became the spouse of the grantor after the creation, but only for periods after the individual became the spouse. (Code Sec. 672(e)(1)) This rule applies only to transfers in trust made after Mar. 1, '86.[18]

---

10. ¶C-4101
11. ¶C-4100 *et seq.*
12. ¶C-5800; ¶C-9850
13. ¶C-5200 *et seq.*
14. ¶C-5216

15. ¶C-5201
16. ¶C-5207 *et seq.*
17. ¶C-5209 *et seq.*
18. ¶C-5204 *et seq.*

A "defective grantor trust" is a trust intentionally structured so that the grantor, rather than the trust or its beneficiaries, will be taxed on the trust's income without the trust being included in the grantor's estate. A defective grantor trust can lower income taxes where the grantor is in a lower bracket than the beneficiary or some income would be accumulated in the trust and taxed at the highly compressed trust tax brackets. The grantor's payment of income tax on trust income taxed to the grantor isn't a gift to the beneficiaries. If a defective grantor trust or applicable state law requires the trustee to reimburse the grantor for the income tax on trust income, the full value of the trust property will be included in the grantor's gross estate for trusts created after Oct. 3, 2004.[19]

¶ 3952   Grantor's power to revoke—grantor trust rules.

Under Code Sec. 671 and Code Sec. 676, if the grantor of a trust reserves the power to take back title to the trust funds, the grantor is considered the owner of the trust, whether or not the grantor actually exercises that power. The power to get back the trust funds may be a power to revoke, terminate, alter or amend, or to appoint. (Reg § 1.676(a)-1)

The grantor is taxed if the grantor can exercise the power alone, if it can be exercised only by another who is regarded as a "nonadverse party" (see below), or if it can be exercised by both the grantor and a "nonadverse party" together. (Code Sec. 676(a))[20] The grantor isn't taxed if the power can be exercised only by or with consent of an adverse party. (Code Sec. 672(a), Code Sec. 676(a); Reg § 1.676(a)-1)[21]

An "adverse party" is any person with a substantial beneficial interest in the trust (including a general power of appointment over trust property) which would be adversely affected by the exercise or non-exercise of his or her power with regards to the trust. (Code Sec. 672(a)) A beneficiary is ordinarily an adverse party. (Reg § 1.672(a)-1(b)) A "nonadverse party" has either no beneficial interest, or one that isn't substantial, or one which wouldn't be adversely affected by the exercise of his or her power with regard to the trust. (Code Sec. 672(b); Reg § 1.672(b)-1)[22]

¶ 3953   Income for grantor, spouse or dependent—grantor trust rules.

Under Code Sec. 677(a), the grantor of a trust is treated as its owner and taxed on its income, if the trust income is:

. . . distributed actually or constructively to the grantor or the grantor's spouse;

. . . held or accumulated for future distribution to the grantor or the grantor's spouse; or

. . . applied to pay premiums on life insurance policies taken out on the life of the grantor or the grantor's spouse (and not irrevocably payable to charities).

The income isn't taxable to the grantor if the application of the income to any of these purposes requires the approval of an adverse party (¶3952). (Reg § 1.677(a)-1(b))[23]

If trust income is *actually* used to support a beneficiary (other than the grantor's spouse) whom the grantor is legally obligated to support, such as the grantor's minor children, the grantor is taxable on that income. But the mere fact that trust income *may* be so used doesn't make the grantor taxable, unless the use is discretionary with the grantor as an *individual* (not trustee). (Reg § 1.677(b)-1(d), Reg § 1.677(b)-1(e), Reg § 1.677(b)-1(f))[24]

---

19. ¶C-5200
20. ¶C-5301
21. ¶C-5303

22. ¶C-5312 *et seq.*
23. ¶C-5401
24. ¶C-5423

¶ 3954   Reversionary interests—grantor trust rules.

Under Code Sec. 673(a), for transfers in trust made after Mar. 1, '86, the grantor of a trust is generally taxable as the owner on its income if the grantor has a reversionary interest in the corpus or income and, as of the inception of the trust, the value of that interest is more than 5% of the value of the trust. The value of the reversionary interest must be determined by assuming the maximum exercise of discretion in favor of the grantor. (Code Sec. 673(c))

Any postponement of the date specified for the reacquisition of possession or enjoyment of the reversionary interest is treated as a new transfer in trust starting with the date the postponement is effective and terminating with the date prescribed by the postponement. However, income for any period isn't included in income of the grantor by reason of this rule if it wouldn't be includible in the absence of the postponement. (Code Sec. 673(d))

The grantor isn't treated as the owner where the reversionary interest takes effect on the death before age 21 of a beneficiary who (1) is a lineal descendant of the grantor, and (2) holds all present interests in the trust. (Code Sec. 673(b))[25]

¶ 3955   Power to control beneficial enjoyment (including "sprinkling" and "spray" powers)—grantor trust rules.

Under Code Sec. 674, trust income is generally taxable to the grantor as the owner of the trust property if the beneficial enjoyment of trust corpus or income is subject to a power of disposition that may be exercised by the grantor personally, or by a nonadverse party (¶3952), or both, and requires no consent or approval of an adverse party (¶3952).[26]

Similarly, the grantor will be taxed if he or she retains certain administrative powers, such as borrowing powers and dealing with the trust for less than full consideration. (Code Sec. 675)[27]

But certain relatively broad powers to shift benefits may be given to 'independent' trustees without causing the grantor to be treated as owner. These so called 'sprinkling' and 'spray' powers permit the trustee to distribute, apportion or accumulate income, or to pay out corpus to or among beneficiaries (Code Sec. 674(c)), but not to add beneficiaries except to include after-born or after-adopted children. These powers vested solely in trustees won't cause the grantor to be taxed as the owner of the trust if the grantor isn't eligible as a trustee or co-trustee and no more than half the trustees vested with the power are related or subordinate parties subservient to the grantor's wishes. (Code Sec. 674(c), Code Sec. 674(d); Reg § 1.674(d)-2(b))

Also, a power to distribute, apportion or accumulate income won't subject the grantor to tax if the grantor and the grantor's spouse (living with the grantor) are ineligible to exercise the power as trustee or co-trustee and the power is limited by a reasonably definite external standard set forth in the trust instrument. (Code Sec. 674(d); Reg § 1.674(d)-1)[28]

¶ 3956   Person other than the grantor as owner of trust (including 'Crummey' powers)—grantor trust rules.

Under Code Sec. 678, a trustee, beneficiary, or some other person may be taxable on the income as the owner, if that person:

. . . has a power exercisable solely by him or her to vest the corpus, or income from it, in

---

25. ¶C-5450 *et seq.*
26. ¶C-5531

27. ¶C-5551 *et seq.*
28. ¶C-5542 *et seq.*

himself or herself; or

. . . has previously modified or released such a power and afterward retains control which would make the grantor taxable under the rules discussed at ¶3951 *et seq.*[29]

A holder of a "Crummey" power (see ¶5048) is treated as owner under the above rule.[30]

¶ 3957 Foreign trust grantors or other transferors—Form 3520, Form 3520-A.

Under Code Sec. 679(a)(1), if a U.S. person (e.g., a grantor) makes a transfer to a foreign trust with a U.S. beneficiary, the income of the trust (including foreign source income) will be taxed currently to the transferor as the owner of the trust. (Code Sec. 679(a)(1); Reg § 1.679-1) This rule doesn't apply where the transfer is: (a) by reason of death, (b) for fair market value, or (c) to a foreign employee-benefit or charitable trust. (Code Sec. 679(a); Reg § 1.679-4)

A trust is treated as having a U.S. beneficiary for a tax year unless (1) under the terms of the trust, no part of the trust's income or corpus may be paid or accumulated during the tax year to or for the benefit of a U.S. person, and (2) if the trust is terminated at any time during the tax year, no part of the income or corpus could be paid to or for the benefit of a U.S. person. An amount is treated as accumulated for the benefit of a U.S. person even if the U.S. person's interest in the trust is contingent on a future event. (Code Sec. 679(c)(1))

If a U.S. person directly or indirectly transfers property to a foreign trust, there is a rebuttable presumption that the trust has a U.S. beneficiary unless the U.S. person submits information as required by IRS and demonstrates to its satisfaction that requirements (1) and (2) in the above paragraph are met. (Code Sec. 679(d)) If any person has the discretion to make a distribution from a trust to, or for the benefit of, any person, the trust is treated as having a U.S. beneficiary unless: (i) the trust terms specifically identify the class of persons to whom the distributions may be made; and (ii) none of those persons is a U.S. person during the tax year. (Code Sec. 679(c)(4)) If any U.S. person who directly or indirectly transfers property to the trust is directly or indirectly involved in any agreement or understanding that may result in the income or corpus of the trust being paid or accumulated to or for the benefit of a U.S. person, that agreement or understanding is treated as a term of the trust. (Code Sec. 679(c)(5)) For purposes of determining whether a foreign trust has a U.S. beneficiary, a loan of cash or marketable securities (or the use of any other trust property) directly or indirectly to or by any U.S. person (whether or not the U.S. person is a beneficiary under the terms of the trust) is treated as paid or accumulated for the benefit of a U.S. person, unless the U.S. person repays the loan at a market rate of interest (or pays the fair market value of the use of the property) within a reasonable period of time. (Code Sec. 679(c)(6))[31]

The above rules also apply to (1) certain foreign persons who transfer property to a foreign trust and later become a U.S. person (Code Sec. 679(a)(4); Reg § 1.679-5(a)) and (2) a U.S. person who transferred property to a domestic trust that becomes a foreign trust during the transferor's life. (Code Sec. 679(a)(5); Reg § 1.679-6(b))[32]

A U.S. person who is treated as an owner of any portion of a foreign trust must provide information as IRS may require with respect to the trust. (Code Sec. 6048(b)(1))

Specifically, a U.S. person (and an executor of the estate of a U.S. decedent) that is treated as the owner of a foreign trust must file Form 3520 to report certain transactions with foreign trusts, ownership of foreign trusts under the grantor trust rules, and receipt of certain large gifts or bequests from certain foreign persons.[33]

---

29. ¶C-5571
30. ¶C-5574
31. ¶C-5600 *et seq.*

32. ¶s C-5603.1, C-5603.2
33. ¶S-3644

Further, a foreign trust with a U.S. owner must file Form 3520-A to satisfy the annual information reporting requirements.[34]

¶ 3958   Beneficiary treated as grantor to the extent of gifts to foreign grantor.

Under Code Sec. 672(f)(5), where a foreign person would ordinarily be treated as the owner of any portion of a trust, *and* the trust has a beneficiary who is a U.S. person, the beneficiary generally is treated as the grantor of that portion to the extent the beneficiary has after Nov. 5, '90, made transfers by gift (directly or indirectly) to the foreign grantor. Gifts which are excluded from the calculation of gift tax under Code Sec. 2503(b) (generally, annual gifts of present interests of up to $16,000 for 2022, and up to $17,000 for 2023); see ¶5048) aren't included. (Code Sec. 672(f)(5); Reg § 1.672(f)-5) This rule applies even if the beneficiary wasn't a U.S. person at the time of the transfer.[35]

¶ 3959   Decedent's Income and Deductions. ▬▬▬▬▬▬

The last tax year of a decedent ends with the date of death. (Reg § 1.451-1(b))[36]

For a *cash basis* decedent, include only the income received, actually or constructively, up to the end of the day of death (Code Sec. 691(a); Reg § 1.451-1(d)(1), Reg § 1.691(a)-1(b)), and deduct expenses only to the extent paid before death (except for the special deduction for the unrecovered investment in an annuity contract, see ¶3960, and certain medical expenses paid within one year after death, see ¶2143).[37]

For an *accrual basis* decedent, include income and deductions computed on the accrual method. But an amount of income or deduction accrued *solely* by reason of death isn't includible on the final return. (Code Sec. 451(b), Code Sec. 461(b))[38]

Post-death income and deductions "in respect of a decedent" must be reported by decedent's estate or others who acquire the decedent's rights or obligations (¶3961 *et seq.*).

¶ 3960   Deduction for unrecovered investment in annuity contract—decedent's income and deductions.

Under Code Sec. 72(b)(3)(A), a decedent's unrecovered investment in an annuity contract is an itemized deduction (*not* subject to the 2%-of-AGI floor) (Code Sec. 67(b)(10)) for the decedent's last tax year, if the annuity payments cease by reason of death.[39]

¶ 3961   Income in respect of a decedent (IRD, after-death income).

IRD covers income (including capital gain) which a decedent had a right to receive but that: (1) wasn't actually or constructively received by a cash basis decedent, or (2) wasn't accrued by an accrual basis decedent. IRD includes insurance renewal commissions, a monthly pension paid to deceased employee's spouse, taxable distributions from a qualified employee plan or IRA, a death benefit under a deferred annuity contract, partnership income of a deceased partner (Reg § 1.742-1) and S corporation income of a deceased shareholder. (Code Sec. 1367(b)(4))[40]

¶ 3962   Installment obligations, including self-cancelling installment notes (SCINs)—income in respect of a decedent (IRD).

Uncollected installment obligations held by the decedent and disposed of at death are

---

34. ¶S-3645.2
35. ¶C-5218.31
36. ¶C-9601
37. ¶s C-9556, C-9605

38. ¶s C-9606, C-9608
39. ¶C-9608
40. ¶C-9505 *et seq.*

income in respect of a decedent (IRD, Code Sec. 453B(c); Reg § 1.691(a)-5(a)) and not reported on the decedent's final return. (Code Sec. 691(a)(4)) The amount of the IRD is the excess of the face amount of the obligation over its basis in the hands of the decedent. (Code Sec. 453B(b), Code Sec. 691(a)(4)) On collecting the face amount, the executor, beneficiary or other recipient includes in gross income the same proportion of the payment that would have been reported by the decedent if he or she had lived and received the payment. (Reg § 1.691(a)-5(a))

If the executor or beneficiary transfers the installment obligation, the amount included in gross income for the tax year of the transfer is the fair market value of the obligation at the time of the transfer plus any excess of sales proceeds over fair market value (if it's sold) minus an amount equal to the basis of the obligation in the hands of the decedent (adjusted to reflect the receipt of any installment payments since the decedent's death). (Code Sec. 691(a)(4); Reg § 1.691(a)-5(b))

If the installment obligation is transferred to the obligor or is cancelled by the executor, any previously unreported gain from the installment sale will be recognized by the seller's estate. (Code Sec. 691(a)(5)) The result is the same where payments due on an installment note are extinguished at the holder's death under a provision contained in the sales agreement and installment note, i.e., a "death-terminating" installment note or a SCIN. [41]

¶ 3963   Who is taxed on income in respect of a decedent (IRD)?

Under Code Sec. 691(a)(1), a decedent's IRD not includible on the decedent's last return must be reported, for the tax year when received, by:

. . . the decedent's estate, if it acquired the right to receive the item of income from the decedent;

. . . the person who, by reason of the decedent's death, acquires the right to the income whenever this right isn't acquired by the decedent's estate from the decedent; or

. . . the person who acquires the right from the decedent by bequest, devise or inheritance, if the amount is received after distribution by the decedent's estate of the right to the income. [42]

The character of IRD is the same as it would have been in the hands of the decedent, if the decedent had lived and received the income. (Code Sec. 691(a)(3); Reg § 1.691(a)-3(a)) [43]

¶ 3964   Decedent's deductions and credits available to estate or beneficiaries.

Under Code Sec. 691(b), deductions for a decedent's business expenses, expenses for the production of income, interest, taxes, depletion and the credit for foreign taxes are available to the decedent's estate if the estate is liable for the obligation giving rise to the deduction or credit, and it isn't allowable in the decedent's final (or any previous) return. If not available to the estate, the deduction or credit may be taken by the person who acquires an interest in the decedent's property from the decedent by reason of the decedent's death, or by bequest, devise or inheritance, subject to the obligation. [44]

¶ 3965   Deduction for estate tax attributable to income in respect of a decedent (IRD).

Under Code Sec. 691(c)(1), the decedent's right to IRD is frequently included in his or her gross estate for federal estate and GST tax purposes although it's taxed as income to the recipient. As a relief, the recipient of the IRD can deduct the estate and GST tax

41. ¶C-9528
42. ¶C-9501
43. ¶C-9506
44. ¶C-9551

attributable to inclusion of the right to income in the gross estate. (Code Sec. 691(c)(1); Reg § 1.691(c)-1(a)) This relief is available to an individual only if he or she itemizes deductions, but the deduction isn't subject to the 2%-of-AGI floor. (Code Sec. 67(b)(8))[45]

If IRD includes capital gains or qualified dividends, the Code in effect treats the deduction as an offset against the capital gains or qualified dividends. For purposes of computing (1) the Code Sec. 1211 limitation on capital losses, (2) the maximum tax on a noncorporate taxpayer's capital gains or qualified dividends under Code Sec. 1(h), (3) the alternative tax on a corporation's capital gains, and (4) the full or partial exclusion of gain realized on the disposition of qualified small business stock, the amount of any gain taken into account that is treated as IRD must be reduced (but not below zero) by the amount of the allowable deduction for estate tax attributable to that gain. (Code Sec. 691(c)(4))[46]

Annuity payments received by the surviving annuitant of a joint and survivor annuity are IRD of the deceased annuitant to the extent that the payments are includible in gross income of the survivor. The portion of the estate tax attributable to the survivor's annuity is allowable as a deduction to the survivor over the survivor's life expectancy (determined under IRS tables). (Code Sec. 691(d); Reg § 1.691(d)-1(c))[47]

¶ 3966   Bankruptcy Estate for Bankrupt Individual.

The bankruptcy estate of an individual is treated as a separate taxable entity for income tax purposes, subject to special rules.

Specifically, the separate entity rules apply if a bankruptcy case involving an *individual* debtor (not a corporation or partnership) is brought under Chapter 7 (relating to liquidations) or Chapter 11 (reorganizations) of Title 11 of the U.S. Code. (Code Sec. 1398(a))[48]

For income tax returns of bankruptcy estates (Form 1040 and Form 1041), see ¶4736.

¶ 3967   Debtor's election to close tax year—individual's bankruptcy estate.

Under Code Sec. 1398(d)(2)(A) and Code Sec. 1398(d)(3), an individual debtor can elect to close his or her tax year as of the day before the date the bankruptcy case commences. If the election is made, the debtor's tax year that otherwise would include the commencement date is divided into two "short" tax years. The first year ends on the day before the commencement date; the second begins on the commencement date. (Code Sec. 1398(d)(2)(A))[49]

¶ 3968   Taxation of individual's bankruptcy estate.

Under Code Sec. 1398(e)(1), the gross income of the bankruptcy estate of an individual consists of: (1) any gross income of the individual debtor (other than any amount received or accrued as income by the debtor before the commencement of the case), that under the substantive law of bankruptcy (Title 11 of the U.S. Code), is property of the bankruptcy estate, and (2) the gross income of the estate beginning on and after the date the case commenced.[50]

Except as otherwise provided, the taxable income of the bankruptcy estate is computed the same as in the case of an individual. (Code Sec. 1398(c)(1))[1] The estate is allowed a personal exemption deduction equal to that of an individual (two exemptions for married debtors jointly filing for bankruptcy)[2] and the same standard deduction as married individuals filing separately. (Code Sec. 1398(c)(3)) The tax rate schedule applicable to the

45. ¶C-9557 *et seq.*
46. ¶C-9563
47. ¶C-9569
48. ¶C-9701

49. ¶C-9802 *et seq.*
50. ¶C-9711
1. ¶C-9708
2. ¶C-9709

estate is the same as for married individuals filing separate returns. (Code Sec. 1398(c)(2))[3]

The estate succeeds to various income tax attributes of the debtor (including certain carryovers and unused passive activity and at-risk losses). (Code Sec. 1398(g); Reg § 1.1398-1, Reg § 1.1398-2)[4]

¶ 3969   Deduction of business and administrative expenses—individual's bankruptcy estate.

Under Code Sec. 1398(e)(3), an amount paid or incurred by the bankruptcy estate is deductible or creditable by the estate to the same extent that the item would be by the debtor had the debtor remained in the same trades, businesses or activities after the case commenced as before and had the debtor paid or incurred the amount.[5]

The estate can deduct: (1) any administrative expense allowed under 11 U.S. Sec. 503 (11 USCS 503), and (2) any court fees and costs assessed against the estate under Chapter 123 of Title 28 of the U.S. Code. (Code Sec. 1398(h)(1))[6]

¶ 3970   Carrybacks and carryovers—individual's bankruptcy estate.

Any deduction for administrative and related expenses not used in the current year can be carried back by the estate three years and carried forward seven years (Code Sec. 1398(h)(2)), but only to a tax year of the *estate,* not of the debtor. (Code Sec. 1398(h)(2)(D))

The administrative expense carrybacks and carryovers that may be carried to a particular tax year are "stacked" after the net operating loss deductions (allowed by Code Sec. 172) are computed for the particular year. (Code Sec. 1398(h)(2)(C))[7]

If the bankruptcy estate itself incurs a net operating loss (apart from losses passing to the estate from the individual debtor), the bankruptcy estate can carry back its net operating losses not only to earlier tax years of the estate, but also to tax years of the debtor before the year in which the case commenced. (Code Sec. 1398(j)(2)(A))[8]

¶ 3971   Tax attributes on termination of estate—individual's bankruptcy estate.

Under Code Sec. 1398(i), on termination of the bankruptcy estate, the debtor generally succeeds to various tax attributes of the estate (including certain carryovers).[9]

---

3. ¶C-9707
4. ¶C-9718
5. ¶C-9714
6. ¶C-9715

7. ¶C-9720
8. ¶C-9721
9. ¶C-9812

Chapter 19   Exempt Organizations

¶ 4100   **Tax-Exempt Organizations, Overview.** ▬▬▬▬▬▬▬▬▬▬▬▬▬▬▬▬

Certain nonprofit organizations are exempt from federal income taxation, but they may be taxable on income from unrelated businesses they conduct.

Exempt organizations include, among other entities:

. . . religious, charitable, scientific, literary and educational organizations, organizations testing for public safety, organizations that foster national or international amateur sports competition, those organized and operated for preventing cruelty to children or animals (¶4102) (Code Sec. 501(c)(3)), qualified charitable risk pools, (Code Sec. 501(n)) cooperative hospital (Code Sec. 501(e)) and educational organization, service organizations; (Code Sec. 501(f))[1]

. . . religious and apostolic organizations (¶4103);

. . . nonprofit civic organizations operated exclusively for social welfare, and local employees' associations whose net earnings are used solely for charitable, educational or recreational purposes (Code Sec. 501(c)(4));[2]

. . . labor, agricultural or horticultural organizations (Code Sec. 501(c)(5), Code Sec. 501(g));[3]

. . . chambers of commerce, business leagues, real estate boards, boards of trade or professional football leagues not organized for profit or private benefit (Code Sec. 501(c)(6));[4]

. . . social clubs organized for pleasure, recreation and other nonprofitable purposes (¶4105) (Code Sec. 501(c)(7)) and fraternal beneficiary societies, orders or associations operating under the lodge system and providing life, sick, accident or other benefits to members and their dependents (Code Sec. 501(c)(8));[5]

. . . voluntary employees' beneficiary associations (VEBAs) providing benefit payments to members and their dependents (Code Sec. 501(c)(9));[6]

. . . supplemental unemployment benefit plans (SUBs) (Code Sec. 501(c)(17));[7]

. . . qualified employee benefit trusts (¶4307);

. . . organizations (including mutual insurance companies) providing worker's compensation (Code Sec. 501(c)(27)(B))[8]; and

. . . state sponsored high-risk health coverage organizations (Code Sec. 501(c)(26)).[9]

¶ 4101   **Rules governing "feeder" organizations—exempt organizations.**

Under Code Sec. 502(a), an organization operated for the primary purpose of carrying on a business for profit (not just holding title to property) is taxable on all its income, even if all its profits are payable to exempt organizations. (Code Sec. 502(a); Reg § 1.502-1(a))[10] But this type of "feeder" organization is exempt if it's controlled by and furnishes its services *solely* to: a single exempt organization, an exempt parent organization and its exempt subs, or exempt subs having a common parent. (Reg § 1.502-1(b))[11]

---

1. ¶D-4070 *et seq.*
2. ¶D-5100 *et seq.*
3. ¶D-4600 *et seq.*
4. ¶D-4800 *et seq.*
5. ¶D-4300 *et seq.*
6. ¶D-4400 *et seq.*

7. ¶D-4500
8. ¶D-6346
9. ¶D-6320
10. ¶D-7101
11. ¶D-7103

References beginning with a single letter are to paragraphs in Federal Tax Coordinator 2d and RIA's Analysis of Federal Taxes: Income.

¶ 4102   Religious, charitable, educational and similar organizations—exempt organizations.

Under Code Sec. 501(c)(3), a corporation, community chest, fund, foundation, or other organization is exempt if:

. . . it's both organized *and* operated exclusively for: religious, charitable, scientific, literary or educational (including certain child care) purposes; public safety testing; prevention of cruelty to children or animals; or fostering national or international amateur sports competition; (Code Sec. 501(c)(3); Reg § 1.501(c)(3)-1(a))

. . . no part of its net earnings inures to benefit any private shareholder or individual; *and*

. . . no substantial part of its activities consists of carrying on propaganda or otherwise attempting to influence legislation, i.e., lobbying (for an election, see ¶4110), or intervening in any political campaign for or against any candidate. (Code Sec. 501(c)(3))[12]

Special qualification requirements apply to any Code Sec. 501(c)(3) organization that operates at least one hospital facility. (Code Sec. 501(r),[13] Code Sec. 6033(b))

¶ 4103   Religious or apostolic associations—exempt organizations.

Under Code Sec. 501(d), even if an organization carries on business activities so that it can't be exempt under Code Sec. 501(c)(3) (as *exclusively* for exempt purposes), it still can be exempt as a *religious or apostolic association*. The organization may thus be exempt if it has a common or community treasury, and if its income (whether or not distributed) is taxed pro rata to its members, as a dividend received, for the organization's tax year ending with or within the member's tax year. (Code Sec. 501(d); Reg § 1.501(d)-1)[14]

¶ 4104   Civic leagues for social welfare—exempt organizations.

Under Code Sec. 501(c)(4), a civic league is exempt if it isn't organized or operated for profit; it is operated exclusively for the promotion of social welfare; no part of its net earnings inures to the benefit of any private shareholder or individual; and (Code Sec. 501(m)(1)) no substantial part of its activities consists of providing commercial-type insurance.[15]

¶ 4105   Social clubs; 35%/15% tests—exempt organizations.

Under Code Sec. 501(c)(7), for a social club to be exempt, it must be organized and operated substantially for pleasure, recreation or other nonprofit purposes, its governing instruments or written policies can't provide for discrimination based on color, race or religion, and no part of its earnings may benefit any private shareholder.[16]

Up to 35% of a social club's gross receipts (including investment income) may be from sources outside of its membership. Within this 35%, not more than 15% of gross receipts may be from the general public's (i.e., not members or their guests) use of the club's facilities or services.[17]

If the club fails the 35% or 15% tests (and a facts and circumstances test) in any tax year, all of its income, even amounts (reduced by allocable costs) received from members, is subject to tax in that year. (Code Sec. 277)[18]

---

12. ¶D-4008
13. ¶D-4152 *et seq.*
14. ¶D-5601
15. ¶D-5100 *et seq.*
16. ¶D-4201
17. ¶D-4206
18. ¶D-4206

¶ 4106　Nondiscrimination requirements for voluntary employees' beneficiary associations (VEBAs) and supplemental unemployment benefit trusts (SUBs).

Under Code Sec. 501(c)(17)(A), Code Sec. 505(a)(1), and Code Sec. 505(b)(1), a VEBA or SUB won't be exempt unless it satisfies nondiscrimination rules similar to those applicable to qualified employee benefit plans (¶4314).[19]

¶ 4107　Political organizations—Forms 1120-POL, 990, 8871, 8872, 8453-X—exempt organizations.

Under Code Sec. 527(e)(1), Code Sec. 527(e)(2), and Code Sec. 527(g), a political organization is a party, committee, association, fund (including certain newsletter funds) or other organization (whether or not incorporated) that's organized and operated primarily to accept contributions and/or make expenditures for an "exempt function," e.g., influencing or attempting to influence the selection, nomination, election or appointment of any individual to public office.[20] Subject to exceptions, political organizations must (1) give notice of status electronically (use Form 8871 and Form 8453-X), (2) provide periodic reports of contributions and expenditures, electronically (use Form 8872), and (3) file annual returns. Although generally tax-exempt (Code Sec. 527(a)), a political organization is taxed, at the *highest* corporate rate, on income (minus connected expenses) that isn't from its exempt function. (Code Sec. 527(b), Code Sec. 527(c))[21] A political organization, whether or not tax-exempt, that has more than $100 of taxable income must file an annual income tax return on Form 1120-POL. (Code Sec. 6012(a)(6)) Subject to exceptions, a tax-exempt political organization (other than a qualified state or local political organization) with $25,000 or more of annual gross receipts must file Form 990. Qualified state or local political organizations must file Form 990 (see ¶4126) if they have annual gross receipts of $100,000 or more. (Code Sec. 6033(g)(1)).[22]

¶ 4108　Homeowners' associations—Form 1120-H—exempt organizations.

Under Code Sec. 528(a), Code Sec. 528(c), associations for the management of residential real estate and condominiums and timeshare associations (but not cooperative housing corporations) that meet an organization and operation test and an income test may elect (by filing Form 1120-H) to be treated as exempt organizations.[23] Electing associations are taxed at a 30% (32% for timeshare associations) rate on income other than amounts received as dues, fees or assessments from members. (Code Sec. 528(b))[24] This taxable income must be reported on Form 1120-H.[25]

¶ 4109　Loss of exemption for exempt employee trusts engaging in prohibited transactions.

Under Code Sec. 503(a)(1), some employee trusts (including church and governmental plans) lose or are denied their exemption from income tax (and are subject to an excise tax, see ¶4337) if they engage in "prohibited transactions." [26]

A prohibited transaction occurs if a trust engages in an activity with its creator, a substantial contributor, or person related to either, in which it (1) lends any part of its income or corpus without receiving adequate security and a reasonable rate of interest; (2)

---

19. ¶D-4418, D-4501
20. ¶s D-5002, D-5021
21. ¶D-5008
22. ¶S-1921

23. ¶D-5701 *et seq.*
24. ¶D-5712
25. ¶S-1922
26. ¶D-6700 *et seq.*

pays any compensation in excess of a reasonable allowance for personal services actually rendered; (3) makes any part of its services available on a preferential basis; (4) makes any substantial purchase of securities or any other property for more than adequate consideration; (5) sells any substantial part of its securities or any other property for less than adequate consideration; or (6) engages in any other transaction that results in a substantial diversion of its income or corpus. (Code Sec. 503(b))[27] :

¶ 4110   Lobbying expenditures election for Code Sec. 501(c)(3) organizations—Form 5768.

Under Code Sec. 501(h), certain Code Sec. 501(c)(3) organizations (other than church-related ones or private foundations) may elect (on Form 5768) to make limited lobbying expenditures without losing their exempt status.[28] The election is effective for all tax years that end after it's made, and that begin before it's revoked. (Code Sec. 501(h)(6))[29]

An electing charity's permissible lobbying expenditures for any tax year can't exceed ("general limit") the *lesser of:* (1) $1 million, or (2) the sum of 20% of the first $500,000 it paid or incurred for exempt purposes (including related administrative costs) for the year, plus 15% of the second $500,000, plus 10% of the third $500,000, plus 5% of any additional such expenditures. (Code Sec. 4911(c)(2); Reg § 56.4911-1(c)(1)) Also, only 25% of this lobbying amount may go to influencing legislation ("grass roots expenditures"). (Code Sec. 4911(c)(4); Reg § 56.4911-1(c)(2))[30] Charities must keep records of these expenditures (and show them on their annual returns, see ¶4126). (Reg § 56.4911-6)[31]

In any tax year an electing charity's lobbying expenditures exceed either the general or the grass roots limit, a 25% excise tax is imposed on that excess. If both limits are exceeded, the tax is imposed on the greater excess. (Code Sec. 4911(a), Code Sec. 4911(b))[32] Pay the tax on Form 4720. Use Form 8868 for an extension (¶4126).[33] Also, an electing charity can lose its tax exemption if its lobbying expenditures over a 4-year period exceed 150% of either limit. (Code Sec. 501(h)(1), Code Sec. 501(h)(2))[34]

¶ 4111   Excise tax on Code Sec. 501(c)(3) organizations' political and lobbying expenditures—Form 4720.

Under Code Sec. 4955, a Code Sec. 501(c)(3) organization is subject to a 2-tier excise tax on its *political expenditures.* An initial tax of 10% of the expenditure is imposed on the organization, and an initial 2.5% tax (up to $5,000 per expenditure) is imposed on any organization manager who willfully and without reasonable cause agreed to the expenditure. (Code Sec. 4955(a), Code Sec. 4955(c)(2); Reg § 53.4955-1(b))[35] Use Form 4720 to report these taxes, and Form 8868 for an extension. (¶4126)[36] Additional taxes are imposed on both the organization (100%) and management (50%, up to $10,000 per expenditure) if the expenditure isn't corrected within a reasonable time. (Code Sec. 4955(b), Code Sec. 4955(c)(2))[37]

A Code Sec. 501(c)(3) organization (other than charities making the lobbying expense election (¶4110), private foundations and church-related organizations) whose *lobbying expenditures* for a tax year cause it to lose its tax exemption is subject to a 5% tax on those disqualifying amounts. The 5% tax also is imposed on any organization manager who agreed to the expenditure knowing that disqualification could result. (Code Sec. 4912)[38][39]

---

27. ¶D-6702 *et seq.*
28. ¶D-6500 *et seq.*, ¶D-6571
29. ¶D-6501
30. ¶D-6507 *et seq.*
31. ¶D-6571
32. ¶D-6532 *et seq.*
33. ¶S-2512
34. ¶D-6572 *et seq.*
35. ¶D-6421 *et seq.*
36. ¶S-2512
37. ¶D-6421 *et seq.*
38. ¶D-6417 *et seq.*
39. ¶S-2512

IRS may also seek to enjoin a Code Sec. 501(c)(3) organization from engaging in flagrant political activities. (Code Sec. 7409(a); Reg § 301.7409-1(a))[40]

¶ 4112 Excise tax on excess benefit transactions by disqualified persons and organization managers—Form 4720—exempt organizations.

Under Code Sec. 4958(a), penalty excise taxes are imposed on disqualified persons and organization managers who benefit from an excess benefit transaction with a Code Sec. 501(c)(3) or Code Sec. 501(c)(4) organization (other than a private foundation), or that was such an organization at any time within five years before the transaction. (Code Sec. 4958(a); Reg § 53.4958-1) An excess benefit transaction is one in which the exempt organization provides a benefit directly or indirectly to or for the use of a disqualified person (any person in a position to exercise substantial influence over the organization at any time during the five years before the transaction (Code Sec. 4958(f); Reg § 53.4958-4)), or certain related parties, that exceeds the value of the consideration, including services, received in exchange. (Code Sec. 4958(c))[41]

The disqualified person is liable for a tax of 25% of the excess benefit (200% if the transaction is not corrected by the time a deficiency notice is mailed or the tax is assessed). (Code Sec. 4958(a)(1), Code Sec. 4958(b); Reg § 53.4958-1)[42] An organization manager (officer, director, trustee, etc.) who knowingly participates in an excess benefit transaction is liable for a tax of the lesser of 10% or $20,000. (Code Sec. 4958(a)(2), Code Sec. 4958(d)(2))[43] Distributions from a donor advised fund to a donor, donor advisor, or related person are automatically treated as excess benefit transactions. (Code Sec. 4958(c)(2)) Excess benefit transactions of Code Sec. 509(a)(3) supporting organizations are determined under special rules. (Code Sec. 4958(c)(3))[44] IRS may abate the first-tier taxes for reasonable cause. (Code Sec. 4962(b))[45] Persons liable for excess benefit transaction excise taxes report them on Form 4720. (Reg § 53.6071-1(f)) Use Form 8868 for an extension (¶4126).

¶ 4113 Excise tax on tax-exempt organizations that pay "excess compensation."

Under Code Sec. 4960, an "applicable tax-exempt organization" is liable for a 21% excise tax on remuneration exceeding $1 million paid to a "covered employee," and on "excess parachute payments" made to a covered employee. An applicable tax-exempt organization is generally one exempt from tax under Code Sec. 501(a), a farmer's cooperative organization under Code Sec. 521(b)(1), a state or political subdivision that has income excluded from tax under Code Sec. 115(1), or a political organization under Code Sec. 527(e)(1). (Code Sec. 4960(c)(1)) A covered employee is any current or former employee of an applicable tax-exempt organization if the employee is (a) one of the five highest compensated employees of the organization for the tax year, or (b) was a covered employee of the organization, or any predecessor of the organization, for any tax year beginning after Dec. 31, 2016. (Code Sec. 4960(c)(2))[46]

Regs provide guidance on the excess compensation rules. Under the regs, taxpayers may base their positions on a good faith, reasonable interpretation of Code Sec. 4960. (Reg § 53.4960-1 *et seq.*)[47]

An excess parachute payment is the amount by which a parachute payment (defined in Code Sec. 4960(c)(5)(B)) exceeds the base amount (determined under rules similar to Code

---

40. ¶V-2721
41. ¶D-6650 *et seq.*
42. ¶D-6652 *et seq.*
43. ¶D-6653 *et seq.*

44. ¶D-6654 *et seq.*
45. ¶D-8201
46. ¶D-4046
47. ¶D-4046

Sec. 280G(b)(3); ¶1533) allocated to it. (Code Sec. 4960(c)(5)(A))[48]

¶ 4114 Excise tax on investment income of private colleges and universities—exempt organizations.

Under Code Sec. 4968, a 1.4% excise tax is imposed on net investment income of certain private colleges and universities with at least 500 tuition-paying students during the preceding tax year, more than 50% of whom are located in the U.S., and with assets at the end of the preceding tax year (other than those used directly in carrying out the institution's exempt purpose) of at least $500,000 per student. Reg § 53.4968-1 provides definitions for several of the necessary terms, and additional clarification, for determining this excise tax.[49]

¶ 4115 Excise tax on entities that are parties to, and managers who knowingly approve, prohibited tax shelter transactions—exempt organizations.

Excise taxes are imposed on (1) certain tax-exempt entities that are parties to "prohibited tax shelter transactions" (Code Sec. 4965(a)(1)) and (2) "entity managers" of tax-exempt entities who approve the entity as a party (or otherwise cause the entity to be a party) to a prohibited tax shelter transaction and know or have reason to know that the transaction is a prohibited tax shelter transaction. (Code Sec. 4965(a)(2); Reg § 53.4965-1 through Reg § 53.4965-9)[50]

¶ 4116 Mandatory disclosure of participation in prohibited tax shelter transactions—Form 8886-T—exempt organizations.

Under Code Sec. 6033(a)(2), every tax-exempt entity described in Code Sec. 4965(c) that is a party to a prohibited tax shelter transaction (¶4115) must disclose to IRS (on Form 8886-T): (a) that the entity is a party to the prohibited tax shelter transaction; and (b) the identity of any other party to the transaction which is known to such tax-exempt entity.[1] For 2022, the penalty for failing to comply is $110 ($120 for 2023) for each day during which such failure continues, not to exceed $56,000 ($60,000 for 2023) for any one disclosure. IRS may make a written demand on any entity or manager subject to the penalty for nondisclosure, specifying a reasonable future date by which the required disclosure must be filed. For 2022, failure to comply with the demand is subject to an additional penalty of $110 ($120 for 2023) for each day after the expiration of the time specified in the demand during which such failure continues, not to exceed $11,000 ($12,000 for 2023) for any one disclosure. (Code Sec. 6652(c)(3)(B)(ii))[2]

Any taxable party to a prohibited tax shelter transaction must disclose, by statement, to any tax-exempt entity that is a party to the transaction that it's a prohibited tax shelter transaction. (Code Sec. 6011(g))[3]

¶ 4117 Donee acknowledgment of qualified vehicle donations—Form 1098-C—exempt organizations.

Under Code Sec. 170(f)(12)(B), an organization that receives a charitable contribution of a "qualified vehicle" (¶2138) must provide the donor with a contemporaneous written acknowledgment of the contribution if the claimed value is more than $500, and report the information to IRS (use Form 1098-C) or face a penalty, which also applies for furnishing a false or fraudulent acknowledgment. It also must indicate whether the donee provided any

---

48. ¶D-4047
49. ¶D-8171 *et seq.*
50. ¶D-8301

1. ¶S-2895
2. ¶V-2535
3. ¶S-4433

goods or services in consideration for the vehicle, and, if so, a description and good faith estimate of their value, or, if they consist solely of intangible religious benefits, a statement to that effect.[4]

¶ 4118 Application for exemption—advance rulings—Forms 1023, Form 1023-EZ, Form 1024, Form 8976—exempt organizations.

An organization must apply (on Form 1023 for Code Sec. 501(c)(3) organizations, Form 1024 for most others, and with the appropriate user fee, but see below for Code Sec. 501(c)(4) organizations) for an IRS ruling or determination that it's exempt from federal income tax. (Reg § 1.501(a)-1(a)(2)) Form 1023 must be submitted electronically, and beginning Jan. 3, 2022 (subject to a 90-day transitional period), Form 1024 must be submitted online at Pay.gov. A parent organization's exemption doesn't cover its subsidiary.[5] But organizations under the general control of a central organization may apply on a group basis.[6] When applying for tax-exempt status, sponsoring organizations must notify IRS of any donor advised fund they maintain or intend to maintain. (Code Sec. 508(f))[7] Small charities (U.S. charities with assets of $250,000 or less, and annual gross receipts of $50,000 or less) may use Form 1023-EZ to apply for Code Sec. 501(c)(3) tax-exempt status.[8]

Newly-formed organizations seeking to operate under Code Sec. 501(c)(4) are to provide IRS with the required notice of their intent to operate as such by filing Form 8976 (online) within 60 days of their formation. IRS, in turn, must acknowledge receipt of the Form 8976 within 60 days after it is submitted. (Code Sec. 506; Reg § 1.506-1)[9]

¶ 4119 Modification or revocation of exemption—exempt organizations.

IRS may modify or revoke rulings and determination letters that granted exempt status to an organization. (Reg § 601.201(n)(6)) The revocation may be retroactive, in which case deficiencies and penalties may be imposed for open years.[10]

¶ 4120 Disclosure of nondeductibility of contributions—exempt organizations.

Under Code Sec. 6113, certain exempt organizations that aren't eligible to receive deductible contributions must expressly state that fact (in a conspicuous and easily recognizable format) in every fund-raising solicitation.[11]

¶ 4121 Disclosure requirement for quid pro quo contributions—exempt organizations.

Under Code Sec. 6115, certain charities that are eligible to receive deductible contributions must, in connection with soliciting or receiving a quid pro quo contribution in excess of $75, inform the donor in writing that the donor's charitable deduction is limited to the excess of the donor's contribution over the value of the goods or services provided by the charity (with a good faith estimate of the value of those goods and services). (Code Sec. 6115; Reg § 1.6115-1)[12]

¶ 4122 Disclosure of annual return and exemption application—Form 990s, 990-PF, 990-T, 4720—exempt organizations.

Under Code Sec. 6104, a Code Sec. 501(c) or Code Sec. 501(d) organization must make

4. ¶K-3948.2
5. ¶T-10450 *et seq.*
6. ¶T-10481
7. ¶T-10462.1
8. ¶T-10461.1

9. ¶D-5101.1
10. ¶s T-10485, T-10486
11. ¶V-2703
12. ¶K-3126 *et seq.*

available for inspection during business hours a copy of its annual returns (Form 990) for the last three years and its exempt status application and supporting documents; religious or apostolic organizations don't have to make K-1s available. (Code Sec. 6104(a), Code Sec. 6104(b), Code Sec. 6104(d); Reg § 301.6104(a)-1)[13] The organization must provide a copy of the application without charge, except reasonable reproduction and mailing costs, to any individual who requests it. Copies must be provided within 30 days for written requests, or immediately for in-person requests. (Code Sec. 6104(d)(1)) Requests don't have to be honored if the information has been made widely available or if the request is determined by IRS to be part of a harassment campaign. (Code Sec. 6104(d)(4); Reg § 301.6104(d)-3) These rules apply to annual information returns (Form 990-PF and Form 4720) of private foundations, which also must disclose names and addresses of contributors. (Reg § 301.6104(d)-1(b)(4)(ii))[14] Returns of certain political organizations (¶4107) also are subject to disclosure rules. (Code Sec. 6104(a), Code Sec. 6104(b), Code Sec. 6104(d))[15] Code Sec. 501(c)(3) organizations (¶4102) must make available for public inspection copies of their unrelated business income tax (UBIT) returns (Form 990-T) for the 3-year period after the return's filing. (Code Sec. 6104(d)(1)(A)(ii)) Any annual return that must be e-filed under Code Sec. 6033(n) (¶4126) must be made available by IRS to the public as soon as practicable in machine readable form. (Code Sec. 6104(b))[16]

¶ 4123 Unrelated business income tax (UBIT)—Form 990-T—exempt organizations.

Exempt organizations (other than U.S. corporate instrumentalities and certain other exempt organizations) are subject to a tax on income (¶4124) from any unrelated business (defined below). (Code Sec. 511(a), Code Sec. 512(a), Code Sec. 512(b)(12); Reg § 1.511-2(a)(1))[17] Form 990-T is used to report and pay UBIT. (Reg § 1.6012-2(e), Reg § 1.6012-3(a)(5)) Organizations required to file a return relating to any tax on UBTI must file the return electronically. (Code Sec. 6011(h)) Thus, any 2022 Forms 990-T with a due date on or after Apr. 15, 2023 must be filed electronically.[18] Imposition of UBIT doesn't affect the organization's exempt status. (Code Sec. 501(b), Code Sec. 511)[19]

An unrelated business is a trade or business (i.e., carried on for the production of income, whether or not profit results) regularly carried on (including seasonally) by the organization, that isn't substantially related (aside from providing funds) to the exercise or performance of its exempt purpose or function. (Code Sec. 513(a), Code Sec. 513(c); Reg § 1.513-1)[20] An unrelated trade or business doesn't include the activity of soliciting and receiving qualified sponsorship payments (payments from a person engaged in a trade or business for which the person won't get any substantial return benefit other than the use or acknowledgment of the donor's name or logo as part of a sponsored event or certain goods or services that have an insubstantial value). (Code Sec. 513(i); Reg § 1.513-4)[21]

For exempt Supplemental Unemployment Benefit trusts (SUBs), qualified employee pension, etc., trusts, and nonexempt trusts, *any* business regularly carried on is "unrelated." (Code Sec. 513(b))[22] But an unrelated business doesn't include an activity where substantially all the work is performed for the organization without compensation, e.g., by volunteers. (Code Sec. 513(a)(1))[23]

The rules on assessment, collection, and penalties applicable to income tax, including estimated tax and foreign tax credit, apply to UBIT. (Code Sec. 515, Code

---

13. ¶S-6601 *et seq.*
14. ¶S-6603
15. ¶S-6642 *et seq.*
16. ¶S-6627
17. ¶D-6800 *et seq.*
18. ¶S-2101

19. ¶D-6801
20. ¶D-6804 *et seq.*
21. ¶D-6819 *et seq.*
22. ¶D-6807
23. ¶D-6836

Sec. 6655(g)(3)(A); Reg § 1.511-3(a)) The corporate tax rates and filing dates apply if the organization is a corporation, and those for trusts apply if it's a charitable trust. (Code Sec. 511(a), Code Sec. 511(b))[24]

Tax-exempt organizations must make estimated tax payments on their unrelated business taxable income. (Code Sec. 6655(g)(3))[25]

¶ 4124 Unrelated business taxable income (UBTI) defined—exempt organizations.

Under Code Sec. 512(a) and Code Sec. 512(b), UBTI is the gross income derived from any unrelated trade or business (¶4123), less directly connected allowable deductions, but with certain exceptions (below), additions and limitations, including a specific deduction of $1,000.[26] Tax-exempt organizations with more than one unrelated trade or business generally must calculate their UBTI separately for each trade or business, such that losses from one may not be used to offset income of another. (Code Sec. 512(a)(6))[27]

IRS provides guidance for calculating UBTI for separate businesses.[28]

Social clubs, voluntary employees' beneficiary associations (VEBAs), supplemental unemployment benefit plans (SUBs), and veterans organizations are allowed special exclusions. (Code Sec. 512(a)(3))[29] A charitable organization's income or gain from ownership of S corporation stock is UBTI. (Code Sec. 512(e))[30]

Dividends (except certain insurance income received from a controlled foreign corporation (Code Sec. 512(b)(17)), interest, rents, royalties, annuities, payments for securities loans, loan commitment fees, and gains or losses from property dispositions are excluded from UBTI, as are gains or losses from the lapse or termination of options to buy or sell securities or real property, or from the forfeiture of good-faith deposits to buy, sell, or lease real property in connection with the organization's investment activities (Code Sec. 512(b)),[31] and annual dues of up to $178 for 2022 ($191 for 2023) per member received by agricultural or horticultural organizations. (Code Sec. 512(d))[32]

But to the extent the dividends, etc., are attributable to property acquired through debt financing ("debt-financed property," see ¶4125), they *are* included in UBTI. The includible portion (computed separately for each property) equals a percentage (not over 100%) of the dividends, etc., derived from the property during the tax year, based on the ratio of: (1) the average acquisition indebtedness, to (2) the average adjusted basis of debt-financed property, for the year. (Code Sec. 514(a)(1))[33] This same percentage also is used to compute the allowable deductions for that property (other than capital loss carryovers or depreciation). (Code Sec. 514(a)(2), Code Sec. 514(a)(3))[34]

Tax-exempt organizations that paid unrelated business income tax on expenses for qualified transportation fringe benefits, including employee parking, under repealed Code Sec. 512(a)(7) (which provided that such benefits were included in UBTI), should file an amended Form 990-T within the time allowed for refunds. (Information Release 2020-23, 1/28/2020)[35]

---

24. ¶D-6928 *et seq.*
25. ¶S-5421
26. ¶D-6900 *et seq.*
27. ¶D-6922.1
28. ¶D-6922.1
29. ¶D-6929 *et seq.*

30. ¶D-6916.1
31. ¶D-6901 *et seq.*
32. ¶D-6847
33. ¶D-7000 *et seq.*
34. ¶s D-7007, D-7010
35. ¶D-6917.1

¶ 4125 Property acquired through debt financing—"debt-financed property"—exempt organizations.

Under Code Sec. 514(b), debt-financed property, with certain exceptions, is any property held to produce income (including gains from its disposition, as well as rents, dividends and other recurring income) (Code Sec. 514(b); Reg § 1.514(b)-1(a)), for which there's an acquisition indebtedness at any time during the tax year.[36]

"Acquisition indebtedness" for any property generally means: (1) the unpaid amount of indebtedness incurred by the organization in acquiring or improving the property; and (2) indebtedness incurred at other times which *but for* the acquisition or improvement wouldn't have been incurred (if incurred after the acquisition, etc., the debt must have been reasonably foreseeable at that time). (Code Sec. 514(c))[37]

Any mortgage or other lien on the acquired property is considered incurred in that acquisition, whether or not it's assumed by the organization. (Code Sec. 514(c)(2)(A))[38]

¶ 4126 Exempt organization return-filing requirement; exemptions; Forms 990 or 990-EZ, 990-N ("e-Postcard"), 8868, 4720; Form 8868 or Form 7004 (automatic extension); penalty for failure to file Form 990; mandatory e-filing.

In general, under Code Sec. 6033(a)(1), every organization that's exempt from tax or whose exemption application is pending, must file an annual information return (Form 990 series) and keep the records and make sworn statements as required by IRS. Exceptions to the filing requirement (e.g., for churches, and for organizations with gross receipts below a certain threshold) are found in Code Sec. 6033(a)(3) and Reg § 1.6033-2(g)(1). (Code Sec. 6033(a)(1); Reg § 1.6033-2)[39] Code Sec. 509(a)(3) supporting organizations must file annual information returns (Code Sec. 509(a)(3)) containing specific information (Code Sec. 6033(l))[40] Certain exempt organizations that acquired interests in life insurance contracts before Aug. 18, 2008 must file an information return or face a penalty. (Code Sec. 6050V, Code Sec. 6724(d)(1)(B)(xv), Code Sec. 6721(e)(2)(D))[41] For private foundations, see ¶4133.

The return must show the organization's total lobbying and political expenditures for the year (Code Sec. 6033(b)(8)), (except political expenditures of nonpolitical organizations taxed under Code Sec. 527(f) (Code Sec. 6033(e)(1)(B)(iii)) and the total amount of dues and similar receipts to which the expenditures are allocable. There are exceptions for Code Sec. 501(c)(3) organizations' in-house expenditures not exceeding $2,000 (Code Sec. 6033(e)(1))[42] and certain nondeductible dues.[43]

IRS Publication 4839, as well as material on IRS's web site, provide guidance for tax-exempt organizations in filing Form 990 (or 990-EZ) and its schedules.

Form 990-N. An exempt organization (other than a private foundation or Code Sec. 509(a)(3) supporting organization) whose annual gross receipts aren't normally in excess of $50,000 may e-file the simpler Form 990-N (the "e-Postcard") instead of Form 990 or 990-EZ. (Reg § 1.6033-2(g)(1)(iii); Reg § 1.6033-2(g)(5))[44]

Information returns of parent tax-exempt organizations must include information about transactions with controlled entities. (Code Sec. 6033(h))[45]

---

36. ¶D-7012 *et seq.*
37. ¶D-7040 *et seq.*
38. ¶D-7043
39. ¶S-2801 *et seq.*
40. ¶S-2823
41. ¶S-2896
42. ¶S-2853; ¶s S-2858.1, S-2858.2
43. ¶S-2858.3
44. ¶S-2820
45. ¶S-2862.2

Sponsoring organizations must disclose information about donor advised funds on information returns. (Code Sec. 6033(k))[46]

Form 990 must be for the organization's annual accounting period or, if it has none, the calendar year. (Reg § 1.6033-2(b)) It must be filed on or before the 15th day of the fifth full calendar month after the close of the annual accounting period. (Reg § 1.6033-2(e))[47]

An exempt organization required to file a return on Form 990, Form 1041-A, Form 4720, Form 5227, Form 6069, Form 1120-POL, or Form 8870 may obtain an automatic 6-month filing extension by filing on or before the return due date a Form 8868 (Form 7004 for Form 1120-POL) showing the full amount properly estimated as tax, and remitting the full unpaid amount. (Reg § 1.6081-9(a))[48]

An exempt organization that fails to file the required information return or notice for three consecutive years will automatically lose its exempt status and must reapply to be recognized as an exempt organization. If an organization fails to file for two consecutive years, IRS must provide a notice to the organization; the notice must include information on how to comply with the filing requirements.[49] Organizations that lost their exempt status for this reason may have their tax-exempt status retroactively reinstated.[50]

Most exempt organizations must file an information return (with Form 990) on liquidation, dissolution, termination or contraction if they were exempt for any of their last five years. (Code Sec. 6043(b))[1]

Penalty for failure to file Form 990. Failure to file an annual information return (Form 990), or failure to include the required information, may result in a penalty of $20 per day (as adjusted for inflation, see below) that the failure continues. For returns required to be filed in 2022, the penalty is $20 per day ($20 for 2023) , subject to a maximum of $11,000 for 2022 ($12,000 for 2023), or 5% of the gross receipts of the organization for the year. However, for an organization that has gross receipts of more than $1,129,000 for the year ($1,208,500 for the year for 2023), the penalty for failure to file a return required to be filed for that year is $110 in 2022 ($120 for 2023) for each day the failure continues, and the maximum penalty for all failures with respect to any one return can't exceed $56,000 for 2022 ($60,000 for 2023). (Code Sec. 6652(c)(1)(A))[2]

Mandatory e-filing. Any organization that must file a return (see above) must file electronically. (Code Sec. 6033(n); Reg § 301.6033-4)[3]

IRS Publication 4779 provides information on the steps to be taken when an exempt organization is merged or terminated.

¶ 4127   Private Foundations and Donor Advised Funds. ▄▄▄▄▄▄

Private foundations are generally exempt from income tax, but are subject to excise taxes, notification requirements and other restrictions.

Under Code Sec. 509(a), a private foundation is any domestic or foreign religious, scientific, charitable, etc., organization described in Code Sec. 501(c)(3) (¶4102) *other than* organizations that:

(1) are "50% charities" (¶2124), Code Sec. 170(b)(1)(A)(i) through Code Sec. 170(b)(1)(A)(vi) or Code Sec. 170(b)(1)(A)(ix), including include churches, schools, hospitals, medical research organizations, agricultural research organizations, states and their subdivisions, and government supported charities; (Code Sec. 509(a)(1));[4]

(2) meet detailed public support tests (Code Sec. 509(a)(2), Code Sec. 509(d));[5]

46. ¶S-2862.3
47. ¶S-4928
48. ¶S-5034.1
49. ¶S-2802
50. ¶S-2802.1B

1. ¶S-2883
2. ¶V-2722
3. ¶S-2821
4. ¶D-7203
5. ¶s D-7204, D-7207, D-7209

(3) operate exclusively for the benefit of one or more of the above organizations (as Type I, Type II, or Type III supporting organizations) and aren't controlled by disqualified persons (¶4129, other than foundation managers) (Code Sec. 509(a)(3)); and[6]

(4) are organized and operated exclusively for testing for public safety. (Code Sec. 509(a)(4))[7]

Strict accountability requirements apply to qualify as a Type III supporting organization (Code Sec. 509(f)(1), Reg § 1.509(a)-4(f)(5), Reg § 1.509(a)-4(i));[8] and Type I and Type III supporting organizations lose their status as non-private foundations if they accept gifts from prohibited persons. (Code Sec. 509(f)(2)(A))[9]

A Code Sec. 501(c)(3) organization (other than a church or an organization whose annual gross receipts don't exceed $5,000) is presumed to be a private foundation unless it notifies IRS to the contrary (Code Sec. 508(b), Code Sec. 508(c))[10] on Form 1023 within 15 months from the end of the month it was organized. (Reg § 1.508-1(b)(2))[11]

IRS has established a specific procedure for organizations classified as supporting organizations under Code Sec. 509(a)(3) that seek reclassification under Code Sec. 509(a)(1) or Code Sec. 509(a)(2).[12]

Donor advised funds (¶4131 *et seq.*—funds or accounts that meet certain requirements) are subject to excise taxes.

¶ 4128 Taxable trusts and foreign organizations subject to private foundation rules—Forms 1041-A, 5227.

Under Code Sec. 4947 and Code Sec. 4948, certain charitable trusts and split interest trusts, and foreign organizations meeting the private foundation definition (¶4127), may be subject to the private foundation excise taxes (¶4129) and rules on prohibited acts, but not the notification requirements. File Form 1041-A for a split interest trust. Use Form 8868 for an extension, see ¶4126. Use Form 5227 to report the financial activities of a split-interest trust and to determine if it is treated as a private foundation and is subject to excise tax.[13]

¶ 4129 Excise taxes on private foundations: net investment income, self-dealing, etc.—Forms 990-PF, 4720.

Private foundations may be subject to the following excise taxes:

Net investment income. An *exempt* private foundation is liable for an excise tax of 1.39% on its net investment income for the tax year. (Code Sec. 4940(a); Reg § 53.4940-1)[14] The tax doesn't apply for certain operating foundations. (Code Sec. 4940(d))[15] For a *taxable* foundation, the excise tax equals the amount (if any) by which: (1) the sum of 1.39% of its net investment income (computed as if it were exempt) plus the unrelated business income tax (¶4124) that would have been imposed on it had it been exempt, *exceeds* (2) the income tax actually imposed on it for the tax year. (Code Sec. 4940(b))[16] Report the tax on Form 990-PF. (Reg § 53.6011-1(d))[17]

Self-dealing. An excise tax is imposed when a disqualified person (substantial contributors, foundation managers, and specified owners, family members and related entities of these, as well as government officials) (Code Sec. 4946(a)(1)) engages in any of certain acts

6. ¶D-7212 *et seq.*
7. ¶D-7202
8. ¶D-7211; ¶D-7213 *et seq.*
9. ¶D-7213.3
10. ¶s D-7216, D-7217
11. ¶T-10464
12. ¶T-10492
13. ¶s D-7300 *et seq.*, D-7400 *et seq.*
14. ¶D-7501
15. ¶D-7505
16. ¶D-7506
17. ¶S-2511

of self-dealing with a private foundation.[18]

For *each* act of self-dealing (Code Sec. 4941(a), Code Sec. 4941(b)),[19] the disqualified person (except a foundation manager) is subject to an initial tax of 10% on the amount involved (Code Sec. 4941(a)(1); Reg § 53.4941(a)-1(a))[20] and a 200% additional tax if the self-dealing isn't timely corrected. (Code Sec. 4941(b)(1))[21] Any foundation manager who knowingly participates in the act is subject to an initial 5% tax. (Code Sec. 4941(a)(2))[22] and, if he or she refuses to agree with all or part of the correction, an additional 50% tax. (Code Sec. 4941(b)(2))[23] Managers may be jointly and severally liable, but their maximum liability for any one act is $20,000 in initial tax and $20,000 in additional tax. (Code Sec. 4941(c))[24] Report the initial taxes on Form 4720. (Reg § 53.6011-1(b))

Failure to distribute income. A foundation (other than an operating foundation) that fails to distribute its income for a tax year by the end of the *next* year is subject to an initial tax equal to 30% of the income (based on a 5% minimum investment return) (Code Sec. 4942(a); Code Sec. 4942(e); Reg § 53.4942(a)-1(a); Reg § 53.4942(a)-2), which IRS may abate for reasonable cause (Code Sec. 4962(a))[25] and a 100% additional tax if the foundation fails to distribute the income by the date the initial tax is assessed or IRS issues a 90-day letter for it. (Code Sec. 4942(b))[26] Distributions by nonoperating private foundations to certain supporting organizations are not qualifying distributions. (Code Sec. 4942(g)(4))[27] Report the initial taxes on Form 4720. (Reg § 53.6011-1(b))

Excess business holdings. A foundation that has any excess business holdings is subject to an initial tax (which IRS may abate for reasonable cause) equal to 10% of those excess holdings, based on their value on the day during the tax year when those holdings were the greatest. (Code Sec. 4943(a), Code Sec. 4962)[28] An exception applies if the foundation owns all of the business enterprise's voting stock at all times during the tax year and acquired its interests other than by purchase, the business distributes all net operating income for a tax year to the foundation within 120 days after the close of that year, and other requirements are met. (Code Sec. 4943(g))[29] If the foundation fails to timely correct its holdings, an additional 200% tax is imposed. (Code Sec. 4943(b))[30] The excess business holding tax applies to donor advised funds (Code Sec. 4943(e))[31] and the excess business holdings rules apply to certain supporting organizations. (Code Sec. 4943(f))[32] Report the initial taxes on Form 4720. (Reg § 53.6011-1(b))

Investments that jeopardize a foundation's charitable purpose. An excise tax is imposed if a foundation makes investments that jeopardize its charitable purpose. An initial tax of 10% of the amount invested is imposed on the foundation *and* on any foundation manager who knowingly participated in the investment. (Code Sec. 4944(a))[33] Additional taxes are imposed on the foundation (25%) if the investment is not timely removed from jeopardy (Code Sec. 4944(b)(1))[34] and on any manager (5%) who refuses to agree to removing the investment from jeopardy. (Code Sec. 4944(b)(2))[35] Foundation managers may be jointly and severally liable for these taxes, but the initial tax on management for any one investment is limited to $10,000, and the additional tax to $20,000. (Code Sec. 4944(d))[36] The initial taxes are reported on Form 4720. (Reg § 53.6011-1(b))

Propaganda, legislative activities and other taxable expenditures. An excise tax is imposed for engaging in propaganda or legislative activities or for making other taxable

---

18. ¶D-7600 *et seq.*
19. ¶s D-7606, D-7608
20. ¶D-7601
21. ¶D-7602
22. ¶D-7601
23. ¶D-7602
24. ¶s D-7603, D-7604
25. ¶D-7701, D-7704, D-8201
26. ¶s D-7701, D-7706
27. ¶D-7718

28. ¶s D-7800 *et seq.*, D-8201
29. ¶D-7804.5
30. ¶D-7801
31. ¶D-7804.4
32. ¶D-7804.3
33. ¶s D-7901, D-7903
34. ¶D-7905
35. ¶D-7906
36. ¶D-7907

expenditures. An initial tax equal to 20% of the amount of the taxable expenditure is imposed on the foundation, and a 5% initial tax is imposed on any foundation manager who willfully agreed to the expenditure. (Code Sec. 4945(a))[37] An additional tax is imposed on the foundation (100%) if the expenditure isn't timely corrected, and on any foundation manager (50%) who refuses to agree to part or all of the correction. (Code Sec. 4945(b))[38] Foundation managers may be jointly and severally liable, but the maximum tax that may be imposed on them for any one taxable expenditure is $10,000 of initial tax and $20,000 of additional tax. (Code Sec. 4945(c))[39] These taxes don't apply if the political expenditures tax (¶4111) applies. (Code Sec. 4955(e))[40] Report the initial taxes on Form 4720. (Reg § 53.6011-1(b))

Use Form 8868 for an extension to file the above forms, see ¶4126.

¶ 4130 Termination of private foundation status; termination tax—Form 990-PF.

Under Code Sec. 507(a), except as otherwise provided below, an organization's status as a private foundation may terminate only if either: (1) the organization notifies IRS of its intent to terminate, or (2) the organization is guilty of willful repeated acts or omissions or of a willful and flagrant act or omission resulting in liability for any of the excise taxes on private foundations (see ¶4129), and IRS notifies the organization that it's liable for tax on termination of its status as a private foundation.[41]

The organization must pay a tax (use Form 990-PF, see ¶4133) on termination of its private foundation status. Unless abated by IRS, the tax equals the lesser of: (1) the aggregate tax benefit (as adequately substantiated by the foundation) resulting from its Code Sec. 501(c)(3) status, or (2) the value of its net assets. (Code Sec. 507(c), Code Sec. 507(g))[42]

Absent willful repeated acts or omissions or willful and flagrant acts or omissions resulting in private foundation excise tax liability, a private foundation's status may be terminated without imposition of the tax on termination if: (a) it distributes all its net assets to one or more public charities that have been in existence as such for at least 60 calendar months before the distribution; or (b) it notifies IRS of its intent to terminate, and the organization becomes a public charity for a continuous 60-month period. (Code Sec. 507(b))[43]

¶ 4131 Excise tax on taxable distributions from donor advised funds—Form 4720.

Under Code Sec. 4966(a), if a taxable distribution is made from a donor advised fund (defined below):

(1) a tax equal to 20% of the amount distributed is imposed and must be paid by the donor advised fund's sponsoring organization (Code Sec. 4966(a)(1)); and

(2) a tax equal to 5% of the amount distributed is imposed if any fund manager agreed to the making of a distribution knowing that it was a taxable distribution. The tax must be paid by any fund manager who agreed to the making of the distribution. (Code Sec. 4966(a)(2))[44]

The maximum amount of tax imposed under item (2) as to any one taxable distribution is $10,000. (Code Sec. 4966(b)(2))[45]

---

37. ¶D-8001
38. ¶D-8001
39. ¶D-8002.2; ¶D-8003
40. ¶D-8000
41. ¶s D-7220, D-7222

42. ¶D-7228; ¶D-7234
43. ¶D-7223; ¶D-7225
44. ¶D-8152 *et seq.*
45. ¶D-8152

Subject to exceptions, a *donor advised fund* is a fund or account: (1) that's separately identified by reference to contributions of a donor or donors, (2) that's owned and controlled by a sponsoring organization, and (3) as to which a donor (or any person appointed or designated by the donor) has, or reasonably expects to have, advisory privileges as to the distribution or investment of amounts held in the fund or account by reason of the donor's status as a donor. (Code Sec. 4966(d)(2))[46]

¶ 4132 Excise taxes on prohibited benefits received by a donor, donor advisor, or related person from a donor advised fund—Form 4720.

If a distribution from a donor advised fund (¶4131) results in a donor, donor advisor, or a related person ("Subsection (d) person," as set forth in Code Sec. 4967(d)) receiving directly or indirectly a more than incidental benefit as a result of the distribution:

(1) A tax equal to 125% of the amount of the prohibited benefit is imposed on the advice of any Subsection (d) person who recommended the distribution, payable by that Subsection (d) person or the person who benefited from it. (Code Sec. 4967(a)(1))

(2) A tax equal to 10% of the amount of the prohibited benefit (not to exceed $10,000) is imposed on the agreement of any fund manager to knowingly make such a distribution, payable by that fund manager. (Code Sec. 4967(a)(2), Code Sec. 4967(c)(2))[47]

The above taxes are not imposed for any distribution subject to tax under Code Sec. 4958 (i.e., the excess benefit transaction rules, ¶4112). (Code Sec. 4967(b))

¶ 4133 Annual return required for private foundations—Form 990-PF; due date.

A private foundation must file an annual information return on Form 990-PF (Reg § 1.6033-2(a)(2)(i)) on or before the fifteenth day of the fifth month following the close of the tax year. (Reg § 1.6033-2(e))[48] For return disclosure requirements, see ¶4122. For electronic filing requirements, see ¶4126. (Reg § 301.6033-4)

---

46. ¶D-8155
47. ¶D-8160 *et seq.*

48. ¶s S-2801, S-4928

Chapter 20   RICs (Mutual Funds), REITs, REMICs, Banks and Other Special Corporations

¶ 4200   Special Corporations and Other Entities. ▬▬▬▬▬

Regulated investment companies (¶4201), real estate investment trusts (¶4202), and real estate mortgage investment conduits (¶4204) are generally not subject to tax, but serve as pass-through entities.

Other corporations that are subject to special tax treatment include Small Business Investment companies (¶4205), cooperatives (¶4206), banks and other financial institutions (¶4209), common trust funds maintained by banks or trust companies (¶4210), and insurance companies (¶4211).

¶ 4201   Regulated investment companies (RICs)—mutual funds—Form 1120-RIC.

A RIC (Code Sec. 851(a)) is a domestic corporation that at all times in the tax year is registered with the SEC as a management company or unit investment trust, has an election in effect to be treated as a business development company under the '40 Investment Company Act, or is a mutual or common trust fund other than an "investment company" under that Act.[1] It must also meet gross income, (Code Sec. 851(b)(2))[2] diversification, (Code Sec. 851(b)(3))[3] and E&P tests, (Code Sec. 852(a)(2))[4] satisfy the distribution requirement (Code Sec. 852(a)(1))[5] *and* elect on its return (Form 1120-RIC) to be taxed as a RIC. (Code Sec. 851(b)(1))[6]

If it makes the required distributions, a RIC is taxed only on: (1) the undistributed portion of its ordinary net income, at the regular corporate rates; and (2) the undistributed portion of its net long-term capital gains, at the corporate capital gains rate. (Code Sec. 852(b))[7] The RIC isn't taxed on the amounts it distributes to shareholders, thus allowing it to pass through ordinary income, net capital gains, qualified dividend income eligible for capital gain treatment (see ¶1288), dividend income eligible for the corporate dividends-received deduction, and certain other items to them (see ¶1298) without any tax at the RIC level (if requirements are met). (Code Sec. 852(b))[8] For "late-paid" and year-end dividends, see ¶4203.

The RIC's *undistributed* capital gains may also be designated (on Form 2439) and passed through to the shareholders (but the RIC pays tax (on Form 2438) on the retained gains). The effects of designation are that the shareholders: (1) include their shares of the undistributed capital gains in income, (2) get a credit or refund for their shares of the tax the RIC paid on these amounts (so that only one tax is paid), and (3) get a basis step-up in their shares equal to the difference between the amount of the includible capital gains from the dividend and the tax the shareholder is deemed to have paid with respect to those shares. (Code Sec. 852(b)(3)(D))[9]

The RIC must report capital gains distributions or undistributed capital gains by specifying the rate group of the capital gains passed through to the shareholder, i.e., as 20% rate gain, 25% rate gain for unrecaptured Code Sec. 1250 gains, 28% rate gain for collectibles gains, and Code Sec. 1202 gain for gains on the sale of qualified small business stock held for more than five years.[10]

---

1. ¶E-6001 *et seq.*
2. ¶E-6003
3. ¶E-6007, E-6010
4. ¶E-6021
5. ¶E-6101

6. ¶E-6002
7. ¶E-6100 *et seq.*
8. ¶E-6150
9. ¶E-6157
10. ¶E-6153

References beginning with a single letter are to paragraphs in Federal Tax Coordinator 2d and RIA's Analysis of Federal Taxes: Income.

¶ 4202   Real estate investment trusts (REITs)—Form 1120-REIT.

A REIT must be a calendar-year (Code Sec. 859) corporation, trust or association that meets certain requirements as to the source of income, earnings and profits, type of its investments, nature of its activities, and its relationships with financially interested parties (Code Sec. 856(a)), and certain recordkeeping and distribution requirements. (Code Sec. 857(a)) And it must elect on its return (Form 1120-REIT) to be a REIT. (Code Sec. 856(c)(1); Reg § 1.856-2(b))[11]

REITs are generally taxed only on amounts not distributed to their shareholders or beneficiaries, as follows: (1) at *regular* corporate rates on undistributed earnings and profits and net capital gains, and (2) at the *highest* corporate rate on net income from foreclosure property. (Code Sec. 857(b))[12] A REIT may pass through the character of its capital gains and qualified dividend income eligible for capital gain treatment (see ¶1288) to its shareholders, see ¶1299. In addition, a REIT's *undistributed* capital gains may be passed through to the shareholders (on Form 2439). The REIT pays tax on the retained gains (on Form 2438) and the shareholders: (1) include their shares of the undistributed capital gains in income, (2) get a credit or refund for their shares of the tax the REIT paid on these amounts (so that only one tax is paid), and (3) get a basis step-up in their shares equal to the difference between the amount of the includible capital gains from the dividend and the tax the shareholder is deemed to have paid with respect to those shares. (Code Sec. 857(b)(3)(C))[13] For "late-paid" and year-end dividends, see ¶4203.

¶ 4203   RIC (mutual fund) and REIT dividends paid after close of tax year ("late-paid dividends")—election; treatment of year-end dividends.

Under Code Sec. 855(a) and Code Sec. 858(a), a RIC (¶4201) or REIT (¶4202) may elect to treat all or part of any dividend paid after the end of a tax year ("late-paid dividends") as paid during the year, if the dividend is declared and paid within the required statutory periods.[14]

A dividend declared by a RIC or REIT in October, November or December of any calendar year, that's payable to shareholders of record on a specified date in one of those months, is considered to have been paid on Dec. 31 if the dividend is actually paid during January of the following calendar year. (Code Sec. 852(b)(7), Code Sec. 857(b)(9))[15]

For shareholders' tax on these dividends, see ¶1298 (RICs) and ¶1299 (REITs).

¶ 4204   Real estate mortgage investment conduits (REMICs)—Form 1066; penalty taxes.

REMICs are fixed mortgage pools with multiple classes ("regular" and "residual") (Code Sec. 860G(a)(1), Code Sec. 860G(a)(2); Reg § 1.860G-1)) of investment interests that have elected REMIC status (on Form 1066). (Code Sec. 860D; Reg § 1.860D-1)[16] REMICs, which are treated as partnerships for procedural purposes (Code Sec. 860F(e)),[17] generally aren't taxable. (Code Sec. 860A(a))[18] The REMIC's income is allocated to, and taken into account by, the holders of its interests. (Code Sec. 860A(b)) REMICs report on Form 1066.[19]

Although not subject to federal *income* tax, a REMIC is subject to penalty taxes on: income from foreclosure property (Code Sec. 860G(c)), contributions after the start-up date

---

11. ¶E-6501, E-6506 *et seq.*
12. ¶E-6600 *et seq.*
13. ¶E-6617.7
14. ¶s E-6201, E-6701
15. ¶s E-6202, E-6704

16. ¶s E-6901, E-6903
17. ¶E-6927
18. ¶E-6917
19. ¶E-7000 *et seq.*

(Code Sec. 860G(d)), and prohibited transactions (Code Sec. 860F(a)), and an excise tax (reported on Form 8831) on certain transfers of residual interests. (Code Sec. 860E(e))[20]

¶ 4205 Small business investment companies (SBICs): special tax rules.

SBICs are licensed and operated under the Small Business Investment Act of '58.[21] They are subject to these special tax rules:

. . . Loss on stock received through the conversion of convertible debentures originally acquired for long-term equity capital supplied to small business concerns is a fully deductible ordinary loss. (Code Sec. 1243)[22]

. . . An SBIC's gain or loss on sale of bonds, debentures, etc., (regardless of issuer) is ordinary gain or loss. (Code Sec. 582(c); Reg § 1.582-1(d))[23]

. . . Dividends the SBIC receives from taxable domestic corporations are 100% deductible. (Code Sec. 243(a)(2))[24]

. . . An SBIC is exempt from personal holding company tax (¶3324 *et seq.*), unless at any time in the tax year any shareholder of the SBIC owns, directly or indirectly, a 5%-or-more interest in the companies financed by the SBIC. (Code Sec. 542(c)(7))[25]

¶ 4206 Cooperatives (co-ops), exempt and non-exempt; deductions.

A co-op (Code Sec. 1382) is an entity in which the same persons are both owners and customers. Although some co-ops are *classified* as "exempt," most co-ops are taxed like any ordinary business corporation, and at the regular corporate rates, but with a specific deduction for patronage dividends (¶4207). (Code Sec. 1382(b)) "Exempt" farmers' co-ops also may deduct certain nonpatronage distributions (¶4208). (Code Sec. 1382(c))[26]

¶ 4207 Patronage dividends and per-unit retain allocations—cooperatives.

Under Code Sec. 1381(a) and Code Sec. 1382(b), both "exempt" farmers' co-ops and nonexempt co-ops exclude (deduct) from their income amounts paid as patronage dividends or per-unit retain allocations.[27] For deduction of nonpatronage dividends, see ¶4208. For how the patrons or shareholders treat these amounts, see ¶1300.

A patronage dividend represents distributions of net earnings among the cooperators and other patrons on the basis of each person's patronage. (Code Sec. 1388(a))[28] It may be paid in money, a certificate of indebtedness, or other property, including a qualified written notice of allocation.[29]

A per-unit retain allocation is an allocation by a co-op to a patron with respect to products marketed for him or her. (Code Sec. 1388(f))[30]

A written notice of allocation must disclose the dollar amount allocated to the patron and the portion that is a patronage dividend. (Code Sec. 1388(b); Reg § 1.1388-1(b))[31]

¶ 4208 Nonpatronage distributions deductible by exempt co-ops.

In addition to patronage distributions (¶4207), an "exempt" farmers' co-op may also deduct: dividends paid during the tax year on its capital stock and on any other evidence of proprietary interest in the co-op, (Code Sec. 1382(c)(1); Reg § 1.1382-3(b)) distributions to

20. ¶E-6920 *et seq.*; ¶E-7106
21. ¶I-9541
22. ¶I-9542
23. ¶I-9544
24. ¶D-2243
25. ¶D-3311
26. ¶E-1100 *et seq.*
27. ¶E-1100 *et seq.*
28. ¶E-1104
29. ¶E-1120
30. ¶E-1126
31. ¶E-1123

patrons on a patronage basis out of earnings from nonpatronage sources, (Code Sec. 1382(c)(2)(A); Reg § 1.1382-3(c), Reg § 1.1382-3(c)(3)) and payments in redemption of nonqualified written notices of allocation issued to patrons on a patronage basis with respect to earnings from nonpatronage sources. (Code Sec. 1382(c)(2)(B); Reg § 1.1382-3(d))[32]

¶ 4209   Taxation of banks and other financial institutions.

Banks are generally taxed like regular corporations (Reg § 1.581-1), except that:[33]

Gains and losses from sales or exchanges of bonds, debentures, notes or certificates or other evidences of indebtedness (including any regular or residual interest in a REMIC, see ¶4204) are treated as ordinary gains and losses. (Code Sec. 582(c)(1)) Sales of stock and securities are subject to the regular wash sale provisions (¶2456).[34]

Interest paid or credited on deposits or CDs is deductible (special rules apply to frozen deposits).[35] But no deduction is allowed for any portion of interest expense that's allocable (comparing the bank's adjusted bases in taxable and exempt investments) to investment in tax-exempts. (Code Sec. 265(b)(1), Code Sec. 265(b)(2))[36] However, interest allocable to tax-exempts acquired (or treated as acquired) before Aug. 8, '86, is 80% deductible (100% deductible if acquired before '83). (Code Sec. 291(a)(3), Code Sec. 291(e)(1)(B))[37]

Bad debts. Banks generally must treat bad debts (e.g., losses on loans) by taking a specific deduction ("charge-off") for the debt, but non-large banks can choose to deduct additions to bad debt reserves. (Code Sec. 585(a))[38] Banks using reserves must use the experience method to compute the additions. Under this method, the additions can't bring the reserve above the bank's loans outstanding at year-end, times a six-year moving average percentage (ratio of total bad debts to total outstanding loans). (Code Sec. 585(b))[39]

Losses a bank incurs on account of its deposits in other banks must be specifically deducted, whether or not it uses the reserve method for other bad debts.[40]

Worthless securities. A bad debt deduction is allowed to banks for total or partial worthlessness (¶1772) of debts evidenced by securities. (Code Sec. 582(a)) Under the charge-off method, a bank's debt is conclusively presumed to be worthless where the charge-off is made under specific orders or in conformance with established policies, of federal or state supervisory authorities, or is in accordance with a properly made "conformity" election. (Reg § 1.166-2(d))[41]

Mutual savings banks or stock associations, savings and loan associations, building and loan associations, and cooperative banks are subject to special tax rules.[42] Gain or loss from the sale or exchange of any qualifying Fannie Mae and Freddie Mac preferred stock by any applicable financial institution (those referred to in Code Sec. 582(c) or financial institution holding companies) is treated as ordinary income or loss. (§ 301 of Division A, P.L. 110-343, 10/3/2008)[43]

¶ 4210   Common trust funds—tax treatment.

A common trust fund isn't subject to tax (Code Sec. 584(b)) but must file a return (on Form 1065) and pass through its income or loss and other items attributable to each participant. (Reg § 1.6032-1)[44] A common trust fund is a fund maintained by a bank or

---

32. ¶s E-1140, E-1141, E-1142
33. ¶E-3000 *et seq.*, ¶E-3300 *et seq.*
34. ¶E-3022 *et seq.*
35. ¶E-3105
36. ¶E-3108
37. ¶s E-3111, E-3124
38. ¶E-3201, ¶E-3224

39. ¶E-3227
40. ¶E-3139
41. ¶E-3201 *et seq.*
42. ¶E-3300 *et seq.*
43. ¶E-3022.1 *et seq.*
44. ¶s E-3600 *et seq.*, S-4105

trust company exclusively to collectively invest and reinvest moneys that it, in its capacity as a trustee, executor, administrator, guardian or custodian, contributes to the fund. (Code Sec. 584(a))[45]

¶ 4211 Taxation of insurance companies; life and non-life companies.

Life insurance companies (Code Sec. 801(a)) are taxed, at the regular corporate rates, on their "life insurance company taxable income" (LICTI). [46] LICTI is life insurance company gross income minus general deductions. (Code Sec. 803(a), Code Sec. 805)[47] Gain from the redemption at maturity of certain market discount bonds is taxed under a special rule.[48]

A corporation (whether stock, mutual, or mutual benefit) is taxed as a life insurance company if: (1) it's an insurance company, (2) it's engaged in the business of issuing life insurance and annuity contracts, and (3) it meets a reserve test. (Code Sec. 816(a))[49]

Nonlife insurance companies (stock and mutual) are taxed like corporations generally (¶3303 *et seq.*), with certain deductions particular to insurance. Gross income is investment and underwriting income, and gain or loss from property dispositions. (Code Sec. 831, Code Sec. 832)[50] Certain small nonlife insurance companies may elect to be taxed only on investment income, (Code Sec. 831(b))[1] and others may be exempt. (Code Sec. 501(c)(15))[2]

45. ¶E-3600 *et seq.*
46. ¶E-4801
47. ¶E-4801 *et seq.*
48. ¶E-4819

49. ¶E-5401
50. ¶E-5500 *et seq.*
1. ¶E-5503
2. ¶D-5901

Chapter 21 Pension and Profit-Sharing Plans—401(k) Plans—IRAs—Roth IRAs—Roth 401(k) Programs—Deemed IRAs—SEPs—SIMPLE Plans

¶ 4300   Employee Benefit Plans, Overview.

Qualified pension, profit-sharing and stock bonus plans offer substantial tax benefits to sponsor-employers and their employees.

The principal tax advantages are:

. . . the employer gets an immediate deduction for contributions under the plan (Code Sec. 404);[1]

. . . income earned by funds held under the plan is tax-exempt (Code Sec. 501(a));[2]

. . . employees generally aren't taxed on their share of the fund until amounts are distributed to them (usually after retirement), ¶4328 *et seq.*, (Code Sec. 402; Reg § 1.402(a)-1);[3]

. . . amounts transferred in a direct trustee-to-trustee transfer are excluded from income (¶4349) (Code Sec. 402(e)(6)) and eligible rollover distributions can be rolled over tax-free to eligible retirement plans (¶4349) (Code Sec. 402(c)(1));[4]

. . . tax is deferred on qualifying distributions of appreciated employer stock until the stock is sold, see ¶4330. (Code Sec. 402(e)(4))[5]

For the small-employer retirement plan start-up tax credit, see ¶2329. For the small-employer auto-enrollment credit, see ¶2333.

¶ 4301   Pension plans, overview: defined benefit plans, money-purchase plans, hybrid plans.

A qualified pension plan provides systematically for the payment of definitely determinable benefits to employees (and their beneficiaries) after retirement over a period of years, usually for life.[6] Pension benefits are generally measured by such factors as years of the employee's service and compensation received. (Reg § 1.401-1(b)(1)(i))[7] Benefits under a defined benefit plan are "definitely determinable" if they are determined actuarially, on a basis that precludes employer discretion. (Code Sec. 401(a)(25))[8] A money-purchase plan—contributions geared to a fixed formula (e.g., 10% of compensation), rather than to profits—is a pension plan if the plan "designates" its intent to be a money purchase pension plan. (Code Sec. 401(a)(27)(B); Reg § 1.401-1(b)(1)(i))[9]

Defined benefit plans also include so-called "hybrid plans," such as cash balance plans and pension equity plans (PEPs). Special rules apply to these plans. (Code Sec. 411(b)(5))[10] ; Reg § 1.411(b)(5)-1(b) through Reg § 1.411(b)(5)-1(e)[11]

---

1. ¶H-10000 *et seq.*
2. ¶H-5315
3. ¶H-11000 *et seq.*
4. ¶H-8250 *et seq.*; ¶H-11400 *et seq.*
5. ¶H-11500 *et seq.*
6. ¶H-5328

7. ¶H-5328
8. ¶H-5328
9. ¶s H-5205, H-5337
10. ¶H-7239.2 *et seq.*
11. ¶H-7239.4 *et seq.*

References beginning with a single letter are to paragraphs in Federal Tax Coordinator 2d and RIA's Analysis of Federal Taxes: Income.

¶ 4302 Profit-sharing and stock bonus plans, overview.

A qualified profit-sharing plan must have a definite, predetermined formula for allocating contributions made under the plan among the participants, and provide for distributing the funds accumulated under the plan only after a fixed number of years, the attainment of a stated age or upon the occurrence of some event (such as disability, retirement, death or severance of employment). (Reg § 1.401-1(b)(1)(ii))[12]

Contributions can be made to a qualified profit-sharing plan whether or not the employer has current or accumulated profits, and even if the employer is a tax-exempt organization. (Code Sec. 401(a)(27)(A))[13]

A qualified stock bonus plan pays benefits in the form of the employer-corporation's own stock. Stock bonus plans must generally satisfy the qualification requirements that apply to profit sharing plans, plus some additional requirements. (Reg § 1.401-1(b)(1)(iii))[14]

¶ 4303 Employee stock ownership plans (ESOPs)—qualified retirement plans.

An ESOP is a qualified defined contribution plan that is either a stock bonus plan, or a combination stock bonus and money purchase plan, that invests primarily in employer securities (Code Sec. 4975(e)(7)), and is formally designated as an ESOP.[15]

To ensure that S corporation ESOPs benefit a broad range of employees, restrictions apply under Code Sec. 409(p) that generally prohibit the accrual or allocation of S corp. stock to certain disqualified persons in an ESOP where 10% owners hold 50% or more of the interests in the S corp. (Code Sec. 409(p); Reg § 1.409(p)-1)[16]

Dividends on employer securities that are distributed from an ESOP under Code Sec. 404(k) must be reported on a Form 1099-R that does not report any other distributions, rather than on Form 1099-DIV.[17]

¶ 4304 Annuity plans—qualified retirement plans.

Under Code Sec. 403(a)(1) and Code Sec. 404(a)(2), the tax advantages of a qualified plan can be obtained without a trust by using contributions to buy retirement annuities directly from an insurance company.[18]

Taxpayers may buy deferred "longevity" annuities ("Qualified Longevity Annuity Contracts," or QLACs) under qualified defined contribution plans, Code Sec. 403 plans, Code Sec. 408 individual retirement annuities and accounts (IRAs), and eligible governmental Code Sec. 457 plans. (Reg § 1.401(a)(9)-5; Reg § 1.401(a)(9)-6; Reg § 1.408-8, Q&A-12; Reg § 1.403(b)-6(e))[19]

¶ 4305 Cash or deferred arrangements (CODAs)/"401(k) plans"—elective deferral—qualified retirement plans.

Cash or deferred arrangements (CODAs), or 401(k) plans (Code Sec. 401(k)), allow employees to elect to have a portion of their pay contributed to a qualified trust under a profit-sharing plan, stock bonus plan, pre-ERISA money purchase plan, or rural cooperative defined contribution pension plan.[20]

For 2022, an employee may elect to defer a maximum of $20,500 ($22,500 for 2023)on a

---

12. ¶H-5337 *et seq.*
13. ¶H-5337
14. ¶H-5209
15. ¶H-9300 *et seq.*
16. ¶H-12112.1 *et seq.*

17. ¶S-3419.1
18. ¶H-5212 *et seq.*
19. ¶H-8280.14 *et seq.*; ¶H-12264.12; ¶H-12290.42A
20. ¶H-8975 *et seq.*

pre-tax basis under a 401(k) plan, SEP, or Code Sec. 403(b) tax-sheltered annuity (¶4375). (Code Sec. 402(g)(1), Code Sec. 402(g)(4))[21] Individuals who attain age 50 by the end of the plan year may make (if their plan permits) additional pre-tax "catch-up" contributions (Reg § 1.414(v)-1(a)) of up to $6,500 for 2022 and $7,500 for 2023. (Code Sec. 414(v)(2)(B)(i), Code Sec. 414(v)(2)(C)) The maximum catch-up amounts apply to all qualified plans, tax-sheltered annuity plans, SEPs and SIMPLE plans of an employer on an aggregated basis, as if all plans were a single plan. (Code Sec. 414(v)(2)(D))[22]

If all the requirements are met, any amount set aside under the CODA isn't taxed to the employee currently but instead is taxed at distribution. But elective deferrals and designated Roth contributions (¶4363) are included in wages for social security and Medicare taxes. (Code Sec. 3121(v)(1)(A))[23]

Excess deferrals are included in the employee's gross income. (Code Sec. 402(g)(1)(A); Reg § 1.402(g)-1(a)) They're taxed again on distribution, unless distributed to the employee in a corrective (nontaxable) distribution during the tax year or by the Apr. 15th after the close of the employee's tax year. (Code Sec. 402(g)(2)(C); Reg § 1.402(g)-1(e)(8))[24]

A 401(k) plan must meet all the normal tax qualification rules (¶4307), including the nondiscrimination rules (¶4314), and, in addition, all of the following requirements:

(1) amounts must not be distributable earlier than: (a) retirement; death; disability; other separation from employment; or (in a lump sum) on a plan termination described in Code Sec. 401(k)(10); (b) hardship (see below) or attainment of age 59½ (for profit-sharing or stock bonus plans); (c) for a qualified reservist distribution (Code Sec. 72(t)(2)(G)(iii)), the date the reservist is called up; or (d) for investments in a lifetime income investment (Code Sec. 401(a)(38)(B)(ii)), 90 days before the lifetime income investment may no longer be an investment option. (Code Sec. 401(k)(2)(B))[25] (for loans from 401(k) plans, see ¶4333);

(2) employer contributions made under the employee's election must be nonforfeitable at all times (Code Sec. 401(k)(2)(C));[26]

(3) an employee must be allowed to make elective deferrals if he or she has worked at least 500 hours per year for at least 3 consecutive years and has reached age 21 by the end of the 3-consecutive-year period (a "long-term part-time employee"); for determining whether the 3-consecutive-year period has been met, the 12-month periods beginning before 2021 won't be taken into account; (Code Sec. 401(k)(2)(D), Code Sec. 401(k)(15))[27]

(4) a covered employee must be able to elect to have the employer make plan contributions on the employee's behalf or make the payment directly to the employee in cash (Code Sec. 401(k)(2)(A))[28] (automatic contributions are permitted for employees who don't affirmatively elect to receive cash, see below);[29]

(5) elective deferrals under the plan (as aggregated with all other plans, etc., of the employer) must be prohibited from exceeding the above indexed dollar limits;[30] and

(6) special nondiscrimination rules that require the plan to satisfy an actual deferral percentage (ADP) test, so highly compensated employees can't elect to defer a disproportionately higher amount of their salary, must be met. (Code Sec. 401(k)(3)(A))[31] A similar actual contribution percentage (ACP) test applies to limit employer matching or employee contributions made on behalf of highly compensated employees. (Code Sec. 401(m))[32] Special rules will apply for "long-term part-time employees" (see (3),

---

21. ¶H-9151
22. ¶H-9246
23. ¶H-4624
24. ¶H-9155 et seq.
25. ¶H-9201 et seq.
26. ¶H-8975.12

27. ¶H-5809
28. ¶H-8975.12
29. ¶H-8975.6; ¶H-9053.1I
30. ¶s H-9150, H-9159
31. ¶H-8976; ¶H-9071.1 et seq.
32. ¶H-6575 et seq.

above) for eligibility for employer nonelective and matching contributions, and for non-discrimination testing relief. (Code Sec. 401(k)(15))[33]

A 401(k) plan is treated as meeting the nondiscrimination requirements if it's a "SIMPLE" plan (¶4369) that meets specified matching or nonelective contribution tests and other requirements. (Code Sec. 401(k)(11))[34]

A nondiscrimination safe harbor to ADP testing that requires minimum employer matching or nonelective contributions is available. (Code Sec. 401(k)(12))[35] Another non-discrimination safe harbor applies for automatic enrollment 401(k) programs (called qualified automatic contribution arrangements, or "QACAs") that meet certain contribution, vesting, and withdrawal requirements. (Code Sec. 401(k)(13))[36]

Similar nondiscrimination safe harbor alternatives to ACP testing of matching contributions are also available. (Code Sec. 401(m)(11); Code Sec. 401(m)(12))[37]

Similar rules apply for 403(b) plans, see ¶4375.

A 401(k) plan can include a qualified Roth contribution program; see ¶4363.

A distribution is on account of hardship (see (1)(b), above) if it: (1) is made on account of an immediate and heavy financial need of the employee, and (2) is necessary to satisfy that need. A distribution is deemed made on account of an immediate and heavy financial need if it's for the items listed in Reg § 1.401(k)-1(d)(3)(ii)(B). These include medical expenses, burial expenses, and losses due to disasters. (Reg § 1.401(k)-1(d)(3))[38] Hardship distributions may be made from the sources listed in Code Sec. 401(k)(14)(A). Plans may impose additional conditions (e.g., that any available plan loans be taken), but cannot require a suspension of elective or employee contributions. (Reg § 1.401(k)-1(d)(3)(iii)(C))[39]

Hardship distributions are not rollover-eligible, see ¶4349.

¶ 4306 "Defined contribution" and "defined benefit" plans—qualified retirement plans.

Certain rules governing employee benefit plans specifically apply either to "defined contribution plans" or to "defined benefit plans."

A "defined contribution plan" provides for individual accounts for participants and for benefits based on those accounts. (Code Sec. 414(i)) Included are money purchase pension plans, profit-sharing plans and stock bonus plans.

A "defined benefit plan" is a pension plan other than a defined contribution plan. (Code Sec. 414(j)) It provides for the payments of definitely determinable benefits to the employee over a period of years, usually for life, after retirement. (Reg § 1.401-1(b)(1)(i))[40]

Employers with 500 or fewer employees may establish a combined defined benefit–401(k) plan (a "DB(k) plan"). (Code Sec. 414(x)(2))[41]

¶ 4307 Qualification requirements for a qualified employee plan.

The chief requirements for tax qualification of an employee benefit plan and tax-exempt trust are:

33. ¶H-6168
34. ¶H-9087
35. ¶H-9053.1
36. ¶H-9053.1I
37. ¶H-6596 *et seq.*

38. ¶H-9211 *et seq.*; ¶H-8978.5
39. ¶H-8978.2
40. ¶H-5200 *et seq.*
41. ¶H-9252

(1) The plan must be a definite written program[42] that's communicated to the employees. (Reg § 1.401-1(a)(2))[43]

(2) The plan must be established by the employer for the *exclusive* benefit of the employees or their beneficiaries. (Code Sec. 401(a))[44]

(3) The plan must generally provide that benefits can't be assigned, except for transfers under a qualified domestic relations order (QDRO) and judgments or settlements for certain ERISA crimes and violations. (Code Sec. 401(a)(13); Reg § 1.401(a)-13(g)(2))[45]

(4) The plan must meet special tests based on coverage and eligibility of employees to participate (¶4312).

(5) The plan must not discriminate in favor of highly compensated employees with respect to contributions or benefits (¶4314).

(6) The plan must meet certain vesting requirements (¶4311).

(7) Defined benefit and money purchase pension plans must be properly funded (¶4319).

(8) Under a defined benefit plan, forfeitures must not be applied to increase the benefits of the employees. (Code Sec. 401(a)(8))[46]

(9) A pension plan (and certain other plans) must in general pay a married participant's benefits in the form of a qualified joint and survivor annuity (QJSA), unless the participant elects otherwise (with written spousal consent). The monthly survivor benefit must be at least 50% of the joint benefit. (Code Sec. 417(b))[47] Plans that offer a QJSA must offer, as an option, a joint and survivor benefit that provides at least a 75% survivor benefit. (Code Sec. 417(a)(1)(A), Code Sec. 417(g)) Plans subject to the QJSA requirements must provide, to a participant who waives the QJSA, the chance to elect a qualified optional survivor annuity (QOSA). (Code Sec. 417(a)(1)(A)(ii))[48]

(10) In the event of a merger or consolidation with, or transfer of assets or liabilities to, any other plan, each participant must be entitled to a termination benefit at least equal to his or her pre-merger termination benefit. (Code Sec. 401(a)(12))[49]

(11) The plan may not provide for contributions or benefits that exceed specified overall limits (Code Sec. 401(a)(16))[50] (¶4317).

(12) The plan must provide that benefit payments begin (unless otherwise elected) no later than the 60th day after the plan year in which occurs the latest of: (a) the date the participant reaches age 65 (or earlier retirement age), (b) the 10th anniversary of the employee's participation in the plan, or (c) the date the participant terminates service. (Code Sec. 401(a)(14); Reg § 1.401(a)-14(a))[1]

Qualified pension plans may allow employees age 59½ or older to receive in-service distributions. Certain pension plans won't lose their status as qualified trusts solely because the plan allows certain employees in the building and construction industries who are not separated from employment to take distributions at age 55. (Code Sec. 401(a)(36); Reg § 1.401(a)-1(b); Notice 2020-68, 2020-38 IRB 567)[2]

(13) The plan must require certain minimum distributions (Code Sec. 401(a)(9) (¶4335).

(14) A pension plan can't allow withdrawal of employer contributions before termination of employment, or of the plan.[3] But employer contributions accumulated in a profit-sharing plan may be distributed after a fixed number of years (not less than two years). (Reg § 1.401-1(b)(1)(ii))[4] A profit-sharing plan may also permit withdrawal of employer

---

42. ¶H-5301
43. ¶H-5303
44. ¶H-5304
45. ¶H-8200 *et seq.*
46. ¶H-7502
47. ¶H-8611
48. ¶H-8623.1 *et seq.*

49. ¶H-8800 *et seq.*
50. ¶H-5901 *et seq.*
1. ¶H-8271
2. ¶H-8273.2
3. ¶H-5310
4. ¶H-5346

contributions for hardship[5] or by participants with at least 60 months of participation.[6]

(15) Every plan must provide that a distributee of an eligible rollover distribution may elect to have the distribution transferred directly to an eligible retirement plan (¶4349). (Code Sec. 401(a)(31)(A); Reg § 1.401(a)(31)-1)[7] Plans also must adhere to certain involuntary cash-out rollover rules (see ¶4349). (Code Sec. 401(a)(31)(B))

(16) The plan can't reduce plan benefits (including death or disability) to account for post-separation social security benefit increases. (Code Sec. 401(a)(15))[8]

(17) A plan may take into account only the first $305,000 for 2022 ($330,000 for 2023). of each employee's annual compensation. (Code Sec. 401(a)(17))[9]

(18) Defined benefit plans other than government plans must meet minimum participation requirements (¶4312) (Code Sec. 401(a)(26)) in addition to the coverage and eligibility requirements (¶4313).[10]

(19) If a plan member elects to have an eligible rollover distribution paid directly to a specified eligible retirement plan, the plan must make the distribution in the form of direct trustee-to-trustee transfer. (Code Sec. 401(a)(31))[11]

(20) A qualified trust that's a retirement plan must provide that the survivors of a participant who dies while performing qualified military service are entitled to any additional benefits (other than benefit accruals relating to the period of qualified military service) under the plan as if the participant had resumed and then terminated employment on account of his or her death. (Code Sec. 401(a)(37))[12]

To help address COVID-related labor shortages, IRS said that employers generally won't jeopardize the tax status of their pension plans if they rehire retirees or permit distributions of retirement benefits to current employees who have reached age 59½ or the plan's normal retirement age. (IR 2021-208, 10/22/2021)

For the cash-out requirements under the minimum survivor annuity rules, which allow participant accounts of $5,000 or less to be distributed, the present value of plan benefits is calculated using the "applicable mortality table" and the "applicable interest rate." (Code Sec. 417(e)(3)) The "applicable interest rate" is the adjusted first, second, and third segment rates for the month before the distribution date (or as IRS regs prescribe).[13] The "applicable mortality table" is a mortality table, modified as appropriate by IRS, based on the mortality table specified for the plan year.[14]

¶ 4308 Qualified retirement plan adopted by filing due date can be treated as in effect at year-end.

For plans adopted for tax years beginning after 2019, an employer may elect to treat a qualified retirement plan adopted after the close of a tax year but before the due date (including extensions) of the employer's tax return for the tax year, as having been adopted as of the last day of the tax year. (Code Sec. 401(b)(2))[15] This does not, however, allow retroactive adoption of a qualified CODA. (Reg § 1.401(k)-1(a)(3)(iii)(A))

¶ 4309 Distributions under domestic relations orders—qualified retirement plans.

Under Code Sec. 401(a)(13)(B), the rules prohibiting the assignment or alienation of

---

5. ¶H-5348
6. ¶H-5346
7. ¶H-8250 *et seq.*
8. ¶H-5311
9. ¶H-5919
10. ¶H-5700 *et seq.*

11. ¶H-8251
12. ¶H-9963 *et seq.*
13. ¶H-8705.1
14. ¶H-8704
15. ¶H-5302.1

qualified plan benefits do not apply to the creation, assignment, or recognition of a right to any benefit payable for a participant under a domestic relations order that is determined to be a "qualified domestic relations order" (i.e., a "QDRO").[16] A domestic relations order is any judgment, decree, or order (including approval of a property settlement agreement) that: (i) relates to the provision of child support, alimony payments, or marital property rights to a spouse, former spouse, child, or other dependent of the participant, and (ii) is made under a state domestic relations law (including a community property law). (Code Sec. 414(p)(1))[17]

A QDRO is a "domestic relations order" (see above) that: (1) creates or recognizes the existence of an alternate payee's right, or assigns to an alternate payee (see below) the right, to receive all or a portion of a plan participant's benefits payable under a plan, (2) clearly specifies certain facts, such as the amount or percentage of, and manner that, the participant's benefits are to be paid to the alternate payee, and (3) does not alter the amount or form of benefit. (Code Sec. 414(p)(1)(A), Code Sec. 414(p)(2), Code Sec. 414(p)(3))[18]

An "alternate payee" includes any spouse, former spouse, child, or other dependent of a participant who is recognized by a QDRO as having a right to receive all, or a portion of, the benefits payable under a plan with respect to the participant. (Code Sec. 414(p)(8))[19]

A spouse (or former spouse) who has a right to receive all or a part of a distribution under a QDRO as an alternate payee, is treated as the distributee of any distribution received under the QDRO. However, a distribution to a participant's non-spouse dependent (who also may be an alternate payee) is taxed to the participant. (Code Sec. 402(e)(1)(A)) Similar rules apply to distributions from Code Sec. 457 plans. (Code Sec. 414(p)(12))[20]

Lump-sum distributions to alternate payees who are spouses (or ex-spouses) of participants are eligible for preferential tax treatment (see ¶4329) if the distributions would qualify for the preferential tax treatment if made to the participant. Further, any amounts paid or distributed under a qualified plan to an alternate payee who is the spouse (or former spouse) of the participant under a QDRO may be rolled over (see ¶4349 *et seq.*) as if the alternate payee were the participant. Thus, a QDRO distribution made to an employee's spouse (or former spouse) as an alternate payee is an eligible rollover distribution. (Code Sec. 402(e)(1)(B))[21]

For a distribution to the spouse (or former spouse) of the plan participant as alternate payee under a QDRO, net employee contributions (together with other amounts treated as the participant's investment in the contract) are apportioned between the participant and the alternate payee. The apportionment is made pro rata, on the basis of the present value of all benefits of the participant under the plan and the present value of all benefits of the alternate payee under the plan (as alternate payee with respect to the participant under a QDRO). (Code Sec. 72(m)(10))[22]

¶ 4310   Incidental benefits—qualified retirement plans.

Life or accident and health insurance features that are incidental to the primary benefit of a qualified plan, may be included to a limited extent. (Reg § 1.401-1(b)(1)(i), Reg § 1.401-1(b)(1)(ii))[23] IRS regs address the tax treatment of payments for accident or health insurance made by qualified retirement plans. (Reg § 1.402(a)-1(e))[24]

16. ¶H-8207
17. ¶H-8208
18. ¶H-8209
19. ¶H-8209.1
20. ¶H-11008

21. ¶H-11439
22. ¶H-11049
23. ¶H-8104 *et seq.*
24. ¶H-11076.1

¶ 4311   Vesting of benefits—qualified retirement plans.

Plans must provide that a participant's accrued benefit (defined below) becomes nonforfeitable, i.e., vests, at the minimum rate specified in Code Sec. 411(a), or faster. Benefits derived from employee contributions must be 100% vested at all times. (Code Sec. 411(a); Reg § 1.411(a)-1(a)(2)) Benefits derived from employer contributions must become nonforfeitable when the employee reaches normal retirement age (defined below). (Code Sec. 411(a)) A defined benefit plan also must meet one of two alternative minimum vesting standards for vesting in benefits derived from employer contributions before normal retirement age: (1) a 5-year cliff schedule requiring full vesting after 5 years of service, or (2) a 3-to-7 year graded schedule requiring 20% vesting after 3 years of service and 20% additional vesting in each of the following years. (Code Sec. 411(a)(2)(A)) For a defined contribution plan, slightly faster vesting (3-year cliff or 2-to-6 year graded) is the minimum for all employer contributions (non-elective and matching employer contributions). (Code Sec. 411(a)(2)(B))[25]

For hybrid defined benefit plans (¶4301), IRS regs provide guidance on the accelerated 3-year vesting for employer contributions. (Reg § 1.411(a)(13)-1(c))[26]

Accrued benefit means the participant's annual benefit (or its actuarial equivalent) starting at normal retirement age (defined benefit plans) or the balance in the participant's account (defined contribution plans). (Code Sec. 411(a)(7)(A))[27]

Normal retirement age is the earlier of the time a participant attains normal retirement age under the plan or the later of: (1) the time the participant reaches age 65, or (2) the 5th anniversary of the individual's participation in the plan. (Code Sec. 411(a)(8))[28]

IRS regs allow plans to set normal retirement age lower than age 65, so long as this age isn't earlier than the earliest age that is reasonably representative of the typical age for the industry in which the covered workforce is employed. Age 62 is a safe harbor for this requirement. (Reg § 1.401(a)-1(b)(2))[29]

¶ 4312   Coverage and eligibility requirements—qualified retirement plans.

A qualified plan other than a government plan must meet special tests designed to ensure adequate coverage of rank and file employees and avoid discrimination.

The plan must, on at least one day in each quarter of its tax year, either: (1) benefit 70% of the employees who aren't "highly compensated" (¶4315), (2) benefit a percentage of nonhighly compensated employees that is at least 70% of the highly compensated benefiting, or (3) meet a test under which the average benefit for the nonhighly compensated is at least 70% of the average benefit for the highly compensated. (Code Sec. 410(b)(1)) This "average benefits test" also requires that the plan benefit employees under a nondiscriminatory classification. (Code Sec. 410(b)(2))[30] However, a plan maintained by an employer that has no employees other than highly compensated employees for a year is treated as meeting the coverage requirement for the year. (Code Sec. 410(b)(6)(F))[31]

A qualified plan can't require as a condition of participation that any employee complete a period of service extending beyond the later of the date he: (1) reaches age 21, or (2) completes one year of service (or two years, if the plan provides full and immediate vesting for all participants). (Code Sec. 410(a)(1)(A), Code Sec. 410(a)(1)(B)(i))[32]

25. ¶H-7400 *et seq.*
26. ¶H-7239.22
27. ¶H-7200 *et seq.*
28. ¶H-7404

29. ¶H-7404
30. ¶H-5410 *et seq.*
31. ¶H-5410
32. ¶s H-5804, H-5807 *et seq.*

¶ 4313   Minimum participation requirement—the 50-employee/40% test—qualified retirement plans.

Under Code Sec. 401(a)(26)(A), a defined benefit plan other than a governmental plan isn't qualified unless, on each day of the plan year, the plan benefits at least the lesser of (a) 50 employees of the employer, or (b) the greater of 40% of employees, or 2 employees (or 1 employee if there is only 1 employee).[33] Instead of meeting the test on each day of the plan year, compliance on a single representative "snapshot" day during the year is sufficient. (Reg § 1.401(a)(26)-7(b))[34]

¶ 4314   Contributions or benefits must be nondiscriminatory—qualified retirement plans.

Under Code Sec. 401(a)(4), contributions or benefits under a plan other than a governmental plan must not discriminate in favor of "highly compensated employees," see ¶4315.[35] To comply, a plan must satisfy three requirements: (1) either the contributions or benefits under the plan must be nondiscriminatory in amount, (2) the plan's optional forms of benefit, ancillary benefits (e.g., disability benefits), and other rights and features (e.g., plan loans and investment alternatives) must be made available to employees in a nondiscriminatory manner, and (3) the effect of the plan under certain plan amendments, grants of past service credit, and plan terminations must be nondiscriminatory. (Reg § 1.401(a)(4)-1(b))[36] Defined benefit plans can be cross-tested for discrimination on the basis of equivalent employer contributions to profit-sharing plans, and vice versa. (Reg § 1.401(a)(4)-8) "Catch-up" elective deferrals by older employees (¶4305) are not subject to nondiscrimination requirements, above, but all eligible employees must have the opportunity to make these "catch-up" contributions (the "universal availability" requirement). (Code Sec. 414(v)(3)(B), Code Sec. 414(v)(4))[37]

¶ 4315   Who is a highly compensated employee (HCE)—qualified retirement plans.

Under Code Sec. 414(q), an HCE is an employee (1) who was a 5% owner at any time during the determination year or the preceding year, or (2) whose compensation from the employer for the preceding year exceeded the applicable threshold ($135,000 if the preceding year began in 2022; $150,000 if it began in 2023) and, if the employer elects, also was in the "top-paid group" (top 20%) of employees for that year. [38]

¶ 4316   Plans covering self-employed persons—qualified retirement plans.

Under Code Sec. 401(c)(1), a person who is a "self-employed individual," i.e., derives "earned income" from a business or profession that the individual owns or conducts, or has earned income from a partnership in which the individual is a partner, or has other self-employment income (such as director's fees), can establish and be covered by a qualified retirement plan.[39] Earned income for this purpose consists essentially of earnings attributable to personal services, whether from a sole proprietorship, partnership or other unincorporated venture, derived from the trade or business for which the plan is established. (Code Sec. 401(c)(2), Code Sec. 401(d))[40]

---

33. ¶H-5701 *et seq.*
34. ¶H-5704
35. ¶H-6100 *et seq.*
36. ¶H-6350 *et seq.*

37. ¶H-9247.1
38. ¶H-6702
39. ¶s H-5218, H-9500 *et seq.*
40. ¶H-9513 *et seq.*

¶ 4317 Overall limits on plan contributions and benefits—qualified retirement plans.

A plan can't be qualified if it provides for contributions or benefits that exceed the overall limits described below.

Benefits under a defined benefit plan (DB plan) will disqualify the plan if the "annual benefit" for each participant beginning at age 65 exceeds the lesser of: (1) $245,000 for 2022 ($265,000 for 2023), but actuarially reduced if benefit begins before age 62, and increased if the benefit begins after age 65, or (2) 100% of the participant's average compensation for his or her three high consecutive years of active plan participation. (Code Sec. 415(b); Reg § 1.415(b)-1(a)(1))[41] The maximum dollar benefit is reduced if the employee has less than ten years of plan participation when retirement benefits begin. (Code Sec. 415(b)(5)) This reduction doesn't apply to pro rata benefit increases under a terminating plan if there's no discrimination in favor of highly compensated employees. (Code Sec. 4980(d)(4)(C))[42] Neither the dollar nor the percentage limitation applies if the annual benefit payable under a DB plan doesn't exceed $10,000 and the employer has never had a defined contribution plan (DC plan) in which he or she participated. (Code Sec. 415(b)(4))[43]

Annual additions under a DC plan may not exceed the lesser of: (1) $61,000 for 2022 ($66,000 for 2023), or (2) 100% of the participant's compensation. (Code Sec. 415(c)(1)) Annual additions include employer contributions, employee contributions other than qualified cost-of-living contributions to a DB plan (Code Sec. 415(k)(2)(A)), and employee forfeitures. (Code Sec. 415(c)(2); Reg § 1.415(c)-1(b))[44]

Mandatory employee contributions made to a DB plan are treated as contributions made to a DC plan, and so are subject to the Code Sec. 415(c) contribution limit. An individual medical account that's part of a pension or annuity plan under Code Sec. 401(h), and an account set up to provide post-retirement medical benefits or life insurance for a key employee under Code Sec. 419A(d)(1), are treated as DC plans, so that contributions to these accounts are also subject to the Code Sec. 415(c) limit.[45]

Special rules apply the limits to certain ESOPs. (Code Sec. 415(c)(6); Reg § 1.415(c)-1(f))[46]

Benefits to alternate payees under a qualified domestic relations order (QDRO) relating to a participant's benefits must be aggregated with benefits to the participant from all DB and DC plans in applying the Code Sec. 415 limitations.[47]

Foster care-related payments that are received from an employer and excludable as "difficulty of care" payments (¶1206) are treated as compensation for calculating the DC contribution limits (Notice 2020-68, 2020-38 IRB 567). (Code Sec. 415(c)(8))[48]

¶ 4318 Additional qualification requirements for "top-heavy" plans—qualified retirement plans.

Under Code Sec. 416(a), a "top-heavy" plan is one that primarily favors officers, shareholders, partners and other key employees. If more than 60% of the accrued benefits in a defined benefit plan, or more than 60% of the aggregate of the account balances in a defined contribution plan, are for "key employees," the plan is top-heavy and must meet additional requirements for minimum vesting, and minimum benefits or contributions for

---

41. ¶H-5950
42. ¶H-8907
43. ¶H-5965
44. ¶H-6000 *et seq.*

45. ¶H-6000 *et seq.*
46. ¶H-6016
47. ¶s H-5950, H-6000, H-8217 *et seq.*
48. ¶H-6006.1

non-key employees, in determining contributions or benefits.[49] SIMPLE retirement plans (¶4369) and Code Sec. 401(k) plans that meet safe-harbor nondiscrimination requirements, aren't subject to the top-heavy rules. (Code Sec. 416(g)(4)(G), Code Sec. 416(g)(4)(H))[50]

Top-heavy plans are subject to special vesting rules. (Code Sec. 416(b))[1] Further, top-heavy defined benefit plans must provide non-key employes with a minimum annual benefit that's not integrated with social security. (Code Sec. 416(c)(1))[2] And, for top-heavy defined contribution plans, the employer must make contributions of at least 3% of compensation for each non-key employee (including employer matching contributions). (Code Sec. 416(c)(2))[3]

¶ 4319   Minimum funding requirements for defined benefit plans, money purchase plans; minimum required contribution; contribution due date.

To qualify for tax advantages, defined benefit plans (DB plans) and money purchase plans (including target benefit plans) must meet minimum funding standards. To the extent the minimum funding standard is not met, the employer must pay nondeductible taxes on the amount of the deficiency until the deficiency is eliminated.

A plan is treated as satisfying the minimum funding standard for a plan year if:

(1) for a single-employer DB plan, the employer makes contributions to, or under, the plan for the plan year which, in total, are not less than the Code Sec. 430 minimum required contribution for the plan year;

(2) for a single-employer money purchase plan, the employer makes contributions to, or under, the plan for the plan year, which are required under the plan's terms;

(3) for a multiemployer plan, the employers make contributions to, or under, the plan, for any plan year which, in the aggregate, are sufficient to ensure that the plan does not have an accumulated funding deficiency under Code Sec. 431 as of the end of the plan year. (Code Sec. 412(a)(2))[4]

For single-employer DB plans, the minimum required contribution generally depends on whether the value of plan assets covers the plan's "funding target," i.e., the present value of all benefits accrued, earned, or otherwise allocated to years of service before the first day of the plan year. (Code Sec. 430(d)(1); Reg § 1.430(d)-1(b)(2))[5]

If the value of plan assets (less any prefunding balance or funding standard carryover balance) is less than the funding target, the minimum required contribution is the sum of the plan's target normal cost and the shortfall and waiver amortization charges for the plan year. (Code Sec. 430(a)(1); Reg § 1.430(a)-1(b)) If the value of plan assets (less any prefunding balance or funding standard carryover balance) equals or exceeds the funding target, the minimum required contribution is the plan's target normal cost for the plan year reduced (but not below zero) by the amount of the excess. (Code Sec. 430(a)(2); Reg § 1.430(a)-1(b)(2))

A plan's target normal cost is the present value of the benefits that are expected to accrue or to be earned during the plan year, plus any plan-related expenses expected to be paid from plan assets, and less any mandatory employee contributions expected to be made during the plan year. (Code Sec. 430(b)(1)(A); Reg § 1.430(d)-1(b)(1))[6]

To determine a plan's target normal cost and funding target, plan liabilities are calculated by discounting future payments to present value using required interest rates based on corporate bonds. Plans must discount future liabilities using three different interest

49. ¶H-8000 *et seq.*
50. ¶H-8002 *et seq.*
1. ¶H-7423
2. ¶H-8025
3. ¶H-8032
4. ¶H-7601
5. ¶H-7752.1
6. ¶H-7751.1

rates (segment rates), depending on the length of time until the liabilities must be paid. A short-term interest (segment) rate is used to calculate the present value of liabilities that will come due within 5 years. A midterm interest (segment) rate is used for liabilities that will come due in 5 to 15 years, and a long-term interest (segment) rate is applied to liabilities that will come due in more than 15 years. These rates are derived from a "yield curve" of investment-grade corporate bonds averaged over the most recent 24 months (i.e., the interest rates are "smoothed" over a 24-month period).

If a rate determined under the regular rules (see above) is outside a specified percentage corridor based on 25-year average segment rates, the rate is adjusted. The average segment rate is the average of the segment rates determined under the regular rules for the 25-year period ending Sept. 30 of the calendar year before the calendar year in which the plan year begins. Under the 2021 American Rescue Plan Act (ARPA, Sec. 9706(a), PL 117-2, 3/11/2021), the pension funding stabilization percentages, which were to begin phasing out in 2021, are modified and extended through 2029, and a 5% floor is established on the 25-year interest rate averages. As a result, the corridor is 95% to 105% of the 25-year average for plan years beginning in calendar years 2020 through 2025. Beginning in 2026, the corridor increases by 5 percentage points each year until it attains (and then remains at) 30% in 2030 (making the corridor 70% to 130% of the 25-year average). (Code Sec. 430(h)(2)(C)(iv))[7]

Typically, a plan will have a funding shortfall for a plan year if its funding target for the year exceeds the value of the plan's assets. The shortfall amortization base for a plan year is (1) the plan's funding shortfall, less (2) the present value, determined using one of several permissible rates, of the total of the shortfall amortization installments that have been determined for the current plan year and any succeeding plan years. The total of these installments is referred to as the shortfall amortization charge. The "shortfall amortization installments" are the amounts necessary to amortize the plan's "shortfall amortization base" for any plan year, in level annual installments over the seven-year period beginning with the plan year (i.e., the period including the current plan year and the six succeeding plan years). (Code Sec. 430(c)(2)) However, for plan years beginning after Dec. 31, 2021 (or, if elected plan years beginning after Dec. 31, 2018, Dec. 31, 2019, or Dec. 31, 2020) all shortfall amortization bases in single-employer defined benefit plans for certain plan years, and all shortfall amortization installments determined with respect to those bases, are reduced to zero. Those shortfalls, as recalculated, and all future funding shortfalls, may be amortized over a period of 15 years, rather than over seven years. (Code Sec. 430(c)(8))[8]

Plans in "at risk status" (generally, less than 80% funded) must use additional actuarial assumptions to determine their funding target and target normal cost. (Code Sec. 430(i); Reg § 1.430(i)-1)[9]

Underfunded DB plans must also satisfy funding-based limits on the accrual and payment of benefits, such as plant shutdown benefits, plan amendments that increase liabilities for benefits, the payment of accelerated benefit distributions, etc. (Code Sec. 436; Reg § 1.436-1)[10]

The due date to pay minimum required contributions to DB plans, other than multiemployer plans, is 8½ months after the close of the plan year. Thus, for calendar-year plan years, the due date for payment of the minimum required contribution for plan Year 1 is Sept. 15 of Year 2.[11] A payment made before the first day of the plan year cannot be applied toward the minimum required contribution for that plan year. An accelerated schedule of quarterly installments of a plan's contributions applies where the plan had a

---

7. ¶H-7756.2A
8. ¶H-7751.3; ¶H-7751.2
9. ¶H-7759.1 *et seq.*

10. ¶H-7730.5 *et seq.*
11. ¶H-7770.1A *et seq.*

funding shortfall for the preceding plan year. Any payment of the minimum required contribution made on a date other than the valuation date must be adjusted for interest accruing for the period between (i) the valuation date, and (ii) the payment date, at the plan's effective rate of interest for the plan year, with a special adjustment required for a small plan. (Code Sec. 430(j); Reg § 1.430(j)-1)

IRS has provided guidance on the ARPA changes to the funding rules under Code Sec. 430 for single employer defined-benefit pension plans and ARPA changes affecting the application of the funding-based limits on benefits under Code Sec. 436. (Notice 2021-48, 2021-33 IRB 305)[12]

¶ 4320   Returning veteran's pension rights—qualified retirement plans.

Under Code Sec. 414(u)(8)(B), an employee who returns to a civilian employer following qualified military service is entitled to restoration of certain qualified plan benefits that would have accrued but for the absence due to military service. Qualified military service of a reemployed person can't be treated as a break in service, and must be considered service with the employer for determining the nonforfeitability and the accrual of the individual's benefits.[13] "Make-up" contributions in excess of the usual contribution and deduction limits for the year made, and suspension of plan loan repayment during uniformed service do not cause loss of a plan's qualified status. (Code Sec. 414(u)(1); Code Sec. 414(u)(4))[14] Plans must permit returning employees to make additional elective deferrals and employee contributions, and must make matching contributions that would have been required had the deferral been made during the period of military service. (Code Sec. 414(u)(2)(A)) Report make-up contributions on Form W-2 or a separate statement identifying the type of plan, years involved, and amounts.[15]

For retirement plans that are subject to Code Sec. 414(u): (1) an individual receiving a differential wage payment (¶3005) must be treated as an employee of the employer making the payment; (2) the differential wage payment must be treated as compensation; and (3) the plan won't be treated as failing to meet certain nondiscrimination requirements by reason of any contribution or benefit based on the differential wage payment (but other nondiscrimination requirements apply). (Code Sec. 414(u)(12)(A))

Death benefits. Qualified retirement plans, including Code Sec. 403(b) tax-deferred annuities and Code Sec. 457(b) plans, must provide that, where a plan participant dies while performing qualified military service, the participant's survivors are entitled to any additional benefits (other than benefit accruals relating to the period of qualified military service) that would have been provided under the plan had the participant resumed employment and then terminated employment on account of death. However, benefit accruals for the period of qualified military service are excepted from these additional benefits.[16]

¶ 4321   How to request IRS approval of qualified retirement plan—Form 5300; Form 5307.

Although advance IRS approval isn't required, it's desirable and customary to seek it by requesting an opinion letter (or determination letter) on special forms issued by IRS (e.g., Form 5300). Form 5300 can be submitted electronically; IRS continued to accept paper versions of Form 5300 through June 30, 2022. (IRS Employee Plans Newsletter, May 25, 2022)[17]

IRS limits the issuance of determination letters for individually-designed plans to initial

---

12. ¶H-7756.2J
13. ¶H-9951
14. ¶H-9952 *et seq.*

15. ¶H-9956
16. ¶H-9963 *et seq.*
17. ¶T-10500 *et seq.*

plan qualification, qualification upon plan termination, and certain other limited circumstances. (Rev Proc 2016-37, 2016-29 IRB 136, modified by Rev. Proc. 2021-38, 2021-38 IRB 425; Rev. Proc. 2021-37, 2021-38 IRB 385)[18]

Pre-approved plans. Instead of using individually-designed plans, many employers adopt plan documents that have been prepared by a legal or financial organization—such as a bank, law firm, mutual fund, or insurance company—and received advance approval from the IRS. Employers who adopt such pre-approved documents generally can rely on the opinion letter issued to the document provider. But employers that have modified their pre-approved document may be able to request a IRS determination of their own (Rev. Proc. 2020-40, 2020-38 IRB 575). Such determination requests will be made on Form 5307 or Form 5300, depending on the circumstances (e.g., the extent of the employer's modifications).[19]

For the small-employer retirement plan start-up tax credit, see ¶2329.

¶ 4322 Employee contributions and employer matching contributions—nondiscrimination tests—qualified retirement plans.

A plan may require an employee to contribute to the plan, as a condition to participation, or it may permit such contributions, if no discrimination results.[20]

Employee contributions and employer matching contributions under defined contribution plans (and those under a defined benefit plan treated as made under a defined contribution plan) must meet a nondiscrimination test that restricts the extent to which the actual contribution percentage (ACP) of eligible highly compensated employees can exceed the ACP for all other eligible employees. (Code Sec. 401(m), Code Sec. 414(k)(2)) The current year ACP for highly compensated employees is compared to the previous year's, or, electively, the current year's ACP for other employees. (Code Sec. 401(m)(2)) The ACP test can be satisfied using a safe-harbor. (Code Sec. 401(m)(11), Code Sec. 401(m)(12))[21] "SIMPLE" plans (¶4369) are deemed to satisfy the ACP test. (Code Sec. 401(m)(10))[22]

Qualified Nonelective Contributions (QNECs) and Qualified Matching Contributions (QMACs) are employer contributions, other than elective contributions or matching contributions, that meet certain nonforfeitability requirements and distribution limits, that are designed to allow a 401(k) plan to pass ADP/ACP testing. Employer contributions to a 401(k) plan are treated as QMACs or QNECs if they satisfy the nonforfeitability and distribution conditions when they are allocated to participants' accounts. (Reg § 1.401(k)-6)[23]

¶ 4323 Diversification of investments in employer securities—qualified retirement plans.

Defined contribution plans generally must allow participants to immediately diversify any employee contributions or elective deferrals invested in employer securities into at least 3 other investment options. For employer contributions, other than elective deferrals, invested in employer securities, the same diversification rights must be given to participants with at least 3 years of service, or each beneficiary of such participants or deceased participants. (Code Sec. 401(a)(35)) Individuals with diversification rights must be offered the opportunity to divest the employer securities and reinvest in another investment at least quarterly.[24]

---

18. ¶T-10506 *et seq.*
19. ¶T-10620 *et seq.*
20. ¶H-6556.1 *et seq.*
21. ¶H-6565

22. ¶H-6565.2
23. ¶H-9071.15
24. ¶H-8069*et seq.*

An ESOP won't lose its exemption from the application of the diversification rules just because it receives rollover contributions of amounts from another plan that are held in a separate account. The exemption continues to apply even if those amounts were attributable to contributions that were subject to Code Sec. 401(k) or Code Sec. 401(m) in the other plan.[25]

¶ 4324 Deduction limit for contributions to pension and annuity plans—qualified retirement plans.

Code Sec. 404(a) limits the deduction an employer may take for timely paid (¶4327) qualified retirement plan contributions. The limit for qualified pension and annuity plan contributions differs from the limit for stock bonus and profit-sharing plan contributions.[26]

The deduction limit for single-employer defined benefit (DB) pension and annuity plan contributions for any tax year is the greater of: (i) the excess (if any) of (A) the sum of: the plan's funding target, the plan's target normal cost, and, if the plan is in "at-risk" status, a cushion amount, over (B) the value of the plan's assets (determined under Code Sec. 430(g)(3)) as of the valuation date for the plan year (Code Sec. 404(o)(2)(A)); or (ii) the sum of the minimum required contributions for each plan year ending with or within the plan year. (Code Sec. 404(o))[27]

The deduction limit for contributions to a multiemployer DB plan is determined by:[28]

(1) the minimum funding standard (¶4319), if that exceeds the "level cost" or "normal cost" limit applicable to the plan (Code Sec. 404(a)(1)(A)(i));

(2) the "level cost" limit (if applicable), i.e., the amount necessary to provide for all participating employees the remaining unfunded cost of their past and current service credits, distributed as a level amount (or level percentage of compensation) over the entire future remaining service of each employee, but if the remaining unfunded cost with respect to any three individuals is more than 50% of the total remaining unfunded cost, the unfunded cost attributable to those three must be distributed over at least five tax years (Code Sec. 404(a)(1)(A)(ii));

(3) the "normal cost" limit (if applicable), i.e., an amount equal to (a) the "normal cost" (cost of credits for current services determined as though past service credits had been properly funded), plus (b) an amount necessary to amortize the cost of past service or supplementary or annuity credits provided by the plan in equal annual payments (until fully amortized) over ten years (Code Sec. 404(a)(1)(A)(iii)); or

(4) the full funding limit for the year (Code Sec. 404(a)(1)(A)), if that is less than the foregoing applicable amounts.[29]

Money purchase and target benefit plans are also subject to the 25%-of-compensation deduction limit that applies to profit-sharing plans (¶4325). (Code Sec. 404(a)(3)(A)(v))[30]

Contributions in excess of the amount deductible (except contributions to SIMPLE plans (¶4369) for household workers (Code Sec. 4972(c)(6))) are subject to a nondeductible 10% excise tax in certain cases (Code Sec. 4972), but may be carried over and deducted in later years, subject to the above limitations. (Code Sec. 404(a)(1)(E))[31]

---

25. ¶H-8075
26. ¶H-10000*et seq.*
27. ¶H-10106
28. ¶H-10102 *et seq.*

29. ¶H-10108 *et seq.*
30. ¶H-10101
31. ¶H-10133

¶ 4325   Deduction limit for contributions to profit-sharing and stock bonus plans—qualified retirement plans.

Under Code Sec. 404(a)(3)(A), the deduction limit for contributions under a profit-sharing or stock-bonus plan is 25% of the aggregate compensation (generally exclusive of qualified plan contributions, but see below) paid or accrued during the tax year for all employees participating in the plan. Contributions in excess of this limit may be carried over and deducted in a later year to the extent that contributions for that later year are below the applicable percentage limit for that year. (Code Sec. 404(a)(3)(A)(ii))[32]

The percentage of compensation limit on deductible contributions to a stock bonus or profit-sharing plan for a self-employed individual is 25% of "earned income," i.e., 25% of net earnings from self-employment less the self-employment tax deduction (Code Sec. 164(f)) and the individual's deductible qualified plan contributions. (Code Sec. 404(a)(8)(B))[33]

Elective deferrals (¶4305) are not subject to the deduction limits for stock bonus and profit sharing plans, combination defined contribution and defined benefit plans, or ESOPs. (Code Sec. 404(n))[34] Compensation includes elective deferral amounts, amounts deferred to a cafeteria plan, and certain pre-disability compensation. (Code Sec. 404(a)(12))[35]

¶ 4326   Overall deduction limit for combinations of qualified retirement plans.

Under Code Sec. 404(a)(7)(A), if there's a mixture of one or more defined contribution plans and one or more defined benefit plans, or any combination of two or more pension trusts, annuity plans, and stock bonus or profit-sharing trusts, an overall limit on deductible contributions applies. Under this limit, the total amount deductible for *all* plans is the greater of: (1) 25% of the compensation (generally exclusive of qualified plan contributions, but see below) paid or accrued during the tax year to the beneficiaries of the various trusts or plans, or (2) the total contributions to the trusts or plans to the extent those contributions don't exceed the amount necessary to satisfy the Code Sec. 412 minimum funding standards.[36] The amount necessary to satisfy a single employer plan's Code Sec. 412 minimum funding standard cannot be less than the plan's funding shortfall under Code Sec. 430.

The overall limit does not apply if the only amounts contributed to the defined compensation plan are elective deferrals. (Code Sec. 404(a)(7)(C)(ii))[37] Further, the overall limit applies only to the extent employer contributions to one or more defined contribution plans exceed 6% of the compensation otherwise paid or accrued to plan beneficiaries during the tax year.[38]

In determining the limit on deductions where there is a combination of one or more defined benefit and one or more defined contribution plans, any single employer defined benefit plan guaranteed by the PBGC is not taken into account. (Code Sec. 404(a)(7)(C)(iv))

¶ 4327   Timely payment requirement—qualified retirement plans.

Under Code Sec. 404(a), a contribution must actually be paid to the trust or under the plan to be deductible.[39] However, payments (including those made to "SIMPLE" plans (¶4369) (Code Sec. 404(m)(2)(B)), made after the end of a year are considered paid on the

---

32. ¶H-10202
33. ¶H-10204
34. ¶H-10202
35. ¶H-10203

36. ¶H-10113 *et seq.*
37. ¶H-10118 *et seq.*
38. ¶H-10119
39. ¶H-10010 *et seq.*

last day of the year if paid by the employer no later than the due date of its tax return (including extensions). (Code Sec. 404(a)(6))[40] This applies to both cash and accrual employers, even if other accrual requirements are not met. (Reg § 1.404(a)-1(c))[41]

The plan to which the contribution is made must be in existence by the end of the employer's tax year.[42] Plans adopted after the close of a tax year but before the due date (including extensions) for the employer's tax return may be treated as adopted on the last day of the tax year (¶4308).

¶ 4328 How employees are taxed—qualified retirement plans.

Under Code Sec. 402(a), apart from certain "lump-sum" payments qualifying for preferential tax treatment (¶4329 *et seq.*), and "rollovers" (¶4349), distributions from a qualified plan (reported to recipients on Form 1099-R) generally are taxed to the employee under the annuity rules (¶1352 *et seq.*) in the year distributed or otherwise made available to the employee. (Code Sec. 402(a); Reg § 1.402(a)-1(a)) Taxation under the annuity rules varies depending on the form of payment. A portion of each periodic payment, and of each nonperiodic payment received before an annuity starting date, that represents a return of the employee's investment in the plan (e.g., after-tax contributions) is received tax-free.[43]

Certain early (¶4334) distributions are subject to a 10% additional tax.

¶ 4329 Preferential treatment for certain lump-sum distributions—qualified retirement plans.

Distributions from a qualified plan that are lump-sum distributions (Code Sec. 402(e)(4)(D)) are taxable as ordinary income, subject to special elections that allow pre-'74 capital gain treatment and/or ten-year forward averaging for those born before '36. A lump-sum distribution eligible for these special elections is a distribution or payment from an exempt trust or annuity within one tax year of the recipient of the balance to the credit of the participant (excluding amounts payable to an alternate payee under a qualified domestic relations order (QDRO; see ¶4309), which separately can qualify for lump-sum treatment to the alternate payee): (1) on account of an employee's (other than a self-employed's) separation from service; or (2) after attaining age 59½ (regardless of his or her separation from service); or (3) on account of his or her death; or (4) on account of self-employed's disability. (Code Sec. 402(d)(4)(A) before amend by Sec. 1401(a), PL 104-188, 8/20/1996)[44]

¶ 4330 Lump-sum distributions of employer securities—qualified retirement plans.

Under Code Sec. 402(e)(4)(B), if a lump-sum distribution consists in part of securities of the employer, the net unrealized appreciation in value of the securities while held by the trust is not taxed to the recipient at the time of distribution. But the same amount also is excluded from the recipient's basis in the securities, so that it's taken into account for tax purposes if and when the securities are later disposed of in a taxable transaction. The distributee, however, has the right to elect, on the tax return on which a distribution is required to be included, to have this rule not apply, i.e., to include any net unrealized appreciation in income. (Code Sec. 402(e)(4)(B); Reg § 1.402(a)-1(b)(1))[45] Net unrealized appreciation that isn't included in income at the time of distribution is long-term capital gain when it's realized in a later taxable transaction. (Reg § 1.402(a)-1(b)(1)(i))[46]

---

40. ¶H-10016;
41. ¶H-10017
42. ¶H-10021
43. ¶H-11009 *et seq.*

44. ¶H-11200 *et seq.*
45. ¶s H-11501, H-11503
46. ¶H-11510

¶ 4331   Tax on current payments for life insurance protection—qualified retirement plans.

Under Code Sec. 72(m)(3), the cost of current life insurance protection under a life insurance contract purchased with employer contributions to a qualified plan (or earnings thereon) is income to the insured employee for the tax year of purchase, where the benefits are payable to the employee or beneficiaries. (Code Sec. 72(m)(3); Reg § 1.72-16(b)) The taxable amount is generally determined using "Table 2001" in IRS Notice 2002-8. [47]

¶ 4332   Tax on failure to notify participants of benefit-accrual reduction—qualified retirement plans.

Under Code Sec. 4980F(a), defined benefit plans and individual account plans subject to minimum funding standards are subject to an excise tax of $100 per day per participant, subject to an overall dollar limit, for failure to provide, within a reasonable time, written notice to any participant, alternate payee under a qualified domestic relations order, employee organization, or employer contributing to a multiemployer plan, when the plan is amended to provide for a significant reduction in the rate of future benefit accrual. (Code Sec. 4980F(a); Reg § 54.4980F-1)[48] Plans with fewer than 100 participants or that offer participants the option to choose between a new benefit formula and the old one may be able to use a simplified notice form or be exempted by IRS from the notice requirements. (Code Sec. 4980F(e)(2)(A))[49]

¶ 4333   Loans from qualified plans: repayment, amount, amortization, and use of credit cards; temporary disaster-related loan limit increases and repayment delays.

Under Code Sec. 72(p), a loan from a qualified plan isn't treated as a taxable distribution to the participant if it must be repaid within 5 years (except certain home loans) and, when added to the balance of all other plan loans, it doesn't exceed the *lesser* of: (1) $50,000 (reduced by the excess of the participant's highest outstanding aggregate loan balance in the prior year over the current balance), or (2) the greater of (a) ½ of the present value of the employee's nonforfeitable accrued benefit, or (b) $10,000. If a loan exceeds that limit, the excess is treated (and taxed) as a distribution (¶4328). If a loan isn't required to be repaid within 5 years (except for certain home loans) the entire loan is treated as a distribution.[50] The outstanding balance of a loan is treated as distributed if the borrower fails to make a timely payment. (Reg § 1.72(p)-1, Q&A 10(b))[1] Loan repayments after a deemed distribution increase the participant's investment in the contract (basis). (Reg § 1.72(p)-1, Q&A 21)

A plan loan must be amortized in substantially level payments, at least quarterly, over its term. (Code Sec. 72(p)(2)(C))[2] The level amortization requirement doesn't apply while the employee is on leave without pay for up to one year. (Reg § 1.72(p)-1, Q&A 9)[3]

Plan loans distributed through credit cards or similar arrangements can't meet the above requirements for loan treatment, and are deemed distributions. (Code Sec. 72(p)(2)(D))[4]

The nontaxable loan limit is sometimes temporarily increased (typically by raising the

---

47. ¶H-10507 *et seq.*
48. ¶H-7360 *et seq.*
49. ¶H-7368
50. ¶H-11067 *et seq.*

1. ¶H-11070
2. ¶H-11068;
3. ¶H-11068.1
4. ¶H-11066.8

$50,000 limit to $100,000, and by increasing the 50% limit to 100%) in response to specified disasters. Those temporary increases are usually accompanied by relief allowing delayed loan repayments (typically for up to one year).[5]

¶ 4334   10% additional tax on early distributions—Form 5329; exceptions—qualified retirement plans.

Under Code Sec. 72(t)(1), early withdrawals from a qualified retirement plan, SIMPLE plan, or IRA result in an additional tax (reported on Form 5329) of 10% of the amounts withdrawn that are includible in gross income. The additional tax applies to all withdrawals unless specifically excepted. Exceptions include distributions that are: (i) made on or after age 59½; (ii) made to a beneficiary or estate on or after death; (iii) attributable to disability; (iv) from a qualified plan after an employee's separation from service in or after the year when he or she attains age 55 (not for IRAs); (v) not over the amount allowable as a medical expense deduction for the year, whether or not the distributee itemizes; (vi) that are part of a series of substantially equal periodic (at least annual) payments (after separation from service if from a qualified plan) for the life (or life expectancy) of the employee or the joint lives (or joint life expectancies) of the employee and beneficiary; (vii) from an IRA, not exceeding amounts paid for medical insurance by IRA owners who have received unemployment compensation for at least 12 weeks (or could have if not self-employed); (viii) from an IRA, for qualified higher education expenses; (ix) from an IRA, for qualified "first-home" purchases, subject to $10,000 lifetime cap; (x) from a qualified plan to an alternate payee under a qualified domestic relations order (QDRO ¶4309, but not for IRAs); (xi) made on account of an IRS tax levy; (xii) from a phased or composite retirement annuity under the Federal Phased Retirement Program; (xiii) "qualified birth or adoption distributions" of up to $5,000 per distributee per birth/adoption[6], (xiv) from a gov't plan to a "qualified public safety employee" (e.g., firefighter, police officer, certain federal gov't employees) who separates from service after age 50; and (xv) any "qualified reservist distribution" to those called to active duty for more than 179 days (or an indefinite period). (Code Sec. 72(t)(2), Code Sec. 72(t)(3))[7]

For transfers of an IRA to a spouse (or former spouse) under a divorce or separation instrument, see ¶4347.

Taxpayers who used the annuitization or amortization methods to compute substantially equal payments can make a one-time switch to the required minimum distribution method, which generally requires smaller annual distributions, without triggering the 10% additional tax on early distributions.[8]

The additional tax is 25%, not 10%, on amounts received from a SIMPLE retirement account (¶4369) in the employee's first 2 years of participation. (Code Sec. 72(t)(6))[9]

The tax applies to certain involuntary cash-outs and deemed distributions. It doesn't apply to amounts distributed from unfunded deferred compensation plans of tax-exempt employers or state and local government employees (Code Sec. 457 plans).[10]

¶ 4335   Required minimum distributions (RMDs); post-death RMD rules; effects of 2020 RMD waiver; IRS-provided relief for 2021 and 2022—qualified retirement plans.

Under Code Sec. 401(a)(9), qualified retirement plans (e.g., 401(k), 403(b), or 457(b) plans) are subject to required minimum distribution (RMD) rules which require benefits to

5. ¶H-11066 *et seq.*, ¶H-11067.2, ¶H-11068.3*et seq.*
6. ¶H-11118
7. ¶H-11100 *et seq.*

8. ¶H-11107
9. ¶H-12377
10. ¶H-11101

be distributed or minimum payments to commence not later than the participant's required beginning date (RBD). Similar rules apply to traditional IRAs and individual retirement annuities (see ¶4347). A participant's RBD is generally Apr. 1 of the calendar year following the later of the year in which the participant (a) reaches age 72 (70½ for participants who attained that age on or before Dec. 31, 2019), or (b) retires (except for 5% owners).

Lifetime RMDs. If not fully paid by the participant's RBD, payments must commence by the participant's RBD and be paid over (i) the participant's life, (ii) the participant's life and the life of a designated beneficiary, (iii) a period not longer than the participant's life expectancy, or (iv) a period not longer than the life expectancy of the participant and a designated beneficiary. (Code Sec. 401(a)(9)(A), Code Sec. 401(a)(9)(C))[11]

Post-death RMD rules for defined contribution plans if participant dies after 2019. If a participant dies after 2019, and regardless of whether the participant dies before, on, or after the RBD, the remaining account balance generally must be distributed to the designated beneficiaries within 10 years after the date of death (the "10-year rule") unless the designated beneficiary is an "eligible designated beneficiary" (see below). (Code Sec. 401(a)(9)(H)(i)) Special rules delay the 10-year rule's effective date for governmental plans, collectively bargained plans, and in other circumstances.[12]

An exception to the 10-year rule applies to eligible designated beneficiaries (EDBs), i.e., surviving spouses, children who haven't reached the age of majority, certain chronically ill individuals, and any other individuals who are not more than 10 years younger than the participant. (Code Sec. 401(a)(9)(E)(ii)) Under the exception, after the participant's death, the remaining account balance generally may be distributed (similar to pre-2020 law, above) over the life or life expectancy of the EDB, beginning in the year following the year of death. (Code Sec. 401(a)(9)(B)(iii), Code Sec. 401(a)(9)(H)(ii)) After the death of an EDB, the account balance must be distributed within 10 years after the EDB's death. (Code Sec. 401(a)(9)(H)(iii)) After a child of the participant reaches the age of majority, the balance in the account must be distributed within 10 years after that date. (Code Sec. 401(a)(9)(E)(iii))[13]

Post-death RMD rules that apply if: (1) participant died before 2020, or (2) rule for defined contribution plans (see below) doesn't apply.. If a participant dies after RMDs begin, the remaining interest must be distributed at least as rapidly as under the method used before death. (Code Sec. 401(a)(9)(B)(i)) If an account balance is not being paid as an annuity, distribution of the remaining interest must be completed over the longer of the remaining life expectancy of the designated beneficiary (if there is one) or the participant. (Reg § 1.401(a)(9)-5, Q&A 5)[14] If a participant dies before RMDs begin, the entire interest generally must be distributed within five years after death. (Code Sec. 401(a)(9)(B)(ii); Reg § 1.401(a)(9)-3, Q&A 1) However, if the participant dies before RMDs begin and there is a designated beneficiary, distributions beginning within one year of death (or later date prescribed in regs) can be paid over the life or life expectancy of the designated beneficiary. (Code Sec. 401(a)(9)(B)(iii)) If the participant's beneficiary is the surviving spouse, distributions need not begin until the year the participant would have attained age 72 (70½ for participants who attained that age on or before Dec. 31, 2019). If the surviving spouse dies before distributions begin, the post-death RMD rules apply after the death of the spouse as though the spouse were the participant. (Code Sec. 401(a)(9)(B)(iv))[15]

Designated beneficiary. Designated beneficiaries are those designated as of the participant's death who remain beneficiaries on Sept. 30 of the year after the year of the participant's death. (Reg § 1.401(a)(9)-4, Q&A 4(a)) Except for certain trusts (see below), only an

---

11. ¶H-8275.1 *et seq.*
12. ¶H-8275.1 *et seq.*; ¶H-12289.5
13. ¶H-8279.9; ¶H-12289.5

14. ¶H-8279.8
15. ¶H-8276 *et seq.*

individual may be a designated beneficiary for the RMD rules. (Reg § 1.401(a)(9)-4, Q&A 3)[16]

Trusts as beneficiaries. An underlying beneficiary of a trust may be treated as the participant's designated beneficiary for RMD purposes when the trust is named as the beneficiary of a retirement plan, if certain requirements are met (e.g., documentation of the underlying beneficiaries of the trust must be provided timely to the plan administrator, and beneficiaries of the trust can be identified). (Reg § 1.401(a)(9)-4, Q&A 6(b), Reg § 1.401(a)(9)-4, Q&A 5)[17]

Determining amounts of lifetime RMDs. RMD amounts for defined contribution plans are determined using IRS tables. (Reg § 1.401(a)(9)-5, Q&A 1; Reg § 1.401(a)(9)-9)[18]

Life Expectancy Determinations. Life expectancies for non-annuity-type payouts for distribution calendar years beginning on or after Jan. 1, 2022, are generally determined using the Single Life Table of Reg § 1.401(a)(9)-9, Q&A 1. The tables for earlier distribution calendar years appear in the version of Reg. §1.401(a)(9)-9 set forth in the regulations revised as of Apr. 1, 2020.[19]

Determining amount of annuity-type distributions. Separate rules apply to annuity-type required distributions, namely defined-benefit (i.e., pension) plan RMDs, as well as annuity contracts purchased from firms such as insurance companies to make RMDs from other qualified plans and IRAs. (Reg § 1.401(a)(9)-6) Under these rules, distributions of the participant's entire interest must be paid in the form of periodic annuity payments for the participant's or beneficiary's life (or the joint lives of the participant and beneficiary) or over a comparable period certain. The payments must be nonincreasing or only increase as provided in the regs. (Reg § 1.401(a)(9)-6, Q&A 1)[20]

Penalty. Failure to make required distributions is subject to an excise tax (report on Form 5329) equal to 50% of the minimum amount that should have been distributed over the amount actually distributed. (Code Sec. 4974(a))[21] The excise tax is waived during the first 5 years after the year of the participant's death before the required beginning date if the entire benefit is distributed by the end of the 5th year following the year of death. (Reg § 54.4974-2, Q&A 4)

Effects of 2020 waiver of RMD rules. The RMD requirements generally did not apply for calendar year 2020. (Code Sec. 401(a)(9)(I))[22] For calendar years after 2020, the required beginning date for any individual is determined without regard to the 2020 waiver of RMDs. And if the 5-year rule of Code Sec. 401(a)(9)(B)(ii) applies, the 5-year period is determined without regard to calendar year 2020. (Code Sec. 401(a)(9)(I)(iii))

IRS-provided relief for 2021 and 2022. In Notice 2022-53, IRS said it would not treat a defined contribution plan that failed, in 2021 or 2022, to make certain required RMDs (described in Sec. IV.C of the Notice), as having failed to satisfy the RMD rules on account of that failure. And IRS said it would not assert the excise tax under Code Sec. 4974 (above) against taxpayers who did not take these described RMDs in 2021 or 2022. If a taxpayer already paid the Code Sec. 4974 tax in 2021, the taxpayer may request a refund. (Notice 2022-53)

¶ 4336 Excise tax on employer reversions—Form 5330—qualified retirement plans.

Under Code Sec. 4980(a), Code Sec. 4980(b), Code Sec. 4980(c)(1), and Code Sec. 4980(d),

---

16. ¶H-8278
17. ¶H-8278.4
18. ¶H-8279 *et seq.*
19. ¶H-8279.6

20. ¶H-8280
21. ¶H-8500 *et seq.*
22. ¶H-8275.3 *et seq.*

an "employer reversion" from a terminating qualified plan (except for certain exempt employers and government plans) is, in addition to being includible in the employer's gross income, also subject to a 50% excise tax (20% in certain cases). Pay with Form 5330 filed no later than the last day of the month following the month in which the reversion occurred.[23]

¶ 4337 Excise tax on prohibited transactions—Form 5330—qualified retirement plans.

Under Code Sec. 4975(a) and Code Sec. 4975(b), an excise tax is imposed on a disqualified person who takes part in a prohibited transaction with a qualified plan, IRA, or medical savings account. The tax (report on Form 5330 each year for each transaction (Reg § 54.6011-1(b))) is 15% of the amount involved in the prohibited transaction for each tax year (or part of the year) in the taxable period. And if the prohibited transaction isn't timely corrected, the disqualified person must pay an additional tax of 100% of the amount involved.[24] Neither level of tax is imposed on a fiduciary acting only as such. (Code Sec. 4975(a))[25]

Providing investment advice through an "eligible investment advice arrangement" to participants and beneficiaries of a defined contribution plan who direct the investment of their accounts under the plan and to beneficiaries of IRAs (as well as HSAs, Archer MSAs, and Coverdell education savings accounts) is exempt from the prohibited transaction rules. (Code Sec. 4975(d)(17))[26]

Other transactions also are exempt from the prohibited transaction rules, including certain transactions between plans and service providers, for adequate consideration (Code Sec. 4975(d)(20)), and certain otherwise prohibited transactions involving the sale or exchange of securities and commodities between the plan and a party in interest that are corrected within 14 days (Code Sec. 4975(d)(23)).

¶ 4338 Transfers of excess pension assets to health benefits and applicable life insurance accounts before 2026—qualified retirement plans.

Under Code Sec. 420(a), before Jan. 1, 2026, excess pension assets may be transferred to a retiree health benefit account without the transfer being treated as either a prohibited transaction (¶4337) or a reversion to the employer (¶4336) if certain conditions are met. Transfers of excess pension assets may also be made to buy retiree group-term life insurance (an "applicable life insurance account"). [27]

Single-employer plans can use excess pension assets to fund future retiree health or life insurance benefits by making qualified future transfers to retiree health benefit accounts or applicable life insurance accounts, if certain minimum cost requirements are maintained. Similar rules apply to "collectively bargained transfers" to fund collectively bargained retiree health liabilities or life insurance benefits. A qualified future transfer or collectively bargained transfer must meet the requirements applicable to qualified transfers, with certain modifications to the requirements, one of which is the minimum cost requirement. (Code Sec. 420(f))

Qualified transfers may satisfy the minimum cost requirement by satisfying the minimum cost requirement that applies to a collectively bargained transfer. (Code Sec. 420(c)(3)(A))[28]

Multiemployer plans may transfer excess pension assets to retiree health accounts.

---

23. ¶H-8900 *et seq.*
24. ¶H-12510
25. ¶H-12514 *et seq.*

26. ¶H-12558.1
27. ¶H-8163
28. ¶H-8173

(Code Sec. 420(a); Code Sec. 420(e)(5)) Assets transferred in a qualified transfer to a retiree health account or applicable life insurance account will not be treated as assets in the plan for purpose of the minimum contribution rules. (Code Sec. 430(l))[29]

Generally, only group-term life insurance not in excess of $50,000 may be purchased with excess pension assets.[30]

¶ 4339 Distributions from governmental retirement plans for health and long-term care insurance for public safety officers—exclusion.

Under Code Sec. 402(l), Code Sec. 403(a), Code Sec. 403(b), and Code Sec. 457(a), public safety officers may exclude from income governmental retirement plan distributions that don't exceed accident, health or long-term care insurance premiums for themselves, their spouses, and dependents, if the distributions are paid directly to insurers. The exclusion is limited to $3,000 per year.[31] The accident or health plan receiving the payments of qualified health insurance premiums may be a self-insured plan.[32]

An exception to the rules that generally apply to deferred compensation plans of state and local governments, and tax-exempt organizations, allows a plan paying solely length of service awards to bona fide volunteers (or their beneficiaries), on account of qualified services performed by the volunteers, to make awards of up to $6,500 per year for 2022 ($7,000 for 2023). (Code Sec. 457(e))[33]

¶ 4340 Retirement plans that fail to qualify or that lose qualified status.

The following rules apply to a plan that fails to qualify or that loses its qualified status: First, under Code Sec. 402(b), contributions to the trust by an employer are included in the gross income of the employee. The employee must report the value of his or her interest in the employer's contributions the first time his or her interest isn't subject to substantial risk of forfeiture, or is transferable free of such risk, whichever occurs first. (Reg § 1.402(b)-1)[34]

An employer's contributions to a non-qualified plan are deductible in the tax year in which an amount attributable to the contribution is includible in the gross income of employees participating in the plan (Code Sec. 404(a)(5)), even if the employer is an accrual basis taxpayer.[35]

The amount actually distributed or made available to the employee or other distributee (beneficiary, etc.) is taxable in the year distributed or made available under the regular annuity rules (¶1352 *et seq.*), with a minor exception for distribution of trust income before the annuity is to begin. (Code Sec. 402(b)(2))[36]

Premiums paid by an employer for an annuity contract not purchased under a qualified annuity plan (¶4304), are included in the employee's gross income. Amounts actually paid or made available to any employee-beneficiary under the nonqualified annuity contract are taxed under regular annuity rules. (Code Sec. 403(c))[37]

¶ 4341 Individual Retirement Account (IRAs)—Overview. ■■■■■■■■■■

Employees and self-employed individuals who aren't active participants in an employer-maintained retirement plan can deduct up to $6,000 for 2022 and $6,500 for 2023, plus an additional catch-up contribution for those 50 and over, for contributions to an individual retirement account (IRA), or for the purchase of individual

29. ¶H-8164
30. ¶H-8167
31. ¶H-11089
32. ¶H-11091
33. ¶H-3339.1

34. ¶H-9900 *et seq.*; ¶H-3200 *et seq.*
35. ¶H-3677 *et seq.*
36. ¶H-3246
37. ¶H-3249

retirement annuities or endowment contracts. An individual who is an active participant in an employer plan (or whose spouse is) can't make deductible IRA contributions unless his or her adjusted gross income is below specified levels (¶4342).

An individual retirement account (IRA) is a trust (or custodial account) created or organized in the U.S. with a written governing instrument. The assets of the account must be invested in a trusteed or custodial account with a bank, savings and loan association, credit union or other qualified person. (Code Sec. 408(a)(2))[38]

IRAs may be set up by employers for employees and by unions for members if these employer- and association-sponsored IRAs separately account for the interest of each participant (or spouse). (Code Sec. 408(c); Reg § 1.408-2(c))[39] Qualified retirement plans, tax-sheltered annuities, and government retirement plans may allow employees to make voluntary contributions to separate IRA or Roth IRA accounts or annuities (¶4364). (Code Sec. 408(q))[40]

Individuals who turn age 50 before the year-end may increase the maximum permitted annual contribution by a $1,000 "catch-up" contribution. (Code Sec. 219(b)(5)(B))[41]

Except for rollover contributions (¶4349) the maximum amount that may be contributed to IRAs for any individual for 2022 is $7,000 ($6,000 + $1,000 catch-up contribution) and for 2023 is $7,500 ($6,500 + $1,000 catch-up contribution). (Code Sec. 408(a)(1), Code Sec. 408(b), Code Sec. 219(b)(1)(A), Code Sec. 219(b)(5)(A), Code Sec. 219(b)(5)(C))[42]

IRA funds can't be used to buy life insurance. (Code Sec. 408(a)(3))[43] IRA contributions may not be invested in "collectibles" (except for certain coins and bullion), the acquisition of which is treated as an includible distribution (and possibly subject to early distribution penalties). (Code Sec. 408(m))[44]

Individual retirement annuities are nontransferable flexible premium annuity or endowment contracts issued by an insurance company. (Code Sec. 408(b))[45]

No tax is paid on income earned on contributions until the retirement savings are distributed or retirement bonds are cashed, at which time the distributions or retirement bond proceeds are taxable (Code Sec. 408(d)(1))[46] though the tax-free "rollover" provisions (¶4349) may apply. Rules penalize excess contributions, early (before age 59½) distributions (¶4334), and certain distributions deferred beyond age 72 (70½ for participants who attained that age on or before Dec. 31, 2019) (¶4347).

For deductible contributions, see ¶4342; for nondeductible contributions to traditional IRAs, see ¶4344.

For Roth IRAs, see ¶4357 *et seq.* For the saver's credit for lower-income taxpayers' contributions to IRAs, see ¶2356.

¶ 4342   Deduction for IRA; "compensation"; deadline for establishing.

Under Code Sec. 219(b)(1), an individual who isn't an active participant in certain retirement plans, and whose spouse isn't an active participant, can deduct, for a tax year, cash contributions to an IRA, up to the lesser of: (1) $6,000 for 2022 and $6,500 for 2023, plus a $1,000 catch-up contribution, if eligible (¶4341), or (2) 100% of compensation includible in gross income for the year.[47] For spousal IRAs, see ¶4345.

If the individual (or spouse) is an active plan participant (for any part of a plan year in

---

38. ¶H-12201 *et seq.*
39. ¶s H-12212, H-12213
40. ¶H-12280
41. ¶H-12215
42. ¶H-12215

43. ¶H-12201
44. ¶H-12259
45. ¶H-12208 *et seq.*
46. ¶H-12253, H-12262
47. ¶H-12215

his or her tax year), and has adjusted gross income (AGI) that exceeds an "applicable dollar limit," the IRA deduction limit is reduced (but not below zero) by an amount (rounded to the next lowest multiple of $10) that bears the same ratio to the dollar limit on the deduction that his or her (and spouse's, if joint return) AGI (determined without regard to the IRA deduction and with certain other modifications), minus the applicable dollar limit, bears to $10,000 ($20,000 for joint return filers, except for non-active plan participants whose spouses are active plan participants). (Code Sec. 219(g)(1), Code Sec. 219(g)(2), Code Sec. 219(g)(3)(A), Code Sec. 219(g)(7)(B)) But the maximum IRA deduction can't be reduced below $200 unless the applicable dollar limit is reduced to zero. (Code Sec. 219(g)(2)(B))[48] The applicable dollar limit is higher than the usual limit for an individual who is not an active participant in an employer plan during any part of the year, but whose spouse is an active plan participant. The higher limit does not apply to the active-participant spouse. (Code Sec. 219(g)(7))[49]

The deduction phaseouts are as follows. For joint filers, the deduction phaseout for 2022 begins at modified AGI (MAGI) of $109,000 and is fully phased-out at MAGI of $129,000 (for 2023, the deduction phaseout begins at MAGI of $116,000 and is fully phased-out at MAGI of $136,000). For single filers, or heads of households, the deduction phaseout for 2022 begins at MAGI of $68,000 and is fully phased-out at MAGI of $78,000 (for 2023, the deduction phaseout begins at MAGI of $73,000 and is fully phased-out at MAGI of $83,000). For marrieds filing separately, the deduction phaseout begins at MAGI of zero, and is fully phased-out at MAGI of $10,000 for 2022 and 2023. Finally, for a non-active participant whose spouse is an active participant, the deduction phaseout for 2022 begins at MAGI of $204,000 and is fully phased-out at MAGI of $214,000 (for 2023, the deduction phaseout begins at MAGI of $218,000 and is fully phased-out at MAGI of $228,000).

Spouses who file separate returns and live apart at all times during the year aren't treated as married for the phase-out. (Code Sec. 219(g)(4))[50]

"Compensation" means wages, salaries, commissions, tips, bonuses, professional fees, other amounts received for personal services, and amounts includible in gross income and paid to aid in graduate or postdoctoral study. It doesn't include earnings from property, such as interest, rents and dividends, or pension and annuity payments or other deferred compensation. Only compensation includible in gross income is used. (Code Sec. 219(f)(1))[1] Compensation includes alimony paid under a pre-2019 decree of divorce or separate maintenance. It also includes differential wage payments (¶3005). (Code Sec. 219(f)(1))[2]

The amount shown on Form W-2 as "Wages, tips, other compensation," less any amount shown as distributions from nonqualified plans can be used as "safe harbor" compensation.[3]

The "compensation" of a self-employed individual includes net earnings from self-employment reduced by any allowable deduction for contributions to a tax-qualified plan, e.g., a Keogh plan. (Code Sec. 219(f)(1))[4] A self-employed individual's net earnings from self-employment are also reduced by the deduction allowed for one-half of the self-employment tax (¶1746). (Code Sec. 219(f)(1), Code Sec. 401(c)(2)(A)(vi))[5]

Combat pay excluded under Code Sec. 112 (¶1223) is treated as if it were includible compensation for IRA purposes. (Code Sec. 219(f)(7))[6]

The IRA must be established no later than the due date (*not* including extensions) of the taxpayer's return for the year the deduction is claimed. To be deductible for the preceding tax year, the contribution also must be made by that date. (Code Sec. 219(f)(3))[7]

---

48. ¶H-12217
49. ¶H-12217.2
50. ¶H-12217
1. ¶H-12226
2. ¶H-12232

3. ¶H-12226
4. ¶H-12226
5. ¶s H-9514, H-12228
6. ¶H-12215.1 *et seq.*
7. ¶H-12233; ¶S-4700

No part of a premium (under an IRA endowment policy) used to buy life insurance is deductible. (Code Sec. 219(d)(3))[8]

There's no deduction for a rollover contribution (¶4349) (Code Sec. 219(d)(2))[9] or for any contribution to an "inherited" IRA (i.e., acquired by non-surviving-spouse due to death of IRA owner). (Code Sec. 219(d)(4))[10] Inherited IRAs aren't exempt from a debtor's bankruptcy estate.[11]

¶ 4343   Active participant defined—IRAs.

Under Code Sec. 219(g), an individual who (or whose spouse) is an active participant in a qualified pension, profit-sharing, stock bonus or annuity plan, government plan, tax-sheltered annuity plan, SEP, SIMPLE retirement plan, or certain other trusts can't make deductible IRA contributions unless his or her adjusted gross income falls with the dollar limits at ¶4342.[12]

An individual is an active participant for any tax year in which he or she is eligible to participate in a defined benefit plan, or any year in which employer or employee contributions or forfeitures are added to his or her account in a defined contribution plan.[13]

¶ 4344   Nondeductible IRA contributions—Form 8606.

Under Code Sec. 408(o), an active participant in a qualified plan who may not be eligible to make deductible contributions either in whole or in part to an IRA (see ¶4343), can make (use Form 8606) designated nondeductible contributions (DNCs) to an IRA for a tax year (Code Sec. 408(o)(2)(C)(i)) up to the due date (*without* extensions) for the taxpayer's income tax return for that year. (Code Sec. 408(o)(3))[14]

The amount of any DNCs made in any tax year on behalf of an individual is limited to the excess of: (1) the lesser of $6,000 for 2022 ($6,500 for 2023), plus an additional $1,000 for those 50 and over, see ¶4341, or 100% of compensation (including the higher-earning spouse's compensation (¶4345)), over (2) the amount allowable as a deduction for IRA contributions by active participants. (Code Sec. 408(o)(2)(B)(i))[15]

A taxpayer can elect to treat an otherwise deductible contribution as a DNC, thereby increasing, to that extent, his or her DNC limit for that year. (Code Sec. 408(o)(2)(B)(ii))[16]

DNCs and deductible contributions may be made to the same IRA.[17]

¶ 4345   Special IRA deduction rules for married taxpayers.

Married taxpayers can each make deductible contributions to separate IRAs, subject to the deduction phase-out rules at ¶4342 that apply if either or both are active participants in an employer retirement plan for any part of the tax year.[18]

An individual who files a joint return and has less taxable compensation than his or her spouse may contribute to a spousal IRA and deduct the lesser of (1) $6,000 for 2022 ($6,500 for 2023), plus an additional $1,000 for those 50 and over, see ¶4341, or (2) the sum of (a) that individual's includible compensation for the tax year, plus (b) the includible compensation of the individual's spouse reduced by the sum of the spouse's allowable IRA deduction, designated nondeductible IRA contribution, and Roth IRA contribution for that tax year. (Code Sec. 219(c))[19]

---

8. ¶H-12236
9. ¶H-12235
10. ¶H-12237
11. ¶H-12207.1
12. ¶H-12217 *et seq.*
13. ¶H-12220 *et seq.*

14. ¶s H-12238, H-12240
15. ¶H-12239
16. ¶H-12240
17. ¶H-12238
18. ¶H-12217
19. ¶s H-12230, H-12231

¶ 4346   Penalties for excess contributions—Form 5329—IRAs.

Under Code Sec. 4973(a), an individual who contributes more to an IRA than he or she is entitled to deduct must pay (use Form 5329) a 6% excise tax on the excess *every year*. The tax for any particular year, however, can't exceed 6% of the value of the IRA (as of the close of the tax year).

An excess contribution to an IRA is the sum of: (1) the excess of the amount contributed for the tax year (*other than* a contribution to a Roth IRA or a rollover contribution), over the amount allowable as a deduction for the contribution, plus (2) any excess contribution for the preceding tax year, *reduced by* the sum of taxable distributions for the tax year, distributions for the tax year of excess contributions after the due date of the return, and the excess (if any) of the maximum amount allowable as a deduction for the tax year, over the amount contributed to the IRA for the tax year (without regard to any deduction for a preceding year's excess contribution) *including* the amount contributed to a Roth IRA. (Code Sec. 4973(b))[20]

There's no 6% penalty for the year of the contribution (or any other year) if the taxpayer is allowed no IRA deduction for the excess *and* withdraws the excess (together with any net income earned on it) by the income tax return filing due date for the year the excess contribution was made. (Code Sec. 4973(b))[21]

For tax on excess contributions to Roth IRAs, see ¶4358.

¶ 4347   Distributions from IRAs and individual retirement annuities; "qualified charitable distributions."

Payouts from an IRA can be made without penalty once the participant attains age 59½ (or earlier in the case of death, disability, certain medical-related distributions, higher education expenses, and other exceptions, see ¶4334). These distributions can be made in a lump sum or in installments and are taxable as ordinary income under the annuity rules (see ¶1352 *et seq.*) when received, except that distributions are tax-free if reinvested (i.e., "rolled over," see ¶4349 *et seq.*) within 60 days into that or another IRA. (Code Sec. 408(d)(3)(A))[22] (If not reinvested, the distribution is taxable in the year received, not the year in which the 60-day rollover period ends.)[23] A distribution from a SIMPLE retirement plan (¶4369) can't be rolled over tax-free except to another SIMPLE plan during the employee's first two years of participation in the plan. (Code Sec. 408(d)(3)(G))

Amounts distributed from an IRA are included in gross income under the Code Sec. 72 annuity rules. (Code Sec. 408(d)(1)) In applying the annuity rules, all IRAs (other than Roth IRAs) are treated as one contract, all distributions made during any tax year are treated as one distribution, and the value of the contract, income on the contract, and investment in it are determined at the end of the calendar year in which the tax year begins. (Code Sec. 408(d)(2))[24] Part of an individual's withdrawal from an IRA is excludible if he or she previously made nondeductible IRA contributions. The excludible part is (the amount withdrawn × [aggregate nondeductible IRA contributions ÷ aggregate adjusted balance on the last day of the tax year of all IRAs of the individual]). For the calculation, IRAs include all of the taxpayer's traditional IRAs, SEPs and SIMPLE IRAs.[25]

Up to $100,000 of otherwise taxable distributions that meet the rules for "qualified charitable distributions" (under Code Sec. 408(d)(8)(B)), and are made on or after the date the IRA owner (or Roth IRA owner) reaches age 70½, are excludible from a taxpayer's

---

20. ¶H-12242 *et seq.*
21. ¶H-12247 *et seq.*
22. ¶H-12253

23. ¶s H-11460, H-12253
24. ¶H-12253
25. ¶H-12253

income. But the amount of the exclusion under this rule for a tax year must be reduced by the excess of: (1) the total amount of IRA contribution deductions allowed to the taxpayer for all tax years ending on or after the date the taxpayer attains age 70½, over (2) the total amount of reductions for all tax years before the current tax year. (Code Sec. 408(d)(8))

Losses in an IRA are currently nondeductible due to the suspension of miscellaneous itemized deductions (¶2162).[26]

Distributions from an IRA are reported on Form 1099-R. Distribution recipients who at any time made nondeductible contributions to a IRA (¶4344), must file Form 8606.

The transfer of an interest in an IRA (but not the distribution of funds from an IRA) to a spouse under a divorce or separation instrument isn't taxable (the transferred IRA is treated as the spouse's). (Code Sec. 408(d)(6))[27] Roth IRAs (¶4357 *et seq.*) are treated separately. (Code Sec. 408A(d)(4))

For the tax on early distributions from an IRA, see ¶4334.

Distribution of a participant's entire interest in an IRA (other than a Roth IRA, see ¶4361) must be made under rules similar to the Code Sec. 401(a)(9) required distribution rules for qualified plans (¶4335), (Code Sec. 408(a)(6), Code Sec. 408(b)(3)) except that required distributions from an IRA can't be deferred beyond age 72 (70½ for participants who attained that age on or before Dec. 31, 2019) due to the account owner's not being retired (Code Sec. 401(a)(9)(C)(ii)(II), see ¶4335). While the required minimum distribution must be separately calculated for each IRA an individual has, the amounts may then be totalled, and the total distribution taken from any one or more of the individual's IRAs. Failure to make the required distributions results in a nondeductible excise tax payable (on Form 5329) by the recipient. The tax is 50% of the excess of the minimum amount that should have been distributed over the amount actually distributed. (Code Sec. 4974(a))[28] IRS can waive the 50% tax if the shortfall in the amount distributed is due to "reasonable error" and reasonable corrective steps are taken. (Code Sec. 4974(d))[29]

¶ 4348 Exemption of IRA from tax; IRA owner may not use IRA as loan security.

Under Code Sec. 408(e), income earned by an IRA is tax-exempt until distribution. This tax exemption doesn't apply to the unrelated business income tax, see ¶4123. Engaging in a prohibited transaction causes loss of the exemption.[30] Certain nominal gifts, free banking services, and free group term life insurance offered by banks for opening and contributing to an IRA are exempted from the prohibited transaction rules.[31]

If the owner of an individual retirement annuity borrows any money under, or by use of, the annuity contract, the contract stops being an individual retirement annuity as of the first day of the tax year, and the owner must include in income for that year an amount equal to the fair market value of the contract on the first day of the year. (Code Sec. 408(e)(3))[32] If the individual for whom an IRA is established uses the account or any portion of it as security for a loan, that portion is treated as distributed to that individual. (Code Sec. 408(e)(4))[33]

¶ 4349 Tax-free rollovers from qualified plans; 60-day rollover window—IRAs.

A tax-free rollover from a qualified plan occurs when an employee transfers to an "eligible retirement plan" any portion of the balance of the employee's credit in a qualified trust that was paid to the employee in an "eligible rollover distribution." (Code

26. ¶H-12255
27. ¶H-12261
28. ¶H-8501
29. ¶H-8508
30. ¶H-12214
31. ¶H-12530
32. ¶H-12251
33. ¶H-12252

Sec. 402(c)(1))[34] A distribution must be rolled over within 60 days after receipt to be tax-free, but IRS may waive the 60-day rollover period for equitable reasons (Code Sec. 402(c)(3), Code Sec. 408(d)(3); Reg § 301.7508A-1(c)(1)), if certain conditions are met.[35]

IRS has established a program allowing taxpayers to self-certify that there was reasonable cause for their missing the 60-day IRA rollover window. A taxpayer typically will qualify for a waiver if one of the specified circumstances apply. (Rev. Proc. 2020-46, 2020-45 IRB 995)

Generally, an "eligible rollover distribution" is any distribution to an employee of all or any portion of the balance to the credit of the employee in a qualified trust. (Code Sec. 402(c)(4)) An "eligible rollover distribution" does *not* include:

(1) any distribution that's one of a series of substantially equal periodic payments made (at least annually) for (a) the life (or life expectancy) of the employee, or the joint lives (or joint life expectancies) of the employee and the employee's designated beneficiary, or (b) a specified period of ten years or more (Code Sec. 402(c)(4)(A));

(2) any distribution to the extent it is a required distribution under Code Sec. 401(a)(9); (Code Sec. 402(c)(4)(B); Reg § 1.402(c)-2) and

(3) any hardship distribution. (Code Sec. 402(c)(4)(C), Code Sec. 403(b)(8)(B))[36]

✓caution: An eligible rollover distribution from a qualified plan is subject to 20% withholding, unless there is a direct trustee-to-trustee transfer, see ¶3035.

Amounts transferred in a direct trustee-to-trustee transfer (¶4307) are excludable from income for the tax year of the transfer. (Code Sec. 402(e)(6))[37]

Certain payments can't be rolled over, e.g., corrective distributions of excess 401(k) contributions, loans treated as deemed distributions, and dividends paid on employer securities. (Reg § 1.402(c)-2, Q&A 4) If a participant's accrued benefit is reduced (offset) to repay a loan (e.g., when the loan is in default or treated as such), the plan loan offset amount is an actual distribution that can be an eligible rollover distribution. (Reg § 1.402(c)-2, Q&A 9)[38] The rollover period for certain "qualified plan loan offsets" extends to the tax return due date (including extensions). (Code Sec. 402(c)(3))[39]

An "eligible retirement plan" is: (1) an individual retirement account (not a Roth IRA), (2) an individual retirement annuity (other than an endowment contract), (3) a qualified trust, (4) an annuity plan, (5) a Code Sec. 403(b) annuity, and (6) a governmental section 457 plan. If any portion of an eligible rollover distribution is attributable to payments or distributions from a designated Roth account (see ¶4363), then an eligible retirement plan with respect to that portion includes only (a) another designated Roth account, and (b) a Roth IRA. (Code Sec. 402(c)(8)(B))[40]

If noncash property (e.g., securities) is distributed, the employee can sell the property and roll over the proceeds. There's no gain or loss recognized on the sale if the full proceeds are rolled over. (Code Sec. 402(c)(6)(A))[41] If cash is distributed, it must be recontributed as cash.[42]

Plan administrators must inform recipients of potential rollovers in writing of the applicable rollover rules, no less than 30 days, and no more than 90 days before making an eligible rollover distribution (but the 30-day time period may be waived by a participant in certain cases, and a summary notice procedure also is available). (Code Sec. 402(f); Reg § 1.402(c)-2, Q&A 2, Reg § 1.402(f)-1, Q&A 2(b))[43]

---

34. ¶H-11402
35. ¶H-11452; ¶H-11452.2
36. ¶H-11406
37. ¶H-11403
38. ¶H-11415

39. ¶H-11452
40. ¶H-11440
41. ¶H-11448
42. ¶H-11402
43. ¶H-11458

Plans may provide for the distribution of benefits without the participant's consent, or a spouse's consent (a "mandatory distribution" or an "involuntary cash-out distribution"), when a participant with a small accrued benefit (a nonforfeitable accrued benefit whose present value is $5,000 or less) terminates employment with the plan sponsor. Such mandatory distributions must follow the automatic rollover rules. Under these rules, plans with mandatory distribution provisions must transfer the amount of the distribution to an IRA of a designated trustee or issuer where (i) the distribution of a nonforfeitable accrued benefit is more than $1,000, but no more than $5,000; and (ii) the plan participant (or beneficiary) receiving the distribution does not elect to have the distribution paid directly to another qualified plan or IRA (a direct rollover), and does not elect to receive the distribution personally. (Code Sec. 401(a)(31)(B))[44]

The plan administrator must also notify the distributee in writing that the distribution may be transferred without cost or penalty to another IRA.[45]

For rollovers of after-tax contributions, see ¶4352.

¶ 4350   Additional types of tax-free 60-day rollovers; recontributions of coronavirus-related distributions—IRAs.

Permissible types of tax-free 60-day rollovers, besides those covered at ¶4349, include:

. . . Rollovers from one type of IRA (individual retirement account or individual retirement annuity) to the same or another type. But these rollovers may be made no more than once in a one-year period. (Code Sec. 408(d)(3))[46] Further, the one IRA rollover per year limit applies on an aggregate basis, not on an IRA-by-IRA basis; thus, taxpayers with multiple IRAs can make just one rollover per year for all their IRAs.[47] Qualified rollovers from an IRA to a Roth IRA are disregarded for purposes of the one-year rule. (Code Sec. 408A(e)) However, a distribution from a SIMPLE retirement plan (¶4369) can't be rolled over tax-free except to another SIMPLE plan during the employee's first two years of participation in the plan. (Code Sec. 408(d)(3)(G))

. . . From one type of IRA (individual retirement account or individual retirement annuity) to an eligible retirement plan (¶4349) (limited to amount which would otherwise be included in gross income). (Code Sec. 408(d)(3)(A)(ii))[48]

. . . Eligible rollover distributions from a Code Sec. 403(b) plan to an eligible retirement plan (¶4349) and from an eligible retirement plan to a Code Sec. 403(b) plan. (Code Sec. 402(c)(8)(B), Code Sec. 403(b)(8)(A)(ii))

. . . Eligible rollover distributions from a Code Sec. 457 plan to an eligible retirement plan (¶4349) and from an eligible retirement plan to a Code Sec. 457 plan. (Code Sec. 402(c)(8)(B), Code Sec. 457(e)(16))

. . . Wrongfully levied retirement plan account or benefit returned after Dec. 31, 2017, and any interest on it, if the plan permits, or to an individual retirement plan eligible to receive a rollover distribution from the plan. The rollover must be made by the unextended return due date for the tax year in which the funds were returned, and the contribution is treated as made for that tax year. Any income tax collected on the amount includible in income resulting from the distribution caused by the levy is to be refunded or credited, unless the rollover contribution is made from an eligible retirement plan that is not a Roth IRA or a designated Roth account into a Roth IRA or designated Roth account. (Code Sec. 6343(f))[49]

For taxable rollovers to Roth IRAs, see ¶4353.

---

44. ¶H-8251.3
45. ¶H-8251.3
46. ¶H-11460 *et seq.*

47. ¶H-11463.0
48. ¶H-11463.1
49. ¶V-5141

¶ 4351   Partial rollovers—IRAs.

When an employee elects to roll over less than his or her entire distribution:

(1) the portion not rolled over is taxed under the regular rules for taxing ordinary income;

(2) ten-year forward averaging and/or capital gains treatment, where applicable, for lump-sum distributions (¶4329) don't apply if any part of the lump-sum distribution is rolled over; (Code Sec. 402(c)(1), Code Sec. 402(d)(4)(K) before amend by Sec. 1401(a), PL 104-188, 8/20/96)

(3) the basis recovery rules of Code Sec. 72(e) apply to a distribution that's rolled over under Code Sec. 402(c); and

(4) any net unrealized appreciation in employer securities attributable to nondeductible employee contributions is subject to tax immediately.[50]

¶ 4352   Rollovers of after-tax contributions—IRAs.

Generally, only otherwise taxable amounts of an eligible rollover distribution may be rolled over. However, the "nontaxable" portion of a eligible rollover distribution (attributable to after-tax employee contributions) may be rolled over to the extent that the "taxable" portion is rolled over directly to (1) an IRA, or (2) to a defined contribution plan or tax-sheltered Code Sec. 403(b) annuity that will account separately for the taxable and nontaxable portions. In such a case, the amount transferred is treated as consisting first of the portion of the distribution that would be includible in income were it not for the rollover. (Code Sec. 402(c)(2))[1]

¶ 4353   Qualified plan to Roth IRA rollovers.

Distributions from qualified retirement plans, tax-sheltered Code Sec. 403(b) annuities, and governmental Code Sec. 457 plans may be rolled over directly into a Roth IRA, generally subject to the usual rules that apply to rollovers from a traditional IRA into a Roth IRA (see ¶4360). For example, a rollover from a qualified retirement plan into a Roth IRA is includible in gross income (except to the extent it represents a return of after-tax contributions), and the 10% early distribution tax does not apply. (Code Sec. 408A(e)) A rollover from a qualified plan, etc., to a Roth IRA doesn't count for purposes of the one-rollover-per-year rule.[2] The rollover also can be made through a distribution from the plan that's then contributed (rolled over) to the Roth IRA within 60 days. In either case, the amount rolled over must be an eligible rollover distribution.

For the tax treatment of amounts rolled into a Roth IRA from an eligible retirement plan that are later distributed within 5 years, see ¶4362.

¶ 4354   One-time IRA to HSA rollovers.

Under Code Sec. 408(d)(9), taxpayers may make a one-time-only tax-free rollover, via direct trustee-to-trustee-transfer, from an IRA to a Health Savings Account (HSA) (¶1528).The rollover amount is nondeductible and is limited to the otherwise maximum deductible HSA contribution amount, computed on the basis of the type of coverage under the taxpayer's high deductible health plan (HDHP) at the time of the contribution. The rollover reduces the otherwise allowable HSA contribution amount.

---

50. ¶H-11405 *et seq.*
1. ¶H-11406.1

2. ¶H-11463

Generally, only one rollover may be made during a taxpayer's lifetime, but if one is made during a month in which the taxpayer has self-only coverage as of the first day of the month, an additional rollover may be made during a subsequent month within the tax year in which the taxpayer has family coverage. (Code Sec. 408(d)(9)(C)(ii))

If a taxpayer does not remain an eligible individual (except because of death or disability) during the testing period (begins with the month of the contribution and ends on the last day of the 12th month following that month), the amount of the IRA distribution that would otherwise have been includible (absent the rollover) is taxed and subject to a 10% additional tax. The amount is includible in income for the tax year of the first day during the testing period that the taxpayer is not an eligible individual. (Code Sec. 408(d)(9)(D))[3]

A qualified HSA funding distribution may be made from a traditional IRA or a Roth IRA, but not from an ongoing SIMPLE IRA or SEP IRA. Further, a qualified HSA funding distribution must not exceed the IRA or Roth IRA account owner's maximum annual HSA contribution.[4]

¶ 4355   Surviving spouse's rollover of distribution from decedent—IRAs.

A surviving-spouse beneficiary may elect to treat the entire beneficiary interest in the decedent's IRA as the spouse-beneficiary's own IRA if he or she is the sole beneficiary of the IRA and has an unlimited right to withdraw amounts from it. However, this requirement is not satisfied if a trust is named beneficiary of the IRA even if the spouse is sole beneficiary of the trust. (Reg § 1.408-8, Q&A 5(a)) The election is made by the surviving spouse redesignating the account as an account in his or her name as IRA owner rather than as beneficiary. Alternatively, a surviving spouse is deemed to have made the election if, at any time, either of the following occurs: (1) any amount required to be distributed to the surviving spouse as beneficiary is not timely distributed, or (2) any additional amount is contributed to the IRA. (Reg § 1.408-8, Q&A 5(b)) If the election is made, the surviving spouse is considered the IRA owner for all purposes under the Code. (Reg § 1.408-8, Q&A 5(c))[5]

A surviving spouse may also roll a distribution from a qualified plan, annuity, or IRA over to any other qualified plan, annuity, or IRA in which the surviving spouse participates that accepts rollover contributions. (Code Sec. 402(c)(9), Code Sec. 408(d)(3)(C))[6]

¶ 4356   Rollover by beneficiary other than surviving spouse—IRAs.

Distributions from qualified plans, tax-sheltered annuities (¶4375 *et seq.*), and Code Sec. 457 government plans may be rolled over (in a direct trustee-to-trustee transfer, see ¶4307) to a non-spouse beneficiary's IRA that's established for the purpose of receiving the distribution. This "recipient IRA" is treated as an inherited IRA, and so is subject to the required minimum distribution (RMD) rules that apply to inherited IRAs of nonspouse beneficiaries (¶4335). If a trust is a decedent's named beneficiary, then a plan can make a direct rollover under the nonspouse beneficiary rollover rules to an IRA established with the trust as beneficiary, provided certain rules are met. (Code Sec. 402(c)(11), Code Sec. 403(a)(4)(B), Code Sec. 457(e)(16)(B))[7]

¶ 4357   Overview—Roth IRAs. ▬▬▬▬▬▬▬▬▬▬▬

Under Code Sec. 408A, taxpayers can make nondeductible contributions to Roth IRAs. A Roth IRA is an IRA that is designated as a Roth IRA when it's established (Code Sec. 408A(b)); it's treated as a traditional IRA (¶4341 *et seq.*) except to the

3. ¶H-12253.1C
4. ¶H-12253.1B
5. ¶H-12264.7

6. ¶H-11467 *et seq.*
7. ¶H-11438.1; ¶H-11438.3

extent that special rules apply to it. (Code Sec. 408A(a))

Contributions to a Roth IRA aren't deductible (Code Sec. 408A(c)(1)), and are limited based on modified adjusted gross income (MAGI, ¶4358). Qualified distributions from a Roth IRA aren't included in income (Code Sec. 408A(d)(1)) and other distributions are treated as a return of investment to the extent of contributions to Roth IRAs (¶4361). (Code Sec. 408A(d)(4)) Rollovers from traditional IRAs to Roth IRAs are taxable, but not subject to the 10% additional tax on early distributions. (Code Sec. 408A(d)(3))[8] (Reg § 1.408A-3, Reg § 1.408A-4, Reg § 1.408A-5)

Use Form 5305-R, Form 5305-RA, and Form 5305-RB to set up Roth trust, custodial, and annuity accounts, respectively, with financial institutions.

¶ 4358   Contributions to Roth IRAs.

An individual can make annual nondeductible contributions to a Roth IRA in amounts up to $6,000, plus an additional $1,000 for 2022 ($6,500 plus an additional $1,000 for 2023) for those 50 and older, or 100% of compensation, if less, reduced by the amount of contributions for the tax year made to all other IRAs (Code Sec. 408A(c)(1), Code Sec. 408A(c)(2)) but not reduced by contributions to a SEP (¶4365) or SIMPLE plan (¶4369) (Code Sec. 408A(f)(2); Reg § 1.408A-3, Q&A 3(c))[9] The allowable contribution phases out ratably (in $10 increments) over the following levels of modified adjusted gross income (MAGI):

* For joint filers, $204,000 to $214,000 for 2022 ($218,000 to $228,000 for 2023));
* For married persons filing separately, $0 to $10,000 for 2022 and 2023; and
* For single taxpayers and heads of household, $129,000 to $144,000 for 2022 ($138,000 to $153,000 for 2023).

However, a $200 contribution may be made if the phase-out lowers the contribution limit to under $200 but more than $0. (Code Sec. 408A(c)(3)(A), Code Sec. 408A(c)(3)(B); Reg § 1.408A-3, Q&A 3(b))

AGI for purposes of the Roth IRA contribution phaseout is defined as it is for traditional IRA purposes (¶4342), except that it does not include income resulting from the conversion from a traditional IRA to a Roth IRA (¶4360). (Code Sec. 408A(c)(3)(B)(i); Reg § 1.408A-3, Q&A 5)[10]

observation: The MAGI-based contribution limits for Roth IRAs apply whether or not the taxpayer is a participant in a qualified retirement plan.

Roth IRA contributions for a year must be made by the unextended tax return due date for the contribution year. (Code Sec. 408A(c)(6); Reg § 1.408A-3, Q&A 2(b))[11] For rollover contributions, see ¶4360.

A 6% excise tax is imposed each year on excess contributions to an IRA (¶4346). Similar rules apply to a Roth IRA. (Code Sec. 4973(f))[12]

Any contribution distributed with its net income from a Roth IRA before the due date of the individual's tax return is treated as an amount not contributed. (Code Sec. 4973(f))[13]

For the saver's credit for lower-income taxpayers' contributions to Roth IRAs, see ¶2356.

A recipient of a military death gratuity or Servicemembers' Group Life Insurance (SGLI) proceeds can contribute the amounts received (reduced by any amounts contributed to a Coverdell education savings account, ¶2207) to a Roth IRA as qualified rollover contributions. The requirement that only one tax-free rollover contribution can be made to a Roth

---

8. ¶H-12290 *et seq.*
9. ¶H-12290.7
10. ¶H-12290.9

11. ¶H-12290.14
12. ¶H-12242.1
13. ¶H-12242.1

IRA during any one-year period (¶4350) doesn't apply. The rollover has to be made within one year of receipt of a payment. (Code Sec. 408A(e)(2))[14]

¶ 4359   Recharacterizing (changing the nature of) IRA contributions; election.

Under Code Sec. 408A(d)(6), a taxpayer may elect to recharacterize an IRA *contribution,* that is, treat a contribution to one type of IRA (Roth IRA or traditional IRA) as made to a different type of IRA. (Code Sec. 408A(d)(6); Reg § 1.408A-5)

observation: The recharacterization election allows a contribution to a traditional IRA to be treated as made to a Roth IRA, or a contribution to a Roth IRA to be treated as made to a traditional IRA.

To make the recharacterization election:

... The taxpayer must notify the trustees of the first (distributing) and second (receiving) IRAs of his or her election to recharacterize a contribution (regular or conversion), i.e., that the taxpayer is electing for tax purposes to treat the contribution as having been made to the second IRA, instead of the first IRA. The taxpayer must provide the trustees with specified information (including the type and amount of the contribution being recharacterized) sufficient to effect the recharacterization transfer.

... The contribution (regular or conversion) originally made to first IRA, plus net income (if any) allocable to the contribution (Reg § 1.408A-10, Reg § 1.408A-5, Q&A 2(c)), must be transferred from the first IRA to the second IRA via a trustee-to-trustee transfer.

... The trustee-to-trustee transfer must be made on a timely basis. (Reg § 1.408A-5, Q&A-6)[15]

An IRA contribution for a tax year may be recharacterized as late as six months after the unextended due date for filing the return for that year. (Reg § 301.9100-2(b))[16]

A recharacterization election cannot be revoked after the transfer. (Reg § 1.408A-5, Q&A 6(b))

The contribution that is being recharacterized is treated as having been originally contributed to the second IRA on the same date and (in the case of a regular contribution) for the same tax year that the contribution was made to the first IRA. (Reg § 1.408A-5, Q&A 3)

¶ 4360   Conversions of traditional IRAs to Roth IRAs—Form 8606.

Taxpayers, including marrieds filing separately, may convert amounts in a traditional IRA to amounts in a Roth IRA without regard to their modified adjusted gross income (MAGI) or filing status.[17] The conversion may be done in one of three ways:

(1) Rollover to a Roth IRA of a distribution from a traditional IRA within 60 days of the distribution.

(2) Trustee-to-trustee transfer from the trustee of the traditional IRA to the trustee of the Roth IRA.

(3) Transfer of an amount in a traditional IRA to a Roth IRA maintained by the same trustee. (Code Sec. 408A(d)(3)(C); Reg § 1.408A-4, Q&A 1(b))

Amounts from a SEP-IRA (¶4366) or a SIMPLE IRA (¶4349) also may be converted to a Roth IRA, but a conversion from a SIMPLE IRA may be made only after the 2-year period

---

14. ¶H-12290.19A
15. ¶H-12290.22

16. ¶H-12290.23A
17. ¶H-12290.16A

beginning on the date on which the taxpayer first participated in any SIMPLE IRA maintained by the taxpayer's employer. (Reg § 1.408A-4, Q&A 4)

The conversion is subject to tax (report on Form 8606) as if it were distributed from the traditional IRA and not recontributed to another IRA (¶4347) (Code Sec. 408A(d)(3)(A)(i)), but isn't subject to the 10% early distribution tax. (Code Sec. 408A(d)(3)(A)(ii); Reg § 1.408A-4, Q&A 7)[18]

When a traditional individual retirement annuity is converted to a Roth IRA, the amount treated as distributed is the FMV of the annuity contract on the date it is converted. Similarly, when a traditional IRA holding an annuity contract as an account asset is converted to a Roth IRA, the amount that is treated as distributed with respect to the annuity contract is the FMV of the annuity contract on the date the annuity contract is converted (i.e., distributed or treated as distributed from the traditional IRA). (Reg § 1.408A-4, Q&A 14(a))[19]

¶ 4361   Distributions from Roth IRAs—Form 8606.

Qualified distributions. Under Code Sec. 408A(d)(1), qualified distributions from Roth IRAs aren't included in income. These are distributions made after the 5-tax-year period beginning with the first tax year for which the taxpayer or the taxpayer's spouse made a contribution to a Roth IRA established for the taxpayer, including a qualified rollover contribution from an IRA other than a Roth IRA (Code Sec. 408A(d)(2)(B)), and that are made:

(1) on or after attaining age 59½,

(2) at or after death (to a beneficiary or estate),

(3) on account of disability, or

(4) for a first-time home purchase expense under Code Sec. 72(t)(2)(F). (Code Sec. 408A(d)(2)(A), Code Sec. 408A(d)(5); Reg § 1.408A-6, Q&A 1)[20]

The 5-year period for qualified distributions isn't recalculated when a Roth IRA owner dies. The 5-year period for a beneficiary's inherited Roth IRA is determined independently of the period for any other Roth IRA that the beneficiary may have, except that the 5-year period for a spousal beneficiary with both an inherited Roth IRA and his or her own Roth IRA ends with the earlier of the five-year periods. (Reg § 1.408A-5, Q&A 7)[21]

Corrective distributions made by the return due date, plus extensions, for the tax year of the contribution aren't qualified distributions. (Code Sec. 408A(d)(2)(C); Reg § 1.408A-6, Q&A 2)[22]

Nonqualified distributions. Distributions that aren't qualified distributions are treated as made first from contributions to all of an individual's Roth IRAs and are nontaxable to that extent; distributions in excess of contributions are taxable. (Code Sec. 408A(d)(4))[23]

Order of distributions. Distributions are treated as made from contributions to the Roth IRA to the extent that the distribution, when added to all previous distributions from the Roth IRA, doesn't exceed the total amount of all contributions. (Code Sec. 408A(d)(4)(B)(i)) Contributions are treated as withdrawn in the following order: first, contributions other than qualified rollover contributions (i.e., qualified conversions, see ¶4360); second, qualified rollover contributions (on a FIFO basis); third, a distribution allocable to a qualified rollover contribution is allocated first to the part of the contribution required to be included in gross income. (Code Sec. 408A(d)(4)(B)(ii); Reg § 1.408A-6, Q&A 8)[24] All of a

---

18. ¶H-12290.20
19. ¶H-12290.20A
20. ¶H-12290.28
21. ¶H-12290.30

22. ¶H-12290.33
23. ¶H-12290.34
24. ¶H-12290.35

taxpayer's Roth IRAs are treated as a single Roth IRA. (Code Sec. 408A(d)(4)(A), Code Sec. 408(d)(2))

Losses in a Roth IRA are currently nondeductible due to the suspension of miscellaneous itemized deductions (¶2162).[25]

Report Roth IRA distributions on Form 8606, Part III.

Roth IRAs aren't subject to the required minimum distribution rules of Code Sec. 401(a)(9)(A) (¶4335) or the incidental benefit requirements of Code Sec. 401(a). However, the post-death minimum distribution rules of Code Sec. 401(a)(9)(B) (¶4335) that apply to traditional IRAs, with the exception of the at-least-as-rapidly rule of Code Sec. 401(a)(9)(B)(i), apply to Roth IRAs. The post-death minimum distribution rules apply to the Roth IRA as though the Roth IRA owner died before his or her required beginning date. Thus, for owners who die after Dec. 31, 2019, the entire interest in the Roth IRA generally must be distributed by the end of the 10th calendar year after the year of the owner's death, unless the interest is payable to an eligible designated beneficiary over a period not greater than that beneficiary's life expectancy and distribution begins before the end of the calendar year after the year of death. If the eligible designated beneficiary dies, any remaining interest must be distributed within 10 years. For owners who die on or before Dec. 31, 2019, and whenever the beneficiary is not a designated beneficiary, the distribution deadline is generally the 5th calendar year after the year of the owner's death unless the interest is payable to a designated beneficiary over a period not greater than that beneficiary's life expectancy and distribution begins before the end of the calendar year after the year of death. If the sole beneficiary is the decedent's spouse (whether the owner dies before or after Dec. 31, 2019), the spouse may delay distributions until the decedent would have attained age 72 (70½ for decedents who attained that age on or before Dec. 31, 2019) or may treat the Roth IRA as the spouse's own. (Reg § 1.408A-6, Q&A 14(b)) (Code Sec. 408A(c)(4))[26]

For the 10% additional tax on early distributions, see ¶4362. For distributions from designated Roth accounts, see ¶4363.

¶ 4362 10% additional tax on early Roth IRA distributions.

As with other IRAs (¶4334) the Code Sec. 72(t) 10% additional tax on early distributions applies to the portion of an early withdrawal that is includible in income. In addition, however, a distribution from a Roth IRA is subject to the early withdrawal tax as if it *were* includible in income, if that distribution (or any portion of it): (1) is allocable (under rules at ¶4361) to a "qualified rollover contribution;" and (2) is made within the five-tax year period beginning with the tax year for which the contribution was made. However, the 10% tax applies only to the extent that the amount of the qualified rollover contribution was includible in income. (Code Sec. 408A(d)(3)(F))[27]

¶ 4363 Designated Roth Accounts.

Under Code Sec. 402A, an applicable retirement plan—i.e., a Code Sec. 401(k) plan, Code Sec. 403(b) annuity (¶4375), or governmental Code Sec. 457 plan—may include a qualified Roth contribution program that allows participants to elect to have all or part of their elective deferrals treated as "designated Roth contributions."(Code Sec. 402A(a)(1)) Designated Roth contributions, which are currently includible in income, aren't subject to the AGI-based phaseouts for regular Roth IRA contributions (¶4358). Qualified distributions are excludable from income. (Code Sec. 402A(d))[28]

---

25. ¶H-12255
26. ¶H-12290.42.

27. ¶H-12290.38
28. ¶H-12295.1 *et seq.*

Designated Roth contributions. These are elective deferrals permitted by an applicable retirement plan that are:

(1) irrevocably designated by the employee as designated Roth contributions when the deferral election is made;

(2) treated by the employer as includible in the employee's income when the employee would have received the amount had the employee not made the deferral election (e.g., by treating the contributions as wages subject to applicable withholding requirements); and

(3) maintained by the plan in a separate account. (Code Sec. 402A(b)(2))[29]

Plans can't provide for designated Roth contributions unless it also offers pre-tax elective contributions. (Reg § 1.401(k)-1(f)(1)(i))[30]

A designated Roth contribution must satisfy the other requirements that apply to elective deferrals, including nonforfeitability and distribution restrictions and, in the case of contributions to a Code Sec. 401(k) plan, the actual deferral percentage (ADP) nondiscrimination test (or a safe harbor alternative); see ¶4305. (Reg § 1.401(k)-1(f)(3))[31]

In-plan Roth rollovers. Employers may amend their Roth 401(k), 403(b), or 457 plans to allow participants to transfer an eligible rollover distribution (ERD) to their designated Roth account in the plan. (Code Sec. 402A(c)(4)) An ERD is a distribution (1) from a non-designated Roth account in the same plan, (2) because of an event that triggers an ERD from the plan; and (3) otherwise meets the rollover requirements. For transfers of amounts not otherwise distributable, a plan will not be treated as violating the distribution restrictions of (i) Code Sec. 401(k)(2)(B)(i), (ii) Code Sec. 403(b)(7)(A)(i), (iii) Code Sec. 403(b)(11), (iv) Code Sec. 457(d)(1)(A), or (v) 5 USC §8433, solely because of the transfer. (Code Sec. 402A(c)(4)(E))

Thus, for transfers to designated Roth accounts, IRS timing restrictions on distributions—such as age or severance from employment—need not be met.[32] However, once the ERD has been transferred in an in-plan Roth rollover, the ERD—plus any applicable earnings—is again subject to the distribution restrictions that applied before the transfer. (Notice 2013-74, 2013-52 IRB 819)

The participant must include in gross income the amount that would be includible in gross income if it were not part of a qualified rollover distribution. (Code Sec. 402A(c)(4)(A)(i))[33]

Any distribution from an applicable retirement plan (other than from a designated Roth account) that is contributed in a qualified rollover contribution to the designated Roth account, is not taken into account as a designated Roth contribution (e.g., for purposes of the annual limit on elective deferrals). (Code Sec. 402A(c)(4)(C))[34]

Distributions from designated Roths. A qualified distribution from a designated Roth is excluded from income if it meets the requirements for qualified distributions from Roth IRAs (¶4361), with the following differences:

...A distribution for a first-time home purchase isn't excluded. (Code Sec. 402A(d)(2)(A))[35]

...The five-year period necessary for a distribution to be excluded begins on the first day of the employee's tax year for which the employee first had designated Roth contributions made to the plan. If a direct rollover is made from a designated Roth account under another plan, the five-year period begins on the first day for which the employee

29. ¶H-12295.5
30. ¶H-12295.3
31. ¶H-12295.5B
32. ¶H-12295.5E
33. ¶H-12295.5K
34. ¶H-12295.5A
35. ¶H-12295.6A

first had designated Roth contributions made to the other plan, if earlier. (Reg § 1.402A-1, Q&A 4)[36]

. . . Designated Roth accounts are subject to the lifetime required minimum distribution (RMD) rules of Code Sec. 401(a)(9)(A) and Code Sec. 401(a)(9)(B) (¶4335). (Reg § 1.401(k)-1(f)(4)(i)) By contrast, a regular Roth IRA is not subject to the Code Sec. 401(a)(9)(A) lifetime RMD rules (¶4361).

Where disbursements are made from a taxpayer's designated Roth account to the taxpayer and also to the taxpayer's Roth IRA or designated Roth account in a direct rollover, then pretax amounts will be allocated first to the direct rollover, rather than being allocated pro rata to each destination. Also, a taxpayer may direct the allocation of pretax and after-tax amounts that are included in disbursements from a designated Roth account that are directly rolled over to multiple destinations, applying the same allocation rules to distributions from designated Roth accounts that apply to distributions from other types of accounts. (Reg § 1.402A-1, Q&A-5)[37]

A distribution from a designated Roth account that is not a qualified distribution is taxable to the distributee under the Code Sec. 72 rules, *not* under the regular Roth IRA ordering rules (¶4361). (Reg § 1.402A-1, Q&A 3)[38]

¶ 4364   Deemed IRAs.

Under Code Sec. 408(q), qualified plans, Code Sec. 403(b) annuities (¶4375), and governmental Code Sec. 457 plans may include a deemed IRA, which is a separate account or annuity in a qualified employer plan to which plan participants may make voluntary IRA or Roth IRA contributions.

The qualified plan must elect to allow employees to make voluntary employee contributions (designated as such by the employees) to a separate account or annuity (meeting the requirements for a traditional IRA or Roth IRA) established under the plan. However, the general requirement that IRA assets not be commingled does not apply to deemed IRAs. (Code Sec. 408(q))[39]

SEPs (see ¶4365) and SIMPLE IRAs (¶4369) cannot be used as deemed IRAs. (Reg § 1.408(q)-1(b))[40]

Contributions to a deemed IRA are treated as contributions to an IRA, and not as contributions to the qualified employer plan. Thus, a deemed IRA contribution is in addition to the $20,500 maximum amount for 2022 ($22,500 for 2023) that can be contributed to a Code Sec. 401(k) plan (excluding catch-up contributions). (Code Sec. 408(q)(1))

The ceilings on modified adjusted gross income (MAGI) that limit a taxpayer's ability to make Roth IRA contributions (¶4358) or deductible contributions to a regular IRA (¶4342) also apply to voluntary contributions to a deemed IRA. (Code Sec. 408(q)(1)(B); Reg § 1.408(q)-1(f)(4))[41]

A deemed IRA isn't subject to the rules that apply to the qualified employer plan, so contributions to a deemed IRA are not taken into account in applying those rules to any other contributions under the plan. Thus, deemed IRA contributions don't count against the 100% of income or dollar limit on annual additions to defined contribution plans. (Reg § 1.408(q)-1(c))

¶ 4365   Simplified Employee Pensions (SEPs).

An employer can make deductible contributions on behalf of its employees to a

---

36. ¶H-12295.6B *et seq.*
37. ¶H-12295.7B
38. ¶H-12295.7

39. ¶H-12280
40. ¶H-12280
41. ¶H-12284

simplified employee pension (SEP, Code Sec. 408(k)). These deductible employer contributions are excluded from the gross income of the employee.

¶ 4366   Simplified employee pension (SEP) defined; governing rules.

Under Code Sec. 408(k), a SEP is an individual retirement account or individual retirement annuity (IRA, see ¶4341), established by an employer by filing Form 5305-SEP, in which:

(1) The employer contributions are made only under a definite written allocation formula that is executed within the time for making a deductible contribution (¶4367)[42] that specifies (a) the requirements that an employee must satisfy to share in an allocation, and (b) how the allocated amount is computed. (Code Sec. 408(k)(5))[43]

(2) Employer contributions for a year must be made to each SEP of each employee who has reached age 21, performed service for the employer during at least three of the immediately preceding five years, and received at least $650 in compensation for the year for 2022 (at least $750 for 2023). (Code Sec. 408(k)(2))[44]

(3) The employer contributions don't discriminate in favor of highly compensated employees. (Code Sec. 408(k)(3)(A))[45]

(4) The employer contributions aren't conditional on the retention in the plan of any portion of the amounts contributed. (Code Sec. 408(k)(4))[46]

(5) The employer doesn't restrict employee withdrawals. (Code Sec. 408(k)(4)(B))[47]

(6) If the SEP was established before 1997, it can permit elective deferrals (making it a SARSEP) if the employer did not have more than 25 employees eligible to participate during the prior year, and at least 50% of eligible employees elect to defer. Elective deferrals made by each highly compensated employee may not exceed the average of the deferral percentage of all other eligible employees multiplied by 1.25. (Code Sec. 408(k)(6)(A)(iii))[48]

Employer contributions are discriminatory unless they bear a uniform relationship to the first $305,000 for 2022 ($330,000 for 2023) of the compensation (including self-employed income) of each employee maintaining the SEP. (Code Sec. 408(k)(3)(C))[49]

Employees covered by a collective bargaining agreement and nonresident aliens may be excluded from participation in the plan and from the discrimination test under certain conditions. (Code Sec. 408(k)(3)(B))[50]

Maximum allowable contributions made by an employer to a SEP on behalf of an employee for any year cannot exceed the lesser of: (1) 25% of compensation (limited by the annual compensation limit, see ¶4307) from the employer includible in the employee's gross income for the year (determined without regard to the employer's contributions to the SEP), or (2) the dollar limitation for defined contribution plans ($61,000 for 2022, $66,000 for 2023; see ¶4317). (Special calculations are needed for self-employeds, like those for Keogh plans, see ¶4316.) Employee elective deferrals to a SEP do not count towards the limit. Where the SEP is integrated with social security, the dollar limitation in (2) is reduced by the amount taken into account above the integration level, in the case of a highly compensated employee. (Code Sec. 402(h)(2))[1]

---

42. ¶H-12303
43. ¶H-12310
44. ¶H-12305
45. ¶H-12306
46. ¶H-12309

47. ¶H-12309
48. ¶H-12321.1
49. ¶H-12307
50. ¶H-12306
1. ¶s H-12308, H-12311

¶ 4367   Employer's deduction for contributions to a SEP.

Under Code Sec. 404(h), a contribution by an employer to a SEP is deductible for a tax year if made on account of that year and not later than the time prescribed for filing the return for that year plus extensions.[2] The deduction can't exceed 25% of the compensation paid to the employees during the calendar year, up to the defined contribution plan limit (¶4317). Contributions that exceed this limit can be carried over to, and deducted in, succeeding tax years in order of time. Elective deferrals are not subject to the deduction limit. (Code Sec. 404(h))[3]

An employer may elect to use either the calendar year or, subject to such terms and conditions as IRS may prescribe, its own tax year as the computation period for purposes of determining contributions to a SEP. (Code Sec. 408(k)(7)) If the calendar year is used, contributions made for a year are deductible for the employer's tax year with which or within which the calendar year ends. If the employer's "regular" tax year is used, contributions are deductible for that tax year. For purposes of deductibility, contributions are treated as if they were made for a tax year if the contributions are made on account of the tax year and are made not later than the time prescribed by law for filing the return for the tax year, plus extensions. (Code Sec. 404(h)(1)(A), Code Sec. 404(h)(1)(B))[4] Special rules apply where the employer also contributes to other plans. (Code Sec. 404(h)(2), Code Sec. 404(h)(3))[5]

¶ 4368   Employee's treatment of SEP contributions and withdrawals.

Under Code Sec. 402(h)(1), contributions made to a SEP by an employer on behalf of an employee are excluded from the employee's gross income, up to the deduction limits at ¶4367. Contributions in excess of those limits are taxed to the employee in the year made. (Code Sec. 402(h)(2))[6] Payments made from the SEP are taxed to the recipient under the IRA rules (¶4347). (Code Sec. 402(h)(3))[7]

¶ 4369   "SIMPLE" Retirement Plans. ▬▬▬▬▬▬▬

An eligible employer (¶4370) that doesn't have a qualified plan can establish a "SIMPLE" (savings incentive match plan for employees, Code Sec. 408(p)) retirement plan under which contributions are made to individual retirement accounts or annuities known as SIMPLE retirement accounts or SIMPLE IRAs (defined at ¶4372), without having to meet most of the requirements for qualified plans.

For qualified salary reduction arrangements under SIMPLE plans, see ¶4371. For contributions to SIMPLE plans, see ¶4373; for distributions, see ¶4374.

¶ 4370   Employers eligible to adopt SIMPLE retirement plans.

Under Code Sec. 408(p), a "SIMPLE retirement plan" can be adopted (use Form 5305-SIMPLE, Form 5304-SIMPLE if there is no designated financial institution, or Form 5305-SA for a SIMPLE individual retirement custodial account) by an employer with 100 or fewer employees who received at least $5,000 of compensation from the employer for the preceding year (Code Sec. 408(p)(2)(C)(i)(I)) that doesn't have another employer-sponsored retirement plan (including a SEP or annuity plan), except for a collectively bargained plan covering employees ineligible to participate in the SIMPLE plan, to which contributions were made or benefits accrued for the year. (Code Sec. 408(p)(2)(D))[8] "Employee" includes

---

2. ¶H-12312 *et seq.*
3. ¶H-12315 *et seq.*
4. ¶H-12317
5. ¶H-12318 *et seq.*

6. ¶H-12311
7. ¶H-12319.3
8. ¶H-12351, ¶H-12353

a self-employed individual. (Code Sec. 408(p)(6)(B)) A qualifying employer that maintains a SIMPLE plan but later fails to qualify may continue to maintain the plan for two years after its last year of eligibility, subject to certain restrictions for acquisitions, dispositions and similar transactions. (Code Sec. 408(p)(2)(C)(i)(II), Code Sec. 408(p)(10))[9]

¶ 4371   "Qualified salary reduction arrangements" under SIMPLE plans.

Employees designate contributions to be made to a SIMPLE plan under a "qualified salary reduction arrangement." This is a written arrangement under which an employee may elect to have the employer make elective employer contributions (expressed as a percentage of compensation, or, if the employer permits, a specific dollar amount) to a SIMPLE retirement account on behalf of the employee, or to the employee directly in cash. The amount that an employee may elect for any year can't exceed $14,000 for 2022 ($15,500 for 2023). (Code Sec. 408(p)(2)(A)(i), Code Sec. 408(p)(2)(A)(ii), Code Sec. 408(p)(2)(E))[10] SIMPLE IRA participants who are age 50 or over by the end of the plan year may make additional catch-up contributions of up to $3,000 for 2022 and $3,500 for 2023. (Code Sec. 414(v)(2)(B)(ii), Code Sec. 414(v)(2)(C))[11]

For the saver's credit for lower-income taxpayers' elective contributions to SIMPLE plans, see ¶2356.

The employer must make either:

(1)   a matching contribution equal to the amount the employee contributes, up to 3% (Code Sec. 408(p)(2)(C)(ii)(I)) of the employee's compensation for the year, or, electively, as little as 1% in no more than two out of the previous five years, if the employer timely notifies the employees of the lower percentage (Code Sec. 408(p)(2)(C)(ii)(II))[12] ; or

(2)   a nonelective contribution of 2% of compensation for each employee eligible to participate who has at least $5,000 of compensation from the employer for the year. (Code Sec. 408(p)(2)(B)(i))[13]

No other contributions may be made. (Code Sec. 408(p)(2)(A)(iv), Code Sec. 408(p)(8)) Elective employer contributions must be made no later than 30 days after the month for which the contributions are to be made. (Code Sec. 408(p)(5)(A)(i)) Matching contributions and nonelective contributions must be made by the deductible contribution due date for the year. (Code Sec. 408(p)(5)(A)(ii))[14]

"Compensation" is wages for income tax withholding purposes plus the amount of the employee's elective deferrals (Code Sec. 408(p)(6)(A)(i)) (for a self-employed person, net self-employment earnings (under Code Sec. 1402(a)) without regard to the SIMPLE retirement plan provisions. (Code Sec. 408(p)(6)(A)(ii)) For purposes of determining contributions to a SIMPLE plan, the definition of compensation includes wages paid to domestic workers, even though those amounts are not subject to income tax withholding. (Code Sec. 408(p)(6)(A)(i))

The compensation taken into account for purposes of determining the amount of the 2% nonelective contribution can't exceed the limit on compensation (under Code Sec. 401(a)(17), see ¶4307) that may be taken into account for the year. (Code Sec. 408(p)(2)(B)(ii))[15]

---

9. ¶H-12352.1
10. ¶H-12357
11. ¶H-9244.1
12. ¶H-12359
13. ¶H-12360
14. ¶H-12364
15. ¶H-12358

¶ 4372   SIMPLE retirement account (SIMPLE IRA) defined.

Under Code Sec. 408(p)(1), a "SIMPLE retirement account" (SIMPLE IRA) into which employer contributions under a SIMPLE retirement plan are made is an individual retirement account or annuity that: (1) meets certain vesting, participation and administrative requirements (Code Sec. 408(p)(1)(A)); and (2) can accept only (a) contributions under a qualified salary reduction arrangement (including salary reduction contributions and employer matching or nonelective contributions), and b) various rollovers, including rollovers from an IRA or from another SIMPLE IRA, but only if made after the 2-year period beginning on the date that the employee first participated in a qualified salary reduction arrangement maintained by the employee's employer. (Code Sec. 408(p)(1)(B)).[16]

Employees' rights to all SIMPLE account contributions must be nonforfeitable. (Code Sec. 408(p)(3)) All employees (except those who can be excluded from a qualified plan (Code Sec. 408(p)(4)(B)) who received at least $5,000 in compensation from the employer during any two preceding years (Code Sec. 408(p)(4)(A)(i)), and are reasonably expected to receive at least $5,000 in compensation during the current year (Code Sec. 408(p)(4)(A)(ii)) must be eligible either to elect to make a salary reduction contribution or receive nonelective contributions. (Code Sec. 408(p)(4)(A))[17]

¶ 4373   Contributions to SIMPLE retirement accounts.

Under Code Sec. 404(m)(1) and Code Sec. 404(m)(2)(A), employer contributions to SIMPLE accounts are deductible in the employer's tax year with which (or within which) the calendar year for which the contributions were made ends. Contributions are treated as made for the tax year if they are made (a) on account of that year, and (b) not later than the time for filing that year's tax return (including extensions). (Code Sec. 404(m)(2)(B))[18]

Contributions to SIMPLE plans are excluded from the employee's income similar to the rules for SEPs under Code Sec. 402(h)(1) (¶4368). Employees aren't entitled to a deduction for employer contributions made on their behalf to a SIMPLE retirement account. (Code Sec. 219(b)(4)) Any elective contributions under a SIMPLE retirement plan are included in the sum of elective deferrals, subject to an annual limit on the amount that can be excluded from income. (Code Sec. 402(g)(3)(D))[19] Matching contributions on behalf of self-employed persons aren't treated as employer elective contributions for this purpose. (Code Sec. 408(p)(9))[20]

SIMPLE plans may also incorporate an automatic contribution arrangement (ACA), which permits an employer to make contributions to an employee's SIMPLE IRA without the employee having made an affirmative election to participate in the plan.[21]

¶ 4374   SIMPLE retirement account distributions.

Under Code Sec. 402(k), rules similar to those for distributions from simplified employee pensions (SEPs), apply to SIMPLE retirement accounts. Thus, SIMPLE distributions are taxed under the rules relating to IRAs in the year of distribution. (Code Sec. 402(h)(3))[22] For tax-free rollovers of SIMPLE retirement account distributions, see ¶4347.[23] For early withdrawal penalties for SIMPLE account distributions, see ¶4334.[24]

---

16. ¶H-12361 *et seq.*
17. ¶H-12363
18. ¶H-12372
19. ¶H-12373
20. ¶H-12357

21. ¶H-12365.1
22. ¶H-12374
23. ¶H-12375
24. ¶H-12377

¶ 4375 Tax-Sheltered 403(b) Annuities. ▬▬▬▬▬▬

Under Code Sec. 403(b), employees of tax-exempt educational, charitable, religious, etc., organizations, or public schools get special tax advantages from annuities bought for them by the exempt employers.

Tax-sheltered annuities offer benefits similar to those under a qualified employee plan. The tax isn't imposed when the annuity is bought, but is deferred until payments are received. (Code Sec. 403(b); Reg § 1.403(b)-1)[25] These annuities may be bought only for common law employees of certain exempt educational, charitable, religious, etc., employers, and by or for certain self-employed ministers. (Code Sec. 403(b)(1)(A))[26] The annuity must be nonforfeitable (except for failure to pay premiums) and nontransferable. (Code Sec. 403(b)(1)(C); Reg § 1.401-9(b)(3))[27] Certain elective deferral limits must be met if the annuity is part of a salary reduction arrangement (¶4377). (Code Sec. 403(b)(1)(E))[28] Also, except for annuities bought by church employers, certain nondiscrimination tests must be met. (Code Sec. 403(b)(1)(D), Code Sec. 403(b)(12))[29] Tax-sheltered annuities are treated as defined contribution plans for purposes of the contribution limits (¶4317).[30]

¶ 4376 How tax-sheltered annuity arrangements work.

Under Code Sec. 403(b)(1), employees of a qualifying employer can get a prescribed amount of their compensation in the form of a tax-sheltered annuity. The employee pays no immediate tax on the amount the employer pays for the annuity, but the employee is taxed under the regular annuity rules (¶1352 *et seq.*) when the annuity payments are made.[31]

The tax deferral is denied for distributions attributable to contributions made under a salary reduction agreement (¶4377), unless the annuity provides that payments may be paid only: (1) when the employee attains age 59½, separates from employment, dies, or becomes disabled, or (2) in the case of hardship. (Code Sec. 403(b)(11)) The 10% additional tax on early distributions applies (¶4334). (Code Sec. 72(t)) The contract may not provide for the distribution of any income attributable to such contributions in the case of hardship. (Code Sec. 403(b)(11))[32] Tax-sheltered annuities are subject to the loan rules at ¶4333. (Code Sec. 72(p)(4)(A))[33]

For rollovers to and from Code Sec. 403(b) plans, see ¶4349 and ¶4350.

¶ 4377 Tax-sheltered annuity salary-reduction agreements.

An employee of a qualifying employer can agree to reduce his or her salary or forego an increase as a means of contributing to a 403(b) plan. The rules that apply to cash or deferred arrangements under Code Sec. 401(k) (¶4305) determine how often a salary reduction may be entered into, the compensation to which the agreement applies, and the ability to revoke the agreement.[34]

All of the employer's employees (except those covered by a CODA or an eligible Code Sec. 457 plan) must get a chance to elect to have the employer contribute more than $200 under the salary reduction agreement, on a nondiscriminatory basis, if *any* employee may so elect. (Code Sec. 403(b)(12)(A))[35] The employee's elective deferrals for a year can't exceed the CODA limits, including catch-up contributions for those age 50 or over (¶4305).

25. ¶H-12450 *et seq.*
26. ¶H-12452, H-12453
27. ¶H-12454
28. ¶H-12454 *et seq.*
29. ¶H-12464
30. ¶H-12454 *et seq.*
31. ¶H-12451
32. ¶H-12479
33. ¶H-11066
34. ¶H-12465
35. ¶H-12465

(Code Sec. 403(b)(1)(E); Reg § 1.403(b)-4(c))[36]

A 403(b) plan can include a qualified Roth contribution program (see ¶4363).

The term "salary reduction agreement" includes a plan or arrangement whereby a payment will be made if the employee:

. . . elects to reduce compensation pursuant to a cash or deferred election as defined at Reg § 1.401(k)-1(a)(3);

. . . elects to reduce compensation pursuant to a one-time irrevocable election made at or before the time of initial eligibility to participate in the plan or arrangement (or pursuant to a similar arrangement involving a one-time irrevocable election); or

. . . agrees as a condition of employment (whether the condition is set by statute, contract, or otherwise) to make a contribution that reduces the employee's compensation. (Reg § 31.3121(a)(5)-2(a))[37]

For the saver's credit for lower-income taxpayers' contributions to 403(b) annuities, see ¶2356.

¶ 4378 Tax-sheltered annuity contribution limit.

If a qualifying employer buys a tax-sheltered annuity for an employee and the employee's rights are nonforfeitable, the premium paid is not taxable to the employee at that time, up to the applicable limit for a defined contribution plan under Code Sec. 415 (¶4317). (Code Sec. 403(b)(1), Code Sec. 415(c)(1), Code Sec. 415(k)(4); Reg § 1.403(b)-3(b)(3))[38]

Special limits apply for contributions by church plans. (Code Sec. 415(c)(7))

¶ 4379 "Includible compensation" and "years of service"—tax-sheltered annuities.

A participant's includible compensation is used when applying the defined contribution plan limit under Code Sec. 415 (¶4317) to a Code Sec. 403(b) annuity contract (Code Sec. 415(c)(3)(E)). "Includible compensation" means the amount of compensation received by the employee from an eligible employer (Code Sec. 403(b)(1)(A))[39] that is includible in gross income (disregarding the exclusion for certain foreign source earned income (Code Sec. 911)) for the most recent period ending not later than the close of the employee's tax year that can be counted as one "year of service" and which precedes the tax year by no more than five years (Code Sec. 403(b)(3); Reg § 1.403(b)-2(b)(11)). Amounts contributed by the employer for tax-sheltered annuities are not included. Elective deferrals and any amount contributed or deferred by the employer at the employee's election that is excluded from income under Code Sec. 125 or Code Sec. 457 are included.[40]

The employee's "years of service," which can't be less than one, includes one year for each full year the employee was a full-time employee of the organization buying the annuity for him or her, plus a fraction of each year, as prescribed by regs, for each full year the employee was a part-time employee, or for each part of a year the employee was a full or part-time employee. (Code Sec. 403(b)(4))[41]

An employee's years of service equals the aggregate of the annual work periods during which the employee is employed by the eligible employer. (Reg § 1.403(b)-4(e)(1))

---

36. ¶H-12454
37. ¶H-4650
38. ¶H-12467

39. ¶H-12452
40. ¶H-12468
41. ¶H-12469 *et seq.*

Chapter 22   Farmers

¶ 4500   **Farmers.** ▬▬▬▬▬▬▬▬▬▬▬▬▬▬▬▬▬▬▬▬▬▬▬

Farmers get tax breaks not generally available to others, including: 3-year income averaging (¶4502), a 2-year net operating loss carryback period (¶4503), favorable accounting (¶4505 *et seq.*) and inventory methods (¶4513 *et seq.*), income deferrals (¶4508), capital gain–ordinary loss treatment (¶4524, ¶4526), and the deduction of items normally capitalized (¶4516 *et seq.*).

For tax years before 2026, certain specified agricultural or horticultural cooperatives may also claim a deduction under Code Sec. 199A(g) for a percentage of the cooperative's qualified production activities income (¶1600).

¶ 4501   **Farmers' income and expenses—Schedule F (Form 1040).**

Farm income (and expenses) are reported on Form 1040, Schedule F. A farmer's gross income includes cash and the fair market value of goods received ("barter income") from crops, produce, poultry and livestock. (Reg § 1.61-4(c)) The value of produce consumed by the farmer's family isn't included, but expenses incurred in raising that produce can't be deducted.[1]

Farmers may deduct the ordinary and necessary expenses of operating a farm for profit—e.g., rent, labor, feed (¶4515), fertilizer (¶4516). (Reg § 1.162-12(a))[2] For required capitalization of certain expenses, see ¶4519.

¶ 4502   **Election of three-year averaging for farming or fishing income—Schedule J (Form 1040); elected farm income.**

Under Code Sec. 1301(a), an individual (including a partner in a partnership and a shareholder of an S corporation, but not including an estate or trust) engaged in a farming or fishing business may elect 3-year averaging of "elected farm income" (below) for regular income tax (but not for employment tax) purposes. If the election is made, the tax for the year is equal to the sum of (1) the tax computed on taxable income reduced by elected farm or fishing income, and (2) the increase in tax that would result if taxable income for the three prior tax years were increased by an amount equal to one-third of the elected farm or fishing income. Any adjustment under this provision for any tax year is taken into account in applying this provision for any later tax year. (Code Sec. 1301(a), Code Sec. 1301(b)(3); Reg § 1.1301-1(b)) Taxable income for prior years can be less than zero, but in that case any amount that may provide a benefit in another tax year (such as an NOL) is added back in determining base year taxable income. (Reg § 1.1301-1(d)(2))[3]

Elect by filing Form 1040, Schedule J with a return for the election year (including a late or amended return if the time for filing for a credit or refund hasn't expired). An individual may change or revoke a previous election, if the period of limitation on filing a claim for credit or refund hasn't expired for the election year. (Reg § 1.1301-1(c))

"Elected farm income" means the amount of taxable income for the tax year attributable to any farming or fishing business that's specified in the election to average farm or fishing income (Code Sec. 1301(b)(1)(A); Reg § 1.1301-1(e)(2)), including farm wages paid to an S shareholder (Reg § 1.1301-1(e)(1)), income of fishing-boat crew members compensated by a share of the boat's catch or a share of the catch proceeds (Reg § 1.1301-1(b)(3)), and certain crop-share income. (Reg § 1.1301-1(b)(2)) Gain from the sale or other disposition of property (other than land) regularly used by the taxpayer in a farming or fishing business for a substantial period is treated as attributable to that farming business. (Code

---

1. ¶N-1151
2. ¶N-1301
3. ¶N-1501 *et seq.*

References beginning with a single letter are to paragraphs in Federal Tax Coordinator 2d and RIA's Analysis of Federal Taxes: Income.

Sec. 1301(b)(1)(B); Reg § 1.1301-1(e)(1)(ii)(A))[4] A landlord is engaged in a farming business for farm averaging purposes for rental income based on a share of production (not fixed rent) from a tenant's farming business determined under a written agreement entered into before the tenant begins significant activities on the land. Similar rules apply to fishing-boat lessors who share in the catch. (Reg § 1.1301-1(e)(1)(ii)) Tobacco quota payments don't qualify for income averaging. (Rev. Rul. 2005-57, 2005-32 IRB 267)[5]

Electing income averaging doesn't cause the taxpayer's AMT to increase because regular tax liability for determining the AMT is computed as though the election hadn't been made, see ¶3201.

¶ 4503 "Farming loss" NOL carryback and carryover periods; farmers' election to disregard CARES Act changes.

Although NOLs can be carried forward indefinitely but generally cannot be carried back (¶1818), any part of an NOL that's a "farming loss" can be carried back (under Code Sec. 172(b)(1)(B)(i)) to each of the two tax years preceding the tax year of the loss.[6] A farming loss is the lesser of: (1) the amount that would be the NOL for the tax year if only income and deductions attributable to farming businesses are taken into account, or (2) the amount of the NOL for the tax year. (Code Sec. 172(b)(1)(B)(ii))[7] In determining the order in which NOLs are absorbed, a farming loss for any tax year is treated as a separate NOL for that tax year and is taken into account after the remaining part of that year's NOL. (Code Sec. 172(b)(1)(B)(iii))[8] Farmers may elect to forego the 2-year carryback. The election, which is made as prescribed by IRS and by the return due date (including extensions) for the tax year of the NOL, is irrevocable for the tax year for which it is made. (Code Sec. 172(b)(1)(B)(iv))[9]

For general limitation of NOL deductions to 80% of taxable income, see ¶1816 *et seq.*).

¶ 4504 "Excess business loss" disallowance rule limits deduction of farm losses; post-2028 "excess farm loss" disallowance rule.

Noncorporate taxpayers—including farmers—are subject to the "excess business loss" disallowance rule under Code Sec. 461(l) (see ¶1774). For tax years beginning before Jan. 1, 2029, the excess farm loss disallowance rule under Code Sec. 461(j), which limited (except for C corporations) the amount of farming losses that could be claimed for any tax year in which certain subsidies were received, is suspended.[10]

¶ 4505 Farmers' accounting methods: cash, accrual, crop, and hybrid methods.

Under Reg § 1.61-4, farmers (unless listed at ¶4510) may use the cash method (¶4506), the accrual method (¶4509), the crop method (¶4512), or a "hybrid" method combining any of these methods if it clearly reflects income (¶2813). (Reg § 1.61-4, Reg § 1.446-1(c), Reg § 1.471-6(a))[11]

Farmers aren't required to use inventories (regardless of whether they satisfy the gross receipts test under Code Sec. 448(c); see ¶2814) unless they are subject to the uniform capitalization rules (¶4519). (Reg § 1.471-6(a))[12] But a farmer that does use inventories must use the accrual method at least for purchases and sales.[13]

---

4. ¶N-1515 *et seq.*
5. ¶N-1501 *et seq.*
6. ¶M-4311
7. ¶M-4311
8. ¶M-4303

9. ¶M-4313
10. ¶N-1331 *et seq.*
11. ¶N-1010 *et seq.*
12. ¶N-1100 *et seq.*
13. ¶N-1017

¶ 4506   **Cash-method farmers—when income is included and expenses are deducted.**

Cash method farmers include income in the year actually or constructively received, whichever is earlier (¶2815). Under Reg § 1.61-4(a), gross income includes receipts of: (1) proceeds from sales of *raised* livestock or produce; (2) profits from the sale of any *purchased* property, including livestock, (3) breeding fees, (4) fees from renting teams, machinery or land, (5) taxable subsidy and conservation payments, (6) crop insurance proceeds, and (7) all other gross income. (Reg § 1.61-4(a))[14] For deferral of insurance proceeds and forced livestock sales, see ¶4508.

Expenses are ordinarily deductible in the year paid (other than the cost of animals and plants bought for resale, see ¶4507). (Reg § 1.61-4(a))[15] For feed expenses, see ¶4515, and for pre-paid expenses, see ¶4517. An option to accelerate the receipt of any payment under a production flexibility contract that is payable under the FAIR Act of 1996 as in effect on Dec. 17, '99 won't accelerate the recognition of income unless the option is exercised. (Sec. 525 of P.L. 106-170) The constructive receipt rules also don't apply to options to receive payments under the Farm Security and Rural Investment Act of 2002.[16]

¶ 4507   **Cash method farmer's deduction of costs of purchased animals and plants—election to deduct in year bought or year sold.**

Cash method farmers generally deduct the costs of animals and plants bought for resale in the year they are sold. (Reg § 1.61-4(a)) But for the following animals and plants, a farmer may elect to deduct the costs either for the year they are purchased or for the year they are sold, if the method chosen clearly reflects income:

. . . baby chicks and pullets bought for raising and resale;

. . . hens bought for commercial egg production;

. . . seeds and young plants (other than Christmas trees and timber) bought for further development and cultivation before sale. (Reg § 1.162-12)[17]

The farmer makes the election by deducting the cost for the first year in which the items are bought. Once the farmer elects this option, it must be used consistently until IRS consents to a change (¶2828).[18]

¶ 4508   **One-year deferral elections for cash-method farmers—"disaster" receipts.**

Under Code Sec. 451(f), a cash method farmer can elect to defer reporting certain insurance proceeds and federal disaster payments (including payments under Title II (but not Title I) of the '88 Disaster Assistance Act) until the tax year after the year of the destruction or damage to, or inability to plant, the crops, if the farmer shows that under his or her practice, the income from the crops would have been reported in a later year. To elect, check the box in Part I on Schedule F and attach a statement to the return (or amended return) for the year payments are received. (Code Sec. 451(f); Reg § 1.451-6)[19]

One-year deferral also may be elected for income from livestock sold on account of a drought, flood or other weather-related condition so severe that the sale had to take place in an earlier year than normal. Elect on a statement attached to the return for the sale year. (Code Sec. 451(g)(1); Reg § 1.451-7(g)) However, if the period for buying replacement property for such livestock under the involuntary conversion rules (¶2431) is extended to four years from the end of the year of sale (see ¶2438), the election of one-year deferral is

---

14. ¶N-1013
15. ¶N-1013
16. ¶N-1152.1

17. ¶s N-1021, N-1022
18. ¶N-1022
19. ¶N-1024 *et seq.*

valid if made during that replacement period. (Code Sec. 451(g)(3))[20]

¶ 4509 Accrual-method farmers; when income is included and expenses are deducted; calculation of gross income.

Under Code Sec. 461(h), accrual farmers include farm income for the year earned, regardless of when payment is received, and deduct farm expenses for the year the "all events test" is met (¶2818 *et seq.*). Accrual farmers also must use inventories to determine gross income (¶4513). (Code Sec. 461(h); Reg § 1.61-4(b), Reg § 1.446-1(c))[21] For when the accrual method is mandatory, see ¶4510.

An accrual farmer's gross income for a tax year is the sum of: (1) the sales price of all livestock and other products held for sale that are sold during the year, (2) the inventory value of the livestock, etc. (i.e., the proceeds from the disposition of livestock, etc., during the year, plus the inventory value of livestock, etc., not sold at the end of the year, reduced by the inventory value of livestock, etc., on hand at the start of the year, and by the cost of any livestock, etc., bought during the year and included in inventory), (3) miscellaneous farm receipts, e.g., fees from breeding, (4) all subsidy and conservation payments includible that year, plus (5) gross income from all other sources. Crop shares are included in the year they are reduced to money or its equivalent. (Reg § 1.61-4(b))[22]

¶ 4510 When accrual accounting is mandatory for farmers.

Code Sec. 447(c) provides that the accrual method is *not* required, and the cash method may be used, by farming C corporations (and farming partnerships with a C corporation partner) that satisfy a gross receipts test—i.e., with annual average gross receipts for the three prior tax years that don't exceed $29 million for 2023 or $27 million for 2022. (Code Sec. 447(c))[23]

Farming C corporations (and farming partnerships with a C corporation partner) that don't satisfy the gross receipts test must use the accrual method, unless they qualify under one of the limited exceptions below. The accrual method must also be used by tax shelters, including farm syndicates (¶4511), and by farmers that use inventories (¶4705).

S corporations (Code Sec. 447(c)(1), certain corporations (and partnerships having a corporate partner) described in Code Sec. 447(e),[24] and nurseries, sod farms, and raisers and harvesters of trees (other than fruit and nut trees) (Code Sec. 447(a))[25] aren't required to use the accrual method.

¶ 4511 Tax shelters, including "farming syndicates," must use accrual method.

Under Code Sec. 448(a)(3), all tax shelters, including farming syndicates, must use the accrual method. (Code Sec. 448(a)(3))[26] For pre-paid expenses, see ¶4517. For uniform capitalization rules, see ¶4519. For tax shelter losses for AMT purposes, see ¶3211.

A farming syndicate is any partnership (or other noncorporate enterprise) or S corporation engaged in the business of farming if:

(1) at any time, interests in the partnership, etc., have been offered for sale in an offering required to be registered with any federal or state agency having authority to regulate the offering of securities for sale; (Code Sec. 461(k)(1)(A)or

(2) more than 35% of the losses during any periods are allocable to limited partners or limited entrepreneurs (Code Sec. 461(k)(1)(B)); or

(3) it's a tax shelter. (Code Sec. 461(i)(3), Code Sec. 461(i)(4))[27]

---

20. ¶N-1031 *et seq.*
21. ¶N-1017
22. ¶N-1017
23. ¶N-1037 *et seq.*
24. ¶N-1049
25. ¶N-1036 *et seq.*
26. ¶G-2056
27. ¶G-2457.1

The Court of Appeals for the Fifth Circuit held that Code Sec. 461(j)(2), under which the interest of any individual who has actively participated in the management of any farming trade or business is treated as not held by a limited partner or limited entrepreneur under (2), above, could be met by an individual who actively participated and owned a super-majority interest in a farming partnership through her wholly owned S corp. IRS, however, believes that the active participation exception applies only to an interest held by an individual, and generally won't follow the Fifth Circuit's decision outside of the Fifth Circuit.[28]

¶ 4512 Crop method of accounting—farmers.

Reg § 1.61-4(c) allows a farmer, with IRS consent, to use the crop method to report income from crops (other than timber) for which the process of planting, harvesting and sale isn't completed within the same tax year. (Reg § 1.61-4(c))[29] Under this method, all expenses of the crop (including expenses of seed or young plants) are charged, and all crop receipts are credited, to a crop account. Profit (or loss) is realized and included in (or deducted from) income only in the year the crop is harvested and disposed of. (Reg § 1.61-4(c), Reg § 1.162-12(a))[30]

¶ 4513 Rules that apply to farmers' inventories.

A farmer using inventories (¶4514) *must* inventory:

. . . all livestock and poultry, whether raised or purchased, held primarily for sale (Reg § 1.61-4(b));

. . . all harvested and purchased farm products held for sale, feed, or seed, such as grain, hay ensilage, concentrates, cotton, tobacco;

. . . supplies, unless only small amounts are on hand;

. . . if in the hatchery business, eggs in incubation and growing and pre-market chickens. (Inventories *may* be used for hens primarily held for egg production that are also held for sale after their egg-producing life.)[31]

Livestock held for dairy, breeding, sporting or draft purposes may be inventoried at the taxpayer's election. But raised livestock must be inventoried by farmers using the unit-livestock-price method. (Reg § 1.61-4(b), Reg § 1.471-6(f))[32]

¶ 4514 Inventory valuation methods for farmers—cost method, lower-of-cost-or-market method, farm-price method, and unit-livestock-price method.

Methods that farmers use to value inventory include:

. . . *Cost method* (¶2855). (Reg § 1.471-3)[33]

. . . *Lower-of-cost-or-market method* (¶2856). (Reg § 1.471-4)[34]

. . . *Farm-price method.* Each item, raised or purchased, is valued at its market price less estimated direct cost of disposition. A farmer using this method must use it for all inventory, except that the unit-livestock-price method may be used for livestock at the farmer's election. (Reg § 1.471-6(d))[35]

. . . *Unit-livestock-price method.* Livestock is reasonably classified according to kind and age. A standard unit price is used for each animal within a class. Unit prices must reflect costs capitalized under the uniform capitalization rules (¶4519). Once elected, the "unit-price" method is binding and cannot be changed without IRS's consent. Users of

---

28. ¶G-2457.1
29. ¶N-1018 *et seq.*
30. ¶N-1019
31. ¶N-1102

32. ¶s N-1109, N-1113
33. ¶N-1106
34. ¶N-1107
35. ¶N-1112

this method must annually reevaluate their unit prices and adjust them to reflect increases or decreases in the costs of raising livestock. (Reg § 1.471-6(f))[36]

¶ 4515   Feed expenses of farmers; rules for deducting pre-paid feed.

The cost of feed is a deductible business expense. (Reg § 1.162-12(a))[37] A cash method farmer may deduct, in the year paid, the cost of feed that the farmer's livestock will consume that year. Payments for feed to be used in the next tax year ("pre-paid feed") aren't deductible until the year of consumption, except the farmer may deduct pre-paid feed expenses in the payment year if: (1) the payment represents a purchase and not a deposit, (2) the advance payment is for a business purpose and not merely for tax avoidance, *and* (3) deduction in the payment year doesn't materially distort income.[38] For pre-paid farm expenses generally, see ¶4517.

¶ 4516   Fertilizer, lime, etc. expenses of farmers.

The cost of acquiring fertilizer, lime, marl, and other materials used to enrich, neutralize, or condition farmland, and the costs of applying them, are deductible under Code Sec. 180(a) in the year the costs are paid or incurred if the benefit doesn't last beyond one year. If the benefit lasts substantially more than a year the costs generally are capitalized but the farmer may elect to deduct them in the year paid or incurred (Code Sec. 180(a))[39] by deducting them on his or her return for that year. (Code Sec. 180(c); Reg § 1.180-2)[40] The election to deduct isn't allowable for costs of preparing land not previously used for farming by the taxpayer or by the farmer's tenant. (Code Sec. 180(b); Reg § 1.180-1(b))[41]

If fertilizer expenses are capitalized, the taxpayer may deduct a portion of the capitalized amounts for each year the benefits last.[42]

¶ 4517   Rules limiting deduction of pre-paid farm expenses.

Code Sec. 464(a) limits a cash-method taxpayer's current deduction for pre-paid farm expenses (i.e., for farm supplies that won't be used until a later tax year) to one-half of the other deductible farming expenses for the year (for a special rule for feed, see ¶4515). The "excess" part (i.e., over that one-half amount) isn't deductible until the year the supplies are used. (Code Sec. 464(a); Code Sec. 464(d))[43]

But this limit *doesn't apply* if the taxpayer's (or a family member's) principal home (within the meaning of Code Sec. 121, see ¶2439) is a farm or his or her principal business is farming, if: (1) for the three preceding tax years, the farmer's total pre-paid farm expenses are less than 50% of total other deductible farm expenses, or (2) for the current year, pre-paid farm expenses are more than 50% of other farm expenses because of a change in business operations attributable to extraordinary circumstances. (Code Sec. 464(d)(2))[44]

¶ 4518   Pre-productive period expenses of farmers.

Reg § 1.162-12(a) allows the taxpayer to either deduct or capitalize certain costs of developing and operating his or her farm and crops (e.g., taxes, interest, upkeep) during its pre-productive period (Reg § 1.162-12(a))[45] (subject to the uniform capitalization rules, see ¶4519). But capital expenditures aren't deductible.[46] The pre-productive period begins when the farmer first acquires the seed or plant, and ends when the plant produces marketable quantities, or is reasonably expected to be sold or otherwise disposed of. (Code

---

36. ¶N-1113
37. ¶N-1311
38. ¶N-1312
39. ¶N-1306
40. ¶N-1307
41. ¶N-1307

42. ¶N-1307
43. ¶N-1319 *et seq.*
44. ¶N-1319
45. ¶N-1302
46. ¶N-1303

Sec. 263A(e)(3))[47]

¶ 4519   Application of uniform capitalization (UNICAP) rules to farmers.

Under Code Sec. 263A, farmers and ranchers are subject to UNICAP for taxpayers generally (¶1639) for the production, growing, or raising of property that: (i) is produced by a farmer required to use the accrual method (¶4510), (Code Sec. 263A(a), Code Sec. 263A(d)(1); Reg § 1.263A-4(a), Reg § 1.263A-4(b)) or (ii) has a pre-productive period (¶4518) of more than two years. (Code Sec. 263A(d)(1)(A)(ii))

For taxpayers not required to use the accrual method, UNICAP *doesn't apply* to costs related to any animal, or plant with a pre-productive period of two years or less, which is produced by a taxpayer in a farming business. (Code Sec. 263A(d)(1)(A); Reg § 1.263A-4(a)(2))[48] The pre-productive period is the period before the first marketable crop or yield, for plants that have more than one crop or yield (e.g., the orange tree); the period before a crop or yield is disposed of, for the crop or yield of a plant that will have more than one crop or yield (e.g., the orange); or, for any other plant, the period before it is disposed of. (Reg § 1.263A-4(b)(2)) IRS has provided a list of plants with pre-productive periods in excess of 2 years.[49]

For exception for replanting because of casualties, see ¶4520. For election out of UNICAP, see ¶4521.

¶ 4520   Exception to uniform capitalization (UNICAP) rules for replanting because of casualty.

Code Sec. 263A(d)(2)(A) provides that UNICAP (¶4519) doesn't apply to costs incurred for the replanting, cultivation, maintenance and development of plants bearing edible crops for human consumption (including citrus or almond) that were lost or damaged (while in the taxpayer's hands) by freezing temperatures, disease, drought, pests, or casualty. (Code Sec. 263A(d)(2)(A); Reg § 1.263A-4(e)(1), Reg § 1.263A-4(e)(4))[50]

This casualty exception generally applies to the costs of the owner of the plants at the time of the loss or damage. But costs paid or incurred by another person (payor) in any tax year also may qualify if in that year: (1) the owner has a more-than-50% equity interest in the plants, and (2) the payor owns any of the remaining equity interest in them *and* materially participates in their planting, maintenance, cultivation or development. (Code Sec. 263A(d)(2)(B); Reg § 1.263A-4(e)(2))[1]

For amounts paid or incurred for replanting, etc. before Dec. 23, 2027 for citrus plants lost or damaged due to casualty, the costs may also be deducted by a person other than the taxpayer if (1) the taxpayer has an equity interest of not less than 50% in the replanted citrus plants at all times during the tax year in which the replanting costs are paid or incurred and the other person holds any part of the remaining equity interest, *or* (2) the other person acquires all of the taxpayer's equity interest in the land on which the lost or damaged citrus plants were located at the time of the loss or damage, and the replanting is on that land. (Code Sec. 263A(d)(2)(C)) This temporary allowance removes the material participation requirement to qualify for the exception.[2] IRS has provided automatic consent for farmers to change their method of accounting from applying Code Sec. 263A to citrus replanting costs to instead deducting those costs under Code Sec. 263A(d)(2)(C).[3]

¶ 4521   Farmers' election out of uniform capitalization (UNICAP) rules; effects of election; how to elect.

Except as noted below, under Code Sec. 263A(d)(3)(A), a farmer may elect to have

---

47. ¶N-1074.1
48. ¶N-1071 et seq.
49. ¶N-1074.2A
50. ¶N-1081

1. ¶N-1082
2. ¶N-1082.2
3. ¶G-2203.62A

UNICAP (¶4519) *not* apply to any plant produced in the farmer's farm business. If the election is allowed, a farmer may elect to deduct currently all preproductive costs of plants that would be deductible but for UNICAP. (Code Sec. 263A(d)(3)(A))[4]

If the taxpayer or any related person (as specially defined) makes the election, Code Sec. 168(g)(2) alternative (i.e., straight-line) depreciation must be used for all of the taxpayer's property used predominantly in the farming business that was placed in service in any tax year during which the election is in effect. (Code Sec. 263A(e)(2)(A); Reg § 1.263A-4(d)(4)(ii))[5]

If the election is made, any plant for which amounts would have been capitalized *but for* the election is treated as Code Sec. 1245 property (if it's not otherwise Code Sec. 1245 property). (Code Sec. 263A(e)(1)(A)(i); Reg § 1.263A-4(d)(4)(i)) Deductible amounts that, but for the election, would have been capitalized, are treated as depreciation deductions for Code Sec. 1245 purposes, so that they are recaptured as ordinary income when the product is disposed of, see ¶2674. (Code Sec. 263A(e)(1)(A)(ii); Code Sec. 263A(e)(1)(B); Reg § 1.263A-4(d)(4)(i))[6]

The election can't be made for any item attributable to the planting, cultivation, maintenance or development of any citrus or almond grove (or part of a grove) that's incurred before the close of the 4th tax year beginning with the tax year the trees were planted. For this purpose, the portion of a grove planted in one tax year must be treated separately from the portion planted in another tax year. (Code Sec. 263A(d)(3)(C); Reg § 1.263A-4(d)(2))[7]

A taxpayer makes the election by *not* applying the rules of Code Sec. 263A to determine the capitalized costs of plants produced in a farming business and by applying the rules of Reg § 1.263A-4(d)(4) on the original return for the first tax year capitalization of Code Sec. 263A costs is required. (Code Sec. 263A(d)(3)(D); Reg § 1.263A-4(d)(3)(i))[8] Other than a taxpayer that's no longer eligible for the small business exception to UNICAP (¶1639) and that elects out of UNICAP under Reg § 1.263A-4(d)(1), a taxpayer that doesn't make the automatic election described above must get IRS consent (¶2828) to change accounting methods. (Reg § 1.263A-4(d)(3)(ii))[9] The election can't be made by a corporation, partnership, or tax shelter required to use the accrual method of accounting, see ¶4510 and ¶4511. For partnerships or S corporations, the election is made by the partner, shareholder, or member. (Code Sec. 263A(d)(3)(B))[10]

¶ 4522 Soil and water conservation, anti-erosion, and endangered species recovery costs; election to deduct; how made—farmers.

Code Sec. 175 allows farmers to deduct currently, as business expenses, certain outlays for soil and water conservation or erosion prevention that are incurred to maintain the farm and preserve its normal productivity, and not to increase its value or convert it to a new use. Costs that result in the acquisition of depreciable property must be capitalized.[11]

A farmer may elect to deduct certain nondepreciable expenditures for conservation, etc., of land he or she uses for farming (Code Sec. 175(a)) if the expenditures are consistent with a federal or state approved conservation plan. (Code Sec. 175(c)(3))[12] Qualifying expenditures include (1) costs of: treating or moving earth (e.g., leveling, terracing or restoring fertility); constructing and protecting diversion channels, drainage ditches, earthen dams; eradicating brush; planting windbreaks; producing vegetation primarily to conserve soil or water, or prevent soil erosion, and (2) expenses paid or incurred for endangered species recovery, including site-specific management actions under the Endangered Species Act of '73. (Code Sec. 175(c); Reg § 1.175-2(a), Reg § 1.175-2(b)(2)) Costs of draining or filling

4. ¶N-1084
5. ¶N-1090
6. ¶N-1093
7. ¶N-1084
8. ¶N-1085

9. ¶N-1085
10. ¶N-1084
11. ¶N-1401
12. ¶N-1402

wetlands or for center pivot irrigation systems don't qualify. (Code Sec. 175(c)(3)(B)) Nor does the election apply to depreciable assets. (Reg § 1.175-2(b)(1))[13]

The amount of conservation, etc., expenses a farmer may deduct in any tax year under this election can't exceed 25% of the farmer's gross income from farming for the year. Any excess may be carried over to and deducted in the next tax year (subject to that year's 25% ceiling). (Code Sec. 175(b); Reg § 1.175-5(b))[14]

Elect by deducting the expenses on the return for the first tax year they are incurred. (Reg § 1.175-6(a))[15] IRS consent is needed to elect for a year other than that first year. (Code Sec. 175(d)(2))[16] Once the election is made, a farmer must continue to deduct all qualifying expenditures (subject to the 25% ceiling) unless IRS consents to a change. (Code Sec. 175(e))[17]

A farmer must recapture as ordinary income (use Form 4797) part of the conservation, etc., expenses if the farm land is disposed of after being held for less than 10 years. (Code Sec. 1252)[18]

¶ 4523   Rules that apply to depreciation of farm property—Form 4562.

A farmer may take depreciation deductions (on Form 4562) on property used in a farming business, including: buildings (except the farmer's dwelling); farm machinery; other physical property (not including land); orchards (trees and vines bearing fruits or nuts); and draft, breeding, sporting or dairy livestock (unless inventoried). (Reg § 1.167(a)-6(b))[19]

Most MACRS farming property (subject to certain exceptions; see below) may be depreciated under the 200% declining balance method (¶1921).[20]

observation: Thus, farming property can be depreciated under the 200% declining balance method except for (1) buildings and trees or vines bearing fruits or nuts (to which the straight-line method applies), (2) property for which the taxpayer elects either the straight-line method or 150% declining balance method, (3) 15- or 20-year MACRS property that has to be depreciated under the 150% declining balance method, and (4) property subject to the ADS. Land improvements other than buildings are 15-year property, and fences and grain bins have a 7-year recovery period, and single-purpose agricultural or horticultural structures (e.g., greenhouses, specialized housing for livestock) have a 10-year recovery period.

Machinery and equipment used in agriculture is included within the 5-year MACRS class (¶1913).[21] Certain MACRS property, however, must be depreciated under ADS (¶1927), including any MACRS property with a recovery period of 10 years or more that is held by an "electing farm business"; i.e., one that elects under Code Sec. 163(j)(7)(C) to not be subject to the business interest deduction limitation (¶1710).[22]

observation: A farming business that satisfies an average gross receipts test (see ¶1710) and isn't a tax shelter isn't subject to the business interest deduction limitations. Thus, the taxpayer that owns it doesn't have to decide whether or not to be make the election for that real property trade or business.

recommendation: In deciding whether to make the Code Sec. 163(j)(7)(C) election, a taxpayer with a farming business should compare the overall effect on it of the business interest limitation (which will generally have the result of deferring deductions) to claiming depreciation deductions at a decelerated rate and over a longer period.

The cost of *purchased* dairy, etc., livestock may be recovered under MACRS. The cost of

---

13. ¶N-1407, N-1409
14. ¶N-1415
15. ¶N-1420
16. ¶N-1421
17. ¶N-1422
18. ¶N-1423
19. ¶N-1304
20. ¶L-9402.2
21. ¶N-1361
22. ¶L-9402.2

raised livestock may be either deducted (but costs so deducted can't be included in depreciable basis) (Reg § 1.61-4(a), Reg § 1.162-12(a)) or capitalized as the taxpayer chooses.[23] But accrual method farmers using inventories can't depreciate any purchased dairy, etc., livestock that's inventoried. (Reg § 1.167(a)-6)[24]

¶ 4524 Dispositions of unharvested crop with land.

Gain or loss on an unharvested crop sold, exchanged, or compulsorily or involuntarily converted with the underlying land qualifies under the capital gain-ordinary loss rule of Code Sec. 1231 (¶2666 *et seq.*), if: (1) the land was used in the taxpayer's trade or business and was held for the long-term capital gain holding period (¶2652), *and* (2) the land and crops are sold at the same time and to the same person. (Code Sec. 1231(b)(4)) It doesn't matter how long the crops were held, or their state of maturity. (Reg § 1.1231-1(f))[25]

¶ 4525 Treatment of gain on disposition of farm land that is converted wetlands or highly erodible croplands.

Gain on the disposition of land used for farming that is converted wetland or highly erodible cropland is ordinary income under Code Sec. 1257. Loss is long-term capital loss. (Code Sec. 1257)[26]

¶ 4526 Treatment of gain on dispositions of breeding, dairy, sporting, draft livestock.

Gains and losses from the sale, exchange, or involuntary conversion of animals held for draft, breeding, dairy, or sporting purposes qualify for capital gain-ordinary loss treatment under Code Sec. 1231 (¶2666 *et seq.*) as follows:

. . . cattle and horses held for 24 months or more from the date of acquisition;

. . . other livestock (except poultry) held for 12 months or more from the date of acquisition. (Code Sec. 1231(a), Code Sec. 1231(b)(3); Reg § 1.1231-2(a))[27]

Inventorying the livestock doesn't preclude Code Sec. 1231 treatment if the animal is held for the required purposes and relevant period and not for sale to customers.[28]

¶ 4527 Tax treatment of special farming-related payments—Schedule F (Form 1040); conservation programs; pledges of crops to secure CCC loans.

Conservation programs. Unless the taxpayer elects out (Code Sec. 126(c)), gross income doesn't include the excludable part of payments received under certain cost-sharing conservation programs specified in Code Sec. 126(a)(1) to Code Sec. 126(a)(8). (Code Sec. 126(b))[29] Part or all of the cost-share payments made under the Forest Health Protection Program may qualify for the Code Sec. 126 exclusion.

Pledge of crops to secure CCC loan. Farmers who pledge part or all of their production to secure a Commodity Credit Corporation (CCC) loan can make a special election to treat the loan proceeds as income in the year received and obtain a basis in the commodity for the amount reported as income. Thus, instead of a loan, the money advanced to the farmer may be treated as the sales price of the commodity pledged for the loan. Elect by reporting the CCC loan proceeds as income on Form 1040, Schedule F for the year the loan is received and attaching a statement to the return showing the details of the CCC loan.[30]

---

23. ¶s N-1020, N-1350 *et seq.*
24. ¶N-1351
25. ¶N-1206
26. ¶N-1431 *et seq.*

27. ¶s N-1209, N-1223
28. ¶N-1209
29. ¶N-1181
30. ¶N-1164

Chapter 23 Foreign Income—Foreign Taxpayers—Foreign Currency Transactions

¶ 4600 **Foreign Income of U.S. persons.** ▬▬▬▬▬▬▬▬▬▬▬▬

U.S. persons (Code Sec. 7701(a)(30)) are generally taxable on their worldwide income, subject to a participation exemption for certain corporate taxpayers (see ¶3314). Specific rules apply to U.S. citizens (¶4601), resident aliens (¶4602), and domestic corporations (¶4604). Individual U.S. persons who work or live abroad may be allowed certain exclusions or deductions (see ¶4605 *et seq.*). U.S. persons who conduct businesses through foreign corporations may be taxed on the corporations' undistributed income (see ¶4611 *et seq.*). A foreign tax credit is available to mitigate the risk of double taxation (see ¶2360 *et seq.*). U.S. persons who give up U.S. citizenship or terminate long-term U.S. residency are subject to expatriation tax rules (see ¶4639).

¶ 4601 **Taxation of U.S. citizens on worldwide income.**

U.S. citizens, whether they reside in the U.S. or abroad, are generally subject to U.S. income tax on their income from sources within and without the U.S. (Reg § 1.1-1(b)) A U.S. citizen is every person born or naturalized in the U.S. and subject to its jurisdiction. (Reg § 1.1-1(c))[1] A foreign tax credit is available to mitigate the risk of double taxation (see ¶2360 *et seq.*).[2]

¶ 4602 **Taxation of resident aliens on worldwide income; substantial presence test (Form 8843, Form 8840 to claim exemptions); first-year election to be taxed as resident.**

A resident alien individual generally is subject to U.S. tax in the same manner as a U.S. citizen (¶4601), with certain minor exceptions. (Reg § 1.1-1(b))[3]

An alien individual is treated as a U.S. resident for any calendar year in which he or she (1) is a lawful permanent resident (the green card test), (2) meets a substantial presence test, or (3) makes the first year election. (Code Sec. 7701(b)(1)(A))[4]

Subject to certain exceptions, an individual meets the substantial presence test (i.e., is a U.S. resident) for any calendar (current) year if: (1) he or she is present in the U.S. on at least 31 days during the year, *and* (2) the sum of the number of days he or she was present in the U.S. during the current year and the two preceding calendar years, in each case multiplied by a multiplier (1 for the current year, 1/3 for the first preceding year, and 1/6 for the second preceding year), is at least 183. (Code Sec. 7701(b)(3)(A))

An individual isn't treated as present in the U.S. on any day on which he or she is an exempt individual (e.g., foreign official, teacher), or on which a medical condition (including COVID-19/coronavirus) prevents him or her from leaving the U.S. Form 8843 is used to claim the exemption. (Code Sec. 7701(b)(3)(D); Code Sec. 7701(b)(5)) Further, an individual who otherwise meets the substantial presence test can avoid being treated as a U.S. resident that year if the individual: (1) is present in the U.S. on fewer than 183 days during the year, and (2) files a "closer connection statement" on Form 8840 which establishes that for the year, he or she has a tax home (¶1540) in a foreign country to which he or she has a closer connection than to the U.S. (Code Sec. 7701(b)(3)(B))[5]

A qualifying alien who arrives in the U.S. too late in a calendar year to meet the substantial presence test may under certain circumstances elect (on a statement attached

---

1. ¶O-1001 *et seq.*
2. ¶O-4000 *et seq.*
3. ¶O-1008 *et seq.*

4. ¶O-1051 *et seq.*
5. ¶O-1057 *et seq.*

References beginning with a single letter are to paragraphs in Federal Tax Coordinator 2d and RIA's Analysis of Federal Taxes: Income.

to the return) to be taxed as a U.S. resident for part of that first (election) year if the substantial presence test is met in the *next* calendar year. (Code Sec. 7701(b)(4); Reg § 301.7701(b)-4(c)(3))[6]

¶ 4603   Taxation of bona fide residents of U.S. possessions (Puerto Rico, American Samoa, Guam or CNMI, Virgin Islands)—Forms 1040-PR, 4563.

Puerto Rico. Under Code Sec. 876 and Code Sec. 933, a nonresident alien individual (NRA, ¶4624) who is a bona fide resident of Puerto Rico during the entire tax year is taxed in the same manner as a resident alien individual (¶4602), except that income from Puerto Rico sources (except amounts received for services performed as an employee of the U.S.) is excluded (on Form 1040-PR) from gross income. The exclusion is available to all bona fide residents of Puerto Rico, regardless of U.S. citizenship/residence status. (Code Sec. 876; Code Sec. 933(1); Reg § 1.1-1(b))[7]

American Samoa. An NRA who is a bona fide resident of American Samoa for the entire tax year is taxed in the same manner as a resident alien individual, except that gross income for U.S. income tax purposes doesn't include income from sources within American Samoa, or income effectively connected with the individual's conduct of a trade or business in American Samoa. The exclusion (available to all bona fide residents of American Samoa, regardless of U.S. citizenship/residence status) doesn't apply to amounts received for services performed as an employee if Form 4563 is used for the exclusion of income for bona fide residents of American Samoa. (Code Sec. 876; Code Sec. 931; Reg § 1.1-1(b))[8]

Guam or the CNMI. Bona fide Guam or CNMI residents during the entire tax year, whether or not they are U.S. citizens or resident aliens, file their income tax returns with the possession of which they are bona fide residents, and need not file a U.S. income tax return or pay any U.S. income tax, provided they fully report and pay their taxes to the possession. (former Code Sec. 935)[9]

Virgin Islands (VI). An individual who is a bona fide VI resident for the entire tax year (or files a joint return with such a person) files a VI return and pays VI tax on his or her worldwide income for that year. If the individual properly files and reports all income from all sources on a VI tax return and pays the VI tax, the individual isn't subject to tax in the U.S. A U.S. citizen or resident, other than a bona fide resident of the VI, who has VI source income, files an income tax return for the tax year with both the U.S. and the VI, and pays VI tax on the VI-source income (and receives a credit against U.S. tax for that amount). (Code Sec. 932; Code Sec. 934)[10]

Bona fide resident. A bona fide resident of a possession is a person who is present for at least 183 days during the tax year in that possession, and who doesn't have a tax home (¶1540) outside the specified possession during the tax year and doesn't have a closer connection to the U.S. or a foreign country than to that possession. (Code Sec. 937(a))[11]

¶ 4604   Taxation of domestic corporations (Form 1120); treatment of IC-DISC (Form 4876-A).

Under Code Sec. 11, Code Sec. 61, and Code Sec. 63, a domestic corporation is generally taxed on its taxable income from whatever source derived. A domestic corporation is one created or organized in or under the laws of the U.S. or any state. (Code Sec. 7701(a)(4))[12]

A qualifying domestic corporation that elects on Form 4876-A to be a small interest-charge domestic international sales corporation (IC-DISC) is not subject to tax. Instead, its shareholders are taxed on their pro rata shares of IC-DISC income. An IC-DISC can retain the first $10 million of qualified export receipts tax-free until these are actually distributed

---

6. ¶O-1072 *et seq.*
7. ¶O-1450 *et seq.*
8. ¶O-1430 *et seq.*
9. ¶O-1400 *et seq.*

10. ¶O-1470 *et seq.*
11. ¶O-1085 *et seq.*
12. ¶O-1006

to shareholders, if it pays an interest charge on the accumulated untaxed income. (Code Sec. 991 *et seq.*)[13]

¶ 4605   Partial exclusion for a qualified individual's foreign earned income— Form 2555.

Under Code Sec. 911(a)(1) and Code Sec. 911(b)(2), a qualified individual (¶4608) may elect on Form 2555 to exclude from gross income his or her foreign earned income up to the inflation-adjusted exclusion amount (discussed below) and subject to limitations (¶4609).[14] For a separate exclusion for foreign housing costs, see ¶4606.

An individual's foreign earned income is his or her earned income from foreign countries attributable to services performed during the period he or she was a qualified individual, with certain exceptions, including amounts paid by the U.S. government or its agency or instrumentality to its employees. (Code Sec. 911(b)(1))[15] Earned income means wages and other amounts received as compensation (i.e., not as a distribution of profits) for personal services actually rendered, including the fair market value of compensation paid with property (Code Sec. 911(d)(2)(A); Reg § 1.911-3(b)(1)) and, where both personal services and capital are material income-producing factors in the taxpayer's noncorporate business, a reasonable allowance (up to 30% of his or her share of the net profits) as compensation for personal services. (Code Sec. 911(d)(2)(B))[16]

An individual's foreign earned income exclusion amount for a tax year can't exceed his or her foreign earned income for the year, as computed on a daily basis at an annual rate of $112,000 for 2022 ($120,000 in 2023). (Code Sec. 911(b)(2)(A), Code Sec. 911(b)(2)(D)) For married couples where both spouses are qualified individuals, each chooses whether to elect the exclusion. (Reg § 1.911-5(a)(1)) The amount of the exclusion is computed separately for each spouse based on the income attributable to that spouse's services. If the spouses file separate returns, each may exclude the amount of his or her foreign earned income attributable to services, subject to the ceiling. If the spouses file a joint return, the sum of those separate amounts may be excluded. (Reg § 1.911-5(a)(2))[17]

¶ 4606   Partial exclusion for a qualified individual's foreign housing costs— Form 2555.

Under Code Sec. 911(a)(2), a qualified individual (¶4608) may elect on Form 2555 to exclude from gross income his or her housing cost amount.[18]

The exclusion amount is limited to the lesser of the full amount of the individual's housing cost amount attributable to employer-provided amounts, or the individual's foreign earned income for the tax year. An individual who claims the foreign housing cost amount exclusion must claim the full housing cost amount exclusion, up to the extent allowable (i.e., if both the housing cost amount exclusion and the foreign earned income exclusion (¶4605) are elected, the housing cost amount exclusion must be taken first). (Reg § 1.911-4(d)(1))[19]

The housing cost amount is the excess of: (1) the individual's housing expenses for the tax year (but not exceeding an amount equal to 30% of the taxpayer's foreign earned income exclusion (computed on a daily basis) multiplied by the number of qualifying days in the year), over (2) 16% of the taxpayer's foreign earned income exclusion (computed on a daily basis) multiplied by the number of qualifying days in the tax year. (Code Sec. 911(c)) A qualifying day is a day on which the taxpayer's tax home (¶1540) is in a foreign country and the taxpayer meets the bona fide residence or 330-day test (see ¶4608). For 2022, the maximum amount of the foreign housing cost exclusion is $15,680 (($112,000 × 30%) −

---

13. ¶O-2020 *et seq.*
14. ¶O-1100 *et seq.*, ¶O-1350 *et seq.*
15. ¶O-1104 *et seq.*
16. ¶O-1103

17. ¶O-1101
18. ¶O-1160 *et seq.*, O-1350 *et seq.*
19. ¶O-1168

($112,000 × 16%)). For 2023, it is $16,800 (($120,000 × 30%) – ($120,000 × 16%)). IRS provides a higher adjusted limitation on housing expenses in high-cost localities. (Code Sec. 911(c)(2)(B))[20]

Housing expenses are those reasonable expenses paid or incurred during the tax year by or on behalf of an individual for housing for the individual (and, if they reside with the individual, for spouse and dependents) in a foreign country. (Code Sec. 911(c)(3)(A))[21] For a deduction for housing costs when the taxpayer has income from self-employment (i.e., non-employer provided amounts), see ¶4607.

For married couples where both spouses are qualified individuals, each chooses whether to elect the exclusion. (Reg § 1.911-5(a)(1)) The housing cost amount attributable to employer provided amounts is determined separately for each spouse. (Reg § 1.911-5(a)(3)(iii)) Where spouses reside together and file a joint return, they may compute their exclusion separately or jointly. If they reside together and file separate returns, they must make separate computations, but they may allocate the housing expenses between them. (Reg § 1.911-5(a)(3)(i)) Where spouses reside apart, they both may exclude (or deduct) their respective housing cost amounts if their tax homes aren't within reasonable commuting distance of each other and neither spouse's residence is within a reasonable commuting distance of the other spouse's tax home. If the spouses' tax homes or residences *are* within reasonable commuting distance, only one spouse may exclude (or deduct) the housing cost amount. (Reg § 1.911-5(a)(3)(ii))[22]

¶ 4607   Self-employed qualified individual's deduction for foreign housing expenses—Form 2555.

Under Code Sec. 911(c)(4)(A), a qualified individual (¶4608) may deduct foreign housing expenses that are attributable to self-employment. The deduction is limited to the individual's foreign earned income for the tax year which isn't otherwise excluded from gross income under either the foreign earned income (¶4605) or foreign housing cost (¶4606) exclusions. (Code Sec. 911(c)(4)(B)) Any unused housing expenses may be carried over and deducted in the next tax year, subject to that year's limits. (Code Sec. 911(c)(4)(C))[23] For the exclusion for housing costs where the taxpayer has employer-provided income, see ¶4606.

¶ 4608   Who is a qualified individual for foreign earned income/housing cost exclusions, or housing cost deduction.

Generally, under Code Sec. 911(d)(1), a taxpayer qualifies for the foreign earned income (¶4605) and housing cost (¶4606) exclusions and the housing cost deduction (¶4607) for a tax year if his or her tax home is in a foreign country *and* he or she is either: (1) a U.S. citizen who can establish that he or she has been a bona fide resident of one or more foreign countries for an uninterrupted period which includes the entire tax year;[24] or (2) a U.S. citizen or resident who, during any period of 12 consecutive months, is present in one or more foreign countries during at least 330 full days.[25]

An individual's tax home is his or her home for deducting away-from-home travel expenses (¶1540). Individuals have no tax home in a foreign country for any period their abode is in the U.S. (unless serving in a designated combat zone). (Code Sec. 911(d)(3)) The fact that an individual is temporarily present in the U.S. or maintains a U.S. dwelling (even if used by spouse or dependents) doesn't necessarily mean his or her abode is in the U.S. (Reg § 1.911-2(b))[26] For married couples, qualification is determined separately. (Reg § 1.911-5(a)(1))

20. ¶O-1166
21. ¶O-1162
22. ¶s O-1174, O-1175
23. ¶O-1171, ¶O-1173

24. ¶O-1250 *et seq.*
25. ¶O-1300 *et seq.*
26. ¶O-1202, ¶O-1203

715

The residency requirements are waived for specified countries if taxpayers reasonably expected to meet the eligibility requirements for the foreign earned income and housing cost exclusions, but left the country due to adverse or dangerous conditions. (Code Sec. 911(d)(4))[27]

¶ 4609　Rules that limit the benefit of foreign earned income/housing costs exclusions.

Tax rate adjustment. Under Code Sec. 911(f), a "stacking" rule limits the benefits of the foreign earned income and housing cost exclusions by adding back the excluded amounts to taxable income solely for determining the applicable marginal tax rate. Special rules apply where the net capital gain exceeds the individual's taxable income for a tax year.[28]

Disallowance of deductions and credits allocable to excluded income. No deduction, exclusion or credit, including any credit or deduction for foreign taxes (see ¶2360 *et seq.*), is allowable to the extent the deduction, etc., is allocable to or chargeable against foreign income excluded from gross income under the foreign earned income (¶4605) or housing costs (¶4606) exclusions. (Code Sec. 911(d)(6); Reg § 1.911-6(a))[29]

¶ 4610　Exclusions for certain U.S. government employees and Peace Corps volunteers abroad.

For civilian officers and U.S. government employees, Code Sec. 912 excludes from gross income certain allowances (other than amounts received as post differentials), including cost-of-living allowances received by persons stationed outside the continental U.S. (except Alaska).[30] In addition, gross income doesn't include certain allowances to Peace Corps volunteers or volunteer leaders and family members, other than termination payments, leave allowances, allowances to members of the family of a volunteer leader who is training in the U.S., and the part of an allowance designated as basic compensation. (Code Sec. 912(3))[31]

¶ 4611　Taxation of U.S. shareholders of controlled foreign corporations (CFCs)—Form 5471.

Under Code Sec. 951(a)(1), if a foreign corporation is a CFC (¶4612) at any time during any tax year, every person who is a U.S. shareholder (¶4612) of the corporation, and who owns stock (directly or indirectly) in the corporation on the last day in that year on which the corporation is a CFC, includes in gross income for the U.S. shareholder's tax year in which or with which the tax year of the corporation ends, the U.S. shareholder's pro rata share of: (1) the corporation's subpart F income (¶4613) for that year;[32] and (2) any increase during the tax year in the CFC's earnings invested in U.S. property under Code Sec. 956 (to the extent not attributable to amounts previously taxed as subpart F income).[33]

A U.S. shareholder of any CFC for any tax year of the U.S. shareholder must also include in gross income the U.S. shareholder's global intangible low-taxed income (GILTI) for the tax year, see ¶4614.

The U.S. shareholder reports these amounts on Form 5471.[34]

Amounts included in a U.S. shareholder's gross income under the above rules for (i.e., previously taxed income or PTI) are not included in income a second time when they are later distributed. (Code Sec. 959)[35]

---

27. ¶O-1273
28. ¶O-1109
29. ¶O-1106
30. ¶H-3133, H-3135
31. ¶H-3136

32. ¶O-2400 *et seq.*, ¶O-2470 *et seq.*
33. ¶O-2760 *et seq.*
34. ¶S-3586.1
35. ¶O-2430 *et seq.*

¶ 4612   Controlled foreign corporation (CFC) and U.S. shareholder defined.

Under Code Sec. 957(a) and Code Sec. 957(b), a CFC is a foreign corporation more than 50% (25%, for certain insurance companies) of whose stock by vote or value is, on any day in the corporation's tax year, owned (directly, indirectly, or constructively) by U.S. shareholders.[36]

A U.S. shareholder is, as to any foreign corporation, a U.S. person (generally, a U.S. citizen or resident, or a domestic corporation, partnership, estate or trust), that owns (directly, indirectly or constructively) 10% or more of the combined voting power of all classes of stock of the corporation, or 10% or more of the total value of shares of all classes of stock of the corporation. (Code Sec. 951(b))[37]

Attribution rules apply under which stock owned directly or indirectly by a foreign corporation, domestic or foreign partnership, foreign trust, or foreign estate is treated as owned proportionately by its foreign or domestic shareholders, partners, or beneficiaries. (Code Sec. 958(a)) In addition, constructive ownership rules apply. (Code Sec. 958(a))[38]

¶ 4613   What is subpart F income—controlled foreign corporations.

A controlled foreign corporation's (CFC's) subpart F income consists of:

(1) Insurance income. (Code Sec. 952(a)(1), Code Sec. 953)[39]

(2) Foreign base company income (FBCI). (Code Sec. 952(a)(2), Code Sec. 954; Reg § 1.954-1)[40], which includes:

(a) Foreign personal holding company income (FPHCI), including investment income such as dividends, interest, rents, royalties and annuities; gains from certain property and commodities transactions; certain personal services income; and certain other passive type income. Exceptions apply for certain income received from related parties or as part of an active business, as well as for qualified banking, financing and insurance income. In addition, look-through rules may apply. (Code Sec. 954(c); Reg § 1.954-2)[41]

(b) Foreign base company sales and services income. (Code Sec. 954(d), Code Sec. 954(e); Reg § 1.954-3, Reg § 1.954-4)[42]

(3) Income attributable to operations that constitute participation in or cooperation with an unsanctioned international boycott. (Code Sec. 952(a)(3))[43]

(4) The amount of any illegal (under the U.S. Foreign Corrupt Practices Act) payment made (directly or indirectly) by or for the CFC to a government official, employee or agent. (Code Sec. 952(a)(4))[44] and

(5) Income from foreign countries with which the U.S. doesn't have diplomatic relations or that have been identified as sponsors of terrorism. (Code Sec. 952(a)(5))[45]

In any tax year where the sum of the CFC's FBCI and insurance income exceeds 70% of its gross income, *all* of the CFC's gross income is includible in its subpart F income. However, in any tax year where this sum is less than 5% of the CFC's gross income or $1 million (whichever is less), *none* of the CFC's income is FBCI or insurance income. (Code Sec. 954(b)(3); Reg § 1.954-1(b)) In addition, any item of FBCI or insurance income that is subject to an effective rate of foreign tax that is greater than 90% of the maximum U.S. corporate rate may, at the election of the CFC's controlling U.S. shareholders, be excluded

---

36. ¶O-2302, ¶O-2325
37. ¶O-2303, ¶O-2305 *et seq.*
38. ¶O-2303.1, ¶O-2329 *et seq.*
39. ¶O-2500 *et seq.*
40. ¶O-2520 *et seq.*

41. ¶O-2530 *et seq.*
42. ¶O-2620 *et seq.*, ¶O-2650 *et seq.*
43. ¶O-2731
44. ¶O-2732
45. ¶O-2733

from subpart F income. (Code Sec. 954(b)(4); Reg § 1.954-1(d))[46]

¶ 4614   U.S. shareholders of CFCs are also taxed on global intangible low-taxed income (GILTI)—Form 8992.

Under Code Sec. 951A(a) and Code Sec. 951A(f), a U.S. shareholder (¶4612) of a CFC (¶4612) must include in gross income for a tax year the U.S. shareholder's global intangible low-taxed income (GILTI) in a manner similar to a subpart F inclusion (see ¶4611 *et seq.*). The GILTI is then treated as subpart F income for certain purposes of the Code (such as the PTI rules, see ¶4611) but not others. For a limited foreign tax credit available for GILTI, see ¶2367.

GILTI is, for any U.S. shareholder for the shareholder's tax year, the excess (if any) of the shareholder's net CFC tested income over the shareholder's net deemed tangible income return. (Code Sec. 951A(b)(1); Reg § 1.951A-1(c)(1))

The net CFC tested income is, for any U.S. shareholder, the excess of the aggregate of the U.S. shareholder's pro rata share of the tested income of each CFC for which it is a U.S. shareholder over the aggregate of the U.S. shareholder's pro rata share of the tested loss of each CFC for which it is a U.S. shareholder. (Code Sec. 951A(c)(1); Reg § 1.951A-1(c)(2))

The tested income of a CFC is the excess of its gross income over the deductions (including taxes) properly allocable to gross income, but does not include effectively connected income, subpart F income, highly-taxed foreign income, foreign oil and gas extraction income, or certain related party payments. (Code Sec. 951A(c)(2)(A); Reg § 1.951A-2) A tested loss is the excess of those deductions over that gross income of the CFC. (Code Sec. 951A(c)(2)(B); Reg § 1.951A-2)

The shareholder's net deemed tangible income return is an amount equal to the excess of (i) 10% of the aggregate of the shareholder's pro rata share of the qualified business asset investment (QBAI) of each CFC for which it is a U.S. shareholder; over (ii) the amount of interest expense taken into account under Code Sec. 951A(c)(2)(A)(ii) in determining the shareholder's net CFC tested income for the tax year to the extent the interest income attributable to the expense is not taken into account in determining the shareholder's net CFC tested income. (Code Sec. 951A(b)(2); Reg § 1.951A-1(c)(3))[47]

Reporting rules require the filing of Form 8992, U.S. Shareholder Calculation of Global Intangible Low-Taxed Income. (Reg § 1.6038-5)[48]

A U.S. shareholder that is a domestic corporation is taxed at an effective tax rate of 10.5% on GILTI. This effective tax rate is achieved by means of a 50% deduction on the GILTI amount (plus the attributable Code Sec. 78 gross-up) (see ¶3315). The deduction may be limited based on taxable income. (Code Sec. 250)[49]

¶ 4615   Gain from disposition of foreign corporation stock may be treated as a dividend.

Under Code Sec. 1248(a), if a U.S. person sells or exchanges stock in a foreign corporation, and that person owns (directly, indirectly, or constructively) 10% or more of the combined voting power of all classes of stock of the foreign corporation at any time during the 5-year period ending on the date of the sale when the corporation was a CFC (¶4612), then the gain recognized on the sale is included in the U.S. person's gross income as a dividend, to the extent of the foreign corporation's E&P attributable to that stock.[50]

A sale or exchange includes a redemption of stock under Code Sec. 302(a) (¶3515 *et seq.*), a liquidation under Code Sec. 331(a) (¶3559), and amounts treated as gain from a sale or

---

46. ¶O-2522; ¶O-2524 *et seq.*
47. ¶O-2790 *et seq.*
48. ¶S-3600

49. ¶O-3000 *et seq.*
50. ¶O-2800 *et seq.*

exchange under Code Sec. 301(c)(3) are treated as gain from the sale or exchange of stock. (Reg § 1.1248-1(b))[1]

Dividend treatment may also apply to certain distributions by, and dispositions of, a *domestic* corporation, e.g., where the corporation was formed or availed of principally for holding (directly or indirectly) stock of one or more foreign corporations. (Code Sec. 1248(e), Code Sec. 1248(f))[2]

Dividend treatment under this rule doesn't apply to redemptions to pay death tax under Code Sec. 303 or certain amounts treated as dividends, ordinary income, or short-term capital gains under other Code provisions. (Code Sec. 1248(g))[3]

If the shareholder is an individual, there is a limit on the amount of tax imposed on the dividend portion of his or her gain. (Code Sec. 1248(b))[4]

Under Code Sec. 964(e), gain recognized by a CFC from the sale or exchange of stock in a foreign corporation is treated as a dividend to the same extent that it would have been so treated under Code Sec. 1248(a) if the CFC were a U.S. person. The foreign-source portion of the dividend is treated as subpart F income of the selling CFC for which the deduction under the Code Sec. 245A DRD (¶3314) is available.[5]

¶ 4616　Sales of patents, etc., by U.S. person to foreign corporation that U.S. person controls.

Under Code Sec. 1249, a U.S. person who sells (or exchanges) a patent, invention, model, or design (whether or not patented), a copyright, a secret formula or process or similar property right to a foreign corporation in which the seller owns (directly, indirectly or constructively) stock with over 50% of the combined voting power of all classes of stock, must treat as ordinary income any gain recognized on that sale (or exchange).[6]

¶ 4617　Passive foreign investment company (PFIC) defined.

Under Code Sec. 1297(a), a PFIC is any foreign corporation if: (1) at least 75% of its gross income for its tax year is passive, or (2) at least 50% of the assets it held during the year produce passive income or are held for the production of passive income. The passive assets test is generally applied based on the fair market value (FMV) of the corporation's assets, but assets are valued based on their adjusted basis where the corporation isn't publicly traded and either is a CFC or elects to use the adjusted basis instead of FMV. (Code Sec. 1297(e))[7]

How a U.S. person who is a PFIC shareholder is taxed depends on whether the U.S. person has made a qualified electing fund (QEF) election (¶4619), a mark-to-market election (¶4620), or no election (¶4618).

¶ 4618　Taxation of U.S. persons who are PFIC shareholders in the absence of an election—Form 8621.

Under Code Sec. 1291(a), a U.S. person who is a shareholder in a PFIC (¶4617) that has not made a qualified electing fund (¶4619) or mark-to-market (¶4620) election can defer the U.S. tax with respect to that investment until the shareholder disposes of the PFIC stock or receives an excess distribution. At that time, the shareholder must pay U.S. tax, plus interest based on the value of the tax deferral, at ordinary income rates, and report the amounts on Form 8621. (Code Sec. 1298(f))[8]

An excess distribution is a current year distribution received by a shareholder on PFIC stock, to the extent it does not exceed its ratable portion of the excess (if any) of (i) the total

---

1. ¶O-2801
2. ¶O-2804 *et seq.*
3. ¶O-2803
4. ¶O-2811
5. ¶O-2800.2
6. ¶O-2900 *et seq.*
7. ¶O-2200 *et seq.*
8. ¶O-2220 *et seq.*, ¶O-2258

amount of the distributions received by the taxpayer during the tax year, over (ii) 125% of the average amount received with respect to the stock during the three preceding years (or, if shorter, the shareholder's holding period prior to the tax year). (Code Sec. 1291(b))[9] Portions of distributions that aren't excess distributions are taxed under the normal rules for corporate distributions, see ¶1285 *et seq.*[10]

A U.S. person holding stock in a PFIC is generally not subject to the PFIC rules if the PFIC is also a CFC (¶4612) and the U.S. person is a U.S. shareholder (¶4612). (Code Sec. 1297(d))[11]

¶ 4619   Qualified electing fund (QEF) treatment for passive foreign investment company (PFIC) stock—Form 8621.

Under Code Sec. 1295, a PFIC (¶4617) is treated as a QEF with respect to a particular shareholder if the shareholder so elects and the PFIC complies with the requirements for determining its ordinary earnings and net capital gain and otherwise carrying out the purposes of the election.[12]

A U.S. investor in a PFIC makes the QEF election by attaching a completed Form 8621 to the investor's timely filed income tax return (original or amended, by the due date (as extended) for the original return) for that year, reflecting the information provided by the PFIC in its annual information statement. (Code Sec. 1295(b)(2); Reg § 1.1295-1(e), Reg § 1.1295-1(f))[13]

If the election is made, the electing shareholder is not subject to the deferred tax and interest charge (¶4618). (Code Sec. 1291(d)(1)) Instead, the electing shareholder must currently include in income the shareholder's share of the PFIC's earnings and profits (with appropriate basis adjustments for amounts not distributed and previously taxed distributions). The fund's ordinary income and net capital gain are passed through to the shareholder as ordinary income and long-term capital gain respectively. (Code Sec. 1293)[14] For the availability of the foreign tax credit as to QEF inclusions, see ¶2367.

If a PFIC is also a controlled foreign corporation (CFC), (¶4612), amounts includible in gross income under the CFC rules (¶4611) are not included under the QEF rules. (Code Sec. 951(c))[15]

¶ 4620   Electing mark-to-market treatment for passive foreign investment company (PFIC) stock—Form 8621.

Under Code Sec. 1296 and Code Sec. 1291(d), a U.S. person who is a shareholder in a PFIC may make a mark-to-market election with respect to marketable (i.e., regularly traded) PFIC stock and avoid the otherwise applicable PFIC rules (¶4618).[16] The election is made by filing Form 8621 with the return. (Reg § 1.1296-1(h)(1))[17]

A shareholder that makes the election must report as ordinary income each year the amount by which the fair market value (FMV) of the PFIC stock at the close of the tax year exceeds the shareholder's adjusted basis in the stock. If the stock's basis exceeds the FMV at the end of the year, the shareholder has an ordinary loss deduction to the extent of the lesser of the amount of that excess, or the unreversed inclusions with respect to the PFIC stock. (Code Sec. 1296(a), Code Sec. 1296(c)) The amount of unreversed inclusions equals the sum of all income inclusions in past years, reduced by any deductions allowed in past years. (Code Sec. 1296(d)) Any gain or loss on the actual sale or disposition of the PFIC stock is treated as ordinary income or loss. (Code Sec. 1296(c))[18]

---

9. ¶O-2227
10. ¶O-2225
11. ¶O-2250
12. ¶O-2260 *et seq.*
13. ¶O-2270 *et seq.*

14. ¶O-2261 *et seq.*
15. ¶O-2266
16. ¶O-2290 *et seq.*
17. ¶O-2297
18. ¶O-2290 *et seq.*

¶ 4621 Taxation of U.S. beneficiaries of foreign trusts—Form 3520, Form 4970.

Under Code Sec. 652 and Code Sec. 662, a U.S. beneficiary is taxed on a foreign trust's foreign and U.S.-source income at the time it becomes distributable.[19] Distributions are reported on Form 3520.[20] For the throwback rules applicable to distributions of accumulated trust income to the U.S. beneficiary (including the use of Form 4970 to compute the tax and the nondeductible interest charge that applies to a foreign trust), see ¶3948 *et seq.*

¶ 4622 Recognition of gain on transfers to foreign estates or foreign non-grantor trusts.

Under Code Sec. 684, gain is recognized on a transfer of appreciated property by a U.S. person to a foreign estate or trust to the extent its fair market value (FMV) exceeds its basis in the hands of the transferor. Similarly, if a domestic trust becomes a foreign trust, the trust is treated as having transferred, immediately before becoming a foreign trust, all of its assets to a foreign trust, and must recognize gain on any appreciated assets transferred. (Reg § 1.684-4)

Gain is not recognized on transfers of property by a U.S. person: (a) to foreign grantor trusts, (b) to exempt charitable trusts, (c) by reason of death of the U.S. transferor, (d) to unrelated foreign trusts for FMV, under Code Sec. 1032, and (e) with respect to certain distributions to a trust on an interest held by the trust in certain investment trusts, liquidating trusts, or environmental remediation trusts. (Reg § 1.684-3)[21]

For gain recognition on transfers to a foreign corporation, see ¶3568. For gain recognition on transfers to foreign partnerships, see ¶3707.

¶ 4623 Tax sanctions for international boycott activities—Form 5713.

Under Code Sec. 908(a), Code Sec. 952(a)(3) and Code Sec. 995(b)(1)(F)(ii), if a taxpayer participates in or cooperates with an unsanctioned international boycott or has operations in or related to a country carrying out such a boycott, the taxpayer is denied certain tax benefits, including the foreign tax credit (¶2360), reduced deferral under IC-DISC rules (¶4604) and income deferral under subpart F (¶4613). Taxpayers that have operations in a country on the IRS's boycott list or in a country that requires participation or cooperation with an international boycott, namely, Iraq, Kuwait, Lebanon, Libya, Qatar, Saudi Arabia, Syria, and Yemen, must make a report to IRS on Form 5713. (Code Sec. 999)[22]

¶ 4624 Taxation of Nonresident Aliens and Foreign Corporations. ▬▬▬▬

A nonresident alien or foreign corporation is generally only taxed on (i) investment income from U.S.-sources (¶4626) at a 30% or lower treaty rate (see ¶4628), and (ii) if engaged in a U.S. trade or business, net income effectively connected with that business (ECI) at regular U.S. rates (see ¶4630). Tax on ECI may be eliminated or reduced under a treaty, which usually conditions U.S. taxation on the presence of a permanent establishment (or sometimes, a fixed base). Income from U.S. real estate investments may be taxed as ECI (see ¶4629). A foreign taxpayer also may be subject to the accumulated earnings tax (¶3320 *et seq.*), a branch profits tax (¶4633), and/or a transportation tax (¶4637). A nonresident alien may exclude from income compensation received for services as an employee of a foreign government or international organization if certain conditions are met (Code Sec. 893)[23]

A nonresident alien individual is an individual who isn't a U.S. citizen or resident (¶4601, ¶4602). (Code Sec. 7701(b)(1)(B))[24]

---

19. ¶C-3021
20. ¶S-3644
21. ¶C-1020 *et seq.*

22. ¶O-3500 *et seq.*
23. ¶O-10100 *et seq.*, O-10200 *et seq.*, O-11829
24. ¶O-1086

A foreign corporation is one that's created or organized outside the U.S. or under any law other than that of the U.S., a state, or the District of Columbia. (Code Sec. 7701(a)(5))[25]

Corporations organized in a possession are not treated as foreign corporations under certain circumstances and for certain purposes. (Code Sec. 881(b); Reg § 1.881-5)[26]

¶ 4625   Taxation of nonresident aliens and foreign corporations under tax treaties—Form 8833.

The U.S. has income tax treaties with a number of foreign countries under which residents or citizens of those countries are taxed at a reduced rate or are exempt from U.S. income tax on certain U.S.-source income. Code Sec. 894 addresses income affected by those treaties.[27] With limited exceptions, a taxpayer who takes a return position that a treaty overrules or otherwise modifies, and reduces any U.S. tax incurred at any time, must disclose that return position on Form 8833 attached to the return. (Code Sec. 6114(a); Reg § 301.6114-1)[28]

¶ 4626   Determining whether income is U.S.-source or foreign-source income.

Specific rules are used to determine the source of the following types of income:

Compensation generally is sourced where the services were performed, except in the case of nonresident aliens temporarily present in the U.S. (Code Sec. 861(a)(3), Code Sec. 862(a)(3); Reg § 1.861-4)[29]

Rents and royalties are sourced where the leased or licensed property is located or used. (Code Sec. 861(a)(4), Code Sec. 862(a)(4))[30]

Income from the sale of intangible property, when payment is contingent on the use or productivity of the property, is sourced as royalty income (i.e., sourced at the place of use). (Code Sec. 865(d))[31]

Proceeds from the sale of noninventory personal property generally are sourced where the seller resides. (Code Sec. 865(a))[32]

Proceeds from the sale of inventory generally are sourced on the basis of place of sale for purchased inventory, and on the basis of production activities for produced inventory. (Code Sec. 861(a)(6), Code Sec. 862(a)(6), Code Sec. 863(b), Code Sec. 865(b))[33]

Proceeds from sales of real property are sourced at the location of the property. (Code Sec. 861(a)(5), Code Sec. 862(a)(5))[34]

Dividends generally are sourced where the corporation is incorporated. However, dividends received from a foreign corporation are treated in part as from U.S.-sources if 25% or more of the corporation's gross income was effectively connected with the conduct of a U.S. business for the 3-year period (or shorter period of its existence) ending with the close of its tax year preceding the declaration of the dividends. (Code Sec. 861(a)(2), Code Sec. 862(a)(2))[35]

Dividend equivalents determined by reference to the payment of a U.S.-source dividend are treated as U.S.-source dividends. (Code Sec. 871(m))[36]

Interest generally is sourced where the debtor is located. (Code Sec. 861(a)(1), Code Sec. 862(a)(1))[37]

Amounts received for the provision of a guarantee are from U.S.-sources if paid by: (1) a noncorporate U.S. resident or a U.S. corporation for the provision of a guarantee of the

25. ¶F-6011
26. ¶O-10218
27. ¶O-15000 *et seq.*
28. ¶O-15010 *et seq.*
29. ¶O-10931.1 *et seq.*
30. ¶O-10936
31. ¶O-10954

32. ¶O-10948
33. ¶O-10957 *et seq.*
34. ¶O-10945, O-10946
35. ¶O-10926, ¶O-10928
36. ¶O-10930.1
37. ¶O-10906 *et seq.*

resident or corporation; or (2) any foreign person for the provision of a guarantee if the payment is connected with income that is effectively connected, or treated as effectively connected, with the conduct of a U.S. trade or business. (Code Sec. 861(a)(9), Code Sec. 862(a)(9))[38]

Insurance income from insuring U.S. risks is U.S.-source. (Code Sec. 861(a)(7), Code Sec. 862(a)(7))[39]

International communications income derived by a U.S. person from the transmission of communications or data between the U.S. and a foreign country or U.S. possession is half foreign-source and half U.S.-source. A foreign person's international communications income is foreign-source, except where it is attributable to an office or fixed place of business in the U.S. (Code Sec. 863(e)(1))[40]

Space and ocean activity income of a U.S. person is U.S.-source (while that of a foreign person is foreign-source). (Code Sec. 863(d)(1))[41]

Transportation income derived from the use and performance of services directly related to the use of a vessel or aircraft from transportation that either begins or ends in the U.S. is half foreign-source and half U.S.-source. Transportation income attributable to transportation which begins and ends in the U.S. is U.S. source income. (Code Sec. 863(c))[42]

¶ 4627 Allocating and apportioning deductions to determine U.S.-source and foreign-source taxable income; allocation and apportionment of interest expense.

Reg § 1.861-8 *et seq.* provide guidance for determining taxable income of a taxpayer from sources within and without the U.S. with rules for the allocation and apportionment of expenses, losses, and other deductions of the taxpayer. Except for any deductions that are not definitely related to gross income and that, therefore, are ratably apportioned to all gross income, a taxpayer must allocate deductions to a class of gross income and then, if necessary to make the determination required by the relevant provision of the Code, apportion deductions within the class of gross income between the statutory grouping (or groupings) of gross income and the residual grouping of gross income. A statutory grouping of gross income is the gross income from a specific source or activity that must first be determined to arrive at taxable income from the specific source or activity under a Code Section. Gross income from other sources or activities is referred to as the residual grouping of gross income. Allocations and apportionments are made on the basis of the factual relationship of deductions to gross income. (Reg § 1.861-8(a))[43]

Except as otherwise provided in the regs, allocations and apportionments of interest expense (which is considered related to all of a taxpayer's activities and assets) is determined based on the adjusted bases of assets rather than the fair market value of the assets or gross income. (Code Sec. 864(e)(2)), Reg § 1.861-9, Reg § 1.861-9T, Reg § 1.861-10T)[44]

¶ 4628 Certain U.S.-source gross income not effectively connected with a U.S. business taxed to nonresident aliens and foreign corporations at 30% rate.

Nonresident aliens and foreign corporations are taxed at a flat 30% (or lower treaty rate) on the following types of U.S.-source gross income that is not effectively connected with a U.S. business (¶4630):

. . . subject to exceptions discussed below, interest (other than original issue discount, or

---

38. ¶O-10923
39. ¶O-10985
40. ¶O-10984
41. ¶O-10976
42. ¶O-10941
43. ¶O-11000 *et seq.*
44. ¶O-11100 *et seq.*

OID), dividends, rents, salaries, wages, premiums, annuities, compensations, remunerations, emoluments and other fixed or determinable annual or periodical gains, profits and income. (Code Sec. 871(a)(1)(A), Code Sec. 881(a)(1))

. . . gain on the disposition of certain timber, coal, and iron ore mined in the U.S. (Code Sec. 871(a)(1)(B), Code Sec. 881(a)(2))

. . . payments on OID obligations, and gain on the sale of certain OID obligations (¶1312 *et seq.*). (Code Sec. 871(a)(1)(C), Code Sec. 881(a)(3))

. . . gain from the disposition of patents, copyrights, goodwill, etc. to the extent the gain is from payments contingent on the productivity, use, or disposition of that property (Code Sec. 871(a)(1)(D), Code Sec. 881(a)(4))

. . . certain U.S.-source capital gain if the nonresident alien is in the U.S. for at least 183 days during the tax year. (Code Sec. 871(a)(2))

. . . 85% of any social security benefits received. (Code Sec. 871(a)(3))[45]

The following types of income are exempt from the 30% tax otherwise applicable under the rules above:

. . . certain dividends including (i) dividends paid by a foreign corporation with less than 25% effectively connected income that is treated as U.S.-source income, (Code Sec. 871(i)(2)(D)) (ii) dividends paid by an existing 80/20 company, (Code Sec. 871(i)(2)(B)(i)) and (iii) interest-related dividends and short-term capital gains dividends from a regulated investment company (RIC). (Code Sec. 871(k), Code Sec. 881(e))[46]

. . . certain interest including (i) portfolio interest, (Code Sec. 871(h), Code Sec. 881(c)) (ii) interest earned on bank account deposits, (Code Sec. 871(i)(2)(A)) and (iii) interest paid by an existing 80/20 company. (Code Sec. 871(i)(2)(B)(ii))[47]

. . . certain gambling winnings. (Code Sec. 871(j))[48]

For the withholding regime that applies to non-effectively connected income, see ¶4648 *et seq.*

¶ 4629 Nonresident alien individual or foreign corporation may elect to treat real property income as income connected with a U.S. trade or business.

Under Code Sec. 871(d) and Code Sec. 882(d), a nonresident alien individual or foreign corporation may elect to treat certain income from U.S. real property held for investment as effectively connected with the conduct of a U.S. business (¶4630). The electing foreign taxpayer is then taxed at regular U.S. rates (not 30%) on net rather than gross income, and may take depreciation deductions, etc. The election is made on a statement attached to the income tax return for the election year. (Reg § 1.871-10(d)(1)(ii))[49]

¶ 4630 What is income effectively connected with a U.S. trade or business (ECI) of a foreign corporation or nonresident alien.

Under Code Sec. 871(b) and Code Sec. 882, a foreign corporation or nonresident alien (NRA) engaged in a U.S. business (¶4631) at any time during the tax year is taxed at the regular graduated U.S. rates on ECI, i.e., gross income effectively connected with the U.S. business, less allowable deductions (¶4632).[50] U.S. source investment income (generally Code Sec. 871(a) income and U.S.-source capital gains) is effectively connected with a U.S. trade or business only if the activities of the U.S. trade or business were a material factor in the realization of that income, or the income, gain, or loss is derived from assets used in or held for use in the conduct of a U.S. trade or business. Other U.S.-source income is generally treated as ECI. (Code Sec. 864(c)(2), Code Sec. 864(c)(3))[1]

45. ¶O-10200 *et seq.*
46. ¶O-10212 *et seq.*
47. ¶O-10204, O-10211, O-10214
48. ¶O-10202

49. ¶O-10618
50. ¶O-10600 *et seq.*
1. ¶O-10603 *et seq.*

Foreign-source income treated as effectively connected to a U.S. trade or business includes the following, but only to the extent the item is attributable to an office or other fixed place of business in the U.S.:

... Rents or royalties from intangible property derived from an active licensing business.

... Dividends, interest, or guarantee fees derived from an active banking, financing or trading business.

... Certain inventory sales attributable to a U.S. sales office.

... Income or gain that is equivalent to the above items.

Foreign-source income of a foreign insurance company attributable to its U.S. business is also ECI. (Code Sec. 864(c)(4))[2]

Notwithstanding any other tax rules, if an NRA or foreign corporation owns, directly or indirectly, an interest in a partnership engaged in any trade or business in the U.S., gain or loss on the sale or exchange of all (or any portion of) the interest is treated as effectively connected with the conduct of the trade or business to the extent it does not exceed the selling partner's distributive share of partnership gain or loss that would have been effectively connected with the trade or business had the partnership sold all of its assets in a taxable transaction. (Code Sec. 864(c)(8))[3]

¶ 4631 When is a foreign corporation or nonresident alien engaged in a U.S. trade or business.

A foreign corporation or nonresident alien is engaged in a U.S. trade or business if they carry on continuous and regular business activities in the U.S.[4]

The performance of personal services in the U.S. constitutes engaging in a U.S. trade or business unless the performer of services is a nonresident alien individual (i) whose compensation for those services is $3,000 or less, (ii) who is in the U.S. for 90 days or less, and (iii) who works either for a foreign person not engaged in business in the U.S., or for a foreign office of a U.S. person. (Code Sec. 864(b)(1))[5]

Alien students and exchange visitors may be treated as engaging in a U.S. trade or business, and may be subject to tax on their scholarship or fellowship grants. (Code Sec. 871(c))[6]

If a partnership, estate or trust is engaged in a U.S. business, the entity's foreign partners or beneficiaries are considered so engaged. (Code Sec. 875)[7]

The trading of securities and commodities through a resident broker, commission agent, custodian, or other independent agent doesn't constitute engaging in a trade or business as long as the taxpayer doesn't have a U.S. office through which the trading transactions are effected. The trading of securities and commodities for one's own account isn't engaging in a U.S. trade or business, however effected. (Code Sec. 864(b)(2))[8]

¶ 4632 Deductions and credits of foreign corporations and nonresident aliens in calculating income effectively connected with a U.S. trade or business.

Under Code Sec. 873(a) and Code Sec. 882(c)(1)(A), a nonresident alien individual (NRA) and a foreign corporation are generally allowed deductions only if and to the extent that they are connected with against income effectively connected with the conduct of a U.S. trade or business (¶4630). A deduction for charitable contributions, however, is allowed whether or not connected with a U.S. business. In addition, NRAs are allowed a deduction for nonbusiness casualty and theft losses. (Code Sec. 873(b), Code Sec. 882(c)(1)(B))[9]

---

2. ¶O-10609 *et seq.*
3. ¶O-10615 *et seq.*
4. ¶O-10500 *et seq.*
5. ¶O-10502

6. ¶O-10503
7. ¶O-10504
8. ¶O-10505 *et seq.*
9. ¶O-10621 *et seq.*

An NRA or foreign corporation engaged in a U.S. trade or business is entitled to a foreign tax credit for taxes imposed by foreign countries other than the taxpayer's home country with respect to income effectively connected to that business, as well as other credits attributable to income effectively connected with the conduct of the U.S. trade or business beyond those available to other foreign taxpayers. (Code Sec. 874(c), Code Sec. 882(c)(2); Reg § 1.874-1(c), Reg § 1.882-4(b)(1))[10] Generally, a true and accurate return (¶4641 *et seq.*) must be filed in order to get the benefit of an otherwise allowable deduction or credit. (Code Sec. 874(a), Code Sec. 882(c)(2))[11]

¶ 4633   Branch profits tax on foreign corporations—Form 8848.

Under Code Sec. 884, a foreign corporation engaged in a U.S. trade or business through a branch office is liable for a branch profits tax (in addition to regular income tax on ECI, see ¶4630) equal to 30% of the tax year's dividend equivalent amount. The dividend equivalent amount is the corporation's effectively connected earnings and profits (E&P), *reduced* (not below zero) by any increase for the year in its U.S. net equity (i.e., amounts reinvested in the U.S. business), and *increased* (within limits) by any decrease for the year in its U.S. net equity.[12]

If a foreign corporation is subject to the branch profits tax for any tax year, the 30% tax on U.S.-source non-ECI (¶4628) and the related withholding (¶4648 *et seq.*) do not apply to any dividends it pays out of its E&P for that year. (Code Sec. 884(e)(3))[13]

The branch profits tax isn't imposed on a foreign corporation for the year it completely terminates its U.S. trade or business, except where there is a Code Sec. 381(a) corporate liquidation or reorganization, or a Code Sec. 351 incorporation. In order to completely terminate, a corporation must waive the statute of limitations for the year on Form 8848 attached to the income tax return. (Reg § 1.884-2, Reg § 1.884-2T)[14]

The branch profits tax may be reduced or eliminated by an income tax treaty if the taxpayer is a qualified resident of the treaty country. (Code Sec. 884(e))[15]

¶ 4634   Branch-level interest tax—foreign corporations.

Under Code Sec. 884(f)(1)(A), if a foreign corporation is engaged in a U.S. trade or business or has gross income treated as ECI (¶4630), interest paid by the corporation's U.S. trade or business (i.e., its U.S. branch) is treated as if it were paid by a U.S. corporation. In addition, if the interest allocable to the branch exceeds the interest actually paid by the branch, the difference is treated as interest paid by a U.S. subsidiary to its foreign parent and the foreign parent is subject to the 30% tax on that amount. (Code Sec. 884(f)(1)(B)) The branch-level interest tax may be reduced or eliminated by treaty. (Code Sec. 884(f)(3))[16]

¶ 4635   Tax treatment under FIRPTA of disposition of U.S. real property interests (USRPIs) by foreign corporations and nonresident aliens (NRAs).

Under Code Sec. 897(a)(1)—part of the Foreign Investment in Real Property Tax Act (FIRPTA)—gain or loss of an NRA or foreign corporation from the disposition of a USRPI is taxed as income effectively connected (¶4630) with a U.S. trade or business.[17]

Such income is also subject to reporting and withholding requirements, see ¶4646 and ¶4659.

A USRPI includes: (1) an interest in real property located in the U.S. or the Virgin Islands, and (2) any interest (other than solely as a creditor) in any U.S. corporation unless the corporation is shown *not* to have been a U.S. real property holding corporation

---

10. ¶O-10627
11. ¶O-10628
12. ¶O-11300 *et seq.*
13. ¶O-11315

14. ¶O-11316 *et seq.*
15. ¶O-11314, O-11334 *et seq.*
16. ¶O-11326 *et seq.*
17. ¶O-10700 *et seq.*

(USRPHC) during the 5-year period ending on the date of disposition (or, if shorter, the period held by the taxpayer). (Code Sec. 897(c)(1)(A)) An interest in a U.S. corporation is no longer a USRPI if it no longer holds USRPIs. (Code Sec. 897(c)(1)(B)) If the U.S. corporation is regularly traded, it is only treated as a USRPI for certain more-than-5% shareholders. (Code Sec. 897(c)(3))[18]

A USRPI does *not* include interests in domestically controlled real estate investment trusts (REITs) or certain domestically controlled regulated investment companies (RICs). (Code Sec. 897(h))[19] Special rules apply to foreign taxpayers that receive distributions from RICs and REITs. (Code Sec. 897(h))[20]

A USRPHC is any corporation, if the fair market value of its USRPIs on any applicable determination date is 50% or more of the fair market value of its USRPIs, its interests in non-U.S. real property, plus any other business assets. (Code Sec. 897(c)(2))[21]

Foreign taxpayers that hold USRPIs indirectly through an interest in a partnership, estate or trust are subject to U.S. tax on any gain attributable to the entity's USRPIs upon the disposition of their interest in the entity. (Code Sec. 897(g))[22]

¶ 4636 A foreign corporation's election to be treated as a U.S. corporation for FIRPTA purposes.

A foreign corporation may elect to be treated as a U.S. corporation for purposes of the FIRPTA rules (¶4635), including reporting and withholding (¶4646 and ¶4659), if the corporation: (i) holds a U.S. real property interest (USRPI) (¶4635) at the time of the election, (ii) is entitled to nondiscriminatory treatment under an income tax treaty, (iii) would have qualified as a U.S. real property holding corporation (¶4635), and (iv) makes a timely and proper election. (Code Sec. 897(i); Reg § 1.897-3, Reg § 1.897-8T(b))[23]

¶ 4637 4% tax on U.S. source gross transportation income of foreign corporations and nonresident aliens.

Under Code Sec. 887, a 4% tax is imposed on the U.S.-source gross transportation income of foreign corporations and nonresident aliens. Income subject to this 4% gross-basis tax isn't subject to the 30% tax on non-effectively connected income (¶4628) or the regular U.S. tax on effectively connected income (¶4630). (Code Sec. 887(c))[24]

¶ 4638 2% excise tax on certain federal procurement payments to foreign corporations and nonresident aliens.

Under Code Sec. 5000C, a 2% excise tax applies to specified federal procurement payments to foreign persons, i.e., payments made under a contract with the U.S. for the provision of goods manufactured or produced, or services provided, in any country which is not a party to an international procurement agreement with the U.S. The excise tax is enforced by withholding. Certain foreign vendors (e.g., vendors protected under a nondiscrimination clause of a treaty) and certain transactions (e.g., small purchases at or under $250,000) are exempt. (Reg § 1.5000C-1, Reg § 1.5000C-2, Reg § 1.5000C-3)[25]

¶ 4639 Tax treatment of U.S. citizens and long-term residents who expatriate— Form 8854.

Under Code Sec. 877A, a covered expatriate is subject to a mark-to-market rule under which his or her property is generally treated as sold on the day before the expatriation

---

18. ¶O-10705 *et seq.*
19. ¶O-10709
20. ¶O-10703 *et seq.*
21. ¶O-10711 *et seq.*

22. ¶O-10702
23. ¶O-10725
24. ¶O-11500 *et seq.*
25. ¶O-13350 *et seq.*

date for fair market value (FMV).[26]

The gain from the deemed sale is taken into account at that time without regard to other Code provisions, and any loss generally is taken into account to the extent otherwise provided in the Code, except that the wash sale rules of Code Sec. 1091 don't apply. (Code Sec. 877A(a)(2)) However, any net gain on the deemed sale is taxed only to the extent it exceeds an inflation adjusted amount that is $767,000 for 2022 ($821,000 for 2023). (Code Sec. 877A(a)(3)) Subsequent gains or losses that are realized are adjusted for the gains and losses taken into account under the deemed sale rules without regard to this exemption. (Code Sec. 877A(a)(2))[27]

The mark-to-market deemed sale rule does not apply to deferred compensation items, interests in nongrantor trusts, and specified tax deferred accounts. (Code Sec. 877A(c))[28]

Covered expatriates are U.S. citizens who relinquish citizenship and long-term residents who terminate U.S. residency, if they meet any of the following tests:

(1) the individual's average annual net income tax for the period of five tax years ending before the date of the loss of U.S. citizenship was greater than an inflation adjusted amount that is $178,000 for losses of citizenship in 2022 ($190,000 for 2023) (the "average annual net income tax" test);

(2) the individual's net worth as of that date was $2 million or more (the "net worth" test); or

(3) the individual: (i) fails to certify under penalty of perjury that he or she has met the requirements of the Code for the five preceding tax years, or (ii) fails to submit evidence of compliance as IRS may require. The certification is made on Form 8854. (Code Sec. 877A(g)(1)(A), Code Sec. 877A(g)(2))

However, an individual will not be treated as a covered expatriate under the average annual net income tax or net worth tests if he: (1) became at birth a citizen of the U.S. and a citizen of another country and, as of the expatriation date, continues to be a citizen of, and is taxed as a resident of, the other country, and has been a U.S. resident (under the substantial presence test) for not more than 10 tax years during the 15 tax-year period ending with the tax year in which the expatriation date occurs; or (2) gives up U.S. citizenship before becoming 18½ years old and was a U.S. resident for not more than 10 tax years before the relinquishment date. (Code Sec. 877A(g)(1)(B))[29]

Election to defer tax on expatriation. An individual may irrevocably elect, on a property-by-property basis, to defer payment of the mark-to-market tax imposed on the deemed sale of property. Interest is charged for the period the tax is deferred. The deferred tax generally is due when the return is due for the tax year in which the property is disposed of. (Code Sec. 877A(b))[30]

¶ 4640   Tax treatment of corporate and partnership inversions (restructurings to achieve expatriation).

Under Code Sec. 7874, if (i) a foreign corporation (surrogate foreign corporation) directly or indirectly acquires substantially all of the properties held by a domestic corporation or substantially all of the properties constituting a trade or business of a domestic partnership (each an expatriated entity), and (ii) the expanded affiliated group (EAG) that includes the surrogate foreign corporation doesn't have substantial business activities in the country in which the surrogate foreign corporation was created or organized, then, after the transaction, if the former owners of the expatriated entity own:

... 80% or more of the interests in the surrogate foreign corporation, the surrogate foreign corporation is taxed as a domestic entity.

... 60% or more of the interests in the surrogate foreign corporation, the expatriated

---

26. ¶O-11650 *et seq.*
27. ¶O-11651.1 *et seq.*
28. ¶O-11654

29. ¶O-11659
30. ¶O-11653

entity must recognize taxable income at least equal to the inversion gain (defined below) for the tax year.[31]

Inversion gain is any income or gain recognized by reason of the expatriated entity's transfer during a 10-year period after the transfer of stock or other properties, and any income received or accrued during that period by reason of a license of any property by an expatriated entity as part of the inversion (or after the inversion, if the transfer or license is to a foreign related person). Inversion gain generally can't be offset by credits or NOLs. (Code Sec. 7874(d)(2), Code Sec. 7874(e))[32]

An EAG has substantial business activities in the foreign country only if at least 25% of (i) the group employees and their compensation are based, (ii) the value of the group's total assets are located, and (iii) the group's income is derived, in the relevant country. However, an EAG cannot have substantial business activities in the foreign country unless the foreign acquiring corporation is liable to tax as a resident of the foreign country. (Reg § 1.7874-3)[33]

Special rules address transactions that are structured to avoid the purposes of the inversion rules. Thus, in determining stock ownership, disqualified stock (Reg § 1.7874-4), certain transferred stock (Reg § 1.7874-5 and Reg § 1.7874-6), stock attributable to passive assets (Reg § 1.7874-7), stock attributable to multiple domestic entity acquisitions (Reg § 1.7874-8), certain third-country transactions (Reg § 1.7874-9) and non-ordinary course distributions (Reg § 1.7874-10) are disregarded.[34]

¶ 4641   Returns Relating to Foreign Taxpayers.

U.S. income tax returns must be filed by nonresident alien individuals (¶4642) and foreign corporations engaged in a U.S. business (¶4644). An income tax return is also required for a partnership with gross income from U.S.-sources or that is effectively connected with the conduct of a U.S. trade or business (¶4645). Information returns are required for certain foreign transactions (¶4646).

¶ 4642   Return of nonresident alien individual (NRA)—Forms 1040NR and 1040NR-EZ.

An NRA individual must file a U.S. tax return (Form 1040-NR, or, for certain NRAs with no dependents, Form 1040NR-EZ) if they have income subject to the income tax or if they were engaged in business in the U.S. (¶4631) or deemed to be so engaged at any time during the tax year, even if they have no income effectively connected to that trade or business (¶4630), no other U.S.-source income, or their income is tax-exempt (by treaty or otherwise). (Reg § 1.6012-1(b)(1)) However, if the NRA is at no time during the year engaged in a U.S. trade or business, they are not required to file a return if their tax liability is fully satisfied by withholding. (Reg § 1.6012-1(b)(2))[35] In general, an NRA won't get the benefit of otherwise allowable deductions and credits if they do not file a true and accurate return, see ¶4632.

Form 1040NR and Form 1040NR-EZ are due by the 15th day of the sixth month (i.e., June 15), or fourth month (April 15) if the alien had wages subject to wage withholding, after the close of the tax year. (Code Sec. 6072(c); Reg § 1.6072-1(c))[36]

¶ 4643   Departing alien—certificate of tax compliance—Forms 1040C, 2063.

Under Code Sec. 6851(d)(1), an alien (resident or nonresident) cannot leave the U.S. without obtaining a certificate of compliance with income tax law (sailing or departure permit), except most tourists, students, trainees, and foreign government personnel and their family members aren't required to get a certificate of compliance. (Reg § 1.6851-

---

31. ¶F-5700 *et seq.*
32. ¶F-5724, F-5725
33. ¶F-5706
34. ¶F-5711 *et seq.*
35. ¶S-1750 *et seq.*
36. ¶S-4703

2(a)(2)) The alien files either Form 1040C (if the alien has income subject to U.S. tax) or Form 2063 (if the alien has no such income) in order to receive the certificate. (Reg § 1.6851-2(b))[37]

¶ 4644   Return of foreign corporation—Form 1120F.

A foreign corporation must file a U.S. income tax return (Form 1120F) if it has income subject to the income tax or if it was engaged in business in the U.S. (¶4631) during the tax year (or deemed to be so engaged), even if (i) the corporation has no income effectively connected to such business (¶4630) or other U.S.-source income, or (ii) its income is tax-exempt (by treaty or otherwise). However, if the foreign corporation has no gross income for the tax year, it is not required to complete the return schedules. A foreign corporation which is not engaged in business in the U.S. at any time during the tax year is not required to make a return if its tax liability is fully satisfied by withholding. (Reg § 1.6012-2(g))[38] In general, the foreign corporation won't get the benefit of otherwise allowable deductions and credits if it does not file a true and accurate return, see ¶4632.

Foreign corporations that have no U.S. office or place of business must file their return by the 15th day of June following the close of the tax year (in the case of a fiscal year-based return, on or before the 15th day of the sixth month following the end of the fiscal year). (Code Sec. 6072(c))[39]

¶ 4645   Return of foreign partnership—Form 1065.

Under Code Sec. 6031(e), a foreign partnership isn't required to file a partnership return (Form 1065), unless it has gross income that is (or is treated as) effectively connected with the conduct of a trade or business within the U.S. (ECI, see ¶4630) or has gross income from sources within the U.S. (U.S.-source income). (Reg § 1.6031(a)-1(b)(1)) A foreign partnership, other than a withholding foreign partnership, that has $20,000 or less of U.S.-source income and has no ECI during its tax year need not file a partnership return if, at no time during the partnership tax year, 1% or more of any item of partnership income, gain, loss, deduction, or credit is allocable in the aggregate to direct U.S. partners. The U.S. partners must directly report their shares of the allocable items of partnership income, gain, loss, deduction, and credit. (Reg § 1.6031(a)-1(b)(2)) A foreign partnership (other than a withholding foreign partnership) with no ECI which files any required Form 1042 and Form 1042-S and fully pays the associated withholding tax, and that has no U.S. partners, is not required to file a partnership return. If the partnership does have U.S. partners, it must file a partnership return, but it need only file Schedules K-1 for its direct U.S. partners and for its pass-through partners through which U.S. partners hold an interest in the foreign partnership. (Reg § 1.6031(a)-1(b)(3))[40]

¶ 4646   Information returns related to foreign taxpayers—Forms 926, 5471, 5472, 8865, 8938, 8975, FinCEN Form 114 (FBAR).

Under Code Sec. 6038(a)(1), a U.S. person must provide certain information (on Form 5471) for each foreign corporation that person controls. (Code Sec. 6038; Reg § 1.6038-2)[41] Similarly, a U.S. partner that controls a foreign partnership must also furnish IRS with information on Form 8865. (Code Sec. 6038; Reg § 1.6038-3)[42]

The ownership of, or acquisition of, 10% or more of the stock in, a foreign corporation may trigger a reporting obligation on Form 5471 by certain U.S. shareholders, officers and directors. (Code Sec. 6046)[43] The acquisition, disposition or substantial change in size of an interest in a foreign partnership must be reported on Form 8865 by a U.S. person if the U.S. person holds a 10% or greater interest in the partnership either before or after the

37. ¶S-1760 *et seq.*
38. ¶S-1910 *et seq.*
39. ¶S-4704
40. ¶S-2712 *et seq.*
41. ¶S-3586 *et seq.*
42. ¶S-3585.0 *et seq.*
43. ¶S-3602 *et seq.*

acquisition/disposition or if the change in size of the interest is at least 10%. (Code Sec. 6046A)[44]

A U.S. corporation at least 25% of which is owned by one foreign person (including, for these purposes, a U.S. disregarded entity wholly owned by a foreign person), or a foreign corporation engaged in a U.S. trade or business, must maintain records and furnish IRS with certain information on Form 5472 regarding transactions with related parties during the tax year. (Code Sec. 6038A, Code Sec. 6038C; Reg § 1.6038A-1(c)(1), Reg § 1.6038A-2(a)(1), Reg § 301.7701-2(c)(2)(vi)(A))[45]

Each U.S. person (i) transferring property to a foreign corporation (or a partnership under certain conditions) in specified tax-free exchanges, or (ii) distributing property in complete liquidation to a non-U.S. person, must report the transfer to IRS on Form 926 for corporations, Form 8865 for partnerships. (Code Sec. 6038B)[46]

Any individual who, during the tax year, holds any interest in a specified foreign financial asset as defined in Reg § 1.6038D-3, must attach to the income tax return for that tax year required information on Form 8938 for each specified foreign financial asset if the aggregate value of all the individual's specified foreign financial assets exceeds $50,000 (higher thresholds apply in certain cases under the regs). These same rules apply to any domestic entity formed or availed of for purposes of holding specified foreign financial assets. (Code Sec. 6038D; Reg § 1.6038D-1, Reg § 1.6038D-2)[47]

To the extent provided in future regs, foreign investors in U.S. real property will be required to report their direct ownership interests to IRS. (Code Sec. 6039C)[48]

Except for certain corporations with annual revenues of less than $850 million, every U.S. person that is the ultimate parent entity of a U.S. multinational enterprise (MNE) group must make an annual return on Form 8975 (Country-by-Country Report or CbCR) setting forth the required information. (Reg § 1.6038-4)[49]

Foreign bank and financial accounts (including on-line poker accounts) are reported on Financial Crimes Enforcement Network (FinCEN) Form 114 (FBAR) by any person (including a person acting as an agent) with a financial interest in or signature authority over the account, if the aggregate value of these accounts exceeds $10,000 at any time during the calendar year. FBAR is due by Apr. 15 of the year following the year that the account holder meets the $10,000 threshold, but is eligible for an automatic 6-month extension. IRS has provided information on completing and filing an FBAR. (IR 2022-73, 3/31/2022; FS-2022-24, 3/31/2022) The deadline for filing a 2022 FBAR is Apr. 15, 2022. (IR 2022-73, 3/31/2022; FS-2022-24, 3/31/2022)[50]

¶ 4647 Tax Withholding on Payments to Foreign Taxpayers. ▬▬▬

Several withholding regimes enforce the imposition of tax and/or reporting requirements on foreign taxpayers. These include (i) withholding at a 30% or lower rate on the gross amount of U.S.-source fixed and determinable income items (chapter 3 or "FDAP" withholding, see ¶4648 *et seq.*), (ii) 30% withholding on certain withholdable payments under the Foreign Account Tax Compliance Act if the payee doesn't provide the required documentation (FATCA withholding, see ¶4653 *et seq.*), (iii) wage withholding (¶4656), (iv) withholding on effectively connected income of foreign partners in a partnership (¶4657), and (v) withholding on the disposition of U.S. real property interests (¶4659).

¶ 4648 Which foreign taxpayers are subject to FDAP withholding?

Nonresident alien individuals and foreign partnerships are subject to FDAP withholding (¶4647) (Code Sec. 1441(a)), as are foreign corporations (Code Sec. 1442(a)), foreign trusts,

---

44. ¶S-3643 *et seq.*
45. ¶D-1166, ¶S-3485 *et seq.*, ¶S-3510 *et seq.*
46. ¶S-3629 *et seq.*
47. ¶S-3650.1 *et seq.*

48. ¶S-3481 *et seq.*
49. ¶S-3490 *et seq.*
50. ¶S-3650

foreign estates, foreign branches of U.S. financial institutions for which a QI agreement (¶4651) is in effect (but only for withholding purposes), and any other person that is not a U.S. person. (Reg § 1.1441-1(b), Reg § 1.1441-1(c)(2), Reg § 1.1441-1(c)(12)) An alien individual who made an election to be treated as a resident of the U.S. is nevertheless treated as a nonresident alien individual for withholding purposes. (Reg § 1.1441-1(c)(3)(ii)) A corporation organized in the Virgin Islands, American Samoa, Guam, or the Commonwealth of the Northern Mariana Islands is not a foreign corporation for withholding purposes if certain tests are met. (Code Sec. 1442(c))[1]

¶ 4649   What income is subject to FDAP withholding on foreign taxpayers?

The amounts subject to FDAP withholding (¶4647) are U.S.-source amounts that are either fixed or determinable annual or periodical income (FDAP income) or certain gains from the disposition of timber, coal or domestic iron ore, and from contingent payment sales of intangible property. FDAP income includes all gross income except for gains derived from the sale of property (including market discount and option premiums, but not including original issue discount (OID)), namely interest (other than OID), dividends, rent, salaries, wages, premiums, annuities, compensations, remunerations, emoluments, payments on and gain on sale of OID obligations, social security benefits to the extent of 85% of those benefits, excess inclusions of holders of real estate mortgage investment conduit (REMIC) residual interests, dividend equivalents, patronage dividends, and alimony payments. (Code Sec. 1441(b), Code Sec. 1441(g), Code Sec. 860G(b)(1); Reg § 1.1441-2)[2]

Items exempt from FDAP withholding include (but are not limited to):

. . . income (other than compensation for personal services) which is effectively connected with the conduct of a U.S. business and taxed at regular U.S. tax rates. (Code Sec. 1441(c)(1))

. . . portfolio interest, substitute interest payments, certain kinds of deposit interest, interest and OID on short-term obligations. (Code Sec. 1441(c); Reg § 1.1441-1(b)(4))

. . . compensation for personal services of a nonresident alien individual if such compensation is effectively connected with the conduct of a trade or business within the U.S. *and* it: (i) is subject to the wage withholding regime (see ¶4656), (ii) would be subject to the wage withholding regime, except that it is specifically exempted from the definition of wages for these purposes, (iii) is for services performed by Canadian or Mexican residents who enter or leave the U.S. at frequent intervals, (iv) is exempt from tax by law or treaty, (v) is paid as a commission or rebate by a ship supplier under certain circumstances; or (vi) is exempt from withholding under a statutory "all-or-nothing" rule if the employee and employer enter into a voluntary nonwage withholding agreement. (Code Sec. 1441(c)(4); Reg § 1.1441-4(b))

. . . regulated investment company (RIC) dividends that are paid out of interest that would not be subject to withholding, and certain short-term capital gains under Code Sec. 871(k). (Code Sec. 1441(c)(12))[3]

¶ 4650   Rate of FDAP withholding on foreign taxpayers.

The amount of tax to be withheld on an item of FDAP income (¶4649) is generally 30%, except that the rate is reduced to 14% on certain scholarship or fellowship amounts received by a nonresident alien individual temporarily present in the U.S. (Code Sec. 1441(a), Code Sec. 1441(b))[4]

The rate of withholding on non-compensation income may be reduced to the extent provided under an income tax treaty in effect between the U.S. and a foreign country (see ¶4651 for required documentation). (Reg § 1.1441-6(a))[5]

1. ¶O-11900 *et seq.*
2. ¶O-11902 *et seq.*
3. ¶O-11960 *et seq.*
4. ¶O-11901, ¶O-11998
5. ¶O-12032

¶ **4651** **Documentation to be provided to the FDAP withholding agent—Forms W-9, W-8, 8233—withholding on foreign taxpayers.**

The withholding agent. Under Code Sec. 1441(a) and Code Sec. 1442(a), any person having the control, receipt, custody, disposal, or payment of an item of income subject to FDAP withholding (¶4649) of a foreign person (¶4648) is a FDAP withholding agent. (Reg § 1.1441-7(a)) The withholding agent must withhold at a 30% rate on that income unless it can reliably associate the payment with documentation upon which it can rely to treat the payment as made to a payee that is a U.S. person or as made to a foreign beneficial owner entitled to a reduced rate of withholding (see below). However, a withholding agent need not withhold if the foreign person assumes responsibility for withholding (i) as a qualified intermediary (QI, ¶4655), (ii) as a U.S. branch of a foreign person, or (iii) as a withholding foreign partnership or withholding foreign trust (¶4655). FDAP withholding is also not required if FATCA withholding (¶4653) was applied to the payment. (Reg § 1.1441-1(b)(1))[6]

A U.S. partnership must withhold as a FDAP withholding agent on an amount subject to withholding that is includible in the gross income of a partner that is a foreign person. Similarly, a U.S. trust is required to withhold as a FDAP withholding agent on the distributable net income (DNI) includible in the gross income of a foreign beneficiary to the extent the DNI is an amount subject to withholding. (Reg § 1.1441-5(b))[7]

Documentation of U.S. status of beneficial owner or payee. Absent actual knowledge or reason to know otherwise, a withholding agent may treat a payee as a U.S. person if (i) the payee is required to furnish a Form W-9 and furnishes it under the backup withholding rules, and it includes the payee's taxpayer identification number (TIN) or (ii) the payee is not required to furnish the Form W-9 but provides the withholding agent with a Form W-9 (or a substitute form) that contains the payee's name, address, and TIN. The form must be signed under penalties of perjury. (Reg § 1.1441-1(d)) A withholding agent that makes a payment to an intermediary, flow-through entity, or U.S. branch or territory financial institution may treat the payment as made to a U.S. payee to the extent that, prior to the payment, the withholding agent can reliably associate the payment with: (a) a Form W-9 attached to a valid intermediary, flow-through, or U.S. branch withholding certificate; or (b) a Form W-8 that evidences an agreement to treat a U.S. branch as a U.S. person. (Reg § 1.1441-1(d)(4))[8]

Documentation of entitlement to reduced rate of withholding under tax treaty. Absent actual knowledge or reason to know otherwise, a withholding agent may rely on a claim that a beneficial owner is entitled to a reduced rate of withholding under a treaty if, before the payment, the withholding agent can reliably associate the payment with a Form W-8BEN beneficial owner withholding certificate that includes the required information, representations and certifications. (Reg § 1.1441-6(b)(1))[9]

In the case of compensation income, the form used is Form 8233 containing the required information. (Reg § 1.1441-4(b)(2))[10]

Documentation that income is effectively connected. Absent actual knowledge or reason to know otherwise, a withholding agent may rely on a claim of exemption from withholding for income effectively connected with a U.S. trade or business if, prior to the payment to the foreign person, the withholding agent can reliably associate the payment with a valid Form W-8ECI. To be valid, in addition to other applicable requirements, the form must include the TIN and represent, under penalties of perjury, that the amounts for which the certificate is furnished are effectively connected with the conduct of a trade or business in the U.S. and includable in the beneficial owner's gross income for the tax year. (Reg § 1.1441-4(a)(2)(i))[11]

---

6. ¶O-11901, ¶O-11914 *et seq.*
7. ¶O-12005.1, ¶O-12010
8. ¶O-11929.6

9. ¶O-12032
10. ¶O-11991.1
11. ¶O-11968

¶ 4652   Reporting FDAP withholding amounts—Forms 1042, 1042-S—withholding on foreign taxpayers.

A withholding agent must file an annual income tax return on Form 1042 for income paid during the preceding calendar year that the withholding agent is required to report on an information return on Form 1042-S (see below). The income tax return must be filed with IRS on or before Mar. 15 of the calendar year following the year in which the income was paid, even if no tax was required to be withheld during the preceding calendar year. A single Form 1042 may be filed by a withholding agent to report FDAP and FATCA (¶4653) amounts, including tax withheld. (Reg § 1.1461-1(b)(1))[12]

A withholding agent (other than an individual who is not acting in the course of a trade or business with respect to a payment) must also file an information return on Form 1042-S to report the amounts subject to reporting that were paid during the preceding calendar year. However, a person that withholds or is required to withhold must file a Form 1042-S for the payment withheld on whether that person is engaged in a trade or business and whether the payment is an amount subject to reporting. A Form 1042-S must be prepared for each recipient of an amount subject to reporting and for each single type of income payment. One copy of the form must be filed with IRS on or before Mar. 15 of the calendar year following the year in which the amount subject to reporting was paid, another copy must be furnished to the recipient for whom the form is prepared on or before the same date, and a third copy must be retained by the withholding agent. (Reg § 1.1461-1(c)(1))[13]

Amounts subject to reporting. Subject to certain exceptions, the amounts subject to reporting are the amounts subject to withholding (as described in ¶4649) paid to a foreign payee, even if no amount is withheld from the payment because of a treaty or Code exception to taxation, or because an amount withheld was reimbursed to the payee under certain adjustment procedures. In addition, amounts subject to reporting include any amounts paid to a foreign payee on which a withholding agent actually withheld (either under the FDAP provisions or the backup withholding provisions (see ¶3043 *et seq.*)), whether or not the amount is subject to withholding. (Reg § 1.1461-1(c)(2))[14]

¶ 4653   FATCA withholding on foreign banks, other foreign entities—Forms 8966, 8957.

Under Code Sec. 1471 through Code Sec. 1474, in order to encourage reporting on certain U.S.-owned foreign accounts, the Foreign Account Tax Compliance Act (FATCA) requires a withholding agent (as defined in Reg § 1.1473-1(d)) to withhold at a 30% rate on withholdable payments to (i) foreign financial institutions (FFIs; as defined in Reg § 1.1471-5(d)) that do not meet certain reporting, compliance and withholding requirements for their U.S. accounts, and (ii) nonfinancial foreign entities (NFFEs) unless they has no substantial U.S. owners or any substantial U.S. owners are identified.[15]

Withholding on payments to FFIs. An FFI isn't subject to withholding if it: (i) enters into an FFI agreement with IRS under which it assumes specific compliance and reporting (on Form 8966) obligations (a "participating FFI"), or (ii) is deemed to comply with the compliance and reporting requirements (a "deemed-compliant FFI"). An FFI may satisfy the compliance and reporting requirements but elect to be withheld upon rather than to withhold. An FFI registers on Form 8957 via an online FATCA registration system in order to enter into its FFI agreement. (Code Sec. 1471; Reg § 1.1471-2(a))[16]

Withholding on payments to NFFEs. An NFFE isn't subject to withholding if (i) the beneficial owner of the payment is the NFFE or any other NFFE, (ii) the payee or the beneficial owner provides the withholding agent with either a certification that the foreign

---

12. ¶S-3471
13. ¶S-3471.2
14. ¶S-3477

15. ¶O-13070 *et seq.*
16. ¶O-13072 *et seq.*

entity does not have a substantial U.S. owner or the name, address and taxpayer identification number (TIN) of each substantial U.S. owner; and (iii) certain reporting requirements are met. Withholding also does not apply to excepted NFFEs. (Code Sec. 1472; Reg § 1.1472-1)[17]

Withholdable payments. Withholdable payments are non-effectively connected (i) payments of U.S.-source interest (including any original issue discount), dividends, rents, salaries, wages, premiums, annuities, compensations, remunerations, emoluments, and other fixed or determinable annual or periodical gains, profits; and (ii) gross proceeds from the sale or other disposition of any property of a type that can produce U.S.-source interest or dividends. However, payments on certain obligations outstanding on July 1, 2014 (grandfathered obligations) are exempt from withholding tax altogether. (Code Sec. 1473(1); Reg § 1.1471-2(b), Reg § 1.1473-1(a)) Proposed regulations, on which taxpayers may rely, eliminate withholding on payments of gross proceeds. (Prop Reg. § 1.1473-1(a)(1))[18]

¶ 4654 Reporting FATCA withholding on foreign banks, other foreign entities—Forms 1042, 1042-S.

Every FATCA withholding agent (¶4653) must file an income tax return on Form 1042 to report reportable amounts (generally, withholdable payments (¶4653) including those reportable under the FDAP provisions (see ¶4652)). This income tax return is filed on the same income tax return used to report amounts subject to withholding under the FDAP withholding provisions (¶4652). A Form 1042 must be filed even if no tax was required to be withheld under the FATCA provisions during the preceding calendar year. (Reg § 1.1474-1(c), Reg § 1.1474-1(d)(2))[19]

Every FATCA withholding agent must file an information return on Form 1042-S to report to IRS reportable amounts that were paid to a recipient during the preceding calendar year. Except as otherwise provided in the regs, a separate Form 1042-S must be filed with IRS for each recipient of an amount subject to reporting and for each separate type of payment made to a single recipient. One copy of the form must be filed with IRS on or before Mar. 15 of the calendar year following the year in which the amount subject to reporting was paid, another copy must be furnished to the recipient (and certain intermediaries) on or before the same date, and the withholding agent must retain a third copy. (Reg § 1.1474-1(d)(1))[20]

¶ 4655 Qualified intermediary (QI), withholding foreign partnership (WFP), and withholding foreign trust (WFT) agreements—FATCA and FDAP withholding.

QIs. A QI is a foreign entity (typically, a financial institution) that enters into an agreement with IRS under which it acts as an agent on behalf of persons for whom it receives payment and subjects itself to the withholding and reporting provisions applicable to withholding agents under the FDAP (¶4648 *et seq.*) and FATCA (¶4653 *et seq.*) provisions, and to payors under the backup withholding (¶3043 *et seq.*) and information reporting (¶4737 *et seq.*) rules, in addition to other withholding rules, except to the extent provided under the agreement. The QI furnishes a QI withholding certificate instead of transmitting to the withholding agent the withholding certificates or other documentation it has obtained from the payees. A QI may assume the primary obligation to withhold, deposit, and report amounts under the FATCA and FDAP provisions and/or under the backup withholding and information reporting provisions if it meets the relevant requirements. A QI that assumes primary withholding responsibility for payments made to an

---

17. ¶O-13074, O-13093
18. ¶O-13078 *et seq.*

19. ¶S-3471.1, ¶S-3478.1
20. ¶S-3471.2

account under the FDAP provisions is also required to assume primary withholding responsibility under the FATCA provisions. If the QI has assumed primary withholding responsibility for the payment, the withholding agent is not required to withhold on the payment and is not required to determine that the QI actually performs its primary withholding responsibilities. (Reg § 1.1441-1(e)(5))[21]

WFPs and WFTs. Foreign trusts and partnerships may similarly enter into agreements with IRS under which they may act as withholding agents. (Reg § 1.1441-5(c)(2), Reg § 1.1441-5(e)(5)(v))[22]

¶ 4656   Withholding on effectively connected wages of a nonresident alien individual.

Compensation paid for personal services performed by a nonresident alien individual which meets the definition of "wages" (¶3005), and which is effectively connected with a U.S. trade or business, is subject to regular graduated income tax withholding with certain adjustments under Code Sec. 3402. (Reg § 31.3401(a)(6)-1(a))[23]

The following aren't wages subject to the wage withholding regime:

(1) Wages paid for services performed outside the U.S. by a nonresident alien individual other than a resident of Puerto Rico (PR). (Reg § 31.3401(a)(6)-1(b))

(2) Remuneration paid to Canadian and Mexican residents who enter or leave the U.S. at frequent intervals and are engaged in transportation service or in service on international projects. (Reg § 31.3401(a)(6)-1(c))

(3) Wages paid (i) to PR residents for services performed in PR for an employer other than the U.S. government, (ii) for services performed outside the U.S., but not in PR, by a PR resident for an employer other than the U.S. government if the individual does not expect to be a PR resident during the entire tax year, or (iii) for services performed outside the U.S. by a nonresident alien individual who is a PR resident as an employee of the U.S. government, if the individual does not expect to be a PR resident during the entire tax year. (Reg § 31.3401(a)(6)-1(d))

(4) Wages exempt from tax by law or treaty. (Reg § 31.3401(a)(6)-1(f))[24]

 observation: Compensation paid to self-employed individuals that doesn't meet the above definition of wages, is generally subject to withholding under the FDAP provisions (¶4647 *et seq.*) unless an exception (¶4649) applies.

¶ 4657   Withholding by partnerships with respect to foreign partners—Forms 8813, 8804, 8805.

Under Code Sec. 1446(a), a partnership must pay a withholding tax if it has effectively connected taxable income for the tax year (whether or not the income is distributed), any part of which is allocable to a foreign partner. Unless the partner can show that the tax should be lower, the partnership must withhold at the highest rate of U.S. (corporate or individual, as applicable) tax to which the foreign partner would be subject on that allocable income. (Code Sec. 1446(b); Reg § 1.1446-3, Reg § 1.1446-6) The partnership must determine the status of its partners based on the Form W-8 or Form W-9 filed by the partners. In the absence of documentation of a partner's status, the partnership must follow the presumptions in the regs. (Reg § 1.1446-1) Special rules apply to publicly traded partnerships and tiered partnerships. (Reg § 1.1446-4, Reg § 1.1446-5)[25]

The partnership must pay the withheld amount in installments together with a Form 8813, report the partnership's total withholding liability for its year on Form 8804, and

---

21. ¶O-12700 *et seq.*
22. ¶O-12770 *et seq.*, ¶O-12820 *et seq.*
23. ¶H-4436

24. ¶H-4436.1
25. ¶O-12100 *et seq.*

notify each foreign partner of his or her share thereof on Form 8805. (Reg § 1.1446-3)[26]

¶ 4658 Withholding on amounts realized on dispositions of partnership interests—Forms 8288, 8288-A.

Under Code Sec. 1446(f)(1), if any portion of the gain on the disposition of a partnership interest would be treated as effectively connected with the conduct of a U.S. trade or business (¶4630), the transferee must withhold 10% of the amount realized on the disposition. Taxpayers must use the principles applicable to withholding on U.S. real property interests (¶4659), including the use of Form 8288 and Form 8288-A. However, no withholding is required if the transferor provides a nonforeign affidavit. (Code Sec. 1446(f)(2); Reg § 1.1446(f)-2(b)) Special rules apply for transfers of publicly traded partnership interests.[27]

¶ 4659 Withholding on U.S. real property interest (USRPI) dispositions by foreign persons—Forms 8288, 8288-A.

Under Code Sec. 1445(a), any person who acquires a USRPI (¶4635) from a foreign person must generally withhold a tax of 15% on the amount realized by the transferor foreign person. (Reg § 1.1445-1(a); Reg § 1.1445-1(b)) The amount realized is the sum of cash received, the fair market value of any other property received, and any liability assumed by the transferee (e.g., buyer) or to which the USRPI was subject. (Reg § 1.1445-1(g)(5)) The amount required to be withheld can't exceed the transferor's maximum tax liability with respect to the transfer (i.e., the maximum amount of U.S. income tax that could be imposed with respect to the disposition, plus any unsatisfied withholding liability of the transferor with respect to USRPI). (Code Sec. 1445(c), Code Sec. 1445(f)(4))[28]

To the extent provided in the regs, the transferee of a partnership interest or of a beneficial interest in a trust or estate is required to deduct and withhold 15% of the amount realized on a disposition where the entity directly or indirectly owns a USRPI. (Code Sec. 1445(e)(5); Reg § 1.1445-11T(b))[29]

Withholding is not required where the transferor gives the transferee a sworn "nonforeign affidavit" which includes his or her U.S. TIN, a sworn "non-USRPHC affidavit" (¶4635) stating the interest is not a USRPI, or a statement from IRS that withholding is not required. Withholding also does not apply if the USRPI is acquired by the transferee as his or her residence, and the amount realized doesn't exceed $300,000; where the amount exceeds $300,000 but is not more than $1 million, a 10% withholding rate applies. (Code Sec. 1445(b); Reg § 1.1445-1(b))[30]

The transferee of the USRPI acquired from a foreign person must report on Form 8288 and Form 8288-A, and pay over to IRS the amounts withheld by the 20th day after transfer. (Reg § 1.1445-1(c))[31]

¶ 4660 Foreign Currency Rules; Functional Currency; Qualified Business Units. ▬

Under Code Sec. 985(a), U.S. taxpayers must generally make all federal income tax determinations, including those stemming from transactions involving foreign currency, in their functional currency.[32]

A U.S. taxpayer's functional currency is generally the U.S. dollar (Code Sec. 985(b)(1)(A)), except in the case of a qualified business unit (QBU) that uses the currency of the economic environment in which a significant part of its activities are conducted and which is used to keep its books and records. (Code Sec. 985(b)(1)(B)). A QBU may elect to use the U.S. dollar instead if it meets certain requirements. (Code

26. ¶S-2716
27. ¶O-12116 *et seq.*
28. ¶O-13000 *et seq.*
29. ¶O-13037

30. ¶O-13010 *et seq.*
31. ¶O-13002.1
32. ¶G-6900 *et seq.*

Sec. 985(b)(3))[33]

A QBU is any separate and clearly identified unit (or activity) of a trade or business of a taxpayer which maintains separate books and records. (Code Sec. 989(a)) A corporation is a QBU. A partnership is a QBU of a partner. A trust or estate is a QBU of a beneficiary. An individual is not a QBU. (Reg § 1.989(a)-1(b)(2)(i))[34] If a U.S. taxpayer has one or more QBUs with non-dollar functional currencies, profits and losses are computed separately for each unit in its functional currency and then translated into dollars at the appropriate exchange rate. (Code Sec. 987)[35]

¶ 4661   Treatment of foreign currency gains and losses from "section 988 transactions."

Under Code Sec. 988(a)(1)(A), foreign currency gain or loss attributable to a "section 988 transaction" must generally be computed separately for each transaction and treated as ordinary income or expense, as the case may be. But a taxpayer may elect to treat the foreign currency gain or loss attributable to certain forward contracts, futures contracts, or options as capital gain or loss. (Code Sec. 988(a)(1)(B))[36] A section 988 transaction is (i) the acquisition of a debt instrument or becoming the obligor under a debt instrument, (ii) the accruing (or otherwise taking into account) of an item of expense or gross income or receipts which is to be paid or received after the accrual date, or (iii) the entering into or acquiring of a forward contract, futures contract, option, or similar financial instrument; if the amount the taxpayer is entitled to receive, or required to pay, by reason of such transaction, is either: (1) denominated in terms of a nonfunctional currency; or (2) determined by reference to the value of one or more nonfunctional currencies. The disposition of nonfunctional currency is also treated as a section 988 transaction. (Code Sec. 988(c)(1))[37]

The source of currency gains and losses treated as ordinary income or loss is determined by reference to the residence of the taxpayer or qualified business unit (QBU) on whose books the relevant asset, liability, or item of income or expense is properly reflected. A special source rule applies for certain related party loans. (Code Sec. 988(a)(3))[38]

Two or more separate transactions may be integrated into a single "988 hedging transaction" which is taxed in accordance with its economic substance. (Code Sec. 988(d); Reg § 1.988-5)[39]

The Code Sec. 988 rules do not apply if nonfunctional currency is disposed of by an individual in a personal transaction (any transaction entered into by an individual, except to the extent that expenses properly allocable to it qualify as deductible business or investment expenses), unless the currency gain that would otherwise be recognized exceeds $200. (Code Sec. 988(e))[40]

33. ¶G-6901, G-6906, G-6918
34. ¶G-6912
35. ¶G-6978 *et seq.*
36. ¶G-7001, G-7024
37. ¶G-6988 *et seq.*
38. ¶G-7029
39. ¶G-7037
40. ¶G-7047, ¶G-7048

Chapter 24   Returns and Payment of Tax

¶ 4700   **Returns and Payment of Tax.** ▪▪▪▪▪▪▪▪

Under Code Sec. 6012(f), an individual taxpayer must file an income tax return if his or her gross income equals or exceeds a specified amount (¶4701). Married taxpayers may file a joint return (¶4704). Corporations (¶4724 *et seq.*), and trusts and estates (¶4732 *et seq.*) also file income tax returns. A partnership files an information return (¶4731). Payors and others must file information returns to report specified payments, sales, etc. (¶4737 *et seq.*).

¶ 4701   **Income tax return-filing thresholds for individuals, 2018 – 2025.**

The filing requirement rules of Code Sec. 6012(a) (based on exemption amount and standard deduction) don't apply for tax years beginning before Jan. 1, 2026. Instead, every individual who has gross income for the tax year must file an income tax return, except:

(1)   an unmarried (Code Sec. 7703) individual who has gross income for the tax year that doesn't exceed the standard deduction (¶3110) for that individual for that tax year (Code Sec. 6012(f)(1)); or

(2)   an individual entitled to file jointly if: (i) the individual's gross income, when combined with the spouse's gross income, doesn't exceed, for the tax year, the standard deduction (¶3110) that would apply to the taxpayer for the tax year if the individual and spouse filed jointly; (ii) the individual and spouse have the same household as their home at the end of the tax year; (iii) the spouse doesn't file separately; and (iv) neither the individual nor spouse is an individual for whom a dependency deduction may be claimed by another taxpayer, who has income (other than earned income) in excess of the limited deduction allowed for dependents (Code Sec. 6012(f)(2)) ($1,150 for 2022 and $1,250 for 2023).[1]

Filing threshold chart, 2022–2023.   The following chart may be used to determine filing requirements for 2022 and 2023.

An individual who's *single, divorced, or legally separated* (and who isn't claimed as a dependent on another's return) must file a return if that individual:

- Uses single filing status, is under 65, and has gross income of at least $12,950 for 2022 ($13,850 for 2023).
- Uses single filing status, is 65 or older, and has gross income of at least $14,700 for 2022 ($15,700 for 2023).
- Uses head-of-household (HOH) filing status, is under 65, and has gross income of at least $19,400 for 2022 ($20,800 for 2023).
- Uses HOH filing status, is 65 or older, and has gross income of at least $21,150 for 2022 ($22,650 for 2023).

A married individual with a dependent child who's living apart from the spouse during the last six months of the tax year (and who isn't claimed as a dependent on another's return) must file a return if that individual:

- Uses HOH filing status, is under 65, and has gross income of at least $19,400 for 2022 ($20,800 for 2023).
- Uses HOH filing status, is 65 or older, and has gross income of at least $21,150 for 2022 ($22,650 for 2023).

A married couple in which the spouses are living together at the end of the tax year, or in which the spouses lived together on the date one spouse died (and where neither spouse is

---

1. ¶A-2805

References beginning with a single letter are to paragraphs in Federal Tax Coordinator 2d and RIA's Analysis of Federal Taxes: Income.

claimed as a dependent on another's return) must file a return if:

- They use married-filing-jointly (MFJ) status, are both under 65, and they have gross income of at least $25,900 for 2022 ($27,700 for 2023).
- They use MFJ status, one spouse is 65 or older, and they have gross income of at least $27,300 for 2022 ($29,200 for 2023).
- They use MFJ status, both spouses are 65 or older, and they have gross income of at least $28,700 for 2022 ($30,700 for 2023).
- They use married-filing-separately (MFS) status, are any age, and they have gross income of at least $5.

A married couple in which the spouses are not living together at the end of the tax year, or not living together on the date one spouse died (and where neither spouse is claimed as a dependent on another's return) must file a return if:

- They use either MFJ of MFS status, they are any age, and they have gross income of at least $5.

An individual who is widowed before the end of the tax year and not remarried in the tax year (and where neither spouse is claimed as a dependent on another's return) must file a return if the individual:

- Uses single filing status, is under 65, and has gross income of at least $12,950 for 2022 ($13,850 for 2023).
- Uses single filing status, is 65 or older, and has gross income of at least $14,700 for 2022 ($15,700 for 2023).
- Uses HOH filing status, is under 65, and has gross income of at least $19,400 for 2022 ($20,800 for 2023).
- Uses HOH filing status, is 65 or older, and has gross income of at least $21,150 for 2022 ($22,650 for 2023).
- Uses surviving-spouse (SS) filing status, is under 65, and has gross income of at least $25,900 for 2022 ($27,700 for 2023).
- Uses SS filing status, is 65 or older, and has gross income of at least $27,300 for 2022 ($29,200 for 2023).[2]

Other filing requirements. The following may have to file an income tax return even though they have gross income below the levels listed above: individuals receiving tips (whether reported to employer or not) from which social security tax wasn't withheld[3]; individuals owing AMT[4]; employees who receive more than $108.28 of wages from a church or church-controlled organization that is exempt from payroll taxes[5]; individuals receiving income from U.S. possessions[6]; nonresident aliens (NRAs)[7]; individuals who change their citizenship or country of residence during the year[8]; individuals who must pay a tax with respect to an IRA or other tax-favored account (if filing only for this reason, use Form 5329 by itself)[9]; or with respect to their health savings accounts, Archer medical savings accounts, or Medicare Advantage MSAs[10]; individuals who owe uncollected payroll tax on group-term life insurance and additional taxes on health savings accounts[11]; individuals who owe recapture tax on certain credits[12]; individuals receiving advance payment of the premium tax credit (PTC or "premium assistance credit")[13]; and certain self-employed individuals (¶4713).

The individual filing thresholds for a decedent's final return aren't reduced or

---

2. ¶A-2806, ¶S-1702
3. ¶S-1709
4. ¶S-1716
5. ¶S-1718
6. ¶S-1704.3
7. ¶S-1750 *et seq.*

8. ¶S-1758
9. ¶S-1708.1
10. ¶S-1708.1
11. ¶S-1708.1
12. ¶S-1708.1
13. ¶S-1708.1

prorated.[14]

Guardians or fiduciaries should file returns for minors and others who are incapable of filing their own returns. A minor may make his or her own return. (Reg § 1.6012-3(b)(3))[15] For the election to claim a child's income on a parent's return, see ¶3132.

¶ 4702   Individual income tax returns: Form 1040, Form 1040-SR.

U.S. citizens and residents use Form 1040 (Reg § 1.6012-1(a)(6)) or Form 1040-SR.

All individual taxpayers (other than those using Form 1040-SR, see below) must use the Form 1040, which can be supplemented with additional schedules if needed, including the following:

Schedule 1—additional income (e.g., Schedule C income, unemployment compensation) and adjustments to income such as the deductible part of self-employment tax, IRA deduction, or educator expenses.

Schedule 2—alternative minimum tax, excess advance premium tax credit repayment, and other taxes (e.g., self-employment tax, household employment taxes, and additional tax on IRAs).

Schedule 3—refundable and nonrefundable credits and other payments not entered on Form 1040 or Form 1040-SR.[16]

Individuals age 65 and older at the end of the tax year can use Form 1040-SR which is similar to the prior-law Form 1040- EZ but not restricted based on income, along with Schedule A if claiming itemized deductions. Thus, taxpayers can include social security benefits, distributions from retirement plans, annuities and other deferred pay arrangements, interest and dividends, and adjusted net capital gain.[17]

All taxpayers filing Form 1040, Form 1040-SR or Form 1040-NR for 2021—even those not engaged in a transaction involving virtual currency/cryptocurrency in 2021—were required to check a box answering either "Yes" or "No" to the virtual currency question at the top of those forms. (IR 2022-61, 03/18/2022)[18]

caution: Taxpayers should check the 2022 Form 1040 instructions when available to see whether this requirement applies to 2022 returns as well.

¶ 4703   E-filing of individual returns; mandatory e-filing for preparers; electronic signatures (Form 8879); e-signatures allowed on many non-e-filable forms, during COVID-19/coronavirus pandemic.

Current-year returns can be e-filed (but not after Oct. 15, even with a filing extension), as can Form 4868 automatic filing extensions for individual taxpayers, including returns that show a balance due.[19] Amended returns can be e-filed;[20] however, returns that cover fiscal-year tax periods, and certain other returns, cannot be e-filed.[21]

Preparers reasonably expected to file more than 10 individual tax returns must e-file those returns. (Code Sec. 6011(e)(3)) IRS may waive the e-filing requirement for preparers who are unable to meet it due to lack of internet access. (Code Sec. 6011(e)(3)(D))[22]

An electronic return may be a composite return consisting of electronically transmitted data and of paper documents (filed later) that can't be electronically transmitted, or it may be completely paperless.[23] There are procedures for accepting digital or electronic signatures (Code Sec. 6061(b)).[24] All taxpayers who e-file their returns must use electronic

14. ¶C-9616 *et seq.*
15. ¶S-1704.1
16. ¶S-1714
17. ¶S-1704.4A
18. ¶I-2153
19. ¶S-1600 *et seq.*
20. ¶S-1605
21. ¶S-1604
22. ¶S-1601.1 *et seq.*
23. ¶S-1608 *et seq.*
24. ¶S-4518 *et seq.*

signatures under either the self-select Personal Identification Number (PIN) or practitioner PIN methods. Practitioner PINs require use of Form 8879, which is retained by the practitioner; taxpayers who use this method and enter their own PINs in the electronic return record after reviewing the completed return must still sign the Form 8879 signature authorization form. If a taxpayer doesn't have and isn't eligible to get a Social Security number (SSN), the taxpayer's IRS Individual Taxpayer Identification Number (ITIN) can be entered instead wherever an SSN is requested on Form 8879.[25] For submitting payments, see ¶4720. For the requirement to use ID.me to sign in to IRS online accounts and verify identity in order to obtain or retrieve an Identity Protection PIN, see ¶4757.

An ERO must obtain and retain a separately completed and executed Form 8879 for each return (original or amended) the ERO transmits to the IRS. Each return the ERO transmits to IRS should have its own completed and executed Form 8879, which must include, in Part I, Tax Return Information, the tax year for the particular return the ERO will transmit. An ERO should not accept one Form 8879 as authorization to file multiple years' returns for the same taxpayer.[26]

Due to the COVID-19/coronavirus pandemic, IRS temporarily (through Oct. 31, 2023) allows digital signatures on many forms that can't be e-filed.[27]

¶ 4704   Spouses may file joint or separate returns; effect of joint or separate filing.

Under Code Sec. 6013(a) and Code Sec. 1(d), married persons (¶4705) can choose to file a joint return (reporting their combined taxable income)[28] or a separate return.[29]

Neither a return prepared and executed by IRS nor a Form 870 waiver is a valid election to file a joint return.[30]

observation: Filing separately may save taxes due to the adjusted-gross-income floors on some deductions (e.g., medical expenses). If either spouse has high amounts of these expenses, measuring them against a separate AGI can produce a larger deduction. But any advantages may be offset by the many restrictive rules for separate filers.

Separate returns. Each spouse is liable only for his or her own tax and penalties.[31]

Joint returns. Except as noted at ¶4709 to ¶4711, each spouse is jointly and severally liable for the full amount of the tax, penalties (other than civil fraud (¶4865)), and interest arising out of their joint return, regardless of the amount of his or her separate taxable income. (Code Sec. 6013(d)(3))[32] Only the spouse committing fraud can be subjected to fraud penalties.[33]

¶ 4705   "Married" defined for joint return and other tax purposes.

To file a joint return (¶4704), individuals must be legally married as of the *end* of the tax year or at the time of death of a spouse who dies before the close of the tax year. (Code Sec. 6013(d))[34] If spouses file a joint return and later get an annulment, they must re-file as separate unmarried persons.[35]

The terms "spouse," "husband," and "wife" mean an individual lawfully married to another individual. IRS recognizes a marriage of two individuals, regardless of gender, if the marriage is recognized by the state, possession, or territory of the U.S. in which it was entered into, regardless of domicile. Marriage does *not* include a registered domestic partnership, civil union, or other similar formal relationship recognized under state law that is

25. ¶S-1613; ¶S-1617.3
26. ¶S-1608.2
27. ¶S-4518.1
28. ¶S-1801
29. ¶A-1502
30. ¶S-1832

31. ¶V-8501.1
32. ¶V-8501
33. ¶V-8502
34. ¶S-1803
35. ¶A-1609

not denominated as a marriage.[36]

¶ 4706   Qualifying to file joint returns: accounting methods, accounting periods, nonresident aliens.

Under Code Sec. 6013(a), spouses can file a joint return even if only one has income[37] and even if they have different accounting *methods*.

A joint return *can't* be filed if: (a) *either spouse was a nonresident alien* (NRA) at any time during the tax year (Code Sec. 6013(a)(1)),[38] but where 1 spouse is an NRA for the entire year (Code Sec. 6013(g)) or where an NRA spouse becomes a U.S. resident during the tax year (Code Sec. 6013(h)), spouses can file jointly if they agree to subject their worldwide income to U.S. tax;[39] or (b) *the spouses have different tax years,* except when 1 spouse dies, see ¶4708.

¶ 4707   Changing from joint to separate filing status and vice versa.

Once a joint return has been filed, spouses can revoke it (by filing separate returns) up until the return's due date. After the due date, they can't switch. (Reg § 1.6013-1(a))[40]

A married couple who filed separate returns can switch to a joint return after the due date if: (a) the joint return is filed within 3 years from the original due date (without extension), and (b) neither spouse has, for a previously filed separate return, petitioned the Tax Court, filed a suit for refund, or entered into a closing agreement or final compromise. (Code Sec. 6013(b); Reg § 1.6013-2(b))[41]

¶ 4708   Joint return for year spouse dies.

Under Code Sec. 6013(a)(2), a joint return may be filed for spouses where their tax years start on the same day and end on different days because of the death of either or both (unless the surviving spouse (SS) remarries before the end of his or her tax year or the tax year of either spouse is a "short" year because of a change in accounting period). The joint return must be made for the tax year of each.[42] For when to file, see ¶4716.

SS may file a joint return if: the deceased spouse (DS) hasn't already filed a return for the tax year; an executor wasn't appointed when the joint return is made; and an executor hasn't been appointed before the extended due date for filing SS's return. (Code Sec. 6013(a)(3))[43]

✔observation: The return for the year before the year of death also is subject to these rules if DS died before filing a return for that year.

If an executor or administrator is appointed by the filing due date, SS *can't* file a joint return for DS. Only the fiduciary can act for DS, so both the fiduciary and SS must sign the joint return. Even if SS properly filed a joint return (because no fiduciary had been appointed by the due date), the fiduciary may disaffirm (revoke) the joint return by filing a *separate* return for DS within 1 year after the extended due date. Any joint return improperly filed by SS or disaffirmed by the fiduciary is treated as SS's *separate* return. (Code Sec. 6013(a)(3))[44] For when SS can use joint return rates, see ¶3125.

¶ 4709   Elective relief from joint tax liability (innocent spouse rule)—Form 8857.

Under Code Sec. 6015(a)(1), unless an exception (¶4712) applies, an individual who has filed a joint return may elect relief from joint and several liability (¶¶4704) under innocent

---

36. ¶A-1603; A-1603.1
37. ¶S-1801
38. ¶S-1802
39. ¶A-1800 *et seq.*
40. ¶S-1831

41. ¶S-1829; ¶S-1830
42. ¶S-1805
43. ¶S-1806
44. ¶S-1806

spouse rules. An individual is relieved of liability for tax, interest, penalties, etc. for a tax year to the extent the liability is due to an understatement if: (a) a joint return was filed for the tax year; (b) there's an understatement of tax on the return due to the other spouse's erroneous items; (c) the individual shows that, in signing the return, he or she didn't know or have reason to know of the understatement; (d) under the facts and circumstances, it would be inequitable to hold the individual liable for the deficiency; and (e) the individual elects the benefits of the innocent spouse rules, by filing Form 8857 (separately from the tax return) and the required attached statement, no later than 2 years after IRS has begun collection activities against the individual. (Code Sec. 6015(b)(1))[45]

> **✓observation:** Innocent spouse relief isn't available for unpaid liabilities that were properly reported on a joint return, because in that situation there's no understatement of tax. However, equitable relief (¶4711) may be available.

Spouses who knew or had reason to know of the understatement, but show that they didn't know or have reason to know of its *extent*, can be relieved of liability to the extent of the understatement of which they didn't know or have reason to know. (Code Sec. 6015(b)(2))[46]

Special innocent spouse relief applies to a spouse of a partner in a partnership subject to unified partnership audit procedures (¶4827).

Any determination of innocent spouse relief is made without regard to community property laws. (Reg § 1.6015-1(f)(1))[47] For a spouse's separate liability election, see ¶4710.

On receipt of a request for relief (¶4710; ¶4711), IRS must send a notice to the nonrequesting spouse's last known address informing that spouse of the requesting spouse's claim for relief. (Reg § 1.6015-6(a)(1)) The nonrequesting spouse may file a protest and receive an IRS appeals conference regarding a determination.[48] IRS's procedures protect domestic abuse victims who fear retaliation for applying for innocent spouse relief.[49] The nonrequesting spouse may also intervene to support the requesting spouse's innocent spouse claim.[50]

The Tax Court reviews denied claims under a de novo standard. (Code Sec. 6015(e)(7))[1]

¶ 4710 Separate liability ("allocation of liability") election for joint filer—Form 8857.

Under Code Sec. 6015(a)(2) and Code Sec. 6015(c), an individual who files a joint return and meets the eligibility requirements can elect to limit liability for a deficiency. The separate liability election may be made in addition to the innocent spouse election (¶4709).[2] The relief is available only for unpaid liabilities from understatements; refunds aren't allowed. (Reg § 1.6015-3(c)(1))[3]

An individual can elect only if, when the election is filed, he or she is no longer married to, or is legally separated from, the spouse with whom the joint return was filed, or wasn't a member of the same household as that spouse at any time during the previous 12-month period. If IRS shows that assets were transferred between spouses in a fraudulent scheme joined in by both spouses, a separate liability election by either spouse is invalid. (Code Sec. 6015(c)(3)(A))[4]

To elect, file Form 8857 (separately from the return), with specified attachments, no later than 2 years after IRS begins collection against the electing spouse. (Code Sec. 6015(c)(3)(B); Reg § 1.6015-5)[5] For equitable claims, see ¶4711.

---

45. ¶V-8506 *et seq.*
46. ¶V-8510.1
47. ¶V-8504
48. ¶V-8506.3 *et seq.*
49. ¶V-8506.2
50. ¶U-2152

1. ¶U-2148.2
2. ¶V-8533
3. ¶T-5513
4. ¶V-8534
5. ¶V-8536

Except as provided below, an electing spouse's liability for a deficiency that IRS assesses won't exceed the portion of the deficiency properly allocable to that spouse. (Code Sec. 6015(c)(1), Code Sec. 6015(d)(3)(A))[6] The liability is generally allocated between the spouses in proportion to the net items taken into account in determining the deficiency as if separate returns were filed. (Code Sec. 6015(d)(1))[7] But, the limitation on an electing spouse's tax liability is increased by the value of property transferred to that spouse by the nonelecting spouse principally to avoid tax, which is reputably presumed (except for divorce or separate maintenance transfers) to be the case for transfers made anytime after 1 year before the first letter of proposed deficiency is sent. (Code Sec. 6015(c)(4))[8] Also, except where a joint return was signed under duress, the election doesn't apply to the extent that IRS has evidence that the electing spouse had *actual* knowledge of an item giving rise to all or part of a deficiency allocable to the other spouse. (Code Sec. 6015(c)(3)(C))[9]

¶ 4711   Equitable relief from joint liability for spouses—Form 8857.

Under Code Sec. 6015(f)(1), if, under all the facts and circumstances, it's inequitable to hold a spouse liable for any portion of any unpaid tax or deficiency, and relief isn't available under the innocent spouse (¶4709) or separate liability election (¶4710) rules, IRS may relieve that spouse of liability for that unpaid tax or deficiency (Code Sec. 6015(f)(1); Reg § 1.6015-4) and in limited cases may issue a refund. A request for equitable relief under Code Sec. 6015(f) may be made for any portion of any liability that: (1) hasn't been paid, as long as the request is made before the expiration of the applicable period of limitation on collection under Code Sec. 6502 (see ¶4891), or (2) has been paid, as long as the request is made during the period (see ¶4838) in which the individual could submit a timely claim for refund or credit of that payment. (Code Sec. 6015(f)(2)) To request equitable relief, file Form 8857 (separately from the tax return) with specified attached statement. (Reg § 1.6015-5(a))[10]

Threshold conditions must be met for equitable relief, such as that the requesting spouse filed a joint return for the tax year for which relief is sought, and that relief isn't available under Code Sec. 6015(b) or Code Sec. 6015(c).[11] IRS makes a streamlined determination if certain threshold requirements are met.[12] The Tax Court reviews denied claims under a *de novo* standard (without reference to legal conclusions or assumptions of the previous court). (Code Sec. 6015(e)(7))[13]

¶ 4712   Exceptions to innocent spouse relief.

Innocent spouse relief (¶4709, ¶4710, ¶4711) isn't available: (1) for liabilities other than income taxes, (e.g. "nanny" taxes, see ¶3030), that are reported on a joint federal income tax return (Reg § 1.6015-1(a)(3));[14] (2) for a tax year for which the spouse seeking relief has entered into an offer in compromise or a closing agreement with IRS that disposes of the liability (Reg § 1.6015-1(c));[15] or (3) if a spouse transferred assets to the other spouse as part of a fraudulent scheme to defraud IRS or another third party. (Reg § 1.6015-1(d))[16]

¶ 4713   Self-employed individuals' returns—Form 1040 and Schedule SE.

Under Code Sec. 6017, individuals (except nonresident aliens) who have $400 or more in net earnings from self-employment (¶3135) have to file Form 1040 (including Schedule SE), even if the individual's gross income is less than the filing thresholds (¶4701). Report self-employment tax (¶3133) on Form 1040.[17]

---

6. ¶V-8537
7. ¶V-8539
8. ¶V-8538
9. ¶V-8549.1
10. ¶V-8553
11. ¶V-8554

12. ¶V-8555
13. ¶U-2148.2
14. ¶V-8501
15. ¶V-8505
16. ¶V-8535
17. ¶S-1717

¶ 4714　Decedent's final return, filing requirement.

Under Code Sec. 6012(b)(1), a final income tax return is filed for a decedent who would be required to file if alive, for the part of the year up to the date of death. A decedent's final return is filed by the person entrusted with his or her property (e.g., the estate's executor).[18] For the income and deductions reportable on the return, see ¶3959.

¶ 4715　U.S. military and civilian employees dying in combat/terrorist attacks—income tax exemption.

Under Code Sec. 692(c)(1), if a U.S. military or civilian employee dies due to wounds or injury sustained in a terrorist or military action, income tax won't apply for the year of death and any earlier year beginning with the last year ending before the year when the wounds or injury were sustained. IRS has provided procedures for determining whether a terrorist or military action has occurred. Refund of withheld or estimated taxes may be claimed by filing Form 1040, or, on an amended return (Form 1040X). On joint returns, the tax liability is allocated between the deceased and surviving spouses.[19]

¶ 4716　Extension of due dates for individual returns.

Under Code Sec. 6072(a), income tax returns (including self-employment tax returns and a decedent's final return) of U.S. citizens and resident aliens must be filed by the 15th day of the 4th month following the end of the tax year (Apr. 15 for calendar year taxpayers). (Code Sec. 6072(a); Reg § 1.6072-1(a)(1), Reg § 1.6072-1(b))[20] However, as Apr. 15 falls on a Saturday in 2023, individual returns are due Apr. 17, 2023—and calendar year taxpayers in the District of Columbia have until Apr. 18, 2023 to file their 2022 returns because of the Emancipation Day holiday, and calendar year taxpayers in Maine and Massachusetts have until Apr. 18, 2023 to file their 2022 returns because of the Patriots' Day holiday in those states.[21] For a nonresident alien's return, see ¶4642.

A "short period return" must be filed by the 15th day of the 4th month following the end of the short period. (Reg § 1.6071-1(b))[22]

A final return for a decedent, covering the part of the year during which he or she was alive, is due by the 15th day of the 4th month following the date the decedent's tax year would have ended. Reg § 1.6072-1(b))[23]

¶ 4717　Extensions of time for filing individual returns—Form 4868.

File Form 4868 to get an automatic 6-month filing extension (until Oct. 15 for a calendar year taxpayer). (Reg § 1.6081-4)[24] The form must show the full amount properly estimated as tax for the year but it doesn't have to include payment of the balance of the tax estimated to be due. (Reg § 1.6081-4(b))[25] Failure to include the balance due won't affect the extension, but interest and penalties apply.[26] Extension requests may be e-filed.[27] For payment extensions, see ¶4721. IRS can terminate extensions on 10 days' notice. (Reg § 1.6081-4(d))[28]

Extensions can't exceed 6 months unless the taxpayer is abroad. (Code Sec. 6081(a))[29]

---

18. ¶C-9601, S-1704.2
19. ¶C-9660 *et seq.*
20. ¶S-4701 *et seq.*; ¶S-5100 *et seq.*
21. ¶T-10796
22. ¶S-4710
23. ¶S-4702

24. ¶S-5011
25. ¶S-5013
26. ¶s S-5010, S-5011
27. ¶S-1606
28. ¶S-5009
29. ¶S-5003

¶ 4718 **Extension for citizen or resident with non-U.S. tax home—Forms 4868, 2350.**

A U.S. citizen or resident whose tax home and abode is outside the U.S. and Puerto Rico (Reg § 1.6081-5(a)(5)) and a U.S. citizen or resident in military or naval service on duty outside the U.S. and Puerto Rico (Reg § 1.6081-5(a)(6)) get automatic extensions until the 15th day of the sixth month after the end of the tax year. A statement must be attached to the return that shows the taxpayer qualified for the extension. (Reg § 1.6081-5(b))[30] The automatic 6-month extension for individuals (¶4717) runs concurrently with the 2-month extension of time to file. (Reg § 1.6081-4(a))[31]

U.S. citizens and resident aliens who expect to qualify for the foreign earned income and/or housing cost exclusion (¶4605), can request an extension (in addition to the automatic extension) until after the completion of the qualifying period for claiming the exclusion or deduction on Form 2350. (Reg § 1.911-7(c)(2), Rev Proc 78-31, 1978-2 CB 531)[32]

¶ 4719 **Filing extensions: combat zone, declared disaster, significant fire, terrorist or military action; 60-day extension for disasters; collection deferral for servicemember's income tax**

Under Code Sec. 7508(a), an extension of time is provided for an individual serving in the U.S. Armed Forces, or serving in support of the Armed Forces, in an area designated by the President as a "combat zone" (¶1223) or when deployed outside the U.S. away from the individual's permanent duty station while participating in an operation designated by the Secretary of Defense as a contingency operation. Individuals serving in a "qualified hazardous duty area" are also granted this extension.[33] Various tax-related acts (e.g., filing of returns, paying of tax, and filing of Tax Court petition) are covered under the Code Sec. 7508(a) extension.[34] Generally, the period of extension includes: (1) the period during which the individual served in a designated "combat zone" or "contingency operation"; (2) any period of continuous hospitalization due to injury while serving in the combat zone; (3) time in missing-in-action status; and (4) 180 days after the end of service or hospitalization. If an act must be performed within a certain period of time, and the taxpayer enters a combat zone before that period begins, then in addition to the periods discussed in (1) through (4), above, the deadline is extended by the entire period of time the taxpayer has to take the action. For IRS's tax collection, there's *no* suspension for hospitalization or the next 180 days.[35]

IRS may allow taxpayers affected by a Code Sec. 165(i)(5) "federally declared" disaster, a significant fire, or a Code Sec. 692(c)(2) terrorist or military action to extend for up to 1 year: (1) the timely performance of acts described in Code Sec. 7508(a)(1) (e.g., filing a return); (2) the amount of interest, penalty, additional amount, or addition to tax due for periods after the disaster date; and (3) the amount of any tax credit or refund.[36] (Code Sec. 7508A) IRS has specified acts subject to postponement,[37] (Reg § 301.7508A-1) including for disasters occurring in 2022. A federally-declared disaster includes both a major disaster and an emergency declared under Section 401 or 501 of the Stafford Act. (Reg § 1.165-11(b)(1)) A significant fire is any fire with respect to which assistance is provided under section 420 of the Stafford Act. (Code Sec. 7508A(e))[38]

In addition to the discretionary up-to-one-year period (above), a mandatory and automatic 60-day filing deadline extension applies to "qualified taxpayers" (generally, those in a disaster area (an area in which a major disaster for which the President provides financial assistance under section 408 of the Stafford Act occurs)), see Code

30. ¶S-5064
31. ¶S-5065
32. ¶S-5020
33. ¶S-8007
34. ¶S-8012

35. ¶S-8011
36. ¶S-8502
37. ¶S-8012
38. ¶S-8501.50 *et seq.*

Sec. 7508A(d)(2)). (Code Sec. 7508A(d))[39] If multiple declarations relating to a disaster area are issued in a 60-day period, a separate period is determined for each declaration. (Code Sec. 7508A(d)(6)) Regs clarify what time-sensitive acts are to be postponed and how the mandatory 60-day postponement period is to be calculated. (Reg § 1.165-11(b)(1); Reg § 301.7508A-1(g))[40]

On notice to IRS, the collection of income tax from a member of the uniformed services— i.e., a member of: the armed forces, the commissioned corps of the National Oceanic and Atmospheric Administration, or the commissioned corps of the Public Health Service— falling due before or during military service, is deferred for not more than 180 days after the member's termination of or release from military service, if a member's ability to pay that income tax is materially affected by military service. No interest or penalty accrues for the deferment period on a deferred amount. Also, running of the limitations period for collection of any deferred amount is suspended for the period of service plus 270 days.[41] For tax relief for U.S. military and civilian employees dying in combat or terrorist attacks, see ¶4715.

¶ 4720   Individuals' tax payment due date; ways of paying tax (Form 1040-V, etc.).

Under Code Sec. 6151(a), the tax is due on the original due date for filing the return despite any extensions of time for *filing* the return. (Code Sec. 6151(a); Reg § 1.6151-1(a))[42] If IRS computes the tax, the tax due date is the later of the 30th day after the date IRS mails the tax bill or the tax return due date. (Reg § 1.6151-1(b))[43] The automatic filing extension for taxpayers with a tax home and abode, or in military service, outside the U.S. (¶4718), also extends the time for payment. (Reg § 1.6081-5(a))[44] For treatment of extension requests without full payment, see ¶4717.

For the payment extension for corporations, see ¶4729.

Taxpayers with a balance due on a return can pay via: (1) check or money order with Form 1040-V (free), (2) a debit card, credit card, or digital wallet payment by phone or online, (3) Electronic Funds Withdrawal (when using tax prep software and e-filing a return) (free), (4) Direct Pay (free), (5) the IRS2Go mobile app, (6) Electronic Federal Tax Payment System (EFTPS) (free), or (7) cash, using PayNearMe. IRS has provided guidance on payment methods, as well as online payment plans, deferred collection, and offers in compromise (see ¶4813). (IR 2022-63, 03/22/2022)[45] Receipt of the check is payment, if the check is honored. IRS will accept personal checks or money orders drawn on any U.S. financial institution if the check or money order is collectible in U.S. currency. Express, telegraphic, and similar money orders are also acceptable. (Reg § 301.6311-1)[46]

Taxes (including interest and penalties) can be paid by any commercially acceptable means that IRS deems appropriate by regs, including approved credit or debit cards as provided in IRS forms, etc. (Code Sec. 6311(a), Code Sec. 6311(d)(1); Reg § 301.6311-2) Taxpayers can: (1) authorize IRS to debit a bank account for the unpaid balance, or (2) make credit or debit card payments through tax software, by phone, or on-line. IRS doesn't set or collect any fees for credit or debit card payments, but convenience fees are charged by these service providers: payUSAtax (855-508-0159); Pay1040.com (888-658-5465); and ACI Payments, Inc. (https://fed.acipayonline.com) (888-872-9829). The option to pay taxes by credit or debit card also applies to payments with automatic extensions and to estimated tax payments. Taxpayers who charge a payment with an automatic extension request or who charge an estimated tax payment don't need to file paper Form 4868 or Form 1040-ES.[47]

---

39. ¶S-8505
40. ¶S-8011 *et seq.*
41. ¶S-8001, ¶S-8005
42. ¶S-5451
43. ¶S-5454

44. ¶S-5064
45. ¶S-5454.1
46. ¶S-5752
47. ¶S-5756.1A *et seq.*, ¶S-1629.1, ¶S-5010

Tax payment by credit or debit card is deemed made when the issuer properly authorizes the transaction, provided payment is actually received by IRS in the ordinary course of business and isn't returned due to error resolution processing. (Reg § 301.6311-2(b))[48]

Where quarterly estimated tax payments (¶3145) aren't necessary, payments are generally made with the individual's return (¶4716).[49]

¶ 4721 Extension of time for paying individual income tax—Form 1127.

Code Sec. 6161(a)(1) allows IRS to grant a reasonable extension of time (not to exceed 6 months, unless taxpayer is abroad) to pay the tax. (Code Sec. 6161(a)(1)) Apply on Form 1127 by the due date for payment. (Reg § 1.6161-1(c)) IRS grants extensions, generally within 30 days, only on a satisfactory showing that payment on the due date will result in undue hardship (more than an inconvenience), e.g., that taxpayer would have to sell property at a great financial sacrifice (i.e., below fair market value) to pay the tax. (Reg § 1.6161-1(b))[50]

¶ 4722 Installment agreement for payments of individual income tax—Forms 9465, 433-A, 433-D; 433-F.

To request an installment agreement, attach Form 9465 to the front of a balance-due return or submit an on-line payment application. A fee of $225 for a regular installment agreement ($107 for a direct debit agreement; $149 for an online payment agreement; $31 for a direct debit online payment agreement; and $43 for low-income taxpayers to enter any type of agreement except direct debit online, for which the lower $31 rate applies). (Reg § 300.1(b)) To restructure/reinstate an installment agreement: the fee is $89, but for low-income taxpayers, the fee is $43. The $43 fee is waived if the taxpayer agrees to make electronic payments through a debit instrument. For low-income taxpayers unable to make electronic payments through a debit instrument, the $43 fee is reimbursed on completion of the installment agreement.[1] Interest, and a late-payment penalty (see ¶4857) apply. For the requirement to use ID.me to sign in to IRS online accounts and verify identity in order to apply for a payment plan online, see ¶4757.

IRS must enter into an installment agreement (guaranteed installment agreement) requested by an *individual* whose aggregate tax liability (without interest, penalties, additions to tax, and additional amounts) isn't more than $10,000; and who (or whose spouse for joint return liability) hasn't failed to file or to pay income tax, or entered into another installment agreement, during any of the preceding 5 tax years, if IRS determines that the taxpayer is financially unable to pay the liability in full when due (and the taxpayer submits information that IRS may require to make this determination). The agreement must require full payment within 3 years, and the taxpayer must agree to comply with all Code provisions while it's in effect. (Code Sec. 6159(c); Reg § 301.6159-1(c))[2] IRS grants streamlined installment agreement requests to taxpayers who agree to pay a balance due of $50,000 or less within a 6-year period, without requiring a collection manager's approval. Taxpayers seeking installment agreements exceeding $50,000 have to supply IRS with Form 433-A or Form 433-F.[3]

IRS may (but isn't required to, except as noted above) enter into an installment agreement if it determines that the agreement will facilitate full or partial collection of the tax. (Code Sec. 6159(a); Reg § 301.6159-1(a)) IRS may disregard frivolous submissions of installment payment applications. (Code Sec. 7122(g))[4]

An individual who had an automatic 6-month extension of time to file without paying the tax estimated to be due (¶4717), but can't pay by the extended due date, should use

---

48. ¶S-5756.4
49. ¶S-5200 *et seq.*
50. ¶S-5851
1. ¶T-10021, T-10022

2. ¶V-5012
3. ¶V-5013
4. ¶T-9612

Form 9465 and Form 433-D to arrange an installment agreement.[5]

¶ 4723   Amended income tax returns—Form 1040X.

Amended income tax returns (on Form 1040X) may be filed to claim a refund (¶4833) after an original return has been filed if the period of limitations is open. (Reg § 301.6402-3(a)(2))[6]

¶ 4724   Requirement to file corporate income tax return—Form 1120 series.

Under Code Sec. 6012(a)(2), every corporation subject to income tax, and in existence during any portion of a tax year, must file an income tax return (on the Form 1120 series) for that year (or portion), regardless of the amount of its gross income or whether it has taxable income. (Code Sec. 6012(a)(2); Reg § 1.6012-2(a))[7] A corporation that has merely received a charter doesn't have to file if it furnishes a statement to IRS that it hasn't perfected its organization, transacted any business, or received income from any source. (Reg § 1.6012-2(a)(2))[8]

After a corporation ceases business and dissolves, retaining no assets, it must file a return for that part of the year during which it was in existence. But retention of even a small amount of cash keeps the corporation alive for filing purposes until the cash is distributed or paid. (Reg § 1.6012-2(a)(2))[9] A receiver, bankruptcy trustee, etc. that has control and custody of all (or substantially all) of a corporation's business or property must make the return in the same manner as the corporation would. (Code Sec. 6012(b)(3))[10]

If a corporation doesn't file a required return, IRS may make its return. (Code Sec. 6020)[11]

¶ 4725   Who signs corporate returns.

Under Code Sec. 6062, the return and all related documents requiring a signature on a corporation's behalf, must be signed by the president, vice-president, treasurer, assistant treasurer, chief accounting officer (controller) or any other officer duly authorized to sign. If an LLC treated as a corporation doesn't have any of the specific officers listed above, the managing member or another individual authorized to act for the company can sign the return. If a return is made for the corporation by a trustee, receiver, etc., that fiduciary must sign.[12]

¶ 4726   Corporate forms—Form 1120; Form 1120-S; Schedules L, M-1, M-2, and M-3; Schedule UTP; Forms 1125-A, 1125-E; mandatory e-filing rules.

Most domestic corporations file Form 1120 as their income tax return. (Reg § 1.6012-2(a)) Form 1120, Schedule PH must be attached if the corporation is a personal holding company (¶3324 *et seq.*). (Reg § 1.6012-2(b))[13] (For foreign corporation returns, see ¶4644.)

A regulated investment company (mutual fund) uses Form 1120-RIC,[14] a real estate investment trust, Form 1120-REIT,[15] a political organization, Form 1120-POL, a homeowners association, Form 1120-H,[16] and a designated settlement fund, Form 1120-SF.[17] Insurance companies use Form 1120L (life) or Form 1120-PC (property and casualty).[18]

S corporations use Form 1120S, including Schedule K-2 and K-3, which must show information on actual and constructive distributions to shareholders. (Code Sec. 6037(a); Reg § 1.6012-2(h)) The corporation must, by the date it files the return, furnish this

---

5. ¶s S-5020, V-5010 *et seq.*
6. ¶S-5151.5
7. ¶S-1900, S-1901, S-1908
8. ¶S-1908
9. ¶S-1909
10. ¶S-2014
11. ¶S-1004

12. ¶S-4508
13. ¶S-1902, S-1903
14. ¶S-1920
15. ¶S-1919
16. ¶S-1921, ¶S-1922
17. ¶S-1925
18. ¶S-1904

information to anyone who was a shareholder during the tax year. (Code Sec. 6037(b))[19]

Small corporations (less than $250,000 in gross receipts and less than $250,000 in assets) don't have to complete Schedules L, M-1, and M-2 of Form 1120; or Schedules L and M-1 of Form 1120S.[20] Large corporations (reporting total assets of $10 million or more on Form 1120, Schedule L) and large partnerships (¶4731) must file the more detailed Schedule M-3 instead of M-1. On the M-3, research and development costs have to be separately stated. A supporting schedule must be attached with a description, the expense per income, temporary and permanent differences, and deduction per the tax return. Corporations and partnerships with at least $10 million but less than $50 million in total assets at year end can file Schedule M-1 in place of Schedule M-3, Parts II and III, but they must file Schedule M-3, Part I. Corporations and partnerships filing Forms 1120, 1120-C, 1120-F, 1120S, and 1065 with $10 million to $50 million in total assets need not file Form 1120, Schedule B, Form 1065, Schedule C, or Form 8916-A.[21]

Corporations (filing Form 1120), insurance companies (filing Form 1120L or Form 1120PC), and foreign corporations (filing Form 1120F) with both uncertain tax positions and at least $10 million of assets have to file Schedule UTP if they or a related party issued audited financial statements. (Reg § 1.6012-2(a)(4)) Schedule UTP requires a concise description of each uncertain *federal* tax position for which the taxpayer or a related entity recorded a reserve on financial statements (or for which no reserve was recorded because of an expectation to litigate).[22]

If the corporation deducts: (a) the cost of goods sold, it must file Form 1125-A or (b) officer compensation and has $500,000 of receipts, it must file Form 1125-E.[23] A corporation uses Form 8822-B to notify IRS of a new business address or location.[24]

E-filing. A corporation that files at least 250 returns of any kind in the aggregate, including information returns, during the calendar year ending with or within its tax year must e-file its income tax return (i.e., the Form 1120 and Form 1120S series) if it has assets of $10 million or more. Exemptions apply for forms that can't be e-filed and where IRS waives the requirement for undue hardship. A corporation can request a written request for a waiver. All members of a controlled group must e-file if the controlled group in the aggregate files at least 250 returns (including information returns). Failure to e-file when required to do so is deemed to be a failure to file a return. (Reg § 301.6011-5) IRS allows a filer 10 calendar days from the date of first transmission to perfect a rejected e-file return for resubmission. For returns that can't be accepted for processing electronically, the filer generally has 10 days to file a paper return.[25]

¶ 4727 When to file corporate returns; C corps. with June 30 fiscal year; S corps.; short-period returns.

Domestic corporations (including RICs, REITs, but not S corporations; see below) generally must file their returns by the 15th day of the *4th* month after the end of the tax year (Apr. 15 for a calendar year corporation). However, under a special rule, C corporations with fiscal years ending on June 30 file by the 15th day of the *3rd* month after the end of the tax year until their first tax year beginning after Dec. 31, 2025, at which point they must file by the 15th day of the fourth month following the end of the tax year.[26]

S corporations must file their returns by the 15th day of the *3rd* month after the end of the tax year (Mar. 15 for a calendar year S corporation). (Code Sec. 6072(a), Code Sec. 6072(b); Reg § 1.6037-1(b); Reg § 1.6072-2(a)(1)(ii))[27]

"Short period" returns must be filed by the 15th day of the 4th month (3rd month for S corporations and C corporations with fiscal years ending on June 30) after the end of the

---

19. ¶S-1905, S-1906
20. ¶S-1902, ¶S-1905
21. ¶S-1902.1
22. ¶S-4460.1, ¶S-4460.4 *et seq.*
23. ¶S-1902

24. ¶S-1582A
25. ¶S-1941
26. ¶S-4704
27. ¶S-4923

short period.[28]

File as directed on the form's instructions. (Code Sec. 6091(b)(2)(A); Reg § 1.6091-2(c)) Hand-carried returns may be filed with any person assigned the responsibility to receive hand-carried returns in the local IRS office (i.e., the office in which the corporation has its principal place of business). (Code Sec. 6091(b)(4); Reg § 1.6091-2(d)(2))[29]

For extensions, see ¶4728.

¶ 4728 Corporate return filing extension (Form 7004); automatic extension; tax year ending June 30; blanket extension.

Automatic extensions, Form 7004. Under Code Sec. 6081(b), except as otherwise provided, a corporation (including an S corporation, an affiliated group planning to file a consolidated return (¶3338), and a foreign corporation with a U.S. office) can get an automatic 6-month extension by filing Form 7004 that shows its estimated tax liability by the original due date. For any return for a tax year of a C corporation that ends on June 30 and begins before Jan. 1, 2026, the automatic extension period is 7 months (not 6 months). (Code Sec. 6081(b); Reg § 1.6081-3)[30]

A filing extension won't extend the time for *paying* the tax, see ¶4729. (Reg § 1.6081-3(c))[31] IRS can terminate an extension on 10 days' notice. (Code Sec. 6081(b); Reg § 1.6081-3(d))[32]

Blanket extensions. A domestic corporation that does business and keeps its records outside the U.S. or Puerto Rico, or whose principal income is from sources within U.S. possessions, and a resident foreign corporation, may file its return up to the 15th day of the sixth month after the end of the tax year. A statement setting forth the qualifying facts must be attached to the return. (Reg § 1.6081-5(a)(2), Reg § 1.6081-5(a)(4), Reg § 1.6081-5(b))[33]

¶ 4729 Payment of corporate tax, due date; loss carrybacks—Forms 1127, 1138.

Under Code Sec. 6151(a)), corporations must pay in full by the due date (without extension) for filing the return (¶4727).[34] For corporate estimated tax, see ¶3343 *et seq.*

Six-month extension for undue hardship—Form 1127. IRS may grant an extension (up to 6 months) for paying corporate income tax at the taxpayer's request (on Form 1127) by the payment due date if undue hardship is shown (¶4721). Late applications won't be considered. (Code Sec. 6161(a); Reg § 1.6161-1)[35]

Loss carryback expected—Form 1138. A corporation that expects a net operating loss in a current year can get an extension for paying the *preceding* year's tax based on the expected carryback (Code Sec. 6164(a)), by filing Form 1138. (Reg § 1.6164-1) The extension expires the last day of the month for filing the current year return or, if an application for a tentative carryback refund (Form 1139, see ¶4834) is filed before that date, on the date IRS sends notice that the refund is allowed or disallowed. (Code Sec. 6164(d))[36]

¶ 4730 Electronic tax deposits required for corporations.

Unless an exemption applies, a corporation must make electronic deposits of all depository taxes using the Electronic Federal Tax Payment System (EFTPS). (Reg § 31.6302-1(h)(2)(iii)) For how taxpayers make tax deposits by Automated Clearing House (ACH) payments or by telephone, see ¶3028. Also, if corporations are unwilling or unable to use EFTPS, it can arrange for a tax professional, financial institution, payroll service, etc. to

---

28. ¶S-4710
29. ¶S-5104
30. ¶S-5024 *et seq.*
31. ¶S-5027
32. ¶S-5009

33. ¶S-5064
34. ¶S-5451
35. ¶S-5850 *et seq.*, ¶S-5862 *et seq.*
36. ¶S-5861 *et seq.*

make a deposit on its behalf using a master account. It can also arrange for its financial institution to initiate a same-day tax wire payment on its behalf.[37]

Corporations make their income and estimated tax payments by depositing them by the return due date (¶4727) (Code Sec. 6302; Reg § 1.6302-1(a)) and reporting the deposits on the return.[38] For de minimis rule for deposits of employment taxes, see ¶3027.

¶ 4731   Partnership return-filing requirements, due date—Form 1065, Schedule K-1; Form 7004; Form 1125-A; exemptions from filing.

Under Code Sec. 6031(a) and Code Sec. 6031(e), partnerships (except foreign partnerships with no or de minimis U.S. source gross income and no gross income effectively connected with a U.S. trade or business) (Reg § 1.6031(a)-1(b)) must file Form 1065 to report income and deductions. (Reg § 1.6031(a)-1(a))[39] Certain tax-exempt bond partnerships are exempt from filing.[40] (Reg § 1.6031(a)-1(a)(3)(ii)) A foreign partnership that is otherwise exempt from filing must file a return to make an election, (Reg § 1.6031(a)-1(b)) and a foreign or domestic partnership must file to elect out of the Code's partnership rules. (Reg § 1.6031(a)-1(c))[41]

A partnership needn't file a partnership return for any period before it has taxable income or incurs deductible expenses. (Reg § 1.6031(a)-1(a)(3))[42] Nor does it file if it doesn't have any gross income that is effectively connected with the conduct of a U.S. trade or business, or any U.S. source gross income. (Reg § 1.6031(a)-1(b)(1))[43]

Form 1065 is due on the 15th day of the 3rd month after the end of the partnership's tax year (Mar. 15 for a calendar year partnership). (Code Sec. 6072(b));[44] and regs provide an automatic extension of 6 months (to Sept. 15 for a calendar year partnership). (Reg § 1.6081-2(a)).[45]

Every partnership required to file a return must furnish (by the extended return due date) Form 1065, Schedule K-1, containing the information specified in the regs, to every person who was a partner (or who held a partnership interest as a nominee for another person) at any time during the partnership's tax year. (Code Sec. 6031(b); Reg § 1.6031(b)-1T(a))[46] (The nominee must in turn give the information it gets to the other person (Code Sec. 6031(c)(2); Reg § 1.6031(c)-1T(h)) and furnish the partnership with specified information about that person.) (Code Sec. 6031(c)(1); Reg § 1.6031(c)-1T(a))[47] Certain U.S. persons with interests in foreign partnerships must file Form 1065, Schedule K-2 and Form 1065, Schedule K-3 to report necessary information with respect to the international tax aspects of the Internal Revenue Code.[48] If a partnership deducts the cost of goods sold, it must file Form 1125-A.[49] For large partnerships that have to file Form 1065, Schedule M-3, see ¶4726

For mandatory e-filing rules for partnerships, see ¶4753.

IRS has provided additional guidance on completing Form 1065, Schedule K-2 and K-3, both of which report items of international tax relevance. (https://www.irs.gov/businesses/schedules-k-2-and-k-3-frequently-asked-questions-forms-1065-1120s-and-8865)

¶ 4732   Returns of trusts and estates—Forms 1041, K-1, 7004, 8453-FE; due date; automatic extension.

Trusts (¶4733) and estates (¶4734) must file income tax and information returns.[50]

---

37. ¶S-5623, S-5628
38. ¶S-5600 *et seq.*
39. ¶S-2701
40. ¶S-2708
41. ¶S-2705
42. ¶S-2701
43. ¶S-2712

44. ¶S-4923
45. ¶S-5030
46. ¶S-2710, ¶S-2714
47. ¶S-2724
48. ¶S-1906
49. ¶S-2701
50. ¶S-2004, S-2007

If there are *joint* fiduciaries, a return by one will suffice if he or she states in the return that he or she has sufficient knowledge of the facts to make the return and that it is true to the best of his or her knowledge and belief. (Reg § 1.6012-3(c))[1]

A fiduciary who prepares the trust's or estate's return must provide beneficiaries (or nominees) receiving distributions, or to whom an income item is allocated, a Form 1041, Schedule K-1, containing the same information. This must be furnished on or before a return is filed, and a copy must be filed with Form 1041. (Code Sec. 6034A(a)) If a nominee is given the information, he or she must furnish it to the beneficiary, and furnish to the estate or trust specified information about the beneficiary. (Code Sec. 6034A(b))[2]

Income tax returns that must be filed by estates, domestic trusts, and foreign trusts having a U.S. office or place of business, are due by the 15th day of the 4th month following the end of the tax year. (Reg § 1.6072-1(a)(1)) Foreign trusts and estates of nonresident aliens that don't have an office or place of business in the U.S. must file by the 15th day of the 6th month following the end of the tax year. (Reg § 1.6072-1(c))[3]

Fiduciaries use Form 8453-FE to e-file Form 1041.[4]

Under regs, non-bankruptcy estates and trusts get an automatic 5½-month extension to file Form 1041 by filing Form 7004 showing the full amount properly estimated as tax by the return's due date. (Reg § 1.6081-6)[5] IRS can terminate an automatic extension on 10 days' notice. (Reg § 1.6081-6(e))[6] For *payment* extensions, see ¶4721.

¶ 4733　Filing threshold for filing trust returns (Form 1041); grantor trusts; split-interest trusts (Form 5227).

Under Code Sec. 6012(a)(4) and Code Sec. 6012(a)(5), a trustee files Form 1041 if the trust isn't tax-exempt and if the trust has: (a) any taxable income for the year; (b) gross income of $600 or more; or (c) any beneficiary who is a nonresident alien.[7]

Trust income taxable to the grantor or other "owner" is reported on a separate attachment to Form 1041, but alternative reporting methods are available. The alternatives depend on whether the trust is treated as owned by 1 grantor, or by 2 or more grantors. (The latter may require a trustee to provide Form 1099 and a statement showing trust income items, deductions and credits). (Reg § 1.671-4(b))[8]

Split-interest trusts file Form 5227, even if they must currently distribute all net income. (Code Sec. 6034(a))[9]

¶ 4734　Filing threshold for filing estate returns—Form 1041.

Under Code Sec. 6012(a), the executor or administrator must file Form 1041 if gross income for the estate's tax year is $600 or more (Code Sec. 6012(a)(3)) *or* if any beneficiary is a nonresident alien. (Code Sec. 6012(a); Reg § 1.6012-3(a)(1)(iii))[10] A fiduciary doesn't have to file a copy of the will for income tax purposes unless IRS *requests* a copy. (Reg § 1.6012-3(a)(2))[11]

The executor who probates the entire will (in the state the decedent was domiciled) files Form 1041 reporting all the income. Any out-of-state (i.e., ancillary) executor *also* files a Form 1041, but it shows only the gross income received by the ancillary fiduciary and the deductions attributable to that income. (Reg § 1.6012-3(a)(3))[12]

1. ¶S-2002
2. ¶S-2019, S-2020
3. ¶S-4707
4. ¶S-1632
5. ¶S-5032
6. ¶S-5009

7. ¶S-2007
8. ¶S-2009 *et seq.*
9. ¶S-2806
10. ¶S-2004
11. ¶S-2006
12. ¶S-2005

¶ 4735 **Extensions for taxpayers making elections—automatic and non-automatic.**

Two automatic extensions are available for taxpayer elections, if the taxpayer takes corrective action within the extension period:

(1)   An automatic *12-month extension* for certain regulatory elections specified in Reg § 301.9100-2(a)(2). The more widely applicable ones are: the election to use a tax year other than the required tax year (¶2810); the election to use the LIFO inventory method (¶2859); and the election to adjust basis on partnership transfers and distributions (¶3769). The extension is available regardless of whether the taxpayer timely filed its return for the year the election should have been made. (Reg § 301.9100-2(a)(1))[13]

(2)   An automatic *6-month extension* for regulatory elections and statutory elections required to be made by the due date of the return or the due date of the return *including extensions,* for taxpayers who timely filed the return for the year in which the election should have been made. (Reg § 301.9100-2(b))[14]

Nonautomatic extensions of time are available for regulatory elections that don't qualify for an automatic extension, if the taxpayer shows IRS that he or she acted reasonably and in good faith, and that granting relief won't prejudice IRS's interests. (Reg § 301.9100-3(a)) A request for a nonautomatic extension is generally a request for a letter ruling, and is submitted under those procedures, with the applicable user fee. (Reg § 301.9100-3(e)(5))[15]

The grant of an extension of time to make an election isn't a determination that the taxpayer is otherwise eligible to make the election. (Reg § 301.9100-1(a))[16]

¶ 4736 **Returns of individuals' bankruptcy estates (Form 1041); filing thresholds; extensions (Form 7004).**

Under Code Sec. 6012(a)(8), the debtor-in-possession or trustee (if appointed) for an individual's Chapter 7 or 11 bankruptcy estate must file an income tax return (Form 1041) if the estate's gross income equals at least the sum of the exemption amount plus the basic standard deduction for unmarried taxpayers who weren't surviving spouses or heads of household. This amount is $12,950 for 2022 ($13,850 for 2023).[17] File Form 7004 for an automatic 6-month extension. (Reg § 1.6081-6(a)(2))[18]

¶ 4737 **Overview of information returns—Form 1099, etc.—due dates.**

Taxpayers report certain activities with third parties on information returns and statements. These are filed with IRS and in some cases furnished to third parties (¶4742).[19] For e-filing, see ¶4753. Payors (including nominees, see ¶4738) report their payments for a calendar year by filing an appropriate Form 1099 (or permitted substitute form) for payee (with a Form 1096 transmittal statement) after Sept. 30 of the calendar year of the payment (but not before the payor's final payments for the year) and by the next Feb. 28. (Reg § 1.6042-2(c), Reg § 1.6044-2(d)), except for nonemployee compensation returns for which the due date is Jan. 31. (Code Sec. 6071(c)[20] And returns filed electronically, other than nonemployee compensation returns, aren't due until Mar. 31 after the end of the calendar year to which they relate. (Code Sec. 6071(b))[21] For extensions, see ¶4747.

---

13. ¶S-4819
14. ¶S-4821
15. ¶S-4823, ¶S-4827
16. ¶S-4815.1
17. ¶C-9700 *et seq.*, S-2016

18. ¶S-5032
19. ¶S-2900 *et seq.*, S-4930
20. ¶S-4930
21. ¶S-1305; ¶S-4930

¶ 4738   Nominees (banks, dealers, brokers, etc.) and middleman—information returns—Forms 1099, 1099-DIV.

Under Code Sec. 6042(a)(1)(B) and Code Sec. 6049(a)(2), if reportable interest or dividends are paid to any person who, as middleman or nominee, then pays them over to the actual (beneficial) owner, the original payor (corporation, bank, etc.) must file an information return (Form 1099 or Form 1099-DIV for dividends) for the nominee, who must file another Form 1099 (or Form 1099-DIV) for the actual owner. (Code Sec. 6042(a)(1)(B), Code Sec. 6049(a)(2); Reg § 1.6042-2(a)(1)(iii), Reg § 1.6049-4(b)(3))[22]

A nominee is a payee who isn't the actual owner of the dividend or interest, but who would be required to furnish his or her TIN (¶4752) to the payor for inclusion on the *payor's* return. Nominees include banks, etc., and, for dividends, dealers and brokers. (Reg § 1.6042-2(a)(2), Reg § 1.6049-1(a)(2))[23] Special reporting rules apply to payments to joint payees (Reg § 1.6041-1(c)); and payments on behalf of another. (Reg § 1.6041-1(e))

¶ 4739   Dividend reporting—Forms 1099-DIV, 5452; cooperatives (1099-PATR)—information returns.

Under Code Sec. 6042(a), a payor (including nominees, see ¶4738) must file a Form 1099-DIV for each person to whom it pays "reportable" dividends aggregating $10 or more during the calendar year. (Code Sec. 6042(a), Reg § 1.6042-2(a)(1)) Dividends qualifying for preferential tax rates must be differentiated from nonqualified dividends.[24] For payee statements, see ¶4742.

Reportable dividends are corporate "dividends" (¶1285 *et seq.*) and substitute dividends (e.g., payments in lieu of dividends that brokers pay on short sales). (Code Sec. 6042(b)(1))[25] Nontaxable dividends are reported on Form 5452.[26]

Cooperatives (¶4206) report *patronage dividends* aggregating $10 or more to any payee in a calendar year on Form 1099-PATR. (Code Sec. 6044(a)(1); Reg § 1.6044-2(b))[27]

¶ 4740   Interest reporting—Forms 1099-INT, 1042-S; nonresident aliens—information returns.

Under Code Sec. 6049(a)(1)and Code Sec. 6049(d), every person (including nominees, see ¶4738) who pays $10 or more of reportable interest to any person (except certain payees) in a calendar year reports the payments on Form 1099-INT.[28] For payee statements, see ¶4742.

Reportable interest is interest on: (a) obligations issued publicly or in registered form (other than a short-term obligation held by a corporation), (b) deposits with banks or brokers, and (c) amounts held by insurance or investment companies. (Code Sec. 6049(b)(1))[29] Reportable interest also includes original issue discount (¶4741); amounts includible in gross income with respect to regular real estate mortgage investment conduits interests (¶4204) (Code Sec. 6049(d)(6)(A)(i), Code Sec. 6049(d)(7)(A));[30] and interest paid on tax-exempt bonds. But interest on obligations issued by a natural person isn't "reportable." (Code Sec. 6049(b)(2))[31]

A payor reports on Form 1042-S interest aggregating $10 or more that is paid to a nonresident alien individual (NRA) on deposits maintained at U.S. offices of financial institutions if the NRA lives in a country with which the U.S. has in effect an information exchange agreement. A payor can elect to report all interest paid to all NRAs.

22. ¶S-2904 *et seq.*
23. ¶s S-2904 *et seq.*, S-3003 *et seq.*
24. ¶S-2901, ¶S-2910
25. ¶S-2910, S-3724
26. ¶S-2914

27. ¶S-2951
28. ¶S-3001 *et seq.*
29. ¶S-3011 *et seq.*, ¶S-3023 *et seq.*
30. ¶s S-3073, S-3087
31. ¶S-3038, S-3040, S-3042

(Reg § 1.6049-4(b)(5), Reg § 1.6049-8)[32]

IRS' Form 1042-S Data Integrity Tool performs a quality review before data is submitted to IRS. IRS will consider a withholding agent's use of the tool when making enforcement and penalty determinations. (IR 2021-223, 11/15/2021)

¶ 4741 Information-return reporting of original issue discount (OID)—Form 1099-OID; one-time filing (Form 8281); brokers' reporting of bond premium, acquisition premium; tax-exempt obligations.

Under Code Sec. 6049(d)(6), an issuer (or nominee, see ¶4738) reports OID of at least $10 on any obligation as an interest payment. Form 1099-OID is used to report the OID and any interest actually paid on the obligation.[33] Form 8281 must be filed by certain issuers of publicly-offered debt instruments having OID within 30 days after issuance. (Code Sec. 1275(c)(2); Reg § 1.1275-3(c))[34]

observation: The one-time reporting requirement on Form 8281 is in addition to the annual information reporting on Form 1099-OID.

If a broker has to file a statement for a debt instrument (statements to recipients of interest payments and holders of obligations for attributed OID), the broker generally reports any bond premium (under Reg § 1.171-1(d), see ¶2165) or acquisition premium (under Reg § 1.1272-2(b)(3), see ¶2621) for the calendar year.[35]

For tax-exempt obligations acquired after 2016, a payer must report the daily portions of OID on a tax-exempt obligation. (Reg § 1.6049-10)[36]

¶ 4742 Payee statements must be furnished by payors required to file information returns; due date—Form 1099, Form 1042-S.

Under Code Sec. 6042(c), payors of reportable dividends (and payments in lieu of dividends) and (under Code Sec. 6049) interest (including OID) must furnish payees with specified written statements of the amount reported to IRS (i.e., Copy B of Form 1099 sent to IRS). This generally must be done, either in person or in a "statement mailing," by Jan. 31 of the year following the calendar year for which the payor's Form 1099 was required. (Reg § 1.6042-4(d)(1), Reg § 1.6044-5(b), Reg § 1.6049-3(c)(1)) Payees can consent to receiving Form 1099 and Form 1042-S statements electronically. (Reg § 1.6049-6(e)(4))[37]

¶ 4743 Information reporting for business payments of $600 or more; gambling winnings—Form 1099-MISC.

Under Code Sec. 6041, with limited exceptions, every person, corporate or otherwise, engaged in a trade or business who, in the course of that business, makes payments aggregating $600 or more to another person (e.g., an independent contractor) in a calendar year must file Form 1099-MISC setting forth the payee's name and address and the amount paid, and furnish a statement to the payee. Any return or statement reporting nonemployee compensation must be filed by Jan. 31 of the year following the calendar year to which the returns relate.[38] Reportable payments are: rent, salaries, wages, premiums, annuities, compensations, remunerations, emoluments, prizes or awards (that aren't for services rendered), or other fixed or determinable gains, profits and income. (Code Sec. 6041; Reg § 1.6041-1) Payments made using virtual currency/cryptocurrency (¶2402), such as Bitcoin, are subject to these requirements.[39] This rule doesn't apply to transactions covered by other information return rules (e.g., dividends, see ¶4739), or most payments to corporations (including LLCs that elect to be treated as corporations, ¶3701).

32. ¶S-3012.1; ¶S-3012.1A
33. ¶S-3073, S-3074
34. ¶S-3080 *et seq.*
35. ¶S-3078.1

36. ¶S-3040
37. ¶S-1376; ¶S-2927 *et seq.*; ¶S-3002; ¶S-3071 *et seq.*
38. ¶S-3658
39. ¶S-3655 *et seq.*, ¶S-3658

Payments of bills for merchandise, telegrams, telephone, freight, storage, and similar charges are exempt from the return requirement. (Reg § 1.6041-3(c)) But a taxpayer must report certain payments to doctors or corporations engaged in providing medical care (including veterinary care) if the payment is made in the course of the taxpayer's trade or business. (Reg § 1.6041-3(p)) Also, persons who, in the course of a trade or business, pay reportable gambling winnings, must make an information return for those payments (for winnings of $1,200 and above for bingo and slot machines; $1,500 and above for keno). A separate information return is required for each payment. (Reg § 1.6041-10)[40]

Lenders who have filed or furnished Forms 1099-MISC reporting certain payments on loans subsidized by the Small Business Administration as income of the borrower must file and furnish corrected Forms 1099-MISC that exclude those payments, as they aren't includible in borrowers' gross income. (Notice 2021-6, 2021-6 IRB 822; Ann. 2021-2, 2021-8 IRB 892)[41]

¶ 4744   Information reporting of mortgage interest (and points) received (Form 1098); HUD and state HFAs.

Under Code Sec. 6050H, an "interest recipient" who receives interest, or reimburses interest overpayments, aggregating $600 or more for a calendar year on a mortgage must report (on Form 1098) those receipts or reimbursements, even if the interest is received on behalf of another. This applies to any person (including cooperative housing corporations) who, in the course of a trade or business (except governmental recipients), receives interest on a mortgage secured all or in part by real property, if the payor of record is an individual. (Code Sec. 6050H; Reg § 1.6050H-1, Reg § 1.6050H-2(a))[42] The return must also include any points received in the year that were paid directly by the buyer (including certain points paid by or charged to the seller). (Code Sec. 6050H(b)(2)(C); Reg § 1.6050H-1(f))[43] For 2011-2021, HUD and state housing finance authorities (State HFAs) can report payments made to or on behalf of financially distressed homeowners under programs such as Emergency-Homeowners' Loan Program (EHLP) or similar programs designed by State HFAs on Form 1098-MA or on a statement containing the required information.[44]

¶ 4745   Information-reporting rules for payor, recipient, of qualified residence interest on seller-provided financing—Form 1040, Schedule A; Form 1040, Schedule B.

Under Code Sec. 6109(h), a return on which taxpayer claims a deduction for qualified residence interest (¶1729) on seller-provided financing must show the name, address and TIN of the person (the seller) to whom the interest is paid or accrued on Form 1040, Schedule A. And any person who receives or accrues interest from seller-provided financing must include on Form 1040, Schedule B for the tax year in which the interest is so received or accrued the name, address and TIN of the person liable for the interest.[45]

¶ 4746   Miscellaneous information return requirements.

. . . *Abandonment or foreclosure of property held as security* for a business loan must be reported by the lender on Form 1099-A (Code Sec. 6050J; Reg § 1.6050J-1T) (unless related to a discharge of debt reported on Form 1099-C, below).[46]

. . . *Accelerated death benefits* paid to any individual must be reported by the payor (Code Sec. 6050Q) on Form 1099-LTC.[47]

. . . *Acquiring corporation in taxable acquisition* must file information returns with IRS

---

40. ¶S-3676, S-3667, S-3697.1
41. ¶S-3676
42. ¶S-3901 *et seq.*
43. ¶S-3907 *et seq.*

44. ¶V-1810.4 *et seq.*
45. ¶S-1524 *et seq.*
46. ¶S-4200 *et seq.*
47. ¶S-3440

and furnish statements to shareholders if a shareholder of the acquired corporation recognizes gain or loss in whole or in part due to the acquisition. (Code Sec. 6043A(a))[48]

...*Alcohol and biodiesel fuel tax benefits, Code Sec. 34 credit for farming, off-highway and certain other nontaxable uses of fuel*—information return required by persons claiming alcohol or biodiesel fuel tax benefits or a Code Sec. 34 credit, providing information on the benefits or credit. (Code Sec. 4104(a))[49]

...*Attorney's fees* paid in the course of a trade or business that aren't reportable as wages or under Code Sec. 6041 (or would have to be reported under Code Sec. 6041 but for the $600 limitation, see ¶4743), whether or not the services are performed for the payor (Code Sec. 6045(f); Reg § 1.6045-5) and whether or not the attorney is the exclusive payee, on Form 1099-MISC. (Reg § 1.6045-5)[50]

...*Applicable large employers* (ALEs) must offer their full-time employees and their dependents the opportunity to enroll in minimum essential coverage (MEC), ¶4879) under an eligible employer-sponsored plan have to report insurance coverage (including health reimbursement accounts) on Form 1094-C and Form 1095-C. Use Form 8809 to request an extension. (Code Sec. 6056; Reg § 301.6056-1)[1]

...*Banks and on-line payment networks* (payment settlement entities (PSEs) or third party settlement organizations (TPSOs)) have to report credit card sales to IRS and "participating payees" on Form 1099-K. (Code Sec. 6050W, Reg § 1.6050W-1) TPSOs have to only report payments made in settlement of third party network transactions if the transactions exceed $600. (Code Sec. 6050W(e) as amended by ARPA Sec. 9674)[2]

...*Barter exchanges* having at least 100 exchanges of property or services are made in the calendar year are reported on Form 1099-B. (Code Sec. 6045; Reg § 1.6045-1(e))[3]

...*Basis information, regarding property acquired from decedents,* must be provided by executors and/or certain beneficiaries to persons who acquire property from a decedent. (Code Sec. 6035(a))[4]

...*Brokers* (including, for returns that must be filed after 2023, those responsible for regularly effectuating transfers of digital assets on behalf of someone else—e.g., cryptocurrency exchanges) must report each sale of securities, commodities, regulated futures contracts, foreign currency contracts, forward contracts, and debt instruments the broker effects for its customers, on Form 1099-B (and, for transactions occurring after Jan. 1, 2023, must report digital assets (Code Sec. 6045(g)(3)(D))—e.g., cryptocurrency—transactions on Form 1099-B). (Code Sec. 6045; Reg § 1.6045-1(c), Reg § 1.6045-2)[5] Brokers also must report customer's adjusted basis (determined under Reg § 1.6045-1(n)(6)) and character of gain or loss for sales of "covered securities" (as defined in Code Sec. 6045(g)(3) and Reg § 1.6045-1(a)(15)). Brokers can treat all securities as covered securities to simplify reporting.[6] Also, brokers that transfer covered securities to other brokers have to provide statements to other brokers. (Code Sec. 6045A; Reg § 1.6045A-1)[7]

...*Cash of more than $10,000,* including certain cash equivalents (e.g., cashier's checks, foreign currency, and, for returns due after 2023, digital assets (e.g., cryptocurrency, see Code Sec. 6045(g)(3)(D))), received in connection with a trade or business must be reported by the recipient (Code Sec. 6050I(a), Code Sec. 6050I(d); Reg § 1.6050I-1(a)(1), Reg § 1.6050I-1(c)(1)) within 15 days after receipt. Use Form 8300 (Reg § 1.6050I-1(e)), except that banks file Financial Crimes Enforcement Network (FinCEN) Form 104 and casinos, under special rules (Reg § 1.6050I-1(d)(2)), file FinCEN Form 103 (certain Nevada casinos file Form 8852) to report cash from gaming activities.[8] Recipients in U.S. territories must report.[9] Special rules apply for cash installment payments.

---

48. ¶S-4317
49. ¶S-4466
50. ¶S-3851
1. ¶S-3331
2. ¶S-3699.19
3. ¶S-3731 *et seq.*

4. ¶S-2309
5. ¶S-3700 *et seq.*
6. ¶S-3741 *et seq.*
7. ¶S-3761 *et seq.*
8. ¶S-4000 *et seq.*
9. ¶S-4012

(Reg § 1.6050I-1(b))[10]

. . . *Change in control or recapitalization of a corporation* generally must be reported on Form 8806 showing the parties to the transaction, the fees involved, the changes in capital structure and any other information IRS requires. (Code Sec. 6043(c); Reg § 1.6043-4)[11]

. . . *Charitable organization required to acknowledge gift of auto, plane, or boat* (¶2138) must provide the information required on Form 1098-C to IRS. (Code Sec. 170(f)(12)(D))[12]

. . . *Charitable property disposition* by the donee within 3 years of contribution must be reported on Form 8282 by the charity, if the deduction claimed for the property exceeds $5,000 (but disposition of items appraised for $500 or less doesn't have to be reported). (Code Sec. 6050L; Reg § 1.6050L-1)[13]

. . . *Commodity Credit Corporation (CCC)* must report market gain associated with the repayment of a CCC loan, regardless of whether the taxpayer repays the loan with cash or uses CCC certificates in repayment of the loan, on Form 1099-G. (Code Sec. 6039J)[14]

. . . *Crowdfunding* websites or payment processors must file and furnish a Form 1099-K if, during a calendar year, the total of all payments distributed to a person exceeds $600 in gross payments, regardless of the number of transactions or donations.[15]

. . . *Direct sales of consumer goods* of $5,000 or more to any 1 buyer in a calendar year must be reported by the seller (Code Sec. 6041A) on Form 1099-MISC.[16]

. . . *Discharge of debt (including student loans) by banks, and other financial entities and organizations having a significant lending trade or business* of $600 or more is reported to IRS, on Form 1099-C. (Code Sec. 6050P; Reg § 1.6050P-1, Reg § 1.6050P-2)[17]

. . . *Donee of qualified intellectual property* (¶2106) must file annual information return (Form 8899) of net income from property for each specified tax year of the donee. (Code Sec. 6050L(b)(1); Reg § 1.6050L-2)[18]

. . . *Education-related payments* received (or billed) by higher education institutions for qualified tuition and related expenses; qualified tuition refunds (Form 1098-T) (Reg § 1.6050S-1); and interest of $600 or more received from an individual for a calendar year on an educational loan (Form 1098-E) are reported. (Code Sec. 6050S; Reg § 1.6050S-3)[19] For educational loans, lenders report amounts (in addition to all other interest paid) attributable to capitalized interest and loan origination fees.[20] Certain statements to students and borrowers may be provided electronically. (Reg § 1.6050S-2(a)(1), Reg § 1.6050S-4(a))[21]

. . . *Education savings distributions* (certain) from Coverdell ESAs[22] and qualified tuition programs or 529 plans are reported on Form 1099-Q.[23]

. . . *Employer-owned life insurance contracts* issued after Aug. 17, 2006, must be reported on Form 8925 by applicable policyholders. (Code Sec. 6039I; Reg § 1.6039I-1)[24]

. . . *Fishing boat operators* report crew payments on Form 1099-MISC. (Code Sec. 6050A; Reg § 1.6050A-1)[25]

. . . *Fish bought for resale* for cash (of $600 or more) are reported on Form 1099-MISC for each seller by persons engaged in the trade or business of buying fish for resale. (Code Sec. 6050R)[26]

. . . *Foreign bank and financial accounts* (including on-line poker accounts) are reported on Financial Crimes Enforcement Network (FinCEN) Form 114 (FBAR) by any person

---

10. ¶S-4019 *et seq.*　　　　　　　　19. ¶S-3430 *et seq.*
11. ¶S-4308　　　　　　　　　　　　20. ¶S-3432.11
12. ¶K-3948.1; ¶S-2872.1　　　　　21. ¶S-1370
13. ¶S-2873　　　　　　　　　　　　22. ¶S-3428
14. ¶N-1171.1　　　　　　　　　　　23. ¶S-3422
15. ¶J-1009.1　　　　　　　　　　　24. ¶S-3231
16. ¶S-3677　　　　　　　　　　　　25. ¶S-3695
17. ¶S-4251 *et seq.*　　　　　　　　26. ¶S-3695.1
18. ¶S-2882.1

(including a person acting as an agent) with a financial interest in or signature authority over the account, if the aggregate value of these accounts exceeds $10,000 at any time during the calendar year. FBAR is due by Apr. 15 of the year following the year that the account holder meets the $10,000 threshold, but is eligible for an automatic 6-month extension. IRS has provided information on completing and filing an FBAR. (IR 2021-83, 04/09/2021; FS-2021-7, 04/2021; IR 2022-73, 3/31/2022; FS-2022-24, 3/31/2022) The deadline for filing a 2021 FBAR is Apr. 18, 2022. (IR 2022-73, 3/31/2022; FS-2022-24, 3/31/2022) The deadline for filing a 2022 FBAR is Apr. 17, 2023.[27]

... *Individuals and specified domestic entities holding any interest in specified foreign financial assets* have to attach the information required on Form 8938 to their income tax returns if the aggregate value of those assets exceed $50,000 ($100,000 for certain married individuals) or a higher amount prescribed by IRS. Specified foreign financial assets include stock, securities, financial instruments, and contracts that are held for investment, are not held in an account maintained by a financial institution, and are issued by a person organized under the laws of a U.S. possession. The maximum fair market value for a specified foreign financial asset with no positive value during the year is treated as zero. (Code Sec. 6038D; Reg § 1.6038D-1; Reg § 1.6038D-2; Reg § 1.6038D-3; Reg § 1.6038D-5)[28]

... *Insurers* (including self-insured employers) that provide minimal essential coverage (MEC), ¶4879) to any individual during a calendar year report health insurance coverage information for coverage on Form 1095-B. Proposed reliance regs provide guidance under Code Sec. 6055 relating to Form 1095-B. (Code Sec. 6055; Reg § 1.6055-1; Prop Reg. § 1.6055-1 ("Taxpayers may rely")) [29]

... *IRA (and Roth IRA) contributions and withdrawals* must be reported by the IRA trustees or issuer (Code Sec. 408(i), Code Sec. 408A(d)(3)(D)), on Form 5498.[30] The trustee also reports on Form 5498 that a required minimum distribution (but not the amount) is required for an IRA for a calendar year. (Reg § 1.408-8, Q&10)[31] For required distributions, information is provided to the IRA owner by Jan. 31 of the required distribution year.[32]

... *Issuers* of specified securities (i.e., stocks, bonds, commodity contracts, etc.) report organizational actions (e.g., stock splits, mergers, acquisitions, etc.) affecting basis on Form 8937. It is due within 45 days of the action or, if earlier, by Jan. 15 of the next calendar year. But, the issuer can post the form on its primary public website in a readily accessible format by the due date (instead of filing). (Code Sec. 6045B; Reg § 1.6045B-1)[33]

... *Life insurance contracts:* Information reporting requirements (Form 1099-LS) are imposed on the acquirer of a life insurance contract in a "reportable policy sale." Also, issuers must satisfy reporting requirements concerning the seller's basis in the contract in a reportable policy sale and the transferor's basis in the contract in certain foreign transfers. There are also reporting requirements imposed on the payor in the case of reportable death benefits made under a contract transferred in a reportable policy sale.[34]

... *Liquidating corporations* report the adoption of the plan of liquidation on Form 966,[35] and liquidating distributions of $600 or more (Code Sec. 6043(a)) on Form 1099-DIV.[36]

... *Long-term care payments* made under a long-term care insurance contract to any individual must be reported by the payor (Code Sec. 6050Q) on Form 1099-LTC.[37]

... *Medical savings account and health savings account contributions and distributions* are reported by a trustee on Form 5498-SA and Form 1099-SA. (Code Sec. 220(h))[38]

... *Mortgage credit certificate* (MCC) information is reported (on Form 8329) by each

27. ¶S-3650
28. ¶S-3650.1; S-3650.2
29. ¶S-3321
30. ¶S-3391
31. ¶S-3392.1
32. ¶S-3392.2
33. ¶S-3781, S-3786
34. ¶S-3240 *et seq.*
35. ¶S-4314
36. ¶S-4315
37. ¶S-3435.1 *et seq.*
38. ¶H-1328.1

person who makes a "certified indebtedness" loan under an MCC program. (Reg § 1.25-8T(a))[39] Each state or political subdivision with MCC programs reports (on Form 8330) the amount of MCCs issued each quarter. (Code Sec. 25(g); Reg § 1.25-4T)[40]

...*Mortgage insurance premiums* aggregating $600 or more for any calendar year must be reported on Form 1098 by any person who, in the course of a trade or business, received the premiums. (Code Sec. 6050H(h)(1), Reg § 1.6050H-3)[41]

...*Outbound Code Sec. 355 distributions* (¶3545) and outbound Code Sec. 332 corporate liquidations (Reg § 1.6038B-1(e))[42] are reported on Form 926.[43]

...*Parent tax-exempt organizations* that are controlling organizations (Code Sec. 512(b)(3)) report transactions with controlled entities on Form 990-T. (Code Sec. 6033(h))[44]

...*Partnership interest sales or exchanges* due to unrealized receivables, inventory, collectibles, or Code Sec. 1250 gain are reported by partnerships on Form 8308. (Code Sec. 6050K; Reg § 1.6050K-1(a)(1))[45] A partnership doesn't have to file until it's notified of the exchange (Code Sec. 6050K(c)(2)), i.e., when it receives written notification required from the transferor, or has knowledge of it. (Reg § 1.6050K-1)[46]

...*Pension, profit-sharing plans* file annual return/report forms in the Form 5500 series (Code Sec. 6058(a)),[47] file Form 5310A to notify IRS of plan mergers, consolidations, or divisions, (Code Sec. 6057(b)(4))[48] and make returns and reports of designated Roth contributions. (Code Sec. 6047(f)) Form 5500 series is due no later than the last day of the 7th month after the plan year ends (July 31 for calendar year plans). There is an automatic 2 1/2 month extension to file certain Form 5500.[49] Form 8955-SSA is used to report information about separated participants with deferred vested benefits.[50] A short Form 5500-SF may be filed by plans: covering fewer than 100 participants at the beginning of the plan year; not holding employer securities; investing 100% in certain secure, easy to value assets; eligible for a waiver under DOL annual examination and report rules; and not multiemployer plans.[1] 1-participant plan with total assets of $250,000 or less are exempt from filing the annual return. If that plan must file a return, it can file a paper Form 5500-EZ (or Form 5500-SF e-file).[2] All other annual reports—including any statements and schedules—are filed electronically with DOL using EFAST2.[3] Use Form 5558 to request extensions for filing Form 5500 and Form 8955-SSA.[4]

...*Political organizations* except for certain state and local committees under Code Sec. 527 must file an initial notice of status (Form 8871) (Code Sec. 527(i)),[5] and periodic reports of contributions and expenditures (Form 8872) (Code Sec. 527(j)(2)), which can be filed on-line with an IRS-supplied user ID and password.[6]

...*Premium and advance payment* information is reported by an Exchange on Form 1095-A, see ¶2343. IRS announced that Exchanges may, but aren't required to, report information relating to catastrophic health plan coverage enrolled in through an Exchange for coverage years after 2017. (Code Sec. 6055)[7]

...*Real estate* reporting persons (as defined in Code Sec. 6045(e)(2)) must report real estate transactions on Form 1099-S, including the sale of a condominium unit or stock in a cooperative housing unit. For a residential transactions, the return includes any portion of real property tax treated as imposed on the buyer. Reporting isn't required for sales of principal residences for $250,000 or less ($500,000 or less for married sellers) (regs can permit higher amounts) if the reporting person receives specified written assurances (on IRS's certification form) from the seller by Jan. 31 following the year of

39. ¶S-4206
40. ¶S-4207
41. ¶S-3923
42. ¶S-3640.1; ¶S-3640.1A
43. ¶S-3630
44. ¶S-2862.2
45. ¶S-2725 *et seq.*
46. ¶S-2719 *et seq.*
47. ¶S-3351
48. ¶S-3383, S-3384

49. ¶S-3400.1; S-3366.1
50. ¶S-3369
1. ¶S-3355.1
2. ¶S-3357
3. ¶S-3351
4. ¶S-5057
5. ¶S-2858.7
6. ¶S-2858.9
7. ¶S-3321

sale. (Code Sec. 6045(e); Reg § 1.6045-4)[8] Reportable real estate transactions also include sales or exchanges of standing timber for lump-sum payments. (Reg § 1.6045-4(b)(2)(i)(E), Reg § 1.6045-4(s))[9]

. . . *Receipt of fines, penalties, etc. by government and other agencies of $50,000 or more for law violations.* Officials of governments, government entities and certain non-governmental entities that are charged with controlling suits, investigations, or inquiries for a violation or potential violation of any law (or are specifically assigned the tax reporting responsibility) must report to IRS and the taxpayer the amount of each settlement agreement or order entered into on or after Jan. 1, 2022. The threshold amount that requires reporting is $600 under the Code, raised to $50,000 by regs. (Form 1098-F). (Code Sec. 6050X; Reg § 1.6050X-1(g))[10]

. . . *Refunds of state and local income tax* of $10 or more must be reported by the state or local tax authority/payor on Form 1099-G. (Code Sec. 6050E; Reg § 1.6050E-1)[11]

. . . *Royalty payments* of $10 or more per year per payee (including nominees) must be reported unless the payee is a corporation, exempt organization or government (Code Sec. 6050N), on Form 1099-MISC. Where a publisher pays royalties to an author's agent and the agent subtracts his or her commission and expenses, both parties report the gross royalties on Form 1099-MISC, unreduced by the subtracted amounts.[12]

. . . *Transfers under incentive stock options (ISOs) and employee stock purchase plans (ESPPs)* are reported by corporations on Form 3921 and Form 3922. (Code Sec. 6039(a); Reg § 1.6039-1)[13]

. . . *Sick pay* (nonwage) paid by a third party to an employee must be reported by the third party to the employee's employer. An employer or third party files Form 8922 if the employer is including the employer FICA tax on sick pay wages on the employer's Form 941 but the third party is including the employee FICA tax on the same sick pay wages on the third party's Form 941 (split liability). Whether the employer or the third party is required to file the Form 8922 depends on which entity is filing Form W-2 for the sick pay. (Code Sec. 6051(f)(1); Reg § 31.6051-3(a))[14]

. . . *Simplified employee pension (SEP) contributions* are reported by the SEP trustee or issuer of a SEP endowment contract (Code Sec. 408(l); Reg § 1.408-7) on Form 5498.[15]

. . . *Sponsoring organizations* (under Code Sec. 4966(d)(1), ¶4131), on their annual information returns (Form 990-T), must include information relating to donor advised funds (DAFs), ¶4127) owned by an organization at the end of the tax year. (Code Sec. 6033(k))[16]

. . . *Supporting organizations* (Code Sec. 509(a)(3)) must file annual information returns listing supported organizations, the type of supporting organization, certify that the organization isn't controlled by 1 or more disqualified persons. (Code Sec. 6033(l))[17]

. . . *Tips* must be reported by employees to employers on Form 4070. (Code Sec. 6053(a); Reg § 31.6053-1(b)(2))[18] Large food and beverage establishments (more than 10 employees on a typical business day) must report to IRS (on Form 8027) and to employees tips reported by the employees to the employer plus the excess (as specially allocated) of 8% of the establishment's gross receipts (as specially defined) over the amount of tips reported by the employees. The 8% can be reduced to not below 2%, on application to IRS. (Code Sec. 6053(c)(3); Reg § 31.6053-3)[19] An employer doesn't have to report tips that aren't reported to the employer until it receives a Code Sec. 3121(q) Notice and Demand. Then, the employer reports them on its next Form 941.[20]

. . . *Unemployment insurance benefit* payments of $10 or more must be reported by the payor on Form 1099-G. (Code Sec. 6050B; Reg § 1.6050B-1)[21]

---

8. ¶S-3800 *et seq.*
9. ¶S-3813
10. ¶S-4271
11. ¶S-3690
12. ¶S-3684 *et seq.*
13. ¶S-3206.1 *et seq.*
14. ¶S-3173

15. ¶S-3399 *et seq.*
16. ¶S-2862.3
17. ¶S-2823
18. ¶H-4344
19. ¶S-3250 *et seq.*; ¶S-3303;
20. ¶H-4714.1
21. ¶S-3694

¶ 4747 Extension of time for information returns, automatic and non-automatic—Form 8809.

Use Form 8809 to request a 30-day extension to file the following forms: W-2G, 1042-S, 1094-C, 1095-B, 1095-C, 3921, 3922, 8027, 1097 series, 1098 series, 1099 series (except forms reporting nonemployee compensation) and 5498 series. Approval is automatic for 30-day extension requests (no signature or explanation needed). Detailed explanation and signature are required for requests beyond the original 30-day extension. Anyone required to file Form W-2 series returns (except Form W-2G) or a form reporting nonemployee compensation is only allowed to request a single 30-day "non-automatic" extension. (Reg § 1.6081-8)[22] "Non-automatic" extensions are also available to file Social Security Administration's copy of Forms W-2 and W-3. (Reg § 31.6081(a)-1)[23]

¶ 4748 "Material advisors" must disclose reportable transactions, and maintain lists—Forms 8918, 13976; due date.

Under Code Sec. 6111(a), each material advisor, for any reportable transaction (Code Sec. 6707A(c), ¶4874), files Form 8918 setting out: information identifying and describing a transaction and its expected tax benefits, and any other information IRS requests. (Code Sec. 6111(a); Reg § 301.6111-3(a)) Form 8918 is due by the last day of the month after the calendar quarter when a person becomes a material advisor or when an amended disclosure statement becomes necessary.[24] For penalties, see ¶4876.

A material advisor is any person who provides any material aid, assistance, or advice for organizing, managing, promoting, selling, implementing, insuring, or carrying out any reportable transaction, and who directly or indirectly derives gross income in excess of a threshold amount (or such other amount prescribed by IRS) for that assistance or advice. (Code Sec. 6111(b)(1)(A); Reg § 301.6111-3(b)) A person becomes a material advisor on: (1) making a tax statement, (2) receiving (or expecting to receive) the minimum fees, and (3) the taxpayer's entering into the transaction.[25]

The threshold amount is $50,000 for a reportable transaction substantially all of the tax benefits from which are provided to natural persons, and $250,000 in any other case. (Code Sec. 6111(b)(1)(B); Reg § 301.6111-3(b)(3))[26]

Each material advisor must maintain a list with respect to any reportable transaction. The list must identify each person for whom the advisor acted as a material advisor for the transaction and contain any other information as IRS regs may require. The list may (but is not required to) be kept on Form 13976. (Code Sec. 6112(a); Reg § 301.6112-1)[27]

¶ 4749 Participation in tax shelter reportable transactions, reporting requirements—Form 8886; due date.

Taxpayers must disclose (on Form 8886, due with an original or amended return reporting participation) their participation in "reportable transactions," "listed transactions," "confidential transactions," "transactions with contractual protection," certain loss transactions, and "transactions of interest" (see Reg § 1.6011-4(b)), by attaching an information statement to their income tax returns. (Reg § 1.6011-4)[28]

A copy of Form 8886 must be sent to the IRS Office of Tax Shelter Analysis (OTSA) at the time of the first filing of a disclosure. (Reg § 1.6011-4(d)) For penalties, see ¶4874. Taxpayers also must disclose participation in listed transactions involving estate tax (Reg § 20.6011-4), gift tax (Reg § 25.6011-4), employment tax (Reg § 31.6011-4), excise

---

22. ¶S-5049
23. ¶S-5052, S-5054
24. ¶S-4401, ¶S-4413
25. ¶S-4413

26. ¶S-4406
27. ¶S-4414, S-4416
28. ¶S-4429, ¶S-4445

764

tax related to private foundations and certain other tax exempts (Reg § 53.6011-4), excise taxes relating to qualified pension and other plans under Code Sec. 4971 through Code Sec. 4980F (Reg § 54.6011-4), and excise taxes relating to public charities. (Reg § 56.6011-4) Disclosure means, among other things, the expected tax treatment of and all potential tax benefits expected from the transaction, a sufficiently detailed description of the transaction, and the identity of all parties involved in the transaction. (Reg § 1.6011-4(d)) Confidential corporate tax shelters also are subject to the tax shelter registration rules of Code Sec. 6111. (Reg § 301.6111-2)[29]

¶ 4750 Return preparer's duties; PTINs; mandatory e-filing; IRS's voluntary AFSP program; IRS's directory of preparers.

A tax return preparer (¶4751) must:

. . . *sign the return* as prescribed by IRS in forms, instructions, etc. (Code Sec. 6695(b)) If the return isn't signed electronically, he or she must sign a completed return before it is presented to a taxpayer for signature. If the preparer is unavailable for signature, another preparer must review the entire return and sign it. (Reg § 1.6695-1(b)(1)) Preparers may sign original or amended returns, or extension requests, as a return preparer with a stamp, mechanical device, or computer software program. The method used must contain either a facsimile of the preparer's signature or his or her printed name.[30]

. . . *enter a preparer tax ID number (PTIN).* (Code Sec. 6109(a)(4)) All compensated preparers (including those who already have PTINs) must register on the on-line registration system (on the Tax Professionals page at irs.gov) or submit a paper Form W-12 (4 to 6 weeks of response time). Preparers must renew PTINs annually. User fees apply. (Reg § 1.6109-2; Reg § 300.0(b)(12); Reg § 300.12)[31] An enrolled retirement plan agent (ERPA) needs a PTIN if, for compensation, he or she prepares, or assists in the preparation of, all or substantially all of any tax return or claim for refund that is not an exempt form; Form 5300 and Form 5500 are exempt forms.[32]

. . . *enter an address where the return was prepared* on any return he or she prepares; if there's a partnership or employment arrangement between 2 or more preparers, the identifying number of the partnership or employer must also appear on the return or claim for refund. The identifying number of a preparer (whether an individual, corporation, or partnership) who employs or engages 1 or more persons to prepare returns or refund claims is that preparer's employer identification number (EIN). (Reg § 1.6109-2A(b)(1))[33]

. . . *furnish the taxpayer with a completed copy of any tax return* no later than when the return is presented for signature. (Code Sec. 6107(a)) The same rule applies to a return prepared for a nontaxable entity (i.e., partnership or S corporation). (Reg § 1.6107-1(a))[34]

. . . *retain for 3 years a completed copy of each return* or a list of the name and TIN of each taxpayer for whom a return was prepared (Code Sec. 6107(b));[35]

. . . *retain a record of the name, TIN, and principal place of work of each income tax return preparer* employed or engaged by the preparer/employer during each July 1-June 30 period. (Reg § 1.6060-1(a)(1))[36]

. . . *e-file* individual income tax returns (and estate and trust returns), unless the preparer neither files nor reasonably expects to file 10 or more individual income tax returns in a calendar year. (Code Sec. 6011(e); Reg § 301.6011-7) E-filing is mandatory for preparers anticipating filing 11 or more federal individual or trust tax returns. Firms have to compute the number of returns in the aggregate that they reasonably expect to file as a firm. Clients can independently choose to file paper returns. Preparers should

---

29. ¶S-4438
30. ¶S-4603, ¶S-4604
31. ¶S-1522 *et seq.*
32. ¶S-1522.1

33. ¶S-1101
34. ¶S-1102
35. ¶V-2675
36. ¶S-1106, V-2676

document each client's choice to file a paper return and keep a copy of the signed statement on file. Use Form 8944 to request hardship waivers from e-filing.[37]

IRS established a voluntary education program (Annual Filing Season Program, or AFSP) for return preparers (other than attorneys, CPAs, EAs, etc.). Applicants apply for AFSP in the same manner as applying for a PTIN.[38]

IRS has published an on-line directory of preparers who have satisfied the requirements for AFSP or who have recognized credentials (e.g., an attorney, CPA, enrolled agents) at https://irs.treasury.gov/rpo/rpo.jsf.

For penalties on return preparers related to the above duties, see ¶4871.

¶ 4751 Tax return preparer defined (for return preparers' duties); signing and non-signing preparer.

Under Code Sec. 7701(a)(36)(A), a tax return preparer is any person, including a partnership or corporation, who, in return for compensation, prepares, or employs or engages another to prepare, all or a substantial portion of any federal tax return or refund claim. A *signing* tax return preparer is the individual tax return preparer who has the primary responsibility for the overall substantive accuracy of the preparation of the return or refund claim. (Reg § 301.7701-15(b)(1))

A *nonsigning* tax return preparer is any tax return preparer who is not a signing tax return preparer but who prepares all or a substantial portion of a return or claim for refund for events that have occurred at the time the advice is rendered. Time spent on advice that is given after events have occurred that represents less than 5% of the individual's aggregate time for the position giving rise to the understatement isn't taken into account. Examples of nonsigning tax return preparers are preparers who provide advice to a taxpayer or another preparer when that advice leads to a position or entry that is a substantial portion of the return. (Reg § 301.7701-15(b)(2)(i))[39]

A person may also be a "preparer" of a related return if an entry on a return he or she actually prepared (e.g., partnership or S corporation return) is directly reflected on the related return (e.g., partner's or shareholder's return), and the entry is a substantial portion of the related return. (Reg § 301.7701-15(b)(3)(iii))[40]

A portion of a return prepared by a nonsigning tax return preparer won't be "substantial" if, aggregating all schedules, etc., he or she prepared, that portion involves amounts of gross income, deductions, or amounts on which credits are based that are: (1) less than $10,000, or (2) less than $400,000 *and* less than 20% of the gross income (AGI, for individuals) as shown on the return. (Reg § 301.7701-15(b)(3)(ii)(A))[41]

A tax consultant is a "preparer" even though he or she may do no more than review a return already prepared by the taxpayer.[42] A person is a "preparer" if he or she supplies enough information and advice so that completion of a return is a mere mechanical or clerical matter (Reg § 301.7701-15(c))[43] but not if he or she merely furnishes typing, reproducing or other mechanical assistance with respect to preparing a return. (Code Sec. 7701(a)(36)(B)(i); Reg § 301.7701-15(f)(1)(viii)) A person who provides a computerized return preparation service is a preparer if his or her computer programs provide substantive tax determinations, but not if his or her services are limited to mechanical calculations and processing.[44]

---

37. ¶S-1601
38. ¶T-10906.1
39. ¶S-1107
40. ¶S-1117
41. ¶S-1116
42. ¶S-1109
43. ¶S-1109
44. ¶S-1110

¶ **4752**   **Taxpayer identification numbers (TINs) must be included where required; SSNs; truncated TINs; ITINs; EINs; ATINs; BINs—Forms SS-5; W-7, W-9.**

Under Code Sec. 6109(a)(1), any person who files a return, statement, or other document must include his or her own TIN[45] and the TIN of any other person, as required by the form or instructions to the form. (Code Sec. 6109(a)(3); Reg § 301.6109-1(c))[46]

A TIN is either a social security number (SSN), an IRS individual taxpayer identification number (ITIN), an employer identification number (EIN), or an IRS adoption taxpayer identification number (ATIN). (Reg § 301.6109-1(a)(1)(i))[47] Once a taxpayer is issued an SSN, IRS says it must be used to file the return, even if the SSN doesn't authorize employment, or if the SSN does authorize employment but the taxpayer loses his or her employment authorization. And taxpayers who previously used ITINs must stop using them, and use the SSN, once the SSN is issued.[48]

Thus, for divorce or separation instruments executed before Jan. 1, 2019, an alimony payor's return must include the payee's TIN. (Use Form W-9 to request another person's TIN.)[49] For the requirement to include the parent's TIN where a child is subject to the kiddie tax rules, see ¶3130. For the requirement to include a Social Security number (SSN) for each qualifying child for whom a child tax credit is claimed from 2018 to 2025, see ¶2349.

SSNs are used to identify individuals, sole proprietors not otherwise required to use EINs, and grantor trusts. (Code Sec. 6109(d); Reg § 301.6109-1(a))[50] To get an SSN, file Form SS-5. (Reg § 301.6109-1(d)(1))[1] Information return filers can use a truncated TIN (TTIN) on paper and electronic payee statements (e.g., Form 1098, Form 1099, Form 5498). (Reg § 301.6109-4)[2]

Aliens who aren't eligible for SSNs use ITINs requested on Form W-7 in accordance with IRS procedures. (Reg § 301.6109-1(a))[3] Prospective adoptive parents who have had a child placed lawfully with them for legal adoption may apply (use Form W-7A) for a temporary (2-year) ATIN for the child (unless the child is an alien eligible to get an ITIN) to satisfy filing requirements (but not for earned income credit purposes (¶2337)). (Reg § 301.6109-3)[4]

Other entities use EINs. (Reg § 301.6109-1(a)) Taxpayers can request an EIN instantly on-line (if present in the U.S. or a U.S. possession) by entering the required information or by phone, mail, or fax. Persons issued an EIN must provide IRS with any updated application information that IRS requires. (Reg § 301.6109-1(d))[5] All employers (corporations, partnerships or sole proprietors) must use EINs for reporting employment and excise taxes.[6] Large food and beverage establishments use an identifying number for tip reporting. (Reg § 31.6053-3(a)(5))[7]

Buildings that have been or will be allocated a low-income housing credit must be assigned a building identification number (BIN) by the applicable state housing credit agency.[8]

Foreign transferors of U.S. real property interests (and transferees where applicable) must provide their TINs on withholding tax returns, applications for withholding certificates, etc. Foreign persons must have TINs for placement on any return, statement, or other document required by the regs under Code Sec. 897 or Code Sec. 1445. (Reg § 301.6109-1(b)(2)(vi))[9]

---

45. ¶S-1502
46. ¶S-1531
47. ¶S-1501
48. ¶S-1501.1
49. ¶S-1535
50. ¶S-1505
1. ¶S-1581
2. ¶S-1501A

3. ¶S-1508.1; S-1582.1 et seq.
4. ¶S-1504.6 *et seq.*
5. ¶S-1582 *et seq.*
6. ¶S-1505
7. ¶S-3289
8. ¶S-1521
9. ¶S-1508

¶ 4753　Mandatory e-filing: information returns (Form 4419), employee benefit plans, partnership returns, and taxpayers with 25 or more heavy vehicles (Form 2290); e-filing due date; hardship waivers (Form 8508).

Under Code Sec. 6011(e)(2)(A), subject to hardship waivers (see below), filers of at least the "applicable number" of information returns during a calendar year —including the Form 1099 series and the Form W-2 series—must file electronically. Forms required to be filed electronically include forms specified in the regs.

✓caution: Reg § 301.6011-2, below, doesn't reflect replacement of the prior-law "250-return" minimum for mandatory e-filing, with the "applicable number" rule. But its guidance on what is an information return should retain validity.

(Code Sec. 6011(e)(2)(A); Reg § 301.6011-2; Reg § 301.6058-2; Reg § 301.6059-2)[10]

For the information-return threshold discussed above, the "applicable number" (except for partnerships, see (a) below) is: (1) "100" for calendar year 2021; and (2) "10" for calendar years after 2021. For a partnership, for any calendar year before 2022, the "applicable number" is: (a) "50" for calendar year 2021. (Code Sec. 6011(e)(5))[11]

illustration: IRS has indicated that the applicable number remains at 250 for 2022, pending the issuance of final regs.

The applicable-number threshold doesn't apply to any return filed by a financial institution for tax for which the institution is liable as a withholding agent under Code Sec. 1461 (withholding of tax on nonresident aliens and foreign corporations) or Code Sec. 1474(a) (FATCA). (Code Sec. 6011(e)(4))[12]

All annual reports—including any statements and schedules—for employee benefit plans must be filed electronically under the EFAST2 program (¶4746).[13]

Submit Form 4419 at least 45 days before the return due date to apply to transmit information returns electronically.[14] The general due date for e-filing information returns is Mar. 31; however, for W-2, W-3 and nonemployee compensation returns and statements, the due date is Jan. 31.[15]

Hardship waivers (Form 8508) are requested by submitting written requests 45 days before the due date. (Code Sec. 6011(e)(2)(B))[16]

Partnerships with more than 100 partners (counting any person who is a partner at any time during its tax year) must file their partnership returns electronically. (Code Sec. 6011(e)(6); Reg § 301.6011-3)[17]

Individuals and organizations with 25 or more trucks, tractors or other heavy vehicles used on highways must file excise tax Form 2290 electronically.[18]

¶ 4754　Timely mailing as timely filing and paying.

Under Code Sec. 7502(c)(1), a return, claim, statement, document or payment (except a tax deposit) that must be filed or made by a certain date generally is considered timely filed or made if it has a timely postmark.[19] This rule also applies to claims for credit or refund made on a late-filed original return, but not to an amended return showing additional tax. (Reg § 301.7502-1(f))[20] For the timely mailing rule to apply, the return, etc., must be: (1) deposited in the U.S. mail in a properly addressed envelope or wrapper with

---

10. ¶S-1301
11. ¶S-1302
12. ¶S-1302
13. ¶S-3351; ¶S-3353
14. ¶S-1311
15. ¶S-1305

16. ¶S-1314
17. ¶S-1350
18. ¶W-6456
19. ¶T-10751
20. ¶T-10752; ¶T-10752.1

enough postage; (Code Sec. 7502(a)(2)(B)) (2) postmarked by the prescribed filing or payment date (Code Sec. 7502(a)(2)(A)) (returns postmarked after the due date are considered filed when received by IRS); and (3) actually delivered by U.S. mail to the proper place. (Code Sec. 7502(a)(1))[21] Some courts permit delivery to be proven by a common-law "mailbox rule" (i.e., when mail is properly addressed and deposited in the U.S. mail, with prepaid postage, there is a rebuttable presumption that the addressee received it in the ordinary course of the mail).[22] However, the Court of Federal Claims has held that when an envelope doesn't contain a postmark, the taxpayer can't use extrinsic evidence to prove when they mailed it. (McCaffery v. U.S., (Ct Fed Cl 08/09/2021) 128 AFTR 2d ¶2021-5115.[23]

The timely-mailing rule applies to private delivery services (PDSs) such as: *DHL Express:* DHL Express 9:00, DHL Express 10:30, DHL Express 12:00, DHL Express Worldwide, DHL Express Envelope, DHL Import Express 10:30, DHL Import Express 12:00, and DHL Import Express Worldwide. *UPS:* UPS Next Day Air Early A.M., UPS Next Day Air, UPS Next Day Air Saver, UPS 2nd Day Air, UPS 2nd Day Air A.M., UPS Worldwide Express Plus, and UPS Worldwide Express. *FedEx:* FedEx First Overnight, FedEx Priority Overnight, FedEx Standard Overnight, FedEx 2 Day, FedEx International First Next Flight Out, FedEx International Priority, FedEx International First, and FedEx International Economy. (Code Sec. 7502(f); Reg § 301.7502-1(c)(3))[24]

The postmark stamp date on the mailing envelope overrides the postmark stamp date on a Certificate of Mailing (P.S. Form 3817).[25] If a private postage meter is used (including a Stamps.com postage label), the postmark isn't enough. The document must actually be received by the proper office or officer not later than the time the postmark indicates it ordinarily would be received. If it is actually received later, taxpayer can prove timely mailing only by showing: (1) that the document was deposited in the mail before the last collection that was postmarked (by the U.S.P.S.) on the last day for filing; and (2) that the delay in receiving the document was due to delay in transmission of the mail; and (3) the cause of the delay. (Reg § 301.7502-1(c)(1)(iii)(B))[26]

An e-filed return (¶4703) isn't considered filed until IRS acknowledges the electronic portion of the return as accepted and a signature has been received either electronically or on Form 8453 (used to transmit paper schedules or forms that can't be e-filed).[27]

¶ 4755 Effect of registered or certified mail on timely filing.

Under Code Sec. 7502(c)(1), the registration date is considered the postmark date, and registration is prima facie evidence the return, etc., was delivered to the addressee.[28] The U.S. postmark date on the sender's receipt is treated as the postmark date of a document sent by certified mail (Reg § 301.7502-1(c)(2)), and proof that a properly postmarked certified mail sender's receipt was properly issued and that the envelope or wrapper was properly addressed is prima facie evidence that the document was properly delivered. (Reg § 301.7502-1(e)(2))[29]

¶ 4756 Due date on Saturday, Sunday or holiday—effect on timely filing.

Under Code Sec. 7503, if a due date falls on Sat., Sun. or legal holiday, there is an automatic extension of time to the next succeeding day that isn't a Sat., Sun. or legal holiday. The rule applies to *all acts* required to be performed under the Code both by the *taxpayer* and IRS. "Legal holiday" includes: (1) the legal holidays throughout the state or possession where the office at which the act to be performed is located even if not a legal holiday in the state or possession where the taxpayer resides, and (2) all legal holidays in

21. ¶T-10751 *et seq.*
22. ¶T-10774 *et seq.*
23. ¶T-10762.2
24. ¶T-10781, ¶T-10787
25. ¶T-10762

26. ¶T-10763, T-10765
27. ¶S-1609, ¶S-1617.3
28. ¶T-10762.3
29. ¶T-10776.1

the District of Columbia (D.C.), i.e.: New Year's Day (Jan. 1); Inauguration Day (Jan. 20, every 4th year); Martin Luther King, Jr.'s birthday (3rd Mon. in Jan.); Washington's birthday (3rd Mon. in Feb.); Emancipation Day (Apr. 16); Memorial Day (last Mon. in May); Independence Day; Labor Day (first Mon. in Sept.); Columbus Day (second Mon. in Oct.); Veterans Day (Nov. 11); Thanksgiving Day (4th Thurs. in Nov.); and Christmas Day (Dec. 25). If a holiday in D.C. falls on Sunday, the next day is a holiday in D.C.; if the holiday (other than Inauguration Day) falls on a Sat., it's treated as falling on the preceding Fri.[30]

¶ 4757   Obtaining copies of tax returns, or return transcripts—Forms 4506, 4506-C, 4506T-EZ; Online Account.

Code Sec. 6103(p)(2)(A) requires IRS to provide copies of returns or return information to taxpayers, when requested. (Code Sec. 6103(p)(2)(A)) To obtain an actual photocopy of a tax return, taxpayers must use Form 4506, and pay a $43 fee (unless the taxpayer is a disaster victim, see below). (Reg § 601.702(d)(1)) To obtain one of the various types of tax transcripts that IRS provides—often for free—to requesting individual or business taxpayers, the taxpayer can either: (1) order the type of transcript desired online or by mail, using IRS's "Get Transcript" service (for individuals) (https://www.irs.gov/individuals/get-transcript); (2) file a Form Form 4506-C or, for free transcripts, a Form 4506T-EZ; or (3) use IRS's automated phone transcript service at 800-908-9946 to order a tax return or tax account transcript to be sent by mail.[31]

A "masked" transcript, which partially obscures taxpayer's personal information, is available. IRS doesn't fax transcripts, nor does it mail them to third parties. In addition to the above ways of obtaining transcript information, taxpayers and representatives can call IRS and ask for information to be provided verbally. Before response, IRS requires proper authentication of identity and entitlement to receive the information.[32] There's a waiver of the usual fee for requests for copies of tax returns by affected taxpayers located in a federally declared disaster area.[33]

Online Account. Online Account is an online portal that allows individual taxpayers to access their tax account information (including tax balances and payment history); set up payment plans for outstanding balances; and get copies of their tax transcripts. (IRS.gov/View Your Account Information; https://www.irs.gov/payments/frequently-asked-questions-about-online-account). IRS announced a new identity verification process using ID.me that taxpayers will use to access IRS online services, such as the Child Tax Credit Update Portal, Online Account, Get Transcript Online, Get an Identity Protection PIN (IP PIN) and Online Payment Agreement. Help setting up an ID.me account is found at the ID.me IRS Help Site. The IRS has also incorporated its new ID verification process into some applications used by tax professionals, including those used to request powers of attorney or tax information authorizations online using Tax Pro Account or to submit Forms 2848 and 8821 online. (IR 2021-228, 11/17/2021) In addition, taxpayers can use a new option in IRS's authentication system to sign up for IRS online accounts without the use of any biometric data, including facial recognition, by verifying their identity during a live, virtual interview with IRS agents (although taxpayers will still be able to verify their identity automatically through ID.me's self-assistance tool if they choose). (https://www.irs.gov/newsroom/irs-statement-new-features-put-in-place-for-irs-online-account-registration-process-strengthened-to-ensure-privacy-and-security)[34]

30. ¶T-10790 *et seq.*
31. ¶S-6407
32. ¶S-6407; ¶S-6409

33. ¶S-8500 *et seq.*
34. ¶S-6408; ¶T-10163.1

¶ 4800   Tax Audits, Deficiencies and Assessments. ▬▬▬▬▬

IRS preliminarily checks every return filed (¶4801 *et seq.*) and selects returns for
audit based on various criteria (¶4802). Once IRS finishes an audit, a taxpayer has
various alternatives (¶4810 *et seq.*) for resolving any disputed items.

**¶ 4801   Mathematical, etc., check of all returns; summary assessment; request
for abatement—IRS audits.**

IRS checks each return for math errors and computes tax using the amounts on the
return. If the taxpayer made an error resulting in a tax underpayment, IRS sends a
corrected computation and a notice and demand for payment of any balance due (which
doesn't entitle the taxpayer to petition the Tax Court), (Code Sec. 6213(b)(1)) or reduces
the refund. (Reg § 601.105(a))[1]

The failure to include a correct taxpayer identification number (TIN) on a return as
required under Code Sec. 21 (child care credit), Code Sec. 24(e) (child credit), and Code
Sec. 25A(g)(1) (higher education credit), Code Sec. 32 (earned income credit (EIC)) and
Code Sec. 151 (deductions for personal exemptions). (Code Sec. 6213(g)(2)) are among the
items counted as mathematical errors.[2]

A taxpayer has 60 days from the date the notice is sent to file a request for an abatement
of the summary assessment. IRS can't collect on the assessment until the taxpayer agrees
or the 60-day period expires. After the abatement period has expired, IRS can reassess the
tax by following the regular deficiency procedures and issuing a 90-day letter (¶4815).
(Code Sec. 6213(b)(2))[3]

Adjustments to make an S corporation shareholder's return consistent with the corporation's return are treated as resulting from math or clerical error. (Code Sec. 6037(c)(3))[4]
Similar rules apply to estate and trust beneficiary returns. (Code Sec. 6034A(c)(3))[5]

Taxpayers' federal income and estate tax returns may also be checked against their
state or foreign tax returns.[6]

**¶ 4802   IRS check of taxpayer's return against information returns (matching
program); selection of returns for audit.**

IRS compares the taxpayers' income tax returns against information returns under its
document matching program. If there is a mismatch, IRS sends the taxpayer a computer-
generated notice (CP-2000), which must describe the basis for, and identify, any amounts
of taxes, additions, interest or penalties claimed to be due. (Code Sec. 7522(a); Code
Sec. 7522(b)(2)) The notice, which isn't a demand for payment, can be challenged by the
taxpayer, who has the burden of proof. IRS also matches information filed by pass-through
entities (partnerships, S corporations, and trusts) to what the partners, shareholders, and
beneficiaries report on their own returns.[7]

IRS selects returns for examination, e.g., based on discrepancy with information returns,
the filing of frivolous returns, random sampling, etc. IRS attempts to select tax returns for
audit that have the greatest audit potential.[8]

1. ¶T-3622 *et seq.*; ¶T-1000 *et seq.*
2. ¶T-3628
3. ¶T-3902.1
4. ¶D-1801
5. ¶C-3081; ¶C-9081
6. ¶T-1005; ¶T-1006
7. ¶s T-1003, T-1004
8. ¶T-1023, T-1060 *et seq.*

References beginning with a single letter are to paragraphs in Federal Tax Coordinator 2d and RIA's Analysis of Federal Taxes: Income.

771

¶ 4803   IRS's voluntary disclosure program; settlement initiatives—IRS audits.

Taxpayers (both offshore and domestic) who are noncompliant and concerned about criminal exposure, can, by participating in IRS's voluntary disclosure program, come into compliance and potentially avoid criminal prosecution; mitigation of civil penalty exposure is also possible.[9] Such taxpayers can use Form 14457 to voluntarily disclose previously undisclosed information to IRS. Form 14457 has been revised includes a section on reporting virtual currency/cryptocurrency.[10]

Other programs are available to noncompliant taxpayers who are not concerned about criminal liability or substantial civil penalties due to willfulness.[11]

IRS has at times offered "settlement initiatives," allowing qualifying taxpayers in specified classes—e.g., participants in certain types of tax shelters—to settle on terms more favorable than those that would result from litigation.

¶ 4804   Types of audits; time and place of audit; limits on "financial status" audits; one-examination rule; unnecessary audits.

IRS fixes the time and method of examination, which must be reasonable under the circumstances. (Code Sec. 7605(a); Reg § 301.7605-1(a)) An examination may be at: (1) an IRS office, with the taxpayer bringing (office audit) or mailing (correspondence audit) tax records (Reg § 601.105(b)(2)(ii)), or (2) the office of the taxpayer (or representative) (field audit) (Reg § 601.105(b)(3)). Taxpayers or their representatives may make written requests to change the place that IRS has set for an examination. (Reg § 301.7605-1(e)(1))[12]

In a regular income tax audit, an IRS agent examines the taxpayer's books, papers, records, or other data to determine whether the records support the income reported and the deductions taken by the taxpayer. (Code Sec. 7602)[13]

Limits on "financial status" audits. IRS is limited in its ability to conduct a "financial status" examination or an "economic reality" examination, to determine the existence of unreported income. (Code Sec. 7602(e)) Financial status or economic reality audit techniques are IRS indirect methods of examination, such as the bank deposits method (¶2844).[14]

One-audit rule; unnecessary audits. Under Code Sec. 7605(b), IRS can't conduct unnecessary examinations of a taxpayer and can make only one inspection of a taxpayer's books and records a tax year unless the taxpayer requests otherwise, IRS gives notice *in writing* that an additional inspection (i.e., reexamination) is necessary,[15] or IRS suspects fraud.[16]

¶ 4805   Taxpayer's rights in an IRS audit.

Under Code Sec. 7521(b)(1), before or at an initial in-person interview (other than criminal investigations), IRS must give the taxpayer an explanation (written or oral) of the audit process (and assessment and collection) and his or her rights under that process.[17] A taxpayer has the right to: be represented by an advisor (¶4806); make certain audio (but generally not video) recordings of meetings (on advance notice) with the IRS agent (Code Sec. 7521(a)(1)); claim additional deductions not claimed on the return; ask that a particular technical question raised in the examination be referred to IRS's National Office for technical advice; not be subjected to unnecessary examinations (¶4804); and claim constitutional rights if questioned about possible criminal violations.[18]

---

9. ¶V-3850 *et seq.*
10. ¶V-3850.02
11. ¶V-3867 *et seq.*
12. ¶T-1090 *et seq.*, ¶T-1102
13. ¶T-1181*et seq.*

14. ¶T-1076
15. ¶T-1425 *et seq.*
16. ¶T-1443 *et seq.*
17. ¶T-1122 *et seq.*
18. ¶s T-1120 *et seq.*, T-1129 *et seq.*

¶ 4806   Who can represent taxpayers before IRS? Privileged communications.

The taxpayer's representative may be an attorney, CPA, enrolled agent, enrolled actuary or any other person permitted (under Treas Dept Circ No. 230, Sec. 10.3) to represent taxpayers before IRS, who isn't disbarred or suspended from practice before IRS, and who has a written power of attorney (on Form 2848) executed by the taxpayer. Absent a summons, IRS can't require the taxpayer to accompany the representative. (Code Sec. 7521(c))[19] IRS must suspend an interview if the taxpayer clearly states a desire to consult with a representative. (Code Sec. 7521(b)(2))[20]

Attorney-client privilege extends to attorney-client communications made in confidence by the client, that encompass legal advice from an attorney in that capacity, unless the client waives the protection.[21] For non-criminal tax matters and proceedings, the attorney-client privilege also applies to communications between a taxpayer and any federally authorized tax practitioner, for tax advice (except for tax shelters), to the extent the communication would be privileged if made between taxpayer and attorney. (Code Sec. 7525)[22] The work product privilege applies to materials prepared by attorneys and their agents and representatives for anticipated litigation. Only a strong showing of necessity and inability to get the information without undue hardship overcomes the privilege.[23]

¶ 4807   IRS's power to summons persons and records; enforcement; third-party summons; summons for tax-related software.

Under Code Sec. 7602(a), where there is a legitimate purpose for an investigation, IRS can issue a summons for testimony, books, records, or other data that are potentially relevant to a particular tax inquiry.[24] The summons (Form 2039) must describe with reasonable certainty the records sought (Code Sec. 7603). It also must set the time for appearance before IRS, which must be not less than ten days from summons date. (Code Sec. 7605(a))[25] If the taxpayer intentionally disregards the summons, IRS can apply to the district court (or a U.S. Commissioner) for an order directing compliance. (Code Sec. 7604(b))[26]

Third-party summons. IRS may enforce a summons ("third-party summons") on a person other than the taxpayer for testimony and records. (Certain communications (see ¶4806) are privileged.) IRS must send a notice of the summons, including a copy and an explanation of the taxpayer's right to institute a suit to quash the summons to any person identified in the summons other than the summoned party. (Code Sec. 7609(a)(1); Reg § 301.7609-1)[27]

Taxpayer intervention in a proceeding to enforce the summons or a taxpayer proceeding to quash a summons results in a suspension of the assessment period. (Code Sec. 7609(e)(1); Reg § 301.7609-5(b))[28]

Summons for tax-related software. IRS may only issue, or begin an action to enforce, a summons for tax-related computer software source code under certain circumstances. (Code Sec. 7612)[29]

¶ 4808   National Taxpayer Advocate (NTA)—Taxpayer Assistance Orders (TAOs).

The Office of the Taxpayer Advocate is headed by the NTA, who reports directly to the

19. ¶s T-1124, T-1127
20. ¶T-1127
21. ¶T-1314
22. ¶T-1334
23. ¶T-1330; ¶T-1334.1
24. ¶T-1201, T-1212

25. ¶T-1354; ¶T-1099
26. ¶T-1357
27. ¶T-1252
28. ¶T-1250 *et seq.*; ¶V-3714
29. ¶T-1290 *et seq.*

Commissioner. (Code Sec. 7803(c)(1)) Its functions are to assist taxpayers in resolving problems with IRS, identify areas where taxpayers have problems dealing with IRS, propose changes in IRS administrative practices to mitigate these identified problems, and identify potential legislative changes that may do so. (Code Sec. 7803(c)(2)(A)) A taxpayer can make, in a manner prescribed by regs, an application to request that NTA issue a TAO in cases involving significant hardship because of IRS's administration of the tax laws. (Code Sec. 7811(a)(1); Reg § 301.7811-1(b))[30]

¶ 4809 User fees for IRS rulings or determinations.

IRS charges taxpayers a separate user fee (Code Sec. 7528(a)) for each request for a ruling, opinion letter, determination letter, or other similar request. User fees must be paid electronically.[31]

¶ 4810 Proposed deficiency, revenue agent's report (RAR), "30-day letter"; taxpayer's options.

An IRS auditor may propose adjustments to a taxpayer's return before determining a deficiency (¶4814).[32] The taxpayer can agree to the adjustments or argue they should be modified before the examiner submits the RAR. Once the RAR is submitted, along with a proposed deficiency letter (the "30-day letter," see below), the taxpayer has 30 days to choose from options at (1) through (3), below. (Reg § 601.105(d)(1))[33]

The RAR that IRS sends, along with a "30-day letter," to a taxpayer who rejects the examiner's findings, must show the basis for and amount of any proposed adjustments. (Code Sec. 7522(a), Code Sec. 7522(b)(3)) The letter also explains appeal procedures and asks a taxpayer to indicate within 30 days whether he or she will: (1) accept the findings and sign a waiver of restrictions on assessment (Form 870, which allows IRS to collect the deficiency without issuing a 90-day letter (¶4815), and limits the taxpayer's appeal to a claim or suit for refund (no Tax Court petition)); (2) request an Independent Appeals Office conference (¶4811); or (3) do nothing and IRS will send a 90-day letter. (Reg § 601.105(d)(1)) IRS must include an explanation of this process, that allows taxpayer an opportunity for administrative review, with any first letter of proposed deficiency.[34]

¶ 4811 Independent Appeals conference; how to request; rights of taxpayer, duties of IRS; requirements for protest; nonbinding mediation, arbitration; settlement with no concessions—Forms 870, 890; settlement with concessions—Forms 870-AD, 890-AD.

The taxpayer can get an Appeals conference by sending a written request (in response to a 30-day letter, see ¶4810) and any required protest (discussed below) to IRS.[35] The conference is informal, and testimony isn't under oath, although taxpayer may be asked to submit affidavits. (Reg § 601.106(c))[36] The conference is available after IRS has issued a 90-day letter (¶4815), discussed below. (Reg § 601.106(b))[37]

Under Code Sec. 7123(a), a taxpayer may request early referral of one or more unresolved issues, from either the examination or collection division, to Independent Appeals.[38]

Under Code Sec. 7803(e)(4), the right of appeal is, with exceptions, available to all

---

30. ¶T-10205 *et seq.*
31. ¶T-10000 *et seq.*
32. ¶T-1550 *et seq.*
33. ¶T-1600 *et seq.*
34. ¶T-1601 *et seq.*

35. ¶T-1711
36. ¶T-1720
37. ¶T-1702 *et seq.*
38. ¶T-1709 *et seq.*

taxpayers.[39] Limits apply to IRS's denials of appeal requests of taxpayers who have received a 90-day letter (¶4815). (Code Sec. 7803(e)(5))[40] Independent Appeals must have access to unbiased legal assistance and advice from the Office of Chief Counsel about cases pending there. (Code Sec. 7803(e)(6))[41] Appeals must ensure that "specified taxpayers" (i.e., individuals whose adjusted gross income (AGI) doesn't exceed $400,000 for the tax year, or entities whose gross receipts do not exceed $5 million for the tax year) are provided access to nonprivileged portions of the case file, not later than 10 days before the conference. (Code Sec. 7803(e)(7))[42]

An oral request is enough to get Independent Appeals consideration in all office or correspondence audit cases. In a field audit case, a written protest is: required if the total amount of the proposed increase in tax (including penalties), proposed overassessment or claimed refund, or compromise offer exceeds $10,000 for any tax period; optional (but a statement of issues is required) if that total amount is between $2,500 and $10,000; and not required if it is less than $2,500. (Reg § 601.106(a)(1)(iii)(a))[43] The 30-day letter (¶4810) contains instructions for the protest (Reg § 601.105(d)(2)) and spells out the required information.[44]

The Independent Appeals Office has authority to settle all factual and legal issues raised by the examiner's report (RAR, see ¶4810) or the taxpayer's protest.(Reg § 601.106(f)(2))[45] as long as the case isn't docketed in the Tax Court. (Reg § 601.106(a)(2))[46] If no settlement is reached, IRS will prepare a 90-day letter (¶4815).[47] Under IRS procedures, either the taxpayer or Appeals can request nonbinding mediation on any issue still unresolved after the end of appeals procedures or unsuccessful attempts to enter into a closing agreement or a compromise. (Code Sec. 7123(b)(1))[48] In addition, a taxpayer and IRS can jointly request binding arbitration of factual issues unresolved after the end of appeals procedures or after unsuccessful attempts to enter into a closing agreement or a compromise. (Code Sec. 7123(b)(2))[49]

If the taxpayer accepts IRS's position in full, with no concessions, he or she signs a Form 870 (Form 890, in gift, estate or generation-skipping transfer tax cases), waiving restrictions on assessment (¶4818). (Reg § 601.106(d)(2))[50]

If the Independent Appeals Office makes any concessions, a Form 870-AD (Form 890-AD, in estate tax cases) is executed stating that: the settlement is subject to acceptance by IRS; on acceptance, it won't be reopened by IRS absent fraud, malfeasance, concealment or misrepresentation of a material fact, an important mathematical mistake, or an excessive tentative net operating loss (NOL) carryback; *and* the taxpayer waives the right to file a claim for refund (other than from an NOL carryback) for any years covered by the agreement.[1]

¶ 4812   Final closing agreements—Forms 866, 906—IRS audits.

The taxpayer and IRS may conclusively settle a tax dispute by entering into a final agreement to close either a tax year that has ended (use Form 866) (Code Sec. 7121(a); Reg § 301.7121-1(b)(2), Reg § 601.202(a)(2))[2] or a specific transaction, past or future (use Form 906). (Reg § 601.202(b))[3] The agreement is irrevocable (except for fraud, malfeasance or misrepresentation of a material fact) and binds both parties. (Code Sec. 7121(b)) User fees (¶4809) apply.[4]

---

39. ¶T-1700.2
40. ¶T-1700.5
41. ¶T-1700.1
42. ¶T-1700.6
43. ¶T-1713
44. ¶T-1717
45. ¶T-1721
46. ¶T-1725

47. ¶T-1732
48. ¶T-1733
49. ¶T-1756
50. ¶T-1731
1. ¶T-3402
2. ¶T-9500 *et seq.*
3. ¶T-9521
4. ¶T-9507

¶ 4813   Offer in compromise (OIC)—Forms 656, 656-L, 433-A, 433-B.

Under Code Sec. 7122(a), civil or criminal tax cases can be compromised by IRS, after assessment, before referral to the Department of Justice (after referral, compromise can be only by the Attorney General). (Code Sec. 7122(a))[5] IRS may compromise tax liabilities on any of these grounds: (1) doubt as to collectibility, (2) doubt as to liability, (3) to promote effective tax administration because either (a) collection of the full amount would cause economic hardship for the taxpayer, or (b) compelling public policy or equity justify compromise. (Reg § 301.7122-1(b)) To make an offer, file Form 656, Form 433-A (individuals) or Form 433-B (businesses) (sole proprietors must file both)—and pay the $205 processing fee. (Reg § 301.7122-1(d)(1); Reg § 300.3(b)(1)) Taxpayers should file Form 656-L for offers based solely on doubt as to liability. The processing fee doesn't apply to low-income taxpayers or if an offer is based solely on doubt as to liability. (Code Sec. 7122(c)(3); Reg § 300.3(b)(1))[6] IRS may disregard frivolous offer submissions. (Code Sec. 7122(f))[7]

¶ 4814   Determining amount of deficiency.

Under Code Sec. 6211(a) and Code Sec. 6213(b), a deficiency is the amount by which a taxpayer's correct tax liability is more than the excess of: (1) tax shown on the return (except that math and clerical errors are corrected), plus (2) amounts previously assessed (or collected without assessment) as a deficiency, over (3) the amount of any rebates (credits, refunds, or other repayments).[8]

In determining a deficiency, any excess of certain specified credits over the tax imposed by subtitle A (without taking into account those credits) and any excess of those credits shown by the taxpayer on the return over the amount shown as tax on the return (without taking into account those credits) is taken into account as a negative amount of tax. (Code Sec. 6211(b)(4))[9]

If no return was filed, or if a return doesn't show any tax, the deficiency equals the entire amount of the correct tax. (Reg § 301.6211-1(a))[10]

¶ 4815   Notice of deficiency—"90-day letter"; taxpayer's options on receipt.

Under Code Sec. 6212(a), a statutory notice of deficiency ("90-day letter"), which must be sent by certified or registered mail to the taxpayer's last known address, tells the taxpayer that IRS has determined a deficiency (in income, estate or gift tax, or excise tax on private foundations or pension plans).[11] The letter must describe the basis for and identify the amounts (if any) of tax, interest, additional amounts, additions to tax and assessable penalties. (Code Sec. 7522(a))[12] After receiving the letter, the taxpayer can: pay the deficiency, not pay and seek to rescind it, pay and file a refund claim (¶4833), take no action (let tax be assessed) and then file a compromise offer (¶4813), or file a Tax Court petition (¶4843).[13]

¶ 4816   Assessment of deficiency—procedures IRS must follow; assessment of interest and penalties; assessment and collection of court-ordered restitution.

Under Code Sec. 6213(a), unless the taxpayer and IRS sign a closing agreement (¶4812), the taxpayer pays the deficiency or signs a Form 870 (¶4810), IRS determines collection is in jeopardy (¶4817), or the rules for court-ordered restitution (discussed below) apply, IRS

---

5. ¶T-9600; T-9649
6. ¶T-9617.2, T-10024
7. ¶T-9612
8. ¶T-1500*et seq.*
9. ¶T-1501 *et seq.*

10. ¶T-1506*et seq.*
11. ¶T-2700 *et seq.*
12. ¶T-2714 *et seq.*
13. ¶T-2738

can't assess deficiencies in income, estate, and gift taxes, and the excise taxes on private foundations and qualified pension, etc., plans until after the taxpayer has had an opportunity to make a Tax Court appeal.[14]

Assessment of interest. Under Code Sec. 6601(g), interest may be assessed when the underlying tax is collectible.[15]

Assessment of penalties. For income, estate, gift and certain excise taxes, the negligence and fraud penalties are assessed like deficiencies. So are the delinquency penalties (¶4856, ¶4857), but only if attributable to a deficiency and not if measured by the tax shown on the return. (Code Sec. 6665(b))[16] The penalty for estimated tax underpayments (¶3154, ¶3348) is assessed as a deficiency only if no return is filed. (Code Sec. 6665(b)(2))

The normal assessment and collection rules don't apply to the penalties for promoting an abusive tax shelter (¶4872), aiding and abetting a tax understatement (¶4868), filing a frivolous return (¶4881). A taxpayer may delay collection of these penalties by paying at least 15% of the penalty and filing a claim for refund of it, within 30 days of notice and demand for payment. If IRS denies the claim, the taxpayer has 30 days to sue for refund in a district court (where IRS may counterclaim for the unpaid penalty amount). (Code Sec. 6703(b), Code Sec. 6703(c))[17]

Court-ordered restitution. Under Code Sec. 6201(a)(4), IRS can assess and collect restitution for unpaid taxes owed by defendants in criminal tax cases as if it were a tax.[18] Court-ordered restitution can be assessed, or a court proceeding for the amount can be begun without assessment, at any time. (Code Sec. 6501(c)(11))[19] A tax liability under a restitution order is not subject to the deficiency procedures (¶4815). (Code Sec. 6201(a)(4)(C))

IRS may not collect criminal restitution and a civil tax liability for the same period. Where a taxpayer makes payments to satisfy a restitution-based assessment, IRS must also apply the payment to satisfy the civil tax liability for the same tax period.[20]

¶ 4817 IRS jeopardy assessments and termination assessments; rules for immediate assessments in bankruptcy or receivership.

Jeopardy assessments. Under Code Sec. 6861(a), if IRS believes assessment or collection of a deficiency will be jeopardized by delay, it can immediately assess the deficiency (plus interest and penalties) and demand payment. (Code Sec. 6861(a); Reg § 301.6861-1(a)) But, within 60 days after the assessment, IRS must issue the taxpayer a 90-day letter (¶4815). (Code Sec. 6861(b))[21] IRS Chief Counsel must pre-approve these "jeopardy assessments." (Code Sec. 7429(a)(1)(A))[22] Collection is in jeopardy if (1) taxpayers are or appear to be designing quickly to leave the U.S. or conceal themselves and/or place property beyond IRS's reach, or (2) taxpayers' financial solvency is or appears to be imperiled. (Code Sec. 6861; Reg § 301.6861-1(a); Reg § 1.6851-1(a))[23]

Termination assessments. IRS can also terminate a tax year and demand immediate payment of income taxes for the current and preceding year, if it finds that taxpayers plan to leave or remove property from the U.S., conceal themselves or their property in the U.S., or otherwise impair collection of those taxes ("termination assessment"). Within 60 days, IRS must issue a 90-day letter for the full year. (Code Sec. 6851(a), Code Sec. 6852(a))[24]

Procedures for jeopardy and termination assessments. There are procedures for administrative and judicial review of jeopardy and termination assessments (Code

---

14. ¶T-3602
15. ¶T-3646
16. ¶T-3638 *et seq.*
17. ¶V-5650
18. ¶T-3639
19. ¶T-4172
20. ¶T-3639
21. ¶T-3700 *et seq.*
22. ¶T-3733.1
23. ¶T-3701 *et seq.*
24. ¶T-3717 *et seq.*

Sec. 7429)[25] and for stay of collection. (Code Sec. 6863)[26]

Immediate assessment in bankruptcy or receivership. Under Code Sec. 6871(a) and Code Sec. 6871(b), IRS may make an immediate assessment of any deficiency, whether or not a 90-day letter (¶4815) has been issued: (1) on the debtor's estate in a Title 11 bankruptcy case; (2) on the debtor, but only if the tax liability becomes res judicata under a Title 11 bankruptcy case; or (3) on appointment of a receiver for the taxpayer in a receivership proceeding.[27]

¶ 4818   General 3-year statute of limitations on IRS assessments; rules for pass-through entities; burden of proof.

Under Code Sec. 6501(a), generally (for exceptions, see ¶4819, ¶4822), all taxes must be assessed: (1) within 3 years after the date the return was filed (below), or (2) if the tax is payable by stamp, within 3 years after the date any part of the tax was paid.[28] A return filed before the deadline is considered filed on the due date. (Code Sec. 6501(b)(1))[29] But a return of tax withheld (from wages or at source) for any period ending with or within a calendar year is, if filed before Apr. 15 of the next calendar year, considered filed *on* Apr. 15. (Code Sec. 6501(b)(2); Reg § 301.6501(b)-1(b))[30] The assessment period for a late-filed return starts on the day after actual filing. (Code Sec. 6501(a))[31] If, within 60 days before the limitations period expires, IRS receives an amended return that shows an increase in tax liability, IRS has 60 days from the receipt to assess the additional tax. (Code Sec. 6501(c)(7))[32]

Rules for pass-through entities. The assessment period for items of an S corporation, trust or estate that are passed through to and reported by the shareholders or beneficiaries, is based on their returns (not the entity's). (Code Sec. 6501(a))[33] Special limitations period rules apply under the BBA partnership assessment rules (Code Sec. 6235(a)),[34] unless a partnership has elected out of the BBA partnership rules, ¶4828, which the general rule for entities (Code Sec. 6501(a), above) applies.

Burden of proof. A taxpayer who claims that the assessment of a tax is barred by the expiration of the limitations period must raise the issue and has the burden of proof.[35]

¶ 4819   6-year limitations period on assessments: over-25% omission, PHC tax, foreign financial assets.

Over-25% omissions. Under Code Sec. 6501(e), the assessment period is 6 years where taxpayers omit items from gross income (or an estate omits items includible in the gross estate) in an amount that exceeds 25% of the amount of gross income stated on the return. For this purpose, "omissions" don't include amounts for which adequate information is given on the return or attached statements.[36]

Personal holding company tax on a personal holding company (PHC) that didn't file a PHC schedule with its income tax return may be assessed within 6 years after the income tax return was filed. (Code Sec. 6501(f))[37]

Understatements due to foreign financial assets. A 6-year limitations period applies for assessment of tax on understatements of income attributable to foreign financial assets if there is an omission of gross income in excess of $5,000 attributable to an asset for which information reports are required under Code Sec. 6038D or would be required if certain Code Sec. 6038D exceptions didn't apply. (Code Sec. 6501(e)(1)(A)(ii))[38]

25. ¶T-3735 *et seq.*
26. ¶T-3757 *et seq.*
27. ¶T-3802
28. ¶T-4001
29. ¶T-4002
30. ¶T-4010
31. ¶T-4003
32. ¶T-4209.1
33. ¶T-4021 *et seq.*
34. ¶T-2431
35. ¶T-4030
36. ¶T-4201 *et seq.*
37. ¶T-4218
38. ¶T-4210.1

¶ 4820   Assessment limitations period for carrybacks and carryovers.

Under Code Sec. 6501(h) and Code Sec. 6501(j), a deficiency attributable to a taxpayer's carryback of a net operating loss (NOL), capital loss, or business credit may be assessed at any time before expiration of the period applicable to the year the loss was sustained or the credit earned.[39] A deficiency attributable to a foreign tax credit carryback may be assessed up to one year after the credit year's assessment period expires. (Code Sec. 6501(i))[40]

¶ 4821   Assessment period for unreported listed transactions.

If a taxpayer fails to include on a return or statement for a tax year information about a listed transaction (¶4874) required under Code Sec. 6011, the time for assessment of tax for that transaction won't expire before one year after the earlier of: (1) the date the required information is furnished to IRS, or (2) the date a material advisor meets the list-maintenance requirements with respect to a request by IRS under Code Sec. 6112(b) related to that transaction. (Code Sec. 6501(c)(10); Reg § 301.6501(c)-1(g))[41]

¶ 4822   When the assessment limitations period remains open.

Under Code Sec. 6501, the assessment period is open indefinitely in a number of situations, including where a taxpayer:

. . . fails to file a required return (Code Sec. 6501(c)(3)), but the assessment period starts to run if a trust or partnership return is filed by a taxpayer later held to be a corporation (Code Sec. 6501(g)(1)) or an exempt organization return is filed by an organization later held to be taxable (Code Sec. 6501(g)(2));[42]

. . . files a false or fraudulent income, gift or estate tax return with intent to evade tax. (Code Sec. 6501(c)(1)) The courts disagree as to whether, to keep the assessment period open, the taxpayer must have the fraudulent intent (Tax Court and the Federal Circuit) or whether the fraudulent intent of another party—e.g., income tax preparer, accountant, tax shelter promoter—suffices (2nd Circuit).[43]

. . . willfully attempts in any manner to defeat and evade taxes (Code Sec. 6501(c)(2));[44]

. . . fails to pay any part of a tax required to be paid by stamp (Code Sec. 6501(a); Reg § 301.6501(a)-1);[45]

. . . for gift tax, fails to show or adequately disclose (1) any gift of property (or increase in taxable gifts) whose value is determined under the special valuation rules or (2) any post-Aug. 5, '97 gift. (Code Sec. 6501(c)(9); Reg § 301.6501(c)-1(e), Reg § 301.6501(c)-1(f))[46] Filing an amended return with required information will get the limitation period running for a prior gift that wasn't adequately disclosed.[47]

. . . is subject to the tax for termination of private foundation status, see ¶4130.[48]

. . . fails to notify IRS of an election not to take, or to revoke, certain credits, in which case the assessment of a deficiency attributable to such an election remains open until one year after IRS is notified of the election or revocation. (Code Sec. 6501(m))[49]

For information required under certain provisions, the assessment period for tax as to any tax return, event or period to which the information relates won't expire before the date that is 3 years after the information is given to IRS. The provisions include Code Sec. 1295(b), Code Sec. 1298(f), Code Sec. 6038, Code Sec. 6038A, Code Sec. 6038B, Code Sec. 6038D, Code Sec. 6046, Code Sec. 6046A, and Code Sec. 6048. However, if the failure

39. ¶T-4034
40. ¶T-4042
41. ¶T-4163
42. ¶T-4101 *et seq.*
43. ¶T-4127
44. ¶T-4141

45. ¶T-4122
46. ¶T-4147
47. ¶T-4162
48. ¶T-4143
49. ¶T-4014.1

to furnish the information required under these Code sections is due to reasonable cause and not willful neglect, the suspension of the assessment limitations period will apply only to the items related to that failure. (Code Sec. 6501(c)(8))[50]

The penalties for promoting abusive tax shelters, or for aiding and abetting an understatement, can be assessed at any time,[1] as can the penalty (but not the tax) imposed on a return preparer for willful tax understatements,[2] and certain restitution in criminal tax cases (see ¶4816).[3]

¶ 4823 Voluntary extension of assessment period; indefinite and restricted consent—Form 872.

Under Code Sec. 6501(c)(4), at any time *before* expiration of the assessment period (¶4818), a taxpayer and IRS can agree in writing (usually on a form in the Form 872 series) to extend the assessment period (except for estate taxes). They can also enter into successive agreements further extending the period.[4]

observation: IRS refers to Form 872 as a *"consent,"* while practitioners may refer to it as a *"waiver,"* which actually means a Form 870 (see ¶4811).

Restricted consent. A restricted consent postpones the close of the tax year with respect to an unsettled issue. It is used where some issues are resolved, but settlement of others must await the establishment of an IRS position through a court decision, etc., or where other equally meritorious circumstances exist.[5]

Indefinite consent—Form 872-A. A taxpayer whose case is before the Independent Appeals Office (¶4811) can execute Form 872-A, which is an indefinite extension.[6] It expires 90 days after: (1) Independent Appeals receives notice (on Form 872-T) of the taxpayer's desire to terminate the extension, (2) IRS mails Form 872-T to the taxpayer, or (3) IRS mails a 90-day letter.[7]

IRS must notify the taxpayer of his or her right to refuse to extend the assessment limitations period, or to limit the extension to particular issues or a particular time period, on each occasion the taxpayer is requested to provide consent. (Code Sec. 6501(c)(4)(B))[8]

¶ 4824 Suspension of assessment period by 90-day letter, TAO, issuance of designated summons in certain corporate audits.

Under Code Sec. 6503(a), a 90-day letter (¶4815) suspends the assessment period. The assessment period stops running on the date IRS mails the letter, and doesn't resume until 60 days after: (1) the 90-day period (150 days if the letter is addressed to a person outside the U.S.) if no petition is filed, or (2) the Tax Court's decision becomes final if a petition is filed.[9] Taxpayer's application for a Taxpayer Assistance Order (¶4808) also suspends the assessment period, up to the date the National Taxpayer Advocate makes a decision. (Code Sec. 7811(d))[10]

The assessment period is suspended in Tax Court employment tax determinations. (Code Sec. 7436(d)(1))[11]

For returns of corporations being examined under the coordinated industry case program or a successor program, the issuance of a "designated summons" or a related summons also suspends the assessment period, pending final resolution of its enforcement. (Code Sec. 6503(j); Reg § 301.6503(j)-1)[12]

---

50. ¶T-4146
1. ¶s T-4125, T-4126
2. ¶T-4145
3. ¶T-4172
4. ¶T-4400 *et seq.*; ¶S-4518
5. ¶T-4445
6. ¶T-4402

7. ¶T-4457 *et seq.*
8. ¶T-4403
9. ¶T-4300 *et seq.*
10. ¶T-4325
11. ¶T-4301.2
12. ¶T-4333 *et seq.*

¶ 4825 Request for prompt assessment reduces 3-year assessment period—Form 4810.

Under Code Sec. 6501(d), the normal 3-year assessment period can be cut to 18 months *at the taxpayer's request* (use Form 4810) for an income tax return of a decedent or an estate, or for a return of a dissolved or dissolving corporation.[13]

¶ 4826 "Mitigation" and judicial relief after limitations periods on assessment/refund have run.

Under Code Sec. 1311, Code Sec. 1312, and Code Sec. 1313, after the period for assessment or refund has run, a closed year may be reopened under the Code's "mitigation" provisions.[14]

In addition, relief from the limitation periods may be available, even if the statutory mitigation conditions aren't met, under the doctrines of equitable recoupment,[15] estoppel,[16] or election.[17]

¶ 4827 BBA Unified Audit and Review for Partnerships. ▬▬▬

Under Code Sec. 6221(a), part of the Bipartisan Budget Act (BBA) centralized partnership audit regime, in general, for a "partnership-related item" (¶4828), the following is done at the partnership level: any adjustment is determined; any attributable tax is assessed and collected; and applicability of any penalty, addition to tax, or additional amount due to an adjustment to any such item is determined.

¶ 4828 BBA partnership audit procedures—"partnership-related item"; partnership adjustment; partnership representative; election out; liquidating partnership distributions.

Under Code Sec. 6221(a) and Code Sec. 6223, in general, any adjustment to a "partnership-related item" (below) is determined, and any tax attributable thereto will be assessed and collected, and any penalty, addition to tax, or additional amount relating to an adjustment to any such item will be determined, at the partnership level.[18]

If IRS makes a partnership adjustment under the partnership audit rules: (1) if the adjustment results in an imputed underpayment (¶4829), the partnership must pay the amount of the imputed underpayment in the adjustment year; and (2) if the adjustment doesn't result in an imputed underpayment, the adjustment must be taken into account by the partnership in the adjustment year. (Code Sec. 6225(a))[19]

A partnership adjustment is an adjustment to a partnership-related item, i.e., an adjustment to: (i) any item or amount relating to the partnership that's relevant in determining the income tax liability of any person, (ii) any partner's distributive share of any such item or amount, and (iii) any imputed underpayment. (Code Sec. 6241(2)(B); Reg § 301.6241-1(a)(6)(ii)) The regs include a list of partnership-related items. (Reg § 301.6241-1(a)(6)(v))[20]

These rules generally apply to any partnership required to file a partnership return (Form 1065) and, to the extent provided in regs, where a partnership return is filed by an entity for a tax year but it is determined that the entity is not a partnership (or that there is no entity) for such year. (Code Sec. 6241(1); Code Sec. 6241(8); Reg § 301.6241-5)[21]

13. ¶T-4500 *et seq.*
14. ¶T-5000 *et seq.*
15. ¶T-5200 *et seq.*
16. ¶T-5300 *et seq.*
17. ¶T-5400 *et seq.*
18. ¶T-2401 *et seq.*
19. ¶T-2409
20. ¶T-2409
21. ¶T-2407

A partnership must designate (in the way set forth in regs) a partner or other person with a substantial presence in the U.S. as the partnership representative with the sole authority to act on behalf of the partnership for the partnership audit rules. Where no designation is in effect, IRS may select any person as the partnership representative. (Code Sec. 6223; Reg § 301.6223-1)[22]

Partnerships may elect out of the partnership audit rules if: (1) they're required to furnish 100 or fewer statements to partners or nominees under Code Sec. 6031(b); and (2) each statement is furnished to a partner that's an individual, a C corporation, an "eligible foreign entity," an S corporation, or an estate of a deceased partner. All partners must be notified of the election in the time and manner provided in regs. (Code Sec. 6221(b); Reg § 301.6221(b)-1(b))[23]

¶ 4829   Imputed underpayments; modification; push-out election (Form 8988)— BBA partnership audit procedures.

Under Code Sec. 6225(a), if IRS adjusts any partnership-related items (referred to as a partnership adjustment, see ¶4828), the partnership, rather than the partners, is subject to the liability for any imputed underpayment.[24] The imputed underpayment is determined by grouping (Reg § 301.6225-1(c)) and netting partnership adjustments, and applying the highest rate of tax in effect for that year under Code Sec. 1 or Code Sec. 11. (Code Sec. 6225(b))[25]

IRS regs set forth rules and procedures under which a partnership may modify the imputed underpayment, with IRS's approval. (Code Sec. 6225(c); Reg § 301.6225-2)[26]

As an alternative to taking IRS audit adjustments into account at the partnership level, a partnership can elect (on Form 8988) to "push out" the adjustments to its partners (in a manner specified in regs, and revocable only with IRS's consent) not later than 45 days after the date of the notice of final partnership adjustment. If the election is made, each partner takes his or her share of the partnership adjustments that relate to an imputed underpayment. (Code Sec. 6226; Reg § 301.6226-1; Reg § 301.6226-2(g))[27]

¶ 4830   Partnership-level assessment and review procedures—BBA partnership audit procedures.

Under Code Sec. 6231(a), for any administrative proceeding under the partnership audit procedures, the following notices must be mailed to the partnership and the partnership representative: (i) notice of any administrative proceeding (Letters 5893 and 5893-A) initiated at the partnership level as to an adjustment to any partnership-related item for a partnership tax year, or any partner's distributive share thereof; (ii) notice of any proposed partnership adjustment resulting from the proceeding; and (iii) notice of any final partnership adjustment (FPA) resulting from the proceeding. (Code Sec. 6231(a); Reg § 301.6231-1)[28] A notice of an FPA can't be mailed earlier than 270 days after the date on which the notice of the proposed partnership adjustment is mailed, unless the partnership waives this limitation. (Code Sec. 6231(b)(2)(A))[29]

Special limitation periods apply for partnership assessments. (Code Sec. 6235(a))[30]

Any imputed underpayment is assessed and collected as if it were an income tax, except that the deficiency procedures don't apply—i.e., no notice of deficiency (¶4815) is required and the restrictions on assessment (¶4816) don't apply. (Code Sec. 6232(a)(1); Reg § 301.6232-1)[31]

---

22. ¶T-2404
23. ¶T-2408
24. ¶T-2409
25. ¶T-2411 *et seq.*
26. ¶T-2419 *et seq.*

27. ¶T-2424 *et seq.*
28. ¶T-2429
29. ¶T-2429
30. ¶T-2431
31. ¶T-2430

A partnership has 90 days from the mailing of the notice of an FPA to file a petition for a readjustment for the tax year with (i) the Tax Court, (ii) the U.S. district court for the district in which the partnership's principal place of business is located, or (iii) the Court of Federal Claims. However, a petition in a U.S. district court or the Court of Federal Claims may be filed only if the partnership deposits with IRS the amount of the imputed underpayment, and penalties. (Code Sec. 6234)[32]

¶ 4831 Recovering Overpayments by Refund or Credit; Tax Litigation. ▄▄▄▄

A taxpayer can recover an overpayment as a credit or a refund by properly filing a claim (¶4833) and, if the claim is denied, bringing suit (¶4842 *et seq.*). A taxpayer who has been issued a 90-day letter (¶4815) can go to Tax Court without first paying the disputed tax.

An overpayment is the excess of the amount paid (or withheld) as tax over the taxpayer's correct tax liability. It includes the part of a correct tax paid after the applicable assessment period has run. (Code Sec. 6401)[33] An overpayment can be recovered as a refund or credit, generally only by the taxpayer who paid the tax, but IRS may first credit the overpayment (including interest) against *any* of the taxpayer's past due tax liability (including interest, additions, penalties). (Code Sec. 6402(a); Reg § 301.6402-3(a)(5))[34] For offset against nontax debts, see ¶4832.

No credit or refund for an overpayment is made to a taxpayer before the 15th day of the second month after the close of that tax year, if the taxpayer claimed the earned income tax credit or additional child tax credit. (Code Sec. 6402(m))[35]

Electronic filers may elect (on Form 8453) to have their refunds deposited directly into their bank accounts. Paper filers elect direct deposit by filling in the appropriate blanks on the "Refund" lines of Form 1040. In either case, use Form 8888 to direct deposit a refund into two or three accounts including IRAs.[36]

A refund may be claimed for a deceased taxpayer. Attach Form 1310 (not needed for surviving spouse filing jointly with decedent) to the decedent's final return (¶4714).[37]

¶ 4832 Overpayments applied to child support and other non-tax debts.

Under Code Sec. 6402(c), if a state notifies IRS that a taxpayer owes any child support payments, it must first apply the taxpayer's overpayment (including earned income amounts) to those past-due obligations, before making any refund or credit.[38] If a federal agency notifies the Treasury of any past-due, legally enforceable non-tax debt a taxpayer owes the agency, IRS must apply the balance (i.e., after the child support offset) of the taxpayer's overpayment to that non-tax debt. (Code Sec. 6402(d))[39] After these reductions, refunds can be reduced by state income tax debts, (Code Sec. 6402(e))[40] or reduced to recover debts to states for certain overpayments of unemployment compensation. (Code Sec. 6402(f))[41]

¶ 4833 Refund claim rules.

To get a refund, a taxpayer must file a timely (¶4838) written claim. For income, gift and federal unemployment taxes, a separate claim must be made for each tax year or period. (Reg § 301.6402-2(a), Reg § 301.6402-2(d)) To claim their refund, individuals who have filed Form 1040 must use Form 1040X, and corporations who have filed Form 1120 must use Form 1120X. Where a form other than Form 1040 or Form 1120 was filed, a refund claim must be made on the appropriate amended income tax return.

---

32. ¶T-2432
33. ¶T-5500 *et seq.*
34. ¶T-5600 *et seq.*, T-5700 *et seq.*
35. ¶T-5605
36. ¶T-5610 *et seq.*

37. ¶T-5710
38. ¶T-6013 *et seq.*
39. ¶T-6023 *et seq.*
40. ¶T-6038
41. ¶T-6045.1

(Reg § 301.6402-3(a)) Form 843 is used for refunds of most non-income taxes other than certain excise taxes. (Reg § 601.105(e)(1))[42]

Although taxpayers should file a refund claim on official IRS forms, certain informal claims have been ruled sufficient.[43]

IRS must provide the taxpayer with an explanation for the disallowance of a refund claim. (Code Sec. 6402(l))[44]

¶ 4834   Quick refund for carrybacks and "claim of right" adjustments—Forms 1045, 1139.

Under Code Sec. 6411(a), a taxpayer who reports a carryback of a net operating loss (NOL), capital loss, business credit, or capital loss from a Code Sec. 1256 contract under Code Sec. 1212(c) on his or her return, can quickly recover a refund based on the carryback by filing Form 1045 (individuals) or Form 1139 (corporations) on or after the date the return for the loss or credit year is filed, and within 12 months after the end of the tax year from which the carryback is made. (Code Sec. 6411(a); Reg § 1.6411-1(b)(1))[45] This procedure also applies to overpayments attributable to a "claim of right" adjustment (¶2848), where the amount of repayment in any one year exceeds $3,000. (Code Sec. 6411(d))[46] IRS has 90 days from the later of the date the claim is filed or the last day of the month the loss year return is due (with extensions), to make any credit or refund. (Code Sec. 6411(b); Reg § 1.6411-3)[47] IRS's determination is tentative. If the claim is rejected, the taxpayer can't sue but must first file a standard refund claim. (Code Sec. 6411(b); Reg § 1.6411-3(c)) Even if IRS grants the refund, it can later examine the loss year return and the refund application. IRS may assess any part of the refund it finds excessive, without issuing a 90-day letter. (Code Sec. 6213(b)(3))[48]

¶ 4835   Quick refunds of corporate estimated tax overpayments—Form 4466.

Under Code Sec. 6425(b)(1) and Code Sec. 6425(b)(2), a corporation that overpaid estimated tax (¶3343 *et seq.*) can get a refund within 45 days after filing Form 4466. (Code Sec. 6425(b)(1), Code Sec. 6425(b)(2); Reg § 1.6425-1(b)) The form must be filed *after* the corporation's tax year ends and *on or before* the 15th day of the fourth month after the year ends (or before the corporation first files its income tax return for that year, if earlier); but for C corporations with a tax year ending on June 30, for tax years beginning before Jan. 1, 2026, the deadline is the 15th day of the *third* month. (Code Sec. 6425(a)(1)) The corporation's estimated tax overpayment must be at least 10% of its revised expected annual tax, *and* at least $500. (Code Sec. 6425(b)(3)) If a corporate estimated tax overpayment refund is excessive, an addition to tax equal to the underpayment interest rate (¶4849), times the excessive amount is imposed. (Code Sec. 6655(h))[49]

¶ 4836   Protective refund claims.

A protective refund claim is a regular refund claim (see ¶4833) filed merely to keep a particular claim alive. It is generally used where IRS has a settled view adverse to a taxpayer on an issue being litigated by other taxpayers. A protective refund claim is usually filed just before the refund claim period expires. It will keep the taxpayer's claim alive (i.e., protect his or her right to sue) for the additional period from the date of filing to the date of rejection plus the refund suit period.[50]

---

42. ¶T-6700 *et seq.*
43. ¶T-6721
44. ¶T-5618.1
45. ¶T-6501 *et seq.*
46. ¶T-6522

47. ¶T-6509
48. ¶T-3633
49. ¶T-6600 *et seq.*
50. ¶T-6742

¶ 4837 Interest paid on overpayments; period for interest; grace period; interest rate; deposits of tax.

Under Code Sec. 6611(a), IRS pays interest on overpayments. The interest (compounded daily) runs from the date of the overpayment to a date not more than 30 days before the refund is made (or to the (unextended) return due date for the amount against which the overpayment is credited). (Code Sec. 6611(b))[1]

No interest is payable on a refund arising from an original income, employment, excise, estate or gift tax return made within 45 days after the later of the return due date (without extensions) or the date it was filed. (Code Sec. 6611(e)(1); Reg § 301.6611-1(j))[2] If a refund arising from an amended return or refund claim is issued within 45 days, no interest is payable for that up-to-45-day period. (Code Sec. 6611(e)(2))[3] For refunds or credits arising from an adjustment initiated by IRS, the interest period is reduced by 45 days. (Code Sec. 6611(e)(3))[4] The grace period during which the government isn't required to pay interest on overpayments is increased from 45 days to 180 days for overpayments resulting from excess amounts deducted and withheld under Chapter 3 of the Code (Code Sec. 1441 through Code Sec. 1464 (withholding on nonresident aliens and foreign corporations)) or Chapter 4 of the Code (Code Sec. 1471 through Code Sec. 1474). (Code Sec. 6611(e)) For returns filed after the due date (with extensions), no interest is payable for the period preceding the actual filing date. (Code Sec. 6611(b)(3))[5] And, no interest is payable on an estate's overpayment unless it shows that the interest (and refund) won't escheat to the state. (Code Sec. 6408)[6] IRS also won't pay interest when it refunds a conditional or advance payment of taxes.[7]

The overpayment rate for individuals is the short-term applicable federal rate (AFR) plus 3 percentage points (same as the underpayment rate, see ¶4849). The overpayment rate for corporations (including non-profit corporations) is generally the short-term AFR plus 2 percentage points. However, the rate for C corporations is reduced to the short-term AFR plus 0.5 percentage points, to the extent the overpayment for any period exceeds $10,000. (Code Sec. 6621(a)(1))[8]

For noncorporate taxpayers, the overpayment rate is 6% for the period Oct. 1, 2022 – Dec. 31, 2022, 5% for the period July 1, 2022 – Sept. 30, 2022, 4% for the period Apr. 1, 2022 – June 30, 2022, and 3% for the period July 1, 2020 – Mar. 31, 2022.[9]

For the period Oct. 1, 2022 – Dec. 31, 2022: the overpayment rate for regular corporate overpayments is 5%, and for the portion of corporate overpayments exceeding $10,000, the rate is 3.5%. For the period July 1, 2022 – Sept. 30, 2022: the overpayment rate for regular corporate overpayments is 4%, and for the portion of corporate overpayments exceeding $10,000, the rate is 2.5%. For the period Apr. 1, 2022 - June 30, 2022: the overpayment rate for regular corporate overpayments is 3%, and for the portion of corporate overpayments exceeding $10,000, the rate is 1.5%.[10]

A deposit (¶4851) that's returned to a taxpayer is treated as a payment of tax for any period to the extent (and only to the extent) attributable to a disputable tax for that period. (Code Sec. 6603(d)(1)) But the interest on the return of such a deposit is payable only at the short-term AFR rate compounded daily. (Code Sec. 6603(d)(4))[11] The overpayment date for taxes withheld or paid as estimated taxes is the unextended due date of the return. (Code Sec. 6513(b))[12] Overpayments resulting from the carryback of an NOL, net capital loss, business credit, or foreign tax credit, are considered not to have been made before the "filing date" for the tax year when the loss or credit arose or the foreign tax was paid or

---

1. ¶s T-8008, T-8031, T-8034
2. ¶T-8024
3. ¶T-8027
4. ¶T-8028
5. ¶T-8008
6. ¶s T-8063, T-8065

7. ¶T-8046
8. ¶T-8002, ¶T-8002.1
9. ¶T-8003
10. ¶T-8003.1, T-8003.2
11. ¶S-5804.3
12. ¶T-7530

accrued. (Code Sec. 6611(f))[13] Similarly, where a business credit carryback is attributable to an NOL, etc., carryback from a later year, the overpayment is considered not to have been made before the filing date for that later year. (Code Sec. 6611(f)(3))[14]

¶ 4838 Deadline (limitations period) for filing refund claims; when longer period applies.

Under Code Sec. 6511(a), a claim for credit or refund of a tax paid by *return* generally must be filed within the later of: (1) three years from the date the return was timely or untimely filed (or the due date if filed earlier than the due date), or (2) two years from the date the tax was paid. If the required return wasn't filed, the claim must be filed within two years from when the tax was paid.[15] For the prohibited transaction excise tax (¶4337), the relevant return is the plan's annual Form 5500, not Form 5330 on which the tax is reported.[16]

A longer refund claim period applies in these cases:

. . . If a taxpayer and IRS execute one of the Form 872 series extending the assessment period (see ¶4823), the claim can be filed within six months after the expiration of the extended assessment period. (Code Sec. 6511(c)(1))[17]

. . . For an overpayment resulting from carryback of an NOL, net capital loss, or business credit, the period expires three years after the time the return is due (including extensions) for the year the loss or credit arose, not the year to which it's carried back. (Code Sec. 6511(d)(2), Code Sec. 6511(d)(4))[18] If the overpayment is attributable to a carryback from a later year, the period expires three years after the time for filing the return (including extensions) for that later year. (Code Sec. 6511(d)(4))[19]

. . . For an overpayment resulting from the payment or accrual of foreign taxes for which a foreign tax credit is allowed, the claim period is ten years. (Code Sec. 6511(d)(3))[20]

. . . For an overpayment resulting from a bad debt or from worthless securities, the claim period is seven years. (Code Sec. 6511(d)(1))[21]

. . . For self-employment tax claims attributable to Tax Court employment status proceedings, the claim period is two years after the calendar year the Tax Court determination becomes final. (Code Sec. 6511(d)(7))[22]

. . . For credit or refund claims for retired military personnel who receive disability determinations from the Dept. of Veterans Affairs (VA), the refund claim filing period is extended for one year after the date of a disability determination from the VA (if later than the time allowed under the general refund limitations period). The extended time period doesn't apply for any tax year beginning more than five years before the date of the disability determination. (Code Sec. 6511(d)(8))[23]

. . . If certain requirements are met, the limitations period may be suspended during any period an individual is unable to manage his or her financial affairs by reason of a medically-determinable physical or mental impairment. (Code Sec. 6511(h))[24]

¶ 4839 Refund suit limitations period; Form 2297 (waiver of notice); agreement to extend period.

Under Code Sec. 6532(a)(1), a refund suit can't be started *before* six months from filing the refund claim (unless IRS acts on the claim in that period), or *after* two years from the date IRS mails a notice of disallowance of the claim. The taxpayer can waive (on Form

---

13. ¶T-8049 *et seq.*
14. ¶T-8051
15. ¶T-7500 *et seq.*
16. ¶T-7524
17. ¶T-7574
18. ¶T-7554

19. ¶T-7563
20. ¶T-7569
21. ¶T-7552
22. ¶T-7573.1
23. ¶T-7573.2
24. ¶T-7506

2297) issuance of this notice, and the 2-year period will start on the date the waiver is filed. (Code Sec. 6532(a)(3)) Under Code Sec. 7422(a), a taxpayer *must* file a refund claim with IRS before starting a suit for refund (or credit).[25] The taxpayer and IRS can execute a Form 907 extending the 2-year period. (Code Sec. 6532(a)(2))[26]

¶ 4840   Limits on amount of refund or credit.

Under Code Sec. 6511(b)(2)(A), if a claim is filed within three years from the time the return was filed, the refund or credit is limited to the portion of tax paid during the three years (plus the period of any filing extension) immediately preceding the filing of the claim.[27] If the claim wasn't filed within the three-year period, the refund or credit is limited to the portion of the tax paid during the two years immediately preceding the filing of the claim. (Code Sec. 6511(b)(2)(B)) This two-year limitation also applies if a claim, but no return, was filed. (Reg § 301.6511(b)-1(b)(1)(iii))[28] Where no claim is filed and a refund or credit is allowed within three years from the time the return was filed, the refund or credit is limited to the portion of the tax paid during the three years immediately before the allowance. If the refund or credit is not allowed within that three-year period, it's limited to the portion of the tax paid during the two years immediately before the allowance. (Code Sec. 6511(b)(2)(C))[29] For purposes of determining the amount of an individual taxpayer's refund or credit under these rules, the refund claim periods described above are suspended during any period when the individual is unable to manage his or her financial affairs (see ¶4838). (Code Sec. 6511(h))[30]

¶ 4841   Refundable-credit refunds aren't income for determining eligibility for benefits.

Under Code Sec. 6409, any refund or advance payment of a refundable credit made to an individual isn't taken into account as income, and isn't taken into account as resources for a period of 12 months from receipt, in determining the eligibility of the recipient or any other individual for benefits or assistance, or the amount or extent of benefits or assistance, under any federal program or any state or local program financed in whole or part with federal funds.[31]

¶ 4842   Tax litigation: available courts; burden of proof.

A taxpayer may go to:

. . . the Tax Court: to set aside a deficiency determined by IRS (¶4843) (Code Sec. 6214(a));[32] to review appeals of Collection Due Process hearings (¶4887 *et seq.*) (Code Sec. 6330(d)(1));[33] to determine worker classification in certain cases and, according to Tax Court, the correct amount of employment taxes that relate to such determinations (Code Sec. 7436);[34] to review IRS's failure to abate interest to taxpayers within certain net worth limits who bring an action within 180 days of IRS's final adverse determination, and to order abatement if IRS abused its discretion (Code Sec. 6404(h));[35] for a declaratory judgment on retirement plan qualification (Code Sec. 7476(a));[36] for eligibility for deferral of estate tax on a closely held business interest (Code Sec. 7479);[37] for the value of certain gifts made (Code Sec. 7477; Reg § 301.7477-1);[38] to redetermine transferee liability (¶4896) (Code Sec. 6901);[39] over actions for administrative costs

25. ¶T-6701
26. ¶T-9034
27. ¶T-7537
28. ¶s T-7546, T-7547
29. ¶T-7548
30. ¶T-7506
31. ¶A-4249
32. ¶U-2100 *et seq.*

33. ¶V-5272, ¶V-6015
34. ¶U-2143
35. ¶U-2129.1
36. ¶U-3700 *et seq.*
37. ¶U-3851 *et seq.*
38. ¶U-3880;
39. ¶V-9200 *et seq.*

787

(Code Sec. 7430);[40] to determine innocent spouse relief when a deficiency has been issued and the taxpayer elects regular or separate innocent spouse relief or requests equitable relief (but the Tax Court can't rule on the timeliness of an assessment in reviewing a denial of innocent spouse relief) (Code Sec. 6015(e));[41] to review awards to whistleblowers (Code Sec. 7623(b)(4));[42] to determine liability in proceedings for determination of employment status, including IRS's determination denying a taxpayer's request for participation in the Voluntary Classification Settlement Program;[43] and for other matters;

. . . a U.S. district court to enjoin IRS from assessing and collecting a tax in certain cases (¶4892), or to get damages for IRS's unauthorized collection activities or failure to release a lien; (Code Sec. 7432, Code Sec. 7433)[44]

. . . a bankruptcy court to sue for up to $1 million in damages for willful IRS violations of automatic stay or discharge in bankruptcy. (Code Sec. 7433(e))[45]

. . . a U.S. district court or the U.S. Court of Federal Claims: to recover an overpayment of taxes (after filing a refund claim); (Code Sec. 6532(a))[46] or to determine the correct amount of (or for a refund of) the estate's estate tax liability, even if it wasn't fully paid due to a Code Sec. 6166 election; (Code Sec. 7422(j)(1))[47]

. . . the Tax Court, the district court for the DC Circuit, or the U.S. Court of Federal Claims for a declaratory judgment on the tax status of exempt organizations and foundations. (Code Sec. 7428(a))[48]

. . . the Tax Court, a U.S. district court or the U.S. Court of Federal Claims, to review partnership adjustments under BBA partnership audit procedures (also, U.S. District Court, or U.S. Claims Court); (Code Sec. 6234);[49]

For taxpayers other than certain large partnerships, corporations, and trusts, IRS has the burden of proof in any court proceeding for any factual issue relevant to ascertaining a taxpayer's liability for any tax imposed by subtitle A or B of the Code, e.g., income and self-employment, gift, estate, and generation-skipping transfer taxes, if the taxpayer: introduces credible evidence on the issue; has complied with the substantiation requirements; has maintained all required records; and has cooperated with reasonable IRS requests. (Code Sec. 7491(a))[50] IRS has the burden of production (i.e., to come forward initially with evidence) in any court proceeding on the liability of any individual for any penalty imposed by the Code. (Code Sec. 7491(c))[1]

¶ 4843   Tax Court review of deficiencies; jurisdiction.

Under Code Sec. 6213(a), to get Tax Court review of a deficiency, a taxpayer must file a petition with the Tax Court in Washington, D.C., in response to a 90-day letter (see ¶4815) from IRS, within 90 days (150 days if the letter is addressed to a person outside the U.S.) after the letter is mailed (i.e., postmarked). A petition is timely if it's filed with the Tax Court on or before the last date specified by IRS in the 90-day letter for filing it.[2] For the types of matters within the Tax Court's jurisdiction, see ¶4842.

The Tax Court's jurisdiction is generally limited to the review (without a jury) of deficiencies asserted by IRS (and not paid when the 90-day letter is issued). It can order payment of a refund if it determines the taxpayer overpaid. (Code Sec. 6512(b)) But it can't grant equitable relief. The Tax Court has jurisdiction to order a refund of any amount collected while IRS was prohibited from collecting a deficiency by levy or court proceeding but only if a timely petition for a redetermination of the deficiency has been filed and only

---

40. ¶U-1241
41. ¶U-2148
42. ¶U-2154
43. ¶ U-2143
44. ¶s V-5801, V-6113
45. ¶V-5820 *et seq.*
46. ¶s U-4000 *et seq.*, U-6000 *et seq.*

47. ¶T-9007.1
48. ¶s U-3800 *et seq.*, U-4116, U-6005
49. ¶T-2432
50. ¶U-1351
1. ¶U-1331
2. ¶U-2300 *et seq.*

with respect to the deficiency at issue. (Code Sec. 6213(a))[3] The Tax Court is generally barred from determining whether the tax for any period not before it has been overpaid or underpaid. However, it may apply the doctrine of equitable recoupment. (Code Sec. 6214(b))[4]

¶ 4844   Settlement after Tax Court petition is filed.

IRS District Counsel refers all docketed Tax Court cases to Independent Appeals for consideration of settlement (unless Independent Appeals issued the deficiency notice, in which case there will be no referral if there is little likelihood that the case can be settled in a reasonable period of time). Counsel and Independent Appeals can agree otherwise, work together, or transfer the case back and forth to promote efficient disposition of the case. The taxpayer-petitioner and/or representative is notified as to who has the case and the settlement authority.[5] If the taxpayer and IRS agree on a settlement, they enter into a written agreement stipulating the amount of any deficiency or overpayment. This stipulation is filed with the Tax Court which will enter a decision in accordance with it. (Reg § 601.106(d)(3)(i))[6]

¶ 4845   Small tax claims in Tax Court.

Under Code Sec. 7463, special informal procedures apply, at a taxpayer's election and with the Tax Court's concurrence, to any Tax Court case where neither the amount (including any additions to tax, additional amounts and penalties) of the deficiency disputed nor of any claimed overpayment exceeds $50,000 (the Tax Court has held that the limit includes tax, interest and penalties and applies to the total owed for all years in a single proceeding). The taxpayer thus gets the Court's decision faster and more easily, but gives up the right to appeal.[7]

¶ 4846   Appeals from Tax Court, district court and U.S. Court of Federal Claims: U.S. Courts of Appeal.

Decisions of the Tax Court and U.S. district courts are appealable to the U.S. Court of Appeals.[8] The appeal is made in the circuit where the taxpayer's legal residence (for appeals from Tax Court)[9] or the trial court (for appeals from district courts) is located.[10] U.S. Court of Federal Claims decisions may be appealed to the Court of Appeals for the Federal Circuit.[11] Appeals from U.S. Courts of Appeals are to the U.S. Supreme Court.[12]

¶ 4847   Recovery of attorneys' fees and costs in tax disputes.

Under Code Sec. 7430, taxpayers whose net worth doesn't exceed specified limits, who meet other requirements, and who prevail against the U.S. in court (or at the administrative level) may be awarded reasonable litigation and administrative costs (including the costs of recovering the award). The inflation-adjusted limit on attorney fee recoveries is $220 per hour for 2022 and $230 for 2023. (Code Sec. 7430(c)(1)(B)(iii))[13] To avoid an award of fees, IRS must show its position was substantially justified. (Code Sec. 7430(c)(4)(B)) Administrative costs can be awarded from the date IRS sends the "30-day letter" (¶4810) (Code Sec. 7430(c)(2)) When a taxpayer is represented on a pro bono basis, the fees recoverable may exceed the amounts that the taxpayer paid or incurred. (Code Sec. 7430(c)(3)(B)) IRS losses on similar issues in other circuits are taken into account in determining whether its position was substantially justified (Code

---

3. ¶U-2134.1
4. ¶U-2138
5. ¶T-1902 *et seq.*
6. ¶T-1909
7. ¶U-3600 *et seq.*
8. ¶s U-3417, U-5000 *et seq.*

9. ¶U-5202
10. ¶U-5401
11. ¶U-6001
12. ¶s U-5700 *et seq.*, U-7000 *et seq.*
13. ¶U-1267

Sec. 7430(c)(4)(B)(iii)), and costs can be awarded where IRS rejects a taxpayer's offer and later gets a judgment not exceeding the offer. (Code Sec. 7430(c)(4)(E)(i); Reg § 301.7430-7)[14]

¶ 4848   Interest and Penalties. ▬▬▬▬▬

Under Code Sec. 6601(a), interest is charged on underpayments of tax (¶4849 *et seq.*). Various civil and criminal penalties are imposed on taxpayers (and/or return preparers) who violate the tax law (¶4855 *et seq.*).

¶ 4849   Interest on underpayments; when payable; interest rate; large corporate underpayments.

Under Code Sec. 6601(a), interest is generally payable whenever any tax or civil penalty isn't paid when due (Code Sec. 6601(a)), even if the taxpayer has been granted an extension of time to pay the tax. (Code Sec. 6601(b)(1); Reg § 301.6601-1(a))[15]

There's no interest on late payments of estimated tax (Code Sec. 6601(h))—but for comparable penalty computations, see ¶3154 (individuals) and ¶3348 (corporations)—or unemployment tax. (Code Sec. 6601(i))[16] Interest is payable on an erroneous refund or credit. (Code Sec. 6602)[17]

The rate of interest on tax underpayments and penalties is the short-term applicable federal rate (AFR) plus 3 percentage points. (Code Sec. 6621(a)(2))[18] For Oct. 1, 2022– Dec. 31, 2022, the rate is 6%. For July 1, 2022– Sept. 30, 2022, the rate is 5%. For Apr. 1, 2022 - Jun. 30, 2022, the rate is 4%. For Jul. 1, 2020 – Mar. 31, 2022, the rate is 3%.[19]

If a C corporation's tax underpayment for any tax period exceeds $100,000, a higher interest rate applies for the period after the 30th day after a notice (or proposed notice) of deficiency. For Oct. 1, 2022– Dec. 31, 2022, the rate is 8%. For July 1, 2022– Sept. 30, 2022, the rate is 7%. For Apr. 1, 2022 - Jun. 30, 2022, the rate is 6%. For Jul. 1, 2020 – Mar. 31, 2022, the rate is 5%. (Code Sec. 6621(c); Reg § 301.6621-3)[20] A net interest rate of zero applies to equivalent amounts of underpayments and overpayments by the same taxpayer. (Code Sec. 6621(d)) Interest netting is requested on Form 843.[21]

¶ 4850   Interest accrual period—interest on underpayments and penalties.

Under Code Sec. 6601, *interest on unpaid tax liabilities* runs from the last day prescribed by the Code for payment (disregarding extensions or any installment payment agreement) (Code Sec. 6601(b)(1)), to the date paid. (Code Sec. 6601(a)) However, where the tax is paid within 21 days after notice and demand (10 business days if the amount is $100,000 or more), interest stops on the date of the notice and demand. (Code Sec. 6601(e)(3))[22] (For payments to stop interest, see ¶4851.) Also, where a taxpayer consents to immediate assessment (by signing one of the Form 870 series, see ¶4811) and IRS doesn't make notice and demand for payment within 30 days of the filing of that consent, interest stops running during the period beginning immediately after that 30th day and ending with the date of the notice and demand. (Code Sec. 6601(c))[23]

Interest on civil penalties runs from the date of notice and demand if not paid within 21 days after that date (10 business days for amounts of $100,000 or more). (Code Sec. 6601(e)(2)(A)) But for the penalties for failure to file, valuation misstatement (income tax) or understatement (estate or gift tax), substantial understatement, negligence, and fraud, the interest period begins on the *return* due date (with extensions). In either case,

---

14. ¶U-1240 *et seq.*
15. ¶V-1000 *et seq.*; ¶V-1201
16. ¶V-1000 *et seq.*
17. ¶T-9108
18. ¶V-1100 *et seq.*

19. ¶V-1102
20. ¶V-1106 *et seq.*
21. ¶V-1303 *et seq.*
22. ¶V-1200 *et seq.*, ¶V-1300
23. ¶V-1311

the interest stops on the date the penalty is paid. (Code Sec. 6601(e)(2)(B))[24]

¶ 4851 Deposits to prepay and/or stop the running of interest on underpayments.

Under Code Sec. 6603(a), a cash deposit made under IRS rules may be used to pay income, gift, estate, or generation-skipping tax or certain excise taxes that have not yet been assessed at the time of the deposit. The amount of the deposit later used by IRS to pay tax is treated as a tax payment at the time of the deposit, for determining whether the taxpayer owes interest on an underpayment. (Code Sec. 6603(b)) Interest may be allowed on the return of all or part of such a deposit, see ¶4837.[25]

¶ 4852 How NOLs, other carryovers, and overpayments affect interest on underpayments.

Under Code Sec. 6601(d), interest on a deficiency isn't eliminated when the deficiency is eliminated by a net operating loss (NOL), net capital loss, foreign tax credit or business credit carryback. It accrues from its original due date to the filing date for the tax year when the carryback arose (or, for any portion of a credit carryback attributable to a carryback from a later year, to the filing date for that later year).[26]

An underpayment of tax in one year may be paid by crediting against it an overpayment of tax in another year. (Code Sec. 6402(a)) No interest accrues on any part of the underpayment so paid for any period after the return due date (without extension) for the overpayment year or, if later, when the offsetting return is filed. This rule doesn't apply to the extent the zero rate (¶4849) applies. (Code Sec. 6601(f))[27] When a taxpayer elects to apply an overpayment to the following year's estimated taxes, the overpayment will be applied to unpaid installments of estimated tax due on or after the date the overpayment arose, in the order in they are required to be paid to avoid an estimated tax penalty. IRS assesses interest on a later determined deficiency for the overpayment year only from the date the overpayment is applied to the following year's estimated taxes.[28]

¶ 4853 Abatement of interest and penalties; abatement where IRS unreasonably delayed, etc., or in case of erroneous written advice; IRS's first-time abatement for certain penalties—Form 843.

Under Code Sec. 6404(e)(1), IRS has discretion to abate interest assessed because of a deficiency attributable to any unreasonable error or delay by an IRS employee in performing a managerial or ministerial act. (Code Sec. 6404(e)(1); Reg § 301.6404-2)[29]

IRS must abate any portion of any penalty or addition to tax attributable to erroneous written advice (as defined in Reg § 301.6404-3(c)(1)) that the taxpayer reasonably relied on that was furnished to the taxpayer by an IRS employee in response to a specific written request. (Code Sec. 6404(f)(1), Code Sec. 6404(f)(2)(A)), (Code Sec. 6404(f)(2)(B))[30] To obtain such an abatement, a taxpayer must make an abatement request on Form 843 (with certain required attachments). (Reg § 301.6404-3(d))[31]

First-time abatement. IRS, when considering requests for relief from failure-to-file penalties (¶4856), failure-to-pay penalties (¶4857), or failure-to-the deposit penalty (¶4881), should determine whether the taxpayer is eligible for a first-time abatement (FTA) administrative waiver. For FTA to apply, it must be the first time a taxpayer is subject to one of the above penalties, for a single return; also, the taxpayer must be compliant, having filed (or extended) all required returns, and paid, or arranged to pay, any tax; and for the 3

24. ¶V-1218
25. ¶S-5804 *et seq.*
26. ¶V-1302
27. ¶V-1301
28. ¶V-1210
29. ¶T-3951 *et seq.*
30. ¶T-3908 *et seq.*
31. ¶T-3914 *et seq.*

791

preceding years, either the taxpayer can't have been required to file the same return, or the taxpayer must have no penalties (other than the estimated tax penalty).[32]

For taxpayers affected by a federally declared disaster or a terroristic or military action, IRS may postpone the deadlines for performing various tax acts for a period of up to one year. (Code Sec. 7508A(a)(2))[33]

¶ 4854 Interest and penalty suspension for IRS failure to notify individual of liability.

Under Code Sec. 6404(g), if an individual taxpayer files an income tax return on or before the return due date (with extensions), IRS must generally suspend interest and penalty for any taxpayer failure relating to that return if IRS doesn't—during the 36-month period beginning on the date the return is filed or, if later, the due date (without extensions)—notify the taxpayer, specifying the liability and the basis for it. Exceptions to this rule include interest or penalty in a case of fraud or for any (i) tax liability shown on a return, (ii) gross misstatement, (iii) reportable transaction not meeting the applicable disclosure requirements, or (iv) listed transaction. The suspension period begins on the day after the end of the 36-month period and ends on the date that's 21 days after IRS provides the notice. Where a taxpayer files an amended return (or other written document) showing additional tax liability, the above 36-month period is restarted. (Code Sec. 6404(g); Reg § 301.6404-4)[34]

¶ 4855 When reasonable cause excuses civil penalties.

Certain civil penalties won't be imposed if the taxpayer's failure to perform the required act was due to reasonable cause—e.g., reliance on tax expert or IRS advice, irregularities in mail delivery, death or serious illness, unavoidable absence, casualty, disaster. The taxpayer generally has the burden of showing that the failure was due to reasonable cause and not willful neglect.[35]

No accuracy-related (¶4858 *et seq.*) or fraud (¶4865) penalty applies to any portion of an underpayment for which the taxpayer shows reasonable cause and good faith. (Code Sec. 6664(c)(1); Reg § 1.6664-4) The failure to disclose a reportable transaction (¶4749) is a strong indication of failure to act in good faith. (Reg § 1.6664-4(d))[36]

¶ 4856 Penalty for failure to file income, estate or gift tax returns when due (late-filing penalty); relief for certain taxpayers filing returns and statements for 2019 and 2020.

Under Code Sec. 6651(a)(1), the failure-to-file penalty is 5% of the amount of tax required to be shown on the return (less any earlier payments and credits) for the first month, plus an additional 5% for each month (or fraction of a month) the failure continues without reasonable cause (¶4855), but not more than 25%. (Code Sec. 6651(a)(1))[37]

The penalty for failure to file any income tax return within 60 days of the due date (including extensions) is the lesser of $485 (for returns required to be filed during 2023; $450 for 2022) or the amount required to be shown as tax on the return. (Code Sec. 6651(a) (last sentence); Code Sec. 6651(j))[38]

The Code Sec. 6651(a)(1) penalty is reduced (but not below the minimum) by the amount of any failure-to-pay penalty (0.5%, see ¶4857) for that month. (Code Sec. 6651(c)(1)) The 25% ceiling applies to each penalty before this reduction.[39] If the failure to file is fraudulent, the penalty increases to 15% per month (or fraction of month), up to a 75% cap. (Code

32. ¶V-1620 *et seq.*
33. ¶S-8502
34. ¶V-1401, ¶V-1601.2
35. ¶V-1776 *et seq.*, ¶V-2750 *et seq.*
36. ¶V-2060
37. ¶V-1750 *et seq.*
38. ¶V-1752
39. ¶V-1791

Sec. 6651(f))[40]

Penalties for late-filing certain tax returns, as well as penalties for not reporting certain required information on Form 1065 or Form 1120-S, are waived or abated if the relevant return was filed on or before Sept. 30, 2022. (Notice 2022-36, 2022-36 IRB 188) But individuals and households that reside or have a business in recently declared FEMA disaster areas have postponed deadlines (to either Nov. 15, 2022, or Feb. 15, 2023, depending on the location of the disaster area) to file the return to get this relief. (IR 2022-185, 10/19/2022)[41]

¶ 4857   Penalty for failure to pay tax.

Under Code Sec. 6651(a), a penalty is imposed on a taxpayer who, without reasonable cause (¶4855) fails to pay the tax shown on a return or an assessed deficiency of that tax by the prescribed date. The penalty is 0.5% of tax shown (or assessed) for each month (or fraction of a month) that it isn't paid (but not more than 25%). (Code Sec. 6651(a)(2), Code Sec. 6651(a)(3))[42] A substitute return prepared by IRS is a "return." (Code Sec. 6651(g)(2); Reg § 301.6020-1(b)(3))[43] The penalty is increased to 1% per month (or fraction of a month), up to 25% penalty maximum, if the tax isn't paid within ten days after IRS serves notice of levy. (Code Sec. 6651(d))[44] The penalty is reduced to 0.25% per month for individuals paying in installments. (Code Sec. 6651(h))[45] An individual who gets an automatic extension of time for *filing* is subject to the penalty (absent reasonable cause) if any additional payment due with the extended return *either*: (1) exceeds 10% of the total shown on Form 1040, *or* (2) isn't paid by the extended filing date. (Reg § 301.6651-1(c)(3))[46] If a subsequent event results in a decrease in the amount required to be shown on a return, the penalty will be computed using this lesser amount.[47]

¶ 4858   Accuracy-related penalty.

Under Code Sec. 6662(a) , Code Sec. 6662(b), and Code Sec. 6664(c)(1), an "accuracy-related" civil penalty applies if any portion of an understatement of tax on a tax return is due (absent reasonable cause, see ¶4855) to: negligence (¶4859), substantial income tax valuation misstatements (¶4860), income tax understatements (¶4861), estate or gift tax valuation understatements (¶4863), pension liability overstatements (¶4864), disallowance of benefits due to lack of economic substance (¶4878), overstatement of the Code Sec. 170(p) deduction (non-itemizers charitable deduction for 2021, ¶2100), or undisclosed foreign financial asset understatements (¶4862). (Code Sec. 6662(a), Code Sec. 6662(b), Code Sec. 6664(c)(1); Reg § 1.6662-2(a))[48] The accuracy-related penalty doesn't apply to any part of an underpayment for which the fraud penalty (¶4865) is imposed or to the part of any underpayment attributable to a reportable transaction understatement on which the Code Sec. 6662A reportable transaction understatement penalty is imposed, except: (i) for purposes of determining whether an underpayment is substantial or (ii) where the 40% gross valuation misstatement penalty applies. (Code Sec. 6662(b))[49] Also, it only applies if a return is filed by the taxpayer (not by IRS). (Code Sec. 6664(b); Reg § 1.6662-2(a))[50]

¶ 4859   "Negligence" for accuracy-related penalty.

Under Code Sec. 6662(a) and Code Sec. 6662(b), the "accuracy-related" penalty is imposed if any part of an underpayment is due either to negligence or to disregard of rules or regs but without intent to defraud. The penalty is 20% of the portion of the underpayment

40. ¶V-1753
41. ¶V-1750.1
42. ¶V-1671 *et seq.*
43. ¶V-1685
44. ¶V-1683
45. ¶V-1684
46. ¶V-1681
47. ¶V-1672
48. ¶V-2000 *et seq.*
49. ¶V-2002
50. ¶V-2051

attributable to the negligence, etc. (Code Sec. 6662(a), Code Sec. 6662(b)(1)) For rules common to all accuracy-related penalties, see ¶4858. "Negligence" includes failure to reasonably attempt to comply with the law or to exercise ordinary and reasonable care in preparing a return, as well as failure to keep adequate books and records or properly substantiate. "Disregard" includes any careless, reckless or intentional disregard. (Code Sec. 6662(c); Reg § 1.6662-3(b))[1] The penalties are not imposed for a position (other than for a reportable transaction) contrary to a published revenue ruling or a notice (other than proposed rulemaking), if the position has a realistic possibility of being sustained on its merits. (Reg § 1.6662-3(a)) The penalty for disregard of rules or regs isn't imposed where a position is contrary to a rule or reg if the position is disclosed and has a reasonable basis, the taxpayer keeps adequate books and records and substantiates items properly; and, for a position contrary to a reg, the position represents a good faith challenge to the reg. (Reg § 1.6662-3(c), Reg § 1.6662-7(c))[2]

¶ 4860   Misstating value or basis of property on income tax return—accuracy-related penalty.

Under Code Sec. 6662(a), Code Sec. 6662(b)(3), and Code Sec. 6662(e), the accuracy-related penalty is imposed on a taxpayer who makes any of these "substantial valuation misstatements":

. . . any value (or adjusted basis) claimed on an income tax return that is 150% or more of the correct figure (Code Sec. 6662(e)(1)(A));

. . . Code Sec. 482 transfer price adjustments where the price for any property (or its use) or services on an income tax return is 200% or more, or 50% or less, of the correct figure—transactional penalty (Code Sec. 6662(e)(1)(B)(i); Reg § 1.6662-6(b));

. . . a net increase in taxable income for a tax year (without regard to carryovers) resulting from all Code Sec. 482 adjustments in the transfer price of any property (or its use) or services, that (with certain adjustments) exceeds the lesser of $5 million or 10% of the taxpayer's gross receipts—net adjustment penalty. (Code Sec. 6662(e)(1)(B)(ii), Code Sec. 6662(e)(3); Reg § 1.6662-6(c))[3]

The penalty equals 20% of the portion of any income tax underpayment that results from the misstatement (except to the extent the fraud penalty is imposed) (Code Sec. 6662(a), Code Sec. 6662(b))—40% if the misstatement is gross (the above 200%, 150%, 50% and $5 million/10% figures are, respectively, 400%, 200%, 25% or $20 million/20%, or the correct value or basis is zero). (Code Sec. 6662(h); Reg § 1.6662-5(g))[4] The penalty doesn't apply unless the amount of the underpayment for the tax year attributable to all these misstatements for the year exceeds $5,000 ($10,000 for corporations other than S corporations or personal holding companies). (Code Sec. 6662(e)(2))[5] Reasonable cause (¶4855) excuses the penalty. There's no disclosure exception. (Code Sec. 6664(c)(1); Reg § 1.6662-5(a))[6] Strict appraisal requirements apply to overvalued charitable gifts. (Code Sec. 6664(c)(3))[7]

¶ 4861   Penalty on substantial understatements of income tax—accuracy-related penalty.

Under Code Sec. 6662(a) and Code Sec. 6662(b)(2), the 20% accuracy-related penalty is imposed on any portion of an underpayment of tax that (absent reasonable cause, see ¶4855) is attributable to any substantial understatement of income tax (or self-employment tax, see ¶3133 *et seq.*).[8] For rules common to all accuracy-related penalties, see ¶4858. For corporate taxpayers (other than S corporations and personal holding companies), an understatement is substantial if the amount of the understatement exceeds the

1. ¶V-2105
2. ¶V-2106 *et seq.*
3. ¶V-2200 *et seq.*
4. ¶V-2206 *et seq.*

5. ¶V-2205
6. ¶V-2234
7. ¶V-2237
8. ¶V-2150 *et seq.*

lesser of (1) 10% of the tax required to be shown on the return for that tax year (or $10,000, if that is greater), or (2) $10 million. For other taxpayers, an understatement is substantial if it exceeds the greater of $5,000 or 10% of the tax required to be shown on the return (5% if the deduction under Code Sec. 199A for qualified business income (¶1593 *et seq.*) is claimed). (Code Sec. 6662(d)(1); Reg § 1.6662-4(b)(1))[9] An understatement is the excess of (a) the tax amount required to be shown on the return, over (b) the tax amount that's shown (or withheld) reduced by any rebate. (Code Sec. 6662(d)(2)(A); Reg § 1.6662-4(b)(2), Reg § 1.6662-4(b)(3))[10] The understatement is reduced to the extent attributable to an item (other than tax shelter items, see below) for which: (a) there is or was substantial authority for how the taxpayer treated it (Code Sec. 6662(d)(2)(B)(i)), or (b) the relevant facts affecting the item's tax treatment are adequately disclosed on the return (IRS lists which items on the return qualify) or on a Form 8275 (Form 8275-R if the taxpayer's position is contrary to a reg) attached to the return *and* there's a reasonable basis (¶4859) for the taxpayer's treatment of the item. (Code Sec. 6662(d)(2)(B)(ii); Reg § 1.6662-4(f))[11]

Substantial authority exists only if the weight of the authorities supporting the treatment is substantial related to the weight of contrary authorities. (Reg § 1.6662-4(d)(3)(i))[12]

¶ 4862 Penalty on undisclosed foreign financial assets understatement.

Under Code Sec. 6662(j)(3), a 40% penalty is imposed on any understatement attributable to an undisclosed foreign financial asset. "Undisclosed foreign financial asset" includes all assets subject to information reporting requirements under Code Sec. 6038 (return of U.S. person who controls a foreign corporation or partnership), Code Sec. 6038B (return of U.S. person making "outbound" transfers to foreign entities), Code Sec. 6038D (self-reporting required for "specified foreign financial assets"), Code Sec. 6046A (return of U.S. person who acquires, disposes of, or has substantial changes in, foreign partnership interests), or Code Sec. 6048 (information reporting for foreign trusts) for which the required information wasn't provided by the taxpayer as required under the reporting rules. (Code Sec. 6662(j)(2)) An understatement is attributable to an undisclosed foreign financial asset if it's attributable to any transaction involving the asset. (Code Sec. 6662(j)(1))[13]

¶ 4863 Penalty for understating value of property on gift or estate tax return.

Under Code Sec. 6662(a), Code Sec. 6662(b)(5), and Code Sec. 6662(g)(1), if the value of any property claimed on any gift or estate tax return is 65% or less of the correct value, the 20% accuracy-related penalty (¶4858) is imposed on an underpayment attributable to that understatement. The penalty is increased to 40% for gross misstatements—i.e., the claimed value is 40% or less of the correct figure. (Code Sec. 6662(h)(1), Code Sec. 6662(h)(2)(C))[14] The penalty applies only if the portion of the underpayment attributable to all these undervaluations for the tax period exceeds $5,000. (Code Sec. 6662(g)(2))[15]

¶ 4864 Overstatement of pension liabilities—accuracy-related penalty.

Under Code Sec. 6662(a), Code Sec. 6662(b)(4), and Code Sec. 6662(f)(2), a taxpayer who (absent reasonable cause, see ¶4855) substantially overstates pension liabilities for a tax year is subject to the accuracy-related penalty (¶4858) if the overstatement results in an income tax underpayment of $1,000 or more.[16] The penalty equals 20% of the underpayment (40% for "gross" overstatements). (Code Sec. 6662(a), Code Sec. 6662(h)(1))[17] Pension liabilities are substantially overstated if the actuarial determination of the liabilities taken into account in computing the contribution deduction (¶4324) is at least 200% of the

---

9. ¶V-2159
10. ¶V-2154
11. ¶s V-2154, V-2167 et seq.
12. ¶V-2161, ¶V-2163
13. ¶V-2276

14. ¶s V-2251, V-2252
15. ¶V-2251
16. ¶V-2260 *et seq.*
17. ¶V-2262

correct amount. (Code Sec. 6662(f)(1)) The overstatement is "gross" if it's 400% or more of the correct figure. (Code Sec. 6662(h)(2)(B))[18]

¶ 4865   Civil fraud penalty.

Under Code Sec. 6663(a), fraudulent underpayment of tax required to be shown on a return results in a civil penalty of 75% of the portion of the underpayment attributable to fraud.[19] The fraud penalty can be imposed only if a return is filed (not by IRS). (Code Sec. 6664(b))[20] It won't be imposed where the taxpayer shows reasonable cause (¶4855) and good faith. (Code Sec. 6664(c)(1))[21] Imposition of the fraud penalty on any part of an underpayment precludes imposition of any of the accuracy-related penalties (¶4858) on that same part. (Code Sec. 6662(b))[22] If IRS establishes that any part of an underpayment is attributable to fraud, the entire underpayment is treated as attributable to fraud, except for any part the taxpayer establishes (by a preponderance of the evidence) isn't so attributable. (Code Sec. 6663(b))[23]

¶ 4866   Trust fund recovery penalty for responsible persons; IRS postponement of assessment where penalty affected by certain COVID-related tax benefits.

Under Code Sec. 6672, willful failure to collect or account for and pay over a tax or willful attempt to evade or defeat a tax, by a "responsible person" required to collect, account for, and pay over the tax carries a civil "trust fund recovery penalty" equal to 100% of the total tax evaded or not accounted for and paid over. IRS can't assess the penalty without notifying a responsible person of its intent to do so at least 60 days before making notice and demand for the penalty (unless collection is in jeopardy). (Code Sec. 6672(b)) A "responsible person" is an officer or employee of the corporation, or a partner or employee of a partnership, who is under a duty to perform the act at issue. (Code Sec. 6671(b))[24] A responsible person also includes any person who is connected or associated with an employer in such a manner that he or she has the power to see that the taxes are paid.[25] Unpaid volunteer board members of exempt organizations who aren't involved in day-to-day financial activities and don't know about the penalized failure are exempt from the penalty, unless that results in no one being liable for it. (Code Sec. 6672(e))[26] IRS must disclose, at the written request of a responsible person, the names of other responsible persons and collection activities against them. (Code Sec. 6103(e)(9))[27] Responsible persons who pay more than their proportionate share of tax have the right to recover the excess from other responsible persons. (Code Sec. 6672(d))[28]

Postponement of assessment in certain COVID-related cases. For certain affected payroll periods in 2020 and 2021, IRS is postponing assessment of the trust fund recovery penalty until **after Jan. 3, 2023,** in cases that are affected by: employer tax deferrals of payroll tax under Sec. 2302 of the CARES Act; deferral of the employee portion of payroll tax under Notice 2021-11 and Notice 2020-65; the employee retention credit under Sec. 2301(m)DivA, PL 116-136, 3/27/2020, as amended by Sec. 207(a)(1)DivEE, PL 116-260, 12/27/2020; and the credit for sick and family leave wages under Code Sec. 3131(a) and Code Sec. 3132(a). The postponement doesn't apply in cases of exigent circumstances, offers in compromise, or bankruptcy. (SBSE-05-0222-0015)[29]

---

18. ¶V-2263
19. ¶V-2300 *et seq.*
20. ¶V-2051
21. ¶V-2060
22. ¶V-2002
23. ¶V-2302

24. ¶V-1700 *et seq.*
25. ¶V-1704
26. ¶V-1703.1
27. ¶S-6313.1
28. ¶V-1730
29. ¶V-1724

¶ 4867   Penalty for refund claim that's for "excessive amount."

Under Code Sec. 6676(a), if a claim for refund or credit of income tax is for an "excessive amount," the claimant is liable for a penalty of 20% of the excessive amount. "Excessive amount" is the amount by which the claimed refund or credit exceeds the allowable amount. (Code Sec. 6676(b)) The penalty doesn't apply if it's shown that the claim for the excessive amount is due to a reasonable cause. (Code Sec. 6676(a)) But the reasonable cause exception doesn't apply to transactions that lack economic substance (¶4878). (Code Sec. 6676(c)) The penalty doesn't apply to any portion of the excessive amount that's subject to an accuracy-related penalty under Code Sec. 6662 (¶4858) or Code Sec. 6662A (¶4875) or a fraud penalty under Code Sec. 6663 (¶4865). (Code Sec. 6676(c))[30]

¶ 4868   Penalty for aiding and abetting understatement of tax liability.

Under Code Sec. 6701(a) and Code Sec. 6701(b), a penalty of $1,000 ($10,000 for a corporation)[31] is imposed on any person who aids or assists, procures or advises with respect to the preparation or presentation of any part of a return, affidavit, claim or other document connected with any matter arising under the internal revenue laws, and who knows (or has reason to believe) that the part will be used in connection with any material matter arising under those laws, and knows that an understatement of another person's tax would result from that use, even if there is no actual understatement.[32] The penalty applies whether or not the taxpayer knew of or gave consent to the understatement. (Code Sec. 6701(d))[33] The term "advises" includes the actions of lawyers and accountants who counsel a particular course of action[34] and appraisers who falsely or fraudulently overstate the value of property in a qualified appraisal (see ¶2137). (Reg § 1.170A-13(c)(3)(iii))[35]

observation: The aiding and abetting penalty applies regardless of whether a fee is charged by the adviser.

¶ 4869   Return preparer understatement penalties.

Under Code Sec. 6694(a)(1), if a tax return preparer prepares returns or refund claims for which any part of a tax liability understatement is due to an "unreasonable position," and the preparer knew or should have known of the position, the preparer must pay a penalty for each return or claim, equal to the greater of $1,000 or 50% of the income derived (or to be derived) by the preparer for the return or claim. If the position is for a reportable transaction (to which Code Sec. 6662A applies, ¶4875) or for a tax shelter, a position is unreasonable if it wasn't reasonable to believe that the position would more likely than not be sustained on its merits. In other cases, a position is unreasonable if (1) there wasn't substantial authority for it or (2) for a position that was disclosed in the return or in a statement attached to the return (under Code Sec. 6662(d)(2)(B)(ii)(I)), there was no reasonable basis for it. (Code Sec. 6694(a)(2); Reg § 1.6694-2(a)(1)) However, there's no penalty if it's shown that there was reasonable cause for the understatement and the preparer acted in good faith. (Code Sec. 6694(a)(3); Reg § 1.6694-2(e))

"Tax return preparer" means any person who is a tax return preparer under the rules at ¶4751. An individual is a tax return preparer if he or she is primarily responsible for the position on the return or claim for refund giving rise to an understatement. There's only one individual in a firm primarily responsible for each position on the return or refund claim giving rise to an understatement. If there's a signing preparer under the rules at ¶4751, he or she will generally be the person primarily responsible for the positions on the return or refund claim unless it's concluded that the signing tax return preparer isn't

---

30. ¶V-2291
31. ¶V-2352
32. ¶V-2351 *et seq.*

33. ¶V-2354
34. ¶V-2353
35. ¶V-2351

primarily responsible for the position. (Reg § 1.6694-1(b))[36]

A preparer who prepares returns or refund claims for which any part of a tax liability understatement is due to willful or reckless conduct must pay a penalty for each return or claim equal to the greater of (1) $5,000; or (2) 75% of the income derived (or to be derived) by the tax return preparer for preparing the return or claim. (Code Sec. 6694(b); Reg § 1.6694-3(a)) "Willful or reckless conduct" is conduct by the tax return preparer which is a willful attempt to understate the tax liability on the return or claim, or a reckless or intentional disregard of rules or regulations. (Code Sec. 6694(b)(2); Reg § 1.6694-3(b), Reg § 1.6694-3(c)) A penalty due to willful or reckless conduct in connection with a return or refund claim is reduced by the penalty paid due to an unreasonable position. (Code Sec. 6694(b)(3); Reg § 1.6694-3(f))[37]

IRS has provided lists of the documents covered by the above penalties.[38]

¶ 4870   Penalty for valuation misstatements attributable to incorrect appraisals.

Under Code Sec. 6695A(a), a penalty is imposed where: (A) a person prepares a property appraisal and knows, or reasonably should have known, that the appraisal would be used in connection with a return or a refund claim, and (B) the claimed property value on the return or refund claim based on the appraisal results in a substantial valuation misstatement under Code Sec. 6662(e), a gross valuation misstatement under Code Sec. 6662(h) (¶4860), or a substantial estate or gift tax valuation understatement under Code Sec. 6662(g).[39]

¶ 4871   Penalties on tax return preparers; failure to comply with rules; improper disclosure; injunctions.

For 2023, a return preparer is subject to inflation-adjusted civil penalties under Code Sec. 6695, as follows:

. . . $60 ($55 in 2022) for each failure to furnish completed copy of return to the taxpayer subject to a maximum penalty of $30,000 ($28,000 in 2022). (Code Sec. 6695(a))[40]

. . . $60 ($55 in 2022) for each failure to sign a return as required subject to a maximum penalty of $30,000 ($28,000 in 2022). (Code Sec. 6695(b))[41]

. . . $60 ($55 in 2022) for each failure to show his or her taxpayer ID number or preparer tax identification number as required subject to a maximum penalty of $30,000 ($28,000 in 2022). (Code Sec. 6695(c))[42]

. . . $60 ($55 in 2022) for each failure to retain a copy of a prepared return or to include it on a list of prepared returns subject to a maximum penalty of $30,000 ($28,000 in 2022). (Code Sec. 6695(d))[43]

. . . $60 ($55 in 2022) for each failure to file, or include a required item on, an information return mandated by Code Sec. 6060 (which requires that a record be made and maintained of the preparers employed or engaged during a return period) subject to a maximum penalty of $30,000 ($28,000 in 2022). (Code Sec. 6695(e))[44]

. . . $600 for 2023 ($560 in 2022), with no maximum, for each tax-related check issued to a taxpayer that the preparer endorses or otherwise negotiates, except where the preparer is a bank and deposits the check to the taxpayer's account in the bank. (Code Sec. 6695(f))[45]

. . . $600 for 2023 ($560 in 2022), with no maximum, for each failure to follow regulatory due diligence requirements in claiming the earned income credit, child tax credit, Hope

36. ¶V-2632 *et seq.*
37. ¶V-2630
38. ¶V-2631.3
39. ¶V-2691
40. ¶V-2674
41. ¶V-2673
42. ¶V-2677
43. ¶V-2675
44. ¶V-2676
45. ¶V-2671

Scholarship Credit, and eligibility for head-of-household filing status. To avoid the penalty, Form 8867 must be submitted with the return or refund claim claiming the credit. (Code Sec. 6695(g); Reg § 1.6695-2)[46]

Improper disclosure or use of information by return preparers is subject to a civil penalty of $250 for each improper disclosure or use ($10,000 maximum per calendar year), (Code Sec. 6713(a))[47] as well as a criminal penalty if the disclosure is done knowingly or recklessly. (Code Sec. 7216)[48] A bigger penalty applies where an improper disclosure or use is connected to identity theft: $1,000 for each improper disclosure or use ($50,000 maximum per calendar year). (Code Sec. 6713(b))[49] The criminal penalty is also enhanced for disclosures connected to identity theft. (Code Sec. 7216(a))[50] Regs provide exceptions to these penalties (Reg § 301.7216-1(a), Reg § 301.7216-2)[1] and additional exceptions where the taxpayer consents.

IRS may get a district court to enjoin a preparer from engaging in misconduct, but only if an injunction is appropriate to prevent recurrence. If a court finds that a preparer continually engaged in misconduct, and an injunction isn't enough to prevent interference with proper tax administration, it can enjoin him or her from practicing. (Code Sec. 7407)[2]

¶ 4872 Abusive tax shelter promoter penalties; injunctions.

Under Code Sec. 6700(a), a person who promotes an abusive tax shelter is subject to a penalty equal to the lesser of $1,000 or 100% of the gross income derived or to be derived from the activity. However, if an activity on which the penalty is imposed involves a false or fraudulent statement, the penalty equals 50% of the gross income derived or to be derived by that person from the activity.[3] IRS may seek an injunction to stop any action or failure to take action:

(1) that is subject to penalty under Code Sec. 6700, Code Sec. 6701 (aiding or abetting an understatement, see ¶4868), Code Sec. 6707 (failure to furnish information regarding reportable transactions, see ¶4876), and Code Sec. 6708 (failure to provide list of advisees with respect to reportable transactions, see ¶4873) or

(2) in violation of any requirement imposed by regs issued under Section 330 of Title 31 of the U.S. Code (rules regulating the practice of taxpayer representatives before the Department of the Treasury), i.e., the Circular 230 rules. (Code Sec. 7408)[4]

¶ 4873 Penalty for failure to provide reportable transaction advisee list.

Under Code Sec. 6708(a), any person required under Code Sec. 6112 to maintain a list of advisees for reportable transactions (see ¶4748), who fails to make that list available to IRS within 20 business days after IRS's written request, is liable for a $10,000-per-day penalty for each day of that failure after the 20th day. This penalty isn't imposed for any day that the failure is due to reasonable cause. In certain circumstances, IRS has the discretion to extend the 20-day production period. (Reg § 301.6708-1)[5]

¶ 4874 Penalty for failure to report reportable transactions.

Under Code Sec. 6707A(a), a penalty is imposed on any person who fails to include on any return or statement any information required to be disclosed under Code Sec. 6011 (¶4749) for a reportable transaction. (Code Sec. 6707A(a); Reg § 301.6707A-1(a)) The penalty is 75% of the "decrease in tax" shown on the return from the transaction (or which would have resulted if the transaction were respected) subject to a maximum of $10,000 for

46. ¶V-2677.1; ¶S-1106.1
47. ¶V-2678
48. ¶V-3308
49. ¶V-2678.1
50. ¶V-3308

1. ¶V-2678; ¶V-3309 *et seq.*
2. ¶V-2680 *et seq.*
3. ¶V-2403
4. ¶V-2451
5. ¶V-2503

natural persons and $50,000 for others (increased to $100,000 and $200,000 respectively if a listed transaction is involved). (Reg § 301.6707A-1(d)(1)(i)) The minimum penalty per transaction is $5,000 for natural persons and $10,000 for others. (Code Sec. 6707A(b)) The status of transactions as reportable/listed transactions is determined under regs under Code Sec. 6011. (Code Sec. 6707A(c); Reg § 1.6011-4(b))

IRS can rescind all or a portion of a Code Sec. 6707A penalty if (a) the violation relates to a reportable transaction that isn't a listed transaction and (b) rescission would promote compliance with the Code and effective tax administration. (Code Sec. 6707A(d)) Regs list factors considered in determining whether to grant rescission requests. (Reg § 301.6707A-1(d)) IRS procedures establish how to request rescission.[6]

¶ 4875   Penalty for reportable/listed transaction understatements.

Under Code Sec. 6662A(a), a 20% accuracy-related penalty applies for reportable transaction understatements. The penalty is increased to 30% for any portion of any reportable transaction understatement for which Code Sec. 6664(d)(3)(A) disclosure rules are not met. (Code Sec. 6662A(c)) A reportable transaction understatement is the sum of (1) the increase in taxable income resulting from a difference between (a) the proper tax treatment of an item subject to the penalty rules and (b) the taxpayer's treatment of the item (on the taxpayer's tax return), multiplied by the highest noncorporate rate (or corporate tax rate, in the case of a corporation), and (2) the amount of the decrease (if any) in the total amount of income tax credits which results from a difference between (a) the taxpayer's treatment of an item subject to the penalty rules (on the taxpayer's tax return) and (b) the proper tax treatment of the item. (Code Sec. 6662A(b)(1)) The penalty doesn't apply to any part of an understatement on which the 40% penalty for transactions that lack economic substance (¶4878) is imposed. (Code Sec. 6662A(e)(2)(B))[7] For this purpose, any reduction in the excess of deductions allowed in the tax year over gross income for the year, and any reduction in the amount of capital losses which would (without regard to the capital loss carryover rules) be allowed for the year, is treated as an increase in taxable income. (Code Sec. 6662A(b)(1))

An item is subject to the penalty rules if it's attributable to any listed transaction and any reportable transaction (other than a listed transaction) if a significant purpose of the transaction is federal income tax avoidance or evasion. (Code Sec. 6662A(b)(2)(B)) Listed and reportable transactions are defined under the Code Sec. 6707A penalty rules for reportable transactions for which disclosure is required (see ¶4874) (Code Sec. 6662A(d)) A limited reasonable cause exception applies if certain disclosure, substantial authority and reasonable belief requirements are met. (Code Sec. 6662A(d))[8] But this exception doesn't apply to any part of a reportable transaction understatement attributable to a transaction lacking economic substance under Code Sec. 7701(o) or failing to meet the requirements of any similar rule of law (¶4878). (Code Sec. 6664(d)(2))[9]

¶ 4876   Material advisor's penalty for not reporting reportable/listed transactions.

Under Code Sec. 6707(a)and Code Sec. 6707(b), a material advisor who fails to file a timely information return required under Code Sec. 6111(a) (¶4748), or who files a false or incomplete information return, for a reportable transaction (including a listed transaction) is subject to a penalty of $50,000 for each failure. If the failure relates to a listed transaction, the penalty increases to the greater of: (1) $200,000, or (2) 50% of the gross income received by the advisor that is attributable to aid, assistance, or advice provided for the listed transaction before the date the advisor files an information return including the transaction. If the reporting failure is intentional, the 50% of gross income penalty amount

---

6. ¶V-2531 *et seq.*
7. ¶V-2281

8. ¶V-2284
9. ¶V-2284

(item 2 above) is increased to 75% of gross income. Reportable and listed transactions are defined under Code Sec. 6707A(c) (see ¶4874). (Code Sec. 6707(d))

IRS can rescind all or a portion of a Code Sec. 6707 penalty under rules that are similar to the rescission rules that apply to taxpayers under Code Sec. 6707A (see ¶4874). (Code Sec. 6707(c); Reg § 301.6707-1)[10]

¶ 4877 Penalties for tax-exempts acting as tax shelter accommodation parties.

Under Code Sec. 6033(a)(2) and Code Sec. 6652(c)(3), with limited exceptions, a tax-exempt entity that is a party to a prohibited tax shelter transaction (see ¶4115) must disclose to IRS: (a) that the entity is a party to the prohibited tax shelter transaction; and (b) the identity of any other party to the transaction which is known to such tax-exempt entity. For 2023, the penalty for failure to comply is $120 per day, subject to a maximum of $60,000 for 2023. For 2022, the penalty for failing to comply is $110 per day, subject to a maximum of $56,000 for 2022.[11]

¶ 4878 Penalty for transaction lacking economic substance.

Under Code Sec. 6662(b)(6), a 20% penalty applies to an underpayment attributable to any disallowance of claimed tax benefits because of a transaction lacking economic substance (defined in Code Sec. 7701(o), see below), or failing to meet the requirements of any similar rule. The penalty is increased to 40% if the taxpayer doesn't adequately disclose the relevant facts affecting the tax treatment. (Code Sec. 6662(i)(1)) An amended return or supplement to a return is not taken into account if filed after the taxpayer has been contacted for audit or such other date as IRS specifies. (Code Sec. 6662(i)(3)) No reasonable cause and good faith exception applies. (Code Sec. 6664(c)(2)) This provision doesn't apply to personal transactions of individuals, only to transactions entered into in connection with a trade or business or an activity engaged in for the production of income. (Code Sec. 7701(o)(5)(B)) The penalty also doesn't apply to the part of an underpayment on which a fraud penalty is imposed (¶4865).[12]

Economic substance. A transaction is treated as having economic substance only if (apart from Federal income tax effects): (1) the transaction changes in a meaningful way the taxpayer's economic position, and (2) the taxpayer has a substantial purpose for entering into the transaction. (Code Sec. 7701(o)(1)) Any State or local income tax effect related to a Federal income tax effect is treated in the same manner as a Federal income tax effect. (Code Sec. 7701(o)(3)) A taxpayer may rely on factors other than profit potential to show that a transaction results in a meaningful change in the taxpayer's economic position or that the taxpayer has a substantial non-Federal-income-tax purpose for entering the transaction. Code Sec. 7701(o) doesn't require a minimum return that will meet the profit potential test. But, if a taxpayer relies on profit potential, the present value of the reasonably expected pre-tax profit must be substantial in relation to the present value of the expected net tax benefits that would be allowed if the transaction were respected ("the pre-tax profit to tax benefit ratio test"). (Code Sec. 7701(o)(2)(A)) IRS will continue to rely on relevant case law under the common-law economic substance doctrine in applying the two-prong conjunctive test at items (1) and (2) above.[13]

¶ 4879 Health-care-related penalties.

Employer mandate. An applicable large employer (i.e., one with at least 50 full-time, including full-time equivalent employees) must pay an assessable payment (the "employer shared responsibility payment"; "employer mandate") if at least one full-time employee has been certified to the employer as having purchased health insurance through a state

---

10. ¶V-2500 *et seq.*
11. ¶V-2535

12. ¶V-2271
13. ¶M-5901

exchange for which an applicable premium tax credit or cost-sharing reduction is allowed or paid to the employee, and the employer either (1) doesn't offer health care coverage for its full-time employees, or (2) offers minimum essential coverage that is unaffordable or does not provide minimum value. (Code Sec. 4980H)[14]

Regs clarify the application of these rules and certain nondiscrimination rules to health reimbursement arrangements (HRAs, see ¶1373) and other account-based group health plans integrated with individual health insurance coverage or Medicare (individual coverage HRAs). (Reg § 54.4980H-5)[15]

Employers (including applicable large employers) are subject to the Code Sec. 4980D excise tax if they maintain group health plans that don't satisfy detailed rules.[16] "Small employer health reimbursement arrangements" are exempt. (Code Sec. 9831(d)(1), Code Sec. 9831(d)(2))[17]

¶ 4880 Failure to file information returns and provide payee statements—penalties.

Under Code Sec. 6721 and Code Sec. 6722—subject to several exceptions, including reasonable cause—a payor who fails to timely file a required information return, furnish a payee statement (¶4337), or include all required information, or who provides incorrect information, is subject to penalties. The amount of the penalty depends on the time frame within which the failure is remedied. Where the taxpayer's average gross receipts for the most recent 3 tax years before the calendar year of the failure don't exceed $5 million, the annual maximum penalty is less.

For returns and statements required to be filed in 2023, for persons with average annual gross receipts for the most recent 3 tax years of more than $5 million, for failure to file correct information returns: (a) under Code Sec. 6721's general rule, $310 per return ($290 in 2022) subject to a $3,783,000 calendar-year maximum ($3,533,000 in 2022); (b) if corrected on or before 30 days after the required filing date under Code Sec. 6721(b)(1), $60 per return ($50 in 2022) subject to a $630,500 calendar-year maximum ($588,500 in 2022); and (c) if corrected after the 30th day but on or before Aug. 1 under Code Sec. 6721(b)(2), $120 per return ($110 in 2022) subject to a $1,891,500 calendar-year maximum ($1,766,500 in 2022).

For returns and statements required to be filed in 2023, for persons with average gross receipts for the most recent 3 tax years of $5 million or less, for failure to file correct information returns: (a) under Code Sec. 6721(d)(1)(A)'s general rule, $310 per return ($290 in 2022) subject to a $1,261,000 calendar-year maximum ($1,177,500 in 2022); (b) if corrected on or before 30 days after the required filing date under Code Sec. 6721(d)(1)(B), $60 per return ($50 in 2022) subject to a $220,500 calendar-year maximum ($206,000 in 2022); and (c) if corrected after the 30th day but on or before Aug. 1 under Code Sec. 6721(d)(1)(C), $120 per return ($110 in 2022) subject to a $630,500 calendar-year maximum ($588,500 in 2022).[18]

For 2023, for failure to file correct information returns due to intentional disregard: (a) under Code Sec. 6721(e)(2)(A), for a return other than under Code Sec. 6045(a), Code Sec. 6041A(b), Code Sec. 6050H, Code Sec. 6050I, Code Sec. 6050J, Code Sec. 6050K, and Code Sec. 6050L, the per-return penalty equals the greater of $630 ($580 in 2022) or 10% of the aggregate number of items required to be reported correctly, with no limit; (b) under Code Sec. 6721(e)(2)(B), for a return under Code Sec. 6045(a), Code Sec. 6050K, or Code Sec. 6050L, the per-return penalty equals the greater of $630 ($580 in 2022) or 5% of the aggregate number of items required to be reported correctly, with no limit; (c) under Code

---

14. ¶H-1170 *et seq.*
15. ¶H-1184.1
16. ¶H-1325.34

17. ¶H-1349.18 *et seq.*
18. ¶V-1803 *et seq.*

Sec. 6721(e)(2)(C), for a return under Code Sec. 6050I(a), the per-return penalty equals the greater of $31,520 or the amount of cash received, up to $126,000 ($29,440 and $117,500, respectively, for 2022); and (d) under Code Sec. 6721(e)(2)(D), for a return under Code Sec. 6050V, the per-return penalty equals the greater of (i) $630, or (ii) 10% of the value of the benefit of any contract for which information must be included on the return, with no limit.[19]

Definition of information return. The comprehensive list of "information returns" that are included for the penalty is contained in Code Sec. 6724(d)(1). (Code Sec. 6724(d)(1))[20]

Definition of payee statement. The term "payee statement," for purposes of the penalty, means any statement required to be furnished under a provisions enumerated in Code Sec. 6724(d)(2). (Code Sec. 6724(d)(2))[21]

¶ 4881 Miscellaneous civil penalties for information reporting, other items; relief for certain taxpayers filing returns and statements for 2019 and 2020.

Other civil penalties are provided for:

... failure to file information returns for dividend payments under $10 (Code Sec. 6652(a));[22]

... failure to file actuarial report of pension plan (¶4746) (Code Sec. 6652(e));[23]

... failure to file annual return for a pension plan (¶4746) (Code Sec. 6652(e));[24]

... failure to file annual return for an exempt organization or private foundation (¶4126) (Code Sec. 6652(c));[25]

... failure by split-interest trust to file an information return (Code Sec. 6652(c)(2)(C));[26]

... failure by an exempt organization to report excise tax on personal benefit contracts (Code Sec. 170(f)(10)(F)(iii));[27]

... failure by any person, under a duty to comply with Code Sec. 6104(d) requirements relating to public inspection of, and provision of copies of, exempt organization annual returns or exempt status application materials (Code Sec. 6652(c)(1)(C), Code Sec. 6652(c)(1)(D));[28]

... failure to file fringe benefit plan return (Code Sec. 6652(e));[29]

... failure to provide a written explanation to the recipient of a qualified rollover distribution (Code Sec. 6652(i));[30]

... failure to file notification of change of status of pension plan (Code Sec. 6652(d)(2));[31]

... failure to file registration statement of pension plan (¶4746) (Code Sec. 6652(d)(1)),[32] or to furnish correct statement to deferred compensation plan participants (Code Sec. 6690);[33]

... failure to provide notice of a transfer of qualified stock to a qualified employee as required by Code Sec. 83(i)(6) (Code Sec. 6652(i));[34]

... failure to file individual retirement account, simple retirement account reports, Archer MSA, HSA, CESA, and qualified tuition program, reports (Code Sec. 6693);[35]

... overstatement reported on return by IRA participant of the amount of designated nondeductible contributions (Code Sec. 6693(b));[36]

... failure to keep records for reporting on pension, annuity, etc., payments subject to

---

19. ¶V-1811 *et seq.*, V-1816 *et seq.*
20. ¶V-1804
21. ¶V-1815
22. ¶V-1841
23. ¶V-1971
24. ¶V-1971
25. ¶V-2722
26. ¶V-2726
27. ¶V-2728
28. ¶V-2727
29. ¶V-1973
30. ¶V-1984
31. ¶V-1971
32. ¶V-1971
33. ¶V-1972
34. ¶V-1989
35. ¶V-1974 *et seq.*
36. ¶V-1981

withholding (Code Sec. 6704(a));[37]

. . . failure by a corporation that issues qualified small business stock to make prescribed reports to IRS (Code Sec. 6652(k));[38]

. . . failure to provide notice to eligible employees with respect to small employer health reimbursement arrangements (Code Sec. 6652(o));[39]

. . . failure to file certain returns for foreign corporations, partnerships (Code Sec. 6679),[40] and trusts (Code Sec. 6677);[41]

. . . failure to file information returns in connection with foreign corporations and partnerships (¶4646) (Code Sec. 6038(b), Code Sec. 6038(c), Code Sec. 6038A(d), Code Sec. 6038B(c), Code Sec. 6038C(c);[42]

. . . failure to include tax information with passport or green card applications (Code Sec. 6039E(c));[43]

. . . failure to keep records, furnish information, or file domestic international sales corporation (DISC, ¶4604) or former foreign sales corporation (FSC) returns (Code Sec. 6686);[44]

. . . failure to meet FIRPTA reporting requirements (Code Sec. 6652(f));[45]

. . . failure to file notice of redetermination of certain foreign taxes (Code Sec. 6689);[46]

. . . failure to disclose a treaty-based position taken on a return that overrules or otherwise modifies the tax law (¶4625) (Code Sec. 6712);[47]

. . . failure by individual who loses U.S. citizenship or terminates U.S. residency (¶4639) to file expatriate information statement (Code Sec. 6039G(a));[48]

. . . failure by an exempt organization to disclose that information it is offering to sell or soliciting money for is available free from the federal government (Code Sec. 6711);[49]

. . . failure by an exempt organization to disclose that fund-raising solicitations are nondeductible as charitable contributions (¶4121) (Code Sec. 6710);[50]

. . . failure by an exempt organization to make the required disclosure for quid pro quo contributions of $75 or more (¶4121) (Code Sec. 6714);[1]

. . . willful failure to make available for inspection or provide copies of, a return or application for exemption of certain exempt organizations (Code Sec. 6685);[2]

. . . any repeated or willful and flagrant act or failure to act by any person who becomes liable for any excise tax on a private foundation by reason of the act or failure to act (Code Sec. 6684);[3]

. . . making a negligent or fraudulent misstatement in connection with the issuance of a mortgage credit certificate or failing to file the required report (¶4746) (Code Sec. 6709);[4]

. . . failure to file a partnership return (¶4731) (Code Sec. 6698);[5]

. . . failure to file an S corporation return (Code Sec. 6699);[6]

. . . failure to file returns with respect to qualified rental housing projects (Code Sec. 42(l)(2), Code Sec. 6652(j));[7]

. . . failure to deposit taxes (an IRS procedure explains how IRS applies deposits in determining the penalty when there is a shortfall) (Code Sec. 6656(a))[8] (including deposits required to be made by electronic funds transfer (EFT, see ¶3028);[9]

---

37. ¶V-1986
38. ¶V-1843
39. ¶V-1988
40. ¶V-1903
41. ¶V-1901
42. ¶V-1903; V-1931; V-1951; V-1961 *et seq.*
43. ¶V-1910
44. ¶V-1912
45. ¶V-1909
46. ¶V-1983
47. ¶V-1908
48. ¶V-1911

49. ¶V-2713
50. ¶V-2701
1. ¶V-2710
2. ¶V-2727
3. ¶V-2731
4. ¶V-1998
5. ¶V-1762 *et seq.*
6. ¶V-1763.3
7. ¶V-1996
8. ¶V-1650 *et seq.*; ¶V-1652
9. ¶V-1658

. . . use of any commercially acceptable instrument to pay taxes, if the amount isn't duly paid (Code Sec. 6657);[10]

. . . failure to pay stamp taxes (Code Sec. 6653);[11]

. . . claiming excessive gasoline tax rebates (Code Sec. 6675);[12]

. . . filing a frivolous income tax return or submitting a position identified as frivolous on IRS's list of frivolous positions (Code Sec. 6702);[13]

. . . use of Tax Court primarily for delay or where taxpayer's position is frivolous or groundless, he or she hasn't exhausted administrative remedies or has instituted a frivolous or groundless claim for damages against the U.S. (Code Sec. 6673);[14]

. . . failure to comply with a specified information reporting requirement, including providing taxpayer identification numbers (Code Sec. 6723; Reg § 301.6723-1(a));[15]

. . . failure to report tips (¶4746) (Code Sec. 6652(b));[16]

. . . failure by broker to provide back-up withholding notice (Code Sec. 6705);[17]

. . . failure to meet FBAR (FinCEN Report 114) reporting requirements on interests in foreign bank and financial accounts. (31 USCS 5321)[18]

. . . failure to file information return for change in control or recapitalization of corporation (¶4746) (Code Sec. 6652(l));[19] and

. . . making a false statement that results in reduced amounts of withholding (Code Sec. 6682),[20] or relates to the applicability of backup withholding. (Code Sec. 6682)[21]

Penalties for late-filing certain tax returns, as well as penalties for not reporting certain required information on Form 1065 or Form 1120-S, are waived or abated if the relevant return was filed on or before Sept. 30, 2022. (Notice 2022-36, 2022-36 IRB 188) But individuals and households that reside or have a business in recently declared FEMA disaster areas have postponed deadlines (to either Nov. 15, 2022, or Feb. 15, 2023, depending on the location of the disaster area) to file the return to get this relief. (IR 2022-185, 10/19/2022)[22]

¶ 4882 Damages for filing fraudulent information return.

Under Code Sec. 7434, if any person willfully files a fraudulent information return as to payments purported to be made to any other person, that other person may sue the filer for damages for the greater of (1) $5,000, or (2) actual damages plus costs, and, in the court's discretion, reasonable attorney's fees.[23]

¶ 4883 Criminal tax evasion.

Tax evasion (Code Sec. 7201) is a felony punishable by a fine of up to $100,000 ($500,000 for a corp.) and/or up to 5 years' imprisonment, plus costs of prosecution. The elements of the crime are willfulness, attempt to evade tax, and additional tax due.[24]

¶ 4884 Criminal penalties other than tax evasion.

Under Code Sec. 7206(2), any person who willfully aids or assists in, or procures, counsels or advises the preparation or presentation of a materially false or fraudulent return, affidavit, claim or other document, is subject to a criminal penalty of up to $100,000

---

10. ¶V-1687
11. ¶V-2732
12. ¶V-2736
13. ¶V-2551; ¶V-2571
14. ¶V-2601 *et seq.*
15. ¶V-1821 *et seq.*
16. ¶V-1745
17. ¶V-1842
18. ¶V-1813.4
19. ¶V-1845
20. ¶V-1741
21. ¶V-1743
22. ¶V-1750.1
23. ¶S-4470 *et seq.*
24. ¶V-4100 *et seq.*

($500,000 for a corporation) and/or up to three years' imprisonment, plus costs of prosecution.[25] Other criminal penalties (fines and/or imprisonment) are imposed for willful failure to: (1) file a return (Code Sec. 7203);[26] (2) pay a tax (Code Sec. 7203);[27] (3) collect or pay over a tax as required (Code Sec. 7202);[28] (4) keep proper records (Code Sec. 7203);[29] (5) supply tax information (Code Sec. 7203);[30] or (6) furnish a W-2 to employees in the manner, at the time or with the information required, or willful filing of a false or fraudulent W-2. (Code Sec. 7204)[31] Criminal penalties are also imposed for: willful filing of a false or fraudulent return (Code Sec. 7207);[32] failure to obey a summons (Code Sec. 7210);[33] and various other offenses.[34]

¶ 4885 Revocation or denial of passport—taxpayer with seriously delinquent tax debt.

Under Code Sec. 7345(a), if an individual is certified as having a seriously delinquent tax debt—i.e., an assessed tax liability, including interest and penalties, over $59,000 for 2023 (up from $55,000 for 2022), for which a notice of lien (for which administrative rights have been exhausted or have lapsed) has been filed, or for which a levy has been made—IRS must transmit the certification to the State Department for the denial, revocation, or limitation of that individual's passport. Exceptions from the certification process - e.g., for a debt being paid under an installment agreement or compromise agreement—are listed in Code Sec. 7345(b)(2).[35]

¶ 4886 Tax Collection, Overview.

IRS has broad tax collection powers, including seizure and sale of a taxpayer's property (Code Sec. 6331(a))—i.e., levy and distraint, ¶4887—and liens (Code Sec. 6321), ¶4893.

Before IRS can start administrative collection proceedings, it must, within 60 days after a tax has been assessed, send the taxpayer a notice of the amount assessed and a demand for payment. (Code Sec. 6303(a), Code Sec. 6331(a))[36] The taxpayer usually gets at least ten days from a date stated in the notice and demand, to pay the tax, unless IRS finds that collection is in jeopardy. (Code Sec. 6331(a); Reg § 301.6331-1(a)(3))[37] Taxpayers suffering undue hardship can get an extension of time for paying the assessed taxes.[38] IRS must send delinquent taxpayers a written notice of the amount of the delinquency at least annually. (Code Sec. 7524)[39]

For installment agreements, see ¶4722.

¶ 4887 Seizure and sale of taxpayer's property; exemptions; Collection Due Process (CDP) hearing (Form 12153)—IRS collection.

Under Code Sec. 6331, IRS can seize any property, other than specified exempt property, of a delinquent taxpayer, sell it, and apply the proceeds to pay the unpaid taxes.[40] The property seized may be real, personal, tangible, or intangible, including receivables, evidences of debt, securities (Code Sec. 6331(a)) and, to the extent they exceed a specified amount, present and future wages. (Reg § 301.6331-2(c)) There are exemptions for certain kinds of income (Code Sec. 6334(d)) and property (e.g., clothing, tools) (Code Sec. 6334(a)), and a complete exemption for a taxpayer's principal residence unless a judge or magistrate

25. ¶V-3113
26. ¶V-3002
27. ¶V-3001
28. ¶V-3017
29. ¶V-3007
30. ¶V-3008
31. ¶V-3013
32. ¶V-3120 *et seq.*
33. ¶V-3503
34. ¶V-3500 *et seq.*
35. ¶V-3507 *et seq.*
36. ¶s V-5003, V-5004
37. ¶V-5007
38. ¶V-5009
39. ¶V-5009.2
40. ¶V-5100 *et seq.*

approves the levy in writing. (Code Sec. 6334(a)(13)(B)) Levy is prohibited where an installment agreement is pending or in effect. (Code Sec. 6331(k); Reg § 301.6331-4) Regs enumerate various categories of exemptions. (Reg § 301.6334-1)[41][42]

A penalty (plus costs and interest) applies if the person fails or refuses to surrender the property. (Code Sec. 6332(d))[43]

Salary and wages and certain other payments are subject to continuous levy. (Code Sec. 6331(e); Code Sec. 6331(h)(1))[44] However, in an internal memo, IRS stated that it will exclude from such levies Social Security disability insurance payments.[45]

CDP hearing. Subject to exceptions, IRS may not levy against a person's property or property right unless it gives the person a notification in writing of his or her right to, and the opportunity for, a pre-levy CDP hearing with IRS. (Code Sec. 6330(a)(1); Reg § 301.6330-1(a)(1)) The exceptions relate to jeopardy levies (¶4817), levies to collect from state tax refunds, federal contractor levies, and persons subject to employment tax levies who made a previous recent hearing request as to unpaid employment taxes. (Code Sec. 6330(f)) The notice—the CDP Notice—must be given at least 30 days before the day of the first levy for the unpaid tax for the tax period. (Code Sec. 6330(a)(2)) A person who receives a CDP Notice may request a hearing (use Form 12153) with the IRS Office of Appeals within the 30-day period beginning on the day after the date of the CDP Notice. (Code Sec. 6330(b)(1); Reg § 301.6330-1(b)(1), Reg § 301.6330-1(c)(1)) A person who requests a CDP hearing can, within 30 days of the date it was made, appeal the hearing's determination. (Code Sec. 6330(d); Reg § 301.6330-1(f)) The Tax Court has sole jurisdiction over all CDP appeals. (Code Sec. 6330(d)(1)) IRS can disregard frivolous requests for a CDP hearing. (Code Sec. 6330(g))[46]

¶ 4888   Wrongful seizures—IRS collection.

Under Code Sec. 6343(b), if IRS wrongfully levies on property, it may, on written request, return the specific property seized (or the proceeds from its sale) or the amount of money levied on (Code Sec. 6343(b)), with interest (Code Sec. 6343(c)). IRS may also return (without interest) property, including money deposited in the Treasury, that has been levied on if IRS determines that: (1) the levy was premature or otherwise not in accordance with its administrative procedures (Code Sec. 6343(d)(2)(A)); (2) the taxpayer has agreed to pay off the underlying tax liability in installments, unless the agreement provides otherwise (Code Sec. 6343(d)(2)(B)); (3) the return of the property will make collection of the underlying tax liability easier (Code Sec. 6343(d)(2)(C)); or (4) the return of the property is in the taxpayer's best interests, as determined by the National Taxpayer Advocate (¶4808), and IRS, and the taxpayer or the National Taxpayer Advocate consent. (Code Sec. 6343(d)(2)(D); Reg § 301.6343-3)[47]

An amount equal to the money levied on or the money received from a sale of the property may be returned within two years from the date of the levy. (Code Sec. 6343(b))[48]

For treatment of returned wrongfully levied retirement plan assets, see ¶4350.

¶ 4889   Third-party remedies for wrongful seizures of property—tax collection.

Under Code Sec. 7426, if IRS wrongfully seizes property of a person other than the taxpayer, the third party may sue for its return (or the sale proceeds, if it has been sold) (Code Sec. 7426), but must start the suit within two years of the levy. (Code Sec. 6532(c)(1)) The Supreme Court held that Code Sec. 7426(a)(1) is the exclusive remedy for third-party levy claims.[49] The third party may also recover damages (subject to limits,

41. ¶V-5200 *et seq.*
42. ¶V-5231 *et seq.*
43. ¶V-5116
44. ¶V-5214, ¶V-5216
45. ¶V-5217

46. ¶V-5271 *et seq.*
47. ¶V-5136, ¶V-5137
48. ¶V-5127
49. ¶V-5120, ¶V-5126

see ¶4890) if the action results in a finding that any IRS officer or employee recklessly, intentionally, or negligently disregarded any Code or reg provision. (Code Sec. 7426(h)) Regs spell out procedures for claiming damages. (Reg § 301.7426-2)[50] The owner (or heirs, etc.) of any realty sold to satisfy a tax liability can redeem the property at any time within 180 days after the sale. (Code Sec. 6337(b)(1))[1]

¶ 4890 Damages for unauthorized IRS collection.

Under Code Sec. 7433(b), if any IRS officer or employee recklessly, intentionally or negligently disregards a Code or reg in connection with collection of tax, the taxpayer may bring a civil suit for damages against the U.S. in a district court. Damages are limited to the lesser of (1) $1 million ($100,000 for negligence) or (2) the actual, direct economic damages sustained plus the costs of the action. (Code Sec. 7433(b); Reg § 301.7433-1)[2] A taxpayer may petition a bankruptcy court for damages (subject to the above limits) if, in connection with any collection of tax, an IRS officer or employee willfully violates any provision of 11 USC 362 (automatic stay when a debtor files for bankruptcy) or 11 USC 524 (effect of a bankruptcy discharge as an injunction against commencement or continuation of actions to collect a discharged debt as a personal liability of the debtor). (Code Sec. 7433(e); Reg § 301.7433-2)[3]

¶ 4891 Period within which IRS must begin collection.

Under Code Sec. 6502(a), IRS must generally start distraint or court proceedings within ten years after assessment (Code Sec. 6502(a)). But if no return is filed, a collection suit may be brought at any time, without assessment. (Code Sec. 6501(c)(3))[4] The collection period may be extended in connection with installment agreements (Code Sec. 6502(a); Reg § 301.6502-1)[5] or suspended under various circumstances. (Code Sec. 6330(e)(1); Reg § 301.6330-1(g))[6]

¶ 4892 Suits for injunctions against tax collection.

Under Code Sec. 7421(a), injunctions against collection of taxes are generally barred. But exceptions apply, e.g., during the period allowed to file a Tax Court petition or, where a petition has been filed, before the Tax Court's decision becomes final, and where an individual other than the taxpayer sues to recover property wrongfully seized and in other cases. (Code Sec. 7421(a))[7]

¶ 4893 Federal tax liens; notice; Collection Due Process (CDP) hearing—IRS collection.

Federal tax liens (Code Sec. 6321) are claims against a taxpayer's property for payment of delinquent taxes (including any interest, additional amounts, additions to tax, assessable penalties, or accrued costs).[8] There are various federal tax liens, including:

. . . general tax lien, which applies to all property, both real and personal, tangible and intangible including a tenancy by the entirety and an heir's interest in an estate even though he or she later attempts to disclaim it (Code Sec. 6321; Reg § 301.6321-1);[9]

. . . gift tax lien (Code Sec. 6324(b); Reg § 301.6324-1(b));[10]

. . . estate tax lien (Code Sec. 6324(a); Reg § 301.6324-1(a));[11]

---

50. ¶V-5135
1. ¶V-5424
2. ¶V-5800 *et seq.*
3. ¶V-5820
4. ¶V-5600 *et seq.*
5. ¶V-5604 *et seq.*
6. ¶V-5277
7. ¶V-5701
8. ¶V-5900 *et seq.*
9. ¶V-5902 *et seq.*
10. ¶V-6042
11. ¶V-6044

. . . special lien for deferred estate tax attributable to a farm or other closely held business (Code Sec. 6324A; Reg § 20.6324A-1, Reg § 301.6324A-1);[12]

. . . special lien for recapture of estate tax attributable to special use valuation of a farm or closely held business (Code Sec. 6324B; Reg § 20.6324B-1);[13]

. . . generation-skipping transfer tax lien. (Code Sec. 2661; Reg § 26.2662-1(f))[14]

IRS must give written notice of its filing of a notice of lien (NFTL), to the person whose property is to be subject to the lien, not more than five days after it files the notice of lien. (Code Sec. 6320(a); Reg § 301.6320-1(a))[15] IRS must hold a Collection Due Process hearing with respect to the filing if the taxpayer timely requests one (use Form 12153). (Code Sec. 6320(b)(1); Reg § 301.6320-1(b)) But IRS can disregard frivolous requests for a hearing before a lien is filed. (Code Sec. 6320(c))[16] Regs explain how a request for a withdrawal of a federal tax lien is made. (Reg § 301.6323(j)-1)[17]

¶ 4894　Priority of tax liens—IRS collection.

Priority of tax liens (Code Sec. 6323(a)) is governed by federal, not state, law.[18] The general rule is that a lien first in time is first in right.[19] But a tax lien is subordinated to certain later liens that arise before notice of the tax lien (Form 668) is filed. This protects judgment lien creditors, mechanic's lienors, and certain qualifying purchasers and holders of security interests. (Code Sec. 6323(a); Reg § 301.6323(a)-1)[20] Another exception protects certain interests arising even after the notice of the tax lien was filed, e.g., attorney's liens and certain security interests. (Code Sec. 6323(b); Reg § 301.6323(b)-1)[21]

The special gift and estate tax liens don't have to be filed to be superior to claims arising after the special lien arises. But certain later purchasers and creditors are protected. (Code Sec. 6324A(d)(3), Code Sec. 6324B(c)(1))[22]

IRS may withdraw a notice of lien if it was filed prematurely or otherwise not in accordance with its administrative procedures, and for certain other reasons. (Code Sec. 6323(j)(1)) At the taxpayer's request, IRS must make reasonable efforts to notify credit reporting agencies and creditors specified by the taxpayer of the withdrawal of the notice. (Code Sec. 6323(j)(2))[23]

¶ 4895　Taxes in bankruptcy or receivership proceedings—IRS collection.

Under Code Sec. 6036, a receiver in a receivership proceeding must give IRS notice of the receivership. (Code Sec. 6036) (Use Form 56) But a bankruptcy trustee, debtor-in-possession, or other like fiduciary in a bankruptcy proceeding needn't give notice (Reg § 301.6036-1(a)(1)(i)) because notice under the Bankruptcy Rules is sufficient.[24] The filing of a federal bankruptcy petition (but not the start of a state receivership proceeding) automatically stays any Tax Court proceedings against the taxpayer-debtor.[25] The running of the assessment statute of limitations is suspended from the date a bankruptcy or receivership proceeding is instituted until 30 days after IRS has received notice of the proceeding, but the suspension may not exceed two years. (Code Sec. 6872; Reg § 301.6872-1)[26]

Although a taxpayer's bankruptcy triggers an immediate assessment (see ¶4817) collection of the tax is stayed while the taxpayer-debtor's assets are under the control of a court in bankruptcy or receivership proceedings.[27] There is no general bar to discharge of taxes

12. ¶V-6046
13. ¶V-6051
14. ¶V-6053
15. ¶V-6001
16. ¶V-6005
17. ¶V-6134
18. ¶V-6324
19. ¶V-6301

20. ¶V-6400 *et seq.*
21. ¶V-6426
22. ¶s V-6455, V-6456
23. ¶V-6134
24. ¶S-4103
25. ¶U-1220
26. ¶T-4323.1
27. ¶V-7301 *et seq.*

in bankruptcy, but there are broad rules barring discharge of taxes in certain circumstances.[28]

¶ 4896 Transferee's liability for transferor's unpaid taxes—IRS collection.

A transferee is liable for a taxpayer-transferor's unpaid taxes (and interest and penalties) where: (1) the transfer is void or voidable under rules of equity,[29] (2) transferee liability is imposed by statute,[30] or (3) transferee liability arises under contract.[31] Transferees include a donee, heir, legatee, devisee or distributee of a decedent's estate, a shareholder of a dissolved corporation, the assignee or donee of an insolvent person, certain fiduciaries, a successor in a tax-free corporate reorganization, and various other classes of distributees. (Code Sec. 6901(h); Reg § 301.6901-1(b))[32] IRS must assess the (first) transferee within one year after the limitations period against the transferor has run. (Code Sec. 6901(c)(1))[33][34]

¶ 4897 Early discharge of executor's personal liability; Form 5495—IRS collection.

Under Code Sec. 2204(a), an executor or administrator can be discharged from personal liability for estate tax as early as nine months after the estate tax return is due (or filed, if later) if he or she makes a written request to IRS to determine the estate tax liability, and any tax determined to be due is paid (or a bond is posted if the payment period was extended). (Code Sec. 2204(a))[35] A trustee or other fiduciary can get a similar discharge. (Code Sec. 2204(b))[36] An executor or administrator can also request (on Form 5495) early discharge from personal liability for a decedent's income and gift taxes. (Code Sec. 6905(a))[37]

---

28. ¶V-7360 *et seq.*
29. ¶s V-9100 *et seq.*, V-9200 *et seq.*
30. ¶V-9300 *et seq.*
31. ¶V-9400 *et seq.*
32. ¶V-9001

33. ¶V-9801
34.
35. ¶s T-4511, T-4512
36. ¶T-4513
37. ¶T-4518

Chapter 26   Estate, Gift and Generation-Skipping Transfer Taxes

¶ 5000   Estate Tax, Overview. ▬▬▬▬▬▬▬▬▬▬▬▬▬▬▬▬▬▬

The federal estate tax (Code Sec. 2001) is imposed on the transfer of an individual's property at death and on other transfers considered to be the equivalent of transfers at death. The tax is imposed on the "taxable estate" (¶5018), which is the value of the total property transferred or considered transferred at death (the "gross estate"), reduced by various deductions. The tax is computed (¶5034) under a unified rate schedule under which lifetime taxable gifts and transfers at death are taxed on a cumulative basis.

The maximum estate and gift tax rate, and, the generation-skipping transfer (GST) tax rate, is 40%. (Code Sec. 2001(c); ¶1114) The basic exclusion amount is $10 million, as indexed for inflation. (Code Sec. 2010(c)(3)) The basic exclusion amount for gifts and estates, and the exemption amount for generation-skipping transfers, is $12,060,000 for gifts made and decedents dying in 2022 ($12,920,000 for 2023, see ¶5028).

In determining the tax on estates of individuals who at death were citizens or residents of the U.S., the entire estate is considered. (Code Sec. 2033; Reg § 20.0-2(b)(1))[1] For nonresident aliens, see ¶5039.

¶ 5001   Property owned by decedent—gross estate for estate tax.

Under Code Sec. 2033, the gross estate of a decedent who was a U.S. citizen or resident at the time of death includes the value of all property in which the decedent had an interest at the time of death, to the extent of the interest beneficially owned by the decedent. (Code Sec. 2033; Reg § 20.2033-1(a))[2]

The gross estate of a nonresident alien includes property "situated in the U.S." (see ¶5039).

¶ 5002   Gifts within 3 years of death—Form 706, Schedule G—gross estate for estate tax.

Under Code Sec. 2035, an individual who transferred an interest in, or relinquished a power over, any property within three years of death must include the value of the property in the gross estate (on Form 706, Schedule G) to the extent it would have been included in the gross estate under Code Sec. 2036 (transfers with retained life estate, etc., ¶5004), Code Sec. 2037 (transfers taking effect at death, ¶5006), Code Sec. 2038 (revocable transfers, ¶5007), or Code Sec. 2042 (life insurance proceeds, ¶5014), if the interest or relinquished power had been retained. (Code Sec. 2035(a))[3] This rule doesn't apply to any bona fide sale for full and adequate consideration. (Code Sec. 2035(d))

¶ 5003   Gift tax "gross-up" (gift tax paid by decedent)—Form 706, Schedule G—gross estate for estate tax.

Under Code Sec. 2035(b), gift tax paid by the decedent, the decedent's estate or the decedent's donees, on gifts made by decedent or his or her spouse within three years of decedent's death—including, according to the Ninth Circuit and Tax Court, deemed gifts under Code Sec. 2519 (¶5050)—is included in the gross estate (on Form 706, Schedule G).

---

1. ¶R-1010 *et seq.*, ¶R-2000 *et seq.*   3. ¶R-2201 *et seq.*
2. ¶R-2001

References beginning with a single letter are to paragraphs in Federal Tax Coordinator 2d and RIA's Analysis of Federal Taxes: Income.

But, gift tax paid by the spouse on the spouse's share of decedent's gifts under the gift-splitting rules isn't included. (Code Sec. 2035(b))[4] The gift tax gross-up rule does not apply to the payment of a gift tax by a nonresident alien within three years of death.[5]

¶ 5004 Retained rights in transferred property—Form 706, Schedule G—gross estate for estate tax.

Under Code Sec. 2036(a), a decedent's gross estate includes transfers under which he or she retained the possession or enjoyment of, or the right to the income from, the transferred property (on Form 706, Schedule G). (Code Sec. 2036(a)(1); Reg § 20.2036-1)[6]

The decedent's gross estate also includes transfers where he or she retained the right to designate the person(s) to possess or enjoy the transferred property or its income. (Code Sec. 2036(a)(2))[7]

These rules don't apply to any bona fide sale for full and adequate consideration. (Code Sec. 2036(a))

A decedent who transfers property during life to a trust and retains the right to an annuity, unitrust, or other income payment from, or retains the use of an asset in, the trust has retained the right to income from all or a specific portion of the property transferred. The includible amount is that portion of the trust corpus, valued as of the decedent's death (or the alternate valuation date, if applicable) necessary to yield that annual payment (or use) applying the appropriate Code Sec. 7520 interest rate in effect on the date of death (or alternate valuation date). The regs also provide guidance on the portion of trust property includible in the grantor's gross estate where the grantor has a "graduated retained interest." (Reg § 20.2036-1(c)(2))[8]

¶ 5005 Retained voting rights in stock of controlled corporation—Form 706, Schedule G—gross estate for estate tax.

Under Code Sec. 2036(b), retention of voting rights in stock of a controlled corporation is a retention of the enjoyment of the transferred stock. The value of the transferred stock is included in the decedent's gross estate (on Form 706, Schedule G). (Code Sec. 2036(b))[9]

¶ 5006 Transfers taking effect at death—Form 706, Schedule G—gross estate for estate tax.

Under Code Sec. 2037, if a decedent transfers property during life, but the transferee can't possess or enjoy the property except by surviving the decedent, and the decedent retained a significant reversionary interest (exceeding 5% of the value of the transferred property immediately before the decedent's death), then the property is includible in decedent's gross estate (on Form 706, Schedule G). This rule doesn't apply to bona fide sales for full and adequate consideration. (Code Sec. 2037)[10]

¶ 5007 Revocable transfers—Form 706, Schedule G—gross estate for estate tax.

Under Code Sec. 2038(a), the decedent's gross estate includes (on Form 706, Schedule G) lifetime transfers if the enjoyment of the transferred property was subject at death to any change through the exercise by the decedent of a power to alter, amend, revoke or

---

4. ¶R-2210 *et seq.*
5. ¶R-8006
6. ¶R-2400 *et seq.*
7. ¶R-2450

8. ¶R-2408.1
9. ¶R-2436
10. ¶R-2500 *et seq.*

terminate. This includes any power affecting the time or manner of enjoyment of property or its income. (Code Sec. 2038(a)(1)) This rule doesn't apply to any bona fide sale for full and adequate consideration.[11]

Includible revocable transfers include savings bank (Totten) trusts that are revocable in form,[12] and custodial accounts where the donor is custodian.[13]

¶ 5008 Qualified terminable interest property (QTIP)—inclusion in estate for estate tax.

Under Code Sec. 2044, qualified terminable interest property (QTIP) for which the estate tax (¶5023) or gift tax (¶5050) marital deduction was elected is includible in the estate of the donee spouse at its then fair market value unless the donee disposed of any part of the qualifying income interest for life. (Code Sec. 2044) The property is treated as passing from the surviving spouse. (Code Sec. 2044(c))[14]

The surviving spouse's executor may recover the estate taxes caused by the inclusion from the persons to whom the property passes at the surviving spouse's death, unless the surviving spouse's will specifically indicates an intent to waive the right of recovery. (Code Sec. 2207A(a))[15]

¶ 5009 Powers of appointment—Form 706, Schedule H—gross estate for estate tax.

Under Code Sec. 2041(a), if the decedent possessed a general power of appointment (created after Oct. 21, '42) at the time of death, the property subject to the power is included in the gross estate (on Form 706, Schedule H). (Code Sec. 2041(a))[16] A "general" power is one exercisable in favor of the decedent, the decedent's estate, the decedent's creditors, or the creditors of the decedent's estate. (Code Sec. 2041(b)(1))[17]

¶ 5010 Jointly held property—Form 706, Schedule E—gross estate for estate tax.

Under Code Sec. 2040, the gross estate includes the value of property held jointly with right of survivorship by the decedent and another person. The amount included depends on how the property was acquired and, if owned jointly by individuals who created the joint ownership, whether the "consideration furnished" test, or the spouses' joint property rule, applies. (Code Sec. 2040)[18]

Joint ownership acquired through gift, bequest, devise, or inheritance from another. The decedent's fractional share of the property is included in the gross estate (on Form 706, Schedule E). (Reg § 20.2040-1(a)(1))[19]

Joint ownership created by co-owners. Except for spouse tenancies (¶5011), the *entire* value of the property is included in the co-owner's gross estate except the part, if any, attributable to the consideration in money or money's worth furnished by the other joint owner(s). Consideration furnished by the surviving joint owner(s) doesn't include money or property acquired from the decedent for less than full and adequate consideration in money or money's worth. (Reg § 20.2040-1(a)(2))[20]

Tenancy in common. Only the value of decedent's undivided share of the property is

11. ¶R-2600 *et seq.*
12. ¶R-2621
13. ¶R-2620
14. ¶R-2900 *et seq.*
15. ¶R-6439 *et seq.*
16. ¶R-3000 *et seq.*
17. ¶R-3006
18. ¶R-2705
19. ¶s R-2705, R-2709
20. ¶R-2700 *et seq.*

included in the gross estate.[21]

¶ 5011 Spouses' jointly held property—Form 706, Schedule E—gross estate for estate tax.

Under Code Sec. 2040(b), if an interest in property created after 1976 is held by a decedent and spouse as tenants by the entirety or joint tenants with right of survivorship (if decedent and spouse are the only joint tenants), one-half of the value of the jointly owned interest is included in the estate of the decedent spouse regardless of which spouse furnished the original consideration (on Form 706, Schedule E). (Code Sec. 2040(b)) Where the surviving spouse isn't a U.S. citizen, this rule applies only if the property passes in a qualified domestic trust (QDOT, ¶5026). (Code Sec. 2056(d)(1)(B), Code Sec. 2056(d)(2))[22]

¶ 5012 Community property—gross estate for estate tax.

The value of the interest in community property vested in the decedent by state law—ordinarily, half of the community property—is included in the decedent spouse's estate.[23]

¶ 5013 Annuities—Form 706, Schedule I—gross estate for estate tax.

Under Code Sec. 2039(a), the value of an annuity or other payment receivable by a beneficiary is included in the decedent's gross estate (on Form 706, Schedule I) if, under the contract or agreement, either:

(1) an annuity or other payment was payable to decedent, either alone or with another person(s), for decedent's life or for any period not ascertainable without reference to the decedent's death or for any period that doesn't in fact end before death; or

(2) the decedent possessed, for one of the periods in (1), above, the right to receive such an annuity or other payment, either alone or with another. (Code Sec. 2039(a))

The amount included is an amount proportionate to the part of the purchase price contributed by the decedent. Contributions made by an employer are considered made by the employee if made by reason of employment. (Code Sec. 2039(b))[24]

¶ 5014 Life insurance—Form 706, Schedule D—gross estate for estate tax.

Under Code Sec. 2042(1), proceeds of insurance on the decedent's life receivable by the executor or administrator, or payable to the decedent's estate, are includible in the gross estate (on Form 706, Schedule D). (Code Sec. 2042(1)) The estate needn't be specifically named as the beneficiary. (Reg § 20.2042-1(b)(1))[25]

Proceeds of insurance on the decedent's life not receivable by or for the benefit of the estate are includible if the decedent possessed at death or transferred within three years of death any incidents of ownership in the policy, exercisable either alone or with any other person. (Code Sec. 2042(2)) "Incidents of ownership" include the power to change the beneficiary, to revoke an assignment, to pledge the policy for a loan, etc. (Reg § 20.2042-1(c)(2)), and certain reversionary interests. (Reg § 20.2042-1(c)(3))[26]

¶ 5015 Group term life insurance—Form 706, Schedule D—gross estate for estate tax.

Under Code Sec. 2042, an employee can prevent inclusion in his or her estate (under the

21. ¶R-2707
22. ¶R-2724 *et seq.*
23. ¶R-2800 *et seq.*

24. ¶R-4401 *et seq.*
25. ¶R-4002 *et seq.*
26. ¶R-4006 *et seq.*

rule at ¶5014, on Form 706, Schedule D) of the proceeds of group term life insurance furnished by the employer by transferring the insurance before death, if: (1) the group policy and applicable state law permit the employee to make an absolute assignment of all the employee's incidents of ownership, and (2) the employee irrevocably assigns all policy rights.[27]

¶ 5016 Value of property included in gross estate; alternate valuation date; qualified conservation easements—estate tax.

Under Code Sec. 2031, the value of property included in the gross estate is the fair market value (FMV) of the property at the date of the decedent's death (or at the alternate valuation date, see below). (Code Sec. 2031; Reg § 20.2031-1)[28]

Regs provide rules for valuing specific types of properties, including: stocks and bonds (Reg § 20.2031-2); business interests (Reg § 20.2031-3); notes (Reg § 20.2031-4); household and personal effects (Reg § 20.2031-6); and life insurance and annuity contracts. (Reg § 20.2031-8)

An executor may elect (on Form 706, Schedule U) to exclude from the gross estate up to 40% of the value of land subject to a qualified conservation easement meeting certain requirements and subject to a dollar cap of $500,000. (Code Sec. 2031(c))[29]

The FMV of annuities (other than commercial annuities), life estates, term of years, remainders, and reversions is determined under IRS tables, which include an interest rate component and, if applicable, a mortality component. The interest rate component changes monthly and this can affect planning strategies (e.g., lower interest rates favor private annuities and GRATs, ¶5056).

The executor can elect (irrevocably, on Form 706) to use an alternate valuation date rather than the decedent's date of death to value the property included in the gross estate. This alternate date is generally six months after decedent's death or earlier date of sale or distribution. (Code Sec. 2032(a))[30] Alternate valuation can be elected only if its use decreases both the value of the gross estate and the combined estate and GST tax liability. (Code Sec. 2032(c); Reg § 20.2032-1(b)(1))[31]

¶ 5017 Special-use valuation of farm or other business real property—Form 706, Schedule A-1—estate tax.

Under Code Sec. 2032A, if certain conditions are met, an executor may elect (irrevocably, on Form 706, Schedule A-1) to value qualified real property used for farming purposes or in a trade or business on the basis of the property's value for its actual use, rather than on its highest and best use. The total decrease in the value of all real property under this election may not exceed $1,230,000 for individuals dying in 2022 ($1,310,000 for individuals dying in 2023). (Code Sec. 2032A)[32]

One condition for electing special use valuation is that at least 25% of the adjusted value of the gross estate must consist of the adjusted value of real property meeting certain requirements. Under Reg § 20.2032A-8(a)(2), special use valuation may be elected for less than all of an estate's qualified real property, if the partial election covers enough property to satisfy the at-least-25% rule. But a district court held this reg invalid to the extent it bars a partial special use valuation election covering less than 25% of the adjusted value of the gross estate.[33]

27. ¶R-4033
28. ¶R-1006
29. ¶R-4700 *et seq.*
30. ¶R-5002
31. ¶R-5001
32. ¶R-5200 *et seq.*
33. ¶R-5256

The resulting estate tax savings from special use valuation may be recaptured (use Form 706-A) under certain conditions. (Code Sec. 2032A(c))[34]

¶ 5018   Computing the taxable estate; deductions—estate tax.

Under Code Sec. 2053(a), the following are deducted from the gross estate (¶5000 *et seq.*) to arrive at the taxable estate:[35]

. . . Funeral expenses. (Code Sec. 2053(a)(1))

. . . Administration expenses, such as executors' and administrators' commissions, attorneys', accountants' and appraisers' fees, and court costs. (Code Sec. 2053(a)(2); Reg § 20.2053-3)

. . . Claims against the estate, including property taxes accrued before the decedent's death, unpaid income and gift taxes, and medical expenses of the decedent paid by the estate after death (to the extent not claimed as an income tax deduction, see ¶2143). (Code Sec. 2053(a)(3); Reg § 20.2053-6)

. . . Transfers in satisfaction of claims by the decedent's former spouse. (Code Sec. 2043(b)(2))

. . . Indebtedness on property if the total value of the property is included in the gross estate. (Code Sec. 2053(a)(4))

. . . Casualty and theft losses. (Code Sec. 2054)

. . . Transfers to charitable and similar organizations (Code Sec. 2055), see ¶5020.

. . . Transfers to surviving spouse (marital deduction) (Code Sec. 2056), see ¶5021.

. . . State death taxes (Code Sec. 2058), see ¶5027.

To be deductible as a debt, claim, or expense, an amount must be allowable by the jurisdiction in which the estate is being administered. (Code Sec. 2053(a))[36] Post-death events are taken into account in determining the deductible amount of a claim or other expense, and deductions generally are limited to amounts actually paid by the estate to satisfy deductible claims and expenses. Exceptions apply for claims against the estate for which there's an asset or claim includible in the gross estate that's substantially related to the claim against the estate, and for claims against the estate that, collectively, don't exceed $500,000 (not including those deductible as ascertainable amounts). But in each case, the deduction is subject to adjustment to reflect post-death events. (Reg § 20.2053-1, Reg § 20.2053-4)

Form 706 has a Schedule PC—Protective Claim for Refund, which an estate can file to preserve its right to a refund of estate taxes paid when a claim or expense that is the subject of unresolved controversy at the time of filing the return later becomes deductible.[37]

¶ 5019   Income vs. estate tax deduction for computation of taxable estate— estate tax.

Under Code Sec. 642(g), if an estate administration expense can qualify as both an estate tax deduction and an income tax deduction, the estate is entitled to an income tax deduction or offset only if an estate tax deduction for the item is waived. (Code Sec. 642(g))[38] For the election to take an income tax or estate tax deduction, see ¶3920.

---

34. ¶R-5301
35. ¶R-5400 *et seq.*
36. ¶R-5404

37. ¶R-5403
38. ¶R-5507

¶ 5020   Deductions for charitable bequests in computing the taxable estate—Form 706, Schedule O—estate tax.

Under Code Sec. 2055(a), deductions are allowed (on Form 706, Schedule O) for the value of property included in the gross estate and transferred by a decedent during life or by will to or for the use of the U.S., any state, political subdivision thereof, or the District of Columbia, and to various types of charitable organizations (Code Sec. 2055(a)), including foreign ones.[39]

The charitable deduction is for the amount actually received by the charity.[40]

Strict requirements apply where the charitable bequest is of an income interest or a remainder interest. (Code Sec. 2055(e))[41]

¶ 5021   Marital deduction—Form 706, Schedule M—estate tax.

Under Code Sec. 2056(a), a marital deduction is allowed (on Form 706, Schedule M) for the value of all property included in the gross estate that passes to the decedent's surviving spouse in a manner qualifying for the deduction. (Code Sec. 2056(a))[42]

A surviving spouse's dower or curtesy interest (or statutory interest in lieu thereof) is treated as passing from the decedent to the surviving spouse for the marital deduction. (Code Sec. 2056(c)(3), Reg § 20.2056(c)-1(a)(3))[43]

For terminable interests, see ¶5022. For where the surviving spouse isn't a U.S. citizen, see ¶5026.

¶ 5022   Terminable interests and the marital deduction—Form 706, Schedule M—estate tax.

Under Code Sec. 2056(b)(1), with certain exceptions (see, e.g., ¶5023), a terminable interest does not qualify for the marital deduction (on Form 706, Schedule M) if another interest in the same property passed from the decedent to some other person for less than adequate and full consideration and, because of its passing, that other person or his or her heirs may enjoy part of the property after the termination of the interest of the surviving spouse. (Code Sec. 2056(b)(1); Reg § 20.2056(b)-1(c)) A terminable interest is one that will terminate or fail after a certain period of time, the happening of some contingency, or the failure of some event to occur. (Reg § 20.2056(b)-1(b))[44]

¶ 5023   Qualified terminable interest property (QTIP) election—marital deduction—Form 706, Schedule M—estate tax.

Under Code Sec. 2056(b)(7), property in which a spouse is given only a life estate may qualify for the marital deduction as an exception to the terminable interest rule (¶5022) if the executor elects (by listing the property on Form 706, Schedule M and deducting its value) to have all or part of the property so qualify and the surviving spouse has a "qualifying income interest for life." A surviving spouse has such an interest if:

(1) the surviving spouse is entitled for life to all the income from the property, payable at least annually, or the spouse has a usufruct interest for life in the property; and

(2) no person (including the spouse) has a power to appoint any part of the property to any person other than the surviving spouse during the surviving spouse's life. (Code

---

39. ¶R-5700 *et seq.*
40. ¶P-6015
41. ¶R-5735 *et seq.*

42. ¶R-6000 *et seq.*
43. ¶R-6017
44. ¶R-6300 *et seq.*

Sec. 2056(b)(7))[45]

A surviving spouse's interest can meet the "all income" requirement if the spouse is entitled to income as determined by applicable local law that provides for a reasonable apportionment between the income and remainder beneficiaries of the trust's total return. (Reg § 20.2056(b)-5(f)(1), Reg § 20.2056(b)-7(d)(2))[46]

QTIP treatment isn't defeated merely because the spouse's income interest is contingent on the executor making a QTIP election. (Reg § 20.2056(b)-7(d)(3))[47]

An annuity, including one arising under community property law, where only the surviving spouse has the right to receive payments before the death of that surviving spouse, is a qualifying income interest for life, and the QTIP election is treated as made for that interest unless the executor otherwise elects. (Code Sec. 2056(b)(7)(C))[48]

Certain individual retirement accounts (IRAs) qualify. (Reg § 20.2056(b)-7(h), Ex 10)[49]

Partial QTIP elections that relate to a fractional or percentage share of the property are allowed. (Reg § 20.2056(b)-7(b)(2))[50] Protective QTIP elections are possible. (Reg § 20.2056(b)-7(c))[1]

For inclusion of the QTIP in the surviving spouse's estate, see ¶5008.

¶ 5024 Effect of death taxes on amount of marital deduction—estate tax.

Under Code Sec. 2056(b)(4)(A), federal estate or other death taxes payable out of the marital share reduce the amount of the bequest that qualifies for the marital deduction. (Code Sec. 2056(b)(4)(A))

The surviving spouse's interest can be completely absolved from the burden of the tax by a provision in decedent's will that is effective under local law. In this case, death taxes won't affect the amount of the deduction.[2]

¶ 5025 Effect of administration expenses on amount of marital deduction—estate tax.

The marital deduction is reduced by estate transmission expenses paid from the marital share (Reg § 20.2056(b)-4(d)(2)), but not by estate management expenses attributable to and paid from the marital share unless those expenses are deducted on the estate tax return under Code Sec. 2053. (Reg § 20.2056(b)-4(d)(3)) The marital deduction is reduced to the extent estate management expenses are paid from the marital share and are attributable to other property. (Reg § 20.2056(b)-4(d)(4)) Estate transmission expenses are expenses that wouldn't have been incurred but for the necessity of collecting the decedent's assets, paying any debts and death taxes, and distributing the decedent's property. They include any administration expense that is not a management expense. (Reg § 20.2056(b)-4(d)(1)(ii)) Management expenses are those incurred in connection with the investment of estate assets or with their preservation or maintenance during a reasonable period of administration. (Reg § 20.2056(b)-4(d)(1)(i))[3]

¶ 5026 Marital deduction where surviving spouse isn't U.S. citizen—qualified domestic trust (QDOT) requirement—estate tax.

Under Code Sec. 2056(d)(1)(A) and Code Sec. 2056(d)(2), no marital deduction is allowed

45. ¶R-6393
46. ¶R-6355
47. ¶R-6400
48. ¶R-6413 *et seq.*
49. ¶R-6421
50. ¶R-6431
1. ¶R-6430
2. ¶R-6612 *et seq.*
3. ¶R-6608

if the surviving spouse isn't a U.S. citizen (Code Sec. 2056(d)(1)(A); Reg § 20.2056A-1(a)), unless the property passes (or is treated as passing) to the spouse in a QDOT (Code Sec. 2056(d)(2))—a trust that satisfies certain requirements (Code Sec. 2056A; Reg § 20.2056A-2)—or the spouse timely becomes a citizen. (Code Sec. 2056(d)(4); Reg § 20.2056A-1(b))[4]

An estate tax is imposed (use Form 706-QDT) on any distribution (other than an income or a hardship distribution (Reg § 20.2056A-5(c))) from the trust before the date of the surviving spouse's death and on the value of the property remaining in the trust on the date of death of the surviving spouse (Code Sec. 2056A(b)(1)) (or the date the trust ceases to qualify). (Code Sec. 2056A(b)(3))[5]

¶ 5027   Deduction for state death taxes—estate tax.

Under Code Sec. 2058, the value of the taxable estate is determined by deducting from the gross estate any estate, inheritance, legacy, or succession taxes actually paid to any state or the District of Columbia for any property included in the gross estate, but not including any taxes paid for the estate of a person other than the decedent. (Code Sec. 2058)[6]

¶ 5028   Applicable exclusion amount, basic exclusion amount, and applicable credit amount—estate tax.

Under Code Sec. 2010(c)(2), the applicable exclusion amount equals the decedent's basic exclusion (see below) and, for a surviving spouse, the deceased spousal unused exclusion (DSUE) amount (see ¶5029), if any. (Code Sec. 2010(c)(2); Reg § 20.2010-1(e)(2))

The basic exclusion amount is adjusted annually for inflation. For decedents dying in 2022, the basic exclusion amount is $12,060,000. For decedents dying in 2023, the basic exclusion amount is $12,920,000. (Code Sec. 2010(c)(3); Reg § 20.2010-1(e)(3))[7]

The applicable credit amount equals the amount of the tentative tax that would be owed under the rate schedule set forth at ¶1114 on an amount equal to the applicable exclusion amount. (Code Sec. 2010(c)(1); Reg § 20.2010-1(e)(1)) For 2022, the applicable credit amount is $4,769,800, which is the tax that would otherwise be imposed on $12,060,000. For 2023, the applicable credit amount is $5,113,800, which is the tax that would otherwise be imposed on $12,920,000.[8]

¶ 5029   Deceased spousal unused exclusion (DSUE) amount—"portability" of unused part of exclusion—Form 706, Part 6—estate tax.

Under Code Sec. 2010(c)(4), for a surviving spouse of a deceased spouse, the DSUE amount, used in computing the applicable credit amount against estate tax, see ¶5028, is the lesser of (1) the basic exclusion amount (see ¶5028), or (2) the excess of (a) the applicable exclusion amount of the last deceased spouse of the surviving spouse (below), over (b) the amount on which the tentative tax on the estate of the deceased spouse is determined.[9]

A surviving spouse may not use the DSUE amount unless the executor of the deceased spouse's estate makes an election allowing the surviving spouse to do so. (Code Sec. 2010(c)(5)(A); Reg § 20.2010-2(a))[10]

A relaxed reporting rule applies for executors who aren't required to file Form 706 but who are filing to elect portability of the DSUE amount to the surviving spouse.

---

4. ¶R-6201 *et seq.*
5. ¶R-7081 *et seq.*
6. ¶R-6901
7. ¶R-7101

8. ¶R-7101
9. ¶R-7107 *et seq.*
10. ¶R-7110

(Reg § 20.2010-2(a)(7)(ii))[11]

If the executor elects transfer or portability of the DSUE amount, the surviving spouse can apply the DSUE amount received from the estate of his or her last deceased spouse (see ¶5030) against any tax liability arising from later lifetime gifts (by completing Schedule C of Form 709) and transfers at death. (Code Sec. 2010(c)(4), Reg § 20.2010-3)[12]

¶ 5030 "Last deceased spouse" for deceased spousal unused exclusion (DSUE) amount—estate tax.

For determining the DSUE amount under Code Sec. 2010(c)(4) (¶5029), the "last deceased spouse" is the most recently deceased individual who, at that individual's death after Dec. 31, 2010, was married to the surviving spouse. (Reg § 20.2010-1(e)(5)) Later remarriage or divorce doesn't change the identity of the last deceased spouse. (Reg § 20.2010-3(a))[13]

¶ 5031 Deceased spousal unused exclusion (DSUE) amount for non-citizen surviving spouse—estate tax.

If a surviving spouse is not a U.S. citizen on the date of the last deceased spouse's (¶5030) death, but the surviving spouse becomes a U.S. citizen after the death of the last deceased spouse, then the DSUE amount of the surviving spouse's last deceased spouse is available to the surviving spouse on the date the surviving spouse becomes a U.S. citizen. This rule applies when the property of the last deceased spouse does not pass to the surviving spouse in a qualified domestic trust (QDOT, see ¶5026). Reg § 20.2010-3(c)(2)[14]

When property passes from a decedent for the benefit of a non-citizen surviving spouse in a QDOT, and portability is elected, the DSUE amount must be redetermined upon the occurrence of the final distribution or other event (generally the death of the surviving spouse or the earlier termination of all QDOTs for that surviving spouse) on which estate tax is imposed. Reg § 20.2010-2(c)(4)(i)[15]

Where a QDOT has been validly established, if the non-citizen surviving spouse beneficiary becomes a citizen of the U.S. after the death of the last deceased spouse, then the DSUE amount will become available to the surviving spouse (without redetermination, as described above) as of the date the surviving spouse becomes a U.S. citizen. (Reg § 20.2010-3(c)(3))[16]

¶ 5032 Credit for tax on prior transfers—Form 706, Schedule Q—estate tax.

Under Code Sec. 2013, credit is allowed (on Form 706, Schedule Q) against the estate tax, for federal estate tax paid by the estate of another decedent (the transferor) on the transfer of property to the present decedent, where the transferor died within ten years before, or within two years after, the present decedent's death. (Code Sec. 2013)[17]

Where a transferor decedent was denied a marital deduction because the surviving spouse wasn't a U.S. citizen or where the estate tax on qualified domestic trust distributions applied (see ¶5026), the surviving spouse decedent is allowed a credit for the estate tax paid by the transferor decedent, or by the trust, without regard to when the transferor decedent died. (Code Sec. 2056(d)(3))[18]

11. ¶R-7111
12. ¶R-7109
13. ¶R-7109
14. ¶R-7112
15. ¶R-7108
16. ¶R-7112
17. ¶R-7300 *et seq.*
18. ¶R-7301

¶ 5033   Credit for foreign death taxes—Form 706, Schedule P—estate tax.

Under Code Sec. 2014, credit is allowed (on Form 706, Schedule P), subject to certain limits, against the estate tax for estate, inheritance, legacy, or succession taxes actually paid to any foreign country or U.S. possession. (Code Sec. 2014)[19]

¶ 5034   Computation of estate tax—Form 706.

To compute the estate tax under Code Sec. 2001(b), first compute a tentative tax under the unified rate schedule at ¶1114 (which applies a maximum tax rate of 40% for 2022 and 2023 transfers) on the total of: (1) the amount of the taxable estate (¶5018), and (2) the total amount of adjusted taxable gifts made by the decedent after 1976 that aren't includible in the gross estate. (Code Sec. 2001(b)(1))[20] Then reduce this tentative tax amount by the amount of gift tax that would have been payable on the decedent's post-1976 gifts if the rates in effect at the time of the decedent's death had applied, and not the amount actually paid based on the rates in effect at the time of the gift. Regs provide rules for when there's a difference between the basic exclusion amount that applied on the date of a donor' s gift, and the basic exclusion amount that applied on the date of death. (Code Sec. 2001(b)(2); Code Sec. 2001(g); Reg § 20.2010-1(c))[21]

The net estate tax payable is the gross estate tax minus the applicable credit amount (¶5028, previously called the unified credit) and allowable credits for gift taxes on pre-1977 gifts, estate taxes on earlier transfers, and foreign death taxes (¶5028 *et seq.*). (Code Sec. 2010, Code Sec. 2012, Code Sec. 2013, Code Sec. 2014)[22]

The estate of a "qualified decedent" who was an armed forces member, victim of terrorism, or astronaut, and who died in the line of duty, may compute estate tax using a special, lower, rate schedule. (Code Sec. 2201)[23]

¶ 5035   Return requirements—Form 706—estate tax.

Under Code Sec. 6018(a), an executor must file an estate tax return (Form 706) if the decedent's gross estate at death exceeds the basic exclusion amount for the calendar year of death ($12,060,000 for estates of individuals dying in 2022; $12,920,000 for 2023, see ¶5028). This dollar amount is reduced by certain gifts made by the decedent. (Code Sec. 6018(a)(1), Code Sec. 6018(a)(3))[24]

¶ 5036   When to file estate tax return—Form 706, Form 4768 (extension).

Under Code Sec. 6075(a), generally, an estate must file an estate tax return within nine months after the date of death. (Code Sec. 6075(a))[25]

IRS grants an automatic 6-month extension to file Form 706, and may grant a 6-month discretionary filing extension (1) for estates that didn't seek an automatic extension, (2) to file Form 706-NA for the estates of nonresident alien, and (3) to file specialized estate tax forms for various recapture estate taxes (e.g., Form 706-A for recapture of special use valuation). (use Form 4768 for all extensions). An executor who is abroad can request a longer discretionary extension. (Reg § 20.6081-1)[26]

---

19. ¶R-7400 *et seq.*
20. ¶R-7001 *et seq.*
21. ¶R-7009
22. ¶R-7001 *et seq.*

23. ¶R-7011
24. ¶S-2300 *et seq.*
25. ¶S-4902
26. ¶S-5035.1

¶ 5037   When to pay estate tax; estate tax deferral elections.

The estate tax must be paid at the time for filing the return (see ¶5036). Filing extensions don't extend the time for payment (Reg § 20.6151-1),[27] but extensions of time to pay can be granted (use Form 4768) for reasonable cause. (Code Sec. 6161(a)(1))[28]

Special estate tax deferrals (elected on Form 706) are available where a future interest is included in the estate (6-month deferral) (Code Sec. 6163)[29] or where the estate consists largely of a closely held business (up to five years' deferral). (Code Sec. 6166)

Tax deferred under Code Sec. 6166 can be accelerated on certain events,[30] but IRS privately ruled that a change in the form of doing business doesn't result in acceleration.[31]

The estate tax on distributions made from qualified domestic trusts (QDOTs, see ¶5026), before the surviving spouse's death is due on Apr. 15 of the year following the calendar year the taxable event occurs. (Code Sec. 2056A(b)(5))[32]

¶ 5038   Request for estate tax closing letter or account transcript (Form 4506-T).

To confirm that IRS examination of an estate tax return is completed and is closed, estates or representatives may either request an estate tax closing letter (IRS Letter 627), or request an account transcript (on Form 4506-T). Receipt of an account transcript with a transaction code of "421," like receipt of a closing letter, confirms the closing of the IRS examination of the estate tax return.[33] There is a $67 fee on requests for issuance of IRS Letter 627. (TD 9957, 9/28/2021)[34]

¶ 5039   Estates of nonresident aliens; expatriates—Form 706-NA—estate tax.

Under Code Sec. 2103, decedents who were neither U.S. citizens nor U.S. residents are taxed only on the transfer of property situated within the U.S. (on Form 706-NA). With that exception, the make-up of the gross estate is the same as that for a U.S. citizen or resident. (Code Sec. 2103)[35]

The same rate schedule that applies to the estates of U.S. citizens (¶1114) applies to the estates of nonresident aliens. (Code Sec. 2101(b))[36]

A marital deduction is allowed under the regular marital deduction rules (¶5021 *et seq.*), for U.S. property. (Code Sec. 2106(a)(3))[37] Estates of nonresident aliens may deduct a portion of certain expenses and losses, such as funeral and administration expenses and debts with respect to property included in the gross estate. The portion is determined by the proportion of the value of the gross estate situated in the U.S. to the value of all estate property, wherever situated. (Code Sec. 2106)[38]

An applicable credit of $13,000 is allowed against the estate tax of nonresident aliens, with an alternative credit computation for estates of certain residents of U.S. possessions (Code Sec. 2102(b)(1), Code Sec. 2102(b)(2)), and to the extent required under certain treaty obligations of the U.S. (Code Sec. 2102(b)(3)(A)) The $13,000 is reduced by any gift tax applicable credit allowed. (Code Sec. 2102(b)(3)(B))[39]

Credits are also allowed for estate tax on prior transfers and gift tax on certain pre-1977 gifts. (Code Sec. 2102(b)(5))[40]

---

27. ¶S-5455
28. ¶S-5900 *et seq.*
29. ¶S-5910
30. ¶S-6100 *et seq.*
31. ¶S-6116
32. ¶R-7086
33. ¶T-4511

34. ¶T-10003.2
35. ¶R-8000 *et seq.*
36. ¶R-8000 *et seq.*
37. ¶R-8023
38. ¶R-8022
39. ¶R-8026 *et seq.*
40. ¶R-8031

An estate tax return on Form 706-NA must be filed for the estate of every nonresident not a U.S. citizen if the value of the part of the estate in the U.S. exceeds $60,000 (Code Sec. 6018(a)(2)), reduced by: (1) the amount of adjusted taxable gifts made by the decedent after 1976, and (2) the amount of any pre-1977 specific exemption allowed for gifts made by the decedent after Sept. 8, 1976. (Code Sec. 6018(a)(3))[41] The time for filing the return is the same as for U.S. citizens or residents, see ¶5036.

Expatriates and former long-term residents who gave up citizenship or terminated residency after June 16, 2008. A special transfer tax (the Code Sec. 2801 tax) is imposed on any U.S. citizen or resident who receives any "covered gift or bequest" from a "covered expatriate," see ¶4639. (Code Sec. 2801(a)) The tax applies to any covered gift or bequest valued in excess of the annual exclusion amount in effect for gift tax purposes in the year of the transfer. (Code Sec. 2801(c)) The amount of the Code Sec. 2801 tax is determined by multiplying the value of the covered gift or bequest by the greater of (i) the highest estate tax rate listed in the Code Sec. 2001(c) rate table in effect on the date the transferee receives the covered gift or bequest, or (ii) the highest gift tax rate listed in the Code Sec. 2502(a) rate table in effect on that date. (Code Sec. 2801(a))[42]

¶ 5040 Gift Tax, Overview.

Under Code Sec. 2501, the gift tax is integrated with the estate tax under a "unified" rate schedule (¶1114) that imposes a single tax on transfers during life and at death (see ¶5000) which effectively imposes no tax on gifts unless the total amount of taxable gifts for the year and all prior years exceeds $12,060,000 for 2022 ($12,920,000 for 2023).

The tax is imposed on the transfer, not on the property transferred. It applies even though the property transferred may be exempt from income or other taxes. (Code Sec. 2501(a); Reg § 25.2501-1, Reg § 25.2511-1(a), Reg § 25.2511-2)[43]

For who must pay the gift tax, see ¶5041; what a gift is, ¶5042 *et seq.*; allowable exclusions and deductions, ¶5048 *et seq.*; credits against the tax, ¶5052; how the tax is computed, ¶5053 *et seq.*; and return requirements, ¶5057.

¶ 5041 Who must pay gift tax?

Under Code Sec. 2501(a), the gift tax must be paid by the person (the donor) who makes the gift. (Code Sec. 2501(a); Reg § 25.2511-2(f)) It applies only to donors who are individuals (Reg § 25.2501-1(b)), but a gift by a corporation may be treated as a gift by the shareholders. (Reg § 25.2511-1(h)(1))[44]

If the donor fails to pay the tax when due, the donee is also liable for the tax to the extent of the value of the gift (Code Sec. 6324(b); Reg § 25.2502-2, Reg § 301.6324-1(b)), and potentially for interest on that amount.[45]

These rules apply to a U.S. citizen or resident no matter where the gift property (tangible or intangible) is situated. (Code Sec. 2501(a); Reg § 25.2501-1(a), Reg § 25.2511-3(a))[46]

A nonresident who's not a U.S. citizen is subject to gift tax only if the gift property is real estate or tangible personal property and is situated in the U.S. at the time of the gift. (Code Sec. 2501(a), Code Sec. 2511(a); Reg § 25.2511-1(b), Reg § 25.2511-3(a))[47] A nonresident generally isn't subject to tax on a gift of intangible property. (Code Sec. 2501(a)(2))[48]

For a special transfer tax for recipients of gifts and bequests from expatriates and former

41. ¶S-2302
42. ¶R-8101
43. ¶Q-1000 *et seq.*
44. ¶s Q-1000 *et seq.*, Q-2400 *et seq.*

45. ¶V-9301
46. ¶Q-1016
47. ¶Q-4001
48. ¶Q-4001; ¶Q-4010

long-term residents who gave up citizenship or terminated residency after June 16, 2008, see ¶5039.

¶ 5042   What is a gift for the gift tax; parting with dominion and control; gifts to organizations.

Transactions where property or property rights are gratuitously bestowed on another are gifts. (Reg § 25.2511-1(c))

A gift isn't complete until the donor parts with dominion or control over the transferred property or property interest. The donor must be left without power to change the disposition of the property either for the donor's own benefit or for that of others. (Reg § 25.2511-2(b))[49]

A transfer of property by a shareholder to a corporation for less than adequate consideration represents gifts to the other individual shareholders of the corporation to the extent of their proportionate interests. (Reg § 25.2511-1(h)(1))

There's no gift tax on a transfer to a political organization. (Code Sec. 2501(a)(4))[50] Also, there is no gift tax on contributions to certain tax-exempt organizations, including: nonprofit civic organizations operated exclusively for social welfare and local employees' associations whose net earnings are used solely for charitable, educational or recreational purposes that are exempt under Code Sec. 501(c)(4); labor, agricultural or horticultural organizations that are exempt under Code Sec. 501(c)(5); and chambers of commerce, business leagues, real estate boards, boards of trade or professional football leagues not organized for profit or private benefit that are exempt under Code Sec. 501(c)(6). (Code Sec. 2501(a)(6))[1]

¶ 5043   Below-market loans—"gift loans"—gift tax.

Under Code Sec. 7872, if a below-market (or interest-free) loan is a "gift loan" (that is, a below-market loan where the forgoing of interest is in the nature of a gift), it's treated as: (1) a loan to the borrower/donee in exchange for an interest-paying note, and (2) a gift to the borrower of the funds to pay the interest. The amount of the gift equals:

. . . the forgone interest—excess of interest payable at the applicable federal rate (AFR, ¶1117) over actual interest payable—if the loan is a demand loan; or

. . . the excess of the amount loaned over the present value (using a discount rate equal to the AFR) of all payments required under the terms of the loan, if the gift loan is a term loan. (Code Sec. 7872)[2]

For demand loans, the gift is treated as made on the last day of the calendar year. (Code Sec. 7872(a)) For term loans, the gift is treated as made on the date the loan was made. (Code Sec. 7872(b))[3]

These rules don't apply to certain gift loans between individuals that don't exceed $10,000. (Code Sec. 7872(c)(2))[4]

If the outstanding balance of a gift loan made between individuals is $100,000 or less, the amount of interest treated as retransferred by the borrower to the lender each year doesn't exceed the borrower's net investment income for that year. If the net investment income is $1,000 or less, the amount treated as retransferred is zero. (Code Sec. 7872(d)(1))[5]

---

49. ¶Q-3004
50. ¶Q-3201
1. ¶Q-3203
2. ¶Q-2150 *et seq.*

3. ¶Q-2150
4. ¶Q-2165
5. ¶J-2905

¶ 5044　　**Property placed in joint ownership—gift tax.**

A gift may result where property is placed in joint ownership with someone other than a spouse or where joint ownership with someone other than a spouse ends.[6]

If an individual buys property with his or her own funds and has the title conveyed to him/herself and others as joint tenants with rights of survivorship, but these rights may be defeated by any joint tenant severing their interest, there is an immediate gift to the other joint tenants of equal shares of the property. (Reg § 25.2511-1(h)(5))[7]

An individual doesn't make a gift by merely opening a bank account held jointly with another person, using the individual's own funds, from which the individual can regain all of the funds without the other person's consent; rather, a gift is made only when the other person withdraws money for that other person's own benefit.[8]

¶ 5045　　**Qualified disclaimers—gift tax.**

Under Code Sec. 2518, a qualified disclaimer (an irrevocable and unqualified refusal to accept ownership, made in writing by a specified deadline) with respect to any interest in property has the effect of treating that interest, for gift (and estate and generation-skipping transfer tax) purposes, as if it had never been transferred to the disclaimant. (Code Sec. 2518) And the disclaimant isn't treated as having made a gift to the person to whom the interest passes by reason of the disclaimer. (Reg § 25.2518-1(b))[9]

¶ 5046　　**Amount of gift; "net gift" (donee must pay tax); certain transfers of partnership or corporation interests—gift tax.**

Under Code Sec. 2512(a), the amount of the gift is the money given or, if property is given, the property's value as of the date of the gift, less any consideration received. (Code Sec. 2512(a))[10] For a "net gift," i.e., a gift conditioned on the gift tax being paid by the donee, the value of the gift is reduced by the gift tax amount. The Tax Court has held that a donee's agreement to pay the potential estate tax liability under Code Sec. 2035(b) (¶5003) reduces the value of the gift.[11]

The market value of annuities (other than commercial annuities), unitrust interests, life estates, term of years, remainders, and reversions transferred by gift is determined by use of standard or special Code Sec. 7520 actuarial factors. (Reg § 25.2512-5(a), Reg § 25.7520-1(a)) These factors are derived by using the appropriate Code Sec. 7520 interest rate[12] and, if applicable, the mortality component for the valuation date of the interest that's being valued. These factors appear in IRS-issued tables. (Reg § 25.2512-5(d)(1))[13]

A taxable gift can also occur under Code Sec. 2701 (certain transfers of partnership or corporation interests), even though there may not be a taxable gift under normal tax rules. The amount of the gift is determined under the valuation rules of that Code section.[14]

¶ 5047　　**Taxable gifts—gift tax.**

Under Code Sec. 2503(a), taxable gifts are the gifts made during the calendar year after applying the annual exclusion (¶5048), and reduced by allowable deductions (¶5050, ¶5051). (Code Sec. 2503(a), Code Sec. 2503(b))[15]

---

6. ¶Q-2900 *et seq.*
7. ¶Q-2906
8. ¶Q-2921 *et seq.*
9. ¶Q-2350 *et seq.*
10. ¶Q-1200

11. ¶Q-1210.1
12. ¶P-6619
13. ¶P-6615
14. ¶Q-3402
15. ¶Q-1000

¶ 5048   Annual exclusion; gifts to minors—gift tax.

For 2022, the first $16,000 (and for 2023, the first $17,000) of gifts of a present interest made by a donor *to each donee* is excluded (Code Sec. 2503(b)) from the amount of the donor's taxable gifts. (Code Sec. 2503(b))[16] For 2022, the first $164,000 of gifts made by a donor to a spouse who isn't a U.S. citizen is excluded ($175,000 for 2023). (Code Sec. 2523(i)(2))[17]

No annual exclusion is allowed for gifts of future interests (Code Sec. 2503(b); Reg § 25.2503-2), e.g., reversions or remainders. (Reg § 25.2503-3)[18]

A "Crummey" power (in general, a trust beneficiary's noncumulative right to withdraw a specified amount of trust principal within a limited period) makes a transfer to the trust a gift of a present interest, but not if the Crummey power is unenforceable in a state court.[19]

A transfer for the benefit of a *minor* isn't considered a gift of a future interest if the property and its income:

(1) may be expended by or for the benefit of the minor before the minor reaches 21, and

(2) any balance not so expended *will pass to the minor* when the minor reaches 21, or if the minor dies before 21 will go either to the minor's *estate* or as the minor may appoint under a general power of appointment. (Code Sec. 2503(c); Reg § 25.2503-4(a))[20]

Gifts to minors made through custodians designated under Uniform Acts for gifts or transfers to minors qualify for the annual exclusion.[21]

¶ 5049   Educational or medical payment exclusion; contributions to qualified tuition programs and Coverdell Education Savings Accounts—gift tax.

Under Code Sec. 2503(e), the gift tax doesn't apply to amounts paid by one individual:

(1) on behalf of another individual directly to a qualifying educational organization as tuition for that other individual. (Code Sec. 2503(e); Reg § 25.2503-6(b)(2))

(2) on behalf of another individual directly to a provider of medical care as payment for that medical care. (Code Sec. 2503(e); Reg § 25.2503-6(b)(3)) Payments for medical insurance qualify for this exclusion. (Reg § 25.2503-6(b)(3))

These exclusions are available in addition to the annual gift tax exclusion (¶5048). (Reg § 25.2503-6(a))[22] No gift tax return is required. (Code Sec. 6019)[23]

Contributions to qualified tuition programs (QTPs, ¶2209 *et seq.*) and Coverdell Education Savings Accounts (CESAs, ¶2205 *et seq.*) don't qualify for the Code Sec. 2503(e) tuition exclusion, but are instead treated as present gifts that can qualify for the gift tax annual exclusion including by electively spreading contributions in a single year over a five-year period. A contributor isn't subject to gift tax on distributions from QTPs and CESAs. (Code Sec. 529(c), Code Sec. 530(d)(3))[24] A transfer by reason of a change in the designated beneficiary under a QTP, or a rollover to the account of a new beneficiary, is subject to gift and generation-skipping transfer taxes unless the new beneficiary is: (1) assigned to the same generation as, or a higher generation than, the old beneficiary; and (2) a member of the old beneficiary's family. (Code Sec. 529(c)(5)(B))[25]

---

16. ¶Q-5000 *et seq.*
17. ¶Q-5003
18. ¶Q-5100 *et seq.*
19. ¶Q-5112
20. ¶Q-5201 *et seq.*

21. ¶Q-5212
22. ¶Q-5250 *et seq.*
23. ¶S-2201
24. ¶Q-1910.1 *et seq.*; ¶Q-1910.2
25. ¶Q-1910.1C

¶ 5050   Marital deduction; QTIP property—gift tax.

Under Code Sec. 2523, a marital deduction is allowed for the value of all qualifying gifts made by one spouse to the other if the donee spouse is a U.S. citizen (with some exceptions) and the gift isn't a nondeductible "terminable interest." (Code Sec. 2523)[26]

Qualified terminable interest property (QTIP) qualifies for the deduction if the donee spouse receives income payments for life and no person has a power to appoint any part of the property to anyone other than the donee spouse during that spouse's life. (Code Sec. 2523(f))[27]

For an increased exclusion for transfers to noncitizen spouses, see ¶5048.

If an estate (¶5023) or gift tax QTIP marital deduction is taken, the QTIP property is included in the spouse's estate on death (¶5008). However, transfer tax is accelerated if the spouse makes a gift of the income interest. Under Code Sec. 2519, if a spouse makes a gift of any portion of the qualifying income interest in the QTIP trust, the spouse is deemed to make a transfer of the entire value of the remainder.[28]

¶ 5051   Charitable gifts—gift tax.

Under Code Sec. 2522, charitable gifts and certain similar gifts are deducted in arriving at taxable gifts for the calendar year. (Code Sec. 2522)[29] A number of Courts of Appeal have upheld the use of defined value formula clauses to limit the gift tax liability resulting from transfers of hard-to-value assets (e.g., closely held stock or family limited partnership interests), by reallocating the transferred assets among charitable and noncharitable donees when the value of the assets is increased on audit of the gift tax return.[30]

¶ 5052   Applicable credit—gift tax.

For gifts made in 2022, the applicable credit (Code Sec. 2505) is $4,769,800 (the amount that exempts the $12,060,000 basic exclusion amount for 2022 from gift tax). For 2023, the applicable credit amount is $5,113,800, which is the tax that would otherwise be imposed on $12,920,000. See ¶5028.

The applicable credit against tax on gifts in a calendar year is reduced by the sum of all amounts allowable as a credit in preceding calendar periods. In determining this reduction, the gift tax rates that are in effect for the calendar year of the gift (instead of the rates in effect for the preceding calendar periods) are used in determining the amounts allowable as a credit for all preceding calendar periods. (Code Sec. 2505)[31] The instructions to Form 709 contain a worksheet to determine the amount of the applicable credit amount used for post-1976 gifts where prior gifts total more than $500,000.

¶ 5053   How to compute gift tax if no gifts made before current year.

Under Code Sec. 2504, if a person has *not* made any taxable gifts (in excess of annual exclusions and deductions and the pre-1977 specific lifetime exemption) before the calendar year for which the tax is being computed, the gift tax is computed as follows:[32]

(1) Determine the aggregate value of the total gifts made during the calendar year for which the tax is being computed. If the donor is married, and the donor and the donor's spouse have consented to split their gifts to third parties, only half of the gifts the donor

---

26. ¶Q-6100 *et seq.*
27. ¶Q-6300 *et seq.*
28. ¶Q-6315
29. ¶Q-6000 *et seq.*
30. ¶Q-1983.2
31. ¶Q-8005
32. ¶Q-8010 *et seq.*

made to third parties plus half of the gifts, if any, the donor's spouse made to third parties are included in computing the donor's total gifts. (A separate gift tax computation is made for the spouse, and the other half of the donor's gifts to third parties plus the other half of the spouse's gifts to third parties are included in computing the spouse's total gifts.)

(2) Deduct from the amount in (1), above, any amounts qualifying for the year's annual exclusion (¶5048).

(3) From the excess of (1) over (2), above, subtract the amount of charitable (¶5051) and marital (¶5050) gifts.

(4) Compute a gift tax on the excess of (1) over the sum of (2) and (3); for gifts made during 2022 or 2023, use the rate schedule at ¶1114.

(5) Subtract from the gift tax computed in (4) the allowable unified credit (now called the applicable credit amount).

¶ 5054 Cumulative computation where gifts were made before current year—gift tax.

Under Code Sec. 2502, previous taxable gifts affect the amount of gift tax imposed on gifts made in the current year. These taxable gifts are taken into account whether they were made before 1977 or after 1976. (Code Sec. 2502) In general, the gift tax (before the applicable credit amount) is the excess of: (1) a tentative tax computed under the unified rate schedules on the aggregate sum of taxable gifts for the current calendar year for which the tax is being computed *and* taxable gifts for all preceding years, over (2) a tentative tax (determined on the basis of the gift tax rates in effect for the current year, see ¶5052) on the aggregate sum of the taxable gifts for all of the years preceding the current calendar year for which the tax is being computed. (Code Sec. 2502(a)) The gift tax payable is the excess of the tentative tax in (1) over the tentative tax in (2), reduced by the applicable credit amount allowable.[33]

¶ 5055 Split gifts to third parties by married donors—gift tax.

Under Code Sec. 2513(a), spouses may consent to have their gifts to others treated as if made one-half by each (Code Sec. 2513(a); Reg § 25.2513-1) if:

... both spouses are U.S. citizens or residents on the date of the gift (Code Sec. 2513(a));

... both spouses consent (on Form 709) to have all gifts made to others in the calendar year treated as split gifts (Code Sec. 2513(a), Code Sec. 2513(b), Code Sec. 2513(c); Reg § 25.2513-1(b)(5)); and

... the consenting spouses are married to each other on the date of the gift and don't remarry during the remainder of the calendar year. (Code Sec. 2513(a))[34]

Each spouse is liable, jointly and severally, for the *entire* gift tax for the period in which he or she consents to split gifts. (Code Sec. 2513(d); Reg § 25.2513-4)[35]

Gifts of community property to a third party are generally considered to have been made one half by each spouse.[36]

¶ 5056 Gift tax rules for "estate freeze" transfers (Chapter 14 rules).

An estate freeze—a technique to reduce the value of an asset for estate tax purposes, typically by having an older-generation transferor retain a non-appreciating interest in a

33. ¶Q-8011
34. ¶Q-7000 *et seq.*

35. ¶V-8503
36. ¶Q-2929 *et seq.*

business, while transferring the interest that will appreciate to a younger-generation transferee—is subject to the special rules in Code Sec. 2701, Code Sec. 2702, Code Sec. 2703, and Code Sec. 2704. These special rules generally disregard, for *gift tax* valuation purposes, interests retained by the transferor after a transfer to a family member. This insures that a high gift tax will be imposed on the transferred interest at the time of the transfer.

The transactions that the special rules apply to are: (1) transfers of interests in corporations and partnerships;[37] (2) transfers of interests in trusts;[38] (3) buy-sell agreements and options;[39] and (4) lapsing rights.[40]

¶ 5057 Gift tax returns—Form 709; extensions (Form 8892).

Under Code Sec. 6019, any individual who makes gifts to any one donee during a calendar year that aren't fully excluded under the annual exclusion (see ¶5048) must file a gift tax return (Form 709). A return must be filed even if no tax is payable. (Reg § 25.6019-1(f)) But, no return is required to report a qualified transfer for educational or medical costs (¶5049), most charitable transfers, or a transfer that qualifies for the marital deduction (¶5050) (Code Sec. 6019), except that a return must be filed to make a QTIP (¶5050) election. (Reg § 25.6019-1(a))[41] The return is due on Apr. 15 of the year following the year the gifts were made. (Code Sec. 6075) A different rule applies if the donor has died.[42] An extension for filing the income tax return automatically extends the time for filing the gift tax return for the same calendar year. (Code Sec. 6075(b)(2)) Use Form 8892 to request an extension of time to file Form 709 when not applying for an extension to file an income tax return or to make a payment of gift (or GST) tax when applying for an extension of time to file Form 709. (Reg § 25.6081-1)[43]

¶ 5058 Generation-Skipping Transfer (GST) Tax, Overview. ▬▬▬▬▬

Under Code Sec. 2641, a GST tax is imposed on transfers outright or in trust to beneficiaries more than one generation below the transferor's generation at a rate equal to the maximum gift and estate tax rate, which is 40% (Code Sec. 2001(c)), multiplied by the "inclusion ratio." (Code Sec. 2641)[44]

The GST tax generally applies to GSTs made after Oct. 22, 1986, but not to any GST from a "grandfathered" trust that was irrevocable on Sept. 25, 1985, unless the transfer is made out of corpus added to the trust after Sept. 25, 1985. (TRA 1986 §1433(b)(2)(A))

A GST is any one of three taxable events: (1) a *taxable termination* of an interest in a trust if, after the termination, all interests in the trust are held by or for the benefit of persons two or more generations below that of the transferor (trustee pays the GST tax on taxable terminations on Form 706GS(T)), (2) a *taxable distribution* of income or principal from a trust to or for the benefit of a person two or more generations below that of the transferor (transferee pays the tax on Form 706GS(D), the trustee must file Form 706GS(D-1)), and (3) a *direct skip,* which is a transfer of an interest in property to or for the benefit of a person two or more generations below that of the transferor (transferor pays tax with Form 709 for lifetime direct skips, executor pays with Form 706 and attached Form 706, Schedule R or Form 706, Schedule R-1, for direct skips occurring at death). (Code Sec. 2611(a), Code Sec. 2612) (Use Form 8892 to request an extension of time to file Form 709 when not applying for an extension to file an income tax return or to make a payment of GST tax when applying for an extension of time to file Form 709.)

In determining whether there is a GST, a special rule "steps up" the generation of an

---

37. ¶Q-3400 *et seq.*
38. ¶Q-3500 *et seq.*
39. ¶Q-3600 *et seq.*
40. ¶Q-3443 *et seq.*

41. ¶S-2200 *et seq.*
42. ¶S-4901
43. ¶S-5035
44. ¶R-9575

individual (or the descendants of an individual) with a deceased parent that's a descendant of the transferor's parent. (Code Sec. 2651(e)(1); Reg § 26.2651-1)[45]

¶ 5059 Exemption from tax (estate tax basic exclusion)—generation-skipping transfer tax.

Under Code Sec. 2631, an individual is allowed an exemption equal to the estate tax basic exclusion ($12,060,000 for 2022, $12,920,000 for 2023; see ¶5028), which may be allocated to any property transferred. (Code Sec. 2631) Married couples may treat transfers as made one-half by each spouse, in effect giving them a combined $24,120,000 exemption for transfers in 2022 ($25,840,000 in 2023). (Code Sec. 2652(a)(2))[46] Once a transfer is designated as exempt, all later appreciation in the value of the exempt property is also exempt.[47] The tax doesn't apply to lifetime transfers (except for certain transfers in trust) that are exempt from gift tax because of the annual exclusion (¶5048) or the exclusion for certain tuition and medical expense payments (¶5049). (Code Sec. 2642(c)(3)) For lifetime transfers, the available GST exemption is automatically allocated to a direct skip under Code Sec. 2632(b), and to indirect skips made after Dec. 31, 2000 under Code Sec. 2632(c), unless the individual elects out of the automatic allocation under Code Sec. 2632(b)(3) and Code Sec. 2632(c)(5), respectively. The automatic allocation under Code Sec. 2632(c) also applies to an indirect skip occurring upon the post-2000 termination of an estate tax inclusion period. (Code Sec. 2632(c)(4)) Regs provide details about these elections. (Reg § 26.2632-1)[48]

¶ 5060 Computation of GST tax—Form 706, Schedule R—generation-skipping transfer tax.

Under Code Sec. 2602, the amount of GST tax imposed on any GST is the "taxable amount" multiplied by the "applicable rate." (Code Sec. 2602) The calculation of the GST tax is made on Form 706, Schedule R.

The "taxable amount" is the value of the property subject to GST tax and depends on what type of GST is involved (see ¶5058).[49]

The "applicable rate" is the product of the maximum federal estate tax rate (40%) and the "inclusion ratio," which is determined according to the amount of the GST exemption allocated to the trust (or allocated to the property transferred in the skip in cases of a direct skip).[50]

---

45. ¶R-9500 *et seq.*
46. ¶R-9551
47. ¶R-9557
48. ¶R-9501 *et seq.*
49. ¶R-9571 *et seq.*
50. ¶R-9575 *et seq.*

B

Backup withholding

Employee business expenses — Cont'd
. home office deduction 1618
. impairment-related work expenses 1617
. performing artists 3105
. reimbursements of expenses . . . . 1557 et seq.;
         3007; 3104
. related employers and employees, reim-
    bursed expenses 1563
. state and local officials 3106
. statutory employees 3103
. substantiation requirements . . . . 1559 et seq.
. transportation expenses . . . . 1548 et seq.
. travel expenses . . . . 1539 et seq.
. unreimbursed, deduction for 1551; 1615;
         3104
Employee leasing companies 3002
Employees. *See also "Government officials*
    and employees"; "Highly compensated
    employees"; "Statutory employees"
. bargain purchases from employer 1215
. below market interest rate loans to 1212
. benefit associations 4100
. classification of 4842
. . IRS determination of status 3004
. "qualified employee"
. . qualified equity grants, election to defer
     income from 1218
. . restricted stock unit (RSU) 1218
. recreational, social, or similar activities for
    the benefit of 1555
. residence of, employer's rental of space in 1625
. withholding on wages . . . . 3000 et seq.
Employee stock ownership plan (ESOP)
. generally 4303
. basis of replacement for stock sold to 2499
. diversification rules, exemption from 4323
. dividends on employer securities owned by . . . 1288
. sales of employer stock to 2428
Employee stock purchase plan 1220; 1275;
         1524; 3007;
         4746
Employer identification number (EIN) 3351; 4752
Employer-owned life insurance 1351
Employer-provided child care credit 2328
Employer reversions 4336
Employers, withholding by . . . . 3000 et seq.
Employment-related expenses, child and
    dependent care credit 2347
Employment taxes. *See also*
    "Self-employment tax"; "Unemployment
    tax"
. accrual basis taxpayers, time for deduction . . . 1536
. assessment period 4824
. deposit of
. . electronic funds transfer 3028
. . monthly depositors 3026
. . safe harbor and de minimis rules 3027
. . semi-weekly depositors 3026
. . time for 3026
. employer failure to collect, deposit, and/or
    report income or 3025
. household employees 3030
. levy for 4887
. motion picture industry 3029
. professional employer organizations 3002; 3026
. separate accounting for 3025
. statement required to be furnished to em-
    ployee
. . generally 3021
. . nonreceipt of statement 3022
Empowerment zones. *See also "Enterprise*
    zones"
. exclusion of gain on sale of empowerment
    zone stock 2638
. rollover of gain on qualified zone assets 2425

Endangered species recovery costs 4522
Endowment contracts. *See "Life insurance*
    and endowment contracts"
Energy conservation
. subsidies, rate reduction or credit from utili-
    ty 1206
Energy credits
. generally 2310
. advanced coal projects, qualifying 2312
. advanced energy project credit, qualifying . . . 2313
. alcohol fuel credit 4746
. basis of energy credit property 2472
. biodiesel fuel credit 4746
. "energy percentage"
. . 6% energy percentage 2310
. . 2% energy percentage 2310
. "energy property" 2310
. enhanced oil recovery credit 2322
. gasification projects, qualifying 2312
. grant in lieu of credit 1206
. increase of credits to 30% or 10% 2310
. new energy-efficient home credit for eligible
    contractors, pre-2033
. . "50% manufactured home" 2342
. pre-2023 nonbusiness energy property
    credit/post-2022 energy efficient home
    improvement credit 2352
. renewable electricity production credit 2324
. . base credit rate 2324
. research credit 2319
. solar and wind facilities in certain
    low-income communities, increased
    credit (2023 and 2024) for 2311
Energy efficient commercial building
    property
. deduction 2470
. recapture rules for Section 1245 property . . . 2674
Energy property. *See also "Energy efficient*
    commercial building property"
. credits for. *See "Energy credits"*
. depreciation, generally 1913
. smart electric meters or grid systems
. . advanced energy project credit 2313
. . depreciation 1915; 1921
Enhanced oil recovery credit 2322
. qualified costs paid or incurred in 2022 is
    phased-out completely 2322
Enterprise zones
. carryovers, corporate acquisitions 3550
Entertainment expenses. *See also "Meals*
    and lodging"; "Travel expenses"
. business meetings 1555
. as charitable contribution 2104
. deductibility . . . . 1554 et seq.
. exceptions to nondeductibility 1555
. percentage limitation, deductible expenses . . . 1556 et seq.
. support, as 3118
Environmental remediation
. carbon oxide/carbon dioxide sequestration
    credit 2316
. cleanup costs 1634; 1639
. expensing deduction 2674
Equipment. *See "Machinery and equipment"*
Equitable relief, liability of spouses 1203; 4711;
         4843
Equity *vs. debt* 1709
Erroneous returns
. mathematical or clerical errors, assess-
    ments 4801
Escheat, as involuntary conversion 2431
Escrow payments
. generally 2407
. like-kind exchanges 2419
ESOP. *See "Employee stock ownership plan*
    (ESOP)"

G

References are to paragraph [¶] numbers.

References are to paragraph [¶] numbers.